Less managing. More teaching. Greater learning.

INSTRUCTORS...

Would you like your **students** to show up for class more **prepared**? *(Let's face it, class is much more fun if everyone is engaged and prepared...)*

Want ready-made application-level **interactive assignments,** student progress reporting, and auto-assignment grading? *(Less time grading means more time teaching...)*

Want an **instant view of student or class performance** relative to learning objectives? *(No more wondering if students understand...)*

Need to **collect data and generate reports** required for administration or accreditation? *(Say goodbye to manually tracking student learning outcomes...)*

Want to **record and post your lectures** for students to view online?

With McGraw-Hill's *Connect™ Operations Management*,

INSTRUCTORS GET:

- Interactive Applications – **book-specific interactive assignments** that require students to APPLY what they've learned.
- Simple **assignment management**, allowing you to spend more time teaching.
- **Auto-graded** assignments, quizzes, and tests.
- **Detailed Visual Reporting** where student and section results can be viewed and analyzed.
- Sophisticated **online testing** capability.
- A **filtering and reporting** function that allows you to easily assign and report on materials that are correlated to accreditation standards, learning outcomes, and Bloom's taxonomy.
- An easy-to-use **lecture capture** tool.

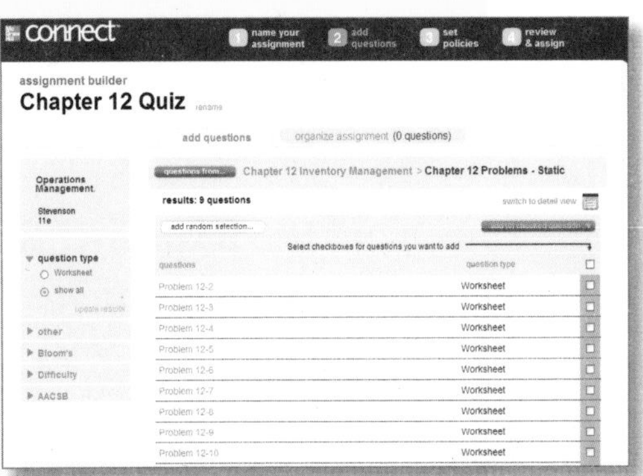

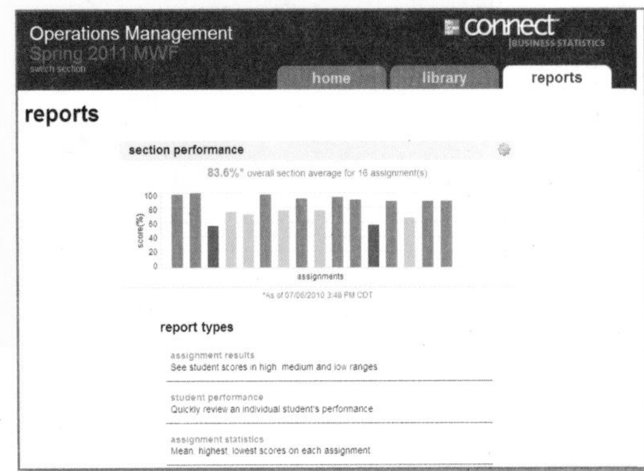

STUDENTS...

Want an online, **searchable version** of your textbook?

Wish your textbook could be **available online** while you're doing your assignments?

Connect™ Plus Operations Management eBook

If you choose to use *Connect™ Plus Operations Management*, you have an affordable and searchable online version of your book integrated with your other online tools.

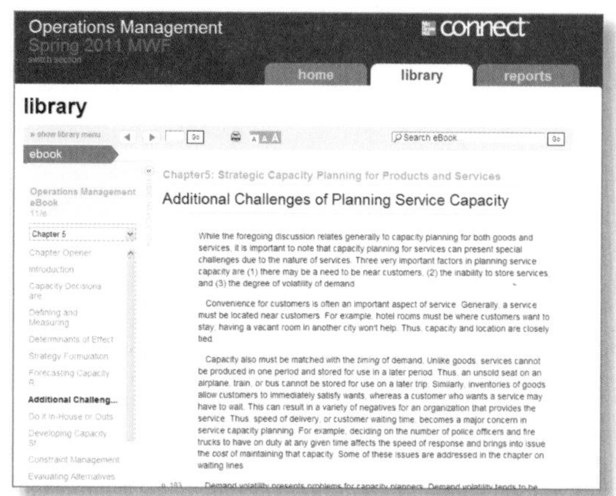

Connect™ Plus Operations Management eBook offers features like:

- Topic search
- Direct links from assignments
- Adjustable text size
- Jump to page number
- Print by section

STUDENTS...

Want to get more **value** from your textbook purchase?

Think learning operations management should be a bit more **interesting**?

Check out the STUDENT RESOURCES section under the *Connect™* Library tab.

Here you'll find a wealth of resources designed to help you achieve your goals in the course. You'll find things like **quizzes, PowerPoints, and Internet activities** to help you study. Every student has different needs, so explore the STUDENT RESOURCES to find the materials best suited to you.

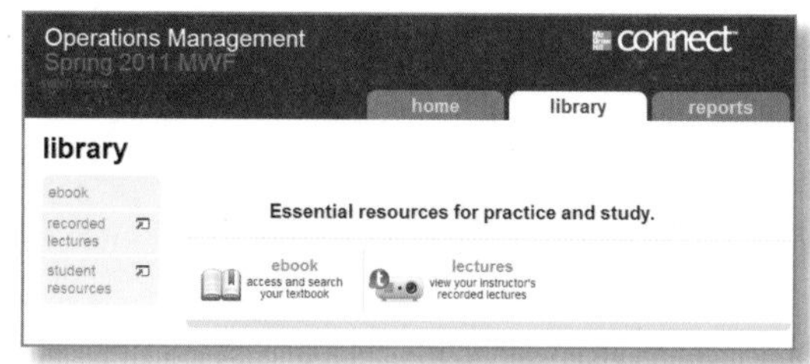

Operations Management

eleventh edition

William J. Stevenson
Rochester Institute of Technology

McGraw-Hill
Irwin

This book is dedicated to you.

OPERATIONS MANAGEMENT

Published by McGraw-Hill/Irwin, a business unit of The McGraw-Hill Companies, Inc., 1221 Avenue of the Americas, New York, NY, 10020.

This book is printed on acid-free paper.

2 3 4 5 6 7 8 9 0 DOW/DOW 1 0 9 8 7 6 5 4 3 2 1

ISBN 978-0-07-352525-9
MHID 0-07-352525-1

Vice president and editor-in-chief: *Brent Gordon*
Editorial director: *Stewart Mattson*
Publisher: *Tim Vertovec*
Executive editor: *Richard T. Hercher, Jr.*
Executive director of development: *Ann Torbert*
Managing development editor: *Gail Korosa*
Vice president and director of marketing: *Robin J. Zwettler*
Marketing director: *Brad Parkins*
Marketing manager: *Katie White*
Vice president of editing, design, and production: *Sesha Bolisetty*
Senior project manager: *Bruce Gin*
Buyer II: *Debra R. Sylvester*
Interior designer: *Laurie J. Entringer*
Senior photo research coordinator: *Keri Johnson*
Photo researcher: *Bill Van Werden*
Lead media project manager: *Kerry Bowler*
Media project manager: *Ron Nelms*
Cover design: © *Design Pics/Bilderbuch*
Typeface: *10/12 Times New Roman*
Compositor: *Laserwords Private Limited*
Printer: *R. R. Donnelley*

Library of Congress Cataloging-in-Publication Data

Stevenson, William J.
Operations management/William J. Stevenson.—11th ed.
p. cm.
Includes bibliographical references and index.
ISBN-13: 978-0-07-352525-9 (alk. paper)
ISBN-10: 0-07-352525-1 (alk. paper)
1. Production management. I. Title.
TS155.S7824 2012
658.5—dc22 2010051901

www.mhhe.com

The McGraw-Hill/Irwin Series Operations and Decision Sciences

Operations Management

Beckman and Rosenfield, **Operations Strategy: Competing in the 21st Century,** *First Edition*

Benton, **Purchasing and Supply Chain Management,** *Second Edition*

Bowersox, Closs, and Cooper, **Supply Chain Logistics Management,** *Third Edition*

Brown and Hyer, **Managing Projects: A Team-Based Approach,** *First Edition*

Burt, Petcavage, and Pinkerton, **Supply Management,** *Eighth Edition*

Cachon and Terwiesch, **Matching Supply with Demand: An Introduction to Operations Management,** *Second Edition*

Finch, **Interactive Models for Operations and Supply Chain Management,** *First Edition*

Fitzsimmons and Fitzsimmons, **Service Management: Operations, Strategy, Information Technology,** *Seventh Edition*

Gehrlein, **Operations Management Cases,** *First Edition*

Harrison and Samson, **Technology Management,** *First Edition*

Hayen, **SAP R/3 Enterprise Software: An Introduction,** *First Edition*

Hill, **Manufacturing Strategy: Text & Cases,** *Third Edition*

Hopp, **Supply Chain Science,** *First Edition*

Hopp and Spearman, **Factory Physics,** *Third Edition*

Jacobs, Berry, Whybark, and Vollmann, **Manufacturing Planning & Control for Supply Chain Management,** *Sixth Edition*

Jacobs and Chase, **Operations and Supply Management: The Core,** *Second Edition*

Jacobs and Chase, **Operations and Supply Chain Management,** *Thirteenth Edition*

Jacobs and Whybark, **Why ERP?** *First Edition*

Johnson, Leenders, and Flynn, **Purchasing and Supply Management,** *Fourteenth Edition*

Larson and Gray, **Project Management: The Managerial Process,** *Fifth Edition*

Olson, **Introduction to Information Systems Project Management,** *Second Edition*

Schroeder, Goldstein, and Rungtusanatham, **Operations Management: Contemporary Concepts and Cases,** *Fifth Edition*

Simchi-Levi, Kaminsky, and Simchi-Levi, **Designing and Managing the Supply Chain: Concepts, Strategies, Case Studies,** *Third Edition*

Sterman, **Business Dynamics: Systems Thinking and Modeling for a Complex World,** *First Edition*

Stevenson, **Operations Management,** *Eleventh Edition*

Swink, Melnyk, Cooper, and Hartley, **Managing Operations Across the Supply Chain,** *First Edition*

Thomke, **Managing Product and Service Development: Text and Cases,** *First Edition*

Ulrich and Eppinger, **Product Design and Development,** *Fourth Edition*

Zipkin, **Foundations of Inventory Management,** *First Edition*

Quantitative Methods and Management Science

Hillier and Hillier, **Introduction to Management Science: A Modeling and Case Studies Approach with Spreadsheets,** *Fourth Edition*

Stevenson and Ozgur, **Introduction to Management Science with Spreadsheets,** *First Edition*

Preface

The material in this book is intended as an introduction to the field of operations management. The topics covered include both strategic issues and practical applications. Among the topics are forecasting, product and service design, capacity planning, management of quality and quality control, inventory management, scheduling, supply chain management, and project management.

My purpose in revising this book continues to be to provide a clear presentation of the concepts, tools, and applications of the field of operations management. Operations management is evolving and growing, and I have found updating and integrating new material to be both rewarding and challenging, particularly due to the plethora of new developments in the field, while facing the practical limits on the length of the book.

This Eleventh Edition Contains a Considerable Amount of Material . . .

much more than one could hope to cover in a single semester. However, there is also considerable flexibility in terms of what material to cover. This allows instructors to select the chapters, or portions of chapters, that are most relevant for their purposes. That flexibility also extends to the choice of relative weighting of the qualitative or quantitative aspects of the material.

As in previous editions, there are major pedagogical features designed to help students learn and understand the material. This section describes the key features of the book, the chapter elements, the supplements that are available for teaching the course, highlights of the eleventh edition, and suggested applications for classroom instruction. By providing this support, it is our hope that instructors and students will have the tools to make this learning experience a rewarding one.

What's New in This Edition

This edition has been revised to incorporate and integrate changes in the field of Operations Management, and the many suggestions for improvement received from instructors around the world who are using the text. The following are key among the revisions:

- The sequence of chapters has been changed to improve the flow.
- A tutorial has been added on working with the normal distribution.
- A list of key points has been added to every chapter.
- New material and more emphasis have been devoted to these topics:

    Service
    Supply chain management
    Ethical conduct
    Sustainability
    Step-by-step problem solving
- Linear programming is now a chapter rather than a chapter supplement, to allow more flexibility on when and where it is used.
- There is added emphasis on ethics in every chapter.
- Throughout the text, there are new, updated readings and photos to provide students with a motivating view of the critical importance of operations management today.
- Available for instructors, OM Video/DVD series Volumes 1–16 document the latest innovations in operations at companies such as Zappos.com, Xerox, Burton Snowboards, FedEx, Honda, and more.

Acknowledgments

I want to thank the many contributors to this edition. Over the recent editions, reviewers and adopters of the text have provided a "continuously improving" wealth of ideas and suggestions. It is encouraging to me as an author. I hope all reviewers and readers will know their suggestions were valuable, were carefully considered, and are sincerely appreciated. The list includes post-publication reviewers, focus group participants, and manuscript reviewers: Vikas Agrawal, Fayetteville State University; Bahram Alidaee, University of Mississippi; Chen Chung, University of Kentucky; Robert Clark, Stony Brook University; Kathy Dhanda, DePaul University; Richard Ehrhardt, University of North Carolina at Greensboro; Warren Fisher, Stephen F. Austin State University; Seung-Lae Kim, Drexel University; Jooh Lee, Rowan University; Gita Mathur, San Jose State University; Kaushic Sengupta, Hofstra University; Kenneth Shaw, Oregon State University; Michael Shurden, Lander University; John Simon, Governors State University; Young Son, Bernard M. Baruch College; Timothy Vaughan, University of Wisconsin at Eau Claire; Pamela Zelbst, Sam Houston State University; Tekle Wanorie, Northwest Missouri State University.

Other contributors included accuracy checkers: Michael Godfrey, University of Wisconsin at Oshkosh and Pamela Zelbst, Sam Houston State University; Test Bank: Alan Cannon, University of Texas at Arlington; Power Points: David Cook, Old Dominion University; Data Sets: Mehdi Kaighobadi, Florida Atlantic University; Excel Templates and

ScreenCam tutorials: Lee Tangedahl, University of Montana; Instructors Manual: Michael Godfrey and Pamela Zelbst.

Special thanks goes out to those subject matter experts who helped design and develop content in *Connect™ Operations Management* for this edition: Ronny Richardson of Southern Polytechnic State University who created Guided Examples and Shyam Jha, University of Arizona, Nancy Lambe, University of South Alabama, and Andrew Manikas, University of Wisconsin at Oshkosh, who designed the new assignable interactive applications.

Finally I would like to thank all the people at McGraw-Hill/Irwin for their efforts and support. It is always a pleasure to work with such a professional and competent group of people. Special thanks go to Dick Hercher, Executive Editor; Gail Korosa, Managing Developmental Editor; Bruce Gin, Project Manager; Debra Sylvester, Buyer II; Katie White, Marketing Manager; Laurie Entringer, Designer; Kerry Bowler and Ron Nelms, Media Project Managers; Keri Johnson, Photo Research and many others who worked "behind the scenes."

I would also like to thank the many reviewers of previous editions for their contributions. Ardavan Asef-Faziri, California State University at Northridge; Prabir Bagchi, George Washington State University; Gordon F. Bagot, California State University at Los Angeles; Ravi Behara, Florida Atlantic University; Michael Bendixen, Nova Southeastern; Ednilson Bernardes, Georgia Southern University; Prashanth N. Bharadwaj, Indiana University of Pennsylvania; Greg Bier, University of Missouri at Columbia; Joseph Biggs, Cal Poly State University; Kimball Bullington, Middle Tennessee State University; Alan Cannon, University of Texas at Arlington; Injazz Chen, Cleveland State University; Alan Chow, University of Southern Alabama at Mobile; Chrwan-Jyh, Oklahoma State University; Loretta Cochran, Arkansas Tech University; Lewis Coopersmith, Rider University; Richard Crandall, Appalachian State University; Dinesh Dave, Appalachian State University; Scott Dellana, East Carolina University; Xin Ding, University of Utah; Ellen Dumond, California State University at Fullerton; Kurt Engemann, Iona College; Diane Ervin, DeVry University; Farzaneh Fazel, Illinois State University; Wanda Fennell, University of Mississippi at Hattiesburg; Joy Field, Boston College; Lillian Fok, University of New Orleans; Charles Foley, Columbus State Community College; Matthew W. Ford, Northern Kentucky University; Phillip C. Fry, Boise State University; Charles A. Gates Jr., Aurora University; Tom Gattiker, Boise State University; Damodar Golhar, Western Michigan University; Robert Graham, Jacksonville State University; Angappa Gunasekaran, University of Massachusetts at Dartmouth; Haresh Gurnani, University of Miami; Terry Harrison, Penn State University; Vishwanath Hegde, California State University at East Bay; Craig Hill, Georgia State University; Jim Ho, University of Illinois at Chicago; Jonatan Jelen, Mercy College; Prafulla Joglekar, LaSalle University; Vijay Kannan, Utah State University; Sunder Kekre, Carnegie-Mellon University; Jim Keyes, University of Wisconsin at Stout; Beate Klingenberg, Marist College; John Kros, East Carolina University; Vinod Lall, Minnesota State University at Moorhead; Kenneth Lawrence, New Jersey Institute of Technology; Anita Lee-Post, University of Kentucky; Karen Lewis, University of Mississippi; Bingguang Li, Albany State University; Cheng Li, California State University at Los Angeles; Maureen P. Lojo, California State University at Sacramento; F. Victor Lu, St. John's University; Janet Lyons, Utah State University; James Maddox, Friends University; Mark McComb, Mississippi College; George Mechling, Western Carolina University; Scott Metlen, University of Idaho; Douglas Micklich, Illinois State University; Ajay Mishra, SUNY at Binghamton; Scott S. Morris, Southern Nazarene University; Philip F. Musa, University of Alabama at Birmingham; Seong Hyun Nam, University of North Dakota; Roy Nersesian, Monmouth University; John Olson, University of St. Thomas; Jeffrey Ohlmann, University of Iowa at Iowa City; Ozgur Ozluk, San Francisco State University; Kenneth Paetsch, Cleveland State University; Taeho Park, San Jose State University; Allison Pearson, Mississippi State University; Patrick Penfield, Syracuse University; Steve Peng, California State University at Hayward; Richard Peschke, Minnesota State University at Moorhead; Andru Peters, San Jose State University; Charles Phillips, Mississippi State University; Frank Pianki, Anderson University; Sharma Pillutla, Towson University; Zinovy Radovilsky, California State University at Hayward; Stephen A. Raper, University of Missouri at Rolla; Pedro Reyes, Baylor University; Buddhadev Roychoudhury, Minnesota State University at Mankato; Narendra Rustagi, Howard University; Herb Schiller, Stony Brook University; Dean T. Scott, DeVry University; Scott J. Seipel, Middle Tennessee State University; Raj Selladurai, Indiana University; Dooyoung Shin, Minnesota State University at Mankato; Raymond E. Simko, Myers University; Jake Simons, Georgia Southern University; Charles Smith, Virginia Commonwealth University; Kenneth Solheim, DeVry University; Victor Sower, Sam Houston State University; Jeremy Stafford, University of North Alabama; Donna Stewart, University of Wisconsin at Stout; Dothang Truong, Fayetteville State University; Mike Umble, Baylor University; Javad Varzandeh, California State University at San Bernardino; Emre Veral, Baruch College; Mark Vroblefski, University of Arizona; Gustavo Vulcano, New York University; Walter Wallace, Georgia State University; James Walters, Ball State University; John Wang, Montclair State University; Jerry Wei, University of Notre Dame; Michael Whittenberg, University of Texas; Geoff Willis, University of Central Oklahoma; Jiawei Zhang, NYU; Zhenying Zhao, University of Maryland; Yong-Pin Zhou, University of Washington.

William J. Stevenson

Walkthrough

MAJOR STUDY AND LEARNING FEATURES

A number of key features in this text have been specifically designed to help introductory students learn, understand, and apply Operations concepts and problem-solving techniques.

Examples with Solutions

Throughout the text, wherever a quantitative or analytic technique is introduced, an example is included to illustrate the application of that technique. These are designed to be easy to follow.

EXAMPLE 7

A furniture manufacturer wants to predict quarterly demand for a certain loveseat for periods 15 and 16, which happen to be the second and third quarters of a particular year. The series consists of both trend and seasonality. The trend portion of demand is projected using the equation $F_t = 124 + 7.5t$. Quarter relatives are $SR_1 = 1.20$, $SR_2 = 1.10$, $SR_3 = 0.75$, and $SR_4 = 0.95$.

a. Use this information to deseasonalize sales for quarters 1 through 8.

b. Use this information to predict demand for periods 15 and 16.

SOLUTION

a.

Period	Quarter	Sales	÷	Quarter Relative	=	Deseasonalized Sales
1	1	132	÷	1.20	=	110.00
2	2	140	÷	1.10	=	127.27
3	3	146	÷	0.75	=	194.67
4	4	153	÷	0.95	=	161.05
5	1	160	÷	1.20	=	133.33
6	2	168	÷	1.10	=	152.73
7	3	176	÷	0.75	=	234.67
8	4	185	÷	0.95	=	194.74

b. The trend values at $t = 15$ and $t = 16$ are:

$F_{15} = 124 + 7.5(15) = 236.5$

$F_{16} = 124 + 7.5(16) = 244.0$

Multiplying the trend value by the appropriate quarter relative yields a forecast that includes both trend and seasonality. Given that $t = 15$ is a third quarter and $t = 16$ is a fourth quarter, the forecasts are

Period 15: $236.5(0.75) = 177.38$

Period 16: $244.0(0.95) = 231.80$

Solved Problems

At the end of chapters and chapter supplements, "solved problems" are provided to illustrate problem solving and the core concepts in the chapter. These have been carefully prepared to enhance student understanding as well as to provide additional examples of problem solving. The Excel logo indicates that a spreadsheet is available on the text's Web site, to help solve the problem.

SOLVED PROBLEMS

Problem 1

www.mhhe.com/stevenson11e

A firm's manager must decide whether to make or buy a certain item used in the production of vending machines. Making the item would involve annual lease costs of $150,000. Cost and volume estimates are as follows:

	Make	Buy
Annual fixed cost	$150,000	None
Variable cost/unit	$60	$80
Annual volume (units)	12,000	12,000

a. Given these numbers, should the firm buy or make this item?

b. There is a possibility that volume could change in the future. At what volume would the manager be indifferent between making and buying?

Solution

a. Determine the annual cost of each alternative:

Total cost = Fixed cost + Volume × Variable cost

Make: $150,000 + 12,000($60) = $870,000
Buy: 0 + 12,000($80) = $960,000

Because the annual cost of making the item is less than the annual cost of buying it, the manager would reasonably choose to make the item. *Note:* If the unit cost to buy had been *less than* the *variable cost* to make, there would be no need to even consider fixed costs; it would simply have

...ume at which the two choices would be equivalent, set the two total costs ...nd solve for volume: $TC_{make} = TC_{buy}$. Thus, $150,000 + Q($60) = 0 + ... = 7,500 units. Therefore, at a volume of 7,500 units a year, the manager ...etween making and buying. For lower volumes, the choice would be to buy, ...es, the choice would be to make.

Excel solution:

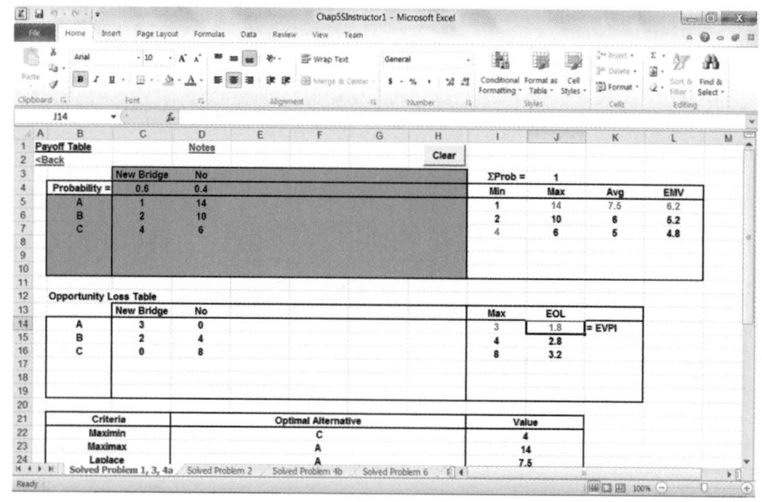

Placing the problem data in the cell positions shown, the expected monetary value (EMV) for each alternative is shown in column J.

Then, the overall EMV is obtained in column J as the maximum of the values in J5, J6, and J7.

The EVPI is obtained using the Opportunity Loss Table by summing the product of the maximum in column C2 and the probability in C4, and the product of the maximum in column D and the probability in D4.

Excel Spreadsheet Solutions

Where applicable, the examples and solved problems include screen shots of a spreadsheet solution. Many of these were taken from the Excel templates, which are on the text's Web site. Templates are programmed to be fully functional in Excel 2007 and Excel 2003.

CHAPTER ELEMENTS

Within each chapter, you will find the following elements that are designed to facilitate study and learning. All of these have been carefully developed over eleven editions and have proven to be successful.

Chapter Outlines

Every chapter and supplement includes an outline of the topics covered.

CHAPTER

Introduction to Operations Management

CHAPTER OUTLINE

LEARNING OBJECTIVES

After completing this chapter, you should be able to:

1 Define the term *operations management.*
2 Identify the three major functional areas of organizations and describe how they interrelate.
3 Identify similarities and differences between production and service operations.
4 Describe the operations function and the nature of the operations manager's job.
5 Summarize the two major aspects of process management.
6 Explain the key aspects of operations management decision making.
7 Briefly describe the historical evolution of operations management.
8 Characterize current trends in business that impact operations management.

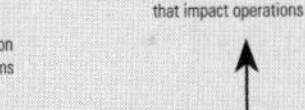

Recalls of automobiles, eggs, produce, toys, and other products; major oil spills; and even dysfunctional state legislatures are all examples of operations failures. They underscore the need for effective operations management.

This book is about operations management. The subject matter is fascinating and timely: Productivity, quality, e-business, global competition, and customer service are very much in the news, and all are part of operations management. This first chapter presents an introduction and overview of operations management. Among the issues it addresses are: What is operations management? Why is it important? What do operations management professionals do?

The chapter also provides a brief description of the historical evolution of operations management and a discussion of the trends and issues that impact operations management.

More specifically, you will learn about (1) the economic balance that every business organization seeks to achieve; (2) the condition that generally exists that makes achieving the economic balance challenging; (3) the line function that is the core of every business organization; (4) key steps in the history and evolution of operations management; (5) the differences and similarities between producing products and delivering services; (6) what a supply chain is, and why it is important to manage it; and (7) the key issues for today's business operations.

Learning Objectives

Every chapter and supplement lists the learning objectives as a short guide to studying the chapter.

Opening Vignettes

Each chapter opens with an introduction to the important operations topics covered in the chapter. Students need to see the relevance of operations management in order to actively engage in learning the material.

Figures and Photos

The text includes photographs and graphic illustrations to support student learning and provide interest and motivation. Approximately 100 carefully selected photos highlight the eleventh edition. Many of the photos provide additional examples of companies that use operations and supply chain concepts. More than 400 graphic illustrations, more than any other text in the field, are included and all are color coded with pedagogical consistency to assist students in understanding concepts.

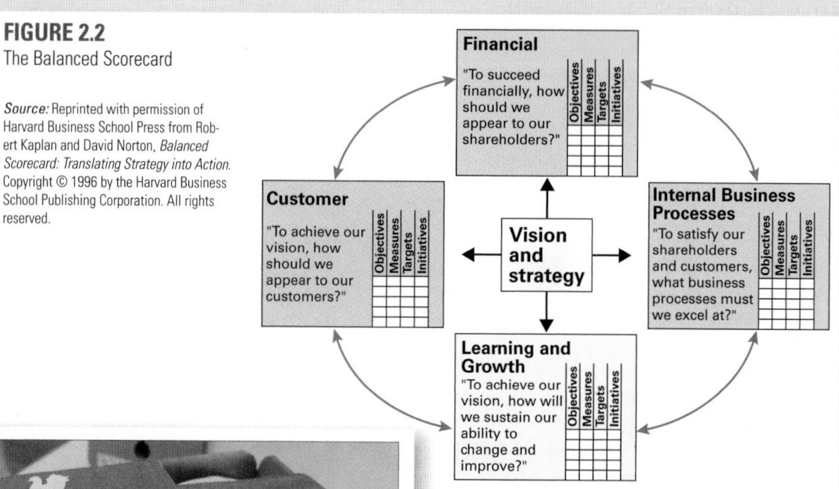

FIGURE 2.2
The Balanced Scorecard

Source: Reprinted with permission of Harvard Business School Press from Robert Kaplan and David Norton, *Balanced Scorecard: Translating Strategy into Action.* Copyright © 1996 by the Harvard Business School Publishing Corporation. All rights reserved.

Puma's "Clever Little Bag" changes the idea of the shoebox by wrapping footwear in a cardboard structure with 65 percent less cardboard. It uses a bag made of recycled plastic as the outer layer that holds the inner cardboard structure together. Puma expects to cut carbon dioxide emissions by 10,000 tons per year and water, energy, and diesel use by 60 percent by using fewer materials—8,500 fewer tons of paper to be specific—and the new packaging's lighter weight.

Icons

Icons are included throughout the text, to point out relevant applications in a discussion or concept. These include: Service icons to alert students to examples that are service oriented; Supply chain icons to indicate that the text refers to the supply chain; Excel icons to point out Excel applications; and ScreenCam Tutorial icons to link to the tutorials on the text's Web site.

SERVICE

SUPPLY CHAIN

SCREENCAM TUTORIAL

Operations Strategies

Throughout the text, whenever the concepts being presented have significant strategic implications for firms, a distinctive heading is placed to signify that text will relate to strategic issues.

OPERATIONS STRATEGY

Forecasts are the basis for many decisions and an essential input for matching supply and demand. Clearly, the more accurate an organization's forecasts, the better prepared it will be to take advantage of future opportunities and reduce potential risks. A worthwhile strategy can be to work to improve short-term forecasts. Better short-term forecasts will not only enhance profits through lower inventory levels, fewer shortages, and improved customer service, they also will enhance forecasting *credibility* throughout the organization: If short-term forecasts are inaccurate, why should other areas of the organization put faith in long-term forecasts? Also, the sense of confidence accurate short-term forecasts would generate would allow allocating more resources to strategic and medium- to longer-term planning and less on short-term, tactical activities.

Maintaining accurate, up-to-date information on prices, demand, and other variables can have a significant impact on forecast accuracy. An organization also can do other things to improve forecasts. These do not involve searching for improved techniques but relate to the inverse relation of accuracy to the forecast horizon: Forecasts that cover shorter time frames tend to be more accurate than longer-term forecasts. Recognizing this, management might choose to devote efforts to *shortening the time horizon that forecasts must cover.* Essentially, this means shortening the *lead time* needed to respond to a forecast. This might involve building *flexibility* into operations to permit rapid response to changing demands for products and services, or to changing volumes in quantities der
obtain supplies, equipment, and raw materials or
ees; or shortening the time needed to *develop* nev

Lean systems are demand driven; goods are pr
inventory until demand arises. Consequently, the
casts than more traditional systems.

Readings

Throughout the text, and in the assignment sections of some chapters, are readings. These highlight important real-world applications, provide examples of production/operations issues, and offer further elaboration of the text material. They also provide a basis for classroom discussion and generate interest in the subject matter. Many of the end-of-chapter readings include assignment questions.

Kraft Foods' Recipe for Sustainability

READING

The threat of global warming and the desire to protect the environment has many companies embracing sustainability initiatives. And they are finding that in many instances, there are cost savings in doing so. Among them is the Kraft Foods company, whose well-known brands include Cool Whip, Philadelphia Cream Cheese, DiGiorno pizza, Oscar Mayer, Oreo cookies, and Kraft cheeses and salad dressings. Kraft is the world's second largest food company with 100,000 employees and annual revenues of $42 billion. The company is a member of the Dow Jones Sustainability Index and the Ethibel Sustainability Index.

The company has set some ambitious goals that it wants to achieve:

- Reduce plant energy usage by 25 percent.
- Reduce plant energy-related carbon dioxide emissions by 25 percent.
- Reduce plant water consumption by 15 percent.
- Reduce plant waste by 15 percent.
- Eliminate 150 million pounds of packaging material from the supply chain.

Some of Kraft's successes have come from redesigned packaging. The goal is ambitious. It will require more efficient packaging and a reduction in the amount of packaging material used. Kraft believes that the greatest opportunity to reduce the environmental impact of a package is early in the design phase. Their packaging designers worldwide critically consider the amount of packaging used, how much postconsumer material can be used, how much energy is used to create the packing materials, how much CO_2 is generated as the materials are created and formed, and how well the package fits the product physically. According to Kraft's press releases, examples and benefits of recent packaging redesigns include:

- DiGiorno and California Pizza Kitchen pizzas: Using slimmer cartons that allow shipment of two extra pizza boxes per case and 14 percent more pizzas per pallet. This leads to a savings of approximately 1.4 million pounds of packaging per year, and the ability to load more pizzas on each truck means there are fewer trucks on the road and less fuel consumed.
- Oscar Mayer Deli Creations: Using 30 percent less paperboard than the previous design results in 1.2 million fewer pounds of packaging going to landfills.

Kraft Natural Cheese new packaging zipper eliminates more than one million pounds of packaging per year.

- Kraft salad dressing: Using 19 percent less plastic per bottle translates to 3 million pounds fewer annually. Additionally the new design allows more bottles to be shipped per truckload, leading to an increase in transportation efficiency of 18 percent.

The company is also working to help the environment, reduce water pollution/soil erosion, and support biodiversity. Considering these successes, Kraft's recipe for sustainability is one that other companies should emulate.

END-OF-CHAPTER RESOURCES

For student study and review, the following items are provided at the end of each chapter or chapter supplement.

Summaries

Chapters contain summaries that provide an overview of the material covered.

Key Points

The key points of the chapter are emphasized.

KEY POINTS

1. A range of factors can cause an organization to design or redesign a product or service, including economic, legal, political, social, technological, and competitive pressures. Furthermore, an important cause of operations failures can be traced to faulty design.
2. Every area of a business organization, and its supply chain, is connected to, and influenced by, its products and/or services, so the potential impact on each area must be taken into account when products or services are redesigned or new products or services are to be designed.
3. Central issues relate to the actual or expected demand for a product or service, the organization's capabilities, the cost to produce or provide, the desired quality level, and the cost and availability of necessary resources.
4. Among considerations that are generally important are legal, ethical, and environmental.
5. Although there are some basic differences between product design and service design, there are many similarities between the two.

Key Terms

Key terms are highlighted in the text and then repeated in the margin with brief definitions for emphasis. They are listed at the end of each chapter (along with page references) to aid in reviewing.

Taking Stock and Critical Thinking Exercises

These activities encourage analytical thinking and help broaden conceptual understanding. A question related to ethics is included in the Critical Thinking Exercises.

TAKING STOCK

1. Explain the trade-off between responsiveness and stability in a forecasting system that uses time series data.
2. Who needs to be involved in preparing forecasts?
3. How has technology had an impact on forecasting?

CRITICAL THINKING EXERCISES

1. It has been said that forecasting using exponential smoothing is like driving a car by looking in the rear-view mirror. What are the conditions that would have to exist for driving a car that are analogous to the assumptions made when using exponential smoothing?
2. What capability would an organization have to have to not need forecasts?
3. When a new business is started, or a patent idea needs funding, venture capitalists or investment bankers will want to see a business plan that includes forecast information related to a profit and loss statement. What type of forecasting information do you suppose would be required?
4. Discuss how you would manage a poor forecast.
5. Omar has heard from some of his customers that they will probably cut back on order sizes in the next quarter. The company he works for has been reducing its sales force due to falling demand and he worries that he could be next if his sales begin to fall off. Believing that he may be able to convince his customers not to cut back on orders, he turns in an optimistic forecast of his next quarter sales to his manager. Is that ethical?

Discussion and Review Questions

Each chapter and each supplement have a list of discussion and review questions. These precede the problem sets and are intended to serve as a student self-review or as class discussion starters.

Problem Sets

Each chapter includes a set of problems for assignment. The problems have been refined over many editions and are intended to be challenging but doable for students. Check-answers to most of the problems are included in Appendix A so that students can see immediately how they are progressing.

PROBLEMS

1. Examine and compare one of the following product sets. Base your comparison on such factors as features, costs, convenience, ease of use, ease and/or cost of repair, and safety.
   a. VCR players versus DVD players.
   b. Cell phones versus landlines.
   c. Wide-screen versus traditional television sets.
   d. Standard gasoline automobile engines versus hybrids.
   e. Standard wooden mousetraps versus new plastic mousetraps.
   f. Satellite television versus cable.
2. Use the Internet to obtain recent crash-safety ratings for passenger vehicles. Then answer these questions:
   a. Which vehicles received the highest ratings? The lowest ratings?
   b. How important are crash-safety ratings to new car buyers? Does the degree of importance depend on the circumstances of the buyer?
   c. Which types of buyers would you expect to be the most concerned with crash-safety ratings?
   d. Are there other features of a new car that might sway a buyer from focusing solely on crash safety? If so, what might they be?
3. Prepare a service blueprint for each of these banking transactions:
   a. Make a savings deposit using a teller.
   b. Apply for a home equity loan.

Operations Tours

These provide a simple "walkthrough" of an operation for students, describing the company, its product or service, and its process of managing operations. Companies featured include Wegmans Food Markets, Morton Salt, Stickley Furniture, and Boeing.

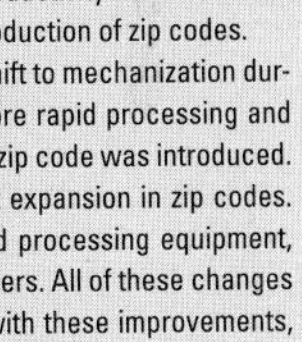

The U.S. Postal Service — OPERATIONS TOUR

"Neither rain, nor snow . . ."

The U.S. Postal Service (USPS) is the largest postal service in the world, handling about 41 percent (630 million pieces a day) of the world's mail volume. The second largest is Japan's, which handles only about 6 percent of the world's mail. The USPS is huge by any standard. It employs over 760,000 workers, making it the largest civilian employer in the United States. It has over 300,000 mail collection boxes, 38,000 post offices, 130 million mail delivery points, more than 300 processing plants to sort and ship mail, and more than 75,000 pieces of mail processing equipment. It handles over 100 billion pieces of first-class mail a year, and ships about 3 billion pounds of mail on commercial airline flights, making it the airlines' largest shipper.

Processing First-Class Mail

The essence of processing the mail is sorting, which means organizing the mail into smaller and smaller subgroups to facilitate its timely delivery. Sorting involves a combination of manual and automatic operations. Much of the mail that is processed is first-class mail.

Most first-class mail is handled using automated equipment. A

Productivity

Over the years, the USPS has experienced an ever-increasing volume of mail. Productivity has been an important factor for the USPS in keeping postal rates low and maintaining rapid delivery service. Two key factors in improved productivity have been the increased use of automation and the introduction of zip codes.

Mail processing underwent a major shift to mechanization during the 1950s and 1960s, which led to more rapid processing and higher productivity. In 1978, an expanded zip code was introduced. That was followed in 1983 by a four-digit expansion in zip codes. These changes required new, automated processing equipment, and the use of bar codes and optical readers. All of these changes added greatly to productivity. But even with these improvements, the USPS faced increasing competitive pressures.

Competition

In the late 1980s, the USPS experienced a slowdown in the volume of mail. Some of this was due to a slowing of the economy, but most of it was the result of increasing competition. Delivery giants FedEx and UPS, as well as other companies that offer speedy delivery and package tracking, gave businesses and the general public conve-
...tives for some mail services. At the same time, there
...g use of fax machines and electronic communications
...d use of alternate forms of advertising such as cable
...ch cut into the volume of mail. Early in this century,
...tomated bill paying also cut into mail volume.

Outsourcing of Hospital Services — CASE

Due to financial pressures that many hospitals face, the Deaconess Clinic in Billings, Montana, decided to outsource a number of services, although in somewhat different ways.

First, the hospital outsourced its cafeteria food service. Although the food service employees were hired by the outside firm, they still felt a sense of ownership of their jobs, and still felt connected to the hospital because of the family atmosphere in the kitchen and the cafeteria.

When the hospital tried the same thing with housekeeping, employee turnover became a problem. An investigation revealed that because the housekeeping employees were more isolated in their work, they lost what little feeling of being connected to the hospital they had. The problem was solved by hiring the employees back but using the outsource company to manage housekeeping.

The hospital also decided to outsource its laundry service. This time the hospital approached a rival hospital about joining it in outsourcing laundry service.

Questions

1. In some instances the outsourced service occurs in a different location, while in others it takes place inside the organization doing the outsourcing, as the food service did in this case. What advantages were there in having the outsourced work performed within the hospital? Suppose a different hospital outsourced its food service but decided not to have the work performed in-house. What might its rationale be?
2. In the housekeeping situation, why not just forget about outsourcing, especially since the hospital ended up rehiring its employees anyway?
3. For laundry service, what might have been the rationale for asking another hospital to join it?

Source: Based on Norm Friedman, "Is Outsourcing the Solution?" www.hpnonline.com/inside/June04/outsourcing.htm.

Cases

The text includes short cases. The cases were selected to provide a broader, more integrated thinking opportunity for students without taking a full case approach.

ASSURANCE OF LEARNING READY

Many educational institutions today are focused on the notion of *assurance of learning,* an important element of some accreditation standards. *Operations Management* is designed specifically to support your assurance of learning initiatives with a simple, yet powerful, solution.

Each test bank question for *Operations Management* maps to a specific chapter learning outcome/objective listed in the text. You can use our test bank software, EZ Test and EZ Test Online, or Connect Operations Management to easily query for learning outcomes/objectives that directly relate to the learning objectives for your course. You can then use the reporting features of EZ Test to aggregate student results in similar fashion, making the collection and presentation of assurance of learning data simple and easy.

AACSB STATEMENT

The McGraw-Hill Companies is a proud corporate member of AACSB International. Understanding the importance and value of AACSB accreditation, *Operations Management* recognizes the curricula guidelines detailed in the AACSB standards for business accreditation by connecting selected questions in the test bank to the six general knowledge and skill areas in the AACSB's Assessment of Learning Standards.

The statements contained in *Operations Management* are provided only as a guide for the users of this textbook. The AACSB leaves content coverage and assessment within the purview of individual schools, the mission of the school, and the faculty. While *Operations Management* and the teaching package make no claim of any specific AACSB qualification or evaluation, we have within the test bank labeled questions according to the six general knowledge and skill areas.

FOR INSTRUCTORS

Instructor Resource CD-ROM (ISBN 0077327446)

This all-in-one resource incorporates the Instructor's Manual, Test Bank, EZ Test, PowerPoint slides, Instructor PowerPoint slides, Excel Lecture Scripts, Data Sets, Textbook Art Files, and Chapter Study Outlines.

Instructor's Manual

Prepared by William J. Stevenson, Michael Godfrey, and Pamela Zelbst, this manual includes "teaching notes" for each chapter and complete solutions to all text problems. Also included are several enrichment modules that cover such topics as Simplex, Vogel's Approximation, Distance Measurement, and Emergency Facility Location.

Test Bank and EZ Test

Prepared by Alan Cannon, the Test Bank includes over 2,000 questions and problems for exams. All of these have been class tested by the author or contributors. EZ Test is a flexible electronic testing program.

PowerPoint Lecture Slides

Prepared by David Cook, Old Dominion University, the PowerPoint slides draw on the highlights of each chapter and provide an opportunity for the instructor to emphasize the more relevant visuals in class discussions.

Excel Lecture Scripts

Prepared by Lee Tangedahl, University of Montana, the scripts provide suggestions on using Excel and the templates in classroom lectures.

Online Learning Center (OLC)—Text's Web Site www.mhhe.com/stevenson11e

The Online Learning Center includes faculty teaching supplements such as

- Instructor's Manual
- PowerPoint Lecture Slides for instructors
- Test Bank
- Lecture Scripts – How to demonstrate OM concepts using Excel
- Updates and Errata
- Supplementary Problems and Solutions
- Excel Solution Templates

FOR STUDENTS

Online Learning Center (OLC)—Text's Web Site www.mhhe.com/stevenson11e

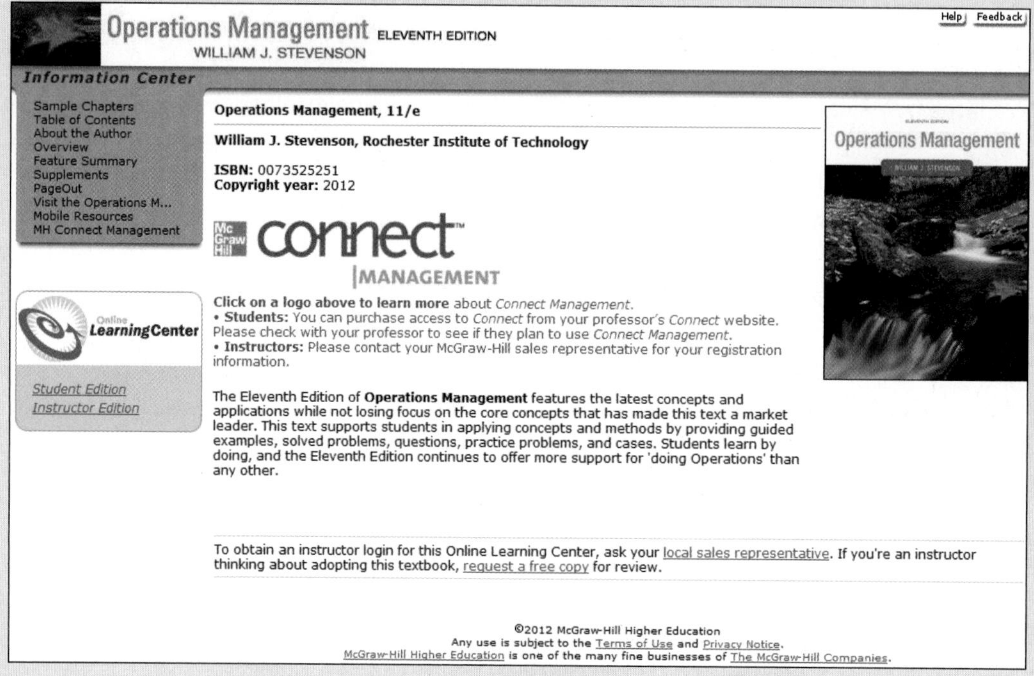

The Online Learning Center provides a wealth of materials for study and review, as well as enrichment.

- Excel Template/Data Files
- Multiple Choice Quizzes
- PowerPoint Slides for students
- Advanced Topics
- Interactive Operations Management (IOM) Java applets
- ScreenCam Tutorials
- Updates and Errata
- Chapter Study Outlines
- Memo-writing Exercises
- Experiential Exercises

(All of these are also included in the Instructor's Edition of the Online Learning Center.)

ScreenCam Tutorials

These screen "movies" and voiceover tutorials explain key chapter content, using Excel and other software platforms.

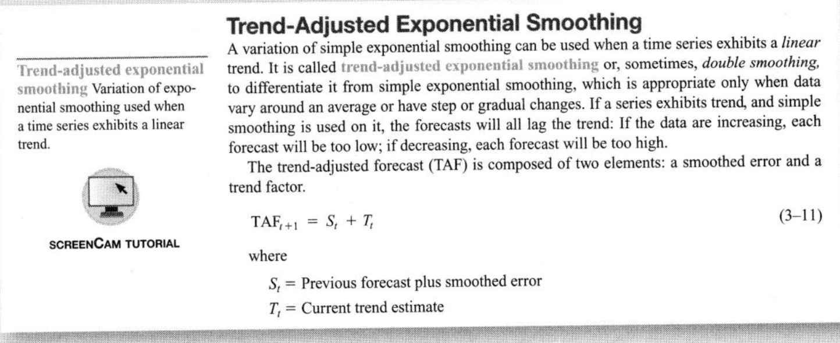

Trend-Adjusted Exponential Smoothing

Trend-adjusted exponential smoothing Variation of exponential smoothing used when a time series exhibits a linear trend.

SCREENCAM TUTORIAL

A variation of simple exponential smoothing can be used when a time series exhibits a *linear* trend. It is called **trend-adjusted exponential smoothing** or, sometimes, *double smoothing,* to differentiate it from simple exponential smoothing, which is appropriate only when data vary around an average or have step or gradual changes. If a series exhibits trend, and simple smoothing is used on it, the forecasts will all lag the trend: If the data are increasing, each forecast will be too low; if decreasing, each forecast will be too high.

The trend-adjusted forecast (TAF) is composed of two elements: a smoothed error and a trend factor.

$$TAF_{t+1} = S_t + T_t \quad (3\text{–}11)$$

where

S_t = Previous forecast plus smoothed error

T_t = Current trend estimate

Excel Templates

Templates created by Lee Tangedahl, University of Montana, are included on the OLC. The templates, over 70 total, include dynamically linked graphics and variable controls. They allow you to solve a number of problems in the text or additional problems. All templates have been revised to allow formatting of all cells, hiding rows or columns, and entering data or calculations in blank cells. Many of the templates have been expanded to accommodate solving larger problems and cases.

TABLE 3.1 Excel Solution for Example 5

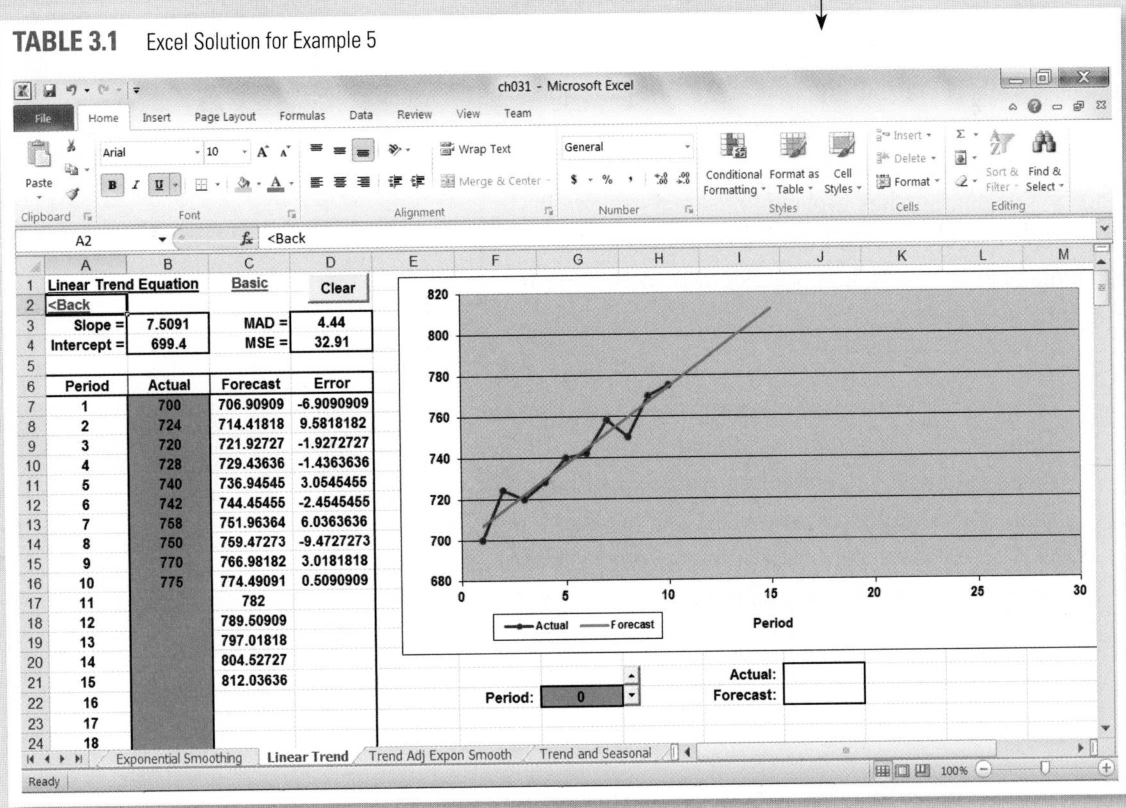

	A	B	C	D
1	Linear Trend Equation		Basic	Clear
2	<Back			
3	Slope =	7.5091	MAD =	4.44
4	Intercept =	699.4	MSE =	32.91
5				
6	Period	Actual	Forecast	Error
7	1	700	706.90909	-6.9090909
8	2	724	714.41818	9.5818182
9	3	720	721.92727	-1.9272727
10	4	728	729.43636	-1.4363636
11	5	740	736.94545	3.0545455
12	6	742	744.45455	-2.4545455
13	7	758	751.96364	6.0363636
14	8	750	759.47273	-9.4727273
15	9	770	766.98182	3.0181818
16	10	775	774.49091	0.5090909
17	11		782	
18	12		789.50909	
19	13		797.01818	
20	14		804.52727	
21	15		812.03636	
22	16			
23	17			
24	18			

McGraw-Hill *Connect Operations Management* is an online assignment and assessment solution that connects your students with the tools and resources needed to achieve success through faster learning, more efficient studying, and higher retention of knowledge.

Online Assignments: *Connect Operations Management* helps students learn more efficiently by providing feedback and practice material when they need it, where they need it. *Connect* grades homework automatically and gives immediate feedback on any questions students may have missed.

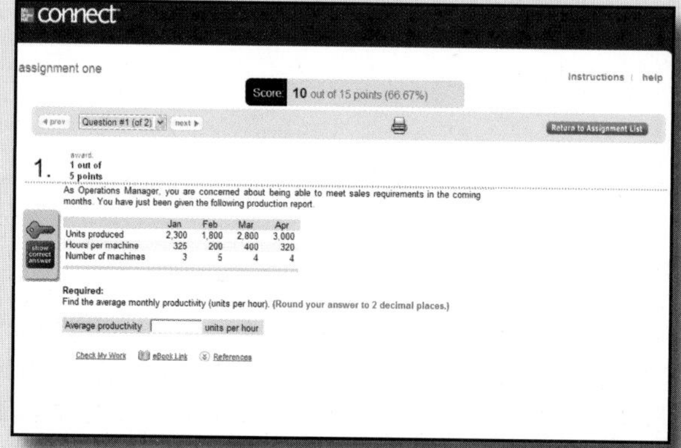

Interactive Presentations: The interactive presentations provide engaging narratives of all chapter learning objectives in an interactive online format. The presentations are tied specifically to *Operations Management,* 11e. They follow the structure of the text and are organized to match the learning objectives within each chapter. While the interactive presentations are not meant to replace the textbook in this course, they provide additional explanation and enhancement of material from the text chapter, allowing students to learn, study, and practice with instant feedback at their own pace.

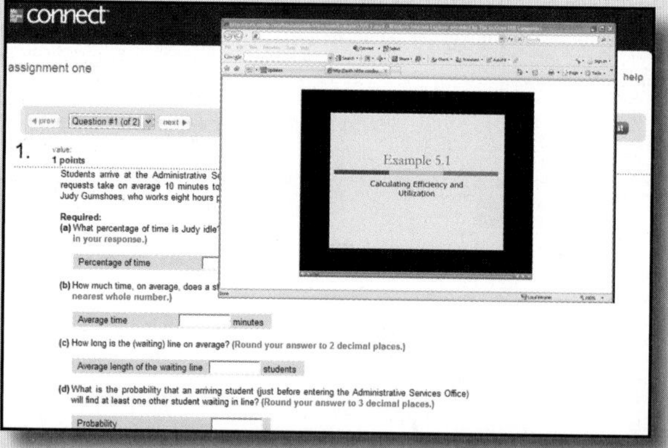

Student Resource Library: The *Connect Operations Management* Student Study Center gives access to additional resources such as recorded lectures, PowerPoint slides, Excel templates and data sets, video library, online practice materials, an eBook, and more.

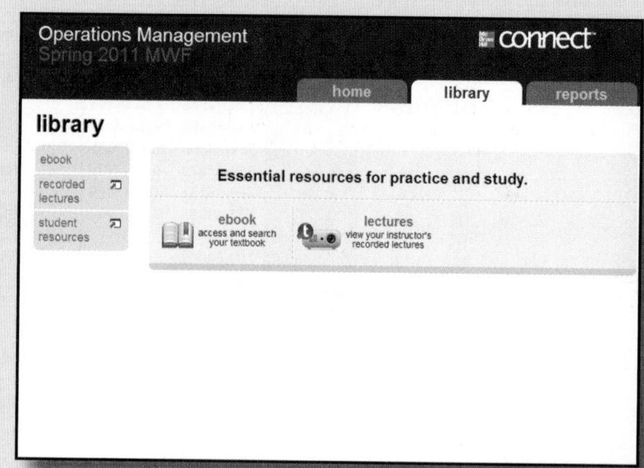

Connect Operations Management offers a number of powerful tools and features to make managing assignments easier, so faculty can spend more time teaching. With *Connect Operations Management*, students can engage with their coursework anytime and anywhere, making the learning process more accessible and efficient.

Simple Assignment Management and Smart Grading

With *Connect Operations Management*, creating assignments is easier than ever, so you can spend more time teaching and less time managing. *Connect Operations Management* enables you to:

- Create and deliver assignments easily with select end-of-chapter problems and test bank items.
- Go paperless with the eBook and online submission and grading of student assignments.
- Have assignments scored automatically, giving students immediate feedback on their work and side-by-side comparisons with correct answers.
- Reinforce and preview classroom concepts with practice tests and instant quizzes.

Student Reporting

Connect Operations Management keeps instructors informed about how each student, section, and class is performing, allowing for more productive use of lecture and office hours. The reporting function enables you to:

- View scored work immediately and track individual or group performance with assignment and grade reports.
- Access an instant view of student or class performance relative to learning objectives.
- Collect data and generate reports required by many accreditation organizations, such as the AACSB.

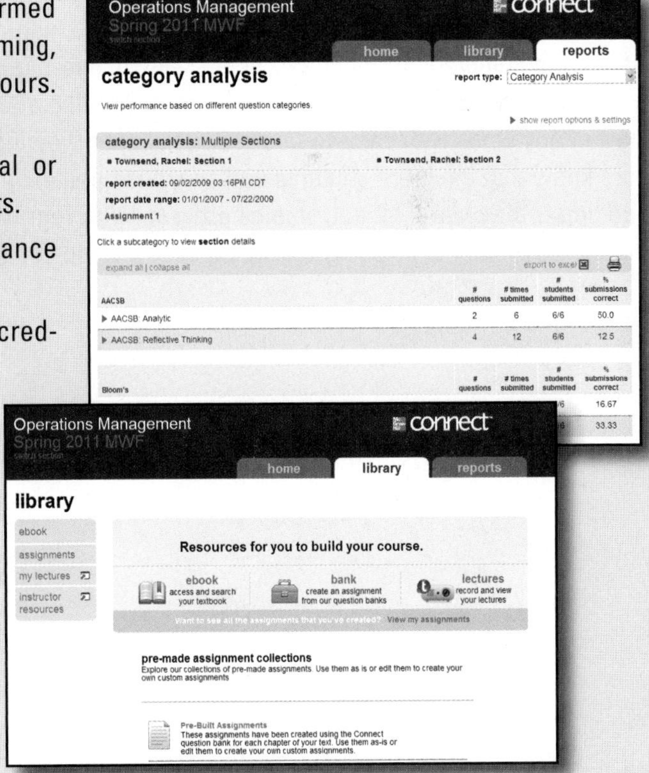

Instructor Library

The *Connect Operations Management* Instructor Library is your repository for additional resources to improve student engagement in and out of class. You can select and use any asset that enhances your course approach. The *Connect Operations Management* Instructor Library includes: access to the eBook version of the text, PowerPoint files, Instructor's Manual, and Test Bank.

McGraw-Hill *Connect Plus Operations Management*

- An integrated eBook, allowing for anytime, anywhere access to the textbook.
- Dynamic links between the problems or questions you assign to your students and the location in the eBook where that problem or question is covered.
- A powerful search function to pinpoint and connect key concepts in a snap.

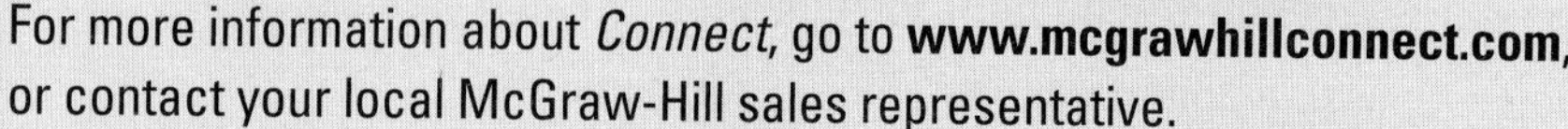
For more information about *Connect*, go to **www.mcgrawhillconnect.com**, or contact your local McGraw-Hill sales representative.

TEGRITY CAMPUS: LECTURES 24/7

Tegrity Campus is a service that makes class time available 24/7 by automatically capturing every lecture in a searchable format for students to review when they study and complete assignments. With a simple one-click start-and-stop process, you capture all computer screens and corresponding audio. Students can replay any part of any class with easy-to-use browser-based viewing on a PC or Mac. Educators know that the more students can see, hear, and experience class resources, the better they learn. In fact, studies prove it. With Tegrity Campus, students quickly recall key moments by using Tegrity Campus's unique search feature.

Operations Management Center (OMC)

The OM Center, edited and maintained by Byron Finch, provides additional operations management resources for both students and instructors. Please consider this as your site for pedagogical support or reference and for getting current OM information. To explore, visit http://www.mhhe.com/pom.

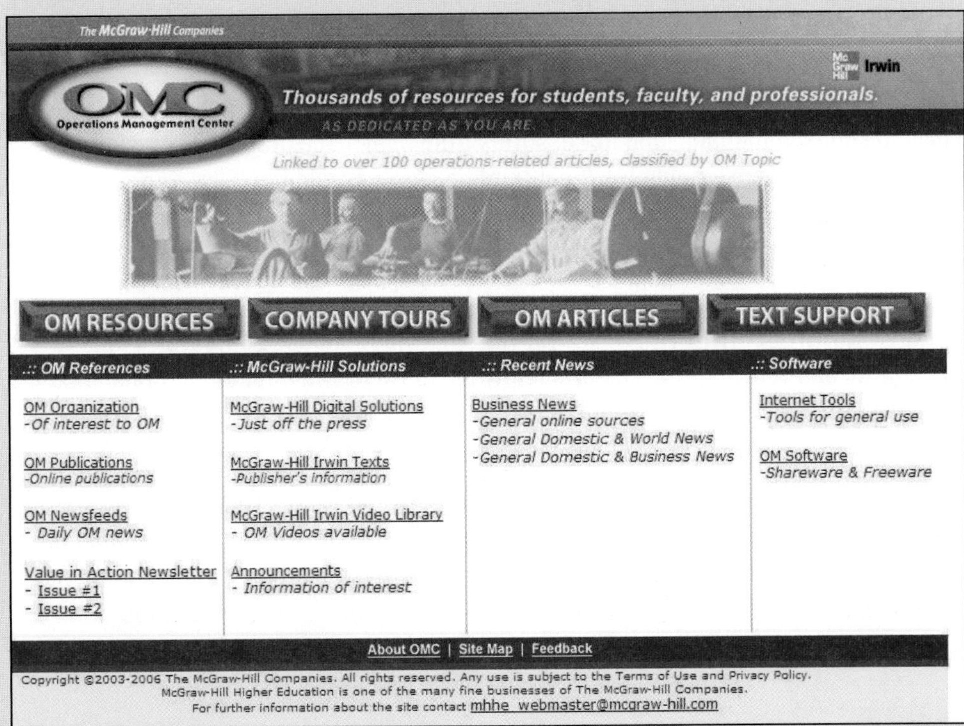

VIDEO LIBRARY

The OM Video Series includes professionally developed videos showing students real applications of key manufacturing and service topics. For a full description of all volumes, visit http://www.mhhe.com/pom/video-frames.htm.

Volume 14 (ISBN 0073278785), DVD

Service at Zappos.com (13:14) Zappos.com currently stocks more than 3 million shoes, handbags, and accessories from over 1,100 brands. Their slogan, "Powered by Service" highlights their emphasis on a service culture. Featured in this video is the company's random access inventory system and distinctive spider-merge conveyor system which speeds shipping time.

Green Manufacturing at Xerox (9:42) This video focuses on Xerox's goal to use energy and raw materials as efficiently as possible while reducing the amount of waste through sustainable product design.

Burton Snowboards—Manufacturing Design (19:34) This segment takes the viewer on a plant tour of the Burton Snowboards factory in Vermont, showcasing their unique manufacturing and design process. Focusing on their "Just enough system" and built-to-order process, the step-by-step, hand-customized board build process is presented in depth.

Volume 15 (ISBN 007336486X), DVD

Noodles & Company—Service Process Design (8:17) Noodles & Company uses business processes to provide quality food in a speedy manner. Everything from location to layout is designed to improve the order process. Line flow for customers and line flow for the food are examined. Division of tasks and failsafing each station allows team members to succeed. FIFO and JIT are also discussed.

Honda-Green Product Design and PHILL (8:25) The Honda Civic GX is similar to the Civic, but is powered by natural gas for environmental and cost efficiencies. They share most of the same components and can use the same assembly line for efficient operations and to meet demand.

FedEx—Logistics and Customer Service (7:20) FedEx has long been known for its small package delivery service. This video focuses on the logistics in freight shipments involving FedEx's vast plane and ground network and technology. Customer service is a high priority, developed in its Customer Critical Service Center.

Volume 16 (ISBN 0077248341), DVD "Profitable Sustainability" featuring Subaru of Indiana

Segment 1 Reduce (8:02) At Subaru the first and most cost-effective sustainability initiative is reduction—bringing less onsite. This segment provides examples such as reducing sealant, based on associate (employee) suggestions. Another example is using new technology to analyze the internal structure of welds, thus reducing the normal destruction method of testing and examining the welds. As a result of these and other initiatives, Subaru sends no waste to landfills.

Segment 2 Reuse (7:47) Subaru's goal is to reuse all materials that are not leaving the plant within a finished automobile. Examples include reusing containers and packaging. In some cases, packaging for engine blocks has been shipped back and forth from suppliers as many as seven or eight times before being recycled. All plastic, paper, wood, and even fluorescent lightbulbs are recycled. Over 95 percent of wood pallets are returned multiple times to vendors—an annual cost saving of $1.3 million.

Segment 3 Recycle (7:58) Recycling includes setting up sorting systems that match recycler input. For example, different plastics are sorted on the spot to specifically match different recycler needs and to be a better "supplier" to them. Hazardous waste contained in fluorescent lightbulbs is prepped for recycling by way of a "bulb eater" that compresses glass and metal and separates them from hazardous waste such as mercury. Even floor sweepings at welding stations are packaged for metal recyclers.

Note to the Student

The material in this text is part of the core knowledge in your education. Consequently, you will derive considerable benefit from your study of operations management, *regardless of your major.* Practically speaking, operations is a course in *management.*

This book describes principles and concepts of operations management. You should be aware that many of these principles and concepts are applicable to other aspects of your professional and personal life. You can expect the benefits of your study of operations management to serve you in those other areas as well.

Some students approach this course with apprehension, and perhaps even some negative feelings. It may be that they have heard that the course contains a certain amount of quantitative material that they feel uncomfortable with, or that the subject matter is dreary, or that the course is about "factory management." This is unfortunate, because the subject matter of this book is interesting and vital for all business students. While it is true that some of the material is quantitative, numerous examples, solved problems, and answers at the back of the book will help you with the quantitative material. As for "factory management," there is material on manufacturing as well as on services. Manufacturing is important, and something that you should know about for a number of reasons. Look around you. Most of the "things" you see were manufactured: cars, trucks, planes, clothing, shoes, computers, books, pens and pencils, desks, and cell phones. And these are just the tip of the iceberg. So it makes sense to know something about how these things are produced. Beyond all that is the fact that manufacturing is largely responsible for the high standard of living people have in industrialized countries.

After reading each chapter or supplement in the text, attending related classroom lectures, and completing assigned questions and problems, you should be able to do each of the following:

1. *Identify the key features* of that material.
2. *Define and use terminology.*
3. *Solve typical problems.*
4. *Recognize applications* of the concepts and techniques covered.
5. *Discuss the subject matter* in some depth, including its relevance, managerial considerations, and advantages and limitations.

You will encounter a number of chapter supplements. Check with your instructor to determine whether to study them.

This book places an emphasis on problem solving. There are many examples throughout the text illustrating solutions. In addition, at the end of most chapters and supplements you will find a group of solved problems. The examples within the chapter itself serve to illustrate concepts and techniques. Too much detail at those points would be counterproductive. Yet, later on, when you begin to solve the end-of-chapter problems, you will find the solved problems quite helpful. Moreover, those solved problems usually illustrate more and different details than the problems within the chapter.

I suggest the following approach to increase your chances of getting an "A" in the course:

1. Look over the chapter outline and learning objectives.
2. Read the chapter summary, and then skim the chapter.
3. Read the chapter and take notes.
4. Look over and try to answer the discussion and review questions.
5. Solve the problems, referring to the solved problems and chapter examples as needed.
6. Take the quizzes on the text's Web site.

Note that the answers to many problems are given at the end of the book. Try to solve each problem before turning to the answer. Remember—tests don't come with answers.

An Online Learning Center (www.mhhe.com/stevenson11e) is also available, containing many of the same study tools found in the text.

And here is one final thought: Homework is on the Highway to Happiness! Enjoy the journey!

W.J.S.

Brief Contents

Contents

Operations Management

Introduction to Operations Management

CHAPTER OUTLINE

LEARNING OBJECTIVES

After completing this chapter, you should be able to:

1. Define the term *operations management.*
2. Identify the three major functional areas of organizations and describe how they interrelate.
3. Identify similarities and differences between production and service operations.
4. Describe the operations function and the nature of the operations manager's job.
5. Summarize the two major aspects of process management.
6. Explain the key aspects of operations management decision making.
7. Briefly describe the historical evolution of operations management.
8. Characterize current trends in business that impact operations management.

Recalls of automobiles, eggs, produce, toys, and other products; major oil spills; and even dysfunctional state legislatures are all examples of operations failures. They underscore the need for effective operations management.

This book is about operations management. The subject matter is fascinating and timely: Productivity, quality, e-business, global competition, and customer service are very much in the news, and all are part of operations management. This first chapter presents an introduction and overview of operations management. Among the issues it addresses are: What is operations management? Why is it important? What do operations management professionals do?

The chapter also provides a brief description of the historical evolution of operations management and a discussion of the trends and issues that impact operations management.

More specifically, you will learn about (1) the economic balance that every business organization seeks to achieve; (2) the condition that generally exists that makes achieving the economic balance challenging; (3) the line function that is the core of every business organization; (4) key steps in the history and evolution of operations management; (5) the differences and similarities between producing products and delivering services; (6) what a supply chain is, and why it is important to manage it; and (7) the key issues for today's business operations.

INTRODUCTION

Goods Physical items produced by business organizations.

Services Activities that provide some combination of time, location, form, and psychological value.

SERVICE

Operations is that part of a business organization that is responsible for producing goods and/or services. **Goods** are physical items that include raw materials, parts, subassemblies such as motherboards that go into computers, and final products such as cell phones and automobiles. **Services** are activities that provide some combination of time, location, form, or psychological value. Examples of goods and services are found all around you. Every book you read, every video you watch, every e-mail you send, every telephone conversation you have, and every medical treatment you receive involves the operations function of one or more organizations. So does everything you wear, eat, travel in, sit on, and access the Internet with. The operations function in business can also be viewed from a more far-reaching perspective: The collective success or failure of companies' operations functions has an impact on the ability of a nation to compete with other nations, and on the nation's economy.

The ideal situation for a business organization is to achieve a match of supply and demand. Having excess supply or excess capacity is wasteful and costly; having too little means lost opportunity and possible customer dissatisfaction. The key functions on the supply side are operations and supply chains, and sales and marketing on the demand side.

While the operations function is responsible for producing products and/or delivering services, it needs the support and input from other areas of the organization. Business organizations have three basic functional areas, as depicted in Figure 1.1: finance, marketing, and operations. It doesn't matter whether the business is a retail store, a hospital, a manufacturing firm, a car wash, or some other type of business; all business organizations have these three basic functions.

Finance is responsible for securing financial resources at favorable prices and allocating those resources throughout the organization, as well as budgeting, analyzing investment proposals, and providing funds for operations. Marketing and operations are the primary, or "line," functions. Marketing is responsible for assessing consumer wants and needs, and selling and promoting the organization's goods or services. Operations is responsible for producing the goods or providing the services offered by the organization. To put this into perspective, if a business organization were a car, operations would be its engine. And just as the engine is the core of what a car does, in a business organization, operations is the core of what the organization does. Operations management is responsible for managing that core. Hence, **operations management** is the management of systems or processes that create goods and/or provide services.

Operations management The management of systems or processes that *create goods and/or provide services.*

Supply chain A sequence of activities and organizations involved in producing and delivering a good or service.

Operations and supply chains are intrinsically linked and no business organization could exist without both. A **supply chain** is the sequence of organizations—their facilities, functions, and activities—that are involved in producing and delivering a product or service. The sequence begins with basic suppliers of raw materials and extends all the way to the final customer, as seen in Figure 1.2. Facilities might include warehouses, factories, processing centers, offices, distribution centers, and retail outlets. Functions and activities include forecasting, purchasing, inventory management, information management, quality assurance, scheduling, production, distribution, delivery, and customer service. Figure 1.3 provides another illustration of a supply chain: a chain that begins with wheat growing on a farm and ends with a customer buying a loaf of bread in a supermarket. Notice that the value of the product increases as it moves through the supply chain.

SUPPLY CHAIN

FIGURE 1.1
The three basic functions of business organizations

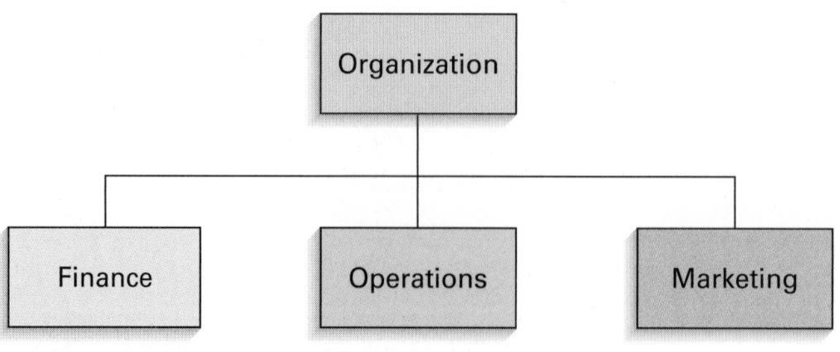

FIGURE 1.2
A simple product supply chain

Supply chains are both external and internal to the organization. The external parts of a supply chain provide raw materials, parts, equipment, supplies, and/or other inputs to the organization, and they deliver outputs that are goods to the organization's customers. The internal parts of a supply chain are part of the operations function itself, supplying operations with parts and materials, performing work on products and/or services, and passing the work on to the next step in the process.

The creation of goods or services involves transforming or converting inputs into outputs. Various inputs such as capital, labor, and information are used to create goods or services using one or more *transformation processes* (e.g., storing, transporting, repairing). To ensure that the desired outputs are obtained, an organization takes measurements at various points in the transformation process (*feedback*) and then compares them with previously established standards to determine whether corrective action is needed (*control*). Figure 1.4 depicts the conversion system.

Table 1.1 provides some examples of inputs, transformation processes, and outputs. Although goods and services are listed separately in Table 1.1, it is important to note that goods and services often occur jointly. For example, having the oil changed in your car is a service, but the oil that is delivered is a good. Similarly, house painting is a service, but the

FIGURE 1.3
A supply chain for bread

FIGURE 1.4
The operations function involves the conversion of inputs into outputs

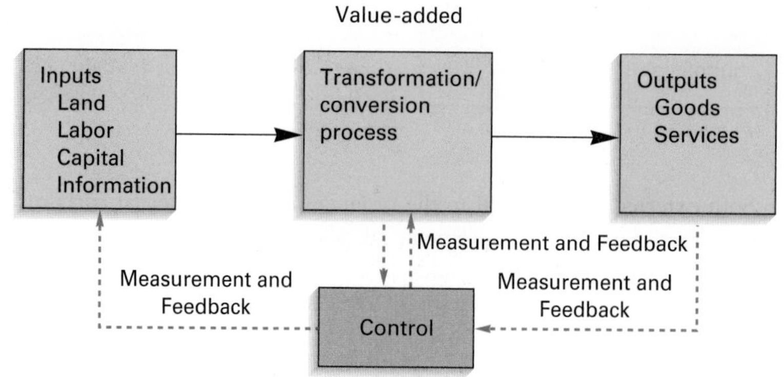

paint is a good. The goods–service combination is a continuum. It can range from primarily goods, with little service, to primarily service, with few goods. Figure 1.5 illustrates this continuum. Because there are relatively few pure goods or pure services, companies usually sell *product packages,* which are a combination of goods and services. There are elements of both goods production and service delivery in these product packages. This makes managing operations more interesting, and also more challenging.

Table 1.2 provides some specific illustrations of the transformation process.

Value-added The difference between the cost of inputs and the value or price of outputs.

The essence of the operations function is to *add value* during the transformation process: **Value-added** is the term used to describe the difference between the cost of inputs and the value or price of outputs. In nonprofit organizations, the value of outputs (e.g., highway construction,

TABLE 1.1
Examples of inputs, transformation, and outputs

Inputs	Transformation	Outputs
Land	Processes	High goods percentage
Human	Cutting, drilling	Houses
Physical labor	Transporting	Automobiles
Intellectual labor	Teaching	Clothing
Capital	Farming	Computers
Raw materials	Mixing	Machines
Water	Packing	Televisions
Metals	Copying, faxing	Food products
Wood	Analyzing	Textbooks
Equipment	Developing	CD players
Machines	Searching	High service percentage
Computers	Researching	Health care
Trucks	Repairing	Entertainment
Tools	Innovating	Car repair
Facilities	Debugging	Legal
Hospitals	Selling	Banking
Factories		Communication
Retail stores		
Energy		
Other		
Information		
Time		
Legal constraints		
Government regulations		

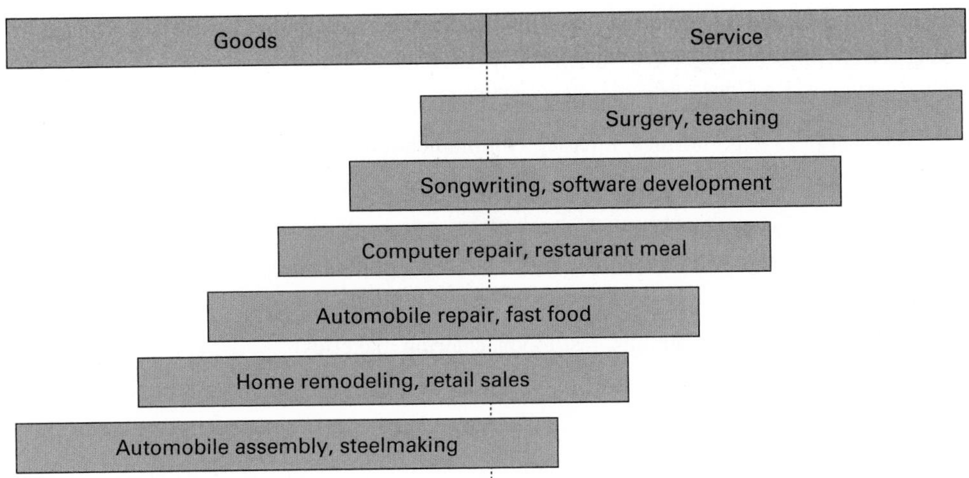

FIGURE 1.5
The goods–service continuum

police and fire protection) is their value to society; the greater the value-added, the greater the effectiveness of these operations. In for-profit organizations, the value of outputs is measured by the prices that customers are willing to pay for those goods or services. Firms use the money generated by value-added for research and development, investment in new facilities and equipment, worker salaries, and *profits.* Consequently, the greater the value-added, the greater the amount of funds available for these purposes. Value can also be psychological, as in *branding.*

Many factors affect the design and management of operations systems. Among them are the degree of involvement of customers in the process and the degree to which technology is used to produce and/or deliver a product or service. The greater the degree of customer involvement, the more challenging it can be to design and manage the operation. Technology choices can have a major impact on productivity, costs, flexibility, and quality and customer satisfaction.

Production of Goods versus Delivery of Services

Although goods and services often go hand in hand, there are some very basic differences between the two, differences that impact the management of the goods portion versus management of the service portion. There are also many similarities between the two.

Production of goods results in a *tangible output,* such as an automobile, eyeglasses, a golf ball, a refrigerator—anything that we can see or touch. It may take place in a factory, but can occur elsewhere. For example, farming produces *nonmanufactured* goods. Delivery of service, on the other hand, generally implies an *act.* A physician's examination, TV and auto

TABLE 1.2
Illustrations of the transformation process

	Inputs	Processing	Output
Food Processor	Raw vegetables	Cleaning	Canned vegetables
	Metal sheets	Making cans	
	Water	Cutting	
	Energy	Cooking	
	Labor	Packing	
	Building	Labeling	
	Equipment		
Hospital	Doctors, nurses	Examination	Treated patients
	Hospital	Surgery	
	Medical supplies	Monitoring	
	Equipment	Medication	
	Laboratories	Therapy	

repair, lawn care, and the projection of a film in a theater are examples of services. The majority of service jobs fall into these categories:

Professional services (e.g., financial, health care, legal).
Mass services (e.g., utilities, Internet, communications).
Service shops (e.g., tailoring, appliance repair, car wash, auto repair/maintenance).
Personal care (e.g., beauty salon, spa, barbershop).
Government (e.g., Medicare, mail, social services, police, fire).
Education (e.g., schools, universities).
Food service (e.g., restaurants, fast foods, catering, bakeries).
Services within organizations (e.g., payroll, accounting, maintenance, IT, HR, janitorial).
Retailing and wholesaling.
Shipping and delivery (e.g., truck, railroad, boat, air).
Residential services (e.g., lawn care, painting, general repair, remodeling, interior design).
Transportation (e.g., mass transit, taxi, airlines, ambulance).
Travel and hospitality (e.g., travel bureaus, hotels, resorts).
Miscellaneous services (e.g., copy service, temporary help).

Manufacturing and service are often different in terms of *what* is done but quite similar in terms of *how* it is done.

Consider these points of comparison:

Degree of customer contact. Many services involve a high degree of customer contact, although services such as Internet providers, utilities, and mail service do not. When there is a high degree of contact, the interaction between server and customer becomes a "moment of truth" that will be judged by the customer every time the service occurs.

Labor content of jobs. Services often have a higher degree of labor content than manufacturing jobs do, although automated services are an exception.

Uniformity of inputs. Service operations are often subject to a higher degree of variability of inputs. Each client, patient, customer, repair job, and so on presents a somewhat unique situation that requires assessment and flexibility. Conversely, manufacturing operations often have a greater ability to control the variability of inputs, which leads to more-uniform job requirements.

Measurement of productivity. Measurement of productivity can be more difficult for service jobs due largely to the high variations of inputs. Thus, one doctor might have a higher level of routine cases to deal with, while another might have more-difficult cases. Unless a careful analysis is conducted, it may appear that the doctor with the difficult cases has a much lower productivity than the one with the routine cases.

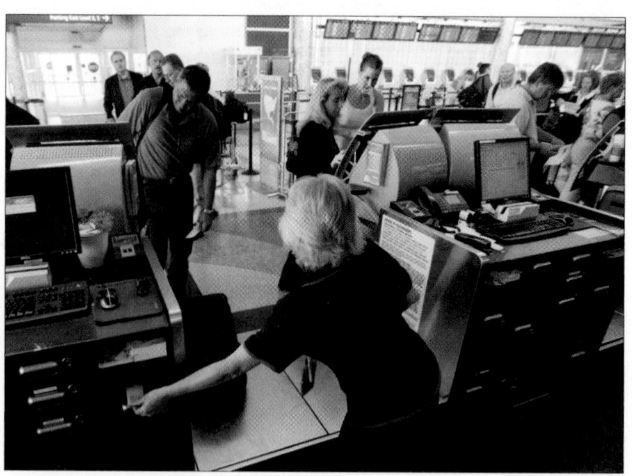

Quality assurance. Quality assurance is usually more challenging for services due to the higher variation in input, and because delivery and consumption occur at the same time. Unlike manufacturing, which typically occurs away from the customer and allows mistakes that are identified to be corrected, services have less opportunity to avoid exposing the customer to mistakes.

Inventory. Many services tend to involve less use of inventory than manufacturing operations, so the costs of having inventory on hand are lower than they are for manufacturing. However, unlike manufactured goods, services cannot be stored. Instead, they must be provided "on demand."

Wages. Manufacturing jobs are often well paid, and have less wage variation than service jobs, which can range from highly paid professional services to minimum-wage workers.

Ability to patent. Product designs are often easier to patent than service designs, and some services cannot be patented, making them easier for competitors to copy.

There are also many similarities between managing the production of products and managing services. In fact, most of the topics in this book pertain to both. When there are important service considerations, these are highlighted in separate sections. Here are some of the primary factors for both:

a. Forecasting and capacity planning to match supply and demand.
b. Process management.
c. Managing variations.
d. Monitoring and controlling costs and productivity.
e. Supply chain management.
f. Location planning, inventory management, quality control, and scheduling.

SUPPLY CHAIN

Note that many service activities are essential in goods-producing companies. These include training, human resource management, customer service, equipment repair, procurement, and administrative services.

Table 1.3 provides an overview of the differences between production of goods and service operations. Remember, though, that most systems involve a blend of goods and services.

PROCESS MANAGEMENT

A key aspect of operations management is process management. A **process** consists of one or more actions that transform inputs into outputs. In essence, the central role of all management is process management.

Process One or more actions that transform inputs into outputs.

TABLE 1.3
Typical differences between production of goods and provision of services

Characteristic	Goods	Services
Output	Tangible	Intangible
Customer contact	Low	High
Labor content	Low	High
Uniformity of input	High	Low
Measurement of productivity	Easy	Difficult
Opportunity to correct problems before delivery	High	Low
Inventory	Much	Little
Wages	Narrow range	Wide range
Patentable	Usually	Not usually

Businesses are composed of many interrelated processes. Generally speaking, there are three categories of business processes:

1. **Upper-management processes.** These govern the operation of the entire organization. Examples include organizational governance and organizational strategy.
2. **Operational processes.** These are the core processes that make up the value stream. Examples include purchasing, production and/or service, marketing, and sales.
3. **Supporting processes.** These support the core processes. Examples include accounting, human resources, and IT (information technology).

Business processes, large and small, are composed of a series of supplier–customer relationships, where every business organization, every department, and every individual operation is both a customer of the previous step in the process and a supplier to the next step in the process. Figure 1.6 illustrates this concept.

SUPPLY CHAIN

A major process can consist of many subprocesses, each having its own goals that contribute to the goals of the overall process. Business organizations and supply chains have many such processes and subprocesses and they benefit greatly when management is using a process perspective. Business process management (BPM) activities include process design, process execution, and process monitoring. Two basic aspects of this for operations and supply chain management are managing processes to meet demand and dealing with process variability.

Managing a Process to Meet Demand

Ideally, the capacity of a process will be such that its output just matches demand. Excess capacity is wasteful and costly; too little capacity means dissatisfied customers and lost revenue. Having the right capacity requires having accurate forecasts of demand, the ability to translate forecasts into capacity requirements, and a process in place capable of meeting expected demand. Even so, process variation and demand variability can make the achievement of a match between process output and demand difficult. Therefore, to be effective, it is also necessary for managers to be able to deal with variation.

Process Variation

Variation occurs in all business processes. It can be due to variety or variability. For example, random variability is inherent in every process; it is always present. In addition, variation can occur as the result of deliberate management choices to offer customers variety.

There are four basic sources of variation:

1. **The variety of goods or services being offered.** The greater the variety of goods and services, the greater the variation in production or service requirements.
2. **Structural variation in demand.** These variations, which include trends and seasonal variations, are generally predictable. They are particularly important for capacity planning.
3. **Random variation.** This natural variability is present to some extent in all processes, as well as in demand for services and products, and it cannot generally be influenced by managers.
4. **Assignable variation.** These variations are caused by defective inputs, incorrect work methods, out-of-adjustment equipment, and so on. This type of variation can be reduced or eliminated by analysis and corrective action.

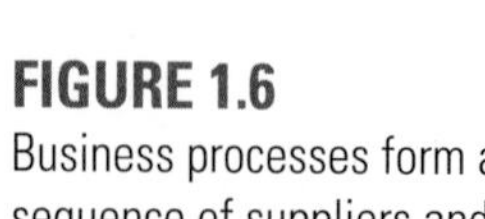

FIGURE 1.6
Business processes form a sequence of suppliers and customers

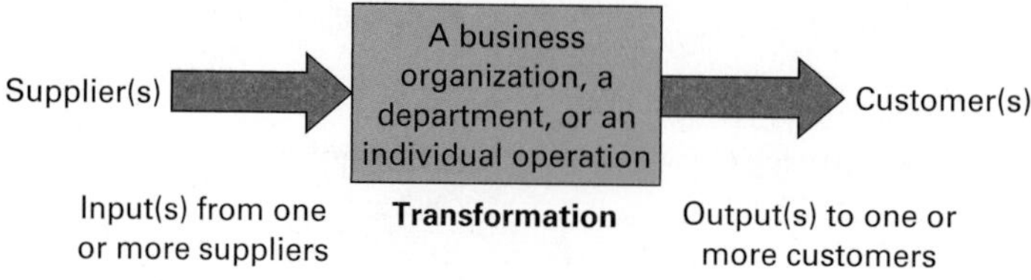

Variations can be disruptive to operations and supply chain processes, interfering with optimal functioning. Variations result in additional cost, delays and shortages, poor quality, and inefficient work systems. Poor quality and product shortages or service delays can lead to dissatisfied customers and damage an organization's reputation and image. It is not surprising, then, that the ability to deal with variability is absolutely necessary for managers.

Throughout this book, you will learn about some of the tools managers use to deal with variation. An important aspect of being able to deal with variation is to use metrics to describe it. Two widely used metrics are the *mean* (average) and the *standard deviation.* The standard deviation quantifies variation around the mean. The mean and standard deviation are used throughout this book in conjunction with variation. So, too, is the normal distribution. Because you will come across many examples of how the normal distribution is used, you may find the overview on working with the normal distribution in the appendix at the end of the book helpful.

THE SCOPE OF OPERATIONS MANAGEMENT

The scope of operations management ranges across the organization. Operations management people are involved in product and service design, process selection, selection and management of technology, design of work systems, location planning, facilities planning, and quality improvement of the organization's products or services.

The operations function includes many interrelated activities, such as forecasting, capacity planning, scheduling, managing inventories, assuring quality, motivating employees, deciding where to locate facilities, and more.

We can use an airline company to illustrate a service organization's operations system. The system consists of the airplanes, airport facilities, and maintenance facilities, sometimes spread out over a wide territory. The activities include:

Forecasting such things as weather and landing conditions, seat demand for flights, and the growth in air travel.

Capacity planning, essential for the airline to maintain cash flow and make a reasonable profit. (Too few or too many planes, or even the right number of planes but in the wrong places, will hurt profits.)

Scheduling planes, cargo, and flight and ground crews is an operations function for an airline.

Facilities and layout, important in achieving effective use of workers and equipment.

Scheduling of planes for flights and for routine maintenance; scheduling of pilots and flight attendants; and scheduling of ground crews, counter staff, and baggage handlers.

Managing inventories of such items as foods and beverages, first-aid equipment, in-flight magazines, pillows and blankets, and life preservers.

Assuring quality, essential in flying and maintenance operations, where the emphasis is on safety, and important in dealing with customers at ticket counters, check-in, telephone and electronic reservations, and curb service, where the emphasis is on efficiency and courtesy.

Motivating and training employees in all phases of operations.

Locating facilities according to managers' decisions on which cities to provide service for, where to locate maintenance facilities, and where to locate major and minor hubs.

Now consider a bicycle factory. This might be primarily an *assembly* operation: buying components such as frames, tires, wheels, gears, and other items from suppliers, and then assembling bicycles. The factory also might do some of the *fabrication* work itself, forming frames, making the gears and chains, and it might buy mainly raw materials and a few parts and materials such as paint, nuts and bolts, and tires. Among the key management tasks in either case are scheduling production, deciding which components to make and which to buy, ordering parts and materials, deciding on the style of bicycle to produce and how many, purchasing new equipment to replace old or worn out equipment, maintaining equipment, motivating workers, and ensuring that quality standards are met.

SERVICE

Obviously, an airline company and a bicycle factory are completely different types of operations. One is primarily a service operation, the other a producer of goods. Nonetheless, these two operations have much in common. Both involve scheduling activities, motivating employees, ordering and managing supplies, selecting and maintaining equipment, satisfying quality standards, and—above all—satisfying customers. And in both businesses, the success of the business depends on short- and long-term planning.

The operations function consists of all activities *directly* related to producing goods or providing services. Hence, it exists both in manufacturing and assembly operations, which are *goods-oriented,* and in areas such as health care, transportation, food handling, and retailing, which are primarily *service-oriented.*

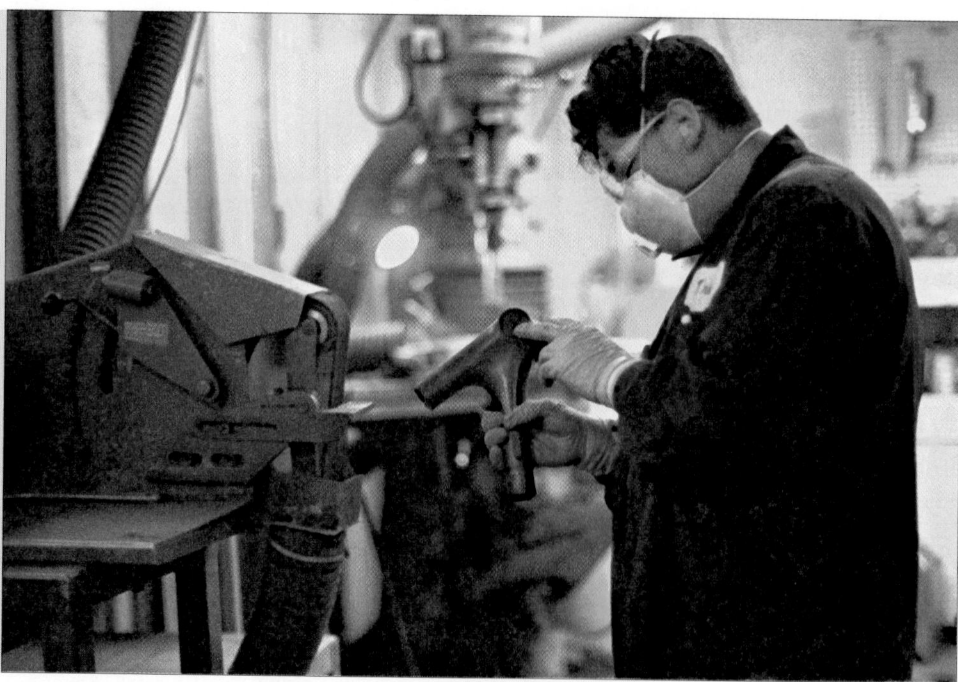

A worker is making the bottom bracket lug for a Trek OCLV carbon road bike at Trek Bicycle Company in Waterloo, Wisconsin, world headquarters for Trek. Trek is a world leader in bicycle products and accessories, with 1,500 employees worldwide. Designers and engineers incorporate the most advanced technology into Trek products, resulting in award-winning bikes and components.

A primary function of an operations manager is to guide the system by decision making. Certain decisions affect the *design* of the system, and others affect the *operation* of the system.

System design involves decisions that relate to system capacity, the geographic location of facilities, arrangement of departments and placement of equipment within physical structures, product and service planning, and acquisition of equipment. These decisions usually, but not always, require long-term commitments. Moreover, they are typically *strategic* decisions. *System operation* involves management of personnel, inventory planning and control, scheduling, project management, and quality assurance. These are generally *tactical* and *operational* decisions. Feedback on these decisions involves *measurement* and *control.* In many instances, the operations manager is more involved in day-to-day operating decisions than with decisions relating to system design. However, the operations manager has a vital stake in system design because *system design essentially determines many of the parameters of system operation.* For example, costs, space, capacities, and quality are directly affected by design decisions. Even though the operations manager is not responsible for making all design decisions, he or she can provide those decision makers with a wide range of information that will have a bearing on their decisions.

A number of other areas are part of, or support, the operations function. They include purchasing, industrial engineering, distribution, and maintenance.

> **Purchasing** has responsibility for procurement of materials, supplies, and equipment. Close contact with operations is necessary to ensure correct quantities and timing of purchases. The purchasing department is often called on to evaluate vendors for quality, reliability, service, price, and ability to adjust to changing demand. Purchasing is also involved in receiving and inspecting the purchased goods.
>
> **Industrial engineering** is often concerned with scheduling, performance standards, work methods, quality control, and material handling.
>
> **Distribution** involves the shipping of goods to warehouses, retail outlets, or final customers.
>
> **Maintenance** is responsible for general upkeep and repair of equipment, buildings and grounds, heating and air-conditioning; removing toxic wastes; parking; and perhaps security.

The operations manager is the key figure in the system: He or she has the ultimate responsibility for the creation of goods or provision of services.

The kinds of jobs that operations managers oversee vary tremendously from organization to organization largely because of the different products or services involved. Thus, managing a banking operation obviously requires a different kind of expertise than managing a steelmaking operation. However, in a very important respect, the jobs are the same: They are both essentially *managerial.* The same thing can be said for the job of any operations manager regardless of the kinds of goods or services being created.

SERVICE

The service sector and the manufacturing sector are both important to the economy. The service sector now accounts for more than 70 percent of jobs in the United States, and it is growing in other countries as well. Moreover, the number of people working in services is increasing, while the number of people working in manufacturing is not. (See Figure 1.7.) The reason for the decline in manufacturing jobs is twofold: As the operations function in manufacturing companies finds more productive ways of producing goods, the companies are able to maintain or even increase their output using fewer workers. Furthermore, some manufacturing work has been *outsourced* to more productive companies, many in other countries, that are able to produce goods at lower costs. Outsourcing and productivity will be discussed in more detail in this and other chapters.

Many of the concepts presented in this book apply equally to manufacturing and service. Consequently, whether your interest at this time is on manufacturing or on service, these concepts will be important, regardless of whether a manufacturing example or service example is used to illustrate the concept.

The reading on page 14 gives another reason for the importance of manufacturing jobs.

FIGURE 1.7
U.S. manufacturing versus service employment, 1940–2010
Source: U.S. Bureau of Labor Statistics.

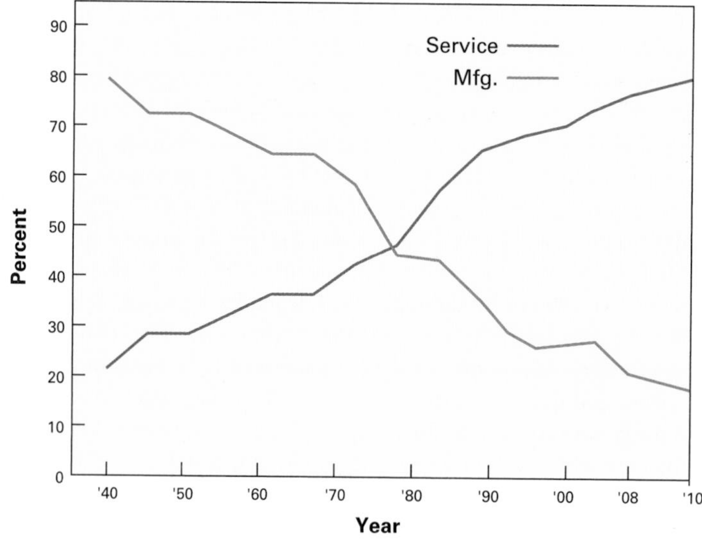

Why Manufacturing Matters

READING

The U.S. economy is becoming more and more service-based. The percentage of employment in manufacturing continues to decrease while the percentage employed in services continues to increase. However, it would be unwise to assume that manufacturing isn't important to the economy, or that service is more important. Let's see why.

Not only is the percentage of manufacturing jobs decreasing, but the actual number of manufacturing jobs is also decreasing. There are two main reasons for the decline: increases in productivity which means fewer workers are needed to maintain manufacturing output; and outsourcing, especially to countries that have much lower wages, an attractive option for companies seeking to maintain their competitiveness and boost their bottom lines.

However, when companies outsource part (or in some cases, all) of their manufacturing to lower-cost countries, the loss of jobs results in the loss of service jobs as well. Some are lost in the community in retail businesses patronized by the manufacturing workers. Also included in that figure are factory service workers (e.g., workers who do machine repairs, maintenance, material handling, packaging, and so on). General estimates are that three service jobs are lost for each manufacturing job lost.

As the manufacturing base shrinks, workers who lose their manufacturing job are finding it tougher to find another opening in manufacturing. Instead they join the ranks of the unemployed, or take a service job, usually at a lower wage rate than what manufacturing paid.

From a national perspective, not only is work transferred to a foreign country, intellectual knowledge is transferred. Moreover, as time passes, the domestic base of manufacturing skills and know-how is lost.

There are important consequences for taxes as well. Unemployment benefits are costly, and the erosion of federal, state, and local tax bases results in lower tax revenues collected from individuals and from corporations.

At the Montana Economic Development Summit in Butte, Montana on Monday, September 13, 2010, GE CEO Jeffery Immelt said that since the 1970s the economy has been driven by consumer credit and a misguided notion of building a service economy. "It was just wrong. It was stupid. It was insane," Immelt said of the push for a service-based economy. Instead, he said, in the future the economy has to be as an exporter, and that manufacturing, with an aim to reduce the trade deficit, is the key.

Questions

1. How important is the loss of manufacturing jobs to the nation?
2. Can you suggest some actions the government (federal, state, or local) can take to stem the job loss?

WHY LEARN ABOUT OPERATIONS MANAGEMENT?

There are many career-related reasons for wanting to learn about operations management, whether you plan to work in the field of operations or not. This is because every aspect of business affects or is affected by operations. Operations and sales are the two line functions

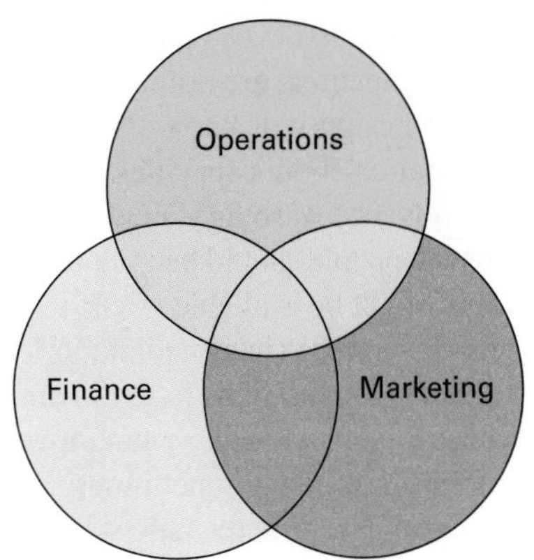

FIGURE 1.8
The three major functions of business organizations overlap

in a business organization. All other functions—accounting, finance, marketing, IT, and so on—support the two line functions. Among the service jobs that are closely related to operations are financial services (e.g., stock market analyst, broker, investment banker, and loan officer), marketing services (e.g., market analyst, marketing researcher, advertising manager, and product manager), accounting services (e.g., corporate accountant, public accountant, and budget analyst), and information services (e.g., corporate intelligence, library services, management information systems design services).

Apart from the career-related reasons is a not so obvious one: Through learning about operations and supply chains, you will have a much better understanding of the world you live in, the global dependencies of companies and nations, some of the reasons that companies succeed or fail, and the importance of working with others.

Working together successfully means that all members of the organization understand not only their own role, but they also understand the roles of others. This is precisely why all business students, regardless of their particular major, are required to take a common core of courses that will enable them to learn about all aspects of business. Because operations management is central to the functioning of every business organization, it is included in the core of courses business students are required to take. And even though individual courses have a narrow focus (e.g., accounting, marketing), in practice, there is significant interfacing and *collaboration* among the various functional areas, involving *exchange of information* and *cooperative decision making.* For example, although the three primary functions in business organizations perform different activities, many of their decisions impact the other areas of the organization. Consequently, these functions have numerous interactions, as depicted by the overlapping circles shown in Figure 1.8.

Finance and operations management personnel cooperate by exchanging information and expertise in such activities as the following:

1. **Budgeting.** Budgets must be periodically prepared to plan financial requirements. Budgets must sometimes be adjusted, and performance relative to a budget must be evaluated.
2. **Economic analysis of investment proposals.** Evaluation of alternative investments in plant and equipment requires inputs from both operations and finance people.
3. **Provision of funds.** The necessary funding of operations and the amount and timing of funding can be important and even critical when funds are tight. Careful planning can help avoid cash-flow problems.

Marketing's focus is on selling and/or promoting the goods or services of an organization. Marketing is also responsible for assessing customer wants and needs, and for communicating those to operations people (short term) and to design people (long term). That is, operations needs information about demand over the short to intermediate term so that it can plan accordingly (e.g., purchase materials or schedule work), while design people need information that relates to improving current products and services and designing new ones. Marketing, design, and production must work closely together to successfully implement design changes and to develop and produce new products. Marketing can provide valuable insight on what competitors are doing. Marketing also can supply information on consumer preferences so that design will know the kinds of products and features needed; operations can supply information about capacities and judge the *manufacturability* of designs. Operations will also have advance warning if new equipment or skills will be needed for new products or services. Finance people should be included in these exchanges in order to provide information on what funds might be available (short term) and to learn what funds might be needed for new products or services (intermediate to long term). One important piece of information marketing needs from operations is the manufacturing or service **lead time** in order to give customers realistic estimates of how long it will take to fill their orders.

Lead time The time between ordering a good or service and receiving it.

Thus, marketing, operations, and finance must interface on product and process design, forecasting, setting realistic schedules, quality and quantity decisions, and keeping each other informed on the other's strengths and weaknesses.

People in every area of business need to appreciate the importance of managing and coordinating operations decisions that affect the supply chain and the matching of supply and demand, and how those decisions impact other functions in an organization.

Operations also interacts with other functional areas of the organization, including legal, management information systems (MIS), accounting, personnel/human resources, and public relations, as depicted in Figure 1.9.

The *legal* department must be consulted on contracts with employees, customers, suppliers, and transporters, as well as on liability and environmental issues.

Accounting supplies information to management on costs of labor, materials, and overhead, and may provide reports on items such as scrap, downtime, and inventories.

Management information systems (MIS) is concerned with providing management with the information it needs to effectively manage. This occurs mainly through designing systems to capture relevant information and designing reports. MIS is also important for managing the control and decision-making tools used in operations management.

The *personnel* or *human resources* department is concerned with recruitment and training of personnel, labor relations, contract negotiations, wage and salary administration, assisting in manpower projections, and ensuring the health and safety of employees.

Public relations has responsibility for building and maintaining a positive public image of the organization. Good public relations provides many potential benefits. An obvious one is in the marketplace. Other potential benefits include public awareness of the organization as a good place to work (labor supply), improved chances of approval of zoning change requests, community acceptance of expansion plans, and instilling a positive attitude among employees.

FIGURE 1.9
Operations interfaces with a number of supporting functions

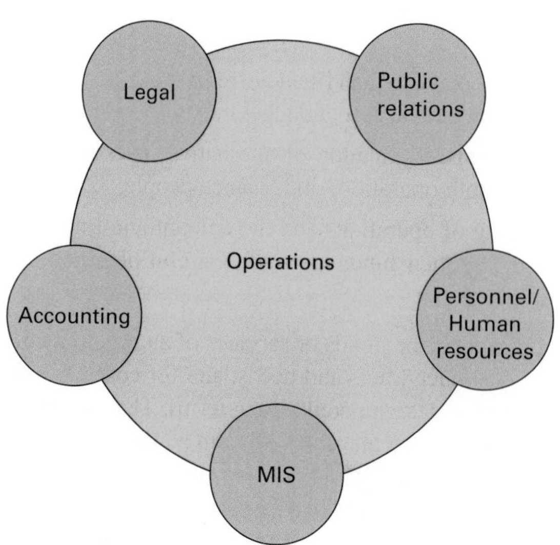

Career Opportunities and Professional Societies

There are many career opportunities in the operations management and supply chain fields. Among the numerous job titles are operations manager, production analyst, production manager, industrial engineer, time study analyst, inventory manager, purchasing manager, schedule coordinator, distribution manager, supply chain manager, quality analyst, and quality manager.

People who work in the operations field should have a skill set that includes both people skills and knowledge skills. People skills include political awareness; mentoring ability; and collaboration, negotiation, and communication skills. Knowledge skills, necessary for credibility and good decision making, include product and/or service knowledge, process knowledge, industry and global knowledge, and financial and accounting skills.

If you are thinking of a career in operations management, you can benefit by joining one or more of the professional societies.

APICS, the Association for Operations Management
8430 West Bryn Mawr Avenue, Suite 1000, Chicago, Illinois 60631 www.apics.org

American Society for Quality (ASQ)
230 West Wells Street, Milwaukee, Wisconsin 53203 www.asq.org

Institute for Supply Management (ISM)
2055 East Centennial Circle, Tempe, Arizona 85284 www.ism.ws

Institute for Operations Research and the Management Sciences (INFORMS)
901 Elkridge Landing Road, Linthicum, Maryland 21090-2909 www.informs.org

The Production and Operations Management Society (POMS)
College of Engineering, Florida International University, EAS 2460,
10555 West Flagler Street, Miami, Florida 33174 www.poms.org

The Project Management Institute (PMI)
4 Campus Boulevard, Newtown Square, Pennsylvania 19073-3299 www.pmi.org

Council of Supply Chain Management Professionals (CSCMP)
333 East Butterfield Road, Suite 140, Lombard, Illinois 60148 http//cscmp.org

APICS, ASQ, ISM, and other professional societies offer a practitioner certification examination that can enhance your qualifications. Information about job opportunities can be obtained from all of these societies as well as from other sources, such as the Decision Sciences Institute (University Plaza, Atlanta, Georgia 30303) and the Institute of Industrial Engineers (25 Technology Park, Norcross, Georgia 30092).

OPERATIONS MANAGEMENT AND DECISION MAKING

The chief role of an operations manager is that of planner/decision maker. In this capacity, the operations manager exerts considerable influence over the degree to which the goals and objectives of the organization are realized. Most decisions involve many possible alternatives that can have quite different impacts on costs or profits. Consequently, it is important to make *informed* decisions.

Operations management professionals make a number of key decisions that affect the entire organization. These include the following:

What: What resources will be needed, and in what amounts?

When: When will each resource be needed? When should the work be scheduled? When should materials and other supplies be ordered? When is corrective action needed?

Where: Where will the work be done?

How: How will the product or service be designed? How will the work be done (organization, methods, equipment)? How will resources be allocated?

Who: Who will do the work?

Throughout this book, you will encounter the broad range of decisions that operations managers must make, and you will be introduced to the tools necessary to handle those decisions. This section describes general approaches to decision making, including the use of models, quantitative methods, analysis of trade-offs, establishing priorities, ethics, and the systems approach. Models are often a key tool used by all decision makers.

Models

Model An abstraction of reality; a simplified representation of something.

A **model** is an abstraction of reality, a simplified representation of something. For example, a child's toy car is a model of a real automobile. It has many of the same visual features (shape, relative proportions, wheels) that make it suitable for the child's learning and playing. But the toy does not have a real engine, it cannot transport people, and it does not weigh 2,000 pounds.

Other examples of models include automobile test tracks and crash tests; formulas, graphs and charts; balance sheets and income statements; and financial ratios. Common statistical models include descriptive statistics such as the mean, median, mode, range, and standard deviation, as well as random sampling, the normal distribution, and regression equations.

Models are sometimes classified as physical, schematic, or mathematical:

Physical models look like their real-life counterparts. Examples include miniature cars, trucks, airplanes, toy animals and trains, and scale-model buildings. The advantage of these models is their visual correspondence with reality.

Schematic models are more abstract than their physical counterparts; that is, they have less resemblance to the physical reality. Examples include graphs and charts, blueprints, pictures, and drawings. The advantage of schematic models is that they are often relatively simple to construct and change. Moreover, they have some degree of visual correspondence.

Mathematical models are the most abstract: They do not look at all like their real-life counterparts. Examples include numbers, formulas, and symbols. These models are usually the easiest to manipulate, and they are important forms of inputs for computers and calculators.

The variety of models in use is enormous. Nonetheless, all have certain common features: They are all decision-making aids and simplifications of more complex real-life phenomena. Real life involves an overwhelming amount of detail, much of which is irrelevant for any particular problem. Models omit unimportant details so that attention can be concentrated on the most important aspects of a situation.

Because models play a significant role in operations management decision making, they are heavily integrated into the material of this text. For each model, try to learn (1) its purpose, (2) how it is used to generate results, (3) how these results are interpreted and used, and (4) what assumptions and limitations apply.

The last point is particularly important because virtually every model has an associated set of assumptions or conditions under which the model is valid. Failure to satisfy all of the assumptions will make the results suspect. Attempts to apply the results to a problem under such circumstances can lead to disastrous consequences.

Managers use models in a variety of ways and for a variety of reasons. Models are beneficial because they

1. Are generally easy to use and less expensive than dealing directly with the actual situation.
2. Require users to organize and sometimes quantify information and, in the process, often indicate areas where additional information is needed.

3. Increase understanding of the problem.
4. Enable managers to analyze what-if questions.
5. Serve as a consistent tool for evaluation and provide a standardized format for analyzing a problem.
6. Enable users to bring the power of mathematics to bear on a problem.

This impressive list of benefits notwithstanding, models have certain limitations of which you should be aware. The following are three of the more important limitations:

1. Quantitative information may be emphasized at the expense of qualitative information.
2. Models may be incorrectly applied and the results misinterpreted. The widespread use of computerized models adds to this risk because highly sophisticated models may be placed in the hands of users who are not sufficiently knowledgeable to appreciate the subtleties of a particular model; thus, they are unable to fully comprehend the circumstances under which the model can be successfully employed.
3. The use of models does not guarantee good decisions.

Quantitative Approaches

Quantitative approaches to problem solving often embody an attempt to obtain mathematically optimal solutions to managerial problems. *Linear programming* and related mathematical techniques are widely used for optimum allocation of scarce resources. *Queuing techniques* are useful for analyzing situations in which waiting lines form. *Inventory models* are widely used to control inventories. *Project models* such as PERT (program evaluation and review technique) and CPM (critical path method) are useful for planning, coordinating, and controlling large-scale projects. *Forecasting techniques* are widely used in planning and scheduling. *Statistical models* are currently used in many areas of decision making.

In large measure, *quantitative approaches* to decision making in operations management (and in other functional business areas) have been accepted because of calculators and computers capable of handling the required calculations. Computers have had a major impact on operations management. Moreover, the growing availability of software packages for quantitative techniques has greatly increased management's use of those techniques.

Although quantitative approaches are widely used in operations management decision making, it is important to note that managers typically use a combination of qualitative and quantitative approaches, and many important decisions are based on qualitative approaches.

Performance Metrics

All managers use metrics to manage and control operations. There are many metrics in use, including those related to profits, costs, quality, productivity, flexibility, assets, inventories, schedules, and forecast accuracy. As you read each chapter, note the metrics being used and how they are applied to manage operations.

Analysis of Trade-Offs

Operations personnel frequently encounter decisions that can be described as *trade-off* decisions. For example, in deciding on the amount of inventory to stock, the decision maker must take into account the trade-off between the increased level of customer service that the additional inventory would yield and the increased costs required to stock that inventory.

Throughout this book you will be presented with decision models that reflect these kinds of trade-offs. Decision makers sometimes deal with these decisions by listing the advantages and disadvantages—the pros and cons—of a course of action to better understand the consequences of the decisions they must make. In some instances, decision makers add weights to the items on their list that reflect the relative importance of various factors. This can help them "net out" the potential impacts of the trade-offs on their decision.

Degree of Customization

A major influence on the entire organization is the degree of customization of products or services being offered to its customers. Providing highly customized products or services such as home remodeling, plastic surgery, and legal counseling tends to be more labor intensive than providing standardized products such as those you would buy "off the shelf" at a mall store or a supermarket or standardized services such as public utilities and Internet services. Furthermore, production of customized products or provision of customized services is generally more time consuming, requires more highly skilled people, and involves more flexible equipment than what is needed for standardized products or services. Customized processes tend to have a much lower volume of output than standardized processes, and customized output carries a higher price tag. The degree of customization has important implications for process selection and job requirements. The impact goes beyond operations and supply chains. It affects marketing, sales, accounting, finance, and information systems.

A Systems Approach

System A set of interrelated parts that must work together.

A systems viewpoint is almost always beneficial in decision making. A **system** can be defined as a set of interrelated parts that must work together. In a business organization, the organization can be thought of as a system composed of subsystems (e.g., marketing subsystem, operations subsystem, finance subsystem), which in turn are composed of lower subsystems. The systems approach emphasizes interrelationships among subsystems, but its main theme is that *the whole is greater than the sum of its individual parts.* Hence, from a systems viewpoint, the output and objectives of the organization as a whole take precedence over those of any one subsystem. An alternative approach is to concentrate on efficiency within subsystems and thereby achieve overall efficiency. But that approach overlooks the facts that organizations must operate in an environment of scarce resources and that subsystems are often in direct competition for those scarce resources, so that an orderly approach to the allocation of resources is called for.

The big picture—a Systems view.

A systems approach is essential whenever something is being designed, redesigned, implemented, improved, or otherwise changed. It is important to take into account the impact on all parts of the system. For example, if the upcoming model of an automobile will add antilock brakes, a designer must take into account how customers will view the change, instructions for using the brakes, chances for misuse, the cost of producing the new brakes, installation procedures, recycling worn-out brakes, and repair procedures. In addition, workers will need training to make and/or assemble the brakes, production scheduling may change, inventory procedures may have to change, quality standards will have to be established, advertising must be informed of the new features, and parts suppliers must be selected.

Global competition and outsourcing are increasing the length of companies' supply chains, making it more important than ever for companies to use a systems approach to take the "big picture" into account in their decision making.

SUPPLY CHAIN

Establishing Priorities

In virtually every situation, managers discover that certain issues or items are more important than others. Recognizing this enables the managers to direct their efforts to where they will do the most good.

Pareto phenomenon A few factors account for a high percentage of the occurrence of some event(s).

Typically, a relatively few issues or items are very important, so that dealing with those factors will generally have a disproportionately large impact on the results achieved. This well-known effect is referred to as the **Pareto phenomenon.** The implication is that a manager should examine each situation, searching for the few factors that will have the greatest impact, and give them the highest priority. This is one of the most important and pervasive concepts in operations management. In fact, this concept can be applied at all levels of management and to every aspect of decision making, both professional and personal.

THE HISTORICAL EVOLUTION OF OPERATIONS MANAGEMENT

Systems for production have existed since ancient times. The production of goods for sale, at least in the modern sense, and the modern factory system had their roots in the Industrial Revolution.

The Industrial Revolution

The Industrial Revolution began in the 1770s in England and spread to the rest of Europe and to the United States during the 19th century. Prior to that time, goods were produced in small shops by craftsmen and their apprentices. Under that system, it was common for one person to be responsible for making a product, such as a horse-drawn wagon or a piece of furniture, from start to finish. Only simple tools were available; the machines in use today had not been invented.

Then, a number of innovations in the 18th century changed the face of production forever by substituting machine power for human power. Perhaps the most significant of these was the steam engine, because it provided a source of power to operate machines in factories. Ample supplies of coal and iron ore provided materials for generating power and making machinery. The new machines, made of iron, were much stronger and more durable than the simple wooden machines they replaced.

In the earliest days of manufacturing, goods were produced using **craft production:** highly skilled workers using simple, flexible tools produced goods according to customer specifications.

Craft production System in which highly skilled workers use simple, flexible tools to produce small quantities of customized goods.

Craft production had major shortcomings. Because products were made by skilled craftsmen who custom fitted parts, production was slow and costly. And when parts failed, the replacements also had to be custom made, which was also slow and costly. Another shortcoming was that production costs did not decrease as volume increased; there were no *economies of scale,* which would have provided a major incentive for companies to expand. Instead, many small companies emerged, each with its own set of standards.

A major change occurred that gave the Industrial Revolution a boost: the development of standard gauging systems. This greatly reduced the need for custom-made goods. Factories began to spring up and grow rapidly, providing jobs for countless people who were attracted in large numbers from rural areas.

Despite the major changes that were taking place, management theory and practice had not progressed much from early days. What was needed was an enlightened and more systematic approach to management.

Scientific Management

The scientific management era brought widespread changes to the management of factories. The movement was spearheaded by the efficiency engineer and inventor Frederick Winslow Taylor, who is often referred to as the father of scientific management. Taylor believed in a "science of management" based on observation, measurement, analysis and improvement of work methods, and economic incentives. He studied work methods in great detail to identify the best method for doing each job. Taylor also believed that management should be responsible for planning, carefully selecting and training workers, finding the best way to perform each job, achieving cooperation between management and workers, and separating management activities from work activities.

Taylor's methods emphasized maximizing output. They were not always popular with workers, who sometimes thought the methods were used to unfairly increase output without a corresponding increase in compensation. Certainly some companies did abuse workers in their quest for efficiency. Eventually, the public outcry reached the halls of Congress, and hearings were held on the matter. Taylor himself was called to testify in 1911, the same year in which his classic book, *The Principles of Scientific Management,* was published. The publicity from those hearings actually helped scientific management principles to achieve wide acceptance in industry.

A number of other pioneers also contributed heavily to this movement, including the following:

Frank Gilbreth was an industrial engineer who is often referred to as the father of motion study. He developed principles of motion economy that could be applied to incredibly small portions of a task.

Henry Gantt recognized the value of nonmonetary rewards to motivate workers, and developed a widely used system for scheduling, called Gantt charts.

Harrington Emerson applied Taylor's ideas to organization structure and encouraged the use of experts to improve organizational efficiency. He testified in a congressional hearing that railroads could save a million dollars a day by applying principles of scientific management.

Henry Ford, the great industrialist, employed scientific management techniques in his factories.

During the early part of the 20th century, automobiles were just coming into vogue in the United States. Ford's Model T was such a success that the company had trouble keeping up with orders for the cars. In an effort to improve the efficiency of operations, Ford adopted the scientific management principles espoused by Frederick Winslow Taylor. He also introduced the *moving assembly line,* which had a tremendous impact on production methods in many industries.

Mass production System in which low-skilled workers use specialized machinery to produce high volumes of standardized goods.

Among Ford's many contributions was the introduction of **mass production** to the automotive industry, a system of production in which large volumes of standardized goods are produced by low-skilled or semiskilled workers using highly specialized, and often costly, equipment. Ford was able to do this by taking advantage of a number of important concepts. Perhaps the

Row of "Tin Lizzies," or Model T's, being manufactured on the Ford assembly line.

ASSEMBLY LINES

Assembly lines are one of several approaches to the production of goods and delivering services. But the importance of assembly lines to business and society is hard to overstate. Often associated with Henry Ford's automobile production, they were the hallmark of mass production, achieving high volumes of standardized products. As such, they played a pivotal role in the development of what we now refer to as industrialized nations. By shifting from craft production methods to assembly lines, producers were able to successfully employ large numbers of unskilled workers. By using assembly lines, they achieved tremendous gains in industrial productivity, produced affordable products, and in the process greatly increased the standard of living of people in industrial nations. As you will learn later in the book, assembly lines also play an important role in a newer approach to operations called lean production or, more generally, lean operations.

key concept that launched mass production was **interchangeable parts,** sometimes attributed to Eli Whitney, an American inventor who applied the concept to assembling muskets in the late 1700s. The basis for interchangeable parts was to standardize parts so that any part in a batch of parts would fit any automobile coming down the assembly line. This meant that parts did not have to be custom fitted, as they were in craft production. The standardized parts could also be used for replacement parts. The result was a tremendous decrease in assembly time and cost. Ford accomplished this by standardizing the gauges used to measure parts during production and by using newly developed processes to produce uniform parts.

Interchangeable parts Parts of a product made to such precision that they do not have to be custom fitted.

A second concept used by Ford was the **division of labor,** which Adam Smith wrote about in *The Wealth of Nations* (1776). Division of labor means that an operation, such as assembling an automobile, is divided up into a series of many small tasks, and individual workers are assigned to one of those tasks. Unlike craft production, where each worker was responsible for doing many tasks, and thus required skill, with division of labor the tasks were so narrow that virtually no skill was required.

Division of labor The breaking up of a production process into small tasks, so that each worker performs a small portion of the overall job.

Together, these concepts enabled Ford to tremendously increase the production rate at his factories using readily available inexpensive labor. Both Taylor and Ford were despised by many workers, because they held workers in such low regard, expecting them to perform like robots. This paved the way for the human relations movement.

The Human Relations Movement

Whereas the scientific management movement heavily emphasized the technical aspects of work design, the human relations movement emphasized the importance of the human element in job design. Lillian Gilbreth, a psychologist and the wife of Frank Gilbreth, worked with her husband, focusing on the human factor in work. (The Gilbreths were the subject of a classic 1950s film, *Cheaper by the Dozen.*) Many of her studies in the 1920s dealt with worker fatigue. In the following decades, there was much emphasis on motivation. During the 1930s, Elton Mayo conducted studies at the Hawthorne division of Western Electric. His studies revealed that in addition to the physical and technical aspects of work, worker motivation is critical for improving productivity. During the 1940s, Abraham Maslow developed motivational theories, which Frederick Hertzberg refined in the 1950s. Douglas McGregor added Theory X and Theory Y in the 1960s. These theories represented the two ends of the spectrum of how employees view work. Theory X, on the negative end, assumed that workers do not like to work, and have to be controlled—rewarded and punished—to get them to do good work. This attitude was quite common in the automobile industry and in some other industries, until the threat of global competition forced them to rethink that approach. Theory Y, on the other end of the spectrum, assumed that workers enjoy the physical and mental aspects of work and become committed to work. The Theory X approach resulted in an adversarial environment, whereas the Theory Y approach resulted in empowered workers and a more cooperative spirit. In the 1970s, William Ouchi added Theory Z, which combined the Japanese approach with such features as lifetime employment, employee problem solving, and consensus building, and the traditional Western approach that features short-term employment, specialists, and individual decision making and responsibility.

Decision Models and Management Science

The factory movement was accompanied by the development of several quantitative techniques. F. W. Harris developed one of the first models in 1915: a mathematical model for inventory order size. In the 1930s, three coworkers at Bell Telephone Labs, H. F. Dodge, H. G. Romig, and W. Shewhart, developed statistical procedures for sampling and quality control. In 1935, L.H.C. Tippett conducted studies that provided the groundwork for statistical-sampling theory.

At first, these quantitative models were not widely used in industry. However, the onset of World War II changed that. The war generated tremendous pressures on manufacturing output, and specialists from many disciplines combined efforts to achieve advancements in the military and in manufacturing. After the war, efforts to develop and refine quantitative tools for decision making continued, resulting in decision models for forecasting, inventory management, project management, and other areas of operations management.

During the 1960s and 1970s, management science techniques were highly regarded; in the 1980s, they lost some favor. However, the widespread use of personal computers and user-friendly software in the workplace contributed to a resurgence in the popularity of these techniques.

The Influence of Japanese Manufacturers

A number of Japanese manufacturers developed or refined management practices that increased the productivity of their operations and the quality of their products, due in part to the influence of Americans W. Edwards Deming and Joseph Juran. This made them very competitive, sparking interest in their approaches by companies outside Japan. Their approaches emphasized quality and continual improvement, worker teams and empowerment, and achieving customer satisfaction. The Japanese can be credited with spawning the "quality revolution" that occurred in industrialized countries, and with generating widespread interest in lean production.

The influence of the Japanese on U.S. manufacturing and service companies has been enormous and promises to continue for the foreseeable future. Because of that influence, this book will provide considerable information about Japanese methods and successes.

Table 1.4 provides a chronological summary of some of the key developments in the evolution of operations management.

OPERATIONS TODAY

Advances in information technology and global competition have had a major influence on operations management. While the *Internet* offers great potential for business organizations, the potential as well as the risks must be clearly understood in order to determine if and how to exploit this potential. In many cases, the Internet has altered the way companies compete in the marketplace.

E-business Use of the Internet to transact business.

E-commerce Consumer-to-business transactions.

Electronic business, or **e-business,** involves the use of the Internet to transact business. E-business is changing the way business organizations interact with their customers and their suppliers. Most familiar to the general public is **e-commerce,** consumer–business transactions such as buying online or requesting information. However, business-to-business transactions such as e-procurement represent an increasing share of e-business. E-business is receiving increased attention from business owners and managers in developing strategies, planning, and decision making.

Technology The application of scientific discoveries to the development and improvement of goods and services.

The word **technology** has several definitions, depending on the context. Generally, *technology* refers to the application of scientific discoveries to the development and improvement of goods and services. It can involve knowledge, materials, methods, and equipment. The term *high technology* refers to the most advanced and developed machines and methods. Operations management is primarily concerned with three kinds of technology: product and service technology, process technology, and information technology (IT). All three can have a major impact on costs, productivity, and competitiveness.

> ***Product and service technology*** refers to the discovery and development of new products and services. This is done mainly by researchers and engineers, who use the scientific approach to develop new knowledge and translate that into commercial applications.

TABLE 1.4
Historical summary of operations management

Approximate Date	Contribution/Concept	Originator
1776	Division of labor	Adam Smith
1790	Interchangeable parts	Eli Whitney
1911	Principles of scientific management	Frederick W. Taylor
1911	Motion study, use of industrial psychology	Frank and Lillian Gilbreth
1912	Chart for scheduling activities	Henry Gantt
1913	Moving assembly line	Henry Ford
1915	Mathematical model for inventory ordering	F. W. Harris
1930	Hawthorne studies on worker motivation	Elton Mayo
1935	Statistical procedures for sampling and quality control	H. F. Dodge, H. G. Romig, W. Shewhart, L.H.C. Tippett
1940	Operations research applications in warfare	Operations research groups
1947	Linear programming	George Dantzig
1951	Commercial digital computers	Sperry Univac, IBM
1950s	Automation	Numerous
1960s	Extensive development of quantitative tools	Numerous
1960s	Industrial dynamics	Jay Forrester
1975	Emphasis an manufacturing strategy	W. Skinner
1980s	Emphasis on flexibility, time-based competition, lean production	T. Ohno, S. Shingo, Toyota
1980s	Emphasis on quality	W. Edwards Deming, J. Juran, K. Ishikawa
1990s	Internet, supply chain management	Numerous
2000s	Applications service providers and outsourcing	Numerous

Process technology refers to methods, procedures, and equipment used to produce goods and provide services. They include not only processes within an organization but also supply chain processes.

Information technology (IT) refers to the science and use of computers and other electronic equipment to store, process, and send information. Information technology is heavily ingrained in today's business operations. This includes electronic data processing, the use of bar codes to identify and track goods, obtaining point-of-sale information, data transmission, the Internet, e-commerce, e-mail, and more.

Management of technology is high on the list of major trends, and it promises to be high well into the future. For example, computers have had a tremendous impact on businesses in many ways, including new product and service features, process management, medical diagnosis, production planning and scheduling, data processing, and communication. Advances in materials, methods, and equipment also have had an impact on competition and productivity. Advances in information technology also have had a major impact on businesses. Obviously there have been—and will continue to be—many benefits from technological advances. However, technological advance also places a burden on management. For example, management must keep abreast of changes and quickly assess both their benefits and risks. Predicting advances can be tricky at best, and new technologies often carry a high price tag and usually a high cost to operate or repair. And in the case of computer operating systems, as new systems are introduced, support for older versions is discontinued, making periodic upgrades necessary. Conflicting technologies can exist that make technological choices even more difficult. Technological innovations in both *products* and *processes* will continue to change the way businesses operate, and hence require continuing attention.

The North American Free Trade Agreement (NAFTA) opened borders for trade between the United States and Canada and Mexico. The General Agreement on Tariffs and Trade (GATT) of 1994 reduced tariffs and subsidies in many countries, expanding world trade. The resulting global competition and global markets have had an impact on the strategies and operations of businesses large and small around the world. One effect is the importance business organizations are giving to management of their supply chains.

SUPPLY CHAIN

Globalization and the need for global supply chains have broadened the scope of supply chain management. However, tightened border security in certain instances has slowed some movement of goods and people. Moreover, in some cases, organizations are reassessing their use of offshore outsourcing.

Competitive pressures and changing economic conditions have caused business organizations to put more emphasis on

Operations strategy.

Working with fewer resources.

Revenue management.

Process analysis and improvement, and quality improvement.

Agility

Lean production.

During the 1970s and 1980s, many companies neglected to include *operations strategy* in their corporate strategy. Some of them paid dearly for that neglect. Now more and more companies are recognizing the importance of operations strategy on the overall success of their business as well as the necessity for relating it to their overall business strategy.

Working with fewer resources due to layoffs, corporate downsizing, and general cost cutting is forcing managers to make trade-off decisions on resource allocation, and to place increased emphasis on cost control and productivity improvement.

Revenue management is a method used by some companies to maximize the revenue they receive from fixed operating capacity by influencing demand through price manipulation. Also known as yield management, it has been successfully used in the travel and tourism industries by airlines, cruise lines, hotels, amusement parks, and rental car companies, and in other industries such as trucking and public utilities.

Six sigma A process for reducing costs, improving quality, and increasing customer satisfaction.

Process analysis and improvement includes cost and time reduction, productivity improvement, process yield improvement, and quality improvement and increasing customer satisfaction. This is sometimes referred to as a **six sigma** process.

Given a boost by the "quality revolution" of the 1980s and 1990s, *quality* is now ingrained in business. Some businesses use the term *total quality management (TQM)* to describe their quality efforts. A quality focus emphasizes *customer satisfaction* and often involves *teamwork. Process improvement* can result in improved quality, cost reduction, and *time reduction.* Time relates to costs and to competitive advantage, and businesses seek ways to reduce the time to bring new products and services to the marketplace to gain a competitive edge. If two companies can provide the same product at the same price and quality, but one can deliver it four weeks earlier than the other, the quicker company will invariably get the sale. Time reductions are being achieved in many companies now. Kodak was able to cut in half the time needed to bring a new camera to market; Union Carbide was able to cut $400 million of fixed expenses; and Bell Atlantic was able to cut the time needed to hook up long-distance carriers from 15 days to less than 1, at a savings of $82 million.

Agility The ability of an organization to respond quickly to demands or opportunities.

Agility refers to the ability of an organization to respond quickly to demands or opportunities. It is a strategy that involves maintaining a flexible system that can quickly respond to changes in either the volume of demand or changes in product/service offerings. This is particularly important as organizations scramble to remain competitive and cope with increasingly shorter product life cycles and strive to achieve shorter development times for new or improved products and services.

Lean production, a new approach to production, emerged in the 1990s. It incorporates a number of the recent trends listed here, with an emphasis on quality, flexibility, time reduction, and teamwork. This has led to a *flattening* of the organizational structure, with fewer levels of management.

Lean system System that uses minimal amounts of resources to produce a high volume of high-quality goods with some variety.

Lean systems are so named because they use much less of certain resources than typical mass production systems use—space, inventory, and workers—to produce a comparable amount of output. Lean systems use a highly skilled workforce and flexible equipment. In effect, they incorporate advantages of both mass production (high volume, low unit cost) and craft production (variety and flexibility). And quality is higher than in mass production. This approach has now spread to services, including health care, offices, and shipping and delivery.

The skilled workers in lean production systems are more involved in maintaining and improving the system than their mass production counterparts. They are taught to stop an operation if they discover a defect, and to work with other employees to find and correct the cause of the defect so that it won't recur. This results in an increasing level of quality over time and eliminates the need to inspect and rework at the end of the line.

Because lean production systems operate with lower amounts of inventory, additional emphasis is placed on anticipating when problems might occur *before* they arise and avoiding those problems through planning. Even so, problems can still occur at times, and quick resolution is important. Workers participate in both the planning and correction stages.

Compared to workers in traditional systems, much more is expected of workers in lean production systems. They must be able to function in teams, playing active roles in operating and improving the system. Individual creativity is much less important than team success. Responsibilities also are much greater, which can lead to pressure and anxiety not present in traditional systems. Moreover, a flatter organizational structure means career paths are not as steep in lean production organizations. Workers tend to become generalists rather than specialists, another contrast to more traditional organizations.

KEY ISSUES FOR TODAY'S BUSINESS OPERATIONS

There are a number of issues that are high priorities of many business organizations. Although not every business is faced with these issues, many are. Chief among the issues are the following:

Economic conditions. The lingering recession and slow recovery in various sectors of the economy has made managers cautious about investment and rehiring workers that had been laid off during the recession.

Innovating. Finding new or improved products or services are only two of the many possibilities that can provide value to an organization. Innovations can be made in processes, the use of the Internet, or the supply chain that reduce costs, increase productivity, expand markets, or improve customer service.

SUPPLY CHAIN

Quality problems. The numerous operations failures mentioned at the beginning of the chapter underscore the need to improve the way operations are managed. That relates to product design and testing, oversight of suppliers, risk assessment, and timely response to potential problems.

Risk management. The need for managing risk is underscored by recent events that include the crisis in housing, product recalls, oil spills, and natural and man-made disasters, and economic ups and downs. Managing risks starts with identifying risks, assessing vulnerability and potential damage (liability costs, reputation, demand), and taking steps to reduce or share risks.

Competing in a global economy. Low labor costs in third-world countries have increased pressure to reduce labor costs. Companies must carefully weigh their options, which include outsourcing some or all of their operations to low-wage areas, reducing costs internally, changing designs, and working to improve productivity.

Three other key areas require more in-depth discussion: environmental concerns, ethical conduct, and managing the supply chain.

Environmental Concerns

Concern about global warming and pollution has had an increasing effect on how businesses operate.

Stricter environmental regulations, particularly in developed nations, are being imposed. Furthermore, business organizations are coming under increasing pressure to reduce their carbon footprint (the amount of carbon dioxide generated by their operations and their supply chains) and to generally operate sustainable processes. **Sustainability** refers to service and production processes that use resources in ways that do not harm ecological systems that support both current and future human existence. Sustainability measures often go beyond traditional environmental and economic measures to include measures that incorporate social criteria in decision making.

Sustainability Using resources in ways that do not harm ecological systems that support human existence.

All areas of business will be affected by this. Areas that will be most affected include product and service design, consumer education programs, disaster preparation and response, supply chain waste management, and outsourcing decisions. Note that outsourcing of goods production increases not only transportation costs, but also fuel consumption and carbon released into the atmosphere. Consequently, sustainability thinking may have implications for outsourcing decisions.

Because they all fall within the realm of operations, operations management is central to dealing with these issues. Sometimes referred to as "green initiatives," the possibilities include reducing packaging, materials, water and energy use, and the environmental impact of the supply chain, including buying locally. Other possibilities include reconditioning used equipment (e.g., printers and copiers) for resale, and recycling.

Puma's "Clever Little Bag" changes the idea of the shoebox by wrapping footwear in a cardboard structure with 65 percent less cardboard. It uses a bag made of recycled plastic as the outer layer that holds the inner cardboard structure together. Puma expects to cut carbon dioxide emissions by 10,000 tons per year and water, energy, and diesel use by 60 percent by using fewer materials—8,500 fewer tons of paper to be specific—and the new packaging's lighter weight.

Universities Embrace Sustainability

READING

Universities and colleges are increasingly embracing sustainability, linking it to global warming, biodiversity, and global commerce. Some are building sustainability into existing courses, while others are offering new courses, certificate programs, or degree programs. And some, such as Arizona State University and the Rochester Institute of Technology, are offering advanced degree programs.

Some universities are also "practicing what they preach," by applying sustainable practices in their operations. Among them are Dartmouth College, Harvard University, Stanford, Williams College, and the University of British Columbia, which was named by the environmental magazine *Grist* as one of the top 15 universities in the world in reducing greenhouse gas emissions and being energy efficient.

Source: Based on "The Sustainable University: Saving the Planet by Degrees," *Chronicle of Higher Education,* Special Report, October 20, 2006, Stanford News Service, January 2007, and "B.C.'s School of Greener Learning," *Toronto Globe and Mail,* August 25, 2007, p. A6.

The following reading suggests that even our choice of diet can affect the environment.

Diet and the Environment: Vegetarian vs. Nonvegetarian

READING

It is interesting to examine the environmental impact of dietary choices. There's ample evidence that agricultural practices pollute the soil, air, and water. Factors range from the distance food travels to get to the consumer, to the amount of water and fertilizer used. Of particular concern is the environmental impact of a diet high in animal protein. The Food and Agricultural Organization (FAO) of the United Nations recently reported that livestock production is one of the major causes of global warming and air and water pollution. Using a methodology that considers the entire supply chain, the FAO estimated that livestock accounts for 18 percent of greenhouse gas emissions.

A Vegetarian versus Nonvegetarian Diet and the Environment The eco-friendliness of a meat eater's diet was the subject of a "study conducted by researchers from the Departments of Environmental Health and Nutrition of Loma Linda University in California. They compared the environmental effects of a vegetarian vs. nonvegetarian diet in California in terms of agricultural production inputs, including pesticides and fertilizers, water and energy.

"The study results showed that for the combined production of 11 food items the nonvegetarian diet required 2.9 times more water, 2.5 times more primary energy, 13 times more fertilizer, and 1.4 times more pesticides than did the vegetarian diet. The biggest differences came from including beef in the diet."

Source: Based on "Finding a Scientific Connection Between Food Choices and the Environment," *Environmental Nutrition Newsletter,* October 2009, p. 3.

Ethical Conduct

The need for ethical conduct in business is becoming increasingly obvious, given numerous examples of questionable actions in recent history. In making decisions, managers must consider how their decisions will affect shareholders, management, employees, customers, the community at large, and the environment. Finding solutions that will be in the best interests of all of these stakeholders is not always easy, but it is a goal that all managers should strive to achieve. Furthermore, even managers with the best intentions will sometimes make mistakes. If mistakes do occur, managers should act responsibly to correct those mistakes as quickly as possible, and to address any negative consequences.

The Fair Trade Certified™ label guarantees to consumers that strict economic, social, and environmental criteria were met in the production and trade of an agricultural product.

Operations managers, like all managers, have the responsibility to make ethical decisions. Ethical issues arise in many aspects of operations management, including

- Financial statements: accurately representing the organization's financial condition.
- Worker safety: providing adequate training, maintaining equipment in good working condition, maintaining a safe working environment.
- Product safety: providing products that minimize the risk of injury to users or damage to property or the environment.
- Quality: honoring warranties, avoiding hidden defects.
- The environment: not doing things that will harm the environment.
- The community: being a good neighbor.
- Hiring and firing workers: avoiding false pretenses (e.g., promising a long-term job when that is not what is intended).
- Closing facilities: taking into account the impact on a community, and honoring commitments that have been made.
- Workers' rights: respecting workers' rights, dealing with workers' problems quickly and fairly.

Ethics A standard of behavior that guides how one should act in various situations.

Many organizations have developed *codes of ethics* to guide employees' or members' conduct. **Ethics** is a standard of behavior that guides how one should act in various situations. The Markula Center for Applied Ethics at Santa Clara University identifies five principles for thinking ethically:

- The **Utilitarian Principle** is that the good done by an action or inaction should outweigh any harm it causes or might cause. An example is not allowing a person who has had too much to drink to drive.
- The **Rights Principle** is that actions should respect and protect the moral rights of others. An example is not taking advantage of a vulnerable person.
- The **Fairness Principle** is that equals should be held to, or evaluated by, the same standards. An example is equal pay for equal work.
- The **Common Good Principle** is that actions should contribute to the common good of the community. An example is an ordinance on noise abatement.
- The **Virtue Principle** is that actions should be consistent with certain ideal virtues. Examples include honesty, compassion, generosity, tolerance, fidelity, integrity, and self-control.

Ethical framework A sequence of steps intended to guide thinking and subsequent decision or action.

The center expands these principles to create a framework for ethical conduct. An **ethical framework** is a sequence of steps intended to guide thinking and subsequent decisions or actions. Here is the one developed by the Markula Center for Applied Ethics:

1. Recognize an ethical issue by asking if an action could be damaging to a group or an individual. Is there more to it than just what is legal?
2. Make sure the pertinent facts are known, such as who will be impacted, and what options are available.
3. Evaluate the options by referring to each of the preceding five ethical principles.
4. Identify the "best" option and then further examine it by asking how someone you respect would view it.
5. In retrospect, consider the effect your decision had and what you can learn from it.

More detail is available at the Center's Web site: http://www.scu.edu/ethics/practicing/decision/framework.html.

The Need to Manage the Supply Chain

Supply chain management is being given increasing attention as business organizations face mounting pressure to improve management of their supply chains. In the past, most organizations did little to manage their supply chains. Instead, they tended to concentrate on their own

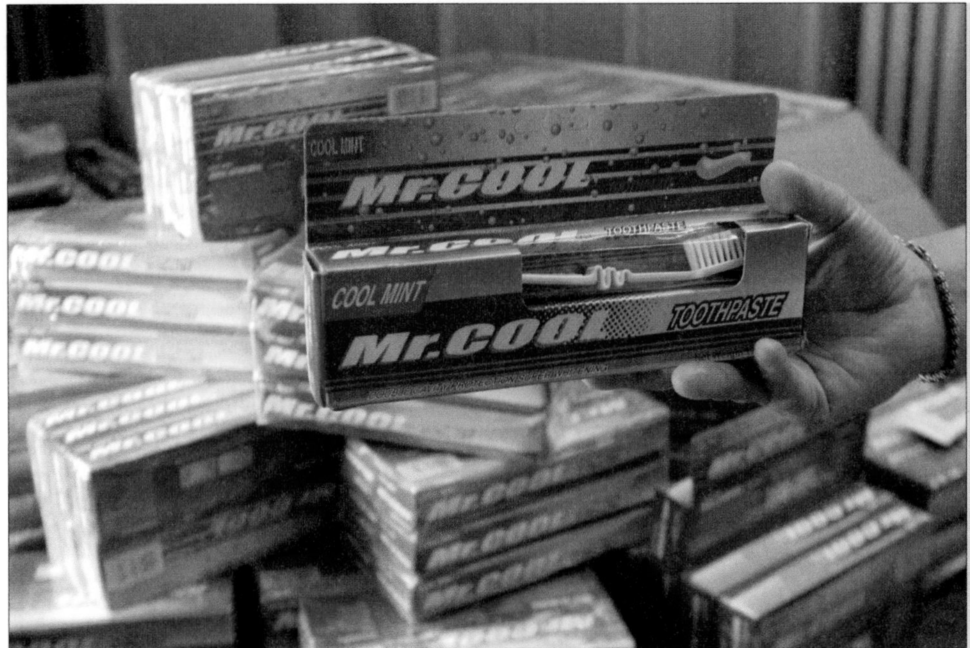

Chinese-made Mr. Cool tainted toothpaste is displayed at the Ministry of Health in San Jose, Costa Rica. China said it was investigating reports that toothpaste containing a potentially deadly chemical had been exported to Central America, one in a series of scandals involving tainted Chinese products. Costa Rica has ordered the removal of Chinese toothpaste and other brands from store shelves.

operations and on their immediate suppliers. Moreover, the planning, marketing, production and inventory management functions in organizations in supply chains have often operated independently of each other. As a result, supply chains experienced a range of problems that were seemingly beyond the control of individual organizations. The problems included large oscillations of inventories, inventory stockouts, late deliveries, and quality problems. These and other issues now make it clear that management of supply chains is essential to business success. The other issues include the following:

1. **The need to improve operations.** During the last decade, many organizations adopted practices such as lean operation and total quality management (TQM). As a result, they were able to achieve improved quality while wringing much of the excess costs out of their systems. Although there is still room for improvement, for many organizations, the major gains have been realized. Opportunity now lies largely with procurement, distribution, and logistics—the supply chain.

2. **Increasing levels of outsourcing.** Organizations are increasing their levels of **outsourcing**, buying goods or services instead of producing or providing them themselves. As outsourcing increases, organizations are spending increasing amounts on supply-related activities (wrapping, packaging, moving, loading and unloading, and sorting). A significant amount of the cost and time spent on these and other related activities may be unnecessary. Issues with imported products, including tainted food products, toothpaste, and pet foods, as well as unsafe tires and toys, have led to questions of liability and the need for companies to take responsibility for monitoring the safety of outsourced goods.

Outsourcing Buying goods or services instead of producing or providing them in-house.

3. **Increasing transportation costs.** Transportation costs are increasing, and they need to be more carefully managed.

4. **Competitive pressures.** Competitive pressures have led to an increasing number of new products, shorter product development cycles, and increased demand for customization. And in some industries, most notably consumer electronics, product life cycles are relatively short. Added to this are adoption of quick-response strategies and efforts to reduce lead times.

5. **Increasing globalization.** Increasing globalization has expanded the physical length of supply chains. A global supply chain increases the challenges of managing a supply chain. Having far-flung customers and/or suppliers means longer lead times and greater opportunities for disruption of deliveries. Often currency differences and monetary fluctuations are factors, as well as language and cultural differences. Also, tightened border security in some instances has slowed shipments of goods.

6. **Increasing importance of e-business.** The increasing importance of e-business has added new dimensions to business buying and selling and has presented new challenges.

7. **The complexity of supply chains.** Supply chains are complex; they are dynamic, and they have many inherent uncertainties that can adversely affect them, such as inaccurate forecasts, late deliveries, substandard quality, equipment breakdowns, and canceled or changed orders.

8. **The need to manage inventories.** Inventories play a major role in the success or failure of a supply chain, so it is important to coordinate inventory levels throughout a supply chain. Shortages can severely disrupt the timely flow of work and have far-reaching impacts, while excess inventories add unnecessary costs. It would not be unusual to find inventory shortages in some parts of a supply chain and excess inventories in other parts of the same supply chain.

Elements of Supply Chain Management

Supply chain management involves coordinating activities across the supply chain. Central to this is taking customer demand and translating it into corresponding activities at each level of the supply chain.

SUPPLY CHAIN

The key elements of supply chain management are listed in Table 1.5. The first element, customers, is the driving element. Typically, marketing is responsible for determining what customers want as well as forecasting the quantities and timing of customer demand. Product and service design must match customer wants with operations capabilities.

Processing occurs in each component of the supply chain: it is the core of each organization. The major portion of processing occurs in the organization that produces the product or service for the final customer (the organization that assembles the computer, services the car, etc.). A major aspect of this for both the internal and external portions of a supply chain is scheduling.

Inventory is a staple in most supply chains. Balance is the main objective; too little causes delays and disrupts schedules, but too much adds unnecessary costs and limits flexibility.

Purchasing is the link between an organization and its suppliers. It is responsible for obtaining goods and or services that will be used to produce products or provide services for the organization's customers. Purchasing selects suppliers, negotiates contracts, establishes alliances, and acts as liaison between suppliers and various internal departments.

The supply portion of a value chain is made up of one or more suppliers, all links in the chain, and each one capable of having an impact on the effectiveness—or the ineffectiveness—of the supply chain. Moreover, it is essential that the planning and execution be carefully coordinated between suppliers and all members of the demand portion of their chains.

TABLE 1.5
Elements of supply chain management

Element	Typical Issues	Chapter(s)
Customers	Determining what products and/or services customers want	3, 4
Forecasting	Predicting the quantity and timing of customer demand	3
Design	Incorporating customers, wants, manufacturability, and time to market	4
Capacity planning	Matching supply and demand	5, 11
Processing	Controlling quality, scheduling work	10, 16
Inventory	Meeting demand requirements while managing the costs of holding inventory	12, 13, 14
Purchasing	Evaluating potential suppliers, supporting the needs of operations on purchased goods and services	15
Suppliers	Monitoring supplier quality, on-time delivery, and flexibility; maintaining supplier relations	15
Location	Determining the location of facilities	8
Logistics	Deciding how to best move information and materials	15

Location can be a factor in a number of ways. Where suppliers are located can be important, as can location of processing facilities. Nearness to market, nearness to sources of supply, or nearness to both may be critical. Also, delivery time and cost are usually affected by location.

Two types of decisions are relevant to supply chain management—strategic and operational. The strategic decisions are the design and policy decisions. The operational decisions relate to day-to-day activities: managing the flow of material and product and other aspects of the supply chain in accordance with strategic decisions.

The major decision areas in supply chain management are location, production, distribution, and inventory. The *location* decision relates to the choice of locations for both production and distribution facilities. Production and transportation costs and delivery lead times are important. *Production* and *distribution* decisions focus on what customers want, when they want it, and how much is needed. Outsourcing can be a consideration. Distribution decisions are strongly influenced by transportation cost and delivery times, because transportation costs often represent a significant portion of total cost. Moreover, shipping alternatives are closely tied to production and inventory decisions. For example, using air transport means higher costs but faster deliveries and less inventory in transit than sea, rail, or trucking options. Distribution decisions must also take into account capacity and quality issues. Operational decisions focus on scheduling, maintaining equipment, and meeting customer demand. Quality control and workload balancing are also important considerations. *Inventory* decisions relate to determining inventory needs and coordinating production and stocking decisions throughout the supply chain. Logistics management plays the key role in inventory decisions.

Operations Tours

Throughout the book you will discover operations tours that describe operations in all sorts of companies. The tour you are about to read is Wegmans Food Markets, a major regional supermarket chain and one of the largest privately held companies in the United States. Wegmans has been consistently ranked high on *Fortune* magazine's list of the 100 Best Companies to Work For since the inception of the survey a decade ago. In 2005 Wegmans was ranked number one on the list.

Wegmans Food Markets

OPERATIONS TOUR

SERVICE

Wegmans Food Markets, Inc., is one of the premier grocery chains in the United States. Headquartered in Rochester, New York, Wegmans operates over 70 stores, mainly in Rochester, Buffalo, and Syracuse. There are also a handful of stores elsewhere in New York State and in New Jersey, Pennsylvania, and Virginia. The company employs over 37,000 people, and has annual sales of over $3 billion.

Wegmans has a strong reputation for offering its customers high product quality and excellent service. Through a combination of market research, trial and error, and listening to its customers, Wegmans has evolved into a very successful organization. Its sales per square foot are 50 percent higher than the industry average.

Superstores

Many of the company's stores are giant 100,000-square-foot superstores, double or triple the size of average supermarkets. You can get an idea about the size of these stores from this: they usually have between 25 and 35 checkout lanes, and during busy periods, all of the checkouts are in operation. A superstore typically employs from 500 to 600 people.

Individual stores differ somewhat in terms of actual size and some special features. Aside from the features normally found in supermarkets, they generally have a full-service deli (typically a 40-foot display case), a 500-square-foot fisherman's wharf that has perhaps 10 different fresh fish offerings most days, a large bakery section (each store bakes its own bread, rolls, cakes, pies, and pastries), and extra-large produce sections. They also offer film processing, a complete pharmacy, a card shop, video rentals, and an Olde World Cheese section. In-store floral shops range in size up to 800 square feet of floor space and offer a wide variety of fresh-cut flowers, flower arrangements, vases, and plants. In-store card shops cover over 1,000 square feet of floor space. The bulk foods department provides customers with the opportunity to select the quantities they desire from a vast array of foodstuffs and some nonfood items such as birdseed and pet food.

(continued)

Each store is a little different. Among the special features in some stores are a dry cleaning department, a wokery, and a salad bar. Some stores feature a Market Café that has different food stations, each devoted to preparing and serving a certain type of food. For example, one station will have pizza and other Italian specialties, and another oriental food, and still another chicken or fish. There also will be a sandwich bar, a salad bar, and a dessert station. Customers often wander among stations as they decide what to order. In some Market Cafés, diners can have wine with their meals and have brunch on Sundays. In several affluent locations, customers can stop in on their way home from work and choose from a selection of freshly prepared dinner entrees such as medallions of beef with herb butter, chicken Marsala, stuffed flank steak with mushrooms, Cajun tuna, crab cakes, and accompaniments such as roasted red potatoes, grilled vegetables, and Caesar salad. Many Wegmans stores offer ready-made sandwiches as well as made-to-order sandwiches. Some stores have a coffee-shop section with tables and chairs where shoppers can enjoy regular or specialty coffees and a variety of tempting pastries.

Produce Department

The company prides itself on fresh produce. Produce is replenished as often as 12 times a day. The larger stores have produce sections that are four to five times the size of a produce section in an average supermarket. Wegmans offers locally grown produce in season. Wegmans uses a "farm to market" system whereby some local growers deliver their produce directly to individual stores, bypassing the main warehouse. That reduces the company's inventory holding costs and gets the produce into the stores as quickly as possible. Growers may use specially designed containers that go right onto the store floor instead of large bins. This avoids the bruising that often occurs when fruits and vegetables are transferred from bins to display shelves and the need to devote labor to transfer the produce to shelves.

Meat Department

In addition to large display cases of both fresh and frozen meat products, many stores have a full-service butcher shop that offers a variety of fresh meat products and where butchers are available to provide customized cuts of meat for customers.

Meat department employees attend Wegmans' "Meat University," where they learn about different cuts of meat and how to best prepare them. They also learn about other items to pair with various meats, and suggest side dishes, breads, and wine. This helps instill a "selling culture" among employees, who often spend 75 percent of their time talking with customers.

Wegmans continually analyzes store operations to improve processes. In the meat department, a change from in-store cutting and traditional packaging to using a centralized meat processing facility and vacuum packaging extended the shelf life of meats and reduced staffing requirements in meat departments, reducing costs and providing customers with an improved product.

Ordering

Each department handles its own ordering. Although sales records are available from records of items scanned at the checkouts, they are not used directly for replenishing stock. Other factors—such as pricing, special promotions, and local circumstances (e.g., festivals, weather conditions)—must all be taken into account.

(continued)

Wegmans' Patisserie is an authentic French pastry shop.

However, for seasonal periods, such as holidays, managers often check scanner records to learn what past demand was during a comparable period.

The superstores typically receive one truckload of goods per day from the main warehouse. During peak periods, a store may receive two truckloads from the main warehouse. The short lead time greatly reduces the length of time an item might be out of stock, unless the main warehouse is also out of stock.

The company exercises strict control over suppliers, insisting on product quality and on-time deliveries.

Inventory Management

Wegmans uses a companywide system to keep track of inventory. Departments take a monthly inventory count to verify the amount shown in the companywide system. Departments receive a periodic report indicating how many days of inventory the department has on hand. Having an appropriate amount on hand is important to department managers: If they have too much inventory on hand, that will add to their department's costs, whereas having too little inventory will result in shortages and thus lost sales and dissatisfied customers.

Employees

The company recognizes the value of good employees. It typically invests an average of $7,000 to train each new employee. In addition to learning about store operations, new employees learn the importance of good customer service and how to provide it. The employees are helpful, cheerfully answering customer questions or handling complaints. Employees are motivated through a combination of compensation, profit sharing, and benefits. Employee turnover for full-time workers is about 6 percent, compared to the industry average of about 20 percent.

Quality

Quality and customer satisfaction are utmost in the minds of Wegmans' management and its employees. Private-label food items as well as name brands are regularly evaluated in test kitchens, along with potential new products. Managers are responsible for checking and maintaining product and service quality in their departments. Moreover, employees are encouraged to report problems to their managers.

If a customer is dissatisfied with an item, and returns it, or even a portion of the item, the customer is offered a choice of a replacement or a refund. If the item is a Wegmans brand food item, it is then sent to the test kitchen to determine the cause of the problem. If the cause can be determined, corrective action is taken.

Technology

Wegmans continues to adopt new technologies to maintain its competitive edge, including new approaches to tracking inventory and managing its supply chain, and new ways to maintain freshness in the meat and produce departments.

Sustainability

Wegmans began replacing incandescent light bulbs with compact fluorescent bulbs in 2007, and the company expects this will result in generating 3,000 fewer tons of carbon dioxide each year. Also the company installed sensors in its dairy cases that reduced the time the cooling systems run by 50 percent.

(continued)

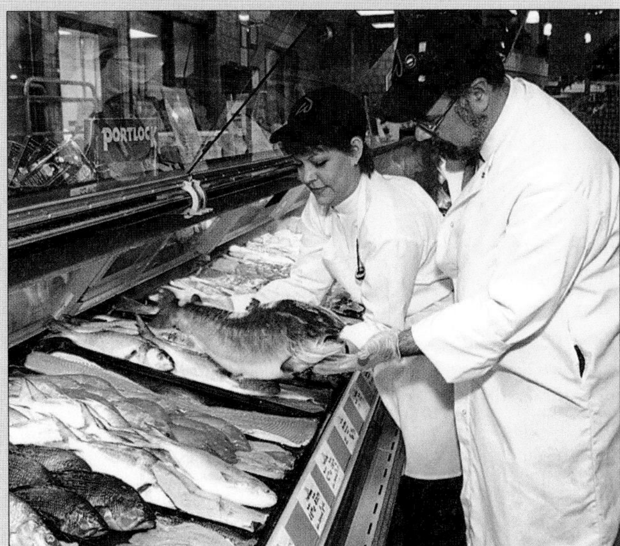

Fresh seafood is delivered daily, often direct from boat to store the same day it was caught.

Wegmans' chefs fill the Chef's Case with ready-to-eat and ready-to-heat entrees, side dishes, and salads.

(concluded)

Questions

1. How do customers judge the quality of a supermarket?
2. Indicate how and why each of these factors is important to the successful operation of a supermarket:
   a. Customer satisfaction.
   b. Forecasting.
   c. Capacity planning.
   d. Location.
   e. Inventory management.
   f. Layout of the store.
   g. Scheduling.
3. What are some of the ways Wegmans uses technology to gain an edge over its competition?

SUMMARY

The operations function in business organizations is responsible for producing goods and providing services. It is a core function of every business. Supply chains are the sequential system of suppliers and customers that begins with basic sources of inputs and ends with final customers of the system. Operations and supply chains are interdependent—one couldn't exist without the other, and no business organization could exist without both.

Operations management involves system design and operating decisions related to product and service design, capacity planning, process selection, location selection, work management, inventory and supply management, production planning, quality assurance, scheduling, and project management.

The historical evolution of operations management provides interesting background information on the continuing evolution of this core business function.

The Operations Tours and Readings included in this and subsequent chapters provide insights into actual business operations.

KEY POINTS

1. The operations function is that part of every business organization that produces products and/or delivers services.
2. Operations consists of processes that convert inputs into outputs. Failure to manage those processes effectively will have a negative impact on the organization.
3. A key goal of business organizations is to achieve an economic matching of supply and demand. The operations function is responsible for providing the supply or service capacity for expected demand.
4. All processes exhibit variation that must be managed.
5. Although there are some basic differences between services and products that must be taken into account from a managerial standpoint, there are also many similarities between the two.
6. Environmental issues will increasingly impact operations decision making.
7. Ethical behavior is an integral part of good management practice.
8. All business organizations have, and are part of, a supply chain that must be managed.

KEY TERMS

agility, 26
craft production, 21
division of labor, 23
e-business, 24
e-commerce, 24
ethical framework 30
ethics, 30
goods, 4
interchangeable parts, 23
lead time, 16
lean system, 27
mass production, 22
model, 18
operations management, 4
outsourcing, 31
Pareto phenomenon, 20
process, 9
services, 4
six sigma, 26
supply chain, 4
sustainability, 28
system, 20
technology, 24
value-added, 6

DISCUSSION AND REVIEW QUESTIONS

1. Briefly describe the term *operations management.*
2. Identify the three major functional areas of business organizations and briefly describe how they interrelate.
3. Describe the operations function and the nature of the operations manager's job.

4. List five important differences between goods production and service operations; then list five important similarities.
5. Briefly discuss each of these terms related to the historical evolution of operations management:
   a. Industrial Revolution
   b. Scientific management
   c. Interchangeable parts
   d. Division of labor
6. Why are services important? Why is manufacturing important? What are nonmanufactured goods?
7. What are models and why are they important?
8. Why is the degree of customization an important consideration in process planning?
9. List the trade-offs you would consider for each of these decisions:
   a. Driving your own car versus public transportation.
   b. Buying a computer now versus waiting for an improved model.
   c. Buying a new car versus buying a used car.
   d. Speaking up in class versus waiting to get called on by the instructor.
   e. A small business owner having a Web site versus newspaper advertising.
10. Describe each of these systems: craft production, mass production, and lean production.
11. Why might some workers prefer not to work in a lean production environment?
12. Discuss the importance of each of the following:
    a. Matching supply and demand
    b. Managing a supply chain
13. List and briefly explain the four basic sources of variation, and explain why it is important for managers to be able to effectively deal with variation.
14. Why do people do things that are unethical?
15. Explain the term *value-added.*
16. Discuss the various impacts of outsourcing.
17. Discuss the term *sustainability,* and its relevance for business organizations.

TAKING STOCK

This item appears at the end of each chapter. It is intended to focus your attention on three key issues for business organizations in general, and operations management in particular. Those issues are trade-off decisions, collaboration among various functional areas of the organization, and the impact of technology. You will see three or more questions relating to these issues. Here is the first set of questions:

1. What are trade-offs? Why is careful consideration of trade-offs important in decision making?
2. Why is it important for the various functional areas of a business organization to collaborate?
3. In what general ways does technology have an impact on operations management decision making?

CRITICAL THINKING EXERCISES

This item also will appear in every chapter. It allows you to critically apply information you learned in the chapter to a practical situation. Here is the first set of exercises:

1. Many organizations offer a combination of goods and services to their customers. As you learned in this chapter, there are some key differences between production of goods and delivery of services. What are the implications of these differences relative to managing operations?
2. Why is it important to match supply and demand? If a manager believes that supply and demand will not be equal, what actions could the manager take to increase the probability of achieving a match?
3. One way that organizations compete is through technological innovation. However, there can be downsides for both the organization and the consumer. Explain.
4. a. What are some possible reasons a business person would make an unethical decision?
   b. What are the risks of doing so?

Hazel

CASE

Hazel had worked for the same Fortune 500 company for almost 15 years. Although the company had gone through some tough times, things were starting to turn around. Customer orders were up, and quality and productivity had improved dramatically from what they had been only a few years earlier due to a company-wide quality improvement program. So it came as a real shock to Hazel and about 400 of her coworkers when they were suddenly terminated following the new CEO's decision to downsize the company.

After recovering from the initial shock, Hazel tried to find employment elsewhere. Despite her efforts, after eight months of searching she was no closer to finding a job than the day she started. Her funds were being depleted and she was getting more discouraged. There was one bright spot, though: She was able to bring in a little money by mowing lawns for her neighbors. She got involved quite by chance when she heard one neighbor remark that now that his children were on their own, nobody was around to cut the grass. Almost jokingly, Hazel asked him how much he'd be willing to pay. Soon Hazel was mowing the lawns of five neighbors. Other neighbors wanted her to work on their lawns, but she didn't feel that she could spare any more time from her job search.

However, as the rejection letters began to pile up, Hazel knew she had to make a decision. On a sunny Tuesday morning, she decided, like many others in a similar situation, to go into business for herself—taking care of neighborhood lawns. She was relieved to give up the stress of job hunting, and she was excited about the prospect of being her own boss. But she was also fearful of being completely on her own. Nevertheless, Hazel was determined to make a go of it.

At first, business was a little slow, but once people realized Hazel was available, many asked her to take care of their lawns. Some people were simply glad to turn the work over to her; others switched from professional lawn care services. By the end of her first year in business, Hazel knew she could earn a living this way. She also performed other services such as fertilizing lawns, weeding gardens, and trimming shrubbery. Business became so good that Hazel hired two part-time workers to assist her and, even then, she believed she could expand further if she wanted to.

Questions

1. In what ways are Hazel's customers most likely to judge the quality of her lawn care services?
2. Hazel is the operations manager of her business. Among her responsibilities are forecasting, inventory management, scheduling, quality assurance, and maintenance.
   a. What kinds of things would likely require forecasts?
   b. What inventory items does Hazel probably have? Name one inventory decision she has to make periodically.
   c. What scheduling must she do? What things might occur to disrupt schedules and cause Hazel to reschedule?
   d. How important is quality assurance to Hazel's business? Explain.
   e. What kinds of maintenance must be performed?
3. What are some of the trade-offs that Hazel probably considered relative to:
   a. Working for a company instead of for herself?
   b. Expanding the business?
   c. Launching a Web site?
4. The town is considering an ordinance that would prohibit putting grass clippings at the curb for pickup because local landfills cannot handle the volume. What options might Hazel consider if the ordinance is passed? Name two advantages and two drawbacks of each option.
5. Hazel decided to offer the students who worked for her a bonus of $25 for ideas on how to improve the business, and they provided several good ideas. One idea that she initially rejected now appears to hold great promise. The student who proposed the idea has left, and is currently working for a competitor. Should Hazel send that student a check for the idea? What are the possible trade-offs?
6. All managers have to cope with variation.
   a. What are the major sources of variation that Hazel has to contend with?
   b. How might these sources of variation impact Hazel's ability to match supply and demand?
   c. What are some ways she can cope with variation?
7. Hazel is thinking of making some of her operations sustainable. What are some ideas she might consider?

SELECTED BIBLIOGRAPHY AND FURTHER READINGS

Bowie, Norman E., ed. *The Blackwell Guide to Business Ethics.* Malden, MA: Blackwell, 2002.

Colvin, Geoffrey. "Managing in the Info Era." *Fortune,* March 6, 2000, pp. F6–F9.

Crainer, Stuart. *The Management Century.* New York: Jossey-Bass, 2000.

Fitzsimmons, James, and Mona Fitzsimmons. *Service Management,* 4th ed. New York: McGraw-Hill/Irwin, 2004.

Hanke, John E. and Dean W. Wichern. *Business Forecasting,* 9th ed. Upper Saddle River, NJ: Pearson Prentice-Hall, 2009.

Shinn, Sharon. "What About the Widgets?" *BizEd,* November–December 2004, pp. 30–35.

Womack, James P., Daniel Jones, and Daniel Roos. *The Machine That Changed the World.* New York: Harper Perennial, 1991, 2007.

Wisner, Joel D., and Linda L. Stanley. *Process Management: Creating Value Along the Supply Chain.* Mason, OH: Thomson South-Western, 2008.

Competitiveness, Strategy, and Productivity

CHAPTER OUTLINE

LEARNING OBJECTIVES

After completing this chapter, you should be able to:

1 List the three primary ways that business organizations compete.
2 Explain five reasons for the poor competitiveness of some companies.
3 Define the term *strategy* and explain why strategy is important.
4 Discuss and compare organization strategy and operations strategy, and explain why it is important to link the two.
5 Describe and give examples of *time-based* strategies.
6 Define the term *productivity* and explain why it is important to organizations and to countries.
7 Provide some of the reasons for poor productivity and some ways of improving it.

This chapter discusses competitiveness, strategy, and productivity, three separate but related topics that are vitally important to business organizations. *Competitiveness* relates to the effectiveness of an organization in the marketplace relative to other organizations that offer similar products or services. Operations and marketing have a major impact on competitiveness. *Strategy* relates to the plans that determine how an organization pursues its goals. Operations strategy is particularly important in this regard. *Productivity* relates to the effective use of resources, and it has a direct impact on competitiveness. Operations management is chiefly responsible for productivity.

THE COLD HARD FACTS

The name of the game is competition. The playing field is global. Those who understand how to play the game will succeed; those who don't are doomed to failure. And don't think the game is just companies competing with each other. In companies that have multiple factories or divisions producing the same good or service, factories or divisions sometimes find themselves competing with each other. When a competitor—another company or a sister factory or division in the same company—can turn out products better, cheaper, and faster, that spells real trouble for the factory or division that is performing at a lower level. The trouble can be layoffs or even a shutdown if the managers can't turn things around. The bottom line? Better quality, higher productivity, lower costs, and the ability to quickly respond to customer needs are more important than ever, and the bar is getting higher. Business organizations need to develop solid strategies for dealing with these issues.

INTRODUCTION

In this chapter you will learn about the different ways companies compete and why some firms do a very good job of competing. You will learn how effective strategies can lead to competitive organizations, and you will learn what productivity is, why it is important, and what organizations can do to improve it.

COMPETITIVENESS

Competitiveness How effectively an organization meets the wants and needs of customers relative to others that offer similar goods or services.

Companies must be competitive to sell their goods and services in the marketplace. **Competitiveness** is an important factor in determining whether a company prospers, barely gets by, or fails.

Business organizations compete through some combination of their marketing and operations functions. Marketing influences competitiveness in several ways, including identifying consumer wants and needs, pricing, and advertising and promotion.

1. **Identifying consumer wants and/or needs** is a basic input in an organization's decision-making process, and central to competitiveness. The ideal is to achieve a perfect match between those wants and needs and the organization's goods and/or services.
2. **Price and quality** are key factors in consumer buying decisions. It is important to understand the trade-off decision consumers make between price and quality.
3. **Advertising and promotion** are ways organizations can inform potential customers about features of their products or services, and attract buyers.

Operations has a major influence on competitiveness through product and service design, cost, location, quality, response time, flexibility, inventory and supply chain management, and service. Many of these are interrelated.

1. **Product and service design** should reflect joint efforts of many areas of the firm to achieve a match between financial resources, operations capabilities, supply chain capabilities, and consumer wants and needs. Special characteristics or features of a product or service can be a key factor in consumer buying decisions. Other key factors include **innovation** and the **time-to-market** for new products and services.
2. **Cost** of an organization's output is a key variable that affects pricing decisions and profits. Cost-reduction efforts are generally ongoing in business organizations. **Productivity** (discussed later in the chapter) is an important determinant of cost. Organizations with higher productivity rates than their competitors have a competitive cost advantage. A company may outsource a portion of its operation to achieve lower costs, higher productivity, or better quality.
3. **Location** can be important in terms of cost and convenience for customers. Location near inputs can result in lower input costs. Location near markets can result in lower transportation costs and quicker delivery times. Convenient location is particularly important in the retail sector.
4. **Quality** refers to materials, workmanship, design, and service. Consumers judge quality in terms of how well they think a product or service will satisfy its intended purpose. Customers are generally willing to pay more for a product or service if they perceive the product or service has a higher quality than that of a competitor.
5. **Quick response** can be a competitive advantage. One way is quickly bringing new or improved products or services to the market. Another is being able to quickly deliver existing products and services to a customer after they are ordered, and still another is quickly handling customer complaints.
6. **Flexibility** is the ability to respond to changes. Changes might relate to alterations in design features of a product or service, or to the volume demanded by customers, or the

Indian employees at a call center provide service support to international customers. The hiring frenzy in India is the flip side of the United States and Britain, where thousands of software and back-office jobs are being cut as companies take advantage of cheap communications offshore to drive down costs. This industry in India already provides one million jobs.

mix of products or services offered by an organization. High flexibility can be a competitive advantage in a changeable environment.

7. **Inventory management** can be a competitive advantage by effectively matching supplies of goods with demand.
8. **Supply chain management** involves coordinating internal and external operations (buyers and suppliers) to achieve timely and cost-effective delivery of goods throughout the system.
9. **Service** might involve after-sale activities customers perceive as value-added, such as delivery, setup, warranty work, and technical support. Or it might involve extra attention while work is in progress, such as courtesy, keeping the customer informed, and attention to details. **Service quality** can be a key differentiator; and it is one that is often sustainable. Moreover, businesses rated highly by their customers for service quality tend to be more profitable, and grow faster, than businesses that are not rated highly.
10. **Managers** and **workers** are the people at the heart and soul of an organization, and if they are competent and motivated, they can provide a distinct competitive edge by their skills and the ideas they create. One often overlooked skill is answering the telephone. How complaint calls or requests for information are handled can be a positive or a negative. If a person answering is rude or not helpful, that can produce a negative image. Conversely, if calls are handled promptly and cheerfully, that can produce a positive image and, potentially, a competitive advantage.

SERVICE

Why Some Organizations Fail

Organizations fail, or perform poorly, for a variety of reasons. Being aware of those reasons can help managers avoid making similar mistakes. Among the chief reasons are the following:

1. Neglecting operations strategy.
2. Failing to take advantage of strengths and opportunities, and/or failing to recognize competitive threats.
3. Putting too much emphasis on short-term financial performance at the expense of research and development.

4. Placing too much emphasis on product and service design and not enough on process design and improvement.
5. Neglecting investments in capital and human resources.
6. Failing to establish good internal communications and cooperation among different functional areas.
7. Failing to consider customer wants and needs.

The key to successfully competing is to determine what customers want and then directing efforts toward meeting (or even exceeding) customer expectations. Two basic issues must be addressed. First: What do the customers want? (Which items on the preceding list of the ways business organizations compete are important to customers?) Second: What is the best way to satisfy those wants?

Operations must work with marketing to obtain information on the relative importance of the various items to each major customer or target market.

Understanding competitive issues can help managers develop successful strategies.

MISSION AND STRATEGIES

Mission The reason for the existence of an organization.

Mission statement States the purpose of an organization.

Goals Provide detail and scope of the mission.

An organization's **mission** is the reason for its existence. It is expressed in its **mission statement.** For a business organization, the mission statement should answer the question "What business are we in?" Missions vary from organization to organization, depending on the nature of their business. Table 2.1 provides several examples of mission statements.

A mission statement serves as the basis for organizational **goals,** which provide more detail and describe the scope of the mission. The mission and goals often relate to how an organization wants to be perceived by the general public, and by its employees, suppliers, and customers. Goals serve as a foundation for the development of organizational strategies. These, in turn, provide the basis for strategies and tactics of the functional units of the organization.

Strategies Plans for achieving organizational goals.

Organizational strategy is important because it guides the organization by providing direction for, and alignment of, the goals and **strategies** of the functional units. Moreover, strategies can be the main reason for the success or failure of an organization.

There are three basic business strategies:

- Low cost.
- Responsiveness.
- Differentiation from competitors.

TABLE 2.1
Selected portions of company mission statements

Microsoft	To help people and businesses throughout the world to realize their full potential.
Nike	To bring inspiration and innovation to every athlete in the world.
Verizon	To help people and businesses communicate with each other.
Walt Disney	To be one of the world's leading producers and providers of entertainment and information.

IS IT A STRATEGIC, TACTICAL, OR OPERATIONAL ISSUE?

Sometimes the same issue may apply to all three levels. However, a key difference is the time frame. From a strategic perspective, long-term implications are most relevant. From tactical and operational perspectives, the time frames are much shorter. In fact, the operational time frame is often measured in days.

Responsiveness relates to ability to respond to changing demands. Differentiation can relate to product or service features, quality, reputation, or customer service. Some organizations focus on a single strategy while others employ a combination of strategies. One company that

Amazon's service helped propel the company to double-digit sales in each quarter of 2009. Amazon started same-day shipping in seven major cities, launched a program to urge manufacturers to drop frustrating packaging, and extended its service reach by acquiring free-shipping pioneer Zappos.com.

has multiple strategies is Amazon.com. Not only does it offer low cost and quick, reliable deliveries, it also excels in customer service.

AMAZON Tops in Customer Service

READING

Amazon received the top spot in customer service in a recent *BusinessWeek* ranking. Although most Amazon customers never talk with an employee, when something goes wrong, Amazon excels in dealing with the problem. In one case, when a New Jersey woman received a workbook she ordered that was described as "like new," she was surprised to discover that it wasn't even close to new—worksheets had already been filled in. She complained to the merchant but didn't get a response. Then she complained to Amazon. She promptly received a refund, even though she had paid the merchant, not Amazon. And she wasn't asked to return the book.

Amazon sees its customer service as a way to enhance customer experience, and as a way to identify potential problems with merchants. In fact, if merchants have problems with more than 1 percent of their orders, that can get them removed from the site.

Source: Based on "How Amazon Aims to Keep You Clicking," *BusinessWeek,* March 2009, p. 34.

Strategies and Tactics

If you think of goals as destinations, then strategies are the roadmaps for reaching the destinations. Strategies provide *focus* for decision making. Generally speaking, organizations have overall strategies called *organizational strategies,* which relate to the entire organization. They also have *functional strategies,* which relate to each of the functional areas of the organization. The functional strategies should support the overall strategies of the organization, just as the organizational strategies should support the goals and mission of the organization.

Tactics are the methods and actions used to accomplish strategies. They are more specific than strategies, and they provide guidance and direction for carrying out actual *operations,* which need the most specific and detailed plans and decision making in an organization. You might think of tactics as the "how to" part of the process (e.g., how to reach the destination, following the strategy roadmap) and operations as the actual "doing" part of the process. Much of this book deals with tactical operations.

Tactics The methods and actions taken to accomplish strategies.

It should be apparent that the overall relationship that exists from the mission down to actual operations is *hierarchical.* This is illustrated in Figure 2.1.

A simple example may help to put this hierarchy into perspective.

FIGURE 2.1
Planning and decision making are hierarchical in organizations

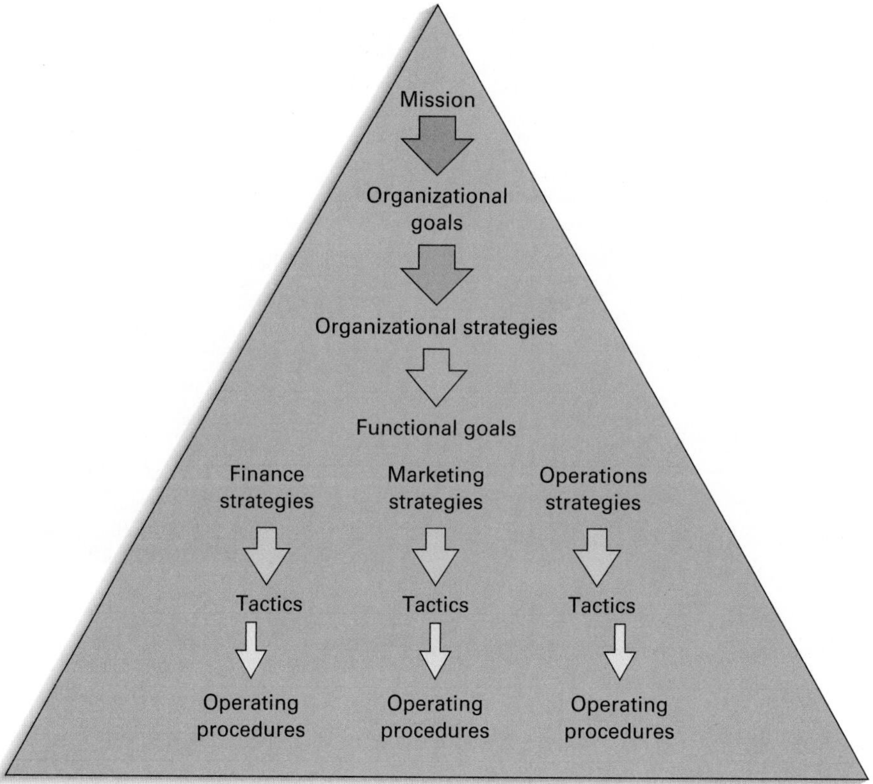

EXAMPLE 1

Rita is a high school student in Southern California. She would like to have a career in business, have a good job, and earn enough income to live comfortably.

A possible scenario for achieving her goals might look something like this:

Mission: Live a good life.

Goal: Successful career, good income.

Strategy: Obtain a college education.

Tactics: Select a college and a major; decide how to finance college.

Operations: Register, buy books, take courses, study.

Here are some examples of different strategies an organization might choose from:

Low cost. Outsource operations to third-world countries that have low labor costs.

Scale-based strategies. Use capital-intensive methods to achieve high output volume and low unit costs.

Specialization. Focus on narrow product lines or limited service to achieve higher quality.

Newness. Focus on innovation to create new products or services.

Flexible operations. Focus on quick response and/or customization.

High quality. Focus on achieving higher quality than competitors.

Service. Focus on various aspects of service (e.g., helpful, courteous, reliable, etc.).

Sustainability. Focus on environmental-friendly and energy-efficient operations.

A wide range of business organizations are beginning to recognize the strategic advantages of sustainability, not only in economic terms, but also in promotional benefit by publicizing their sustainability efforts and achievements.

Sometimes organizations will combine two or more of these or other approaches into their strategy. However, unless they are careful, they risk losing focus and not achieving advantage in any category. Generally speaking, strategy formulation takes into account the way organizations compete and a particular organization's assessment of its own strengths and weaknesses in order to take advantage of its **core competencies**—those special attributes or abilities possessed by an organization that give it a *competitive edge.*

Core competencies The special attributes or abilities that give an organization a competitive edge.

The most effective organizations use an approach that develops core competencies based on customer needs as well as on what the competition is doing. Marketing and operations work closely to match customer needs with operations capabilities. Competitor competencies are important for several reasons. For example, if a competitor is able to supply high-quality products, it may be necessary to meet that high quality as a baseline. However, merely *matching* a competitor is usually not sufficient to gain market share. It may be necessary to exceed the quality level of the competitor or gain an edge by excelling in one or more other dimensions, such as rapid delivery or service after the sale. Walmart, for example, has been very successful in managing its supply chain, which has contributed to its competitive advantage.

To be effective, strategies and core competencies need to be aligned. Table 2.2 lists examples of strategies and companies that have successfully employed those strategies.

Strategy Formulation

Strategy formulation is almost always critical to the success of a strategy. Walmart discovered that when it opened stores in Japan. Although Walmart thrived in many countries on its reputation for low-cost items, Japanese consumers associated low cost with low quality, causing Walmart to rethink its strategy in the Japanese market. And many felt that Hewlett-Packard (HP) committed a strategic error when it acquired Compaq Computers at a cost of $19 billion. HP's share of the computer market was less after the merger than the sum of the shares of the separate companies before the merger. In another example, U.S. automakers adopted a strategy in the early 2000s of offering discounts and rebates on a range of cars and SUVs, many of which were on low-margin vehicles. The strategy put a strain on profits, but customers began to expect those incentives, and the companies maintained them to keep from losing additional market share.

On the other hand, Coach, the maker of leather handbags and purses, successfully changed its longtime strategy to grow its market by creating new products. Long known for its highly durable leather goods in a market where women typically owned few handbags, Coach created a new market for itself by changing women's view of handbags by promoting "different handbags for different occasions" such as party bags, totes, clutches, wristlets, overnight bags, purses, and day bags. And Coach introduced many fashion styles and colors.

To formulate an effective strategy, senior managers must take into account the core competencies of the organizations, and they must *scan the environment.* They must determine what competitors are doing, or planning to do, and take that into account. They must critically examine other factors that could have either positive or negative effects. This is sometimes referred to as the **SWOT** approach (strengths, weaknesses, opportunities, and threats). Strengths and weaknesses have an internal focus and are typically evaluated by operations people. Threats and opportunities have an external focus and are typically evaluated by marketing people. SWOT is often regarded as the link between organizational strategy and operations strategy.

SWOT Analysis of strengths, weaknesses, opportunities, and threats.

In formulating a successful strategy, organizations must take into account both order qualifiers and order winners. **Order qualifiers** are those characteristics that potential customers perceive as minimum standards of acceptability for a product to be considered for purchase. However, that may not be sufficient to get a potential customer to purchase from the organization. **Order winners** are those characteristics of an organization's goods or services that cause them to be perceived as better than the competition.

Order qualifiers Characteristics that customers perceive as minimum standards of acceptability to be considered as a potential for purchase.

Order winners Characteristics of an organization's goods or services that cause it to be perceived as better than the competition.

Characteristics such as price, delivery reliability, delivery speed, and quality can be order qualifiers or order winners. Thus, quality may be an order winner in some situations, but in

TABLE 2.2
Examples of operations strategies

Organization Strategy	Operations Strategy	Examples of Companies or Services
Low price	Low cost	U.S. first-class postage
		Walmart
		Southwest Airlines
Responsiveness	Short processing time	McDonald's restaurants
		Express Mail, UPS, FedEx
		One-hour photo
	On-time delivery	Domino's Pizza
		FedEx
Differentiation: High quality	High-performance design and/or high-quality processing	Sony TV
		Lexus
		Disneyland
		Five-star restaurants or hotels
	Consistent quality	Coca-Cola, PepsiCo
		Kodak, Xerox, Motorola
		Electrical power
Differentiation: Newness	Innovation	3M, Apple
		Google
Differentiation: Variety	Flexibility	Burger King ("Have it your way")
		Hospital emergency room
	Volume	McDonald's ("Buses welcome")
		Toyota
		Supermarkets (additional checkouts)
Differentiation: Service	Superior customer service	Disneyland
		Amazon
		Hewlett-Packard
		IBM
		Nordstrom
Differentiation: Location	Convenience	Supermarkets, dry cleaners
		Mall stores
		Service stations
		Banks, ATMs

others only an order qualifier. Over time, a characteristic that was once an order winner may become an order qualifier, and vice versa.

Obviously, it is important to determine the set of order qualifier characteristics and the set of order winner characteristics. It is also necessary to decide on the relative importance of each characteristic so that appropriate attention can be given to the various characteristics. Marketing must make that determination and communicate it to operations.

Environmental scanning
The monitoring of events and trends that present threats or opportunities for a company.

Environmental scanning is the monitoring of events and trends that present either threats or opportunities for the organization. Generally these include competitors' activities; changing consumer needs; legal, economic, political, and environmental issues; the potential for new markets; and the like.

Another key factor to consider when developing strategies is technological change, which can present real opportunities and threats to an organization. Technological changes occur in products (high-definition TV, improved computer chips, improved cellular telephone systems, and improved designs for earthquake-proof structures); in services (faster order processing, faster delivery); and in processes (robotics, automation, computer-assisted processing, point-of-sale scanners, and flexible manufacturing systems). The obvious benefit is a competitive edge; the risk is that incorrect choices, poor execution, and higher-than-expected operating costs will create competitive *disadvantages.*

Important factors may be internal or external. The following are key external factors:

1. **Economic conditions.** These include the general health and direction of the economy, inflation and deflation, interest rates, tax laws, and tariffs.
2. **Political conditions.** These include favorable or unfavorable attitudes toward business, political stability or instability, and wars.
3. **Legal environment.** This includes antitrust laws, government regulations, trade restrictions, minimum wage laws, product liability laws and recent court experience, labor laws, and patents.
4. **Technology.** This can include the rate at which product innovations are occurring, current and future process technology (equipment, materials handling), and design technology.
5. **Competition.** This includes the number and strength of competitors, the basis of competition (price, quality, special features), and the ease of market entry.
6. **Markets.** This includes size, location, brand loyalties, ease of entry, potential for growth, long-term stability, and demographics.

The organization also must take into account various *internal factors* that relate to possible strengths or weaknesses. Among the key internal factors are the following:

1. **Human resources.** These include the skills and abilities of managers and workers; special talents (creativity, designing, problem solving); loyalty to the organization; expertise; dedication; and experience.
2. **Facilities and equipment.** Capacities, location, age, and cost to maintain or replace can have a significant impact on operations.
3. **Financial resources.** Cash flow, access to additional funding, existing debt burden, and cost of capital are important considerations.
4. **Customers.** Loyalty, existing relationships, and understanding of wants and needs are important.
5. **Products and services.** These include existing products and services, and the potential for new products and services.
6. **Technology.** This includes existing technology, the ability to integrate new technology, and the probable impact of technology on current and future operations.
7. **Suppliers.** Supplier relationships, dependability of suppliers, quality, flexibility, and service are typical considerations.
8. **Other.** Other factors include patents, labor relations, company or product image, distribution channels, relationships with distributors, maintenance of facilities and equipment, access to resources, and access to markets.

After assessing internal and external factors and an organization's distinctive competence, a strategy or strategies must be formulated that will give the organization the best chance of success. Among the types of questions that may need to be addressed are the following:

What role, if any, will the Internet play?

Will the organization have a global presence?

To what extent will *outsourcing* be used?

What will the supply chain management strategy be?

SUPPLY CHAIN

To what extent will new products or services be introduced?

What rate of growth is desirable and *sustainable?*

What emphasis, if any, should be placed on lean production?

How will the organization differentiate its products and/or services from competitors'?

The organization may decide to have a single, dominant strategy (e.g., be the price leader) or to have multiple strategies. A single strategy would allow the organization to concentrate on one particular strength or market condition. On the other hand, multiple strategies may be needed to address a particular set of conditions.

Many companies are increasing their use of outsourcing to reduce overhead, gain flexibility, and take advantage of suppliers' expertise. Dell Computers provides a great example of some of the potential benefits of outsourcing as part of a business strategy.

Growth is often a component of strategy, especially for new companies. A key aspect of this strategy is the need to seek a growth rate that is sustainable. In the 1990s, fast-food company Boston Markets dazzled investors and fast-food consumers alike. Fueled by its success, it undertook rapid expansion. By the end of the decade, the company was nearly bankrupt; it had overexpanded. In 2000, it was absorbed by fast-food giant McDonald's.

Companies increase their risk of failure not only by missing or incomplete strategies; they also fail due to poor execution of strategies. And sometimes they fail due to factors beyond their control, such as natural or man-made disasters, major political or economic changes, or competitors that have an overwhelming advantage (e.g., deep pockets, very low labor costs, less rigorous environmental requirements).

A useful resource on successful business strategies is the Profit Impact of Market Strategy (PIMS) database (www.pimsonline.com). The database contains profiles of over 3,000 businesses located primarily in the United States, Canada, and western Europe. It is used by companies and academic institutions to guide strategic thinking. It allows subscribers to answer strategy questions about their business. Moreover, they can use it to generate benchmarks and develop successful strategies.

In 1984, Michael Dell, then a college student, started selling personal computers from his dorm room. He didn't have the resources to make computer components, so he let others do that, choosing instead to concentrate on selling the computers. And, unlike the major computer producers, he didn't sell to dealers. Instead, he sold directly to PC buyers, eliminating some intermediaries, which allowed for lower cost and faster delivery. Although direct selling of PCs is fairly commonplace now, in those days it was a major departure from the norm.

What did Dell do that was so different from the big guys? To start, he bought components from suppliers instead of making them. That gave him tremendous leverage. He had little inventory, no R&D expenditures, and relatively few employees. And the risks of this approach were spread among his suppliers. Suppliers were willing to do this because Dell worked closely with them, and kept them informed. And because he was in direct contact with his customers, he gained tremendous insight into their expectations and needs, which he communicated to his suppliers.

Having little inventory gave Dell several advantages over his competitors. Aside from the lower costs of inventory, when new, faster computer chips became available, there was little inventory to work off, so he was able to offer the newer models much sooner than competitors with larger inventories. Also, when the prices of various components dropped, as they frequently did, he was able to take advantage of the lower prices, which kept his average costs lower than competitors'.

Today the company is worth billions, and so is Michael Dell.

STRATEGY FORMULATION

The key steps in strategy formulation are:

1. Link strategy directly to the organization's mission or vision statement.
2. Assess strengths, weaknesses, threats and opportunities, and identify core competencies.
3. Identify order winners and order qualifiers.
4. Select one or two strategies (e.g., low cost, speed, customer service) to focus on.

According to the PIMS Web site,

> The *database* is a collection of statistically documented experiences drawn from thousands of businesses, designed to help understand what kinds of strategies (e.g. quality, pricing, vertical integration, innovation, advertising) work best in what kinds of business environments. The data constitute a key resource for such critical management tasks as evaluating business performance, analyzing new business opportunities, evaluating and reality testing new strategies, and screening

business portfolios. *The primary role* of the PIMS Program of the Strategic Planning Institute is to help managers understand and react to their business environment. PIMS does this by assisting managers as they develop and test strategies that will achieve an acceptable level of winning as defined by various strategies and financial measures.

Supply Chain Strategy

A supply chain strategy specifies how the supply chain should function to achieve supply chain goals. The supply chain strategy should be aligned with the business strategy. If it is well executed, it can create value for the organization. It establishes how the organization should work with suppliers and policies relating to customer relationships and sustainability. Supply chain strategy is covered in more detail in a later chapter.

Sustainability Strategy

Society is placing increasing emphasis on corporate sustainability practices in the form of governmental regulations and interest groups. For these and other reasons, business organizations are or should be devoting attention to sustainability goals. To be successful, they will need a sustainability strategy. That requires elevating sustainability to the level of organizational governance; formulating goals for products and services, for processes, and for the entire supply chain; measuring achievements and striving for improvements; and possibly linking executive compensation to the achievement of sustainability goals.

Global Strategy

As globalization increased, many companies realized that strategic decisions with respect to globalization must be made. One issue companies must face is that what works in one country or region will not necessarily work in another, and strategies must be carefully crafted to take these variabilities into account. Another issue is the threat of political or social upheaval. Still another issue is the difficulty of coordinating and managing far-flung operations. Indeed, "In today's global markets, you don't have to go abroad to experience international competition. Sooner or later the world comes to you."[1]

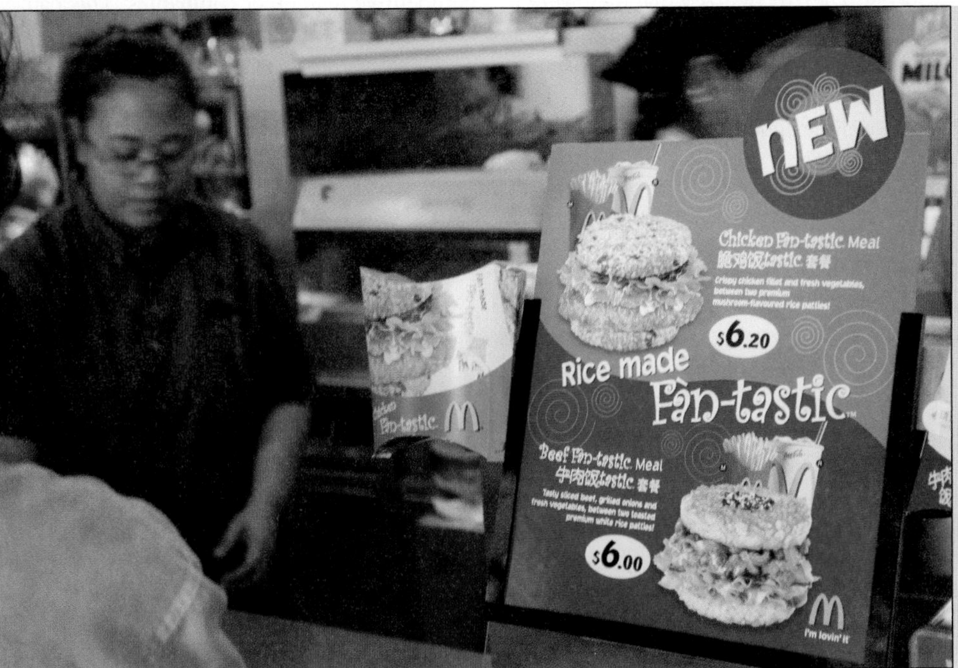

At this McDonalds in Singapore, one variable is the use of rice as a staple of the Chinese diet. This ad highlights rice burgers.

[1] Christopher A. Bartlett and Sumantra Ghoshal, "Going Global: Lessons from Late Movers," *Harvard Business Review,* March–April 2000, p. 139.

OPERATIONS STRATEGY

Operations strategy The approach, consistent with the organization strategy, that is used to guide the operations function.

The organization strategy provides the overall direction for the organization. It is broad in scope, covering the entire organization. **Operations strategy** is narrower in scope, dealing primarily with the operations aspect of the organization. Operations strategy relates to products, processes, methods, operating resources, quality, costs, lead times, and scheduling. Table 2.3 provides a comparison of an organization's mission, its overall strategy, and its operations strategy, tactics, and operations.

In order for operations strategy to be truly effective, it is important to link it to organization strategy; that is, the two should not be formulated independently. Rather, formulation of organization strategy should take into account the realities of operations' strengths and weaknesses, capitalizing on strengths and dealing with weaknesses. Similarly, operations strategy must be consistent with the overall strategy of the organization, and with the other functional units of the organization. This requires that senior managers work with functional units to formulate strategies that will support, rather than conflict with, each other and the overall strategy of the organization. As obvious as this may seem, it doesn't always happen in practice. Instead, we may find power struggles between various functional units. These struggles are detrimental to the organization because they pit functional units against each other rather than focusing their energy on making the organization more competitive and better able to serve the customer. Some of the latest approaches in organizations, involving teams of managers and workers, may reflect a growing awareness of the synergistic effects of working together rather than competing internally.

In the 1970s and early 1980s, operations strategy in the United States was often neglected in favor of marketing and financial strategies. That may have occurred because many chief executive officers did not come from operations backgrounds and perhaps did not fully appreciate the importance of the operations function. Mergers and acquisitions were common; leveraged buyouts were used, and conglomerates were formed that joined dissimilar operations. These did little to add value to the organization; they were purely financial in nature. Decisions were often made by individuals who were unfamiliar with the business, frequently to the detriment of that business. Meanwhile, foreign competitors began to fill the resulting vacuum with a careful focus on operations strategy.

In the late 1980s and early 1990s, many companies began to realize this approach was not working. They recognized that they were less competitive than other companies. This caused them to focus attention on operations strategy. A key element of both organization strategy and operations strategy is strategy formulation.

Operations strategy can have a major influence on the competitiveness of an organization. If it is well designed and well executed, there is a good chance that the organization will be successful; if it is not well designed or executed, the chances are much less that the organization will be successful.

TABLE 2.3 Comparison of mission, organization strategy, and operations strategy

		Management Level	Time Horizon	Scope	Level of Detail	Relates to
The overall organization	Mission	Top	Long	Broad	Low	Survival, profitability
	Strategy	Senior	Long	Broad	Low	Growth rate, market share
Operations	Strategic	Senior	Moderate to long	Broad	Low	Product design, choice of location, choice of technology, new facilities
	Tactical	Middle	Moderate	Moderate	Moderate	Employment levels, output levels, equipment selection, facility layout
	Operational	Low	Short	Narrow	High	Scheduling personnel, adjusting output rates, inventory management, purchasing

TABLE 2.4
Strategic operations management decisions

Decision Area	What the Decisions Affect
1. Product and service design	Costs, quality, liability and environmental issues
2. Capacity	Cost structure, flexibility
3. Process selection and layout	Costs, flexibility, skill level needed, capacity
4. Work design	Quality of work life, employee safety, productivity
5. Location	Costs, visibility
6. Quality	Ability to meet or exceed customer expectations
7. Inventory	Costs, shortages
8. Maintenance	Costs, equipment reliability, productivity
9. Scheduling	Flexibility, efficiency
10. Supply chains	Costs, quality, agility, shortages, vendor relations
11. Projects	Costs, new products, services, or operating systems

Strategic Operations Management Decision Areas

Operations management people play a strategic role in many strategic decisions in a business organization. Table 2.4 highlights some key decision areas. Notice that most of the decision areas have cost implications.

Two factors that tend to have universal strategic operations importance relate to quality and time. The following section discusses quality and time strategies.

Quality and Time Strategies

Traditional strategies of business organizations have tended to emphasize cost minimization or product differentiation. While not abandoning those strategies, many organizations have embraced strategies based on *quality* and/or *time.*

Quality-based strategy Strategy that focuses on quality in all phases of an organization.

Quality-based strategies focus on maintaining or improving the quality of an organization's products or services. Quality is generally a factor in both attracting and retaining customers. Quality-based strategies may be motivated by a variety of factors. They may reflect an effort to overcome an image of poor quality, a desire to catch up with the competition, a desire to maintain an existing image of high quality, or some combination of these and other factors. Interestingly enough, quality-based strategies can be part of another strategy such as cost reduction, increased productivity, or time, all of which benefit from higher quality.

Time-based strategy Strategy that focuses on reduction of time needed to accomplish tasks.

Time-based strategies focus on reducing the time required to accomplish various activities (e.g., develop new products or services and market them, respond to a change in customer demand, or deliver a product or perform a service). By doing so, organizations seek to improve service to the customer and to gain a competitive advantage over rivals who take more time to accomplish the same tasks.

Productivity Gains Curb Inflation

READING

Wage increases can lead to inflationary pressure. They can cause the prices consumers pay for products and services to rise—unless, that is, they are offset by gains in productivity, which lead to an increase in profits. If that happens, a portion of the resulting profits can be used to cover the wage increases without having to raise prices.

Some Burger Kings were able to increase the starting pay of new workers by $1 by achieving productivity gains. The restaurants restructured the menu, combining items into meal packages such as a burger, fries, and soft drink. This enabled the counter staff to enter orders with a single keystroke instead of multiple keystrokes on their point-of-sale machines, reducing the time needed to take an order. That, in turn, enabled them to take orders more quickly, increasing productivity and, consequently, reducing labor requirements, which produced higher profits.

Source: Based on "Despite Pay Increases, Gains in Productivity, Profits Curb Inflation," *The Wall Street Journal,* May 22, 1997, p. A1.

Time-based strategies focus on reducing the time needed to conduct the various activities in a process. The rationale is that by reducing time, costs are generally less, productivity is higher, quality tends to be higher, product innovations appear on the market sooner, and customer service is improved.

Organizations have achieved time reduction in some of the following:

Planning time: The time needed to react to a competitive threat, to develop strategies and select tactics, to approve proposed changes to facilities, to adopt new technologies, and so on.

Product/service design time: The time needed to develop and market new or redesigned products or services.

Processing time: The time needed to produce goods or provide services. This can involve scheduling, repairing equipment, methods used, inventories, quality, training, and the like.

Changeover time: The time needed to change from producing one type of product or service to another. This may involve new equipment settings and attachments, different methods, equipment, schedules, or materials.

Delivery time: The time needed to fill orders.

Response time for complaints: These might be customer complaints about quality, timing of deliveries, and incorrect shipments. These might also be complaints from employees about working conditions (e.g., safety, lighting, heat or cold), equipment problems, or quality problems.

It is essential for marketing and operations personnel to collaborate on strategy formulation in order to ensure that the buying criteria of the most important customers in each market segment are addressed.

Agile operations is a strategic approach for competitive advantage that emphasizes the use of flexibility to adapt and prosper in an environment of change. Agility involves a blending of several distinct competencies such as cost, quality, and reliability along with flexibility. Processing aspects of flexibility include quick equipment changeovers, scheduling, and innovation. Product or service aspects include varying output volumes and product mix.

Successful agile operations requires careful planning to achieve a system that includes people, flexible equipment, and information technology. Reducing the time needed to perform work is one of the ways an organization can improve a key metric: *productivity.*

IMPLICATIONS OF ORGANIZATION STRATEGY FOR OPERATIONS MANAGEMENT

Organization strategy has a major impact on operations and supply chain management strategies. For example, organizations that use a low-cost, high-volume strategy limit the amount of variety offered to customers. As a result, variations for operations and the supply chain are minimal, so they are easier to deal with. Conversely, a strategy to offer a wide variety of products or services, or to perform customized work, creates substantial operational and supply chain variations and, hence, more challenges in achieving a smooth flow of goods and services throughout the supply chain, thus making the matching of supply to demand more difficult. Similarly, increasing service reduces the ability to compete on price. Table 2.5 provides a brief overview of variety and some other key implications.

TRANSFORMING STRATEGY INTO ACTION: THE BALANCED SCORECARD

The Balanced Scorecard (BSC) is a top-down *management system* that organizations can use to clarify their vision and strategy and transform them into action. It was introduced in the early 1990s by Robert Kaplan and David Norton,[2] and it has been revised and improved since

[2]Robert S. Kaplan and David P. Norton, *Balanced Scorecard: Translating Strategy into Action* (Harvard Business School Press, 1996).

TABLE 2.5
Organization strategies and their implications for operations management

Organization Strategy	Implications for Operations Management
Low price	Requires low variation in products/services and a high-volume, steady flow of goods results in maximum use of resources through the system. Standardized work, material, and inventory requirements.
High quality	Entails higher initial cost for product and service design, and process design, and more emphasis on assuring supplier quality.
Quick response	Requires flexibility, extra capacity, and higher levels of some inventory items.
Newness/innovation	Entails large investment in research and development for new or improved products and services plus the need to adapt operations and supply processes to suit new products or services.
Product or service variety	Requires high variation in resource and more emphasis on product and service design; higher worker skills needed, cost estimation more difficult; scheduling more complex; quality assurance more involved; inventory management more complex; and matching supply to demand more difficult.
Sustainability	Affects location planning, product and service design, process design, outsourcing decisions, returns policies, and waste management.

then. The idea was to move away from a purely financial perspective of the organization and integrate other perspectives such as customers, internal business processes, and learning and growth. Using this approach, managers develop objectives, metrics, and targets for each objective and initiatives to achieve objectives, and they identify links among the various perspectives. Results are monitored and used to improve strategic performance results. Figure 2.2 illustrates the conceptual framework of this approach. Many organizations employ this or a similar approach.

As seen in Figure 2.2, the four perspectives are intended to balance not only financial and nonfinancial performance, but also internal and external performance as well as past and future performance. This approach can also help organizations focus on how they differ from the competition in each of the four areas if their vision is realized.

A major key to Apple's continued success is its ability to keep pushing the boundaries of innovation. Apple has demonstrated how to create growth by dreaming up products so new and ingenious that they have upended one industry after another.

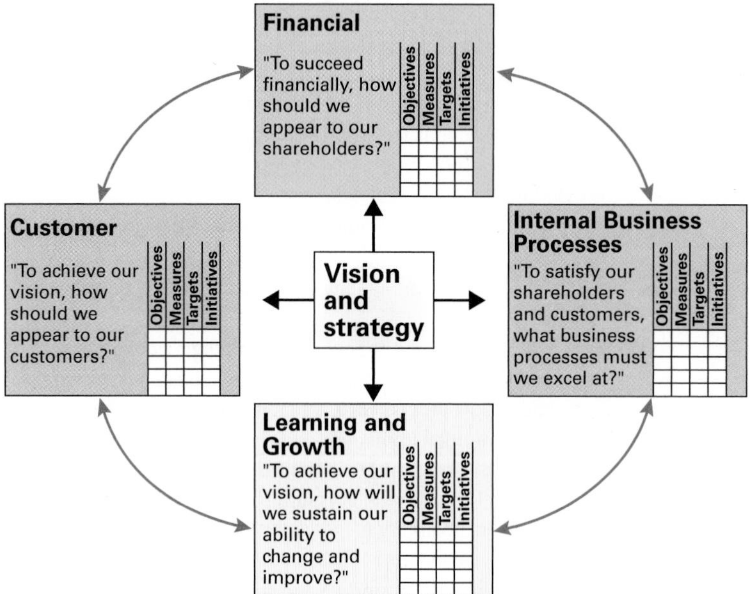

FIGURE 2.2
The Balanced Scorecard

Source: Reprinted with permission of Harvard Business School Press from Robert Kaplan and David Norton, *Balanced Scorecard: Translating Strategy into Action.* Copyright © 1996 by the Harvard Business School Publishing Corporation. All rights reserved.

Although the Balanced Scorecard helps focus managers' attention on strategic issues and the implementation of strategy, it is important to note that it has no role in strategy formulation. Moreover, this approach pays little attention to suppliers and government regulations, and community, environmental, and sustainability issues are missing. These are closely linked and business organizations need to be aware of the impact they are having in these areas and respond accordingly. Otherwise, organizations may be subject to attack by pressure groups and risk damage to their reputation.

PRODUCTIVITY

Productivity A measure of the effective use of resources, usually expressed as the ratio of output to input.

One of the primary responsibilities of a manager is to achieve *productive use* of an organization's resources. The term *productivity* is used to describe this. **Productivity** is an index that measures output (goods and services) relative to the input (labor, materials, energy, and other resources) used to produce it. It is usually expressed as the ratio of output to input:

$$\text{Productivity} = \frac{\text{Output}}{\text{Input}} \tag{2–1}$$

Although productivity is important for all business organizations, it is particularly important for organizations that use a strategy of low cost, because the higher the productivity, the lower the cost of the output.

A productivity ratio can be computed for a single operation, a department, an organization, or an entire country. In business organizations, productivity ratios are used for planning workforce requirements, scheduling equipment, financial analysis, and other important tasks.

Productivity has important implications for business organizations and for entire nations. For nonprofit organizations, higher productivity means lower costs; for profit-based organizations, productivity is an important factor in determining how competitive a company is. For a nation, the rate of *productivity growth* is of great importance. Productivity growth is the increase in productivity from one period to the next relative to the productivity in the preceding period. Thus,

$$\text{Productivity growth} = \frac{\text{Current productivity} - \text{Previous productivity}}{\text{Previous productivity}} \times 100 \tag{2–2}$$

Productivity can be enhanced by the use of robotic equipment. The robot carves a styrofoam car mock-up designed by Ford engineers in Detroit. Robots can operate for long periods with consistent precision and speed.

For example, if productivity increased from 80 to 84, the growth rate would be

$$\frac{84 - 80}{80} \times 100 = 5\%$$

Productivity growth is a key factor in a country's rate of inflation and the standard of living of its people. Productivity increases add value to the economy while keeping inflation in check. Productivity growth was a major factor in the long period of sustained economic growth in the United States in the 1990s.

Computing Productivity

Productivity measures can be based on a single input (partial productivity), on more than one input (multifactor productivity), or on all inputs (total productivity). Table 2.6 lists some examples of productivity measures. The choice of productivity measure depends primarily on the purpose of the measurement. If the purpose is to track improvements in labor productivity, then labor becomes the obvious input measure.

Partial measures are often of greatest use in operations management. Table 2.7 provides some examples of partial productivity measures.

TABLE 2.6
Some examples of different types of productivity measures

Partial measures	$\frac{\text{Output}}{\text{Labor}}$	$\frac{\text{Output}}{\text{Machine}}$	$\frac{\text{Output}}{\text{Capital}}$	$\frac{\text{Output}}{\text{Energy}}$
Multifactor measures	$\frac{\text{Output}}{\text{Labor + Machine}}$		$\frac{\text{Output}}{\text{Labor + Capital + Energy}}$	
Total measure	$\frac{\text{Goods or services produced}}{\text{All inputs used to produce them}}$			

TABLE 2.7
Some examples of partial productivity measures

Labor productivity	Units of output per labor hour
	Units of output per shift
	Value-added per labor hour
	Dollar value of output per labor hour
Machine productivity	Units of output per machine hour
	Dollar value of output per machine hour
Capital productivity	Units of output per dollar input
	Dollar value of output per dollar input
Energy productivity	Units of output per kilowatt-hour
	Dollar value of output per kilowatt-hour

The units of output used in productivity measures depend on the type of job performed. The following are examples of labor productivity:

$$\frac{\text{Yards of carpet installed}}{\text{Labor hours}} = \text{Yards of carpet installed per labor hour}$$

$$\frac{\text{Number of motel rooms cleaned}}{\text{Number of workers}} = \text{Number of motel rooms cleaned per worker}$$

Similar examples can be listed for *machine productivity* (e.g., the number of pieces per hour turned out by a machine).

EXAMPLE 2

Determine the productivity for these cases:

a. Four workers installed 720 square yards of carpeting in eight hours.

b. A machine produced 70 pieces in two hours. However, two pieces were unusable.

SOLUTION

a.
$$\begin{aligned}\text{Productivity} &= \frac{\text{Yards of carpet installed}}{\text{Labor hours worked}} \\ &= \frac{\text{720 square yards}}{\text{4 workers} \times \text{8 hours/worker}} \\ &= \frac{\text{720 yards}}{\text{32 hours}} \\ &= \text{22.5 yards/hour}\end{aligned}$$

b.
$$\begin{aligned}\text{Productivity} &= \frac{\text{Usable pieces}}{\text{Production time}} \\ &= \frac{70 - 2 = \text{68 usable pieces}}{\text{2 hours}} \\ &= \text{34 pieces/hour}\end{aligned}$$

Calculations of multifactor productivity measure inputs and outputs using a common unit of measurement, such as cost. For instance, the measure might use cost of inputs and units of the output:

$$\frac{\text{Quantity of production}}{\text{Labor cost} + \text{Materials cost} + \text{Overhead}} \qquad (2\text{–}3)$$

Note: The unit of measure must be the same for all factors in the denominator.

Determine the multifactor productivity for the combined input of labor and machine time using the following data:

Output: 7,040 units
Input
Labor: \$1,000
Materials: \$520
Overhead: \$2,000

SOLUTION

$$\text{Multifactor productivity} = \frac{\text{Output}}{\text{Labor} + \text{Materials} + \text{Overhead}}$$

$$= \frac{7,040 \text{ units}}{\$1,000 + \$520 + \$2,000} = 2 \text{ units per dollar input}$$

Productivity measures are useful on a number of levels. For an individual department or organization, productivity measures can be used to track performance *over time.* This allows managers to judge performance and to decide where improvements are needed. For example, if productivity has slipped in a certain area, operations staff can examine the factors used to compute productivity to determine what has changed and then devise a means of improving productivity in subsequent periods.

Productivity measures also can be used to judge the performance of an entire industry or the productivity of a country as a whole. These productivity measures are *aggregate* measures.

In essence, productivity measurements serve as scorecards of the effective use of resources. Business leaders are concerned with productivity as it relates to *competitiveness:* If two firms both have the same level of output but one requires less input because of higher productivity, that one will be able to charge a lower price and consequently increase its share of the market. Or that firm might elect to charge the same price, thereby reaping a greater profit. Government leaders are concerned with national productivity because of the close relationship between productivity and a nation's standard of living. High levels of productivity are largely responsible for the relatively high standards of living enjoyed by people in industrial nations. Furthermore, wage and price increases not accompanied by productivity increases tend to create inflationary pressures on a nation's economy.

Why Productivity Matters

READING

It is sometimes easy to overlook the importance of productivity. National figures are often reported in the media. They may seem to be ho-hum; there's nothing glamorous about them to get our attention. But make no mistake; they are key economic indicators—barometers, if you will, that affect everybody. How? High productivity and high standard of living go hand-in-hand. If a country becomes more service-based, as the United States has become, some (but not all) high-productivity manufacturing jobs are replaced by lower-productivity service jobs. That makes it more difficult to support a high standard of living.

Productivity levels are also important for industries and companies. For companies, a higher productivity relative to their competitors gives them a competitive advantage in the marketplace. With a higher productivity, they can afford to undercut competitors' prices to gain market share, or charge the same prices but realize greater profits! For an industry, higher relative productivity means it is less likely to be supplanted by foreign industry.

Questions

1. Why is high productivity important for a nation?
2. Why do you suppose that service jobs have lower productivity than manufacturing jobs?
3. How can a company gain a competitive advantage by having higher productivity than its competitors have?

Productivity growth in the United States in the 1970s and 1980s lagged behind that of other leading industrial countries, most notably Japan, Korea, the United Kingdom, and West Germany. That caused concern among government officials and business leaders. Although U.S. productivity was still among the highest in the world, it was losing ground to other nations. Moreover, a significant portion of U.S. productivity could be attributed to high *agricultural* productivity; *manufacturing* productivity tended to be lower. It slowed during the late 1970s and early 1980s, but it was strong in the mid to late 1990s. (See Figure 2.3.) In 2007, it was the highest in the world!

Productivity in the Service Sector

Service productivity is more problematic than manufacturing productivity. In many situations, it is more difficult to measure, and thus to manage, because it involves intellectual activities and a high degree of variability. Think about medical diagnoses, surgery, consulting, legal services, customer service, and computer repair work. This makes productivity improvements more difficult to achieve. Nonetheless, because service is becoming an increasingly large portion of our economy, the issues related to service productivity will have to be dealt with. It is interesting to note that government statistics normally do not include service firms.

A useful measure closely related to productivity is *process yield.* Where products are involved, process yield is defined as the ratio of output of good product (i.e., defective product is not included) to the quantity of raw material input. Where services are involved, process yield measurement is often dependent on the particular process. For example, in a car rental agency, a measure of yield is the ratio of cars rented to cars available for a given day. In education, a measure for college and university admission yield is the ratio of student acceptances to the total number of students approved for admission. For subscription services, yield is the ratio of new subscriptions to the number of calls made or the number of letters mailed. However, not all services lend themselves to a simple yield measurement. For example, services such as automotive, appliance, and computer repair don't readily lend themselves to such measures.

Factors That Affect Productivity

Numerous factors affect productivity. Generally, they are methods, capital, quality, technology, and management.

FIGURE 2.3 U.S. multifactor productivity, 1976–2010

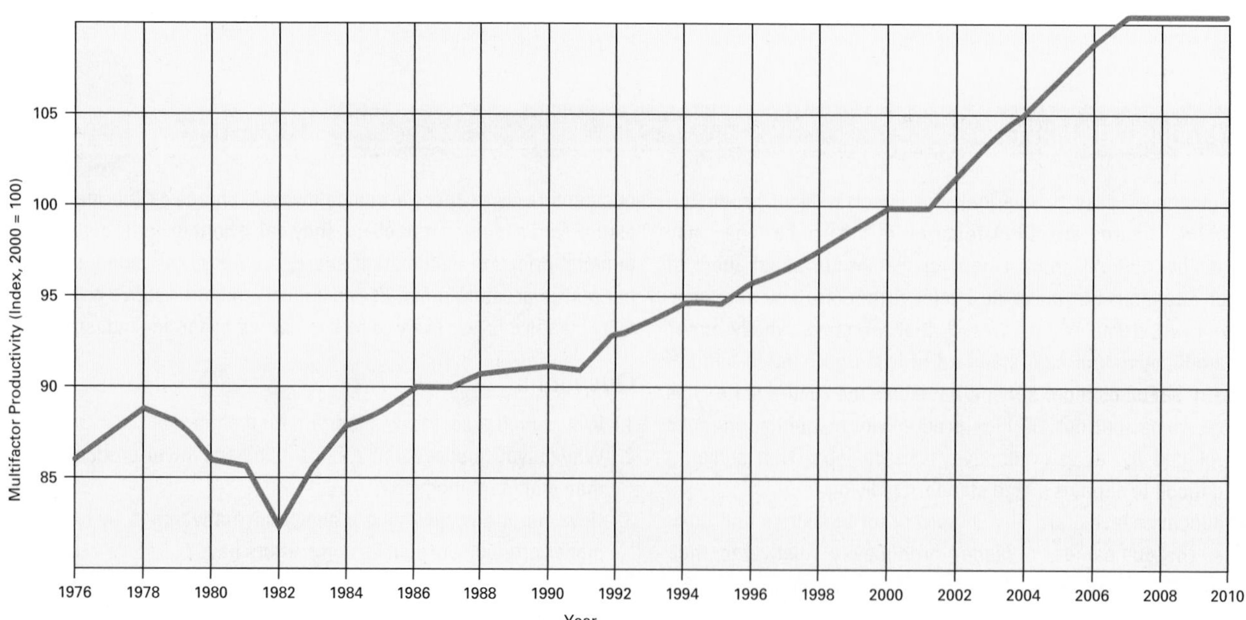

A commonly held misconception is that workers are the main determinant of productivity. According to that theory, the route to productivity gains involves getting employees to work harder. However, the fact is that many productivity gains in the past have come from *technological* improvements. Familiar examples include

Fax machines	Automation
Copiers	Calculators
The Internet, search engines	Computers
Voice mail, cellular phones	E-mail
	Software

However, technology alone won't guarantee productivity gains; it must be used wisely and thoughtfully. Without careful planning, technology can actually *reduce* productivity, especially if it leads to inflexibility, high costs, or mismatched operations. Another current productivity pitfall results from employees' use of computers for nonwork-related activities (playing games or checking stock prices or sports scores on the Internet). Beyond all of these is the dip in productivity that results while employees learn to use new equipment or procedures that will eventually lead to productivity gains after the learning phase ends.

Other factors that affect productivity include the following:

Standardizing processes and procedures wherever possible to reduce variability can have a significant benefit for both productivity and quality.

Quality differences may distort productivity measurements. One way this can happen is when comparisons are made over time, such as comparing the productivity of a factory now with one 30 years ago. Quality is now much higher than it was then, but there is no simple way to incorporate quality improvements into productivity measurements.

Use of the Internet can lower costs of a wide range of transactions, thereby increasing productivity. It is likely that this effect will continue to increase productivity in the foreseeable future.

Computer viruses can have an immense negative impact on productivity.

Searching for lost or misplaced items wastes time, hence negatively affecting productivity.

Scrap rates have an adverse effect on productivity, signaling inefficient use of resources.

New workers tend to have lower productivity than seasoned workers. Thus, growing companies may experience a productivity lag.

Safety should be addressed. Accidents can take a toll on productivity.

A shortage of information technology workers and other technical workers hampers the ability of companies to update computing resources, generate and sustain growth, and take advantage of new opportunities.

Layoffs often affect productivity. The effect can be positive and negative. Initially, productivity may increase after a layoff, because the workload remains the same but fewer workers do the work—although they have to work harder and longer to do it. However, as time goes by, the remaining workers may experience an increased risk of burnout, and they may fear additional job cuts. The most capable workers may decide to leave.

Labor turnover has a negative effect on productivity; replacements need time to get up to speed.

Design of the workspace can impact productivity. For example, having tools and other work items within easy reach can positively impact productivity.

Incentive plans that reward productivity increases can boost productivity.

And there are still other factors that affect productivity, such as *equipment breakdowns* and *shortages* of parts or materials. The education level and training of workers and their health can greatly affect productivity. The opportunity to obtain lower costs due to higher productivity elsewhere is a key reason many organizations turn to *outsourcing.* Hence, an alternative to outsourcing can be improved productivity. Moreover, as a part of their strategy for quality, the best organizations strive for *continuous improvement.* Productivity improvements can be an important aspect of that approach.

Improving Productivity

A company or a department can take a number of key steps toward improving productivity:

1. Develop productivity measures for all operations. Measurement is the first step in managing and controlling an operation.
2. Look at the system as a whole in deciding which operations are most critical. It is overall productivity that is important. Managers need to reflect on the value of potential productivity improvements *before* okaying improvement efforts. The issue is *effectiveness.* There are several aspects of this. One is to make sure the result will be something customers want. For example, if a company is able to increase its output through productivity improvements, but then is unable to sell the increased output, the increase in productivity isn't effective. Second, it is important to adopt a systems viewpoint: A productivity increase in one part of an operation that doesn't increase the productivity of the system would not be effective. For example, suppose a system consists of a sequence of two operations, where the output of the first operation is the input to the second operation, and each operation can complete its part of the process at a rate of 20 units per hour. If the productivity of the first operation is increased, but the productivity of the second operation is not, the output of the system will still be 20 units per hour.
3. Develop methods for achieving productivity improvements, such as soliciting ideas from workers (perhaps organizing teams of workers, engineers, and managers), studying how other firms have increased productivity, and reexamining the way work is done.
4. Establish reasonable goals for improvement.
5. Make it clear that management supports and encourages productivity improvement. Consider incentives to reward workers for contributions.
6. Measure improvements and publicize them.

Don't confuse productivity with *efficiency.* Efficiency is a narrower concept that pertains to getting the most out of a *fixed* set of resources; productivity is a broader concept that pertains to effective use of overall resources. For example, an efficiency perspective on mowing a lawn given a hand mower would focus on the best way to use the hand mower; a productivity perspective would include the possibility of using a power mower.

Productivity Improvement

READING

In April 1999, Stryker Howmedica set up a team to improve the running of its packaging line. A strategy focus on productivity improvement was used. The team adopted an approach based on the production system of Toyota. The goal was to satisfy the customer expectations for delivery and quality, while achieving gains in productivity. After the team identified needs and set objectives, a number of improvements were implemented. A one-piece flow was established that reduced bottlenecks in the flow of devices through a clean room and the total time spent blister sealing devices was lowered. Within a short time, productivity nearly doubled from 36 devices per hour to 60 devices per hour, work-in-progress inventory fell, and a 10 percent reduction in the standard cost of product was achieved.

Source: Based on Lauraine Howley, "A Strategy for Company Improvement," *Medical Device Technology* 11, no. 2 (March 2000), p. 33.

SUMMARY

Competition is the driving force in many organizations. It may involve price, quality, special features or services, time, or other factors. To develop effective strategies for business, it is essential for organizations to determine what combinations of factors are important to customers, which factors are order qualifiers, and which are order winners.

It is essential that goals and strategies be aligned with the organization's mission. Strategies are plans for achieving organizational goals. They provide focus for decision making. Strategies must take into account present and future customer wants, as well as the organization's strengths and weaknesses, threats and opportunities. These can run the gamut from what competitors are doing, or are likely to do, to technology, supply chain management, and e-business. Organizations generally have overall strategies that pertain to the entire organization and strategies that pertain to each of the functional areas. Functional strategies are narrower in scope and should be linked to overall strategies. Time-based strategies and quality-based strategies are among the most widely used strategies business organizations employ to serve their customers and to become more productive. The chapter includes a description of the Balanced Scorecard approach, which can be helpful for transforming strategies into actions, and the implications of organization strategy for operations management.

Productivity is a measure of the use of resources. There is considerable interest in productivity both from an organizational standpoint and from a national standpoint. Business organizations want higher productivity because it yields lower costs and helps them to become more competitive. Nations want higher productivity because it makes their goods and services more attractive, offsets inflationary pressures associated with higher wages, and results in a higher standard of living for their people.

KEY POINTS

1. Competitive pressure often means that business organizations must frequently assess their competitors' strengths and weaknesses, as well as their own, to remain competitive.
2. Strategy formulation is critical because strategies provide direction for the organization, so they can play a role in the success or failure of a business organization.
3. Functional strategies and supply chain strategies need to be aligned with the goals and strategies of the overall organization.
4. The three primary business strategies are low cost, responsiveness, and differentiation.
5. Productivity is a key factor in the cost of goods and services. Increases in productivity can become a competitive advantage.
6. High productivity is particularly important for organizations that have a strategy of low costs.

KEY TERMS

competitiveness, 42
core competencies, 47
environmental scanning, 48
goals, 44
mission, 44
mission statement, 44
operations strategy, 52
order qualifiers, 47
order winners, 47
productivity, 56
quality-based strategy, 53
strategies, 44
SWOT, 47
tactics, 45
time-based strategy, 53

SOLVED PROBLEMS

Problem 1

excel
www.mhhe.com/stevenson11e

A company that processes fruits and vegetables is able to produce 400 cases of canned peaches in one-half hour with four workers. What is labor productivity?

Solution

$$\text{Labor productivity} = \frac{\text{Quantity produced}}{\text{Labor hours}} = \frac{400 \text{ cases}}{4 \text{ workers} \times 1/2 \text{ hour/worker}}$$
$$= 200 \text{ cases per labor hour}$$

Problem 2

excel
www.mhhe.com/stevenson11e

A wrapping-paper company produced 2,000 rolls of paper one day. Labor cost was $160, material cost was $50, and overhead was $320. Determine the multifactor productivity.

Solution

$$\text{Multifactor productivity} = \frac{\text{Quantity produced}}{\text{Labor cost} + \text{Material cost} + \text{Overhead}}$$

$$= \frac{2{,}000 \text{ rolls}}{\$160 + \$50 + \$320} = 3.77 \text{ rolls per dollar input}$$

A variation of the multifactor productivity calculation incorporates the standard price in the numerator by multiplying the units by the standard price.

Problem 3

www.mhhe.com/stevenson11e

Compute the multifactor productivity measure for an eight-hour day in which the usable output was 300 units, produced by three workers who used 600 pounds of materials. Workers have an hourly wage of $20, and material cost is $1 per pound. Overhead is 1.5 times labor cost

Solution

$$\text{Multifactor productivity} = \frac{\text{Usable output}}{\text{Labor cost} + \text{Material cost} + \text{Overhead cost}}$$

$$= \frac{300 \text{ units}}{(3 \text{ workers} \times 8 \text{ hours} \times \$20/\text{hour}) + (600 \text{ pounds} \times \$1/\text{pound}) + (3 \text{ workers} \times 8 \text{ hours} \times \$20/\text{hour} \times 1.50)}$$

$$= \frac{300 \text{ units}}{\$480 + \$600 + \$720}$$

$$= .167 \text{ units of output per dollar of input}$$

Problem 4

www.mhhe.com/stevenson11e

A health club has two employees who work on lead generation. Each employee works 40 hours a week, and is paid $20 an hour. Each employee identifies an average of 400 possible leads a week from a list of 8,000 names. Approximately 10 percent of the leads become members and pay a one-time fee of $100. Material costs are $130 per week, and overhead costs are $1,000 per week. Calculate the multifactor productivity for this operation in fees generated per dollar of input.

Solution

$$\text{MFP} = \frac{(\text{Possible leads})(\text{No. of workers})(\text{Fee})(\text{Conversion percentage})}{\text{Labor cost} + \text{Material cost} + \text{Overhead cost}}$$

$$= \frac{(400)(2)(\$100)(.10)}{2(40)(\$20) + \$130 + \$1{,}000} = \frac{\$8{,}000}{\$2{,}730} = 2.93$$

DISCUSSION AND REVIEW QUESTIONS

1. From time to time, various groups clamor for import restrictions or tariffs on foreign-produced goods, particularly automobiles. How might these be helpful? Harmful?
2. List the key ways that organizations compete.
3. Explain the importance of identifying and differentiating order qualifiers and order winners.
4. Select two stores you shop at, and state how they compete.
5. What is the Balanced Scorecard and how is it useful?
6. Contrast the terms *strategies* and *tactics.*
7. Contrast *organization strategy* and *operations strategy.*
8. Explain the term *time-based strategies* and give three examples.
9. Productivity should be a concern of every business organization.
   a. How is productivity defined?
   b. How are productivity measures used?
   c. Why is productivity important?
   d. What part of the organization has primary responsibility for productivity?
   e. How is efficiency different from productivity?
10. List some factors that can affect productivity and some ways that productivity can be improved.
11. It has been said that a typical Japanese automobile manufacturer produces more cars with fewer workers than its U.S. counterpart. What are some possible explanations for this, assuming that U.S. workers are as hardworking as Japanese workers?
12. Boeing's strategy appears to focus on its 777 midsize plane's ability to fly into smaller, nonhub airports. Rival European Airbus's strategy appears to focus on large planes. Compare the advantages and disadvantages of these two strategies.

13. Name 10 ways that banks compete for customers.
14. Explain the rationale of an operations strategy that seeks to increase the opportunity for use of technology by reducing variability in processing requirements.
15. Identify two companies that have time-based strategies, and two that have quality-based strategies.

TAKING STOCK

1. Who needs to be involved in formulating organizational strategy?
2. Name some of the competitive trade-offs that might arise in a fast-food restaurant.
3. How can technology improve
   a. Competitiveness?
   b. Productivity?

CRITICAL THINKING EXERCISES

1. In the past there was concern about a "productivity paradox" related to IT services. More recently, there have been few references to this phenomenon. Using the Internet, explain the term "productivity paradox." Why do you think that the discussion of that topic has faded?
2. A U.S. company has two manufacturing plants, one in the United States and one in another country. Both produce the same item, each for sale in their respective countries. However, their productivity figures are quite different. The analyst thinks this is because the U.S. plant uses more automated equipment for processing while the other plant uses a higher percentage of labor. Explain how that factor can cause productivity figures to be misleading. Is there another way to compare the two plants that would be more meaningful?
3. While it is true that increases in efficiency generate productivity increases, it is possible to get caught in an "efficiency improvement trap." Explain what this means.
4. It is common knowledge that Sam's boss Dom has been fudging the weekly productivity figures. Several employees, including Sam, have spoken to him about this, but he continues to do it. Sam has observed a drop in morale among his coworkers due to this. Sam is thinking about sending an anonymous note to Dom's boss. Would that be ethical? What would you do if you were Sam?
5. Give two examples of what would be considered unethical involving competition and the ethical principles (see Chapter 1) that would be violated.

PROBLEMS

1. A catering company prepared and served 300 meals at an anniversary celebration last week using eight workers. The week before, six workers prepared and served 240 meals at a wedding reception.

   a. For which event was the labor productivity higher? Explain.
   b. What are some possible reasons for the productivity differences?

2. The manager of a crew that installs carpeting has tracked the crew's output over the past several weeks, obtaining these figures:

Week	Crew Size	Yards Installed
1	4	96
2	3	72
3	4	92
4	2	50
5	3	69
6	2	52

Compute the labor productivity for each of the weeks. On the basis of your calculations, what can you conclude about crew size and productivity?

3. Compute the multifactor productivity measure for each of the weeks shown for production of chocolate bars. What do the productivity figures suggest? Assume 40-hour weeks and an hourly wage of $12. Overhead is 1.5 times weekly labor cost. Material cost is $6 per pound.

Week	Output (units)	Workers	Material (lbs)
1	30,000	6	450
2	33,600	7	470
3	32,200	7	460
4	35,400	8	480

4. A company that makes shopping carts for supermarkets and other stores recently purchased some new equipment that reduces the labor content of the jobs needed to produce the shopping carts. Prior to buying the new equipment, the company used five workers, who produced an average of 80 carts per hour. Workers receive $10 per hour, and machine cost was $40 per hour. With the new equipment, it was possible to transfer one of the workers to another department, and equipment cost increased by $10 per hour while output increased by four carts per hour.

a. Compute labor productivity under each system. Use carts per worker per hour as the measure of labor productivity.
b. Compute the multifactor productivity under each system. Use carts per dollar cost (labor plus equipment) as the measure.
c. Comment on the changes in productivity according to the two measures, and on which one you believe is the more pertinent for this situation.

5. An operation has a 10 percent scrap rate. As a result, 72 pieces per hour are produced. What is the potential increase in labor productivity that could be achieved by eliminating the scrap?

6. A manager checked production records and found that a worker produced 160 units while working 40 hours. In the previous week, the same worker produced 138 units while working 36 hours. Did the worker's productivity increase, decrease, or remain the same? Explain.

7. The following table shows data on the average number of customers processed by several bank service units each day. The hourly wage rate is $25, the overhead rate is 1.0 times labor cost, and material cost is $5 per customer.

Unit	Employees	Customers Processed/Day
A	4	36
B	5	40
C	8	60
D	3	20

a. Compute the labor productivity and the multifactor productivity for each unit. Use an eight-hour day for multifactor productivity.
b. Suppose a new, more standardized procedure is to be introduced that will enable each employee to process one additional customer per day. Compute the expected labor and multifactor productivity rates for each unit.

8. A property title search firm is contemplating using online software to increase its search productivity. Currently an average of 40 minutes is needed to do a title search. The researcher cost is $2 per minute. Clients are charged a fee of $400. Company A's software would reduce the average search time by 10 minutes, at a cost of $3.50 per search. Company B's software would reduce the average search time by 12 minutes at a cost of $3.60 per search. Which option would have the highest productivity in terms of revenue per dollar of input?

9. A company offers ID theft protection using leads obtained from client banks. Three employees work 40 hours a week on the leads, at a pay rate of $25 per hour per employee. Each employee identifies an average of 3,000 potential leads a week from a list of 5,000. An average of 4 percent actually sign up for the service, paying a one-time fee of $70. Material costs are $1,000 per week, and overhead costs are $9,000 per week. Calculate the multifactor productivity for this operation in fees generated per dollar of input.

An American Tragedy: How a Good Company Died

CASE

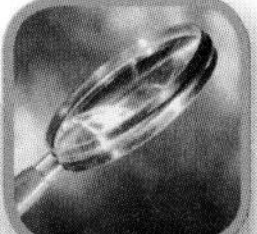

Zachary Schiller

The Rust Belt is back. So say bullish observers as U.S. exports surge, long-moribund industries glow with newfound profits, and unemployment dips to lows not seen in a decade. But in the smokestack citadels, there's disquiet. Too many machine-tool and auto parts factories are silent; too many U.S. industries still can't hold their own.

What went wrong since the heyday of the 1960s? That's the issue Max Holland, a contributing editor of *The Nation,* takes up in his nutsy-boltsy but fascinating study, *When the Machine Stopped.**

The focus of the story is Burgmaster Corp., a Los Angeles–area machine-tool maker founded in 1944 by Czechoslovakian immigrant Fred Burg. Holland's father worked there for 29 years, and the author interviewed 22 former employees. His shop-floor view of this small company is a refreshing change from academic treatises on why America can't compete.

The discussions of spindles and numerical control can be tough going. But Holland compensates by conveying the excitement and innovation of the company's early days and the disgust and cynicism accompanying its decline. Moreover, the fate of Burgmaster and its brethren is crucial to the U.S. industrial economy: Any

(continued)

*Max Holland, *When the Machine Stopped: A Contemporary Tale from Industrial America* (Boston: Harvard Business School Press, 1988).

(concluded)

manufactured item is either made by a machine tool or by a machine made by a machine tool.

Producing innovative turret drills used in a wide variety of metal working tasks, Burgmaster was a thriving enterprise by 1965, when annual sales amounted to about $8 million. The company needed backing to expand, however, so it sold out to Buffalo-based conglomerate Houdaille Industries Inc. Houdaille was in turn purchased in a 1979 leveraged buyout (LBO) led by Kohlberg Kravis Roberts & Co. By 1982, when debt, competition, and a sickly machine-tool market had battered Burgmaster badly, Houdaille went to Washington with a petition to withhold the investment tax credit for certain Japanese-made machine tools.

Thanks to deft lobbying, the Senate passed a resolution supporting Houdaille's position, but President Reagan refused to go along. Houdaille's subsequent attempt to link Burgmaster up with a Japanese rival also failed, and Burgmaster was closed.

Holland uses Burgmaster's demise to explore some key issues of economic and trade policy. Houdaille's charge that a cartel led by the Japanese government had injured U.S. toolmakers, for example, became a rallying point for those who would blame a fearsome Japan Inc. for the problems of U.S. industry.

Holland describes the Washington wrangling over Houdaille in painful detail. But he does show that such government decisions are often made without much knowledge of what's going on in industry. He shows, too, that Japanese producers succeeded less because of government help than because they made better, cheaper machines.

For those who see LBOs as a symptom of what ails the U.S. economy, Holland offers plenty of ammunition. He argues persuasively that the LBO crippled Burgmaster by creating enormous pressure to generate cash. As Burgmaster pushed its products out as fast as possible, he writes, it routinely shipped defective machines. It promised customers features that engineers hadn't yet designed. And although KKR disputes the claim, Holland concludes that the LBO choked off Burgmaster's investment funds just when foreign competition made them most necessary. As for Houdaille, it was recapitalized and sold to Britain's Tube Investments Group.

But Burgmaster's problems had started even before the LBO. Holland's history of the company under Houdaille is a veritable catalog of modern management techniques that flopped. One of the most disastrous was a system for computerizing production scheduling that was too crude for complex machine-tool manufacturing. Holland gives a dramatic depiction of supply snafus that resulted in delays and cost increases.

As an independent company, "Burgmaster thrived because the Burgs knew their business," Holland writes. Their departure under Houdaille was followed by an "endless and ultimately futile search for a better formula." But, he concludes: "No formula was a substitute for management involvement on the shop floor."

In the end, however, Holland puts most of the blame for the industry's decline on government policy. He targets tax laws and macroeconomic policies that encourage LBOs and speculation instead of productive investment. He also criticizes Pentagon procurement policies for favoring exotic, custom machines over standard, low-cost models. This adds up to an industrial policy, Holland writes—a bad one.

The point is well taken, but Holland gives it excessive weight. Like their brethren in Detroit and Pittsburgh, domestic tool-makers in the 1970s were too complacent when imports seized the lower end of the product line. The conservatism that had for years served them in their cyclical industry left them ill-prepared for change. Even now some of the largest U.S. tool-makers are struggling to restructure. Blame the government, yes. But blame the industry, too.

Questions

1. Write a brief report that outlines the reasons (both internal and external) for Burgmaster's demise, and whether operations management played a significant role in the demise.
2. Do you think that inadequate strategic planning was a factor that resulted in the company's asking for trade protection?
3. Can you think of a strategy that could have increased Burgmaster's chance of survival? Explain why you think that strategy would have been effective.

Source: Reprinted from April 17, 1989, issue of *BusinessWeek* by special permission, copyright © 1989 by The McGraw-Hill Companies.

Home-Style Cookies

CASE

The Company

The baking company is located in a small town in New York State. The bakery is run by two brothers. The company employs fewer than 200 people, mainly blue-collar workers, and the atmosphere is informal.

The Product

The company's only product is soft cookies, of which it makes over 50 varieties. Larger companies, such as Nabisco, Sunshine, and Keebler, have traditionally produced biscuit cookies, in which most of the water has been baked out, resulting in crisp cookies. The cookies have no additives or preservatives. The high quality of the cookies has enabled the company to develop a strong market niche for its product.

The Customers

The cookies are sold in convenience stores and supermarkets throughout New York, Connecticut, and New Jersey. The company

(continued)

(continued)
markets its cookies as "good food"—no additives or preservatives—and this appeals to a health-conscious segment of the market. Many customers are over 45 years of age, and prefer a cookie that is soft and not too sweet. Parents with young children also buy the cookies.

The Production Process

The company has two continuous band ovens that it uses to bake the cookies. The production process is called a batch processing system. It begins as soon as management gets orders from distributors. These orders are used to schedule production. At the start of each shift, a list of the cookies to be made that day is delivered to the person in charge of mixing. That person checks a master list, which indicates the ingredients needed for each type of cookie, and enters that information into the computer. The computer then determines the amount of each ingredient needed, according to the quantity of cookies ordered, and relays that information to storage silos located outside the plant where the main ingredients (flour, sugar, and cake flour) are stored. The ingredients are automatically sent to giant mixing machines where the ingredients are combined with proper amounts of eggs, water, and flavorings. After the ingredients have been mixed, the batter is poured into a cutting machine where it is cut into individual cookies. The cookies are then dropped onto a conveyor belt and transported through one of two ovens. Filled cookies, such as apple, date, and raspberry, require an additional step for filling and folding.

The nonfilled cookies are cut on a diagonal rather than round. The diagonal-cut cookies require less space than straight-cut cookies, and the result is a higher level of productivity. In addition, the company recently increased the length of each oven by 25 feet, which also increased the rate of production.

As the cookies emerge from the ovens, they are fed onto spiral cooling racks 20 feet high and 3 feet wide. As the cookies come off the cooling racks, workers place the cookies into boxes manually, removing any broken or deformed cookies in the process. The boxes are then wrapped, sealed, and labeled automatically.

Inventory

Most cookies are loaded immediately onto trucks and shipped to distributors. A small percentage are stored temporarily in the company's warehouse, but they must be shipped shortly because of their limited shelf life. Other inventory includes individual cookie boxes, shipping boxes, labels, and cellophane for wrapping. Labels are reordered frequently, in small batches, because FDA label requirements are subject to change, and the company does not want to get stuck with labels it can't use. The bulk silos are refilled two or three times a week, depending on how quickly supplies are used.

Cookies are baked in a sequence that minimizes downtime for cleaning. For instance, light-colored cookies (e.g., chocolate chip) are baked before dark-colored cookies (e.g., fudge), and oatmeal cookies are baked before oatmeal raisin cookies. This permits the company to avoid having to clean the processing equipment every time a different type of cookie is produced.

Quality

The bakery prides itself on the quality of its cookies. Cookies are sampled randomly by a quality control inspector as they come off the line to assure that their taste and consistency are satisfactory, and that they have been baked to the proper degree. Also, workers on the line are responsible for removing defective cookies when they spot them. The company has also installed an X-ray machine on the line that can detect small bits of metal filings that may have gotten into cookies during the production process. The use of automatic equipment for transporting raw materials and mixing batter has made it easier to maintain a sterile process.

Scrap

The bakery is run very efficiently and has minimal amounts of scrap. For example, if a batch is mixed improperly, it is sold for dog food. Broken cookies are used in the oatmeal cookies. These practices reduce the cost of ingredients and save on waste disposal costs. The company also uses heat reclamation: The heat that escapes from the two ovens is captured and used to boil the water that supplies the heat to the building. Also, the use of automation in the mixing process has resulted in a reduction in waste compared with the manual methods used previously.

New Products

Ideas for new products come from customers, employees, and observations of competitors' products. New ideas are first examined to determine whether the cookies can be made with existing equipment. If so, a sample run is made to determine the cost and time requirements. If the results are satisfactory, marketing tests are conducted to see if there is a demand for the product.

Potential Improvements

There are a number of areas of potential improvement at the bakery. One possibility would be to automate packing the cookies into boxes. Although labor costs are not high, automating the process might save some money and increase efficiency. So far, the owners have resisted making this change because they feel an obligation to the community to employ the 30 women who now do the boxing manually. Another possible improvement would be to use suppliers who are located closer to the plant. That would reduce delivery lead times and transportation costs, but the owners are not convinced that local suppliers could provide the same good quality. Other opportunities have been proposed in recent years, but the owners rejected them because they feared that the quality of the product might suffer.

Questions

1. Briefly describe the cookie production process.
2. What are two ways that the company has increased productivity? Why did increasing the length of the ovens result in a faster output rate?

(continued)

(concluded)

3. Do you think that the company is making the right decision by not automating the packing of cookies? Explain your reasoning. What obligation does a company have to its employees in a situation such as this? What obligation does it have to the community? Is the size of the town a factor? Would it make a difference if the company was located in a large city? Is the size of the company a factor? What if it were a much larger company?
4. What factors cause the company to carry minimal amounts of certain inventories? What benefits result from this policy?
5. As a consumer, what things do you consider in judging the quality of cookies you buy in a supermarket?
6. What advantages and what limitations stem from the company's not using preservatives in cookies?
7. Briefly describe the company's strategy.

Hazel Revisited

CASE

(Refer to p. 38 for the Hazel Case.)

1. What competitive advantage does Hazel have over a professional lawn care service?
2. Hazel would like to increase her profits, but she doesn't believe that it would be wise to raise her prices considering the current state of the local economy. Instead, she has given some thought to increasing productivity.
   a. Explain how increased productivity could be an alternative to increased prices.
   b. What are some ways that Hazel could increase productivity?
3. Hazel is thinking about the purchase of new equipment. One would be power sidewalk edgers. She believes edgers will lead to an increase in productivity. Another would be a chain saw, which would be used for tree pruning. What trade-offs should she consider in her analysis?
4. Hazel has been fairly successful in her neighborhood, and now wants to expand to other neighborhoods, including some that are five miles away. What would be the advantages and disadvantages of doing this?
5. Hazel does not have a mission statement or a set of objectives. Take one of the following positions and defend it:
   a. Hazel doesn't need a formal mission statement and objectives. Many small businesses don't have them.
   b. She definitely needs a mission statement and a set of objectives. They would be extremely beneficial.
   c. There may be some benefit to Hazel's business, and she should consider developing one.

"Your Garden Gloves"

CASE

Joseph Murray, Grand Valley State University

"Your Garden Gloves" is a small gardening business located in Michigan. The company plants and maintains flower gardens for both commercial and residential clients. The company was founded about five years ago, and has since grown substantially, averaging about 10 new clients and one new employee a year. The company currently employs eight seasonal employees who are responsible for a certain number of clients.

Each morning crews are assigned to jobs by the owner. Crew sizes range from two to four workers. Crew size and composition are a function of the square footage of the garden and requirements of the job. The owner feels that large jobs should be assigned to crews of four workers in order to complete the job in a reasonable amount of time.

From time to time, the owner noticed that some jobs, especially the largest ones, took longer than she had estimated, based on the square footage of the garden space involved. The owner's son, Joe, decided to investigate. He kept records of job times and crew sizes, and then used those records to compute labor productivity. The results were:

Crew Size	Average Productivity per Crew
2	4,234 square feet per day
3	5,352 square feet per day
4	7,860 square feet per day

The company operates on a small profit margin, so it is especially important to take worker productivity into account.

Questions

1. Which crew size had the highest productivity? Which crew size had the lowest productivity? What are some possible explanations for these results?
2. After a recent storm, a customer called in a panic, saying that she had planned a garden party for the upcoming weekend and her garden was in shambles. The owner decided to send a crew of four workers, even though a two-worker crew would have a higher productivity. Explain the rationale for this decision.
3. What is a possible qualitative issue that may very well influence productivity levels that the productivity ratios fail to take into account?

"Neither rain, nor snow . . ."

The U.S. Postal Service (USPS) is the largest postal service in the world, handling about 41 percent (630 million pieces a day) of the world's mail volume. The second largest is Japan's, which handles only about 6 percent of the world's mail. The USPS is huge by any standard. It employs over 760,000 workers, making it the largest civilian employer in the United States. It has over 300,000 mail collection boxes, 38,000 post offices, 130 million mail delivery points, more than 300 processing plants to sort and ship mail, and more than 75,000 pieces of mail processing equipment. It handles over 100 billion pieces of first-class mail a year, and ships about 3 billion pounds of mail on commercial airline flights, making it the airlines' largest shipper.

Processing First-Class Mail

The essence of processing the mail is sorting, which means organizing the mail into smaller and smaller subgroups to facilitate its timely delivery. Sorting involves a combination of manual and automatic operations. Much of the mail that is processed is first-class mail.

Most first-class mail is handled using automated equipment. A small portion that cannot be handled by automated equipment must be sorted by hand, just the way it was done in colonial times.

The majority of first-class mail begins at the advanced facer canceling system. This system positions each letter so that it is face up, with the stamp in the upper corner, checks to see if the address is handwritten, and pulls the hand-addressed letters off the line. It also rejects letters that have the stamp covered by tape, have no postage, are third-class mail, or have meter impressions that are too light to read. The rejects are handled manually. The remaining letters are cancelled and date stamped, and then sorted to one of seven stackers.

Next the letters go to the multiline optical character readers, which can handle both printed and pre–bar-coded mail, but not hand-addressed mail. The optical reader sprays a bar code on the mail that hasn't been pre–bar-coded, which represents up to an 11-digit zip code. For hand-addressed mail, a camera focuses on the front of the letter, and the image is displayed on a remote terminal, often in another city, where an operator views the image and provides the information that the optical readers could not determine so that a bar code can be added.

Bar-code readers then sort the mail into one of 96 stackers, doing this at a rate of more than 500 a minute. The mail goes through another sort using manually controlled mechanical equipment. At that point, the mail is separated according to whether it is local or out-of-town mail. The out-of-town mail is placed into appropriate sacks according to its destination, and moved to the outgoing send area where it will be loaded on trucks.

The local mail is moved to another machine that not only sorts the mail into local carrier delivery routes, it sorts it according to delivery walk sequence!

Small parcels, bundles of letters, and bundles of flats are sorted by a bundle-sorting machine.

Productivity

Over the years, the USPS has experienced an ever-increasing volume of mail. Productivity has been an important factor for the USPS in keeping postal rates low and maintaining rapid delivery service. Two key factors in improved productivity have been the increased use of automation and the introduction of zip codes.

Mail processing underwent a major shift to mechanization during the 1950s and 1960s, which led to more rapid processing and higher productivity. In 1978, an expanded zip code was introduced. That was followed in 1983 by a four-digit expansion in zip codes. These changes required new, automated processing equipment, and the use of bar codes and optical readers. All of these changes added greatly to productivity. But even with these improvements, the USPS faced increasing competitive pressures.

Competition

In the late 1980s, the USPS experienced a slowdown in the volume of mail. Some of this was due to a slowing of the economy, but most of it was the result of increasing competition. Delivery giants FedEx and UPS, as well as other companies that offer speedy delivery and package tracking, gave businesses and the general public convenient alternatives for some mail services. At the same time, there was a growing use of fax machines and electronic communications and increased use of alternate forms of advertising such as cable TV, all of which cut into the volume of mail. Early in this century, e-mail and automated bill paying also cut into mail volume.

Strategies and Tactics Used to Make the Postal Service More Competitive

To meet these challenges, the USPS developed several strategies to become more competitive. These included reorganizing, continuing to seek ways to keep costs down, increasing productivity, and emphasizing quality and customer service. Here is an overview of the situation and the strategies and tactics used by the USPS.

The USPS began working more closely with customers to identify better ways to meet their needs and expanded customer conveniences such as stamps on consignment. With the help of business mailers, the USPS continued support for rates reflecting customer work-sharing features, many tied to automation, to give customers more flexibility. At the same time, the USPS began forming Customer Advisory Councils—groups of citizens who volunteered to work with local postal management on postal issues of interest to the community. In 1990, the USPS awarded two contracts to private firms to measure first-class mail service and customer satisfaction. In 1992, the USPS stepped up its quest to become more competitive by reducing bureaucracy and overhead in order to improve service and customer satisfaction, and to reduce the need to increase postage rates.

To help accomplish these goals, the USPS underwent a reorganization. Layers of management were eliminated and overhead positions were cut by about 30,000. Five regions and 73 field divisions were replaced by 10 areas, each with a manager for customer

(continued)

(concluded)

services and a manager for processing and distribution. Ten customer service areas were established, with managers for customer service and processing and distribution in each area, as well as a marketing and sales office. The new structure allowed postal managers to be focused, improved communications, and empowered employees to meet customer needs. The USPS also took other steps to improve service. In 1993 it implemented improvements in processing and mail delivery at major postal facilities, expanded retail hours, and developed a more user-friendly Domestic Mail Manual. In cooperation with business customers, the USPS began to develop new services to meet specific mailer needs and to overhaul and simplify its complex rate structure. It also awarded contracts for two more external tracking systems, one to measure satisfaction levels of business mailers, and the other to measure service performance of third-class mail.

The reorganization eliminated some programs, cut costs, attracted new business, and reduced the USPS's projected deficit.

Questions

1. Why is it important for the USPS to have a high volume of mail to process?
2. What caused productivity to increase?
3. What impact did competitive pressures have on the USPS?
4. What measures did the USPS adopt to increase competitiveness?
5. What results were achieved by the USPS's changes?
6. What effect does the increased use of e-mail have on postal productivity?
7. How does the use of standard shipping containers and flat-rate mailers help competitiveness?

SELECTED BIBLIOGRAPHY AND FURTHER READINGS

Bartlett, Christopher A., and Sumantra Ghoshal. "Going Global: Lessons from Late Movers." *Harvard Business Review,* March–April 2000, pp. 132–42.

Bernstein, Aaron. "Backlash: Behind the Anxiety of Globalization." *BusinessWeek,* April 24, 2000, pp. 38–44.

Blackburn, Joseph D., ed. *Time-Based Competition.* Homewood, IL: Business One Irwin, 1991.

Colvin, Geoffrey. "Managing in the Info Era." *Fortune,* March 6, 2000, pp. F6–F9.

Hachman, Mark. "Supply-Chain Program Boosts Productivity at Seagate Tech." *Electronic Buyers News,* January 17, 2000.

Hammer, Michael, and Steven Stanton. "Ignore Operations at Your Peril." *Harvard Business Review,* 6565, April 2004.

Hill, Terry. *Manufacturing Strategy: Text and Cases,* 3rd ed. New York: McGraw-Hill, 2000.

Holstein, William J. "Are Raises Bad for America?" *U.S. News & World Report,* August 30, 1999, pp. 48–50.

Ingold, Anthony, Ian Yeoman, and Una McMahon-Beattie, eds. *Yield Management: Strategies for the Service Industries,* 2nd ed. London: Continuum, 2001.

Roach, Stephen. "In Search of Productivity." *Harvard Business Review,* September–October 1998, p. 153.

Ross, D. F. *Competing Through Supply Chain Management.* New York: Chapman and Hall, 1998.

Stalk, George, P. Evans, and L. E. Shulman. "Competing on Capabilities: The New Rules of Corporate Strategy." *Harvard Business Review,* March–April 1992, pp. 57–69.

Werbach, Adam. *Strategy for Sustainability: A Business Manifesto.* Boston: Harvard Business Press, 2009.

Forecasting

CHAPTER

CHAPTER OUTLINE

LEARNING OBJECTIVES

After completing this chapter, you should be able to:

1 List the elements of a good forecast.
2 Outline the steps in the forecasting process.
3 Evaluate at least three qualitative forecasting techniques and the advantages and disadvantages of each.
4 Compare and contrast qualitative and quantitative approaches to forecasting.
5 Describe averaging techniques, trend and seasonal techniques, and regression analysis, and solve typical problems.
6 Explain three measures of forecast accuracy.
7 Compare two ways of evaluating and controlling forecasts.
8 Assess the major factors and trade-offs to consider when choosing a forecasting technique.

Weather forecasts are one of the many types of forecasts used by some business organizations. Although some businesses simply rely on publicly available weather forecasts, others turn to firms that specialize in weather-related forecasts. For example, Home Depot, Gap, and JCPenney use such firms to help them take weather factors into account for estimating demand.

Many new car buyers have a thing or two in common. Once they make the decision to buy a new car, they want it as soon as possible. They usually don't want to order it and then have to wait six weeks or more for delivery. If the car dealer they visit doesn't have the car they want, they'll look elsewhere. Hence, it is important for a dealer to *anticipate* buyer wants and to have those models, with the necessary options, in stock. The dealer who can correctly forecast buyer wants, and have those cars available, is going to be much more successful than a competitor who guesses instead of forecasting—and guesses wrong—and gets stuck with cars customers don't want. So how does the dealer know how many cars of each type to stock? The answer is, the dealer *doesn't* know for sure, but by analyzing previous buying patterns, and perhaps making allowances for current conditions, the dealer can come up with a reasonable *approximation* of what buyers will want.

Planning is an integral part of a manager's job. If uncertainties cloud the planning horizon, managers will find it difficult to plan effectively. Forecasts help managers by reducing some of the uncertainty, thereby enabling them to develop more meaningful plans. A **forecast** is a statement about the future value of a variable such as demand. That is, forecasts are predictions about the future. The better those predictions, the more informed decisions can be. Some forecasts are long range, covering several years or more. Long-range forecasts are especially important for decisions that will have long-term consequences for an organization or for a town, city, country, state, or nation. One example is deciding on the right capacity for a planned power plant that will operate for the next 20 years. Other forecasts are used to determine if there is a profit potential for a new service or a new product: Will there be sufficient demand to make the innovation worthwhile? Many forecasts are short term, covering a day or week. They are especially helpful in planning and scheduling day-to-day operations. This chapter provides a survey of business forecasting. It describes the elements of good forecasts, the necessary steps in preparing a forecast, basic forecasting techniques, and how to monitor a forecast.

INTRODUCTION

Forecast A statement about the future value of a variable of interest.

Forecasts are a basic input in the decision processes of operations management because they provide information on future demand. The importance of forecasting to operations management cannot be overstated. The primary goal of operations management is to match supply to demand. Having a forecast of demand is essential for determining how much capacity or supply will be needed to meet demand. For instance, operations needs to know what capacity will be needed to make staffing and equipment decisions, budgets must be prepared, purchasing needs information for ordering from suppliers, and supply chain partners need to make their plans.

Two aspects of forecasts are important. One is the expected level of demand; the other is the degree of accuracy that can be assigned to a forecast (i.e., the potential size of forecast error). The expected level of demand can be a function of some structural variation, such as a trend or seasonal variation. Forecast accuracy is a function of the ability of forecasters to correctly model demand, random variation, and sometimes unforeseen events.

Forecasts are made with reference to a specific time horizon. The time horizon may be fairly short (e.g., an hour, day, week, or month), or somewhat longer (e.g., the next six months, the next year, the next five years, or the life of a product or service). Short-term forecasts pertain to ongoing operations. Long-range forecasts can be an important strategic planning tool. Long-term forecasts pertain to new products or services, new equipment, new facilities, or something else that will require a somewhat long lead time to develop, construct, or otherwise implement.

Forecasts are the basis for budgeting, planning capacity, sales, production and inventory, personnel, purchasing, and more. Forecasts play an important role in the planning process because they enable managers to anticipate the future so they can plan accordingly.

Forecasts affect decisions and activities throughout an organization, in accounting, finance, human resources, marketing, and management information systems (MIS), as well as in operations and other parts of an organization. Here are some examples of uses of forecasts in business organizations:

Accounting. New product/process cost estimates, profit projections, cash management.

Finance. Equipment/equipment replacement needs, timing and amount of funding/borrowing needs.

The Walt Disney World forecasting department has 20 employees who formulate forecasts on volume and revenue for the theme parks, water parks, resort hotels, as well as merchandise, food, and beverage revenue by location.

Human resources. Hiring activities, including recruitment, interviewing, and training; layoff planning, including outplacement counseling.

Marketing. Pricing and promotion, e-business strategies, global competition strategies.

MIS. New/revised information systems, Internet services.

Operations. Schedules, capacity planning, work assignments and workloads, inventory planning, make-or-buy decisions, outsourcing, project management.

Product/service design. Revision of current features, design of new products or services.

In most of these uses of forecasts, decisions in one area have consequences in other areas. Therefore, it is very important for all affected areas to agree on a common forecast. However, this may not be easy to accomplish. Different departments often have very different perspectives on a forecast, making a consensus forecast difficult to achieve. For example, salespeople, by their very nature, may be overly optimistic with their forecasts, and may want to "reserve" capacity for their customers. This can result in excess costs for operations and inventory storage. Conversely, if demand exceeds forecasts, operations and the supply chain may not be able to meet demand, which would mean lost business and dissatisfied customers.

Forecasting is also an important component of *yield management,* which relates to the percentage of capacity being used. Accurate forecasts can help managers plan tactics (e.g., offer discounts, don't offer discounts) to match capacity with demand, thereby achieving high yield levels.

There are two uses for forecasts. One is to help managers *plan the system,* and the other is to help them *plan the use of the system.* Planning the system generally involves long-range plans about the types of products and services to offer, what facilities and equipment to have, where to locate, and so on. Planning the use of the system refers to short-range and intermediate-range planning, which involve tasks such as planning inventory and workforce levels, planning purchasing and production, budgeting, and scheduling.

Business forecasting pertains to more than predicting demand. Forecasts are also used to predict profits, revenues, costs, productivity changes, prices and availability of energy and raw materials, interest rates, movements of key economic indicators (e.g., gross domestic product, inflation, government borrowing), and prices of stocks and bonds. For the sake of simplicity, this chapter will focus on the forecasting of demand. Keep in mind, however, that the concepts and techniques apply equally well to the other variables.

In spite of its use of computers and sophisticated mathematical models, forecasting is not an exact science. Instead, successful forecasting often requires a skillful blending of science and intuition. Experience, judgment, and technical expertise all play a role in developing useful forecasts. Along with these, a certain amount of luck and a dash of humility can be helpful, because the worst forecasters occasionally produce a very good forecast, and even the best forecasters sometimes miss completely. Current forecasting techniques range from the mundane to the exotic. Some work better than others, but no single technique works all the time.

FEATURES COMMON TO ALL FORECASTS

A wide variety of forecasting techniques are in use. In many respects, they are quite different from each other, as you shall soon discover. Nonetheless, certain features are common to all, and it is important to recognize them.

1. Forecasting techniques generally assume that the same underlying causal system that existed in the past will continue to exist in the future.

Comment A manager cannot simply delegate forecasting to models or computers and then forget about it, because unplanned occurrences can wreak havoc with forecasts. For instance, weather-related events, tax increases or decreases, and changes in features or prices of competing products or services can have a major impact on demand. Consequently, a manager must be alert to such occurrences and be ready to override forecasts, which assume a stable causal system.

2. Forecasts are not perfect; actual results usually differ from predicted values; the presence of randomness precludes a perfect forecast. Allowances should be made for forecast errors.
3. Forecasts for groups of items tend to be more accurate than forecasts for individual items because forecasting errors among items in a group usually have a canceling effect. Opportunities for grouping may arise if parts or raw materials are used for multiple products or if a product or service is demanded by a number of independent sources.
4. Forecast accuracy decreases as the time period covered by the forecast—the *time horizon*—increases. Generally speaking, short-range forecasts must contend with fewer uncertainties than longer-range forecasts, so they tend to be more accurate.

An important consequence of the last point is that flexible business organizations—those that can respond quickly to changes in demand—require a shorter forecasting horizon and, hence, benefit from more accurate short-range forecasts than competitors who are less flexible and who must therefore use longer forecast horizons.

ELEMENTS OF A GOOD FORECAST

A properly prepared forecast should fulfill certain requirements:

1. The forecast should be **timely.** Usually, a certain amount of time is needed to respond to the information contained in a forecast. For example, capacity cannot be expanded overnight, nor can inventory levels be changed immediately. Hence, the forecasting horizon must cover the time necessary to implement possible changes.
2. The forecast should be **accurate,** and the degree of accuracy should be stated. This will enable users to plan for possible errors and will provide a basis for comparing alternative forecasts.
3. The forecast should be **reliable;** it should work consistently. A technique that sometimes provides a good forecast and sometimes a poor one will leave users with the uneasy feeling that they may get burned every time a new forecast is issued.
4. The forecast should be expressed in **meaningful units.** Financial planners need to know how many *dollars* will be needed, production planners need to know how many *units* will be needed, and schedulers need to know what *machines* and *skills* will be required. The choice of units depends on user needs.
5. The forecast should be **in writing.** Although this will not guarantee that all concerned are using the same information, it will at least increase the likelihood of it. In addition, a written forecast will permit an objective basis for evaluating the forecast once actual results are in.
6. The forecasting technique should be **simple to understand and use.** Users often lack confidence in forecasts based on sophisticated techniques; they do not understand either the circumstances in which the techniques are appropriate or the limitations of the techniques. Misuse of techniques is an obvious consequence. Not surprisingly, fairly simple forecasting techniques enjoy widespread popularity because users are more comfortable working with them.
7. The forecast should be **cost-effective:** The benefits should outweigh the costs.

FORECASTING AND THE SUPPLY CHAIN

Accurate forecasts are very important for the supply chain. Inaccurate forecasts can lead to shortages and excesses throughout the supply chain. Shortages of materials, parts, and services can lead to missed deliveries, work disruption, and poor customer service. Conversely, overly optimistic forecasts can lead to excesses of materials and/or capacity, which increase costs. Both shortages and excesses in the supply chain have a negative impact not only on customer service but also on profits. Furthermore, inaccurate forecasts can result in temporary increases and decreases in orders to the supply chain, which can be misinterpreted by the supply chain.

Organizations can reduce the likelihood of such occurrences in a number of ways. One, obviously, is by striving to develop the best possible forecasts. Another is through collaborative planning and forecasting with major supply chain partners. Yet another way is through information sharing among partners and perhaps increasing supply chain visibility by allowing supply chain partners to have real-time access to sales and inventory information. Also important is rapid communication about poor forecasts as well as about unplanned events that disrupt operations (e.g., flooding, work stoppages), and changes in plans.

SUPPLY CHAIN

STEPS IN THE FORECASTING PROCESS

There are six basic steps in the forecasting process:

1. **Determine the purpose of the forecast.** How will it be used and when will it be needed? This step will provide an indication of the level of detail required in the forecast, the amount of resources (personnel, computer time, dollars) that can be justified, and the level of accuracy necessary.
2. **Establish a time horizon.** The forecast must indicate a time interval, keeping in mind that accuracy decreases as the time horizon increases.
3. **Obtain, clean, and analyze appropriate data.** Obtaining the data can involve significant effort. Once obtained, the data may need to be "cleaned" to get rid of outliers and obviously incorrect data before analysis.
4. **Select a forecasting technique.**
5. **Make the forecast.**
6. **Monitor the forecast.** A forecast has to be monitored to determine whether it is performing in a satisfactory manner. If it is not, reexamine the method, assumptions, validity of data, and so on; modify as needed; and prepare a revised forecast.

Note too that additional action may be necessary. For example, if demand was much less than the forecast, an action such as a price reduction or a promotion may be needed. Conversely, if demand was much more than predicted, increased output may be advantageous. That may involve working overtime, outsourcing, or taking other measures.

FORECAST ACCURACY

Accuracy and control of forecasts is a vital aspect of forecasting, so forecasters want to minimize forecast errors. However, the complex nature of most real-world variables makes it almost impossible to correctly predict future values of those variables on a regular basis. Moreover, because random variation is always present, there will always be some residual error, even if all other factors have been accounted for. Consequently, it is important to include an indication of the extent to which the forecast might deviate from the value of the variable that actually occurs. This will provide the forecast user with a better perspective on how far off a forecast might be.

SCREENCAM TUTORIAL

Decision makers will want to include accuracy as a factor when choosing among different techniques, along with cost. Accurate forecasts are necessary for the success of daily activities of every business organization. Forecasts are the basis for an organization's schedules, and unless the forecasts are accurate, schedules will be generated that may provide for too few or too many resources, too little or too much output, the wrong output, or the wrong timing of output, all of which can lead to additional costs, dissatisfied customers, and headaches for managers.

Some forecasting applications involve a series of forecasts (e.g., weekly revenues), whereas others involve a single forecast that will be used for a one-time decision (e.g., the size of a power plant). When making periodic forecasts, it is important to monitor forecast errors to determine if the errors are within reasonable bounds. If they are not, it will be necessary to take corrective action.

"I recommend our 'wild' expectations be downgraded to 'great.'"

Error Difference between the actual value and the value that was predicted for a given period.

Forecast **error** is the difference between the value that occurs and the value that was predicted for a given time period. Hence, Error = Actual − Forecast:

$$e_t = A_t - F_t \tag{3–1}$$

where

t = Any given time period

Positive errors result when the forecast is too low, negative errors when the forecast is too high. For example, if actual demand for a week is 100 units and forecast demand was 90 units, the forecast was too low; the error is 100 − 90 = +10.

Forecast errors influence decisions in two somewhat different ways. One is in making a choice between various forecasting alternatives, and the other is in evaluating the success or failure of a technique in use. We shall begin by examining ways to summarize forecast error over time, and see how that information can be applied to compare forecasting alternatives.

High Forecasts Can Be Bad News

READING

Overly optimistic forecasts by retail store buyers can easily lead retailers to overorder, resulting in bloated inventories. When that happens, there is pressure on stores to cut prices in order to move the excess merchandise. Although customers delight in these markdowns, retailer profits generally suffer. Furthermore, retailers will naturally cut back on new orders while they work off their inventories, creating a ripple effect that hits the entire supply chain, from shippers, to producers, to suppliers of raw materials. Moreover, the cutbacks to the supply chain could be misinterpreted. The message is clear: Overly optimistic forecasts can be bad news.

Mean absolute deviation (MAD) The average absolute forecast error.

Mean squared error (MSE) The average of squared forecast errors.

Summarizing Forecast Accuracy

Forecast accuracy is a significant factor when deciding among forecasting alternatives. Accuracy is based on the historical error performance of a forecast.

Three commonly used measures for summarizing historical errors are the **mean absolute deviation (MAD),** the **mean squared error (MSE),** and the **mean absolute percent error (MAPE).** MAD is the average absolute error, MSE is the average of squared errors, and

Mean absolute percent error (MAPE) The average absolute percent error.

MAPE is the average absolute percent error. The formulas used to compute MAD,[1] MSE, and MAPE are as follows:

$$\text{MAD} = \frac{\Sigma|\text{Actual}_t - \text{Forecast}_t|}{n} \quad (3\text{–}2)$$

$$\text{MSE} = \frac{\Sigma(\text{Actual}_t - \text{Forecast}_t)^2}{n-1} \quad (3\text{–}3)$$

$$\text{MAPE} = \frac{\Sigma\dfrac{|\text{Actual}_t - \text{Forecast}_t|}{\text{Actual}_t} \times 100}{n} \quad (3\text{–}4)$$

Example 1 illustrates the computation of MAD, MSE, and MAPE.

EXAMPLE 1

eXcel www.mhhe.com/stevenson11e

SCREENCAM TUTORIAL

Compute MAD, MSE, and MAPE for the following data, showing actual and forecasted numbers of accounts serviced.

Period	Actual	Forecast	(A − F) Error	|Error|	Error²	[|Error| ÷ Actual] × 100
1	217	215	2	2	4	.92%
2	213	216	−3	3	9	1.41
3	216	215	1	1	1	.46
4	210	214	−4	4	16	1.90
5	213	211	2	2	4	.94
6	219	214	5	5	25	2.28
7	216	217	−1	1	1	.46
8	212	216	−4	4	16	1.89
			−2	22	76	10.26%

SOLUTION

Using the figures shown in the table,

$$\text{MAD} = \frac{\Sigma|e|}{n} = \frac{22}{8} = 2.75$$

$$\text{MSE} = \frac{\Sigma e^2}{n-1} = \frac{76}{8-1} = 10.86$$

$$\text{MAPE} = \frac{\Sigma\left[\dfrac{|e|}{\text{Actual}} \times 100\right]}{n} = \frac{10.26\%}{8} = 1.28\%$$

From a computational standpoint, the difference between these measures is that MAD weights all errors evenly, MSE weights errors according to their *squared* values, and MAPE weights according to relative error.

One use for these measures is to compare the accuracy of alternative forecasting methods. For instance, a manager could compare the results to determine one which yields the *lowest* MAD, MSE, or MAPE for a given set of data. Another use is to track error performance over time to decide if attention is needed. Is error performance getting better or worse, or is it staying about the same?

[1]The absolute value, represented by the two vertical lines in Formula 3–2, ignores minus signs; all data are treated as positive values. For example, −2 becomes +2.

In some instances, historical error performance is secondary to the ability of a forecast to respond to changes in data patterns. Choice among alternative methods would then focus on the cost of not responding quickly to a change relative to the cost of responding to changes that are not really there (i.e., random fluctuations).

Overall, the operations manager must settle on the relative importance of historical performance versus responsiveness and whether to use MAD, MSE, or MAPE to measure historical performance. MAD is the easiest to compute, but weights errors linearly. MSE squares errors, thereby giving more weight to larger errors, which typically cause more problems. MAPE should be used when there is a need to put errors in perspective. For example, an error of 10 in a forecast of 15 is huge. Conversely, an error of 10 in a forecast of 10,000 is insignificant. Hence, to put large errors in perspective, MAPE would be used.

APPROACHES TO FORECASTING

There are two general approaches to forecasting: qualitative and quantitative. Qualitative methods consist mainly of subjective inputs, which often defy precise numerical description. Quantitative methods involve either the projection of historical data or the development of associative models that attempt to utilize *causal (explanatory) variables* to make a forecast.

Qualitative techniques permit inclusion of *soft* information (e.g., human factors, personal opinions, hunches) in the forecasting process. Those factors are often omitted or downplayed when quantitative techniques are used because they are difficult or impossible to quantify. Quantitative techniques consist mainly of analyzing objective, or *hard,* data. They usually avoid personal biases that sometimes contaminate qualitative methods. In practice, either approach or a combination of both approaches might be used to develop a forecast.

The following pages present a variety of forecasting techniques that are classified as judgmental, time-series, or associative.

Judgmental forecasts Forecasts that use subjective inputs such as opinions from consumer surveys, sales staff, managers, executives, and experts.

Time-series forecasts Forecasts that project patterns identified in recent time-series observations.

Associative model Forecasting technique that uses explanatory variables to predict future demand.

Judgmental forecasts rely on analysis of subjective inputs obtained from various sources, such as consumer surveys, the sales staff, managers and executives, and panels of experts. Quite frequently, these sources provide insights that are not otherwise available.

Time-series forecasts simply attempt to project past experience into the future. These techniques use historical data with the assumption that the future will be like the past. Some models merely attempt to smooth out random variations in historical data; others attempt to identify specific patterns in the data and project or extrapolate those patterns into the future, without trying to identify causes of the patterns.

Associative models use equations that consist of one or more *explanatory* variables that can be used to predict demand. For example, demand for paint might be related to variables such as the price per gallon and the amount spent on advertising, as well as to specific characteristics of the paint (e.g., drying time, ease of cleanup).

QUALITATIVE FORECASTS

In some situations, forecasters rely solely on judgment and opinion to make forecasts. If management must have a forecast quickly, there may not be enough time to gather and analyze quantitative data. At other times, especially when political and economic conditions are changing, available data may be obsolete and more up-to-date information might not yet be available. Similarly, the introduction of new products and the redesign of existing products or packaging suffer from the absence of historical data that would be useful in forecasting. In such instances, forecasts are based on executive opinions, consumer surveys, opinions of the sales staff, and opinions of experts.

Executive Opinions

A small group of upper-level managers (e.g., in marketing, operations, and finance) may meet and collectively develop a forecast. This approach is often used as a part of long-range planning and new product development. It has the advantage of bringing together the considerable knowledge and talents of various managers. However, there is the risk that the view of one person will prevail, and the possibility that diffusing responsibility for the forecast over the entire group may result in less pressure to produce a good forecast.

Salesforce Opinions

Members of the sales staff or the customer service staff are often good sources of information because of their direct contact with consumers. They are often aware of any plans the customers may be considering for the future. There are, however, several drawbacks to using salesforce opinions. One is that staff members may be unable to distinguish between what customers would *like* to do and what they actually *will* do. Another is that these people are sometimes overly influenced by recent experiences. Thus, after several periods of low sales, their estimates may tend to become pessimistic. After several periods of good sales, they may tend to be too optimistic. In addition, if forecasts are used to establish sales quotas, there will be a conflict of interest because it is to the salesperson's advantage to provide low sales estimates.

Consumer Surveys

Because it is the consumers who ultimately determine demand, it seems natural to solicit input from them. In some instances, every customer or potential customer can be contacted. However, usually there are too many customers or there is no way to identify all potential customers. Therefore, organizations seeking consumer input usually resort to consumer surveys, which enable them to *sample* consumer opinions. The obvious advantage of consumer surveys is that they can tap information that might not be available elsewhere. On the other hand, a considerable amount of knowledge and skill is required to construct a survey, administer it, and correctly interpret the results for valid information. Surveys can be expensive and time-consuming. In addition, even under the best conditions, surveys of the general public must contend with the possibility of irrational behavior patterns. For example, much of the consumer's thoughtful information gathering before purchasing a new car is often undermined by the glitter of a new car showroom or a high-pressure sales pitch. Along the same lines, low response rates to a mail survey should—but often don't—make the results suspect.

If these and similar pitfalls can be avoided, surveys can produce useful information.

Other Approaches

A manager may solicit opinions from a number of other managers and staff people. Occasionally, outside experts are needed to help with a forecast. Advice may be needed on political or economic conditions in the United States or a foreign country, or some other aspect of importance with which an organization lacks familiarity.

Another approach is the **Delphi method**, an iterative process intended to achieve a consensus forecast. This method involves circulating a series of questionnaires among individuals who possess the knowledge and ability to contribute meaningfully. Responses are kept anonymous, which tends to encourage honest responses and reduces the risk that one person's opinion will prevail. Each new questionnaire is developed using the information extracted from the previous one, thus enlarging the scope of information on which participants can base their judgments.

Delphi method An iterative process in which managers and staff complete a series of questionnaires, each developed from the previous one, to achieve a consensus forecast.

The Delphi method has been applied to a variety of situations, not all of which involve forecasting. The discussion here is limited to its use as a forecasting tool.

As a forecasting tool, the Delphi method is useful for *technological* forecasting, that is, for assessing changes in technology and their impact on an organization. Often the goal is to predict *when* a certain event will occur. For instance, the goal of a Delphi forecast might be to predict when video telephones might be installed in at least 50 percent of residential homes or when a vaccine for a disease might be developed and ready for mass distribution. For the most part, these are long-term, single-time forecasts, which usually have very little hard information to go by or data that are costly to obtain, so the problem does not lend itself to analytical techniques. Rather, judgments of experts or others who possess sufficient knowledge to make predictions are used.

FORECASTS BASED ON TIME-SERIES DATA

Time series A time-ordered sequence of observations taken at regular intervals.

A **time series** is a time-ordered sequence of observations taken at regular intervals (e.g., hourly, daily, weekly, monthly, quarterly, annually). The data may be measurements of demand, earnings, profits, shipments, accidents, output, precipitation, productivity, or the consumer price index. Forecasting techniques based on time-series data are made on the assumption that future values of the series can be estimated from past values. Although no attempt is made to identify variables that influence the series, these methods are widely used, often with quite satisfactory results.

Analysis of time-series data requires the analyst to identify the underlying behavior of the series. This can often be accomplished by merely *plotting the data* and visually examining the plot. One or more patterns might appear: trends, seasonal variations, cycles, or variations around an average. In addition, there will be random and perhaps irregular variations. These behaviors can be described as follows:

Trend A long-term upward or downward movement in data.

Seasonality Short-term regular variations related to the calendar or time of day.

Cycle Wavelike variations lasting more than one year.

Irregular variation Caused by unusual circumstances, not reflective of typical behavior.

Random variations Residual variations after all other behaviors are accounted for.

1. **Trend** refers to a long-term upward or downward movement in the data. Population shifts, changing incomes, and cultural changes often account for such movements.
2. **Seasonality** refers to short-term, fairly regular variations generally related to factors such as the calendar or time of day. Restaurants, supermarkets, and theaters experience weekly and even daily "seasonal" variations.
3. **Cycles** are wavelike variations of more than one year's duration. These are often related to a variety of economic, political, and even agricultural conditions.
4. **Irregular variations** are due to unusual circumstances such as severe weather conditions, strikes, or a major change in a product or service. They do not reflect typical behavior, and their inclusion in the series can distort the overall picture. Whenever possible, these should be identified and removed from the data.
5. **Random variations** are residual variations that remain after all other behaviors have been accounted for.

These behaviors are illustrated in Figure 3.1. The small "bumps" in the plots represent random variability.

The remainder of this section describes the various approaches to the analysis of time-series data. Before turning to those discussions, one point should be emphasized: A demand forecast should be based on a time series of past *demand* rather than unit sales. Sales would not truly reflect demand if one or more *stockouts* occurred.

Naive Methods

Naive forecast A forecast for any period that equals the previous period's actual value.

A simple but widely used approach to forecasting is the naive approach. A **naive forecast** uses a single previous value of a time series as the basis of a forecast. The naive approach can be used with a stable series (variations around an average), with seasonal variations, or with trend. With a stable series, the last data point becomes the forecast for the next period. Thus, if demand for a product last week was 20 cases, the forecast for this week is 20 cases. With seasonal variations, the forecast for this "season" is equal to the value of the series last "season." For example, the forecast for demand for turkeys this Thanksgiving season is equal to demand for turkeys last Thanksgiving; the forecast of the number of checks cashed at a bank on the first day of the month next month is equal to the number of checks cashed on the first day of this month; and the forecast for highway traffic volume this Friday is equal to the highway traffic volume last Friday. For data with trend, the forecast is equal to the last value of the series plus or minus the difference between the last two values of the series. For example, suppose the last two values were 50 and 53. The next forecast would be 56:

Period	Actual	Change from Previous Value	Forecast
1	50		
2	53	+3	
3			53 + 3 = 56

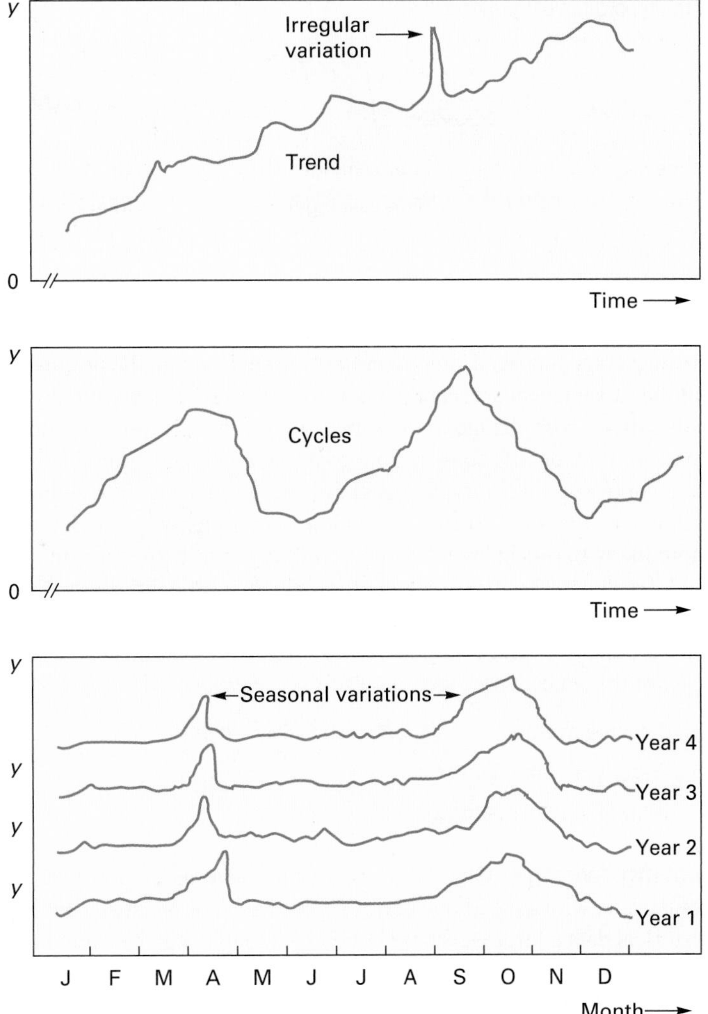

FIGURE 3.1
Trend, cyclical, and seasonal data plots, with random and irregular variations

Although at first glance the naive approach may appear *too* simplistic, it is nonetheless a legitimate forecasting tool. Consider the advantages: It has virtually no cost, it is quick and easy to prepare because data analysis is nonexistent, and it is easily understandable. The main objection to this method is its inability to provide highly accurate forecasts. However, if resulting accuracy is acceptable, this approach deserves serious consideration. Moreover, even if other forecasting techniques offer better accuracy, they will almost always involve a greater cost. The accuracy of a naive forecast can serve as a standard of comparison against which to judge the cost and accuracy of other techniques. Thus, managers must answer the question: Is the increased accuracy of another method worth the additional resources required to achieve that accuracy?

Techniques for Averaging

Historical data typically contain a certain amount of random variation, or *white noise,* that tends to obscure systematic movements in the data. This randomness arises from the combined influence of many—perhaps a great many—relatively unimportant factors, and it cannot be reliably predicted. Averaging techniques smooth variations in the data. Ideally, it would be desirable to completely remove any randomness from the data and leave only "real" variations, such as changes in the demand. As a practical matter, however, it is usually impossible to distinguish between these two kinds of variations, so the best one can hope for is that the small variations are random and the large variations are "real."

SCREENCAM TUTORIAL

FIGURE 3.2 Averaging applied to three possible patterns

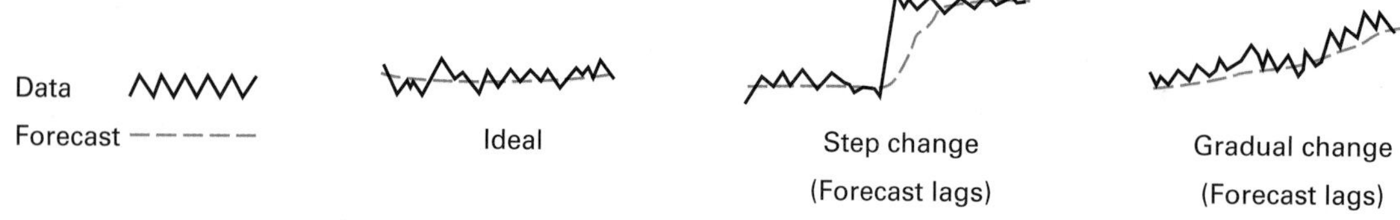

Averaging techniques smooth fluctuations in a time series because the individual highs and lows in the data offset each other when they are combined into an average. A forecast based on an average thus tends to exhibit less variability than the original data (see Figure 3.2). This can be advantageous because many of these movements merely reflect random variability rather than a true change in the series. Moreover, because responding to changes in expected demand often entails considerable cost (e.g., changes in production rate, changes in the size of a workforce, inventory changes), it is desirable to avoid reacting to minor variations. Thus, minor variations are treated as random variations, whereas larger variations are viewed as more likely to reflect "real" changes, although these, too, are smoothed to a certain degree.

Averaging techniques generate forecasts that reflect recent values of a time series (e.g., the average value over the last several periods). These techniques work best when a series tends to vary around an average, although they also can handle step changes or gradual changes in the level of the series. Three techniques for averaging are described in this section:

1. Moving average.
2. Weighted moving average.
3. Exponential smoothing.

Moving Average. One weakness of the naive method is that the forecast just *traces* the actual data, with a lag of one period; it does not smooth at all. But by expanding the amount of historical data a forecast is based on, this difficulty can be overcome. A **moving average** forecast uses a *number* of the most recent actual data values in generating a forecast. The moving average forecast can be computed using the following equation:

Moving average Technique that averages a number of recent actual values, updated as new values become available.

$$F_t = \text{MA}_n = \frac{\sum_{i=1}^{n} A_{t-i}}{n} = \frac{A_{t-n} + \cdots + A_{t-2} + A_{t-1}}{n} \tag{3–5}$$

where

F_t = Forecast for time period t
MA_n = n period moving average
A_{t-i} = Actual value in period $t - i$
n = Number of periods (data points) in the moving average

For example, MA_3 would refer to a three-period moving average forecast, and MA_5 would refer to a five-period moving average forecast.

EXAMPLE 2

www.mhhe.com/stevenson11e

Compute a three-period moving average forecast given demand for shopping carts for the last five periods.

Period	Demand	
1	42	
2	40	
3	43	the 3 most recent demands
4	40	
5	41	

SOLUTION

$$F_6 = \frac{43 + 40 + 41}{3} = 41.33$$

If actual demand in period 6 turns out to be 38, the moving average forecast for period 7 would be

$$F_7 = \frac{40 + 41 + 38}{3} = 39.67$$

Note that in a moving average, as each new actual value becomes available, the forecast is updated by adding the newest value and dropping the oldest and then recomputing the average. Consequently, the forecast "moves" by reflecting only the most recent values.

In computing a moving average, including a *moving total* column—which gives the sum of the n most current values from which the average will be computed—aids computations. To update the moving total: Subtract the oldest value from the newest value and add that amount to the moving total for each update.

Figure 3.3 illustrates a three-period moving average forecast plotted against actual demand over 31 periods. Note how the moving average forecast *lags* the actual values and how *smooth* the forecasted values are compared with the actual values.

The moving average can incorporate as many data points as desired. In selecting the number of periods to include, the decision maker must take into account that the number of data points in the average determines its sensitivity to each new data point: The fewer the data points in an average, the more sensitive (responsive) the average tends to be. (See Figure 3.4A.)

If responsiveness is important, a moving average with relatively few data points should be used. This will permit quick adjustment to, say, a step change in the data, but it also will cause the forecast to be somewhat responsive even to random variations. Conversely, moving averages based on more data points will smooth more but be less responsive to "real" changes. Hence, the decision maker must weigh the cost of responding more slowly to changes in the data against the cost of responding to what might simply be random variations. A review of forecast errors can help in this decision.

The advantages of a moving average forecast are that it is easy to compute and easy to understand. A possible disadvantage is that all values in the average are weighted equally. For instance, in a 10-period moving average, each value has a weight of 1/10. Hence, the oldest value has the *same weight* as the most recent value. If a change occurs in the series, a moving

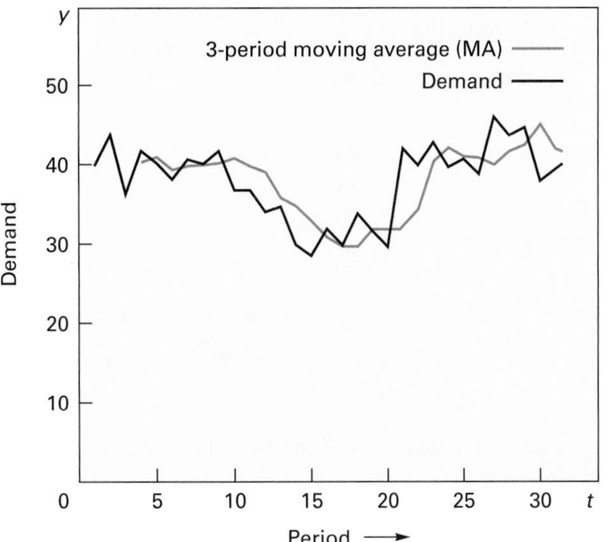

FIGURE 3.3
A moving average forecast tends to smooth and lag changes in the data

FIGURE 3.4A

The more periods in a moving average, the greater the forecast will lag changes in the data.

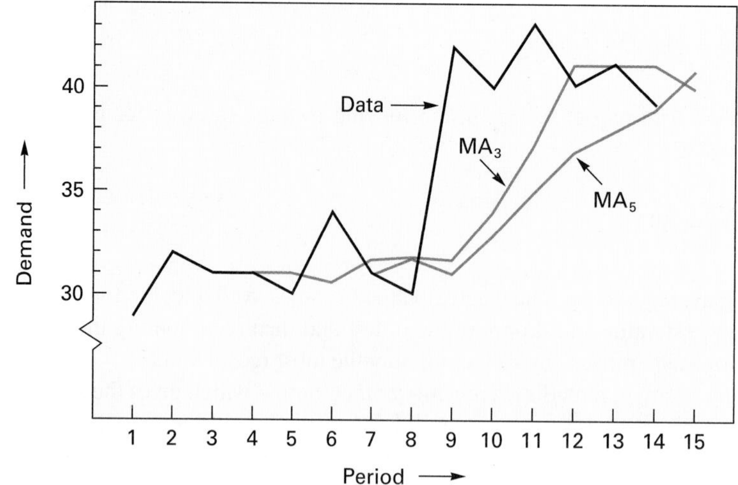

average forecast can be slow to react, especially if there are a large number of values in the average. Decreasing the number of values in the average increases the weight of more recent values, but it does so at the expense of losing potential information from less recent values.

Weighted average More recent values in a series are given more weight in computing a forecast.

Weighted Moving Average. A **weighted average** is similar to a moving average, except that it assigns more weight to the most recent values in a time series. For instance, the most recent value might be assigned a weight of .40, the next most recent value a weight of .30, the next after that a weight of .20, and the next after that a weight of .10. Note that the weights must sum to 1.00, and that the heaviest weights are assigned to the most recent values.

$$F_t = w_t(A_t) + w_{t-1}(A_{t-1}) + \cdots + w_{t-n}(A_{t-n}) \qquad (3\text{–}6)$$

where

w_t = Weight for the period t, w_{t-1} = Weight for period $t - 1$, etc.

A_t = Actual value in period t, A_{t-1} = Actual value for period $t - 1$, etc.

EXAMPLE 3

Given the following demand data,

a. Compute a weighted average forecast using a weight of .40 for the most recent period, .30 for the next most recent, .20 for the next, and .10 for the next.

b. If the actual demand for period 6 is 39, forecast demand for period 7 using the same weights as in part *a*.

Period	Demand
1	42
2	40
3	43
4	40
5	41

SOLUTION

a. $F_6 = .10(40) + .20(43) + .30(40) + .40(41) = 41.0$

b. $F_7 = .10(43) + .20(40) + .30(41) + .40(39) = 40.2$

Note that if four weights are used, only the *four most recent* demands are used to prepare the forecast.

The advantage of a weighted average over a simple moving average is that the weighted average is more reflective of the most recent occurrences. However, the choice of weights is somewhat arbitrary and generally involves the use of trial and error to find a suitable weighting scheme.

Exponential Smoothing. Exponential smoothing is a sophisticated weighted averaging method that is still relatively easy to use and understand. Each new forecast is based on the previous forecast plus a percentage of the difference between that forecast and the actual value of the series at that point. That is:

Exponential smoothing A weighted averaging method based on previous forecast plus a percentage of the forecast error.

SCREENCAM TUTORIAL

$$\text{Next forecast} = \text{Previous forecast} + \alpha(\text{Actual} - \text{Previous forecast})$$

where (Actual − Previous forecast) represents the forecast error and α is a percentage of the error. More concisely,

$$F_t = F_{t-1} + \alpha(A_{t-1} - F_{t-1}) \qquad (3\text{–}7a)$$

where

F_t = Forecast for period t

F_{t-1} = Forecast for the previous period (i.e., period $t - 1$)

α = Smoothing constant (percentage)

A_{t-1} = Actual demand or sales for the previous period

The smoothing constant α represents a percentage of the forecast error. Each new forecast is equal to the previous forecast plus a percentage of the previous error. For example, suppose the previous forecast was 42 units, actual demand was 40 units, and $\alpha = .10$. The new forecast would be computed as follows:

$$F_t = 42 + .10(40 - 42) = 41.8$$

Then, if the actual demand turns out to be 43, the next forecast would be

$$F_t = 41.8 + .10(43 - 41.8) = 41.92$$

An alternate form of Formula 3–7a reveals the weighting of the previous forecast and the latest actual demand:

$$F_t = (1 - \alpha)F_{t-1} + \alpha A_{t-1} \qquad (3\text{–}7b)$$

For example, if $\alpha = .10$, this would be

$$F_t = .90F_{t-1} + .10A_{t-1}$$

The quickness of forecast adjustment to error is determined by the smoothing constant, α. The closer its value is to zero, the slower the forecast will be to adjust to forecast errors (i.e., the greater the smoothing). Conversely, the closer the value of α is to 1.00, the greater the responsiveness and the less the smoothing. This is illustrated in Figure 3.4B.

Selecting a smoothing constant is basically a matter of judgment or trial and error, using forecast errors to guide the decision. The goal is to select a smoothing constant that balances the benefits of smoothing random variations with the benefits of responding to real changes if and when they occur. Commonly used values of α range from .05 to .50. Low values of α are used when the underlying average tends to be stable; higher values are used when the underlying average is susceptible to change.

Some computer packages include a feature that permits automatic modification of the smoothing constant if the forecast errors become unacceptably large.

Exponential smoothing is one of the most widely used techniques in forecasting, partly because of its ease of calculation and partly because of the ease with which the weighting scheme can be altered—simply by changing the value of α.

Note Exponential smoothing should begin several periods back to enable forecasts to adjust to the data, instead of starting one period back. A number of different approaches can be used to obtain a *starting forecast,* such as the average of the first several periods, a subjective estimate, or the first actual value as the forecast for period 2 (i.e., the naive approach). For simplicity, the naive approach is used in this book. In practice, using an average of, say, the first three values as a forecast for period 4 would provide a better starting forecast because that would tend to be more representative.

FIGURE 3.4B
The closer α is to zero, the greater the smoothing

Period (t)	Actual Demand	α = .10 Forecast	α = .40 Forecast
1	42 (starting forecast)	—	—
2	40	42	42
3	43	41.8	41.2
4	40	41.92	41.92
5	41	41.73	41.15
6	39	41.66	41.09
7	46	41.39	40.25
8	44	41.85	42.55
9	45	42.07	43.13
10	38	42.35	43.88
11	40	41.92	41.53
12		41.73	40.92

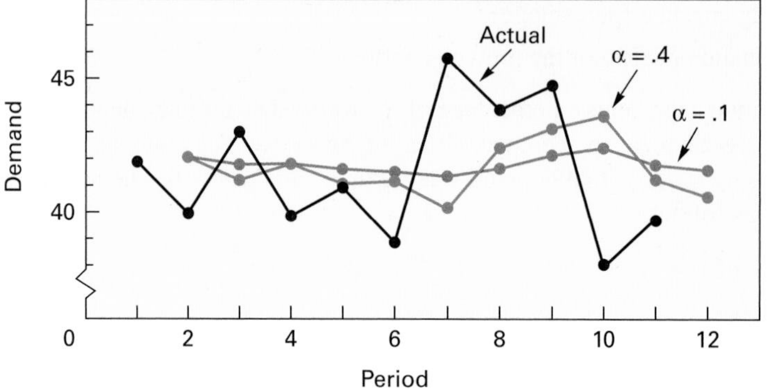

EXAMPLE 4

Compare the error performance of these three forecasting techniques using MAD, MSE, and MAPE: a naive forecast, a two-period moving average, and exponential smoothing with α = .10 *for periods 3 through 11,* using the data shown in Figure 3.4B.

SOLUTION

		Naive		Two-period MA		Exponential Smoothing	
Period, t	**Demand**	**Forecast**	**Error**	**Forecast**	**Error**	**Forecast**	**Error**
1	42	—	—				
2	40	42	−2			42	−2
3	43	40	3	41	2	41.8	1.2
4	40	43	−3	41.5	−1.5	41.92	−1.92
5	41	40	1	41.5	−0.5	41.73	−0.73
6	39	41	−2	40.5	−1.5	41.66	−2.66
7	46	39	7	40	6	41.39	4.61
8	44	46	−2	42.5	1.5	41.85	2.15
9	45	44	1	45	0	42.07	2.93
10	38	45	−7	44.5	−6.5	42.36	−4.36
11	40	38	2	41.5	−1.5	41.92	−1.92
	MAD		3.11		2.33		2.50
	MSE		16.25		11.44		8.73
	MAPE		7.49%		5.64%		5.98%

If lowest MAD is the criterion, the two-period moving average forecast has the greatest accuracy; if lowest MSE is the criterion, exponential smoothing works best; and if lowest MAPE is the criterion, the two-period moving average method is again best. Of course, with other data, or with different values of α for exponential smoothing, and different moving averages, the best performers could be different.

Other Forecasting Methods

You may find two other approaches to forecasting interesting. They are briefly described in this section.

Focus Forecasting. Some companies use forecasts based on a "best current performance" basis. This approach, called focus forecasting, was developed by Bernard T. Smith, and is described in several of his books.[2] It involves the use of several forecasting methods (e.g., moving average, weighted average, and exponential smoothing) all being applied to the last few months of historical data after any irregular variations have been removed. The method that has the highest accuracy is then used to make the forecast for the next month. This process is used for each product or service, and is repeated monthly. Example 4 illustrates this kind of comparison.

Diffusion Models. When new products or services are introduced, historical data are not generally available on which to base forecasts. Instead, predictions are based on rates of product adoption and usage spread from other established products, using mathematical diffusion models. These models take into account such factors as market potential, attention from mass media, and word of mouth. Although the details are beyond the scope of this text, it is important to point out that diffusion models are widely used in marketing and to assess the merits of investing in new technologies.

Techniques for Trend

Analysis of trend involves developing an equation that will suitably describe trend (assuming that trend is present in the data). The trend component may be linear, or it may not. Some commonly encountered nonlinear trend types are illustrated in Figure 3.5. A simple plot of the data often can reveal the existence and nature of a trend. The discussion here focuses exclusively on *linear* trends because these are fairly common.

SCREENCAM TUTORIAL

There are two important techniques that can be used to develop forecasts when trend is present. One involves use of a trend equation; the other is an extension of exponential smoothing.

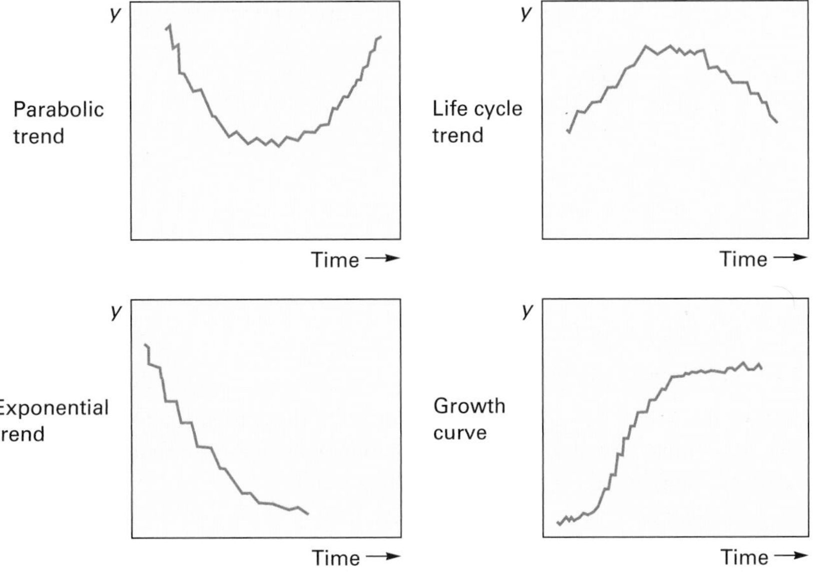

FIGURE 3.5
Graphs of some nonlinear trends

[2]See, for example, Bernard T. Smith and Virginia Brice, *Focus Forecasting: Computer Techniques for Inventory Control Revised for the Twenty-First Century* (Essex Junction, VT: Oliver Wight., 1984).

Linear trend equation $F_t = a + bt$, used to develop forecasts when trend is present.

Trend Equation. A **linear trend equation** has the form

$$F_t = a + bt \tag{3–8}$$

where

F_t = Forecast for period t

a = Value of F_t at $t = 0$

b = Slope of the line

t = Specified number of time periods from $t = 0$

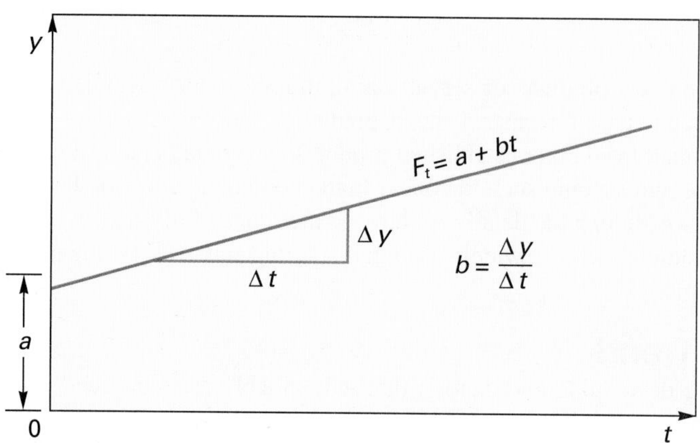

For example, consider the trend equation $F_t = 45 + 5t$. The value of F_t when $t = 0$ is 45, and the slope of the line is 5, which means that, on the average, the value of F_t will increase by five units for each time period. If $t = 10$, the forecast, F_t, is $45 + 5(10) = 95$ units. The equation can be plotted by finding two points on the line. One can be found by substituting some value of t into the equation (e.g., $t = 10$) and then solving for F_t. The other point is a (i.e., F_t at $t = 0$). Plotting those two points and drawing a line through them yields a graph of the linear trend line.

The coefficients of the line, a and b, are based on the following two equations:

$$b = \frac{n\Sigma ty - \Sigma t\Sigma y}{n\Sigma t^2 - (\Sigma t)^2} \tag{3–9}$$

$$a = \frac{\Sigma y - b\Sigma t}{n} \text{ or } \bar{y} - b\bar{t} \tag{3–10}$$

where

n = Number of periods

y = Value of the time series

Note that these two equations are identical to those used for computing a linear regression line, except that t replaces x in the equations. Values for the trend equation can be obtained easily by using the Excel template for linear trend.

EXAMPLE 5

Cell phone sales for a California-based firm over the last 10 weeks are shown in the table below. Plot the data, and visually check to see if a linear trend line would be appropriate. Then determine the equation of the trend line, and predict sales for weeks 11 and 12.

Week	Unit Sales
1	700
2	724
3	720
4	728
5	740
6	742
7	758
8	750
9	770
10	775

SOLUTION

a. A plot suggests that a linear trend line would be appropriate:

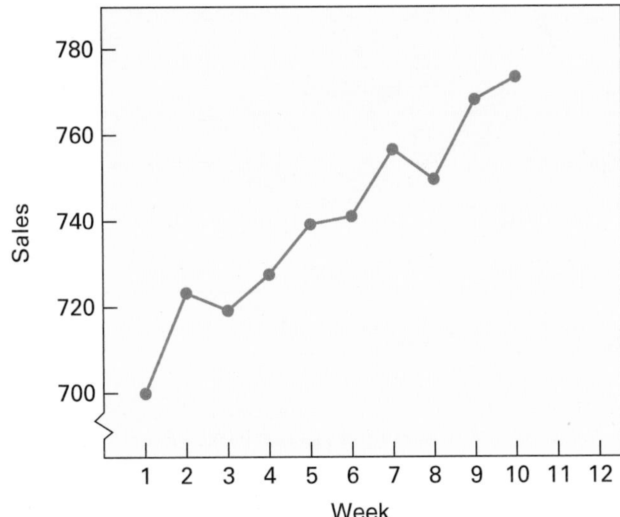

b. The solution obtained by using the Excel template for linear trend is shown in Table 3.1.
$b = 7.51$ and $a = 699.40$
The trend line is $F_t = 699.40 + 7.51t$, where $t = 0$ for period 0.

c. Substituting values of t into this equation, the forecasts for the next two periods (i.e., $t = 11$ and $t = 12$) are:

$$F_{11} = 699.40 + 7.51(11) = 782.01$$
$$F_{12} = 699.40 + 7.51(12) = 789.52$$

d. For purposes of illustration, the original data, the trend line, and the two projections (forecasts) are shown on the following graph:

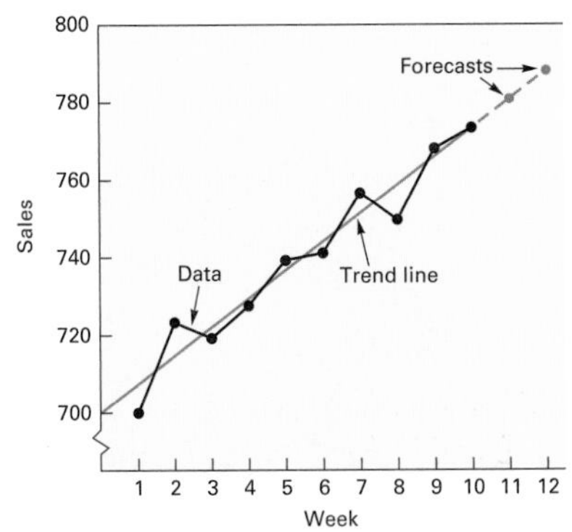

TABLE 3.1 Excel Solution for Example 5

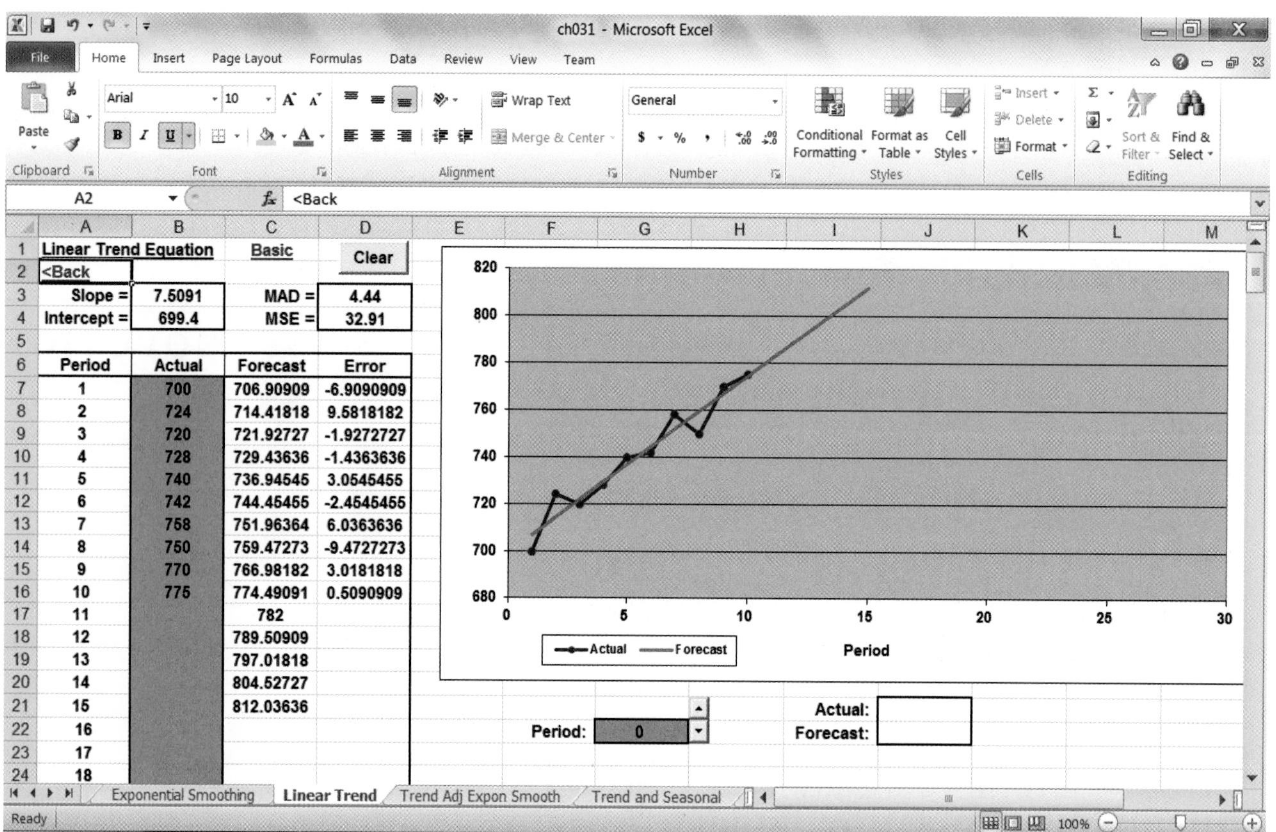

Period	Actual	Forecast	Error
1	700	706.90909	-6.9090909
2	724	714.41818	9.5818182
3	720	721.92727	-1.9272727
4	728	729.43636	-1.4363636
5	740	736.94545	3.0545455
6	742	744.45455	-2.4545455
7	758	751.96364	6.0363636
8	750	759.47273	-9.4727273
9	770	766.98182	3.0181818
10	775	774.49091	0.5090909
11		782	
12		789.50909	
13		797.01818	
14		804.52727	
15		812.03636	
16			
17			
18			

Trend-Adjusted Exponential Smoothing

Trend-adjusted exponential smoothing Variation of exponential smoothing used when a time series exhibits a linear trend.

SCREENCAM TUTORIAL

A variation of simple exponential smoothing can be used when a time series exhibits a *linear* trend. It is called **trend-adjusted exponential smoothing** or, sometimes, *double smoothing,* to differentiate it from simple exponential smoothing, which is appropriate only when data vary around an average or have step or gradual changes. If a series exhibits trend, and simple smoothing is used on it, the forecasts will all lag the trend: If the data are increasing, each forecast will be too low; if decreasing, each forecast will be too high.

The trend-adjusted forecast (TAF) is composed of two elements: a smoothed error and a trend factor.

$$\text{TAF}_{t+1} = S_t + T_t \tag{3–11}$$

where

S_t = Previous forecast plus smoothed error
T_t = Current trend estimate

and

$$S_t = \text{TAF}_t + \alpha(A_t - \text{TAF}_t)$$
$$T_t = T_{t-1} + \beta(\text{TAF}_t - \text{TAF}_{t-1} - T_{t-1}) \tag{3–12}$$

where

α = Smoothing constant for average
β = Smoothing constant for trend

In order to use this method, one must select values of α and β (usually through trial and error) and make a starting forecast and an estimate of trend.

Using the cell phone data from the previous example (where it was concluded that the data exhibited a linear trend), use trend-adjusted exponential smoothing to obtain forecasts for periods 6 through 11, with $\alpha = .40$ and $\beta = .30$.

SOLUTION

The initial estimate of trend is based on the net change of 28 for the *three changes* from period 1 to period 4, for an average of 9.33. The Excel spreadsheet is shown in Table 3.2. Notice that an initial estimate of trend is estimated from the first four values and that the starting forecast (period 5) is developed using the previous (period 4) value of 728 plus the initial trend estimate:

$$\text{Starting forecast} = 728 + 9.33 = 737.33$$

Unlike a linear trend line, trend-adjusted smoothing has the ability to adjust to *changes* in trend. Of course, trend projections are much simpler with a trend line than with trend-adjusted forecasts, so a manager must decide which benefits are most important when choosing between these two techniques for trend.

Techniques for Seasonality

Seasonal variations in time-series data are regularly repeating upward or downward movements in series values that can be tied to recurring events. *Seasonality* may refer to regular annual variations. Familiar examples of seasonality are weather variations (e.g., sales of winter and summer sports equipment) and vacations or holidays (e.g., airline travel, greeting card sales, visitors at tourist and resort centers). The term *seasonal variation* is also applied to daily, weekly, monthly, and other regularly recurring patterns in data. For example, rush hour traffic occurs twice a day—incoming in the morning and outgoing in the late afternoon. Theaters and restaurants often experience weekly demand patterns, with demand higher later in the week. Banks may experience daily seasonal variations (heavier traffic during the noon hour and just before closing), weekly variations (heavier toward the end of the week), and monthly variations (heaviest around the beginning of the month because of Social Security, payroll, and welfare checks being cashed or deposited). Mail volume; sales of toys, beer, automobiles, and turkeys; highway usage; hotel registrations; and gardening also exhibit seasonal variations.

Seasonal variations Regularly repeating movements in series values that can be tied to recurring events.

TABLE 3.2 Using the Excel template for trend-adjusted smoothing

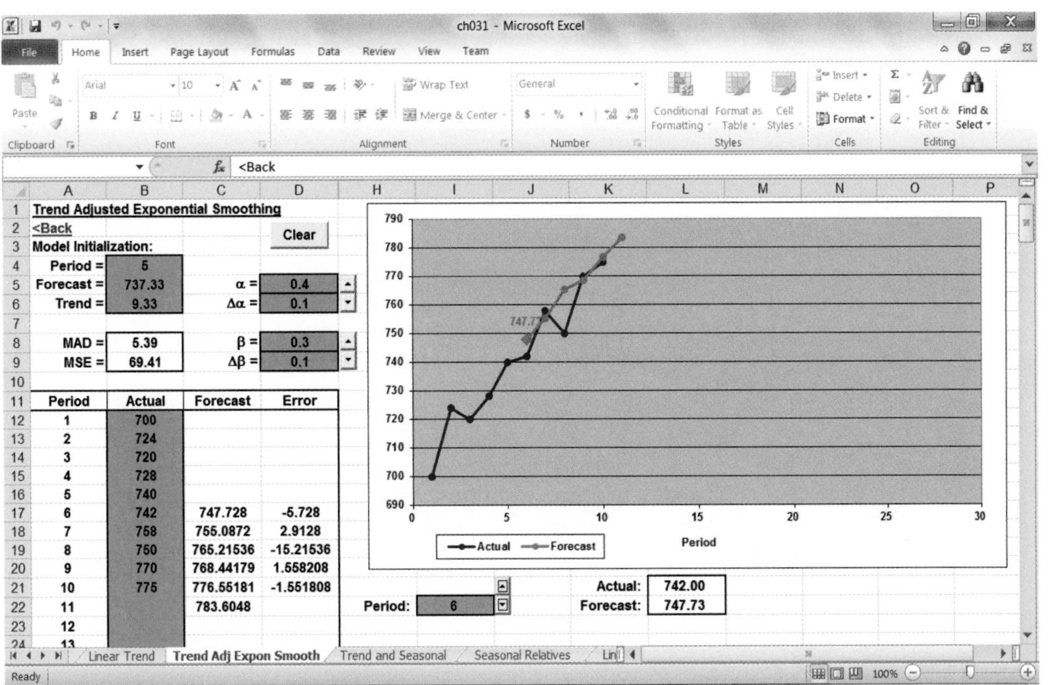

Seasonality in a time series is expressed in terms of the amount that actual values deviate from the *average* value of a series. If the series tends to vary around an average value, then seasonality is expressed in terms of that average (or a moving average); if trend is present, seasonality is expressed in terms of the trend value.

There are two different models of seasonality: additive and multiplicative. In the *additive* model, seasonality is expressed as a *quantity* (e.g., 20 units), which is added to or subtracted from the series average in order to incorporate seasonality. In the *multiplicative* model, seasonality is expressed as a *percentage* of the average (or trend) amount (e.g., 1.10), which is then used to multiply the value of a series to incorporate seasonality. Figure 3.6 illustrates the two models for a linear trend line. In practice, businesses use the multiplicative model much more widely than the additive model, because it tends to be more representative of actual experience, so we shall focus exclusively on the multiplicative model.

Seasonal relative Percentage of average or trend.

The seasonal percentages in the multiplicative model are referred to as **seasonal relatives** or *seasonal indexes.* Suppose that the seasonal relative for the quantity of toys sold in May at a store is 1.20. This indicates that toy sales for that month are 20 percent above the monthly average. A seasonal relative of .90 for July indicates that July sales are 90 percent of the monthly average.

Knowledge of seasonal variations is an important factor in retail planning and scheduling. Moreover, seasonality can be an important factor in capacity planning for systems that must be designed to handle peak loads (e.g., public transportation, electric power plants, highways, and bridges). Knowledge of the extent of seasonality in a time series can enable one to *remove* seasonality from the data (i.e., to seasonally adjust data) in order to discern other patterns or the lack of patterns in the series. Thus, one frequently reads or hears about "seasonally adjusted unemployment" and "seasonally adjusted personal income."

The next section briefly describes how seasonal relatives are used.

Using Seasonal Relatives. Seasonal relatives are used in two different ways in forecasting. One way is to *deseasonalize data;* the other way is to *incorporate seasonality in a forecast.*

FIGURE 3.6
Seasonality: the additive and multiplicative models compared using a linear trend

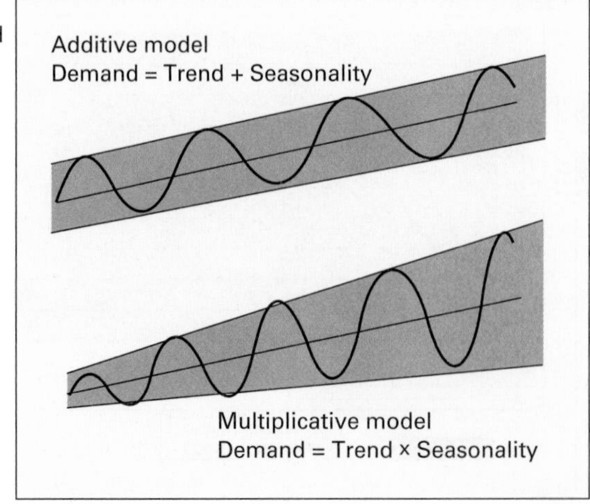

To deseasonalize data is to remove the seasonal component from the data in order to get a clearer picture of the nonseasonal (e.g., trend) components. Deseasonalizing data is accomplished by *dividing* each data point by its corresponding seasonal relative (e.g., divide November demand by the November relative, divide December demand by the December relative, and so on).

Incorporating seasonality in a forecast is useful when demand has both trend (or average) and seasonal components. Incorporating seasonality can be accomplished in this way:

1. Obtain trend estimates for desired periods using a trend equation.
2. Add seasonality to the trend estimates by *multiplying* (assuming a multiplicative model is appropriate) these trend estimates by the corresponding seasonal relative (e.g., multiply the November trend estimate by the November seasonal relative, multiply the December trend estimate by the December seasonal relative, and so on).

Example 7 illustrates these two techniques.

A coffee shop owner wants to estimate demand for the next two quarters for hot chocolate. Sales data consist of trend and seasonality.

a. Quarter relatives are 1.20 for the first quarter, 1.10 for the second quarter, 0.75 for the third quarter, and 0.95 for the fourth quarter. Use this information to deseasonalize sales for quarters 1 through 8.

b. Using the appropriate values of quarter relatives and the equation $F_t = 124 + 7.5t$ for the trend component, estimate demand for periods 9 and 10.

SOLUTION

a.

Period	Quarter	Sales (gal.)	÷	Quarter Relative	=	Deseasonalized Sales
1	1	158.4	÷	1.20	=	132.0
2	2	153.0	÷	1.10	=	139.1
3	3	110.0	÷	0.75	=	146.7
4	4	146.3	÷	0.95	=	154.0
5	1	192.0	÷	1.20	=	160.0
6	2	187.0	÷	1.10	=	170.0
7	3	132.0	÷	0.75	=	176.0
8	4	173.8	÷	0.95	=	182.9

b. The trend values are:

Period 9: $F_t = 124 + 7.5(9) = 191.5$

Period 10: $F_t = 124 + 7.5(10) = 199.0$

Period 9 is a first quarter and period 10 is a second quarter. Multiplying each trend value by the appropriate quarter relative results in:

Period 9: $191.5(1.20) = 229.8$

Period 10: $199.0(1.10) = 218.9$

Computing Seasonal Relatives. A widely used method for computing seasonal relatives involves the use of a **centered moving average.** This approach effectively accounts for any trend (linear or curvilinear) that might be present in the data. For example, Figure 3.7 illustrates how a three-period centered moving average closely tracks the data originally shown in Figure 3.3.

Centered moving average A moving average positioned at the center of the data that were used to compute it.

Manual computation of seasonal relatives using the centered moving average method is a bit cumbersome, so use of software is recommended. Manual computation is illustrated in Solved Problem 4 at the end of the chapter. The Excel template (on the Web site) is a simple and convenient way to obtain values of seasonal relatives (indexes). Example 8A illustrates this approach.

FIGURE 3.7
A centered moving average closely tracks the data

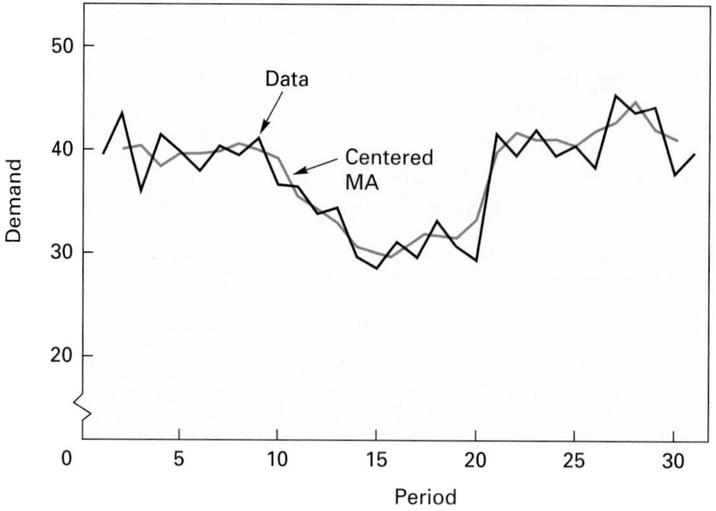

EXAMPLE 8A

The manager of a call center recorded the volume of calls received between 9 and 10 a.m. for 21 days and wants to obtain a seasonal index for each day for that hour.

Day	Volume	Day	Volume	Day	Volume
Tues	67	Tues	60	Tues	64
Wed	75	Wed	73	Wed	76
Thurs	82	Thurs	85	Thurs	87
Fri	98	Fri	99	Fri	96
Sat	90	Sat	86	Sat	88
Sun	36	Sun	40	Sun	44
Mon	55	Mon	52	Mon	50

SOLUTION

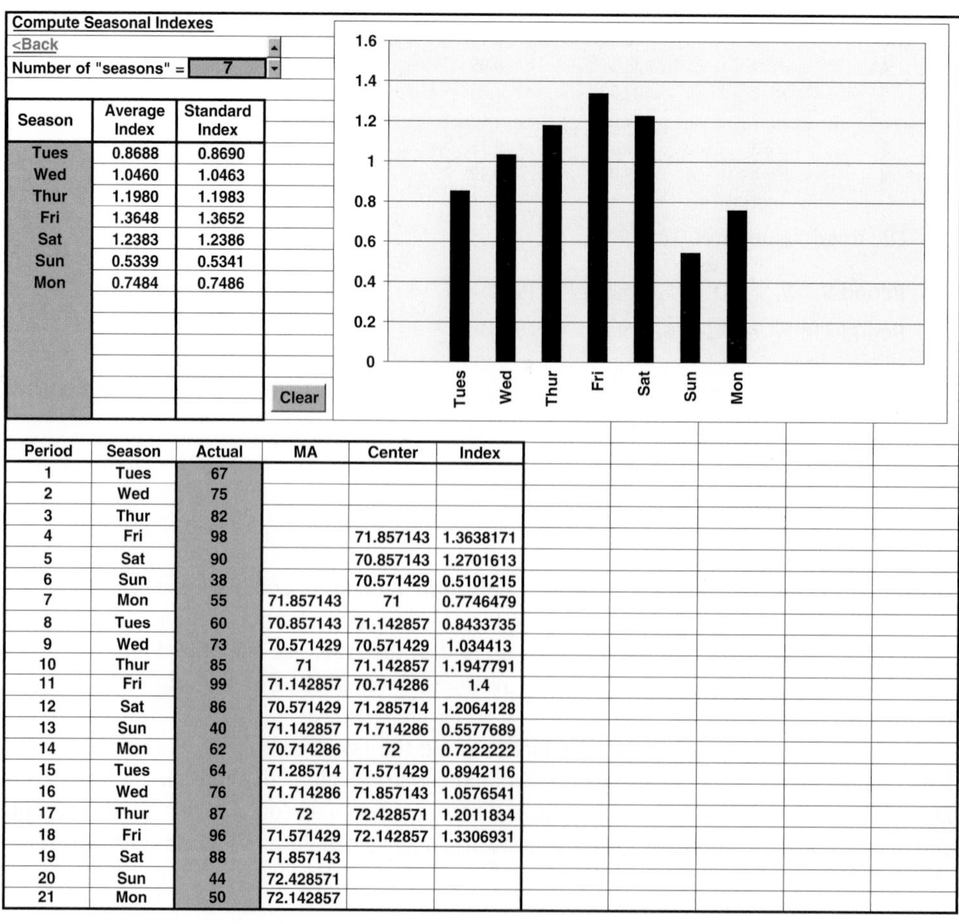

Compute Seasonal Indexes
<Back
Number of "seasons" = 7

Season	Average Index	Standard Index
Tues	0.8688	0.8690
Wed	1.0460	1.0463
Thur	1.1980	1.1983
Fri	1.3648	1.3652
Sat	1.2383	1.2386
Sun	0.5339	0.5341
Mon	0.7484	0.7486

Clear

Period	Season	Actual	MA	Center	Index
1	Tues	67			
2	Wed	75			
3	Thur	82			
4	Fri	98		71.857143	1.3638171
5	Sat	90		70.857143	1.2701613
6	Sun	38		70.571429	0.5101215
7	Mon	55	71.857143	71	0.7746479
8	Tues	60	70.857143	71.142857	0.8433735
9	Wed	73	70.571429	70.571429	1.034413
10	Thur	85	71	71.142857	1.1947791
11	Fri	99	71.142857	70.714286	1.4
12	Sat	86	70.571429	71.285714	1.2064128
13	Sun	40	71.142857	71.714286	0.5577689
14	Mon	62	70.714286	72	0.7222222
15	Tues	64	71.285714	71.571429	0.8942116
16	Wed	76	71.714286	71.857143	1.0576541
17	Thur	87	72	72.428571	1.2011834
18	Fri	96	71.571429	72.142857	1.3306931
19	Sat	88	71.857143		
20	Sun	44	72.428571		
21	Mon	50	72.142857		

For practical purposes, you can round the relatives to two decimal places. Thus, the seasonal (standard) index values are:

Day	Index
Tues	0.87
Wed	1.05
Thurs	1.20
Fri	1.37
Sat	1.24
Sun	0.53
Mon	0.75

Computing Seasonal Relatives Using the Simple Average Method. The simple average (SA) method is an alternative way t o compute seasonal relatives. Each seasonal relative is the average for that season divided by the average of all seasons. This method is illustrated in Example 8B, where the seasons are days. Note that there is no need to standardize the relatives when using the SA method.

EXAMPLE 8B

Compute seasonal relatives for the data given in Example 8A.

SOLUTION

Step 1: Compute the season averages

Step 3: Compute the SA relatives

Season	Week 1	Week 2	Week 3	Season Average	SA Index	MA Index Comparison
Tues	67	60	64	63.667	63.667/71.571 = 0.8896	0.8690
Wed	75	73	76	74.667	74.667/71.571 = 1.0432	1.0463
Thurs	82	85	87	84.667	84.667/71.571 = 1.1830	1.1983
Fri	98	99	96	97.667	97.667/71.571 = 1.3646	1.3652
Sat	90	86	88	88.000	88.000/71.571 = 1.2295	1.2386
Sun	36	40	44	40.000	40.000/71.571 = 0.5589	0.5341
Mon	55	52	50	52.333	52.333/71.571 = 0.7312	0.7486
				71.571		

Step 2: Compute the overall average

The obvious advantage of the SA method compared to the centered MA method is the simplicity of computations. When the data have a stationary mean (i.e., variation around an average), the SA method works quite well, providing values of relatives that are quite close to those obtained using the centered MA method, which is generally accepted as accurate. Conventional wisdom is that the SA method should not be used when linear trend is present in the data. However, it can be used to obtain fairly good values of seasonal relatives as long as the variations (seasonal and random) around the trend line are large relative to the slope of the line.

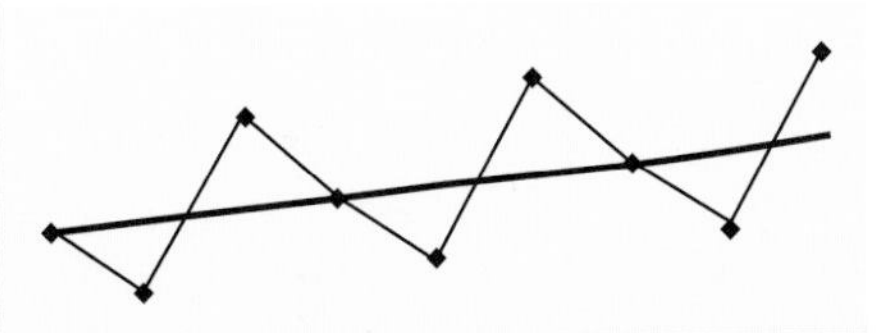

Variations are large relative to the slope of the line, so it is okay to use the SA method.

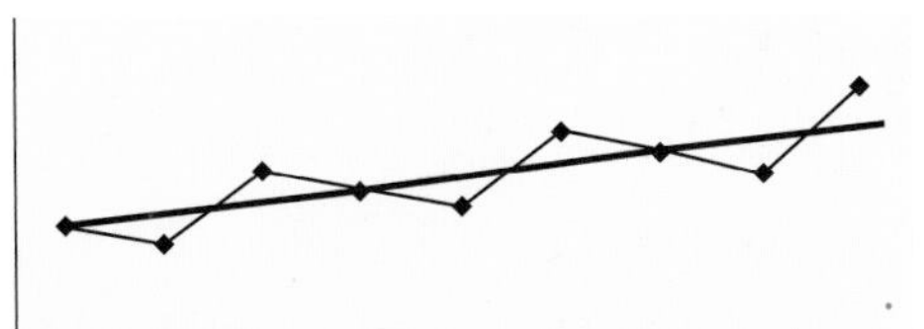

Variations are small relative to the slope of the line, so it is not okay to use the SA method.

Techniques for Cycles

Cycles are up-and-down movements similar to seasonal variations but of longer duration—say, two to six years between peaks. When cycles occur in time-series data, their frequent irregularity makes it difficult or impossible to project them from past data because turning points are difficult to identify. A short moving average or a naive approach may be of some value, although both will produce forecasts that lag cyclical movements by one or several periods.

The most commonly used approach is explanatory: Search for another variable that relates to, and *leads,* the variable of interest. For example, the number of housing starts (i.e., permits to build houses) in a given month often is an indicator of demand a few months later for products and services directly tied to construction of new homes (landscaping; sales of washers and dryers, carpeting, and furniture; new demands for shopping, transportation, schools). Thus, if an organization is able to establish a high correlation with such a *leading variable* (i.e., changes in the variable precede changes in the variable of interest), it can develop an equation that describes the relationship, enabling forecasts to be made. It is important that a persistent relationship exists between the two variables. Moreover, the higher the correlation, the better the chances that the forecast will be on target.

ASSOCIATIVE FORECASTING TECHNIQUES

Associative techniques rely on identification of related variables that can be used to predict values of the variable of interest. For example, sales of beef may be related to the price per pound charged for beef and the prices of substitutes such as chicken, pork, and lamb; real estate prices are usually related to property location and square footage; and crop yields are related to soil conditions and the amounts and timing of water and fertilizer applications.

The essence of associative techniques is the development of an equation that summarizes the effects of **predictor variables.** The primary method of analysis is known as **regression.** A brief overview of regression should suffice to place this approach into perspective relative to the other forecasting approaches described in this chapter.

Predictor variables Variables that can be used to predict values of the variable of interest.

Regression Technique for fitting a line to a set of points.

Simple Linear Regression

The simplest and most widely used form of regression involves a linear relationship between two variables. A plot of the values might appear like that in Figure 3.8. The object in linear regression is to obtain an equation of a straight line that minimizes the sum of squared vertical deviations of data points from the line (i.e., the *least squares criterion*). This **least squares line** has the equation

Least squares line Minimizes the sum of the squared vertical deviations around the line.

$$y_c = a + bx \tag{3–13}$$

FIGURE 3.8
A straight line is fitted to a set of sample points

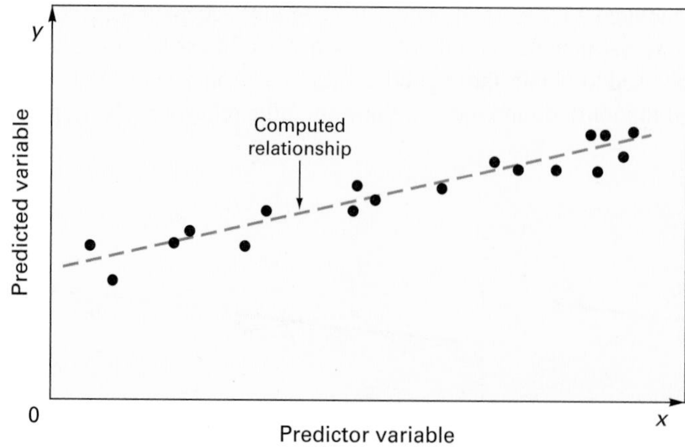

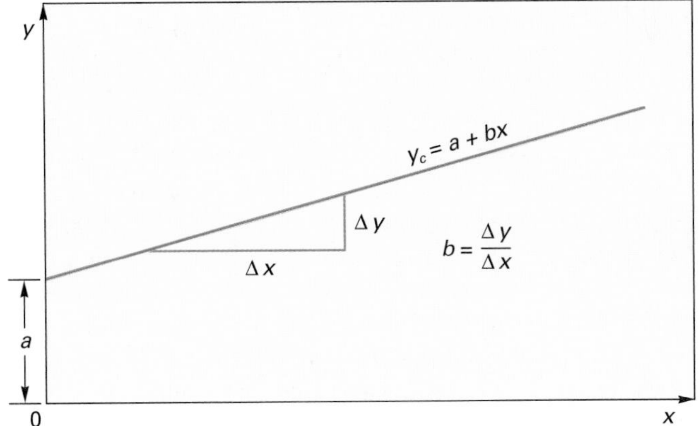

The line intersects the y axis where $y = a$. The slope of the line = b.

FIGURE 3.9
Equation of a straight line: The line represents the average (expected) values of variable y given values of variable x

where

y_c = Predicted (dependent) variable
x = Predictor (independent) variable
b = Slope of the line
a = Value of y_c when $x = 0$ (i.e., the height of the line at the y intercept)

(*Note:* It is conventional to represent values of the predicted variable on the y axis and values of the predictor variable on the x axis.) Figure 3.9 is a general graph of a linear regression line.

The coefficients a and b of the line are based on the following two equations:

$$b = \frac{n(\Sigma xy) - (\Sigma x)(\Sigma y)}{n(\Sigma x^2) - (\Sigma x)^2} \tag{3–14}$$

$$a = \frac{\Sigma y - b\Sigma x}{n} \text{ or } \bar{y} - b\bar{x} \tag{3–15}$$

where

n = Number of paired observations

EXAMPLE 9

www.mhhe.com/stevenson11e

Healthy Hamburgers has a chain of 12 stores in northern Illinois. Sales figures and profits for the stores are given in the following table. Obtain a regression line for the data, and predict profit for a store assuming sales of $10 million.

Unit Sales, x (in \$ millions)	Profits, y (in \$ millions)
$7	$0.15
2	0.10
6	0.13
4	0.15
14	0.25
15	0.27
16	0.24
12	0.20
14	0.27
20	0.44
15	0.34
7	0.17

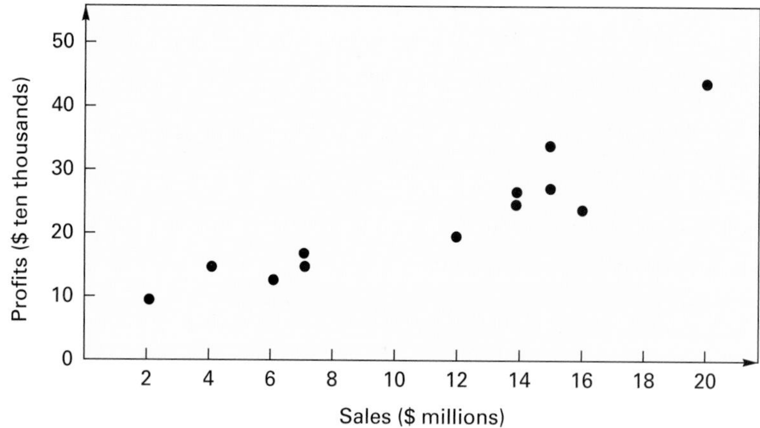

FIGURE 3.10
A linear model seems reasonable

SOLUTION

First, plot the data and decide if a linear model is reasonable. (That is, do the points seem to scatter around a straight line? Figure 3.10 suggests they do.) Next, using the appropriate Excel template on the text Web site, obtain the regression equation $y_c = 0.0506 + 0.0159x$ (see Table 3.3). For sales of $x = 10$ (i.e., 10 million), estimated profit is $y_c = 0.0506 + 0.0159(10) = .2099$, or $209,900. (Substituting $x = 0$ into the equation to produce a predicted profit of $50,600 may appear strange because it seems to suggest that amount of profit will occur with no sales. However, the value of $x = 0$ is *outside the range of observed values.* The regression line should be used only for the range of values from which it was developed; the relationship may be nonlinear outside that range. The purpose of the a value is simply to establish the height of the line where it crosses the y axis.)

One indication of how accurate a prediction might be for a linear regression line is the amount of scatter of the data points around the line. If the data points tend to be relatively close to the line, predictions using the linear equation will tend to be more accurate than if the data points are widely scattered. The scatter can be summarized using the **standard error of estimate.** It can be computed by finding the vertical difference between each data point and the computed value of the regression equation for that value of x, squaring each difference, adding the squared differences, dividing by $n - 2$, and then finding the square root of that value.

Standard error of estimate A measure of the scatter of points around a regression line.

TABLE 3.3 Using the Excel template for linear regression

Simple Linear Regression
<Back
Clear

Slope =	0.0159	r =	0.9166657
Intercept =	0.0506008	r^2 =	0.840276

x	y	Forecast	Error
7	0.15	0.1621124	−0.0121124
2	0.1	0.0824612	0.0175388
6	0.13	0.1461822	−0.0161822
4	0.15	0.1143217	0.0356783
14	0.25	0.273624	−0.023624
15	0.27	0.2895543	−0.0195543
16	0.24	0.3054845	−0.0654845
12	0.2	0.2417636	−0.0417636
14	0.27	0.273624	−0.003624
20	0.44	0.3692054	0.0707946
15	0.34	0.2895543	0.0504457
7	0.17	0.1621124	0.0078876

Y: 0 – 0.5; X: 0 – 25; 0.21; • y — Forecast

x =	10	Forecast:	0.2099031
Δx =	1		

$$S_e = \sqrt{\frac{\Sigma(y - y_c)^2}{n - 2}} \tag{3–16}$$

where

S_e = Standard error of estimate
y = y value of each data point
n = Number of data points

For the data given in Table 3.3, the error column shows the $y - y_c$ differences. Squaring each error and summing the squares yields .01659. Hence, the standard error of estimate is

$$S_e = \sqrt{\frac{.01659}{12 - 2}} = .0407 \text{ million}$$

One application of regression in forecasting relates to the use of indicators. These are uncontrollable variables that tend to lead or precede changes in a variable of interest. For example, changes in the Federal Reserve Board's discount rate may influence certain business activities. Similarly, an increase in energy costs can lead to price increases for a wide range of products and services. Careful identification and analysis of indicators may yield insight into possible future demand in some situations. There are numerous published indexes and Web sites from which to choose.[3] These include:

Net change in inventories on hand and on order.

Interest rates for commercial loans.

Industrial output.

Consumer price index (CPI).

The wholesale price index.

Stock market prices.

Other potential indicators are population shifts, local political climates, and activities of other firms (e.g., the opening of a shopping center may result in increased sales for nearby businesses). Three conditions are required for an indicator to be valid:

1. The relationship between movements of an indicator and movements of the variable should have a logical explanation.
2. Movements of the indicator must precede movements of the dependent variable by enough time so that the forecast isn't outdated before it can be acted upon.
3. A fairly high correlation should exist between the two variables.

Correlation measures the strength and direction of relationship between two variables. Correlation can range from −1.00 to +1.00. A correlation of +1.00 indicates that changes in one variable are always matched by changes in the other; a correlation of −1.00 indicates that increases in one variable are matched by decreases in the other; and a correlation close to zero indicates little *linear* relationship between two variables. The correlation between two variables can be computed using the equation

Correlation A measure of the strength and direction of relationship between two variables.

$$r = \frac{n(\Sigma xy) - (\Sigma x)(\Sigma y)}{\sqrt{n(\Sigma x^2) - (\Sigma x)^2}\sqrt{n(\Sigma y^2) - (\Sigma y)^2}} \tag{3–17}$$

The square of the correlation coefficient, r^2, provides a measure of the percentage of variability in the values of y that is "explained" by the independent variable. The possible values of r^2 range from 0 to 1.00. The closer r^2 is to 1.00, the greater the percentage of explained variation. A high value of r^2, say .80 or more, would indicate that the independent variable is a good predictor of values of the dependent variable. A low value, say .25 or less, would indicate a poor predictor, and a value between .25 and .80 would indicate a moderate predictor.

[3]See, for example, *The National Bureau of Economic Research, The Survey of Current Business, The Monthly Labor Review,* and *Business Conditions Digest.*

Comments on the Use of Linear Regression Analysis

Use of simple regression analysis implies that certain assumptions have been satisfied. Basically, these are as follows:

1. Variations around the line are random. If they are random, no patterns such as cycles or trends should be apparent when the line and data are plotted.
2. Deviations around the average value (i.e., the line) should be normally distributed. A concentration of values close to the line with a small proportion of larger deviations supports the assumption of normality.
3. Predictions are being made only within the range of observed values.

If the assumptions are satisfied, regression analysis can be a powerful tool. To obtain the best results, observe the following:

1. Always plot the data to verify that a linear relationship is appropriate.
2. The data may be time-dependent. Check this by plotting the dependent variable versus time; if patterns appear, use analysis of time series instead of regression, or use time as an independent variable as part of a *multiple regression analysis.*
3. A small correlation may imply that other variables are important.

In addition, note these weaknesses of regression:

1. Simple linear regression applies only to linear relationships with *one* independent variable.
2. One needs a considerable amount of data to establish the relationship—in practice, 20 or more observations.
3. All observations are weighted equally.

EXAMPLE 10

www.mhhe.com/stevenson11e

Sales of new houses and three-month lagged unemployment are shown in the following table. Determine if unemployment levels can be used to predict demand for new houses and, if so, derive a predictive equation.

Period	1	2	3	4	5	6	7	8	9	10	11
Units sold	20	41	17	35	25	31	38	50	15	19	14
Unemployment % (three-month lag)	7.2	4.0	7.3	5.5	6.8	6.0	5.4	3.6	8.4	7.0	9.0

SOLUTION

1. Plot the data to see if a *linear* model seems reasonable. In this case, a linear model seems appropriate *for the range of the data.*

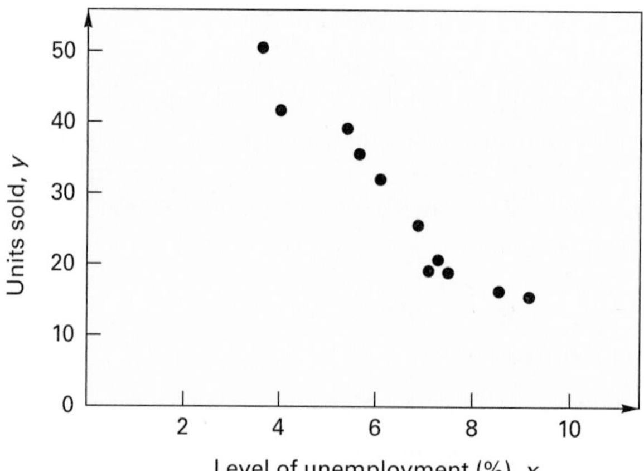

2. Check the correlation coefficient to confirm that it is not close to zero using the Web site template, and then obtain the regression equation:

   $r = -.966$

   This is a fairly high negative correlation. The regression equation is

   $y = 71.85 - 6.91x$

   Note that the equation pertains only to unemployment levels in the range 3.6 to 9.0, because sample observations covered only that range.

Nonlinear and Multiple Regression Analysis

Simple linear regression may prove inadequate to handle certain problems because a linear model is inappropriate or because more than one predictor variable is involved. When nonlinear relationships are present, you should employ nonlinear regression; models that involve more than one predictor require the use of multiple regression analysis. While these analyses are beyond the scope of this text, you should be aware that they are often used. The computations lend themselves more to computers than to hand calculation. Multiple regression forecasting substantially increases data requirements. In each case, it is necessary to weigh the additional cost and effort against potential improvements in accuracy of predictions.

MONITORING THE FORECAST

Many forecasts are made at regular intervals (e.g., weekly, monthly, quarterly). Because forecast errors are the rule rather than the exception, there will be a succession of forecast errors. Tracking the forecast errors and analyzing them can provide useful insight on whether forecasts are performing satisfactorily.

There are a variety of possible sources of forecast errors, including the following:

1. The model may be inadequate due to (*a*) the omission of an important variable, (*b*) a change or shift in the variable that the model cannot deal with (e.g., sudden appearance of a trend or cycle), or (*c*) the appearance of a new variable (e.g., new competitor).
2. Irregular variations may occur due to severe weather or other natural phenomena, temporary shortages or breakdowns, catastrophes, or similar events.
3. The forecasting technique may be used incorrectly, or the results misinterpreted.
4. Random variations. Randomness is the inherent variation that remains in the data after all causes of variation have been accounted for. There are always random variations.

A forecast is generally deemed to perform adequately when the errors exhibit only random variations. Hence, the key to judging when to reexamine the validity of a particular forecasting technique is whether forecast errors are random. If they are not random, it is necessary to investigate to determine which of the other sources is present and how to correct the problem.

Control chart A visual tool for monitoring forecast errors.

A very useful tool for detecting nonrandomness in errors is a **control chart.** Errors are plotted on a control chart in the order that they occur, such as the one depicted in Figure 3.11. The centerline of the chart represents an error of zero. Note the two other lines, one above and one below the centerline. They are called the upper and lower control limits because they represent the upper and lower ends of the range of acceptable variation for the errors.

FIGURE 3.11 Conceptual representation of a control chart

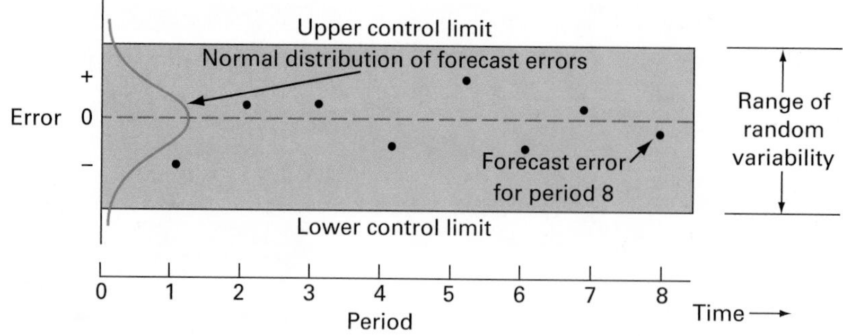

FIGURE 3.12 Examples of nonrandomness

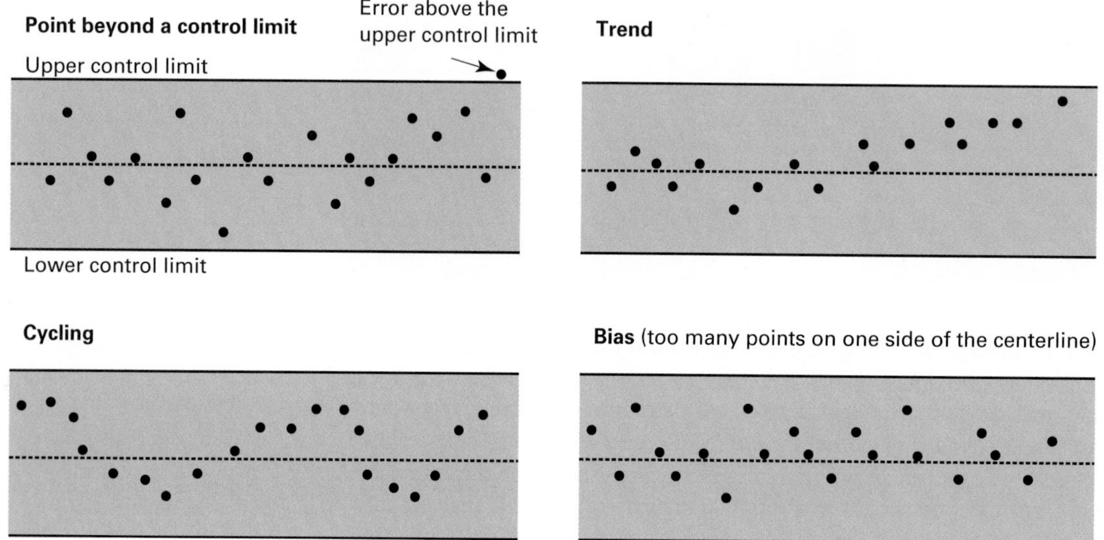

In order for the forecast errors to be judged "in control" (i.e., random), two things are necessary. One is that all errors are within the control limits. The other is that no patterns (e.g., trends, cycles, noncentered data) are present. Both can be accomplished by inspection. Figure 3.12 illustrates some examples of nonrandom errors.

Technically speaking, one could determine if any values exceeded either control limit without actually plotting the errors, but the visual detection of patterns generally requires plotting the errors, so it is best to construct a control chart and plot the errors on the chart.

To construct a control chart, first compute the MSE. The square root of MSE is used in practice as an estimate of the standard deviation of the distribution of errors.[4] That is,

$$s = \sqrt{\text{MSE}} \tag{3–18}$$

Control charts are based on the assumption that when errors are random, they will be distributed according to a normal distribution around a mean of zero. Recall that for a normal distribution, approximately 95.5 percent of the values (errors in this case) can be expected to fall within limits of $0 \pm 2s$ (i.e., 0 ± 2 standard deviations), and approximately 99.7 percent of the values can be expected to fall within $\pm 3s$ of zero. With that in mind, the following formulas can be used to obtain the upper control limit (UCL) and the lower control limit (LCL):

$$\text{UCL: } 0 + z\sqrt{\text{MSE}}$$

$$\text{LCL: } 0 - z\sqrt{\text{MSE}}$$

where

z = Number of standard deviations from the mean

Combining these two formulas, we obtain the following expression for the control limits:

$$\text{Control limits: } 0 \pm z\sqrt{\text{MSE}} \tag{3–19}$$

[4]The actual value could be computed as $s = \sqrt{\dfrac{\Sigma(e - \bar{e})^2}{n - 1}}$.

Compute 2s control limits for forecast errors when the MSE is 9.0.

$$s = \sqrt{\text{MSE}} = 3.0$$
$$\text{UCL} = 0 + 2(3.0) = +6.0$$
$$\text{LCL} = 0 - 2(3.0) = -6.0$$

Another method is the **tracking signal.** It relates the cumulative forecast error to the average absolute error (i.e., MAD). The intent is to detect any **bias** in errors over time (i.e., a tendency for a sequence of errors to be positive or negative). The tracking signal is computed period by period using the following formula:

$$\text{Tracking signal}_t = \frac{\Sigma(\text{Actual}_t - \text{Forecast}_t)}{\text{MAD}_t} \tag{3–20}$$

Tracking signal The ratio of cumulative forecast error to the corresponding value of MAD, used to monitor a forecast.

Bias Persistent tendency for forecasts to be greater or less than the actual values of a time series.

Values can be positive or negative. A value of zero would be ideal; limits of ± 4 or ± 5 are often used for a range of acceptable values of the tracking signal. If a value outside the acceptable range occurs, that would be taken as a signal that there is bias in the forecast, and that corrective action is needed.

After an initial value of MAD has been determined, MAD can be updated and smoothed (SMAD) using exponential smoothing:

$$\text{SMAD}_t = \text{MAD}_{t-1} + \alpha\left(|\text{Actual} - \text{Forecast}|_t - \text{MAD}_{t-1}\right) \tag{3–21}$$

EXAMPLE 12

www.mhhe.com/stevenson11e

Monthly attendance at financial planning seminars for the past 24 months, and forecasts and errors for those months, are shown in the following table. Determine if the forecast is working using these approaches:

1. A tracking signal, beginning with month 10, updating MAD with exponential smoothing. Use limits of ± 4 and $\alpha = .2$.
2. A control chart with 2s limits. Use data from the first eight months to develop the control chart, and then evaluate the remaining data with the control chart.

Month	*A* (Attendance)	*F* (Forecast)	*A* − *F* (Error)	|*e*|	Cumulative |*e*|
1	47	43	4	4	4
2	51	44	7	7	11
3	54	50	4	4	15
4	55	51	4	4	19
5	49	54	−5	5	24
6	46	48	−2	2	26
7	38	46	−8	8	34
8	32	44	−12	12	46
9	25	35	−10	10	56
10	24	26	−2	2	58
11	30	25	5	5	
12	35	32	3	3	
13	44	34	10	10	
14	57	50	7	7	
15	60	51	9	9	
16	55	54	1	1	
17	51	55	−4	4	
18	48	51	−3	3	
19	42	50	−8	8	
20	30	43	−13	13	
21	28	38	−10	10	
22	25	27	−2	2	
23	35	27	8	8	
24	38	32	6	6	
			−11		

SOLUTION

1. The sum of absolute errors through the 10th month is 58. Hence, the initial MAD is 58/10 = 5.8. The subsequent MADs are updated using the formula $MAD_{new} = MAD_{old} + \alpha(|e| - MAD_{old})$. The results are shown in the following table.

   The tracking signal for any month is

$$\frac{\text{Cumulative error at that month}}{\text{Updated MAD at that month}}$$

t (Month)	$\|e\|$	$MAD_t = MAD_{t-1} + .2(\|e\| - MAD_{t-1})$	Cumulative Error	Tracking Signal = Cumulative $Error_t \div MAD_t$
10			−20	−20/5.800 = −3.45
11	5	5.640 = 5.8 + .2(5 − 5.8)	−15	−15/5.640 = −2.66
12	3	5.112 = 5.640 + .2(3 − 5.64)	−12	−12/5.112 = −2.35
13	10	6.090 = 5.112 + .2(10 − 5.112)	−2	−2/6.090 = −0.33
14	7	6.272 = 6.090 + .2(7 − 6.090)	5	5/6.272 = 0.80
15	9	6.817 = 6.272 + .2(9 − 6.272)	14	14/6.817 = 2.05
16	1	5.654 = 6.818 + .2(1 − 6.818)	15	15/5.654 = 2.65
17	4	5.323 = 5.654 + .2(4 − 5.654)	11	11/5.323 = 2.07
18	3	4.858 = 5.323 + .2(3 − 5.323)	8	8/4.858 = 1.65
19	8	5.486 = 4.858 + .2(8 − 4.858)	0	0/5.486 = 0.00
20	13	6.989 = 5.486 + .2(13 − 5.486)	−13	−13/6.989 = −1.86
21	10	7.591 = 6.989 + .2(10 − 6.989)	−23	−23/7.591 = −3.03
22	2	6.473 = 7.591 + .2(2 − 7.591)	−25	−25/6.473 = −3.86
23	8	6.778 = 6.473 + .2(8 − 6.473)	−17	−17/6.778 = −2.51
24	6	6.622 = 6.778 + .2(6 − 6.778)	−11	−11/6.622 = −1.66

   Because the tracking signal is within ± 4 every month, there is no evidence of a problem.

2. a. Make sure that the average error is approximately zero, because a large average would suggest a biased forecast.

$$\text{Average error} = \frac{\Sigma \text{ errors}}{n} = \frac{-11}{24} = -.46$$

   b. Compute the standard deviation:

$$s = \sqrt{MSE} = \sqrt{\frac{\Sigma e^2}{n-1}}$$

$$= \sqrt{\frac{4^2 + 7^2 + 4^2 + 4^2 + (-5)^2 + (-2)^2 + (-8)^2 + (-12)^2}{8-1}} = 6.91$$

   c. Determine 2*s* control limits:

$$0 \pm 2s = 0 \pm 2(6.91) = -13.82 \text{ to } +13.82$$

   d. (1) Check that all errors are within the limits. (They are.)
      (2) Plot the data (see the following graph), and check for nonrandom patterns. Note the strings of positive and negative errors. This suggests nonrandomness (and that an improved forecast is possible). The tracking signal did not reveal this.

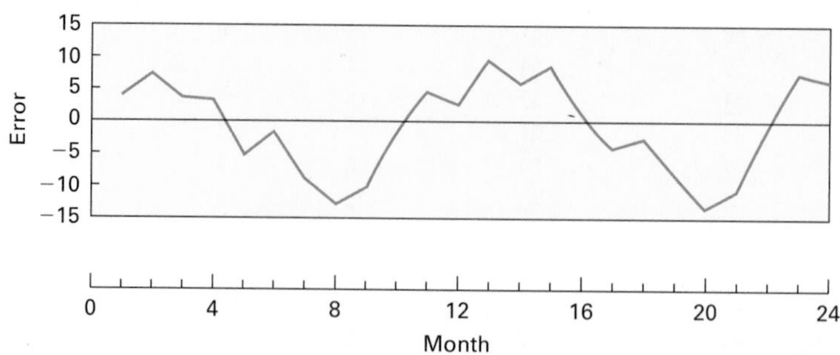

A plot helps you to visualize the process and enables you to check for possible patterns (i.e., nonrandomness) *within the limits* that suggest an improved forecast is possible.[5]

Like the tracking signal, a control chart focuses attention on deviations that lie outside predetermined limits. With either approach, however, it is desirable to check for possible patterns in the errors, even if all errors are within the limits.

If nonrandomness is found, corrective action is needed. That will result in less variability in forecast errors, and, thus, in narrower control limits. (Revised control limits must be computed using the resulting forecast errors.) Figure 3.13 illustrates the impact on control limits due to decreased error variability.

Comment The control chart approach is generally superior to the tracking signal approach. A major weakness of the tracking signal approach is its use of cumulative errors: Individual errors can be obscured so that large positive and negative values cancel each other. Conversely, with control charts, every error is judged individually. Thus, it can be misleading to rely on a tracking signal approach to monitor errors. In fact, the historical roots of the tracking signal approach date from before the first use of computers in business. At that time, it was much more difficult to compute standard deviations than to compute average deviations; for that reason, the concept of a tracking signal was developed. Now computers and calculators can easily provide standard deviations. Nonetheless, the use of tracking signals has persisted, probably because users are unaware of the superiority of the control chart approach.

CHOOSING A FORECASTING TECHNIQUE

Many different kinds of forecasting techniques are available, and no single technique works best in every situation. When selecting a technique, the manager or analyst must take a number of factors into consideration.

The two most important factors are *cost* and *accuracy*. How much money is budgeted for generating the forecast? What are the possible costs of errors, and what are the benefits that might accrue from an accurate forecast? Generally speaking, the higher the accuracy, the higher the cost, so it is important to weigh cost–accuracy trade-offs carefully. The best forecast is not necessarily the most accurate or the least costly; rather, it is some combination of accuracy and cost deemed best by management.

Other factors to consider in selecting a forecasting technique include the availability of historical data; the availability of computer software; and the time needed to gather and analyze data and to prepare the forecast. When gasoline prices increased dramatically in 2005, due in part to hurricane damage, makers of gas-guzzling SUVs had no historical data to predict demand for those vehicles under those conditions. Consequently, they had to resort to qualitative approaches to predict demand. The forecast horizon is important because some techniques are more suited to long-range forecasts while others work best for the short range. For example, moving averages and exponential smoothing are essentially short-range techniques, since they produce forecasts for the *next* period. Trend equations can be used to project over much longer time periods. When using time-series data, *plotting the data* can be very helpful in choosing an appropriate method. Several of the qualitative techniques are well suited to long-range forecasts because they do not require historical data. The Delphi

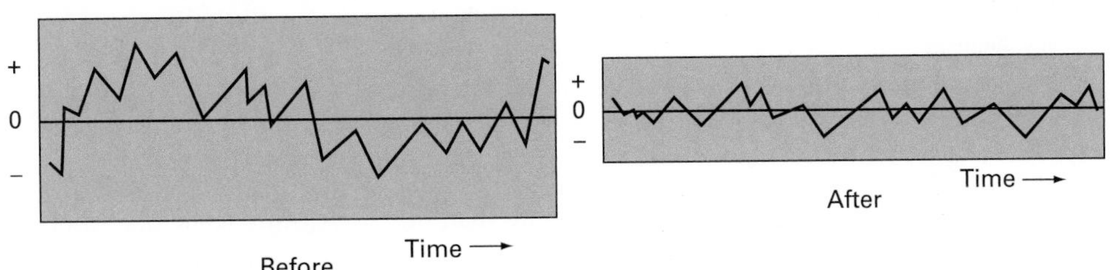

FIGURE 3.13
Removal of a pattern usually results in less variability, and, hence, narrower control limits

[5]The theory and application of control charts and the various methods for detecting patterns in the data are covered in more detail in Chapter 10, on quality control.

method and executive opinion methods are often used for long-range planning. New products and services lack historical data, so forecasts for them must be based on subjective estimates. In many cases, experience with similar items is relevant. Table 3.4 provides a guide for selecting a forecasting method. Table 3.5 provides additional perspectives on forecasts in terms of the time horizon.

TABLE 3.4 A guide to selecting an appropriate forecasting method

Forecasting Method	Amount of Historical Data	Data Pattern	Forecast Horizon	Preparation Time	Personnel Background
Moving average	2 to 30 observations	Data should be stationary	Short	Short	Little sophistication
Simple exponential smoothing	5 to 10 observations	Data should be stationary	Short	Short	Little sophistication
Trend-adjusted exponential smoothing	10 to 15 observations	Trend	Short to medium	Short	Moderate sophistication
Trend models	10 to 20; for seasonality at least 5 per season	Trend	Short to medium	Short	Moderate sophistication
Seasonal	Enough to see 2 peaks and troughs	Handles cyclical and seasonal patterns	Short to medium	Short to moderate	Little sophistication
Causal regression models	10 observations per independent variable	Can handle complex patterns	Short, medium, or long	Long development time, short time for implementation	Considerable sophistication

Source: Adapted from J. Holton Wilson and Deborah Allison-Koerber, "Combining Subjective and Objective Forecasts Improves Results," *Journal of Business Forecasting,* Fall 1992, p. 4.

TABLE 3.5
Forecast factors, by range of forecast

Factor	Short Range	Intermediate Range	Long Range
1. Frequency	Often	Occasional	Infrequent
2. Level of aggregation	Item	Product family	Total output Type of product/service
3. Type of model	Smoothing Projection Regression	Projection Seasonal Regression	Managerial judgment
4. Degree of management involvement	Low	Moderate	High
5. Cost per forecast	Low	Moderate	High

In some instances, a manager might use more than one forecasting technique to obtain independent forecasts. If the different techniques produced approximately the same predictions, that would give increased confidence in the results; disagreement among the forecasts would indicate that additional analysis may be needed.

USING FORECAST INFORMATION

A manager can take a *reactive* or a *proactive* approach to a forecast. A reactive approach views forecasts as probable future demand, and a manager reacts to meet that demand (e.g., adjusts production rates, inventories, the workforce). Conversely, a proactive approach seeks to actively influence demand (e.g., by means of advertising, pricing, or product/service changes).

Generally speaking, a proactive approach requires either an explanatory model (e.g., regression) or a subjective assessment of the influence on demand. A manager might make two forecasts: one to predict what will happen under the status quo and a second one based on a "what if" approach, if the results of the status quo forecast are unacceptable.

COMPUTER SOFTWARE IN FORECASTING

Computers play an important role in preparing forecasts based on quantitative data. Their use allows managers to develop and revise forecasts quickly, and without the burden of manual computations. There is a wide range of software packages available for forecasting. The Excel templates on the text Web site are an example of a spreadsheet approach. There are templates for moving averages, exponential smoothing, linear trend equation, trend-adjusted exponential smoothing, and simple linear regression. Some templates are illustrated in the Solved Problems section at the end of the chapter.

SCREENCAM TUTORIAL

OPERATIONS STRATEGY

Forecasts are the basis for many decisions and an essential input for matching supply and demand. Clearly, the more accurate an organization's forecasts, the better prepared it will be to take advantage of future opportunities and reduce potential risks. A worthwhile strategy can be to work to improve short-term forecasts. Better short-term forecasts will not only enhance profits through lower inventory levels, fewer shortages, and improved customer service, they also will enhance forecasting *credibility* throughout the organization: If short-term forecasts are inaccurate, why should other areas of the organization put faith in long-term forecasts? Also, the sense of confidence accurate short-term forecasts would generate would allow allocating more resources to strategic and medium- to longer-term planning and less on short-term, tactical activities.

Maintaining accurate, up-to-date information on prices, demand, and other variables can have a significant impact on forecast accuracy. An organization also can do other things to improve forecasts. These do not involve searching for improved techniques but relate to the inverse relation of accuracy to the forecast horizon: Forecasts that cover shorter time frames tend to be more accurate than longer-term forecasts. Recognizing this, management might choose to devote efforts to *shortening the time horizon that forecasts must cover.* Essentially, this means shortening the *lead time* needed to respond to a forecast. This might involve building *flexibility* into operations to permit rapid response to changing demands for products and services, or to changing volumes in quantities demanded; shortening the lead time required to obtain supplies, equipment, and raw materials or the time needed to train or retrain employees; or shortening the time needed to *develop* new products and services.

Lean systems are demand driven; goods are produced to fulfill orders rather than to hold in inventory until demand arises. Consequently, they are far less dependent on short-term forecasts than more traditional systems.

In certain situations forecasting can be very difficult when orders have to be placed far in advance. This is the case, for example, when demand is sensitive to weather conditions, such as the arrival of spring, and there is a narrow window for demand. Orders for products or

(continued)

(concluded)

services that relate to this (e.g., garden materials, advertising space) often have to be placed many months in advance—far beyond the ability of forecasters to accurately predict weather conditions and, hence, the timing of demand. In such cases, there may be pressures from salespeople who want low quotas and financial people who don't want to have to deal with the cost of excess inventory to have conservative forecasts. Conversely, operations people may want more optimistic forecasts to reduce the risk of being blamed for possible shortages.

Sharing forecasts or demand data throughout the supply chain can improve forecast quality in the supply chain, resulting in lower costs and shorter lead times. For example, both Hewlett-Packard and IBM require resellers to include such information in their contracts.

The following reading provides additional insights on forecasting and supply chains.

Gazing at the Crystal Ball

READING

Ram Reddy

Disregarding Demand Forecasting Technologies during Tough Economic Times Can Be a Costly Mistake

It's no secret that the IT sector has felt the brunt of the economic downturn. Caught up in the general disillusionment with IT has been demand forecasting (DF) technologies. Many companies blame DF technologies for supply chain problems such as excess inventory. Pinning the blame on and discontinuing DF technologies is the equivalent of throwing out the baby with the bathwater. The DF misunderstanding stems from the fact that, despite sophisticated mathematical models and underlying technologies, the output from these systems is, at best, an educated guess about the future.

A forecast from these systems is only as good as the assumptions and data used to build the forecast. Even the best forecast fails when an unexpected event—such as a recession—clobbers the underlying assumptions. However, this doesn't imply that DF technologies aren't delivering the goods. But, unfortunately, many DF and supply chain technology implementations have recently fallen victim to this mindset. DF is part science and part art (or intuition)—having the potential to significantly impact a company's bottom line. In this column, you'll find an overview of how DF is supposed to work and contrast that with how most companies actually practice it. I'll conclude with suggestions on how to avoid common mistakes implementing and using this particular class of technologies.

The Need for DF Systems

DF is crucial to minimizing working capital and associated expenses and extracting maximum value from a company's capital investments in property, plant, and equipment (PPE). It takes a manufacturing company a lot of lead time to assemble and stage the raw materials and components to manufacture a given number of products per day. The manufacturing company, in turn, generates its sales forecast numbers using data from a variety of sources such as distribution channels, factory outlets, value-added resellers, historical sales data, and general macroeconomic data. Manufacturing companies can't operate without a demand forecast because they won't know the quantities of finished goods to produce. The manufacturing company wants to make sure all or much of its finished product moves off the store shelves or dealer lots as quickly as possible. Unsold products represent millions of dollars tied up in inventory.

The flip side of this equation is the millions of dollars invested in PPE to manufacture the finished products. The company and its supporting supply chain must utilize as close to 100 percent of its PPE investments. Some manufacturing plants make products in lots of 100 or 1,000. Generally, it's cost prohibitive to have production runs of one unit. So how do you extract maximum value from your investments and avoid having money tied up in unsold inventory?

DF and supply chain management (SCM) technologies try to solve this problem by generating a production plan to meet forecasted demand and extract maximum value from PPE, while reducing the amount of capital tied up in inventory. Usually, the demand forecast is pretty close to the actual outcomes, but there are times when demand forecasts don't match the outcomes. In addition to unforeseen economic events, a new product introduction may be a stellar success or an abysmal failure. In the case of a phenomenal success, the manufacturing plant may not be able to meet demand for its product.

Consider the case of the Chrysler PT Cruiser. It succeeded way beyond the demand forecast's projections. Should it have started with manufacturing capacity to fulfill the runaway demand? Absolutely not. Given the additional millions of dollars of investment in PPE necessary to add that capacity, it would've backfired if the PT Cruiser had been a flop. The value provided by DF and supporting SCM technologies in this instance was the ability to add capacity to meet the amended forecast based on actual events. Demand forecasts can and do frequently miss their targets. The point

(continued)

to underscore here is that the underlying DF and supporting SCM technologies are critical to a company's ability to react and respond in a coordinated manner when market conditions change.

The manufacturing company and its supply chain are able to benefit from sharing information about the changed market conditions and responding to them in a coordinated manner. Despite best practices embedded in DF and SCM technologies to support this manner of collaboration, it plays out differently in the real world.

How It Works in Real Life—Worst Practices

A company prepares its forecast by taking into account data about past sales, feedback from distribution channels, qualitative assessments from field sales managers, and macroeconomic data. DF and SCM technologies take these inputs and add existing capacities within the company and across the supply chain to generate a production plan for optimum financial performance.

There's been incredible pressure on executives of publicly traded companies to keep up stock prices. This pressure, among other reasons, may cause manufacturing company executives to make bold projections to external financial analysts (or Wall Street) about future sales without using the demand forecast generated from the bottom up. When the company realizes this disparity between the initial projection and the forecast, the forecast is changed to reflect the projections made by the company's officers, negating its accuracy.

The company arbitrarily sets sales targets for various regions to meet Wall Street numbers that are totally out of sync with input provided by the regional sales managers for the DF process. Even though the regional sales managers' input may have a qualitative element (art), they tend to be more accurate, given their proximity to the customers in the region. Unfortunately, the arbitrary sales targets make their way back to the supply chain, and the result is often excessive inventory build-up starting at the distribution channels to the upstream suppliers.

Seeing the inventory pile up, the manufacturing company may decide to shut down a production line. This action affects upstream suppliers who had procured raw materials and components to meet the executive-mandated production numbers, which may cause them to treat any future forecasted numbers with suspicion. Most cost efficiencies that could be obtained through planned procurement of raw materials and components go out the window. It's very likely that the companies try to blame DF and SCM technologies for failing to provide a responsive and efficient supply chain, even though the fault may lie in the company's misuse of the technologies and not the technologies themselves.

Guarding against the Extremes

Earlier in this column, I said that DF is part art or intuition and part science. The art/intuition part comes in when subject-matter experts (SMEs) make educated estimates about future sales. These SMEs could range from distribution outlet owners to sales and marketing gurus and economists. Their intuition is typically combined with data (such as historical sales figures) to generate the forecast for the next quarter or year. During a recession, the SMEs tend to get overly pessimistic. The demand forecasts generated from this mindset lead to inventory shortages when the economy recovers. Similarly, during an economic expansion, the SMEs tend to have an overly rosy picture of the future. This optimism leads to inventory gluts when the economy starts to slow down. In both instances, blaming and invalidating DF and SCM technologies is counterproductive in the long run.

It's very rare that a demand forecast and the actual outcome match 100 percent. If it's close enough to avoid lost sales or create an excess inventory situation, it's deemed a success. DF and supporting SCM technologies are supposed to form a closed loop with actual sales at the cash register providing a feedback mechanism. This feedback is especially essential during economic upturns or downturns. It provides the necessary information to a company and its supply chain to react in a coordinated and efficient manner.

Don't let the current disillusionment with DF and SCM technologies impede the decision-making process within your company. The intelligent enterprise needs these technologies to effectively utilize its capital resources and efficiently produce to meet its sales forecasts.

Ram Reddy is the author of *Supply Chains to Virtual Integration* (McGraw-Hill, 2001). He is the president of Tactica Consulting Group, a technology and business strategy consulting company.

Source: Ram Reddy, "Gazing at the Crystal Ball," *Intelligent Enterprise*, June 13, 2002.

SUMMARY

Forecasts are vital inputs for the design and the operation of the productive systems because they help managers to anticipate the future.

Forecasting techniques can be classified as qualitative or quantitative. Qualitative techniques rely on judgment, experience, and expertise to formulate forecasts; quantitative techniques rely on the use of historical data or associations among variables to develop forecasts. Some of the techniques are simple, and others are complex. Some work better than others, but no technique works all the time. Moreover, all forecasts include a certain degree of inaccuracy, and allowance should be made for this. The techniques generally assume that the same underlying causal system that existed in the past will continue to exist in the future.

The qualitative techniques described in this chapter include consumer surveys, salesforce estimates, executive opinions, and manager and staff opinions. Two major quantitative approaches are described: analysis of time-series data and associative techniques. The time-series techniques rely strictly on the examination of historical data; predictions are made by projecting past movements of a variable into the future without considering specific factors that might influence the variable. Associative techniques attempt to explicitly identify influencing factors and to incorporate that information into equations that can be used for predictive purposes.

All forecasts tend to be inaccurate; therefore, it is important to provide a measure of accuracy. It is possible to compute several measures of forecast accuracy that help managers to evaluate the performance of a given technique and to choose among alternative forecasting techniques. Control of forecasts involves deciding whether a forecast is performing adequately, typically using a control chart.

When selecting a forecasting technique, a manager must choose a technique that will serve the intended purpose at an acceptable level of cost and accuracy.

The various forecasting techniques are summarized in Table 3.6. Table 3.7 lists the formulas used in the forecasting techniques and in the methods of measuring their accuracy. Note that the Excel templates on the text Web site that accompanies this book are especially useful for tedious calculations.

KEY POINTS

1. Demand forecasts are essential inputs for many business decisions; they help managers decide how much supply or capacity will be needed to match expected demand, both within the organization and in the supply chain.
2. Because of random variations in demand, it is likely that the forecast will not be perfect, so managers need to be prepared to deal with forecast errors.
3. Other, nonrandom factors might also be present, so it is necessary to monitor forecast errors to check for nonrandom patterns in forecast errors.
4. It is important to choose a forecasting technique that is cost-effective, and one that minimizes forecast error.

TABLE 3.6 Forecasting approaches

	Approaches	Brief Description
Judgment/opinion:	Consumer surveys	Questioning consumers on future plans
	Direct-contact composites	Joint estimates obtained from salespeople or customer service people
	Executive opinion	Finance, marketing, and manufacturing managers join to prepare forecast
	Delphi technique	Series of questionnaires answered anonymously by knowledgeable people; successive questionnaires are based on information obtained from previous surveys
	Outside opinion	Consultants or other outside experts prepare the forecast
Statistical:	Time series:	
	Naive	Next value in a series will equal the previous value in a comparable period
	Moving averages	Forecast is based on an average of recent values
	Exponential smoothing	Sophisticated form of weighted moving average
	Associative models:	
	Simple regression	Values of one variable are used to predict values of a dependent variable
	Multiple regression	Two or more variables are used to predict values of a dependent variable

TABLE 3.7
Summary of formulas

Technique	Formula	Definitions
MAD	$\text{MAD} = \dfrac{\sum^{n} \lvert e \rvert}{n}$	MAD = Mean absolute deviation e = Error, $A - F$ n = Number of errors
MSE	$\text{MSE} = \dfrac{\sum^{n} e^2}{n-1}$	MSE = Mean squared error n = Number of errors

Technique	Formula	Definitions
MAPE	$\text{MAPE} = \dfrac{\sum^{n}\left[\dfrac{\lvert e_t \rvert}{\text{Actual}_t} \times 100\right]}{n}$	MAPE = Mean absolute percent error n = Number of errors
Moving average forecast	$F_t = \dfrac{\sum_{i=1}^{n} A_{t-i}}{n}$	A = Demand in period $t - i$ n = Number of periods
Weighted average	$F_t = w_t(A_t) + w_{t-1}(A_{t-1}) + \cdots + w_{t-n}(A_{t-n})$	w_t = Weight for the period t A_t = Actual value in period t
Exponential smoothing forecast	$F_t = F_{t-1} + \alpha(A_{t-1} - F_{t-1})$	α = Smoothing factor
Linear trend forecast	$F_t = a + b_t$ where $b = \dfrac{n\Sigma ty - \Sigma t \Sigma y}{n\Sigma t^2 - (\Sigma t)^2}$ $a = \dfrac{\Sigma y - b\Sigma t}{n}$ or $\bar{y} - b\bar{t}$	a = y intercept b = Slope
Trend-adjusted forecast	$\text{TAF}_{t+1} = S_t + T_t$ where $S_t = \text{TAF}_t + \alpha(A_t - \text{TAF}_t)$ $T_t = T_{t-1} + \beta(\text{TAF}_t - \text{TAF}_{t-1} - T_{t-1})$	t = Current period TAF_{t+1} = Trend-adjusted forecast for next period S = Previous forecast plus smoothed error T = Trend component
Linear regression forecast	$Y_c = a + bx$ where $b = \dfrac{n(\Sigma xy) - (\Sigma x)(\Sigma y)}{n(\Sigma x^2) - (\Sigma x)^2}$ $a = \dfrac{\Sigma y - b\Sigma x}{n}$ or $\bar{y} - b\bar{x}$	y_c = Computed value of dependent variable x = Predictor (independent) variable b = Slope of the line a = Value of y_c when $x = 0$
Standard error of estimate	$S_e = \sqrt{\dfrac{\Sigma(y - y_c)^2}{n - 2}}$	S_e = Standard error of estimate y = y value of each data point n = Number of data points
Tracking signal	$\text{TS} = \dfrac{\sum^{n} e}{\text{MAD}}$	
Control limits	$\text{UCL} = 0 + z\sqrt{\text{MSE}}$ $\text{LCL} = 0 - z\sqrt{\text{MSE}}$	$\sqrt{\text{MSE}}$ = standard deviation z = Number of standard deviations; 2 and 3 are typical values

KEY TERMS

associative model, 80
bias, 105
centered moving average, 95
control chart, 103
correlation, 101
cycle, 82
Delphi method, 81
error, 78
exponential smoothing, 87
forecast, 74
irregular variation, 82
judgmental forecasts, 80
least squares line, 98
linear trend equation, 90
mean absolute deviation (MAD), 78
mean absolute percent error (MAPE), 79
mean squared error (MSE), 78
moving average, 84
naive forecast, 82
predictor variables, 98
random variations, 82
regression, 98
seasonal relative, 94
seasonal variations, 93
seasonality, 82
standard error of estimate, 100
time series, 82
time-series forecasts, 80
tracking signal, 105
trend, 82
trend-adjusted exponential smoothing, 92
weighted average, 86

SOLVED PROBLEMS

Problem 1

Forecasts based on averages. Given the following data:

Period	Number of Complaints
1	60
2	65
3	55
4	58
5	64

Prepare a forecast for period 6 using each of these approaches:

a. The appropriate naive approach.

b. A three-period moving average.

c. A weighted average using weights of .50 (most recent), .30, and .20.

d. Exponential smoothing with a smoothing constant of .40.

Solution

Step by step

a. Plot the data to see if there is a pattern. Variations around an average (i.e., no trend or cycles). Therefore, the most recent value of the series becomes the next forecast: 64.

b. Use the latest values. $MA_3 = \dfrac{55 + 58 + 64}{3} = 59$

c. $F = .20(55) + .30(58) + .50(64) = 60.4$

d. Start with period 2. Use the data in period 1 as the forecast for period 2, and then use exponential smoothing for successive forecasts.

Period	Number of Complaints	Forecast	Calculations
1	60 →		[The previous value of the series is used
2	65	60	as the starting forecast.]
3	55	62	60 + .40(65 − 60) = 62
4	58	59.2	62 + .40(55 − 62) = 59.2
5	64	58.72	59.2 + .40(58 − 59.2) = 58.72
6		60.83	58.72 + .40(64 − 58.72) = 60.83

You also can obtain the forecasts and a plot using an Excel template, as shown:

www.mhhe.com/stevenson11e

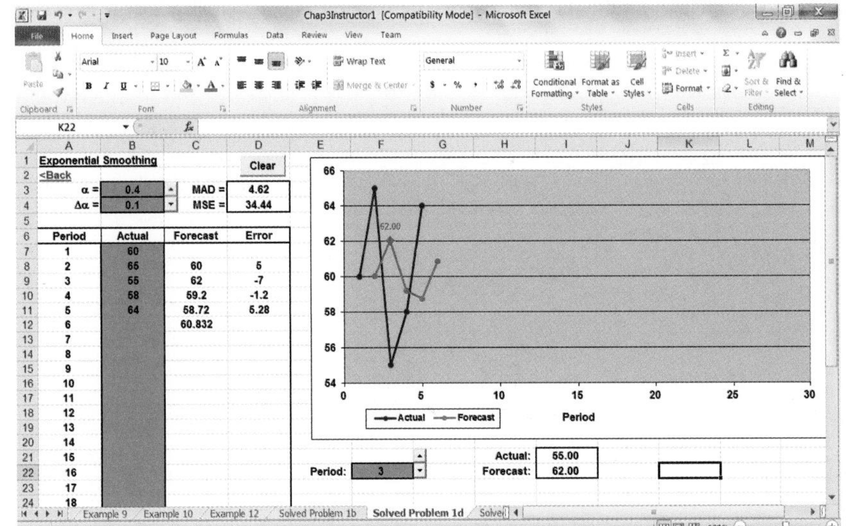

Problem 2

www.mhhe.com/stevenson11e

Using seasonal relatives. Apple's Citrus Fruit Farm ships boxed fruit anywhere in the world. Using the following information, a manager wants to forecast shipments for the first four months of next year.

Month	Seasonal Relative	Month	Seasonal Relative
Jan.	1.2	Jul.	0.8
Feb.	1.3	Aug.	0.6
Mar.	1.3	Sep.	0.7
Apr.	1.1	Oct.	1.0
May.	0.8	Nov.	1.1
Jun.	0.7	Dec.	1.4

The monthly forecast equation being used is:

$$F_t = 402 + 3t$$

where

t_0 = January of *last* year
F_t = Forecast of shipments for month t

Solution

a. Determine trend amounts for the first four months of *next* year: January, $t = 24$; February, $t = 25$; etc. Thus,

$$F_{\text{Jan}} = 402 + 3(24) = 474$$
$$F_{\text{Feb}} = 402 + 3(25) = 477$$
$$F_{\text{Mar}} = 402 + 3(26) = 480$$
$$F_{\text{Apr}} = 402 + 3(27) = 483$$

b. Multiply each monthly trend by the corresponding seasonal relative for that month.

Month	Seasonal Relative	Forecast
Jan.	1.2	474(1.2) = 568.8
Feb.	1.3	477(1.3) = 620.1
Mar.	1.3	480(1.3) = 624.0
Apr.	1.1	483(1.1) = 531.3

Problem 3

Linear trend line. Plot the data on a graph, and verify visually that a linear trend line is appropriate. Develop a linear trend equation for the following data. Then use the equation to predict the next two values of the series.

Period	Demand
1	44
2	52
3	50
4	54
5	55
6	55
7	60
8	56
9	62

Solution

A plot of the data indicates that a linear trend line is appropriate:

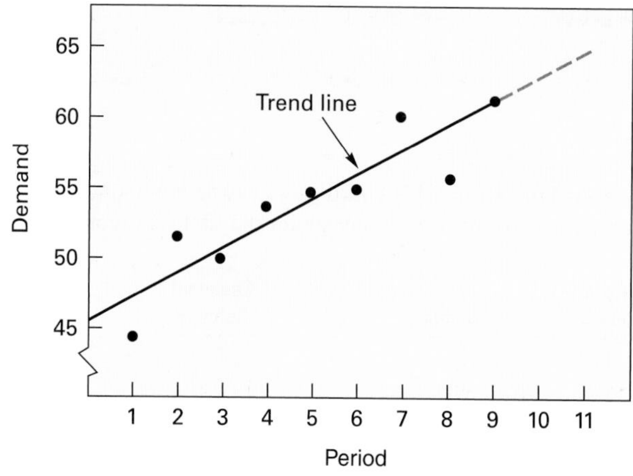

Period, t	Demand, y	ty
1	44	44
2	52	104
3	50	150
4	54	216
5	55	275
6	55	330
7	60	420
8	56	448
9	62	558
	488	2,545

From Table 3.1, with $n = 9$,

$\Sigma t = 45$ and $\Sigma t^2 = 285$

$$b = \frac{n\Sigma ty - \Sigma t\Sigma y}{n\Sigma t^2 - (\Sigma t)^2} = \frac{9(2{,}545) - 45(488)}{9(285) - 45(45)} = 1.75$$

$$a = \frac{\Sigma y - b\Sigma t}{n} = \frac{488 - 1.75(45)}{9} = 45.47$$

Thus, the trend equation is $Ft = 45.47 + 1.75t$. The next two forecasts are:

$$F_{10} = 45.47 + 1.75(10) = 62.97$$
$$F_{11} = 45.47 + 1.75(11) = 64.72$$

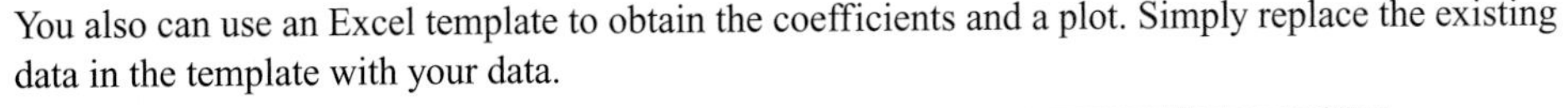

You also can use an Excel template to obtain the coefficients and a plot. Simply replace the existing data in the template with your data.

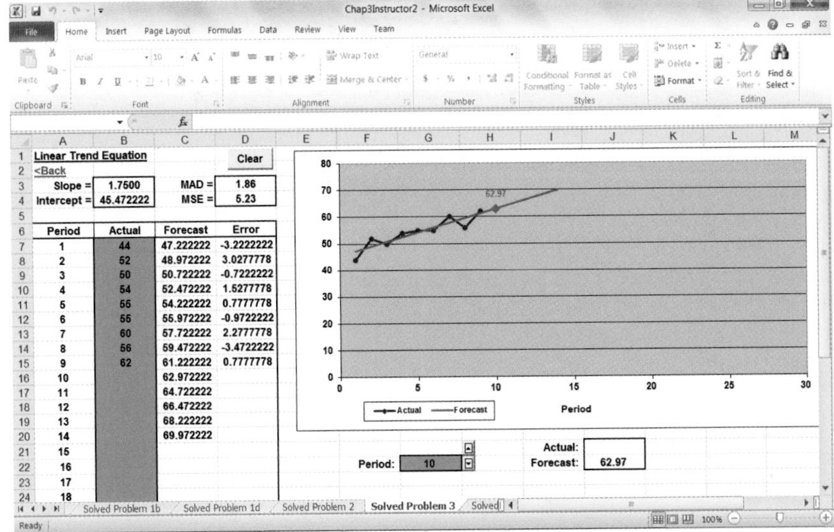

Problem 4

www.mhhe.com/stevenson11e

Seasonal relatives. Obtain estimates of quarter relatives for these data using the centered moving average method:

YEAR	1				2				3				4
Quarter:	1	2	3	4	1	2	3	4	1	2	3	4	1
Demand:	14	18	35	46	28	36	60	71	45	54	84	88	58

Solution

Note that each season has an *even* number of data points. When an even-numbered moving average is used (in this case, a four-period moving average), the "centered value" will not correspond to an actual data point; the center of 4 is *between* the second and third data points. To correct for this, a *second* set of moving averages must be computed using the MA_4 values. The MA_2 values are centered between the MA_4 and "line up" with actual data points. For example, the first MA_4 value is 28.25. It is centered between 18 and 35 (i.e., between quarter 2 and quarter 3). When the average of the first two MA_4 values is taken (i.e., MA_2) and centered, it lines up with the 35 and, hence, with quarter 3.

So, whenever an even-numbered moving average is used as a centered moving average (e.g., MA_4, MA_{12}), a second moving average, a two-period moving average, is used to achieve correspondence with periods. This procedure is not needed when the number of periods in the centered moving average is odd.

Year	Quarter	Demand	MA_4	MA_2	Demand/MA_2
1	1	14			
	2	18	28.25		
	3	35	31.75	30.00	1.17
	4	46	36.25	34.38	1.35
2	1	28	42.50	39.38	0.71
	2	36	48.75	45.63	0.79
	3	60	53.00	50.88	1.18
	4	71	57.50	55.25	1.29
3	1	45	63.50	60.50	0.74
	2	54	67.75	65.63	0.82
	3	84	71.00	69.38	1.21
	4	88			
4	1	58			

	QUARTER			
	1	**2**	**3**	**4**
	0.71	0.79	1.17	1.35
	0.74	0.82	1.18	1.29
	1.45	1.61	1.21	2.64
			3.56	
Average for the quarter:	0.725	0.805	1.187	1.320

The sum of these relatives is 4.037. Multiplying each by 4.00/4.037 will standardize the relatives, making their total equal 4.00. The resulting relatives are quarter 1, .718; quarter 2, .798; quarter 3, 1.176; quarter 4, 1.308.

Problem 5

Regression line. A large midwestern retailer has developed a graph that summarizes the effect of advertising expenditures on sales volume. Using the graph, determine an equation of the form $y = a + bx$ that describes this relationship.

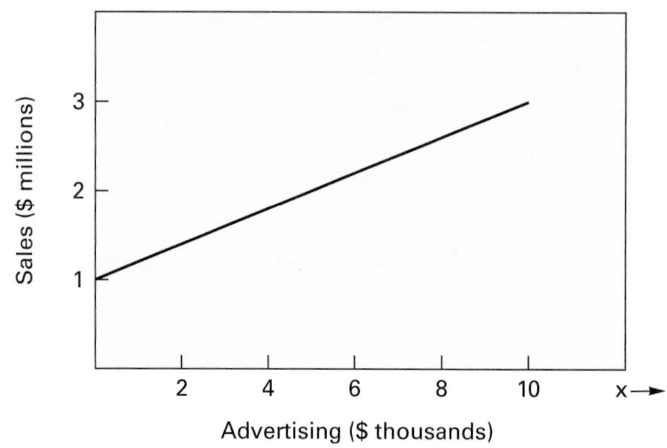

Solution

The linear equation has the form $y = a + bx$, where a is the value of y when $x = 0$ (i.e., where the line intersects the y axis) and b is the slope of the line (the amount by which y changes for a one-unit change in x).

Accordingly, $a = 1$ and $b = (3 - 1)/(10 - 0) = .2$, so $y = a + bx$ becomes $y = 1 + .2x$. [*Note:* $(3 - 1)$ is the change in y, and $(10 - 0)$ is the change in x.]

Problem 6

Regression analysis. The owner of a small hardware store has noted a sales pattern for window locks that seems to parallel the number of break-ins reported each week in the newspaper. The data are:

Sales:	46	18	20	22	27	34	14	37	30
Break-ins:	9	3	3	5	4	7	2	6	4

a. Plot the data to determine which type of equation, linear or nonlinear, is appropriate.

b. Obtain a regression equation for the data.

c. Estimate average sales when the number of break-ins is five.

Solution

a.

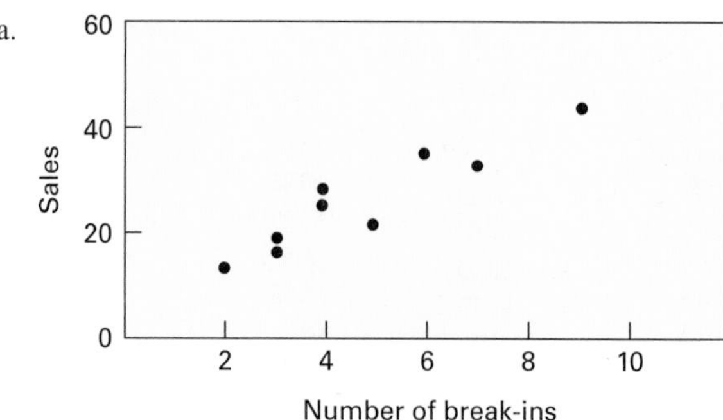

The graph supports a linear relationship.

b. You can obtain the regression coefficients using the appropriate Excel template. Simply replace the existing data for x and y with your data. *Note:* Be careful to enter the values for the variable you want to predict as y values. In this problem, the objective is to predict sales, so the sales values are entered in the y column. The equation is $y_c = 7.129 + 4.275x$.

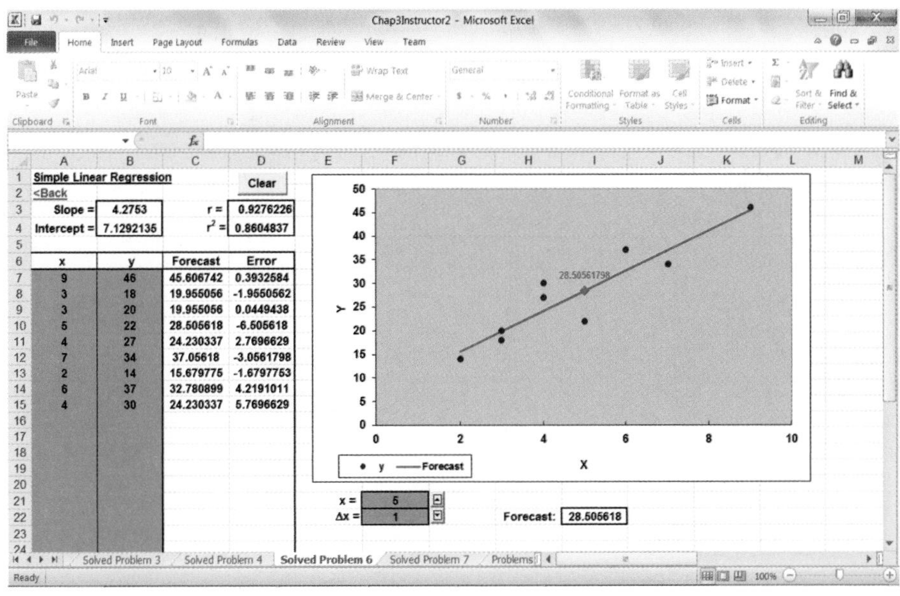

c. For $x = 5$, $y_c = 7.129 + 4.275(5) = 28.50$.

Problem 7

Accuracy of forecasts. The manager of a large manufacturer of industrial pumps must choose between two alternative forecasting techniques. Both techniques have been used to prepare forecasts for a six-month period. Using MAD as a criterion, which technique has the better performance record?

		FORECAST	
Month	**Demand**	**Technique 1**	**Technique 2**
1	492	488	495
2	470	484	482
3	485	480	478
4	493	490	488
5	498	497	492
6	492	493	493

Solution

Check that each forecast has an average error of approximately zero. (See computations that follow.)

Month	Demand	Technique 1	e	$\|e\|$	Technique 2	e	$\|e\|$
1	492	488	4	4	495	−3	3
2	470	484	−14	14	482	−12	12
3	485	480	5	5	478	7	7
4	493	490	3	3	488	5	5
5	498	497	1	1	492	6	6
6	492	493	−1	1	493	−1	1
			−2	28		+2	34

$$\text{MAD}_1 = \frac{\Sigma|e|}{n} = \frac{28}{6} = 4.67$$

$$\text{MAD}_2 = \frac{\Sigma|e|}{n} = \frac{34}{6} = 5.67$$

Technique 1 is superior in this comparison because its MAD is smaller, although six observations would generally be too few on which to base a realistic comparison.

Problem 8

Control chart. Given the demand data that follow, prepare a naive forecast for periods 2 through 10. Then determine each forecast error, and use those values to obtain $2s$ control limits. If demand in the next two periods turns out to be 125 and 130, can you conclude that the forecasts are in control?

Period:	1	2	3	4	5	6	7	8	9	10
Demand:	118	117	120	119	126	122	117	123	121	124

Solution

For a naive forecast, each period's demand becomes the forecast for the next period. Hence, the forecasts and errors are:

Period	Demand	Forecast	Error	Error^2
1	118	—	—	—
2	117	118	−1	1
3	120	117	3	9
4	119	120	−1	1
5	126	119	7	49
6	122	126	−4	16
7	117	122	−5	25
8	123	117	6	36
9	121	123	−2	4
10	124	121	3	9
			+6	150

$$s = \sqrt{\frac{\Sigma \text{Error}^2}{n-1}} = \sqrt{\frac{150}{9-1}} = 4.33 \qquad (n = \text{Number of errors})$$

The control limits are $2(4.33) = \pm 8.66$.

The forecast for period 11 was 124. Demand turned out to be 125, for an error of $125 - 124 = +1$. This is within the limits of ± 8.66. If the next demand is 130 and the naive forecast is 125 (based on the period 11 demand of 125), the error is +5. Again, this is within the limits, so you cannot conclude the forecast is not working properly. With more values—at least five or six—you could plot the errors to see whether you could detect any patterns suggesting the presence of nonrandomness.

DISCUSSION AND REVIEW QUESTIONS

1. What are the main advantages that quantitative techniques for forecasting have over qualitative techniques? What limitations do quantitative techniques have?
2. What are some of the consequences of poor forecasts? Explain.
3. List the specific weaknesses of each of these approaches to developing a forecast:
   a. Consumer surveys.
   b. Salesforce composite.
   c. Committee of managers or executives.
4. Briefly describe the Delphi technique. What are its main benefits and weaknesses?
5. What is the purpose of establishing control limits for forecast errors?
6. What factors would you consider in deciding whether to use wide or narrow control limits for forecasts?
7. Contrast the use of MAD and MSE in evaluating forecasts.
8. What advantages as a forecasting tool does exponential smoothing have over moving averages?
9. How does the number of periods in a moving average affect the responsiveness of the forecast?
10. What factors enter into the choice of a value for the smoothing constant in exponential smoothing?
11. How accurate is your local five-day weather forecast? Support your answer with actual data.
12. Explain how using a centered moving average with a length equal to the length of a season eliminates seasonality from a time series.
13. Contrast the terms *sales* and *demand.*

14. Contrast the reactive and proactive approaches to forecasting. Give several examples of types of organizations or situations in which each type is used.
15. Explain how flexibility in production systems relates to the forecast horizon and forecast accuracy.
16. How is forecasting in the context of a supply chain different from forecasting for just a single organization? List possible supply chain benefits and discuss potential difficulties in doing supply chain forecasting.
17. Which type of forecasting approach, qualitative or quantitative, is better?
18. Suppose a software producer is about to release a new version of its popular software. What information do you think it would take into account in forecasting initial sales?
19. Choose the type of forecasting technique (survey, Delphi, averaging, seasonal, naive, trend, or associative) that would be most appropriate for predicting
    a. Demand for Mother's Day greeting cards.
    b. Popularity of a new television series.
    c. Demand for vacations on the moon.
    d. The impact a price increase of 10 percent would have on sales of orange marmalade.
    e. Demand for toothpaste in a particular supermarket.

TAKING STOCK

1. Explain the trade-off between responsiveness and stability in a forecasting system that uses time-series data.
2. Who needs to be involved in preparing forecasts?
3. How has technology had an impact on forecasting?

CRITICAL THINKING EXERCISES

1. It has been said that forecasting using exponential smoothing is like driving a car by looking in the rear-view mirror. What are the conditions that would have to exist for driving a car that are analogous to the assumptions made when using exponential smoothing?
2. What capability would an organization have to have to not need forecasts?
3. When a new business is started, or a patent idea needs funding, venture capitalists or investment bankers will want to see a business plan that includes forecast information related to a profit and loss statement. What type of forecasting information do you suppose would be required?
4. Discuss how you would manage a poor forecast.
5. Omar has heard from some of his customers that they will probably cut back on order sizes in the next quarter. The company he works for has been reducing its sales force due to falling demand and he worries that he could be next if his sales begin to fall off. Believing that he may be able to convince his customers not to cut back on orders, he turns in an optimistic forecast of his next quarter sales to his manager. What are the pros and cons of doing that?
6. Give three examples of unethical conduct involving forecasting and the ethical principle each violates.

PROBLEMS

1. A commercial bakery has recorded sales (in dozens) for three products, as shown below:

Day	Blueberry Muffins	Cinnamon Buns	Cupcakes
1	30	18	45
2	34	17	26
3	32	19	27
4	34	19	23
5	35	22	22
6	30	23	48
7	34	23	29
8	36	25	20
9	29	24	14
10	31	26	18
11	35	27	47
12	31	28	26
13	37	29	27
14	34	31	24
15	33	33	22

a. Predict orders for the following day for each of the products using an appropriate naive method. *Hint:* Plot each data set.
b. What should the use of *sales* data instead of *demand* imply?

2. National Scan, Inc., sells radio frequency inventory tags. Monthly sales for a seven-month period were as follows:

Month	Sales (000 units)
Feb.	19
Mar.	18
Apr.	15
May	20
Jun.	18
Jul.	22
Aug.	20

a. Plot the monthly data on a sheet of graph paper.
b. Forecast September sales volume using each of the following:
   (1) A linear trend equation.
   (2) A five-month moving average.
   (3) Exponential smoothing with a smoothing constant equal to .20, assuming a March forecast of 19(000).
   (4) The naive approach.
   (5) A weighted average using .60 for August, .30 for July, and .10 for June.
c. Which method seems least appropriate? Why? (*Hint:* Refer to your plot from part *a.*)
d. What does use of the term *sales* rather than *demand* presume?

3. A dry cleaner uses exponential smoothing to forecast equipment usage at its main plant. August usage was forecasted to be 88 percent of capacity; actual usage was 89.6 percent of capacity. A smoothing constant of .1 is used.
a. Prepare a forecast for September.
b. Assuming actual September usage of 92 percent, prepare a forecast for October usage.

4. An electrical contractor's records during the last five weeks indicate the number of job requests:

Week:	1	2	3	4	5
Requests:	20	22	18	21	22

Predict the number of requests for week 6 using each of these methods:
a. Naive.
b. A four-period moving average.
c. Exponential smoothing with $\alpha = .30$. Use 20 for week 2 forecast.

5. A cosmetics manufacturer's marketing department has developed a linear trend equation that can be used to predict annual sales of its popular Hand & Foot Cream.

$$F_t = 80 + 15t$$

where

F_t = Annual sales (000 bottles)
t = 0 corresponds to 1990

a. Are annual sales increasing or decreasing? By how much?
b. Predict annual sales for the year 2006 using the equation.

6. From the following graph, determine the equation of the linear trend line for time-share sales for Glib Marketing, Inc.

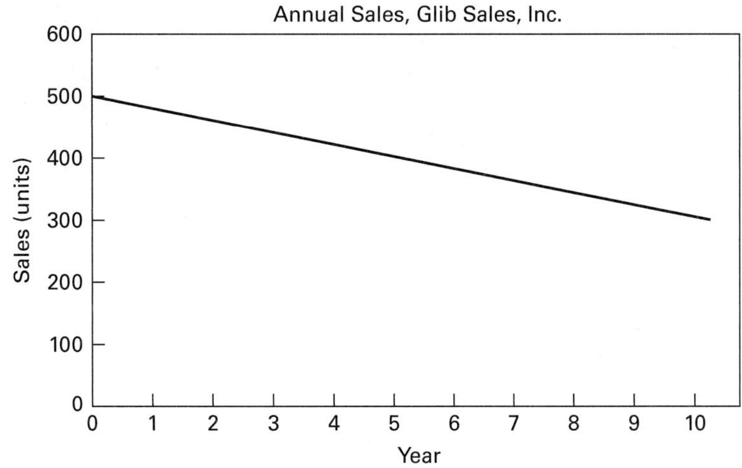

7. Freight car loadings over a 12-year period at a busy port are as follows:

Week	Number	Week	Number	Week	Number
1	220	7	350	13	460
2	245	8	360	14	475
3	280	9	400	15	500
4	275	10	380	16	510
5	300	11	420	17	525
6	310	12	450	18	541

a. Determine a linear trend line for expected freight car loadings.

b. Use the trend equation to predict expected loadings for weeks 20 and 21.

c. The manager intends to install new equipment when the volume exceeds 800 loadings per week. Assuming the current trend continues, the loading volume will reach that level in approximately what week?

8. a. Obtain the linear trend equation for the following data on new checking accounts at Fair Savings Bank and use it to predict expected new checking accounts for periods 16 through 19.

Period	New Accounts	Period	New Accounts	Period	New Accounts
1	200	6	232	11	281
2	214	7	248	12	275
3	211	8	250	13	280
4	228	9	253	14	288
5	235	10	267	15	310

b. Use trend-adjusted smoothing with $\alpha = .3$ and $\beta = .2$ to smooth the new account data in part *a*. What is the forecast for period 16?

9. After plotting demand for four periods, an emergency room manager has concluded that a trend-adjusted exponential smoothing model is appropriate to predict future demand. The initial estimate of trend is based on the net change of 30 for the *three* periods from 1 to 4, for an average of +10 units. Use $\alpha = .5$ and $\beta = .4$, and TAF of 250 for period 5. Obtain forecasts for periods 6 through 10.

Period	Actual	Period	Actual
1	210	6	265
2	224	7	272
3	229	8	285
4	240	9	294
5	255	10	

10. A manager of a store that sells and installs spas wants to prepare a forecast for January, February, and March of next year. Her forecasts are a combination of trend and seasonality. She uses the following equation to estimate the trend component of monthly demand: $Ft = 70 + 5t$, where $t = 0$ in June of last year. Seasonal relatives are 1.10 for January, 1.02 for February, and .95 for March. What demands should she predict?

11. The following equation summarizes the trend portion of quarterly sales of condominiums over a long cycle. Sales also exhibit seasonal variations. Using the information given, prepare a forecast of sales for each quarter of next year (not this year), and the first quarter of the year following that.

$$F_t = 40 - 6.5t + 2t^2$$

where

F_t = Unit sales

$t = 0$ at the first quarter of last year

Quarter	Relative
1	1.1
2	1.0
3	.6
4	1.3

12. A tourist center is open on weekends (Friday, Saturday, and Sunday). The owner-manager hopes to improve scheduling of part-time employees by determining seasonal relatives for each of these days. Data on recent traffic at the center have been tabulated and are shown in the following table:

	WEEK					
	1	2	3	4	5	6
Friday	149	154	152	150	159	163
Saturday	250	255	260	268	273	276
Sunday	166	162	171	173	176	183

a. Develop seasonal relatives for the shop using the centered moving average method.
b. Develop seasonal relatives for the shop using the SA method (see Example 8B).
c. Explain why the results of the two methods correlate the way they do.

13. The manager of a fashionable restaurant open Wednesday through Saturday says that the restaurant does about 35 percent of its business on Friday night, 30 percent on Saturday night, and 20 percent on Thursday night. What seasonal relatives would describe this situation?

14. Air travel on Mountain Airlines for the past 18 weeks was:

Week	Passengers	Week	Passengers
1	405	10	440
2	410	11	446
3	420	12	451
4	415	13	455
5	412	14	464
6	420	15	466
7	424	16	474
8	433	17	476
9	438	18	482

a. Explain why an averaging technique would not be appropriate for forecasting.
b. Use an appropriate technique to develop a forecast for the expected number of passengers for the next three weeks.

15. Obtain estimates of daily relatives for the number of customers at a restaurant for the evening meal, given the following data.
a. Use the centered moving average method. (*Hint:* Use a seven-day moving average.)
b. Use the SA method.

Day	Number Served	Day	Number Served
1	80	15	84
2	75	16	78
3	78	17	83
4	95	18	96
5	130	19	135
6	136	20	140
7	40	21	44
8	82	22	87
9	77	23	82
10	80	24	88
11	94	25	99
12	131	26	144
13	137	27	144
14	42	28	48

16. A pharmacist has been monitoring sales of a certain over-the-counter pain reliever. Daily sales during the last 15 days were

Day:	1	2	3	4	5	6	7	8	9
Number sold:	36	38	42	44	48	49	50	49	52
Day:	10	11	12	13	14	15			
Number sold:	48	52	55	54	56	57			

a. Which method would you suggest using to predict future sales—a linear trend equation or trend-adjusted exponential smoothing? Why?

b. If you learn that on some days the store ran out of the specific pain reliever, would that knowledge cause you any concern? Explain.

c. Assume that the data refer to demand rather than sales. Using trend-adjusted smoothing with an initial forecast of 50 for week 8, an initial trend estimate of 2, and $\alpha = \beta = .3$, develop forecasts for days 9 through 16. What is the MSE for the eight forecasts for which there are actual data?

17. New car sales for a dealer in Cook County, Illinois, for the past year are shown in the following table, along with monthly indexes (seasonal relatives), which are supplied to the dealer by the regional distributor.

Month	Units Sold	Index	Month	Units Sold	Index
Jan.	640	0.80	Jul.	765	0.90
Feb.	648	0.80	Aug.	805	1.15
Mar.	630	0.70	Sept.	840	1.20
Apr.	761	0.94	Oct.	828	1.20
May	735	0.89	Nov.	840	1.25
Jun.	850	1.00	Dec.	800	1.25

a. Plot the data. Does there seem to be a trend?

b. Deseasonalize car sales.

c. Plot the deseasonalized data on the same graph as the original data. Comment on the two graphs.

d. Assuming no proactive approach on the part of management, discuss (no calculations necessary) how you would forecast sales for the first three months of the next year.

e. What action might management consider based on your findings in part *b?*

18. The following table shows a tool and die company's quarterly sales for the current year. What sales would you predict for the first quarter of next year? Quarter relatives are $SR_1 = 1.10$, $SR_2 = .99$, $SR_3 = .90$, and $SR_4 = 1.01$.

Quarter	1	2	3	4
Sales	88	99	108	141.4

19. Compute seasonal relatives for this quarterly data.

a. Use the SA method.
b. Use the centered moving average method.
c. Which set of relatives is better? Why?

	YEAR		
Quarter	**1**	**2**	**3**
1	11	14	17
2	20	23	26
3	29	32	35
4	38	41	44

20. An analyst must decide between two different forecasting techniques for weekly sales of roller blades: a linear trend equation and the naive approach. The linear trend equation is $F_t = 124 + 2t$, and it was developed using data from periods 1 through 10. Based on data for periods 11 through 20 as shown in the table, which of these two methods has the greater accuracy if MAD and MSE are used?

t	Units Sold
11	147
12	148
13	151
14	145
15	155
16	152
17	155
18	157
19	160
20	165

21. Two different forecasting techniques (F1 and F2) were used to forecast demand for cases of bottled water. Actual demand and the two sets of forecasts are as follows:

		PREDICTED DEMAND	
Period	**Demand**	**F1**	**F2**
1	68	66	66
2	75	68	68
3	70	72	70
4	74	71	72
5	69	72	74
6	72	70	76
7	80	71	78
8	78	74	80

a. Compute MAD for each set of forecasts. Given your results, which forecast appears to be more accurate? Explain.
b. Compute the MSE for each set of forecasts. Given your results, which forecast appears to be more accurate?
c. In practice, *either* MAD *or* MSE would be employed to compute forecast errors. What factors might lead a manager to choose one rather than the other?
d. Compute MAPE for each data set. Which forecast appears to be more accurate?

22. Two independent methods of forecasting based on judgment and experience have been prepared each month for the past 10 months. The forecasts and actual sales are as follows:

Month	Sales	Forecast 1	Forecast 2
1	770	771	769
2	789	785	787
3	794	790	792
4	780	784	798
5	768	770	774
6	772	768	770
7	760	761	759
8	775	771	775
9	786	784	788
10	790	788	788

a. Compute the MSE and MAD for each forecast. Does either forecast seem superior? Explain.
b. Compute MAPE for each forecast.
c. Prepare a naive forecast for periods 2 through 11 using the given sales data. Compute each of the following; (1) MSE, (2) MAD, (3) tracking signal at month 10, and (4) $2s$ control limits. How do the naive results compare with the other two forecasts?

23. Long-Life Insurance has developed a linear model that it uses to determine the amount of term life insurance a family of four should have, based on the current age of the head of the household. The equation is:

$$y = 150 - .1x$$

where

y = Insurance needed ($000)

x = Current age of head of household

a. Plot the relationship on a graph.
b. Use the equation to determine the amount of term life insurance to recommend for a family of four if the head of the household is 30 years old.

24. Timely Transport provides local delivery service for a number of downtown and suburban businesses. Delivery charges are based on distance and weight involved for each delivery: 10 cents per pound and 15 cents per mile. Also, there is a $10 handling fee per parcel.
a. Develop an expression that summarizes delivery charges.
b. Determine the delivery charge for transporting a 40-pound parcel 26 miles.

25. The manager of a seafood restaurant was asked to establish a pricing policy on lobster dinners. Experimenting with prices produced the following data:

Average Number Sold per Day, y	Price, x	Average Number Sold per Day, y	Price, x
200	$6.00	155	$8.25
190	6.50	156	8.50
188	6.75	148	8.75
180	7.00	140	9.00
170	7.25	133	9.25
162	7.50		
160	8.00		

a. Plot the data and a regression line on the same graph.
b. Determine the correlation coefficient and interpret it.

26. The following data were collected during a study of consumer buying patterns:

Observation	x	y	Observation	x	y
1	15	74	8	18	78
2	25	80	9	14	70
3	40	84	10	15	72
4	32	81	11	22	85
5	51	96	12	24	88
6	47	95	13	33	90
7	30	83			

a. Plot the data.
b. Obtain a linear regression line for the data.
c. What percentage of the variation is explained by the regression line?
d. Use the equation determined in part *b* to predict the expected value of y for $x = 41$.

27. Lovely Lawns, Inc., intends to use sales of lawn fertilizer to predict lawn mower sales. The store manager estimates a probable six-week lag between fertilizer sales and mower sales. The pertinent data are:

Period	Fertilizer Sales (tons)	Number of Mowers Sold (six-week lag)	Period	Fertilizer Sales (tons)	Number of Mowers Sold (six-week lag)
1	1.6	10	8	1.3	7
2	1.3	8	9	1.7	10
3	1.8	11	10	1.2	6
4	2.0	12	11	1.9	11
5	2.2	12	12	1.4	8
6	1.6	9	13	1.7	10
7	1.5	8	14	1.6	9

a. Determine the correlation between the two variables. Does it appear that a relationship between these variables will yield good predictions? Explain.
b. Obtain a linear regression line for the data.
c. Predict expected lawn mower sales for the first week in August, given fertilizer sales six weeks earlier of 2 tons.

28. The manager of a travel agency has been using a seasonally adjusted forecast to predict demand for packaged tours. The actual and predicted values are as follows:

Period	Demand	Predicted
1	129	124
2	194	200
3	156	150
4	91	94
5	85	80
6	132	140
7	126	128
8	126	124
9	95	100
10	149	150
11	98	94
12	85	80
13	137	140
14	134	128

a. Compute MAD for the fifth period, then update it period by period using exponential smoothing with $\alpha = .3$.
b. Compute a tracking signal for periods 5 through 14 using the initial and updated MADs. If limits of $\pm$ 4 are used, what can you conclude?

29. Refer to the data in problem 22.

a. Compute a tracking signal for the 10th month for each forecast using the cumulative error for months 1 to 10. Use action limits of $\pm$ 4. Is there bias present? Explain.

b. Compute 2*s* control limits for each forecast.

30. The classified department of a monthly magazine has used a combination of quantitative and qualitative methods to forecast sales of advertising space. Results over a 20-month period are as follows:

Month	Error	Month	Error
1	−8	11	1
2	−2	12	6
3	4	13	8
4	7	14	4
5	9	15	1
6	5	16	−2
7	0	17	−4
8	−3	18	−8
9	−9	19	−5
10	−4	20	−1

a. Compute a tracking signal for months 11 through 20. Compute an initial value of MAD for month 11, and then update it for each month using exponential smoothing with $\alpha = .1$. What can you conclude? Assume limits of $\pm$ 4.

b. Using the first half of the data, construct a control chart with 2*s* limits. What can you conclude?

c. Plot the last 10 errors on the control chart. Are the errors random? What is the implication of this?

31. A textbook publishing company has compiled data on total annual sales of its business texts for the preceding nine years:

Year:	1	2	3	4	5	6	7	8	9
Sales (000):	40.2	44.5	48.0	52.3	55.8	57.1	62.4	69.0	73.7

a. Using an appropriate model, forecast textbook sales for each of the next five years.

b. Prepare a control chart for the forecast errors using the original data. Use 2*s* limits.

c. Suppose actual sales for the next five years turn out as follows:

Year:	10	11	12	13	14
Sales (000):	77.2	82.1	87.8	90.6	98.9

Is the forecast performing adequately? Explain.

32. A manager has just received an evaluation from an analyst on two potential forecasting alternatives. The analyst is indifferent between the two alternatives, saying that they should be equally effective.

Period:	1	2	3	4	5	6	7	8	9	10
Data:	37	39	37	39	45	49	47	49	51	54
Alt. 1:	36	38	40	42	46	46	46	48	52	55
Alt. 2:	36	37	38	38	41	52	47	48	52	53

a. What would cause the analyst to reach this conclusion?

b. What information can you add to enhance the analysis?

33. A manager uses this equation to predict demand for landscaping services: $F_t = 10 + 5t$. Over the past eight periods, demand has been as follows:

Period, *t*:	1	2	3	4	5	6	7	8
Demand:	15	21	23	30	32	38	42	47

Is the forecast performing adequately? Explain.

34. A manager uses a trend equation plus quarterly relatives to predict demand. Quarter relatives are $SR_1 = .90$, $SR_2 = .95$, $SR_3 = 1.05$, and $SR_4 = 1.10$. The trend equation is: $Ft = 10 + 5t$. Over the past nine quarters, demand has been as follows:

Period, *t*:	1	2	3	4	5	6	7	8	9
Demand:	14	20	24	31	31	37	43	48	52

Is the forecast performing adequately? Explain.

M&L Manufacturing

CASE

M&L Manufacturing makes various components for printers and copiers. In addition to supplying these items to a major manufacturer, the company distributes these and similar items to office supply stores and computer stores as replacement parts for printers and desktop copiers. In all, the company makes about 20 different items. The two markets (the major manufacturer and the replacement market) require somewhat different handling. For example, replacement products must be packaged individually whereas products are shipped in bulk to the major manufacturer.

The company does not use forecasts for production planning. Instead, the operations manager decides which items to produce and the batch size, based on orders and the amounts in inventory. The products that have the fewest amounts in inventory get the highest priority. Demand is uneven, and the company has experienced being overstocked on some items and out of others. Being understocked has occasionally created tensions with the managers of retail outlets. Another problem is that prices of raw materials have been creeping up, although the operations manager thinks that this might be a temporary condition.

Because of competitive pressures and falling profits, the manager has decided to undertake a number of changes. One change is to introduce more formal forecasting procedures in order to improve production planning and inventory management.

With that in mind, the manager wants to begin forecasting for two products. These products are important for several reasons. First, they account for a disproportionately large share of the company's profits. Second, the manager believes that one of these products will become increasingly important to future growth plans; and third, the other product has experienced periodic out-of-stock instances.

The manager has compiled data on product demand for the two products from order records for the previous 14 weeks. These are shown in the following table.

Week	Product 1	Product 2
1	50	40
2	54	38
3	57	41
4	60	46
5	64	42
6	67	41
7	90*	41
8	76	47
9	79	42
10	82	43
11	85	42
12	87	49
13	92	43
14	96	44

*Unusual order due to flooding of customer's warehouse.

Questions

1. What are some of the potential benefits of a more formalized approach to forecasting?
2. Prepare a weekly forecast for the next four weeks for each product. Briefly explain why you chose the methods you used. (*Hint:* For product 2, a simple approach, possibly some sort of naive/intuitive approach, would be preferable to a technical approach in view of the manager's disdain of more technical methods.)

Highline Financial Services, Ltd.

CASE

Highline Financial Services provides three categories of service to its clients. Managing partner Freddie Mack is getting ready to prepare financial and personnel hiring (or layoff) plans for the coming year. He is a bit perplexed by the following printout he obtained, which seems to show oscillating demand for the three categories of services over the past eight quarters:

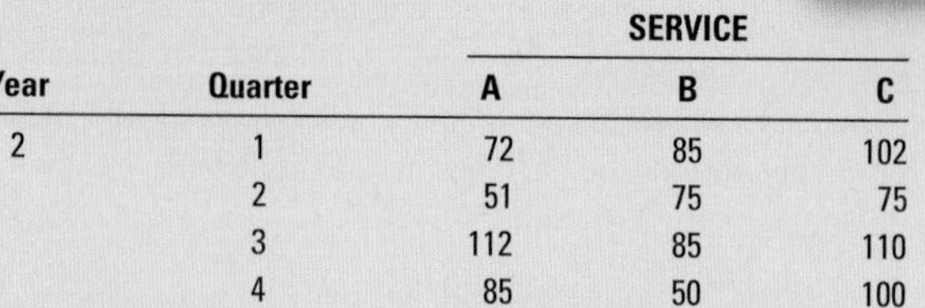

Year	Quarter	SERVICE A	B	C
1	1	60	95	93
	2	45	85	90
	3	100	92	110
	4	75	65	90
2	1	72	85	102
	2	51	75	75
	3	112	85	110
	4	85	50	100

Examine the demand that this company has experienced for the three categories of service it offers over the preceding two years. Assuming nothing changes in terms of advertising or promotion, and competition doesn't change, predict demand for the services the company offers for the next four quarters. Note that there are not enough data to develop seasonal relatives. Nonetheless, you should be able to make reasonably good, approximate *intuitive* estimates of demand. What general observations can you make regarding demand? Should Freddie have any concerns? Explain.

SELECTED BIBLIOGRAPHY AND FURTHER READINGS

Delurgio, Stephen. *Forecasting Principles and Applications.* New York: Irwin/McGraw-Hill, 1998.

Hopp, Wallace J., and Mark L. Spearman. *Factory Physics.* 2nd ed. New York: Irwin/McGraw-Hill, 2001.

"The Impact of Forecasting on Return of Shareholder Value." *Journal of Business Forecasting,* Fall 1999.

Rowe, G., and G. Wright. "The Delphi Technique as a Forecasting Tool: Issues and Analysis." *International Journal of Forecasting* 15, no. 4 (October 1999). See also in the same issue: several commentaries on this article.

"Selecting the Appropriate Forecasting Method." *Journal of Business Forecasting,* Fall 1997.

Wilson, J. Holton, and Barry Keating. *Business Forecasting.* New York: McGraw-Hill, 1998.

Product and Service Design

CHAPTER

CHAPTER OUTLINE

LEARNING OBJECTIVES

After completing this chapter, you should be able to:

1. Explain the *strategic* importance of product and service design.
2. Identify some key reasons for design or redesign.
3. Recognize the key questions of product and service design.
4. List some of the main sources of design ideas.
5. Discuss the importance of legal, ethical, and sustainability considerations in product and service design.
6. Explain the purpose and goal of life cycle assessment.
7. Explain the phrase "the 3 Rs."
8. Briefly describe the phases in product design and development.
9. Name several key issues in manufacturing design.
10. Recognize several key issues in service design.
11. Name the phases in service design.
12. List the characteristics of well-designed service systems.
13. Assess some of the challenges of service design.

The essence of a business organization is the products and services it offers, and every aspect of the organization and its supply chain are structured around those products and services. Organizations that have well-designed products or services are more likely to realize their goals than those with poorly designed products or services. Hence, organizations have a strategic interest in product and service design. Product or service design should be closely tied to an organization's strategy. It is a major factor in cost, quality, time-to-market, customer satisfaction, and competitive advantage. Consequently, marketing, finance, operations, accounting, IT, and HR need to be involved. Demand forecasts and projected costs are important, as is the expected impact on the supply chain. It is significant to note that an important cause of operations failures can be traced to faulty design. Designs that have not been well thought out, or incorrectly implemented, or instructions for assembly or usage that are wrong or unclear, can be the cause of product and service failures, leading to lawsuits, injuries and deaths, products recalls, and damaged reputations.

The introduction of new products or services, or changes to product or services designs, can have impacts throughout the organization as well as the entire supply chain. Some processes may change very little, while others may have to change considerably in terms of what they do or how and when they do it. New processes may have to be added, and some current ones may be eliminated. New suppliers and distributors may need to be found and integrated into the system, and some current suppliers and distributors may no longer be an appropriate fit. Moreover, it is necessary to take into account projected impact on demand as well as financial, marketing, and distribution implications. Because of the potential for widespread effects, taking a "big picture" systems approach early and throughout the design or redesign process is imperative to reduce the chance of missing some implications and costs, and to understand the time it will take. Likewise, input from engineering, operations, marketing, finance, accounting, and supply chains is crucial.

In this chapter you will discover insights into the design process that apply to both product and service design.

Design as a Business Strategy

READING

As businesses continue to reduce costs to achieve competitive advantage, design issues are becoming increasingly important aspects of business strategy. Because product and service design touches every part of a business organization, from operations and supply chains to finance, marketing, accounting, and information systems, design decisions have far-reaching implications for the organization and its success in the marketplace. Product and service innovation is becoming a key avenue in pursuing a competitive edge, and sustainability issues are being given increasing importance in business decisions.

Some companies, such as Steelcase, Inc., have adopted "design thinking" to integrate design strategy throughout the company. The idea is to predicate design on insights into user wants and needs—not really a new concept, but one that is put forth in a way that becomes the focal point of how the company makes design decisions.

Source: Based on "Sustaining the Dream," *BusinessWeek,* October 15, 2007, p. 60.

INTRODUCTION

This section discusses what product and service designers do, the reasons for design (or redesign), and key questions that management must address.

What Does Product and Service Design Do?

The various activities and responsibilities of product and service design include the following (functional interactions are shown in parentheses):

1. Translate customer wants and needs into product and service requirements. (marketing, operations)
2. Refine existing products and services. (marketing)
3. Develop new products and/or services. (marketing, operations)
4. Formulate quality goals. (marketing, operations)
5. Formulate cost targets. (accounting, finance, operations)
6. Construct and test prototypes. (operations, marketing, engineering)
7. Document specifications.
8. Translate product and service specifications into *process* specifications. (engineering, operations)

Product and service design involves or affects nearly every functional area of an organization. However, marketing and operations have major involvement.

Key Questions

From a buyer's standpoint, most purchasing decisions entail two fundamental considerations; one is cost and the other is quality or performance. From the organization's standpoint, the key questions are:

1. **Is there demand for it?** What is the potential size of the market, and what is the expected demand profile (will demand be long term or short term, will it grow slowly or quickly)?
2. **Can we do it?** Do we have the necessary knowledge, skills, equipment, capacity, and supply chain capability? For products, this is known as **manufacturability;** for services, this is known as **serviceability.** Also, is outsourcing some or all of the work an option?
3. **What level of quality is appropriate?** What do customers expect? What level of quality do competitors provide for similar items? How would it fit with our current offerings?
4. **Does it make sense from an economic standpoint?** What are the potential liability issues, ethical considerations, sustainability issues, costs, and profits? For nonprofits, is the cost within budget?

Manufacturability The capability of an organization to produce an item at an acceptable profit.

Serviceability The capability of an organization to provide a service at an acceptable cost or profit.

Reasons for Product and Service Design or Redesign

Product and service design has typically had *strategic* implications for the success and prosperity of an organization. Furthermore, it has an impact on future activities. Consequently, decisions in this area are some of the most fundamental that managers must make.

Organizations become involved in product and service design or redesign for a variety of reasons. The main forces that initiate design or redesign are market opportunities and threats. The factors that give rise to market opportunities and threats can be one or more *changes:*

- **Economic** (e.g., low demand, excessive warranty claims, the need to reduce costs).
- **Social and demographic** (e.g., aging baby boomers, population shifts).
- **Political, liability, or legal** (e.g., government changes, safety issues, new regulations).
- **Competitive** (e.g., new or changed products or services, new advertising/promotions).
- **Cost or availability** (e.g., of raw materials, components, labor, water, energy).
- **Technological** (e.g., in product components, processes).

While each of these factors may seem obvious, let's reflect a bit on technological changes, which can create a need for product or service design changes in several different ways. An obvious way is new technology that can be used directly in a product or service (e.g., a faster, smaller microprocessor that spawns a new generation of personal digital assistants or cell phones). Technology also can indirectly affect product and service design: Advances in processing technology may require altering an existing design to make it compatible with the new processing technology. Still another way that technology can impact product design is illustrated by new digital recording technology that allows television viewers to skip commercials when they view a recorded program. This means that advertisers (who support a television program) can't get their message to viewers. To overcome this, some advertisers have adopted a strategy of making their products an integral part of a television program, say by having their products prominently displayed and/or mentioned by the actors as a way to call viewers' attention to their products without the need for commercials.

The following reading suggests another potential benefit of product redesign.

Product Redesign, Not Offshoring, Holds Cost Advantage for U.S. Manufacturers — READING

Redesign, not offshoring production to countries such as China, holds the greatest promise of cost advantage for U.S. manufacturers, according to a new study that attacks longstanding assumptions about product costs that have troubled manufacturers for decades, both in the United States and worldwide.

The study, "Improved Product Design Practices Would Make U.S. Manufacturing More Cost Effective: A Case to Consider Before Outsourcing to China," suggests that U.S. companies should do a much better job of integrating cost analysis into product design. If rigorous cost analysis were to be instituted as a foundation for product design, U.S. manufacturers would be able to develop innovative products that are more economical to produce in the United States, assert the report's coauthors, Nicholas P. Dewhurst and David G. Meeker.

Dewhurst is executive vice president of Boothroyd Dewhurst, a solution provider specializing in software for design for manufacture and assembly (DFMA). Meeker is a DFMA consultant.

One of the more provocative conclusions of the study is that it can be more advantageous for U.S. manufacturers to lower costs by redesigning products than by outsourcing production to other countries such as China. In many instances, the study shows, redesigning a product and manufacturing it in the United States is a better option for saving money.

To support this idea, the authors identify two principles of design best practices that, they said, many U.S. manufacturing companies overlook when making outsourcing decisions:

- First, it is possible to redesign products to reduce part count and cost. As an illustration, the study features an in-depth, quantitative analysis showing how the redesign of an electric drill would eliminate the cost advantage of offshore manufacturing and justify a decision not to outsource production.
- And second, it is necessary to account for all the additional costs associated with offshore manufacturing and to apply those additional costs to the product. The study warns that companies may not be accounting for the full costs of outsourcing when they consider sending production overseas to

(continued)

(concluded)

countries with very low labor rates such as China. The authors identify a number of hidden costs, including shipping and logistics, that can add an estimated 24 percent to labor and material costs at the offshore location.

The study seeks to demonstrate that if companies consider the potential for design improvement along with a realistic estimate of the full costs of outsourcing, it often makes more sense to manufacture products in the United States.

"We know, from years of consulting with design engineers, that U.S. manufacturers have very little visibility into what their products should cost to make," said Dewhurst. "Companies historically do a poor job of integrating cost analysis into early product design. Many companies now rushing to outsource manufacturing still do not understand that the design of the product determines the final cost."

Dewhurst warned that outsourcing should not be the first step in lowering product costs. "Considering the competitive nature of the global economy and the many hidden risks associated with outsourcing ventures, U.S. companies should scour product designs for efficiency before resorting to offshore production," he said. "We hope this study encourages the U.S. manufacturing industry to take another look at design cost analysis."

Source: "Product Redesign, Not Offshoring, Holds Cost Advantage for U.S. Manufacturers," *Supply & Demand Chain Executive,* September 8, 2004.

Dutch Boy Brushes Up Its Paints

READING

Sherwin-Williams' Dutch Boy Group has put a revolutionary spin on wall/house painting with its new square-shaped Twist & Pour™ paint-delivery container for the Dirt Fighter interior latex paint line. The four-piece square container could be the first major change in how house paint is packaged in decades. Lightweight but sturdy, the Twist & Pour "bucket" is packed with so many conveniences, it's next to impossible to mess up a painting project.

Winning Best of Show in an AmeriStar packaging competition sponsored by the Institute of Packaging Professionals, the exclusive, all-plastic paint container stands almost 7½ in. tall and holds 126 oz., a bit less than 1 gal. Rust-resistant and moisture-resistant, the plastic bucket gives users a new way to mix, brush, and store paint.

A hollow handle on one side makes it comfortable to pour and [carry]. A convenient, snap-in pour spout neatly pours paint into a tray with no dripping but can be removed if desired, to allow a wide brush to be dipped into the 5¾-in.-dia. mouth. Capping the container is a large, twist-off lid that requires no tools to open or close. Molded with two lugs for a snug-finger-tight closing, the threaded cap provides a tight seal to extend the shelf life of unused paint.

While the lid requires no tools to access, the snap-off carry bail is assembled on the container in a "locked-down position" and can be pulled up after purchase for toting or hanging on a ladder. Large, nearly 4½-in.-tall label panels allow glossy front and back labels printed and UV-coated to wrap around the can's rounded corners, for an impressive display.

Jim MacDonald, co-designer of the Twist & Pour and a packaging engineer at Cleveland-based Sherwin-Williams, tells *Packaging Digest* that the space-efficient, square shape is easier to ship and for retailers to stack in stores. It can also be nested, courtesy of a recess in the bottom that mates with the lid's top ring. "The new design allows for one additional shelf facing on an eight-foot rack or shelf area."

The labels are applied automatically, quite a feat, considering their complexity, size, and the hollow handle they likely encounter during application. MacDonald admits, "Label application was a challenge. We had to modify the bottle several times to accommodate the labeling machinery available."

Source: "Dutch Boy Brushes Up Its Paints," *Packaging Digest,* October 2002.

IDEA GENERATION

Ideas for new or redesigned products or services can come from a variety of sources, including customers, the supply chain, competitors, employees, and research. Customer input can come from surveys, focus groups, complaints, and unsolicited suggestions for improvement. Input from suppliers, distributors, and employees can be obtained from interviews, direct or indirect suggestions, and complaints.

One of the strongest motivators for new and improved products or services is competitors' products and services. By studying a competitor's products or services and how the competitor operates (pricing policies, return policies, warranties, location strategies, etc.), an organization can glean many ideas. Beyond that, some companies purchase a competitor's product and then carefully dismantle and inspect it, searching for ways to improve their own product. This is called **reverse engineering.** The Ford Motor Company used this tactic in developing its highly successful Taurus model: It examined competitors' automobiles, searching for best-in-class components (e.g., best hood release, best dashboard display, best door handle). Sometimes reverse engineering can enable a company to leapfrog the competition by developing an even better product. Suppliers are still another source of ideas, and with increased emphasis on supply chains and supplier partnerships, suppliers are becoming an important source of ideas.

Reverse engineering Dismantling and inspecting a competitor's product to discover product improvements.

Research is another source of ideas for new or improved products or services. **Research and development (R&D)** refers to organized efforts that are directed toward increasing scientific knowledge and product or process innovation. Most of the advances in semiconductors, medicine, communications, and space technology can be attributed to R&D efforts at colleges and universities, research foundations, government agencies, and private enterprises.

Research and development (R&D) Organized efforts to increase scientific knowledge or product innovation.

R&D efforts may involve *basic research, applied research,* or *development.*

Basic research has the objective of advancing the state of knowledge about a subject, without any near-term expectation of commercial applications.

Applied research has the objective of achieving commercial applications.

Development converts the results of applied research into useful commercial applications.

Basic research, because it does not lead to near-term commercial applications, is generally underwritten by the government and large corporations. Conversely, applied research and development, because of the potential for commercial applications, appeals to a wide spectrum of business organizations.

The benefits of successful R&D can be tremendous. Some research leads to patents, with the potential of licensing and royalties. However, many discoveries are not patentable, or companies don't wish to divulge details of their ideas so they avoid the patent route. Even so, the first organization to bring a new product or service to the market generally stands to profit from it before the others can catch up. Early products may be priced higher because a temporary monopoly exists until competitors bring their versions out.

The costs of R&D can be high. Some companies spend more than $1 million *a day* on R&D. Large companies in the automotive, computer, communications, and pharmaceutical industries spend even more. For example, IBM spends about $5 billion a year, Hewlett-Packard about $4 billion a year, and Toshiba about $3 billion a year. Even so, critics say that many U.S. companies spend too little on R&D, a factor often cited in the loss of competitive advantage.

It is interesting to note that some companies are now shifting from a focus primarily on *products* to a more balanced approach that explores both product and *process* R&D. Also, there is increasing recognition that technologies often go through life cycles, the same way that many products do. This can impact R&D efforts on two fronts. Sustained economic growth requires constant attention to competitive factors over a life cycle, and it also requires planning to be able to participate in the next-generation technology.

In certain instances, however, research may not be the best approach. The following reading illustrates a research success.

Vlasic on a Roll with Huge Pickle Slices

READING

Michele Darnell

Many were skeptical of Frank Meczkowski's plan to develop a pickle so big that a single slice could cover a hamburger.

After all, whoever saw a pickle that big—except maybe in the *Guinness Book of World Records?*

Meczkowski and his team of food researchers at Vlasic Foods International were convinced the project—given the code name Frisbee—could fly.

For about four years, they labored to cultivate a jumbo cucumber with the taste, shape and crunch to be a perfect pickle.

Made only at the company's plant in Millsboro, the monster-sized slices seem to have captured the pickle lover's fancy. They've become one of Vlasic's best-selling products since their introduction in supermarkets. And the better-than-anticipated sales have helped to reverse a three-year decline in consumption of Vlasic pickles.

Hamburger Stackers are about 10 times bigger than traditional pickle chips and come in dill and bread-and-butter varieties.

"They said it just couldn't be done."

Making a bigger pickle may not sound like that big of a deal. You just grow a bigger cucumber, right?

There is more to it than that. The folks at Vlasic soon learned how tough it was to deal with gigantic cucumbers as they developed the new product and as they retooled the Delaware plant.

Meczkowski came up with the idea for the mammoth pickle slices soon after Vlasic's introduction of its Sandwich Stackers—regular-size pickles sliced lengthwise so they can be draped on sandwiches.

Sandwich Stackers currently account for 20 percent of all Vlasic pickle sales.

Vlasic is the No. 1 seller of pickles in the United States, with a 32 percent share of the $800 million retail pickle market, beating out brands such as Claussen, Heinz, and Peter Piper's.

To develop Hamburger Stackers, Meczkowski worked with seed researchers and others to scour the globe looking for oversized varieties of cucumbers. Most weren't in commercial production.

Vlasic's team grew different varieties in greenhouses, looking for one that would get big enough yet still make a good pickle.

It had to taste like a regular cucumber, stay crisp when pickled, have a small seed cavity and be straight enough so that it could be cut mechanically.

"We wanted it to really be a cucumber," said Meczkowski, who has worked as a food researcher for 22 years and is based at Vlasic's headquarters in New Jersey.

He said Vlasic also had to decide just how big Hamburger Stackers should be. At one point, it asked consumers who were participating in focus groups to bring in their own homemade burgers so the company could determine the perfect size for its new pickles.

Eventually, Vlasic officials found what they were looking for—a now-patented cucumber that grows 3.25 inches in diameter, easily reaches 12 to 16 inches in length, and weighs about five pounds.

The Hamburger Stacker on the burger at left dwarfs a traditional pickle slice. Stackers are genetically designed using cucumbers that grow to over 3 inches in diameter and weigh 5 pounds.

It looks like the watermelon's skinny runt brother.

Once the company settled on a cucumber, it had to work out details of how to get Hamburger Stackers into commercial production. One challenge was to grow the cucumbers in fields, rather than in a greenhouse.

Randy Spence, Vlasic's manager of manufacturing services, said the jumbo cucumbers grew quicker than anyone expected.

"Early on, we expected the bigger ones to grow slower, but that hasn't been the case," he said.

These days, most of the gigantic cucumbers are grown in Florida, where they are handpicked because of their size. Depending on the weather, they take about 54 days from seed to harvest.

Once harvested, they're shipped to Vlasic's plant in Sussex County. The plant employs about 260 workers year-round and 300 to 400 others from April to November.

Steven McNulty, director of plant operations at the nearly 30-year-old Millsboro facility, said the size of the new cucumbers meant they couldn't be handled in the same manner as the smaller versions used to make pickle spears and sweet gherkins.

That became obvious when Vlasic tried to process its first batch of the somewhat fragile, jumbo-sized cucumbers.

Officials didn't end up with the Hamburger Stackers they envisioned. Instead, they ended up with a batch of broken big cucumbers.

"On the first run, we broke every one," Spence said.

But it taught the company a lot about some of the retooling they'd have to do to the plant in Millsboro.

Officials at the plant began making months worth of adjustments so one of the facility's four production lines could handle the jumbo cucumbers.

"We've learned a lot," McNulty said. "And we're still learning."

(continued)

(concluded)

Making Hamburger Stackers requires a mix of automation and the human touch. The process starts when the big cucumbers arrive by truck and are rushed into a cold-storage facility to preserve their flavor.

Once cooled, the cucumbers can be loaded onto the production line and checked for bad spots and other flaws.

They're washed by machine a couple times and sliced.

Then they're sized. Jiggling along a conveyor belt, slices that are too small are weeded out by a worker and a machine. Those that are too big also are sorted out.

Too big?

Yes, the monster-sized cucumbers can get a little too big to fit in the jar.

The cucumber slices that make the cut are mechanically stacked into jars and then topped off by hand.

Ella Mae Wilkerson, who has worked at the Vlasic plant in Millsboro for 17 years, said it takes some fast hands to make certain that outgoing jars have enough pickles packed in.

"The bigger the jar, the harder it is," she said as containers of sweet gherkins being jarred on another production line zipped by on a conveyor belt.

After being packed with pickle slices, the jars of Hamburger Stackers are filled with a combination of water, vinegar, salt, and other flavorings and colorings. They are capped, vacuum-sealed, and pasteurized before being labeled and packed for global distribution.

Some details of how Hamburger Stackers are made are kept secret. McNulty said that is because the company is certain its rivals would love to figure out how to make their own Hamburger Stackers.

Vlasic is the only pickle-making company with such a product on the market. "We think the competition loves the idea," McNulty said.

Apparently, so does the pickle-eating public.

About $13 million worth of Hamburger Stackers were sold in the first five months after they were introduced.

The company is optimistic that the product will continue to grow in popularity with U.S. consumers who eat about 3.5 billion hamburgers at home annually.

Source: *Rochester Democrat and Chronicle,* December 13, 1999.

LEGAL AND ETHICAL CONSIDERATIONS

Designers must be careful to take into account a wide array of legal and ethical considerations. Moreover, if there is a potential to harm the environment, then those issues also become important. Most organizations are subject to numerous government agencies that regulate them. Among the more familiar federal agencies are the Food and Drug Administration, the Occupational Health and Safety Administration, the Environmental Protection Agency, and various state and local agencies. Bans on cyclamates, red food dye, phosphates, and asbestos have sent designers scurrying back to their drawing boards to find alternative designs that were acceptable to both government regulators and customers. Similarly, automobile pollution standards and safety features, such as seat belts, air bags, safety glass, and energy-absorbing bumpers and frames, have had a substantial impact on automotive design. Much attention also has been directed toward toy design to remove sharp edges, small pieces that can cause choking, and toxic materials. The government further regulates construction, requiring the use of lead-free paint, safety glass in entranceways, access to public buildings for individuals with disabilities, and standards for insulation, electrical wiring, and plumbing.

Product liability can be a strong incentive for design improvements. **Product liability** is the responsibility of a manufacturer for any injuries or damages caused by a faulty product because of poor workmanship or design. Many business firms have faced lawsuits related to their products, including Firestone Tire & Rubber, Ford Motor Company, General Motors, tobacco companies, and toy manufacturers. Manufacturers also are faced with the implied warranties created by state laws under the **Uniform Commercial Code**, which says that products carry an implication of *merchantability* and *fitness;* that is, a product must be usable for its intended purposes.

Product liability The responsibility of a manufacturer for any injuries or damages caused by a faulty product.

Uniform Commercial Code Products carry an implication of merchantability and fitness.

The suits and potential suits have led to increased legal and insurance costs, expensive settlements with injured parties, and costly recalls. Moreover, increasing customer awareness of product safety can adversely affect product image and subsequent demand for a product.

Thus, it is extremely important to design products that are reasonably free of hazards. When hazards do exist, it is necessary to install safety guards or other devices for reducing accident potential, and to provide adequate warning notices of risks. Consumer groups,

U.S. Consumer Product Safety Commission investigator points out design flaws in a baby crib which would allow infants to become trapped, as shown by a pair of dolls, during a news conference. National safety officials encouraged thrift stores and consignment shops to find out if they had recalled items like outdated playpens or car seats that could injure or kill children.

business firms, and various government agencies often work together to develop industrywide standards that help avoid some of the hazards.

Ethical issues often arise in the design of products and services; it is important for managers to be aware of these issues and for designers to adhere to ethical standards. Designers are often under pressure to speed up the design process and to cut costs. These pressures often require them to make trade-off decisions, many of which involve ethical considerations. One example of what can happen is "vaporware," when a software company doesn't issue a release of software as scheduled as it struggles with production problems or bugs in the software. The company faces the dilemma of releasing the software right away or waiting until most of the bugs have been removed—knowing that the longer it waits, the more time will be needed before it receives revenues and the greater the risk of damage to its reputation.

Organizations generally want designers to adhere to guidelines such as the following:

- Produce designs that are consistent with the goals of the organization. For instance, if the company has a goal of high quality, don't cut corners to save cost, even in areas where it won't be apparent to the customer.
- Give customers the value they expect.
- Make health and safety a primary concern. At risk are employees who will produce goods or deliver services, workers who will transport the products, customers who will use the products or receive the services, and the general public, which might be endangered by the products or services.

HUMAN FACTORS

Human factor issues often arise in the design of consumer products. Safety and liability are two critical issues in many instances, and they must be carefully considered. For example, the crashworthiness of vehicles is of much interest to consumers, insurance companies, automobile producers, and the government.

Another issue for designers to take into account is adding new features to their products or services. Companies in certain businesses may seek a competitive edge by adding new features. Although this can have obvious benefits, it can sometimes be "too much of a good thing," and be a source of customer dissatisfaction. This "creeping featurism" is particularly evident in electronic products such as handheld devices that continue to offer new features, and more complexity, even while they are shrinking in size. This may result in low consumer ratings in terms of "ease of use."

CULTURAL FACTORS

Product designers in companies that operate globally also must take into account any cultural differences of different countries or regions related to the product. This can result in different designs for different countries or regions, as illustrated by the following reading.

Do You Want Pickled Beets with That?

READING

John Kelly

Since the first McDonald's opened in the United States in 1955, the fast food restaurant has spread around the world.

The company now has locations in 121 countries. In fact, of the 30,000 McDonald's restaurants scattered around the globe, there are more in foreign countries (17,000) than in the good old United States (13,000).

The food you can order at many of these Mickey D's is different from what you'll find at the one down the street. Here's a sample of some of the treats that await you should you pull up to the drive-through window in some faraway places:

India: McAloo Tikki Burger. A totally vegetarian sandwich with regular bun, a crispy, breaded spicy potato and vegetable patty, eggless tomato mayonnaise, two slices of tomatoes and shredded onion.

France: Croque McDo. Cheese and ham between two thin pieces of toasted bread.

Italy: McPink. Two pork patties with a slice of yellow cheese.

New Zealand: Kiwi Burger. A hamburger with a fried egg and a slice of pickled beet.

Turkey: Kofte Burger. A spicy meat patty inside a flavored bun, enriched with a special yogurt mix and spiced tomato sauce.

Philippines: McSpaghetti. Pasta in a red sauce with frankfurter bits.

South Korea: Bulgogi Burger. Pork patty on a bun with lettuce and spicy garlic bulgogi sauce.

China: Hong Dou Pie. A dessert pie filled with red bean paste.

Argentina: McNifica. Hamburger sandwich with cheese, tomato, onion and lettuce.

Egypt: McFalafel. Fried patties of ground beans flavored with spices.

Israel: Seven of the 80 or so McDonald's are kosher, meaning they follow strict Jewish dietary rules so there are no cheeseburgers, milkshakes or sundaes.

United Kingdom: Mega Button Blast. Vanilla ice cream that you eat after breaking through a Cadbury chocolate lid.

Greece: Greek Mac. Pita bread sandwich with two beef patties and some yogurt sauce.

Japan: Teriyaki Burger. Chicken cutlet patty marinated in teriyaki sauce, with sweet mayonnaise and sliced lettuce on a sesame bun.

Germany: Gemuse Mac. A veggie burger with lettuce, tomatoes and special "wurzcreme" sauce.

Questions

1. What effects do cultural differences have on the design of fast food offerings in this reading?
2. What functions in the organization are impacted by the differences in product offerings among different countries?

Source: From *The Washington Post*, December 2, 2002

GLOBAL PRODUCT AND SERVICE DESIGN

Traditionally, product design has been conducted by members of the design team who are located in one facility or a few nearby facilities. However, organizations that operate globally are discovering advantages in global product design, which uses the combined efforts of a team of designers who work in different countries and even on different continents. Such

SERVICE

virtual teams can provide a range of comparative advantages over traditional teams such as engaging the best human resources from around the world without the need to assemble them all in one place, and operating on a 24-hour basis, thereby decreasing the time-to-market. The use of global teams also allows for customer needs assessment to be done in more than one country with local resources, opportunities, and constraints to be taken into account. Global product design can provide design outcomes that increase the marketability and utility of a product. The diversity of an international team may yield different points of view and ideas and information to enrich the design process. However, care must be taken in managing the diversity, because if it is mismanaged, that can lead to conflicts and miscommunications.

Advances in information technology have played a key role in the viability of global product design teams by enabling team members to maintain continual contact with each other and to instantaneously share designs and progress, and to transmit engineering changes and other necessary information.

ENVIRONMENTAL FACTORS: SUSTAINABILITY

Product and service design is a focal point in the quest for sustainability. Key aspects include cradle-to-grave assessment, end-of-life programs, reduction of costs and materials used, reuse of parts of returned products, and recycling.

Cradle-to-Grave Assessment

Cradle-to-grave assessment The assessment of the environmental impact of a product or service throughout its useful life.

Cradle-to-grave assessment, also known as life cycle analysis , is the assessment of the environmental impact of a product or service throughout its useful life, focusing on such factors as global warming (the amount of carbon dioxide released into the atmosphere), smog formation, oxygen depletion, and solid waste generation. For products, cradle-to-grave analysis takes into account impacts in every phase of a product's life cycle, from raw material extraction from the earth, or the growing and harvesting of plant materials, through fabrication of parts and assembly operations, or other processes used to create products, as well as the use or consumption of the product, and final disposal at the end of a product's useful life. It also considers energy consumption, pollution and waste, and transportation in all phases. Although services generally involve less use of materials, cradle-to-grave assessment of services is nonetheless important, because services consume energy and involve many of the same or similar processes that products involve.

The goal of cradle-to-grave assessment is to choose products and services that have the least environmental impact while still taking into account economic considerations. The procedures of cradle-to-grave assessment are part of the ISO 14000 environmental management standards, which are discussed in Chapter 9.

End-of-Life Programs

End-of-life (EOL) programs deal with products that have reached the end of their useful lives. The products include both consumer products and business equipment. The purpose of these programs is to reduce the dumping of products, particularly electronic equipment, in landfills or third-world countries, as has been the common practice, or incineration, which converts materials into hazardous air and water emissions and generates toxic ash. Although the programs are not limited to electronic equipment, that equipment poses problems because the equipment typically contains toxic materials such as lead, cadmium, chromium, and other heavy metals. IBM provides a good example of the potential of EOL programs. Over the last 15 years, it has collected about 2 billion pounds of product and product waste.

Best Buy Wants Your Junk

READING

Electronic junk, that is. The giant electronics retailer sees its recycling program as a way to get customers into its stores while building a green reputation. While old TVs, desktop computers, and other outmoded electronics come in, out go flat-screen TVs, netbooks, and iPhones.

The company decided that being a good corporate citizen makes business sense. Best Buy's commitment to corporate responsibility fits nicely with the company's strategy and business model. To set itself apart from its biggest competitors, Walmart and Amazon, the company wants to do more than sell consumer electronics. It would like to help customers get better use out of technology, whether they are buying, installing, fixing, or disposing of their hardware. Since 2009, when Best Buy began offering free recycling of electronic equipment, millions of pounds of In Store Take Back (ISTB) have found their way to the company's 1,044 U.S. stores, making Best Buy America's biggest collector of electronic junk.

Best Buy's interest in the social and environmental impact of electronic goods that had reached the end of their useful life came at the urging of its workers and customers. "Employees wanted to know what Best Buy was doing to become more environmentally sustainable." Some customers—enough to matter—said they preferred buying from retailers that demonstrated an interest in their community. The company audits the factories of its suppliers to make sure they don't exploit workers or pollute the environment. It actually severed ties with 26 of about 200 factories in 2008. Best Buy CEO, Brian Dunn, strives to stay connected to staff and customers, posting questions on an employee Web site called the Water Cooler, tracking consumer sentiment on Facebook and Twitter (BBYCEO), attending focus groups, and inviting customers to the company's leadership meetings.

TVs account for the majority of items. This is somewhat of a mixed blessing. TVs with picture tubes can't be resold; they have to be taken away and disassembled before the materials are melted down for reuse. Unlike plastics, which might end up in lawn furniture or other products, the innards of TVs aren't of much value. In many states manufacturers are required by take-back laws to help finance recycling, and companies like Samsung and Sony share the costs of disposing of old TVs.

Even though there may not be a clear economic case for doing so, at least for TVs, the take-back program could also be beneficial by encouraging innovative design and new business models. Manufacturers that know they will be responsible for the end of life of their products will design them so that they can be disassembled and recycled easily. Computer maker Dell, for instance, reduced the number of screws in its computers to make them easier to dismantle.

Source: Based on "Best Buy Wants Your Electronic Junk," *Fortune* magazine, December 7, 2009.

The Three Rs: Reduce, Reuse, and Recycle

Designers often reflect on three particular aspects of potential cost saving and reducing environmental impact: reducing the use of materials through value analysis; refurbishing and then reselling returned goods that are deemed to have additional useful life, which is referred to as remanufacturing; and reclaiming parts of unusable products for recycling.

Reduce: Value Analysis

Value analysis refers to an examination of the *function* of parts and materials in an effort to reduce the cost and/or improve the performance of a product. Typical questions that would be asked as part of the analysis include: Could a cheaper part or material be used? Is the function necessary? Can the function of two or more parts or components be performed by a single part for a lower cost? Can a part be simplified? Could product specifications be relaxed, and would this result in a lower price? Could standard parts be substituted for nonstandard parts? Table 4.1 provides a checklist of questions that can guide a value analysis.

Value analysis Examination of the function of parts and materials in an effort to reduce cost and/or improve product performance.

The following reading describes how Kraft foods is working to reduce water and energy use, CO_2 and plant waste, and packaging.

Reuse: Remanufacturing

An emerging concept in manufacturing is the remanufacturing of products. **Remanufacturing** refers to refurbishing used products by replacing worn-out or defective components, and reselling the products. This can be done by the original manufacturer, or another company. Among the products that have remanufactured components are automobiles, printers, copiers, cameras, computers, and telephones.

Remanufacturing Refurbishing used products by replacing worn-out or defective components.

Kraft Foods' Recipe for Sustainability

READING

The threat of global warming and the desire to protect the environment has many companies embracing sustainability initiatives. And they are finding that in many instances, there are cost savings in doing so. Among them is the Kraft Foods company, whose well-known brands include Cool Whip, Philadelphia Cream Cheese, DiGiorno pizza, Oscar Mayer, Oreo cookies, and Kraft cheeses and salad dressings. Kraft is the world's second largest food company with 100,000 employees and annual revenues of $42 billion. The company is a member of the Dow Jones Sustainability Index and the Ethibel Sustainability Index.

The company has set some ambitious goals that it wants to achieve:

- Reduce plant energy usage by 25 percent.
- Reduce plant energy-related carbon dioxide emissions by 25 percent.
- Reduce plant water consumption by 15 percent.
- Reduce plant waste by 15 percent.
- Eliminate 150 million pounds of packaging material from the supply chain.

Some of Kraft's successes have come from redesigned packaging. The goal is ambitious. It will require more efficient packaging and a reduction in the amount of packaging material used. Kraft believes that the greatest opportunity to reduce the environmental impact of a package is early in the design phase. Their packaging designers worldwide critically consider the amount of packaging used, how much postconsumer material can be used, how much energy is used to create the packaging materials, how much CO_2 is generated as the materials are created and formed, and how well the package fits the product physically. According to Kraft's press releases, examples and benefits of recent packaging redesigns include:

- DiGiorno and California Pizza Kitchen pizzas: Using slimmer cartons that allow shipment of two extra pizza boxes per case and 14 percent more pizzas per pallet. This leads to a savings of approximately 1.4 million pounds of packaging per year, and the ability to load more pizzas on each truck means there are fewer trucks on the road and less fuel consumed.
- Oscar Mayer Deli Creations: Using 30 percent less paperboard than the previous design results in 1.2 million fewer pounds of packaging going to landfills.

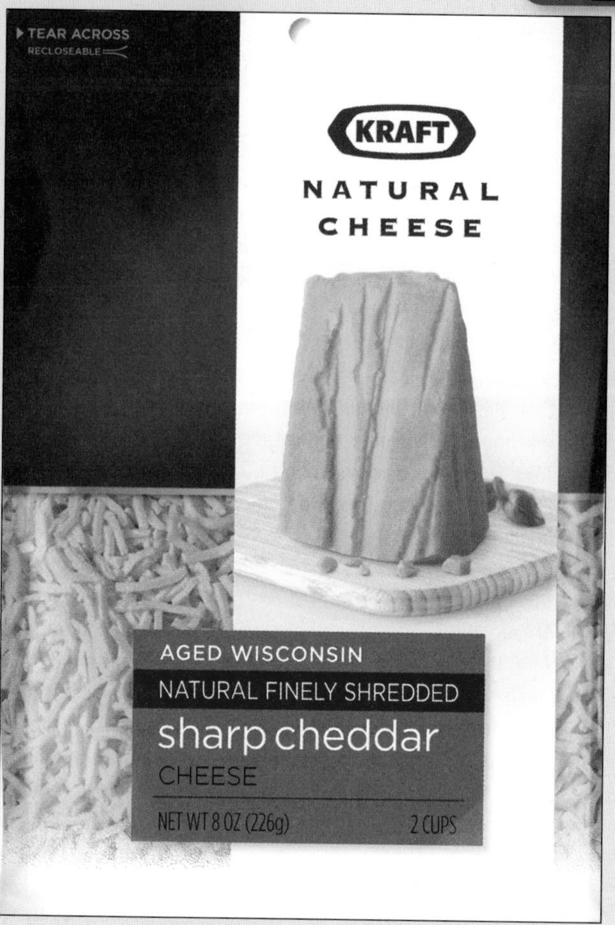

Kraft Natural Cheese new packaging zipper eliminates more than one million pounds of packaging per year.

- Kraft salad dressing: Using 19 percent less plastic per bottle translates to 3 million pounds fewer annually. Additionally the new design allows more bottles to be shipped per truckload, leading to an increase in transportation efficiency of 18 percent.

The company is also working to help the environment, reduce water pollution/soil erosion, and support biodiversity. Considering these successes, Kraft's recipe for sustainability is one that other companies should emulate.

There are a number of important reasons for doing this. One is that a remanufactured product can be sold for about 50 percent of the cost of a new product. Another is that the process requires mostly unskilled and semiskilled workers. And in the global market, European lawmakers are increasingly requiring manufacturers to take back used products, because this means fewer products end up in landfills and there is less depletion of natural resources such as raw materials and fuel.

Design for disassembly (DFD) Design so that used products can be easily taken apart.

Designing products so that they can be more easily taken apart has given rise to yet another design consideration: **Design for disassembly (DFD).**

TABLE 4.1
Overview of value analysis

1. Select an item that has a high annual dollar volume. This can be material, a purchased item, or a service.
2. Identify the function of the item.
3. Obtain answers to these kinds of questions:
   a. Is the item necessary; does it have value; can it be eliminated?
   b. Are there alternative sources for the item?
   c. Can the item be provided internally?
   d. What are the advantages of the present arrangement?
   e. What are the disadvantages of the present arrangement?
   f. Could another material, part, or service be used instead?
   g. Can specifications be less stringent to save cost or time?
   h. Can two or more parts be combined?
   i. Can more/less processing be done on the item to save cost or time?
   j. Do suppliers/providers have suggestions for improvements?
   k. Do employees have suggestions for improvements?
   l. Can packaging be improved or made less costly?
4. Analyze the answers obtained as well as answers to other questions that arise, and make recommendations.

Recycle

Recycling is sometimes an important consideration for designers. **Recycling** means recovering materials for future use. This applies not only to manufactured parts but also to materials used during production, such as lubricants and solvents. Reclaimed metal or plastic parts may be melted down and used to make different products.

Recycling Recovering materials for future use.

Companies recycle for a variety of reasons, including

1. Cost savings.
2. Environment concerns.
3. Environmental regulations.

An interesting note: Companies that want to do business in the European Union must show that a specified proportion of their products are recyclable.

The pressure to recycle has given rise to the term **design for recycling (DFR),** referring to product design that takes into account the ability to disassemble a used product to recover the recyclable parts.

Design for recycling (DFR) Design that facilitates the recovery of materials and components in used products for reuse.

Xerox Diverts 2 Billion Pounds of Waste from Landfills through Green Initiatives

READING

By recycling yet one more 5-pound toner cartridge from a Xerox multifunction system, Xerox Corporation announced today it has surpassed a major sustainability milestone by diverting more than 2 billion pounds of electronic waste from landfills around the world through waste-free initiatives that create sustainability benefits for the company and its customers.

Launched in 1991, long before sustainability was on most companies' radar screens, Xerox's environmental program achieved the 2-billion-pound milestone by waste avoidance in two areas: reuse and recycling in imaging supplies and product take-back and recycling and parts reuse. In addition, Xerox integrates innovative environmental priorities into manufacturing operations to add to its recycling efforts.

"Xerox's experience with reuse, recycling and remanufacturing has not only kept waste out of landfills, but saved the company more than $2 billion as it did so," said Patricia Calkins, Xerox vice president, Environment, Health and Safety. "If that amount of waste were loaded into garbage trucks, it would fill more than 160,000 trucks, stretching more than 1,000 miles, from Seattle to the Mexican border. We believe sustainability is an integral part of developing products, serving customers and posting profits."

Source: Xerox Press Release, November 9, 2007.

Maria's Market is the main supermarket in Recycle City. Maria tries to stock items and provide services in her store that reduce the amount of material going into the waste stream and encourage reuse and recycling.

Maria realized that the first and best thing she should do was to reduce the amount of waste her customers had to throw away after they bought products at her market.

Maria

To reduce the amount of waste and its impact on the environment, Maria began to stock items in the store that contained fewer harmful ingredients and used less packaging. To reduce packaging and wasted food, she created a section in the store where shoppers could buy food in bulk, measuring out the exact amounts they needed.

Maria also set up a program to reuse those things that could be reused, such as cardboard boxes that shoppers could use to carry their purchases and bring back to the store on their next visit. She also gave customers discounts for returning their plastic bags the next time they shopped and for bringing their own cloth sacks to carry groceries home.

Finally, Maria made sure that many of the items in the store could be easily recycled. She set up well-marked collection containers to make it easy for shoppers to participate in the market's recycling program. Maria knows that recycling keeps useful materials from going into landfills, helping to preserve the land in and around Recycle City for other uses, like parks and schools.

Paper or Plastic?

Should you ask for a paper or plastic bag at the checkout counter? There's no easy answer. The materials needed to make either bag come from our natural resources.

- Paper comes from wood, which comes from trees, which grow in the earth's soil.
- Plastic is made from petroleum, also known as fossil fuel. Petroleum is made by the decomposition (breaking down) of ancient plants and animals inside the earth.

The trees needed to make paper are considered renewable resources. That means more trees can be planted to take the place of trees that are cut down to make paper and other products. But, trees take many years to replace because they grow slowly. Once paper is made, it can be recycled and used to create more paper goods. Making it into new paper, however, uses water and energy.

Petroleum needed to make plastic is considered a nonrenewable resource. Like aluminum, tin, and steel, petroleum is not renewable because it is the result of geological processes that take millions of years to complete. When used up, the earth's petroleum reserves will be gone for a long, long time. While plastic bags are easy to reuse, they're seldom recycled, and lots and lots of them get dumped into landfills.

Re-use this bag
the next time you shop
and
receive
5¢
credit
towards your purchase.

The best solution is to use a cloth bag or knapsack for grocery shopping, or to bring your old plastic or paper bag back to the store when you shop again. (Some stores, like Maria's Market in Recycle City, credit your grocery bill for reusing old bags because they don't have to buy as many new ones.) If you only purchase one or two items, you might not need a bag at all.

Recycling Igloos

In many parts of the country, supermarkets place recycling containers near the store to encourage their customers to recycle. (They can be any shape really, but Recycle City uses these brightly colored igloos because they're fun.)

These igloos are used to collect bottles, cans, and plastic from Maria's Market shoppers. Twice a week, trucks from the local Materials Recovery Facility come by to empty the igloos and take the items for recycling.

Cardboard Boxes

The cardboard boxes used to ship food to Maria's Market can be put to a variety of other uses once the food has been unpacked. The folks at the market let Recycle City residents come by and pick up cartons for storing things or moving to a new home. Any cartons that aren't claimed by the residents are broken down and put into a pile so they can be collected, recycled, and made into other things, like new boxes, paper bags, building insulation, animal bedding, or packaging materials.

Reduced Packaging

When the buyers at Maria's Market place orders to restock the store, they try to order items with very little packaging, or that use ecological packaging (ones requiring as little energy and as few resources as possible to produce).

Maria's buyers also try to stock products that come in refillable containers. Products that don't harm the environment and come in ecologically friendly packages are called green products.

(continued)

(concluded)

Packaging that isn't environmentally friendly includes products that are wrapped in several layers of plastic, use plastic foam, or have individually wrapped packages inside of a larger wrapped package.

Maria's buyers let the manufacturers who make products for the grocery shelves know that they and their Recycle City customers would rather buy products wrapped in environmentally friendly packages than ones that aren't. Using this kind of packaging is good for the manufacturer's business.

Bulk and Fresh Foods

Packaging materials make up more than 30 percent of all consumer waste. Maria's Market offers shoppers many fresh foods and bulk foods to help reduce the amount of waste from too much packaging.

Fresh foods, such as bananas, oranges, and nuts, come in their own natural packaging and are excellent sources of nutrition.

Bulk items and food purchased in bulk quantities allow Maria's shoppers to decide exactly how much they want to keep on hand. For small needs, folks measure out the exact quantity they want, helping to reduce food waste. For larger needs, they can buy bulk quantities, which usually use less packaging material and cost less.

When purchasing fresh foods or buying in bulk, shoppers can put their purchases into refillable containers they bring to the store or into the recyclable or reusable bags Maria provides.

Paper Towels and Other Paper Items

Many paper products on the shelves today have already been recycled. Buying recycled products saves valuable natural resources and helps to create a market for those materials. When manufacturers know that shoppers want recyclable goods, they will make more of them.

In Maria's Market, the popularity of paper towels and toilet paper made from recycled materials ensures that fewer new trees have to be cut down to produce new products.

Source: Excerpted from http://www.eps.gov/recyclecity/print/supermarket.htm.

OTHER DESIGN CONSIDERATIONS

Aside from legal, ethical, environmental, and human considerations designers must also take into account product or service life cycles, how much standardization to incorporate, product or service reliability, and the range of operating conditions under which a product or service must function. These topics are discussed in this section. We begin with life cycles.

Strategies for Product or Service Life Stages

Most, but not all, products and services go through a series of stages over their useful life, sometimes referred to as their life cycle, as shown in Figure 4.1. Demand typically varies by phase. Different phases call for different strategies. In every phase, forecasts of demand and cash flow are key inputs for strategy.

When a product or service is introduced, it may be treated as a curiosity item. Many potential buyers may suspect that all the bugs haven't been worked out and that the price may drop after the introductory period. Strategically, companies must carefully weigh the trade-offs in getting all the bugs out versus getting a leap on the competition, as well as getting to the market at an advantageous time. For example, introducing new high-tech products or features

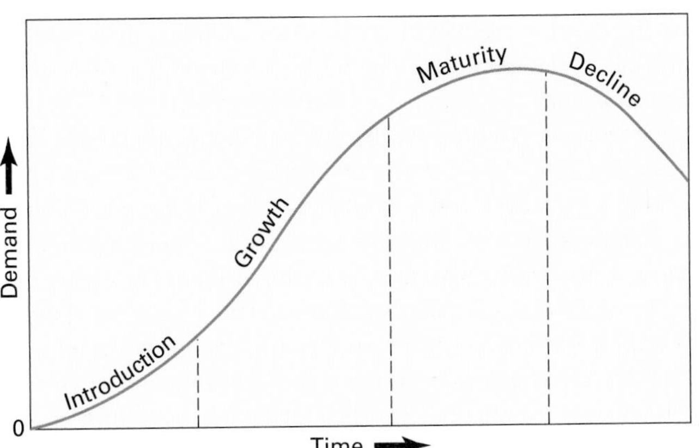

FIGURE 4.1
Products or services often go through stages over time

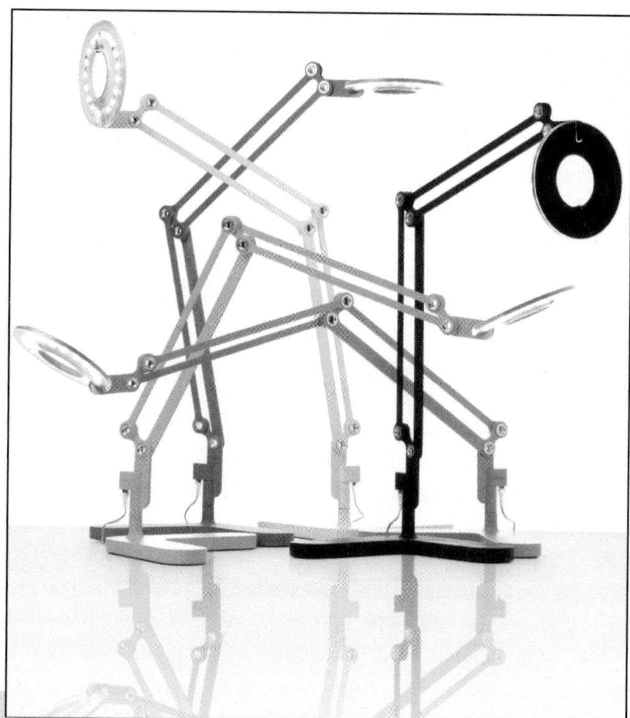

International Design Excellence Award Winners: This performance basketball shoe is made from manufacturing waste. It incorporates leftover materials—leather, foam, and rubber—into new shoes without sacrificing any of the performance aspects from shoes made from virgin materials. The task lamp puts the light right where you need it. A concentrated array of 15 high-power LEDs provides a brighter light output than most other lamps. Its 180-degree movement allows precise adjustability without taking up valuable work space

during peak back-to-school buying periods or holiday buying periods can be highly desirable. It is important to have a reasonable forecast of initial demand so an adequate supply of product or an adequate service capacity is in place.

Over time, design improvements and increasing demand yield higher reliability and lower costs, leading the growth in demand. In the growth phase, it is important to obtain accurate projections of the demand growth rate and how long that will persist, and then to ensure that capacity increases coincide with increasing demand.

In the next phase, the product or service reaches maturity, and demand levels off. Few, if any, design changes are needed. Generally, costs are low and productivity is high. An accurate forecast of how long this phase will last before the market becomes saturated and the decline phase begins is important.

In the decline phase, decisions must be made on whether to discontinue a product or service and replace it with new ones or abandon the market, or to attempt to find new uses or new users for the existing product or service. For example, duct tape and baking soda are two products that have been employed well beyond their original uses of taping heating and cooling ducts and cooking. The advantages of keeping existing products or services can be tremendous. The same workers can produce the product or provide the service using much of the same equipment, the same supply chain, and perhaps the same distribution channels. Consequently, costs tend to be very low, and additional resource needs and training needs are low.

Some products do not exhibit life cycles: wooden pencils; paper clips; nails; knives, forks, and spoons; drinking glasses; and similar items. However, most new products do.

Some service life cycles are related to the life cycles of products. For example, as older products are phased out, services such as installation and repair of the older products also phase out.

Wide variations exist in the amount of time a particular product or service takes to pass through a given phase of its life cycle: some pass through various stages in a relatively short period; others take considerably longer. Often it is a matter of the basic *need* for the item and the *rate of technological change.* Some toys, novelty items, and style items have a life cycle of less than one year, whereas other, more useful items, such as clothes washers and dryers, may last for many years before yielding to technological change.

Degree of Standardization

An important issue that often arises in both product/service design and process design is the degree of standardization. **Standardization** refers to the extent to which there is absence of variety in a product, service, or process. Standardized products are made in large quantities of identical items; calculators, computers, and 2 percent milk are examples. Standardized service implies that every customer or item processed receives essentially the same service. An automatic car wash is a good example; each car, regardless of how clean or dirty it is, receives the same service. Standardized processes deliver standardized service or produce standardized goods.

Standardization Extent to which a product, service, or process lacks variety.

Standardization carries a number of important benefits as well as certain disadvantages. Standardized products are immediately available to customers. Standardized products mean *interchangeable parts,* which greatly lower the cost of production while increasing productivity and making replacement or repair relatively easy compared with that of customized parts. Design costs are generally lower. For example, automobile producers standardize key components of automobiles across product lines; components such as brakes, electrical systems, and other "under-the-skin" parts would be the same for all car models. By reducing variety, companies save time and money while increasing quality and reliability of their products.

Another benefit of standardization is reduced time and cost to train employees and reduced time to design jobs. Similarly, scheduling of work, inventory handling, and purchasing and accounting activities become much more routine, and quality is more consistent.

Lack of standardization can at times lead to serious difficulties and competitive struggles. For example, the use by U.S. manufacturers of the English system of measurement, while most of the rest of the world's manufacturers use the metric system, has led to problems in selling U.S. goods in foreign countries and in buying foreign machines for use in the United States. This may make it more difficult for U.S. firms to compete in the European Union.

Standardization also has disadvantages. A major one relates to the reduction in variety. This can limit the range of customers to whom a product or service appeals. And that creates a risk that a competitor will introduce a better product or greater variety and realize a competitive advantage. Another disadvantage is that a manufacturer may freeze (standardize) a design prematurely and, once the design is frozen, find compelling reasons to resist modification.

Obviously, designers must consider important issues related to standardization when making choices. The major advantages and disadvantages of standardization are summarized in Table 4.2.

Designing for Mass Customization

Companies like standardization because it enables them to produce high volumes of relatively low-cost products, albeit products with little variety. Customers, on the other hand, typically prefer more variety, although they like the low cost. The question for producers is how to resolve these issues without (1) losing the benefits of standardization and (2) incurring a host

TABLE 4.2
Advantages and disadvantages of standardization

Advantages	1. Fewer parts to deal with in inventory and in manufacturing.
	2. Reduced training costs and time.
	3. More routine purchasing, handling, and inspection procedures.
	4. Orders fillable from inventory.
	5. Opportunities for long production runs and automation.
	6. Need for fewer parts justifies increased expenditures on perfecting designs and improving quality control procedures.
Disadvantages	1. Designs may be frozen with too many imperfections remaining.
	2. High cost of design changes increases resistance to improvements.
	3. Decreased variety results in less consumer appeal.

of problems that are often linked to variety. These include increasing the resources needed to achieve design variety; increasing variety in the production process, which would add to the skills necessary to produce products, causing a decrease in productivity; creating an additional inventory burden during and after production, by having to carry replacement parts for the increased variety of parts; and adding to the difficulty of diagnosing and repairing product failures. The answer, at least for some companies, is **mass customization,** a strategy of producing standardized goods or services, but incorporating some degree of customization in the final product or service. Several tactics make this possible. One is *delayed differentiation,* and another is *modular design.*

Mass customization A strategy of producing basically standardized goods, but incorporating some degree of customization.

Delayed differentiation The process of producing, but not quite completing, a product or service until customer preferences are known.

Delayed differentiation is a *postponement* tactic: the process of producing, but not quite completing, a product or service, postponing completion until customer preferences or specifications are known. There are a number of variations of this. In the case of goods, almost-finished units might be held in inventory until customer orders are received, at which time customized features are incorporated, according to customer requests. For example, furniture makers can produce dining room sets, but not apply stain, allowing customers a choice of stains. Once the choice is made, the stain can be applied in a relatively short time, thus eliminating a long wait for customers, giving the seller a competitive advantage. Similarly, various e-mail or Internet services can be delivered to customers as standardized packages, which can then be modified according to the customer's preferences. Hewlett-Packard printers that are made in the United States but intended for foreign markets are mostly completed in domestic assembly plants and then finalized closer to the country of use. The result of delayed differentiation is a product or service with customized features that can be quickly produced, appealing to the customers' desire for variety and speed of delivery, and yet one that for the most part is standardized, enabling the producer to realize the benefits of standardized production. This technique is not new. Manufacturers of men's clothing, for example, produce suits with pants that have legs that are unfinished, allowing customers to tailor choices as to the exact length and whether to have cuffs or no cuffs. What is new is the extent to which business organizations are finding ways to incorporate this concept into a broad range of products and services.

Modular design A form of standardization in which component parts are grouped into modules that are easily replaced or interchanged.

Modular design is a form of standardization. Modules represent groupings of component parts into subassemblies, usually to the point where the individual parts lose their separate identity. One familiar example of modular design is computers, which have modular parts that can be replaced if they become defective. By arranging modules in different configurations, different computer capabilities can be obtained. For mass customization, modular design enables producers to quickly assemble products with modules to achieve a customized configuration for an individual customer, avoiding the long customer wait that would occur if individual parts had to be assembled. Dell Computers has successfully used this concept to become a dominant force in the PC industry by offering consumers the opportunity to configure modules according to their own specifications. Many other computer manufacturers now use a similar approach. Modular design also is found in the construction industry. One firm in Rochester, New York, makes prefabricated motel rooms complete with wiring, plumbing, and even room decorations in its factory and then moves the complete rooms by rail to the construction site, where they are integrated into the structure.

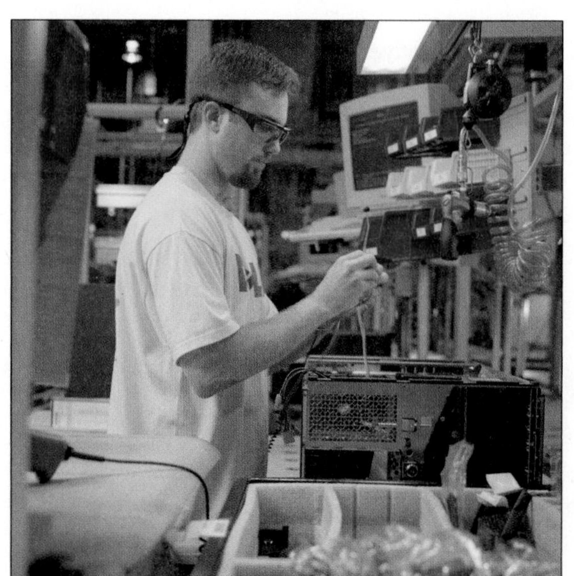

One advantage of modular design of equipment compared with nonmodular design is that failures are often easier to diagnose and remedy because there are fewer pieces to investigate. Similar advantages are found in ease of repair and replacement; the faulty module is conveniently removed and replaced with a good one. The manufacture and assembly of modules generally involve simplifications: Fewer parts are involved, so purchasing and inventory control become more routine, fabrication and assembly operations become more standardized, and training costs often are relatively low.

The main disadvantages of modular design stem from the decrease in variety: The number of possible configurations of modules is much less than the number of possible configurations based on individual components. Another disadvantage that is sometimes encountered is the inability to disassemble a module in order to replace a faulty part; the entire module must be scrapped—usually at a higher cost.

Reliability

Reliability is a measure of the ability of a product, a part, a service, or an entire system to perform its intended function under a prescribed set of conditions. The importance of reliability is underscored by its use by prospective buyers in comparing alternatives and by sellers as one determinant of price. Reliability also can have an impact on repeat sales, reflect on the product's image, and, if it is too low, create legal implications. Reliability is also a consideration for sustainability; the higher the reliability of a product, the fewer the resources that will be needed to maintain it, and the less frequently it will involve the three Rs.

Reliability The ability of a product, part, or system to perform its intended function under a prescribed set of conditions.

The term **failure** is used to describe a situation in which an item does not perform as intended. This includes not only instances in which the item does not function at all, but also instances in which the item's performance is substandard or it functions in a way not intended. For example, a smoke alarm might fail to respond to the presence of smoke (not operate at all), it might sound an alarm that is too faint to provide an adequate warning (substandard performance), or it might sound an alarm even though no smoke is present (unintended response).

Failure Situation in which a product, part, or system does not perform as intended.

Reliabilities are always specified with respect to certain conditions, called **normal operating conditions.** These can include load, temperature, and humidity ranges as well as operating procedures and maintenance schedules. Failure of users to heed these conditions often results in premature failure of parts or complete systems. For example, using a passenger car to tow heavy loads will cause excess wear and tear on the drive train; driving over potholes or curbs often results in untimely tire failure; and using a calculator to drive nails might have a marked impact on its usefulness for performing mathematical operations.

Normal operating conditions The set of conditions under which an item's reliability is specified.

Improving Reliability. Reliability can be improved in a number of ways, some of which are listed in Table 4.3.

Because overall system reliability is a function of the reliability of individual components, improvements in their reliability can increase system reliability. Unfortunately, inadequate production or assembly procedures can negate even the best of designs, and this is often a source of failures. System reliability can be increased by the use of backup components. Failures in actual use often can be reduced by upgrading user education and refining maintenance recommendations or procedures. Finally, it may be possible to increase the overall reliability of the system by simplifying the system (thereby reducing the number of components that could cause the system to fail) or altering component relationships (e.g., increasing the reliability of interfaces).

A fundamental question concerning improving reliability is: How much reliability is needed? Obviously, the reliability needed for a household light bulb isn't in the same category as the reliability needed for an airplane. So the answer to the question depends on the potential benefits of improvements and on the cost of those improvements. Generally speaking, reliability improvements become increasingly costly. Thus, although benefits initially may increase at a much faster rate than costs, the opposite eventually becomes true. The optimal level of reliability is the point where the incremental benefit received equals the incremental cost of obtaining it. In the short term, this trade-off is made in the context of relatively fixed

TABLE 4.3
Potential ways to improve reliability

1. Improve component design.
2. Improve production and/or assembly techniques.
3. Improve testing.
4. Use backups.
5. Improve preventive maintenance procedures.
6. Improve user education.
7. Improve system design.

parameters (e.g., costs). However, in the longer term, efforts to improve reliability and reduce costs can lead to higher optimal levels of reliability.

Robust Design

Some products or services will function as designed only within a narrow range of conditions, while others will perform as designed over a much broader range of conditions. The latter have **robust design.** Consider a pair of fine leather boots—obviously not made for trekking through mud or snow. Now consider a pair of heavy rubber boots—just the thing for mud or snow. The rubber boots have a design that is more *robust* than that of the fine leather boots.

Robust design Design that results in products or services that can function over a broad range of conditions.

The more robust a product or service, the less likely it will fail due to a change in the environment in which it is used or in which it is performed. Hence, the more designers can build robustness into the product or service, the better it should hold up, resulting in a higher level of customer satisfaction.

A similar argument can be made for robust design as it pertains to the production process. Environmental factors can have a negative effect on the quality of a product or service. The more resistant a design is to those influences, the less likely is a negative effect. For example, many products go through a heating process: food products, ceramics, steel, petroleum products, and pharmaceutical products. Furnaces often do not heat uniformly; heat may vary either by position in an oven or over an extended period of production. One approach to this problem might be to develop a superior oven; another might be to design a system that moves the product during heating to achieve uniformity. A robust-design approach would develop a product that is unaffected by minor variations in temperature during processing.

Taguchi's Approach. Japanese engineer Genichi Taguchi's approach is based on the concept of robust design. His premise is that it is often easier to design a product that is insensitive to environmental factors, either in manufacturing or in use, than to control the environmental factors.

The central feature of Taguchi's approach—and the feature used most often by U.S. companies—is *parameter design.* This involves determining the specification settings for both the product and the process that will result in robust design in terms of manufacturing variations, product deterioration, and conditions during use.

The Taguchi approach modifies the conventional statistical methods of experimental design. Consider this example. Suppose a company will use 12 chemicals in a new product it intends to produce. There are two suppliers for these chemicals, but the chemical concentrations vary slightly between the two suppliers. Classical design of experiments would require $2^{12} = 4{,}096$ test runs to determine which combination of chemicals would be optimum. Taguchi's approach would involve only testing a portion of the possible combinations. Relying on experts to identify the variables that would be most likely to affect important performance, the number of combinations would be dramatically reduced, perhaps to, say, 32. Identifying the best combination in the smaller sample might be a near-optimal combination instead of the optimal combination. The value of this approach is its ability to achieve major advances in product or process design fairly quickly, using a relatively small number of experiments.

Critics charge that Taguchi's methods are inefficient and incorrect, and often lead to nonoptimal solutions. Nonetheless, his methods are widely used and have been credited with helping to achieve major improvements in U.S. products and manufacturing processes.

Degree of Newness

Product or service design change can range from the modification of an existing product or service to an entirely new product or service:

1. Modification of an existing product or service.
2. Expansion of an existing product line or service offering.
3. Clone of a competitor's product or service.
4. New product or service.

The degree of change affects the newness to the organization and the newness to the market. For the organization, a low level of newness can mean a fairly quick and easy transition to producing the new product, while a high level of newness would likely mean a slower and more difficult, and therefore more costly, transition. For the market, a low level of newness would mean little difficulty with market acceptance, but possibly low profit potential. Even in instances of low profit potential, organizations might use this strategy to maintain market share. A high level of newness, on the other hand, might mean more difficulty with acceptance, or it might mean a rapid gain in market share with a high potential for profits. Unfortunately, there is no way around these issues. It is important to carefully assess the risks and potential benefits of any design change, taking into account clearly identified customer wants.

Quality Function Deployment

Obtaining input from customers is essential to assure that they will want what is offered for sale. Although obtaining input can be informal through discussions with customers, there is a formal way to document customer wants. **Quality function deployment (QFD)** is a structured approach for integrating the "voice of the customer" into both the product and service development process. The purpose is to ensure that customer requirements are factored into every aspect of the process. Listening to and understanding the customer is the central feature of QFD. Requirements often take the form of a general statement such as, "It should be easy to adjust the cutting height of the lawn mower." Once the requirements are known, they must be translated into technical terms related to the product or service. For example, a statement about changing the height of the lawn mower may relate to the mechanism used to accomplish that, its position, instructions for use, tightness of the spring that controls the mechanism, or materials needed. For manufacturing purposes, these must be related to the materials, dimensions, and equipment used for processing.

Quality function deployment (QFD) An approach that integrates the "voice of the customer" into both product and service development.

The structure of QFD is based on a set of matrices. The main matrix relates customer requirements (what) and their corresponding technical requirements (how). This matrix is illustrated in Figure 4.2. The matrix provides a structure for data collection.

Additional features are usually added to the basic matrix to broaden the scope of analysis. Typical additional features include importance weightings and competitive evaluations. A correlational matrix is usually constructed for technical requirements; this can reveal conflicting technical requirements. With these additional features, the set of matrices has the form illustrated in Figure 4.3. It is often referred to as the *house of quality* because of its houselike appearance.

FIGURE 4.2 An example of the house of quality: the main QFD matrix

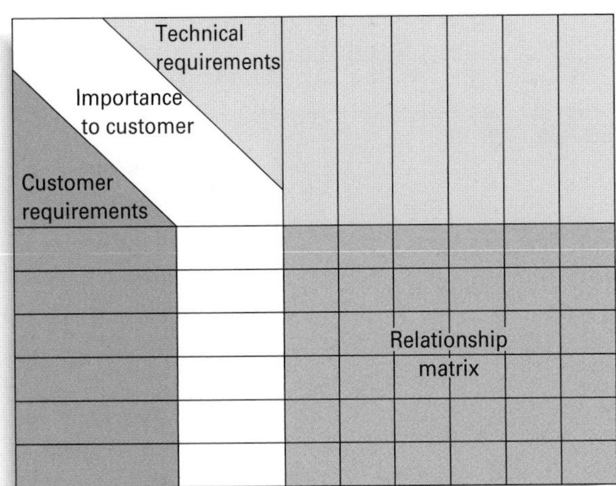

Source: Ernst and Young Consulting Group, *Total Quality* (Homewood, IL: Dow-Jones Irwin, 1991), p. 121. Reprinted by permission.

FIGURE 4.3 The house of quality

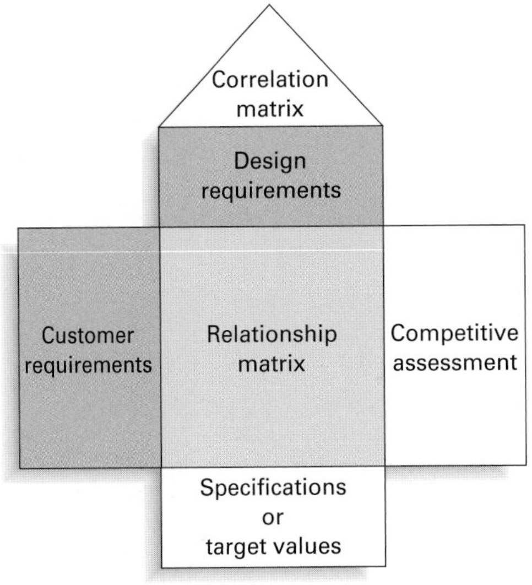

An analysis using this format is shown in Figure 4.4. The data relate to a commercial printer (customer) and the company that supplies the paper. At first glance, the display appears complex. It contains a considerable amount of information for product and process planning. Therefore, let's break it up into separate parts and consider them one at a time. To start, a key part is the list of customer requirements on the left side of the figure. Next, note the technical requirements, listed vertically near the top. The key relationships and their degree of importance are shown in the center of the figure. The circle with a dot inside indicates the strongest positive relationship; that is, it denotes the most important technical requirements for satisfying customer requirements. Now look at the "importance to customer" numbers that are shown next to each customer requirement (3 is the most important). Designers will take into account the importance values and the strength of correlation in determining where to focus the greatest effort.

Next, consider the correlation matrix at the top of the "house." Of special interest is the strong negative correlation between "paper thickness" and "roll roundness." Designers will have to find some way to overcome that or make a trade-off decision.

FIGURE 4.4
An example of the house of quality

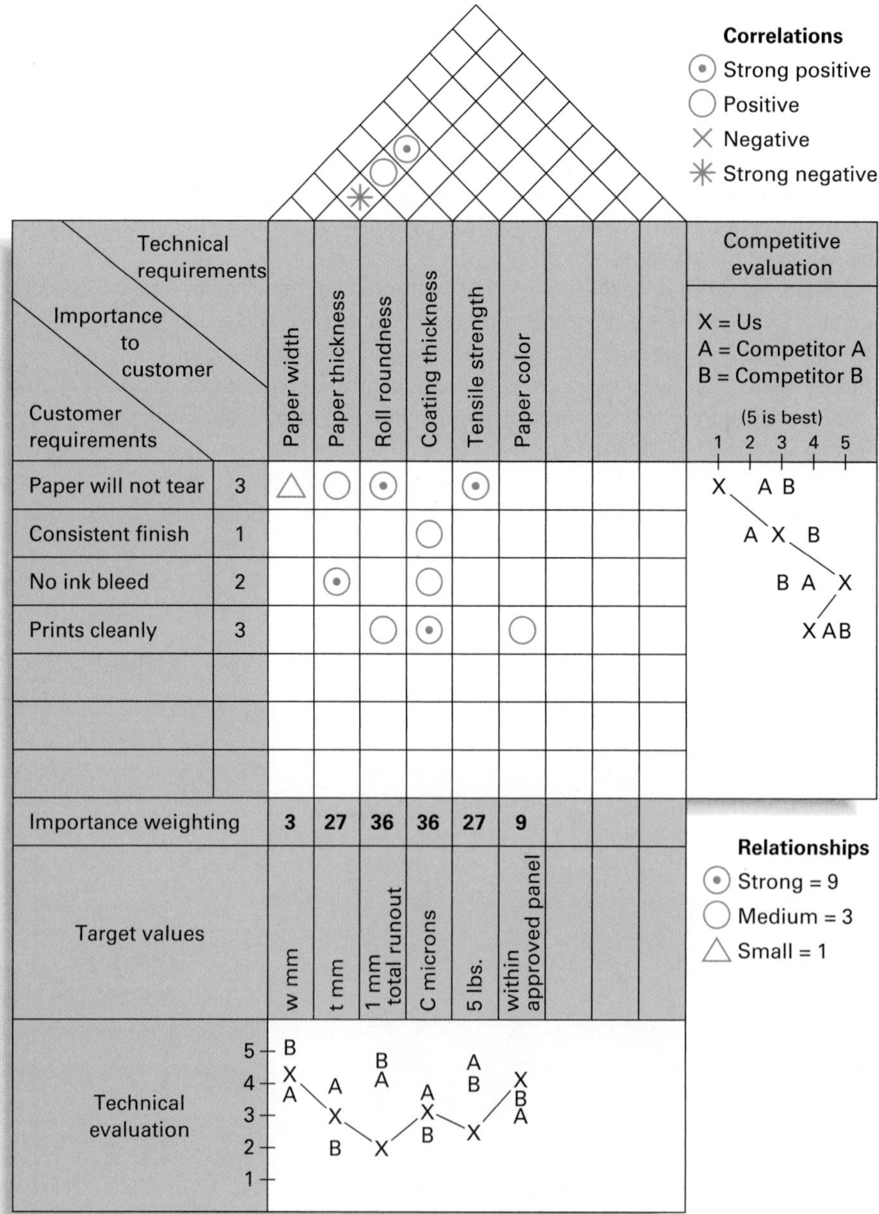

FIGURE 4.5 The house of quality sequence

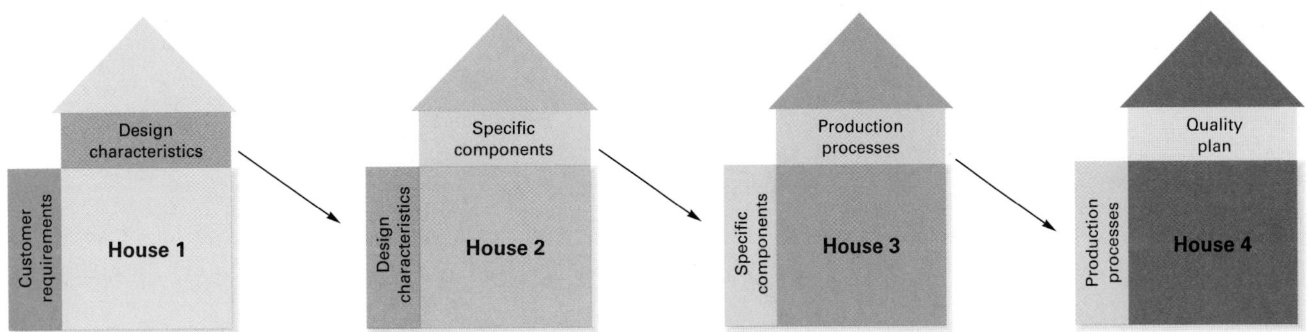

On the right side of the figure is a competitive evaluation comparing the supplier's performance on the customer requirements with each of the two key competitors (A and B). For example, the supplier (X) is worst on the first customer requirement and best on the third customer requirement. The line connects the X performances. Ideally, design will cause all of the Xs to be in the highest positions.

Across the bottom of Figure 4.4 are importance weightings, target values, and technical evaluations. The technical evaluations can be interpreted in a manner similar to that of the competitive evaluations (note the line connecting the Xs). The target values typically contain technical specifications, which we will not discuss. The importance weightings are the sums of values assigned to the relationships (see the lower right-hand key for relationship weights). The 3 in the first column is the product of the importance to the customer, 3, and the small (Δ) weight, 1. The importance weightings and target evaluations help designers focus on desired results. In this example, the first technical requirement has the lowest importance weighting, while the next four technical requirements all have relatively high importance weightings.

The house of quality approach involves a sequence of "houses," beginning with design characteristics, which leads to specific components, then production processes, and finally, a quality plan. The sequence is illustrated in Figure 4.5. Although the details of each house are beyond the scope of this text, Figure 4.5 provides a conceptual understanding of the progression involved.

The Kano Model

The *Kano model* is a theory of product and service design developed by Dr. Noriaki Kano, a Japanese professor, who offered a perspective on customer perceptions of quality different from the traditional view that "more is better." Instead, he proposed different categories of quality and posited that understanding them would better position designers to assess and address quality needs. His model provides insights into the attributes that are perceived to be important to customers. The model employs three definitions of quality: basic, performance, and excitement.

Basic quality refers to customer requirements that have only a limited effect on customer satisfaction if present, but lead to dissatisfaction if not present. For example, putting a very short cord on an electrical appliance will likely result in customer dissatisfaction, but beyond a certain length (e.g., 4 feet), adding more cord will not lead to increased levels of customer satisfaction. Performance quality refers to customer requirements that generate satisfaction or dissatisfaction in proportion to their level of functionality and appeal. For example, increasing the tread life of a tire or the amount of time house paint will last will add to customer satisfaction. Excitement quality refers to a feature or attribute that was unexpected by the customer and causes excitement (the "wow" factor), such as a voucher for dinner for two at the hotel restaurant when checking in. Figure 4.6A portrays how the three definitions of quality influence customer satisfaction or dissatisfaction relative to the degree of implementation. Note that features that are perceived by customers as basic quality result in dissatisfaction if they are missing or at low levels, but do not result in customer satisfaction if they are present, even

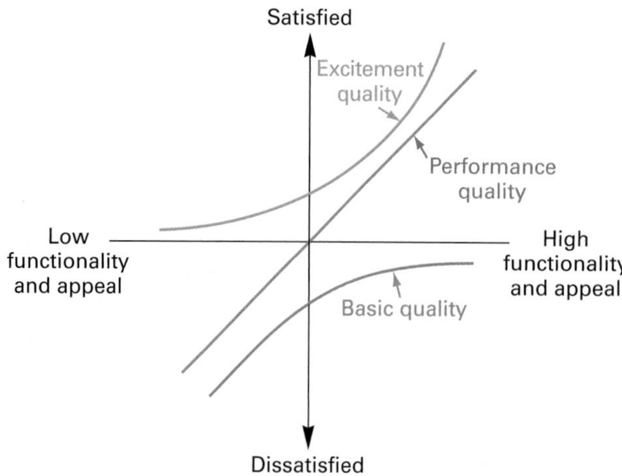

FIGURE 4.6A
The Kano model

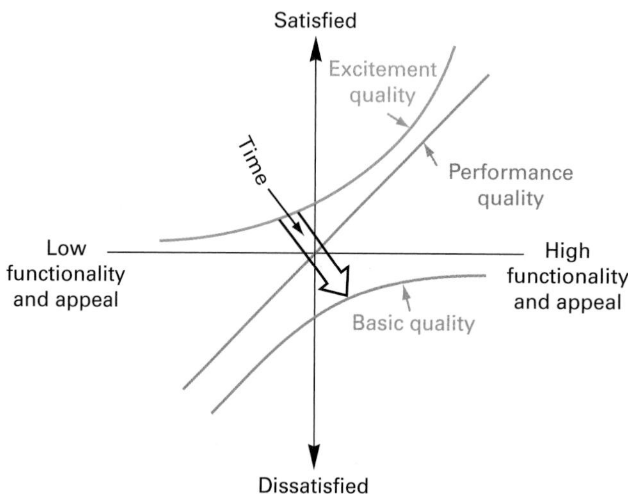

FIGURE 4.6B
As time passes, excitement factors become performance factors, and performance factors become basic factors

at high levels. Performance factors can result in satisfaction or dissatisfaction, depending on the degree to which they are present. Excitement factors, because they are unexpected, do not result in dissatisfaction when they are absent or at low levels, but have the potential for disproportionate levels of satisfaction if they are present.

Over time, features that excited become performance features, and performance features soon become basic quality features, as illustrated in Figure 4.6B. The rates at which various design elements are migrating is an important input from marketing that will enable designers to continue to satisfy and delight customers and not waste efforts on improving what have become basic quality features.

The lesson of the Kano model is that design elements that fall into each aspect of quality must first be determined. Once basic needs have been met, additional efforts in those areas should not be pursued. For performance features, cost–benefit analysis comes into play, and these features should be included as long as the benefit exceeds the cost. Excitement features pose somewhat of a challenge. Customers are not likely to indicate excitement factors in surveys because they don't know that they want them. However, small increases in such factors produce disproportional increases in customer satisfaction and generally increase brand loyalty, so it is important for companies to strive to identify and include these features when economically feasible.

The Kano model can be used in conjunction with QFD as well as in six sigma projects (see Chapter 9 for a discussion of six sigma).

PHASES IN PRODUCT DESIGN AND DEVELOPMENT

Product design and development generally proceeds in a series of phases (see Table 4.4):

Feasibility analysis. Feasibility analysis entails market analysis (demand), economic analysis (development cost and production cost, profit potential), and technical analysis (capacity requirements and availability, and the skills needed). Also, it is necessary to answer the question, Does it fit with the mission? It requires collaboration among marketing, finance, accounting, engineering, and operations.

Product specifications. This involves detailed descriptions of what is needed to meet (or exceed) customer wants, and requires collaboration between legal, marketing, and operations.

Process specifications. Once product specifications have been set, attention turns to specifications for the process that will be needed to produce the product. Alternatives must be weighed in terms of cost, availability of resources, profit potential, and quality. This involves collaboration between accounting and operations.

Prototype development. With product and process specifications complete, one (or a few) units are made to see if there are any problems with the product or process specifications.

Design review. At this stage, any necessary changes are made or the project is abandoned. Marketing, finance, engineering, design, and operations collaborate to determine whether to proceed or abandon.

Market test. A market test is used to determine the extent of consumer acceptance. If unsuccessful, the product returns to the design review phase. This phase is handled by marketing.

Product introduction. The new product is promoted. This phase is handled by marketing.

Follow-up evaluation. Based on user feedback, changes may be made or forecasts refined. This phase is handled by marketing.

DESIGNING FOR PRODUCTION

In this section, you will learn about design techniques that have greater applicability for the design of products than the design of services. Even so, you will see that they do have some relevance for service design. The topics include concurrent engineering, computer-assisted design, designing for assembly and disassembly, and the use of components for similar products.

Concurrent Engineering

To achieve a smoother transition from product design to production, and to decrease product development time, many companies are using *simultaneous development,* or concurrent engineering. In its narrowest sense, **concurrent engineering** means bringing design and manufacturing engineering people together early in the design phase to simultaneously develop the product and the processes for creating the product. More recently, this concept has been enlarged to include manufacturing personnel (e.g., materials specialists) and marketing and purchasing personnel in loosely integrated, cross-functional teams. In addition, the views of suppliers and customers are frequently sought. The purpose, of course, is to achieve product designs that reflect customer wants as well as manufacturing capabilities.

Concurrent engineering Bringing engineering design and manufacturing personnel together early in the design phase.

TABLE 4.4 Phases in the product development process

1. Feasibility analysis	5. Design review
2. Product specifications	6. Market test
3. Process specifications	7. Product introduction
4. Prototype development	8. Follow-up evaluation

Traditionally, designers developed a new product without any input from manufacturing, and then turned over the design to manufacturing, which would then have to develop a process for making the new product. This "over-the-wall" approach created tremendous challenges for manufacturing, generating numerous conflicts and greatly increasing the time needed to successfully produce a new product. It also contributed to an "us versus them" mentality.

For these and similar reasons, the simultaneous development approach has great appeal. Among the key advantages of this approach are the following:

1. Manufacturing personnel are able to identify production capabilities and capacities. Very often, they have some latitude in design in terms of selecting suitable materials and processes. Knowledge of production capabilities can help in the selection process. In addition, cost and quality considerations can be greatly influenced by design, and conflicts during production can be greatly reduced.
2. Design or procurement of critical tooling, some of which might have long lead times, can occur early in the process. This can result in a major shortening of the product development process, which could be a key competitive advantage.
3. The technical feasibility of a particular design or a portion of a design can be assessed early on. Again, this can avoid serious problems during production.
4. The emphasis can be on *problem* resolution instead of *conflict* resolution.

However, despite the advantages of concurrent engineering, a number of potential difficulties exist in this co-development approach. Two key ones are the following:

1. Long-standing boundaries between design and manufacturing can be difficult to overcome. Simply bringing a group of people together and thinking that they will be able to work together effectively is probably naive.
2. There must be extra communication and flexibility if the process is to work, and these can be difficult to achieve.

Hence, managers should plan to devote special attention if this approach is to work.

Computer-Aided Design (CAD)

Computer-aided design (CAD) Product design using computer graphics.

Computers are increasingly used for product design. **Computer-aided design (CAD)** uses computer graphics for product design. The designer can modify an existing design or create a new one on a monitor by means of a light pen, a keyboard, a joystick, or a similar device. Once the design is entered into the computer, the designer can maneuver it on the screen: It can be rotated to provide the designer with different perspectives, it can be split apart to give the designer a view of the inside, and a portion of it can be enlarged for closer examination. The designer can obtain a printed version of the completed design and file it electronically, making it accessible to people in the firm who need this information (e.g., marketing, operations).

A growing number of products are being designed in this way, including transformers, automobile parts, aircraft parts, integrated circuits, and electric motors.

A major benefit of CAD is the increased productivity of designers. No longer is it necessary to laboriously prepare mechanical drawings of products or parts and revise them repeatedly to correct errors or incorporate revisions. A rough estimate is that CAD increases the productivity of designers from 3 to 10 times. A second major benefit of CAD is the creation of a database for manufacturing that can supply needed information on product geometry and dimensions, tolerances, material specifications, and so on. It should be noted, however, that CAD needs this database to function and that this entails a considerable amount of effort.

Some CAD systems allow the designer to perform engineering and cost analyses on proposed designs. For instance, the computer can determine the weight and volume of a part and do stress analysis as well. When there are a number of alternative designs, the computer can quickly go through the possibilities and identify the best one, given the designer's criteria. CAD that includes finite element analysis (FEA) capability can greatly shorten the time to

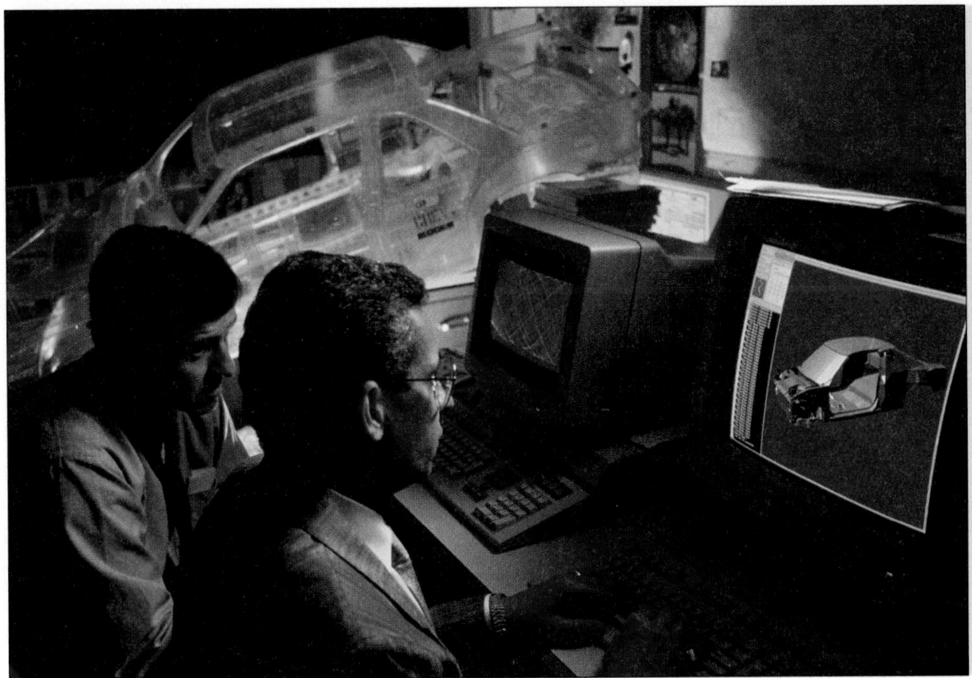

Computer-aided design (CAD) is used to design components and products to exact measurement and detail. At General Motors in Michigan a design team works on a new car design at the computer.

market of new products. It enables developers to perform simulations that aid in the design, analysis, and commercialization of new products. Designers in industries such as aeronautics, biomechanics, and automotives use FEA.

Production Requirements

As noted earlier in the chapter, designers must take into account *production capabilities.* Design needs to clearly understand the capabilities of production (e.g., equipment, skills, types of materials, schedules, technologies, special abilities). This helps in choosing designs that match capabilities. When opportunities and capabilities do not match, management must consider the potential for expanding or changing capabilities to take advantage of those opportunities.

Forecasts of future demand can be very useful, supplying information on the timing and volume of demand, and information on demands for new products and services.

Manufacturability is a key concern for manufactured goods: Ease of fabrication and/or assembly is important for cost, productivity, and quality. With services, ease of providing the service, cost, productivity, and quality are of great concern.

The term **design for manufacturing (DFM)** is used to indicate the designing of products that are compatible with an organization's capabilities. A related concept in manufacturing is **design for assembly (DFA).** A good design must take into account not only how a product will be fabricated, but also how it will be assembled. Design for assembly focuses on reducing the number of parts in an assembly, as well as on the assembly methods and sequence that will be employed. Another, more general term, **manufacturability,** is sometimes used when referring to the ease with which products can be fabricated and/or assembled.

Design for manufacturing (DFM) The designing of products that are compatible with an organization's capabilities.

Design for assembly (DFA) Design that focuses on reducing the number of parts in a product and on assembly methods and sequence.

Manufacturability The ease of fabrication and/or assembly.

Component Commonality

Companies often have multiple products or services to offer customers. Often, these products or services have a high degree of similarity of features and components. This is particularly true of *product families,* but it is also true of many services. Companies can realize significant benefits when a part can be used in multiple products. For example, car manufacturers employ this tactic by using internal components such as water pumps, engines, and transmissions on several automobile nameplates. In addition to the savings in design time, companies reap benefits through standard training for assembly and installation, increased opportunities for savings by buying in bulk from suppliers, and commonality of parts for repair, which reduces the inventory dealers and auto parts stores must carry. Similar benefits accrue in services. For example, in automobile repair, component commonality means less training is needed because the variety of jobs is reduced. The same applies to appliance repair, where commonality and *substitutability* of parts are typical. Multiple-use forms in financial and medical services is another example. Computer software often comprises a number of modules that are commonly used for similar applications, thereby saving the time and cost to write the code for major portions of the software. Tool manufacturers use a design that allows tool users to attach different power tools to a common power source. Similarly, Hewlett-Packard has a universal power source that can be used with a variety of computer hardware.

SERVICE DESIGN

SERVICE

There are many similarities between product and service design. However, there are some important differences as well, owing to the nature of services. One major difference is that unlike manufacturing, where production and delivery are usually separated in time, services are usually created and delivered *simultaneously.*

Service Something that is done to or for a customer.

Service delivery system The facilities, processes, and skills needed to provide a service.

Product bundle The combination of goods and services provided to a customer.

Service package The physical resources needed to perform the service, the accompanying goods, and the explicit and implicit services included.

Service refers to an *act,* something that is done to or for a customer (client, patient, etc.). It is provided by a **service delivery system,** which includes the facilities, processes, and skills needed to provide the service. Many services are not pure services, but part of a **product bundle**—the combination of goods and services provided to a customer. The service component in products is increasing. The ability to create and deliver reliable customer-oriented service is often a key competitive differentiator. Successful companies combine customer-oriented service with their products.

System design involves development or refinement of the overall **service package:**[1]

1. The physical resources needed.
2. The accompanying goods that are purchased or consumed by the customer, or provided with the service.
3. Explicit services (the essential/core features of a service, such as tax preparation).
4. Implicit services (ancillary/extra features, such as friendliness, courtesy).

Overview of Service Design

SERVICE

Service design begins with the choice of a service strategy, which determines the nature and focus of the service, and the target market. This requires an assessment by top management of the potential market and profitability (or need, in the case of a nonprofit organization) of a particular service, and an assessment of the organization's ability to provide the service. Once decisions on the focus of the service and the target market have been made, the customer requirements and expectations of the target market must be determined.

Two key issues in service design are the degree of variation in service requirements and the degree of customer contact and customer involvement in the delivery system. These have an impact on the degree to which service can be standardized or must be customized. The lower the degree of customer contact and service requirement variability, the more standardized the service can be. Service design with no contact and little or no processing variability is very much like product design. Conversely, high variability and high customer contact generally mean the service must be highly customized. A related consideration in service design is the opportunity for selling: The greater the degree of customer contact, the greater the opportunities for selling.

[1]Adapted from James A. Fitzsimmons and Mona J. Fitzsimmons, *Service Management for Competitive Advantage* (New York: McGraw-Hill, 1994). Copyright © 1994 McGraw-Hill Companies, Inc. Used with permission.

Differences between Service Design and Product Design

Service operations managers must contend with issues that may be insignificant or nonexistent for managers in a production setting. These include the following:

1. Products are generally tangible; services are generally intangible. Consequently, service design often focuses more on intangible factors (e.g., peace of mind, ambiance) than does product design.
2. In many instances services are created and delivered at the same time (e.g., a haircut, a car wash). In such instances there is less latitude in finding and correcting errors *before* the customer has a chance to discover them. Consequently, training, process design, and customer relations are particularly important.
3. Services cannot be inventoried. This poses restrictions on flexibility and makes capacity issues very important.
4. Services are highly visible to consumers and must be designed with that in mind; this adds an extra dimension to process design, one that usually is not present in product design.
5. Some services have low barriers to entry and exit. This places additional pressures on service design to be innovative and cost-effective.
6. Location is often important to service design, with convenience as a major factor. Hence, design of services and choice of location are often closely linked.
7. Service systems range from those with little or no customer contact to those that have a very high degree of customer contact. Here are some examples of those different types:

   Insulated technical core; little or no customer contact (e.g., software development).

   Production line; little or no customer contact (e.g., automatic car wash).

   Personalized service (e.g., haircut, medical service).

   Consumer participation (e.g., diet program, dance lessons).

   Self-service (e.g., supermarket).

   If there is little or no customer contact, service system design is like product system design.
8. Demand variability alternately creates waiting lines or idle service resources.

When demand variability is a factor, designers may approach service design from one of two perspectives. One is a cost and efficiency perspective, and the other is a customer perspective.

Basing design objectives on cost and efficiency is essentially a "product design approach" to service design. Because customer participation makes both quality and demand variability more difficult to manage, designers may opt to limit customer participation in the process where possible. Alternatively, designers may use staff flexibility as a means of dealing with demand variability.

In services, a significant aspect of perceived quality relates to the intangibles that are part of the service package. Designers must proceed with caution because attempts to achieve a high level of efficiency tend to depersonalize service and to create the risk of negatively altering the customer's perception of quality. Such attempts may involve the following:

1. Reducing consumer choices makes service more efficient, but it can be both frustrating and irritating for the customer. An example would be a cable company that bundles channels, rather than allowing customers to pick only the channels they want.
2. Standardizing or simplifying certain elements of service can reduce the cost of providing a service, but it risks eliminating features that some customers value, such as personal attention.
3. Incorporating flexibility in capacity management by employing part-time or temporary staff may involve the use of less-skilled or less-interested people, and service quality may suffer.

TABLE 4.5
Phases in service design process

1. Conceptualize.
    - Idea generation
    - Assessment of customer wants/needs (marketing)
    - Assessment of demand potential (marketing)
2. Identify service package components needed (operations and marketing).
3. Determine performance specifications (operations and marketing).
4. Translate performance specifications into design specifications.
5. Translate design specifications into delivery specifications.

Design objectives based on customer perspective require understanding the customer experience, and focusing on how to maintain control over service delivery to achieve customer satisfaction. The customer-oriented approach involves determining consumer wants and needs in order to understand relationships between service delivery and perceived quality. This enables designers to make enlightened choices in designing the delivery system.

Of course, designers must keep in mind that while depersonalizing service delivery for the sake of efficiency can negatively impact perceived quality, customers may not want or be willing to pay for highly personalized service either, so trade-offs may have to be made.

SERVICE

Phases in the Service Design Process

Table 4.5 lists the phases in the service design process. As you can see, they are quite similar to the phases of product design, except that the delivery system also must be designed.

Service Blueprinting

Service blueprint A method used in service design to describe and analyze a proposed service.

A useful tool for conceptualizing a service delivery system is the **service blueprint**, which is a method for describing and analyzing a service process. A service blueprint is much like an architectural drawing, but instead of showing building dimensions and other construction features, a service blueprint shows the basic customer and service actions involved in a service operation. Figure 4.7 illustrates a simple service blueprint for a restaurant. At the

FIGURE 4.7 A simple service blueprint for a restaurant

Customer actions	*Arrive*	*Seated*	*Order*	*Eat*		*Pay and leave*	
line of information							
Contact persons	Greeted by hostess Hostess checks reservation Hostess escorts customers to their table	Greeted by server Server provides menus Server fills water glasses	Server describes specials Server takes orders	Dinners are served	Server occasionally checks to see if any problems	Server brings the check Server receives payment	Busboy clears table
line of visibility							
Backstage contacts			Kitchen staff prepares food				Dishes are washed
line of internal interaction							
Support	Reservation system		Ordering food			Cashier	Laundry service

top of the figure are the customer actions, and just below are the related actions of the direct contact service people. Next are what are sometimes referred to as "backstage contacts"—in this example, the kitchen staff—and below those are the support, or "backroom," operations. In this example support operations include the reservation system, ordering of food and supplies, cashier, and the outsourcing of laundry service. Figure 4.7 is a simplified illustration; typically time estimates for actions and operations would be included.

The major steps in service blueprinting are as follows:

1. Establish boundaries for the service and decide on the level of detail needed.
2. Identify and determine the sequence of customer and service actions and interactions. A flowchart can be a useful tool for this.
3. Develop time estimates for each phase of the process, as well as time variability.
4. Identify potential failure points and develop a plan to prevent or minimize them, as well as a plan to respond to service errors.

Characteristics of Well-Designed Service Systems

There are a number of characteristics of well-designed service systems. They can serve as guidelines in developing a service system. They include the following:

1. Being consistent with the organization mission.
2. Being user-friendly.
3. Being robust if variability is a factor.
4. Being easy to sustain.
5. Being cost-effective.
6. Having value that is obvious to customers.
7. Having effective linkages between back-of-the-house operations (i.e., no contact with the customer) and front-of-the-house operations (i.e., direct contact with customers). Front operations should focus on customer service, while back operations should focus on speed and efficiency.
8. Having a single, unifying theme, such as convenience or speed.
9. Having design features and checks that will ensure service that is reliable and of high quality.

Challenges of Service Design

Variability is a major concern in most aspects of business operations, and it is particularly so in the design of service systems. Requirements tend to be variable, both in terms of differences in what customers want or need, and in terms of the timing of customer requests. Because services generally cannot be stored, there is the additional challenge of balancing supply and demand. This is less of a problem for systems in which the timing of services can be scheduled (e.g., doctor's appointment), but not so in others (e.g., emergency room visit).

Another challenge is that services can be difficult to describe precisely and are dynamic in nature, especially when there is a direct encounter with the customer (e.g., personal services), due to the large number of variables.

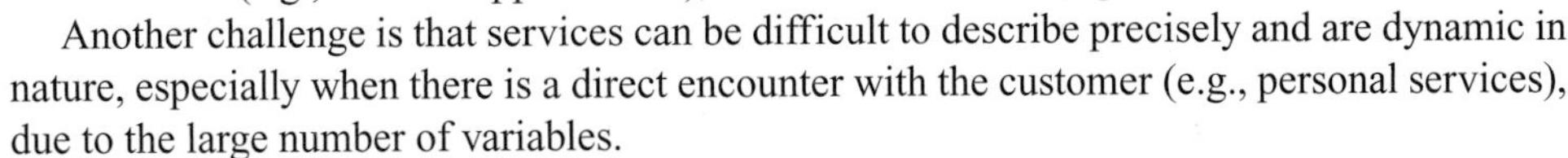

Guidelines for Successful Service Design

1. Define the service package in detail. A service blueprint may be helpful for this.
2. Focus on the operation from the customer's perspective. Consider how customer expectations and perceptions are managed during and after the service.
3. Consider the image that the service package will present both to customers and prospective customers.
4. Recognize that designers' familiarity with the system may give them a quite different perspective than that of the customer, and take steps to overcome this.

5. Make sure that managers are involved and will support the design once it is implemented.
6. Define quality for both tangibles and intangibles. Intangible standards are more difficult to define, but they must be addressed.
7. Make sure that recruitment, training, and reward policies are consistent with service expectations.
8. Establish procedures to handle both predictable and unpredictable events.
9. Establish systems to monitor, maintain, and improve service.

The Challenges of Managing Services

READING

Services can pose a variety of managerial challenges for managers—challenges that in manufacturing are either much less or nonexistent. And because services represent an increasing share of the economy, this places added importance to understanding and dealing with the challenges of managing services. Here are some of the main factors:

1. Jobs in service environments are often less structured than in manufacturing environments.
2. Customer contact is usually much higher in services.
3. In many services, worker skill levels are low compared to those of manufacturing workers.
4. Services are adding many new workers in low-skill, entry-level positions.
5. Employee turnover is often higher, especially in the low-skill jobs.
6. Input variability tends to be higher in many service environments than in manufacturing.
7. Service performance can be adversely affected by workers' emotions, distractions, customers' attitudes, and other factors, many of which are beyond managers' control.

Because of these factors, quality and costs are more difficult to control, productivity tends to be lower, the risk of customer dissatisfaction is greater, and employee motivation is more difficult.

Questions

1. What managerial challenges do services present that manufacturing does not?
2. Why does service management present more challenges than manufacturing?

OPERATIONS STRATEGY

Product and service design is a fertile area for achieving competitive advantage and/or increasing customer satisfaction. Potential sources of such benefits include the following:

- Packaging products and ancillary services to increase sales. Examples include selling PCs at a reduced cost with a two-year Internet access sign-up agreement, offering extended warranties on products, offering installation and service, and offering training with computer software.
- Using multiple-use platforms. Auto manufacturers use the same platform (basic chassis, say) for several nameplates (e.g., Jaguar S type, Lincoln LS, and Ford Thunderbird have shared the same platform). There are two basic computer platforms, PC and Mac, with many variations of computers using a particular platform.
- Implementing tactics that will achieve the benefits of high volume while satisfying customer needs for variety, such as mass customization.
- Continually monitoring products and services for small improvements rather than the "big bang" approach. Often the "little" things can have a positive, long-lasting effect on consumer attitudes and buying behavior.
- Shortening the time it takes to get new or redesigned goods and services to market.

A key competitive advantage of some companies is their ability to bring new products to market more quickly than their competitors. Companies using this "first-to-market" approach are able to enter markets ahead of their competitors, allowing them to set higher selling prices than otherwise due to absence of competition. Such a strategy is also a defense against competition from cheaper "clones" because the competitors always have to play "catch up."

From a design standpoint, reducing the time to market involves

- Using standardized components to create new but reliable products.
- Using technology such as computer-aided design (CAD) equipment to rapidly design new or modified products.
- Concurrent engineering to shorten engineering time.

SUMMARY

Product and service design is a key factor in satisfying the customer. To be successful in product and service design, organizations must be continually aware of what customers want, what the competition is doing, what government regulations are, and what new technologies are available.

The design process involves motivation, ideas for improvement, organizational capabilities, and forecasting. In addition to product life cycles, legal, environmental, and ethical considerations influence design choices. What degree of standardization designers should incorporate into designs is also an important consideration. A key objective for designers is to achieve a product or service design that will meet or exceed customer expectations, within cost or budget and taking into account the capabilities of operations. Although product design and service design are similar in some respects, a number of key differences exist between products and services that influence the way they are designed.

Successful design often incorporates many of these basic principles: Determine what customers want as a starting point; minimize the number of parts needed to manufacture an item or the number of steps to provide a service; simplify assembly or service, standardize as much as possible; and make the design robust. Trade-off decisions are common in design, and they involve such things as development time and cost, product or service cost, special features/performance, and product or service complexity.

Research and development efforts can play a significant role in product and process innovations, although these are sometimes so costly that only large companies or governments can afford to underwrite them.

Reliability of a product or service is often a key dimension in the eyes of the customer. Measuring and improving reliability are important aspects of product and service design, although other areas of the organization also have an influence on reliability.

Quality function deployment is one approach for getting customer input for product or service design.

KEY POINTS

1. A range of factors can cause an organization to design or redesign a product or service, including economic, legal, political, social, technological, and competitive pressures. Furthermore, an important cause of operations failures can be traced to faulty design.
2. Every area of a business organization, and its supply chain, is connected to, and influenced by, its products and/or services, so the potential impact on each area must be taken into account when products or services are redesigned or new products or services are to be designed.
3. Central issues relate to the actual or expected demand for a product or service, the organization's capabilities, the cost to produce or provide, the desired quality level, and the cost and availability of necessary resources.
4. Among considerations that are generally important are legal, ethical, and environmental.
5. Although there are some basic differences between product design and service design, there are many similarities between the two.

KEY TERMS

computer-aided design (CAD), 158
concurrent engineering, 157
cradle-to-grave assessment, 142
delayed differentiation, 150
design for assembly (DFA), 159
design for disassembly (DFD), 144
design for manufacturing (DFM), 159
design for recycling (DFR), 145
failure, 151
manufacturability, 134, 159
mass customization, 150
modular design, 150

normal operating conditions, 151
product bundle, 160
product liability, 139
quality function deployment (QFD), 153
recycling, 145
reliability, 151
remanufacturing, 143
research and development (R&D), 137
reverse engineering, 137
robust design, 152
service, 160
service blueprint, 162
service delivery system, 160
service package, 160
serviceability, 134
standardization, 149
Uniform Commercial Code, 139
value analysis, 143

DISCUSSION AND REVIEW QUESTIONS

1. What are some of the factors that cause organizations to redesign their products or services?
2. Contrast applied research and basic research.
3. What is CAD? Describe some of the ways a product designer can use it.
4. Name some of the main advantages and disadvantages of standardization.
5. What is modular design? What are its main advantages and disadvantages?
6. Explain the term *design for manufacturing* and briefly explain why it is important.
7. What are some of the competitive advantages of concurrent engineering?
8. Explain the term *remanufacturing.*
9. What is meant by the term *life cycle?* Why would this be a consideration in product or service design?
10. Why is R&D a key factor in productivity improvement? Name some ways R&D contributes to productivity improvements.
11. What is *mass customization?*
12. Name two factors that could make service design much different from product design.
13. Explain the term *robust design.*
14. Explain what *quality function deployment* is and how it can be useful.
15. What is reverse engineering? Do you feel this is unethical?
16. What is the purpose of value analysis?
17. What is life cycle assessment, and what is its overall goal?
18. Explain the term "three Rs" and how the three Rs relate to sustainability.

TAKING STOCK

1. Describe some of the trade-offs that are encountered in product and service design.
2. Who needs to be involved in the design of products and services?
3. How has technology had an impact on product and service design?

CRITICAL THINKING EXERCISES

1. A number of fast-food chains, after their success with offering their customers fresh salads, and in an effort to downplay the image of selling unhealthy food, began adding fresh fruit plates to their menus. At about the same time, and seemingly in direct conflict with this "healthy" strategy, several other fast-food chains began offering fat- and calorie-laden items to their menus. Compare these two widely different approaches, and predict the chances of each one's success. Name some other products that are popular, despite known health risks.
2. Think of a new or revised product or service that you would like to see on the market. Discuss the implications of producing that product or service relative to legal, ethical, environmental, profitability, competitive, design, and production issues.
3. How were food producers impacted by the U.S. government's requirement to identify the trans fat content on product labels?
4. Suppose a company intends to offer a new service to some of its internal customers. Briefly discuss how the fact that the customers are internal would change the process of managing the four phases of the service life cycle.
5. A few days before the end of the term of a two-year NDA (non-disclosure agreement) he signed with a startup company related to a possible patent, Frank interviewed with another startup and

divulged information covered by the agreement. The interview had been scheduled for a week later, in which case it wouldn't have been an issue, but had been moved up when another job applicant dropped out and the company had an opening for an earlier interview. Frank reasoned that he had met the spirit of the NDA, and a few days early wouldn't really matter. Besides, as it turned out, the company he interviewed with wasn't interested in that information, although they did hire him. What would you have done if you were Frank?

6. Give two examples of unethical conduct involving product or service design and the ethical principles (see Chapter 1) that are violated.

PROBLEMS

1. Examine and compare one of the following product sets. Base your comparison on such factors as features, costs, convenience, ease of use, ease and/or cost of repair, and safety.
   a. VCR players versus DVD players.
   b. Cell phones versus landlines.
   c. Wide-screen versus traditional television sets.
   d. Standard gasoline automobile engines versus hybrids.
   e. Standard wooden mousetraps versus new plastic mousetraps.
   f. Satellite television versus cable.

2. Use the Internet to obtain recent crash-safety ratings for passenger vehicles. Then answer these questions:
   a. Which vehicles received the highest ratings? The lowest ratings?
   b. How important are crash-safety ratings to new car buyers? Does the degree of importance depend on the circumstances of the buyer?
   c. Which types of buyers would you expect to be the most concerned with crash-safety ratings?
   d. Are there other features of a new car that might sway a buyer from focusing solely on crash safety? If so, what might they be?

3. Prepare a service blueprint for each of these banking transactions:
   a. Make a savings deposit using a teller.
   b. Apply for a home equity loan.

4. Prepare a service blueprint for each of these post office transactions:
   a. Buy stamps from a machine.
   b. Buy stamps from a postal clerk.

5. List the steps involved in getting gasoline into your car for full service and for self-service. Assume that paying cash is the only means of payment. For each list, identify the potential trouble points and indicate a likely problem.

6. Construct a list of steps for making a cash withdrawal from an automated teller machine (ATM). Assume that the process begins at the ATM with your bank card in hand. Then identify the potential failure points (i.e., where problems might arise in the process). For each failure point, state one potential problem.

7. a. Refer to Figure 4.4. What two technical requirements have the highest impact on the customer requirement that the paper not tear?
   b. The following table presents technical requirements and customer requirements for the output of a laser printer. First, decide if any of the technical requirements relate to each customer requirement. Decide which technical requirement, if any, has the greatest impact on that customer requirement.

	TECHNICAL REQUIREMENTS		
Customer Requirements	**Type of Paper**	**Internal Paper Feed**	**Print Element**
Paper doesn't wrinkle			
Prints clearly			
Easy to use			

8. Prepare a table similar to that shown in Problem 7*b* for cookies sold in a bakery. List what you believe are the three most important customer requirements (not including cost) and the three most relevant technical requirements (not including sanitary conditions). Next, indicate by a checkmark which customer requirements and which technical requirements are related.

High Acres Landfill

OPERATIONS TOUR

The High Acres Landfill is located on a 218-acre site outside Fairport, New York. Opened in 1971, it is licensed to handle residential, commercial, and industrial nonhazardous waste. The landfill has 27 employees, and it receives approximately 3,000 tons of waste per day.

The public often has certain preconceived notions about a landfill, chief among them that landfills are dirty and unpleasant. However, a visit to the landfill dispelled some of those misconceptions. The entrance is nicely landscaped. Most of the site is planted with grass and a few trees. Although unpleasant odors can emanate from arriving trucks or at the dump site, the remainder of the landfill is relatively free of odors.

A major portion of the landfill consists of a large hill within which the waste is buried. Initially, the landfill began not as a hill but as a large hole in the ground. After a number of years of depositing waste, the hole eventually was filled. From that point on, as additional layers were added, the landfill began to take the shape of a flattop hill. Each layer is a little narrower than the preceding one, giving the hill a slope. The sides of the hill are planted with grass. Only the "working face" along the top remains unplanted. When the designated capacity is exhausted (this may take another 10 years), the landfill will be closed to further waste disposal. The site will be converted into a public park with hiking trails and picnic and recreation areas, and given to the town.

The construction and operation of landfills are subject to numerous state and federal regulations. For example, nonpermeable liners must be placed on the bottom and sides of the landfill to prevent leakage of liquids into the groundwater. (Independent firms monitor groundwater to determine if there is any leakage into wells placed around the perimeter of the hill.) Mindful of public opinion, every effort is made to minimize the amount of time that waste is left exposed. At the end of each day, the waste that has been deposited in the landfill is compacted and covered with six inches of soil.

The primary source of income for the landfill is the fees it charges users. The landfill also generates income from methane gas, a by-product of organic waste decomposition, that accumulates within the landfill. A collection system is in place to capture and extract the gas from the landfill, and it is then sold to the local power company. Also, the landfill has a composting operation in which leaves and other yard wastes are converted into mulch.

SELECTED BIBLIOGRAPHY AND FURTHER READINGS

Baldwin, Carliss C., and Kim B. Clark. "Managing in the Age of Modularity." *Harvard Business Review,* September–October 1997, pp. 84–93.

Davis, Mark M., and Janelle Heineke. *Managing Services: Using Technology to Create Value.* New York: McGraw-Hill/Irwin, 2003.

Duray, Rebecca, and Glenn W. Milligan. "Improving Customer Satisfaction Through Mass Customization." *Quality Progress,* August 1999, pp. 60–66.

Feitzinger, Edward, and Hau L. Lee. "Mass Customization at Hewlett-Packard: The Power of Postponement." *Harvard Business Review,* January–February 1997, pp. 116–121.

Fitzsimmons, James A., and Mona J. Fitzsimmons. *Service Management for Competitive Advantage.* New York: McGraw-Hill, 1994.

Gilmore, James, and B. Joseph Pine II. "The Four Faces of Mass Customization." *Harvard Business Review,* January–February 1997, pp. 91–101.

Gilmore, James, and B. Joseph Pine II. *Markets of One: Creating Customer-Unique Value through Mass Customization.* Boston: Harvard Business School Press, 2000.

Gorman, Michael E. *Transforming Nature: Ethics, Invention, and Design.* Boston: Kluwer Academic Publishers, 1998.

Groover, Mikell P. *Automation, Production Systems, and Computer-Aided Manufacturing.* 2nd ed. Englewood Cliffs, NJ: Prentice Hall, 2001.

Heskett, James L., W. Earl Sasser Jr., and Leonard A. Schlesinger. *The Service Profit Chain.* New York: Free Press, 1997.

Lovelock, Christopher H. *Service Marketing: People, Technology, Strategy.* 2nd ed. Englewood Cliffs, NJ: Prentice Hall, 2001.

Prasad, Biren. *Concurrent Engineering Fundamentals: Integrated Product Development.* Upper Saddle River, NJ: Prentice Hall, 1997.

Prasad, Biren. *Concurrent Engineering Fundamentals: Integrated Product Development.* Volume II. Upper Saddle River, NJ: Prentice Hall, 1997.

Ternicko, John. *Step-by-Step QFD: Customer-Driven Product Design.* 2nd ed. Boca Raton, FL: CRC Press, 1997.

Ulrich, Karl T., and Steven D. Eppinger. *Product Design and Development.* 3rd ed. New York: McGraw-Hill, 2004.

Vicente, Kim. *The Human Factor.* New York: Routledge, 2004.

SUPPLEMENT TO CHAPTER 4

Reliability

LEARNING OBJECTIVES

After completing this supplement, you should be able to:

1 Define reliability.
2 Perform simple reliability computations.
3 Explain the purpose of redundancy in a system.

SUPPLEMENT OUTLINE

INTRODUCTION

Reliability is a measure of the ability of a product, service, part, or system to perform its intended function under a prescribed set of conditions. In effect, reliability is a *probability*.

Suppose that an item has a reliability of .90. This means that it has a 90 percent probability of functioning as intended. The probability it will fail is 1 − .90 = .10, or 10 percent. Hence, it is expected that, on the average, 1 of every 10 such items will fail or, equivalently, that the item will fail, on the average, once in every 10 trials. Similarly, a reliability of .985 implies 15 failures per 1,000 parts or trials.

Reliability The ability of a product, service, part, or system to perform its intended function under a prescribed set of conditions.

QUANTIFYING RELIABILITY

Engineers and designers have a number of techniques at their disposal for assessing reliability. A discussion of those techniques is not within the scope of this text. Instead, let us turn to the issue of quantifying overall product or system reliability. Probability is used in two ways.

1. The probability that the product or system will function when activated.
2. The probability that the product or system will function for a given length of time.

The first of these focuses on *one point in time* and is often used when a system must operate for one time or a relatively few number of times. The second of these focuses on the *length of service*. The distinction will become more apparent as each of these approaches is described in more detail.

Finding the Probability of Functioning When Activated

The probability that a system or a product will operate as planned is an important concept in system and product design. Determining that probability when the product or system consists of a number of *independent* components requires the use of the rules of probability for independent events. **Independent events** have no relation to the occurrence or nonoccurrence of each other. What follows are three examples illustrating the use of probability rules to determine whether a given system will operate successfully.

Independent events Events whose occurrence or nonoccurrence does not influence each other.

Rule 1. If two or more events are independent and *success* is defined as the probability that all of the events occur, then the probability of success is equal to the product of the probabilities of the events.

Example Suppose a room has two lamps, but to have adequate light both lamps must work (success) when turned on. One lamp has a probability of working of .90, and the other has a probability of working of .80. The probability that both will work is .90 × .80 = .72. Note that the order of multiplication is unimportant: .80 × .90 = .72. Also note that if the room had three lamps, three probabilities would have been multiplied.

This system can be represented by the following diagram:

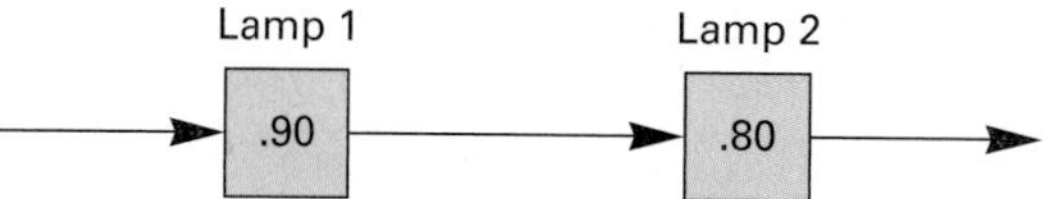

Even though the individual components of a system might have high reliabilities, the system as a whole can have considerably less reliability because all components that are in series (as are the ones in the preceding example) must function. As the number of components in a series increases, the system reliability decreases. For example, a system that has eight components in a series, each with a reliability of .99, has a reliability of only $.99^8 = .923$.

Obviously, many products and systems have a large number of component parts that must all operate, and some way to increase overall reliability is needed. One approach is to use **redundancy** in the design. This involves providing backup parts for some items.

Redundancy The use of backup components to increase reliability.

Rule 2. If two events are independent and *success* is defined as the probability that *at least one* of the events will occur, the probability of success is equal to the probability of either one plus 1.00 minus that probability multiplied by the other probability.

Example There are two lamps in a room. When turned on, one has a probability of working of .90 and the other has a probability of working of .80. Only a single lamp is needed to light for success. If one fails to light when turned on, the other lamp is turned on. Hence, one of the lamps is a backup in case the other one fails. Either lamp can be treated as the backup; the probability of success will be the same. The probability of success is .90 + (1 − .90) × .80 = .98. If the .80 light is first, the computation would be .80 + (1 − .80) × .90 = .98.

This system can be represented by the following diagram:

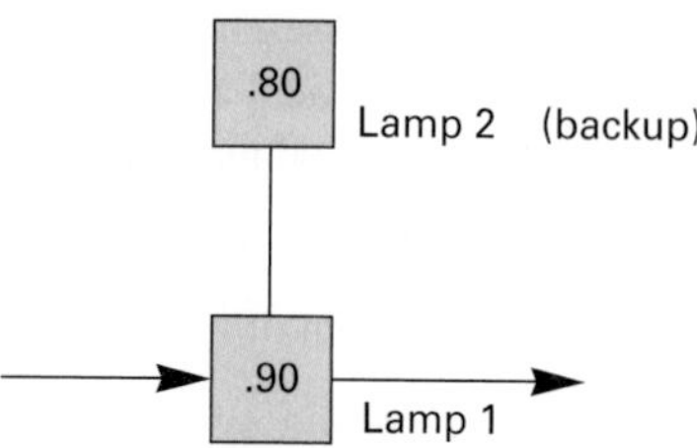

Rule 3. If two or more events are involved and success is defined as the probability that at least one of them occurs, the probability of success is 1 − *P* (all fail).

Example Three lamps have probabilities of .90, .80, and .70 of lighting when turned on. Only one lighted lamp is needed for success; hence, two of the lamps are considered to be backups. The probability of success is

$$1 - [(1 - .90) \times (1 - .80) \times (1 - .70)] = .994$$

This system can be represented by the following diagram:

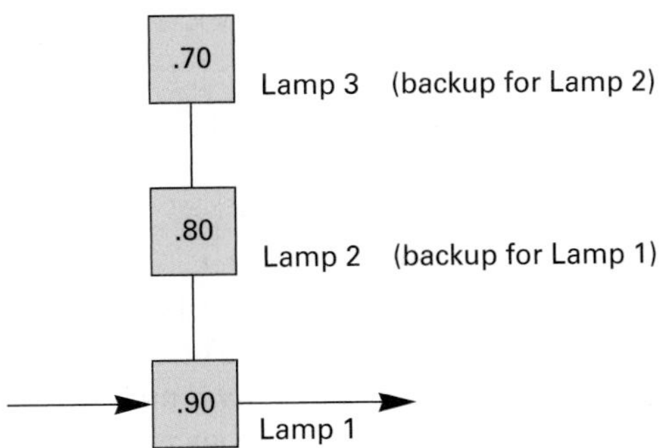

Determine the reliability of the system shown below.

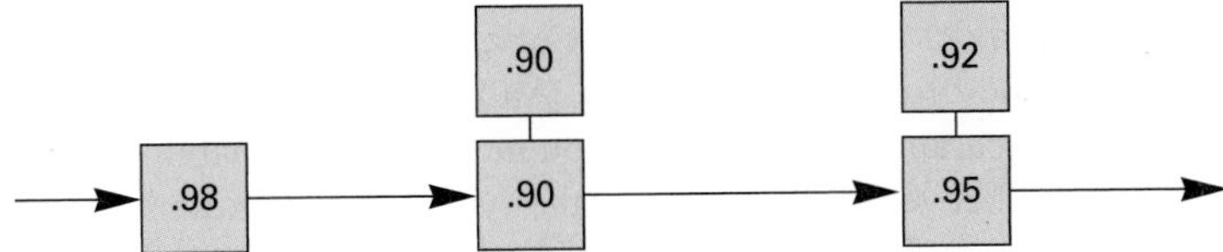

The system can be reduced to a series of three components:

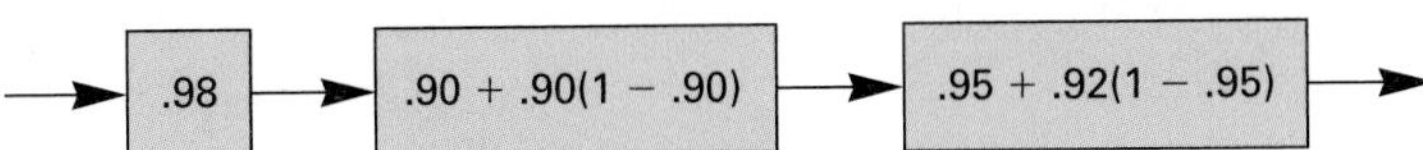

The system reliability is, then, the product of these:

$$.98 \times .99 \times .996 = .966$$

Finding the Probability of Functioning for a Given Length of Time

The second way of looking at reliability considers the incorporation of a time dimension: Probabilities are determined relative to a specified length of time. This approach is commonly used in product warranties, which pertain to a given period of time after purchase of a product.

A typical profile of product failure rate over time is illustrated in Figure 4S.1. Because of its shape, it is sometimes referred to as a bathtub curve. Frequently, a number of products fail shortly after they are put into service, not because they wear out, but because they are defective to begin with. The rate of failures decreases rapidly once the truly defective items are weeded out. During the second phase, there are fewer failures because most of the defective items have been eliminated, and it is too soon to encounter items that fail because they have worn out. In some cases, this phase covers a relatively long time. In the third phase, failures occur because the products are worn out, and the failure rate increases.

Information on the distribution and length of each phase requires the collection of historical data and analysis of those data. It often turns out that the **mean time between failures (MTBF)** in the infant mortality phase can be modeled by a negative exponential distribution, such as that depicted in Figure 4S.2. Equipment failures as well as product failures may occur in this pattern. In such cases, the exponential distribution can be used to determine various

Mean time between failures (MTBF) The average length of time between failures of a product or component.

FIGURE 4S.1
Failure rate is a function of time

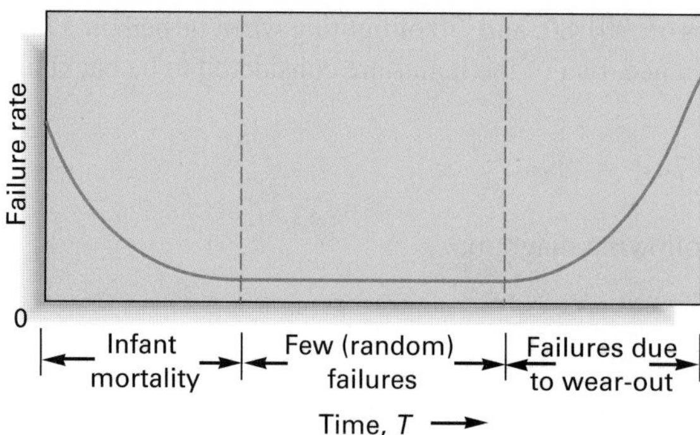

probabilities of interest. The probability that equipment or a product put into service at time 0 will fail *before* some specified time, *T*, is equal to the area under the curve between 0 and *T*. Reliability is specified as the probability that a product will last *at least until* time *T;* reliability is equal to the area under the curve *beyond T*. (Note that the total area under the curve in each phase is treated as 100 percent for computational purposes.) Observe that as the specified length of service increases, the area under the curve to the right of that point (i.e., the reliability) decreases.

Determining values for the area under a curve to the right of a given point, *T*, becomes a relatively simple matter using a table of exponential values. An exponential distribution is completely described using a single parameter, the distribution mean, which reliability engineers often refer to as the mean time between failures. Using the symbol *T* to represent length of service, the probability that failure will *not* occur before time *T* (i.e., the area in the right tail) is easily determined:

$$P(\text{no failure before } T) = e^{-T/\text{MTBF}}$$

where

$$e = 2.7183\ldots$$
$$T = \text{Length of service before failure}$$
$$\text{MTBF} = \text{Mean time between failures}$$

The probability that failure will occur before time *T* is:

$$P(\text{failure before } T) = 1 - e^{-T/\text{MTBF}}$$

Selected values of $e^{-T/\text{MTBF}}$ are listed in Table 4S.1.

FIGURE 4S.2
An exponential distribution

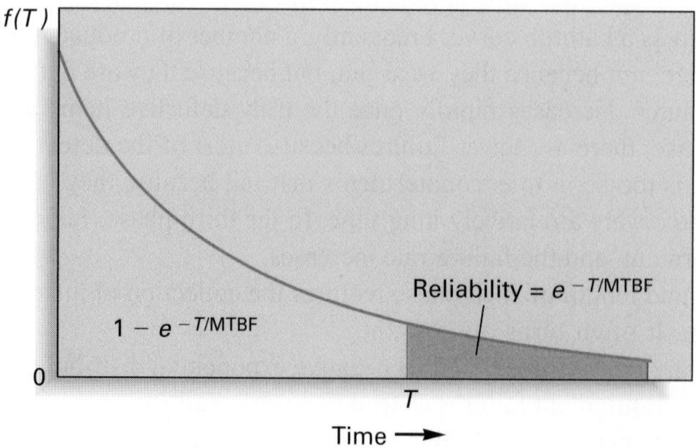

TABLE 4S.1
Values of $e^{-T/\text{MTBF}}$

T/MTBF	$e^{-T/\text{MTBF}}$	T/MTBF	$e^{-T/\text{MTBF}}$	T/MTBF	$e^{-T/\text{MTBF}}$
0.10	.9048	2.60	.0743	5.10	.0061
0.20	.8187	2.70	.0672	5.20	.0055
0.30	.7408	2.80	.0608	5.30	.0050
0.40	.6703	2.90	.0550	5.40	.0045
0.50	.6065	3.00	.0498	5.50	.0041
0.60	.5488	3.10	.0450	5.60	.0037
0.70	.4966	3.20	.0408	5.70	.0033
0.80	.4493	3.30	.0369	5.80	.0030
0.90	.4066	3.40	.0334	5.90	.0027
1.00	.3679	3.50	.0302	6.00	.0025
1.10	.3329	3.60	.0273	6.10	.0022
1.20	.3012	3.70	.0247	6.20	.0020
1.30	.2725	3.80	.0224	6.30	.0018
1.40	.2466	3.90	.0202	6.40	.0017
1.50	.2231	4.00	.0183	6.50	.0015
1.60	.2019	4.10	.0166	6.60	.0014
1.70	.1827	4.20	.0150	6.70	.0012
1.80	.1653	4.30	.0136	6.80	.0011
1.90	.1496	4.40	.0123	6.90	.0010
2.00	.1353	4.50	.0111	7.00	.0009
2.10	.1255	4.60	.0101		
2.20	.1108	4.70	.0091		
2.30	.1003	4.80	.0082		
2.40	.0907	4.90	.0074		
2.50	.0821	5.00	.0067		

EXAMPLE 4S–2

By means of extensive testing, a manufacturer has determined that its Super Sucker Vacuum Cleaner models have an expected life that is exponential with a mean of four years. Find the probability that one of these cleaners will have a life that ends

a. After the initial four years of service.

b. Before four years of service are completed.

c. Not before six years of service.

SOLUTION

MTBF = 4 years

a. $T = 4$ years:

$$T/\text{MTBF} = \frac{4 \text{ years}}{4 \text{ years}} = 1.0$$

From Table 4S.1, $e^{-1.0} = .3679$.

b. The probability of failure before $T = 4$ years is $1 - e^{-1}$, or $1 - .3679 = .6321$.

c. $T = 6$ years:

$$T/\text{MTBF} = \frac{6 \text{ years}}{4 \text{ years}} = 1.50$$

From Table 4S.1, $e^{-1.5} = .2231$.

FIGURE 4S.3
A normal curve

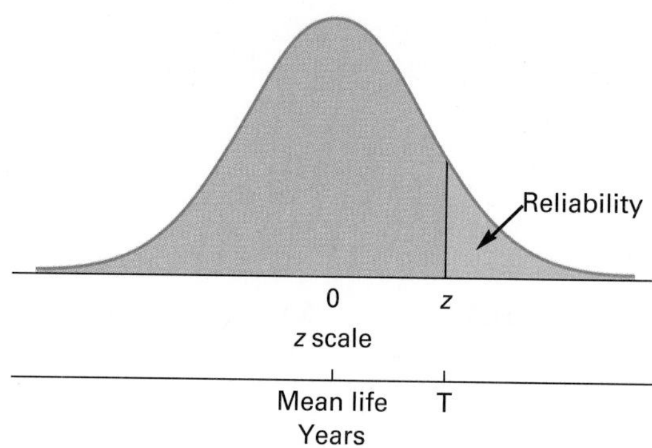

Product failure due to wear-out can sometimes be modeled by a normal distribution. Obtaining probabilities involves the use of a table (refer to Appendix Table B). The table provides areas under a normal curve from (essentially) the left end of the curve to a specified point z, where z is a *standardized* value computed using the formula

$$z = \frac{T - \text{Mean wear-out time}}{\text{Standard deviation of wear-out time}}$$

Thus, to work with the normal distribution, it is necessary to know the mean of the distribution and its standard deviation. A normal distribution is illustrated in Figure 4S.3. Appendix Table B contains normal probabilities (i.e., the area that lies to the left of z). To obtain a probability that service life will not exceed some value T, compute z and refer to the table. To find the reliability for time T, subtract this probability from 100 percent. To obtain the value of T that will provide a given probability, locate the nearest probability under the curve *to the left* in Table B. Then use the corresponding z in the preceding formula and solve for T.

EXAMPLE 4S–3

www.mhhe.com/stevenson11e

The mean life of a certain ball bearing can be modeled using a normal distribution with a mean of six years and a standard deviation of one year. Determine each of the following:

a. The probability that a ball bearing will wear out *before* seven years of service.
b. The probability that a ball bearing will wear out *after* seven years of service (i.e., find its reliability).
c. The service life that will provide a wear-out probability of 10 percent.

SOLUTION

Wear-out life mean = 6 years.
Wear out life standard deviation = 1 year.
Wear-out life is normally distributed.

a. Compute z and use it to obtain the probability directly from Appendix Table B (see diagram).

$$z = \frac{7 - 6}{1} = +1.00$$

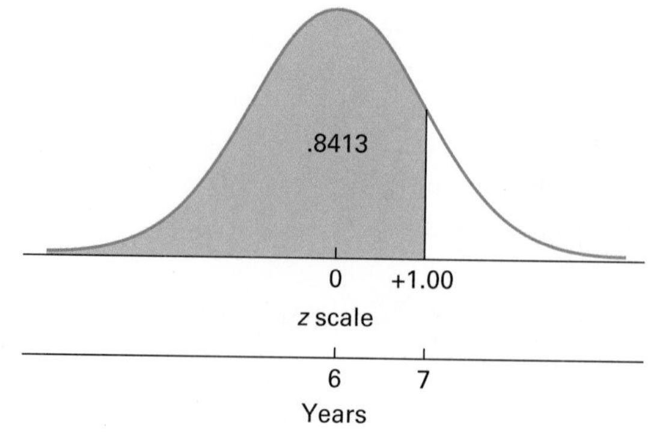

Thus, $P(T < 7) = .8413$.

b. Subtract the probability determined in part *a* from 100 percent (see diagram).

$1.00 - .8413 = .1587$

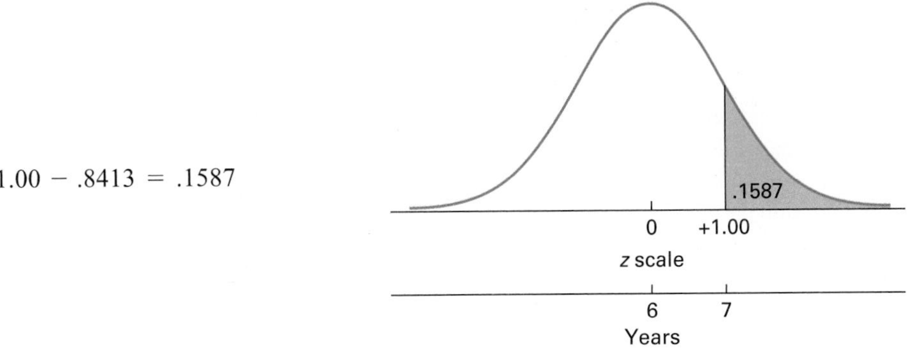

c. Use the normal table and find the value of z that corresponds to an area under the curve of 10 percent (see diagram).

$$z = -1.28 = \frac{T - 6}{1}$$

90%
10%
z = −1.28
0
z scale
4.72
6
Years

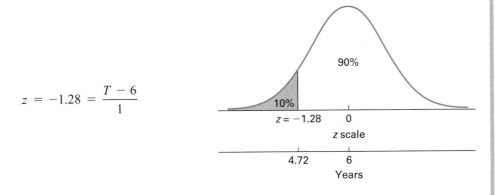

Solving for T, we find $T = 4.72$ years.

AVAILABILITY

A related measure of importance to customers, and hence to designers, is **availability**. It measures the fraction of time a piece of equipment is expected to be operational (as opposed to being down for repairs). Availability can range from zero (never available) to 1.00 (always available). Companies that can offer equipment with a high availability factor have a competitive advantage over companies that offer equipment with lower availability values. Availability is a function of both the mean time between failures and the mean time to repair. The availability factor can be computed using the following formula:

Availability The fraction of time a piece of equipment is expected to be available for operation.

$$\text{Availability} = \frac{\text{MTBF}}{\text{MTBF} + \text{MTR}}$$

where

MTBF = Mean time between failures

MTR = Mean time to repair, including waiting time

EXAMPLE 4S–4

A copier is able to operate for an average of 200 hours between repairs, and the mean repair time is two hours. Determine the availability of the copier.

SOLUTION

MTBF = 200 hours and MTR = 2 hours

$$\text{Availability} = \frac{\text{MTBF}}{\text{MTBF} + \text{MTR}} = \frac{200}{200 + 2} = .99$$

Two implications for design are revealed by the availability formula. One is that availability increases as the mean time between failures increases. The other is that availability also increases as the mean repair time decreases. It would seem obvious that designers would want to design products that have a long time between failures. However, some design options enhance repairability, which can be incorporated into the product. Ink-jet printers, for example, are designed with print cartridges that can easily be replaced.

KEY TERMS

availability, 175
independent events, 170
mean time between failures (MTBF), 171
redundancy, 170
reliability, 169

SOLVED PROBLEMS

Problem 1

A product design engineer must decide if a redundant component is cost-justified in a certain system. The system in question has a critical component with a probability of .98 of operating. System failure would involve a cost of $20,000. For a cost of $100, a switch could be added that would automatically transfer the system to the backup component in the event of a failure. Should the backup be added if the backup probability is also .98?

Solution

Because no probability is given for the switch, we will assume its probability of operating when needed is 100 percent. The expected cost of failure (i.e., without the backup) is $20,000 × (1 − .98) = $400.

With the backup, the probability of *not* failing would be:

$$.98 + .02(.98) = .9996$$

Hence, the probability of failure would be 1 − .9996 = .0004. The expected cost of failure with the backup would be the added cost of the backup component plus the failure cost:

$$\$100 + \$20{,}000(.0004) = \$108$$

Because this is less than the cost without the backup, it appears that adding the backup is definitely cost justifiable.

Problem 2

Due to the extreme cost of interrupting production, a firm has two standby machines available in case a particular machine breaks down. The machine in use has a reliability of .94, and the backups have reliabilities of .90 and .80. In the event of a failure, either backup can be pressed into service. If one fails, the other backup can be used. Compute the system reliability.

Solution

$$R_1 = .94, \quad R_2 = .90, \quad \text{and} \quad R_3 = .80$$

The system can be depicted in this way:

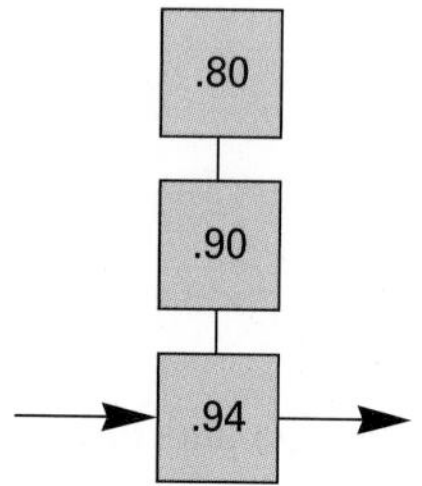

$$\begin{aligned} R_{\text{system}} &= R_1 + R_2(1 - R_1) + R_3(1 - R_2)(1 - R_1) \\ &= .94 + .90(1 - .94) + .80(1 - .90)(1 - .94) = .9988 \end{aligned}$$

Problem 3

A hospital has three *independent* fire alarm systems, with reliabilities of .95, .97, and .99. In the event of a fire, what is the probability that a warning would be given?

Solution

A warning would *not* be given if all three alarms failed. The probability that at least one alarm would operate is $1 - P$ (none operate):

$$P(\text{none operate}) = (1 - .95)(1 - .97)(1 - .99) = .000015$$
$$P(\text{warning}) = 1 - .000015 = .999985$$

Problem 4

A weather satellite has an expected life of 10 years from the time it is placed into earth orbit. Determine its probability of no wear-out before each of the following lengths of service. Assume the exponential distribution is appropriate.

a. 5 years. b. 12 years. c. 20 years. d. 30 years.

Solution

$$\text{MTBF} = 10 \text{ years}$$

Compute the ratio T/MTBF for $T = 5$, 12, 20, and 30, and obtain the values of $e^{-T/\text{MTBF}}$ from Table 4S.1. The solutions are summarized in the following table:

T	MTBF	*T*/MTBF	$e^{-T/\text{MTBF}}$
a. 5	10	0.50	.6065
b. 12	10	1.20	.3012
c. 20	10	2.00	.1353
d. 30	10	3.00	.0498

Problem 5

What is the probability that the satellite described in Solved Problem 4 will fail between 5 and 12 years after being placed into earth orbit?

Solution

$$P(5 \text{ years} < \text{failure} < 12 \text{ years}) = P(\text{failure after 5 years}) - P(\text{failure after 12 years})$$

Using the probabilities shown in the previous solution, you obtain:

$$\begin{array}{r} P(\text{failure after 5 years}) = .6065 \\ -P(\text{failure after 12 years}) = \underline{.3012} \\ .3053 \end{array}$$

The corresponding area under the curve is illustrated as follows:

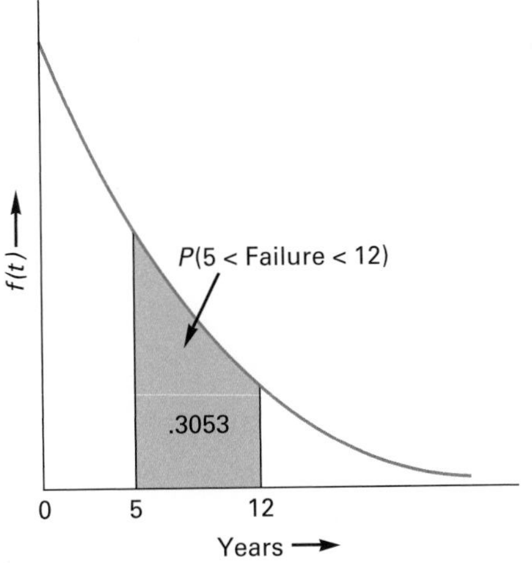

Problem 6

One line of radial tires produced by a large company has a wear-out life that can be modeled using a normal distribution with a mean of 25,000 miles and a standard deviation of 2,000 miles. Determine each of the following:

a. The percentage of tires that can be expected to wear out within ± 2,000 miles of the average (i.e., between 23,000 miles and 27,000 miles).

b. The percentage of tires that can be expected to fail between 26,000 miles and 29,000 miles.

c. For what tire life would you expect 4 percent of the tires to have worn out?

Solution

Notes: (1) Miles are analogous to time and are handled in exactly the same way; (2) the term *percentage* refers to a probability.

a. The phrase "within ± 2,000 miles of the average" translates to within one standard deviation of the mean since the standard deviation equals 2,000 miles. Therefore the range of z is $z = -1.00$, to $z = +1.00$, and the area under the curve between those points is found as the difference between $P(z < +1.00)$ and $P(z < -1.00)$, using values obtained from Appendix Table B.

$$\begin{aligned} P(z < +1.00) &= .8413 \\ -P(z < -1.00) &= .1587 \\ \hline P(-1.00 < z < +1.00) &= .6826 \end{aligned}$$

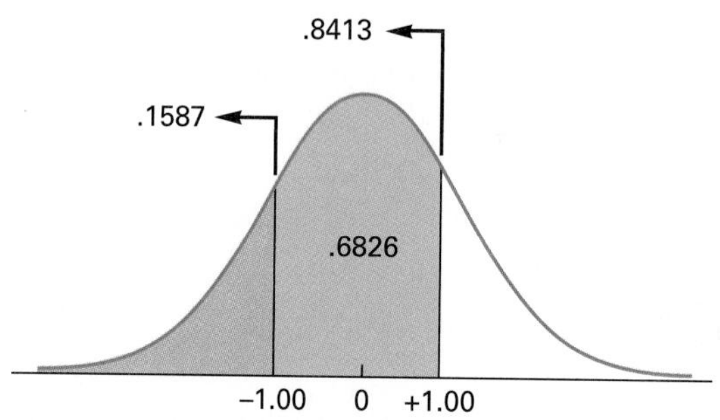

b. Wear-out mean = 25,000 miles
Wear-out standard deviation = 2,000 miles

$P(26{,}000 < \text{Wear-out} < 29{,}000) = P(z < z_{29{,}000}) - P(z < z_{26{,}000})$

$$z_{29{,}000} = \frac{29{,}000 - 25{,}000}{2{,}000} = +2.00 \qquad \text{From Appendix Table B} \quad P = .9772$$

$$z_{26{,}000} = \frac{26{,}000 - 25{,}000}{2{,}000} = +.50 \qquad \text{From Appendix Table B} \quad P = .6915$$

The difference is $.9772 - .6915 = .2857$, which is the expected percent of tires that will wear out between 26,000 miles and 29,000 miles.

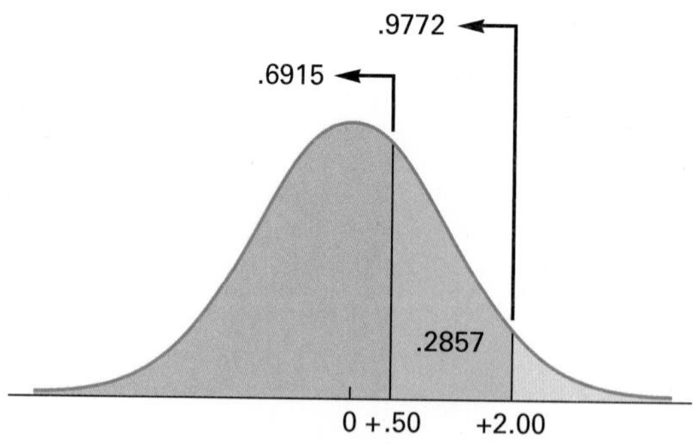

c. Use Appendix Table B.1 to find z for 4 percent: $z = -1.75$.
Find tire life using $\mu + z\sigma$: $25{,}000 - 1.75(2{,}000) = 21{,}500$ miles.

DISCUSSION AND REVIEW QUESTIONS

1. Define the term *reliability*.
2. Explain why a product or system might have an overall reliability that is low even though it is comprised of components that have fairly high reliabilities.
3. What is redundancy and how can it improve product design?

PROBLEMS

1. Consider the following system:

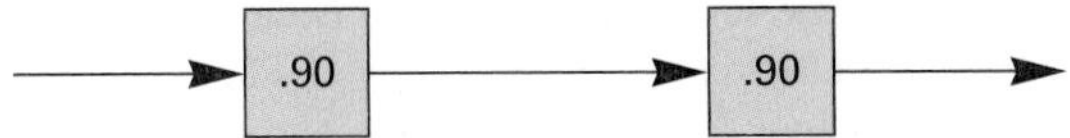

Determine the probability that the system will operate under each of these conditions:

a. The system as shown.
b. Each system component has a backup with a probability of .90 and a switch that is 100 percent reliable.
c. Backups with .90 probability and a switch that is 99 percent reliable.

2. A product is composed of four parts. In order for the product to function properly in a given situation, each of the parts must function. Two of the parts have a .96 probability of functioning, and two have a probability of .99. What is the overall probability that the product will function properly?

3. A system consists of three identical components. In order for the system to perform as intended, all of the components must perform. Each has the same probability of performance. If the system is to have a .92 probability of performing, what is the minimum probability of performing needed by each of the individual components?

4. A product engineer has developed the following equation for the cost of a system component: $C = (10P)^2$, where C is the cost in dollars and P is the probability that the component will operate as expected. The system is composed of two identical components, both of which must operate for the system to operate. The engineer can spend $173 for the two components. To the nearest two decimal places, what is the largest component probability that can be achieved?

5. The guidance system of a ship is controlled by a computer that has three major modules. In order for the computer to function properly, all three modules must function. Two of the modules have reliabilities of .97, and the other has a reliability of .99.

a. What is the reliability of the computer?
b. A backup computer identical to the one being used will be installed to improve overall reliability. Assuming the new computer automatically functions if the main one fails, determine the resulting reliability.
c. If the backup computer must be activated by a switch in the event that the first computer fails, and the switch has a reliability of .98, what is the overall reliability of the system? (*Both* the switch and the backup computer must function in order for the backup to take over.)

6. One of the industrial robots designed by a leading producer of servomechanisms has four major components. Components' reliabilities are .98, .95, .94, and .90. All of the components must function in order for the robot to operate effectively.

a. Compute the reliability of the robot.
b. Designers want to improve the reliability by adding a backup component. Due to space limitations, only one backup can be added. The backup for any component will have the same reliability as the unit for which it is the backup. Which component should get the backup in order to achieve the highest reliability?
c. If one backup with a reliability of .92 can be added to any one of the main components, which component should get it to obtain the highest overall reliability?

7. A production line has three machines A, B, and C, with reliabilities of .99, .96, and .93, respectively. The machines are arranged so that if one breaks down, the others must shut down. Engineers are weighing two alternative designs for increasing the line's reliability. Plan 1 involves adding an identical backup *line,* and plan 2 involves providing a backup for each *machine.* In either case, three machines (A, B, and C) would be used with reliabilities equal to the original three.

a. Which plan will provide the higher reliability?
b. Explain why the two reliabilities are not the same.
c. What other factors might enter into the decision of which plan to adopt?

8. Refer to the previous problem.

a. Assume that the single switch used in plan 1 is 98 percent reliable, while reliabilities of the machines remain the same. Recalculate the reliability of plan 1. Compare the reliability of this plan with the reliability of plan 1 calculated in solving the original problem. How much did the reliability of plan 1 decrease as a result of a 98 percent reliable switch?
b. Assume that the three switches used in plan 2 are all 98 percent reliable, while reliabilities of the machines remain the same. Recalculate the reliability of plan 2. Compare the reliability of this plan with the reliability of plan 2 calculated in solving the original problem. How much did the reliability of plan 2 decrease?

9. A Web server has five major components that must all function in order for it to operate as intended. Assuming that each component of the system has the same reliability, what is the minimum reliability each one must have in order for the overall system to have a reliability of .98?
10. Repeat Problem 9 under the condition that one of the components will have a backup with a reliability equal to that of any one of the other components.
11. Hoping to increase the chances of reaching a performance goal, the director of a research project has assigned three separate research teams the same task. The director estimates that the team probabilities are .9, .8, and .7 for successfully completing the task in the allotted time. Assuming that the teams work independently, what is the probability that the task will not be completed in time?
12. An electronic chess game has a useful life that is exponential with a mean of 30 months. Determine each of the following:
    a. The probability that any given unit will operate for at least (1) 39 months, (2) 48 months, (3) 60 months.
    b. The probability that any given unit will fail sooner than (1) 33 months, (2) 15 months, (3) 6 months.
    c. The length of service time after which the percentage of failed units will approximately equal (1) 50 percent, (2) 85 percent, (3) 95 percent, (4) 99 percent.
13. A manufacturer of programmable calculators is attempting to determine a reasonable free-service period for a model it will introduce shortly. The manager of product testing has indicated that the calculators have an expected life of 30 months. Assume product life can be described by an exponential distribution.
    a. If service contracts are offered for the expected life of the calculator, what percentage of those sold would be expected to fail during the service period?
    b. What service period would result in a failure rate of approximately 10 percent?
14. Lucky Lumen light bulbs have an expected life that is exponentially distributed with a mean of 20,000 hours. Determine the probability that one of these light bulbs will last
    a. At least 24,000 hours.
    b. No longer than 4,000 hours.
    c. Between 4,000 hours and 24,000 hours.
15. Planetary Communications, Inc., intends to launch a satellite that will enhance reception of television programs in Alaska. According to its designers, the satellite will have an expected life of six years. Assume the exponential distribution applies. Determine the probability that it will function for each of the following time periods:
    a. More than 9 years.
    b. Less than 12 years.
    c. More than 9 years but less than 12 years.
    d. At least 21 years.
16. An office manager has received a report from a consultant that includes a section on equipment replacement. The report indicates that scanners have a service life that is normally distributed with a mean of 41 months and a standard deviation of 4 months. On the basis of this information, determine the percentage of scanners that can be expected to fail in the following time periods:
    a. Before 38 months of service.
    b. Between 40 and 45 months of service.
    c. Within $\pm$ 2 months of the mean life.
17. A major television manufacturer has determined that its 19-inch color TV picture tubes have a mean service life that can be modeled by a normal distribution with a mean of six years and a standard deviation of one-half year.
    a. What probability can you assign to service lives of at least (1) Five years? (2) Six years? (3) Seven and one-half years?
    b. If the manufacturer offers service contracts of four years on these picture tubes, what percentage can be expected to fail from wear-out during the service period?
18. Refer to Problem 17. What service period would achieve an expected wear-out rate of
    a. 2 percent?
    b. 5 percent?
19. Determine the availability for each of these cases:
    a. MTBF = 40 days, average repair time = 3 days.
    b. MTBF = 300 hours, average repair time = 6 hours.

20. A machine can operate for an average of 10 weeks before it needs to be overhauled, a process which takes two days. The machine is operated five days a week. Compute the availability of this machine. (*Hint:* All times must be in the same units.)

21. A manager must decide between two machines. The manager will take into account each machine's operating costs and initial costs, and its breakdown and repair times. Machine A has a projected average operating time of 142 hours and a projected average repair time of 7 hours. Projected times for machine B are an average operating time of 65 hours and a repair time of 2 hours. What are the projected availabilities of each machine?

22. A designer estimates that she can (*a*) increase the average time between failures of a part by 5 percent at a cost of $450, or (*b*) reduce the average repair time by 10 percent at a cost of $200. Which option would be more cost-effective? Currently, the average time between failures is 100 hours and the average repair time is 4 hours.

23. Auto batteries have an average life of 2.7 years. Battery life is normally distributed with a mean of 2.7 years and a standard deviation of .3 year. The batteries are warranted to operate for a minimum of 2 years. If a battery fails within the warranty period, it will be replaced with a new battery at no charge. The company sells and installs the batteries. Also, the usual $5 installation charge will be waived.

a. What percentage of batteries would you expect to fail before the warranty period expires?

b. A competitor is offering a warranty of 30 months on its premium battery. The manager of this company is toying with the idea of using the same battery with a different exterior, labeling it as a premium battery, and offering a 30-month warranty on it. How much more would the company have to charge on its "premium" battery to offset the additional cost of replacing batteries?

c. What other factors would you take into consideration besides the price of the battery?

Strategic Capacity Planning for Products and Services

CHAPTER OUTLINE

LEARNING OBJECTIVES

After completing this chapter, you should be able to:

1 Summarize the importance of capacity planning.
2 Discuss ways of defining and measuring capacity.
3 Describe the determinants of effective capacity.
4 Discuss the major considerations related to developing capacity alternatives.
5 Briefly describe approaches that are useful for evaluating capacity alternatives.

Capacity planning is a key strategic component in designing the system. It encompasses many basic decisions with long-term consequences for the organization. In this chapter, you will learn about the importance of capacity decisions, the measurement of capacity, how capacity requirements are determined, and the development and evaluation of capacity alternatives. Note that decisions made in the product or service design stage have major implications for capacity planning. Designs have processing requirements related to volume and degree of customization that affect capacity planning.

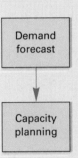

Demand forecast → Capacity planning

INTRODUCTION

Hospitals that not too long ago had what could be described as "facility oversupply" are now experiencing what can be described as a "capacity crisis" in some areas. The way hospitals plan for capacity will be critical to their future success. And the same applies to all sorts of organizations, and at all levels of these organizations. **Capacity** refers to an upper limit or ceiling on the load that an operating unit can handle. The load might be in terms of the number of physical units produced (e.g., bicycles assembled per hour) or the number of services performed (e.g., computers upgraded per hour). The operating unit might be a plant, department, machine, store, or worker. Capacity needs include equipment, space, and employee skills.

Capacity The upper limit or ceiling on the load that an operating unit can handle.

The goal of strategic capacity planning is to achieve a match between the long-term supply capabilities of an organization and the predicted level of long-term demand. Organizations become involved in capacity planning for various reasons. Among the chief reasons are changes in demand, changes in technology, changes in the environment, and perceived threats or opportunities. A gap between current and desired capacity will result in capacity that is out of balance. Overcapacity causes operating costs that are too high, while undercapacity causes strained resources and possible loss of customers.

Excess Capacity Can Be Bad News!

READING

Today, huge gaps between supply and demand have many companies struggling. Excess capacity abounds in such major industries as telecom, airline, and auto manufacturing. The bad news is that some companies are losing millions of dollars a year because of this. In the telecom industry, the increasing reach of cellular technology and other kinds of wireless access is continuing to create more and more supply, requiring telecom companies to cut prices and offer incentives to increase demand.

In the airline industry, air travel is way down, leaving airline companies awash in capacity. And even much of the currently mothballed aircraft are only in storage. Companies have eliminated flights to save money and cut prices to the bone trying to lure passengers.

The auto producers don't have it quite so bad, but for years they've been offering their customers incentives and interest-free financing—in order to keep their excess plants running.

The key questions in capacity planning are the following:

1. What kind of capacity is needed?
2. How much is needed to match demand?
3. When is it needed?

The question of what kind of capacity is needed depends on the products and services that management intends to produce or provide. Hence, in a very real sense, capacity planning is governed by those choices.

Forecasts are key inputs used to answer the questions of how much capacity is needed and when is it needed.

Related questions include:

1. How much will it cost, how will it be funded, and what is the expected return?
2. What are the potential benefits and risks? These involve the degree of uncertainty related to forecasts of the amount of demand and the rate of change in demand, as well as costs, profits, and the time to implement capacity changes. The degree of accuracy that can be attached to forecasts is an important consideration. The likelihood and impact of wrong decisions also need to be assessed.
3. Are there sustainability issues that need to be addressed?
4. Should capacity be changed all at once, or through several (or more) small changes?
5. Can the supply chain handle the necessary changes? Before an organization commits to ramping up its input, it is essential to confirm that its *supply chain* will be able to handle related requirements.

SUPPLY CHAIN

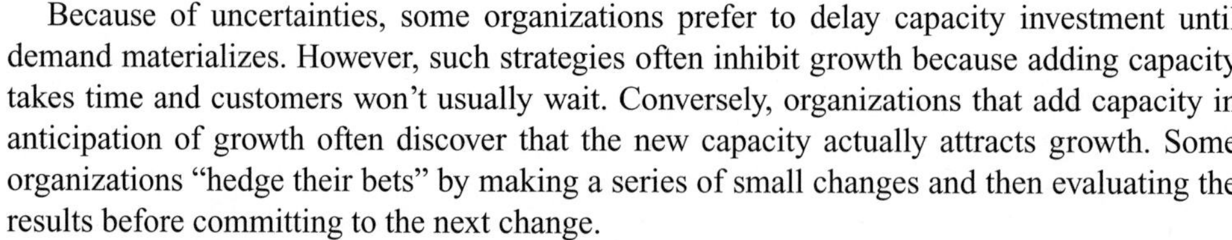

Because of uncertainties, some organizations prefer to delay capacity investment until demand materializes. However, such strategies often inhibit growth because adding capacity takes time and customers won't usually wait. Conversely, organizations that add capacity in anticipation of growth often discover that the new capacity actually attracts growth. Some organizations "hedge their bets" by making a series of small changes and then evaluating the results before committing to the next change.

In some instances, capacity choices are made very infrequently; in others, they are made regularly, as part of an ongoing process. Generally, the factors that influence this frequency are the stability of demand, the rate of technological change in equipment and product design, and competitive factors. Other factors relate to the type of product or service and whether style changes are important (e.g., automobiles and clothing). In any case, management must review product and service choices periodically to ensure that the company makes capacity changes when they are needed for cost, competitive effectiveness, or other reasons.

CAPACITY DECISIONS ARE STRATEGIC

For a number of reasons, capacity decisions are among the most fundamental of all the design decisions that managers must make. In fact, capacity decisions can be *critical* for an organization:

1. Capacity decisions have a real impact on the ability of the organization to meet future demands for products and services; capacity essentially limits the rate of output possible. Having capacity to satisfy demand can often allow a company to take advantage of tremendous benefits. When Microsoft introduced its new Xbox in late 2005, there were insufficient supplies, resulting in lost sales and unhappy customers. And shortages of flu vaccine in some years due to production problems affected capacity, limiting the availability of the vaccine.
2. Capacity decisions affect operating costs. Ideally, capacity and demand requirements will be matched, which will tend to minimize operating costs. In practice, this is not always achieved because actual demand either differs from expected demand or tends to vary (e.g., cyclically). In such cases, a decision might be made to attempt to balance the costs of over- and undercapacity.
3. Capacity is usually a major determinant of initial cost. Typically, the greater the capacity of a productive unit, the greater its cost. This does not necessarily imply a one-for-one relationship; larger units tend to cost *proportionately* less than smaller units.
4. Capacity decisions often involve long-term commitment of resources and the fact that, once they are implemented, those decisions may be difficult or impossible to modify without incurring major costs.
5. Capacity decisions can affect competitiveness. If a firm has excess capacity, or can quickly add capacity, that fact may serve as a barrier to entry by other firms. Then too, capacity can affect *delivery speed,* which can be a competitive advantage.
6. Capacity affects the ease of management; having appropriate capacity makes management easier than when capacity is mismatched.
7. Globalization has increased the importance and the complexity of capacity decisions. Far-flung supply chains and distant markets add to the uncertainty about capacity needs.
8. Because capacity decisions often involve substantial financial and other resources, it is necessary to plan for them far in advance. For example, it may take years for a new power-generating plant to be constructed and become operational. However, this increases the risk that the designated amount of capacity will not match actual demand when the capacity becomes available.

SUPPLY CHAIN

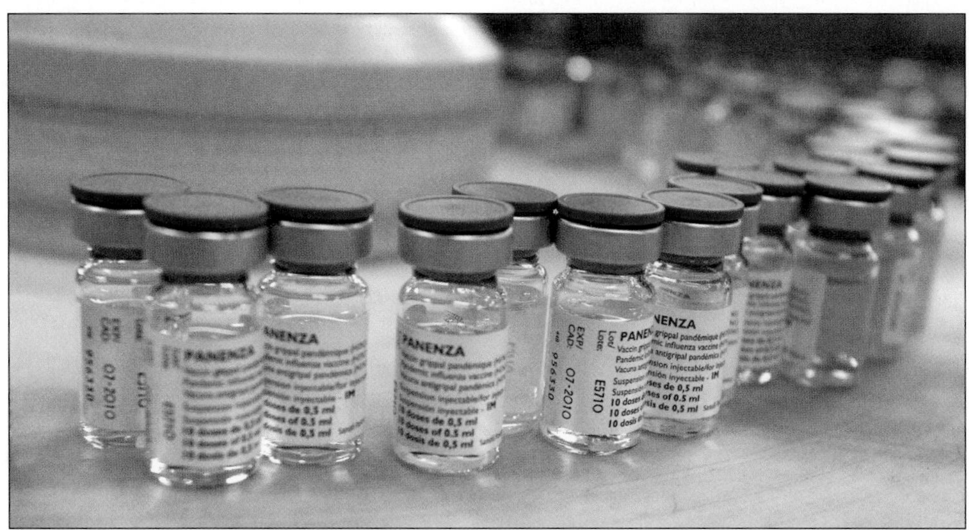

DEFINING AND MEASURING CAPACITY

Capacity often refers to an upper limit on the *rate* of output. Even though this seems simple enough, there are subtle difficulties in actually measuring capacity in certain cases. These difficulties arise because of different interpretations of the term *capacity* and problems with identifying suitable measures for a specific situation.

In selecting a measure of capacity, it is important to choose one that does not require updating. For example, dollar amounts are often a poor measure of capacity (e.g., capacity of $30 million a year) because price changes necessitate updating of that measure.

Where only one product or service is involved, the capacity of the productive unit may be expressed in terms of that item. However, when multiple products or services are involved, as is often the case, using a simple measure of capacity based on units of output can be misleading. An appliance manufacturer may produce both refrigerators and freezers. If the output rates for these two products are different, it would not make sense to simply state capacity in units without reference to either refrigerators or freezers. The problem is compounded if the firm has other products. One possible solution is to state capacities in terms of each product. Thus, the firm may be able to produce 100 refrigerators per day *or* 80 freezers per day. Sometimes this approach is helpful, sometimes not. For instance, if an organization has many different products or services, it may not be practical to list all of the relevant capacities. This is especially true if there are frequent changes in the mix of output, because this would necessitate a frequently changing composite index of capacity. The preferred alternative in such cases is to use a measure of capacity that refers to *availability of inputs*. Thus, a hospital has a certain number of beds, a factory has a certain number of machine hours available, and a bus has a certain number of seats and a certain amount of standing room.

No single measure of capacity will be appropriate in every situation. Rather, the measure of capacity must be tailored to the situation. Table 5.1 provides some examples of commonly used measures of capacity.

Up to this point, we have been using a general definition of capacity. Although it is functional, it can be refined into two useful definitions of capacity:

Design capacity The maximum designed service capacity or output rate.

Effective capacity Design capacity minus personal and other allowances.

1. **Design capacity:** The maximum output rate or service capacity an operation, process, or facility is designed for.
2. **Effective capacity:** Design capacity minus allowances such as personal time, and maintenance.

Design capacity is the maximum rate of output achieved under ideal conditions. Effective capacity is always less than design capacity owing to realities of changing product mix, the need for periodic maintenance of equipment, lunch breaks, coffee breaks, problems in scheduling and balancing operations, and similar circumstances. *Actual output* cannot exceed

TABLE 5.1
Measures of capacity

Business	Inputs	Outputs
Auto manufacturing	Labor hours, machine hours	Number of cars per shift
Steel mill	Furnace size	Tons of steel per day
Oil refinery	Refinery size	Gallons of fuel per day
Farming	Number of acres, number of cows	Bushels of grain per acre per year, gallons of milk per day
Restaurant	Number of tables, seating capacity	Number of meals served per day
Theater	Number of seats	Number of tickets sold per performance
Retail sales	Square feet of floor space	Revenue generated per day

effective capacity and is often less because of machine breakdowns, absenteeism, shortages of materials, and quality problems, as well as factors that are outside the control of the operations managers.

These different measures of capacity are useful in defining two measures of system effectiveness: efficiency and utilization. *Efficiency* is the ratio of actual output to effective capacity. *Capacity utilization* is the ratio of actual output to design capacity.

$$\text{Efficiency} = \frac{\text{Actual output}}{\text{Effective capacity}} \times 100\% \qquad (5\text{–}1)$$

$$\text{Utilization} = \frac{\text{Actual output}}{\text{Design capacity}} \times 100\% \qquad (5\text{–}2)$$

Both measures are expressed as percentages.

It is not unusual for managers to focus exclusively on efficiency, but in many instances this emphasis can be misleading. This happens when effective capacity is low compared to design capacity. In those cases, high efficiency would seem to indicate effective use of resources when it does not. The following example illustrates this point.

EXAMPLE 1

Given the following information, compute the efficiency and the utilization of the vehicle repair department:

Design capacity = 50 trucks per day
Effective capacity = 40 trucks per day
Actual output = 36 trucks per day

SOLUTION

$$\text{Efficiency} = \frac{\text{Actual output}}{\text{Effective capacity}} \times 100\% = \frac{36 \text{ trucks per day}}{40 \text{ trucks per day}} \times 100\% = 90\%$$

$$\text{Utilization} = \frac{\text{Actual output}}{\text{Design capacity}} \times 100\% = \frac{36 \text{ trucks per day}}{50 \text{ trucks per day}} \times 100\% = 72\%$$

Compared to the effective capacity of 40 units per day, 36 units per day looks pretty good. However, compared to the design capacity of 50 units per day, 36 units per day is much less impressive although probably more meaningful.

Because effective capacity acts as a lid on actual output, the real key to improving capacity utilization is to increase effective capacity by correcting quality problems, maintaining equipment in good operating condition, fully training employees, and fully utilizing bottleneck equipment.

Hence, increasing utilization depends on being able to increase effective capacity, and this requires a knowledge of what is constraining effective capacity.

The following section explores some of the main determinants of effective capacity. It is important to recognize that the benefits of high utilization are realized only in instances where there is demand for the output. When demand is not there, focusing exclusively on utilization can be counterproductive, because the excess output not only results in additional variable costs but also generates the costs of having to carry the output as inventory. Another disadvantage of high utilization is that operating costs may increase because of increasing waiting time due to bottleneck conditions.

DETERMINANTS OF EFFECTIVE CAPACITY

Many decisions about system design have an impact on capacity. The same is true for many operating decisions. This section briefly describes some of these factors, which are then elaborated on elsewhere in the book. The main factors relate to facilities, products or services, processes, human considerations, operational factors, the supply chain, and external forces.

Less Trash Leaves Landfills in a Bind

READING

Not too long ago, dire predictions were made about the lack of landfill capacity to handle the growing amounts of trash companies and residences were generating. Now, some landfills around the country are not getting the trash (and the fees) they need to survive. What was once regarded as undercapacity has now turned into overcapacity.

The reasons for this turnaround can be found in strong efforts by the general public to recycle—stronger than most experts had predicted. Companies, too, are recycling more, a result of government regulations and cost-saving measures. They are also incorporating more recyclable and reusable parts and materials in their products, and they are reducing the amount of materials used to package their products.

But landfills, like many other kinds of operations, are designed to operate at a certain level. It is difficult (and in some states illegal) for them to operate above their design capacity, and it is inefficient to operate at levels much below design capacity. The shortfall that some landfills are experiencing underscores the risks involved in long-term capacity planning and the importance of good forecasts of future demand.

Source: Based on Michael Caputo, "Riga Landfill Strains to Survive," *Rochester Democrat and Chronicle*, July 28, 1997.

Facilities. The design of facilities, including size and provision for expansion, is key. Locational factors, such as transportation costs, distance to market, labor supply, energy sources, and room for expansion, are also important. Likewise, layout of the work area often determines how smoothly work can be performed, and environmental factors such as heating, lighting, and ventilation also play a significant role in determining whether personnel can perform effectively or whether they must struggle to overcome poor design characteristics.

SERVICE

Product and Service Factors. Product or service design can have a tremendous influence on capacity. For example, when items are similar, the ability of the system to produce those items is generally much greater than when successive items differ. Thus, a restaurant that offers a limited menu can usually prepare and serve meals at a faster rate than a restaurant with an extensive menu. Generally speaking, the more uniform the output, the more opportunities there are for standardization of methods and materials, which leads to greater capacity. The particular mix of products or services rendered also must be considered since different items will have different rates of output.

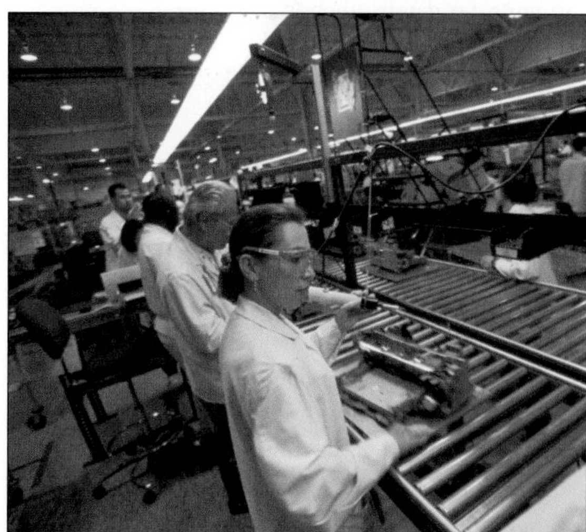

In only 48 hours Solectron in San Jose, California, can build to order, ship, and install a complex computer system. Suppliers hold inventory until it is pulled, thereby increasing manufacturing flexibility.

Making a violin requires precision and skill from an artisan. Capacity is highly limited when items are specialized and produced one at a time.

Process Factors. The quantity capability of a process is an obvious determinant of capacity. A more subtle determinant is the influence of output *quality*. For instance, if quality of output does not meet standards, the rate of output will be slowed by the need for inspection and rework activities. Productivity also affects capacity. Process improvements that increase quality and productivity can result in increased capacity. Also, if multiple products or multiple services are processed in batches, the time to change over equipment settings must be taken into account.

Human Factors. The tasks that make up a job, the variety of activities involved, and the training, skill, and experience required to perform a job all have an impact on the potential and actual output. In addition, employee motivation has a very basic relationship to capacity, as do absenteeism and labor turnover.

Policy Factors. Management policy can affect capacity by allowing or not allowing capacity options such as overtime or second or third shifts.

Operational Factors. Scheduling problems may occur when an organization has differences in equipment capabilities among alternative pieces of equipment or differences in job requirements. Inventory stocking decisions, late deliveries, purchasing requirements, acceptability of purchased materials and parts, and quality inspection and control procedures also can have an impact on effective capacity.

Inventory shortages of even one component of an assembled item (e.g., computers, refrigerators, automobiles) can cause a temporary halt to assembly operations until the components become available. This can have a major impact on effective capacity. Thus, insufficient capacity in one area can affect overall capacity.

Supply Chain Factors. Supply chain factors must be taken into account in capacity planning if substantial capacity changes are involved. Key questions include: What impact will the changes have on suppliers, warehousing, transportation, and distributors? If capacity will be increased, will these elements of the supply chain be able to handle the increase? Conversely, if capacity is to be decreased, what impact will the loss of business have on these elements of the supply chain?

External Factors. Product standards, especially minimum quality and performance standards, can restrict management's options for increasing and using capacity. Thus, pollution standards on products and equipment often reduce effective capacity, as does paperwork required by government regulatory agencies by engaging employees in nonproductive activities. A similar effect occurs when a union contract limits the number of hours and type of work an employee may do.

Table 5.2 summarizes these factors. In addition, *inadequate planning* can be a major limiting determinant of effective capacity.

TABLE 5.2
Factors that determine effective capacity

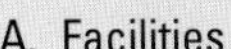

- A. Facilities
  1. Design
  2. Location
  3. Layout
  4. Environment
- B. Product/service
  1. Design
  2. Product or service mix
- C. Process
  1. Quantity capabilities
  2. Quality capabilities
- D. Human factors
  1. Job content
  2. Job design
  3. Training and experience
  4. Motivation
  5. Compensation
  6. Learning rates
  7. Absenteeism and labor turnover
- E. Policy
- F. Operational
  1. Scheduling
  2. Materials management
  3. Quality assurance
  4. Maintenance policies
  5. Equipment breakdowns
- G. Supply chain
- H. External factors
  1. Product standards
  2. Safety regulations
  3. Unions
  4. Pollution control standards

STRATEGY FORMULATION

The three primary strategies are leading, following, and tracking. A leading capacity strategy builds capacity in anticipation of future demand increases. If capacity increases involve a long lead time, this strategy may be the best option. A following strategy builds capacity when demand exceeds current capacity. A tracking strategy is similar to a following strategy, but it adds capacity in relatively small increments to keep pace with increasing demand.

An organization typically bases its capacity strategy on assumptions and predictions about long-term demand patterns, technological changes, and the behavior of its competitors. These typically involve (1) the growth rate and variability of demand, (2) the costs of building and operating facilities of various sizes, (3) the rate and direction of technological innovation, (4) the likely behavior of competitors, and (5) availability of capital and other inputs.

Capacity cushion Extra capacity used to offset demand uncertainty.

In some instances a decision may be made to incorporate a **capacity cushion,** which is an amount of capacity in excess of expected demand when there is some uncertainty about demand. Capacity cushion = capacity − expected demand. Typically, the greater the degree of demand uncertainty, the greater the amount of cushion used. Organizations that have standard products or services generally have smaller capacity cushions. Cost and competitive priorities are also key factors.

Steps in the Capacity Planning Process

1. Estimate future capacity requirements.
2. Evaluate existing capacity and facilities and identify gaps.
3. Identify alternatives for meeting requirements.
4. Conduct financial analyses of each alternative.
5. Assess key qualitative issues for each alternative.
6. Select the alternative to pursue that will be best in the long term.
7. Implement the selected alternative.
8. Monitor results.

Capacity planning can be difficult at times due to the complex influence of market forces and technology.

FORECASTING CAPACITY REQUIREMENTS

Capacity planning decisions involve both long-term and short-term considerations. Long-term considerations relate to overall *level* of capacity, such as facility size; short-term considerations relate to probable *variations* in capacity requirements created by such things as seasonal, random, and irregular fluctuations in demand. Because the time intervals covered by each of these categories can vary significantly from industry to industry, it would be misleading to put times on the intervals. However, the distinction will serve as a framework within which to discuss capacity planning.

Long-term capacity needs require forecasting demand over a time horizon and then converting those forecasts into capacity requirements. Figure 5.1 illustrates some basic demand patterns that might be identified by a forecast. In addition to basic patterns there are more complex patterns, such as a combination of cycles and trends.

When trends are identified, the fundamental issues are (1) how long the trend might persist, because few things last forever, and (2) the slope of the trend. If cycles are identified, interest focuses on (1) the approximate length of the cycles and (2) the amplitude of the cycles (i.e., deviation from average).

Short-term capacity needs are less concerned with cycles or trends than with seasonal variations and other variations from average. These deviations are particularly important because they can place a severe strain on a system's ability to satisfy demand at some times and yet result in idle capacity at other times.

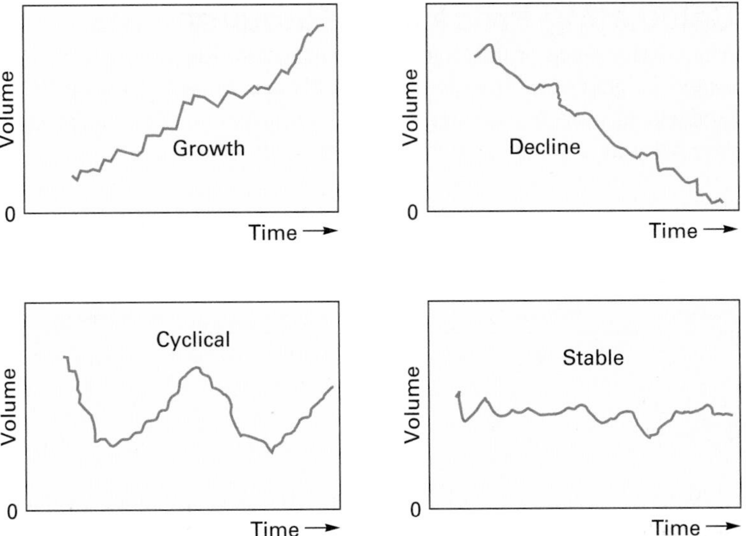

FIGURE 5.1
Common demand patterns

An organization can identify seasonal patterns using standard forecasting techniques. Although commonly thought of as annual fluctuations, seasonal variations are also reflected in monthly, weekly, and even daily capacity requirements. Table 5.3 provides some examples of items that tend to exhibit seasonal demand patterns.

When time intervals are too short to have seasonal variations in demand, the analysis can often describe the variations by probability distributions such as a normal, uniform, or Poisson distribution. For example, we might describe the amount of coffee served during the midday meal at a luncheonette by a normal distribution with a certain mean and standard deviation. The number of customers who enter a bank branch on Monday mornings might be described by a Poisson distribution with a certain mean. It does not follow, however, that *every* instance of random variability will lend itself to description by a standard statistical distribution. Service systems in particular may experience a considerable amount of variability in capacity requirements unless requests for service can be scheduled. Manufacturing systems, because of their typical isolation from customers and the more uniform nature of production, are likely to experience less variations. Waiting-line models and simulation models can be useful when analyzing service systems. These models are described in Chapter 18.

Irregular variations are perhaps the most troublesome: They are difficult or impossible to predict. They are created by such diverse forces as major equipment breakdowns, freak storms that disrupt normal routines, foreign political turmoil that causes oil shortages, discovery of health hazards (nuclear accidents, unsafe chemical dumping grounds, carcinogens in food and drink), and so on.

The link between marketing and operations is crucial to realistic determination of capacity requirements. Through customer contracts, demographic analyses, and forecasts, marketing can supply vital information to operations for ascertaining capacity needs for both the long term and the short term.

TABLE 5.3
Examples of seasonal demand patterns

Period	Items
Year	Beer sales, toy sales, airline traffic, clothing, vacations, tourism, power usage, gasoline consumption, sports and recreation, education
Month	Welfare and social security checks, bank transactions
Week	Retail sales, restaurant meals, automobile traffic, automotive rentals, hotel registrations
Day	Telephone calls, power usage, automobile traffic, public transportation, classroom utilization, retail sales, restaurant meals

Calculating Processing Requirements

A necessary piece of information is the capacity requirements of products that will be processed. To get this information, one must have reasonably accurate demand forecasts for each product and know the standard processing time per unit for each product, the number of workdays per year, and the number of shifts that will be used.

EXAMPLE 2

www.mhhe.com/stevenson11e

A department works one 8-hour shift, 250 days a year, and has these figures for usage of a machine that is currently being considered:

Product	Annual Demand	Standard Processing Time per Unit (hr)	Processing Time Needed (hr)
1	400	5.0	2,000
2	300	8.0	2,400
3	700	2.0	1,400
			5,800

Working one 8-hour shift 250 days a year provides an annual capacity of $8 \times 250 = 2{,}000$ hours per year. Consequently, three of these machines would be needed to handle the required volume:

$$\frac{5{,}800 \text{ hours}}{2{,}000 \text{ hours/machine}} = 2.90 \text{ machines}$$

The task of determining capacity requirements should not be taken lightly. Substantial losses can occur when there are misjudgments on capacity needs. One key reason for those misjudgments can be overly optimistic projections of demand and growth. Marketing personnel are generally optimistic in their outlook, which isn't necessarily a bad thing. But care must be taken so that that optimism doesn't lead to overcapacity, because the resulting underutilized capacity will create an additional cost burden. Another key reason for misjudgments may be focusing exclusively on sales and revenue potential, and not taking into account the *product mix* that will be needed to generate those sales and revenues. To avoid that, marketing and operations personnel must work closely to determine the optimal product mix needed and the resulting cost and profit.

A reasonable approach to determining capacity requirements is to obtain a forecast of future demand, translate demand into both the *quantity and the timing* of capacity requirements, and then decide what capacity changes (increased, decreased, or no changes) are needed.

Long-term capacity alternatives include expansion or contraction of an existing facility, opening or closing branch facilities, and relocation of existing operations. At this point, a decision must be made on whether to make or buy a good, or provide or buy a service.

ADDITIONAL CHALLENGES OF PLANNING SERVICE CAPACITY

SERVICE

While the foregoing discussion relates generally to capacity planning for both goods and services, it is important to note that capacity planning for services can present special challenges due to the nature of services. Three very important factors in planning service capacity are (1) there may be a need to be near customers, (2) the inability to store services, and (3) the degree of volatility of demand.

Convenience for customers is often an important aspect of service. Generally, a service must be located near customers. For example, hotel rooms must be where customers want to stay; having a vacant room in another city won't help. Thus, capacity and location are closely tied.

Capacity also must be matched with the *timing* of demand. Unlike goods, services cannot be produced in one period and stored for use in a later period. Thus, an unsold seat on an airplane, train, or bus cannot be stored for use on a later trip. Similarly, inventories of goods allow customers to immediately satisfy wants, whereas a customer who wants a service may have to wait. This can result in a variety of negatives for an organization that provides the service. Thus, speed of delivery, or customer waiting time, becomes a major concern in service capacity planning. For example, deciding on the number of police officers and fire trucks to have on duty at any given time affects the speed of response and brings into issue the *cost* of maintaining that capacity. Some of these issues are addressed in the chapter on waiting lines.

Demand volatility presents problems for capacity planners. Demand volatility tends to be higher for services than for goods, not only in timing of demand, but also in the amount of time required to service individual customers. For example, banks tend to experience higher volumes of demand on certain days of the week, and the number and nature of transactions tend to vary substantially for different individuals. Then, too, a wide range of social, cultural, and even weather factors can cause major peaks and valleys in demand. The fact that services can't be stored means service systems cannot turn to inventory to smooth demand requirements on the system the way goods-producing systems are able to. Instead, service planners have to devise other methods of coping with demand volatility and cyclical demand. For example, to cope with peak demand periods, planners might consider hiring extra workers, hiring temporary workers, outsourcing some or all of a service, or using pricing and promotion to shift some demand to slower periods.

In some instances, *demand management strategies* can be used to offset capacity limitations. Pricing, promotions, discounts, and similar tactics can help to shift some demand away from peak periods and into slow periods, allowing organizations to achieve a closer match in supply and demand.

DO IT IN-HOUSE OR OUTSOURCE IT?

Once capacity requirements have been determined, the organization must decide whether to produce a good or provide a service itself, or to outsource from another organization. Many organizations buy parts or contract out services, for a variety of reasons. Among those factors are

1. **Available capacity.** If an organization has available the equipment, necessary skills, and *time,* it often makes sense to produce an item or perform a service in-house. The additional costs would be relatively small compared with those required to buy items or subcontract services. On the other hand, outsourcing can increase capacity and flexibility.
2. **Expertise.** If a firm lacks the expertise to do a job satisfactorily, buying might be a reasonable alternative.
3. **Quality considerations.** Firms that specialize can usually offer higher quality than an organization can attain itself. Conversely, unique quality requirements or the desire to closely monitor quality may cause an organization to perform a job itself.
4. **The nature of demand.** When demand for an item is high and steady, the organization is often better off doing the work itself. However, wide fluctuations in demand or small orders are usually better handled by specialists who are able to combine orders from multiple sources, which results in higher volume and tends to offset individual buyer fluctuations.
5. **Cost.** Any cost savings achieved from buying or making must be weighed against the preceding factors. Cost savings might come from the item itself or from transportation cost savings. If there are fixed costs associated with making an item that cannot be reallocated if the service or product is outsourced, that has to be recognized in the analysis. Conversely, outsourcing may help a firm avoid incurring fixed costs.
6. **Risks.** Buying goods or services may entail considerable risks. Loss of direct control over operations, knowledge sharing, and the possible need to disclose proprietary information are three risks. And liability can be a tremendous risk if the products or services of other companies cause harm to customers or the environment, as well as damage to an organization's reputation. Reputation can also be damaged if the public discovers that a supplier operates with substandard working conditions.

In some cases, a firm might choose to perform part of the work itself and let others handle the rest in order to maintain flexibility and to hedge against loss of a subcontractor. If part or all of the work will be done in-house, capacity alternatives will need to be developed.

Outsourcing brings with it a host of supply chain considerations. These are described in Chapter 15.

The following reading describes outsourcing that might surprise you.

My Compliments to the Chef, er, Buyer

READING

Ever wonder how some sit-down restaurants are able to offer a huge variety of menu items, and how they are able to serve everything on that menu quickly? Could they have humongous kitchens and a battery of chefs scurrying around? Or maybe a few amazing chefs whose hands are almost quicker than the eye? Maybe, and maybe not. In fact, that great-tasting restaurant entrée or dessert you are served might have been prepared in a distant kitchen, where it was partially cooked, then flash-frozen or vacuum-packed, and shipped to your restaurant, awaiting your order. Then the entrée was finished cooking, perhaps in a microwave oven, and soon it was served to you—fresh made, so to speak. Surprised? Don't be. Many restaurants, from chains like Fuddruckers and Perkins, to top-quality restaurants, are going the outsourcing route. And companies such as Sara Lee, Land O' Lakes, and Stockpot Soup Company of Redwood, Washington, are only too happy to oblige them. Advertisements in restaurant trade magazines abound, with taglines such as "Hours versus ours" and "Just heat and serve."

Not exactly like mother used to make, but then mother never had to contend with labor costs that run about 30 percent of revenue, or worry about keeping up with the competition.

Questions

1. Explain the meaning of the phrase "Hours versus ours."
2. What advantages are there when restaurants outsource?
3. What are some important disadvantages or limitations of outsourcing for restaurants?
4. Do you consider restaurant outsourcing to be dishonest? Unethical? Explain.
5. Does restaurant outsourcing increase capacity? Explain.

DEVELOPING CAPACITY STRATEGIES

There are a number of ways to enhance development of capacity strategies:

1. **Design flexibility into systems.** The long-term nature of many capacity decisions and the risks inherent in long-term forecasts suggest potential benefits from designing flexible systems. For example, provision for future expansion in the original design of a structure frequently can be obtained at a small price compared to what it would cost to remodel an existing structure that did not have such a provision. Hence, if future expansion of a restaurant seems likely, water lines, power hookups, and waste disposal lines can be put in place initially so that if expansion becomes a reality, modification to the existing structure can be minimized. Similarly, a new golf course may start as a 9-hole operation, but if provision is made for future expansion by obtaining options on adjacent land, it may progress to a larger (18-hole) course. Other considerations in flexible design involve layout of equipment, location, equipment selection, production planning, scheduling, and inventory policies, which will be discussed in later chapters.

2. **Take stage of life cycle into account.** Capacity requirements are often closely linked to the stage of the life cycle that a product or service is in. At the *introduction phase,* it can be difficult to determine both the size of the market and the organization's eventual share of that market. Therefore, organizations should be cautious in making large and/or inflexible capacity investments.

In the *growth phase* the overall market may experience rapid growth. However, the real issue is the rate at which the *organization's* market share grows, which may be more or less than the market rate, depending on the success of the organization's strategies. Organizations generally regard growth as a good thing. They want growth in the overall market for their products or services, and in their share of the market, because they see this as a way of increasing volume, and thus, increasing profits. However, there can also be a downside to this because increasing output levels will require increasing capacity, and that means increasing investment and increasing complexity. In addition, decision makers should take into account possible similar moves by competitors, which would increase the risk of overcapacity in the market, and result in higher unit costs of the output. Another strategy would be to compete on some nonprice attribute of the product by investing in technology and process improvements to make differentiation a competitive advantage.

In the *maturity phase* the size of market levels off, and organizations tend to have stable market shares. Organizations may still be able to increase profitability by reducing costs and making full use of capacity. However, some organizations may still try to increase profitability by increasing capacity if they believe this stage will be fairly long, or the cost to increase capacity is relatively small.

In the *decline phase* an organization is faced with underutilization of capacity due to declining demand. Organizations may eliminate the excess capacity by selling it, or by introducing new products or services. An option that is sometimes used in manufacturing is to transfer capacity to a location that has lower labor costs, which allows the organization to continue to make a profit on the product for a while longer.

3. **Take a "big-picture" (i.e., systems) approach to capacity changes.** When developing capacity alternatives, it is important to consider how parts of the system interrelate. For example, when making a decision to increase the number of rooms in a motel, one should also take into account probable increased demands for parking, entertainment and food, and housekeeping. Also, will suppliers be able to handle the increased volume?

Capacity changes inevitably affect an organization's supply chain. Suppliers may need time to adjust to their capacity, so collaborating with supply chain partners on plans for capacity increases is essential. That includes not only suppliers, but also distributors and transporters.

SUPPLY CHAIN

The risk in not taking a big-picture approach is that the system will be unbalanced. Evidence of an unbalanced system is the existence of a *bottleneck operation.* A **bottleneck operation** is an operation in a sequence of operations whose capacity is lower than the capacities of other operations in the sequence. As a consequence, the capacity of the bottleneck operation limits the system capacity; the capacity of the system is reduced to the capacity of the bottleneck operation. Figure 5.2 illustrates this concept: Four operations generate work that must then be processed by a fifth operation. The four operations each have a capacity of 10 units per hour, for a total capacity of 40 units per hour. However, the fifth operation can only process 30 units per hour. Consequently, the output of the system will only be 30 units per hour. If the other operations operate at capacity, a line of units waiting to be processed by the bottleneck operation will build up at the rate of 10 per hour.

Bottleneck operation An operation in a sequence of operations whose capacity is lower than that of the other operations.

Here is another example. The following diagram illustrates a three-step process, with capacities of each step shown. However, the middle process, because its capacity is lower than that of the others, constrains the system to its capacity of 10 units per hour. Hence it is a bottleneck. In order to increase the capacity of the entire process, it would be necessary to increase the capacity of this bottleneck operation. Note, though, that the potential for

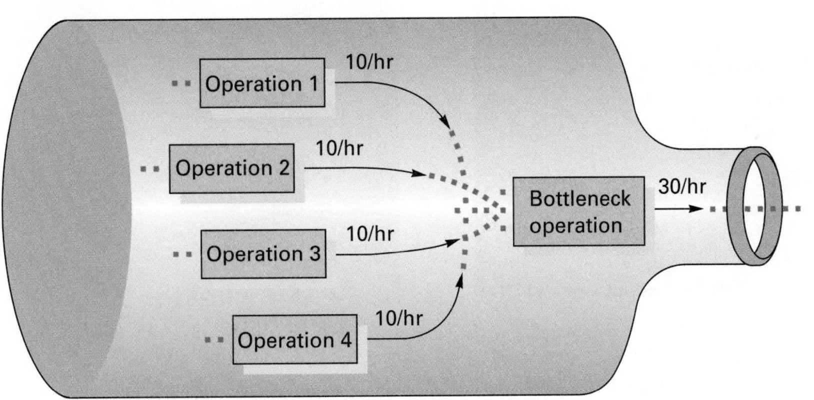

FIGURE 5.2
Bottleneck operation

increasing the capacity of the process is only 5 units, to 15 units per hour. Beyond that, operation 3's capacity would limit process capacity to 15 units/hour.

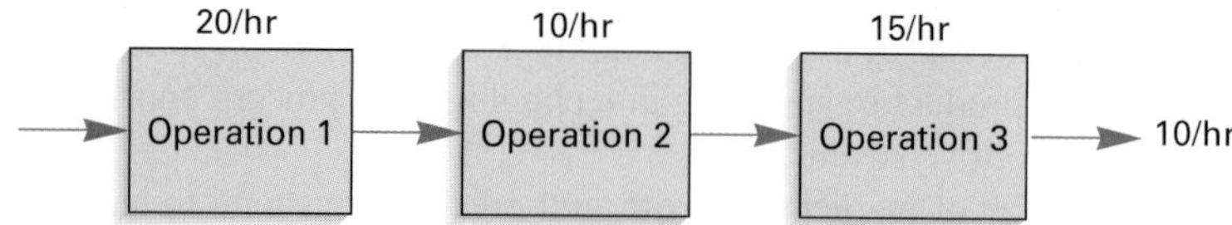

4. **Prepare to deal with capacity "chunks."** Capacity increases are often acquired in fairly large chunks rather than smooth increments, making it difficult to achieve a match between desired capacity and feasible capacity. For instance, the desired capacity of a certain operation may be 55 units per hour, but suppose that machines used for this operation are able to produce 40 units per hour each. One machine by itself would cause capacity to be 15 units per hour short of what is needed, but two machines would result in an excess capacity of 25 units per hour. The illustration becomes even more extreme if we shift the topic—to open-hearth furnaces or to the number of airplanes needed to provide a desired level of capacity.

5. **Attempt to smooth out capacity requirements.** Unevenness in capacity requirements also can create certain problems. For instance, during periods of inclement weather, public transportation ridership tends to increase substantially relative to periods of pleasant weather. Consequently, the system tends to alternate between underutilization and overutilization. Increasing the number of buses or subway cars will reduce the burden during periods of heavy demand, but this will aggravate the problem of overcapacity at other times and certainly add to the cost of operating the system.

We can trace the unevenness in demand for products and services to a variety of sources. The bus ridership problem is weather related to a certain extent, but demand could be considered to be partly random (i.e., varying because of chance factors). Still another source of varying demand is seasonality. Seasonal variations are generally easier to cope with than random variations because they are *predictable.* Consequently, management can make allowances

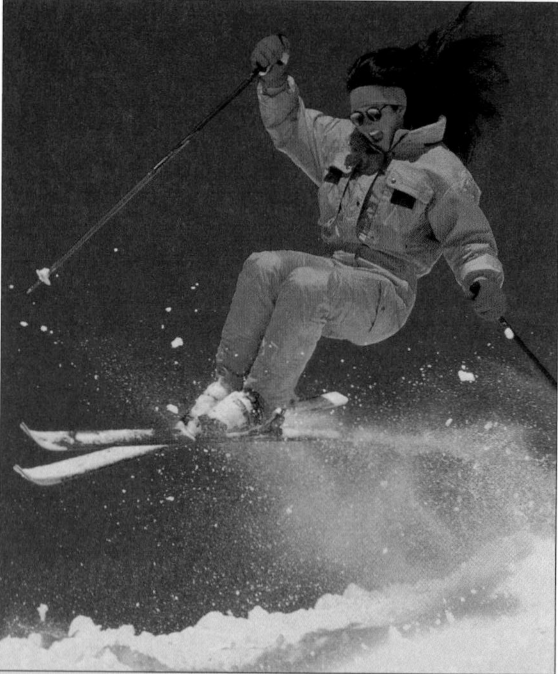

Capacity requirements are affected by seasonal variations. One approach is to identify products that offset each other such as demand for water skis and demand for snow skis.

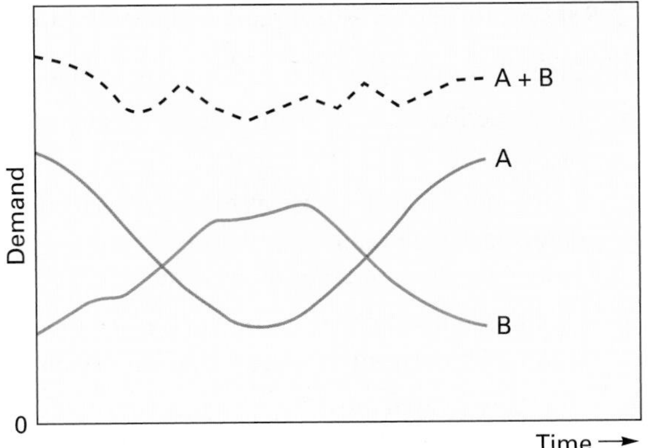

FIGURE 5.3
A and B have complementary demand patterns

in planning and scheduling activities and inventories. However, seasonal variations can still pose problems because of their uneven demands on the system: At certain times the system will tend to be overloaded, while at other times it will tend to be underloaded. One possible approach to this problem is to identify products or services that have complementary demand patterns, that is, patterns that tend to offset each other. For instance, demand for snow skis and demand for water skis might complement each other: Demand for water skis is greater in the spring and summer months, and demand for snow skis is greater in the fall and winter months. The same might apply to heating and air-conditioning equipment. The ideal case is one in which products or services with complementary demand patterns involve the use of the same resources but at different times, so that overall capacity requirements remain fairly stable. Figure 5.3 illustrates complementary demand patterns.

Variability in demand can pose a problem for managers. Simply adding capacity by increasing the size of the operation (e.g., increasing the size of the facility, the workforce, or the amount of processing equipment) is not always the best approach, because that reduces flexibility and adds to fixed costs. Consequently, managers often choose to respond to higher than normal demand in other ways. One way is through the use of overtime work. Another way is to subcontract some of the work. A third way is to draw down finished goods inventories during periods of high demand and replenish them during periods of slow demand. These options and others are discussed in detail in the chapter on aggregate planning.

6. **Identify the optimal operating level.** Production units typically have an ideal or optimal level of operation in terms of unit cost of output. At the ideal level, cost per unit is the lowest for that production unit. If the output rate is less than the optimal level, increasing the output rate will result in decreasing average unit costs. This is known as **economies of scale.** However, if output is increased beyond the optimal level, average unit costs would become increasingly larger. This is known as **diseconomies of scale.** Figure 5.4 illustrates these concepts.

Economies of scale If the output rate is less than the optimal level, increasing the output rate results in decreasing average unit costs.

Diseconomies of scale If the output rate is more than the optimal level, increasing the output rate results in increasing average unit costs.

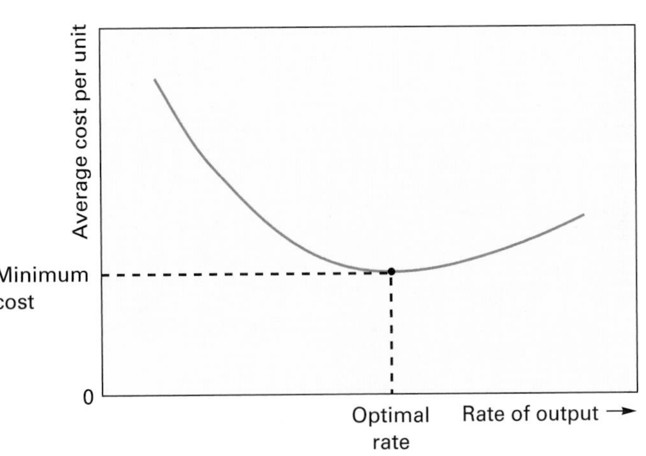

FIGURE 5.4
Production units have an optimal rate of output for minimum cost

Reasons for economies of scale include the following:

a. Fixed costs are spread over more units, reducing the fixed cost per unit.

b. Construction costs increase at a decreasing rate with respect to the size of the facility to be built.

c. Processing costs decrease as output rates increase because operations become more standardized, which reduces unit costs.

Reasons for diseconomies of scale include the following:

a. Distribution costs increase due to traffic congestion and shipping from one large centralized facility instead of several smaller, decentralized facilities.

b. Complexity increases costs; control and communication become more problematic.

c. Inflexibility can be an issue.

d. Additional levels of bureaucracy exist, slowing decision making and approvals for changes.

The explanation for the shape of the cost curve is that at low levels of output, the costs of facilities and equipment must be absorbed (paid for) by very few units. Hence, the cost per unit is high. As output is increased, there are more units to absorb the "fixed" cost of facilities and equipment, so unit costs decrease. However, beyond a certain point, unit costs will start to rise. To be sure, the fixed costs are spread over even more units, so that does not account for the increase, but other factors now become important: worker fatigue; equipment breakdowns; the loss of flexibility, which leaves less of a margin for error; and, generally, greater difficulty in coordinating operations.

Both optimal operating rate and the amount of the minimum cost tend to be a function of the general capacity of the operating unit. For example, as the general capacity of a plant increases, the optimal output rate increases and the minimum cost for the optimal rate decreases. Thus, larger plants tend to have higher optimal output rates and lower minimum costs than smaller plants. Figure 5.5 illustrates these points.

In choosing the capacity of an operating unit, management must take these relationships into account along with the availability of financial and other resources and forecasts of expected demand. To do this, it is necessary to determine enough points for each size facility to be able to make a comparison among different sizes. In some instances, facility sizes are givens, whereas in others, facility size is a continuous variable (i.e., any size can be selected). In the latter case, an ideal facility size can be selected. Usually, management must make a choice from given sizes, and none may have a minimum at the desired rate of output.

7. **Choose a strategy if expansion is involved.** Consider whether incremental expansion or single step is more appropriate. Factors include competitive pressures, market opportunities, costs and availability of funds, disruption of operations, and training requirements. Also, decide whether to lead or follow competitors. Leading is more risky, but it may have greater potential for rewards.

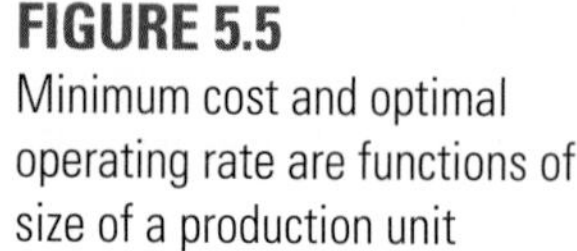

FIGURE 5.5
Minimum cost and optimal operating rate are functions of size of a production unit

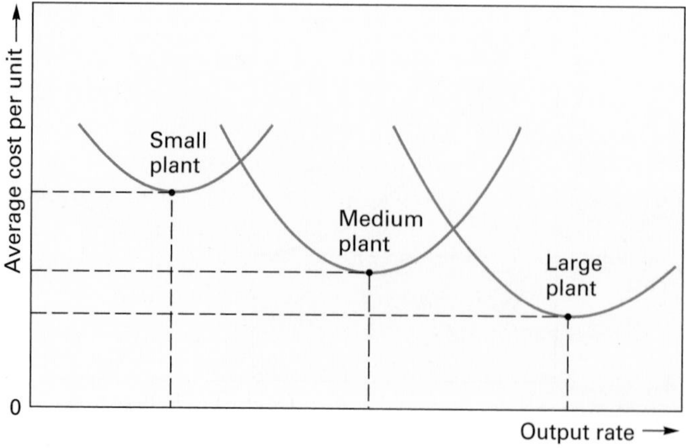

CONSTRAINT MANAGEMENT

A **constraint** is something that limits the performance of a process or system in achieving its goals. Constraint management is often based on the work of Eli Goldratt (*The Theory of Constraints*), and Eli Schragenheim and H. William Dettmer (*Manufacturing at Warp Speed*). There are seven categories of constraints:

Constraint Something that limits the performance of a process or system in achieving its goals.

Market: Insufficient demand.

Resource: Too little of one or more resources (e.g., workers, equipment, and space), as illustrated in Figure 5.2.

Material: Too little of one or more materials.

Financial: Insufficient funds.

Supplier: Unreliable, long lead time, substandard quality.

Knowledge or competency: Needed knowledge or skills missing or incomplete.

Policy: Laws or regulations interfere.

There may only be a few constraints, or there may be more than a few. Constraint issues can be resolved by using the following five steps:[1]

1. Identify the most pressing constraint. If it can easily be overcome, do so, and return to Step 1 for the next constraint. Otherwise, proceed to Step 2.
2. Change the operation to achieve the maximum benefit, given the constraint. This may be a short-term solution.
3. Make sure other portions of the process are supportive of the constraint (e.g., bottleneck operation).
4. Explore and evaluate ways to overcome the constraint. This will depend on the type of constraint. For example, if demand is too low, advertising or price change may be an option. If capacity is the issue, working overtime, purchasing new equipment, and outsourcing are possible options. If additional funds are needed, working to improve cash flow, borrowing, and issuing stocks or bonds may be options. If suppliers are a problem, work with them, find more desirable suppliers, or insource. If knowledge or skills are needed, seek training or consultants, or outsource. If laws or regulations are the issue, working with lawmakers or regulators may be an option.
5. Repeat the process until the level of constraints is acceptable.

EVALUATING ALTERNATIVES

An organization needs to examine alternatives for future capacity from a number of different perspectives. Most obvious are economic considerations: Will an alternative be economically feasible? How much will it cost? How soon can we have it? What will operating and maintenance costs be? What will its useful life be? Will it be compatible with present personnel and present operations?

Less obvious, but nonetheless important, is possible negative public opinion. For instance, the decision to build a new power plant is almost sure to stir up reaction, whether the plant is coal-fired, hydroelectric, or nuclear. Any option that could disrupt lives and property is bound to generate hostile reactions. Construction of new facilities may necessitate moving personnel to a new location. Embracing a new technology may mean retraining some people and terminating some jobs. Relocation can cause unfavorable reactions, particularly if a town is about to lose a major employer. Conversely, community pressure in a new location may arise if the presence of the company is viewed unfavorably (noise, traffic, pollution).

[1]Adapted from Eli Schragenheim and H. William Dettmer, *Manufacturing at Warp Speed* (Boca Raton: St. Lucie Press, 2000).

TABLE 5.4
Cost–volume symbols

FC = Fixed cost
VC = Total variable cost
v = Variable cost per unit
TC = Total cost
TR = Total revenue
R = Revenue per unit
Q = Quantity or volume of output
Q_{BEP} = Break-even quantity
P = Profit

A number of techniques are useful for evaluating capacity alternatives from an economic standpoint. Some of the more common are cost–volume analysis, financial analysis, decision theory, and waiting-line analysis. Cost–volume analysis is described in this section. Financial analysis is mentioned briefly, decision analysis is described in the chapter supplement, and waiting-line analysis is described in Chapter 18.

Cost–Volume Analysis

Cost–volume analysis focuses on relationships between cost, revenue, and volume of output. The purpose of cost–volume analysis is to estimate the income of an organization under different operating conditions. It is particularly useful as a tool for comparing capacity alternatives.

Use of the technique requires identification of all costs related to the production of a given product. These costs are then designated as fixed costs or variable costs. *Fixed costs* tend to remain constant regardless of volume of output. Examples include rental costs, property taxes, equipment costs, heating and cooling expenses, and certain administrative costs. *Variable costs* vary directly with volume of output. The major components of variable costs are generally materials and labor costs. We will assume that variable cost per unit remains the same regardless of volume of output, and that all output can be sold.

Table 5.4 summarizes the symbols used in the cost–volume formulas.

The total cost associated with a given volume of output is equal to the sum of the fixed cost and the variable cost per unit times volume:

$$TC = FC + VC \tag{5–3}$$

$$VC = Q \times v \tag{5–4}$$

where v = variable cost per unit. Figure 5.6A shows the relationship between volume of output and fixed costs, total variable costs, and total (fixed plus variable) costs.

Revenue per unit, like variable cost per unit, is assumed to be the same regardless of quantity of output. Total revenue will have a linear relationship to output, as illustrated in Figure 5.6B. The total revenue associated with a given quantity of output, Q, is

$$TR = R \times Q \tag{5–5}$$

Break-even point (BEP) The volume of output at which total cost and total revenue are equal.

Figure 5.6C describes the relationship between profit—which is the difference between total revenue and total (i.e., fixed plus variable) cost—and volume of output. The volume at which total cost and total revenue are equal is referred to as the **break-even point (BEP).** When volume is less than the break-even point, there is a loss; when volume is greater than the break-even point, there is a profit. The greater the deviation from this point, the greater the profit or loss. Figure 5.6D shows total profit or loss relative to the break-even point. Figure 5.6D can be obtained from Figure 5.6C by drawing a horizontal line through the point where the total cost and total revenue lines intersect. Total profit can be computed using the formula

$$P = TR - TC = R \times Q - (FC + v \times Q)$$

Rearranging terms, we have

$$P = Q(R - v) - FC \tag{5–6}$$

The difference between revenue per unit and variable cost per unit, $R - v$, is known as the *contribution margin.*

The required volume, Q, needed to generate a specified profit is

$$Q = \frac{P + FC}{R - v} \tag{5–7}$$

A special case of this is the volume of output needed for total revenue to equal total cost. This is the break-even point, computed using the formula

FIGURE 5.6 Cost–volume relationships

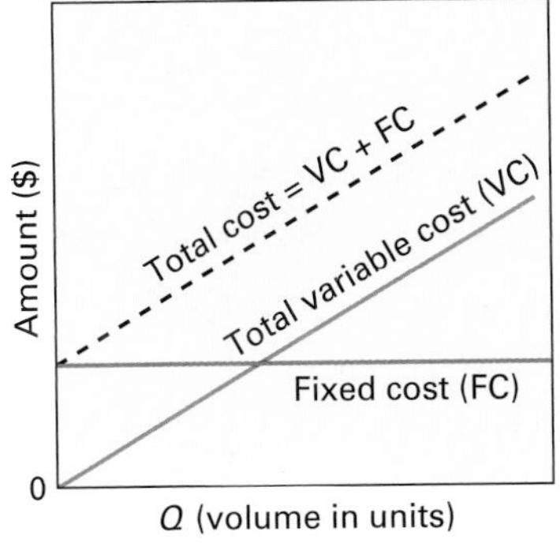

A. Fixed, variable, and total costs

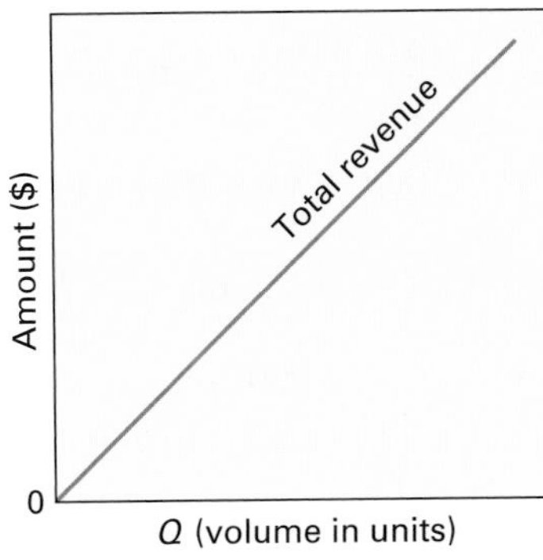

B. Total revenue increases linearly with output

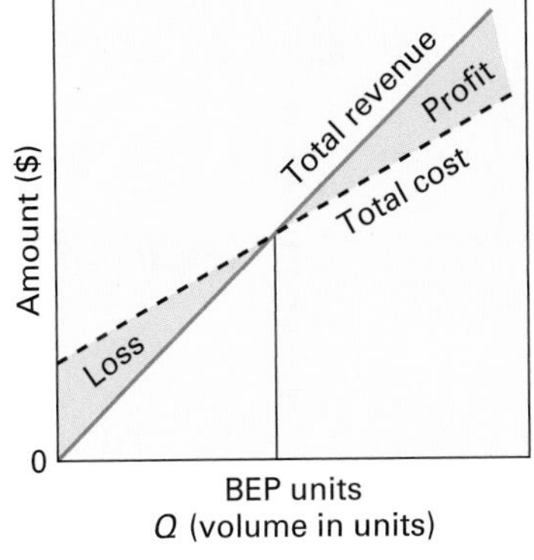

C. Profit = TR – TC

Amount ($)
Profit
0
Loss
Q (volume in units)
BEP

D. Profit versus loss

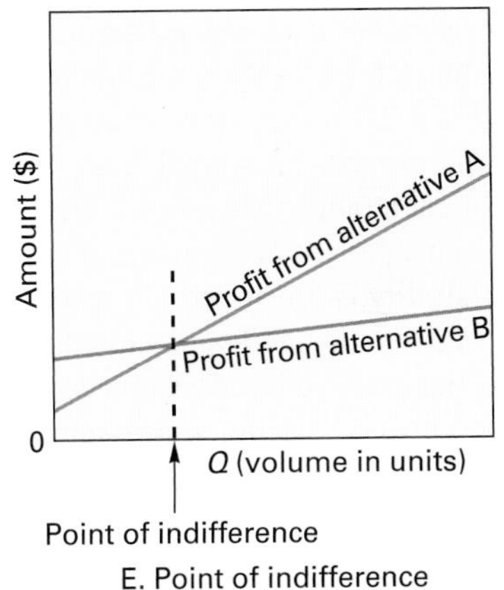

E. Point of indifference for two alternatives

$$Q_{BEP} = \frac{FC}{R - v} \quad (5\text{–}8)$$

Different alternatives can be compared by plotting the profit lines for the alternatives, as shown in Figure 5.6E.

Figure 5.6E illustrates the concept of an **indifference point:** the quantity at which a decision maker would be indifferent between two competing alternatives. In this illustration, a quantity less than the point of indifference would favor choosing alternative B because its profit is higher in that range, while a quantity greater than the point of indifference would favor choosing alternative A.

Indifference point The quantity that would make two alternatives equivalent.

EXAMPLE 3

The owner of Old-Fashioned Berry Pies, S. Simon, is contemplating adding a new line of pies, which will require leasing new equipment for a monthly payment of $6,000. Variable costs would be $2 per pie, and pies would retail for $7 each.

a. How many pies must be sold in order to break even?

b. What would the profit (loss) be if 1,000 pies are made and sold in a month?

c. How many pies must be sold to realize a profit of $4,000?

d. If 2,000 can be sold, and a profit target is $5,000, what price should be charged per pie?

SOLUTION

FC = \$6,000, VC = \$2 per pie, R = \$7 per pie

a. $$Q_{\text{BEP}} = \frac{\text{FC}}{R - \text{VC}} = \frac{\$6{,}000}{\$7 - \$2} = 1{,}200 \text{ pies/month}$$

b. For $Q = 1{,}000$, $P = Q(R - v) - \text{FC} = 1{,}000(\$7 - \$2) - \$6{,}000 = -\$1{,}000$

c. $P = \$4{,}000$; solve for Q using Formula 5–7:

$$Q = \frac{\$4{,}000 + \$6{,}000}{\$7 - \$2} = 2{,}000 \text{ pies}$$

d. $$\text{Profit} = Q(R - v) - \text{FC}$$
$$\$5{,}000 = 2{,}000(R - \$2) - \$6{,}000$$
$$R = \$7.50$$

Capacity alternatives may involve *step costs,* which are costs that increase stepwise as potential volume increases. For example, a firm may have the option of purchasing one, two, or three machines, with each additional machine increasing the fixed cost, although perhaps not linearly. (See Figure 5.7A.) Then fixed costs and potential volume would depend on the number of machines purchased. The implication is that *multiple break-even quantities* may occur, possibly one for each range. Note, however, that the total revenue line might not intersect the fixed-cost line in a particular range, meaning that there would be no break-even point in that range. This possibility is illustrated in Figure 5.7B, where there is no break-even point in the first range. In order to decide how many machines to purchase, a manager must consider projected annual demand (volume) relative to the multiple break-even points and choose the most appropriate number of machines, as Example 4 shows.

EXAMPLE 4

www.mhhe.com/stevenson11e

A manager has the option of purchasing one, two, or three machines. Fixed costs and potential volumes are as follows:

Number of Machines	Total Annual Fixed Costs	Corresponding Range of Output
1	\$ 9,600	0 to 300
2	15,000	301 to 600
3	20,000	601 to 900

Variable cost is \$10 per unit, and revenue is \$40 per unit.

a. Determine the break-even point for each range.

b. If projected annual demand is between 580 and 660 units, how many machines should the manager purchase?

FIGURE 5.7
Break-even problem with step fixed costs

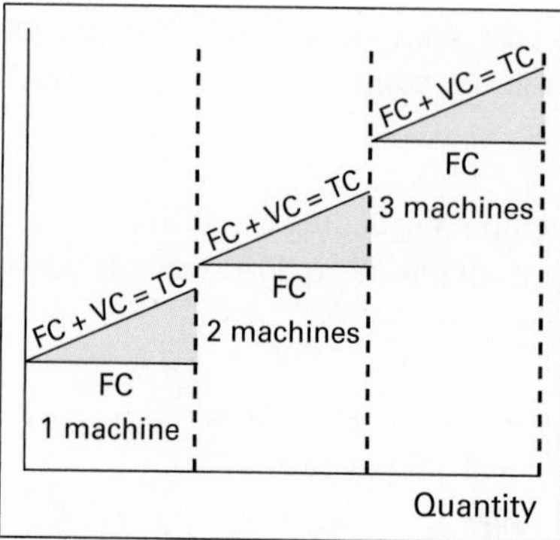

A. Step fixed costs and variable costs

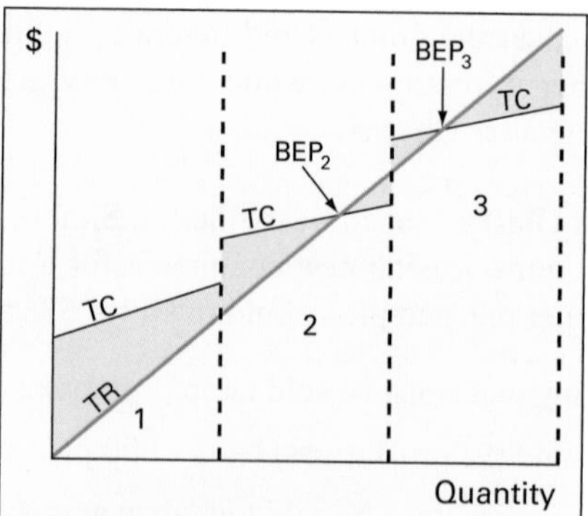

B. Multiple break-even points

SOLUTION

a. Compute the break-even point for each range using the formula $Q_{BEP} = FC/(R - v)$.

For one machine: $Q_{BEP} = \dfrac{\$9,600}{\$40/\text{unit} - \$10/\text{unit}} = 320$ units [not in range, so there is no BEP]

For two machines: $Q_{BEP} = \dfrac{\$15,000}{\$40/\text{unit} - \$10/\text{unit}} = 500$ units

For three machines: $Q_{BEP} = \dfrac{\$20,000}{\$40/\text{unit} - \$10/\text{unit}} = 666.67$ units

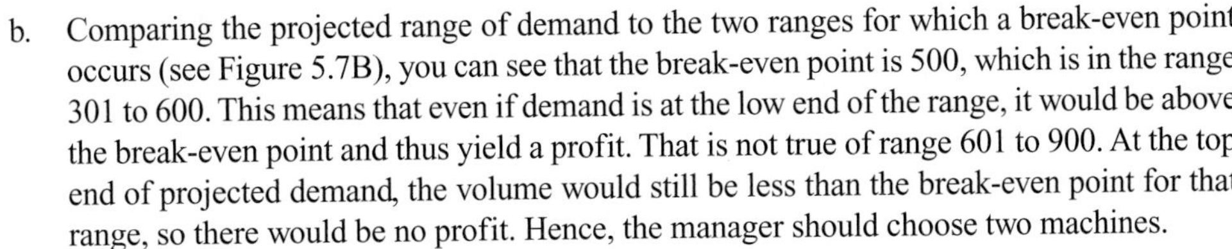

b. Comparing the projected range of demand to the two ranges for which a break-even point occurs (see Figure 5.7B), you can see that the break-even point is 500, which is in the range 301 to 600. This means that even if demand is at the low end of the range, it would be above the break-even point and thus yield a profit. That is not true of range 601 to 900. At the top end of projected demand, the volume would still be less than the break-even point for that range, so there would be no profit. Hence, the manager should choose two machines.

Cost–volume analysis can be a valuable tool for comparing capacity alternatives if certain assumptions are satisfied:

1. One product is involved.
2. Everything produced can be sold.
3. The variable cost per unit is the same regardless of the volume.
4. Fixed costs do not change with volume changes, or they are step changes.
5. The revenue per unit is the same regardless of volume.
6. Revenue per unit exceeds variable cost per unit.

As with any quantitative tool, it is important to verify that the assumptions on which the technique is based are reasonably satisfied for a particular situation. For example, revenue per unit or variable cost per unit is not always constant. In addition, fixed costs may not be constant over the range of possible output. If demand is subject to random variations, one must take that into account in the analysis. Also, cost–volume analysis requires that fixed and variable costs can be separated, and this is sometimes exceedingly difficult to accomplish. Cost–volume analysis works best with one product or a few products that have the same cost characteristics.

A notable benefit of cost–volume considerations is the conceptual framework it provides for integrating cost, revenue, and profit estimates into capacity decisions. If a proposal looks attractive using cost–volume analysis, the next step would be to develop cash flow models to see how it fares with the addition of time and more flexible cost functions.

Financial Analysis

Operations personnel need to have the ability to do *financial analysis.* A problem that is universally encountered by managers is how to allocate scarce funds. A common approach is to use financial analysis to rank investment proposals, taking into account the *time value of money.*

Two important terms in financial analysis are *cash flow* and *present value:*

> **Cash flow** refers to the difference between the cash received from sales (of goods or services) and other sources (e.g., sale of old equipment) and the cash outflow for labor, materials, overhead, and taxes.
>
> **Present value** expresses in current value the sum of all future cash flows of an investment proposal.

Cash flow The difference between cash received from sales and other sources, and cash outflow for labor, material, overhead, and taxes.

Present value The sum, in current value, of all future cash flows of an investment proposal.

The three most commonly used methods of financial analysis are payback, present value, and internal rate of return.

Payback is a crude but widely used method that focuses on the length of time it will take for an investment to return its original cost. For example, an investment with an original cost of $6,000 and a monthly net cash flow of $1,000 has a payback period of six months. Payback ignores the *time value of money.* Its use is easier to rationalize for short-term than for long-term projects.

The *present value (PV)* method summarizes the initial cost of an investment, its estimated annual cash flows, and any expected salvage value in a single value called the *equivalent current value,* taking into account the time value of money (i.e., interest rates).

The *internal rate of return (IRR)* summarizes the initial cost, expected annual cash flows, and estimated future salvage value of an investment proposal in an *equivalent interest rate.* In other words, this method identifies the rate of return that equates the estimated future returns and the initial cost.

These techniques are appropriate when there is a high degree of *certainty* associated with estimates of future cash flows. In many instances, however, operations managers and other managers must deal with situations better described as risky or uncertain. When conditions of risk or uncertainty are present, decision theory is often applied.

Decision Theory

Decision theory is a helpful tool for financial comparison of alternatives under conditions of risk or uncertainty. It is suited to capacity decisions and to a wide range of other decisions managers must make. It involves identifying a set of possible future conditions that could influence results, listing alternative courses of action, and developing a financial outcome for each alternative–future condition combination. Decision theory is described in the supplement to this chapter.

Waiting-Line Analysis

SERVICE

Analysis of lines is often useful for designing or modifying service systems. Waiting lines have a tendency to form in a wide variety of service systems (e.g., airport ticket counters, telephone calls to a cable television company, hospital emergency rooms). The lines are symptoms of bottleneck operations. Analysis is useful in helping managers choose a capacity level that will be cost-effective through balancing the cost of having customers wait with the cost of providing additional capacity. It can aid in the determination of expected costs for various levels of service capacity.

This topic is described in Chapter 18.

Simulation

Simulation can be a useful tool in evaluating what-if scenarios. Simulation is described on the book's Web site.

OPERATIONS STRATEGY

The strategic implications of capacity decisions can be enormous, impacting all areas of the organization. From an operations management standpoint, capacity decisions establish a set of conditions within which operations will be required to function. Hence, it is extremely important to include input from operations management people in making capacity decisions.

Flexibility can be a key issue in capacity decisions, although flexibility is not always an option, particularly in capital-intensive industries. However, where possible, flexibility allows an organization to be agile—that is, responsive to changes in the marketplace. Also, it reduces to a certain extent the dependence on long-range forecasts to accurately predict demand. And flexibility makes it easier for organizations to take advantage of technological and other innovations. Maintaining excess capacity (a capacity cushion) may provide a degree of flexibility, albeit at added cost.

Some organizations use a strategy of maintaining a capacity cushion for the purpose of blocking entry into the market by new competitors. The excess capacity enables them to produce at costs lower than what new competitors can. However, such a strategy means higher-than-necessary unit costs, and it makes it more difficult to cut back if demand slows, or to shift to new product or service offerings.

Bottleneck management can be a way to increase effective capacity, by scheduling non-bottleneck operations to achieve maximum utilization of bottleneck operations.

In cases where capacity expansion will be undertaken, there are two strategies for determining the timing and degree of capacity expansion. One is the *expand-early* strategy (i.e., before demand materializes). The intent might be to achieve economies of scale, to expand market share, or to preempt competitors from expanding. The risks of this strategy include an oversupply that would drive prices down, and underutilized equipment that would result in higher unit costs.

The other approach is the *wait-and-see strategy* (i.e., to expand capacity only after demand materializes, perhaps incrementally). Its advantages include a lower chance of oversupply due to more accurate matching of supply and demand, and higher capacity utilization. The key risks are loss of market share and the inability to meet demand if expansion requires a long lead time.

In cases where capacity contraction will be undertaken, *capacity disposal* strategies become important. This can be the result of the need to replace aging equipment with newer equipment. It can also be the result of outsourcing and downsizing operations. The cost or benefit of asset disposal should be taken into account when contemplating these actions.

SUMMARY

Capacity refers to a system's potential for producing goods or delivering services over a specified time interval. Capacity decisions are important because capacity is a ceiling on output and a major determinant of operating costs.

Three key inputs to capacity planning are the kind of capacity that will be needed, how much will be needed, and when it will be needed. Accurate forecasts are critical to the planning process.

The capacity planning decision is one of the most important decisions that managers make. The capacity decision is strategic and long-term in nature, often involving a significant initial investment of capital. Capacity planning is particularly difficult in cases where returns will accrue over a lengthy period and risk is a major consideration.

A variety of factors can interfere with effective capacity, so effective capacity is usually somewhat less than design capacity. These factors include facilities design and layout, human factors, product/service design, equipment failures, scheduling problems, and quality considerations.

Capacity planning involves long-term and short-term considerations. Long-term considerations relate to the overall level of capacity; short-term considerations relate to variations in capacity requirements due to seasonal, random, and irregular fluctuations in demand. Ideally, capacity will match demand. Thus, there is a close link between forecasting and capacity planning, particularly in the long term. In the short term, emphasis shifts to describing and coping with variations in demand.

Development of capacity alternatives is enhanced by taking a systems approach to planning, by recognizing that capacity increments are often acquired in chunks, by designing flexible systems, and by considering product/service complements as a way of dealing with various patterns of demand.

In evaluating capacity alternatives, a manager must consider both quantitative and qualitative aspects. Quantitative analysis usually reflects economic factors, and qualitative considerations include intangibles such as public opinion and personal preferences of managers. Cost–volume analysis can be useful for analyzing alternatives.

KEY POINTS

1. Capacity decisions can be critical to the success of a business organization because capacity is the supply side of the supply-demand equation, and too little or too much capacity is costly.
2. The key issues in capacity planning relate to determining what kind of capacity is needed, how much is needed, and when it is needed.
3. Volatile demand and long lead times to achieve capacity changes can be challenging.
4. One or more constraints can adversely affect the overall capacity of a system (see, for example, Figure 5.2). Capacity increases can only be achieved by loosening those constraints, not by increasing other resources so it is essential to identify constraining resources and focus efforts on overcoming them.

KEY TERMS

bottleneck operation, 195
break-even point (BEP), 200
capacity, 183
capacity cushion, 190
cash flow, 203
constraint, 199
design capacity, 186
diseconomies of scale, 197
economies of scale, 197
effective capacity, 186
indifference point, 201
present value, 203

SOLVED PROBLEMS

Problem 1

www.mhhe.com/stevenson11e

A firm's manager must decide whether to make or buy a certain item used in the production of vending machines. Making the item would involve annual lease costs of $150,000. Cost and volume estimates are as follows:

	Make	Buy
Annual fixed cost	$150,000	None
Variable cost/unit	$60	$80
Annual volume (units)	12,000	12,000

a. Given these numbers, should the firm buy or make this item?

b. There is a possibility that volume could change in the future. At what volume would the manager be indifferent between making and buying?

Solution

a. Determine the annual cost of each alternative:

Total cost = Fixed cost + Volume × Variable cost

$$\begin{array}{lrl} \text{Make:} & \$150{,}000 + 12{,}000(\$60) & = \$870{,}000 \\ \text{Buy:} & 0 + 12{,}000(\$80) & = \$960{,}000 \end{array}$$

Because the annual cost of making the item is less than the annual cost of buying it, the manager would reasonably choose to make the item. *Note:* If the unit cost to buy had been *less than* the *variable cost* to make, there would be no need to even consider fixed costs; it would simply have been better to buy.

b. To determine the volume at which the two choices would be equivalent, set the two total costs equal to each other and solve for volume: $TC_{make} = TC_{buy}$. Thus, $\$150{,}000 + Q(\$60) = 0 + Q(\$80)$. Solving, $Q = 7{,}500$ units. Therefore, at a volume of 7,500 units a year, the manager would be indifferent between making and buying. For lower volumes, the choice would be to buy, and for higher volumes, the choice would be to make.

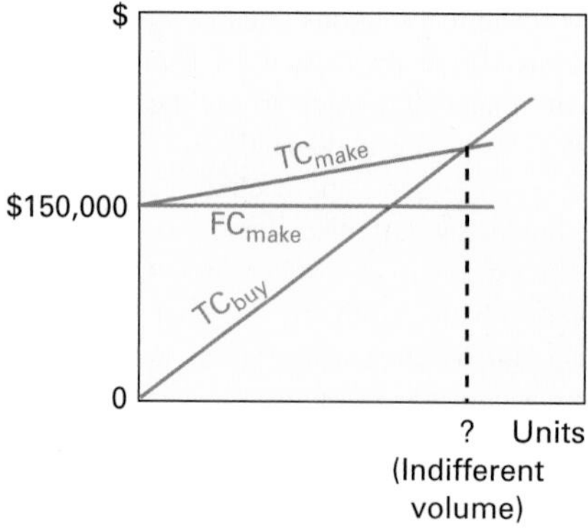

Problem 2

www.mhhe.com/stevenson11e

A small firm produces and sells automotive items in a five-state area. The firm expects to consolidate assembly of its battery chargers line at a single location. Currently, operations are in three widely scattered locations. The leading candidate for location will have a monthly fixed cost of $42,000 and variable costs of $3 per charger. Chargers sell for $7 each. Prepare a table that shows total profits, fixed costs, variable costs, and revenues for monthly volumes of 10,000, 12,000, and 15,000 units. What is the break-even point?

Solution

$$\begin{aligned} \text{Revenue} &= \$7 \text{ per unit} \\ \text{Variable cost} &= \$3 \text{ per unit} \\ \text{Fixed cost} &= \$42,000 \text{ per month} \\ \text{Profit} &= Q(R - v) - \text{FC} \\ \text{Total cost} &= \text{FC} + v \times Q \end{aligned}$$

Volume	Total Revenue	Total VC	Fixed Cost	Total Cost	Total Profit
10,000	$ 70,000	$30,000	$42,000	$72,000	$(2,000)
12,000	84,000	36,000	42,000	78,000	6,000
15,000	105,000	45,000	42,000	87,000	18,000

$$Q_{\text{BEP}} = \frac{\text{FC}}{R - v} = \frac{\$42,000}{\$7 - \$3} = 10,500 \text{ units per month}$$

Problem 3

Refer to Problem 2. Determine profit when volume equals 22,000 units.

Solution

$$\text{Profit} = Q(R - v) - \text{FC} = Q(\$7 - \$3) - \$42,000 = \$4Q - \$42,000$$

For $Q = 22,000$, profit is

$$\$4(22,000) - \$42,000 = \$46,000$$

Problem 4

www.mhhe.com/stevenson11e

A manager must decide which type of equipment to buy, Type A or Type B. Type A equipment costs $15,000 each, and Type B costs $11,000 each. The equipment can be operated eight hours a day, 250 days a year.

Either machine can be used to perform two types of chemical analysis, C1 and C2. Annual service requirements and processing times are shown in the following table. Which type of equipment should be purchased, and how many of that type will be needed? The goal is to minimize total purchase cost.

		PROCESSING TIME PER ANALYSIS (hr)	
Analysis Type	Annual Volume	A	B
C1	1,200	1	2
C2	900	3	2

Solution

Total processing time (Annual volume × Processing time per analysis) needed by type of equipment:

Analysis Type		A	B
C1		1,200	2,400
C2		2,700	1,800
	Total	3,900	4,200

Total processing time available per piece of equipment is 8 hours/day × 250 days/year = 2,000. Hence, one piece can handle 2,000 hours of analysis, two pieces of equipment can handle 4,000 hours, and so on.

Given the total processing requirements, two of Type A would be needed, for a total cost of 2 × $15,000 = $30,000, or three of Type B, for a total cost of 3 × $11,000 = $33,000. Thus, two pieces of Type A would have sufficient capacity to handle the load at a lower cost than three of Type B.

DISCUSSION AND REVIEW QUESTIONS

1. Contrast design capacity and effective capacity.
2. List and briefly explain three factors that may inhibit capacity utilization.
3. How do long-term and short-term capacity considerations differ?
4. Give an example of a good and a service that exhibit these seasonal demand patterns:
   a. Annual
   b. Monthly
   c. Weekly
   d. Daily
5. Give some examples of building flexibility into system design.
6. Why is it important to adopt a big-picture approach to capacity planning?
7. What is meant by "capacity in chunks," and why is that a factor in capacity planning?
8. What kinds of capacity problems do many elementary and secondary schools periodically experience? What are some alternatives to deal with those problems?
9. How can a systems approach to capacity planning be useful?
10. How do capacity decisions influence productivity?
11. Why is it important to match process capabilities with product requirements?
12. Briefly discuss how uncertainty affects capacity decisions.
13. Discuss the importance of capacity planning in deciding on the number of police officers or fire trucks to have on duty at a given time.
14. Why is capacity planning one of the most critical decisions a manager has to make?
15. Why is capacity planning for services more challenging than it is for goods production?
16. What are some capacity measures for each of the following?
    a. University
    b. Hospital
    c. Computer repair shop
    d. Farm
17. What is the benefit to a business organization of having capacity measures?

TAKING STOCK

1. What are the major trade-offs in capacity planning?
2. Who needs to be involved in capacity planning?
3. In what ways does technology have an impact on capacity planning?

CRITICAL THINKING EXERCISES

1. A computer repair service has a design capacity of 80 repairs per day. Its effective capacity, however, is 64 repairs per day, and its actual output is 62 repairs per day. The manager would like to increase the number of repairs per day. Which of the following factors would you recommend that the manager investigate: quality problems, absenteeism, or scheduling and balancing? Explain your reasoning.
2. Compared to manufacturing, service requirements tend to be more time dependent, location dependent, and volatile. In addition, service quality is often directly observable by customers. Find a recent article in a business magazine that describes how a service organization is struggling with one or more of these issues and make recommendations on what an organization needs to do to overcome these difficulties.
3. Identify four potential unethical actions or inactions related to capacity planning, and the ethical principle each violates (see Chapter 1).

PROBLEMS

1. Determine the utilization and the efficiency for each of these situations:
   a. A loan processing operation that processes an average of 7 loans per day. The operation has a design capacity of 10 loans per day and an effective capacity of 8 loans per day.
   b. A furnace repair team that services an average of four furnaces a day if the design capacity is six furnaces a day and the effective capacity is five furnaces a day.
   c. Would you say that systems that have higher efficiency ratios than other systems will always have higher utilization ratios than those other systems? Explain.

2. In a job shop, effective capacity is only 50 percent of design capacity, and actual output is 80 percent of effective output. What design capacity would be needed to achieve an actual output of eight jobs per week?

3. A producer of pottery is considering the addition of a new plant to absorb the backlog of demand that now exists. The primary location being considered will have fixed costs of $9,200 per month and variable costs of 70 cents per unit produced. Each item is sold to retailers at a price that averages 90 cents.

   a. What volume per month is required in order to break even?
   b. What profit would be realized on a monthly volume of 61,000 units? 87,000 units?
   c. What volume is needed to obtain a profit of $16,000 per month?
   d. What volume is needed to provide a revenue of $23,000 per month?
   e. Plot the total cost and total revenue lines.

4. A small firm intends to increase the capacity of a bottleneck operation by adding a new machine. Two alternatives, A and B, have been identified, and the associated costs and revenues have been estimated. Annual fixed costs would be $40,000 for A and $30,000 for B; variable costs per unit would be $10 for A and $11 for B; and revenue per unit would be $15.

   a. Determine each alternative's break-even point in units.
   b. At what volume of output would the two alternatives yield the same profit?
   c. If expected annual demand is 12,000 units, which alternative would yield the higher profit?

5. A producer of felt-tip pens has received a forecast of demand of 30,000 pens for the coming month from its marketing department. Fixed costs of $25,000 per month are allocated to the felt-tip operation, and variable costs are 37 cents per pen.

   a. Find the break-even quantity if pens sell for $1 each.
   b. At what price must pens be sold to obtain a monthly profit of $15,000, assuming that estimated demand materializes?

6. A real estate agent is considering changing her cell phone plan. There are three plans to choose from, all of which involve a monthly service charge of $20. Plan A has a cost of $.45 a minute for daytime calls and $.20 a minute for evening calls. Plan B has a charge of $.55 a minute for daytime calls and $.15 a minute for evening calls. Plan C has a flat rate of $80 with 200 minutes of calls allowed per month and a charge of $.40 per minute beyond that, day or evening.

   a. Determine the total charge under each plan for this case: 120 minutes of day calls and 40 minutes of evening calls in a month.
   b. Prepare a graph that shows total monthly cost for each plan versus daytime call minutes.
   c. If the agent will use the service for daytime calls, over what range of call minutes will each plan be optimal?
   d. Suppose that the agent expects both daytime and evening calls. At what point (i.e., percentage of call minutes for daytime calls) would she be indifferent between plans A and B?

7. A firm plans to begin production of a new small appliance. The manager must decide whether to purchase the motors for the appliance from a vendor at $7 each or to produce them in-house. Either of two processes could be used for in-house production; one would have an annual fixed cost of $160,000 and a variable cost of $5 per unit, and the other would have an annual fixed cost of $190,000 and a variable cost of $4 per unit. Determine the range of annual volume for which each of the alternatives would be best.

8. A manager is trying to decide whether to purchase a certain part or to have it produced internally. Internal production could use either of two processes. One would entail a variable cost of $17 per unit and an annual fixed cost of $200,000; the other would entail a variable cost of $14 per unit and an annual fixed cost of $240,000. Three vendors are willing to provide the part. Vendor A has a price of $20 per unit for any volume up to 30,000 units. Vendor B has a price of $22 per unit for demand of 1,000 units or less, and $18 per unit for larger quantities. Vendor C offers a price of $21 per unit for the first 1,000 units, and $19 per unit for additional units.

   a. If the manager anticipates an annual volume of 10,000 units, which alternative would be best from a cost standpoint? For 20,000 units, which alternative would be best?
   b. Determine the range for which each alternative is best. Are there any alternatives that are never best? Which?

9. A company manufactures a product using two machine cells. Each cell has a design capacity of 250 units per day and an effective capacity of 230 units per day. At present, actual output averages

200 units per cell, but the manager estimates that productivity improvements soon will increase output to 225 units per day. Annual demand is currently 50,000 units. It is forecasted that within two years, annual demand will triple. How many cells should the company plan to produce to satisfy predicted demand under these conditions? Assume 240 workdays per year.

10. A manager must decide which type of machine to buy, A, B, or C. Machine costs are as follows:

Machine	Cost
A	$40,000
B	$30,000
C	$80,000

Product forecasts and processing times on the machines are as follows:

		PROCCESSING TIME PER UNIT (minutes)		
Product	Annual Demand	A	B	C
1	16,000	3	4	2
2	12,000	4	4	3
3	6,000	5	6	4
4	30,000	2	2	1

a. Assume that only purchasing costs are being considered. Which machine would have the lowest total cost, and how many of that machine would be needed? Machines operate 10 hours a day, 250 days a year.

b. Consider this additional information: The machines differ in terms of hourly operating costs: The A machines have an hourly operating cost of $10 each, B machines have an hourly operating cost of $11 each, and C machines have an hourly operating cost of $12 each. Which alternative would be selected, and how many machines, in order to minimize total cost while satisfying capacity processing requirements?

11. A manager must decide how many machines of a certain type to purchase. Each machine can process 100 customers per day. One machine will result in a fixed cost of $2,000 per day, while two machines will result in a fixed cost of $3,800 per day. Variable costs will be $20 per customer, and revenue will be $45 per customer.

a. Determine the break-even point for each range.

b. If estimated demand is 90 to 120 customers per day, how many machines should be purchased?

12. The manager of a car wash must decide whether to have one or two wash lines. One line will mean a fixed cost of $6,000 a month, and two lines will mean a fixed cost of $10,500 a month. Each line would be able to process 15 cars an hour. Variable costs will be $3 per car, and revenue will be $5.95 per car. The manager projects an average demand of between 14 and 18 cars an hour. Would you recommend one or two lines? The car wash is open 300 hours a month.

13. The following diagram shows a 4-step process that begins with Operation 1 and ends with Operation 4. The rates shown in each box represent the effective capacity of that operation.

a. Determine the capacity of this process.

b. Which action would yield the greatest increase in process capacity: (1) increase the capacity of Operation 1 by 15 percent; (2) increase the capacity of Operation 2 by 10 percent; or (3) increase the capacity of Operation 3 by 10 percent?

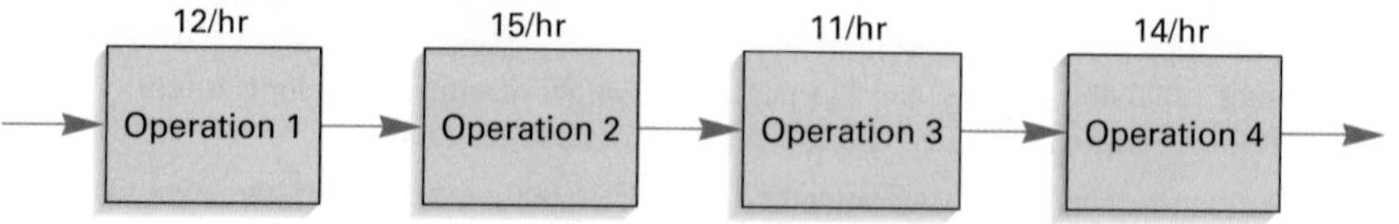

14. The following diagram describes a process that consists of eight separate operations, with sequential relationships and capacities (units per hour) as shown.

a. What is the current capacity of the entire process?
b. If you could increase the capacity of only two operations through process improvement efforts, which two operations would you select, how much additional capacity would you strive for in each of those operations, and what would the resulting capacity of the entire process be?

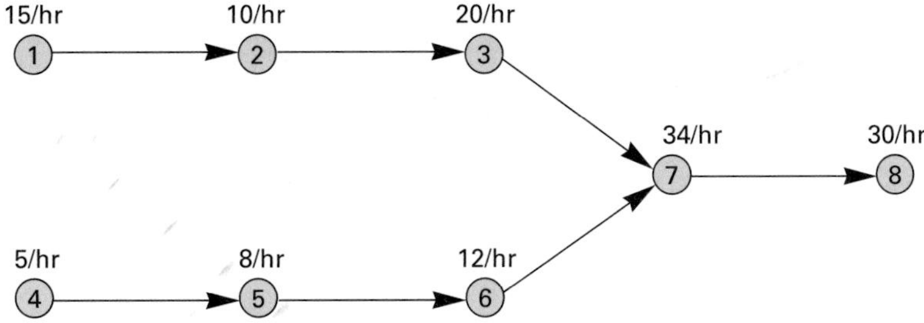

Outsourcing of Hospital Services

CASE

Due to financial pressures that many hospitals face, the Deaconess Clinic in Billings, Montana, decided to outsource a number of services, although in somewhat different ways.

First, the hospital outsourced its cafeteria food service. Although the food service employees were hired by the outside firm, they still felt a sense of ownership of their jobs, and still felt connected to the hospital because of the family atmosphere in the kitchen and the cafeteria.

When the hospital tried the same thing with housekeeping, employee turnover became a problem. An investigation revealed that because the housekeeping employees were more isolated in their work, they lost what little feeling of being connected to the hospital they had. The problem was solved by hiring the employees back but using the outsource company to manage housekeeping.

The hospital also decided to outsource its laundry service. This time the hospital approached a rival hospital about joining it in outsourcing laundry service.

Questions

1. In some instances the outsourced service occurs in a different location, while in others it takes place inside the organization doing the outsourcing, as the food service did in this case. What advantages were there in having the outsourced work performed within the hospital? Suppose a different hospital outsourced its food service but decided not to have the work performed in-house. What might its rationale be?
2. In the housekeeping situation, why not just forget about outsourcing, especially since the hospital ended up rehiring its employees anyway?
3. For laundry service, what might have been the rationale for asking another hospital to join it?

Source: Based on Norm Friedman, "Is Outsourcing the Solution?" www.hpnonline.com/inside/June04/outsourcing.htm.

SELECTED BIBLIOGRAPHY AND FURTHER READINGS

Bakke, N. A., and R. Hellburg. "The Challenges of Capacity Planning." *International Journal of Production Economics* (1993), pp. 243–64.

Goldratt, Eliyahu M. *Theory of Constraints.* Great Barrington, MA: North River Press, 2000.

Hill, Terry. *Manufacturing Strategy.* 2nd ed. Burr Ridge, IL: Richard D. Irwin, 1994.

Ingold, Anthony, Ian Yeoman, and Una McMahon-Beattie, eds. *Yield Management: Strategies for the Service Industries.* 2nd ed. London: Continuum, 2001.

Schragenheim, Eli, and H. William Dettmer. *Manufacturing at Warp Speed.* Boca Raton: St. Lucie Press, 2000.

Upton, David. "What Really Makes Factories Flexible?" *Harvard Business Review,* July–August 1995, 74–84.

SUPPLEMENT TO CHAPTER 5

Decision Theory

LEARNING OBJECTIVES

After completing this supplement, you should be able to:

1. Describe the different environments under which operations decisions are made.
2. Describe and use techniques that apply to decision making under uncertainty.
3. Describe and use the expected-value approach.
4. Construct a decision tree and use it to analyze a problem.
5. Compute the expected value of perfect information.
6. Conduct sensitivity analysis on a simple decision problem.

SUPPLEMENT OUTLINE

INTRODUCTION

Decision theory represents a general approach to decision making. It is suitable for a wide range of operations management decisions. Among them are capacity planning, product and service design, equipment selection, and location planning. Decisions that lend themselves to a decision theory approach tend to be characterized by the following elements:

1. A set of possible future conditions that will have a bearing on the results of the decision.
2. A list of alternatives for the manager to choose from.
3. A known payoff for each alternative under each possible future condition.

To use this approach, a decision maker would employ this process:

1. Identify the possible future conditions (e.g., demand will be low, medium, or high; the competitor will or will not introduce a new product). These are called *states of nature.*
2. Develop a list of possible *alternatives,* one of which may be to do nothing.

3. Determine or estimate the *payoff* associated with each alternative for every possible future condition.
4. If possible, estimate the *likelihood* of each possible future condition.
5. Evaluate alternatives according to some *decision criterion* (e.g., maximize expected profit), and select the best alternative.

The information for a decision is often summarized in a **payoff table**, which shows the expected payoffs for each alternative under the various possible states of nature. These tables are helpful in choosing among alternatives because they facilitate comparison of alternatives. Consider the following payoff table, which illustrates a capacity planning problem.

Payoff table Table showing the expected payoffs for each alternative in every possible state of nature.

	POSSIBLE FUTURE DEMAND		
Alternatives	**Low**	**Moderate**	**High**
Small facility	$10*	$10	$10
Medium facility	7	12	12
Large facility	(4)	2	16

*Present value in $ millions.

The payoffs are shown in the body of the table. In this instance, the payoffs are in terms of present values, which represent equivalent current dollar values of expected future income less costs. This is a convenient measure because it places all alternatives on a comparable basis. If a small facility is built, the payoff will be the same for all three possible states of nature. For a medium facility, low demand will have a present value of $7 million, whereas both moderate and high demand will have present values of $12 million. A large facility will have a loss of $4 million if demand is low, a present value of $2 million if demand is moderate, and a present value of $16 million if demand is high.

The problem for the decision maker is to select one of the alternatives, taking the present value into account.

Evaluation of the alternatives differs according to the degree of certainty associated with the possible future conditions.

CAUSES OF POOR DECISIONS

Despite the best efforts of a manager, a decision occasionally turns out poorly due to unforeseeable circumstances. Luckily, such occurrences are not common. Often, failures can be traced to a combination of mistakes in the decision process, to *bounded rationality,* or to *suboptimization.*

The decision process consists of these steps:

1. Identify the problem.
2. Specify objectives and criteria for a solution.
3. Develop suitable alternatives.
4. Analyze and compare alternatives.
5. Select the best alternative.
6. Implement the solution.
7. Monitor to see that desired result is achieved.

In many cases, managers fail to appreciate the importance of each step in the decision-making process. They may skip a step or not devote enough effort to completing it before jumping to the next step. Sometimes this happens owing to a manager's style of making quick decisions or a failure to recognize the consequences of a poor decision. The manager's ego can be a factor. This sometimes happens when the manager has experienced a series of successes—important decisions that turned out right. Some managers then get the impression that they can do no wrong. But they soon run into trouble, which is usually enough to bring them back down to earth. Other managers seem oblivious to negative results and continue the process they associate with their previous successes, not recognizing that some of that success may have been due more to luck than to any special abilities of their own. A part of the problem may be the manager's unwillingness to admit a mistake. Yet other managers demonstrate an inability to make a decision; they stall long past the time when the decision should have been rendered.

Of course, not all managers fall into these traps—it seems safe to say that the majority do not. Even so, this does not necessarily mean that every decision works out as expected. Another factor with which managers must contend is **bounded rationality**, or the limits imposed on decision making by costs, human abilities, time, technology, and the availability of information. Because of these limitations, managers cannot always expect to reach decisions that are optimal in the sense of providing the best possible outcome (e.g., highest profit, least cost). Instead, they must often resort to achieving a *satisfactory* solution.

Bounded rationality The limitations on decision making caused by costs, human abilities, time, technology, and availability of information.

Still another cause of poor decisions is that organizations typically departmentalize decisions. Naturally, there is a great deal of justification for the use of departments in terms of overcoming span-of-control problems and human limitations. However, **suboptimization** can occur. This is a result of different departments' attempts to reach a solution that is optimum for each. Unfortunately, what is optimal for one department may not be optimal for the organization as a whole. If you are familiar with the theory of constraints (see Chapter 16), suboptimization and local optima are conceptually the same, with the same negative consequences.

Suboptimization The result of different departments each attempting to reach a solution that is optimum for that department.

DECISION ENVIRONMENTS

Operations management decision environments are classified according to the degree of certainty present. There are three basic categories: certainty, risk, and uncertainty.

Certainty means that relevant parameters such as costs, capacity, and demand have known values.

Risk means that certain parameters have probabilistic outcomes.

Uncertainty means that it is impossible to assess the likelihood of various possible future events.

Certainty Environment in which relevant parameters have known values.

Risk Environment in which certain future events have probable outcomes.

Uncertainty Environment in which it is impossible to assess the likelihood of various future events.

Consider these situations:

1. Profit per unit is $5. You have an order for 200 units. How much profit will you make? (This is an example of *certainty* since unit profits and total demand are known.)
2. Profit is $5 per unit. Based on previous experience, there is a 50 percent chance of an order for 100 units and a 50 percent chance of an order for 200 units. What is expected profit? (This is an example of *risk* since demand outcomes are probabilistic.)
3. Profit is $5 per unit. The probabilities of potential demands are unknown. (This is an example of *uncertainty*.)

The importance of these different decision environments is that they require different analysis techniques. Some techniques are better suited for one category than for others.

DECISION MAKING UNDER CERTAINTY

When it is known for certain which of the possible future conditions will actually happen, the decision is usually relatively straightforward: Simply choose the alternative that has the best payoff under that state of nature. Example 5S–1 illustrates this.

EXAMPLE 5S–1

Determine the best alternative in the payoff table on the previous page for each of the cases: It is known with certainty that demand will be (*a*) low, (*b*) moderate, (*c*) high.

SOLUTION

Choose the alternative with the highest payoff. Thus, if we know demand will be low, we would elect to build the small facility and realize a payoff of $10 million. If we know demand will be moderate, a medium factory would yield the highest payoff ($12 million versus either $10 million or $2 million). For high demand, a large facility would provide the highest payoff.

Although complete certainty is rare in such situations, this kind of exercise provides some perspective on the analysis. Moreover, in some instances, there may be an opportunity to consider allocation of funds to research efforts, which may reduce or remove some of the uncertainty surrounding the states of nature, converting uncertainty to risk or to certainty.

DECISION MAKING UNDER UNCERTAINTY

At the opposite extreme is complete uncertainty: No information is available on how likely the various states of nature are. Under those conditions, four possible decision criteria are *maximin, maximax, Laplace,* and *minimax regret.* These approaches can be defined as follows:

Maximin Choose the alternative with the best of the worst possible payoffs.

Maximax Choose the alternative with the best possible payoff.

Laplace Choose the alternative with the best average payoff of any of the alternatives.

Minimax regret Choose the alternative that has the least of the worst regrets.

Maximin—Determine the worst possible payoff for each alternative, and choose the alternative that has the "best worst." The maximin approach is essentially a pessimistic one because it takes into account only the worst possible outcome for each alternative. The actual outcome may not be as bad as that, but this approach establishes a "guaranteed minimum."

Maximax—Determine the best possible payoff, and choose the alternative with that payoff. The maximax approach is an optimistic, "go for it" strategy; it does not take into account any payoff other than the best.

Laplace—Determine the average payoff for each alternative, and choose the alternative with the best average. The Laplace approach treats the states of nature as equally likely.

Minimax regret—Determine the worst *regret* for each alternative, and choose the alternative with the "best worst." This approach seeks to minimize the difference between the payoff that is realized and the best payoff for each state of nature.

The next two examples illustrate these decision criteria.

EXAMPLE 5S–2

Referring to the payoff table on page 213, determine which alternative would be chosen under each of these strategies:

a. Maximin
b. Maximax
c. Laplace

SOLUTION

a. Using maximin, the worst payoffs for the alternatives are as follows:

Small facility:	$10 million
Medium facility:	7 million
Large facility:	−4 million

Hence, since $10 million is the best, choose to build the small facility using the maximin strategy.

b. Using maximax, the best payoffs are as follows:

Small facility:	$10 million
Medium facility:	12 million
Large facility:	16 million

The best overall payoff is the $16 million in the third row. Hence, the maximax criterion leads to building a large facility.

c. For the Laplace criterion, first find the row totals, and then divide each of those amounts by the number of states of nature (three in this case). Thus, we have

	Row Total (in $ millions)	Row Average (in $ millions)
Small facility	$30	$10.00
Medium facility	31	10.33
Large facility	14	4.67

Because the medium facility has the highest average, it would be chosen under the Laplace criterion.

EXAMPLE 5S–3

Determine which alternative would be chosen using a minimax regret approach to the capacity planning program.

SOLUTION

Regret (opportunity loss) The difference between a given payoff and the best payoff for a state of nature.

The first step in this approach is to prepare a table of **regrets** (or **opportunity losses**). To do this, subtract every payoff *in each column* from the best payoff in that column. For instance, in the first column, the best payoff is 10, so each of the three numbers in that column must be subtracted from 10. Going down the column, the regrets will be $10 - 10 = 0$, $10 - 7 = 3$, and $10 - (-4) = 14$. In the second column, the best payoff is 12. Subtracting each payoff from 12 yields 2, 0, and 10. In the third column, 16 is the best payoff. The regrets are 6, 4, and 0. These results are summarized in a regret table:

	REGRETS (in $ millions)			
Alternatives	Low	Moderate	High	Worst
Small facility	$0	$2	$6	$6
Medium facility	3	0	4	4
Large facility	14	10	0	14

The second step is to identify the worst regret for each alternative. For the first alternative, the worst is 6; for the second, the worst is 4; and for the third, the worst is 14.

The best of these worst regrets would be chosen using minimax regret. The lowest regret is 4, which is for a medium facility. Hence, that alternative would be chosen.

Solved Problem 6 at the end of this supplement illustrates decision making under uncertainty when the payoffs represent costs.

The main weakness of these approaches (except for Laplace) is that they do not take into account *all* of the payoffs. Instead, they focus on the worst or best, and so they lose some information. Still, for a given set of circumstances, each has certain merits that can be helpful to a decision maker.

DECISION MAKING UNDER RISK

Between the two extremes of certainty and uncertainty lies the case of risk: The probability of occurrence for each state of nature is known. (Note that because the states are mutually exclusive and collectively exhaustive, these probabilities must add to 1.00.) A widely used approach under such circumstances is the *expected monetary value criterion.* The expected value is computed for each alternative, and the one with the best expected value is selected. The expected value is the sum of the payoffs for an alternative where each payoff is *weighted* by the probability for the relevant state of nature. Thus, the approach is

Expected monetary value (EMV) criterion The best expected value among the alternatives.

Expected monetary value (EMV) criterion—Determine the expected payoff of each alternative, and choose the alternative that has the best expected payoff.

EXAMPLE 5S–4

Using the expected monetary value criterion, identify the best alternative for the previous payoff table for these probabilities: low = .30, moderate = .50, and high = .20.

SOLUTION

excel

www.mhhe.com/stevenson11e

Find the expected value of each alternative by multiplying the probability of occurrence for each state of nature by the payoff for that state of nature and summing them:

$$\begin{aligned} EV_{small} &= .30(\$10) + .50(\$10) + .20(\$10) = \$10 \\ EV_{medium} &= .30(\$7) + .50(\$12) + .20(\$12) = \$10.5 \\ EV_{large} &= .30(\$-4) + .50(\$2) + .20(\$16) = \$3 \end{aligned}$$

Hence, choose the medium facility because it has the highest expected value.

The expected monetary value approach is most appropriate when a decision maker is neither risk averse nor risk seeking, but is risk neutral. Typically, well-established organizations with numerous decisions of this nature tend to use expected value because it provides an indication of the long-run, average payoff. That is, the expected-value amount (e.g., $10.5 million in the last example) is not an actual payoff but an expected or average amount that would be approximated if a large number of identical decisions were to be made. Hence, if a decision maker applies this criterion to a large number of similar decisions, the expected payoff for the total will approximate the sum of the individual expected payoffs.

DECISION TREES

In health care the array of treatment options and medical costs makes tools such as decision trees particularly valuable in diagnosing and prescribing treatment plans. For example, if a 20-year-old and a 50-year-old both are brought into an emergency room complaining of chest pains, the attending physician, after asking each some questions on family history, patient history, general health, and recent events and activities, will use a *decision tree* to sort through the options to arrive at the appropriate decision for each patient.

Decision trees are tools that have many practical applications, not only in health care but also in legal cases and a wide array of management decision making, including credit card fraud; loan, credit, and insurance risk analysis; decisions on new product or service development; and location analysis.

A **decision tree** is a schematic representation of the alternatives available to a decision maker and their possible consequences. The term gets its name from the treelike appearance of the diagram (see Figure 5S.1). Although tree diagrams can be used in place of a payoff table, they are particularly useful for analyzing situations that involve *sequential* decisions. For instance, a manager may initially decide to build a small facility only to discover that demand is much higher than anticipated. In this case, the manager may then be called upon to make a subsequent decision on whether to expand or build an additional facility.

Decision tree A schematic representation of the available alternatives and their possible consequences.

A decision tree is composed of a number of *nodes* that have *branches* emanating from them (see Figure 5S.1). Square nodes denote decision points, and circular nodes denote chance events. Read the tree from left to right. Branches leaving square nodes represent alternatives; branches leaving circular nodes represent chance events (i.e., the possible states of nature).

After the tree has been drawn, it is analyzed from *right to left;* that is, starting with the last decision that might be made. For each decision, choose the alternative that will yield the greatest return (or the lowest cost). If chance events follow a decision, choose the alternative that has the highest expected monetary value (or lowest expected cost).

EXAMPLE 5S–5

A manager must decide on the size of a video arcade to construct. The manager has narrowed the choices to two: large or small. Information has been collected on payoffs, and a decision tree has been constructed. Analyze the decision tree and determine which initial

FIGURE 5S.1
Format of a decision tree

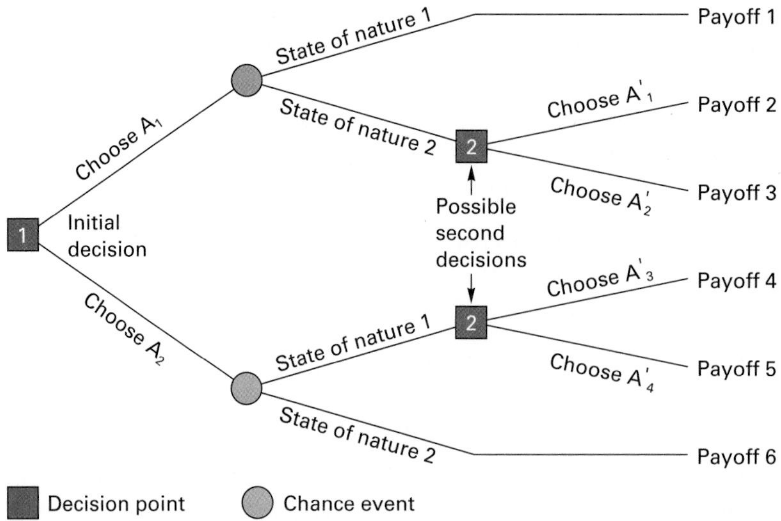

alternative (build small or build large) should be chosen in order to maximize expected monetary value.

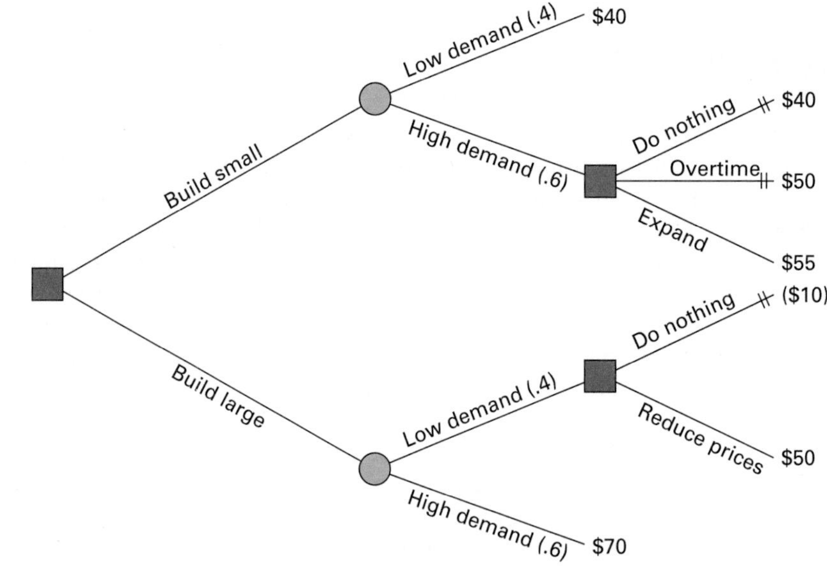

SOLUTION

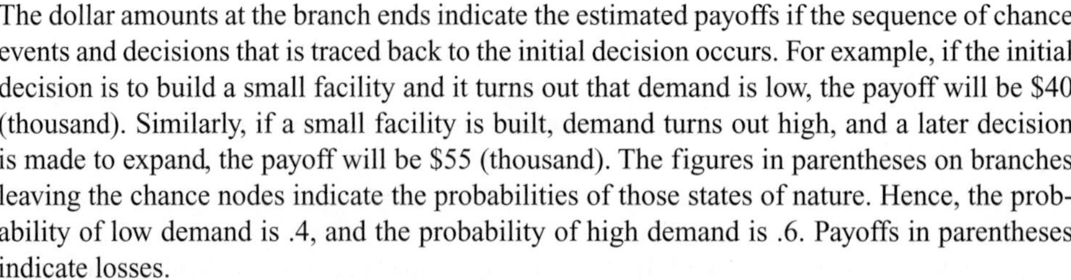

The dollar amounts at the branch ends indicate the estimated payoffs if the sequence of chance events and decisions that is traced back to the initial decision occurs. For example, if the initial decision is to build a small facility and it turns out that demand is low, the payoff will be $40 (thousand). Similarly, if a small facility is built, demand turns out high, and a later decision is made to expand, the payoff will be $55 (thousand). The figures in parentheses on branches leaving the chance nodes indicate the probabilities of those states of nature. Hence, the probability of low demand is .4, and the probability of high demand is .6. Payoffs in parentheses indicate losses.

Analyze the decisions from right to left:

1. Determine which alternative would be selected for each possible second decision. For a small facility with high demand, there are three choices: *do nothing, work overtime,* and *expand.* Because *expand* has the highest payoff, you would choose it. Indicate this by placing a double slash through each of the other alternatives. Similarly, for a large facility

with low demand, there are two choices: *do nothing* and *reduce prices*. You would choose *reduce prices* because it has the higher expected value, so a double slash is placed on the other branch.

2. Determine the product of the chance probabilities and their respective payoffs for the remaining branches:

   Build small

Low demand	.4($40) = $16
High demand	.6($55) = $33

   Build large

Low demand	.4($50) = $20
High demand	.6($70) = $42

3. Determine the expected value of each initial alternative:

Build small	$16 + $33 = $49
Build large	$20 + $42 = $62

   Hence, the choice should be to build the large facility because it has a larger expected value than the small facility.

EXPECTED VALUE OF PERFECT INFORMATION

In certain situations, it is possible to ascertain which state of nature will actually occur in the future. For instance, the choice of location for a restaurant may weigh heavily on whether a new highway will be constructed or whether a zoning permit will be issued. A decision maker may have probabilities for these states of nature; however, it may be possible to delay a decision until it is clear which state of nature will occur. This might involve taking an option to buy the land. If the state of nature is favorable, the option can be exercised; if it is unfavorable, the option can be allowed to expire. The question to consider is whether the cost of the option will be less than the expected gain due to delaying the decision (i.e., the expected payoff *above* the expected value). The expected gain is the **expected value of perfect information,** or **EVPI.**

Expected value of perfect information (EVPI) The difference between the expected payoff with perfect information and the expected payoff under risk.

Other possible ways of obtaining perfect information depend somewhat on the nature of the decision being made. Information about consumer preferences might come from market research, additional information about a product could come from product testing, or legal experts might be called on.

There are two ways to determine the EVPI. One is to compute the expected payoff under certainty and subtract the expected payoff under risk. That is,

$$\begin{array}{c}\text{Expected value of}\\ \text{perfect information}\end{array} = \begin{array}{c}\text{Expected payoff}\\ \text{under certainty}\end{array} - \begin{array}{c}\text{Expected payoff}\\ \text{under risk}\end{array} \qquad (5S\text{–}1)$$

EXAMPLE 5S–6

Using the information from Example 5S–4, determine the expected value of perfect information using Formula 5S–1.

SOLUTION

First, compute the expected payoff under certainty. To do this, identify the best payoff under each state of nature. Then combine these by weighting each payoff by the probability of that state of nature and adding the amounts. Thus, the best payoff under low demand is $10, the best under moderate demand is $12, and the best under high demand is $16. The expected payoff under certainty is, then,

.30($10) + .50($12) + .20($16) = $12.2

The expected payoff under risk, as computed in Example 5S–4, is \$10.5. The EVPI is the difference between these:

$$\text{EVPI} = \$12.2 - \$10.5 = \$1.7$$

This figure indicates the upper limit on the amount the decision maker should be willing to spend to obtain perfect information in this case. Thus, if the cost equals or exceeds this amount, the decision maker would be better off not spending additional money and simply going with the alternative that has the highest expected payoff.

A second approach is to use the regret table to compute the EVPI. To do this, find the expected regret for each alternative. The minimum expected regret is equal to the EVPI.

EXAMPLE 5S–7

www.mhhe.com/stevenson11e

Determine the expected value of perfect information for the capacity-planning problem using the expected regret approach.

SOLUTION

Using information from Examples 5S–2, 5S–3, and 5S–4, we can compute the expected regret for each alternative. Thus:

Small facility	$.30(0) + .50(2) + .20(6) = 2.2$
Medium facility	$.30(3) + .50(0) + .20(4) = 1.7$ [minimum]
Large facility	$.30(14) + .50(10) + .20(0) = 9.2$

The lowest expected regret is 1.7, which is associated with the second alternative. Hence, the EVPI is \$1.7 million, which agrees with the previous example using the other approach.

SENSITIVITY ANALYSIS

Generally speaking, both the payoffs and the probabilities in this kind of a decision problem are estimated values. Consequently, it can be useful for the decision maker to have some indication of how sensitive the choice of an alternative is to changes in one or more of these values. Unfortunately, it is impossible to consider all possible combinations of every variable in a typical problem. Nevertheless, there are certain things a decision maker can do to judge the sensitivity of probability estimates.

Sensitivity analysis Determining the range of probability for which an alternative has the best expected payoff.

Sensitivity analysis provides a range of probability over which the choice of alternatives would remain the same. The approach illustrated here is useful when there are two states of nature. It involves constructing a graph and then using algebra to determine a range of probabilities for which a given solution is best. In effect, the graph provides a visual indication of the range of probability over which the various alternatives are optimal, and the algebra provides exact values of the endpoints of the ranges. Example 5S–8 illustrates the procedure.

EXAMPLE 5S–8

eXcel

www.mhhe.com/stevenson11e

Given the following table, determine the range of probability for state of nature #2, that is, $P(2)$, for which each alternative is optimal under the expected-value approach.

		STATE OF NATURE	
		#1	#2
	A	4	12
Alternative	B	16	2
	C	12	8

SOLUTION

First, plot each alternative relative to $P(2)$. To do this, plot the #1 value on the left side of the graph and the #2 value on the right side. For instance, for alternative A, plot 4 on the left side of the graph and 12 on the right side. Then connect these two points with a straight line. The three alternatives are plotted on the graph as shown below.

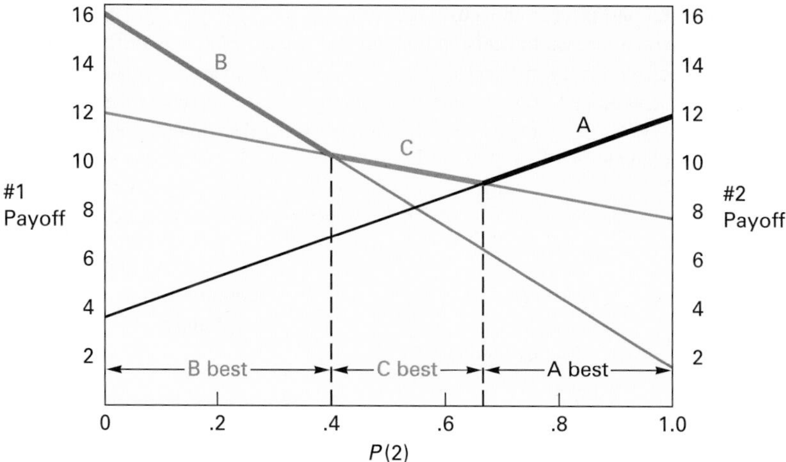

The graph shows the range of values of $P(2)$ over which each alternative is optimal. Thus, for low values of $P(2)$ [and thus high values of $P(1)$, since $P(1) + P(2) = 1.0$], alternative B will have the highest expected value; for intermediate values of $P(2)$, alternative C is best; and for higher values of $P(2)$, alternative A is best.

To find exact values of the ranges, determine where the upper parts of the lines intersect. Note that at the intersections, the two alternatives represented by the lines would be equivalent in terms of expected value. Hence, the decision maker would be indifferent between the two at that point. To determine the intersections, you must obtain the equation of each line. This is relatively simple to do. Because these are straight lines, they have the form $y = a + bx$, where a is the y-intercept value at the left axis, b is the slope of the line, and x is $P(2)$. Slope is defined as the change in y for a one-unit change in x. In this type of problem, the distance between the two vertical axes is 1.0. Consequently, the slope of each line is equal to the right-hand value minus the left-hand value. The slopes and equations are as follows:

	#1	#2	Slope	Equation
A	4	12	12 − 4 = + 8	$4 + 8P(2)$
B	16	2	2 − 16 = −14	$16 - 14P(2)$
C	12	8	8 − 12 = − 4	$12 - 4P(2)$

From the graph, we can see that alternative B is best from $P(2) = 0$ to the point where that straight line intersects the straight line of alternative C, and that begins the region where C is better. To find that point, solve for the value of $P(2)$ at their intersection. This requires setting the two equations equal to each other and solving for $P(2)$. Thus,

$$16 - 14P(2) = 12 - 4P(2)$$

Rearranging terms yields

$$4 = 10P(2)$$

Solving yields $P(2) = .40$. Thus, alternative B is best from $P(2) = 0$ up to $P(2) = .40$. B and C are equivalent at $P(2) = .40$.

Alternative C is best from that point until its line intersects alternative A's line. To find that intersection, set those two equations equal and solve for $P(2)$. Thus,

$$4 + 8P(2) = 12 - 4P(2)$$

Rearranging terms results in

$$12P(2) = 8$$

Solving yields $P(2) = .67$. Thus, alternative C is best from $P(2) > .40$ up to $P(2) = .67$, where A and C are equivalent. For values of $P(2)$ greater than .67 up to $P(2) = 1.0$, A is best.

Note: If a problem calls for ranges with respect to $P(1)$, find the $P(2)$ ranges as above, and then subtract each $P(2)$ from 1.00 (e.g., .40 becomes .60, and .67 becomes .33).

SUMMARY

Decision making is an integral part of operations management.

Decision theory is a general approach to decision making that is useful in many different aspects of operations management. Decision theory provides a framework for the analysis of decisions. It includes a number of techniques that can be classified according to the degree of uncertainty associated with a particular decision problem. Two visual tools useful for analyzing some decision problems are decision trees and graphical sensitivity analysis.

KEY TERMS

bounded rationality, 214
certainty, 214
decision tree, 217
expected monetary value (EMV) criterion, 216
expected value of perfect information (EVPI), 219
Laplace, 215
maximax, 215
maximin, 215
minimax regret, 215
payoff table, 213
regret (opportunity loss), 216
risk, 214
sensitivity analysis, 220
suboptimization, 214
uncertainty, 214

SOLVED PROBLEMS

The following solved problems refer to this payoff table:

		New Bridge Built	No New Bridge
Alternative capacity	A	1	14
for new store	B	2	10
	C	4	6

where A = small, B = medium, and C = large.

Problem 1

www.mhhe.com/stevenson11e

Assume the payoffs represent profits. Determine the alternative that would be chosen under each of these decision criteria:

a. Maximin.

b. Maximax.

c. Laplace.

Solution

	New Bridge	No New Bridge	Maximin (worst)	Maximax (best)	Laplace (average)
A	1	14	1	14 [best]	15 ÷ 2 = 7.5 [best]
B	2	10	2	10	12 ÷ 2 = 6
C	4	6	4 [best]	6	10 ÷ 2 = 5

Thus, the alternatives chosen would be C under maximin, A under maximax, and A under Laplace.

Problem 2

www.mhhe.com/stevenson11e

Using graphical sensitivity analysis, determine the probability for no new bridge for which each alternative would be optimal.

Solution

Plot a straight line for each alternative. Do this by plotting the payoff for new bridge on the left axis and the payoff for no new bridge on the right axis and then connecting the two points. Each line represents the expected profit for an alternative for the entire range of probability of no new bridge. Because the lines represent expected profit, the line that is highest for a given value of P (no new bridge) is optimal. Thus, from the graph, you can see that for low values of this probability, alternative C is best, and for higher values, alternative A is best (B is never the highest line, so it is never optimal).

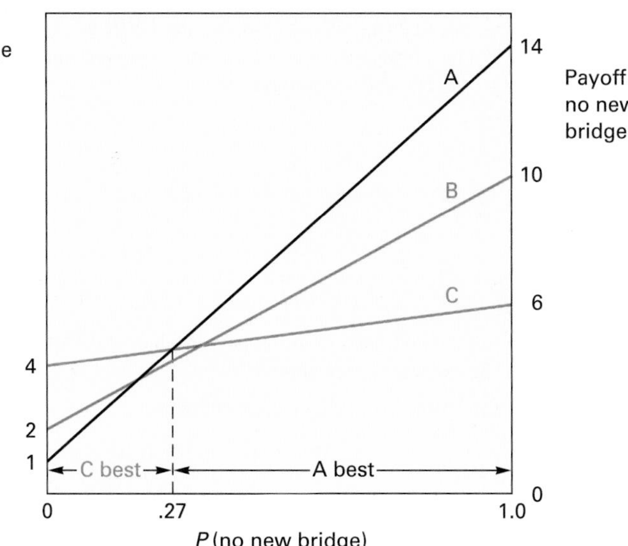

The dividing line between the ranges where C and A are optimal occurs where the two lines intersect. To find that probability, first formulate the equation for each line. To do this, let the intersection with the left axis be the y intercept; the slope equals the right-side payoff minus the left-side payoff. Thus, for C you have $4 + (6 - 4)P$, which is $4 + 2P$. For A, $1 + (14 - 1)P$, which is $1 + 13P$. Setting these two equal to each other, you can solve for P:

$$4 + 2P = 1 + 13P$$

Solving, $P = .27$. Therefore, the ranges for P(no new bridge) are

A: $.27 < P \leq 1.00$

B: never optimal

C: $0 \leq P < .27$

Problem 3

Using the information in the payoff table, develop a table of regrets, and then

a. Determine the alternative that would be chosen under minimax regret.
b. Determine the expected value of perfect information using the regret table, assuming that the probability of a new bridge being built is .60.

Solution

To obtain the regrets, subtract all payoffs in each column from the best payoff in the column. The regrets are

	New Bridge	No New Bridge
A	3	0
B	2	4
C	0	8

a. Minimax regret involves finding the worst regret for each alternative and then choosing the alternative that has the "best" worst. Thus, you would choose A:

	Worst
A	3 [best]
B	4
C	8

b. Once the regret table has been developed, you can compute the EVPI as the *smallest* expected regret. Since the probability of a new bridge is given as .60, we can deduce that the probability of no new bridge is 1.00 − .60 = .40. The expected regrets are

A: .60(3) + .40(0) = 1.80

B: .60(2) + .40(4) = 2.80

C: .60(0) + .40(8) = 3.20

Hence, the EVPI is 1.80.

Problem 4

www.mhhe.com/stevenson11e

Using the probabilities of .60 for a new bridge and .40 for no new bridge

a. Compute the expected value of each alternative in the payoff table, and identify the alternative that would be selected under the expected-value approach.
b. Construct a decision tree for the problem showing expected values.

Solution

a. A: .60(1) + .40(14) = 6.20 [best]

B: .60(2) + .40(10) = 5.20

C: .60(4) + .40(6) = 4.80

b.

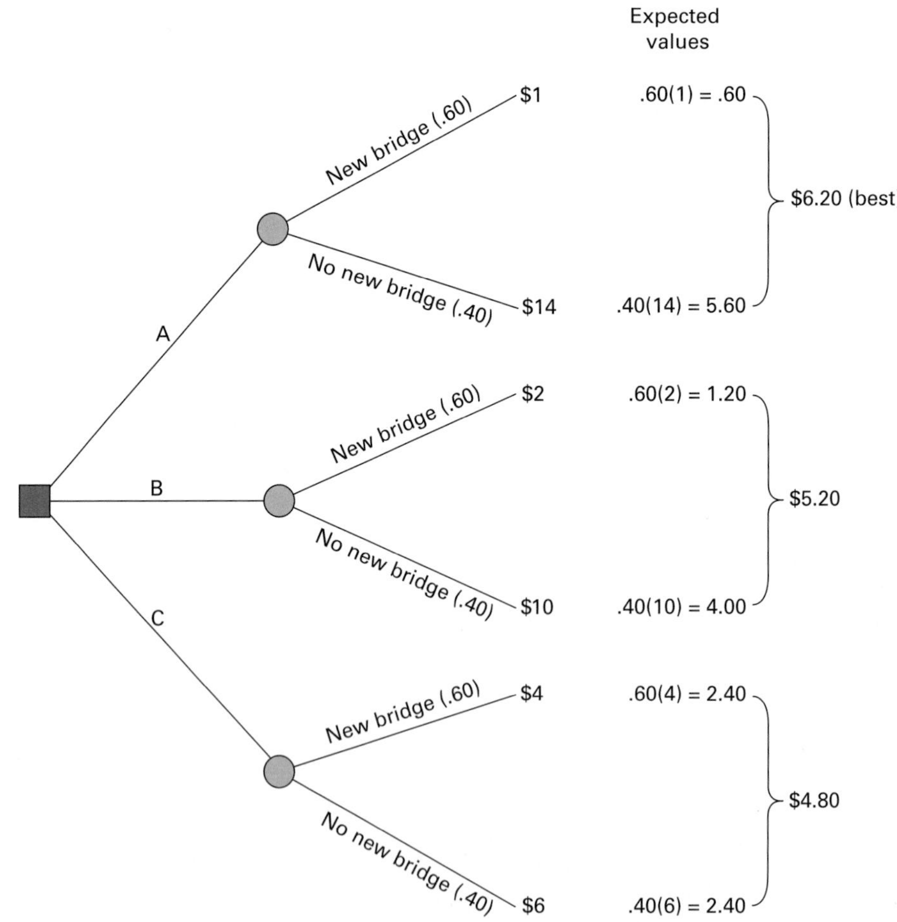

Problem 5

Compute the EVPI using the information from the previous problem.

Solution

Using Formula 5S–1, the EVPI is the expected payoff under certainty minus the maximum expected value. The expected payoff under certainty involves multiplying the best payoff in each column by the column probability and then summing those amounts. The best payoff in the first column is 4, and the best in the second is 14. Thus,

$$\text{Expected payoff under certainty} = .60(4) + .40(14) = 8.00$$

Then

$$\text{EVPI} = 8.00 - 6.20 = 1.80$$

(This agrees with the result obtained in Solved Problem 3*b*.)

Excel solution:

Chap5SInstructor1 - Microsoft Excel

	B	C	D	I	J	K	L
1	Payoff Table		Notes				
2	<Back						
3		New Bridge	No	ΣProb =	1		
4	Probability =	0.6	0.4	Min	Max	Avg	EMV
5	A	1	14	1	14	7.5	6.2
6	B	2	10	2	10	6	5.2
7	C	4	6	4	6	5	4.8
12	Opportunity Loss Table						
13		New Bridge	No	Max	EOL		
14	A	3	0	3	1.8	= EVPI	
15	B	2	4	4	2.8		
16	C	0	8	8	3.2		

Criteria	Optimal Alternative	Value
Maximin	C	4
Maximax	A	14
Laplace	A	7.5

Solved Problem 1, 3, 4a | Solved Problem 2 | Solved Problem 4b | Solved Problem 6

Placing the problem data in the cell positions shown, the expected monetary value (EMV) for each alternative is shown in column J.

Then, the overall EMV is obtained in column J as the maximum of the values in J5, J6, and J7.

The EVPI is obtained using the Opportunity Loss Table by summing the product of the maximum in column C2 and the probability in C4, and the product of the maximum in column D and the probability in D4.

Problem 6

www.mhhe.com/stevenson11e

Suppose that the values in the payoff table represent *costs* instead of profits.

a. Determine the choice that you would make under each of these strategies: maximin, minimin, and Laplace.*

b. Develop the regret table, and identify the alternative chosen using minimax regret. Then find the EVPI if *P*(new bridge) = .60.

c. Using sensitivity analysis, determine the range of *P*(no new bridge) for which each alternative would be optimal.

d. If *P*(new bridge) = .60 and *P*(no new bridge) = .40, find the alternative chosen to minimize expected cost.

**Minimin* is the reverse of maximax; for costs, minimin identifies the lowest (best) cost.

Solution

a.

	New Bridge	No New Bridge	Maximin (worst)	Minimin (best)	Laplace (average)
A	1	14	14	1 [best]	15 ÷ 2 = 7.5
B	2	10	10	2	12 ÷ 2 = 6
C	4	6	6 [best]	4	10 ÷ 2 = 5 [best]

b. Develop the regret table by subtracting the *lowest cost* in each column from each of the values in the column. (Note that none of the values is negative.)

	New Bridge	No New Bridge	Worst
A	0	8	8
B	1	4	4
C	3	0	3 [best]

EVPI = .60(3) + .40(0) = 1.80

c. The graph is identical to that shown in Solved Problem 2. However, the lines now represent expected *costs,* so the best alternative for a given value of *P*(no new bridge) is the *lowest* line. Hence, for very low values of *P*(no new bridge), A is best; for intermediate values, B is best; and for high values, C is best. You can set the equations of A and B, and B and C, equal to each other in order to determine the values of *P*(no new bridge) at their intersections. Thus,

$A = B: 1 + 13P = 2 + 8P$; solving, $P = .20$

$B = C: 2 + 8P = 4 + 2P$; solving, $P = .33$

Hence, the ranges are

A best: $0 \leq P < .20$

B best: $.20 < P < .33$

C best: $.33 < P \leq 1.00$

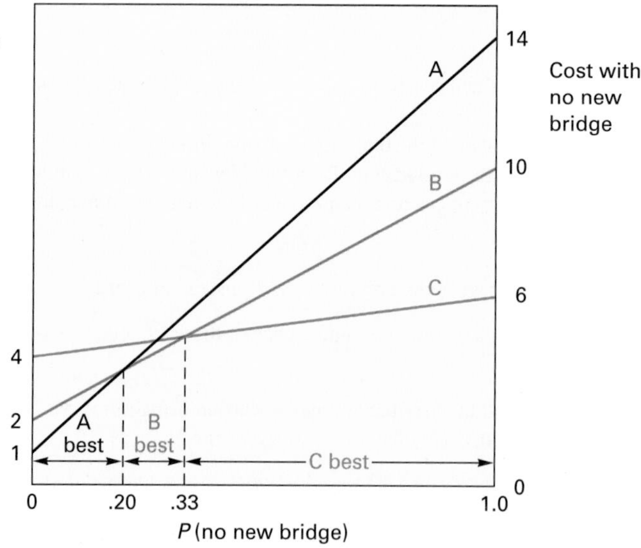

d. Expected-value computations are the same whether the values represent costs or profits. Hence, the expected payoffs for costs are the same as the expected payoffs for profits that were computed in Solved Problem 4. However, now you want the alternative that has the *lowest* expected payoff rather than the one with the highest payoff. Consequently, alternative C is the best because its expected payoff is the lowest of the three.

DISCUSSION AND REVIEW QUESTIONS

1. What is the chief role of the operations manager?
2. List the steps in the decision-making process.
3. Explain the term *bounded rationality.*
4. Explain the term *suboptimization.*
5. What are some of the reasons for poor decisions?
6. What information is contained in a payoff table?
7. What is sensitivity analysis, and how can it be useful to a decision maker?
8. Contrast maximax and maximin decision strategies. Under what circumstances is each appropriate?
9. Under what circumstances is expected monetary value appropriate as a decision criterion? When isn't it appropriate?
10. Explain or define each of these terms:
    a. Laplace criterion.
    b. Minimax regret.
    c. Expected value.
    d. Expected value of perfect information.
11. What information does a decision maker need in order to perform an expected-value analysis of a problem? What options are available to the decision maker if the probabilities of the states of nature are unknown? Can you think of a way you might use sensitivity analysis in such a case?
12. Suppose a manager is using maximum EMV as a basis for making a capacity decision and, in the process, obtains a result in which there is a virtual tie between two of the seven alternatives. How is the manager to make a decision?
13. Identify three potential unethical actions or inactions related to decision analysis and the ethical principle each violates (see Chapter 1).

PROBLEMS

1. A small building contractor has recently experienced two successive years in which work opportunities exceeded the firm's capacity. The contractor must now make a decision on capacity for next year. Estimated profits under each of the two possible states of nature are as shown in the table below. Which alternative should be selected if the decision criterion is

a. Maximax?
b. Maximin?
c. Laplace?
d. Minimax regret?

	NEXT YEAR'S DEMAND	
Alternative	**Low**	**High**
Do nothing	$50*	$60
Expand	20	80
Subcontract	40	70

*Profit in $ thousands.

2. Refer to Problem 1. Suppose after a certain amount of discussion, the contractor is able to subjectively assess the probabilities of low and high demand: *P*(low) = .3 and *P*(high) = .7.

a. Determine the expected profit of each alternative. Which alternative is best? Why?
b. Analyze the problem using a decision tree. Show the expected profit of each alternative on the tree.
c. Compute the expected value of perfect information. How could the contractor use this knowledge?

3. Refer to Problems 1 and 2. Construct a graph that will enable you to perform sensitivity analysis on the problem. Over what range of *P*(high) would the alternative of doing nothing be best? Expand? Subcontract?

4. A firm that plans to expand its product line must decide whether to build a small or a large facility to produce the new products. If it builds a small facility and demand is low, the net present value after deducting for building costs will be $400,000. If demand is high, the firm can either maintain the small facility or expand it. Expansion would have a net present value of $450,000, and maintaining the small facility would have a net present value of $50,000.

If a large facility is built and demand is high, the estimated net present value is $800,000. If demand turns out to be low, the net present value will be −$10,000.

The probability that demand will be high is estimated to be .60, and the probability of low demand is estimated to be .40.

a. Analyze using a tree diagram.
b. Compute the EVPI. How could this information be used?
c. Determine the range over which each alternative would be best in terms of the value of *P* (demand low).

5. Determine the course of action that has the highest expected payoff for this decision tree.

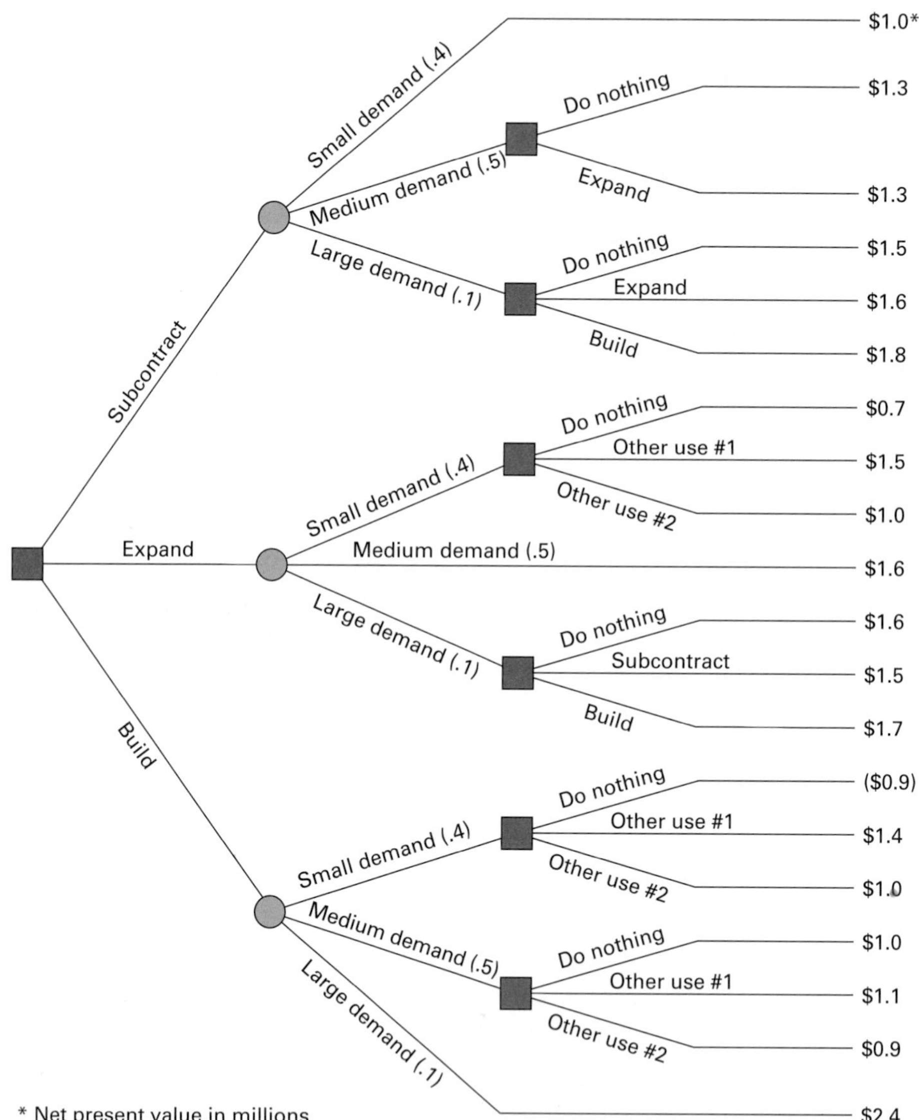

6. The lease of Theme Park, Inc., is about to expire. Management must decide whether to renew the lease for another 10 years or to relocate near the site of a proposed motel. The town planning board is currently debating the merits of granting approval to the motel. A consultant has estimated the net present value of Theme Park's two alternatives under each state of nature as shown on the following page.

What course of action would you recommend using?

a. Maximax.
b. Maximin.
c. Laplace.
d. Minimax regret.

Options	Motel Approved	Motel Rejected
Renew	$ 500,000	$4,000,000
Relocate	5,000,000	100,000

7. Refer to Problem 6. Suppose that the management of Theme Park, Inc., has decided that there is a .35 probability that the motel's application will be approved.

a. If management uses maximum expected monetary value as the decision criterion, which alternative should it choose?
b. Represent this problem in the form of a decision tree.
c. If management has been offered the option of a temporary lease while the town planning board considers the motel's application, would you advise management to sign the lease? The lease will cost $24,000.

8. Construct a graph that can be used for sensitivity analysis for the preceding problem.

a. How sensitive is the solution to the problem in terms of the probability estimate of .35?
b. Suppose that, after consulting with a member of the town planning board, management decides that an estimate of approval is approximately .45. How sensitive is the solution to this revised estimate? Explain.
c. Suppose the management is confident of all the estimated payoffs except for $4 million. If the probability of approval is .35, for what range of payoff for renew/reject will the alternative selected using the maximum expected value remain the same?

9. A firm must decide whether to construct a small, medium, or large stamping plant. A consultant's report indicates a .20 probability that demand will be low and an .80 probability that demand will be high.

If the firm builds a small facility and demand turns out to be low, the net present value will be $42 million. If demand turns out to be high, the firm can either subcontract and realize the net present value of $42 million or expand greatly for a net present value of $48 million.

The firm could build a medium-size facility as a hedge: If demand turns out to be low, its net present value is estimated at $22 million; if demand turns out to be high, the firm could do nothing and realize a net present value of $46 million, or it could expand and realize a net present value of $50 million.

If the firm builds a large facility and demand is low, the net present value will be −$20 million, whereas high demand will result in a net present value of $72 million.

a. Analyze this problem using a decision tree.
b. What is the maximin alternative?
c. Compute the EVPI and interpret it.
d. Perform sensitivity analysis on *P*(high).

10. A manager must decide how many machines of a certain type to buy. The machines will be used to manufacture a new gear for which there is increased demand. The manager has narrowed the decision to two alternatives: buy one machine or buy two. If only one machine is purchased and demand is more than it can handle, a second machine can be purchased at a later time. However, the cost per machine would be lower if the two machines were purchased at the same time.

The estimated probability of low demand is .30, and the estimated probability of high demand is .70.

The net present value associated with the purchase of two machines initially is $75,000 if demand is low and $130,000 if demand is high.

The net present value for one machine and low demand is $90,000. If demand is high, there are three options. One option is to do nothing, which would have a net present value of $90,000. A second option is to subcontract; that would have a net present value of $110,000. The third option is to purchase a second machine. This option would have a net present value of $100,000.

How many machines should the manager purchase initially? Use a decision tree to analyze this problem.

11. Determine the course of action that has the highest EMV for the accompanying tree diagram.

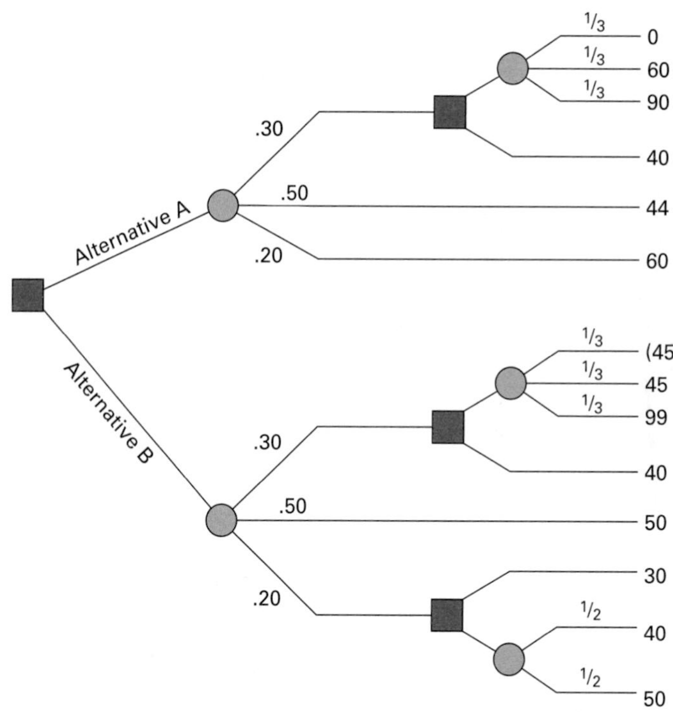

12. A logistics provider plans to have a new warehouse built to handle increasing demands for its services. Although the company is unsure of how much demand there will be, it must decide now on the size (large or small) of the warehouse. Preliminary estimates are that if a small warehouse is built and demand is low, the monthly income will be \$700,000. If demand is high, it will have to either expand the facility or lease additional space. Leasing will result in a monthly income of \$100,000 while expanding will result in a monthly income of \$500,000.

    If a large warehouse is built and demand is low, monthly income will only be \$40,000, while if demand is high, monthly income will be \$2 million.

    a. Construct a tree diagram for this decision.
    b. Using your tree diagram, identify the choice that would be made using each of the four approaches for decision making under uncertainty.

13. The director of social services of a county has learned that the state has mandated additional information requirements. This will place an additional burden on the agency. The director has identified three acceptable alternatives to handle the increased workload. One alternative is to reassign present staff members, the second is to hire and train two new workers, and the third is to redesign current practice so that workers can readily collect the information with little additional effort. An unknown factor is the caseload for the coming year when the new data will be collected on a trial basis. The estimated costs for various options and caseloads are shown in the following table:

	CASELOAD		
	Moderate	**High**	**Very High**
Reassign staff	\$50*	60	85
New staff	60	60	60
Redesign collection	40	50	90

*Cost in \$ thousands.

    Assuming that past experience has shown the probabilities of various caseloads to be unreliable, what decision would be appropriate using each of the following criteria?

    a. Maximin.
    b. Maximax.
    c. Minimax regret.
    d. Laplace.

14. After contemplating the caseload question (see previous problem), the director of social services has decided that reasonable caseload probabilities are .10 for moderate, .30 for high, and .60 for very high.

a. Which alternative will yield the minimum expected cost?
b. Construct a decision tree for this problem. Indicate the expected costs for the three decision branches.
c. Determine the expected value of perfect information using an opportunity loss table.

15. Suppose the director of social services has the option of hiring an additional staff member if one staff member is hired initially and the caseload turns out to be high or very high. Under that plan, the first entry in row 2 of the cost table (see Problem 13) will be 40 instead of 60, the second entry will be 75, and the last entry will be 80. Assume the caseload probabilities are as noted in Problem 14. Construct a decision tree that shows the sequential nature of this decision, and determine which alternative will minimize expected cost.

16. A manager has compiled estimated profits for various capacity alternatives but is reluctant to assign probabilities to the states of nature. The payoff table is as follows:

		STATE OF NATURE	
		#1	**#2**
	A	$ 20*	140
Alternative	B	120	80
	C	100	40

*Profit in $ thousands.

a. Plot the expected-value lines on a graph.
b. Is there any alternative that would never be appropriate in terms of maximizing expected profit? Explain on the basis of your graph.
c. For what range of $P(2)$ would alternative A be the best choice if the goal is to maximize expected profit?
d. For what range of $P(1)$ would alternative A be the best choice if the goal is to maximize expected profit?

17. Repeat all parts of Problem 16, assuming the values in the payoff table are estimated *costs* and the goal is to minimize expected costs.

18. The research staff of a marketing agency has assembled the following payoff table of estimated profits:

		Receive Contract	**Not Receive Contract**
	#1	$10*	−2
Proposal	#2	8	3
	#3	5	5
	#4	0	7

*Cost in $ thousands.

Relative to the probability of not receiving the contract, determine the range of probability for which each of the proposals would maximize expected profit.

19. Given this payoff table:

		STATE OF NATURE	
		#1	**#2**
	A	$120*	20
Alternative	B	60	40
	C	10	110
	D	90	90

*Payoff in $ thousands.

a. Determine the range of $P(1)$ for which each alternative would be best, treating the payoffs as profits.
b. Answer part *a* treating the payoffs as costs.

SELECTED BIBLIOGRAPHY AND FURTHER READINGS

Eppen, G. D., F. J. Gould, C. P. Schmidt, Jeffrey H. Moore, and Larry R. Weatherford. *Introductory Management Science.* 5th ed. Upper Saddle River, NJ: Prentice Hall, 1998.

Stevenson, William J., and Ceyhun Ozgur. *Introduction to Management Science with Spreadsheets.* New York: McGraw-Hill Irwin, 2007.

Taylor, Bernard W. *Introduction to Management Science.* 6th ed. Dubuque, IA: William C. Brown, 1999.

Turban, Efraim, and Jack Meredith. *Fundamentals of Management Science.* New York: McGraw-Hill, 1998.

CHAPTER 6 Process Selection and Facility Layout

CHAPTER OUTLINE

LEARNING OBJECTIVES

After completing this chapter, you should be able to:

1. Explain the strategic importance of process selection.
2. Describe the influence that process selection has on an organization.
3. Compare the basic processing types.
4. Explain the need for management of technology.
5. List some reasons for redesign of layouts.
6. Describe the basic layout types, and the main advantages and disadvantages of each.
7. Solve simple line-balancing problems.
8. Develop simple process layouts.

Product and service choices, capacity planning, process selection, and layout of facilities are among the most basic decisions managers make because they have long-term consequences for business organizations, and they impact a wide range of activities and capabilities.

This chapter is about process selection and facility layout (i.e., the arrangement of the workplace). Processes convert inputs into outputs; they are at the core of operations management. But the impact of process selection goes beyond operations management: It affects the entire organization and its ability to achieve its mission, and it affects the organization's supply chain. So process selection choices very often have strategic significance. Different process types have different capacity ranges, and once a process type is functioning, changing it can be difficult, time consuming, and costly. Obviously, long-term forecasts as well as an organization's mission and goals are important in developing a process strategy.

Process selection has operational and supply chain implications. Operational implications include equipment and labor requirements, operations costs, and both the ability to meet demand and the ability to respond to variations in demand. Supply chain implications relate to the volume and variety of inputs and outputs and the degree of flexibility that is required.

Technology is often a factor in process selection and layout. Three aspects of technology can be factors: product technology, processing technology, and information technology.

Process selection and facility layout are closely tied, and for that reason, these two topics are presented in a single chapter. The first part of the chapter covers the basic options for processing work. This is followed by a discussion of how processes and layout are linked. The remainder of the chapter is devoted to layout design.

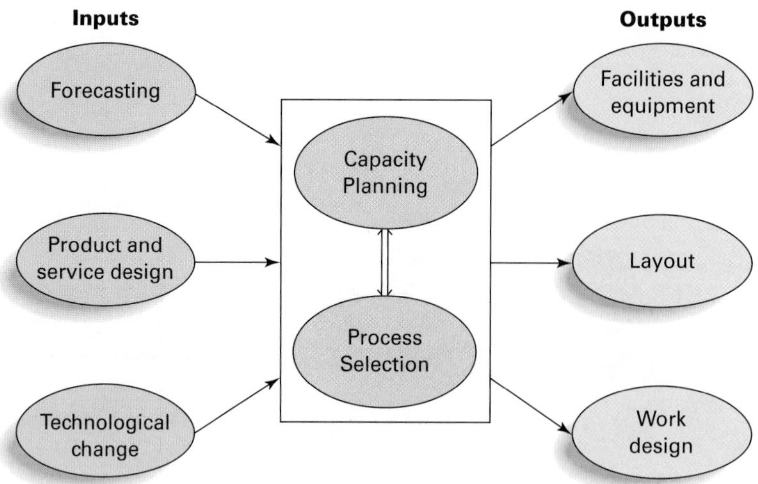

FIGURE 6.1 Process selection and capacity planning influence system design

INTRODUCTION

Process selection refers to deciding on the way production of goods or services will be organized. It has major implications for capacity planning, layout of facilities, equipment, and design of work systems. Process selection occurs as a matter of course when new products or services are being planned. However, it also occurs periodically due to technological changes in products or equipment, as well as competitive pressures. Figure 6.1 provides an overview of where process selection and capacity planning fit into system design. Forecasts, product and service design, and technological considerations all influence capacity planning and process selection. Moreover, capacity and process selection are interrelated, and are often done in concert. They, in turn, affect facility and equipment choices, layout, and work design.

How an organization approaches process selection is determined by the organization's *process strategy.* Key aspects include

- Capital intensity: the mix of equipment and labor that will be used by the organization.
- Process flexibility: the degree to which the system can be adjusted to changes in processing requirements due to such factors as changes in product or service design, changes in volume processed, and changes in technology.

PROCESS SELECTION

Process choice is demand driven. Three primary questions bear on process selection:

1. How much *variety* in products or services will the system need to handle?
2. What degree of equipment *flexibility* will be needed?
3. What is the expected *volume* of output?

Answers to these questions will serve as a guide to selecting an appropriate process.

Process Types

There are five basic process types: job shop, batch, repetitive, continuous, and project.

Job Shop. A job shop usually operates on a relatively small scale. It is used when a low volume of high-variety goods or services will be needed. Processing is *intermittent;* work includes small jobs, each with somewhat different processing requirements. High flexibility using general-purpose equipment and skilled workers are important characteristics of a job shop. A manufacturing example of a job shop is a tool and die shop that is able to produce

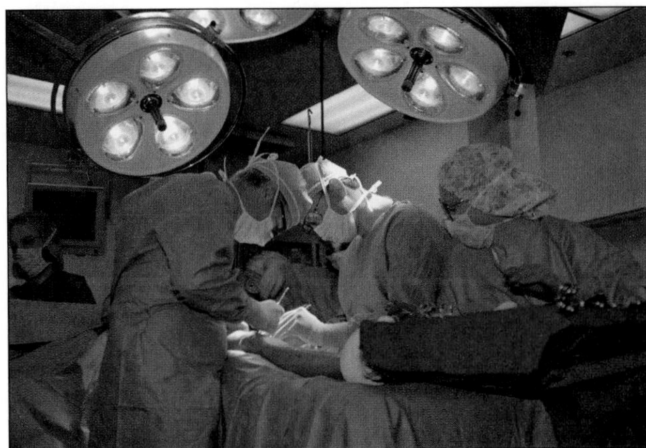

A job shop process: A midwestern hospital medical team performs a diagnostic procedure involving a cardiac catheterization.

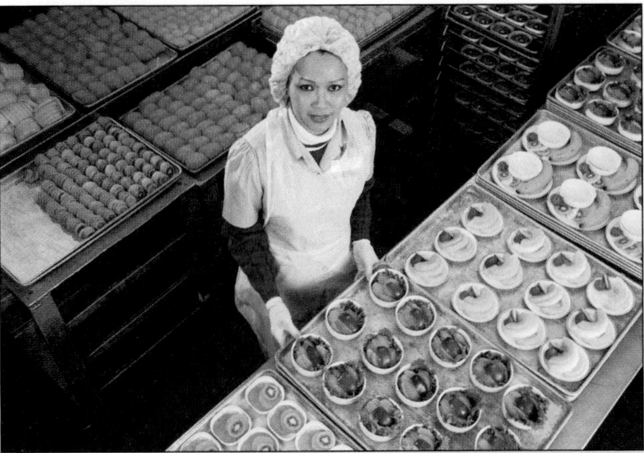

A batch process: Menu items are prepared in batches, in the kitchen of the Spago Restaurant in the Forum at Caesar's Palace, Las Vegas, Nevada.

A repetitive process: Motorcycles on an assembly line with parts added in a sequential order.

A continuous process: An oil refinery performs a continuous process, mixing and separating crude oil into gas, fuel oil, chemicals, and many other products.

one-of-a-kind tools. A service example is a veterinarian's office, which is able to process a variety of animals and a variety of injuries and diseases.

Batch. Batch processing is used when a moderate volume of goods or services is desired, and it can handle a moderate variety in products or services. The equipment need not be as flexible as in a job shop, but processing is still intermittent. The skill level of workers doesn't need to be as high as in a job shop because there is less variety in the jobs being processed. Examples of batch systems include bakeries, which make bread, cakes, or cookies in batches; movie theaters, which show movies to groups (batches) of people; and airlines, which carry planeloads (batches) of people from airport to airport. Other examples of products that lend themselves to batch production are paint, ice cream, soft drinks, beer, magazines, and books. Other examples of services include plays, concerts, music videos, radio and television programs, and public address announcements.

Repetitive. When higher volumes of more standardized goods or services are needed, repetitive processing is used. The standardized output means only slight flexibility of equipment is needed. Skill of workers is generally low. Examples of this type of system include production lines and assembly lines. In fact, this type of process is sometimes referred to as *assembly.* Familiar products made by these systems include automobiles, television sets, pencils, and computers. An example of a service system is an automatic carwash. Other examples of service include cafeteria lines and ticket collectors at sports events and concerts. Also, *mass customization* is an option.

Continuous. When a very high volume of nondiscrete, highly standardized output is desired, a continuous system is used. These systems have almost no variety in output and, hence, no need for equipment flexibility. Workers' skill requirements can range from low to high, depending on the complexity of the system and the expertise workers need. Generally, if equipment is highly specialized, worker skills can be lower. Examples of nondiscrete products made in continuous systems include petroleum products, steel, sugar, flour, and salt. Continuous services include air monitoring, supplying electricity to homes and businesses, and the Internet.

These process types are found in a wide range of manufacturing and service settings. The ideal is to have process capabilities match product or service requirements. Failure to do so can result in inefficiencies and higher costs than are necessary, perhaps creating a competitive disadvantage. Table 6.1 provides a brief description of each process type along with advantages and disadvantages of each.

Figure 6.2 provides an overview of these four process types in the form of a matrix, with an example for each process type. Note that job variety, process flexibility, and unit cost are highest for a job shop and get progressively lower moving from job shop to continuous processing. Conversely, volume of output is lowest for a job shop and gets progressively higher moving from job shop to continuous processing. Note, too, that the examples fall along the diagonal. The implication is that the diagonal represents the ideal choice of processing system for a given set of circumstances. For example, if the goal is to be able to process a small volume of jobs that will involve high variety, job shop processing is most appropriate. For less variety and a higher volume, a batch system would be most appropriate, and so on. Note that combinations far from the diagonal would not even be considered, such as using a job shop for high-volume, low-variety jobs, or continuous processing for low-volume,

TABLE 6.1
Types of processing

	Job Shop	Batch	Repetitive/ Assembly	Continuous
Description	Customized goods or services	Semi-standardized goods or services	Standardized goods or services	Highly standardized goods or services
Advantages	Able to handle a wide variety of work	Flexibility; easy to add or change products or services	Low unit cost, high volume, efficient	Very efficient, very high volume
Disadvantages	Slow, high cost per unit, complex planning and scheduling	Moderate cost per unit, moderate scheduling complexity	Low flexibility, high cost of downtime	Very rigid, lack of variety, costly to change, very high cost of downtime

FIGURE 6.2
Volume, variety, and flexibility of operations processes

	Product or Service and Flexibility Variety and Equipment Flexibility			
	High	Moderate	Low	Very low
Low or very low volume	**Job Shop** repair shop emergency room			
Moderate volume		**Batch** commercial bakery classroom lecture		
High volume			**Repetitive** assembly line automatic car wash	
Very high volume				**Continuous Flow** petroleum refining water treatment

high-variety jobs, because that would result in either higher than necessary costs or lost opportunities.

Another consideration is that products and services often go through *life cycles* that begin with low volume, which increases as products or services become better known. When that happens, a manager must know when to shift from one type of process (e.g., job shop) to the next (e.g., batch). Of course, some operations remain at a certain level (e.g., magazine publishing), while others increase (or decrease as markets become saturated) over time. Again, it is important for a manager to assess his or her products and services and make a judgment on whether to plan for changes in processing over time.

All of these process types (job shop, batch, repetitive, and continuous) are typically ongoing operations. However, some situations are not ongoing but instead are of limited durations. In such instances, the work is often organized as a *project.*

Project. A **project** is used for work that is nonroutine, with a unique set of objectives to be accomplished in a limited time frame. Examples range from simple to complicated, including such things as putting on a play, consulting, making a motion picture, launching a new product or service, publishing a book, building a dam, and building a bridge. Equipment flexibility and worker skills can range from low to high.

Project A nonrepetitive set of activities directed toward a unique goal within a limited time frame.

The type of process or processes used by an organization influences a great many activities of the organization. Table 6.2 briefly describes some of those influences.

Process type also impacts supply chain requirements. Repetitive and continuous processes require steady inputs of high-volume goods and services. Delivery reliability in terms of quality and timing is essential. Job shop and batch processing may mean that suppliers have to be able to deal with varying order quantities and timing of orders. In some instances seasonality is a factor, so suppliers must be able to handle periodic large demand.

SUPPLY CHAIN

The processes discussed do not always exist in their "pure" forms. It is not unusual to find hybrid processes—processes that have elements of other process types embedded in them. For instance, companies that operate primarily in a repetitive mode, or a continuous mode, will often have repair shops (i.e., job shops) to fix or make new parts for equipment that fails. Also, if volume increases for some items, an operation that began, say, in a job shop or as a batch mode may evolve into a batch or repetitive operation. This may result in having some operations in a job shop or batch mode, and others in a repetitive mode.

TABLE 6.2 Process choice affects numerous activities/functions

Activity/Function	Job Shop	Batch	Repetitive	Continuous	Projects
Cost estimation	Difficult	Somewhat routine	Routine	Routine	Simple to complex
Cost per unit	High	Moderate	Low	Low	Very high
Equipment used	General purpose	General purpose	Special purpose	Special purpose	Varied
Fixed costs	Low	Moderate	High	Very high	Varied
Variable costs	High	Moderate	Low	Very low	High
Labor skills	High	Moderate	Low	Low to high	Low to high
Marketing	Promote capabilities	Promote capabilities; semi-standardized goods and services	Promote standardized goods/services	Promote standardized goods/services	Promote capabilities
Scheduling	Complex	Moderately complex	Routine	Routine	Complex, subject to change
Work-in-process inventory	High	High	Low	Low	Varied

Morton Salt

OPERATIONS TOUR

Introduction

Morton Salt is a subsidiary of Morton International, a manufacturer of specialty chemicals, air bags, and salt products. The Morton salt-processing facility in Silver Springs, New York, between Buffalo and Rochester, is one of six similar Morton salt-processing facilities in the United States. The Silver Springs plant employs about 200 people, ranging from unskilled to skilled. It produces salt products for water conditioning, grocery, industrial, and agricultural markets. The grocery business consists of 26-oz. round cans of iodized salt. Although the grocery business represents a relatively small portion of the total output (approximately 15 percent), it is the most profitable.

Salt Production

The basic raw material, salt, is obtained by injecting water into salt caverns that are located some 2,400 feet below the surface. There, the salt deposits dissolve in the water. The resulting brine is pumped to the surface where it is converted into salt crystals. The brine is boiled, and much of the liquid evaporates, leaving salt crystals and some residual moisture, which is removed in a drying process. This process is run continuously for about six weeks at a time. Initially, salt is produced at the rate of 45 tons per hour. But the rate of output decreases due to scale buildup, so that by the sixth week, output is only 75 percent of the initial rate. At that point, the process is halted to perform maintenance on the equipment and remove the scale, after which, salt production resumes.

The salt is stored in silos until it is needed for production, or it is shipped in bulk to industrial customers. Conveyors move the salt to each of the four dedicated production areas, one of which is round can production. (See diagram.) The discussion here focuses exclusively on round can production.

Round Can Production

Annual round can production averages roughly 3.8 million cans. Approximately 70 percent of the output is for the Morton label, and the rest is for private label. There are two parallel, high-speed production lines. The two lines share common processes at the beginning of the lines, and then branch out into two identical lines. Each line is capable of producing 9,600 cans per hour (160 cans per minute). The equipment is not flexible, so the production rate is fixed. The operations are completely standardized; the only variable is the brand label that is applied. One line requires 12 production workers, while both lines together can be operated by 18 workers because of the common processes. Workers on the line perform low-skilled, repetitive tasks.

The plant produces both the salt and the cans the salt is packaged in. The cans are essentially a cylinder with a top and a bottom; they are made of cardboard, except for a plastic pour spout in the top. The cylinder portion is formed from two sheets of chip board that are glued together and then rolled into a continuous tube. The glue not only binds the material, it also provides a moisture barrier. The tube is cut in a two-step process: it is first cut

(continued)

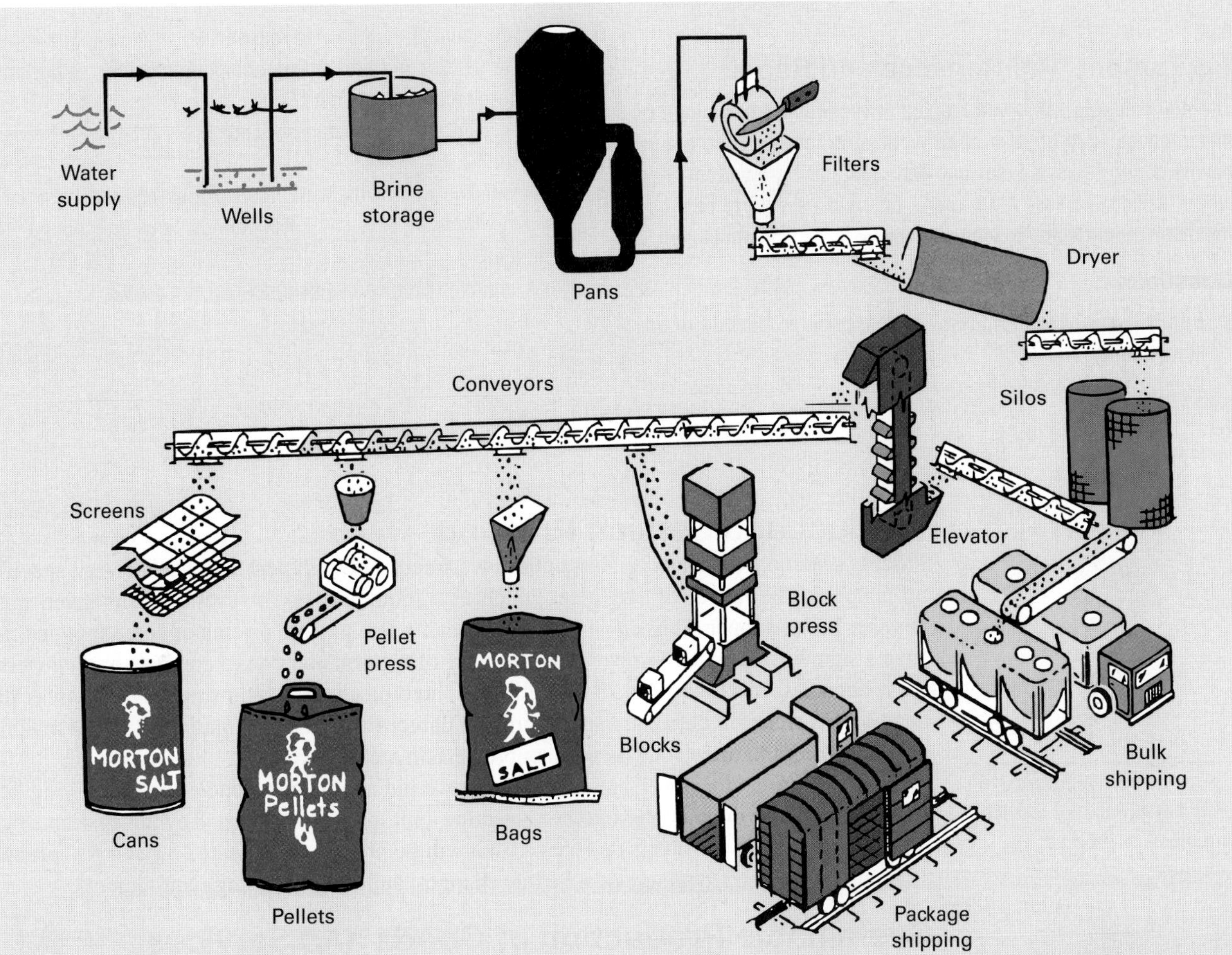

into long sections, and those sections are then cut into can-size pieces. The top and bottom pieces for the cans are punched from a continuous strip of cardboard. The separate pieces move along conveyor belts to the lines where the components are assembled into cans and glued. The cans are then filled with salt and the pour spout is added. Finally, the cans are loaded onto pallets and placed into inventory, ready to be shipped to distributors.

Quality

Quality is checked at several points in the production process. Initially, the salt is checked for purity when it is obtained from the wells. Iodine and an anti-caking compound are added to the salt, and their levels are verified using chemical analysis. Crystal size is important. In order to achieve the desired size and to remove lumps, the salt is forced through a scraping screen, which can cause very fine pieces of metal to mix with the salt. However, these pieces are effectively removed by magnets that are placed at appropriate points in the process. If, for any reason, the salt is judged to be contaminated, it is diverted to a nonfood product.

Checking the quality of the cans is done primarily by visual inspection, including verifying the assembly operation is correct, checking filled cans for correct weight, inspecting cans to see that labels are properly aligned, and checking to see that plastic pour spouts are correctly attached.

The equipment on the production line is sensitive to misshapen or damaged cans, and frequently jams, causing production delays. This greatly reduces the chance of a defective can getting through the process, but it reduces productivity, and the salt in the defective cans must be scrapped. The cost of quality is fairly high, owing to the amount of product that is scrapped, the large number of inspectors, and the extensive laboratory testing that is needed.

Production Planning and Inventory

The plant can sell all of the salt it produces. The job of the production scheduler is to distribute the salt that is stored in the silos to the various production areas, taking into account production capacities in each area and available inventory levels of those products. A key consideration is to make sure there is sufficient storage capacity in the silos to handle the incoming salt from brine production.

(continued)

(concluded)

Equipment Maintenance and Repair

The equipment is 1950s vintage, and it requires a fair amount of maintenance to keep it in good working order. Even so, breakdowns occur as parts wear out. The plant has its own tool shop where skilled workers repair parts or make new parts because replacement parts are no longer available for the old equipment.

Questions

1. Briefly describe salt production, from brine production to finished round cans.
2. Briefly describe quality assurance efforts in round can production.
3. What are some of the possible reasons why the company continues to use the old processing equipment instead of buying new, more modern equipment?
4. Where would you place salt production in the product–process spectrum?
5. Determine the approximate number of tons of salt produced annually. *Hints:* one ton = 2,000 pounds, and one pound = 16 ounces.
6. What improvements can you suggest for the plant?

Product and Service Profiling

SERVICE

Process selection can involve substantial investment in equipment and have a very specific influence on the layout of facilities, which also require heavy investment. Moreover, mismatches between operations capabilities and market demand and pricing or cost strategies can have a significant negative impact on the ability of the organization to compete or, in government agencies, to effectively service clients. Therefore, it is highly desirable to assess the degree of correlation between various process choices and market conditions *before* making process choices in order to achieve an appropriate matching.

Product or service profiling Linking key product or service requirements to process capabilities.

Product or service profiling can be used to avoid any inconsistencies by identifying key product or service dimensions and then selecting appropriate processes. Key dimensions often relate to the range of products or services that will be processed, expected order sizes, pricing strategies, expected frequency of schedule changes, and order-winning requirements.

Sustainable Production of Goods and Services

SERVICE

Business organizations are facing increasing pressure from a variety of sources to operate sustainable production processes. According to the Lowell Center for Sustainable Production (http://sustainableproduction.org), "Sustainable Production is the creation of goods and services using processes and systems that are: non-polluting; conserving of energy and natural resources; economically efficient; safe and healthful for workers, communities, and consumers; and socially and creatively rewarding for all working people." To achieve this, the Lowell Center advocates designing and operating processes in ways that:

- "wastes and ecologically incompatible byproducts are reduced, eliminated or recycled on-site;
- chemical substances or physical agents and conditions that present hazards to human health or the environment are eliminated;
- energy and materials are conserved, and the forms of energy and materials used are most appropriate for the desired ends; and
- work spaces are designed to minimize or eliminate chemical, ergonomic and physical hazard."

To achieve these goals, business organizations must focus on a number of factors that include energy use and efficiency, CO_2 (carbon footprint) and toxic emissions, waste generation, lighting, heating, cooling, ventilation, noise and vibration, and worker health and safety.

Lean Process Design

Lean process design is guided by general principles that are discussed more fully in a later chapter. One principle of particular interest here is waste reduction, which relates to sustainability objectives. Lean design also focuses on variance reduction in workload over the entire process to achieve level production and thereby improve process flow. Successful lean design results in reduced inventory and floor space; quicker response times and shorter lead times; reduced defects, rework, and scrap; and increased productivity. Lean design is often translated into practice using cellular layouts, which are discussed later in this chapter.

Lean process design has broad applications in seemingly diverse areas such as health care delivery systems, manufacturing, construction projects, and process reengineering.

TECHNOLOGY

Technology and technological innovation often have a major influence on business processes. **Technological innovation** refers to the discovery and development of new or improved products, services, or processes for producing or providing them. **Technology** refers to applications of scientific discoveries to the development and improvement of goods and services and/or the processes that produce or provide them. It can involve such factors as knowledge, materials, methods, and equipment. The term *high technology* refers to the most advanced and developed equipment and methods.

Technological innovation The discovery and development of new or improved products, services, or processes for producing or providing them.

Technology The application of scientific discoveries to the development and improvement of products and services and operations processes.

Process technology and information technology can have a major impact on costs, productivity, and competitiveness. *Process technology* includes methods, procedures, and equipment used to produce goods and provide services. This not only involves processes within an organization, it also extends to supply chain processes. *Information technology (IT)* is the science and use of computers and other electronic equipment to store, process, and send information. IT is heavily ingrained in today's business operations. This includes electronic data processing, the use of bar codes and radio frequency tags to identify and track goods, devices used to obtain point-of-sale information, data transmission, the Internet, e-commerce, e-mail, and more.

Technological innovation in processing technology can produce tremendous benefits for organizations by increasing quality, lowering costs, increasing productivity, and expanding processing capabilities. Among the examples are laser technology used in surgery and laser measuring devices, advances in medical diagnostic equipment, high-speed Internet connections, high-definition television, online banking, information retrieval systems, and high-speed search engines. Processing technologies often come through acquisition rather than through internal efforts of an organization.

While process technology can have enormous benefits, it also carries substantial risk unless a significant effort is made to fully understand both the downside as well as the upside of a particular technology. It is essential to understand what the technology will and won't do. Also, there are economic considerations (initial cost, space, cash flow, maintenance, consultants), integration considerations (cost, time, resources), and human considerations (training, safety, job loss).

Automation

A key question in process design is whether to automate. **Automation** is machinery that has sensing and control devices that enable it to operate automatically. If a company decides to automate, the next question is how much. Automation can range from factories that are completely automated to a single automated operation.

Automation Machinery that has sensing and control devices that enable it to operate automatically.

SERVICE

Automated services are also an option. Although not as plentiful as in manufacturing, automated services are becoming increasingly important. Examples range from automated teller machines (ATMs) to automated heating and air conditioning, and include automated inspection, automated storage and retrieval systems, package sorting, mail processing, e-mail, online banking, and E-Z pass.

Automation offers a number of advantages over human labor. It has low variability, whereas it is difficult for a human to perform a task in exactly the same way, in the same amount of time, and on a repetitive basis. In a production setting, variability is detrimental to quality and to meeting schedules. Moreover, machines do not get bored or distracted, nor do they go out on strike, ask for higher wages, or file labor grievances. Still another advantage of automation is reduction of variable costs. In order for automated processing to be an option, job-processing requirements must be *standardized* (i.e., have very little or no variety).

TABLE 6.3
Automation questions

1. What level of automation is appropriate? (Some operations are more suited to being automated than others, so partial automation can be an option.)
2. How would automation affect the flexibility of an operation system?
3. How can automation projects be justified?
4. How should changes be managed?
5. What are the risks of automating?
6. What are some of the likely effects of implementing automation on market share, costs, quality, customer satisfaction, labor relations, and ongoing operations?

Automation is frequently touted as a strategy necessary for competitiveness. However, automation also has certain disadvantages and limitations compared to human labor. To begin with, it can be costly. Technology is expensive; usually it requires high volumes of output to offset high costs. In addition, automation is much less flexible than human labor. Once a process has been automated, there is substantial reason for not changing it. Moreover, workers sometimes fear automation because it might cause them to lose their jobs. That can have an adverse effect on morale and productivity.

Decision makers must carefully examine the issue of whether to automate or the degree to which to automate, so that they clearly understand all the ramifications. Also, much thought and careful planning are necessary to successfully *integrate* automation into a production system. Otherwise, it can lead to major problems. Automation has important implications not only for cost and flexibility, but also for the fit with overall strategic priorities. If the decision is made to automate, care must be taken to remove waste from the system prior to automating, to avoid building the waste into the automated system. Table 6.3 has a list of questions for organizations that are considering automation.

Generally speaking, there are three kinds of automation: fixed, programmable, and flexible.

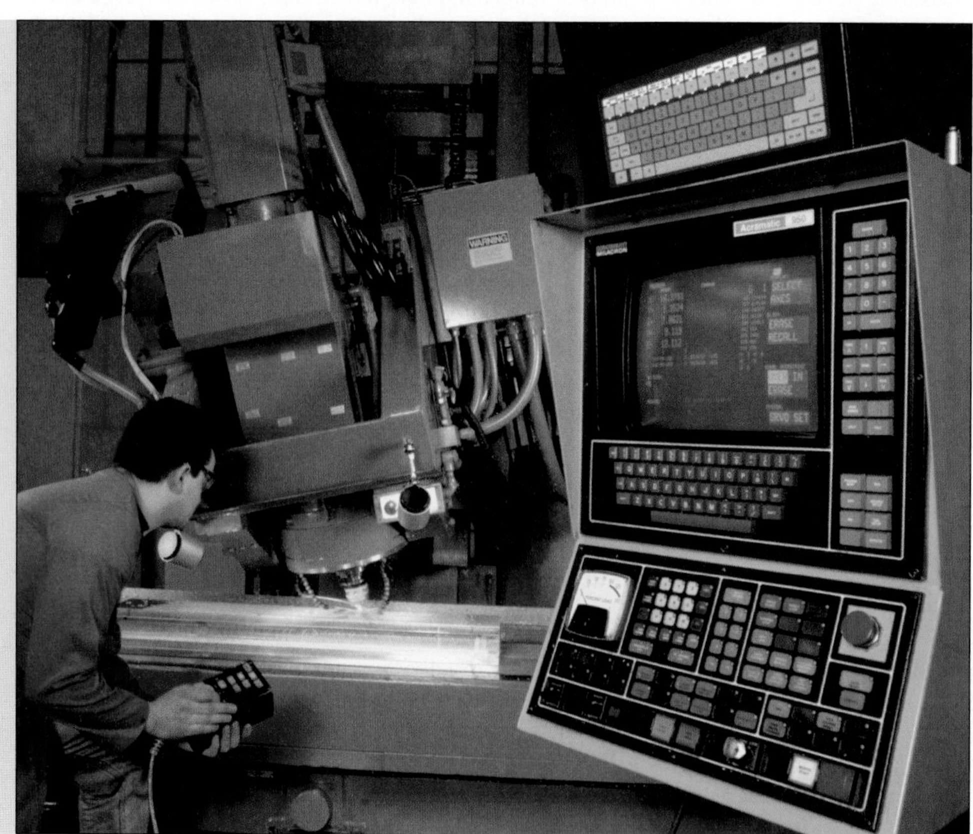

Computer numerical control (CNC) refers to a computer that reads instructions and drives a machine tool. CNC machines are controlled directly from files created by CAM software packages. With increased automation of manufacturing processes with CNC machining, considerable improvements in consistency and quality have been achieved. CNC automation reduces the frequency of errors and provides operators with time to perform additional tasks. The intelligence of CNC controllers has dramatically increased job shop cell production. Some machines might even make 1,000 parts on a weekend with no operator, checking each part with lasers and sensors.

Fixed automation is the least flexible. It uses high-cost, specialized equipment for a fixed sequence of operations. Low cost and high volume are its primary advantages; minimal variety and the high cost of making major changes in either product or process are its primary limitations.

Programmable automation involves the use of high-cost, general-purpose equipment controlled by a computer program that provides both the sequence of operations and specific details about each operation. This type of automation has the capability of economically producing a fairly wide variety of low-volume products in small batches. Numerically controlled (N/C) machines and some robots are applications of programmable automation.

Computer-aided manufacturing (CAM) refers to the use of computers in process control, ranging from robots to automated quality control. **Numerically controlled (N/C) machines** are programmed to follow a set of processing instructions based on mathematical relationships that tell the machine the details of the operations to be performed. The instructions are stored on a device such as magnetic tape, or microprocessor. Although N/C machines have been used for many years, they are an important part of new approaches to manufacturing. Individual machines often have their own computer; this is referred to as *computerized numerical control (CNC).* Or one computer may control a number of N/C machines, which is referred to as *direct numerical control (DNC).*

Computer-aided manufacturing (CAM) The use of computers in process control.

Numerically controlled (N/C) machines Machines that perform operations by following mathematical processing instructions.

N/C machines are best used in cases where parts are processed frequently and in small batches, where part geometry is complex, close tolerances are required, mistakes are costly, and there is the possibility of frequent changes in design. The main limitations of N/C machines are the higher skill levels needed to program the machines and their inability to detect tool wear and material variation.

The use of robots in manufacturing is sometimes an option. Robots can handle a wide variety of tasks, including welding, assembly, loading and unloading of machines, painting, and testing. They relieve humans from heavy or dirty work and often eliminate drudgery tasks.

Some uses of robots are fairly simple, others are much more complex. At the lowest level are robots that follow a fixed set of instructions. Next are programmable robots, which can repeat a set of movements after being led through the sequence. These robots "play back" a mechanical sequence much as a video recorder plays back a visual sequence. At the next level up are robots that follow instructions from a computer. Below are robots that can recognize objects and make certain simple decisions.

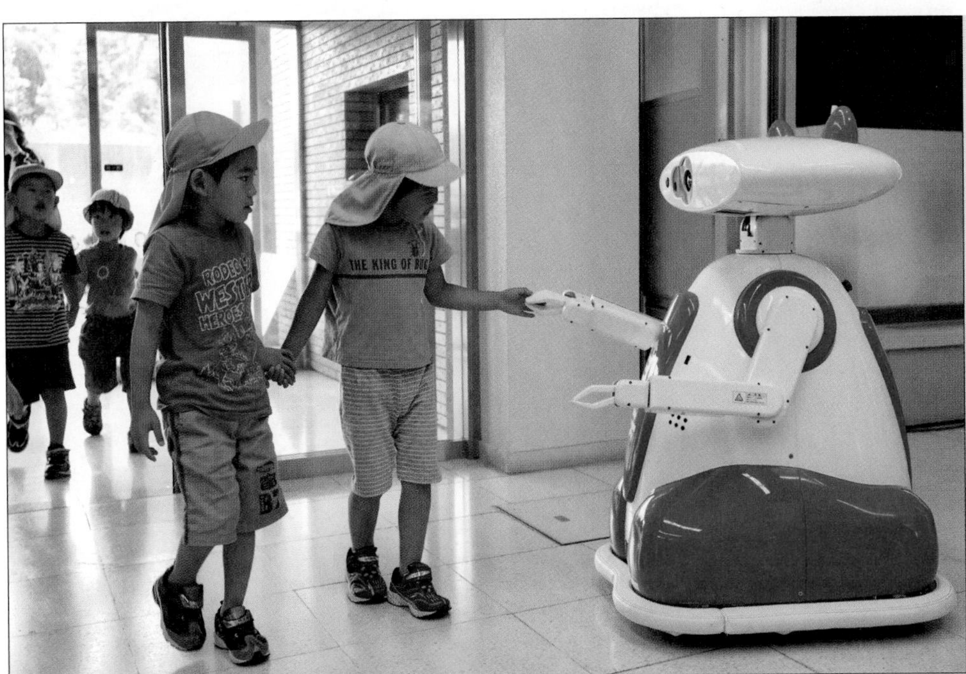

Tmsuk's receptionist robot is used for medical purposes. These robots can guide a hospital visitor to a nearby elevator. If a human touches the panel on the robot's body or speaks to it, the robot can display or print directions.

Flexible automation evolved from programmable automation. It uses equipment that is more customized than that of programmable automation. A key difference between the two is that flexible automation requires significantly less changeover time. This permits almost continuous operation of equipment *and* product variety without the need to produce in batches.

In practice, flexible automation is used in several different formats.

Flexible manufacturing system (FMS) A group of machines designed to handle intermittent processing requirements and produce a variety of similar products.

A **flexible manufacturing system (FMS)** is a group of machines that include supervisory computer control, automatic material handling, and robots or other automated processing equipment. Reprogrammable controllers enable these systems to produce a variety of *similar* products. Systems may range from three or four machines to more than a dozen. They are designed to handle intermittent processing requirements with some of the benefits of automation and some of the flexibility of individual, or stand-alone, machines (e.g., N/C machines). Flexible manufacturing systems offer reduced labor costs and more consistent quality compared with more traditional manufacturing methods, lower capital investment and higher flexibility than "hard" automation, and relatively quick changeover time. Flexible manufacturing systems often appeal to managers who hope to achieve both the flexibility of job shop processing and the productivity of repetitive processing systems.

Although these are important benefits, an FMS also has certain limitations. One is that this type of system can handle a relatively narrow range of part variety, so it must be used for a family of similar parts, which all require similar machining. Also, an FMS requires longer planning and development times than more conventional processing equipment because of its increased complexity and cost. Furthermore, companies sometimes prefer a gradual approach to automation, and FMS represents a sizable chunk of technology.

Computer-integrated manufacturing (CIM) A system for linking a broad range of manufacturing activities through an integrating computer system.

Computer-integrated manufacturing (CIM) is a system that uses an integrating computer system to link a broad range of manufacturing activities, including engineering design, flexible manufacturing systems, purchasing, order processing, and production planning and control. Not all elements are absolutely necessary. For instance, CIM might be as simple as linking two or more FMSs by a host computer. More encompassing systems can link scheduling, purchasing, inventory control, shop control, and distribution. In effect, a CIM system integrates information from other areas of an organization with manufacturing.

The overall goal of using CIM is to link various parts of an organization to achieve rapid response to customer orders and/or product changes, to allow rapid production, and to reduce *indirect* labor costs.

The flexible manufacturing center consists of a flexible manufacturing system and a series of software systems providing fast, accurate production and inspection of a wide variety of materials.

A shining example of how process choices can lead to competitive advantages can be found at Allen-Bradley's computer-integrated manufacturing process in Milwaukee, Wisconsin. The company converted a portion of its factory to a fully automated "factory within a factory" to assemble contactors and relays for electrical motors. A handful of humans operate the factory, although once an order has been entered into the system, the machines do virtually all the work, including packaging and shipping, and quality control. Any defective items are removed from the line, and replacement parts are automatically ordered and scheduled to compensate for the defective items. The humans program the machines, monitor operations, and attend to any problems signaled by a system of warning lights.

As orders come into the plant, computers determine production requirements and schedules and order the necessary parts. Bar-coded labels that contain processing instructions are automatically placed on individual parts. As the parts approach a machine, a sensing device reads the bar code and communicates the processing instructions to the machine. The factory can produce 600 units an hour.

The company has realized substantial competitive advantages from the system. Orders can be completed and shipped within 24 hours of entry into the system, indirect labor costs and inventory costs have been greatly reduced, and quality is very high.

Tour de Force

READING

Gerald Scott

www.chryslercorp.com

DaimlerChrysler's plant that builds Viper and Prowler is the Motor City's "hottest ticket."

The Viper-Prowler plant is not your typical Detroit assembly operation. Instead of mass production techniques using robots, it's "craftsman-style" production for hand-building Vipers and Prowlers. With mass production, DaimlerChrysler can produce up to 75 cars per hour. With late shifts DaimlerChrysler's nearby Jefferson North Assembly Plant can crank out 1,114 Jeep Grand Cherokees in a 24-hour workday. By comparison, the Viper plant produces 13 Vipers a day and has a capacity for 20 Prowlers.

At 392,000 square feet, the Viper plant is a boutique compared to most massive auto plants, such as Saturn Corp.'s Spring Hill, Tenn., manufacturing complex, which is 5 million square feet. The Jefferson North plant has 2.4 million square feet.

"We're not the biggest plant in the area, but we've got the best work force and build the most exciting products—the Plymouth Prowler and Dodge Viper," said Hinckley, who has spent 33 years working in various Detroit auto plants for General Motors and Chrysler and is known for building and driving "kit car" racers. "We're expanding our plant, too. We also are part of the revitalization of Detroit.

"Our plant was about 380,000 square feet and we've just added another 10,000 square feet to improve our process flow and improve our quality. And it provides a little more space since we added the Prowler.

"It will allow us to do a better job of reaching the Prowler's ultimate capacity. It's about a $1 million expansion—for other large plants, that's nothing but for a facility this size it's a lot of money.

"For me it's a dream job. I've been a 'hot rodder' all my life and build race cars and racing engines, and how many hot rodders get to lead the team that runs the only hot-rod plant in the world?"

Conner Avenue is a throwback to early 20th Century, pre–mass assembly techniques. Vipers and Prowlers are built on parallel 720-foot assembly lines, each with a dozen or so workstations, where the cars are hand-assembled. In a rarity, there are no robots in this plant.

When each workstation completes its task, the entire line advances to the next station. So in those 45-minute stops, the employees are relatively free to grab a cup of coffee or talk to tour groups, something they could never do in a plant cranking out 73 units per hour.

The automaker's flexible labor agreement with UAW Local 212 means everybody working in the plant is a "craftsman" and can solve any problem anywhere on the line—in most plants, job categories are sharply defined and protected.

Most large auto assembly plants still require 2,000 or more workers, while the Viper plant needs only 260.

"We do everything from forklift driving to mopping and sweeping, we do it all," says Andrew Stokes, a UAW craftsman who works in underbody and heavy repair.

"I'm one of the first 12 to work on the Prowler," he added. "The Prowler is a little easier to assemble but a little harder to repair. The Viper seems to be a lot more open than the Prowler is—the car seems to be built around the engine and trans and that makes it a little harder to work on."

Thanks to such an interest from car buyers in this plant, Daimler Chrysler allows Viper customers to pick up their car as it comes out of final assembly, to meet the employees who built it and to drive it home from the plant instead of from the dealership.

Questions

1. What is different about this assembly plant compared to more typical auto assembly plants?
2. Why do you suppose there are no robots or other automation?

Source: Excerpts from Gerald Scott, "Tour de Force," *Chicago Tribune.*

PROCESS STRATEGY

Throughout this book, the importance of *flexibility* as a competitive strategy is stressed. However, flexibility does not always offer the best choice in processing decisions. Flexible systems and equipment are often more expensive and not as efficient as less flexible alternatives. In certain instances, flexibility is unnecessary because products are in mature stages, requiring few design changes, and there is a steady volume of output. Ordinarily, this type of situation calls for specialized processing equipment, with no need for flexibility. The implication is clear: Flexibility should be adopted with great care; its applications should be matched with situations in which a *need* for flexibility clearly exists.

In practice, decision makers choose flexible systems for either of two reasons: Demand variety or uncertainty exists about demand. The second reason can be overcome through improved forecasting.

STRATEGIC RESOURCE ORGANIZATION: FACILITIES LAYOUT

Layout refers to the configuration of departments, work centers, and equipment, with particular emphasis on movement of work (customers or materials) through the system. This section describes the main types of layout designs and the models used to evaluate design alternatives.

As in other areas of system design, layout decisions are important for three basic reasons: (1) they require substantial investments of money and effort; (2) they involve long-term commitments, which makes mistakes difficult to overcome; and (3) they have a significant impact on the cost and efficiency of operations.

The need for layout planning arises both in the process of designing new facilities and in redesigning existing facilities. The most common reasons for redesign of layouts include inefficient operations (e.g., high cost, bottlenecks), accidents or safety hazards, changes in the design of products or services, introduction of new products or services, changes in the volume of output or mix of outputs, changes in methods or equipment, changes in environmental or other legal requirements, and morale problems (e.g., lack of face-to-face contact).

SERVICE

Poor layout design can adversely affect system performance. For example, a change in the layout at the Minneapolis–St. Paul International Airport solved a problem that had plagued travelers. In the former layout, security checkpoints were located in the boarding area. That meant that arriving passengers who were simply changing planes had to pass through a security checkpoint before being able to board their connecting flight, along with other passengers whose journeys were originating at Minneapolis–St. Paul. This created excessive waiting times for both sets of passengers. The new layout relocated the security checkpoints, moving them from the boarding area to a position close to the ticket counters. Thus, the need for passengers who were making connecting flights to pass through security was eliminated, and in the process, the waiting time for passengers departing from Minneapolis–St. Paul was considerably reduced.[1]

The basic objective of layout design is to facilitate a smooth flow of work, material, and information through the system. Supporting objectives generally involve the following:

1. To facilitate attainment of product or service quality.
2. To use workers and space efficiently.
3. To avoid bottlenecks.
4. To minimize material handling costs.
5. To eliminate unnecessary movements of workers or materials.

[1]Based on "Airport Checkpoints Moved to Help Speed Travelers on Their Way," *Minneapolis–St. Paul Star Tribune,* January 13, 1995, p. 1B.

6. To minimize production time or customer service time.
7. To design for safety.

The three basic types of layout are product, process, and fixed-position. *Product layouts* are most conducive to repetitive processing, *process layouts* are used for intermittent processing, and *fixed-position layouts* are used when projects require layouts. The characteristics, advantages, and disadvantages of each layout type are described in this section, along with hybrid layouts, which are combinations of these pure types. These include cellular layouts and flexible manufacturing systems.

Repetitive Processing: Product Layouts

Product layouts are used to achieve a smooth and rapid flow of large volumes of goods or customers through a system. This is made possible by highly standardized goods or services that allow highly standardized, repetitive processing. The work is divided into a series of standardized tasks, permitting specialization of equipment and division of labor. The large volumes handled by these systems usually make it economical to invest substantial sums of money in equipment and job design. Because only one or a few very similar items are involved, it is feasible to arrange an entire layout to correspond to the technological processing requirements of the product or service. For instance, if a portion of a manufacturing operation required the sequence of cutting, sanding, and painting, the appropriate pieces of equipment would be arranged in that same sequence. And because each item follows the same sequence of operations, it is often possible to utilize fixed-path material-handling equipment such as conveyors to transport items between operations. The resulting arrangement forms a line like the one depicted in Figure 6.3. In manufacturing environments, the lines are referred to as **production lines** or **assembly lines,** depending on the type of activity involved. In service processes, the term *line* may or may not be used. It is common to refer to a cafeteria line as such but not a car wash, although from a conceptual standpoint the two are nearly identical. Figure 6.4 illustrates the layout of a typical cafeteria serving line. Examples of this type of layout are less plentiful in service environments because processing requirements usually exhibit too much variability to make standardization feasible. Without high standardization, many of the benefits of repetitive processing are lost. When lines are used, certain compromises may be made. For instance, an automatic car wash provides equal treatment to all cars—the same amount of soap, water, and scrubbing—even though cars may differ considerably in cleaning needs.

Product layout Layout that uses standardized processing operations to achieve smooth, rapid, high-volume flow.

Production line Standardized layout arranged according to a fixed sequence of production tasks.

Assembly line Standardized layout arranged according to a fixed sequence of assembly tasks.

Product layouts achieve a high degree of labor and equipment utilization, which tends to offset their high equipment costs. Because items move quickly from operation to operation, the amount of work-in-process is often minimal. Consequently, operations are so closely tied to each other that the entire system is highly vulnerable to being shut down because of mechanical failure or high absenteeism. Maintenance procedures are geared to this. *Preventive maintenance*—periodic inspection and replacement of worn parts or those with high failure rates—reduces the probability of breakdowns during the operations. Of course, no amount

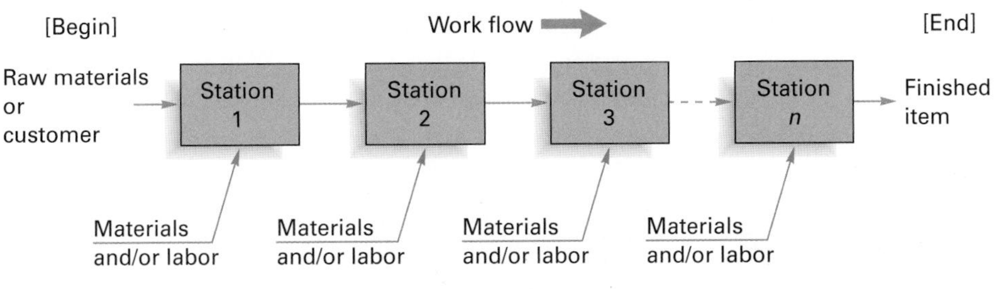

FIGURE 6.3
A flow line for production or service

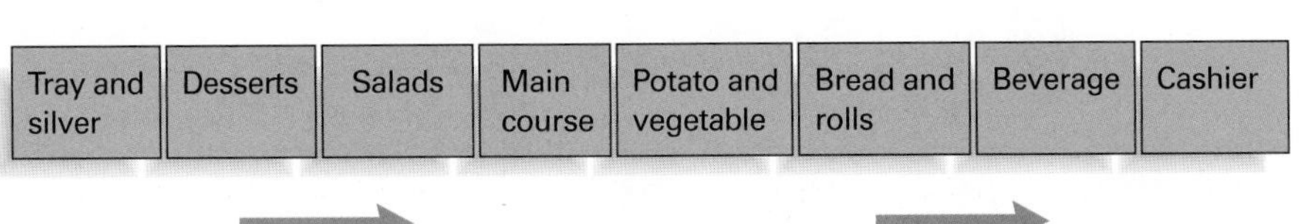

FIGURE 6.4
Cafeteria line

of preventive activity can completely eliminate failures, so management must take measures to provide quick repair. These include maintaining an inventory of spare parts and having repair personnel available to quickly restore equipment to normal operation. These procedures are fairly expensive; because of the specialized nature of equipment, problems become more difficult to diagnose and resolve, and spare-part inventories can be extensive.

Repetitive processing can be machine paced (e.g., automatic car wash, automobile assembly), worker paced (e.g., fast-food restaurants such as McDonald's, Burger King), or even customer paced (e.g., cafeteria line).

The main advantages of product layouts are

1. A high rate of output.
2. Low unit cost due to high volume. The high cost of specialized equipment is spread over many units.
3. Labor specialization, which reduces training costs and time, and results in a wide span of supervision.
4. Low material-handling cost per unit. Material handling is simplified because units follow the same sequence of operations. Material handling is often automated.
5. A high utilization of labor and equipment.
6. The establishment of routing and scheduling in the initial design of the system. These activities do not require much attention once the system is operating.
7. Fairly routine accounting, purchasing, and inventory control.

The primary disadvantages of product layouts include the following:

1. The intensive division of labor usually creates dull, repetitive jobs that provide little opportunity for advancement and may lead to morale problems and to repetitive stress injuries.
2. Poorly skilled workers may exhibit little interest in maintaining equipment or in the quality of output.
3. The system is fairly inflexible in response to changes in the volume of output or changes in product or process design.
4. The system is highly susceptible to shutdowns caused by equipment breakdowns or excessive absenteeism because workstations are highly interdependent.
5. Preventive maintenance, the capacity for quick repairs, and spare-parts inventories are necessary expenses.
6. Incentive plans tied to individual output are impractical since they would cause variations among outputs of individual workers, which would adversely affect the smooth flow of work through the system.

U-Shaped Layouts. Although a straight production line may have intuitive appeal, a U-shaped line (see Figure 6.5) has a number of advantages that make it worthy of consideration. One disadvantage of a long, straight line is that it interferes with cross-travel of workers and vehicles. A U-shaped line is more compact; it often requires approximately half the length

FIGURE 6.5
A U-shaped production line

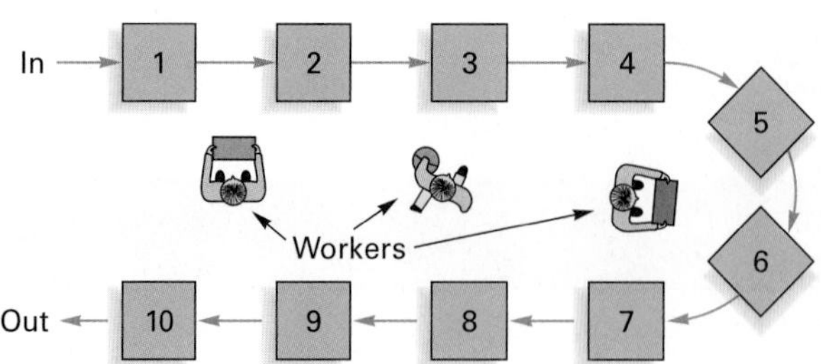

of a straight production line. In addition, a U-shaped line permits increased communication among workers on the line because workers are clustered, thus facilitating teamwork. Flexibility in work assignments is increased because workers can handle not only adjacent stations but also stations on opposite sides of the line. Moreover, if materials enter the plant at the same point that finished products leave it, a U-shaped line minimizes material handling.

Of course, not all situations lend themselves to U-shaped layouts: On highly automated lines there is less need for teamwork and communication. And entry and exit points may be on opposite sides of the building. Also, operations may need to be separated because of noise or contamination factors.

Nonrepetitive Processing: Process Layouts

Process layouts (functional layouts) are designed to process items or provide services that involve a variety of processing requirements. The variety of jobs that are processed requires frequent adjustments to equipment. This causes a discontinuous work flow, which is referred to as **intermittent processing.** The layouts feature departments or other *functional* groupings in which similar kinds of activities are performed. A manufacturing example of a process layout is the *machine shop,* which has separate departments for milling, grinding, drilling, and so on. Items that require those operations are frequently moved in lots or batches to the departments in a sequence that varies from job to job. Consequently, variable-path material-handling equipment (forklift trucks, jeeps, tote boxes) is needed to handle the variety of routes and items. The use of *general-purpose equipment* provides the *flexibility* necessary to handle a wide range of processing requirements. Workers who operate the equipment are usually skilled or semiskilled. Figure 6.6 illustrates the departmental arrangement typical of a process layout.

Process layouts Layouts that can handle varied processing requirements.

Intermittent processing Nonrepetitive processing.

Process layouts are quite common in service environments. Examples include hospitals, colleges and universities, banks, auto repair shops, airlines, and public libraries. For instance, hospitals have departments or other units that specifically handle surgery, maternity, pediatrics, psychiatric, emergency, and geriatric care. And universities have separate schools or departments that concentrate on one area of study such as business, engineering, science, or math.

SERVICE

Because equipment in a process layout is arranged by type rather than by processing sequence, the system is much less vulnerable to shutdown caused by mechanical failure or absenteeism. In manufacturing systems especially, idle equipment is usually available to replace machines that are temporarily out of service. Moreover, because items are often processed in lots (batches), there is considerably less interdependence between successive operations than with a product layout. Maintenance costs tend to be lower because the equipment is less specialized than that of product layouts, and the grouping of machinery permits repair personnel to become skilled in handling that type of equipment. Machine similarity reduces the necessary investment in spare parts. On the negative side, routing and scheduling must be done on a continual basis to accommodate the variety of processing demands typically imposed on these systems. Material handling is inefficient, and unit handling costs are generally much higher than in product layouts. In-process inventories can be substantial due to

FIGURE 6.6 Comparison of process and product layouts

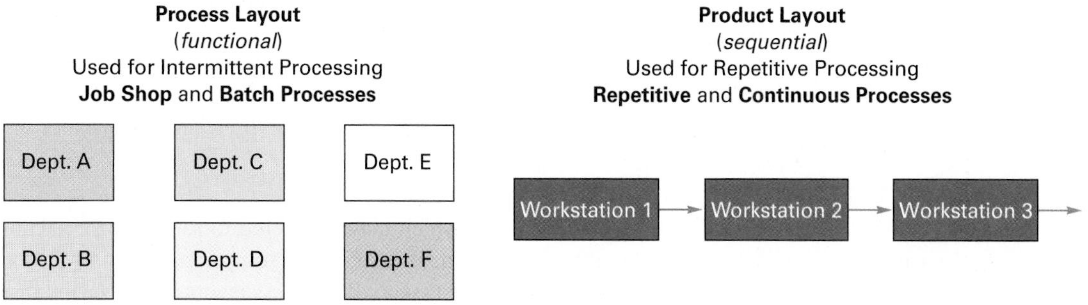

batch processing. Furthermore, it is not uncommon for such systems to have equipment utilization rates under 50 percent because of routing and scheduling complexities related to the variety of processing demands being handled.

In sum, process layouts have both advantages and disadvantages. The advantages of process layouts include the following:

1. The systems can handle a variety of processing requirements.
2. The systems are not particularly vulnerable to equipment failures.
3. General-purpose equipment is often less costly than the specialized equipment used in product layouts and is easier and less costly to maintain.
4. It is possible to use individual incentive systems.

The disadvantages of process layouts include the following:

1. In-process inventory costs can be high if batch processing is used in manufacturing systems.
2. Routing and scheduling pose continual challenges.
3. Equipment utilization rates are low.
4. Material handling is slow and inefficient, and more costly per unit than in product layouts.
5. Job complexities often reduce the span of supervision and result in higher supervisory costs than with product layouts.
6. Special attention necessary for each product or customer (e.g., routing, scheduling, machine setups) and low volumes result in higher unit costs than with product layouts.
7. Accounting, inventory control, and purchasing are much more involved than with product layouts.

Fixed-Position Layouts

Fixed-position layout Layout in which the product or project remains stationary, and workers, materials, and equipment are moved as needed.

In **fixed-position layouts**, the item being worked on remains stationary, and workers, materials, and equipment are moved about as needed. This is in marked contrast to product and process layouts. Almost always, the nature of the product dictates this kind of arrangement: Weight, size, bulk, or some other factor makes it undesirable or extremely difficult to move the product. Fixed-position layouts are used in large construction projects (buildings, power plants, dams), shipbuilding, and production of large aircraft and space mission rockets. In those instances, attention is focused on timing of material and equipment deliveries so as not to clog up the work site and to avoid having to relocate materials and equipment around the work site. Lack of storage space can present significant problems, for example, at construction sites in crowded urban locations. Because of the many diverse activities carried out on large projects and because of the wide range of skills required, special efforts are needed to coordinate the activities, and the span of control can be quite narrow. For these reasons, the administrative burden is often much higher than it would be under either of the other layout types. Material handling may or may not be a factor; in many cases, there is no tangible product involved (e.g., designing a computerized inventory system). When goods and materials are involved, material handling often resembles process-type, variable-path, general-purpose equipment. Projects might require use of earth-moving equipment and trucks to haul materials to, from, and around the work site, for example.

Fixed-position layouts are widely used in farming, firefighting, road building, home building, remodeling and repair, and drilling for oil. In each case, compelling reasons bring workers, materials, and equipment to the "product's" location instead of the other way around.

Combination Layouts

The three basic layout types are ideal models, which may be altered to satisfy the needs of a particular situation. It is not hard to find layouts that represent some combination of these pure types. For instance, supermarket layouts are essentially process layouts, yet we find that

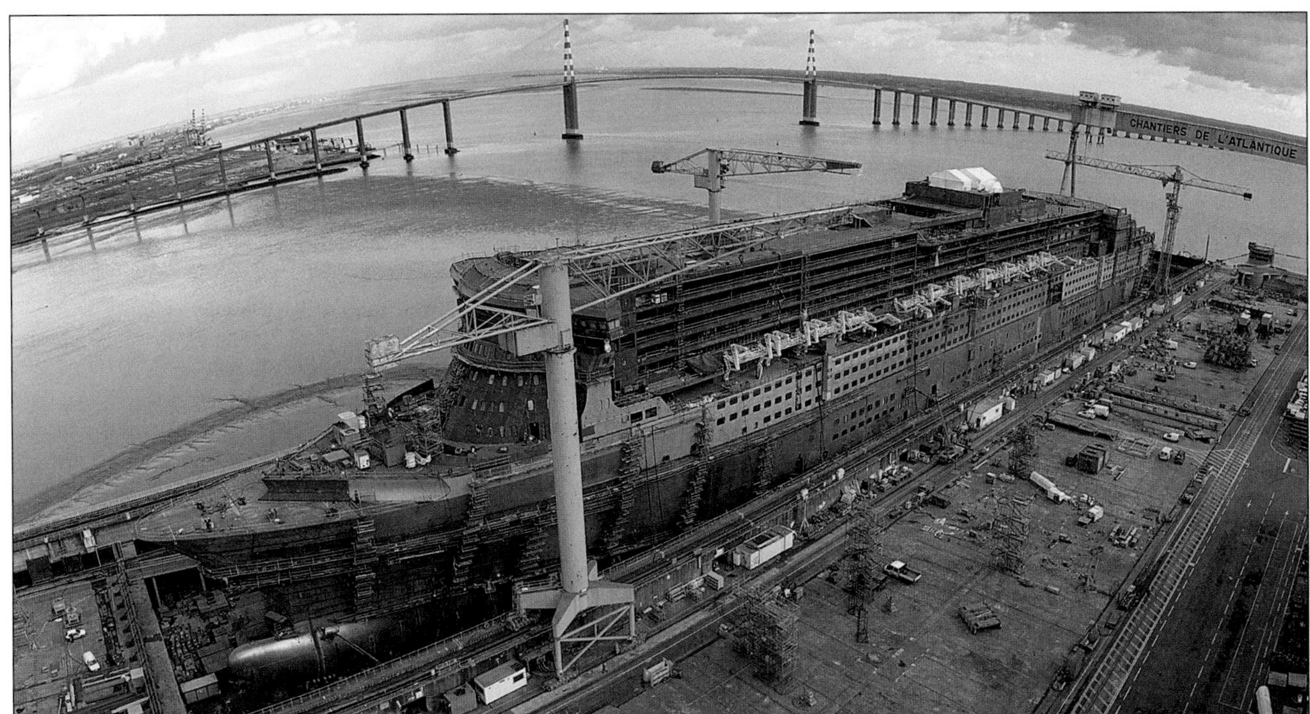

The Queen Mary 2 when under construction at the Chantiers de l'Atlantique shipyard in St. Nazaire, France. When a large project must remain stationary, workers and equipment come to the site. The QM2 weighs 150,000 tons, is 1,132 feet long, and is 147.6 feet wide. Its capacity is 2,620 passengers and 1,253 officers and crew.

most use fixed-path material-handling devices such as roller-type conveyors in the stockroom and belt-type conveyors at the cash registers. Hospitals also use the basic process arrangement, although frequently patient care involves more of a fixed-position approach, in which nurses, doctors, medicines, and special equipment are brought to the patient. By the same token, faulty parts made in a product layout may require off-line reworking, which involves customized processing. Moreover, conveyors are frequently observed in both farming and construction activities.

Process layouts and product layouts represent two ends of a continuum from small jobs to continuous production. Process layouts are conducive to the production of a wider range of products or services than product layouts, which is desirable from a customer standpoint where customized products are often in demand. However, process layouts tend to be less efficient and have higher unit production costs than product layouts. Some manufacturers are moving away from process layouts in an effort to capture some of the benefits of product layouts. Ideally, a system is flexible and yet efficient, with low unit production costs. Cellular manufacturing, group technology, and flexible manufacturing systems represent efforts to move toward this ideal.

Cellular Layouts

Cellular Production. **Cellular production** is a type of layout in which workstations are grouped into what is referred to as a *cell.* Groupings are determined by the operations needed to perform work for a set of similar items, or *part families,* that require similar processing. The cells become, in effect, miniature versions of product layouts. The cells may have no conveyorized movement of parts between machines, or may have a flow line connected by a conveyor (automatic transfer). All parts follow the same route although minor variations (e.g., skipping an operation) are possible. In contrast, the functional layout involves multiple paths for parts. Moreover, there is little effort or need to identify part families.

Cellular production Layout in which workstations are grouped into a cell that can process items that have similar processing requirements.

FIGURE 6.7
Comparison of process and cellular layouts

Source: Adapted from U.S. Environmental Protection Agency, "Lean Manufacturing and the Environment," www.epa.gov/innovation/lean/thinking/cellular.htm.

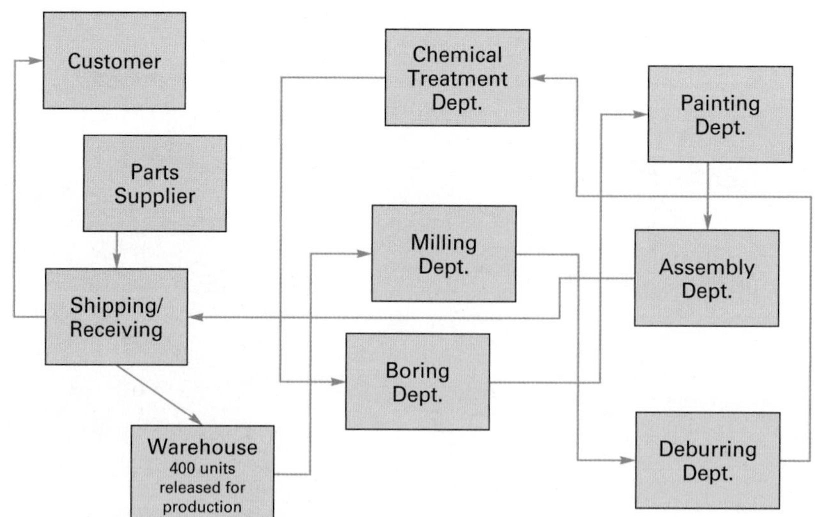

A. Example of an order processed in a traditional process layout.

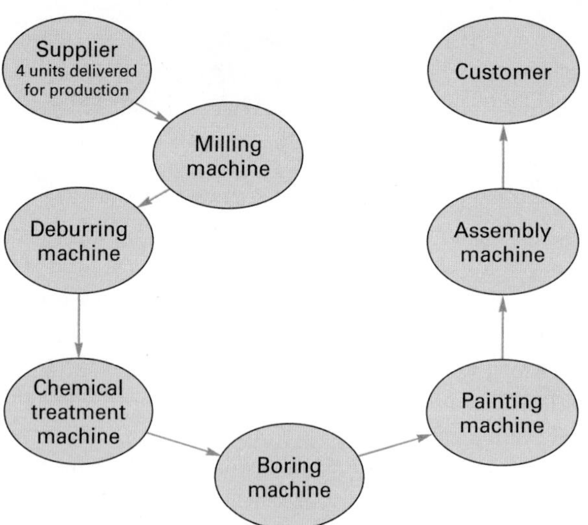

B. The same example of an order processed in a cellular layout.

Cellular manufacturing enables companies to produce a variety of products with as little waste as possible. A cell layout provides a smooth flow of work through the process with minimal transport or delay. Benefits frequently associated with cellular manufacturing include minimal work in process, reduced space requirements and lead times, productivity and quality improvement, and increased flexibility.

Figure 6.7 provides a comparison between a traditional process layout (6.7A) and a cellular layout (6.7B). To get a sense of the advantage of the cellular layout, trace the movement of an order in the traditional layout (6.7A) that is depicted by the path of the arrow. Begin on the bottom left at Shipping/Receiving, then follow the arrow to Warehouse, where a batch of raw material is released for production. Follow the path (shown by the arrows) that the batch takes as it moves through the system to Shipping/Receiving and then to the Customer. Now turn to Figure 6.7B. Note the simple path the order takes as it moves through the system.

Several techniques facilitate effective cellular layout design. Among them are the following two:

Single-minute exchange of die (SMED) enables an organization to quickly convert a machine or process to produce a different (but similar) product type. Thus, a single cell

TABLE 6.4
A comparison of functional (process) layouts and cellular layouts

Dimension	Functional	Cellular
Number of moves between departments	Many	Few
Travel distances	Longer	Shorter
Travel paths	Variable	Fixed
Job waiting time	Greater	Shorter
Throughput time	Higher	Lower
Amount of work in process	Higher	Lower
Supervision difficulty	Higher	Lower
Scheduling complexity	Higher	Lower
Equipment utilization	Lower	Higher

can produce a variety of products without the time-consuming equipment changeover associated with large batch processes, enabling the organization to quickly respond to changes in customer demand.

Right-sized equipment is often smaller than equipment used in traditional process layouts, and mobile, so that it can quickly be reconfigured into a different cellular layout in a different location.

Table 6.4 lists the benefits of cellular layouts compared to functional layouts.

The biggest challenges of implementing cellular manufacturing involve issues of equipment and layout and issues of workers and management. Equipment and layout issues relate to design and cost. The costs of work stoppages during implementation can be considerable, as can the costs of new or modified equipment and the rearrangement of the layout. The costs to implement cellular manufacturing must be weighed against the cost savings that can be expected from using cells. Also, the implementation of cell manufacturing often requires employee training and the redefinition of jobs. Each of the workers in each cell should ideally be able to complete the entire range of tasks required in that cell, and often this means being more multiskilled than they were previously. In addition, cells are often expected to be self-managing, and therefore workers will have to be able to work effectively in teams. Managers have to learn to be less involved than with more traditional work methods.

Group Technology. Effective cellular manufacturing must have groups of identified items with similar processing characteristics. This strategy for product and process design is known as **group technology** and involves identifying items with similarities in either *design characteristics* or *manufacturing characteristics,* and grouping them into *part families.* Design characteristics include size, shape, and function; manufacturing or processing characteristics involve the type and sequence of operations required. In many cases, design and processing characteristics are correlated, although this is not always the case. Thus, design families may be different from processing families. Figure 6.8 illustrates a group of parts with similar processing characteristics but different design characteristics.

Group technology The grouping into part families of items with similar design or manufacturing characteristics.

Once similar items have been identified, items can be classified according to their families; then a system can be developed that facilitates retrieval from a database for purposes of design and manufacturing. For instance, a designer can use the system to determine if there is an existing part similar or identical to one that needs to be designed. It may happen that an existing part, with some modification, is satisfactory. This greatly enhances the productivity of design. Similarly, planning the manufacturing of a new part can include matching it with one of the part families in existence, thereby alleviating much of the burden of specific processing details.

The conversion to group technology and cellular production requires a systematic analysis of parts to identify the part families. This is often a major undertaking; it is a time-consuming job that involves the analysis of a considerable amount of data. Three primary methods for accomplishing this are visual inspection, examination of design and production data, and production flow analysis.

FIGURE 6.8
A group of parts with similar manufacturing process requirements but different design attributes

Source: Mikell P. Groover, *Automation, Production Systems, and Computer-Aided Manufacturing* © 1980, p. 540. Reprinted by permission of Pearson Education Inc., Upper Saddle River, NJ

Visual inspection is the least accurate of the three but also the least costly and the simplest to perform. Examination of design and production data is more accurate but much more time-consuming; it is perhaps the most commonly used method of analysis. Production flow analysis has a manufacturing perspective and not a design perspective, because it examines operations sequences and machine routings to uncover similarities. Moreover, the operation sequences and routings are taken as givens; in reality the existing procedures may be far from optimal.

Conversion to cellular production can involve costly realignment of equipment. Consequently, a manager must weigh the benefits of a switch from a process layout to a cellular one against the cost of moving equipment as well as the cost and time needed for grouping parts.

Flexible manufacturing systems, discussed earlier, are more fully automated versions of cellular manufacturing.

Service Layouts

SERVICE

As is the case with manufacturing, service layouts can often be categorized as product, process, or fixed-position layouts. In a fixed-position service layout (e.g., appliance repair, roofing, landscaping, home remodeling, copier service), materials, labor, and equipment are brought to the customer's residence or office). Process layouts are common in services due mainly to the high degree of variety in customer processing requirements. Examples include hospitals, supermarkets and department stores, vehicle repair centers, and banks. If the service is organized sequentially, with all customers or work following the same or similar sequence, as it is in a car wash or a cafeteria line, a product layout is used.

However, service layout requirements are somewhat different from manufacturing layout requirements. The degree of customer contact and the degree of customization are two key factors in service layout design. If contact and customization are both high, as in health care and personal care, the service environment is a job shop, usually with high labor content and flexible equipment, and a layout that supports this. If customization is high but contact low (e.g., picture framing, tailoring), the layout can be arranged to facilitate workers and equipment. If contact is high but customization is low (e.g., supermarkets, gas stations), self-service is a possibility, in which case layout must take into account ease of obtaining the service as well as customer safety. If the degree of contact and the need for customization are low, the core service and the customer can be separated, making it easier to achieve a high degree of efficiency in operations. Highly standardized services may lend themselves to automation (e.g., Web services, online banking, ATM machines).

Let's consider some of these layouts.

Warehouse and Storage Layouts. The design of storage facilities presents a different set of factors than the design of factory layouts. Frequency of order is an important consideration; items that are ordered frequently should be placed near the entrance to the facility, and those ordered infrequently should be placed toward the rear of the facility. Any correlations between items are also significant (i.e., item A is usually ordered with item B), suggesting that placing those two items close together would reduce the cost and time of *picking* (retrieving) those items. Other considerations include the number and widths of aisles, the height of storage racks, rail and/or truck loading and unloading, and the need to periodically make a physical count of stored items.

Retail Layouts. The objectives that guide design of manufacturing layouts often pertain to cost minimization and product flow. However, with retail layouts such as department stores, supermarkets, and specialty stores, designers must take into account the presence of customers and the opportunity to influence sales volume and customer attitudes through carefully designed layouts. Traffic patterns and traffic flow are important factors to consider. Some large retail chains use standard layouts for all or most of their stores. This has several advantages. Most obvious is the ability to save time and money by using one layout instead of custom designing one for each store. Another advantage is to avoid confusing consumers who visit more than one store. In the case of service retail outlets, especially small ones such as dry cleaners, shoe repair, and auto service centers, layout design is much simpler.

Office Layouts. Office layouts are undergoing transformations as the flow of paperwork is replaced with the increasing use of electronic communications. This lessens the need to place office workers in a layout that optimizes the physical transfer of information or paperwork. Another trend is to create an image of openness; office walls are giving way to low-rise partitions, which also facilitate communication among workers.

Kiosks benefit customers by speeding up tedious processes and reducing waiting time. At McDonald's, kiosks actually increase sales by an average of \$1 over face-to-face purchases. Managers explain this by the kiosk's ability to prompt customers for more purchases by showing pictures of products they might want to buy.

Automation in Services. One way to improve productivity and reduce costs in services is to remove the customer from the process as much as possible. Automated services is one increasingly used alternative. For example, financial services use ATMs, automated call answering, online banking, and electronic funds transfers; retail stores use optical scanning to process sales; and the travel industry uses electronic reservation systems. Other examples of automated services include shipping, mail processing, communication, and health care services.

Automating services means more-standardized services and less need to involve the customer directly. However, service standardization brings trade-off. Generally costs are reduced and productivity increases, but the lack of customization and the inability to deal with a real person raise the risk of customer dissatisfaction.

Designing Supermarkets

READING

David Schardt

The produce is over here, the dairy's over there. The soft drink specials are at the end of the aisles, the candy's at the checkout. Always.

A visit to your local supermarket isn't as haphazard as it seems. It's been laid out so that you spend as much as possible on what the store wants you to buy. And that's often more than you came in for, as we learned when we spoke to supermarket industry insiders.

Here's how a typical supermarket is designed to maximize sales.

On the Edge

The more time you spend shopping along the sides and back of the supermarket, the more money the store makes. About half its profits come from perimeter items like fruits and veggies, milk and cheese, and meat, poultry, and fish. That's also where you'll find the bakery, the salad bar, and the deli. If a store wants to distinguish itself from its competitors, it's got to be here.

Space Eaters

Some foods are so profitable that they command their own aisles. Breakfast cereals bring in more dollars per foot of shelf space than any other product in the interior of the store. So most supermarkets give cereals plenty of space.

Soft drinks aren't as profitable . . . at least not on paper. But beverage manufacturers sweeten the pot with so much free merchandise and cash rebates that carbonated soft drinks end up being one of the biggest moneymakers in a typical store.

The Meating Place

Why are the meat, poultry, and seafood displays almost always along the back of the supermarket? So that you'll see them every time you emerge from an aisle. Not a bad place to put the most profitable sections of the store.

Going to the Dairy

Why are the dairy products usually as far away from the entrance as possible? Most everybody buys milk when they shop. To reach it, they've got to walk through a good chunk of the supermarket, often along the perimeter. That's right where the store wants shoppers.

Also, stores like to "anchor" a display by putting popular items at each end. That's why milk, for example, is often at one end of the dairy case and margarine and butter at the other. You've got to run the gauntlet of cheese, yogurts, dips, etc. to get what you came for.

Paying for Space

Every year, grocery chains are offered more than 15,000 new products, nearly all of which will fail. How do stores decide which ones to stock?

Moolah, in some cases. Large supermarkets often require manufacturers to pay for shelf space. "Slotting fees," as they're called, can range from $5,000 to $25,000 per supermarket chain for each new food. The small local tofu cheese plant seldom has that kind of money to throw around.

In "Prison"

Some supermarket insiders call the aisles of the store the "prison." Once you're in one, you're stuck until you come out the other end. The "prison" is where most of the less-profitable (for the store) national and regional name brands are, so the more time you spend there, the less time you'll spend along the perimeter . . . buying higher-profit items.

Productive Produce

Think it's a coincidence that you almost always have to walk through the produce department when you enter a supermarket? The look of those shiny, neatly stacked fruits and vegetables is *the* most important influence on where people decide to shop.

It also doesn't hurt that produce is the second most profitable section (meat is first). While it occupies a little over 10 percent of the typical supermarket, it brings in close to 20 percent of the store's profits.

DESIGNING PRODUCT LAYOUTS: LINE BALANCING

The goal of a product layout is to arrange workers or machines in the sequence that operations need to be performed. The sequence is referred to as a production line or an assembly line. These lines range from fairly short, with just a few operations, to long lines that have a large number of operations. Automobile assembly lines are examples of long lines. At the assembly line for Ford Mustangs, a Mustang travels about nine miles from start to finish!

Because it is difficult and costly to change a product layout that is inefficient, design is a critical issue. Many of the benefits of a product layout relate to the ability to divide required work into a series of elemental tasks (e.g., "assemble parts C and D") that can be performed quickly and routinely by low-skilled workers or specialized equipment. The durations of these elemental tasks typically range from a few seconds to 15 minutes or more. Most time requirements are so brief that it would be impractical to assign only one task to each worker. For one thing, most workers would quickly become bored by the limited job scope. For another, the number of workers required to complete even a simple product or service would be enormous. Instead, tasks are usually grouped into manageable bundles and assigned to workstations staffed by one or two operators.

The process of deciding how to assign tasks to workstations is referred to as **line balancing**. The goal of line balancing is to obtain task groupings that represent approximately equal time requirements. This minimizes the idle time along the line and results in a high utilization of labor and equipment. Idle time occurs if task times are not equal among workstations; some stations are capable of producing at higher rates than others. These "fast" stations will experience periodic waits for the output from slower stations or else be forced into idleness to avoid buildups of work between stations. Unbalanced lines are undesirable in terms of inefficient utilization of labor and equipment and because they may create morale problems at the slower stations for workers who must work continuously.

Line balancing The process of assigning tasks to workstations in such a way that the workstations have approximately equal time requirements.

Lines that are perfectly balanced will have a smooth flow of work as activities along the line are synchronized to achieve maximum utilization of labor and equipment. The major obstacle to attaining a perfectly balanced line is the difficulty of forming task bundles that have the same duration. One cause of this is that it may not be feasible to combine certain activities into the same bundle, either because of differences in equipment requirements or because the activities are not compatible (e.g., risk of contamination of paint from sanding). Another cause of difficulty is that differences among elemental task lengths cannot always be overcome by grouping tasks. A third cause of an inability to perfectly balance a line is that a required technological sequence may prohibit otherwise desirable task combinations. Consider a series of three operations that have durations of two minutes, four minutes, and two minutes, as shown in the following diagram. Ideally, the first and third operations could be combined at one workstation and have a total time equal to that of the second operation. However, it may not be possible to combine the first and third operations. In the case of an automatic car wash, scrubbing and drying operations could not realistically be combined at the same workstation due to the need to rinse cars between the two operations.

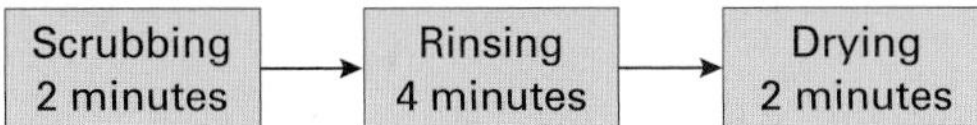

Line balancing involves assigning tasks to workstations. Usually, each workstation has one worker who handles all of the tasks at that station, although an option is to have several workers at a single workstation. For purposes of illustration, however, all of the examples and problems in this chapter have workstations with one worker. A manager could decide to use anywhere from one to five workstations to handle five tasks. With one workstation, all tasks would be done at that station; with five stations, for example, one task would be assigned to each station. If two, three, or four workstations are used, some or all of the stations will have multiple tasks assigned to them. How does a manager decide how many stations to use?

Cycle time The maximum time allowed at each workstation to complete its set of tasks on a unit.

The primary determinant is what the line's **cycle time** will be. The cycle time is the *maximum* time allowed at each workstation to perform assigned tasks before the work moves on. The cycle time also establishes the output rate of a line. For instance, if the cycle time is two minutes, units will come off the end of the line at the rate of one every two minutes. Hence, the line's capacity is a function of its cycle time.

We can gain some insight into task groupings and cycle time by considering a simple example.

Suppose that the work required to fabricate a certain product can be divided up into five elemental tasks, with the task times and precedence relationships as shown in the following diagram:

→ 0.1 min. → 0.7 min. → 1.0 min. → 0.5 min. → 0.2 min. →

The task times govern the range of possible cycle times. The *minimum* cycle time is equal to the *longest* task time (1.0 minute), and the *maximum* cycle time is equal to the sum of the task times (0.1 + 0.7 + 1.0 + 0.5 + 0.2 = 2.5 minutes). The minimum cycle time would apply if there were five workstations. The maximum cycle time would apply if all tasks were performed at a single workstation. The minimum and maximum cycle times are important because they establish the potential range of output for the line, which we can compute using the following formula:

$$\text{Output rate} = \frac{\text{Operating time per day}}{\text{Cycle time}} \tag{6–1}$$

Assume that the line will operate for eight hours per day (480 minutes). With a cycle time of 1.0 minute, output would be

$$\frac{\text{480 minutes per day}}{\text{1.0 minute per unit}} = \text{480 units per day}$$

With a cycle time of 2.5 minutes, the output would be

$$\frac{\text{480 minutes per day}}{\text{2.5 minutes per unit}} = \text{192 units per day}$$

Assuming that no parallel activities are to be employed (e.g., two lines), the output selected for the line must fall in the range of 192 units per day to 480 units per day.

As a general rule, the cycle time is determined by the desired output; that is, a desired output rate is selected, and the cycle time is computed. If the cycle time does not fall between the maximum and minimum bounds, the desired output rate must be revised. We can compute the cycle time using this equation:

$$\text{Cycle time} = \frac{\text{Operating time per day}}{\text{Desired output rate}} \tag{6–2}$$

For example, suppose that the desired output rate is 480 units. Using Formula 6–2, the necessary cycle time is

$$\frac{\text{480 minutes per day}}{\text{480 units per day}} = \text{1.0 minute per unit}$$

The number of workstations that will be needed is a function of both the desired output rate and our ability to combine elemental tasks into workstations. We can determine the *theoretical minimum* number of stations necessary to provide a specified rate of output as follows:

$$N_{\text{min}} = \frac{\Sigma t}{\text{Cycle time}} \tag{6–3}$$

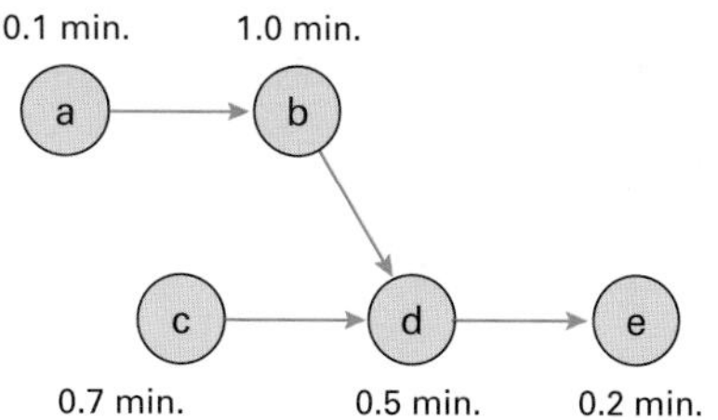

FIGURE 6.9
A simple precedence diagram

where

$$N_{\min} = \text{Theoretical minimum number of stations}$$
$$\Sigma t = \text{Sum of task times}$$

Suppose the desired rate of output is the maximum of 480 units per day.[2] (This will require a cycle time of 1.0 minute.) The minimum number of stations required to achieve this goal is

$$N_{\min} = \frac{2.5 \text{ minutes per unit}}{1 \text{ minute per unit per station}} = 2.5 \text{ stations}$$

Because 2.5 stations is not feasible, it is necessary to *round up* (because 2.5 is the minimum) to three stations. Thus, the actual number of stations used will equal or exceed three, depending on how successfully the tasks can be grouped into work stations.

A very useful tool in line balancing is a **precedence diagram.** Figure 6.9 illustrates a simple precedence diagram. It visually portrays the tasks that are to be performed along with the *sequential* requirements, that is, the *order* in which tasks must be performed. The diagram is read from left to right, so the initial task(s) are on the left and the final task is on the right. In terms of precedence requirements, we can see from the diagram, for example, that the only requirement to begin task *b* is that task *a* must be finished. However, in order to begin task *d*, tasks *b* and *c* must *both* be finished. Note that the elemental tasks are the same ones that we have been using.

Precedence diagram A diagram that shows elemental tasks and their precedence requirements.

Now let's see how a line is balanced. This involves assigning tasks to workstations. Generally, no techniques are available that guarantee an optimal set of assignments. Instead, managers employ *heuristic (intuitive) rules,* which provide good and sometimes optimal sets of assignments. A number of line-balancing heuristics are in use, two of which are described here for purposes of illustration:

1. Assign tasks in order of most following tasks.
2. Assign tasks in order of greatest positional weight. Positional weight is the sum of each task's time and the times of all following tasks.

Arrange the tasks shown in Figure 6.9 into three workstations. Use a cycle time of 1.0 minute. Assign tasks in order of the most number of followers.

SOLUTION

1. Begin with task *a;* it has the most following tasks. Assign it to workstation 1.
2. Next, tasks *b* and *c* each have two following tasks, but only task *c* will fit in the time remaining at workstation 1, so assign task *c* to workstation 1.
3. Task *b* now has the most followers, but it will not fit at workstation 1, so assign it to workstation 2.
4. There is no time left at workstation 2, so we move on to workstation 3, assigning task *d* and then task *e* to that workstation.

[2]At first glance, it might seem that the desired output would logically be the maximum possible output. However, you will see why that is not always the best alternative.

Workstation	Time Remaining	Eligible	Assign Task	Revised Time Remaining	Station Idle Time
1	1.0	a	a	0.9	
	0.9	b, c	c	0.2	
	0.2	none	—		0.2
2	1.0	b	b	0.0	0.0
3	1.0	d	d	0.5	
	0.5	e	e	0.3	
	0.3	—	—		0.3
					0.5

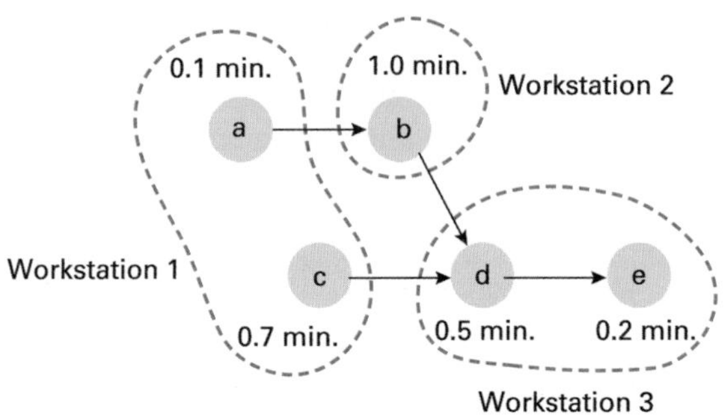

The initial "time remaining" for each workstation is equal to the cycle time. For a task to be eligible, tasks preceding it must have been assigned, and the task's time must not exceed the station's remaining time.

Example 1 is purposely simple; it is designed to illustrate the basic procedure. Later examples will illustrate tiebreaking, constructing precedence diagrams, and the positional weight method. Before considering those examples, let us first consider some measures of effectiveness that can be used for evaluating a given set of assignments.

Two widely used measures of effectiveness are

Balance delay Percentage of idle time of a line.

1. The **percentage of idle time** of the line. This is sometimes referred to as the **balance delay.** It can be computed as follows:

   $$\text{Percentage of idle time} = \frac{\text{Idle time per cycle}}{N_{\text{actual}} \times \text{Cycle time}} \times 100 \qquad (6\text{–}4)$$

   where

   N_{actual} = Actual number of stations

   For the preceding example, the value is

   $$\text{Percentage of idle time} = \frac{.5}{3 \times 1.0} \times 100 = 16.7\%$$

   In effect, this is the average idle time divided by the cycle time, multiplied by 100. Note that cycle time refers to the actual cycle time that is achieved.

2. The **efficiency** of the line. This is computed as follows:

   $$\text{Efficiency} = 100\% - \text{Percent idle time} \qquad (6\text{–}5a)$$

   Here, Efficiency = 100% − 16.7% = 83.3%. Alternatively, efficiency could be computed using Formula 6–5b:

   $$\text{Efficiency} = \frac{N_{\text{actual}} \times \text{Cycle time} - \text{Idle time}}{N_{\text{actual}} \times \text{Cycle time}} \times 100 \qquad (6\text{–}5b)$$

Now let's consider the question of whether the selected level of output should equal the maximum output possible. The minimum number of workstations needed is a function of the desired output rate and, therefore, the cycle time. Thus, a lower rate of output (hence, a longer cycle time) may result in a need for fewer stations. Hence, the manager must consider whether the potential savings realized by having fewer workstations would be greater than the decrease in profit resulting from producing fewer units.

The preceding examples serve to illustrate some of the fundamental concepts of line balancing. They are rather simple; in most real-life situations, the number of branches and tasks is often much greater. Consequently, the job of line balancing can be a good deal more complex. In many instances, the number of alternatives for grouping tasks is so great that it is virtually impossible to conduct an exhaustive review of all possibilities. For this reason, many real-life problems of any magnitude are solved using heuristic approaches. The purpose of a heuristic approach is to reduce the number of alternatives that must be considered, but it does not guarantee an optimal solution.

Some Guidelines for Line Balancing

In balancing an assembly line, tasks are assigned *one at a time* to the line, starting at the first workstation. At each step, the unassigned tasks are checked to determine which are eligible for assignment. Next, the eligible tasks are checked to see which of them will fit in the workstation being loaded. A heuristic is used to select one of the tasks that will fit, and the task is assigned. This process is repeated until there are no eligible tasks that will fit. Then the next workstation can be loaded. This continues until all tasks are assigned. The objective is to minimize the idle time for the line subject to technological and output constraints.

Technological constraints tell us which elemental tasks are *eligible* to be assigned at a particular position on the line. Technological constraints can result from the precedence or ordering relationships among the tasks. The precedence relationships require that certain tasks must be performed before others (and so, must be assigned to workstations before others). Thus, in a car wash, the rinsing operation must be performed before the drying operation. The drying operation is not eligible for assignment until the rinsing operation has been assigned. Technological constraints may also result from two tasks being incompatible (e.g., space restrictions or the nature of the operations may prevent their being placed in the same work center). For example, sanding and painting operations would not be assigned to the same work center because dust particles from the sanding operation could contaminate the paint.

Output constraints, on the other hand, determine the maximum amount of work that a manager can assign to each workstation, and this determines whether an eligible task *will fit* at a workstation. The desired output rate determines the cycle time, and the sum of the task times assigned to any workstation must not exceed the cycle time. If a task can be assigned to a workstation without exceeding the cycle time, then the task will fit.

Once it is known which tasks are *eligible* and *will fit,* the manager can select the task to be assigned (if there is more than one to choose from). This is where the heuristic rules help us decide which task to assign from among those that are eligible and will fit.

To clarify the terminology, *following tasks* are all tasks that you would encounter by following all paths from the task in question through the precedence diagram. *Preceding tasks* are all tasks you would encounter by tracing all paths *backward* from the task in question. In the precedence diagram below, tasks *b, d, e,* and *f* are followers of task *a.* Tasks *a, b,* and *c* are preceding tasks for *e.*

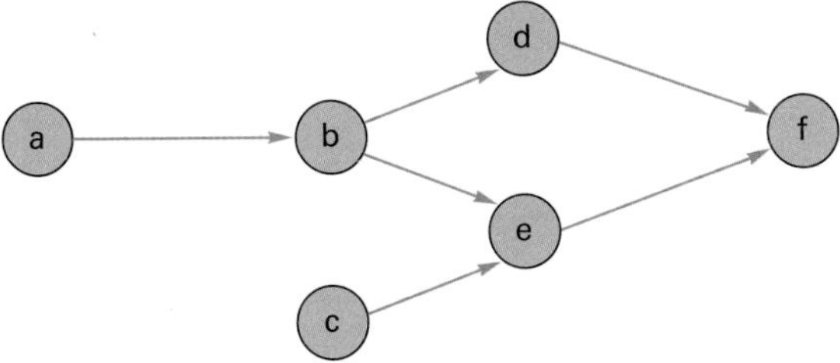

The *positional weight* for a task is the sum of the task times for itself and all its following tasks.

Neither of the heuristics *guarantees* the *best* solution, or even a good solution to the line-balancing problem, but they do provide guidelines for developing a solution. It may be useful to apply several different heuristics to the same problem and pick the best (least idle time) solution out of those developed.

EXAMPLE 2

www.mhhe.com/stevenson11e

Using the information contained in the table shown, do each of the following:

1. Draw a precedence diagram.
2. Assuming an eight-hour workday, compute the cycle time needed to obtain an output of 400 units per day.
3. Determine the minimum number of workstations required.
4. Assign tasks to workstations using this rule: Assign tasks according to greatest number of following tasks. In case of a tie, use the tiebreaker of assigning the task with the longest processing time first.

Task	Immediate Predecessor	Task Time (in minutes)
a	—	0.2
b	a	0.2
c	—	0.8
d	c	0.6
e	b	0.3
f	d, e	1.0
g	f	0.4
h	g	0.3
		$\Sigma t = 3.8$

5. Compute the resulting percent idle time and efficiency of the system.

SOLUTION

1. Drawing a precedence diagram is a relatively straightforward task. Begin with activities with no predecessors. We see from the list that tasks *a* and *c* do not have predecessors. We build from here.

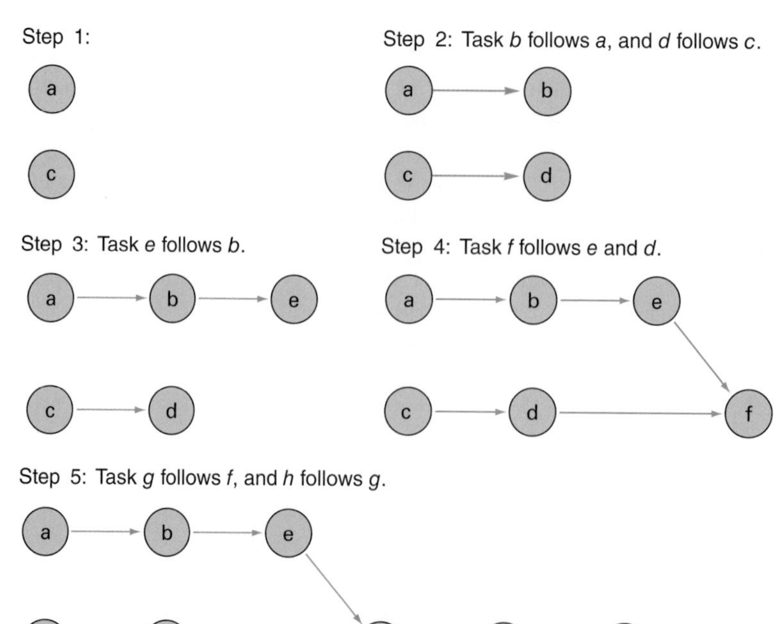

2. $$\text{Cycle time} = \frac{\text{Operating time}}{\text{Desired output rate}} = \frac{480 \text{ minutes per day}}{400 \text{ units per day}} = 1.2 \text{ minutes per cycle}$$

3. $$N_{\min} = \frac{\Sigma t}{\text{Cycle time}} = \frac{3.8 \text{ minutes per unit}}{1.2 \text{ minutes per cycle per station}} = 3.17 \text{ stations (round to 4)}$$

4. Beginning with station 1, make assignments following this procedure: Determine from the precedence diagram which tasks are eligible for assignment. Then determine which of the eligible tasks will fit the time remaining for the station. Use the tiebreaker if necessary. Once a task has been assigned, remove it from consideration. When a station cannot take any more assignments, go on to the next station. Continue until all tasks have been assigned.

Station	Time Remaining	Eligible	Will Fit	Assign (task time)	Revised Time Remaining	Idle
1	1.2	a, c*	a, c*	a (0.2)	1.0	
	1.0	c, b**	c, b**	c (0.8)	0.2	
	0.2	b, d	b	b (0.2)	0.0	
	0	e, d	None	—		0.0
2	1.2	e, d	e, d	d (0.6)	0.6	
	0.6	e	e	e (0.3)	0.3	
	0.3***	f	None	—		0.3
3	1.2	f	f	f (1.0)	0.2	
	0.2	g	None	—		0.2
4	1.2	g	g	g (0.4)	0.8	
	0.8	h	h	h (0.3)	0.5	
	0.5	—	—	—		0.5
						1.0 min.

*Neither *a* nor *c* has any predecessors, so both are eligible. Task *a* was assigned since it has more followers.

**Once *a* is assigned, *b* and *c* are now eligible. Both will fit in the time remaining of 1.0 minute. The tie cannot be broken by the "most followers" rule, so the longer task is assigned.

***Although *f* is eligible, this task will not fit, so station 2 is left with 0.3 minute of idle time per 1.2-minute cycle.

These assignments are shown in the following diagram. *Note:* One should not expect that heuristic approaches will always produce optimal solutions; they merely provide a practical way to deal with complex problems that may not lend themselves to optimizing techniques. Moreover, different heuristics often yield different answers.

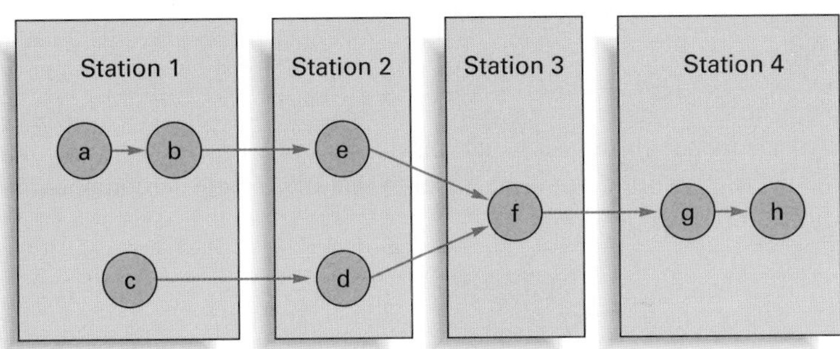

5. $$\text{Percent idle time} = \frac{1.0 \text{ min.}}{4 \times 1.2 \text{ min.}} \times 100 = 20.83\%.$$

$$\text{Efficiency} = 100\% - 20.83\% = 79.17\%$$

Other Factors

The preceding discussion on line balancing presents a relatively straightforward approach to approximating a balanced line. In practice, the ability to do this usually involves additional considerations, some of which are technical.

Technical considerations include skill requirements of different tasks. If skill requirements of tasks are quite different, it may not be feasible to place the tasks in the same workstation. Similarly, if the tasks themselves are incompatible (e.g., the use of fire and flammable liquids), it may not be feasible even to place them in stations that are near each other.

Developing a workable plan for balancing a line may also require consideration of human factors as well as equipment and space limitations.

Although it is convenient to treat assembly operations as if they occur at the same rate time after time, it is more realistic to assume that whenever humans are involved, task completion times will be variable. The reasons for the variations are numerous, including fatigue, boredom, and failure to concentrate on the task at hand. Absenteeism also can affect line balance. Minor variability can be dealt with by allowing some slack along the line. However, if more variability is inherent in even a few tasks, that will severely impact the ability to achieve a balanced line.

For these reasons, lines that involve human tasks are more of an ideal than a reality. In practice, lines are rarely perfectly balanced. However, this is not entirely bad, because some unbalance means that slack exists at points along the line, which can reduce the impact of brief stoppages at some workstations. Also, workstations that have slack can be used for new workers who may not be "up to speed."

Other Approaches

Companies use a number of other approaches to achieve a smooth flow of production. One approach is to use *parallel workstations.* These are beneficial for bottleneck operations which would otherwise disrupt the flow of product as it moves down the line. The bottlenecks may be the result of difficult or very long tasks. Parallel workstations increase the work flow and provide flexibility.

Consider this example.[3] A job has four tasks; task times are 1 minute, 1 minute, 2 minutes, and 1 minute. The cycle time for the line would be 2 minutes, and the output rate would be 30 units per hour:

$$\frac{60 \text{ minutes per hour}}{2 \text{ minutes per unit}} = 30 \text{ units per hour}$$

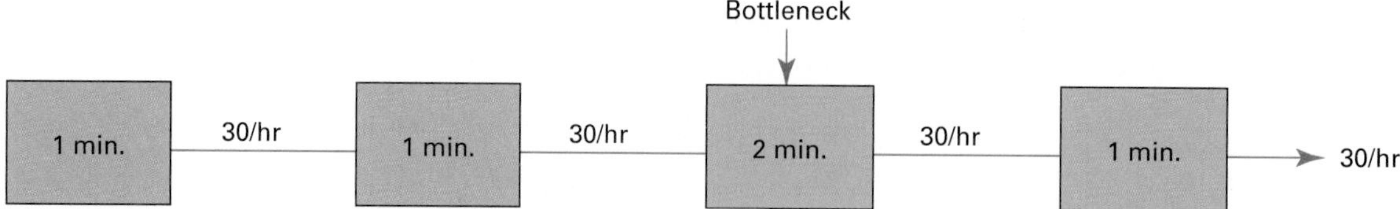

Using parallel stations for the third task would result in a cycle time of 1 minute because the output rate at the parallel stations would be equal to that of a single station and allow an output rate for the line of 60 units per hour:

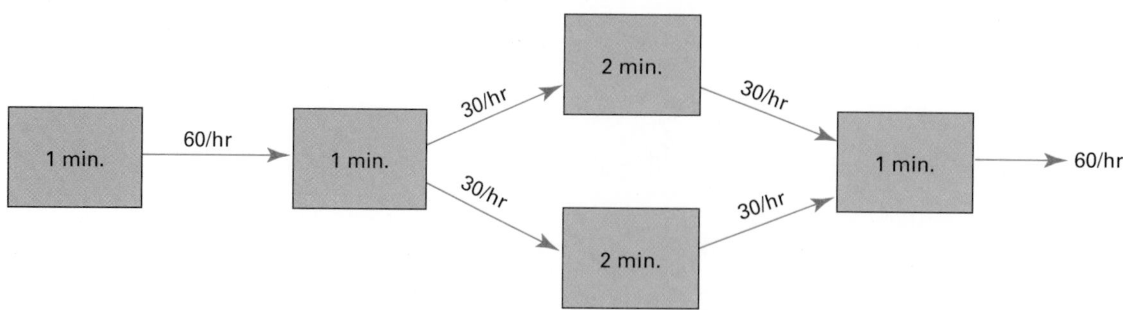

[3]Adapted from Mikell P. Groover, *Automation, Production Systems, and Computer-Aided Manufacturing,* 2nd ed. © 1987. Reprinted by permission of Pearson Education, Inc., Upper Saddle River, NJ

Another approach to achieving a balanced line is to *cross-train* workers so that they are able to perform more than one task. Then, when bottlenecks occur, the workers with temporarily increased idle time can assist other workers who are temporarily overburdened, thereby maintaining an even flow of work along the line. This is sometimes referred to as *dynamic line balancing,* and it is used most often in lean production systems.

Still another approach is to design a line to handle more than one product on the same line. This is referred to as a *mixed model line.* Naturally, the products have to be fairly similar, so that the tasks involved are pretty much the same for all products. This approach offers great flexibility in varying the amount of output of the products. The following reading describes one such line.

BMW's Strategy: Flexibility

READING

The assembly line in Dingolfing, Germany, where BMW assembles its 7-Series, has built-in flexibility that allows it to easily produce multiple models. Rival car producers typically configure their assembly lines to produce just a single model at a time. In order for them to produce a different model, the line must be shut down so that it can be changed over to be able to produce the different model. BMW's production flexibility enables its line to easily respond to market fluctuations while avoiding the costly changeovers that its rivals' more rigid lines require.

Source: Based on "Betting on the S," *The Wall Street Journal,* July 11, 2005, p. B1.

DESIGNING PROCESS LAYOUTS

The main issue in designing process layouts concerns the relative positioning of the departments involved. As illustrated in Figure 6.10, departments must be assigned to locations. The problem is to develop a reasonably good layout; some combinations will be more desirable than others. For example, some departments may benefit from adjacent locations whereas others should be separated. A lab with delicate equipment would not be located near a department that had equipment with strong vibrations. Conversely, two departments that share some of the same equipment would benefit from being close together.

Layouts can also be influenced by external factors such as the location of entrances, loading docks, elevators, windows, and areas of reinforced flooring. Also important are noise levels, safety, and the size and locations of restrooms.

In some instances (e.g., the layouts of supermarkets, gas stations, and fast-food chains), a sufficient number of installations having similar characteristics justify the development of standardized layouts. For example, the use of the same basic patterns in McDonald's fast-food locations facilitates construction of new structures and employee training. Food preparation, order taking, and customer service follow the same pattern throughout the chain. Installation and service of equipment are also standardized. This same concept has been successfully employed in computer software products such as Microsoft Windows and the Macintosh Operating System. Different applications are designed with certain basic features in common, so that a user familiar with one application can readily use other applications without having to start from scratch with each new application.

Locations

A	B	C
D	E	F

Work centers to be assigned

1
2
3
4
5
6

FIGURE 6.10
Work centers must be assigned to locations

The majority of layout problems involve single rather than multiple locations, and they present unique combinations of factors that do not lend themselves to a standardized approach. Consequently, these layouts require customized designs.

A major obstacle to finding the most efficient layout of departments is the large number of possible assignments. For example, there are more than 87 billion different ways that 14 departments can be assigned to 14 locations if the locations form a single line. Different location configurations (e.g., 14 departments in a two-by-seven grid) often reduce the number of possibilities, as do special requirements (e.g., the stamping department may have to be assigned to a location with reinforced flooring). Still, the remaining number of layout possibilities is quite large. Unfortunately, no algorithms exist to identify the best layout arrangement under all circumstances. Often planners must rely on heuristic rules to guide trial-and-error efforts for a satisfactory solution to each problem.

Measures of Effectiveness

One advantage of process layouts is their ability to satisfy a variety of processing requirements. Customers or materials in these systems require different operations and different sequences of operations, which causes them to follow different paths through the system. Material-oriented systems necessitate the use of variable-path material-handling equipment to move materials from work center to work center. In customer-oriented systems, people must travel or be transported from work center to work center. In both cases, transportation costs or time can be significant. Because of this factor, one of the major objectives in process layout is to minimize transportation cost, distance, or time. This is usually accomplished by locating departments with relatively high interdepartmental work flow as close together as possible.

Other concerns in choosing among alternative layouts include initial costs in setting up the layout, expected operating costs, the amount of effective capacity created, and the ease of modifying the system.

In situations that call for improvement of an existing layout, costs of relocating any work center must be weighed against the potential benefits of the move.

Information Requirements

The design of process layouts requires the following information:

1. A list of departments or work centers to be arranged, their approximate dimensions, and the dimensions of the building or buildings that will house the departments.
2. A projection of future work flows between the various work centers.
3. The distance between locations and the cost per unit of distance to move loads between locations.
4. The amount of money to be invested in the layout.
5. A list of any special considerations (e.g., operations that must be close to each other or operations that must be separated).
6. The location of key utilities, access and exit points, loading docks, and so on, in existing buildings.

The ideal situation is to first develop a layout and then design the physical structure around it, thus permitting maximum flexibility in design. This procedure is commonly followed when new facilities are constructed. Nonetheless, many layouts must be developed in existing structures where floor space, the dimensions of the building, location of entrances and elevators, and other similar factors must be carefully weighed in designing the layout. Note that multilevel structures pose special problems for layout planners.

Minimizing Transportation Costs or Distances

The most common goals in designing process layouts are minimization of transportation costs or distances traveled. In such cases, it can be very helpful to summarize the necessary data in *from-to charts* like those illustrated in Tables 6.5 and 6.6. Table 6.5 indicates the distance between each of the locations, and Table 6.6 indicates actual or projected work flow between

TABLE 6.5
Distance between locations (meters)

	LOCATION		
From\To	A	B	C
A		20	40
B			30
C			

TABLE 6.6
Interdepartmental work flow (loads per day)

		DEPARTMENT		
From\To		1	2	3
Dept.	1		30	170
	2			100
	3			

each pair. For instance, the distance chart reveals that a trip from location A to location B will involve a distance of 20 meters. (Distances are often measured between department centers.) Oddly enough, the length of a trip between locations A and B may differ depending on the *direction* of the trip, due to one-way routes, elevators, or other factors. To simplify the discussion, assume a constant distance between any two locations regardless of direction. However, it is not realistic to assume that interdepartmental work flows are equal—there is no reason to suspect that department 1 will send as much work to department 2 as department 2 sends to 1. For example, several departments may send goods to packaging, but packaging may send only to the shipping department.

Transportation costs can also be summarized in from-to charts, but we shall avoid that complexity, assuming instead that costs are a direct, linear function of distance.

EXAMPLE 3

Assign the three departments shown in Table 6.6 to locations A, B, and C, which are separated by the distances shown in Table 6.5, in such a way that transportation cost is minimized. Note that Table 6.6 summarizes the flows in both directions. Use this heuristic: Assign departments with the greatest interdepartmental work flow first to locations that are closest to each other.

SOLUTION

Ranking departments according to highest work flow and locations according to highest interlocation distances helps in making assignments.

Trip	Distance (meters)	Department Pair	Work Flow
A–B	20	1–3	170
B–C	30	2–3	100
A–C	40	1–2	30

From these listings, you can see that departments 1 and 3 have the highest interdepartmental work flow, and that locations A and B are the closest. Thus, it seems reasonable to consider assigning 1 and 3 to locations A and B, although it is not yet obvious which department should be assigned to which location. Further inspection of the work flow list reveals that 2 and 3 have higher work flow than 1 and 2, so 2 and 3 should probably be located more closely than 1 and 2. Hence, it would seem reasonable to place 3 between 1 and 2, or at least centralize that department with respect to the other two. The resulting assignments might appear as illustrated in Figure 6.11.

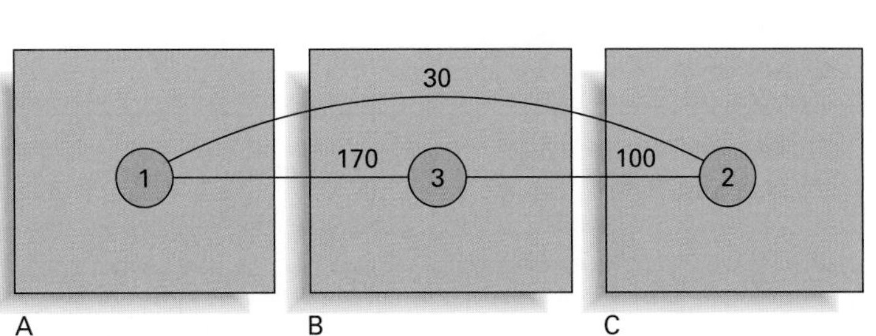

FIGURE 6.11
Interdepartmental work flows for assigned departments

If the cost per meter to move any load is $1, you can compute the total daily transportation cost for this assignment by multiplying each department's number of loads by the trip distance, and summing those quantities:

Department	Number of Loads Between	Location	Distance To:	Loads × Distance
1	2: 30	A	C: 40	30 × 40 = 1,200
	3: 170		B: 20	170 × 20 = 3,400
2	3: 100			
3		B	C: 30	100 × 30 = 3,000
				7,600

At $1 per load meter, the cost for this plan is $7,600 per day. Even though it might appear that this arrangement yields the lowest transportation cost, you cannot be absolutely positive of that without actually computing the total cost for every alternative and comparing it to this one. Instead, rely on the choice of reasonable heuristic rules such as those demonstrated above to arrive at a satisfactory, if not optimal, solution.

Closeness Ratings

Although the preceding approach is widely used, it suffers from the limitation of focusing on only one objective, and many situations involve multiple criteria. Richard Muther developed a more general approach to the problem, which allows for subjective input from analysis or managers to indicate the relative importance of each combination of department pairs.[4] That information is then summarized in a grid like that shown in Figure 6.12. Read the grid in the same way as you would read a mileage chart on a road map, except that letters rather than distances appear at the intersections. The letters represent the importance of closeness for each department pair, with A being the most important and X being an undesirable pairing. Thus, in the grid it is "absolutely necessary" to locate 1 and 2 close to each other because there is an A at the intersection of those departments on the grid. On the other hand, 1 and 4 should not be close together because their intersection has an X. In practice, the letters on the grid are often accompanied by numbers that indicate the reason for each assignment; they are omitted here to simplify the illustration. Muther suggests the following list:

1. They use same equipment or facilities.
2. They share the same personnel or records.
3. Required sequence of work flow.

FIGURE 6.12
A Muther grid

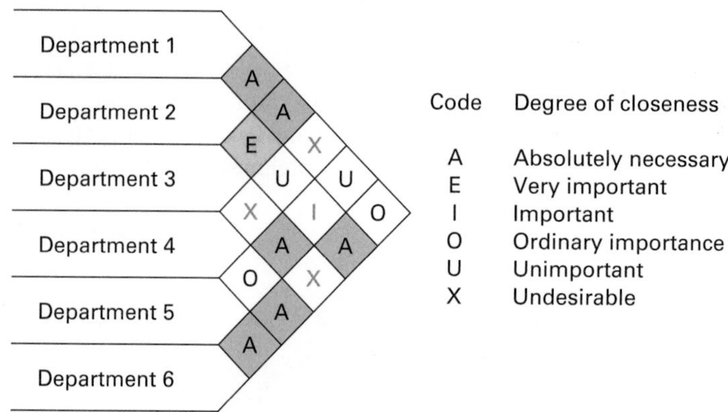

[4]Richard Muther and John Wheeler, "Simplified Systematic Layout Planning," *Factory* 120, nos. 8, 9, and 10 (August, September, October 1962), pp. 68–77, 111–119, 101–113, respectively.

4. Needed for ease of communication.
5. Would create unsafe or unpleasant conditions.
6. Similar work is performed.

EXAMPLE 4

Assign the six departments in Figure 6.12 to a 2×3 set of locations using the heuristic rule: Assign critical departments first, because they are the most important.

SOLUTION

Critical pairs of departments are those with A or X ratings. Prepare a list of those by referring to the grid:

A Links	X Links
1–2	1–4
1–3	3–6
2–6	3–4
3–5	
4–6	
5–6	

Next, form a cluster of A links, beginning with the department that appears most frequently in the A list (in this case, 6). For instance:

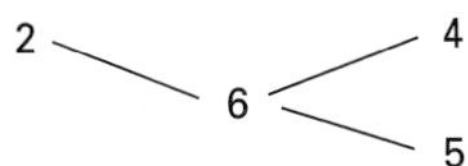

Take the remaining A links in order, and add them to this main cluster where possible, rearranging the cluster as necessary. Form separate clusters for departments that do not link with the main cluster. In this case, all link with the main cluster.

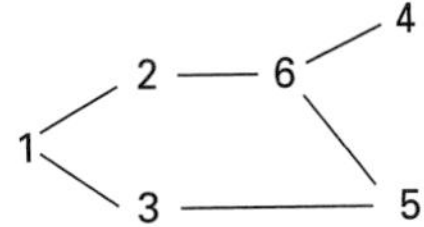

Next, graphically portray the X links:

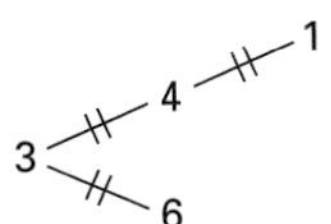

Observe that, as it stands, the cluster of A links also satisfies the X separations. It is a fairly simple exercise to fit the cluster into a 2×3 arrangement:

1	2	6
3	5	4

Note that the lower-level ratings have also been satisfied with this arrangement, even though no attempt was made to explicitly consider the E and I ratings. Naturally, not every problem will yield the same results, so it may be necessary to do some additional adjusting to see if improvements can be made, keeping in mind that the A and X assignments deserve the greatest consideration.

Note that departments are considered close not only when they touch side to side but also when they touch corner to corner.

The value of this rating approach is that it permits the use of multiple objectives and subjective inputs. Its limitations relate to the use of subjective inputs in general: They are imprecise and unreliable.

SUMMARY

Process selection choices often have strategic implications for organizations. They can affect cost, quality, productivity, customer satisfaction, and competitive advantage. Process types include job shop, batch processing, repetitive processing, continuous processing, and projects. Process type determines how work is organized, and it has implications for the entire organization and its supply chain. Process type and layout are closely related.

Layout decisions are an important aspect of the design of operations systems, affecting operating costs and efficiency. Layout decisions are often closely related to process selection decisions.

Product layouts are geared to high-volume output of standardized items. Workers and equipment are arranged according to the technological sequence required by the product or service involved. Emphasis in design is on work flow through the system, and specialized processing and handling equipment is often used. Product layouts are highly vulnerable to breakdowns. Preventive maintenance is used to reduce the occurrence of breakdowns.

Process layouts group similar activities into departments or other work centers. These systems can handle a wide range of processing requirements and are less susceptible to breakdowns. However, the variety of processing requirements necessitates continual routing and scheduling and the use of variable-path material-handling equipment. The rate of output is generally much lower than that of product layouts.

Fixed-position layouts are used when size, fragility, cost, or other factors make it undesirable or impractical to move a product through a system. Instead, workers, equipment, and materials are brought to the product.

The main design efforts in product layout development focus on dividing up the work required to produce a product or service into a series of tasks that are as nearly equal as possible. The goal is to achieve a high degree of utilization of labor and equipment. In process layout, design efforts often focus on the relative positioning of departments to minimize transportation costs or to meet other requirements concerning the proximity of certain department pairs.

The large number of possible alternatives to layout problems prevents an examination of each one. Instead, heuristic rules guide discovery of alternatives. The solutions thus obtained are usually satisfactory although not necessarily optimal. Computer packages are available to reduce the effort required to obtain solutions to layout problems, but these too rely largely on heuristic methods.

KEY POINTS

1. Process choice is demand driven.
2. Process type and layout are a function of expected demand volume and the degree of customization that will be needed.
3. Each process type and layout has advantages and limitations that should be clearly understood when making process selection and layout decisions.
4. Process design is critical in a product-focused system, whereas managing is critical in a process-focused system.

KEY TERMS

assembly line, 249
automation, 243
balance delay, 262
cellular production, 253
computer-aided manufacturing (CAM), 245
computer-integrated manufacturing (CIM), 246
cycle time, 260
fixed-position layout, 252
flexible manufacturing system (FMS), 246
group technology, 255
intermittent processing, 251
line balancing, 259
numerically controlled (N/C) machines, 245
precedence diagram, 261
process layout, 251
product layout, 249
product or service profiling, 242
production line, 249
project, 239
technological innovation, 243
technology, 243

SOLVED PROBLEMS

Problem 1

The tasks shown in the following precedence diagram are to be assigned to workstations with the intent of minimizing idle time. Management has designed an output rate of 275 units per day. Assume 440 minutes are available per day.

a. Determine the appropriate cycle time.

b. What is the minimum number of stations possible?

c. Assign tasks using the "positional weight" rule: Assign tasks with highest following times (including a task's own time) first. Break ties using greatest number of following tasks.

d. Compute efficiency.

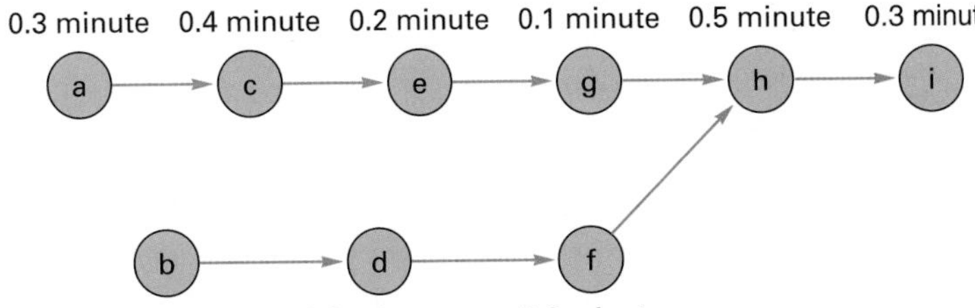

Solution

a. $\text{Cycle time} = \dfrac{\text{Operating time}}{\text{Desired output}} = \dfrac{440 \text{ minutes per day}}{275 \text{ units per day}} = 1.6 \text{ minutes}$

b. $N = \dfrac{\Sigma t}{\text{Cycle time}} = \dfrac{4.2}{1.6 \text{ minutes}} = 2.625 \text{ (round to 3)}$

c. Add positional weights (task time plus the sum of all following times) to the diagram. Start at the right end and work backward:

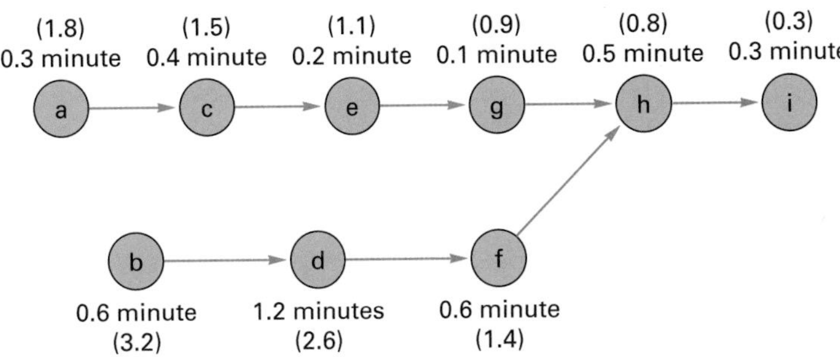

Station	Time Remaining*	Eligible	Will Fit	Assign Task/Time	Station Idle Time
1	1.6	a, b	a, b	b/0.6	
	1.0	a, d	a	a/0.3	
	0.7	c, d	c	c/0.4	
	0.3	e, d	e	e/0.2	
	0.1	g, d	g	g/0.1	
	0	—	—	—	0
2	1.6	d	d	d/1.2	
	0.4	f	none	none	0.4
3	1.6	f	f	f/0.6	
	1.0	h	h	h/0.5	
	0.5	i	i	i/0.3	
	0.2	—	—	—	0.2
					0.6

*The initial time for each station is the cycle time computed in part *a*.

The resulting assignments are shown below.

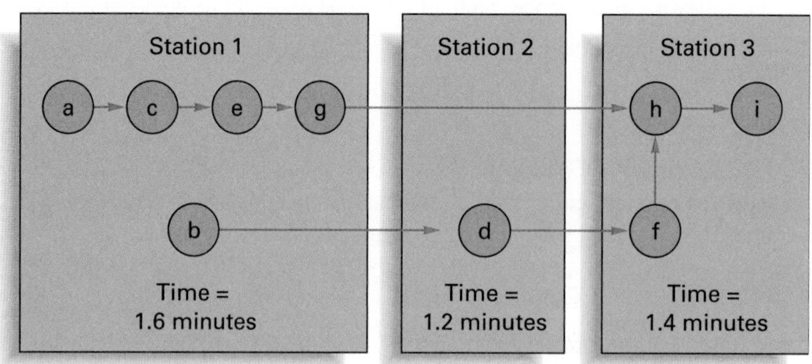

d. Efficiency = 100% − Percent idle time = 100% − $\frac{0.6 \text{ min.}}{3 \times 1.6 \text{ min.}}100 = 87.5\%$.

Problem 2

Assign nine automobile service departments to bays in a 3 × 3 grid so that the closeness ratings in the following matrix are satisfied. (The unimportant and ordinary-importance ratings have been omitted to simplify the example.) The location of department 4 must be in the upper right-hand corner of the grid to satisfy a town ordinance.

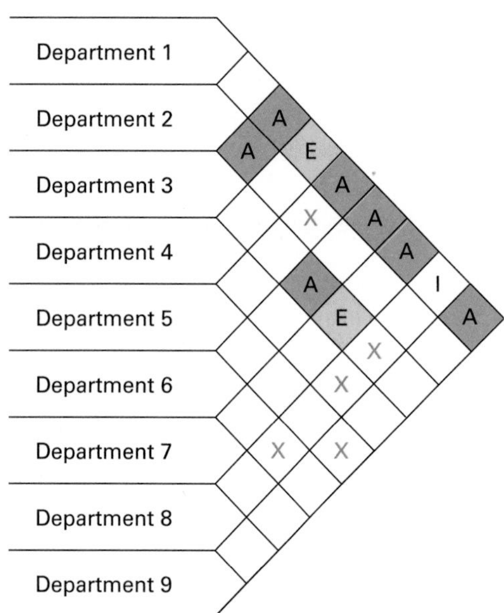

Solution

Note that department 1 has many A ratings, making it a strong candidate for the center position in the grid. We can form a cluster of departments that should be close together:

Next, we can identify departmental pairings that should be avoided:

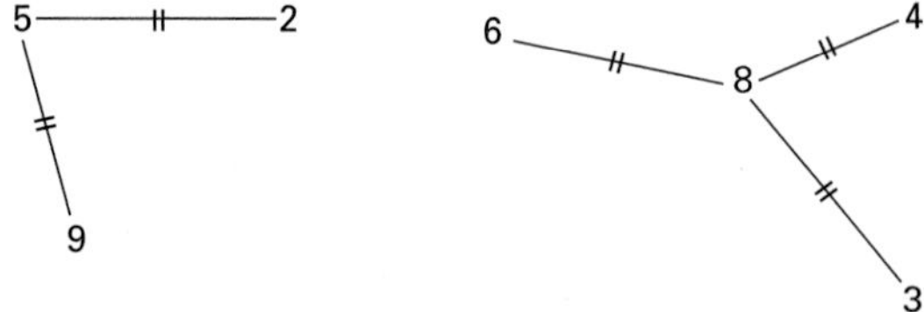

These departments should be spaced around the perimeter of the grid. After a bit of trial and error, the final grid shown below emerged. Check it against the rating matrix to see if it satisfies the ratings.

2	3	4
9	1	6
8	7	5

Problem 3

Five departments are to be assigned to locations B–F in the grid. (For technical reasons, department 6 must be assigned to location A.) Transportation cost is $2 per foot. The objective is to minimize total transportation cost. Information on interdepartmental work flows and distances between locations is shown in the following tables. Assign departments with the greatest interdepartmental work flow first.

DISTANCE BETWEEN LOCATIONS (FEET)

From \ To	A	B	C	D	E	F
A	—	50	100	50	80	130
B		—	50	90	40	70
C			—	140	60	50
D				—	50	120
E					—	50
F						—

NUMBER OF TRIPS PER DAY BETWEEN CENTERS

From \ To	1	2	3	4	5	6
1	—	125	62	64	25	50
2		—	10	17	26	54
3			—	2	0	20
4				—	13	2
5					—	5
6						—

A Dept. 6	B	C
D	E	F

Solution

First either rank or arrange the work flows from high to low. Here they have been arranged from high to low.

Dept.	Work Flow	Dept.	Work Flow
1–2	125	2–4	17
1–4	64	4–5	13
1–3	62	2–3	10
2–6	54	5–6	5
1–6	50	3–4	2
2–5	26	4–6	2
1–5	25	3–5	0
3–6	20		

From this, we can see that departments 1 and 2 have the greatest interdepartmental work flow, so they should be close, perhaps at B and E. Next, work flows for 1–3 and 1–4 are high. Note, though, that the work flow for 3–4 is low, suggesting that they need not be close. Instead, we would place them on either side of department 1. Note also that 3–4 is only 2, 3–5 is 0, while 3–6 is 20 and 4–5 is 13. Hence, place department 3 at location D, department 4 at location F, and department 5 at location C.

A Dept. 6	B Dept. 2	C Dept. 5
D Dept. 3	E Dept. 1	F Dept. 4

Total cost:

Trip	b Distance	c Frequency	(b × c × $2) Cost
1–2	(B–E) 40	125	$10,000
1–3	(D–E) 50	62	6,200
1–4	(F–E) 50	64	6,400
1–5	(E–C) 60	25	3,000
1–6	(A–E) 80	50	8,000
2–3	(B–D) 90	10	1,800
2–4	(B–F) 70	17	2,380
2–5	(B–C) 50	26	2,600
2–6	(A–B) 50	54	5,400
3–4	(F–D) 120	2	480
3–5	(D–C) 140	0	0
3–6	(A–D) 50	20	2,000
4–5	(C–F) 50	13	1,300
4–6	(A–F) 130	2	520
5–6	(A–C) 100	5	1,000
			$51,080

DISCUSSION AND REVIEW QUESTIONS

1. Explain the importance of process selection in system design.
2. Briefly describe the five process types, and indicate the kinds of situations in which each would be used.
3. Briefly discuss the advantages and disadvantages of automation.
4. Briefly describe computer-assisted approaches to production.
5. What is a flexible manufacturing system, and under what set of circumstances is it most appropriate?
6. Why is management of technology important?
7. Why might the choice of equipment that provides flexibility sometimes be viewed as a management cop-out?
8. What are the trade-offs that occur when a process layout is used? What are the trade-offs that occur when a product layout is used?
9. List some common reasons for redesigning layouts.
10. Briefly describe the two main layout types.
11. What are the main advantages of a product layout? The main disadvantages?
12. What are the main advantages of a process layout? The main disadvantages?
13. What is the goal of line balancing? What happens if a line is unbalanced?
14. Why are routing and scheduling continual problems in process layouts?
15. Compare equipment maintenance strategies in product and process layouts.
16. Briefly outline the impact that job sequence has on each of the layout types.
17. The City Transportation Planning Committee must decide whether to begin a long-term project to build a subway system or to upgrade the present bus service. Suppose you are an expert in

fixed-path and variable-path material-handling equipment, and the committee seeks your counsel on this matter. What are the advantages and limitations of the subway and bus systems?

18. Identify the fixed-path and variable-path material-handling equipment commonly found in supermarkets.
19. What are heuristic approaches, and why are they used in designing layouts?
20. Why are product layouts atypical in service environments?
21. According to a study by the Alliance of American Insurers, it costs more than three times the original purchase price in parts and labor to reconstruct a wrecked Chevrolet. Explain the reasons for this large discrepancy in terms of the processes used to assemble the original car and those required to reconstruct the wrecked car.
22. Name some ways that a layout can help or hinder productivity.
23. What is cellular manufacturing? What are its main benefits and limitations?
24. What is group technology?
25. Explain the consequences of task time variability on line balancing.

TAKING STOCK

1. Name three major trade-offs in process selection.
2. What trade-offs are involved when deciding how often to rebalance an assembly line?
3. Who needs to be involved in process selection?
4. Who needs to be involved in layout design?
5. In what ways does technology have an impact on process selection? How can technology impact layout decisions?

CRITICAL THINKING EXERCISES

1. Name two unethical behaviors related to process selection and two related to layout, and the ethical principles they violate (see Chapter 1).
2. Layout decisions affect a wide range of facilities, from factories, supermarkets, offices, department stores, and warehouses, to malls, parking lots and garages, and kitchens. Layout is also important in the design of some products such as the interiors of automobiles and the arrangement of components inside computers and other electronic devices. Select three different items from this list, or other similar items, and explain for each what the four or five key considerations for layout design are.
3. What are the risks of automating a production process? What are the risks for a service process?

PROBLEMS

1. An assembly line with 17 tasks is to be balanced. The longest task is 2.4 minutes, and the total time for all tasks is 18 minutes. The line will operate for 450 minutes per day.

a. What are the minimum and maximum cycle times?
b. What range of output is theoretically possible for the line?
c. What is the minimum number of workstations needed if the maximum output rate is to be sought?
d. What cycle time will provide an output rate of 125 units per day?
e. What output potential will result if the cycle time is (1) 9 minutes? (2) 15 minutes?

2. A manager wants to assign tasks to workstations as efficiently as possible, and achieve an hourly output of 33⅓ units. Assume the shop works a 60-minute hour. Assign the tasks shown in the accompanying precedence diagram (times are in minutes) to workstations using the following rules:

a. In order of most following tasks. Tiebreaker: greatest positional weight.
b. In order of greatest positional weight.
c. What is the efficiency?

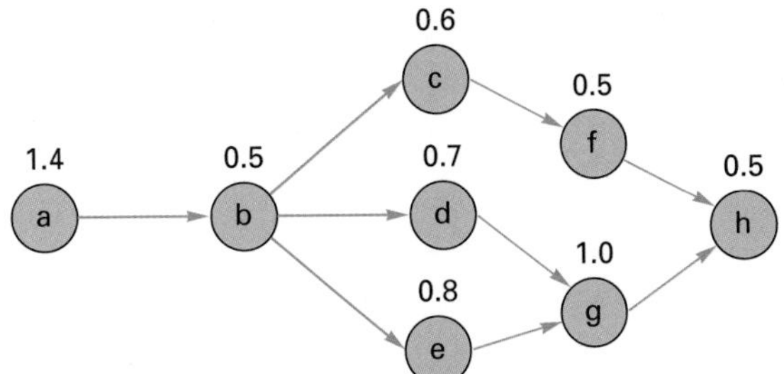

3. A manager wants to assign tasks to workstations as efficiently as possible, and achieve an hourly output of 4 units. The department uses a working time of 56 minutes per hour. Assign the tasks shown in the accompanying precedence diagram (times are in minutes) to workstations using the following rules:

a. In order of most following tasks. Tiebreaker: greatest positional weight.
b. In order of greatest positional weight.
c. What is the efficiency?

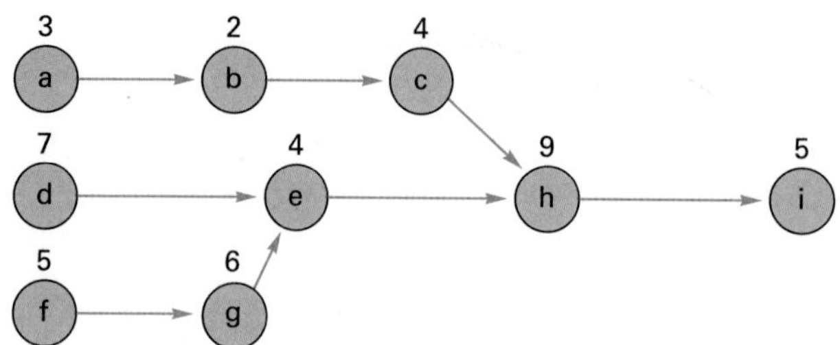

4. A producer of inkjet printers is planning to add a new line of printers, and you have been asked to balance the process, given the following task times and precedence relationships. Assume that cycle time is to be the minimum possible.

Task	Length (minutes)	Immediate Predecessor
a	0.2	—
b	0.4	a
c	0.3	—
d	1.3	b, c
e	0.1	—
f	0.8	e
g	0.3	d, f
h	1.2	g

a. Do each of the following:
 (1) Draw the precedence diagram.
 (2) Assign tasks to stations in order of greatest number of following tasks.
 (3) Determine the percentage of idle time.
 (4) Compute the rate of output in printers per day that could be expected for this line assuming a 420-minute working day.
b. Answer these questions:
 (1) What is the shortest cycle time that will permit use of only two workstations? Is this cycle time feasible? Identify the tasks you would assign to each station.
 (2) Determine the percentage of idle time that would result if two stations were used.
 (3) What is the daily output under this arrangement?
 (4) Determine the output rate that would be associated with the maximum cycle time.

5. As part of a major plant renovation project, the industrial engineering department has been asked to balance a revised assembly operation to achieve an output of 240 units per eight-hour day. Task times and precedence relationships are as follows:

Task	Duration (minutes)	Immediate Predecessor
a	0.2	—
b	0.4	a
c	0.2	b
d	0.4	—
e	1.2	d
f	1.2	c
g	1.0	e, f

Do each of the following:

a. Draw the precedence diagram.
b. Determine the minimum cycle time, the maximum cycle time, and the calculated cycle time.
c. Determine the minimum number of stations needed.
d. Assign tasks to workstations on the basis of greatest number of following tasks. Use longest processing time as a tiebreaker. If ties still exist, assume indifference in choice.
e. Compute the percentage of idle time for the assignment in part *d*.

6. Twelve tasks, with times and precedence requirements as shown in the following table, are to be assigned to workstations using a cycle time of 1.5 minutes. Two heuristic rules will be tried: (1) greatest positional weight, and (2) greatest number of following tasks.

In each case, the tiebreaker will be shortest task time.

Task	Length (minutes)	Immediate Predecessor
a	0.1	—
b	0.2	a
c	0.9	b
d	0.6	c
e	0.1	—
f	0.2	d, e
g	0.4	f
h	0.1	g
i	0.2	h
j	0.7	i
k	0.3	j
l	0.2	k

a. Draw the precedence diagram for this line.
b. Assign tasks to stations under each of the two rules.
c. Compute the percentage of idle time for each rule.

7. For the set of tasks given below, do the following:

a. Develop the precedence diagram.
b. Determine the minimum and maximum cycle times in seconds for a desired output of 500 units in a seven-hour day. Why might a manager use a cycle time of 50 seconds?
c. Determine the minimum number of workstations for output of 500 units per day.
d. Balance the line using the *largest positional weight* heuristic. Break ties with the *most following tasks* heuristic. Use a cycle time of 50 seconds.
e. Calculate the percentage idle time for the line.

Task	Task Time (seconds)	Immediate Predecessor
A	45	—
B	11	A
C	9	B
D	50	—
E	26	D
F	11	E
G	12	C
H	10	C
I	9	F, G, H
J	10	I
	193	

8. A shop works a 400-minute day. The manager of the shop wants an output of 200 units per day for the assembly line that has the elemental tasks shown in the table. Do the following:

a. Construct the precedence diagram.
b. Assign tasks according to the *most following tasks* rule.
c. Assign tasks according to the *greatest positional weight* rule.
d. Compute the balance delay for each rule. Which one yields the better set of assignments in this instance?

Task	Immediate Predecessor	Task Time
a	—	0.5
b	a	1.4
c	a	1.2
d	a	0.7
e	b, c	0.5
f	d	1.0
g	e	0.4
h	g	0.3
i	f	0.5
j	e, i	0.8
k	h, j	0.9
m	k	0.3

9. Arrange six departments into a 2 × 3 grid so that these conditions are satisfied: 1 close to 2, 5 close to 2 and 6, 2 close to 5, and 3 not close to 1 or 2.
10. Using the information given in the preceding problem, develop a Muther-type grid using the letters A, O, and X. Assume that any pair of combinations not mentioned have an O rating.
11. Using the information in the following grid, determine if the department locations shown are appropriate. If not, modify the assignments so that the conditions are satisfied.

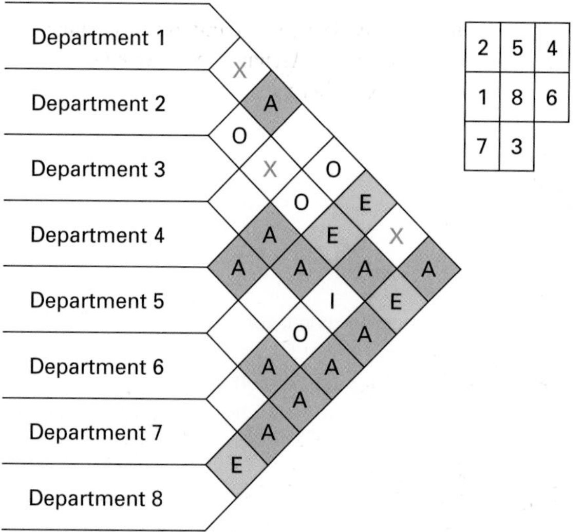

12. Arrange the eight departments shown in the accompanying Muther grid into a 2 × 4 format. *Note:* Department 1 must be in the location shown.

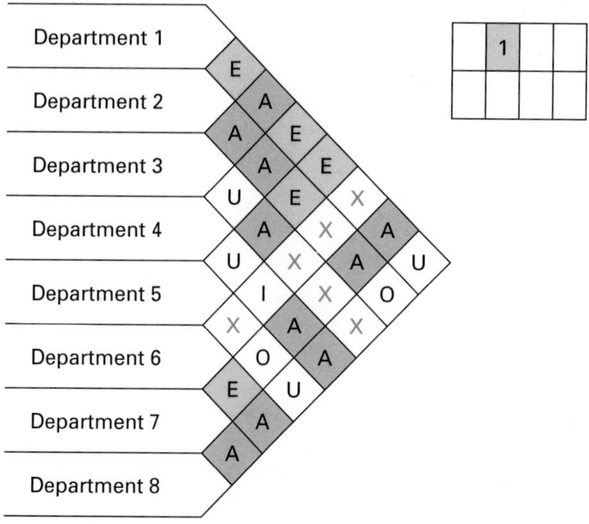

13. Arrange the departments so they satisfy the conditions shown in the following rating grid into a 3×3 format. Place department 5 in the lower left corner of the 3×3 grid.

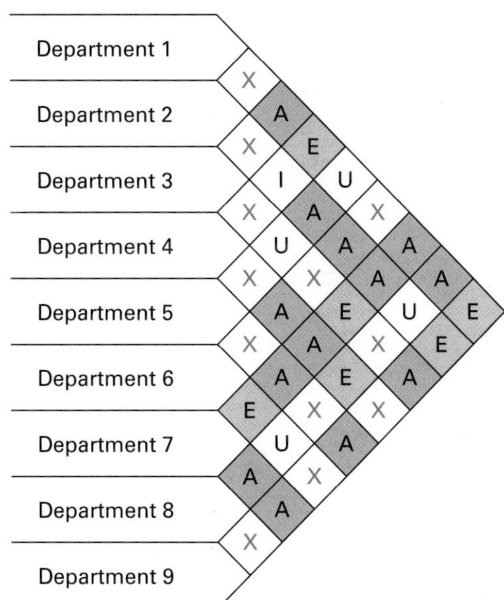

14. a. Determine the placement of departments for a newly designed facility that will minimize total transportation costs using the data in the following tables. Assume that reverse distances are the same. The locations are shown in the grid. Use a cost of $1 per trip yard.

Location A	Location B	Location C
	Location D	

DISTANCE BETWEEN LOCATIONS (yards)

From \ To	A	B	C	D
A	—	40	80	70
B		—	40	50
C			—	60
D				—

NUMBER OF TRIPS PER DAY BETWEEN DEPARTMENTS

From \ To	1	2	3	4
1	—	10	20	80
2		—	40	90
3			—	55
4				—

b. Suppose the company has revised its plans for the processes described in part *a* to accommodate technological process changes. Determine the placement of departments that will now minimize total travel cost. Use the distances shown in part *a*, but use the following new matrix of daily trips between departments.

NUMBER OF TRIPS PER DAY BETWEEN DEPARTMENTS

From \ To	A	B	C	D
1	—	20	20	40
2		—	10	50
3			—	60
4				—

15. Eight work centers must be arranged in an L-shaped building. The locations of centers 1 and 3 are assigned as shown in the accompanying diagram. Assuming transportation costs are $1 per load per meter, develop a suitable layout that minimizes transportation costs using the given information. Compute the total cost. (Assume the reverse distances are the same.)

A 1	B	
C	D	E 3
F	G	H

DISTANCE (meters)

From \ To	A	B	C	D	E	F	G	H
A	—	40	40	60	120	80	100	110
B		—	60	40	60	140	120	130
C			—	45	85	40	70	90
D				—	40	50	40	45
E					—	90	50	40
F						—	40	60
G							—	40
H								—

LOADS PER DAY

From \ To	1	2	3	4	5	6	7	8
1	—	10	5	90	370	135	125	0
2		—	360	120	40	115	45	120
3			—	350	110	40	20	200
4				—	190	70	50	190
5					—	10	40	10
6						—	50	20
7							—	20
8								—

16. Develop a process layout that will minimize the total distance traveled by patients at a medical clinic, using the following information on projected departmental visits by patients and distance between locations. Assume a distance of 35 feet between the reception area and each potential location. Use the format shown.

DISTANCE BETWEEN LOCATIONS (feet)

From \ To	A	B	C	D	E	F
A	—	40	80	100	120	160
B		—	40	60	80	120
C			—	20	40	80
D				—	20	40
E					—	40
F						—

TRIPS BETWEEN DEPARTMENTS (per day)

\ To	Reception	1	2	3	4	5	6
Reception	—	20	50	210	20	10	130
1	10	—	0	40	110	80	50
2	40		—	0	50	40	120
3	10		0	—	10	250	10
4	0				—	40	90
5	10					—	20
6	30						—

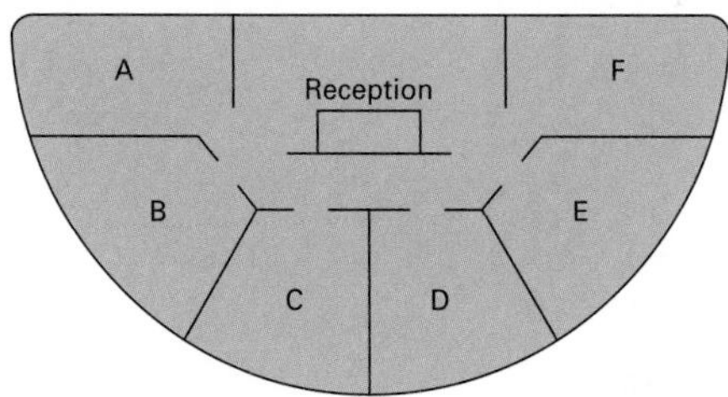

17. Ten labs will be assigned to the circular layout shown. Recalling a similar layout's congestion in the halls, the new lab manager has requested an assignment that will minimize traffic between offices. In addition, movement in the halls is restricted to a counterclockwise route. Develop a suitable layout using the following information.

NUMBER OF TRIPS PER DAY BETWEEN DEPARTMENTS

From \ To	1	2	3	4	5	6	7	8	9	10
1	—	40	51	26	23	9	20	12	11	35
2		—	37	16	27	15	18	18	18	36
3			—	18	20	14	50	18	25	36
4				—	35	14	14	22	23	31
5					—	24	14	13	21	25
6						—	17	44	42	25
7							—	14	33	40
8								—	43	35
9									—	47
10										—

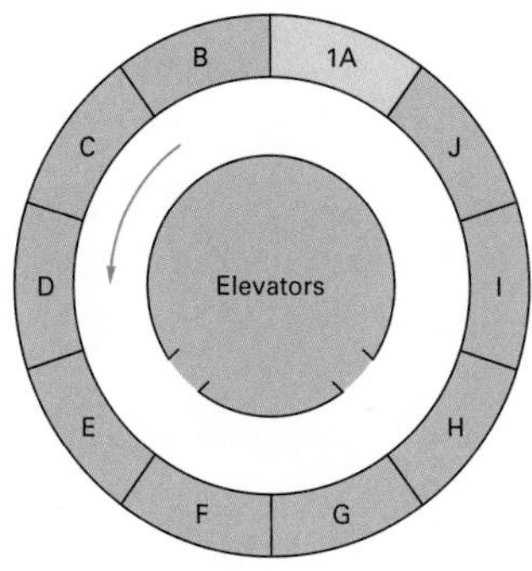

18. Rebalance the assembly line in Problem 7. This time, use the *longest operation time* heuristic. Break ties with the *most following tasks* heuristic. What is the percentage idle time for your line?

SELECTED BIBLIOGRAPHY AND FURTHER READINGS

Cohen, Morris, and Uday M. Apte. *Manufacturing Automation.* Burr Ridge, IL: Richard D. Irwin, 1997.

Francis, Richard L., Leon F. McGinnis Jr., and John A. White. *Facility Layout and Location: An Analytical Approach.* 3rd ed. Upper Saddle River, NJ: Prentice Hall, 1998.

Groover, Mikell P. *Automation, Production Systems, and Computer-Aided Manufacturing.* 2nd ed. Upper Saddle River, NJ: Prentice Hall, 2001.

Hill, Terry. *Manufacturing Strategy.* 3rd ed. Burr Ridge, IL: Richard D. Irwin, 2001.

Kilbridge, M. D., and L. Wester. "A Heuristic Method of Assembly Line Balancing." *Journal of Industrial Engineering* 12 (July–August 1961).

Milas, Gene H. "Assembly Line Balancing . . . Let's Remove the Mystery." *Industrial Engineering,* May 1990, pp. 31–36.

Upton, David. "The Management of Manufacturing Flexibility." *California Management Review* 36, no. 2 (1994), pp. 72–89.

Upton, David. "What Really Makes Factories Flexible." *Harvard Business Review,* July–August 1995, pp. 74–84.

Work Design and Measurement

CHAPTER OUTLINE

LEARNING OBJECTIVES

After completing this chapter, you should be able to:

1 Explain the importance of work design.
2 Compare and contrast the two basic approaches to job design.
3 Discuss the advantages and disadvantages of specialization.
4 Explain the term *knowledge-based pay.*
5 Explain the purpose of methods analysis and describe how methods studies are performed.
6 Compare four commonly used techniques for motion study.
7 Discuss the impact of working conditions on job design.
8 Define a standard time.
9 Describe and compare time study methods and perform calculations.
10 Describe work sampling and perform calculations.
11 Compare stopwatch time study and work sampling.
12 Contrast time and output pay systems.

This chapter has four major sections: quality of work life, job design, methods analysis, and work measurement.

As you read this chapter, note how decisions in other design areas have an impact on work design. For example, product or service design decisions in large measure determine the kinds of activities workers will be involved with. Similarly, layout decisions often influence work design. Process layouts tend to necessitate broader job content than product layouts. The implication of these interrelationships is that it is essential to adopt a systems approach to design; decisions in one area must be related to the overall system.

INTRODUCTION

The importance of work design is underscored by an organization's dependence on human efforts (i.e., work) to accomplish its goals. Furthermore, many of the topics in this chapter are especially relevant for productivity improvement and continuous improvement.

QUALITY OF WORK LIFE

People work for a variety of reasons. Generally people work to earn a living. Also they may be seeking self-realization, status, physical and mental stimulation, and socialization. Quality of work life affects not only workers' overall sense of well-being and contentment, but also worker productivity. Quality of work life has several key aspects. Getting along well with coworkers and having good managers can contribute greatly to the quality of work life. Leadership style is particularly important. Also important are working conditions and compensation, which are addressed here.

Working Conditions

Working conditions are an important aspect of job design. Physical factors such as temperature, humidity, ventilation, illumination, and noise can have a significant impact on worker performance in terms of productivity, quality of output, and accidents. In many instances, government regulations apply.

Temperature and Humidity. Although human beings can function under a fairly wide range of temperatures and humidity, work performance tends to be adversely affected if temperatures or humidities are outside a very narrow *comfort band.* That comfort band depends on how strenuous the work is; the more strenuous the work, the lower the comfort range.

Ventilation. Unpleasant and noxious odors can be distracting and dangerous to workers. Moreover, unless smoke and dust are periodically removed, the air can quickly become stale and annoying.

Illumination. The amount of illumination required depends largely on the type of work being performed; the more detailed the work, the higher the level of illumination needed for adequate performance. Other important considerations are the amount of glare and contrast. From a safety standpoint, good lighting in halls, stairways, and other dangerous points is important. However, because illumination is expensive, high illumination in all areas is not generally desirable.

Noise and Vibrations. Noise is unwanted sound. It is caused by both equipment and humans. Noise can be annoying or distracting, leading to errors and accidents. It also can damage or impair hearing if it is loud enough. Figure 7.1 illustrates loudness levels of some typical sounds.

Vibrations can be a factor in job design even without a noise component, so merely eliminating sound may not be sufficient in every case. Vibrations can come from tools, machines, vehicles, human activity, air-conditioning systems, pumps, and other sources. Corrective measures include padding, stabilizers, shock absorbers, cushioning, and rubber mountings.

Work Time and Work Breaks. Reasonable (and sometimes flexible) work hours can provide a sense of freedom and control over one's work. This is useful in situations where emphasis is on completing work on a timely basis and meeting performance objectives rather than being "on duty" for a given time interval, as is the case for most retail and manufacturing operations.

Work breaks are also important. Long work intervals tend to generate boredom and fatigue. Productivity and quality can both deteriorate. Similarly, periodic vacation breaks can give workers something to look forward to, a change of pace, and a chance to recharge themselves.

Occupational Health Care. Good worker health contributes to productivity, minimizes health care costs, and enhances workers' sense of well-being. Many organizations have exercise and healthy-eating programs designed to improve or maintain employees' fitness and general health.

Safety. Worker safety is one of the most basic issues in job design. This area needs constant attention from management, employees, and designers. Workers cannot be effectively motivated if they feel they are in physical danger.

From an employer standpoint, accidents are undesirable because they are expensive (insurance and compensation); they usually involve damage to equipment and/or products; they

FIGURE 7.1
Decibel values of typical sounds (db)

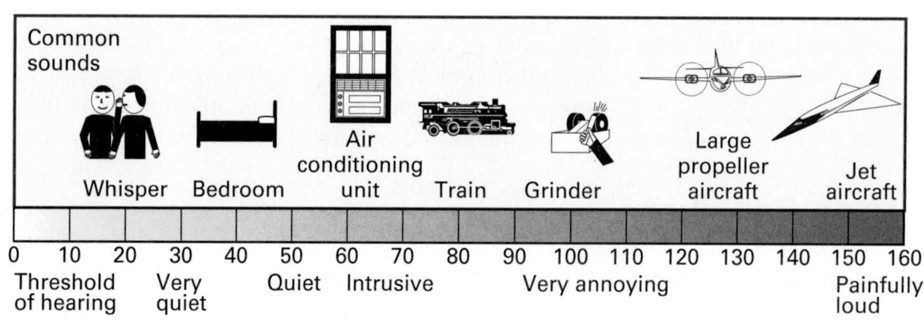

Source: From Benjamin W. Niebel, *Motion and Time Study,* 8th ed. Copyright © 1988 Richard D. Irwin, Inc. Used by permission of McGraw-Hill Companies, Inc., p. 248.

require hiring, training, and makeup work; and they generally interrupt work. From a worker standpoint, accidents mean physical suffering, mental anguish, potential loss of earnings, and disruption of the work routine.

The two basic causes of accidents are worker *carelessness* and accident *hazards.* Under the heading of carelessness come unsafe acts. Examples include failing to use protective equipment, overriding safety controls (e.g., taping control buttons down), disregarding safety procedures, using tools and equipment improperly, and failing to use reasonable caution in danger zones. Unsafe conditions include unprotected pulleys, chains, material-handling equipment, machinery, and so on. Also, poorly lit walkways, stairs, and loading docks constitute hazards. Toxic wastes, gases and vapors, and radiation hazards must be contained. Protection against hazards involves use of proper lighting, clearly marked danger zones, use of protective equipment (hardhats, goggles, earmuffs, gloves, heavy shoes and clothing), safety devices (machine guards, dual control switches that require an operator to use both hands), emergency equipment (emergency showers, fire extinguishers, fire escapes), and thorough instruction in safety procedures and use of regular and emergency equipment. Housekeeping (clean floors, open aisles, waste removal) is another important safety factor.

An effective program of safety and accident control requires the cooperation of both workers and management. Workers must be trained in proper procedures and attitudes, and they can contribute to a reduction in hazards by pointing out hazards to management. Management must enforce safety procedures and use of safety equipment. If supervisors allow workers to ignore safety procedures or look the other way when they see violations, workers will be less likely to take proper precautions. Some firms use contests that compare departmental safety records. However, accidents cannot be completely eliminated, and a freak accident may seriously affect worker morale and might even contribute to additional accidents. Posters can be effective, particularly if they communicate in specific terms how to avoid accidents. For example, the admonition "Be careful" is not nearly as effective as "Wear hardhats," "Walk, don't run," or "Hold on to rail."

The enactment of the Occupational Safety and Health Act in 1970, and the creation of the Occupational Safety and Health Administration **(OSHA),** emphasized the importance of safety considerations in systems design. The law was intended to ensure that workers in all organizations have healthy and safe working conditions. It provides specific safety regulations with inspectors to see that they are adhered to. Inspections are carried out both at random and to investigate complaints of unsafe conditions. OSHA officials are empowered to issue warnings, to impose fines, and even to invoke court-ordered shutdowns for unsafe conditions.

OSHA Occupational Safety and Health Administration, created by the Occupational Safety and Health Act of 1970.

OSHA must be regarded as a major influence on operations management decisions in all areas relating to worker safety. OSHA has promoted the welfare and safety of workers in its role as a catalyst, spurring companies to make changes that they knew were needed but "hadn't gotten around to making."

Ethical Issues. Ethical issues affect operations through work methods, working conditions and employee safety, accurate record keeping, unbiased performance appraisals, fair compensation, and opportunities for advancement.

Compensation

Compensation is a significant issue for the design of work systems. It is important for organizations to develop suitable compensation plans for their employees. If wages are too low, organizations may find it difficult to attract and hold competent workers and managers. If wages are too high, the increased costs may result in lower profits, or may force the organization to increase its prices, which might adversely affect demand for the organization's products or services.

Organizations use a variety of approaches to compensate employees, including *time-based systems, output-based systems,* and *knowledge-based systems.* **Time-based systems,** also known as *hourly* and *measured daywork* systems, compensate employees for the time the employee has worked during a pay period. Salaried workers also represent a form of time-based compensation. **Output-based (incentive) systems** compensate employees according

Time-based system Compensation based on time an employee has worked during a pay period.

Output-based (incentive) system Compensation based on amount of output an employee produced during a pay period.

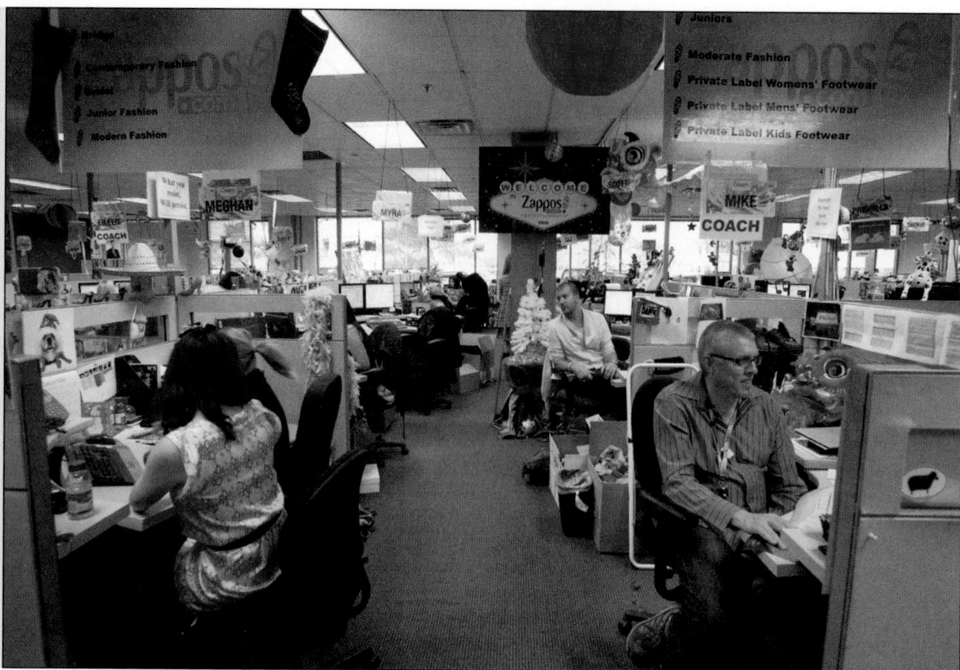

People work for a variety of reasons besides compensation. Online retail giant Zappos' zany culture and work environment make it an appealing place to work.

to the amount of output they produce during a pay period, thereby tying pay directly to performance.

Time-based systems are more widely used than incentive systems, particularly for office, administrative, and managerial employees, but also for blue-collar workers. One reason for this is that computation of wages is straightforward and managers can readily estimate labor costs for a given employee level. Employees often prefer time-based systems because the pay is steady and they know how much compensation they will receive for each pay period. In addition, employees may resent the pressures of an output-based system.

Another reason for using time-based systems is that many jobs do not lend themselves to the use of incentives. In some cases, it may be difficult or impossible to measure output. For example, jobs that require creative or mental work cannot be easily measured on an output basis. Other jobs may include irregular activities or have so many different forms of output that measuring output and determining pay are fairly complex. In the case of assembly lines, the use of *individual* incentives could disrupt the even flow of work; however, *group* incentives are sometimes used successfully in such cases. Finally, *quality* considerations may be as important as *quantity* considerations. In health care, for example, emphasis is generally placed on both the quality of patient care and the number of patients processed.

On the other hand, situations exist where incentives are desirable. Incentives reward workers for their output, presumably causing some workers to produce more than they might under a time-based system. The advantage is that certain (fixed) costs do not vary with increases in output, so the overall cost per unit decreases if output increases. Workers may prefer incentive systems because they see a relationship between their efforts and their pay: An incentive system presents an opportunity for them to earn more money.

On the negative side, incentive systems involve a considerable amount of paperwork, computation of wages is more difficult than under time-based systems, output has to be measured and standards set, cost-of-living increases are difficult to incorporate into incentive plans, and contingency arrangements for unavoidable delays have to be developed.

Table 7.1 lists the main advantages and disadvantages of time-based and output-based plans.

In order to obtain maximum benefit from an incentive plan, the plan should be accurate, easy to understand and apply, fair, and consistent. In addition, there should be an obvious relationship between effort and reward, and no limit on earnings.

Incentive systems may focus on the output of each individual or a group.

TABLE 7.1
Comparison of time-based and output-based pay systems

	Management	Worker
TIME-BASED		
Advantages	1. Stable labor costs 2. Easy to administer 3. Simple to compute pay 4. Stable output	1. Stable pay 2. Less pressure to produce than under output system
Disadvantages	1. No incentive for workers to increase output	1. Extra efforts not rewarded
OUTPUT-BASED		
Advantages	1. Lower cost per unit 2. Greater output	1. Pay related to efforts 2. Opportunity to earn more
Disadvantages	1. Wage computation more difficult 2. Need to measure output 3. Quality may suffer 4. Difficult to incorporate wage increases 5. Increased problems with scheduling	1. Pay fluctuates 2. Workers may be penalized because of factors beyond their control (e.g., machine breakdown)

Individual Incentive Plans. Individual incentive plans take a variety of forms. The simplest plan is *straight piecework.* Under this plan, a worker's pay is a direct linear function of his or her output. In the past, piecework plans were fairly popular. Now minimum wage legislation makes them somewhat impractical. Even so, many of the plans currently in use represent variations of the straight piecework plan. They typically incorporate a base rate that serves as a floor: Workers are guaranteed that amount as a minimum, regardless of output. The base rate is tied to an output standard; a worker who produces less than the standard will be paid at the base rate. This protects workers from pay loss due to delays, breakdowns, and similar problems. In most cases, incentives are paid for output above standard, and the pay is referred to as a *bonus.*

Group Incentive Plans. A variety of group incentive plans, which stress sharing of productivity gains with employees, are in use. Some focus exclusively on output, while others reward employees for output and for reductions in material and other costs.

One form of group incentive is the *team approach,* which many companies are now using for problem solving and continuous improvement. The emphasis is on *team,* not *individual,* performance.

Choosing Incentive Plans

READING

"The right incentive plan properly implemented can drive your business ahead like a rocket ship. But if expectations increase faster than actual payouts—watch out for trouble!"

Incentive Plans Pull Companies Together!

Years ago the only employees offered incentive pay were sales personnel, piece workers, and top executives. Today most large corporations, and many smaller firms, offer an incentive package to all of their employees.

Some kind of incentive pay is an important part of any compensation plan. Incentive pay shows appreciation and creates a sense of participation in the company's well-being that straight salary dollars, no matter how large, don't convey. A well-designed incentive-pay plan can also help pull people together, help point them in the direction you want them to go, and give that extra push that every company needs in today's competitive environment.

(continued)

Profit-Sharing Plans Are Common

Profit-sharing plans are probably the most widespread incentive-pay programs at larger corporations. They are generally company-wide and made available at least to all full-time employees. Usually the company will contribute a small percentage of its pre-tax profitability to a pool, which is then divided among eligible employees. Division is typically prorated according to the base salary of each participant. Profit sharing is generally done on an annual basis. At some firms profit sharing may be directly contributed as pre-tax dollars into a retirement program, such as a 401K program.

Profit plans work best at more established firms with relatively steady earnings. The criteria for the profit plan must be carefully defined in advance.

Profit Plans Don't Always Work

The advantages of a profit-sharing plan include: It pulls people together since everyone is on the same plan; it gets people to focus on profitability; and its cost to the company goes up and down in sync with pre-tax earnings.

The disadvantages include: It echoes the base salary; it does not take into consideration performance during the year; it is focused on a single objective.

For smaller companies with erratic earnings, profit-sharing plans can frustrate and irritate employees by creating expectations that are not fulfilled each year. I switched away from a profit-based incentive plan because I found that a small payout level, following a year of weak profitability, made a low morale situation even worse.

Incentive Programs Award Achievers

Last year we switched to an individual bonus incentive program, where the annual payout is determined by a subjective evaluation of each person's performance.

The advantages are: Unlike a profit-sharing plan, we can dramatically differentiate the payout given to a star performer versus a weaker one; we can differentiate between an individual's performance and the company's performance; and there is complete flexibility for a significant one-time payout if an employee has an extraordinary accomplishment that may not be repeated in future years.

The disadvantages include: The payout is subjective, and employees may feel that they deserve a higher pay-out; it can be divisive when, all too often, a top performer tells other people what a big bonus they got; employees may focus more on "looking good" than on working to increase corporate profits.

Source: Bob Adams, "Streetwise Business Tips," www.businesstown.com.

Knowledge-based pay A pay system used by organizations to reward workers who undergo training that increases their skills.

Knowledge-Based Pay Systems. As companies shift toward lean production, a number of changes have had a direct impact on the work environment. One is that many of the buffers that previously existed are gone. Another is that fewer managers are present. Still another is increased emphasis on quality, productivity, and flexibility. Consequently, workers who can perform a variety of tasks are particularly valuable. Organizations are increasingly recognizing this, and they are setting up pay systems to reward workers who undergo training that increases their skill levels. This is sometimes referred to as **knowledge-based pay.** It is a portion of a worker's pay that is based on the knowledge and skill that the worker possesses. Knowledge-based pay has three dimensions: *Horizontal skills* reflect the variety of tasks the worker is capable of performing; *vertical skills* reflect managerial tasks the worker is capable of; and *depth skills* reflect quality and productivity results.

Management Compensation. Many organizations that traditionally rewarded managers and senior executives on the basis of *output* are now seriously reconsidering that approach. With the new emphasis on customer service and quality, reward systems are being restructured to reflect new dimensions of performance. In addition, executive pay in many companies is being more closely tied to the success of the company or division that executive is responsible for. Even so, there have been news reports of companies increasing the compensation of top executives even as workers were being laid off and the company was losing large amounts of money!

Recent Trends. Many organizations are moving toward compensation systems that emphasize flexibility and performance objectives, with variable pay based on performance. Some are using profit sharing plans, or bonuses based on achieving profit or costs goals. And the increasing cost of employee health benefits is causing organizations to rethink their overall compensation packages. Some are placing more emphasis on quality of work life. An ideal compensation package is one that balances motivation, profitability, and retention of good employees.

JOB DESIGN

Job design involves specifying the content and methods of jobs. Job designers focus on *what* will be done in a job, *who* will do the job, *how* the job will be done, and *where* the job will be done. The objectives of job design include productivity, safety, and quality of work life.

Job design The act of specifying the contents and methods of jobs.

Current practice in job design contains elements of two basic schools of thought. One might be called the *efficiency* school because it emphasizes a systematic, logical approach to job design; the other is called the *behavioral* school because it emphasizes satisfaction of wants and needs.

The efficiency approach, a refinement of Frederick Winslow Taylor's scientific management concepts, received considerable emphasis in the past. The behavioral approach followed and has continued to make inroads into many aspects of job design. It is noteworthy that specialization is a primary issue of disagreement between the efficiency and behavioral approaches.

Specialization

The term **specialization** describes jobs that have a very narrow scope. Examples range from assembly lines to medical specialties. College professors often specialize in teaching certain courses, some auto mechanics specialize in transmission repair, and some bakers specialize in wedding cakes. The main rationale for specialization is the ability to concentrate one's efforts and thereby become proficient at that type of work.

Specialization Work that concentrates on some aspect of a product or service.

Sometimes the amount of knowledge or training required of a specialist and the complexity of the work suggest that individuals who choose such work are very happy with their jobs. This seems to be especially true in the "professions" (e.g., doctors, lawyers, professors). At the other end of the scale are assembly-line workers, who are also specialists, although much less glamorous. The advantage of these highly specialized jobs is that they yield high productivity and relatively low unit costs, and they are largely responsible for the high standard of living that exists today in industrialized nations.

Correct positioning of equipment and tools can help reduce fatigue and increase employee productivity. Here, an ergonomist from Humantech Inc., in Ann Arbor, Michigan, obtains workstation measurements to ensure proper height and accessibility for employees.

TABLE 7.2
Major advantages and disadvantages of specialization in business

Advantages	
For management:	For employees:
1. Simplifies training	1. Low education and skill requirements
2. High productivity	2. Minimum responsibilities
3. Low wage costs	3. Little mental effort needed
Disadvantages	
For management:	For employees:
1. Difficult to motivate quality	1. Monotonous work
2. Worker dissatisfaction, possibly resulting in absenteeism, high turnover, disruptive tactics, poor attention to quality	2. Limited opportunities for advancement
	3. Little control over work
	4. Little opportunity for self-fulfillment

Unfortunately, many of the lower-level jobs can be described as monotonous or downright boring, and are the source of much of the dissatisfaction among many industrial workers. While some workers undoubtedly prefer a job with limited requirements and responsibility for making decisions, others are not capable of handling jobs with greater scopes. Nonetheless, many workers are frustrated and this manifests itself in turnover and absenteeism. In the automotive industry, for example, absenteeism runs as high as 20 percent. Workers may also take out their frustrations through disruptive tactics such as deliberate slowdowns.

The seriousness of these problems caused job designers and others to seek ways of alleviating them. Some of those approaches are discussed in the following sections. Before we turn to them, note that the advantages and disadvantages of specialization are summarized in Table 7.2.

Behavioral Approaches to Job Design

In an effort to make jobs more interesting and meaningful, job designers frequently consider job enlargement, job rotation, job enrichment, and increased use of mechanization.

Job enlargement Giving a worker a larger portion of the total task, by horizontal loading.

Job enlargement means giving a worker a larger portion of the total task. This constitutes *horizontal loading*—the additional work is on the same level of skill and responsibility as the original job. The goal is to make the job more interesting by increasing the variety of skills required and by providing the worker with a more recognizable contribution to the overall output. For example, a production worker's job might be expanded so that he or she is responsible for a *sequence* of activities instead of only one activity.

Job rotation Workers periodically exchange jobs.

Job rotation means having workers periodically exchange jobs. A firm can use this approach to avoid having one or a few employees stuck in monotonous jobs. It works best when workers can be transferred to more interesting jobs; there is little advantage in having workers exchange one boring job for another. Job rotation allows workers to broaden their learning experience and enables them to fill in for others in the event of sickness or absenteeism.

Job enrichment Increasing responsibility for planning and coordination tasks, by vertical loading.

Job enrichment involves an increase in the level of responsibility for planning and coordination tasks. It is sometimes referred to as *vertical loading.* An example of this is to have stock clerks in supermarkets handle reordering of goods, thus increasing their responsibilities. The job enrichment approach focuses on the motivating potential of worker satisfaction.

Job enlargement and job enrichment are also used in *lean operations* (covered in Chapter 14), where workers are cross-trained to be able to perform a wider variety of tasks, and given more authority to manage their jobs.

The importance of these approaches to job design is that they have the potential to increase the motivational power of jobs by increasing worker satisfaction through improvement in the *quality of work life.* Many firms are currently involved in or seriously considering programs related to quality of work life.

Motivation

Motivation is a key factor in many aspects of work life. Not only can it influence quality and productivity, it also contributes to the work environment. People work for a variety of reasons in addition to compensation. Other reasons include socialization, self-actualization, status, the physiological aspects of work, and a sense of purpose and accomplishment. Awareness of these factors can help management to develop a motivational framework that encourages workers to respond in a positive manner to the goals of the organization. A detailed discussion of motivation is beyond the scope of this book, but its importance to work design should be obvious.

Another factor that influences motivation, productivity, and employee–management relations is *trust.* In an ideal work environment, there is a high level of trust between workers and managers. When managers trust employees, there is a greater tendency to give employees added responsibilities. When employees trust management, they are more likely to respond positively. Conversely, when they do not trust management, they are more likely to respond in less desirable ways.

Teams

The efforts of business organizations to become more productive, competitive, and customer-oriented have caused them to rethink how work is accomplished. Significant changes in the structure of some work environments have been the increasing use of teams and the way workers are paid, particularly in lean production systems.

In the past, nonroutine job assignments, such as dealing with customer complaints or improving a process, were typically given to one individual or to several individuals who reported to the same manager. More recently, nonroutine assignments are being given to teams who develop and implement solutions to problems.

There are a number of different forms of teams. One is a short-term team formed to collaborate on a topic such as quality improvement, product or service design, or solving a problem. Team members may be drawn from the same functional area or from several functional areas, depending on the scope of the problem. Other teams are more long term. One form of long-term team that is increasingly being used, especially in lean production settings, is the *self-directed team.*

Self-directed teams Groups empowered to make certain changes in their work processes.

Self-directed teams, sometimes referred to as *self-managed teams,* are designed to achieve a higher level of teamwork and employee involvement. Although such teams are not given absolute authority to make all decisions, they are typically empowered to make changes in the work processes under their control. The underlying concept is that the workers, who are close to the process and have the best knowledge of it, are better suited than management to make the most effective changes to improve the process. Moreover, because they have a vested interest and personal involvement in the changes, they tend to work harder to ensure that the desired results are achieved than they would if management had implemented the changes. For these teams to function properly, team members must be trained in quality, process improvement, and teamwork. Self-directed teams have a number of benefits. One is that fewer managers are necessary; very often one manager can handle several teams. Also, self-directed teams can provide improved responsiveness to problems, they have a personal stake in making the process work, and they require less time to implement improvements.

Generally, the benefits of teams include higher quality, higher productivity, and greater worker satisfaction. Moreover, higher levels of employee satisfaction can lead to less turnover and absenteeism, resulting in lower costs to train new workers and less need to fill in for absent employees. This does not mean that organizations will have no difficulties in applying

TABLE 7.3
Some examples of poor posture

Source: Based on Spine-health.com. "Office Chair Advice" © 1999–2007.

Walking with shoulders hunched
Carrying something heavy on one side of the body
Holding a phone receiver between the neck and shoulder
Leaning forward while sitting in a desk chair
Slouching in a chair

the team concept. Managers, particularly middle managers, often feel threatened as teams assume more of the traditional functions of managers.

Moreover, among the leading problems of teams are conflicts between team members, which can have a detrimental impact on the effectiveness of a team.

Expert Robert Bacal has a list of requirements for successful team building:[1]

1. Clearly stated and commonly held vision and goals.
2. Talent and skills required to meet goals.
3. Clear understanding of team members' roles and functions.
4. Efficient and shared understanding of procedures and norms.
5. Effective and skilled interpersonal relations.
6. A system of reinforcement and celebration.
7. Clear understanding of the team's relationship to the greater organization.

Ergonomics

Ergonomics Incorporation of human factors in the design of the workplace.

Ergonomics (or human factors) is the scientific discipline concerned with the understanding of interactions among humans and other elements of a system, and the profession that applies theory, principles, data and methods to design in order to optimize human well-being and overall system performance. Ergonomists contribute to the design and evaluation of tasks, jobs, products, environments and systems in order to make them compatible with the needs, abilities and limitations of people."[2] In the work environment, ergonomics also helps to increase productivity by reducing worker discomfort and fatigue.

The International Ergonomics Association organizes ergonomics into three domains: physical (e.g., repetitive movements, layout, health, and safety); cognitive (mental workload, decision making, human–computer interaction, and work stress); and organizational (e.g., communication, teamwork, work design, and telework).[3]

Many examples of ergonomics applications can be found in operations management. In the early 1900s, Frederick Winslow Taylor, known as the father of scientific management, found that the amount of coal that workers could shovel could be increased substantially by reducing the size and weight of the shovels. Frank and Lillian Gilbreth expanded Taylor's work, developing a set of motion study principles intended to improve worker efficiency and reduce injury and fatigue. Over the years since then technological changes have broadened the scope of ergonomics, as hand–eye coordination and decision making became more important in the workplace. More recently, the increasing level of human–computer interfacing has again broadened the scope of the field of ergonomics, not only in job design, but also in electronics product design.

Poor posture can lead to fatigue, low productivity, and injuries to the back, neck, and arm. Table 7.3 list some examples of poor posture.

Good posture can help avoid or minimize these problems. Table 7.4 lists some guidelines for good posture when using a computer, and Figure 7.2 illustrates good posture when using a computer.

[1]Robert Bacal, "The Six Deadly Sins of Team-Building," www.performance-appraisals.org.
[2]The International Ergonomics Association (www.iea).
[3]Ibid.

TABLE 7.4
Some guidelines for good posture when using a computer

- "Let your shoulders relax and roll back towards your back.
- Keep your arms on your chair's armrests as often as possible.
- When you are not mousing, return your arm to your armrests; do not keep it hovering on or above the mouse.
- Your back should be slightly angled back so as not to slouch, but not so far that you are leaning way back.
- Your neck position should be upright and at a neutral position—not leaning forward, not turned in either direction.
- Feet should be flat on the ground or if you're short, on a footstool.
- Feet should be positioned about one foot apart from each other.
- Wrists should be straight and neutral (not tilted down or up).
- Do not ever slouch or slump in your seat.
- Adjust the tilt function of your chair, or alter your posture once every two hours.
- Pull your chin in when looking down.
- Always be looking forward at your monitor; do not have it placed to one side.
- Keep your monitor between 18 and 28 inches away from you.
- Your monitor should be raised or lowered so that you can work without raising or lowering your head. Bifocal wearers need to be especially careful that their monitors are positioned to avoid neck strain.
- Keep your chin parallel to the floor and pulled back slightly.
- Get up from your seat and move once an hour."

Source: This work is published under a Creative Commons Attribution-NonCommercial-NoDerivs 3.0 License. Copyright © 2002 CompuMentor.

About the Author: Susan Tenby is Online Community Manager at TechSoup.

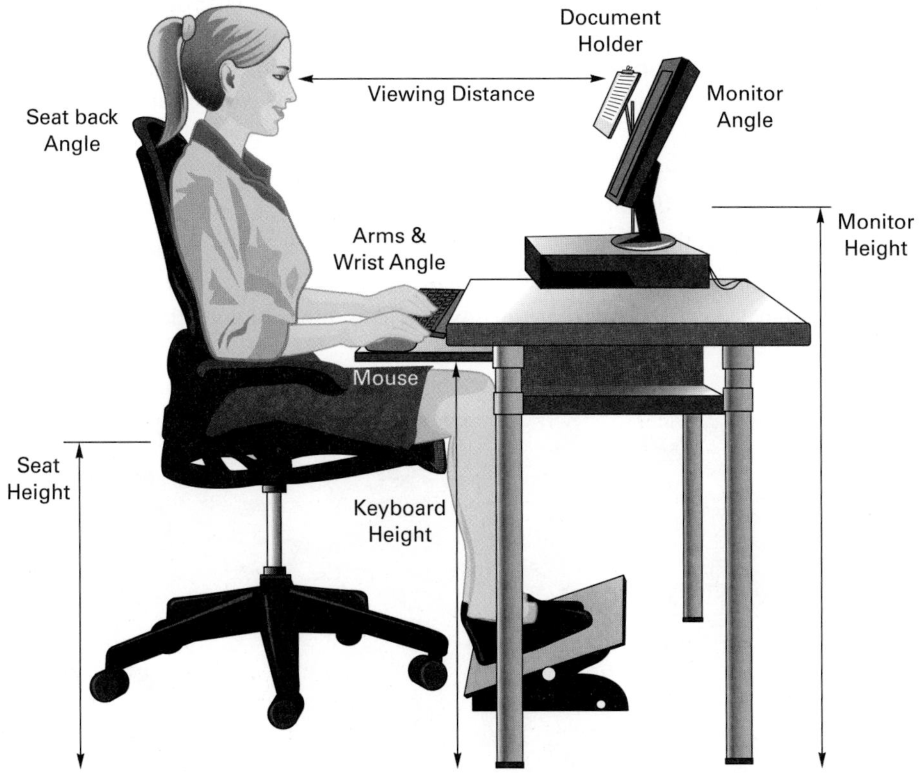

FIGURE 7.2
Components of a comfortable workstation

Source: Copyright 2007 Bennett, Coleman & Co. Ltd. All rights reserved.

METHODS ANALYSIS

One of the techniques used by self-directed teams and work analysts is **methods analysis,** which focuses on how a job is done. Job design often begins with an analysis of the overall operation. It then moves from general to specific details of the job, concentrating on arrangement of the workplace and movements of materials and/or workers. Methods analysis can be a good source of productivity improvements.

Methods analysis Analyzing how a job is done.

The need for methods analysis can come from a number of different sources:

1. Changes in tools and equipment.
2. Changes in product design or introduction of new products.
3. Changes in materials or procedures.
4. Government regulations or contractual agreements.
5. Other factors (e.g., accidents, quality problems).

Methods analysis is done for both existing jobs and new jobs. For a new job it is needed to establish a method. For an existing job the procedure usually is to have the analyst observe the job as it is currently being performed and then devise improvements. For a new job, the analyst must rely on a job description and an ability to visualize the operation.

The basic procedure in methods analysis is as follows:

1. Identify the operation to be studied, and gather all pertinent facts about tools, equipment, materials, and so on.
2. For existing jobs, discuss the job with the operator and supervisor to get their input.
3. Study and document the present method of an existing job using process charts. For new jobs, develop charts based on information about the activities involved.
4. Analyze the job.
5. Propose new methods.
6. Install the new methods.
7. Follow up implementation to assure that improvements have been achieved.

Selecting an Operation to Study. Sometimes a foreman or supervisor will request that a certain operation be studied. At other times, methods analysis will be part of an overall program to increase productivity and reduce costs. Some general guidelines for selecting a job to study are to consider jobs that

1. Have a high labor content.
2. Are done frequently.
3. Are unsafe, tiring, unpleasant, and/or noisy.
4. Are designated as problems (e.g., quality problems, processing bottlenecks).

The most common ergonomic risk factors are awkward postures, excessive force for lifting, pushing, pulling, and gripping, and repetition involving the same group of muscles. On the left, the worker was using a pistol grip driver in a vertical application which was placing her into a poor shoulder posture. She was experiencing increasing pain in her right shoulder. On the right, by modifying the tools being used, the worker is now into a good shoulder posture.

Documenting the Current Method. Use charts, graphs, and verbal descriptions of the way the job is now being performed. This will provide a good understanding of the job and serve as a basis of comparison against which revisions can be judged.

Analyzing the Job and Proposing New Methods. Job analysis requires careful thought about the what, why, when, where, and who of the job. Often, simply going through these questions will clarify the review process by encouraging the analyst to take a devil's advocate attitude toward both present and proposed methods.

Analyzing and improving methods is facilitated by the use of various charts such as *flow process charts* and *worker-machine charts.*

Flow process charts are used to review and critically examine the overall sequence of an operation by focusing on the movements of the operator or the flow of materials. These charts are helpful in identifying nonproductive parts of the process (e.g., delays, temporary storages, distances traveled). Figure 7.3 describes the symbols used in constructing a flow process chart, and Figure 7.4 illustrates a flow process chart.

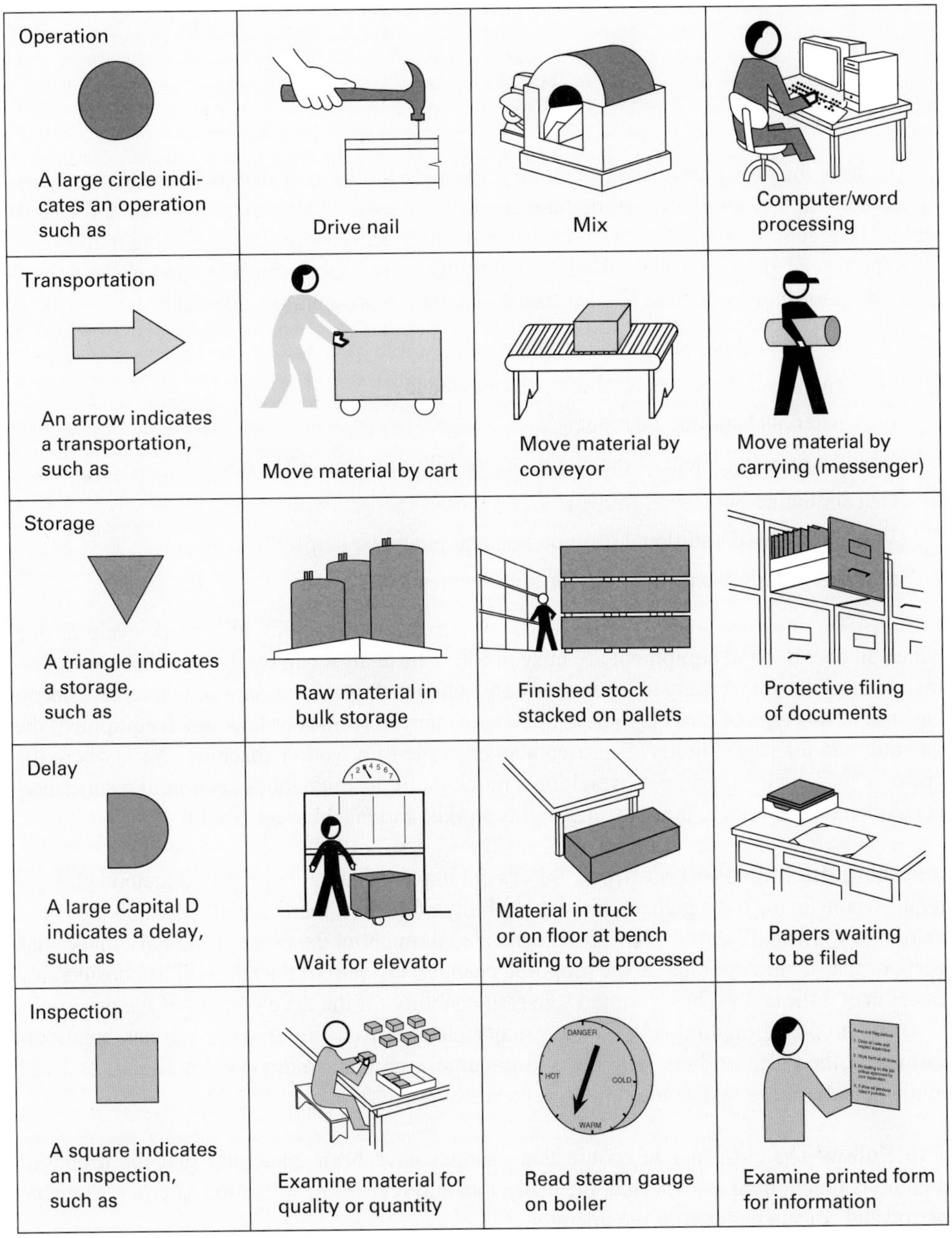

Flow process chart Chart used to examine the overall sequence of an operation by focusing on movements of the operator or flow of materials.

Operation A large circle indicates an operation such as	Drive nail	Mix	Computer/word processing
Transportation An arrow indicates a transportation, such as	Move material by cart	Move material by conveyor	Move material by carrying (messenger)
Storage A triangle indicates a storage, such as	Raw material in bulk storage	Finished stock stacked on pallets	Protective filing of documents
Delay A large Capital D indicates a delay, such as	Wait for elevator	Material in truck or on floor at bench waiting to be processed	Papers waiting to be filed
Inspection A square indicates an inspection, such as	Examine material for quality or quantity	Read steam gauge on boiler	Examine printed form for information

FIGURE 7.3
Process chart symbols

Source: Adapted from Benjamin W. Niebel, *Motion and Time Study,* 8th ed. Copyright © 1988 Richard D. Irwin, Inc. Used by permission of McGraw-Hill Companies, Inc., p. 35.

FIGURE 7.4
Format of a flow process chart

Source: Elias M. Awad, *Systems Analysis and Design,* 4th ed. Copyright © 1985 by Richard D. Irwin, Inc. Used by permission of McGraw-Hill Companies, Inc., p. 113.

FLOW PROCESS CHART Job Requisition of petty cash	ANALYST D. Kolb	PAGE 1 of 2	Operation	Movement	Inspection	Delay	Storage
Details of method							
Requisition made out by department head			●	⇨	□	D	▽
Put in "pick-up" basket			○	⇨	□	◗	▽
To accounting department			○	➡	□	D	▽
Account and signature verified			○	⇨	■	D	▽
Amount approved by treasurer			●	⇨	□	D	▽
Amount counted by cashier			●	⇨	□	D	▽
Amount recorded by bookkeeper			●	⇨	□	D	▽
Petty cash sealed in envelope			●	⇨	□	D	▽
Petty cash carried to department			○	➡	□	D	▽
Petty cash checked against requisition			○	⇨	■	D	▽
Receipt signed			●	⇨	□	D	▽
Petty cash stored in safety box			○	⇨	□	D	▼
			○	⇨	□	D	▽
			○	⇨	□	D	▽
			○	⇨	□	D	▽
			○	⇨	□	D	▽

The uses for flow process charts include studying the flow of material through a department, studying the sequence that documents or forms take, analyzing movement and care of surgical patients, studying layout of department and grocery stores, and handling mail.

Experienced analysts usually develop a checklist of questions they ask themselves to generate ideas for improvements. The following are some representative questions:

1. Why is there a delay or storage at this point?
2. How can travel distances be shortened or avoided?
3. Can materials handling be reduced?
4. Would a rearrangement of the workplace result in greater efficiency?
5. Can similar activities be grouped?
6. Would the use of additional or improved equipment be helpful?
7. Does the worker have any ideas for improvements?

Worker-machine chart Chart used to determine portions of a work cycle during which an operator and equipment are busy or idle.

A **worker-machine chart** is helpful in visualizing the portions of a work cycle during which an operator and equipment are busy or idle. The analyst can easily see when the operator and machine are working independently and when their work overlaps or is interdependent. One use of this type of chart is to determine how many machines or how much equipment the operator can manage. Figure 7.5 presents an example of a worker-machine chart, where the "worker" is actually a customer weighing a purchase in the bulk-foods section of a supermarket. Among other things, the chart highlights worker and machine utilization.

Installing the Improved Method. Successful implementation of proposed method changes requires convincing management of the desirability of the new method and obtaining the cooperation of workers. If workers have been consulted throughout the process and have made suggestions that are incorporated in the proposed changes, this part of the task will be considerably easier than if the analyst has assumed sole responsibility for the development of the proposal.

If the proposed method constitutes a major change from the way the job has been performed in the past, workers may have to undergo a certain amount of retraining, and full implementation may take some time to achieve.

The Follow-Up. In order to ensure that changes have been made and that the proposed method is functioning as expected, the analyst should review the operation after a reasonable period and consult again with the operator.

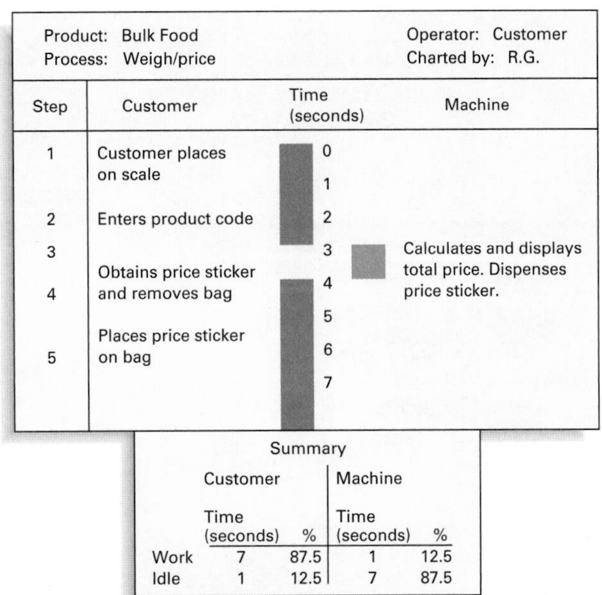

FIGURE 7.5
Worker-machine chart

MOTION STUDY

Motion study is the systematic study of the human motions used to perform an operation. The purpose is to eliminate unnecessary motions and to identify the best sequence of motions for maximum efficiency. Hence, motion study can be an important avenue for productivity improvements. Present practice evolved from the work of Frank Gilbreth, who originated the concepts in the bricklaying trade in the early 20th century. Through the use of motion study techniques, Gilbreth is generally credited with increasing the average number of bricks laid per hour by a factor of 3, even though he was not a bricklayer by trade. When you stop to realize that bricklaying had been carried on for centuries, Gilbreth's accomplishment is even more remarkable.

Motion study Systematic study of the human motions used to perform an operation.

There are a number of different techniques that motion study analysts can use to develop efficient procedures. The most-used techniques are the following:

1. Motion study principles.
2. Analysis of therbligs.
3. Micromotion study.
4. Charts.

Gilbreth's work laid the foundation for the development of **motion study principles,** which are guidelines for designing motion-efficient work procedures. The guidelines are divided into three categories: principles for use of the body, principles for arrangement of the workplace, and principles for the design of tools and equipment. Table 7.5 lists some examples of the principles.

Motion study principles Guidelines for designing motion-efficient work procedures.

In developing work methods that are motion efficient, the analyst tries to

1. Eliminate unnecessary motions.
2. Combine activities.
3. Reduce fatigue.
4. Improve the arrangement of the workplace.
5. Improve the design of tools and equipment.

Therbligs are basic elemental motions. The term *therblig* is Gilbreth spelled backward (except for the *th*). The approach is to break jobs down into basic elements and base improvements on an analysis of these basic elements by eliminating, combining, or rearranging them.

Therbligs Basic elemental motions that make up a job.

Frank Gilbreth was a pioneer in the study of motion. He said, "It is the duty of the educator to apply motion economy to his work." The photo is of a motion efficiency study done in 1914.

Although a complete description of therbligs is outside the scope of this text, a list of some common ones will illustrate the nature of these basic elemental motions:

Search implies hunting for an item with the hands and/or the eyes.

Select means to choose from a group of objects.

Grasp means to take hold of an object.

Hold refers to retention of an object after it has been grasped.

Transport load means movement of an object after hold.

Release load means to deposit the object.

TABLE 7.5
Motion study principles

Source: Adapted from Benjamin W. Niebel, *Motion and Time Study,* 8th ed. Copyright © 1988 Richard D. Irwin, Inc. Used by permission of McGraw-Hill Companies, Inc., pp. 206–207.

A. The use of the human body. Examples:
   1. Both hands should begin and end their basic divisions of accomplishment simultaneously and should not be idle at the same instant, except during rest periods.
   2. The motions made by the hands should be made symmetrically.
   3. Continuous curved motions are preferable to straight-line motions involving sudden and sharp changes in direction.

B. The arrangement and conditions of the workplace. Examples:
   1. Fixed locations for all tools and material should be located to permit the best sequence and to eliminate or reduce the therbligs' search and select.
   2. Gravity bins and drop delivery should reduce reach and move times; wherever possible, ejectors should remove finished parts automatically.

C. The design of tools and equipment. Examples:
   1. All levers, handles, wheels, and other control devices should be readily accessible to the operator and designed to give the best possible mechanical advantage and to utilize the strongest available muscle group.
   2. Parts should be held in position by fixtures.

Some other therbligs are *inspect, position, plan, rest,* and *delay.*

Describing a job using therbligs often takes a substantial amount of work. However, for short, repetitive jobs, therbligs analysis may be justified.

Frank Gilbreth and his wife, Lillian, an industrial psychologist, were also responsible for introducing motion pictures for studying motions, called **micromotion study.** This approach is applied not only in industry but also in many other areas of human endeavor, such as sports and health care. Use of the camera and slow-motion replay enables analysts to study motions that would otherwise be too rapid to see. In addition, the resulting films provide a permanent record that can be referred to, not only for training workers and analysts but also for settling job disputes involving work methods.

Micromotion study Use of motion pictures and slow motion to study motions that otherwise would be too rapid to analyze.

The cost of micromotion study limits its use to repetitive activities, where even minor improvements can yield substantial savings owing to the number of times an operation is repeated, or where other considerations justify its use (e.g., surgical procedures).

Motion study analysts often use charts as tools for analyzing and recording motion studies. Activity charts and process charts such as those described earlier can be quite helpful. In addition, analysts may use a *simo chart* (see Figure 7.6) to study simultaneous motions of the hands. These charts are invaluable in studying operations such as data entry, sewing, surgical and dental procedures, and certain assembly operations.

WORK MEASUREMENT

Job design determines the *content* of a job, and methods analysis determines *how* a job is to be performed. **Work measurement** is concerned with determining the *length of time* it should take to complete the job. Job times are vital inputs for capacity planning, workforce planning, estimating labor costs, scheduling, budgeting, and designing incentive systems. Moreover, from the workers' standpoint, time standards reflect the amount of time it should take to do a given job working under typical conditions. The standards include expected activity time plus allowances for probable delays.

Work measurement Determining how long it should take to do a job.

A **standard time** is the amount of time it should take a qualified worker to complete a specified task, working at a sustainable rate, using given methods, tools and equipment, raw material inputs, and workplace arrangement. Whenever a time standard is developed for a job, it is essential to provide a complete description of the parameters of the job because the actual time to do the job is sensitive to all of these factors; changes in any one of the factors can materially affect time requirements. For instance, changes in product design or changes in job performance brought about by a methods study should trigger a new time study to update the standard time. As a practical matter, though, minor changes are occasionally made that do not justify the expense of restudying the job. Consequently, the standards for many jobs may be slightly inaccurate. Periodic time studies may be used to update the standards.

Standard time The amount of time it should take a qualified worker to complete a specified task, working at a sustainable rate, using given methods, tools and equipment, raw materials, and workplace arrangement.

Organizations develop time standards in a number of different ways. Although some small manufacturers and service organizations rely on subjective estimates of job times, the most commonly used methods of work measurement are (1) stopwatch time study, (2) historical times, (3) predetermined data, and (4) work sampling. The following pages describe each of these techniques in some detail.

Stopwatch Time Study

Stopwatch time study was formally introduced by Frederick Winslow Taylor in the late 19th century. Today it is the most widely used method of work measurement. It is especially appropriate for short, repetitive tasks.

Stopwatch time study is used to develop a time standard based on observations of one worker taken over a number of cycles. That is then applied to the work of all others in the organization who perform the same task. The basic steps in a time study are the following:

Stopwatch time study Development of a time standard based on observations of one worker taken over a number of cycles.

1. Define the task to be studied, and inform the worker who will be studied.
2. Determine the number of cycles to observe.

FIGURE 7.6

A simultaneous motion chart

Source: From Benjamin W. Niebel, *Motion and Time Study,* 8th ed. Copyright © 1988 Richard D. Irwin, Inc. Used by permission of McGraw-Hill Companies, Inc., p. 229.

SIMO CHART

OPERATOR: Ken Reisch
DATE: May 21,
OPERATION: Assembly
PART: Lace Finger
METHOD: Proposed
CHART BY: Joseph Riley

TIME SCALE (winks)	ELEMENT TIME	LEFT-HAND DESCRIPTION	SYMBOL	MOTION CLASS 1 2 3 4 5 5 4 3 2 1	SYMBOL	RIGHT-HAND DESCRIPTION	ELEMENT TIME	TIME SCALE (winks)
4548	12	Reach for finger	RE		RE	Reach for finger	12	4548
4560	19	Grasp finger	G		G	Grasp finger	19	4560
4579	31	Move finger	M		M	Move finger	31	4579
4610	75	Position and release finger	P RL		P RL	Position and release finger	75	4610
4685	15	Reach for clamp	RE		RE	Reach for clamp	15	4685
4700	15	Grasp clamp	G		G	Grasp clamp	15	4700
4715								4715
	12	Grasp assembly	G		G	Grasp assembly	12	
7541	18	Move and release assembly	M RL		M RL	Move and release assembly	18	7541
7559								7559

SUMMARY

%	TIME	LEFT-HAND SUMMARY	SYM.	RIGHT-HAND SUMMARY	TIME	%
8.56	249	Reach	RE	Reach	245	8.4
7.49	218	Grasp	G	Grasp	221	7.6
12.16	354	Move	M	Move	413	14.2
30.47	887	Position	P	Position	1124	38.6
39.33	1145	Use	U	Use	876	30.1
1.03	30	Idle	I	Idle	0	0.0
.96	28	Release	RL	Release	32	1.1
100.0	2911		TOTALS		2911	100.0

3. Time the job, and rate the worker's performance.
4. Compute the standard time.

The analyst who studies the job should be thoroughly familiar with it since it is not unusual for workers to attempt to include extra motions during the study in hope of gaining a standard that allows more time per piece (i.e., the worker will be able to work at a slower pace and still meet the standard). Furthermore, the analyst will need to check that the job is being performed efficiently before setting the time standard.

In most instances, an analyst will break all but very short jobs down into basic elemental motions (e.g., reach, grasp) and obtain times for each element. There are several reasons for this: One is that some elements are not performed in every cycle, and the breakdown enables the analyst to get a better perspective on them. Another is that the worker's proficiency may not be the same for all elements of the job. A third reason is to build a file of elemental times that can be used to set times for other jobs. This use will be described later.

Workers sometimes feel uneasy about being studied and fear changes that might result. The analyst should make an attempt to discuss these things with the worker prior to studying an operation to allay such fears and to enlist the cooperation of the worker.

The number of cycles that must be timed is a function of three things: (1) the variability of observed times, (2) the desired accuracy, and (3) the desired level of confidence for the estimated job time. Very often the desired accuracy is expressed as a percentage of the mean of the observed times. For example, the goal of a time study may be to achieve an estimate that is within 10 percent of the actual mean. The sample size needed to achieve that goal can be determined using this formula:

$$n = \left(\frac{zs}{a\bar{x}}\right)^2 \qquad (7\text{–}1)$$

where

z = Number of normal standard deviations needed for desired confidence

s = Sample standard deviation

a = Desired accuracy percentage

$\bar{x}$ = Sample mean

Typical values of z used in this computation are:[4]

Desired Confidence (%)	z Value
90	1.65
95	1.96
95.5	2.00
98	2.33
99	2.58

Of course, the value of z for any desired confidence can be obtained from the normal table in Appendix B, Table A.

An alternate formula used when the desired accuracy, *e,* is stated as an *amount* (e.g., within one minute of the true mean) instead of a percentage is

$$n = \left(\frac{zs}{e}\right)^2 \qquad (7\text{–}2)$$

where

e = Maximum acceptable amount of time error

To make a preliminary estimate of sample size, it is typical to take a small number of observations (i.e., 10 to 20) and compute values of $\bar{x}$ and s to use in the formula for n. Toward the end of the study, the analyst may want to recompute n using revised estimates of $\bar{x}$ and s based on the increased data available.

Note: These formulas may or may not be used in practice, depending on the person doing the time study. Often, an experienced analyst will rely on his or her judgment in deciding on the number of cycles to time.

[4]Theoretically, a t rather than a z value should be used because the population standard deviation is unknown. However, the use of z is simpler and provides reasonable results when the number of observations is 30 or more, as it generally is. In practice, z is used almost exclusively.

EXAMPLE 1

www.mhhe.com/stevenson11e

A time study analyst wants to estimate the time required to perform a certain job. A preliminary study yielded a mean of 6.4 minutes and a standard deviation of 2.1 minutes. The desired confidence is 95 percent. How many observations will he need (including those already taken) if the desired maximum error is

a. ±10 percent of the sample mean?

b. One-half minute?

SOLUTION

a. $s = 2.1$ minutes $\qquad z = 1.96$

$\bar{x} = 6.4$ minutes $\qquad a = 10\%$

$$n = \left(\frac{zs}{a\bar{x}}\right)^2 = \left(\frac{1.96(2.1)}{.10(6.4)}\right)^2 = 41.36\text{; round up to 42 observations}$$

b. $e = .5$ minute $\quad n = \left(\frac{zs}{e}\right)^2 = \left(\frac{1.96(2.1)}{.5}\right)^2 = 67.77$; round up to 68 observations

Note: When the value of n is noninteger, round up.

Development of a time standard involves computation of three times: the *observed time* (TO), the *normal time* (NT), and the *standard time* (ST).

Observed Time. The observed time is simply the average of the recorded times. Thus,

$$\text{OT} = \frac{\Sigma x_i}{n} \tag{7–3}$$

where

OT = Observed time

Σx_i = Sum of recorded times

n = Number of observations

Note: If a job element does not occur each cycle, its average time should be determined separately and that amount should be included in the observed time, OT.

Normal Time. The normal time is the observed time adjusted for worker performance. It is computed by multiplying the observed time by a *performance rating.* That is,

$$\text{NT} = \text{OT} \times \text{PR} \tag{7–4}$$

where

NT = Normal time

PR = Performance rating

This assumes that a single performance rating has been made for the entire job. If ratings are made on an element-by-element basis, the normal time is obtained by multiplying each element's average time by its performance rating and summing those values:

$$\text{NT} = \Sigma(\bar{x}_j \times \text{PR}_j) \tag{7–5}$$

where

$\bar{x}_j$ = Average time for element j

PR_j = Performance rating for element j

The reason for including this adjustment factor is that the worker being observed may be working at a rate different from a "normal" rate, either to deliberately slow the pace or because his or her natural abilities differ from the norm. For this reason, the observer assigns a performance rating, to adjust the observed times to an "average" pace. A normal rating is 1.00. A performance rating of .9 indicates a pace that is 90 percent of normal, whereas a rating of 1.05 indicates a pace that is slightly faster than normal. For long jobs, each element may be rated; for short jobs, a single rating may be made for an entire cycle.

When assessing performance, the analyst must compare the observed performance to his or her concept of normal. Obviously, there is room for debate about what constitutes normal performance, and performance ratings are sometimes the source of considerable conflict between labor and management. Although no one has been able to suggest a way around these subjective evaluations, sufficient training and periodic *recalibration* of analysts using training films can provide a high degree of consistency in the ratings of different analysts. To avoid any bias, a second analyst may be called in to also do performance ratings. In fact, union shops may require this.

Standard Time. The normal time does not take into account such factors as personal delays (getting a drink of water or going to the restroom), unavoidable delays (machine adjustments and repairs, talking to a supervisor, waiting for materials), or rest breaks. The standard time for a job is the normal time multiplied by an *allowance factor* for these delays.

The standard time is

$$\text{ST} = \text{NT} \times \text{AF} \quad (7\text{–}6)$$

where

ST = Standard time

AF = Allowance factor

Allowances can be based on either job time or time worked (e.g., a workday). If allowances are based on the *job time,* the allowance factor is computed using the following formula:

$$\text{AF}_{\text{job}} = 1 + A, \quad \text{where } A = \text{Allowance percentage based on job time} \quad (7\text{–}7)$$

This is used when different jobs have different allowances. If allowances are based on a percentage of the time worked (i.e., the *workday*), the appropriate formula is

$$\text{AF}_{\text{day}} = \frac{1}{1 - A}, \quad \text{where } A = \text{Allowance percentage based on workday} \quad (7\text{–}8)$$

This is used when jobs are the same or similar and have the same allowance factors.

EXAMPLE 2

Compute the allowance factor for these two cases:

a. The allowance is 20 percent of *job* time.

b. The allowance is 20 percent of *work* time.

SOLUTION

A = .20

a. $\text{AF} = 1 + A = 1.20$, or 120%

b. $\text{AF} = \dfrac{1}{1 - A} = \dfrac{1}{1 - .20} = 1.25$, or 125%

Table 7.6 illustrates some typical allowances. In practice, allowances may be based on the judgment of the time study analyst, work sampling (described later in the chapter), or negotiations between labor and management.

Example 3 illustrates the time study process from observed times to the standard time.

TABLE 7.6 Typical allowance percentages for working conditions

	Percent		Percent
A. Constant allowances:		4. Bad light:	
1. Personal allowance	5	a. Slightly below recommended	0
2. Basic fatigue allowances	4	b. Well below	2
B. Variable allowances:		c. Very inadequate	5
1. Standing allowance	2	5. Atmospheric conditions	
2. Abnormal position allowance:		(heat and humidity)—variable	0–10
a. Slightly awkward	0	6. Close attention:	
b. Awkward (bending)	2	a. Fairly fine work	0
c. Very awkward (lying, stretching)	7	b. Fine or exacting	2
3. Use of force or muscular energy		c. Very fine or very exacting	5
(lifting, pulling, or pushing):		7. Noise level:	
Weight lifted (in pounds):		a. Continuous	0
5	0	b. Intermittent—loud	2
10	1	c. Intermittent—very loud	5
15	2	d. High-pitched—loud	5
20	3	8. Mental strain:	
25	4	a. Fairly complex process	1
30	5	b. Complex or wide span of attention	4
35	7	c. Very complex	8
40	9	9. Monotony:	
45	11	a. Low	0
50	13	b. Medium	1
60	17	c. High	4
70	22	10. Tediousness:	
		a. Rather tedious	0
		b. Tedious	2
		c. Very tedious	5

Source: From Benjamin W. Niebel, *Motion and Time Study,* 8th ed. Copyright © 1988 by Richard D. Irwin, Inc. Used by permission of McGraw-Hill Companies, Inc., p. 416.

EXAMPLE 3

www.mhhe.com/stevenson11e

A time study of an assembly operation yielded the following observed times for one element of the job, for which the analyst gave a performance rating of 1.13 Using an allowance of 20 percent of *job* time, determine the appropriate standard time for this operation.

i Observation	Time, *x* (minutes)	*i* Observation	Time, *x* (minutes)
1	1.12	6	1.18
2	1.15	7	1.14
3	1.16	8	1.14
4	1.12	9	1.19
5	1.15	Total	10.35

$n = 9$ PR $= 1.13$ $A = .20$

SOLUTION

1. $\text{OT} = \frac{\Sigma xi}{n} = \frac{10.35}{9} = 1.15$ minutes.
2. $\text{NT} = \text{OT} \times \text{PR} = 1.15(1.13) = 1.30$ minutes.
3. $\text{ST} = \text{NT} \times (1 + A) = 1.30(1.20) = 1.56$ minutes.

Note: If an abnormally short time has been recorded, it typically would be assumed to be the result of observational error and thus discarded. If one of the observations in Example 3 had been .10, it would have been discarded. However, if an abnormally *long* time has been recorded, the analyst would want to investigate that observation to determine whether some irregularly occurring aspect of the task (e.g., retrieving a dropped tool or part) exists, which should legitimately be factored into the job time.

Despite the obvious benefits that can be derived from work measurement using time study, some limitations also must be mentioned. One limitation is the fact that only those jobs that can be observed can be studied. This precludes most managerial and creative jobs, because these involve mental as well as physical aspects. Also, the cost of the study rules out its use for irregular operations and infrequently occurring jobs. Finally, it disrupts the normal work routine, and workers resent it in many cases.

Standard Elemental Times

Standard elemental times are derived from a firm's own historical time study data. Over the years, a time study department can accumulate a file of elemental times that are common to many jobs. After a while, many elemental times can be simply retrieved from the file, eliminating the need for analysts to go through a complete time study to obtain them.

Standard elemental times Time standards derived from a firm's historical time data.

The procedure for using standard elemental times consists of the following steps:

1. Analyze the job to identify the standard elements.
2. Check the file for elements that have historical times, and record them. Use time study to obtain others, if necessary.
3. Modify the file times if necessary (explained below).
4. Sum the elemental times to obtain the normal time, and factor in allowances to obtain the standard time.

In some cases, the file times may not pertain exactly to a specific task. For instance, standard elemental times might be on file for "move the tool 3 centimeters" and "move the tool 9 centimeters," when the task in question involves a move of 6 centimeters. However, it is often possible to interpolate between values on file to obtain the desired time estimate.

One obvious advantage of this approach is the potential savings in cost and effort created by not having to conduct a complete time study for each job. A second advantage is that there is less disruption of work, again because the analyst does not have to time the worker. A third advantage is that performance ratings do not have to be done; they are generally *averaged* in the file times. The main disadvantage of this approach is that times may not exist for enough standard elements to make it worthwhile, and the file times may be biased or inaccurate.

The method described in the following section is a variation of this approach, which helps avoid some of these problems.

Predetermined Time Standards

Predetermined time standards involve the use of published data on standard elemental times. A commonly used system is *methods-time measurement* (MTM), which was developed in the late 1940s by the Methods Engineering Council. The MTM tables are based on extensive research of basic elemental motions and times. To use this approach, the analyst must divide the job into its basic elements (reach, move, turn, disengage), measure the distances involved (if applicable), rate the difficulty of the element, and then refer to the appropriate table of data to obtain the time for that element. The standard time for the job is obtained by adding the times for all of the basic elements. Times of the basic elements are measured in time measurement units (TMUs); one TMU equals .0006 minute. One minute of work may cover quite a few basic elements; a typical job may involve several hundred or more of these basic elements. The analyst needs a considerable amount of skill to adequately describe the operation and develop realistic time estimates. Table 7.7 presents a portion of the MTM tables, to give you an idea of the kind of information they provide.

Predetermined time standards Published data based on extensive research to determine standard elemental times.

TABLE 7.7 A portion of the MTM tables

Distance Moved (inches)	TIME (TMU) A	B	C	Hand in Motion B	WEIGHT ALLOWANCE Weight (pounds) up to:	Dynamic Factor	Static Constant TMU	Case and Description
3/4 or less	2.0	2.0	2.0	1.7				
1	2.5	2.9	3.4	2.3	2.5	1.00	0	
2	3.6	4.6	5.2	2.9				
3	4.9	5.7	6.7	3.6	7.5	1.06	2.2	**A. Move object to other hand or against stop.**
4	6.1	6.9	8.0	4.3				
5	7.3	8.0	9.2	5.0	12.5	1.11	3.9	
6	8.1	8.9	10.3	5.7				
7	8.9	9.7	11.1	6.5	17.5	1.17	5.6	
8	9.7	10.6	11.8	7.2				
9	10.5	11.5	12.7	7.9	22.5	1.22	7.4	
10	11.3	12.2	13.5	8.6				**B. Move object to approximate or indefinite location.**
12	12.9	13.4	15.2	10.0	27.5	1.28	9.1	
14	14.4	14.6	16.9	11.4				
16	16.0	15.8	18.7	12.8	32.5	1.33	10.8	
18	17.6	17.0	20.4	14.2				
20	19.2	18.2	22.1	15.6	37.5	1.39	12.5	
22	20.8	19.4	23.8	17.0				
24	22.4	20.6	25.5	18.4	42.5	1.44	14.3	**C. Move object to exact location.**
26	24.0	21.8	27.3	19.8				
28	25.5	23.1	29.0	21.2	47.5	1.50	16.0	
30	27.1	24.3	30.7	22.7				
Additional	0.8	0.6	0.85		TMU per inch over 30 inches			

Source: Excerpt from MTM Table.

A high level of skill is required to generate a predetermined time standard. Analysts generally take training or certification courses to develop the necessary skills to do this kind of work.

Among the advantages of predetermined time standards are the following:

1. They are based on large numbers of workers under controlled conditions.
2. The analyst is not required to rate performance in developing the standard.
3. There is no disruption of the operation.
4. Standards can be established even before a job is done.

Although proponents of predetermined standards claim that the approach provides much better accuracy than stopwatch studies, not everyone agrees with that claim. Some argue that many activity times are too specific to a given operation to be generalized from published data. Others argue that different analysts perceive elemental activity breakdowns in different ways, and that this adversely affects the development of times and produces varying time estimates among analysts. Still others claim that analysts differ on the degree of difficulty they assign a given task and thereby obtain different time standards.

Work sampling Technique for estimating the proportion of time that a worker or machine spends on various activities and the idle time.

Work Sampling

Work sampling is a technique for estimating the proportion of time that a worker or machine spends on various activities and the idle time.

Unlike time study, work sampling does not require timing an activity, nor does it even involve continuous observation of the activity. Instead, an observer makes brief observations of a worker or machine at random intervals and simply notes the nature of the activity. For example, a machine may be busy or idle; a secretary may be typing, filing, talking on the telephone, and so on; and a carpenter may be carrying supplies, taking measurements, cutting wood, and so on. The resulting data are *counts* of the number of times each category of activity or nonactivity was observed.

Although work sampling is occasionally used to set time standards, its two primary uses are in (1) ratio-delay studies, which concern the percentage of a worker's time that involves unavoidable delays or the proportion of time a machine is idle, and (2) analysis of nonrepetitive jobs. In a ratio-delay study, a hospital administrator, for example, might want to estimate the percentage of time that a certain piece of X-ray equipment is not in use. In a nonrepetitive job, such as secretarial work or maintenance, it can be important to establish the percentage of time an employee spends doing various tasks.

Nonrepetitive jobs typically involve a broader range of skills than repetitive jobs, and workers in these jobs are often paid on the basis of the highest skill involved. Therefore, it is important to determine the proportion of time spent on the high-skill level. For example, a secretary may do word processing, file, answer the telephone, and do other routine office work. If the secretary spends a high percentage of time filing instead of doing word processing, the compensation will be lower than for a secretary who spends a high percentage of time doing word processing. Work sampling can be used to verify those percentages and can therefore be an important tool in developing the job description. In addition, work sampling can be part of a program for validation of job content that is needed for "bona fide occupational qualifications"—that is, advertised jobs requiring the skills that are specified.

Work sampling estimates include some degree of error. Hence, it is important to treat work sampling estimates as *approximations* of the actual proportion of time devoted to a given activity. The goal of work sampling is to obtain an estimate that provides a specified confidence not differing from the true value by more than a specified error. For example, a hospital administrator might request an estimate of X-ray idle time that will provide a 95 percent confidence of being within 4 percent of the actual percentage. Hence, work sampling is designed to produce a value, $\hat{p}$, which estimates the true proportion, p, within some allowable error, e: $\hat{p} \pm e$. The variability associated with sample estimates of p tends to be approximately normal for large sample sizes. The amount of maximum probable error is a function of both the sample size and the desired level of confidence.

For large samples, the maximum error percent e can be computed using the following formula:

$$e = z\sqrt{\frac{\hat{p}(1 - \hat{p})}{n}} \tag{7–9}$$

where

z = Number of standard deviations needed to achieve desired confidence

$\hat{p}$ = Sample proportion (the number of occurrences divided by the sample size)

n = Sample size

In most instances, management will specify the desired confidence level and amount of allowable error, and the analyst will be required to determine a sample size sufficient to obtain these results. The appropriate value for n can be determined by solving Formula 7–9 for n, which yields

$$n = \left(\frac{z}{e}\right)^2 \hat{p}(1 - \hat{p}) \tag{7–10}$$

EXAMPLE 4

www.mhhe.com/stevenson11e

The manager of a small supermarket chain wants to estimate the proportion of time stock clerks spend making price changes on previously marked merchandise. The manager wants a 98 percent confidence that the resulting estimate will be within 5 percent of the true value. What sample size should she use?

$e = .05 \quad z = 2.33$ (see p. 303) $\hat{p}$ is unknown

SOLUTION

When no sample estimate of p is available, a preliminary estimate of sample size can be obtained using $\hat{p} = .50$. After 20 or so observations, a new estimate of $\hat{p}$ can be obtained from those observations and a revised value of n computed using the new $\hat{p}$. It would be prudent to recompute the value of n at two or three points during the study to obtain a better indication of the necessary sample size. Thus, the initial estimate of n is

$$n = \left(\frac{2.33}{.05}\right)^2 .50(1 - .50) = 542.89, \text{ or } 543 \text{ observations}$$

Suppose that, in the first 20 observations, stock clerks were found to be changing prices twice, making $\hat{p} = 2/20 = .10$. The revised estimate of n at that point would be

$$n = \left(\frac{2.33}{.05}\right)^2 .10(1 - .10) = 195.44, \text{ or } 196 \text{ observations}$$

Suppose a second check is made after a total of 100 observations, and $\hat{p} = .11$ at this point (including the initial 20 observations). Recomputing n yields

$$n = \left(\frac{2.33}{.05}\right)^2 .11(.89) = 212.60, \text{ or } 213 \text{ observations}$$

Note: As before, if the resulting value of n is noninteger, round *up.*

Perhaps the manager might make one more check to settle on a final value for n. If the computed value of n is less than the number of observations already taken, sampling would be terminated at that point.

Determining the sample size is only one part of work sampling. The overall procedure consists of the following steps:

1. Clearly identify the worker(s) or machine(s) to be studied.
2. Notify the workers and supervisors of the purpose of the study to avoid arousing suspicions.
3. Compute an initial estimate of sample size using a preliminary estimate of p, if available (e.g., from analyst experience or past data). Otherwise, use $\hat{p} = .50$.
4. Develop a random observation schedule.
5. Begin taking observations. Recompute the required sample size several times during the study.
6. Determine the estimated proportion of time spent on the specified activity.

Careful problem definition can prevent mistakes such as observing the wrong worker or wrong activity. It is also important to obtain random observations to get valid results.

Observations must be spread out over a period of time so that a true indication of variability is obtained. If observations are bunched too closely in time, the behaviors observed during that time may not genuinely reflect typical performance.

Random number table Table consisting of unordered sequences of numbers, used to determine random observation schedules.

Determination of a random observation schedule involves the use of a **random number table** (see Table 7.8), which consists of *unordered sequences* of numbers (i.e., random). Use of these tables enables the analyst to incorporate randomness into the observation schedule. Numbers obtained from the table can be used to identify observation times for

TABLE 7.8
Portion of a random number table

	1	2	3	4	5	6
1	6912	7264	2801	8901	4627	8387
2	3491	1192	0575	7547	2093	4617
3	4715	2486	2776	2664	3856	0064
4	1632	1546	1950	1844	1123	1908
5	8510	7209	0938	2376	0120	4237
6	3950	1328	7343	6083	2108	2044
7	7871	7752	0521	8511	3956	3957
8	2716	1396	7354	0249	7728	8818
9	2935	8259	9912	3761	4028	9207
10	8533	9957	9585	1039	2159	2438
11	0508	1640	2768	4666	9530	3352
12	2951	0131	4359	3095	4421	3018

a study. Any size number (i.e., any number of digits read as one number) can be obtained from the table. The digits are in groups of four for convenience only. The basic idea is to obtain numbers from the table and to convert each one so that it corresponds to an observation time. There are a number of ways to accomplish this. In the approach used here, we will obtain three sets of numbers from the table for each observation: the first set will correspond to the *day,* the second to the *hour,* and the third to the *minute* when the observation is to be made. The number of digits necessary for any set will relate to the number of days in the study, the number of hours per day, and minutes per hour. For instance, if the study covers 47 days, a two-digit number will be needed; if the activity is performed for eight hours per day, a one-digit number will be needed for hours. Of course, since each hour has 60 minutes, a two-digit number will be needed for minutes. Thus, we need a two-digit number for the day, a one-digit number for the hour, and a two-digit number for minutes. A study requiring observations over a seven-day period in an office that works nine hours per day needs one-digit numbers for days, one-digit numbers for hours, and two-digit numbers for minutes.

Suppose that three observations will be made in the last case (i.e., seven days, nine hours, 60 minutes). We might begin by determining the days on which observations will be made, then the hours, and finally the minutes. Let's begin with the first row in the random number table and read across: The first number is 6, which indicates day 6. The second number is 9. Since it exceeds the number of days in the study, it is simply ignored. The third number is 1, indicating day 1, and the next is 2, indicating day 2. Hence, observations will be made on days 6, 1, and 2. Next we determine the hours. Suppose we read the second row of column 1, again obtaining one-digit numbers. We find

$$3\ (=\text{3rd hour}), 4\ (=\text{4th hour}), 9\ (=\text{9th hour})$$

Moving to the next row and reading two-digit numbers, we find

$$47\ (=\text{47th minute}), 15\ (=\text{15th minute}), 24\ (=\text{24th minute})$$

Combining these results yields the following:

Day	Hour	Minute
6	3	47
1	4	15
2	9	24

This means that on day 6 of the study an observation is to be made during the 47th minute of the 3rd hour; on day 1, during the 15th minute of the 4th hour; and on day 2, during the 24th minute of the 9th hour. For simplicity, these times can be put in chronological order by day. Thus,

Day	Hour	Minute
1	4	15
2	9	24
6	3	47

A complete schedule of observations might appear as follows, after all numbers have been arranged in chronological order, assuming 10 observations per day for two days:

DAY 1

Observation	Time	Busy (✓)	Idle (✓)
1	8:15		
2	9:24		
3	9:02		
4	9:31		
5	9:48		
6	10:05		
7	10:20		
8	11:02		
9	1:13		
10	3:55		

DAY 2

Observation	Time	Busy (✓)	Idle (✓)
1	8:04		
2	9:15		
3	9:24		
4	9:35		
5	10:12		
6	10:27		
7	10:38		
8	10:58		
9	11:50		
10	1:14		

The general procedure for using a random number table is to read the numbers in some sequence (across rows, down or up columns), discarding any that lack correspondence. It is important to vary the starting point from one study to the next to avoid taking observations at the same times, because workers will quickly learn the times that observations are made, and the random feature would be lost. One way to choose a starting point is to use the serial number on a dollar bill to select a starting point.

In sum, the procedure for identifying random times at which to make work sampling observations involves the following steps:

1. Determine the number of days in the study and the number of hours per day. This will indicate the required number of digits for days and hours.
2. Obtain the necessary number of sets for *days,* ignoring any sets that exceed the number of days.
3. Repeat step 2 for *hours.*
4. Repeat step 2 for *minutes.*
5. Link the days, hours, and minutes in the order they were obtained.
6. Place the observation times in chronological order.

Table 7.9 presents a comparison of work sampling and time study. It suggests that a work sampling approach to determining job times is less formal and less detailed, and best suited to nonrepetitive jobs.

TABLE 7.9
Work sampling compared with stopwatch time study

Advantages
1. Observations are spread out over a period of time, making results less susceptible to short-term fluctuations.
2. There is little or no disruption of work.
3. Workers are less resentful.
4. Studies are less costly and less time-consuming, and the skill requirements of the analyst are much less.
5. Studies can be interrupted without affecting the results.
6. Many different studies can be conducted simultaneously.
7. No timing device is required.
8. It is well suited for nonrepetitive tasks.
Disadvantages
1. There is much less detail on the elements of a job.
2. Workers may alter their work patterns when they spot the observer, thereby invalidating the results.
3. In many cases, there is no record of the method used by the worker.
4. Observers may fail to adhere to a random schedule of observations.
5. It is not well suited for short, repetitive tasks.
6. Much time may be required to move from one workplace to another and back to satisfy the randomness requirement.

OPERATIONS STRATEGY

It is important for management to make design of work systems a key element of its operations strategy. Despite the major advances in computers and operations technology, people are still the heart of a business; they can make or break it, regardless of the technology used. Technology is important, of course, but technology alone is not enough.

The topics described in this chapter all have an impact on productivity. Although they lack the glamour of high tech, they are essential to the fundamentals of work design.

Workers can be a valuable source of insight and creativity because they actually perform the jobs and are closest to the problems that arise. All too often, managers overlook contributions and potential contributions of employees, sometimes from ignorance and sometimes from a false sense of pride. Union–management differences are also a factor. More and more, though, companies are attempting to develop a spirit of cooperation between employees and managers.

In the same vein, an increasing number of companies are focusing attention on improving the quality of work life and instilling pride and respect among workers. Many organizations are reaping surprising gains through worker *empowerment,* giving workers more say over their jobs.

SUMMARY

The design of work systems involves quality of work life considerations as well as job design, methods analysis, and work measurement.

Quality of work life includes relationships with managers and co-workers, working conditions, and compensation. Job design is concerned with job content and work methods. In the past, job design tended to emphasize efficiency. More recently, emphasis has expanded to include behavioral considerations and worker satisfaction. Current concerns about productivity have thrust job design into the limelight. However, the jobs usually associated with high productivity are often the same jobs that are the greatest source of worker dissatisfaction, creating somewhat of a paradox for job designers.

TABLE 7.10
Summary of formulas

Time Study		Work Sampling	
A. Sample size		A. Maximum error	
$n = \left(\frac{zs}{a\bar{x}}\right)^2$	(7–1)	$e = z\sqrt{\frac{\hat{p}(1-\hat{p})}{n}}$	(7–9)
$n = \left(\frac{zs}{e}\right)^2$	(7–2)	B. Sample size	
		$n = \left(\frac{z}{e}\right)^2 \hat{p}(1-\hat{p})$	(7–10)
B. Observed time			
$\text{OT} = \frac{\Sigma x_i}{n}$	(7–3)		
C. Normal time			
$\text{NT} = \text{TO} \times \text{PR}$	(7–4)		
$\text{NT} = \Sigma(\bar{x}_j \times \text{PR}_j)$	(7–5)		
D. Standard time			
$\text{ST} = \text{NT} \times \text{AF}$	(7–6)		
E. Allowance factor			
$\text{AF}_{\text{job}} = 1 + A$	(7–7)		
$\text{AF}_{\text{day}} = \frac{1}{1-A}$	(7–8)		

Symbols:

a = Allowable error as percentage of average time
A = Allowance percentage
AF = Allowance factor
e = Maximum acceptable amount of time error
n = Number of observations needed
NT = Normal time
OT = Observed, or average, time
$\hat{p}$ = Sample proportion
PR = Performance rating
s = Standard deviation of observed times
ST = Standard time
x = Sample mean
x_i = Time for ith observation ($i = 1, 2, 3, \ldots, n$)
z = Number of standard deviations needed to achieve desired confidence

Analysts often use methods analysis and motion study techniques to develop the "efficiency" aspects of jobs, but these do not directly address behavioral aspects. Nonetheless, they are an important part of job design. Working conditions are also a notable aspect of job design, not only because of the behavioral and efficiency factors but also because of concern for the health and safety of workers.

Work measurement is concerned with specifying the length of time needed to complete a job. Such information is vital for personnel planning, cost estimating, budgeting, scheduling, and worker compensation. Commonly used approaches include stopwatch time study and predetermined times. A related technique is work sampling, which can also be used to obtain data on activity times. More commonly, work sampling is used to estimate the proportion of time a worker spends on a certain aspect of the job. Table 7.10 provides a summary of the formulas used in time studies and work sampling.

Organizations can choose from a variety of compensation plans. It is important to do so carefully, for compensation is key to both the worker and the organization, and, once adopted, it is usually difficult to substantially change a compensation plan.

KEY POINTS

1. Work design focuses on the core of operations.
2. Job design determines job content; methods analysis and motion study determine how a job is to be performed; and work measurement determines the time it should take to do a job.
3. The information provided by job design, methods analysis, motion study, and time standards is extremely valuable for process and productivity improvement.
4. Quality of work life can be a major factor in maintaining a productive workforce.

KEY TERMS

SOLVED PROBLEMS

Problem 1

A time study analyst timed an assembly operation for 30 cycles, and then computed the average time per cycle, which was 18.75 minutes. The analyst assigned a performance rating of .96, and decided that an appropriate allowance was 15 percent. Assume the allowance factor is based on the *workday.* Determine the following: the observed time (TO), the normal time (NT), and the standard time (ST).

Solution

$$\text{OT} = \text{Average time} = 18.75 \text{ minutes}$$

$$\text{NT} = \text{OT} \times \text{Performance rating} = 18.75 \text{ minutes} \times .96 = 18 \text{ minutes}$$

$$\text{AF} = \frac{1}{1 - A} = \frac{1}{1 - .15} = 1.176$$

$$\text{ST} = \text{NT} \times \text{AF} = 18 \times 1.176 = 21.17 \text{ minutes}$$

Problem 2

A time study analyst wants to estimate the number of observations that will be needed to achieve a specified maximum error, with a confidence of 95.5 percent. A preliminary study yielded a mean of 5.2 minutes and a standard deviation of 1.1 minutes. Determine the total number of observations needed for these two cases:

a. A maximum error of ±6 percent of the sample mean.

b. A maximum error of .40 minute.

Solution

a. $x = 5.2$ minutes $\quad z = 2.00$ for 95.5, from p. 303
$s = 1.1$ minutes $\quad a = .06$

$$n = \left(\frac{zs}{ax}\right)^2 = \left(\frac{2.00(1.1)}{.06(5.2)}\right)^2 = 49.72; \text{ round to 50 observations}$$

b. $e = .40$

$$n = \left(\frac{zs}{e}\right)^2 = \left(\frac{2.00(1.1)}{.40}\right)^2 = 30.25; \text{ round to 31 observations}$$

Problem 3

Work sampling. An analyst has been asked to prepare an estimate of the proportion of time that a turret lathe operator spends adjusting the machine, with a 90 percent confidence level. Based on previous experience, the analyst believes the proportion will be approximately 30 percent.

a. If the analyst uses a sample size of 400 observations, what is the maximum possible error that will be associated with the estimate?

b. What sample size would the analyst need in order to have the maximum error be no more than ±5 percent?

Solution

$\hat{p} = .30 \quad z = 1.65$ for 90 percent confidence from p. 303

a. $$e = z\sqrt{\frac{\hat{p}(1-\hat{p})}{n}} = 1.65\sqrt{\frac{.3(.7)}{400}} = .038$$

b. $$n = \left(\frac{z}{e}\right)^2 \hat{p}(1-\hat{p}) = \left(\frac{1.65}{.05}\right)^2 (.3)(.7) = 228.69, \text{ or } 229$$

DISCUSSION AND REVIEW QUESTIONS

1. What is job design, and why is it important?
2. What are some of the main advantages and disadvantages of specialization from a management perspective? From a worker's perspective?
3. a. Contrast the meanings of the terms *job enlargement* and *job enrichment.*
   b. What is the purpose of approaches such as job enlargement and job enrichment?
4. a. What is ergonomics and why is it important in job design?
   b. Explain how it can relate to quality of work life.
5. Explain the term *knowledge-based pay system.*
6. What are self-directed work teams? What are some potential benefits of using these teams?
7. Some Japanese firms have a policy of rotating their managers among different managerial jobs. In contrast, American managers are more likely to specialize in a certain area (e.g., finance or operations). Discuss the advantages and disadvantages of each of these approaches. Which do you prefer? Why?
8. What are motion study principles? How are they classified?
9. Name some reasons why methods analyses are needed. How is methods analysis linked to productivity improvements?
10. How are devices such as flow process charts and worker-machine charts useful?
11. What is a time standard? What factors must be taken into account when developing standards?
12. What are the main uses of time study information?
13. Could performance rating be avoided by studying a group of workers and averaging their times? Explain briefly.
14. If an average worker could be identified, what advantage would there be in using that person for a time study? What are some reasons why an average worker might not be studied?
15. What are the main limitations of time study?
16. Comment on the following: "At any given instant, the standard times for many jobs will not be strictly correct."
    a. Why is this so?
    b. Does this mean that those standards are useless? Explain.
17. Why do workers sometimes resent time studies?
18. What are the key advantages and disadvantages of:
    a. Time-based pay plans?
    b. Incentive plans?
19. What is work sampling? How does it differ from time study?

TAKING STOCK

1. What are the trade-offs in the following?
   a. Using self-directed teams instead of a more conventional approach with occasional use of teams.
   b. Deciding how often to update standard times due to minor changes in work methods.
   c. Choosing between time study and work sampling for work measurement.
2. Who uses the results of work measurement in an organization, and how do they use them?
3. In what ways does technology have an impact on job design?

CRITICAL THINKING EXERCISE

1. Healthy Hots, a fast-food restaurant that offers heart-healthy food, is experiencing several difficulties with operations. Although customers like the idea of heart-healthy foods, and surveys indicate that customers find the food to be tasty and appealing, business has fallen off in recent weeks. At this point, the restaurant is not making a profit. Customers have complained about slow service, and employee turnover is high.

   Explain briefly how techniques described in this chapter could be used to improve operations. Be specific about which techniques could be used, how they could be used, and why you think those techniques would be helpful.
2. Identify an unethical behavior for each of the five major topics in this chapter, and indicate which ethical principle (see Chapter 1) each violates.

PROBLEMS

1. An analyst has timed a metal-cutting operation for 50 cycles. The average time per cycle was 10.40 minutes, and the standard deviation was 1.20 minutes for a worker with a performance rating of 125 percent. Assume an allowance of 16 percent of job time. Find the standard time for this operation.
2. A job was timed for 60 cycles and had an average of 1.2 minutes per piece. The performance rating was 95 percent, and workday allowances are 10 percent. Determine each of the following:
   a. Observed time.
   b. Normal time.
   c. Standard time.
3. A time study was conducted on a job that contains four elements. The observed times and performance ratings for six cycles are shown in the following table.

		OBSERVATIONS (minutes per cycle)					
Element	**Performance Rating**	**1**	**2**	**3**	**4**	**5**	**6**
1	90%	0.44	0.50	0.43	0.45	0.48	0.46
2	85	1.50	1.54	1.47	1.51	1.49	1.52
3	110	0.84	0.89	0.77	0.83	0.85	0.80
4	100	1.10	1.14	1.08	1.20	1.16	1.26

   a. Determine the average cycle time for each element.
   b. Find the normal time for each element.
   c. Assuming an allowance factor of 15 percent of job time, compute the standard time for this job.
4. Given these observed times (in minutes) for four elements of a job, determine the observed time (OT) for each element. *Note:* The second element only occurs every other cycle.

	CYCLE					
Element	**1**	**2**	**3**	**4**	**5**	**6**
1	4.1	4.0	4.2	4.1	4.1	4.1
2	—	1.5	—	1.6	—	1.4
3	3.2	3.2	3.3	3.2	3.3	3.3
4	2.7	2.8	2.7	2.8	2.8	2.8

5. Given these observed times (in minutes) for five elements of a job, determine the observed time (OT) for each element. Note: Some of the elements occur only periodically.

	CYCLE					
Element	**1**	**2**	**3**	**4**	**5**	**6**
1	2.1	2.0	2.2	2.1	2.1	—
2	—	1.1	—	1.0	—	1.2
3	3.4	3.5	3.3	3.5	3.4	3.3
4	4.0	—	—	4.2	—	—
5	1.4	1.4	1.5	1.5	1.5	1.4

6. Using Table 7.6 (on p. 306), develop an allowance percentage for a job element that requires the worker to lift a weight of 10 pounds while (1) standing in a slightly awkward position, (2) in light that is slightly below recommended standards, and (3) with intermittent loud noises occurring. The monotony for this element is high. Include a personal allowance of 5 percent and a basic fatigue allowance of 4 percent of job time.
7. A worker-machine operation was found to involve 3.3 minutes of machine time per cycle in the course of 40 cycles of stopwatch study. The worker's time averaged 1.9 minutes per cycle, and the worker was given a rating of 120 percent (machine rating is 100 percent). Midway through the study, the worker took a 10-minute rest break. Assuming an allowance factor of 12 percent of work time, determine the standard time for this job.

8. A recently negotiated union contract allows workers in a shipping department 24 minutes for rest, 10 minutes for personal time, and 14 minutes for delays for each four hours worked. A time study analyst observed a job that is performed continuously and found an average time of 6.0 minutes per cycle for a worker she rated at 95 percent. What standard time is applicable for that operation?

9. The data in the table below represent time study observations for a woodworking operation.

a. Based on the observations, determine the standard time for the operation, assuming an allowance of 15 percent of job time.

b. How many observations would be needed to estimate the mean time for element 2 within 1 percent of its true value with a 95.5 percent confidence?

c. How many observations would be needed to estimate the mean time for element 2 within .01 minute of its true value with a 95.5 percent confidence?

		OBSERVATIONS (minutes per cycle)					
Element	Performance Rating	1	2	3	4	5	6
1	110%	1.20	1.17	1.16	1.22	1.24	1.15
2	115	0.83	0.87	0.78	0.82	0.85	1.32*
3	105	0.58	0.53	0.52	0.59	0.60	0.54

*Unusual delay, disregard time.

10. How many observations should a time study analyst plan for in an operation that has a standard deviation of 1.5 minutes per piece if the goal is to estimate the mean time per piece to within .4 minute with a confidence of 95.5 percent?

11. How many work cycles should be timed to estimate the average cycle time to within 2 percent of the sample mean with a confidence of 99 percent if a pilot study yielded these times (minutes): 5.2, 5.5, 5.8, 5.3, 5.5, and 5.1? The standard deviation is .253 minutes per cycle.

12. In an initial survey designed to estimate the percentage of time air-express cargo loaders are idle, an analyst found that loaders were idle in 6 of the 50 observations.

a. What is the estimated percentage of idle time?

b. Based on the initial results, approximately how many observations would you require to estimate the actual percentage of idle time to within 5 percent with a confidence of 95 percent?

13. A job in an insurance office involves telephone conversations with policyholders. The office manager estimates that about half of the employee's time is spent on the telephone. How many observations are needed in a work sampling study to estimate that time percentage to within 6 percent and have a confidence of 98 percent?

14. Design a schedule of work sampling observations in which eight observations are made during one eight-hour day. Using Table 7.8, read the *last digit* going down column 4 for hours (e.g., 1 7 4 4 6 . . .), and read across row 3 from left to right in sets of two for minutes (e.g., 47 15 24 86 . . .). Arrange the times chronologically.

15. The manager of a large office intends to conduct a work sampling of the time the staff spends on the telephone. The observations will be taken over a period of 50 workdays. The office is open five days a week for eight hours a day. Although the study will consist of 200 random observations, in this problem you will be asked to determine times for 11 observations. Use random numbers from Table 7.8.

a. Determine times for 11 observations. For days, read sets of two-digit numbers going across row 4 from left to right (e.g., 16 32 15 46 . . .), and do the same in row 5.

b. For hours, read one-digit numbers going *down,* using the first digit of column 1 (e.g., 6 4 3 1 . . .).

c. For minutes, read two-digit numbers going *up* column 4 using the first two digits (e.g., 30 46 10 . . .), and then repeat for the second two digits going *up* column 4 (e.g., 95 66 39 . . .).

d. Arrange the combinations chronologically by day, hour, and minute.

e. Assume March 1 is a Monday and that there are no holidays in March, April, or May.

Convert your observation days to dates in March, April, and May.

16. A work sampling study is to be conducted on rush-hour traffic (4:00 p.m. to 7:00 p.m.) five days per week. The study will encompass 40 days. Determine the day, hour, and minute for 10 observations using the following procedure and Table 7.8:

a. Read two-digit numbers going *down* the first two digits of column 5 (e.g., 46 20 38 . . .), and then down the second two digits of that column (e.g., 27 93 56 . . .) for days.

b. For hours, read one-digit numbers going from left to right across row 1 and then across row 2. (Read only 4s, 5s, and 6s.)

c. For minutes, read two-digit numbers going *down* column 6, first using the *last* two digits (e.g., 87 17 64 . . .), and, after exhausting those numbers, repeat using the first two digits of that column (e.g., 83 46 00 19 . . .).

Arrange your times chronologically by day, then hour, and then minute.

Making Hotplates

CASE

Edgar F. Huse

A group of 10 workers were responsible for assembling hotplates (instruments for heating solutions to a given temperature) for hospital and medical laboratory use. A number of different models of hotplates were being manufactured. Some had a vibrating device so that the solution could be mixed while being heated. Others heated only test tubes. Still others could heat solutions in a variety of different containers.

With the appropriate small tools, each worker assembled part of a hotplate. The partially completed hotplate was placed on a moving belt, to be carried from one assembly station to the next. When the hotplate was completed, an inspector would check it over to ensure that it was working properly. Then the last worker would place it in a specially prepared cardboard box for shipping.

The assembly line had been carefully balanced by industrial engineers, who had used a time and motion study to break the job down into subassembly tasks, each requiring about three minutes to accomplish. The amount of time calculated for each subassembly had also been "balanced" so that the task performed by each worker was supposed to take almost exactly the same amount of time. The workers were paid a straight hourly rate.

However, there were some problems. Morale seemed to be low, and the inspector was finding a relatively high percentage of badly assembled hotplates. Controllable rejects—those "caused" by the operator rather than by faulty materials—were running about 23 percent.

After discussing the situation, management decided to try something new. The workers were called together and asked if they would like to build the hotplates individually. The workers decided they would like to try this approach, provided they could go back to the old program if the new one did not work well. After several days of training, each worker began to assemble the entire hotplate.

The change was made at about the middle of the year. Productivity climbed quickly. By the end of the year, it had leveled off at about 84 percent higher than during the first half of the year, although no other changes had been made in the department or its personnel. Controllable rejects had dropped from 23 percent to 1 percent during the same period. Absenteeism had dropped from 8 percent to less than 1 percent. The workers had responded positively to the change, and their morale was higher. As one person put it, "Now, it is *my* hotplate." Eventually, the reject rate dropped so low that all routine final inspection was done by the assembly workers themselves. The full-time inspector was transferred to another job in the organization.

Questions

1. What changes in the work situation might account for the increase in productivity and the decrease in controllable rejects?
2. What might account for the drop in absenteeism and the increase in morale?
3. What were the major changes in the situation? Which changes were under the control of the manager? Which were controlled by workers?
4. What might happen if the workers went back to the old assembly line method?

SELECTED BIBLIOGRAPHY AND FURTHER READINGS

Barnes, Ralph M. *Motion and Time Study: Design and Measurement of Work.* 8th ed. New York: John Wiley & Sons, 1980.

Bridger, R. S. *Introduction to Ergonomics.* New York: McGraw-Hill, 1995.

Carlisle, Brian. "Job Design Implications for Operations Managers." *International Journal of Operations and Production Management,* no. 3 (1983), pp. 40–48.

Cascio, Wayne. *Managing Human Resources: Productivity, Quality of Work Life. Profits.* 6th ed. New York: McGraw-Hill, 2003.

Cunningham, J. Barton, and Ted Eberle. "A Guide to Job Enrichment and Redesign." *Personnel,* February 1990, pp. 56–61.

Jorgensen, Karen. *Pay for Results: A Practical Guide to Effective Employee Compensation.* Santa Monica, CA: Merritt, 1996.

Meyers, Fred E. *Motion and Time Study for Lean Manufacturing.* 2nd ed. Upper Saddle River, NJ: Prentice Hall, 1999.

Mundel, Marvin E., and David L. Danner. *Motion and Time Study: Improving Productivity.* 7th ed. Englewood Cliffs, NJ: Prentice Hall, 1994.

Neibel, Benjamin, and Andris Freivalds. *Methods, Standards, and Work Design.* 10th ed. New York: McGraw-Hill, 1999.

SUPPLEMENT TO CHAPTER 7

Learning Curves

LEARNING OBJECTIVES

After completing this supplement, you should be able to:

1 Explain the concept of a learning curve.

2 Make time estimates based on learning curves.

3 List and briefly describe some of the main applications of learning curves.

4 Outline some of the cautions and criticisms of learning curves.

5 Estimate learning rates from data on job times.

SUPPLEMENT OUTLINE

Learning is usually occurring when humans are involved; this is a basic consideration in the design of work systems. It is important to be able to predict how learning will affect task times and costs. This supplement addresses those issues.

THE CONCEPT OF LEARNING CURVES

Human performance of activities typically shows improvement when the activities are done on a repetitive basis: The time required to perform a task decreases with increasing repetitions. *Learning curves* summarize this phenomenon. The degree of improvement and the number of tasks needed to realize the major portion of the improvement is a function of the task being done. If the task is short and somewhat routine, only a modest amount of improvement is likely to occur, and it generally occurs during the first few repetitions. If the task is fairly complex and has a longer duration, improvements will occur over a longer interval (i.e., a larger number of repetitions). Therefore, learning factors have little relevance for planning or scheduling routine activities, but they do have relevance for new or complex repetitive activities.

FIGURE 7S.1 The learning effect: Time per repetition decreases as the number of repetitions increases

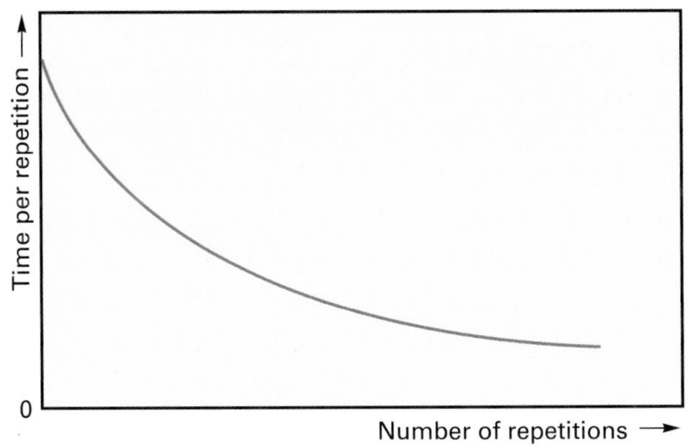

FIGURE 7S.2 Improvements may create a scallop effect in the curve

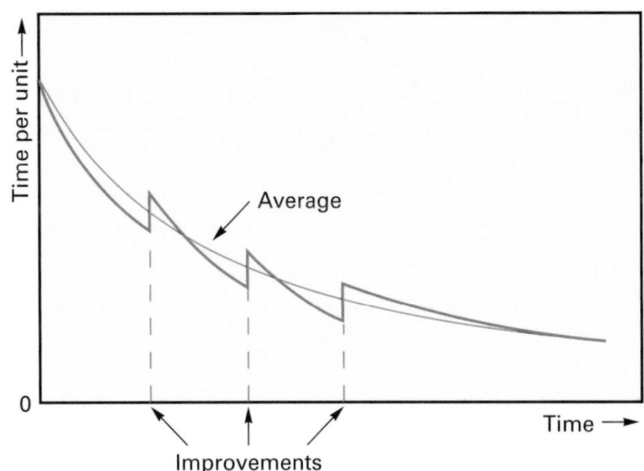

Figure 7S.1 illustrates the basic relationship between increasing repetitions and a decreasing time per repetition. It should be noted that the curve will never touch the horizontal axis; that is, the time per unit will never be zero.

The general relationship is alternatively referred to as an experience curve, a progress function, or an improvement function. Experts agree that the learning effect is the result of other factors in addition to actual worker learning. Some of the improvement can be traced to preproduction factors, such as selection of tooling and equipment, product design, methods analysis, and, in general, the amount of effort expended prior to the start of the work. Other contributing factors may involve changes after production has begun, such as changes in methods, tooling, and design. In addition, management input can be an important factor through improvements in planning, scheduling, motivation, and control.

Changes that are made once production is under way can cause a temporary *increase* in time per unit until workers adjust to the change, even though they eventually lead to an increased output rate. If a number of changes are made during production, the learning curve would be more realistically described by a series of scallops instead of a smooth curve, as illustrated in Figure 7S.2. Nonetheless, it is convenient to work with a smooth curve, which can be interpreted as the *average* effect.

From an organizational standpoint, what makes the learning effect more than an interesting curiosity is its *predictability,* which becomes readily apparent if the relationship is plotted on a log-log scale (see Figure 7S.3). The straight line that results reflects a constant learning percentage, which is the basis of learning curve estimates: Empirical evidence shows that every *doubling* of repetitions results in a *constant percentage* decrease in the time per repetition. This applies both to the *average* and to the *unit* time. Typical decreases range from 10 percent to 20 percent. By convention, learning curves are referred to in terms of the *complements* of their improvement rates. For example, an 80 percent learning curve denotes a 20 percent decrease in unit (or average) time with each doubling of repetitions, and a 90 percent curve denotes a 10 percent improvement rate. Note that a 100 percent curve would imply no improvement at all.

FIGURE 7S.3 On a log-log graph, learning curves are straight lines

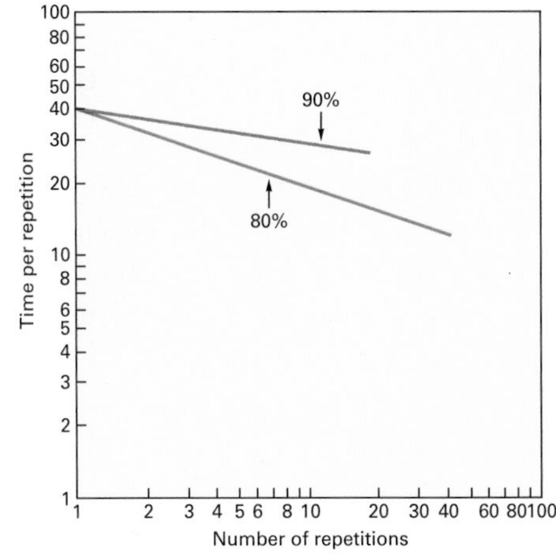

Example 7S–1 illustrates an important point and also raises an interesting question. The point is that the time reduction *per unit* becomes less and less as the number of repetitions increases. For example, the second unit required

EXAMPLE 7S–1

An activity is known to have an 80 percent learning curve. It has taken a worker 10 hours to produce the first unit. Determine expected completion times for these units: the 2nd, 4th, 8th, and 16th (note successive doubling of units).

SOLUTION

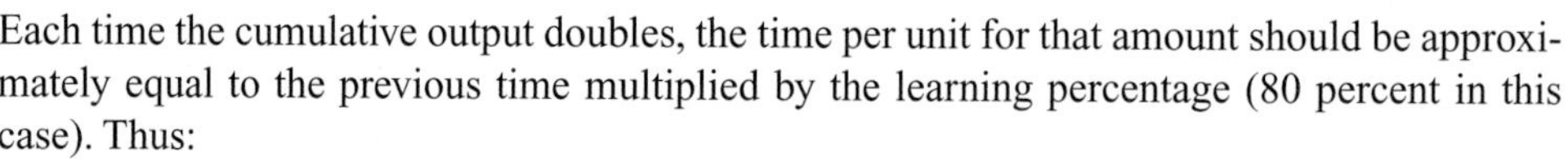

Each time the cumulative output doubles, the time per unit for that amount should be approximately equal to the previous time multiplied by the learning percentage (80 percent in this case). Thus:

Unit	Unit Time (hours)
1	= 10
2	.8(10) = 8
4	.8(8) = 6.4
8	.8(6.4) = 5.12
16	.8(5.12) = 4.096

two hours less time than the first, and the improvement from the 8th to the 16th unit was only slightly more than one hour. The question raised is: How are times computed for values such as three, five, six, seven, and other units that don't fall into this pattern?

There are two ways to obtain the times. One is to use a formula; the other is to use a table of values.

First consider the formula approach. The formula is based on the existence of a linear relationship between the time per unit and the number of units when these two variables are expressed in logarithms.

The unit time (i.e., the number of direct labor hours required) for the nth unit can be computed using the following formula:

$$T_n = T_1 \times n^b \qquad \text{(7S–1)}$$

where

T_n = Time for nth unit

T_1 = Time for first unit

b = ln (Learning percentage) ÷ ln 2; ln stands for the natural logarithm

To use the formula, you need to know the time for the first unit and the learning percentage. For example, for an 80 percent curve with $T_1 = 10$ hours, the time for the third unit would be computed as

$$T_3 = 10(3^{\ln .8/\ln 2}) = 7.02$$

Note: log can be used instead of ln.

The second approach is to use a "learning factor" obtained from a table such as Table 7S.1.

The table shows two things for some selected learning percentages. One is a unit value for the number of repetitions (unit number). This enables us to easily determine how long any unit will take to produce. The other is a cumulative value, which enables us to compute the total number of hours needed to complete any given number of repetitions. The computation for both is a relatively simple operation: Multiply the table value by the time required for the first unit.

To find the time for an individual unit (e.g., the 10th unit), use the formula

$$T_n = T_1 \times \text{Unit time factor} \qquad \text{(7S–2)}$$

Thus, for an 85 percent curve, with $T_1 = 4$ hours, the time for the 10th unit would be $4 \times .583 = 2.33$ hours. To find the time for all units up to a specified unit (e.g., the first 10 units), use the following formula:

TABLE 7S.1 Learning curve coefficients

	70%		75%		80%		85%		90%	
Unit Number	Unit Time	Total Time	Unit Time	Total Time	Unit Time	Total Time	Unit Time	Total Time	Unit Time	Total Time
1	1.000	1.000	1.000	1.000	1.000	1.000	1.000	1.000	1.000	1.000
2	.700	1.700	.750	1.750	.800	1.800	.850	1.850	.900	1.900
3	.568	2.268	.634	2.384	.702	2.502	.773	2.623	.846	2.746
4	.490	2.758	.562	2.946	.640	3.142	.723	3.345	.810	3.556
5	.437	3.195	.513	3.459	.596	3.738	.686	4.031	.783	4.339
6	.398	3.593	.475	3.934	.562	4.299	.657	4.688	.762	5.101
7	.367	3.960	.446	4.380	.534	4.834	.634	5.322	.744	5.845
8	.343	4.303	.422	4.802	.512	5.346	.614	5.936	.729	6.574
9	.323	4.626	.402	5.204	.493	5.839	.597	6.533	.716	7.290
10	.306	4.932	.385	5.589	.477	6.315	.583	7.116	.705	7.994
11	.291	5.223	.370	5.958	.462	6.777	.570	7.686	.695	8.689
12	.278	5.501	.357	6.315	.449	7.227	.558	8.244	.685	9.374
13	.267	5.769	.345	6.660	.438	7.665	.548	8.792	.677	10.052
14	.257	6.026	.334	6.994	.428	8.092	.539	9.331	.670	10.721
15	.248	6.274	.325	7.319	.418	8.511	.530	9.861	.663	11.384
16	.240	6.514	.316	7.635	.410	8.920	.522	10.383	.656	12.040
17	.233	6.747	.309	7.944	.402	9.322	.515	10.898	.650	12.690
18	.226	6.973	.301	8.245	.394	9.716	.508	11.405	.644	13.334
19	.220	7.192	.295	8.540	.388	10.104	.501	11.907	.639	13.974
20	.214	7.407	.288	8.828	.381	10.485	.495	12.402	.634	14.608
21	.209	7.615	.283	9.111	.375	10.860	.490	12.892	.630	15.237
22	.204	7.819	.277	9.388	.370	11.230	.484	13.376	.625	15.862
23	.199	8.018	.272	9.660	.364	11.594	.479	13.856	.621	16.483
24	.195	8.213	.267	9.928	.359	11.954	.475	14.331	.617	17.100
25	.191	8.404	.263	10.191	.355	12.309	.470	14.801	.613	17.713
26	.187	8.591	.259	10.449	.350	12.659	.466	15.267	.609	18.323
27	.183	8.774	.255	10.704	.346	13.005	.462	15.728	.606	18.929
28	.180	8.954	.251	10.955	.342	13.347	.458	16.186	.603	19.531
29	.177	9.131	.247	11.202	.338	13.685	.454	16.640	.599	20.131
30	.174	9.305	.244	11.446	.335	14.020	.450	17.091	.596	20.727

$$\Sigma T_n = T_1 \times \text{Total time factor} \quad (7S\text{–}3)$$

Thus, for an 85 percent curve, with $T_1 = 4$ hours, the total time for all 10 units (including the time for unit 1) would be $4 \times 7.116 = 28.464$ hours.

EXAMPLE 7S–2

Production Airplanes is negotiating a contract for the production of 20 small jet aircraft. The initial jet required the equivalent of 400 days of direct labor. The learning percentage is 80 percent. Estimate the expected number of days of direct labor for

a. The 20th jet.

b. All 20 jets.

c. The average time for 20 jets.

SOLUTION

Using Table 7S.1 with $n = 20$ and an 80 percent learning percentage, you find these factors: Unit time =.381; Total time = 10.485.

a. Expected time for 20th jet: 400(.381) = 152.4 labor days.
b. Expected total time for all 20: 400(10.485) = 4,194 labor days.
c. Average time for 20: 4,194 ÷ 20 = 209.7 labor days.

Use of Table 7S.1 requires a time for the first unit. If for some reason the completion time of the first unit is not available, or if the manager believes the completion time for some later unit is more reliable, the table can be used to obtain an estimate of the initial time.

EXAMPLE 7S–3

www.mhhe.com/stevenson11e

The manager in Example 7S–2 believes that some unusual problems were encountered in producing the first jet and would like to revise that estimate based on a completion time of 276 days for the third jet.

SOLUTION

The unit value for $n = 3$ and an 80 percent curve is .702 (Table 7S.1). Divide the actual time for unit 3 by the table value to obtain the revised estimate for unit 1's time: 276 days ÷ .702 = 393.2 labor days.

APPLICATIONS OF LEARNING CURVES

Learning curve theory has found useful applications in a number of areas, including

1. Manpower planning and scheduling.
2. Negotiated purchasing.
3. Pricing new products.
4. Budgeting, purchasing, and inventory planning.
5. Capacity planning.

Knowledge of output projections in learning situations can help managers make better decisions about how many workers they will need than they could determine from decisions based on initial output rates. Of course, managers obviously recognize that improvement will occur; what the learning curve contributes is a method for quantifying expected future improvements.

Negotiated purchasing often involves contracting for specialized items that may have a high degree of complexity. Examples include aircraft, computers, and special-purpose

FIGURE 7S.4
Worker learning curves can help guide personnel job placement

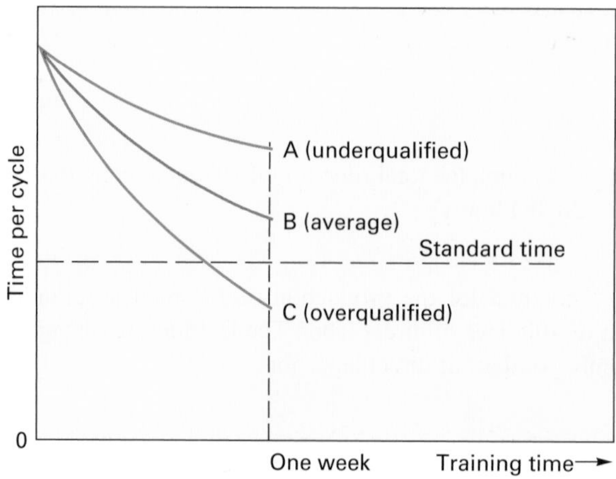

equipment. The direct labor cost per unit of such items can be expected to decrease as the size of the order increases. Hence, negotiators first settle on the number of units and then negotiate price on that basis. The government requires learning curve data on contracts that involve large, complex items. For contracts that are terminated before delivery of all units, suppliers can use learning curve data to argue for an increase in the unit price for the smaller number of units. Conversely, the government can use that information to negotiate a lower price per unit on follow-on orders on the basis of projected additional learning gains.

Managers must establish prices for their new products and services, often on the basis of production of a few units. Generalizing from the cost of the first few units would result in a much higher price than can be expected after a greater number of units have been produced. Actually, the manager needs to use the learning curve to avoid underpricing as well as overpricing. The manager may project initial costs by using the learning progression known to represent an organization's past experience, or else do a regression analysis of the initial results.

The learning curve projections help managers to plan costs and labor, purchasing, and inventory needs. For example, initial cost per unit will be high and output will be fairly low, so purchasing and inventory decisions can reflect this. As productivity increases, purchasing and/or inventory actions must allow for increased usage of raw materials and purchased parts to keep pace with output. Because of learning effects, the usage rate will increase over time. Hence, failure to refer to a learning curve would lead to substantial *overestimates* of labor needs and *underestimates* of the rate of material usage.

The learning principles can sometimes be used to evaluate new workers during training periods. This is accomplished by measuring each worker's performance, graphing the results, and comparing them to an expected rate of learning. The comparison reveals which workers are underqualified, average, and overqualified for a given type of work (see Figure 7S.4). Moreover, measuring a worker's progress can help predict whether the worker will make a quota within a required period of time.

Boeing uses learning curves to estimate weight reduction in new aircraft designs. Weight is a major factor in winning contracts because it is directly related to fuel economy.

EXAMPLE 7S–4

Use learning curve theory to predict the number of repetitions (units) that will be needed for a trainee to achieve a unit time of 6 minutes if the trainee took 10 minutes to do the first unit and a learning curve of 90 percent is operative.

a. Use the learning table.

b. Use the log formula.

SOLUTION

a. The table approach can be used for the learning percentages that are listed across the top of the table, such as the 90 percent curve in this example. The table approach is based on Formula 7S–2:

$$T_n = T_1 \times \text{Unit table factor}$$

Setting T_n equal to the specified time of 6 minutes and solving for the unit table factor yields

$$6 \text{ min} = 10 \text{ min} \times \text{unit table factor.}$$

Solving,

$$\text{unit table factor} = 6 \text{ min} \div 10 \text{ min} = .600$$

From Table 7S.1, under 90% in the Unit Time column, we find .599 at 29 units. Hence, approximately 29 units will be required to achieve the specified time.

b. Using the log formula,

(1) Compute the ratio of specified time to first unit time: 6 min ÷ 10 min = .600.

(2) Compute the ratio of ln learning percentage to ln 2: ln .90 ÷ ln 2 = −0.1053605 ÷ 0.6931472 = −0.1520.

(3) Find n such that $n^{-.1520} = .600$: $\sqrt[-.1520]{.600} = 28.809$. Round to 29. Hence, 29 units (repetitions) will be needed to achieve a time of 6 minutes.

The learning percentage can be estimated from data on repetition times. The procedure for doing this is illustrated in Solved Problem 2.

OPERATIONS STRATEGY

Learning curves often have strategic implications for market entry, when an organization hopes to rapidly gain market share. The use of time-based strategies can contribute to this. An increase in market share creates additional volume, enabling operations to quickly move down the learning curve, thereby decreasing costs and, in the process, gaining a competitive advantage. In some instances, the volumes are sufficiently large that operations will shift from batch mode to repetitive operation, which can lead to further cost reductions.

Learning curve projections can be useful for capacity planning. Having realistic time estimates based on learning curve theory, managers can translate that information into actual capacity needs, and plan on that basis.

CAUTIONS AND CRITICISMS

Managers using learning curves should be aware of their limitations and pitfalls. This section briefly outlines some of the major cautions and criticisms of learning curves.

1. Learning rates may differ from organization to organization and by type of work. Therefore, it is best to base learning rates on empirical studies rather than assumed rates where possible.
2. Projections based on learning curves should be regarded as *approximations* of actual times and treated accordingly.
3. Because time estimates are based on the time for the first unit, considerable care should be taken to ensure that the time is valid. It may be desirable to revise the base time as later times become available. Since it is often necessary to estimate the time for the first unit prior to production, this caution is very important.

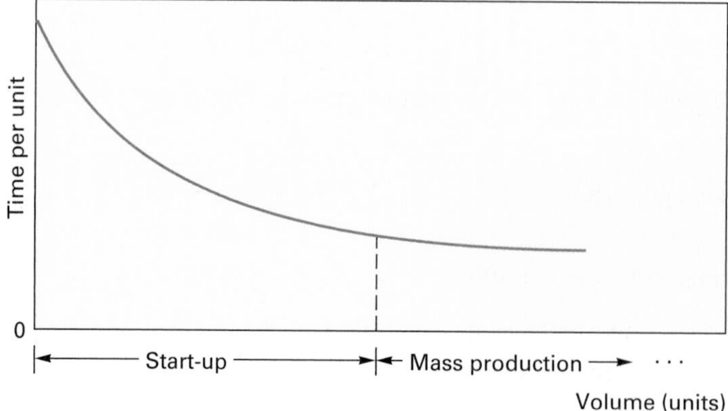

FIGURE 7S.5
Learning curves are useful for production start-up, but not usually for mass production

4. It is possible that at some point the curve might level off or even tip upward, especially near the end of a job. The potential for savings at that point is so slight that most jobs do not command the attention or interest to sustain improvements. Then, too, some of the better workers or other resources may be shifted into new jobs that are starting up.
5. Some of the improvements may be more apparent than real: Improvements in times may be caused in part by *increases* in *indirect* labor costs.
6. In mass production situations, learning curves may be of initial use in predicting how long it will take before the process stabilizes. For the most part, however, the concept does *not* apply to mass production because the decrease in time per unit is imperceptible for all practical purposes (see Figure 7S.5).
7. Users of learning curves sometimes fail to include carryover effects; previous experience with similar activities can reduce activity times, although it should be noted that the *learning rate* remains the same.
8. Shorter product life cycles, flexible manufacturing, and cross-functional workers can affect the ways in which learning curves may be applied.

SOLVED PROBLEMS

Problem 1

An assembly operation has a 90 percent learning curve. The line has just begun work on a new item; the initial unit required 28 hours. Estimate the time that will be needed to complete:

a. The first five units.
b. Units 20 through 25.

Solution

Use the total time factor in the 90 percent column of Table 7S.1.

a. Table value: 4.339.
   Estimated time for five units: 28(4.339) = 121.49 hours.
b. The total time for units 20 through 25 can be determined by subtraction:

		Hours
Total time for 25 units:	28(17.713) =	495.96
−Total time for 19 units:	28(13.974) =	391.27
Total time for units 20 through 25		104.69

Problem 2

A manager wants to determine an appropriate learning rate for a new type of work his firm will undertake. He has obtained completion times for the initial six repetitions of a job of this type. What learning rate is appropriate?

Unit	Completion Time (hours)
1	15.9
2	12.0
3	10.1
4	9.1
5	8.4
6	7.5

Solution

According to theory, the time per unit decreases at a constant rate each time the output *doubles* (e.g., unit 1 to 2, 2 to 4, and 3 to 6). The ratios of these observed times will give us an approximate rate. Thus,

$$\frac{\text{Unit 2}}{\text{Unit 1}} = \frac{12.0}{15.9} = .755 \qquad \frac{\text{Unit 4}}{\text{Unit 2}} = \frac{9.1}{12.0} = .758 \qquad \frac{\text{Unit 6}}{\text{Unit 3}} = \frac{7.5}{10.1} = .743$$

Not surprisingly, there is some variability; the rate is usually a smoothed approximation. Even so, the ratios are fairly close—a rate of 75 percent seems reasonable in this case.

DISCUSSION AND REVIEW QUESTIONS

1. If the learning phenomenon applies to all human activity, why isn't the effect noticeable in mass production or high-volume assembly work?
2. Under what circumstances might a manager prefer a learning rate of approximately 100 percent (i.e., no "learning")?
3. What would a learning percentage of 120 percent imply?
4. Explain how an increase in indirect labor cost can contribute to a decrease in direct labor cost per unit.
5. List the kinds of factors that create the learning effect.
6. Explain how changes in a process, once it is under way, can cause scallops in a learning curve.
7. Name some areas in which learning curves are useful.
8. What factors might cause a learning curve to tip up toward the end of a job?
9. "Users of learning curves sometimes fail to include carryover effects; previous experience with similar activities can reduce initial activity times, although it should be noted that the *learning rate* remains the same." What is the implication of this item from the list of cautions and criticisms?
10. Identify an unethical action that involves the learning rate and the ethical principle it violates.

PROBLEMS

1. An aircraft company has an order to refurbish the interiors of 18 jet aircraft. The work has a learning curve percentage of 80. On the basis of experience with similar jobs, the industrial engineering department estimates that the first plane will require 300 hours to refurbish. Estimate the amount of time needed to complete:
   a. The fifth plane.
   b. The first five planes.
   c. All 18 planes.
2. Estimate the time it will take to complete the 4th unit of a 12-unit job involving a large assembly if the initial unit required approximately 80 hours for each of these learning percentages:
   a. 72 percent
   b. 87 percent
   c. 95 percent
3. A contractor intends to bid on a job installing 30 airport security systems. Because this will be a new line of work for the contractor, he believes there will be a learning effect for the job. After reviewing time records from a similar type of activity, the contractor is convinced that an 85 percent curve is appropriate. He estimates that the first job will take his crew eight days to install. How many days should the contractor budget for
   a. The first 10 installations?
   b. The second 10 installations?
   c. The final 10 installations?
4. A job is known to have a learning percentage equal to 82. If the first unit had a completion time of 20 hours, estimate the times that will be needed to complete the third and fourth units.
5. A manager wants to determine an appropriate learning percentage for processing insurance claims for storm damage. Toward that end, times have been recorded for completion of each of the first six repetitions:

Repetition	1	2	3	4	5	6
Time (minutes)	46	39	35	33	32	30

a. Determine the approximate learning percentage.
b. Using your answer from part *a,* estimate the average completion time per repetition assuming a total of 30 repetitions are planned.

6. Students in an operations management class have been assigned four similar homework problems. One student noted that it took her 50 minutes to complete the first problem. Assume that the four problems are similar and that a 70 percent learning curve is appropriate. How much time can this student plan to spend solving the remaining problems?

7. A subcontractor is responsible for outfitting six satellites that will be used for solar research. Four of the six have been completed in a total of 600 hours. If the crew has a 75 percent learning curve, how long should it take them to finish the last two units?

8. The 5th unit of a 25-unit job took 14.5 hours to complete. If a 90 percent learning curve is appropriate:
   a. How long should it take to complete the last unit?
   b. How long should it take to complete the 10th unit?
   c. Estimate the average time per unit for the 25 units.

9. The labor cost to produce a certain item is $8.50 per hour. Job setup costs $50 and material costs are $20 per unit. The item can be purchased for $88.50 per unit. The learning rate is 90 percent. Overhead is charged at a rate of 50 percent of labor, materials, and setup costs.
   a. Determine the unit cost for 20 units, given that the first unit took 5 hours to complete.
   b. What is the minimum production quantity necessary to make production cost less than purchase cost?

10. A firm has a training program for a certain operation. The progress of trainees is carefully monitored. An established standard requires a trainee to be able to complete the sixth repetition of the operation in six hours or less. Those who are unable to do this are assigned to other jobs.

    Currently, three trainees have each completed two repetitions. Trainee A had times of 9 hours for the first and 8 hours for the second repetition; trainee B had times of 10 hours and 8 hours for the first and second repetitions; and trainee C had times of 12 hours and 9 hours.

    Which trainee(s) do you think will make the standard? Explain your reasoning.

11. The first unit of a job took 40 hours to complete. The work has a learning percentage of 88. The manager wants time estimates for units 2, 3, 4, and 5. Develop those time estimates.

12. A manager wants to estimate the remaining time that will be needed to complete a five-unit job. The initial unit of the job required 12 hours, and the work has a learning percentage of 77. Estimate the total time remaining to complete the job.

13. Kara is supposed to have a learning percentage of 82. Times for the first four units were 30.5, 28.4, 27.2, and 27.0 minutes. Does a learning percentage of 82 seem reasonable? Justify your answer using appropriate calculations.

14. The 5th unit of a 10-unit job took five hours to complete. The 6th unit has been worked on for two hours, but is not yet finished. Estimate the *additional* amount of time needed to finish the 10-unit job if the work has a 75 percent learning rate.

15. Estimate the number of repetitions each of the workers listed in the following table will require to reach a time of 7 hours per unit. Time is in hours.

Trainee	T_1	T_2
Art	11	9.9
Sherry	10.5	8.4
Dave	12	10.2

16. Estimate the number of repetitions that new service worker Irene will require to achieve "standard" if the standard is 18 minutes per repetition. She took 30 minutes to do the initial repetition and 25 minutes to do the next repetition.

17. Estimate the number of repetitions each of the workers listed in the following table will require to achieve a standard time of 25 minutes per repetition. Time is in minutes.

Trainee	T_1	T_2
Beverly	36	31
Max	40	36
Antonio	37	30

18. A research analyst performs database searches for a variety of clients. According to her log, a new search requires approximately 55 minutes. Repeated requests on the same or similar topic take less and less time, as her log shows:

Request no.	1	2	3	4	5	6	7	8
Time (min.)	55.0	41.0	35.2	31.0	28.7	26.1	24.8	23.5

How many more searches will it take until the search time gets down to 19 minutes?

19. A job has an 85 percent learning curve. Estimate the time that will be needed to complete the fifth unit of the job. The time for the first unit is unknown. However, units 2 through 4 took a total of 28.14 hours to complete.

Product Recall

CASE

An automobile manufacturer is conducting a product recall after it was discovered that a possible defect in the steering mechanism could cause loss of control in certain cars. The recall covers a span of three model years. The company sent out letters to car owners promising to repair the defect at no cost at any dealership.

The company's policy is to pay the dealer a fixed amount for each repair. The repair is somewhat complicated, and the company expected learning to be a factor. In order to set a reasonable rate for repairs, company engineers conducted a number of repairs themselves. It was then decided that a rate of $88 per repair would be appropriate, based on a flat hourly rate of $22 per hour and a 90 percent learning rate.

Shortly after dealers began making repairs, the company received word that several dealers were encountering resistance from workers who felt the flat rate was much too low and who were threatening to refuse to work on those jobs. One of the dealers collected data on job times and sent that information to the company: Three mechanics each completed two repairs. Average time for the first unit was 9.6 hours, and average time for the second unit was 7.2 hours. The dealer has suggested a rate of $110 per repair.

You have been asked to investigate the situation and to prepare a report.

Questions

1. Prepare a list of questions that you will need to have answered in order to analyze this situation.
2. Prepare a list of observations regarding the information provided in the case.
3. What preliminary thoughts do you have on solutions/partial solutions to the points you have raised?

SELECTED BIBLIOGRAPHY AND FURTHER READINGS

Argote, Linda, and Dennis Epple. "Learning Curves in Manufacturing." *Science 247* (February 1990), pp. 920–924.

Belkauoi, Ahmed. *The Learning Curve.* Westport, CT: Greenwood, 1986.

Teplitz, Charles J. *The Learning Curve Deskbook.* Westport, CT: Greenwood, 1991.

Location Planning and Analysis

CHAPTER

CHAPTER OUTLINE

LEARNING OBJECTIVES

After completing this chapter, you should be able to:

1 Identify some of the main reasons organizations need to make location decisions.

2 Explain why location decisions are important.

3 Discuss the options that are available for location decisions.

4 Give examples of the major factors that affect location decisions.

5 Outline the decision process for making these kinds of decisions.

6 Use the techniques presented to solve typical problems.

When a well-known real estate broker was asked what the three most important determinants of the value of a property are, he said, "That's easy. Location, location, and location."

In the residential real estate market, location is an important factor. Although the style of house, number of bedrooms and bathrooms, level of maintenance, and modernity of the kitchen undoubtedly enter into the picture, some locations are just more desirable than others.

In many respects, the choice of location for a business organization is every bit as important as it is for a house, although for different reasons.

Location decisions represent a key part of the strategic planning process of virtually every organization. And, although it might appear that location decisions are one-time problems pertaining to new organizations, existing organizations often have a bigger stake in these kinds of decisions than new organizations.

This chapter examines location analysis. It begins with a brief overview of the reasons firms must make location decisions, the nature of these decisions, and a general procedure for developing and evaluating location alternatives.

THE NEED FOR LOCATION DECISIONS

Existing organizations may need to make location decisions for a variety of reasons. Firms such as banks, fast-food chains, supermarkets, and retail stores view locations as part of marketing strategy, and they look for locations that will help them to expand their markets. Basically, the location decisions in those cases reflect the *addition* of new locations to an existing system.

A similar situation occurs when an organization experiences a growth in demand for its products or services that cannot be satisfied by expansion at an existing location. The addition of a new location to complement an existing system is often a realistic alternative.

Some firms face location decisions through depletion of basic inputs. For example, fishing and logging operations are often forced to relocate due to the temporary exhaustion of fish or forests at a given location. Mining and petroleum operations face the same sort of situation, although usually with a longer time horizon.

For other firms, a shift in markets causes them to consider relocation, or the costs of doing business at a particular location reach a point where other locations begin to look more attractive.

THE NATURE OF LOCATION DECISIONS

Location decisions for many types of businesses are made infrequently, but they tend to have a significant impact on the organization. In this section we look at the importance of location decisions, the usual objectives managers have when making location choices, and some of the options that are available to them.

Strategic Importance of Location Decisions

Location decisions are closely tied to an organization's strategies. For example, a strategy of being a low-cost producer might result in locating where labor or material costs are low, or locating near markets or raw materials to reduce transportation costs. A strategy of increasing profits by increasing market share might result in locating in high-traffic areas, and a strategy that emphasizes convenience for the customer might result in having many locations where customers can transact their business or make purchases (e.g., branch banks, ATMs, service stations, fast-food outlets).

Location choices can impact capacity and flexibility. Certain locations may be subject to space constraints that limit future expansion options. Moreover, local restrictions may restrict the types of products or services that can be offered, thus limiting future options for new products or services.

Location decisions are strategically important for other reasons as well. One is that they entail a long-term commitment, which makes mistakes difficult to overcome. Another is that location decisions often have an impact on investment requirements, operating costs and revenues, and operations. A poor choice of location might result in excessive transportation costs, a shortage of qualified labor, loss of competitive advantage, inadequate supplies of raw materials, or some similar condition that is detrimental to operations. For services, a poor location could result in lack of customers and/or high operating costs. For both manufacturing and services, location decisions can have a significant impact on competitive advantage. And another reason for the importance of location decisions is their strategic importance to supply chains.

Objectives of Location Decisions

As a general rule, profit-oriented organizations base their decisions on profit potential, whereas nonprofit organizations strive to achieve a balance between cost and the level of

An aerial view of an oil plant along the Kill Van Kull, Bayonne, New Jersey. Sea transportation was a key consideration in its location. The Kill Van Kull has been one of the most important channels in commerce throughout the region, providing a passage for marine traffic between Manhattan and the industrial towns of New Jersey. It currently provides the principal access for oceangoing container ships to Port Newark–Elizabeth Marine Terminal, the busiest port facility in the eastern United States and the principal marine terminal for New York Harbor.

customer service they provide. It would seem to follow that all organizations attempt to identify the "best" location available. However, this is not necessarily the case.

In many instances, no single location may be significantly better than the others. There may be numerous acceptable locations from which to choose, as shown by the wide variety of locations where successful organizations can be found. Furthermore, the number of possible locations that would have to be examined to find the best location may be too large to make an exhaustive search practical. Consequently, most organizations do not set out with the intention of identifying the *one best* location; rather, they hope to find a number of *acceptable* locations from which to choose.

Location criteria can depend on where a business is in the *supply chain*. For instance, at the retail end of a chain, site selection tends to focus more on accessibility, consumer demographics (population density, age distribution, average buyer income), traffic patterns, and local customs. Businesses at the beginning of a supply chain, if they are involved in supplying raw materials, are often located near the source of the raw materials. Businesses in the middle of the chain may locate near suppliers or near their markets, depending on a variety of circumstances. For example, businesses involved in storing and distributing goods often choose a central location to minimize distribution costs.

Web-based retail businesses are much less dependent on location decisions; they can exist just about anywhere.

Supply Chain Considerations

Supply chain management must address supply chain configuration. This includes determining the number and location of suppliers, production facilities, warehouses, and distribution centers. The location of these facilities can involve a long-term commitment of resources, so known risks and benefits should be considered carefully. A related issue is whether to have centralized or decentralized distribution. Centralized distribution generally yields scale economies as well as tighter control than decentralized distribution, but it sometimes incurs higher transportation costs. Decentralized distribution tends to be more responsive to local needs.

SUPPLY CHAIN

The importance of these decisions is underscored by the fact that they reflect the basic strategy for accessing customer markets, and the decisions will have a significant impact on costs, revenues, and responsiveness.

The quantitative techniques described in this chapter can be helpful in evaluating alternative supply chain configurations. Also, Chapter 15, Supply Chain Management, provides additional insights.

Location Options

Managers of existing companies generally consider four options in location planning.

Expand an existing facility. This option can be attractive if there is adequate room for expansion, especially if the location has desirable features that are not readily available elsewhere. Expansion costs are often less than those of other alternatives.

Add new locations while retaining existing ones. This is done in many retail operations. In such cases, it is essential to take into account what the impact will be on the total system. Opening a new store in a shopping mall may simply draw customers who already patronize an existing store in the same chain, rather than expand the market. On the other hand, adding locations can be a defensive strategy designed to maintain a market share or to prevent competitors from entering a market.

Shut down at one location and move to another. An organization must weigh the costs of a move and the resulting benefits against the costs and benefits of remaining in an existing location. A shift in markets, exhaustion of raw materials, and the cost of operations often cause firms to consider this option seriously.

Do nothing. If a detailed analysis of potential locations fails to uncover benefits that make one of the previous three alternatives attractive, a firm may decide to maintain the status quo, at least for the time being.

GLOBAL LOCATIONS

Globalization has opened new markets, and it has meant increasing dispersion of manufacturing and service operations around the world. In addition, many companies are outsourcing operations to other companies in foreign locations. In the past, companies tended to operate from a "home base" that was located in a single country. Now, companies are finding strategic and tactical reasons to globalize their operations. As they do, some companies are profiting from their efforts, while others are finding the going tough, and all must contend with issues involved in managing global operations.

In this section, we examine some of the reasons for globalization, the benefits, disadvantages, risks, and issues related to managing global operations.

Facilitating Factors

There are a number of factors that have made globalization attractive and feasible for business organizations. Two key factors are trade agreements and technological advances.

Trade Agreements. Barriers to international trade such as tariffs and quotas have been reduced or eliminated with trade agreements such as the North American Free Trade Agreement (NAFTA), the General Agreement on Tariffs and Trade (GATT), and the U.S.–China Trade Relations Act. Also, the European Union has dropped many trade barriers, and the World Trade Organization is helping to facilitate free trade.

Technology. Technological advances in communication and information sharing have been very helpful. These include faxing capability, e-mail, cell phones, teleconferencing, and the Internet.

Benefits

Companies are discovering a wide range of benefits in globalizing their operations. Here is a list of some of the benefits, although it is important to recognize that not all benefits apply to every situation:

Markets. Companies often seek opportunities for expanding markets for their goods and services, as well as better serving existing customers by being more attuned to local needs and having a quicker response time when problems occur.

Cost savings. Among the areas for potential cost saving are transportation costs, labor costs, raw material costs, and taxes. High production costs in Germany have contributed to a number of German companies locating some of their production facilities in lower-cost countries. Among them are industrial products giant Siemens, AG (a semiconductor plant in Britain), drug makers Bayer, AG (a plant in Texas), and Hoechst, AG (a plant in China), and automakers Mercedes (plants in Spain, France, and Alabama) and BMW (a plant in Spartanburg, South Carolina).

Legal and regulatory. There may be more favorable liability and labor laws, and less-restrictive environmental and other regulations.

Financial. Companies can avoid the impact of currency changes that can occur when goods are produced in one country and sold in other countries. Also, a variety of incentives may be offered by national, regional, or local governments to attract businesses that will create jobs and boost the local economy. For example, state incentives, and workforce and land availability and cost, helped convince Nissan to build a huge assembly plant in Canton, Mississippi, and Mercedes to build an assembly plant in Vance, Alabama. An added benefit came when suppliers for these plants also set up facilities in the region.

Other. Globalization may provide new sources of ideas for products and services, new perspectives on operations, and solutions to problems.

Reebok advertisement in the window of Foot Locker in a recently developed Indian shopping mall.

Disadvantages

There are a number of disadvantages of having global operations. These can include the following:

Transportation costs. High transportation costs can occur due to poor infrastructure or having to ship over great distances, and the resulting costs can offset savings in labor and materials costs.

Security costs. Increased security risks and theft can increase costs. Also, security at international borders can slow shipments to other countries.

Unskilled labor. Low labor skills may negatively impact quality and productivity, and the work ethic may differ from that in the home country. Additional employee training may be required.

Import restrictions. Some countries place restrictions on the importation of manufactured goods, so having local suppliers avoids those issues.

Criticisms. Critics may argue that cost savings are being generated through unfair practices such as using sweatshops, in which employees are paid low wages and made to work in poor conditions; using child labor; and operating in countries that have less stringent environmental requirements.

Risks

Political. Political instability and political unrest can create risks for personnel safety and the safety of assets. Moreover, a government might decide to nationalize facilities, taking them over.

Terrorism. Terrorism continues to be a threat in many parts of the world, putting personnel and assets at risk and decreasing the willingness of domestic personnel to travel to or work in certain areas.

Economic. Economic instability might create inflation or deflation, either of which can negatively impact profitability.

Legal. Laws and regulations may change, reducing or eliminating what may have been key benefits.

Ethical. Corruption and bribery, common in some countries, may be illegal in a company's home country (e.g., illegal in the United States). This poses a number of issues. One is how to maintain operations without resorting to bribery. Another is how to prevent employees from doing this, especially when they may be of local origin and used to transacting business in this way.

Cultural. Cultural differences may be more real than apparent. Walmart discovered that fact when it opened stores in Japan. Although Walmart has thrived in many countries on its reputation for low-cost items, Japanese consumers associated low cost with low quality, so Walmart had to rethink its strategy for the Japanese market.

Managing Global Operations

Although global operations offer many benefits, these operations often create new issues for management to deal with. For example, language and cultural differences increase the risk of miscommunication and may also interfere with developing trust that is important in business relationships. Management styles may be quite different, so tactics that work well in one country may not work in another. Increased travel distances and related travel times and costs may result in a decreased tendency for face-to-face meetings and management site visits. Also, coordination of far-flung operations can be more difficult. Managers may have to deal with corruption and bribery as well as differences in work ethic. The level of technology may be lower, and the resistance to technological change may be higher than expected, making the integration of new technologies more difficult. Domestic personnel may resist relocating, even temporarily.

Not-So-Clear Choices: Should You Export, or Manufacture Overseas? — READING

Russ Banham

When the board-games company Bob Moog created in 1985 sought growth through global expansion 2 years later, Moog faced the usual two options: export the product or manufacture it overseas for local distribution. Moog chose the latter.

"We decided for a number of reasons to manufacture our board game, '20 Questions,' in Holland for distribution throughout Europe," said Moog, president of University Games Corp. of Burlingame, CA.

Recently the company expanded into Australia. Unlike the European ventures, however, Moog decided that it was more economical to import its products into Australia from the U.S. manufacturing facility because "anticipated initial sales in Australia just did not warrant a manufacturing operation there at this juncture," Moog said. "If sales pick up down the line, we may then examine local manufacturing."

Moog's dual strategy is not unique. One of the toughest questions a company confronts when pondering an international sales strategy is: to export, or not to export?

While exporting is often the least risky method of selling overseas, it frequently involves significant transportation, logistics, and tax-related costs that may make it uneconomical when compared with foreign manufacturing.

On the other hand, foreign manufacturing, while potentially a more competitive way of entering an overseas market, has its own bugaboos. Political instability, fluctuating market conditions, and the huge capital costs to set up an overseas manufacturing operation are daunting challenges. Determining the best way to go often involves solving a perplexing conundrum. "It boils down to a trade-off between classic cost-and-time considerations and eco-political factors," said Richard Powers, president of Insight Inc., a provider of management support systems based in Bend, OR.

With exporting, a company must evaluate the various modes of transportation that would be involved in getting the goods there, and how this relates to the cycle time of putting the product in the marketplace. Some products are time-sensitive; others are less so.

On the other hand, if a company determines that an overseas manufacturing operation best meets its needs, it must examine the eco-political factors involved, such as tariff and duty drawbacks and international tax issues. "It may be less expensive, given these factors, for a company to incur the logistics costs of exporting than to risk the eco-political costs," Powers explained.

(continued)

Trade-Offs and Traps

In addition to weighing these trade-offs, there are other related factors affecting the decision to either export or locate a plant overseas. To compete in their market, for example, some countries require that some form of local infrastructure be in place.

"Sometimes you run into government contracts where the only way to distribute a product in that country is to have it made locally," said Fred Ehrsam, vice president at Bain & Co., a Boston-based strategy consulting firm. "In China, for instance, you pretty much have to build something there in order to enter that market."

Certain products also dictate the international sales strategy to be taken. "If your company makes drinking glasses, you'll want to manufacture them in whatever country you plan to sell them," observed Scott Setrakian, a director in the San Francisco office of Mercer Management Consulting. "Drinking glasses, generally speaking, are pretty cheap to make and expensive to ship."

Political instability is another guiding force in a company's decision-making process. "If you want to sell in Russia, you're facing political instability as your biggest single operating risk," noted John Koopman, a principal in Mercer's Toronto office. "In Western Europe, this is not an issue. In Asia, there's a little risk, but in Russia it's a given." . . .

The maturity of a company's product affects this decision. A product expected to require design changes, for example, may not fit well with foreign manufacturing plans. "It's pretty hard to implement changes to a product when the product is fairly far removed from the product development and engineering people," Ehrsam continued. "Tactically, you want to be moving products offshore that are relatively stable."

Another factor is the skill of the labor force in the market being considered. "You have to question whether or not the labor pool—no matter how low-cost—can be trained to do the things you need," Ehrsam added.

Many companies enter a foreign market by first exporting there, but with an eye toward building overseas in the future. "Exporting will give you a feel for the product and its market potential," Powers said. "Instead of jumping in the lake head first, exporting allows you to get your toes wet. It may cost more, but you're able to hedge your risks."

But CPC International favors full-scale overseas manufacturing to either foreign product assembly or exporting. "We rely on exporting chiefly as a means of entering a new marketplace," said Gale Griffin, vice president at the Englewood Cliffs, NJ–based food company. "We then like to move from an exporting environment into local manufacturing."

CPC manufactures such well-known food brands as Hellmann's Mayonnaise and the Knorr's line of soups. Altogether, the company manufactures in 62 of the 110 countries in which it markets its products.

CPC uses local personnel and managers almost exclusively when operating overseas. "We look for people who understand the markets and can compete very effectively within them," Griffin said. "They help you understand local government regulations, which can be tricky. We also let our local managers do their own marketing, figuring they know their own markets and how to compete there better than Englewood Cliffs does."

Finding someone qualified to fill these shoes is as easy as calling an executive search firm or accessing the Internet. "There are many qualified people looking to represent all kinds of companies on the Net," Powers noted.

Powers' company, Insight, offers a computer software model that can help companies find the right overseas representatives. Called the Global Supply Chain Model, the software guides companies through the maze of decisions required to develop an international sales strategy, from how many plants [are] needed to satisfy global markets to the best means to source products. The software costs $30,000, excluding consulting services. The task of finding a local rep should not be taken lightly, especially when it concerns finding someone to manage an overseas plant. "Having a plant manager who can create a culture from the ground up with the right discipline and values to develop a solid team of people is crucial to the success of the endeavor," Ehrsam said. "I've seen the best prepared and executed strategies succeed or fall to pieces on the basis of that one individual."

Best-Laid Plans

While some elements making up an international sales strategy can be predicted with a degree of certainty, others—like currency exchange values—are capricious at best. "At Mexx, we planned twice to enter the Italian market," Koopman recalled. "In both cases, one week before we were set to launch our clothing line there, the Italian lira was devalued 20 percent—meaning our prices would increase by 20 percent. Both times we were forced to cancel our plans."

Technology obsolescence and improvements in logistics play similar, unpredictable roles. A company may spend hundreds of thousands of dollars building a foreign facility weeks before a new automated manufacturing system renders its technology a buggy in an age of automobiles.

Moreover, a new way of moving goods faster, more efficiently and less expensively may materialize, reversing the status quo and making exporting a more cost-effective means of reaching a marketplace.

Ultimately, no matter which way a company chooses to enter a foreign market, it needs a pair of fleet feet. "It's very important, especially with new economies, to get in as early as possible," Griffin counseled. "You want to establish market leadership for your brand, and the fact is, the first one there often has the best chance."

Questions

1. What advantages and disadvantages does exporting have?
2. What advantages and disadvantages does foreign manufacturing have?
3. What are the advantages of employing local personnel and managers when operating overseas?
4. What relevance do currency exchange rates have for foreign trade?
5. What other factors might be relevant?

Source: Russ Banham, "Not-So-Clear Choices: Should You Export, or Manufacture Overseas?" *International Business,* November/December 1997, pp. 23–25.

GENERAL PROCEDURE FOR MAKING LOCATION DECISIONS

The way an organization approaches location decisions often depends on its size and the nature or scope of its operations. New or small organizations tend to adopt a rather informal approach to location decisions. New firms typically locate in a certain area simply because the owner lives there. Similarly, managers of small firms often want to keep operations in their backyard, so they tend to focus almost exclusively on local alternatives. Large established companies, particularly those that already operate in more than one location, tend to take a more formal approach. Moreover, they usually consider a wider range of geographic locations. The discussion here pertains mainly to a formal approach to location decisions.

The general procedure for making location decisions usually consists of the following steps:

1. Decide on the criteria to use for evaluating location alternatives, such as increased revenues or community service.
2. Identify important factors, such as location of markets or raw materials.
3. Develop location alternatives:
   a. Identify a country or countries for location.
   b. Identify the general region for a location.
   c. Identify a small number of community alternatives.
   d. Identify site alternatives among the community alternatives.
4. Evaluate the alternatives and make a selection.

Step 1 is simply a matter of managerial preference. Steps 2 through 4 are discussed on the following pages.

Cargo trucks carry containers in and out of the PSA Singapore Terminal. The terminal is the world's largest container hub, handling about one-fifth of the world's total container transshipments. It connects with 200 shipping lines with connections to 600 ports in 123 countries. This includes daily sailings to every major port in the world.

IDENTIFYING A COUNTRY, REGION, COMMUNITY, AND SITE

Many factors influence location decisions. However, it often happens that one or a few factors are so important that they dominate the decision. For example, in manufacturing, the potentially dominating factors usually include availability of an abundant energy and water supply and proximity to raw materials. Thus, nuclear reactors require large amounts of water for cooling, heavy industries such as steel and aluminum production need large amounts of electricity, and so on. Transportation costs can be a major factor. In service organizations, possible dominating factors are market related and include traffic patterns, convenience, and competitors' locations, as well as proximity to the market. For example, car rental agencies locate near airports and midcity, where their customers are. Note, too, that many of the factors discussed pertain to supply chain facilities as well as operations facilities.

SUPPLY CHAIN

Once an organization has determined the most important factors, it will try to narrow the search for suitable alternatives to one geographic region. Then a small number of community-site alternatives are identified and subjected to detailed analysis. Human factors can be very important, as the following reading reveals. These might include the "culture shock" that is often experienced when employees are transferred to an environment that differs significantly from the current location—for instance, a move from a large city to a rural area, or from a rural area to a large city, or a move to an area that has a dramatically different climate.

Innovative MCI Unit Finds Culture Shock in Colorado Springs

READING

Alex Markels

Convinced this town's spectacular setting would inspire his workers, Richard Liebhaber figured "build it, and they will come."

In 1991, the chief technology officer of MCI Communications Corp. decided to relocate MCI's brain trust—the 4,000-employee Systems Engineering division that created numerous breakthrough products—from MCI's Washington, D.C., headquarters to Colorado Springs. An avid skier, he believed the mountains, low crime rate, healthy climate, and rock-bottom real-estate prices would be "a magnet for the best and brightest" computer software engineers.

He rejected warnings from at least half a dozen senior executives that Colorado Springs' isolated and politically conservative setting would actually repel the eclectic, ethnically diverse engineers MCI hoped to attract. Mr. Liebhaber argued that new hires would jump at the chance to live in ski country, while veterans would stay longer, reducing MCI's more than 15% annual turnover rate in Washington. The move, he contended, would also save money by cutting MCI's facilities, labor, and recruiting costs. Besides, four other high-tech companies—including Digital Equipment Corp. and Apple Computer Inc.—had recently moved there. "One of the things that gave me more comfort was the fact that these other guys had selected Colorado Springs," Mr. Liebhaber says.

He was mistaken.

While many rank-and-file MCI employees, buoyed by generous relocation packages, made the move, numerous key executives and engineers, and hundreds of the division's 51% minority population, said no, or fled Colorado Springs soon after relocating.

Living in "Wonder Bread"

"It was like living in a loaf of Wonder Bread," says James Finucane, who is of Japanese descent and whose wife is from Argentina. A veteran senior engineer, Mr. Finucane was considered MCI's top engineer until he took a job with a competitor back east in 1994. "There's no culture, no diversity, no research university, no vitality or resiliency to the job market."

The move isolated MCI's engineers from top management and from marketing colleagues at headquarters, undermining the spontaneous collaborations that had generated some of the company's most innovative products. Meanwhile, the professionals Mr. Liebhaber hoped to recruit from outside proved difficult and expensive to woo, pushing the move's total cost to about $200 million—far more than MCI officials anticipated. "Most of the savings we had hoped for never materialized," says LeRoy Pingho, a senior executive who oversaw the relocation.

Moving Expenses

When the move was announced, many rank-and-file workers were enthusiastic. MCI's relocation policy paid for every expense imaginable. Costing an average of $100,000 per employee, it included up to six months of temporary housing and living expenses, private-school tuition for workers' children and a full month's pay for miscellaneous expenses. And there were exceptional housing bargains. "In Alexandria, [Va.,] we had a tiny place on a 50-by-112-foot

(continued)

(concluded)
lot," says Jerome Sabolik, a senior software engineer. "For the same money, we got a 3,000-square-foot house on 2 ½ acres." Thousands of workers—far more than Mr. Liebhaber expected—took advantage of the offer, undercutting his plans to recruit lower-cost employees in Colorado.

But there was far less enthusiasm among senior managers. James Zucco, Mr. Ditchfield's successor and the head of Systems Engineering, stayed behind and eventually left to join AT&T Corp. Also staying put was Gary Wiesenborn, the division's No. 2 executive, who later moved to Bell Atlantic Corp. Mr. Pingho, who oversaw the division's financial planning and budgeting, declined to move and quit in 1993.

There was also significant fallout among the division's minority population. Although MCI declines to provide specific numbers, it confirms there was a reduction. According to former employees who had access to Equal Employment Opportunity Commission data, there were roughly 1,300 African-Americans on Systems Engineering's staff and a combined 700 Asians and Hispanics before the relocation. Since the relocation, minority representation has been cut almost in half, to about 600 blacks and a combined 500 Asians and Hispanics. "It was a disaster for diversity," Mr. Ditchfield says.

But MCI officials say that despite the reduction, its Colorado division is still more ethnically diverse than other local companies.

Source: Alex Markels, "Innovative MCI Unit Finds Culture Shock in Colorado Springs," *The Wall Street Journal* © 1996 Dow Jones & Company, Inc. Used with permission.

Identifying a Country

Each country carries its own set of potential benefits and risks, and decision makers need to be absolutely clear on what those benefits and risks are as well as their likelihood of occurrence so that they can make an informed judgment on whether locating in that country is desirable. Some important issues have been noted in the previous section on global operations. Table 8.1 provides a listing of factors to consider.

In a report by the Council on Competitiveness and Deloitte Touche Tohmatsu that surveyed 400 global CEOs on their views on manufacturing competitiveness, the top three factors in

TABLE 8.1
Factors relating to foreign locations

Factor	Considerations
Government	a. Policies on foreign ownership of production facilities
	Local content requirements
	Import restrictions
	Currency restrictions
	Environmental regulations
	Local product standards
	Liability laws
	b. Stability issues
Cultural differences	Living circumstances for foreign workers and their dependents
	Ways of doing business
	Religious holidays/traditions
Customer preferences	Possible "buy locally" sentiment
Labor	Level of training and education of workers
	Wage rates
	Labor productivity
	Work ethic
	Possible regulations limiting number of foreign employees
	Language differences
Resources	Availability and quality of raw materials, energy, transportation infrastructure
Financial	Financial incentives, tax rates, inflation rates, interest rates
Technological	Rate of technological change, rate of innovations
Market	Market potential, competition
Safety	Crime, terrorism threat

determining where to locate manufacturing facilities were talent, labor costs, and energy costs.[1] And, in fact, many companies have outsourced some of their operations to foreign suppliers to take advantage of relatively low wage rates. Some U.S. manufacturing companies set up foreign subsidiaries to not only take advantage of low labor rates but also to avoid or delay paying taxes on their profits. With foreign-based subsidiaries, manufacturing companies can ship their products to the United States and pay low tariffs. Furthermore, they can avoid taxes altogether by recording the profits overseas and not returning the earnings to the United States. They can do this through *transfer pricing rules* that allow U.S. companies to establish a price for transfer into the United States that keeps most of the profit in the foreign subsidiary. Those earnings are not subject to U.S. taxes unless or until they are returned as dividends to the U.S. parent corporation.

It is important to take all factors into account when contemplating the advantage of low labor costs. Other costs may negate that advantage. For example, low wage rates may also be accompanied by low *labor productivity,* resulting in a net cost per unit that is actually higher than what could be achieved domestically. Another consideration is transportation costs, which are generally higher for longer distances. Again, that could offset some or all of the low wage benefit. Then, too, longer transport time results in increased supply chain inventory and reduced agility.

Another factor to consider is the *currency and exchange rate risk* that occurs when producing in one country and buying or selling in another country. Companies must transact business in the currency of the country they are involved in. However, because the value of a country's currency fluctuates, exchange rates fluctuate, affecting the cost of supplies and the profits of sales in other countries when converting back to the country the company is located in.

Companies can obtain information about countries of interest from a variety of sources. Here are two useful Web sites:

CIA—https://www.cia.gov/library/publications/the-world-factbook/index.html

World Bank—http://www.doingbusiness.org/ExploreEconomies/?economyid=2

Identifying a Region

The primary regional factors involve raw materials, markets, and labor considerations.

Location of Raw Materials. Firms locate near or at the source of raw materials for three primary reasons: necessity, perishability, and transportation costs. Mining operations, farming, forestry, and fishing fall under *necessity.* Obviously, such operations must locate close to the raw materials. Firms involved in canning or freezing of fresh fruits and vegetables, processing of dairy products, baking, and so on, must consider *perishability* when considering location. *Transportation costs* are important in industries where processing eliminates much of the bulk connected with a raw material, making it much less expensive to transport the product or material after processing. Examples include aluminum reduction, cheese making, and paper production. Where inputs come from different locations, some firms choose to locate near the geographic center of the sources. For instance, steel producers use large quantities of both coal and iron ore, and many are located somewhere between the Appalachian coal fields and iron ore mines. Transportation costs are often the reason that vendors locate near their major customers. Moreover, regional warehouses are used by supermarkets and other retail operations to supply multiple outlets. Often the choice of new locations and additional warehouses reflects the locations of existing warehouses or retail outlets.

Location of Markets. Profit-oriented firms frequently locate near the markets they intend to serve as part of their competitive strategy, whereas nonprofit organizations choose locations relative to the needs of the users of their services. Other factors include distribution costs or the perishability of a finished product.

[1] *Newsweek,* July 19, 2010, p. 15.

Competitive pressures for retail operations can be extremely vital factors. In some cases, a market served by a particular location may be too small to justify two or more competitors (e.g., one hamburger franchise per block), so that a search for potential locations tends to concentrate on locations without competitors. The opposite also might be true; it could be desirable to locate near competitors. Large department stores often locate near each other, and small stores like to locate in shopping centers that have large department stores as anchors. The large stores attract large numbers of shoppers who become potential customers in the smaller stores or in the other large stores.

Some firms must locate close to their markets because of the perishability of their products. Examples include bakeries, flower shops, and fresh seafood stores. For other types of firms, distribution costs are the main factor in closeness to market. For example, sand and gravel dealers usually serve a limited area because of the high distribution costs associated with their products. Still other firms require close customer contact, so they too tend to locate within the area they expect to serve. Typical examples are tailor shops, home remodelers, home repair services, cabinetmakers, rug cleaners, and lawn and garden services.

Locations of many government services are near the markets they are designed to serve. Hence, post offices are typically scattered throughout large metropolitan areas. Police and emergency health care locations are frequently selected on the basis of client needs. For instance, police patrols often concentrate on high crime areas, and emergency health care facilities are usually found in central locations to provide ready access from all directions.

Many foreign manufacturing companies have located manufacturing operations in the United States, because it is a major market for their products. Chief among them are automobile manufacturers, most notably Japanese, but other nations are also represented. Another possible reason that Japanese producers decided to locate in the United States was to offset possible negative consumer sentiment related to job losses of U.S. workers. Thousands of U.S. auto workers are now employed in U.S. manufacturing plants of Japanese and other foreign companies.

Labor Factors. Primary labor considerations are the cost and availability of labor, wage rates in an area, labor productivity and attitudes toward work, and whether unions are a serious potential problem.

Labor costs are very important for labor-intensive organizations. The shift of the textile industry from the New England states to southern states was due partly to labor costs.

Skills of potential employees may be a factor, although some companies prefer to train new employees rather than rely solely on previous experience. Increasing specialization in many industries makes this possibility even more likely than in the past. Although most companies concentrate on the supply of blue-collar workers, some firms are more interested in scientific and technical people as potential employees, and they look for areas with high concentrations of those types of workers.

Worker attitudes toward turnover, absenteeism, and similar factors may differ among potential locations—workers in large urban centers may exhibit different attitudes than workers in small towns or rural areas. Furthermore, worker attitudes in different parts of the country or in different countries may be markedly different.

Some companies offer their current employees jobs if they move to a new location. However, in many instances, employees are reluctant to move, especially when it means leaving families and friends. Furthermore, in families with two wage earners, relocation would require that one wage earner give up a job and then attempt to find another job in the new location.

Other Factors. Climate and taxes sometimes play a role in location decisions. For example, a string of unusually severe winters in northern states may cause some firms to seriously consider moving to a milder climate, especially if delayed deliveries and work disruptions caused by inability of employees to get to work have been frequent. Similarly, the business and personal income taxes in some states reduce their attractiveness to companies seeking new locations. Many companies have been attracted to some Sun Belt states by ample supplies of low-cost energy or labor, the climate, and tax considerations. Also, tax and monetary incentives are major factors in attracting or keeping professional sports franchises.

Identifying a Community

Many communities actively try to attract new businesses, offering financial and other incentives, because they are viewed as potential sources of future tax revenues and new job opportunities. However, communities do not, as a rule, want firms that will create pollution problems or otherwise lessen the quality of life in the community. Local groups may actively seek to exclude certain companies on such grounds, and a company may have to go to great lengths to convince local officials that it will be a "responsible citizen." Furthermore, some organizations discover that even though overall community attitude is favorable, there may still be considerable opposition to specific sites from nearby residents who object to possible increased levels of noise, traffic, or pollution. Examples of this include community resistance to airport expansion, changes in zoning, construction of nuclear facilities, and highway construction.

From a company standpoint, a number of factors determine the desirability of a community as a place for its workers and managers to live. They include facilities for education, shopping, recreation, transportation, religious worship, and entertainment; the quality of police, fire, and medical services; local attitudes toward the company; and the size of the community. Community size can be particularly important if a firm will be a major employer in the community; a future decision to terminate or reduce operations in that location could have a serious impact on the economy of a small community.

Other community-related factors are the cost and availability of utilities, environmental regulations, taxes (state and local, direct and indirect), and often a laundry list of enticements offered by state or local governments that can include bond issues, tax abatements, low-cost loans, grants, and worker training.

Another trend is just-in-time manufacturing techniques (see Chapter 14), which encourage suppliers to locate near their customers to reduce supplier lead times. For this reason, some U.S. firms are reconsidering decisions to locate offshore. Moreover, in light manufacturing (e.g., electronics), low-cost labor is becoming less important than nearness to markets; users of electronics components want suppliers that are close to their manufacturing facilities. One offshoot of this is the possibility that the future will see a trend toward smaller factories located close to markets. In some industries, small, automated **microfactories** with narrow product focuses will be located near major markets to reduce response time.

Microfactory Small factory with a narrow product focus, located near major markets.

A microfactory consisting of an Extrudex machine, which produces fluid tubes of plastic (extrusions) that are turned into designer chairs.

It is likely that advances in information technology will enhance the ability of manufacturing firms to gather, track, and distribute information that links purchasing, marketing, and distribution with design, engineering, and manufacturing. This will reduce the need for these functions to be located close together, thereby permitting a strategy of locating production facilities near major markets.

Ethical Issues. Ethical issues can arise during location searches, so it is important for companies and governments to have policies in place before that happens, and to keep ethical aspects of decisions in mind while negotiating favorable treatment. For example, governments may offer a variety of incentives to companies to locate in their area, usually to obtain promised benefits from the companies. Companies should be careful to not promise more (e.g., jobs, longevity) or less (e.g., noise, traffic) than they can reasonably expect to deliver. Similarly, government negotiators should strive for an agreement that will ultimately benefit taxpayers, and use extreme caution in negotiating long-term arrangements that risk leaving taxpayers "holding the bag." Also at issue are behind-the-scenes payments or favors to make a decision that would otherwise not be rated as highly.

Identifying a Site

The primary considerations related to sites are land, transportation, and zoning or other restrictions.

Evaluation of potential sites may require consulting with engineers or architects, especially in the case of heavy manufacturing or the erection of large buildings or facilities with special requirements. Soil conditions, load factors, and drainage rates can be critical and often necessitate certain kinds of expertise in evaluation.

Because of the long-term commitment usually required, land costs may be secondary to other site-related factors, such as room for future expansion, current utility and sewer capacities—and any limitations on these that could hinder future growth—and sufficient parking space for employees and customers. In addition, for many firms access roads for trucks or rail spurs are important.

Industrial parks may be worthy alternatives for firms involved in light manufacturing or assembly, warehouse operations, and customer service facilities. Typically, the land is already developed—power, water, and sewer hookups have been attended to, and zoning restrictions do not require special attention. On the negative side, industrial parks may place restrictions on the kinds of activities that a company can conduct, which can limit options for future development of a firm's products and services as well as the processes it may consider. Sometimes stringent regulations governing the size, shape, and architectural features of buildings limit managerial choice in these matters. Also, there may not be an adequate allowance for possible future expansion.

For firms with executives who travel frequently, the size and proximity of the airport or train station as well as travel connections can be important, although schedules and connections are subject to change.

Table 8.2 provides a summary of the factors that affect location decisions.

Multiple Plant Manufacturing Strategies

When companies have multiple manufacturing facilities, they can organize operations in several ways. One is to assign different product lines to different plants. Another is to assign different market areas to different plants. And a third is to assign different processes to different plants. Each strategy carries certain cost and managerial implications, as well as competitive advantages.

Product Plant Strategy. With this strategy, entire products or product lines are produced in separate plants, and each plant usually supplies the entire domestic market. This is essentially a decentralized approach, with each plant focusing on a narrow set of requirements that entails specialization of labor, materials, and equipment along product lines. Specialization

TABLE 8.2
Factors affecting location decisions

Level	Factors	Considerations
Regional	Location of raw materials or supplies	Proximity, modes and costs of transportation, quantity available
	Location of markets	Proximity, distribution costs, target market, trade practices/restrictions
	Labor	Availability (general and for specific skills), age distribution of workforce, work attitudes, union or nonunion, productivity, wage scales, unemployment compensation laws
Community	Quality of life	Schools, churches, shopping, housing, transportation, entertainment, recreation, cost of living
	Services	Medical, fire, and police
	Attitudes	Pro/con
	Taxes	State/local, direct and indirect
	Environmental regulations	State/local
	Utilities	Cost and availability
	Development support	Bond issues, tax abatement, low-cost loans, grants
Site	Land	Cost, degree of development required, soil characteristics and drainage, room for expansion, parking
	Transportation	Type (access roads, rail spurs, air freight)
	Environmental/legal	Zoning restrictions

often results in economies of scale and, compared with multipurpose plants, lower operating costs. Plant locations may be widely scattered or clustered relatively close to one another.

Market Area Plant Strategy. With this strategy, plants are designed to serve a particular geographic segment of a market (e.g., the West Coast, the Northeast). Individual plants produce most if not all of a company's products and supply a limited geographical area. Although operating costs tend to be higher than those of product plants, significant savings on shipping costs for comparable products can be made. This arrangement is particularly desirable when shipping costs are high due to volume, weight, or other factors. Such arrangements have the added benefit of rapid delivery and response to local needs. This approach requires centralized coordination of decisions to add or delete plants, or to expand or downsize current plants due to changing market conditions.

Process Plant Strategy. With this strategy, different plants concentrate on different aspects of a process. Automobile manufacturers often use this approach, with different plants for engines, transmissions, body stamping, and even radiators. This approach is best suited to products that have numerous components; separating the production of components results in less confusion than if all production were carried out at the same location.

When an organization uses process plants, coordination of production throughout the system becomes a major issue and requires a highly informed, centralized administration to achieve effective operation. A key benefit is that individual plants are highly specialized and generate volumes that yield economies of scale. However, this approach usually involves additional shipping costs.

General-Purpose Plant Strategy. With this strategy, plants are flexible and capable of handling a range of products. This allows for quick response to product or market changes, although it can be less productive than a more focused approach.

Multiple plants have an additional benefit: the increase in learning opportunities that occurs when similar operations are being done in different plants. Similar problems tend to arise, and solutions to those problems as well as improvements in general in products and processes made at one plant can be shared with other plants.

Geographic Information Systems

Geographic information system (GIS) A computer-based tool for collecting, storing, retrieving, and displaying demographic data on maps.

A **geographic information system (GIS)** is a computer-based tool for collecting, storing, retrieving, and displaying demographic data on maps. A GIS relies on an integrated system of computer hardware, software, data, and trained personnel to make available a wide range of geographically referenced information. Internet mapping programs used to obtain travel directions are an example of a GIS.

Many countries have an abundance of GIS data that can be accessed. For location analysis, a GIS makes it relatively easy to obtain detailed information on factors such as population density, age, incomes, ethnicity, traffic patterns, competitor locations, educational institutions, shopping centers, crime statistics, transportation resources, utilities, recreational facilities, maps and images, and a wealth of other information associated with a given location. Local governments use a GIS to organize, analyze, plan, and communicate information about community resources. And job seekers can use GISes for their searches.

Here are some of the ways businesses use geographical information systems:

- **Logistics companies** use GIS data to plan fleet activities such as routes and schedules based on the locations of their customers.
- **Publishers** of magazines and newspapers use a GIS to analyze circulation and attract advertisers.
- **Real estate** companies rely heavily on a GIS to make maps available online to prospective home and business buyers.
- **Banks** use a GIS to help decide where to locate branch banks and to understand the composition and needs of different market segments.
- **Insurance companies** use a GIS to determine premiums based on population distribution, crime figures, and likelihood of natural disasters such as flooding in various locations, and to manage risk.
- **Retailers** are able to link information about sales, customers, and demographics to geographic locations in planning locations. They also use a GIS to develop marketing strategies and for customer mapping, site selection, sales projections, promotions, and other store portfolio management applications.
- **Utility companies** use a GIS to balance supply and demand, and identify problem areas.
- **Emergency services** use a GIS to allocate resources to locations to provide adequate coverage where they are needed.

SERVICE AND RETAIL LOCATIONS

Service and retail are typically governed by somewhat different considerations than manufacturing organizations in making location decisions. For one thing, nearness to raw materials is usually not a factor, nor is concern about processing requirements. Customer access is sometimes a prime consideration, as it is with banks and supermarkets, but not a consideration in others, such as call centers, catalog sales, and online services. Manufacturers tend to be cost-focused, concerned with labor, energy, and material costs and availability, as well as distribution costs. Service and retail businesses tend to be profit or revenue focused, concerned with demographics such as age, income, and education, population/drawing area, competition, traffic volume/patterns, and customer access/parking.

Retail sales and services are usually found near the center of the markets they serve. Examples include fast-food restaurants, service stations, dry cleaners, and supermarkets. Quite often their products and those of their competitors are so similar that they rely on convenience to attract customers. Hence, these businesses seek locations with high population densities or high traffic. The competition/convenience factor is also important in locating banks, hotels and motels, auto repair shops, drugstores, newspaper kiosks, and shopping centers. Similarly, doctors, dentists, lawyers, barbers, and beauticians typically serve clients who reside within a limited area.

Retail and service organizations typically place traffic volume and convenience high on the list of important factors. Specific types of retail or service businesses may pay more attention to certain factors due to the nature of their business or their customers. If a business is unique, and has its own drawing power, nearness to competitors may not be a factor. However, retail businesses generally prefer locations that are near other retailers because of the higher traffic volumes and convenience to customers. For example, automobile dealerships often tend to locate near each other, and restaurants and specialty stores often locate in and around malls. When businesses locate near similar businesses it is referred to as **clustering.**

Clustering Similar types of businesses locate near each other.

Medical services are often located near hospitals for convenience of patients. Doctors' offices may be located near hospitals, or grouped in other, centralized areas with other doctors' offices. Available public transportation is often a consideration.

Good transportation and/or parking facilities can be vital to retail establishments. Downtown areas have a competitive disadvantage in attracting shoppers compared to malls because malls offer ample free parking and nearness to residential areas.

Customer safety and security can be key factors, particularly in urban settings, for all types of services that involve customers coming to the service location (as opposed, say, to in-home services such as home repair and rug cleaning).

Vying for Patients, Hospitals Think Location, Location

READING

Doreen Carvajal

The mood is as vital as the medicine at the elegant Upper East Side clinic squeezed among the fashionable addresses of Calvin Klein, Ralph Lauren, and Barneys New York.

Silk magnolias bloom in the marble lobby, and abstract oil paintings dominate the pale rose corridors of Columbia-Presbyterian Medical Center's new satellite at East 60th Street and Madison Avenue.

The clinic is one of many ways for Columbia-Presbyterian to draw new patients for routine services as well as to feed its main hospital in Washington Heights for more complicated ones. A free shuttle regularly ferries the clinic's patients northwest along the Hudson River, an indirect route skirting Harlem on the way to the hospital, where the neighbors are not elegant boutiques, but the less fabled Self-Serve Laundromat and El Presidente cafeteria.

Location is becoming fiercely important to hospitals in New York's competitive medical marketplace as managed-care systems, so popular elsewhere, begin to take hold here. In the new world of fixed reimbursements, shorter hospital stays, and tighter rationing of highly specialized services, hospitals must make their money from volume rather than from service fees.

The resulting battle for market share—and for new patients—is being waged not with scalpel and stethoscope, but with hammer and nails, in the neighborhoods where potential customers live.

"New York has been relatively slow to follow the rest of the country toward managed health care because it was so regulated," said Kenneth E. Raske, president of the Greater New York Hospital Association. "But they're here now. And they're going to have a profound influence on redrafting the map of New York health care."

Emerging as hospitals' most promising source of new patients are clinics like Columbia-Presbyterian Eastside, which, in health care jargon, are called "centers," lest potential patients confuse these gleaming outposts with conventional clinics that cater to the poor and uninsured. To attract middle-class patients wary of leaving their protected blocks, the city's huge hospitals are branching out to ethnic enclaves, upscale New York neighborhoods, affluent suburban communities, and even distant American expatriate communities in Eastern Europe.

Columbia-Presbyterian created a satellite in Moscow and more centers are planned for Warsaw, Prague, St. Petersburg, Budapest, and possibly Beijing.

"Our feeling is that there will be no hospitals in the future," said Dr. William T. Speck, president of Columbia-Presbyterian.

Hospital executives contend that satellites, which typically have no beds and no provision for round-the-clock care, are cheaper to operate than highly specialized hospitals, which provide all the incidental services of a hotel. Babies, for instance, can be delivered at alternative sites for half a hospital's $9,000 fee, Dr. Speck said.

Source: Doreen Carvajal, "Vying for Patients, Hospitals Think Location, Location," *The New York Times.*

TABLE 8.3
A comparison of service/retail considerations and manufacturing considerations

Manufacturing/Distribution	Service/Retail
Cost focus	**Revenue focus**
Transportation modes/costs	Demographics: age, income, education
Energy availability/costs	Population/drawing area
Labor cost/availability/skills	Competition
Building/leasing costs	Traffic volume/patterns
	Customer access/parking

Many retail firms have multiple outlets (locations). Among the questions that should be considered in such cases are the following:

1. How can sales, market share, and profit be optimized for the entire set of locations? Solutions might include some combination of upgrading facilities, expanding some sites, adding new outlets, and closing or changing the locations of some outlets.
2. What are the potential sales to be realized from each potential solution?
3. Where should outlets be located to maximize market share, sales, and profits without negatively impacting other outlets? This can be a key cause of friction between the operator of a franchise store and the franchising company.
4. What probable effects would there be on market share, sales, and profits if a competitor located nearby?

Table 8.3 briefly compares service/retail site selection criteria with manufacturing criteria.

More and more, retailers have to decide if they want to have both an online and a physical presence, or only one, and if so, which. The following reading outlines some considerations.

Clicks or Bricks, or Both?

READING

The term "clicks-or-bricks" refers to a business model in which a company has either an online (clicks) or an offline (bricks) presence. Many companies have both. Sometimes that business model is referred to as "clicks-and-mortar" or "clicks-and-bricks." In one version, a chain store may allow a customer to order goods online and pick them up at a local store. In another version, large items such as appliances or furniture may be viewed at a local store and then ordered electronically for home delivery. In both instances, the "bricks" portion necessitates a location decision.

Even companies that are seemingly pure "clicks," selling electronic products such as computers, still have warehousing and delivery facilities behind businesses that trade in material goods. Again, location decisions are necessary.

The choice of which business model to use requires taking into account the costs of having a physical presence and what the balance between the two should be. Of course, customer preferences and shopping patterns are important. For example, some reasons people shop online include ease of price comparison, convenience, availability of hard-to-find items, research recommendations, and elimination of the need to travel. Reasons for offline shopping include immediate possession of an item, ease of returns, the security risks of online shopping, the need to use a credit card, the burden of logistics for returns, and ability to "kick the tires" (e.g., try on clothing or footwear, judge quality).

EVALUATING LOCATION ALTERNATIVES

There are a number of techniques that are helpful in evaluating location alternatives: locational cost-profit-volume analysis, factor rating, and the center of gravity method.

Locational Cost-Profit-Volume Analysis

The economic comparison of location alternatives is facilitated by the use of cost-profit-volume analysis. The analysis can be done numerically or graphically. The graphical approach will be demonstrated here because it enhances understanding of the concept and indicates the ranges over which one of the alternatives is superior to the others.

The procedure for **locational cost-profit-volume analysis** involves these steps:

Locational cost-profit-volume analysis Technique for evaluating location choices in economic terms.

1. Determine the fixed and variable costs associated with each location alternative.
2. Plot the total-cost lines for all location alternatives on the same graph.
3. Determine which location will have the lowest total cost for the expected level of output. Alternatively, determine which location will have the highest profit.

This method assumes the following:

1. Fixed costs are constant for the range of probable output.
2. Variable costs are linear for the range of probable output.
3. The required level of output can be closely estimated.
4. Only one product is involved.

For a cost analysis, compute the total cost for each location:

$$\text{Total cost} = \text{FC} + v \times Q \qquad (8\text{–}1)$$

where

FC = Fixed cost
v = Variable cost per unit
Q = Quantity or volume of output

EXAMPLE 1

Fixed and variable costs for four potential plant locations are shown below:

Location	Fixed Cost per Year	Variable Cost per Unit
A	$250,000	$11
B	100,000	30
C	150,000	20
D	200,000	35

a. Plot the total-cost lines for these locations on a single graph.
b. Identify the range of output for which each alternative is superior (i.e., has the lowest total cost).
c. If expected output at the selected location is to be 8,000 units per year, which location would provide the lowest total cost?

SOLUTION

a. To plot the total-cost lines, select an output that is approximately equal to the expected output level (e.g., 10,000 units per year). Compute the total cost for each location at that level:

	Fixed Cost	+	Variable Cost	=	Total Cost
A	$250,000	+	$11(10,000)	=	$360,000
B	100,000	+	30(10,000)	=	400,000
C	150,000	+	20(10,000)	=	350,000
D	200,000	+	35(10,000)	=	550,000

Plot each location's fixed cost (at Output = 0) and the total cost at 10,000 units; and connect the two points with a straight line. (See the accompanying graph.)

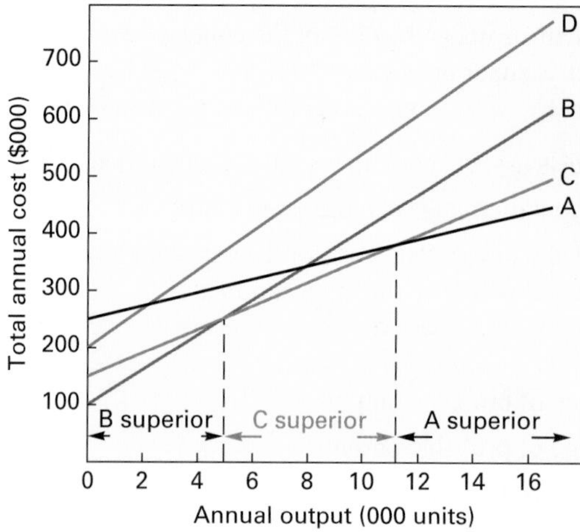

b. The *approximate* ranges for which the various alternatives will yield the lowest costs are shown on the graph. Note that location D is never superior. The *exact* ranges can be determined by finding the output level at which lines B and C and lines C and A cross. To do this, set their total cost equations equal and solve for Q, the break-even output level. Thus, for B and C:

$$\underset{\text{(B)}}{\$100{,}000 + \$30Q} = \underset{\text{(C)}}{\$150{,}000 + \$20Q}$$

Solving, you find $Q = 5{,}000$ units per year.

For C and A:

$$\underset{\text{(C)}}{\$150{,}000 + \$20Q} = \underset{\text{(A)}}{\$250{,}000 + \$11Q}$$

Solving, $Q = 11{,}111$ units per year.

c. From the graph, you can see that for 8,000 units per year, location C provides the lowest total cost.

For a profit analysis, compute the total profit for each location:

$$\text{Total profit} = Q(R - v) - \text{FC} \tag{8–2}$$

where

R = Revenue per unit

Solved Problem 2 at the end of the chapter illustrates profit analysis.

Where the expected level of output is close to the middle of the range over which one alternative is superior, the choice is readily apparent. If the expected level of output is very close to the edge of a range, it means that the two alternatives will yield comparable annual costs, so management would be indifferent in choosing between the two *in terms of total cost.* However, it is important to recognize that, in most situations, other factors besides cost must also be considered. Later in this section, a general scheme for including a broad range of factors is described. First, let's look at another kind of cost often considered in location decisions: transportation costs.

The Transportation Model

Transportation costs sometimes play an important role in location decisions. These can stem from the movement of either raw materials or finished goods. If a facility will be the sole source or destination of shipments, the company can include the transportation costs in a locational cost–volume analysis by incorporating the transportation cost per unit being shipped into the variable cost per unit. (If raw materials are involved, the transportation cost must be converted into cost per unit of *output* in order to correspond to other variable costs.)

When a problem involves shipment of goods from multiple sending points to multiple receiving points, and a new location (sending or receiving point) is to be added to the system, the company should undertake a separate analysis of transportation. In such instances the *transportation model* of linear programming is very helpful. It is a special-purpose algorithm used to determine the minimum transportation cost that would result if a potential new location were to be added to an existing system. It also can be used if a *number* of new facilities are to be added or if an entire new system is being developed. The model is used to analyze each of the configurations considered, and it reveals the minimum costs each would provide. This information can then be included in the evaluation of location alternatives. Solved Problem 1 illustrates how results of a transportation analysis can be combined with the results of a locational cost–volume analysis. See also the chapter supplement.

Factor Rating

Factor rating is a technique that can be applied to a wide range of decisions ranging from personal (buying a car, deciding where to live) to professional (choosing a career, choosing among job offers). Here it is used for location analysis.

A typical location decision involves both qualitative and quantitative inputs, which tend to vary from situation to situation depending on the needs of each organization. **Factor rating** is a general approach that is useful for evaluating a given alternative and comparing alternatives. The value of factor rating is that it provides a rational basis for evaluation and facilitates comparison among alternatives by establishing a *composite* value for each alternative that summarizes all related factors. Factor rating enables decision makers to incorporate their personal opinions and quantitative information in the decision process.

Factor rating General approach to evaluating locations that includes quantitative and qualitative inputs.

The following procedure is used to develop a factor rating:

1. Determine which factors are relevant (e.g., location of market, water supply, parking facilities, revenue potential).
2. Assign a weight to each factor that indicates its relative importance compared with all other factors.
3. Decide on a common scale for all factors (e.g., 1 to 100), and set a minimum acceptable score if necessary.
4. Score each location alternative.
5. Multiply the factor weight by the score for each factor, and sum the results for each location alternative.
6. Choose the alternative that has the highest composite score, unless it fails to meet the minimum acceptable score.

This procedure is illustrated in Example 2.

EXAMPLE 2

A photo-processing company intends to open a new branch store. The following table contains information on two potential locations. Which is the better alternative?

		Scores (Out of 100)		Weighted Scores	
Factor	**Weight**	**Alt. 1**	**Alt. 2**	**Alternative 1**	**Alternative 2**
Proximity to existing store	.10	100	60	.10(100) = 10.0	.10(60) = 6.0
Traffic volume	.05	80	80	.05(80) = 4.0	.05(80) = 4.0
Rental costs	.40	70	90	.40(70) = 28.0	.40(90) = 36.0
Size	.10	86	92	.10(86) = 8.6	.10(92) = 9.2
Layout	.20	40	70	.20(40) = 8.0	.20(70) = 14.0
Operating costs	.15	80	90	.15(80) = 12.0	.15(90) = 13.5
				70.6	82.7

SOLUTION 

Alternative 2 is better because it has the higher composite score.

In some cases, managers may prefer to establish minimum *thresholds* for composite scores. If an alternative fails to meet that minimum, they can reject it without further consideration. If none of the alternatives meets the minimum, this means that either additional alternatives must be identified and evaluated or the minimum threshold must be reevaluated.

The Center of Gravity Method

Center of gravity method Method for locating a distribution center that minimizes distribution cost.

The **center of gravity method** is a method to determine the location of a facility that will minimize shipping costs or travel time to various destinations. For example, community planners use the method to determine the location of fire and public safety centers, schools, community centers, and such, taking into consideration locations of hospitals, senior living centers, population density, highways, airports, and retail businesses. The goal for police and firefighters is often to minimize travel time to answer emergency calls. The center of gravity method is also used for location planning for distribution centers, where the goal is typically to minimize distribution costs. The method treats distribution cost as a linear function of the distance and the quantity shipped. The quantity to be shipped to each destination is assumed to be fixed (i.e., will not change over time). An acceptable variation is that quantities are allowed to change, as long as their relative amounts remain the same (e.g., seasonal variations).

The method includes the use of a map that shows the locations of destinations. The map must be accurate and drawn to scale. A coordinate system is overlaid on the map to determine relative locations. The location of the (0,0) point of the coordinate system, and its scale, is unimportant. Once the coordinate system is in place, you can determine the coordinates of each destination. (See Figure 8.1, parts A and B.)

If the quantities to be shipped to every location are *equal,* you can obtain the coordinates of the center of gravity (i.e., the location of the distribution center) by finding the average of the x coordinates and the average of the y coordinates (see Figure 8.1). These averages can be easily determined using the following formulas:

$$\bar{x} = \frac{\Sigma x_i}{n} \qquad \bar{y} = \frac{\Sigma y_i}{n} \tag{8–3}$$

where

x_i = x coordinate of destination i

y_i = y coordinate of destination i

n = Number of destinations

When the number of units to be shipped is not the same for all destinations (usually the case), a *weighted average* must be used to determine the center of gravity, with the weights being the *quantities* to be shipped. In some cases, the number of trips can be more important than quantities, so that metric would be used instead of quantities.

FIGURE 8.1 Center of gravity method

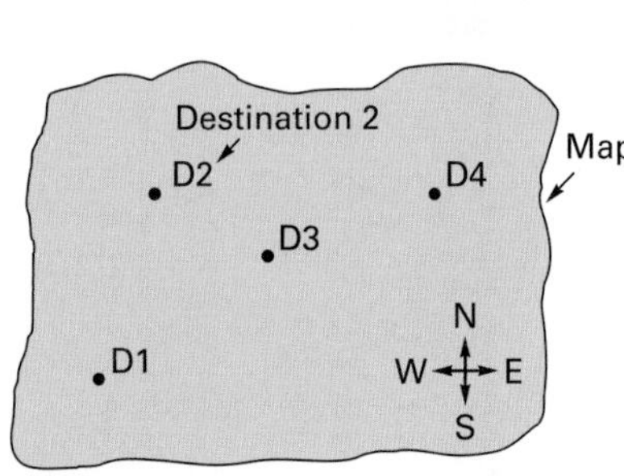

A. Map showing destinations

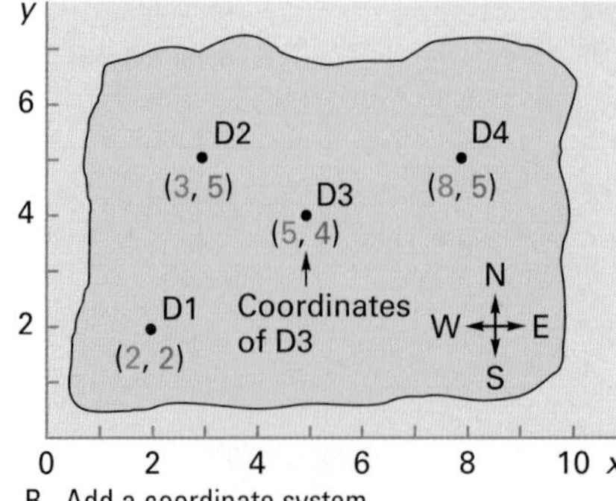

B. Add a coordinate system

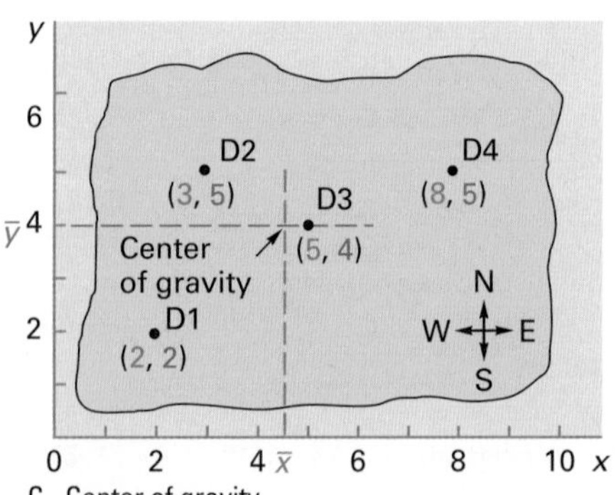

C. Center of gravity

The appropriate formulas are

$$\bar{x} = \frac{\Sigma x_i Q_i}{\Sigma Q_i}$$
$$\bar{y} = \frac{\Sigma y_i Q_i}{\Sigma Q_i} \quad (8\text{–}4)$$

where

Q_i = Quantity to be shipped to destination i

x_i = x coordinate of destination i

y_i = y coordinate of destination i

Determine the coordinates of the center of gravity for the problem depicted in Figure 8.1C. Assume that the shipments from the center of gravity to each of the four destinations will be equal quantities.

SOLUTION

The coordinates of the destinations can be obtained from Figure 8.1B:

Destination	x	y
D1	2,	2
D2	3,	5
D3	5,	4
D4	8,	5
	18	16

$$\bar{x} = \frac{\Sigma x_i}{n} = \frac{18}{4} = 4.5 \qquad \bar{y} = \frac{\Sigma y_i}{n} = \frac{16}{4} = 4$$

Hence, the center of gravity is at (4.5,4), which places it just west of destination D3 (see Figure 8.1).

Suppose that the shipments for the problem depicted in Figure 8.1A are not all equal, but instead are the following:

Destination	x	y	Weekly Quantity
D1	2,	2	800
D2	3,	5	900
D3	5,	4	200
D4	8,	5	100
			2,000

Determine the center of gravity.

Because the quantities to be shipped differ among destinations, you must use the weighted average formulas.

$$\bar{x} = \frac{\Sigma x_i Q_i}{\Sigma Q_i} = \frac{2(800) + 3(900) + 5(200) + 8(100)}{2{,}000} = \frac{6{,}100}{2{,}000} = 3.05 \text{ [round to 3]}$$

$$\bar{y} = \frac{\Sigma y_i Q_i}{\Sigma Q_i} = \frac{2(800) + 5(900) + 4(200) + 5(100)}{2{,}000} = \frac{7{,}400}{2{,}000} = 3.7$$

Hence, the coordinates of the center of gravity are approximately (3,3.7). This would place it south of destination D2, which has coordinates of (3,5). (See Figure 8.2.)

FIGURE 8.2 Center of gravity for Example 4

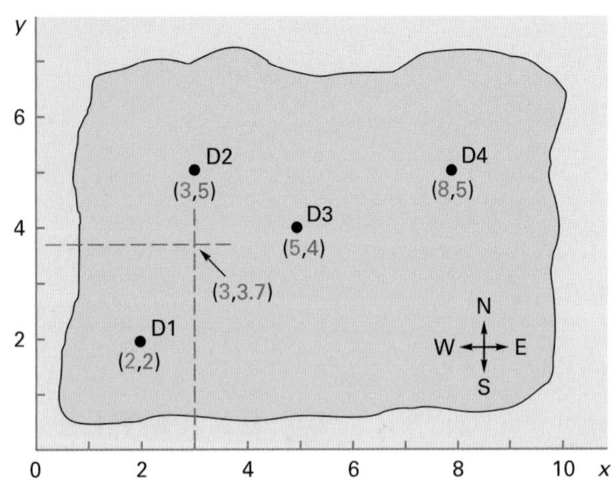

FIGURE 8.3 Solution for Example 4

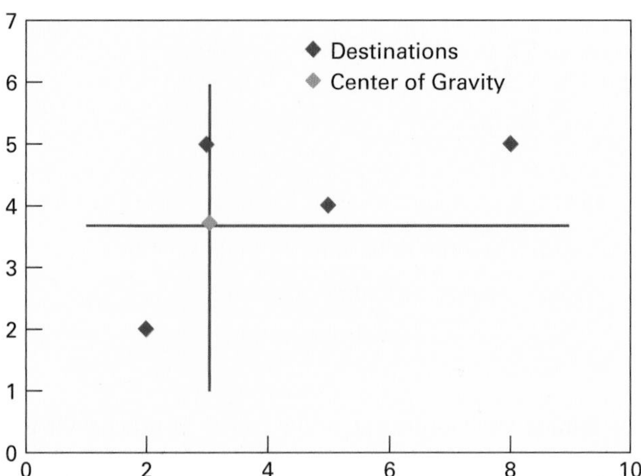

See Figure 8.3 for a graph of the solution to Example 4. The problem can also be solved using the appropriate Excel template that is available on the text Web site.

SUMMARY

Location decisions confront both new and existing organizations. Growth, market shifts, depletion of raw materials, and the introduction of new products and services are among the reasons organizations are concerned with location decisions. The importance of these decisions is underscored by the long-term commitment they typically involve and by their potential impact on the operating system.

The primary location options available to existing organizations are to expand an existing location, move to a new location, maintain existing facilities while adding another facility in a new location, or do nothing.

In practice, the major influences on location decisions are location of raw materials, labor supply, market considerations, community-related factors, site-related factors, and climate. Foreign locations may be attractive in terms of labor costs, abundance of raw materials, or as potential markets for a firm's products or services. Problems organizations sometimes encounter in foreign countries include language differences, cultural differences, bias, and political instability.

A common approach to narrowing the range of location alternatives is to first identify a country or region that seems to satisfy overall needs and then identify a number of community-site alternatives for more in-depth analysis. A variety of methods are used to evaluate location alternatives. Those described in the chapter include locational cost-profit-volume analysis, factor rating, and the center of gravity method. The transportation model was mentioned briefly; the chapter supplement contains a more complete description of that subject.

There are numerous commercial software packages available for location analysis. In addition to the models described, many packages employ linear programming or mixed integer programming algorithms. In addition, some software packages use heuristic approaches to obtain reasonable solutions to location problems.

KEY POINTS

1. Location decisions are strategic; they can have a significant impact on the success or failure of a business.
2. Very often, location decisions are long term and involve substantial cost, so it is important to devote an appropriate amount of effort to selecting a location.
3. Decision makers must not let the attractiveness of a few factors cloud the decision-making process. There are many factors to take into account when selecting a location. It is essential to identify the key factors and their relative importance, and then to use that information to evaluate location alternatives.
4. It is important to also factor in the impact that location choices will have on the supply chain.

KEY TERMS

center of gravity method, 354
clustering, 349
factor rating, 353
geographic information system (GIS), 348
locational cost-profit-volume analysis, 351
microfactory, 345

SOLVED PROBLEMS

Problem 1

Cost analysis. A farm implements dealer is seeking a fourth warehouse location to complement three existing warehouses. There are three potential locations: Charlotte, NC; Atlanta, GA; and Columbia, SC. Charlotte would involve a fixed cost of $4,000 per month and a variable cost of $4 per unit; Atlanta would involve a fixed cost of $3,500 per month and a variable cost of $5 per unit; and Columbia would involve a fixed cost of $5,000 per month and a variable cost of $6 per unit. Use of the Charlotte location would increase system transportation costs by $19,000 per month, Atlanta by $22,000 per month, and Columbia by $18,000 per month. Which location would result in the lowest total cost to handle 800 units per month?

Solution

Given: Volume = 800 units per month

	FC per Month	Variable Cost per Unit, *v*	Transportation Cost per Month
Charlotte	$4,000	$4	$19,000
Atlanta	3,500	5	22,000
Columbia	5,000	6	18,000

Monthly total cost = FC + VC + Transportation cost

Charlotte: $4,000 + $4 per unit × 800 units + $19,000 = $26,200

Atlanta: 3,500 + 5 per unit × 800 units + 22,000 = 29,500

Columbia: 5,000 + 6 per unit × 800 units + 18,000 = 27,800

Hence, Charlotte would have the lowest total cost for this monthly volume.

Problem 2

Profit analysis. A manufacturer of staplers is about to lose its lease, so it must move to another location. Two sites are currently under consideration. Fixed costs would be $8,000 per month at site A and $9,400 per month at site B. Variable costs are expected to be $5 per unit at site A and $4 per unit at site B. Monthly demand has been steady at 8,800 units for the last several years and is not expected to deviate from that amount in the foreseeable future. Assume staplers sell for $6 per unit. Determine which location would yield the higher profit under these conditions.

Solution

$$\text{Profit} = Q(R - v) - \text{FC}$$

Site	Revenue	FC	*v*	Monthly Profit
A	$52,800	$8,000	$44,000	$ 800
B	$52,800	$9,400	$35,200	$8,200

Hence, site B is expected to yield the higher monthly profit.

Problem 3

Factor rating. Determine which location has the highest factor rating given the following information:

		Location Scores	
Factor	Weight	A	B
Labor cost	5	20	40
Material cost	3	10	30
Transportation costs	2	50	10

Solution

Combining the weights with the location scores, we can see that location B has the higher score:

		Location Scores		Weighted Scores	
Factor	Weight	A	B	A	B
Labor cost	5	20	40	5(20) = 100	5(40) = 200
Material cost	3	10	30	3(10) = 30	3(30) = 90
Transportation costs	2	50	10	2(50) = 100	2(10) = 20
				230	310

Note that Location A has very low labor costs compared to Location B, but that is more than offset by its relatively high transportation costs compared to those of Location B.

Problem 4

Center of gravity. Determine the center of gravity location for these destinations:

Destination	*x,y* Coordinates	Weekly Quantity
D1	3,5	20
D2	6,8	10
D3	2,7	15
D4	4,5	15
		60

Solution

If the weekly quantities had all been equal, we could have used the two equations in Formula 8–3 to find the center of gravity. Because the weekly quantities are not all equal, we must use the equations in Formula 8–4.

$$\bar{x} = \frac{\Sigma xQ}{\Sigma Q} = \frac{3(20) + 6(10) + 2(15) + 4(15)}{60} = \frac{210}{60} = 3.5$$

$$\bar{y} = \frac{\Sigma yQ}{\Sigma Q} = \frac{5(20) + 8(10) + 7(15) + 5(15)}{60} = \frac{360}{60} = 6.0$$

Hence, the center of gravity has the coordinates $x = 3.5$ and $y = 6$.

DISCUSSION AND REVIEW QUESTIONS

1. In what ways can the location decision have an impact on the production system?
2. Respond to this statement: "The importance of the location decision is often vastly overrated; the fact that virtually every type of business is located in every section of the country means there should be no problem in finding a suitable location."
3. What community factors influence location decisions?
4. How are manufacturing and nonmanufacturing location decisions similar? Different?
5. What are the potential benefits of locating in foreign countries? Potential drawbacks?
6. What is factor rating, and how does it work?
7. Outline the general approach for developing location alternatives.
8. What are the basic assumptions in locational cost-profit-volume analysis?
9. Discuss recent trends in location and possible future strategies.

TAKING STOCK

1. What trade-offs are involved in deciding to have a single large, centrally located facility instead of several smaller, dispersed facilities?
2. Who needs to be involved in facility location decisions?
3. Name several ways that technology has had an impact on location decisions.

CRITICAL THINKING EXERCISES

1. A company is considering the relocation of its manufacturing plant and administrative offices from a small city in the Midwest to a similar-sized city in the South. Approximately 20 percent of the residents of the city are employed by the company, and many others are employed in businesses such as banks, personal services, restaurants, shopping centers, and supermarkets that would suffer a decline in business if the company decides to relocate. Does the company have a social responsibility to factor into its decision the impact that its move would have on the city? Explain your reasoning.
2. The owner of a fast-food franchise has exclusive rights to operate in a medium-sized metropolitan area. The owner currently has a single outlet open, which has proved to be very popular, and there are often waiting lines of customers. The owner is therefore considering opening one or more outlets in the area. What are the key factors that the owner should investigate before making a final decision? What trade-offs would there be in opening one additional site versus opening several additional sites?
3. Corruption and bribery are common in some countries. Would you avoid locating in such a country, or locate there and deal with it? If the latter, how would you deal with it?
4. Give three examples of unethical behavior involving location selection, and indicate which ethical principle is violated (see Chapter 1).

PROBLEMS

1. A newly formed firm must decide on a plant location. There are two alternatives under consideration: locate near the major raw materials or locate near the major customers. Locating near the raw materials will result in lower fixed and variable costs than locating near the market, but the owners believe there would be a loss in sales volume because customers tend to favor local suppliers. Revenue per unit will be $185 in either case. Using the following information, determine which location would produce the greater profit.

	Omaha	Kansas City
Annual fixed costs ($ millions)	$1.2	$1.4
Variable cost per unit	$36	$47
Expected annual demand (units)	8,000	12,000

2. The owner of Genuine Subs, Inc., hopes to expand the present operation by adding one new outlet. She has studied three locations. Each would have the same labor and materials costs (food, serving containers, napkins, etc.) of $1.76 cents per sandwich. Sandwiches sell for $2.65 each in all locations. Rent and equipment costs would be $5,000 per month for location A, $5,500 per month for location B, and $5,800 per month for location C.
   a. Determine the volume necessary at each location to realize a monthly profit of $10,000.
   b. If expected sales at A, B, and C are 21,000 per month, 22,000 per month, and 23,000 per month, respectively, which location would yield the greatest profits?
3. A small producer of machine tools wants to move to a larger building, and has identified two alternatives. Location A has annual fixed costs of $800,000 and variable costs of $14,000 per unit; location B has annual fixed costs of $920,000 and variable costs of $13,000 per unit. The finished items sell for $17,000 each.
   a. At what volume of output would the two locations have the same total cost?
   b. For what range of output would location A be superior? For what range would B be superior?
4. A company that produces pleasure boats has decided to expand one of its lines. Current facilities are insufficient to handle the increased workload, so the company is considering three alternatives, A (new location), B (subcontract), and C (expand existing facilities).

   Alternative A would involve substantial fixed costs but relatively low variable costs: fixed costs would be $250,000 per year, and variable costs would be $500 per boat. Subcontracting would involve a cost per boat of $2,500, and expansion would require an annual fixed cost of $50,000 and a variable cost of $1,000 per boat.
   a. Find the range of output for each alternative that would yield the lowest total cost.
   b. Which alternative would yield the lowest total cost for an expected annual volume of 150 boats?
   c. What other factors might be considered in choosing between expansion and subcontracting?
5. Rework Problem 4b using this additional information: Expansion would result in an increase of $70,000 per year in transportation costs, subcontracting would result in an increase of $25,000 per year, and adding a new location would result in an increase of $4,000 per year.
6. A firm that has recently experienced an enormous growth rate is seeking to lease a small plant in Memphis, TN; Biloxi, MS; or Birmingham, AL. Prepare an economic analysis of the three locations given the following information: Annual costs for building, equipment, and administration would be $40,000 for Memphis, $60,000 for Biloxi, and $100,000 for Birmingham. Labor and materials are expected to be $8 per unit in Memphis, $4 per unit in Biloxi, and $5 per unit in Birmingham. The Memphis location would increase system transportation costs by $50,000 per year, the Biloxi location by $60,000 per year, and the Birmingham location by $25,000 per year. Expected annual volume is 10,000 units.
7. A retired auto mechanic hopes to open a rustproofing shop. Customers would be local new-car dealers. Two locations are being considered, one in the center of the city and one on the outskirts. The central city location would involve fixed monthly costs of $7,000 and labor, materials, and transportation costs of $30 per car. The outside location would have fixed monthly costs of $4,700 and labor, materials, and transportation costs of $40 per car. Dealer price at either location will be $90 per car.
   a. Which location will yield the greatest profit if monthly demand is (1) 200 cars? (2) 300 cars?
   b. At what volume of output will the two sites yield the same monthly profit?
8. For each of the four types of organizations shown, rate the importance of each factor in terms of making location decisions using L = low importance, M = moderate importance, and H = high importance.

Factor	Local Bank	Steel Mill	Food Warehouse	Public School
Convenience for customers	_____	_____	_____	_____
Attractiveness of building	_____	_____	_____	_____
Nearness to raw materials	_____	_____	_____	_____
Large amounts of power	_____	_____	_____	_____
Pollution controls	_____	_____	_____	_____
Labor cost and availability	_____	_____	_____	_____
Transportation costs	_____	_____	_____	_____
Construction costs	_____	_____	_____	_____

9. Using the following factor ratings, determine which location alternative (A, B, or C) should be chosen on the basis of maximum composite score.

Factor (100 points each)	Weight	Location Score A	B	C
Convenience	.15	80	70	60
Parking facilities	.20	72	76	92
Display area	.18	88	90	90
Shopper traffic	.27	94	86	80
Operating costs	.10	98	90	82
Neighborhood	.10	96	85	75
	1.00			

10. Determine which location has the highest composite score:

Factor	Weight	East #1	East #2	West
Initial cost	8	100	150	140
Traffic	10	40	40	30
Maintenance	6	20	25	18
Dock space	6	25	10	12
Neighborhood	4	12	8	15

11. A manager has received an analysis of several cities being considered for a new office complex. The data (10 points maximum) are as follows:

Factor	Location Score A	B	C
Business services	9	5	5
Community services	7	6	7
Real estate cost	3	8	7
Construction costs	5	6	5
Cost of living	4	7	8
Taxes	5	5	4
Transportation	6	7	8

a. If the manager weights the factors equally, how would the locations stack up in terms of their composite factor rating scores?

b. If business services and construction costs are given weights that are double the weights of the other factors, how would the locations stack up?

12. A toy manufacturer produces toys in five locations throughout the country. Raw materials (primarily barrels of powdered plastic) will be shipped from a new, centralized warehouse whose location is to be determined. The monthly quantities to be shipped to each location are the same. A coordinate system has been established, and the coordinates of each location have been determined as shown. Determine the coordinates of the centralized warehouse.

Location	(x,y)
A	3,7
B	8,2
C	4,6
D	4,1
E	6,4

13. A clothing manufacturer produces women's clothes at four locations in Mexico. Relative locations have been determined, as shown in the table below. The location of a central shipping point for bolts of cloth must now be determined. Weekly quantities to be shipped to each location are also shown in the table. Determine the coordinates of the location that will minimize distribution costs.

Location	(x,y)	Weekly Quantity
A	5,7	15
B	6,9	20
C	3,9	25
D	9,4	30

14. A company that handles hazardous waste wants to minimize the shipping cost for shipments to a disposal center from five receiving stations it operates. Given the locations of the receiving stations and the volumes to be shipped daily, determine the location of the disposal center.

Location of Processing Station, (x,y)	Volume, Tons per Day
10,5	26
4,1	9
4,7	25
2,6	30
8,7	40

15. An analysis of sites for a distribution center has led to two possible sites (L1 and L2 on the map). The sites are comparable on every key factor. The one remaining factor is the center of gravity. Use the center of gravity method to select the better site. Monthly shipments will be the quantities listed in the table.

Destination	Quantity
D1	900
D2	300
D3	700
D4	600
D5	1200

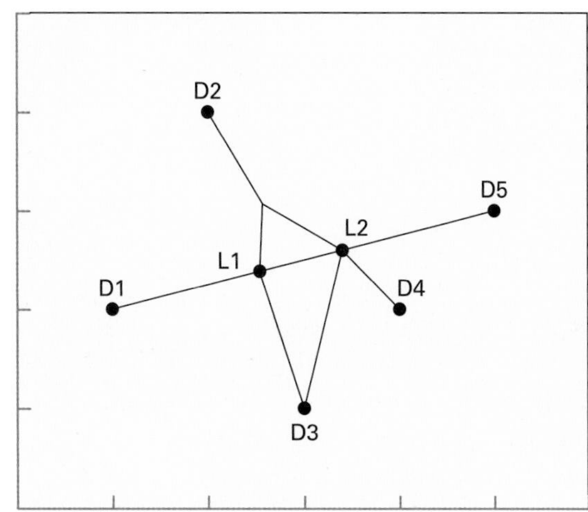

Hello, Walmart?

CASE

Walmart is the largest corporation in the world, and it has obviously enjoyed tremendous success. But while many welcome its location in their communities, others do not. Some complain that its presence has too many negative effects on a community, ranging from traffic congestion to anti-union sentiment to unfair competition.

Suppose Walmart has announced plans to seek approval from the planning commission of a small town to build a new store. Develop a list of the main arguments, pro and con, that could be presented at a public hearing on the matter by members of each of these groups:

1. Owners of small businesses located nearby.
2. Town residents, and residents of nearby towns.

How might a Walmart representative respond to the negative criticisms that might be brought up, and what other benefits could the representative offer the planning board to bolster Walmart's case for gaining the board's approval?

SELECTED BIBLIOGRAPHY AND FURTHER READINGS

Ballou, Ronald H. *Business Logistics Management.* 5th ed. Upper Saddle River, NJ: Prentice Hall, 2004.

De Meirleir, Marcel. *Location, Location, Location: A Plant Location and Site Selection Guide.* London: Routledge, 2008.

Ferdows, Kasra. "Making the Most of Foreign Factories." *Harvard Business Review,* March–April 1997, pp. 73–88.

Francis, Richard L., Leon F. McGinnis Jr., and John A. White. *Layout and Location: An Analytical Approach.* 3rd ed. Upper Saddle River, NJ: Prentice Hall, 1998.

Grimshaw, David J. *Bringing Geographical Information Systems into Business.* New York: John Wiley & Sons, 2000.

Mentzer, John T. "Seven Keys to Facility Location." *Supply Chain Management Review* 12, no.5, May 2008, p. 25.

SUPPLEMENT TO

CHAPTER

8

The Transportation Model

LEARNING OBJECTIVES

After completing this supplement, you should be able to:

1 Describe the nature of a transportation problem.

2 Set up transportation problems in the general linear programming format.

3 Interpret computer solutions.

SUPPLEMENT OUTLINE

Note: The Web site for this book contains a module that provides detailed instruction on problem solving using the transportation method.

The transportation problem involves finding the lowest-cost plan for distributing stocks of goods or *supplies* from multiple origins to multiple destinations that *demand* the goods. For instance, a firm might have three factories, all of which are capable of producing identical units of the same product, and four warehouses that stock or demand those products, as depicted in Figure 8S.1. The *transportation model* can be used to determine how to allocate the supplies available from the various factories to the warehouses that stock or demand those goods, in such a way that total shipping cost is minimized (i.e., the optimal shipping plan). Usually, analysis of the problem will produce a shipping plan that pertains to a certain period of time (day, week), although once the plan is established, it will generally not change unless one or more of the parameters of the problem (supply, demand, unit shipping cost) changes.

SCREENCAM TUTORIAL

INTRODUCTION

Although Figure 8S.1 illustrates the nature of the transportation problem, in real life managers must often deal with allocation problems that are considerably larger in scope. A beer maker may have four or five breweries and hundreds or even thousands of distributors, and an automobile manufacturer may have eight assembly plants scattered throughout the United States and Canada and thousands of dealers that must be supplied with those cars. In such cases, the ability to identify the optimal distribution plan makes the transportation model very important.

FIGURE 8S.1
The transportation problem involves determining a minimum-cost plan for shipping from multiple sources to multiple destinations

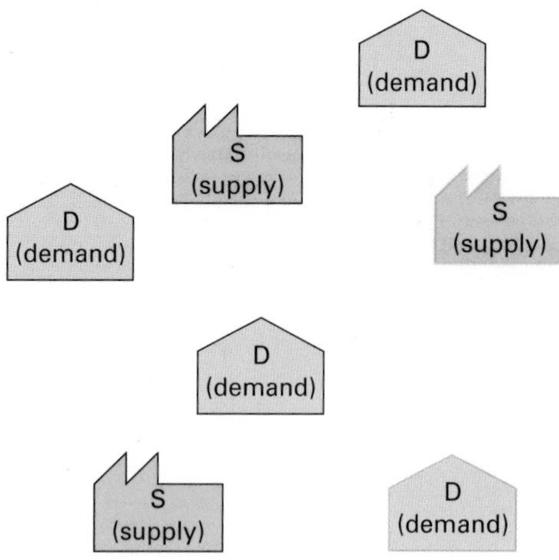

The shipping (supply) points can be factories, warehouses, departments, or any other place from which goods are sent. Destinations can be factories, warehouses, departments, or other points that receive goods. The information needed to use the model consists of the following:

1. A list of the origins and each one's capacity or supply quantity per period.
2. A list of the destinations and each one's demand per period.
3. The unit cost of shipping items from each origin to each destination.

This information is arranged into a *transportation table* (see Table 8S.1).

The transportation model is one of a class of linear programming models, so named because of the linear relationships among variables. In the transportation model, transportation costs are treated as a direct linear function of the number of units shipped.

Use of the transportation model implies that certain assumptions are satisfied. The following are the major ones:

1. The items to be shipped are homogeneous (i.e., they are the same regardless of their source or destination).
2. Shipping cost per unit is the same regardless of the number of units shipped.
3. There is only one route or mode of transportation being used between each origin and each destination.

TABLE 8S.1
A transportation table

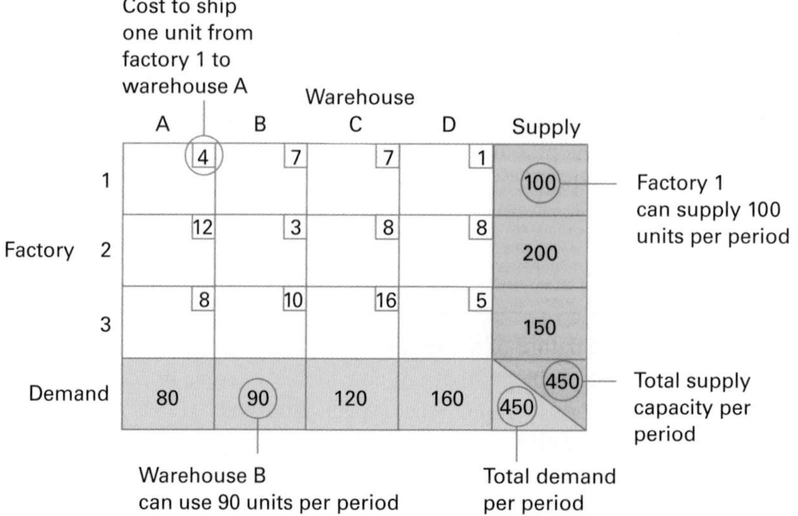

		Warehouse A	Warehouse B	Warehouse C	Warehouse D	Supply
Factory	1	4	7	7	1	100
	2	12	3	8	8	200
	3	8	10	16	5	150
Demand		80	90	120	160	450 / 450

		Warehouse A	Warehouse B	Warehouse C	Warehouse D	Supply
Factory	1	[4]	[7]	[7] 10	[1] 90	100
	2	[12]	[3] 90	[8] 110	[8]	200
	3	[8] 80	[10]	[16]	[5] 70	150
Demand		80	90	120	160	450 / 450

FIGURE 8S.2
Solution for the problem shown in Figure 8S.1

The solution to the problem shown in Figure 8S.1 would look like the one shown in Figure 8S.2. The Web site for this book has instructions for obtaining solutions for transportation problems.

LOCATION DECISIONS

The transportation model can be used to compare location alternatives in terms of their impact on the total distribution costs for a system. The procedure involves working through a separate problem for each location being considered and then comparing the resulting total costs.

If other costs, such as production costs, differ among locations, these can easily be included in the analysis, provided they can be determined on a per-unit basis. In this regard, note that merely adding or subtracting a constant to all cost values in any row or column will not affect the optimum solution; any additional costs should only be included if they have a varying effect within a row or column.

OTHER APPLICATIONS

We have seen how the transportation model can be used to minimize the costs associated with distributing goods, and we have seen how the model can be used for comparing location alternatives. The model is also used in a number of other ways. For example, in a slight variation of the model, profits can be used in place of costs. In such cases, each of the cell profits can be subtracted from the largest profit, and the remaining values (opportunity costs) can be treated in the same manner as shipping costs.

Some of the other uses of the model include production planning (see Chapter 11), problems involving assignment of personnel or jobs to certain departments or machines (see Chapter 16), capacity planning, and transshipment problems.[1]

The use of the transportation model for capacity planning parallels its use for location decisions. An organization can subject proposed capacity alternatives to transportation analysis to determine which one would generate the lowest total shipping cost. For example, it is perhaps intuitively obvious that a factory or warehouse that is close to its market—or has low transportation costs for some other reason—should probably have a larger capacity than other locations. Of course, many problems are not so simple, and they require actual use of the model.

[1]Transshipment relates to problems with major distribution centers that in turn redistribute to smaller market destinations. See, for example, W. J. Stevenson and C. Ozgur, *Introduction to Management Science with Spreadsheets* (New York: McGraw-Hill, 2006).

COMPUTER SOLUTIONS

SCREENCAM TUTORIAL

Although manual solution of transportation problems is fairly straightforward, computer solutions are generally preferred, particularly for moderate or large problems. Many software packages call for data input in the same tabular form used in this supplement. A more general approach is to format the problem as a standard linear programming model (i.e., specify the objective function and a set of constraints). That approach enables one to use the more general version of an LP package to solve a transportation problem. Let's consider this general approach.

The decision variables for a transportation model are the quantities to be shipped. Because each cell represents a potential transportation route, each must have a decision variable. We can use the symbol x_{1A} to represent the decision variable for cell 1A, x_{1B} for cell 1B, and so on. The objective function consists of the cell costs and these cell symbols:

$$\text{Minimize } 4x_{1A} + 7x_{1B} + 7x_{1C} + 1x_{1D} + 12x_{2A} + 3x_{2B} + 8x_{2C} + 8x_{2D} + 8x_{3A} + 10x_{3B} + 16x_{3C} + 5x_{3D}$$

Because the amounts allocated in any row or column must add to the row or column total, each row and column must have a constraint. Thus, we have

Supply (rows)

$$x_{1A} + x_{1B} + x_{1C} + x_{1D} = 100$$
$$x_{2A} + x_{2B} + x_{2C} + x_{2D} = 200$$
$$x_{3A} + x_{3B} + x_{3C} + x_{3D} = 150$$

Demand (columns)

$$x_{1A} + x_{2A} + x_{3A} = 80$$
$$x_{1B} + x_{2B} + x_{3B} = 90$$
$$x_{1C} + x_{2C} + x_{3C} = 120$$
$$x_{1D} + x_{2D} + x_{3D} = 160$$

We do not need a constraint for the total; the row and column constraints take care of this.

If supply and demand are not equal, add an extra (dummy) row or column with the necessary supply (demand) for equality to the table before writing the constraints.

FIGURE 8S.3

Excel template forTable 8S.1

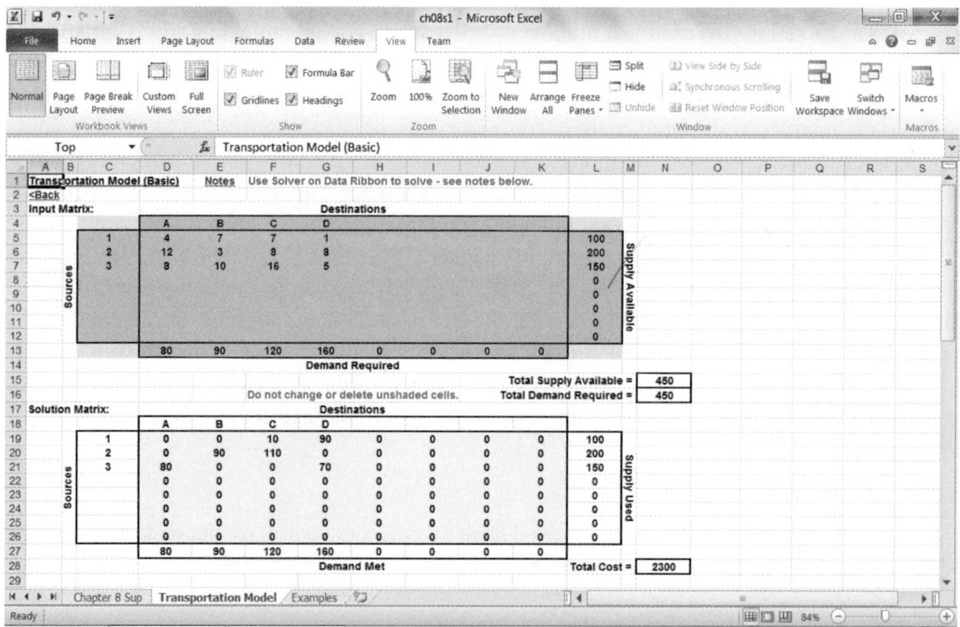

Another approach to transportation problems is to use spreadsheet software. The Excel templates can also be used to solve transportation problems. Figure 8S.3 illustrates the Excel worksheet for the preceding problem.

PROBLEMS

1. Solve this linear programming (LP) problem using the transportation method. Find the optimal transportation plan and the minimum cost. Also, decide if there is an alternate solution. If there is one, identify it.

$$\text{Minimize } 8x_{11} + 2x_{12} + 5x_{13} + 2x_{21} + x_{22} + 3x_{23} + 7x_{31} + 2x_{32} + 6x_{33}$$

$$\begin{aligned}\text{Subject to } \quad x_{11} + x_{12} + x_{13} &= 90\\ x_{21} + x_{22} + x_{23} &= 105\\ x_{31} + x_{32} + x_{33} &= 105\\ x_{11} + x_{21} + x_{31} &= 150\\ x_{12} + x_{22} + x_{32} &= 75\\ x_{13} + x_{23} + x_{33} &= 75\\ \text{All variables} &\geq 0\end{aligned}$$

2. A toy manufacturer wants to open a third warehouse that will supply three retail outlets. The new warehouse will supply 500 units of backyard playsets per week. Two locations are being studied, N1 and N2. Transportation costs for location N1 to stores A, B, and C are \$6, \$8, and \$7 per unit, respectively; for location N2, the costs are \$10, \$6, and \$4, respectively. The existing system is shown in the following table. Which location would result in the lower transportation costs for the system?

Warehouse From:	Store To: A	B	C	Capacity (Units/week)
1	[8]	[3]	[7]	500
2	[5]	[10]	[9]	400
Demand (Units/week)	400	600	350	

3. A large firm is contemplating construction of a new manufacturing facility. The two leading locations are Toledo and Cincinnati. The new factory would have a supply capacity of 160 units per week. Transportation costs from each potential location and existing locations are shown in the following table. Determine which location would provide the lower transportation costs.

From Toledo to	Cost per Unit	From Cincinnati to	Cost per Unit
A	\$18	A	\$ 7
B	8	B	17
C	13	C	13

	A	B	C	Supply (Units/week)
1	[10]	[14]	[10]	210
2	[12]	[17]	[20]	140
3	[11]	[11]	[12]	150
Demand (Units/week)	220	220	220	

4. A large retailer is planning to open a new store. Three locations in California are currently under consideration: South Coast Plaza (SCP), Fashion Island (FI), and Laguna Hills (LH). Transportation costs for the locations and costs, demands, and supplies for existing locations and warehouses (origins), are shown below. Each of the locations has a demand potential of 300 units per week. Which location would yield the lowest transportation costs for the system?

	TO		
From Warehouse	**SCP**	**FI**	**LH**
1	$ 4	$7	$5
2	11	6	5
3	5	5	6

	A	B	Supply (Units/week)
1	(15)	(9)	660
2	(10)	(7)	340
3	(14)	(18)	200
Demand (Units/week)	400	500	

SELECTED BIBLIOGRAPHY AND FURTHER READINGS

Bierman, Harold, Charles P. Bonini, and Warren H. Hausman. *Quantitative Analysis for Business Decisions.* 8th ed. Homewood, IL: Richard D. Irwin, 1991.

Stevenson, William J., and Ceyhun Ozgur. *Introduction to Management Science with Spreadsheets.* New York: McGraw-Hill, 2006.

Management of Quality

CHAPTER

CHAPTER OUTLINE

LEARNING OBJECTIVES

After completing this chapter, you should be able to:

1. Define the term *quality* as it relates to products and as it relates to services.
2. Explain why quality is important and the consequences of poor quality.
3. Identify the determinants of quality.
4. Distinguish the costs associated with quality.
5. Compare the quality awards.
6. Discuss the philosophies of quality gurus.
7. Describe TQM.
8. Give an overview of problem solving.
9. Give an overview of process improvement.
10. Describe and use various quality tools.

This chapter is the first of two chapters on quality. In this chapter you will learn about the evolution of quality management, definitions of quality, the costs of quality and the consequences of poor quality, some quality awards and quality certification, total quality management, and quality tools.

The importance of quality cannot be overstated; two key elements of every purchasing decision are price and quality. Consequently, having a focus on quality and quality improvement should be a part of every business organization, whether the organization's business is making cars, selling electronic goods, providing financial services, providing medical services, or baking cookies.

INTRODUCTION

Broadly defined, **quality** refers to the ability of a product or service to consistently meet or exceed customer requirements or expectations. Different customers will have different requirements, so a working definition of quality is customer-dependent.

Quality The ability of a product or service to consistently meet or exceed customer expectations.

For a decade or so, quality was an important focal point in business. But after a while, the emphasis on quality began to fade, and quality took a backseat to other concerns. However, there has been an upsurge recently in the need for attention to quality. Much of this has been driven by recent experience with costs and adverse publicity associated with wide-ranging recalls that have included automobiles, ground meat, toys, produce, dog food, and pharmaceuticals.

Whatever Happened to Quality?

READING

Quality is more than just a statistical analysis tool for manufacturing lines. When done right, quality should encompass the entire enterprise.

Some 50 years after the advent of the total quality management (TQM) movement championed by W. Edwards Deming, manufacturers of all different sizes and stripes are still being dogged by high-profile manufacturing quality defects. The list is long, and getting longer every week, and crosses every manufacturing vertical. At least a token "quality program" is de rigueur for U.S. manufacturers, but many are still at lip-service level agreement with the means required to reach the necessary ends. However, talk is cheap—recalls are not.

From tainted beef to spinach, from lead-painted toys to poisoned pet food and blood thinners to exploding laptop batteries and malfunctioning medical devices, the costs in scrapped product, consumer lawsuits and lost brand equity from defects and recalls are huge. Persistent, expensive and well-publicized recalls are striking companies with even the most stellar quality reputations. Toyota, the progenitor of a legendary quality-focused production system, has suffered a rash of defects that have caused the company to drop in *Consumer Reports'* Annual Car Reliability Survey ratings—an important market barometer for its consumers.

On a perhaps less dangerous but equally costly front, Microsoft's X-box 360 video gaming platform suffered a high-profile manufacturing defect that at one point had up to one-third of all units suffering from a "fatal error" (device owners called it "the red ring of death") that led at least indirectly to markedly weaker competitive positioning in the crucial holiday selling season, as well as a warranty extension that is estimated at more than $6 billion in unplanned accruals.

Many of these manufacturing problems are coming from global supply chains, which is a failure as much of management as it is the defective products themselves. However bleak the situation may seem, all is not lost. Indeed, the responsibility for quality manufacturing finally seems to be taking hold across all levels of the enterprise.

Quality Goes Upstream

Talk to the manufacturing community about quality's place in today's environment and a clear pattern emerges—companies are finally grasping the "shared responsibility" aspect of Deming's teachings. If quality is truly everyone's responsibility, then the idea goes beyond the shop floor and into the front office, the service department and everywhere else that provides value to customers and shareholders.

Ron Atkinson, chairman of the American Society for Quality (ASQ), has been watching this trend unfold. He describes the path that the idea of quality management in manufacturing has taken over the years.

"When I started in manufacturing 35 years ago, there was a policeman installed at the end of the line who looked at the parts and said, 'That one is OK, that can be shipped and that one can't.' Gradually, it got to, 'Let's find better ways to do the checking,' and then to, 'Let's find a way to predict what the parts are going to look like when they hit the end of the line,' so we started doing defect prevention. Now where we're at is that quality is expanding to cover everything, including outside of the actual manufacturing process, to 'how do we improve the quality of our HR services and support services? How do we improve the quality of the decisions that are made?"

According to Atkinson, concepts crucial to establishing a top-quality manufacturing line have been driven upstream, and expanded to become part of an overall continuous improvement strategy. "Quality has become a systems approach, rather than focusing on one part at a time and whether it's dimensionally correct. Quality is continuous improvement."

Rework and Morale

Larry Coburn, vice president of operations at high-tech audio equipment manufacturer Crown Audio, has seen the need for strong management and employee commitment in his company's recent quality improvements. The market in his industry was driving the development of more complex products that need to be produced more cheaply, and these twin trends put so much pressure on his manufacturing operations that things were breaking down. Their first-pass yields had gotten so bad that their rework inventory had piled up, and even became a major line item on the balance sheet.

"We had areas that were designated for rework that were so large that they were getting on our inventory control list because they were major entities in terms of dollars in inventory," he recounts. In fact, the problem was large enough to conceal what Coburn and his team call 'hidden factories'—millions of dollars of untapped production and sales potential existing within their production line. "We started analyzing these hidden factories and we actually identified $4 million of cost related to poor quality," Coburn says.

To stem the tide of red ink, Crown Audio embarked on a drastic plant-floor triage process that involved stopping production entirely, so as not to generate any more rework. They then analyzed and tested the defective inventory, broke the components up into groups based on the common problems they exhibited, and used those groupings to analyze potential process improvements and defect reduction strategies before plugging them back through the process. Once they finished, they not only had saleable inventory to get out the door, but also had a pretty

(continued)

good handle on the parts of their process that needed changing, says Coburn. "When we started, we had months and sometimes close to a year of backlog that needed to be fixed and repaired," he relates. "Now we are talking in terms of hours of rework in front of us."

However positive and dramatic this change, Coburn and his management team also realized that it wouldn't help much if the scrap and rework inventory piles kept growing, he says, which is where he says the less-tangible "employee engagement" part of the equation comes in.

The first aspect is enabling them to do their jobs. "We're continuing to empower our workers to get real-time data at their fingertips so they're making good decisions without two-week-old data, or without estimating or just evading what they think the problem is," he says. Rather than having his workers hanging their heads, Crown Audio's management team is now in the enviable situation of having different lines and shifts brag about their first-pass yields to each other.

Sustaining this motivated, engaged workforce is itself a team effort, says Coburn, who says that he has learned over the course of Crown Audio's continuing quality initiative that solidly designed manufacturing processes backed up by an engaged and empowered workforce is the essential combination to move any company forward. Quality truly is everyone's responsibility, and everyone appreciates a job well done.

"There is nothing more frustrating than working hard and then knowing that what you did, did not work out or did not come through." Coburn stresses this point in no uncertain terms. "Morale is everything in quality," he says. "People want to do a good job, and we have to enable that."

Source: Excerpted from Brad Kenney, *Industry Week,* April 1, 2008.

INSIGHTS ON QUALITY MANAGEMENT

SUPPLY CHAIN

Successful management of quality requires that managers have insights on various aspects of quality. These include defining quality in operational terms, understanding the costs and benefits of quality, recognizing the consequences of poor quality, and recognizing the need for ethical behavior. We begin with defining quality.

Defining Quality: The Dimensions of Quality

One way to think about quality is the degree to which performance of a product or service meets or exceeds customer expectations. The difference between these two, that is Performance – Expectations, is of great interest. If these two measures are equal, the difference is zero, and expectations have been met. If the difference is negative, expectations have not been met, whereas if the difference is positive, performance has exceeded customer expectations.

Customer expectations can be broken down into a number of categories, or *dimensions,* that customers use to judge the quality of a product or service. Understanding these helps organizations in their efforts to meet or exceed customer expectations. The dimensions used for goods are somewhat different from those used for services.

Product Quality. Product quality is often judged on eight dimensions of quality:[1]

Performance—main characteristics of the product.

Aesthetics—appearance, feel, smell, taste.

Special features—extra characteristics.

Conformance—how well a product corresponds to design specifications.

Reliability—dependable performance.

Durability—ability to perform over time.

Perceived quality—indirect evaluation of quality (e.g., reputation).

Serviceability—handling of complaints or repairs.

[1]Adapted from David Garvin, "Competing on the Eight Dimensions of Quality," *Harvard Business Review* 65, no. 6 (1987). Copyright © 1987 by the Harvard Business School Publishing Corporation; all rights reserved.

TABLE 9.1
Examples of product quality dimensions for a car

Dimension	Examples
1. Performance	Everything works: fit and finish, ride, handling, acceleration
2. Aesthetics	Exterior and interior design
3. Features	Convenience: placement of gauges
	High tech: GPS system
	Safety: anti-skid, airbags
4. Conformance	Car matches manufacturer's specifications
5. Reliability	Infrequent need for repairs
6. Durability	Useful life in miles, resistance to rust
7. Perceived quality	Top-rated
8. Serviceability	Ease of repair

These dimensions are further described by the examples presented in Table 9.1. When referring to a product, a customer sometimes judges the first four dimensions by its *fitness for use.*

Notice that price is *not* a dimension of quality.

SERVICE

Service Quality. The dimensions of product quality don't adequately describe service quality. Instead, service quality is often described using the following dimensions:[2]

Convenience—the availability and accessibility of the service.

Reliability—the ability to perform a service dependably, consistently, and accurately.

Responsiveness—the willingness of service providers to help customers in unusual situations and to deal with problems.

Time—the speed with which service is delivered.

Assurance—the knowledge exhibited by personnel who come into contact with a customer and their ability to convey trust and confidence.

Courtesy—the way customers are treated by employees who come into contact with them.

Tangibles—the physical appearance of facilities, equipment, personnel, and communication materials.

Consistency—The ability to provide the same level of good quality repeatedly.

Table 9.2 illustrates how the dimensions of service quality might apply to having an automobile repaired.

The dimensions of both product and service quality establish a *conceptual* framework for thinking about quality, but even they are too abstract to be applied operationally for purposes of product or service design, or actually producing a product or delivering a service. They must be stated in terms of specific, *measurable* characteristics. For example, when buying a car, a customer would naturally be interested in the car's performance. But what does that mean? In more specific terms, it might refer to a car's estimated miles per gallon, how quickly it can go from 0 to 60 miles per hour, or its stopping distance when traveling at 60 mph. Each of these can be stated in measurable terms (e.g., estimated miles per gallon: city = 25, highway = 30). Similar measurable characteristics can often be identified for each of the other product dimensions, as well as for the service dimensions.

[2]Adapted from Valerie A. Zeithhaml, A. Parasuraman, and Leonard L. Berry, *Delivering Quality Service and Balancing Customer Expectations* (New York: The Free Press, 1990), and J. R. Evans and W. M. Lindsey, *The Management and Control of Quality,* 3rd ed. (St. Paul, MN: West Publishing, 1996).

TABLE 9.2
Examples of service quality dimensions for having a car repaired

Dimension	Examples
1. Convenience	Was the service center conveniently located?
2. Reliability	Was the problem fixed and will the "fix" last?
3. Responsiveness	Were customer service personnel willing and able to answer questions?
4. Time	How long did the customer have to wait?
5. Assurance	Did the customer service personnel seem knowledgeable about the repair?
6. Courtesy	Were customer service personnel and the cashier friendly and courteous?
7. Tangibles	Were the facilities clean? Were personnel neat?
8. Consistency	Was the service quality good, and was it consistent with previous visits?

This is the sort of detailed information that is needed to both design and produce high-quality goods and services.

Information on customer wants in service can sometimes be difficult to pin down, creating challenges for designing and managing service quality. For example, customers may use words such as *friendly, considerate,* and *professional* to describe what they expect from service providers. These and similar descriptors are often difficult to translate into exact service specifications. Moreover in many instances, customer wants are often industry specific. Thus, the expectations would be quite different for health care versus dry cleaning. Furthermore, customer complaints may be due in part to unrelated factors (e.g., customer's mood or general health, the weather).

Other challenges with service quality include the reality that customer expectations often change over time and that different customers tend to have different expectations, so what one customer might view as good service quality, another customer might not be satisfied with at all. Couple these with the fact that each contact with a customer is a "moment of truth" in which service quality is instantly judged, and you begin to understand some of the challenges of achieving a consistently high perception of service quality.

If customers participate in a service system (i.e., self-service), there can be increased potential for a negative perception of quality. Consequently, adequate care must be taken to make the necessary customer acts simple and safe, especially since customers cannot be trained. So error prevention must be designed into the system.

It should also be noted that in most instances, some quality dimensions of a product or service will be more important than others, so it is important to identify customer priorities, especially when it is likely that trade-off decisions will be made at various points in design and production. Quality function deployment (described in Chapter 4) is a tool that can be helpful for that purpose.

The Sounds of Quality

READING

Consumers often associate quiet operation as a sign of product quality, and they are willing to pay extra to get it. Such is the case with clothes washers, dishwashers, air conditioners, shredders, and automobiles. In the case of automobiles, designers know that buyers associate a quiet ride with quality, so doors, hood, windshield and exhaust systems have extra soundproofing and sealing to keep noise out. They also know that buyers value safety, and that buyers associate safety with how solid a car door sounds when it is closed, so designers have given extra attention to those sorts of details. A sign of the growing importance of sound in the auto industry is that J.D. Power & Associates measures "pleasantness of sound" for doors, signals, and engine acceleration in its Initial Quality Study.

Likewise, cell phone manufacturers are giving careful attention to ring tones and other sounds emitted by their products, as are manufacturers of other electronic gadgets.

Source: Based on David Kiley, "Fine-Tuning a Brand's Signature Sound," *BusinessWeek,* August 13, 2007.

Assessing Service Quality

SERVICE

A widely used tool for assessing service quality is SERVQUAL,[3] an instrument designed to obtain feedback on an organization's ability to provide quality service to customers. It focuses on five of the above-mentioned service dimensions that influence customers' perceptions of service quality: tangibles, reliability, responsiveness, assurance, and empathy. The results of this service quality audit help management identify service strengths and weaknesses. Of particular interest are any *gaps* or discrepancies in service quality. There may be discrepancies between:

1. actual customer expectations and management perceptions of those expectations.
2. management perceptions of customer expectations and service-quality specifications.
3. service quality and service actually delivered.
4. service actually delivered and what is communicated about the service to customers.
5. customers' expectations of the service provider and their perceptions of provider delivery.

If gaps are found, they can be related to tangibles or other service quality dimensions to address the discrepancies.

The Determinants of Quality

The degree to which a product or a service successfully satisfies its intended purpose has four primary determinants:

1. Design.
2. How well the product or service conforms to the design.
3. Ease of use.
4. Service after delivery.

Quality of design Intention of designers to include or exclude features in a product or service.

The design phase is the starting point for the level of quality eventually achieved. Design involves decisions about the specific characteristics of a product or service such as size, shape, and location. **Quality of design** refers to the intention of designers to include or exclude certain features in a product or service. For example, many different models of automobiles are on the market today. They differ in size, appearance, roominess, fuel economy, comfort, and materials used. These differences reflect choices made by designers that determine the quality of design. Design decisions must take into account customer wants, production or service capabilities, safety and liability (both during production and after delivery), costs, and other similar considerations.

Designers may determine customer wants from information provided by marketing, perhaps through the use of consumer surveys or other market research. Marketing may organize focus groups of consumers to express their views on a product or service (what they like and don't like, and what they would like to have).

Designers must work closely with representatives of operations to ascertain that designs can be produced; that is, that production or service has the equipment, capacity, and skills necessary to produce or provide a particular design.

A poor design can result in difficulties in production or service. For example, materials might be difficult to obtain, specifications difficult to meet, or procedures difficult to follow. Moreover, if a design is inadequate or inappropriate for the circumstances, the best workmanship in the world may not be enough to achieve the desired quality. Also, we cannot expect a worker to achieve good results if the given tools or procedures are inadequate. Similarly, a superior design usually cannot offset poor workmanship.

Quality of conformance The degree to which goods or services conform to the intent of the designers.

Quality of conformance refers to the degree to which goods and services conform to (i.e., *achieve*) the intent of the designers. This is affected by factors such as the capability of equipment used; the skills, training, and motivation of workers; the extent to which the design lends itself to production; the monitoring process to assess conformance; and the taking of corrective

[3]Valarie A. Zeithaml, A. Parasuraman, and Leonard L. Berry, *Delivering Quality Service: Balancing Customer Perceptions and Expectations* (New York: The Free Press, 1990), p. 26.

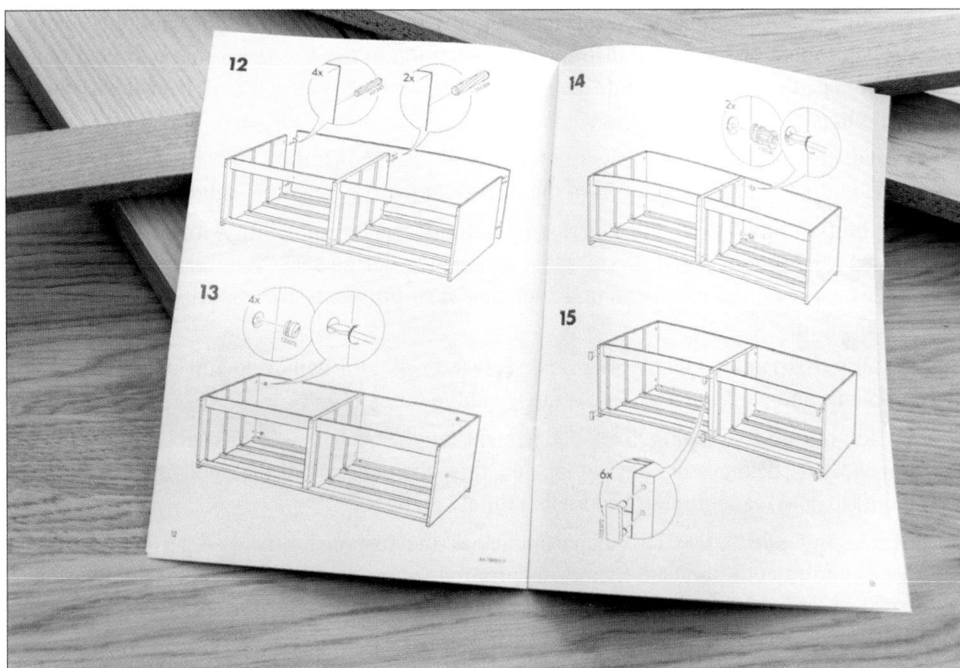

Self-assembly instructions for IKEA flat pack furniture.

action (e.g., through problem solving) when necessary. One important key to quality is reducing the variability in process outputs (i.e., reducing the degree to which individual items or individual service acts vary from one another). This will be discussed in detail in Chapter 10.

The determination of quality does not stop once the product or service has been sold or delivered. *Ease of use* and user instructions are important. They increase the chances, but do not guarantee, that a product will be used for its intended purposes and in such a way that it will continue to function properly and safely. (When faced with liability litigation, companies often argue that injuries and damages occurred because the user misused the product.) Much of the same reasoning can be applied to services. Customers, patients, clients, or other users must be clearly informed on what they should or should not do; otherwise, there is the danger that they will take some action that will adversely affect quality. Some examples include the doctor who fails to specify that a medication should be taken *before* meals and *not* with orange juice and the attorney who neglects to inform a client of a deadline for filing a claim.

Much consumer education takes the form of printed instructions and labeling. Thus, manufacturers must ensure that directions for unpacking, assembling, using, maintaining, and adjusting the product—and what to do if something goes wrong (e.g., flush eyes with water, call a physician, induce vomiting, do not induce vomiting, disconnect set immediately)—are *clearly visible* and *easily understood.*

For a variety of reasons, products do not always perform as expected, and services do not always yield the desired results. Whatever the reason, it is important from a quality standpoint to remedy the situation—through recall and repair of the product, adjustment, replacement or buyback, or reevaluation of a service—and do whatever is necessary to bring the product or service up to standard.

Responsibility for Quality

It is true that all members of an organization have some responsibility for quality, but certain parts of the organization are key areas of responsibility:

Top management. Top management has the ultimate responsibility for quality. While establishing strategies for quality, top management must institute programs to improve quality; guide, direct, and motivate managers and workers; and set an example by being involved in quality initiatives. Examples include taking training in quality, issuing periodic reports on quality, and attending meetings on quality.

Design. Quality products and services begin with design. This includes not only features of the product or service; it also includes attention to the *processes* that will be required to produce the products and/or the services that will be required to deliver the service to customers.

Procurement. The procurement department has responsibility for obtaining goods and services that will not detract from the quality of the organization's goods and services.

Production/operations. Production/operations has responsibility to ensure that processes yield products and services that conform to design specifications. Monitoring processes and finding and correcting root causes of problems are important aspects of this responsibility.

Quality assurance. Quality assurance is responsible for gathering and analyzing data on problems and working with operations to solve problems.

Packaging and shipping. This department must ensure that goods are not damaged in transit, that packages are clearly labeled, that instructions are included, that all parts are included, and that shipping occurs in a timely manner.

Marketing and sales. This department has the responsibility to determine customer needs and to communicate them to appropriate areas of the organization. In addition, it has the responsibility to report any problems with products or services.

Customer service. Customer service is often the first department to learn of problems. It has the responsibility to communicate that information to appropriate departments, deal in a reasonable manner with customers, work to resolve problems, and follow up to confirm that the situation has been effectively remedied.

Poor quality increases certain *costs* incurred by the organization. The following section provides further detail on costs associated with quality.

Benefits of Good Quality

Business organizations with good or excellent quality typically benefit in a variety of ways: an enhanced reputation for quality, the ability to command premium prices, an increased market share, greater customer loyalty, lower liability costs, and fewer production or service problems—which yields higher productivity, fewer complaints from customers, lower production costs, and higher profits. Annual studies by the National Institute of Standards indicate that winners of the Baldrige quality award, described later in the chapter, outperform the S&P 500 Index by a significant amount.[4]

Medical Mistakes Kill Almost 98,000 a Year

READING

Medical mistakes kill tens of thousands of people a year, says a new report by the National Academy of Sciences.

The report said that medical errors kill nearly 98,000 people a year. This exceeds the number of people who die annually from highway accidents (about 43,450), breast cancer (42,300), or AIDS (16,500), the study said.

The group called for a new federal agency to protect patients and said that Congress should require all health care providers to report medical mistakes that cause serious injury or death. The panel said that the United States should strive to reduce medical errors by 50 percent in five years.

Errors range from a simple miscommunication about a drug's name between a doctor and a nurse to the erroneous programming of a complex medical device. They include wrong diagnoses from mislabeled blood tubes, mistaken treatments because of poorly labeled drugs, and improper dosing because of faulty calculations.

Source: Robert Pear, "Group Asking U.S. for New Vigilance in Patient Safety," *New York Times*, November 30, 1999, p. 1a. Copyright © 1999 New York Times Company, Inc. Used with permission.

[4]"'Baldrige Index' Outperforms S&P 500 by Almost 5 to 1," press release, available at www.quality.nist.gov.

The Consequences of Poor Quality

It is important for management to recognize the different ways in which the quality of a firm's products or services can affect the organization and to take these into account in developing and maintaining a quality assurance program. Some of the major areas affected by quality are

1. Loss of business.
2. Liability.
3. Productivity.
4. Costs.

Poor designs or defective products or services can result in *loss of business.* Failure to devote adequate attention to quality can damage a profit-oriented organization's reputation and lead to a decreased share of the market, or it can lead to increased criticism and/or controls for a government agency or nonprofit organization.

In the retail sector, managers might not be fully aware of poor product or service quality because customers do not always report their dissatisfaction. Even so, dissatisfied customers do tend to voice their dissatisfaction to friends and relatives, which can have negative implications for customer perceptions and future business.

Organizations must pay special attention to their potential *liability* due to damages or injuries resulting from either faulty design or poor workmanship. This applies to both products and services. Thus, a poorly designed steering arm on a car might cause the driver to lose control of the car, but so could improper assembly of the steering arm. However, the net result is the same. Similarly, a tree surgeon might be called to cable a tree limb. If the limb later falls and causes damage to a neighbor's car, the accident might be traced to a poorly designed procedure for cabling or to improper workmanship. Liability for poor quality has been well established in the courts. An organization's liability costs can often be substantial, especially if large numbers of items are involved, as in the automobile industry, or if potentially widespread injury or damage is involved (e.g., an accident at a nuclear power plant). Express written warranties as well as implied warranties generally guarantee the product as safe when used as intended. The courts have tended to extend this to *foreseeable* uses, even if these uses were not intended by the producer. In the health care field, medical malpractice claims and insurance costs are contributing to skyrocketing costs and have become a major issue nationwide.

Productivity and quality are often closely related. Poor quality can adversely affect productivity during the manufacturing process if parts are defective and have to be reworked or if an assembler has to try a number of parts before finding one that fits properly. Also, poor quality in tools and equipment can lead to injuries and defective output, which must be reworked or scrapped, thereby reducing the amount of usable output for a given amount of input. Similarly, poor service can mean having to redo the service and reduce service productivity.

Cost to remedy a problem is a major consideration in quality management. The earlier a problem is identified in the process, the cheaper the cost to fix it. The cost to fix a problem at the customer end has been estimated at about five times the cost to fix a problem at the design or production stages.

Hyundai: Kissing Clunkers Goodbye

READING

Moon Ihlwan, with Larry Armstrong and Michael Eidam

When Hyundai Motor Co. Chairman Chung Mong Koo said his company could increase the quality of its cars to "Toyota levels" five years ago, few took him seriously. After all, Hyundai was the butt of talk-show jokes and a target of industry disdain for tinny cars that were about as reliable as a go-kart. So when J. D. Power & Associates Inc. on April 28 said the Korean carmaker had virtually caught up with Toyota in terms of quality, jaws dropped from Detroit to

(continued)

(concluded)

Tokyo. "We still have a long way to go," says Suh Byung Kee, the senior executive vice-president heading Hyundai's quality-control team. "But we have completed the first phase of our task."

The second phase could well be tougher. The eye-opening survey measured initial quality—the number of complaints customers had in the first 90 days of ownership. Hyundai owners reported just 102 problems per 100 cars sold—earning a tie with Honda as the second-best carmaker on the list and falling just below Toyota's tally of 101. And its Sonata sedan was the top-ranked car in the "entry mid-sized" category. On longer-term measures, though, Hyundai remains a laggard: In Power's July, 2003, Vehicle Dependability Study, Hyundai tallied 342 problems per 100 vehicles after three years of ownership, vs. an industry average of 273. Hyundai execs counter that it will take time before the recent improvement shows up in the longer-term statistics.

There's reason to agree with Hyundai's optimism. First wooed by the company's generous warranty—10 years for the drive train and five years for everything else—U.S. consumers are starting to believe that Hyundai is a changed brand. Last year they bought 400,000 of its cars. . . . Jeff Ball, a pharmacist from Laurence Harbor, N.J., has four of them: He and his wife share a Santa Fe SUV and a Sonata sedan ("I call it my Jaguar without the cat," he says), and he has bought smaller models for his sons. Sales like that are helping Hyundai's bottom line. . . .

A Team with Teeth

Hyundai's focus on quality comes straight from the top. Since 1999, Chairman Chung has boosted the quality team to 865 workers from 100, and virtually all employees have had to attend special seminars on improving Hyundai's cars. Chung presides over twice-monthly quality meetings in a special conference room and an adjacent workshop, with vehicle lifts and high-intensity spotlights for comparing Hyundais head-to-head with rivals. And this team has teeth: In the past year, the introduction of three new models was delayed by months as engineers scrambled to boost quality in response to problems found by the team.

The focus is on the details. In 1998, for instance, customers reported faulty warning lights and difficulty starting engines. So Chung set up a $30 million computer center where 71 engineers simulate harsh conditions to test electronics and pinpoint defects. The result: In Power's 2004 initial quality survey, Hyundai had only 9.6 problems in these areas per 100 vehicles, vs. an industry average of 13.8. Three years ago Hyundai had 23.4 problems, vs. the industry's 17.9. "This is not a shotgun approach," says Robert Cosmai, president of the company's U.S. affiliate, Hyundai Motor America.

The big test comes next year when Hyundai is due to begin building redesigned Santa Fes and Sonatas in Alabama. One encouraging sign: DaimlerChrysler and Mitsubishi Motors Corp. plan to use a Hyundai-designed four-cylinder engine in their own small and midsize cars. "This is a vote of confidence for Hyundai's engine quality," says Ahn Soo Woong, an auto analyst at Han-wha Securities Co. Now it's up to consumers to decide whether Hyundai really makes the grade.

Source: "Hyundai: Kissing Clunkers Goodbye," *BusinessWeek,* May 17, 2004.

Recipe for Business Success: Quality

READING

Czech carmaker Skoda is following Hyundai's route to global success, shedding its image of shoddy quality and replacing it with an image of high quality. Not yet ready to supplant quality leader Lexus, Skoda is focusing on the small car, low price sector of the European car market. Once a small regional brand, Skoda teamed with German carmaker Volkswagen to achieve high quality on its way to becoming a global player.

The message for business organizations is clear: Don't underestimate the importance of quality.

Source: Based on Gail Edmondson, "Skoda Means Quality, Really," *BusinessWeek,* October 1, 2007, p. 46.

The Costs of Quality

Any serious attempt to deal with quality issues must take into account the costs associated with quality. Those costs can be classified into three categories: appraisal, prevention, and failure.

Appraisal costs Costs of activities designed to ensure quality or uncover defects.

Appraisal costs relate to inspection, testing, and other activities intended to uncover defective products or services, or to assure that there are none. They include the cost of inspectors, testing, test equipment, labs, quality audits, and field testing.

TABLE 9.3
Summary of quality costs

Category	Description	Examples
Appraisal costs	Costs related to measuring, evaluating, and auditing materials, parts, products, and services to assess conformance with quality standards	Inspection equipment, testing, labs, inspectors, and the interruption of production to take samples
Prevention costs	Costs related to reducing the potential for quality problems	Quality improvement programs, training, monitoring, data collection and analysis, and design costs
Internal failure costs	Costs related to defective products or services before they are delivered to customers	Rework costs, problem solving, material and product losses, scrap, and downtime
External failure costs	Costs related to delivering substandard products or services to customers	Returned goods, reworking costs, warranty costs, loss of goodwill, liability claims, and penalties

Prevention costs relate to attempts to prevent defects from occurring. They include costs such as planning and administration systems, working with vendors, training, quality control procedures, and extra attention in both the design and production phases to decrease the probability of defective workmanship.

Prevention costs Costs of preventing defects from occurring.

Failure costs are incurred by defective parts or products or by faulty services. **Internal failures** are those discovered during the production process; **external failures** are those discovered after delivery to the customer. Internal failures occur for a variety of reasons, including defective material from vendors, incorrect machine settings, faulty equipment, incorrect methods, incorrect processing, carelessness, and faulty or improper material handling procedures. The costs of internal failures include lost production time, scrap and rework, investigation costs, possible equipment damage, and possible employee injury. Rework costs involve the salaries of workers and the additional resources needed to perform the rework (e.g., equipment, energy, raw materials). Beyond those costs are items such as inspection of reworked parts, disruption of schedules, the added costs of parts and materials in inventory waiting for reworked parts, and the paperwork needed to keep track of the items until they can be reintegrated into the process. External failures are defective products or poor service that go undetected by the producer. Resulting costs include warranty work, handling of complaints, replacements, liability/litigation, payments to customers or discounts used to offset the inferior quality, loss of customer goodwill, and opportunity costs related to lost sales.

Failure costs Costs caused by defective parts or products or by faulty services.

Internal failures Failures discovered during production.

External failures Failures discovered after delivery to the customer.

External failure costs are typically much greater than internal failure costs on a per unit basis. Table 9.3 summarizes quality costs.

Internal and external failure costs represent costs related to poor quality, whereas appraisal and prevention costs represent investments for achieving good quality.

An important issue in quality management is the value received from expenditures on prevention. There are two schools of thought on this. One is that prevention costs will be outweighed by savings in appraisal and failure costs. This is espoused by such people as Crosby and Juran, discussed in further detail later in this chapter. They believe that as the costs of defect prevention are increased, the costs of appraisal and failure decrease by much more. What this means, if true, is that the net result is lower total costs, and, thus, as Crosby suggests, quality is free. On the other hand, some managers believe that attempting to go beyond a certain point, such expenditures on quality reduce the funds available for other objectives such as reducing product development times and upgrading technology. The **return on quality** (ROQ) approach focuses on the economics of quality efforts. In this approach, quality improvement projects are viewed as investments, and, as such, they are evaluated like any other investment, using metrics related to return on investment (ROI).

Return on quality An approach that evaluates the financial return of investments in quality.

Ethics and Quality Management

All members of an organization have an obligation to perform their duties in an ethical manner. Ethical behavior comes into play in many situations that involve quality. One major category is substandard work, including defective products and substandard service, poor designs, shoddy workmanship, and substandard parts and raw materials. Having knowledge of this and failing to correct and *report it* in a timely manner is unethical and can have a number of negative consequences. These can include increased costs for organizations in terms of decreased productivity, an increase in the accident rate among employees, inconveniences and injuries to customers, and increased liability costs.

A related issue is how an organization chooses to deal with information about quality problems in products that are already in service. For example, automakers and tire makers in recent years have been accused of withholding information about actual or potential quality problems; they failed to issue product recalls, or failed to divulge information, choosing instead to handle any complaints that arose on an individual basis.

THE EVOLUTION OF QUALITY MANAGEMENT

Prior to the Industrial Revolution, skilled craftsmen performed all stages of production. Pride of workmanship and reputation often provided the motivation to see that a job was done right. Lengthy guild apprenticeships caused this attitude to carry over to new workers. Moreover, one person or a small group of people were responsible for an entire product.

A division of labor accompanied the Industrial Revolution; each worker was then responsible for only a small portion of each product. Pride of workmanship became less meaningful because workers could no longer identify readily with the final product. The responsibility for quality shifted to the foremen. Inspection was either nonexistent or haphazard, although in some instances 100 percent inspection was used.

Frederick Winslow Taylor, the "Father of Scientific Management," gave new emphasis to quality by including product inspection and gauging in his list of fundamental areas of manufacturing management. G. S. Radford improved Taylor's methods. Two of his most significant contributions were the notions of involving quality considerations early in the product design stage and making connections among high quality, increased productivity, and lower costs.

In 1924, Bell Telephone Laboratories introduced statistical control charts that could be used to monitor production. Around 1930, H. F. Dodge and H. G. Romig, also of Bell Labs, introduced tables for sampling. Nevertheless, statistical quality control procedures were not widely used until World War II, when the U.S. government began to require vendors to use them.

World War II caused a dramatic increase in emphasis on quality control. The U.S. Army refined sampling techniques for dealing with large shipments of arms from many suppliers. By the end of the 1940s, the U.S. Army, Bell Labs, and major universities were training engineers in other industries in the use of statistical sampling techniques. About the same time, professional quality organizations were emerging throughout the country. One of these organizations was the American Society for Quality Control (ASQC, now known as ASQ). Over the years, the society has promoted quality with its publications, seminars and conferences, and training programs.

During the 1950s, the quality movement evolved into quality assurance. In the mid-1950s, total quality control efforts enlarged the realm of quality efforts from its primary focus on manufacturing to also include product design and incoming raw materials. One important feature of this work was greater involvement of upper management in quality.

During the 1960s, the concept of "zero defects" gained favor. This approach focused on employee motivation and awareness, and the expectation of perfection from each employee. It evolved from the success of the Martin Company in producing a "perfect" missile for the U.S. Army.

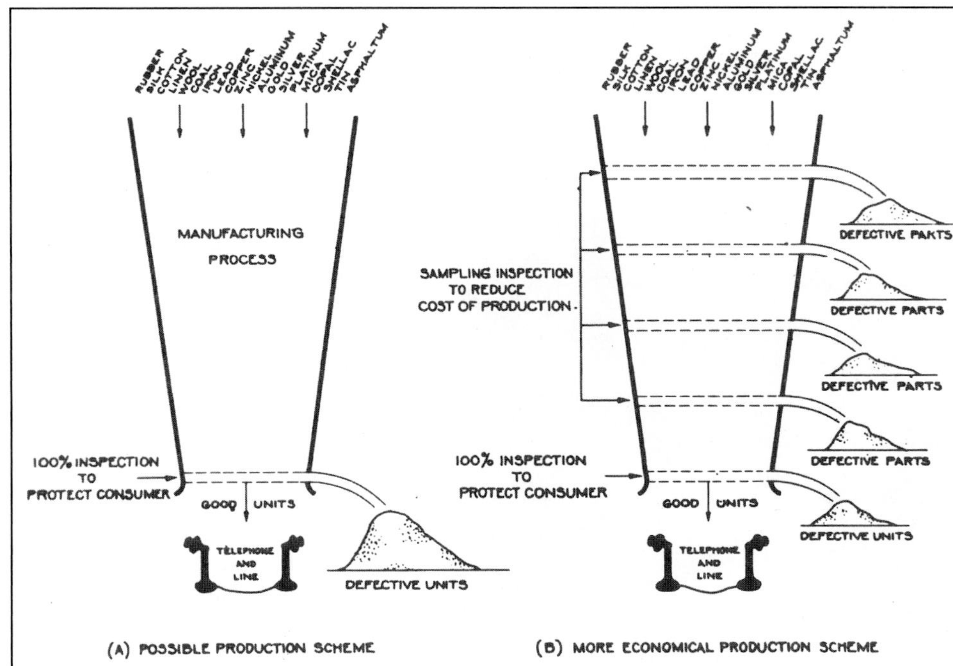

Walter A. Shewhart's 1925 paper in the Journal of American Statistical Association *introduced the control chart to the world. In 1931, he published his classic text,* Economic Control of Quality of Manufactured Product. *Within 25 years the control chart was a basic manufacturing tool used around the world.*

In the 1970s, quality assurance methods gained increasing emphasis in services including government operations, health care, banking, and the travel industry.

Something else happened in the 1970s that had a global impact on quality. An embargo on oil sales instituted by the Organization of Petroleum Exporting Countries (OPEC) caused an increase in energy costs, and automobile buyers became more interested in fuel-efficient, lower-cost vehicles. Japanese auto producers, who had been improving their products, were poised to take advantage of these changes, and they captured an increased share of the automobile market. The quality of their automobiles enhanced the reputation of Japanese producers, opening the door for a wide array of Japanese-produced goods.

American producers, alarmed by their loss of market share, spent much of the late 1970s and the 1980s trying to improve the quality of their goods while lowering their costs.

The evolution of quality took a dramatic shift from quality assurance to a strategic approach to quality in the late 1970s. Up until that time, the main emphasis had been on finding and correcting defective products before they reached the market. It was still a reactive approach. The strategic approach is proactive, focusing on preventing mistakes from occurring in the first place. The idea is to design quality into products, rather than find and correct defects after the fact. This approach has now expanded to include processes and services. Quality and profits are more closely linked. This approach also places greater emphasis on customer satisfaction, and it involves all levels of management as well as workers in a continuing effort to increase quality.

THE FOUNDATIONS OF MODERN QUALITY MANAGEMENT: THE GURUS

A core of quality pioneers shaped current thinking and practice. This section describes some of their key contributions to the field.

Walter Shewhart. Walter Shewhart was a genuine pioneer in the field of quality control, and he became known as the "father of statistical quality control." He developed control charts

W. Edwards Deming

for analyzing output of processes to determine when corrective action was necessary. Shewhart had a strong influence on the thinking of two other gurus, W. Edwards Deming and Joseph Juran.

W. Edwards Deming. Deming, a statistics professor at New York University in the 1940s, went to Japan after World War II to assist the Japanese in improving quality and productivity. The Union of Japanese Scientists, who had invited Deming, were so impressed that in 1951, after a series of lectures presented by Deming, they established the **Deming Prize,** which is awarded annually to firms that distinguish themselves with quality management programs.

Deming Prize Prize established by the Japanese and awarded annually to firms that distinguish themselves with quality management programs.

Although the Japanese revered Deming, he was largely unknown to business leaders in the United States. In fact, he worked with the Japanese for almost 30 years before he gained recognition in his own country. Before his death in 1993, U.S. companies turned their attention to Deming, embraced his philosophy, and requested his assistance in setting up quality improvement programs.

Deming compiled a famous list of 14 points he believed were the prescription needed to achieve quality in an organization (see Table 9.4). His message was that the cause of inefficiency and poor quality is the *system,* not the employees. Deming felt that it was *management's responsibility* to correct the system to achieve the desired results. In addition to the 14 points, Deming stressed the need to reduce variation in output (deviation from a standard), which can be accomplished by distinguishing between *special causes* of variation (i.e., correctable) and *common causes* of variation (i.e., random).

Deming's concept of profound knowledge incorporates the beliefs and values about learning that guided Japan's rise to a world economic power.

Joseph M. Juran. Juran, like Deming, taught Japanese manufacturers how to improve the quality of their goods, and he, too, can be regarded as a major force in Japan's success in quality.

Juran viewed quality as fitness-for-use. He also believed that roughly 80 percent of quality defects are management controllable; thus, management has the responsibility to correct this deficiency. He described quality management in terms of a *trilogy* consisting of quality planning, quality control, and quality improvement. According to Juran, quality planning is necessary to establish processes that are *capable* of meeting quality standards; quality control is necessary in order to know when corrective action is needed; and quality improvement will help to find better ways of doing things. A key element of Juran's philosophy is the commitment of management to continual improvement.

Juran is credited as one of the first to measure the cost of quality, and he demonstrated the potential for increased profits that would result if the costs of poor quality could be reduced.

Armand Feigenbaum. Feigenbaum was instrumental in advancing the "cost of nonconformance" approach as a reason for management to commit to quality. He recognized that

TABLE 9.4
Deming's 14 points

1. Create constancy of purpose toward improvement of product and service.
2. Reduce levels of delays, mistakes, defective materials, and defective workmanship.
3. Cease dependence on mass inspection. (*Prevent* defects rather than *detect* defects.)
4. Eliminate suppliers that cannot qualify with statistical evidence of quality.
5. Find problems. It is management's job to work continually on system improvement.
6. Institute modern methods of training on the job.
7. Emphasize quality instead of volume alone. Management must prepare to take immediate action on reports from foremen concerning barriers such as inherent defects, machines not maintained, poor tools, and fuzzy operational definitions.
8. Drive out fear, so that everyone may work effectively for the company.
9. Break down barriers between departments. People in research, design, sales, and production must work as a team.
10. Eliminate goals and slogans asking for new levels of productivity without providing methods.
11. Eliminate work standards that prescribe numerical quotas.
12. Remove barriers that stand between the hourly worker and his right to pride of workmanship.
13. Institute a vigorous program of education and retraining.
14. Create a structure in top management that will push every day on the above 13 points.

Source: Adapted from W. Edwards Deming, *Out of the Crisis,* pp. 23 and 24. Copyright © 2000 MIT Press. Used with permission.

quality was not simply a collection of tools and techniques, but a "total field." According to Feigenbaum, it is the customer who defines quality.

Philip B. Crosby. Crosby developed the concept of *zero defects* and popularized the phrase "Do it right the first time." He stressed prevention, and he argued against the idea that "there will always be some level of defectives." In 1979, his book *Quality Is Free* was published. The quality-is-free concept is that the costs of poor quality are much greater than traditionally defined. According to Crosby, these costs are so great that rather than viewing quality efforts as costs, organizations should view them as a way to reduce costs, because the improvements generated by quality efforts will more than pay for themselves.

Crosby believes that any level of defects is too high and he maintains that achieving quality can be relatively easy. His book *Quality without Tears: The Art of Hassle-Free Management* was published in 1984.

Kaoru Ishikawa. The late Japanese expert on quality was strongly influenced by both Deming and Juran, although he made significant contributions of his own to quality management. Among his key contributions were the development of the cause-and-effect diagram (also known as a fishbone diagram) for problem solving and the implementation of quality circles, which involve workers in quality improvement. He was the first quality expert to call attention to the *internal customer*—the next person in the process, the next operation, within the organization.

Genichi Taguchi. Taguchi is best known for the Taguchi loss function, which involves a formula for determining the cost of poor quality. The idea is that the deviation of a part from a standard causes a loss, and the combined effect of deviations of all parts from their standards can be large, even though each individual deviation is small.

Taiichi Ohno and Shigeo Shingo. Taiichi Ohno and Shigeo Shingo both developed the philosophy and methods of *kaizen,* a Japanese term for continuous improvement (defined more fully later in this chapter), at Toyota. Continuous improvement is one of the hallmarks of successful quality management.

TABLE 9.5
A summary of key contributors to quality management

Contributor	Key Contributions
Shewhart	Control charts; variance reduction
Deming	14 points; special versus common causes of variation
Juran	Quality is fitness-for-use; quality trilogy
Feigenbaum	Quality is a total field; the customer defines quality
Crosby	Quality is free; zero defects
Ishikawa	Cause-and-effect diagrams; quality circles
Taguchi	Taguchi loss function
Ohno and Shingo	Continuous improvement

Table 9.5 provides a summary of the important contributions of the gurus to modern quality management.

QUALITY AWARDS

Quality awards have been established to generate improvement in quality. The Malcolm Baldrige Award, the European Quality Award, and the Deming Prize are well-known awards given annually to recognize firms that have integrated quality management in their operations.

The Baldrige Award

Baldrige Award Annual award given by the U.S. government to recognize quality achievements of U.S. companies.

Named after the late Malcolm Baldrige, an industrialist and former secretary of commerce, the annual **Baldrige Award** is administered by the National Institute of Standards and Technology. The purpose of the award competition is to stimulate efforts to improve quality, to recognize quality achievements, and to publicize successful programs.

When the award was first presented in 1988, the award categories were manufacturing and small business. A few years later a service category was added, and then categories for education and health care were added a few years after that. The earliest winners included Motorola, Globe Metallurgical, Xerox Corporation, and Milliken & Company. Since then, many companies have been added to the list. For a complete listing of current and former winners, go to www.quality.nist.gov/Award_Recipients.htm.

Applicants are evaluated in seven main areas: leadership, information and analysis, strategic planning, human resource management, customer and market focus, process management, and business results (see Figure 9.1).

Examiners check the extent to which top management incorporates quality values in daily management; whether products or services are at least as good as those of competitors; whether employees receive training in quality techniques; if the business works with suppliers to improve quality; and if customers are satisfied. Even organizations that don't win benefit from applying for the award: All applicants receive a written summary of the strengths and weaknesses of their quality management and suggestions for improvement.

Most states have quality award programs based on the Baldrige criteria. These award programs can serve as an entry point for organizations that want to eventually apply for the national award.

Benefits of the Baldrige competition include the following:

1. Winners achieve financial success.
2. Winners share their knowledge.
3. The process motivates employees.
4. The process provides a well-designed quality system.

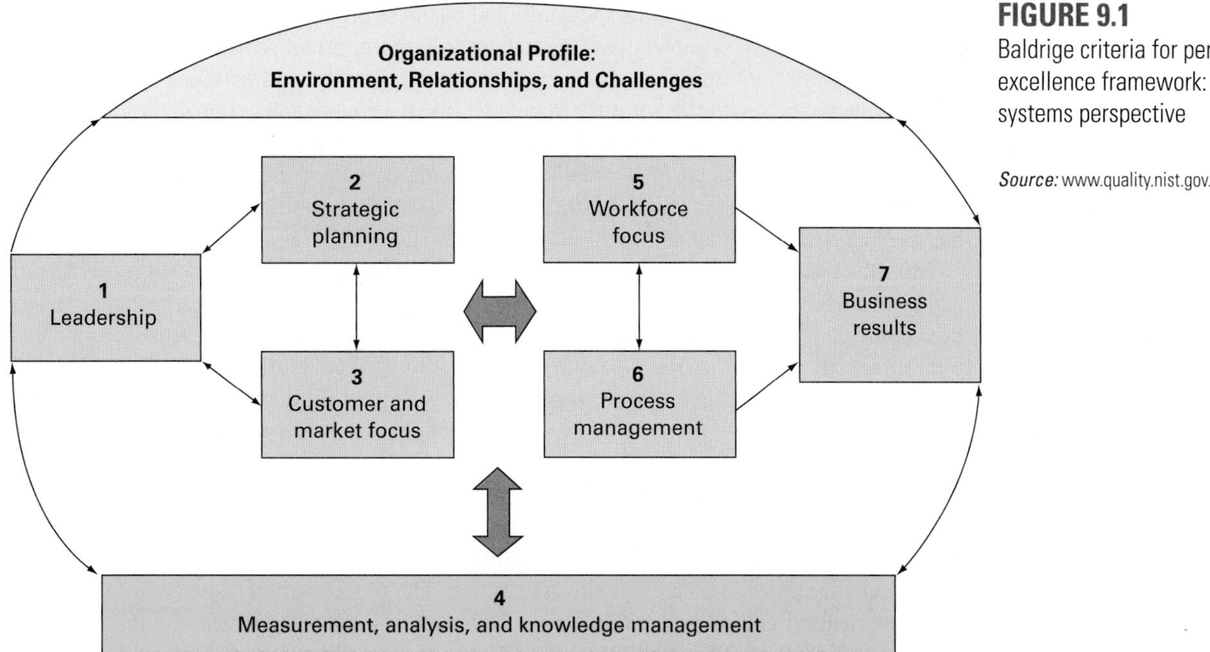

FIGURE 9.1
Baldrige criteria for performance excellence framework: A systems perspective

Source: www.quality.nist.gov.

5. The process requires obtaining data.
6. The process provides feedback.

For more information, visit www.quality.nist.gov.

The European Quality Award

The **European Quality Award** is Europe's most prestigious award for organizational excellence. The European Quality Award sits at the top of regional and national quality awards and applicants have often won one or more of those awards prior to applying for the European Quality Award.

European Quality Award European award for organizational excellence.

The Deming Prize

The Deming Prize, named in honor of the late W. Edwards Deming, is Japan's highly coveted award recognizing successful quality efforts. It is given annually to any company that meets the award's standards. Although typically given to Japanese firms, in 1989, Florida Power and Light became the first U.S. company to win the award.

The major focus of the judging is on statistical quality control, making it much narrower in scope than the Baldrige Award, which focuses more on customer satisfaction. Companies that win the Deming Prize tend to have quality programs that are detailed and well-communicated throughout the company. Their quality improvement programs also reflect the involvement of senior management and employees, customer satisfaction, and training.

Japan also has an additional award, the Japan Prize, fashioned roughly after the Baldrige Award.

QUALITY CERTIFICATION

Many firms that do business internationally recognize the importance of quality certification.

ISO 9000, 14000, and 24700

The International Organization for Standardization (ISO) promotes worldwide standards for the improvement of quality, productivity, and operating efficiency through a series of standards and guidelines. Used by industrial and business organizations, regulatory agencies, governments, and trade organizations, the standards have important economic and social benefits. Not only are they tremendously important for designers, manufacturers, suppliers, service providers, and customers, but the standards make a tremendous contribution to society in general: They increase the levels of quality and reliability, productivity, and safety, while making products and services affordable. The standards help facilitate international trade. They provide governments with a base for health, safety, and environmental legislation. And they aid in transferring technology to developing countries.

ISO 9000 A set of international standards on quality management and quality assurance, critical to international business.

ISO 14000 A set of international standards for assessing a company's environmental performance.

Two of the most well-known of these are ISO 9000 and ISO 14000. **ISO 9000** pertains to quality management. It concerns what an organization does to ensure that its products or services conform to its customers' requirements. **ISO 14000** concerns what an organization does to minimize harmful effects to the environment caused by its operations. Both ISO 9000 and ISO 14000 relate to an organization's *processes* rather than its products and services, and both stress continual improvement. Moreover, the standards are meant to be generic; no matter what the organization's business, if it wants to establish a quality management system or an environmental management system, the system must have the essential elements contained in ISO 9000 or in ISO 14000. The ISO 9000 standards are critical for companies doing business internationally, particularly in Europe. They must go through a process that involves documenting quality procedures and on-site assessment. The process often takes 12 to 18 months. With certification comes *registration* in an ISO directory that companies seeking suppliers can refer to for a list of certified companies. They are generally given preference over unregistered companies. More than 40,000 companies are registered worldwide; three-fourths of them are located in Europe.

A key requirement for registration is that a company review, refine, and map functions such as process control, inspection, purchasing, training, packaging, and delivery. Similar to the Baldrige Award, the review process involves considerable self-appraisal, resulting in problem identification and improvement. Unlike the Baldrige Award, registered companies face an ongoing series of audits, and they must be reregistered every three years.

In addition to the obvious benefits of certification for companies that want to deal with the European Union, the ISO 9000 certification and registration process is particularly helpful for companies that do not currently have a quality management system; it provides guidelines for establishing the system and making it effective.

ISO 9000 standards include the following categories:

System requirements

Management requirements

Resource requirements

Realization of requirements

Remedial requirements

Eight quality management principles form the basis of the latest version of ISO 9000:

1. A customer focus.
2. Leadership.
3. Involvement of people.
4. A process approach.
5. A system approach to management.
6. Continual improvement.
7. Use of a factual approach to decision making.
8. Mutually beneficial supplier relationships.

The standards for ISO 14000 certification bear upon three major areas:

Management systems—systems development and integration of environmental responsibilities into business planning.

Operations—consumption of natural resources and energy.

Environmental systems—measuring, assessing, and managing emissions, effluents, and other waste streams.

ISO 24700 pertains to the quality and performance of office equipment that contains reused components. ISO/IEC 24700 specifies product characteristics for use in an original equipment manufacturer's or authorized third-party's declaration of conformity to demonstrate that a marketed product that contains reused components performs equivalent to new, meeting equivalent-to-new component specifications and performance criteria, and continues to meet all the safety and environmental criteria required by responsibly built products. It is relevant to marketed products whose manufacturing and recovery processes result in the reuse of components.

ISO 24700 A set of international standards that pertains to the quality and performance of office equipment that contains reused components.

If you'd like to learn more about ISO standards, visit the International Organization for Standardization Web site at www.ISO.org/ISO/en/ISOonline.frontpage or the American Society for Quality Web site at www.asq.org.

QUALITY AND THE SUPPLY CHAIN

SUPPLY CHAIN

Business leaders are increasingly recognizing the importance of their supply chains in achieving their quality goals. Achievement requires measuring customer perceptions of quality, identifying problem areas, and correcting those problems.

When dealing with supplier quality in global supply chains, companies are finding a wide range in the degree of sophistication concerning quality assurance. Although developed countries often have a fair level of sophistication, little or no awareness of modern quality practices

The acting chair of the Consumer Product Safety Commission spoke at a press conference on a recall of Mattel Inc. toys manufactured in China. Mattel recalled 18.6 million products around the world because they contained magnets that could fall out and be swallowed by children.

may be found in some less-developed countries. This poses important liability issues for companies that outsource to those areas.

An interesting situation is outsourcing in the pharmaceutical industry. Offshore suppliers offer low prices that domestic producers can't match. However, the cost advantage of offshore producers is not based solely on lower labor costs; a significant "advantage" is the fact that domestic producers undergo strict and costly quality government regulations and unannounced inspections that offshore producers are not subject to. While this lowers the costs to importers, it also increases their liability risks.

Increasingly, the emphasis in supply chain quality management is on reducing outsourcing risk as well as product or service variation and overhead. Risk comes from the use of substandard materials or work methods, which can lead to inferior product quality and potential product liability. Tighter control of vendors and worker training can reduce these risks. Variation results from processes that are not in control; it can be reduced through statistical quality control. Overhead can be reduced by assigning quality assurance responsibility to vendors, while customers operate in a quality audit mode, with some monitoring of vendor quality efforts.

Supply chain quality management can benefit from a collaborative relationship with suppliers that includes helping suppliers with quality assurance efforts as well as information sharing on quality-related matters. Ideally, improving supply chain quality can become part of an organization's continuous improvement efforts.

The following reading offers some guidelines for improving quality and reducing outsourcing risk.

Improving Quality and Reducing Risk in Offshoring

READING

William E. Mitchell, chairman, president and CEO of Arrow Electronics, offered 10 guidelines on how to reduce product quality and related risks in an offshore supply chain. The guidelines were nominally targeted at electronics suppliers, but offer a good starting point for many companies looking to reduce risk and potential quality problems.

1. Source from reputable, well-established companies with tight internal controls.
2. Conduct comprehensive background checks, including checking trade references and past business history, of supply chain partners before conducting business with them.
3. Implement site inspections of supply chain partners and find out what systems have been put in place to track quality.
4. Conduct ongoing performance reviews of supply chain partners and engage in ongoing communications with them to benchmark against preset goals and define improvement plans.
5. Only source from companies that are willing to provide a guarantee for products in writing.
6. Be cautious of buying from companies that do not have franchised relationships with distribution partners to avoid a greater potential risk of counterfeit product.
7. Beware of unusually low pricing.
8. Look for International Organization for Standardization (ISO) or other equivalent, globally recognized certifications in a supply chain partner's operations.
9. Establish relationships with third-party organizations.
10. Translate quality into measurable and clearly defined targets with supply chain partners and ensure these metrics are communicated regularly with employees.

As the *Supply Chain Digest* notes, to do this right will involve greater costs, reducing the relative price advantage of offshore strategies to a degree, and certainly requiring companies to build a substantial infrastructure to develop and maintain these monitoring programs.

Source: Excerpted from "Improving Quality and Reducing Risk in Offshoring," *Supply Chain Digest,* August 7, 2007.

TOTAL QUALITY MANAGEMENT

A primary role of management is to lead an organization in its daily operation and to maintain it as a viable entity into the future. Quality has become an important factor in both of these objectives.

Although ostensibly always an objective of business, customer satisfaction, *in customer terms,* became a specific goal in the late 1980s. Providing high quality was recognized as a key element for success. Most large corporations taking that path have documented their success. First, they survived the strong overseas competition that had set the high quality levels and now have regained some of their former markets. Smaller companies are also adopting similar goals.

Management plays a critical role in TQM. The approach is reflected in an *operating philosophy.* For example, among the 14 Toyota Way Principles is:

> **Principle 1.** Base your management decisions on a long-term philosophy, even at the expense of short-term financial goals. . . . Generate value for the customer, society, and the economy; it is your starting point. Evaluate every function in the company in terms of its ability to achieve this.[5]

The term **total quality management (TQM)** refers to a quest for quality in an organization. There are three key philosophies in this approach. One is a never-ending push to improve, which is referred to as *continuous improvement;* the second is the *involvement of everyone* in the organization; and the third is a goal of *customer satisfaction,* which means meeting or exceeding customer expectations. TQM expands the traditional view of quality—looking only at the quality of the final product or services—to *looking at the quality of every aspect of the process* that produces the product or service. TQM systems are intended to prevent poor quality from occurring.

Total quality management (TQM) A philosophy that involves everyone in an organization in a continual effort to improve quality and achieve customer satisfaction.

We can describe the TQM approach as follows:

1. Find out what customers want. This might involve the use of surveys, focus groups, interviews, or some other technique that integrates the customer's voice in the decision-making process. Be sure to include the *internal customer* (the next person in the process) as well as the *external customer* (the final customer).

> **Sign on the wall of a company cafeteria:**
> Sometimes they can be cranky, and it may sometimes seem like they expect too much, but they do provide our paychecks and our benefits, such as sick leave, maternity leave, health insurance, and three weeks of paid vacation time each year. And what about all the new equipment we've been getting lately? They pay for that, too. And a lot more. So the next time you see them, give them a great big smile to show how much you appreciate them—our *customers!*

2. Design a product or service that will meet (or exceed) what customers want. Make it easy to use and easy to produce.

3. Design processes that facilitate doing the job right the first time. Determine where mistakes are likely to occur and try to prevent them. When mistakes do occur, find out why so that they are less likely to occur again. Strive to make the process "mistake-proof." This is sometimes referred to as a **fail-safing:** Elements are incorporated in product or service design that make it virtually impossible for an employee (or sometimes a customer) to do something incorrectly. The Japanese term for this is *pokayoke.* Examples include parts that fit together one way only and appliance plugs that can be inserted into a wall outlet the correct way only. Another term that is sometimes used is *foolproofing,* but use of this term may be taken to imply that employees (or customers) are fools—not a wise choice!

Fail-safing Incorporating design elements that prevent incorrect procedures.

4. Keep track of results, and use them to guide improvement in the system. Never stop trying to improve.

5. Extend these concepts throughout the supply chain.

Many companies have successfully implemented TQM programs. Successful TQM programs are built through the dedication and combined efforts of everyone in the organization.

[5]From Jeffrey K. Liker, *The Toyota Way* (New York: McGraw-Hill, 2004).

The iPod Shuffle stops playing music when the earphone jack is unplugged. When the earphones are plugged back in, the music resumes right where it left off. This keeps the battery from running down and is an example of mistake proofing.

Top management must be committed and involved. If it isn't, TQM will become just another fad that quickly dies and fades away.

The preceding description provides a good idea of what TQM is all about, but it doesn't tell the whole story. A number of other elements of TQM are important:

1. **Continuous improvement.** The *philosophy* that seeks to improve all factors related to the process of converting inputs into outputs on an ongoing basis is called **continuous improvement.** It covers equipment, methods, materials, and people. Under continuous improvement, the old adage "If it ain't broke, don't fix it" gets transformed into "Just because it isn't broke doesn't mean it can't be improved."

The concept of continuous improvement was not new, but it did not receive much interest in the United States for a while, even though it originated here. However, many Japanese companies used it for years, and it became a cornerstone of the Japanese approach to production. The Japanese use the term ***kaizen*** to refer to continuous improvement. The successes of Japanese companies caused other companies to reexamine many of their approaches. This resulted in a strong interest in the continuous improvement approach.

2. **Competitive benchmarking.** This involves identifying other organizations that are the best at something and studying how they do it to learn how to improve your operation. The company need not be in the same line of business. For example, Xerox used the mail-order company L.L. Bean to benchmark order filling.

3. **Employee empowerment.** Giving workers the responsibility for improvements and the authority to make changes to accomplish them provides strong motivation for employees. This puts decision making into the hands of those who are closest to the job and have considerable insight into problems and solutions.

4. **Team approach.** The use of teams for problem solving and to achieve consensus takes advantage of group synergy, gets people involved, and promotes a spirit of cooperation and shared values among employees.

5. **Decisions based on facts rather than opinions.** Management gathers and analyzes data as a basis for decision making.

Continuous improvement Philosophy that seeks to make never-ending improvements to the process of converting inputs into outputs.

Kaizen Japanese term for continuous improvement.

Quality at the source The philosophy of making each worker responsible for the quality of his or her work.

6. **Knowledge of tools.** Employees and managers are trained in the use of quality tools.

7. **Supplier quality.** Suppliers must be included in quality assurance and quality improvement efforts so that their processes are capable of delivering quality parts and materials in a timely manner.

8. **Champion.** A TQM champion's job is to promote the value and importance of TQM principles throughout the company.

9. **Quality at the source. Quality at the source** refers to the philosophy of making each worker responsible for the quality of his or her work. The idea is to "Do it right the first time." Workers are expected to provide goods or services that meet specifications and to find and correct mistakes that occur. In effect, each worker becomes a quality inspector for his or her work. When the work is passed on to the next operation in the process (the internal customer) or, if that step is the last in the process, to the ultimate customer, the worker is "certifying" that it meets quality standards.

This accomplishes a number of things: (1) it places direct responsibility for quality on the person(s) who directly affect it; (2) it removes the adversarial relationship that often exists between quality control inspectors and production workers; and (3) it motivates workers by giving them control over their work as well as pride in it.

10. **Suppliers** are partners in the process, and long-term relationships are encouraged. This gives suppliers a vital stake in providing quality goods and services. Suppliers, too, are

TABLE 9.6
Comparing the cultures of TQM and traditional organizations

Aspect	Traditional	TQM
Overall mission	Maximize return on investment	Meet or exceed customer expectations
Objectives	Emphasis on short term	Balance of long term and short term
Management	Not always open; sometimes inconsistent objectives	Open; encourages employee input; consistent objectives
Role of manager	Issue orders; enforce	Coach; remove barriers; build trust
Customer requirements	Not highest priority; may be unclear	Highest priority; important to identify and understand
Problems	Assign blame; punish	Identify and resolve
Problem solving	Not systematic; individuals	Systematic; teams
Improvement	Erratic	Continuous
Suppliers	Adversarial	Partners
Jobs	Narrow, specialized; much individual effort	Broad, more general; much team effort
Focus	Product oriented	Process oriented

expected to provide quality at the source, thereby reducing or eliminating the need to inspect deliveries from suppliers.

It would be incorrect to think of TQM as merely a collection of techniques. Rather, TQM reflects a whole new attitude toward quality. It is about the *culture* of an organization. To truly reap the benefits of TQM, the organization must change its culture.

Table 9.6 illustrates the differences between cultures of a TQM organization and a more traditional organization.

Six Sigma

Six sigma A business process for improving quality, reducing costs, and increasing customer satisfaction.

The term **six sigma** has several meanings. Statistically, six sigma means having no more than 3.4 defects per million opportunities in any process, product, or service. Conceptually, the term is much broader, referring to a program designed to reduce the occurrence of defects to achieve lower costs and improved customer satisfaction. It is based on the application of certain tools and techniques to selected projects to achieve strategic business results. In the business world, six-sigma programs have become a key way to improve quality, save time, cut costs, and improve customer satisfaction. Six-sigma programs can be employed in design, production, service, inventory management, and delivery. It is important for six-sigma projects to be aligned with organization strategy.

Motorola pioneered the concept of a six-sigma program in the 1980s. Since then, many other companies have developed their own six-sigma programs, including General Electric, Texas Instruments, Eastman Kodak, and Allied Signal.

There are management and technical components of six-sigma programs. The management component involves providing strong leadership, defining performance metrics, selecting projects likely to achieve business results, and selecting and training appropriate people. The technical component involves improving process performance, reducing variation, utilizing statistical methods, and designing a structured improvement strategy, which involves definition, measurement, analysis, improvement, and control.

For six sigma to succeed in any organization, buy-in at the top is essential. Top management must formulate and communicate the company's overall objectives and lead the program for a successful deployment. Other key players in six-sigma programs are program champions, "master black belts," "black belts," and "green belts." Champions identify and rank potential projects, help select and evaluate candidates, manage program resources, and serve as advocates for the program. Master black belts have extensive training in statistics and use of quality tools. They are teachers and mentors of black belts. Black belts are project team leaders responsible for implementing process improvement projects. They have typically completed four weeks of six-sigma training and have demonstrated mastery of the subject matter through an exam and successful completion of one or more projects. Green belts are members of project teams.

Black belts play a pivotal role in the success of six-sigma programs. They influence change, facilitate teamwork, provide leadership in applying tools and techniques, and convey knowledge and skills to green belts. Black belt candidates generally have a proven strength in either a technical discipline such as engineering or a business discipline. Candidates also must have strong "people skills" and be able to facilitate change. And they must be proficient in applying continuous improvement and statistical methods and tools. A black belt must understand the technical aspects of process improvement as well as the expected business results (time, money, quality improvement).

A six-sigma improvement project typically has one or more objectives such as reducing defects, reducing costs, reducing product and/or process variability, reducing delivery time, increasing productivity, or improving customer satisfaction. The process is to define, measure, analyze, improve, and control (**DMAIC**). The projects involve the use of management science tools as well as statistical tools.[6]

DMAIC A six-sigma process: define, measure, analyze, improve, and control.

Lean/six sigma An approach to continuous improvement that integrates lean operation principles and six-sigma techniques.

Lean/Six Sigma

Lean/six sigma is a balanced approach to process improvement that integrates principles from lean operation and statistical tools for variation reduction from six sigma to achieve speed and quality. Lean/six sigma combines the power of the workers, who are close to the process, and the structured approach of six-sigma methodology. Managers facilitate the creative problem-solving process. The rationale of this approach is that lean principles alone cannot achieve statistical process control, and six sigma alone cannot achieve improved process speed and flow.

The approach is equally applicable to products and services. In fact, some of the earliest applications were in service support functions of General Electric and Caterpillar Finance.

Obstacles to Implementing TQM

Companies have had varying success in implementing TQM. Some have been quite successful, but others have struggled. Part of the difficulty may be with the process by which it is implemented rather than with the principles of TQM. Among the factors cited in the literature are the following:

1. Lack of a companywide definition of quality: Efforts aren't coordinated; people are working at cross-purposes, addressing different issues, and using different measures of success.
2. Lack of a strategic plan for change: Without such a plan the chance of success is lessened and the need to address strategic implications of change is ignored.
3. Lack of a customer focus: Without a customer focus, there is a risk of customer dissatisfaction.
4. Poor intraorganizational communication: The left hand doesn't know what the right hand is doing; frustration, waste, and confusion ensue.
5. Lack of employee empowerment: Not empowering employees gives the impression of not trusting employees to fix problems, adds red tape, and delays solutions.
6. View of quality as a "quick fix": Quality needs to be a long-term, continuing effort.
7. Emphasis on short-term financial results: "Duct-tape" solutions often treat symptoms; spend a little now—a lot more later.

[6]Excerpt from S. L. Ahire, "The Management Science—Total Quality Management Interfaces," *Interfaces* 27, no. 6 (1997), pp. 91–114. Copyright © 1997 The Institute for Operations Research and the Management Sciences (INFORMS). 7240 Parkway Drive, Suite 310, Hanover, MD 21076 USA. Reprinted by permission.

8. Inordinate presence of internal politics and "turf" issues: These can sap the energy of an organization and derail the best of ideas.
9. Lack of strong motivation: Managers need to make sure employees are motivated.
10. Lack of time to devote to quality initiatives: Don't add more work without adding additional resources.
11. Lack of leadership:[7] Managers need to be leaders.

This list of potential problems can serve as a guideline for organizations contemplating implementing TQM or as a checklist for those having trouble implementing it.

What Keeps Six Sigma Practitioners Up at Night? READING

Bill Kowalski

It may be the most widely acclaimed performance improvement system across the business world, yet Six Sigma is not immune to a paradox common to most large-scale change efforts:

> *You can't expect to sustain top executive support without producing consistent bottom-line results . . . yet consistent results aren't likely without sustained top executive support.*

This conundrum is a key finding from a recent survey of more than 240 Six Sigma practitioners across industries and around the globe. Sponsored by Leap Technologies, the survey was conducted anonymously over the web through iSixSigma.com, the leading Six Sigma information portal.

The survey gauged perceptions of Six Sigma practitioners on two primary issues:

1. What causes Six Sigma projects to fail to produce desired results?
2. What would most help to improve Six Sigma project results?

We know these are issues keeping practitioners up at night because these same people are under increasingly heavy pressure to produce and sustain bottom-line results from their projects.

The "Catch 22" for Six Sigma Practitioners

The most often cited reason for Six Sigma project failure was "lack of sustained executive sponsorship and commitment." It is clearly evident that there is no substitute for top leadership support to achieve sustained Six Sigma success. In close second ranking was "lack of buy-in, cooperation and ownership by frontline managers and employees for implementing and sustaining results on Six Sigma project solutions." These top two barriers to success create a classic "Catch 22" for Six Sigma practitioners. On the one hand, executive commitment is critical to the funding and mandate Six Sigma practitioners need to challenge the status quo.

On the other hand, sustaining executive support is nearly impossible without consistent delivery of results. Yet this payoff can't be sustained without active support by those most impacted by Six Sigma solutions . . . *frontline managers and employees!*

Six Sigma is, with its dedicated Belt infrastructure and standardized *DMAIC methodology,* a more sophisticated and effective approach than past quality improvement methods. But, if there is a chink to be found in Six Sigma's armor, it is the issue of non-Belt participation and ownership. This problem, however, rarely surfaces in the first 12 to 18 months of a *Six Sigma Deployment.* In fact, we've observed that, initially, many Six Sigma Deployment Leaders experience a false sense of security about results. Why? Because most of the projects taken on by newly trained Black and Green Belts rarely require high levels of frontline support and, for the most part, don't challenge top management's ingrained cultural biases.

At the same time, it's also not uncommon for organizations adopting Six Sigma to "hit the wall" once "low touch" projects are completed. Top management's appetite for results has been whetted, but the foundational support in terms of skills, experience and commitment may not be there to tackle the projects that present bigger change management challenges.

More Tools Are Needed

According to the Six Sigma practitioners completing the survey, the path to better Six Sigma project results requires equipping practitioners with an expanded set of tools to both tackle more complex projects and improve Belt productivity by getting more non-Belt involvement. This finding is not likely to be a revelation to many of the early pioneers who paved the way to the popularity of Six Sigma. Companies like Motorola, Allied Signal (now merged with Honeywell), and GE, along with other big players, such as DuPont and 3M (among others), have already taken steps to strengthen their Six Sigma Deployments by enhancing the skills of Belts and expanding the tool kit.

At the same time, the survey results indicate there is more work to do in advancing Six Sigma into a robust and sustainable

(continued)

[7]Excerpt from Gary Salegna and Farzaneh Fazel, "Obstacles to Implementing Quality," *Quality Progress,* July 2000, p. 53. Copyright © 2000 American Society for Quality. Reprinted with permission from *Quality Progress* magazine.

(concluded)

method for *transformational change.* The top priority appears to be the expansion of the Six Sigma practitioner's tool kit to break free of the "Catch 22" syndrome. In fact, the integration of *Lean principles* by numerous Six Sigma users is a big step in the right direction. However, in addition to Lean tools there also appears to be a growing recognition that more tools are needed to deal with the *change management* aspects of Six Sigma. Ninety percent of the survey respondents rated the need for a structured tool set for engaging "non-Belts" in projects, particularly those with significant behavior change requirements.

The preceding finding is linked to the second most important reason practitioners stated as the cause for Six Sigma projects falling short (i.e., lack of buy-in, cooperation, or ownership by frontline employees and managers). The relationship between these two findings correlates with the anecdotal evidence from more experienced Six Sigma organizations about the keys to accelerating results and reducing project cycle times. As they move down the experience curve and tackle larger and more complex change projects, the most successful Six Sigma organizations have expanded their tool sets and integrated other improvement disciplines such as Lean seamlessly into deployments.

The Keys to a Better Night's Sleep

Six Sigma practitioners can break free of the "Catch 22" syndrome by designing their deployments to deliver consistent results and sustain consistent executive support. The keys are:

1. Expand the tool set early in deployment with methods to get more non-Belt participation and faster results. The key to avoiding confusion or overload is to integrate Lean, Innovation, and other improvement methods into the DMAIC framework.
2. Engage senior leaders to go beyond the rubber-stamping of project selections to actually designing the project plan with the Belts. The benefits are a more realistic appraisal of project requirements and deeper understanding of where and how to apply other tool sets to drive bigger and faster results.
3. Engage non-Belt managers and employees early on projects where there is existing motivation for change.

Taking actions such as these will provide a steadier stream of results, sustained executive support, and a better night's sleep for Six Sigma practitioners!

Source: Bill Kowalski, "What Keeps Six Sigma Practitioners Up at Night?"

About the Author

Bill Kowalski is a Senior Partner with Leap Technologies, the leading provider of Change Acceleration Tools for Six Sigma Deployment. For more articles and information on accelerating organization change, visit Leap Technologies on the Web at www.actionworkout.com.

Criticisms of TQM

TQM programs are touted as a way for companies to improve their competitiveness, which is a very worthwhile objective. Nonetheless, TQM programs are not without criticism. The following are some of the major criticisms:

1. Overzealous advocates may pursue TQM programs blindly, focusing attention on quality even though other priorities may be more important (e.g., responding quickly to a competitor's advances).
2. Programs may not be linked to the strategies of the organization in a meaningful way.
3. Quality-related decisions may not be tied to market performance. For instance, customer satisfaction may be emphasized to the extent that its cost far exceeds any direct or indirect benefit of doing so.
4. Failure to carefully plan a program before embarking on it can lead to false starts, employee confusion, and meaningless results.
5. Organizations sometimes pursue continuous improvement (i.e., *incremental* improvement) when *dramatic* improvement is needed.
6. Quality efforts may not be tied to results.

Note that there is nothing inherently wrong with TQM; the problem is how some individuals or organizations misuse it. Let's turn our attention to problem solving and process improvement.

PROBLEM SOLVING

Problem solving is one of the basic procedures of TQM. In order to be successful, problem-solving efforts should follow a standard approach. Table 9.7 describes the basic steps in the TQM problem-solving process.

TABLE 9.7
Basic steps in problem solving

Step 1	**Define the problem and establish an improvement goal.** Give problem definition careful consideration; don't rush through this step because this will serve as the focal point of problem-solving efforts.
Step 2	**Develop performance measures and collect data.** The solution must be based on *facts*. Possible tools include check sheet, scatter diagram, histogram, run chart, and control chart.
Step 3	**Analyze the problem.** Possible tools include Pareto chart, cause-and-effect diagram.
Step 4	**Generate potential solutions.** Methods include brainstorming, interviewing, and surveying.
Step 5	**Choose a solution.** Identify the criteria for choosing a solution. (Refer to the goal established in Step 1.) Apply criteria to potential solutions and select the best one.
Step 6	**Implement the solution.** Keep everyone informed.
Step 7	**Monitor the solution to see if it accomplishes the goal.** If not, modify the solution, or return to Step 1. Possible tools include control chart and run chart.

An important aspect of problem solving in the TQM approach is *eliminating* the cause so that the problem does not recur. This is why users of the TQM approach often like to think of problems as "opportunities for improvement."

The Plan-Do-Study-Act Cycle

The **plan-do-study-act (PDSA) cycle,** also referred to as either the Shewhart cycle or the Deming wheel, is the conceptual basis for problem-solving activities. The cycle is illustrated in Figure 9.2. Representing the process with a circle underscores its continuing nature.

Plan-do-study-act (PDSA) cycle A framework for problem solving and improvement activities.

FIGURE 9.2

A. The PDSA cycle B. The PDSA cycle applied to problem solving

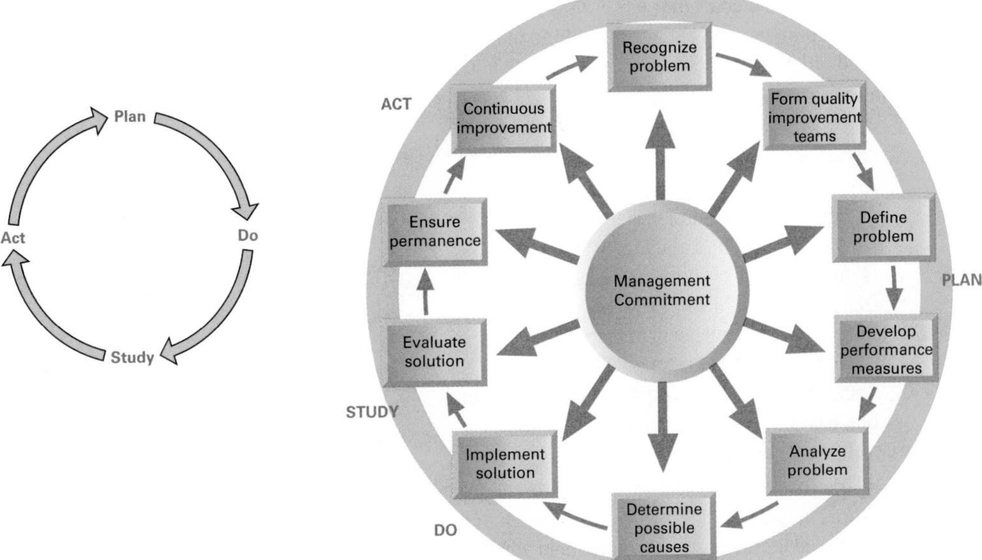

Source: Figure from Donna Summers, *Quality,* 2nd ed., p. 67. Copyright © 2000 Prentice Hall, Inc. Reprinted by permission of Pearson Education, Inc., Upper Saddle River, NJ.

There are four basic steps in the cycle:

Plan. Begin by studying the current process. Document that process. Then collect data on the process or problem. Next, analyze the data and develop a plan for improvement. Specify measures for evaluating the plan.

Do. Implement the plan, on a small scale if possible. Document any changes made during this phase. Collect data systematically for evaluation.

Study. Evaluate the data collection during the *do* phase. Check how closely the results match the original goals of the *plan* phase.

Act. If the results are successful, *standardize* the new method and communicate the new method to all people associated with the process. Implement training for the new method. If the results are unsuccessful, revise the plan and repeat the process or cease this project.

Employing this sequence of steps provides a systematic approach to continuous improvement.

PROCESS IMPROVEMENT

Process improvement A systematic approach to improving a process.

Process improvement is a *systematic* approach to improving a process. It involves documentation, measurement, and analysis for the purpose of improving the functioning of a process. Typical goals of process improvement include increasing customer satisfaction, achieving higher quality, reducing waste, reducing cost, increasing productivity, and reducing processing time.

Table 9.8 provides an overview of process improvement, and Figure 9.3 shows its cyclical nature.

TABLE 9.8
Overview of process improvement

A. Map the process

1. Collect information about the process; identify each step in the process. For each step, determine:
   The inputs and outputs.
   The people involved.
   The decisions that are made.
   Document such measures as time, cost, space used, waste, employee morale and any employee turnover, accidents and/or safety hazards, working conditions, revenues and/or profits, quality, and customer satisfaction, as appropriate.
2. Prepare a flowchart that *accurately* depicts the process; note that too little detail will not allow for meaningful analysis, and too much detail will overwhelm analysts and be counterproductive. Make sure that key activities and decisions are represented.

B. Analyze the process

1. Ask these questions about the process:
   Is the flow logical?
   Are any steps or activities missing?
   Are there any duplications?
2. Ask these questions about each step:
   Is the step necessary? Could it be eliminated?
   Does the step add value?
   Does any waste occur at this step?
   Could the time be shortened?
   Could the cost to perform the step be reduced?
   Could two (or more) steps be combined?

C. Redesign the process

Using the results of the analysis, redesign the process. Document the improvements; potential measures include reductions in time, cost, space, waste, employee turnover, accidents, safety hazards, and increases/improvements in employee morale, working conditions, revenues/profits, quality, and customer satisfaction.

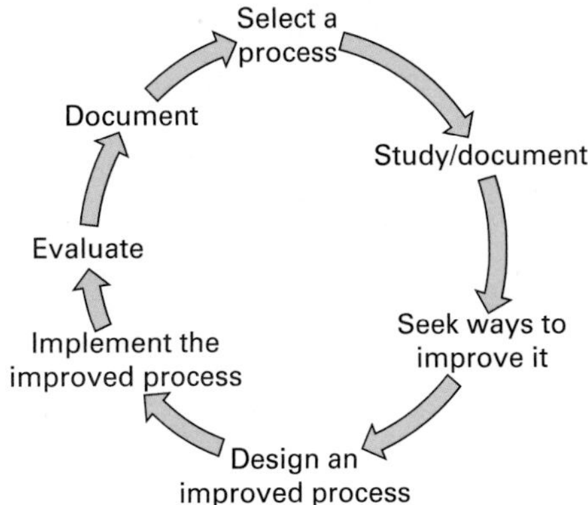

FIGURE 9.3
The process improvement cycle is another version of the plan-do-study-act cycle

QUALITY TOOLS

There are a number of tools that an organization can use for problem solving and process improvement. This section describes eight of these tools. The tools aid in data collection and interpretation, and provide the basis for decision making.

The first seven tools are often referred to as the *seven basic quality tools.* Figure 9.4 provides a quick overview of the seven tools.

Flowcharts. A **flowchart** is a visual representation of a process. As a problem-solving tool, a flowchart can help investigators in identifying possible points in a process where problems occur. Figure 9.5 illustrates a flowchart for catalog telephone orders in which potential failure points are highlighted.

Flowchart A diagram of the steps in a process.

The diamond shapes in the flowchart represent decision points in the process, and the rectangular shapes represent procedures. The arrows show the direction of "flow" of the steps in the process.

To construct a simple flowchart, begin by listing the steps in a process. Then classify each step as either a procedure or a decision (or check) point. Try to not make the flowchart too detailed or it may be overwhelming, but be careful not to omit any key steps.

Check Sheets. A **check sheet** is a simple tool frequently used for problem identification. Check sheets provide a format that enables users to record and organize data in a way that facilitates collection and analysis. This format might be one of simple checkmarks. Check sheets are designed on the basis of what the users are attempting to learn by collecting data.

Check sheet A tool for recording and organizing data to identify a problem.

Many different formats can be used for a check sheet and there are many different types of sheets. One frequently used form of check sheet deals with type of defect, another with location of defects. These are illustrated in Figures 9.6 and 9.7 (on page 401).

Figure 9.6 shows tallies that denote the type of defect and the time of day each occurred. Problems with missing labels tend to occur early in the day and smeared print tends to occur late in the day, whereas off-center labels are found throughout the day. Identifying types of defects and when they occur can help in pinpointing causes of the defects.

Figure 9.7 makes it easy to see where defects on the product—in this case, a glove—are occurring. Defects seem to be occurring on the tips of the thumb and first finger, in the finger valleys (especially between the thumb and first finger), and in the center of the gloves. Again, this may help determine why the defects occur and lead to a solution.

Histograms. A **histogram** can be useful in getting a sense of the distribution of observed values. Among other things, one can see if the distribution is symmetrical, what the range of

Histogram A chart of an empirical frequency distribution.

FIGURE 9.4 The seven basic quality tools

Flowchart

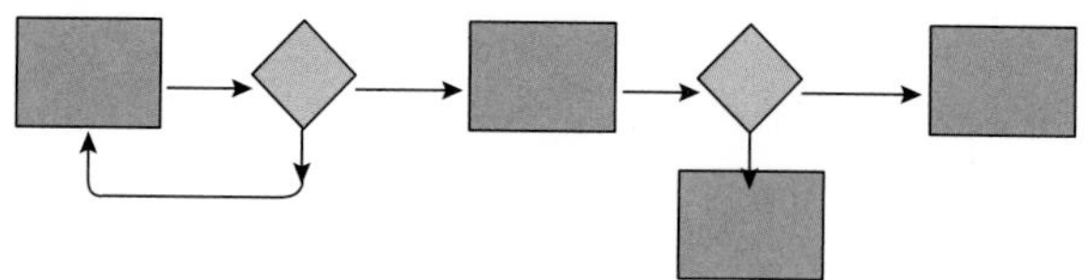

A diagram of the steps in a process

Check sheet

	Day			
Defect	1	2	3	4
A	///		////	/
B	//	/	//	///
C	/	////	//	////

A tool for organizing and collecting data; a tally of problems or other events by category

Histogram

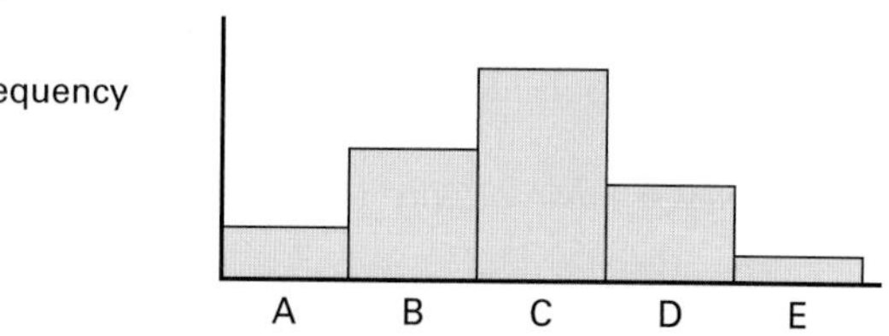

A chart that shows an empirical frequency distribution

Pareto chart

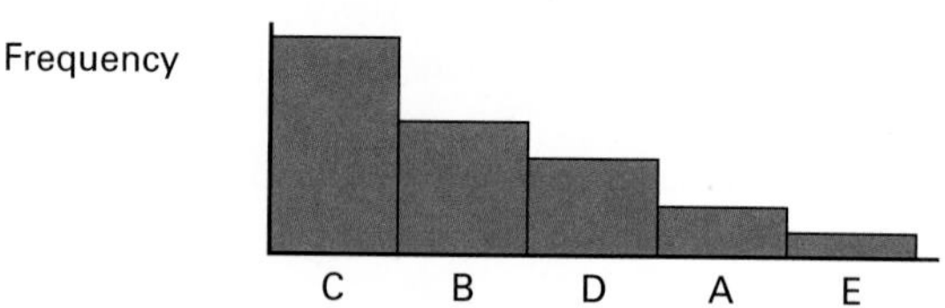

A diagram that arranges categories from highest to lowest frequency of occurrence

Scatter diagram

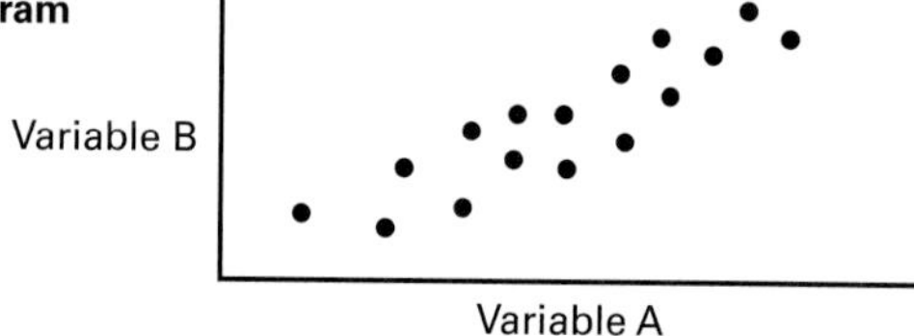

A graph that shows the degree and direction of relationship between two variables

Control chart

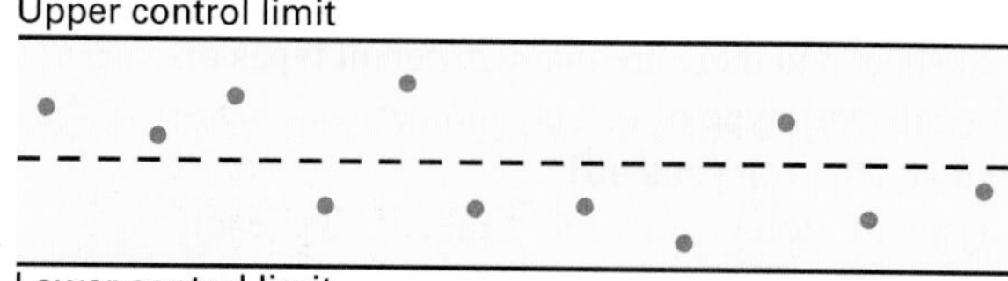

A statistical chart of time-ordered values of a sample statistic (e.g., sample means)

Cause-and-effect diagram

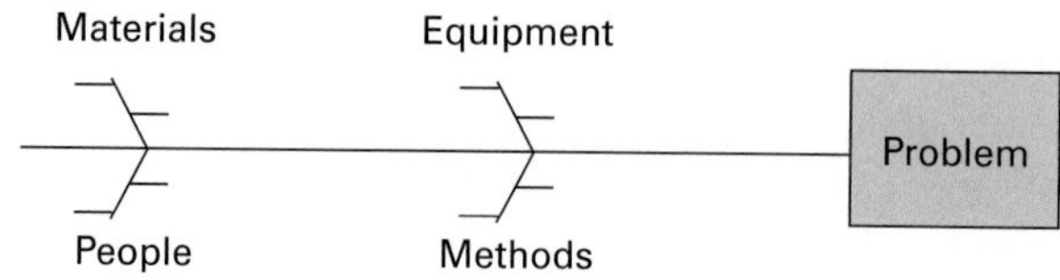

A diagram used to organize a search for the cause(s) of a problem; also known as a *fishbone* diagram

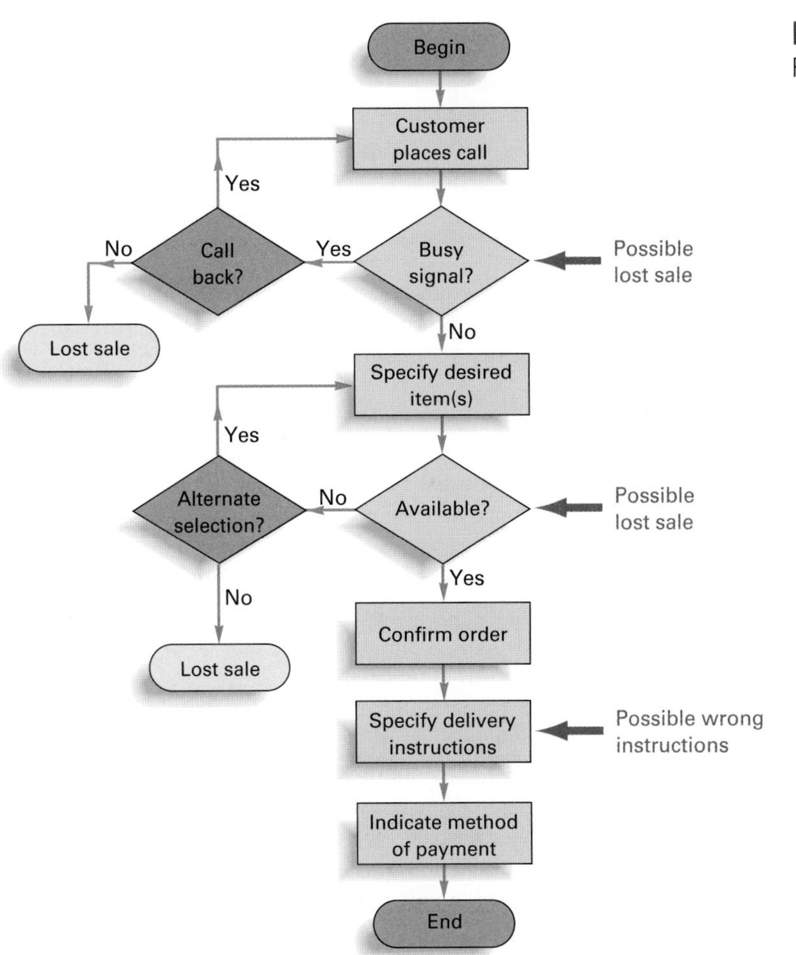

FIGURE 9.5
Flowchart of catalog call

Day	Time	Type of Defect					Total
		Missing label	Off-center	Smeared print	Loose or folded	Other	
M	8–9	IIII	II				6
	9–10		III				3
	10–11	I	III	I			5
	11–12		I		I	I(Torn)	3
	1–2		I				1
	2–3		II	III	I		6
	3–4		II	~~IIII~~ I			8
Total		5	14	10	2	1	32

FIGURE 9.6
An example of a check sheet

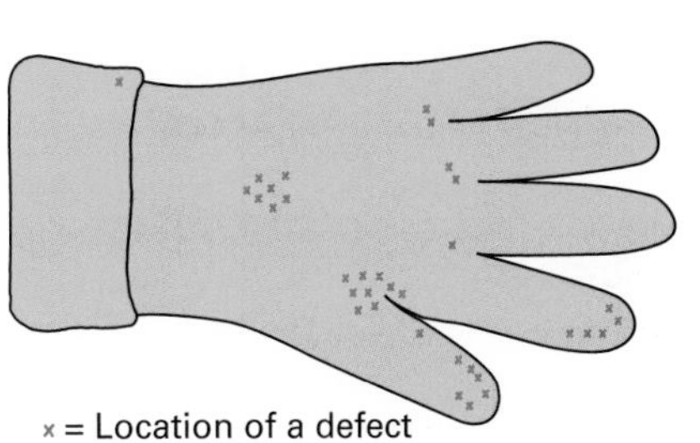

FIGURE 9.7
A special-purpose check sheet

FIGURE 9.8
A histogram

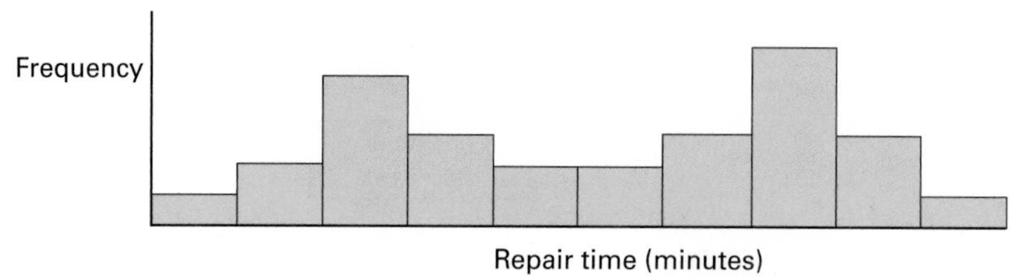

values is, and if there are any unusual values. Figure 9.8 illustrates a histogram. Note the two peaks. This suggests the possibility of *two* distributions with different centers. Possible causes might be two workers or two suppliers with different quality.

Pareto analysis Technique for classifying problem areas according to degree of importance, and focusing on the most important.

Pareto Analysis. **Pareto analysis** is a technique for focusing attention on the most important problem areas. The Pareto concept, named after the 19th-century Italian economist Vilfredo Pareto, is that a relatively few factors generally account for a large percentage of the total cases (e.g., complaints, defects, problems). The idea is to classify the cases according to degree of importance and focus on resolving the most important, leaving the less important. Often referred to as the 80–20 rule, the Pareto concept states that approximately 80 percent of the problems come from 20 percent of the items. For instance, 80 percent of machine breakdowns come from 20 percent of the machines, and 80 percent of the product defects come from 20 percent of the causes of defects.

Often, it is useful to prepare a chart that shows the number of occurrences by category, arranged in order of frequency. Figure 9.9 illustrates such a chart corresponding to the check sheet shown in Figure 9.6. The dominance of the problem with off-center labels becomes apparent. Presumably, the manager and employees would focus on trying to resolve this problem. Once they accomplished that, they could address the remaining defects in similar fashion; "smeared print" would be the next major category to be resolved, and so on. Additional check sheets would be used to collect data to verify that the defects in these categories have been eliminated or greatly reduced. Hence, in later Pareto diagrams, categories such as "off-center" may still appear but would be much less prominent.

Scatter diagram A graph that shows the degree and direction of relationship between two variables.

Scatter Diagrams. A **scatter diagram** can be useful in deciding if there is a correlation between the values of two variables. A correlation may point to a cause of a problem. Figure 9.10

FIGURE 9.9 A Pareto diagram based on data in Figure 9.6

FIGURE 9.10 A scatter diagram

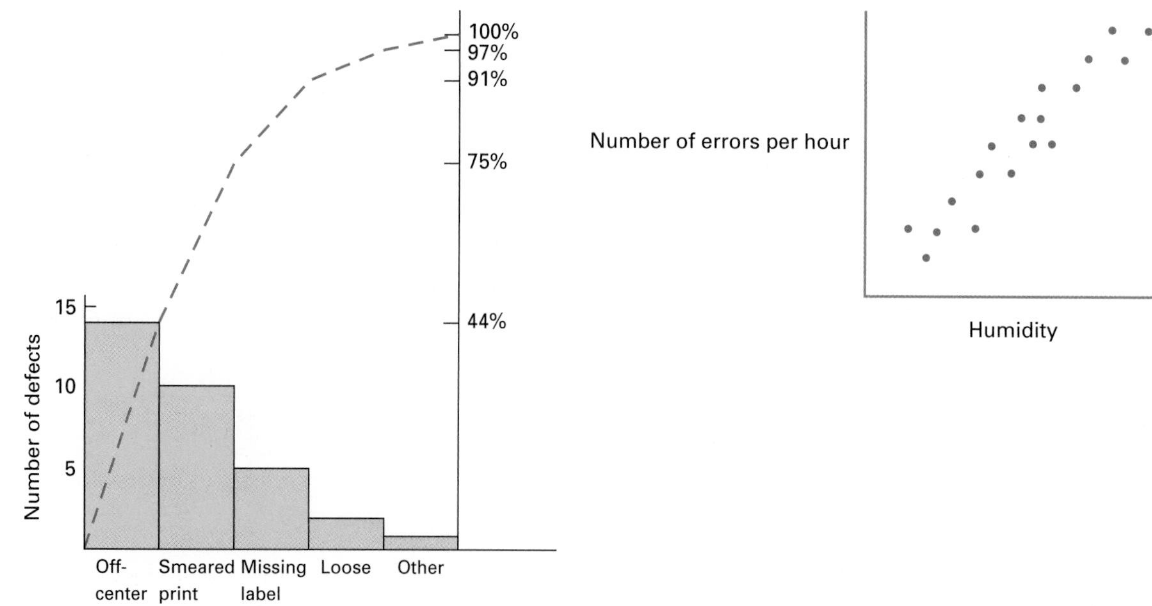

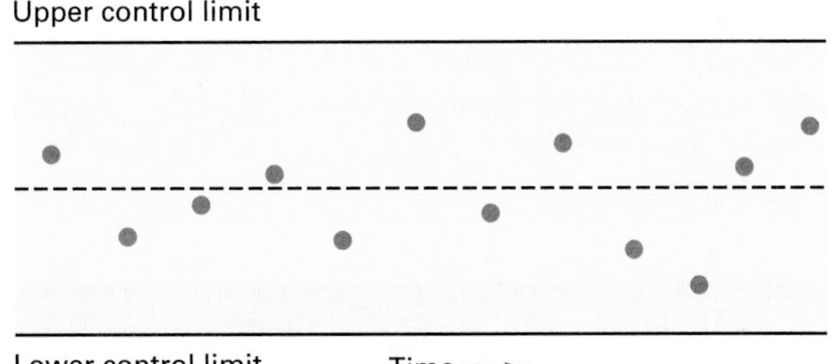

FIGURE 9.11
A control chart

shows an example of a scatter diagram. In this particular diagram, there is a *positive* (upward-sloping) relationship between the humidity and the number of errors per hour. High values of humidity correspond to high numbers of errors, and vice versa. On the other hand, a *negative* (downward-sloping) relationship would mean that when values of one variable are low, values of the other variable are high, and vice versa.

The higher the correlation between the two variables, the less scatter in the points; the points will tend to line up. Conversely, if there were little or no relationship between two variables, the points would be completely scattered. In Figure 9.10, the correlation between humidity and errors seems strong, because the points appear to scatter along an imaginary line.

Control Charts. A **control chart** can be used to monitor a process to see if the process output is random. It can help detect the presence of *correctable* causes of variation. Figure 9.11 illustrates a control chart. Control charts also can indicate when a problem occurred and give insight into what caused the problem. Control charts are described in detail in Chapter 10.

Control chart A statistical chart of time-ordered values of a sample statistic.

Cause-and-Effect Diagrams. A **cause-and-effect diagram** offers a structured approach to the search for the possible cause(s) of a problem. It is also known as a *fishbone diagram* because of its shape, or an *Ishikawa diagram,* after the Japanese professor who developed the approach to aid workers overwhelmed by the number of possible sources of problems when problem solving. This tool helps to organize problem-solving efforts by identifying *categories* of factors that might be causing problems. Often this tool is used after brainstorming sessions to organize the ideas generated. Figure 9.12 illustrates one form of a cause-and-effect diagram.

Cause-and-effect diagram A diagram used to search for the cause(s) of a problem; also called *fishbone diagram.*

An example of an application of such a cause-and-effect diagram is shown in Figure 9.13. Each of the factors listed in the diagram is a potential source of ticket errors. Some are more likely

FIGURE 9.12 One format of a cause-and-effect diagram

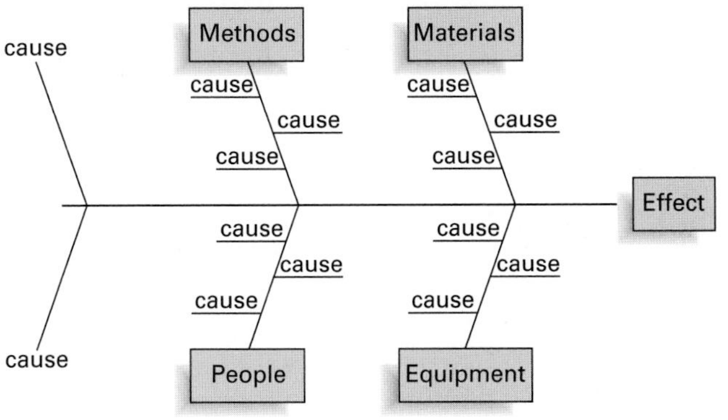

FIGURE 9.13 Cause-and-effect diagram for airline ticket errors

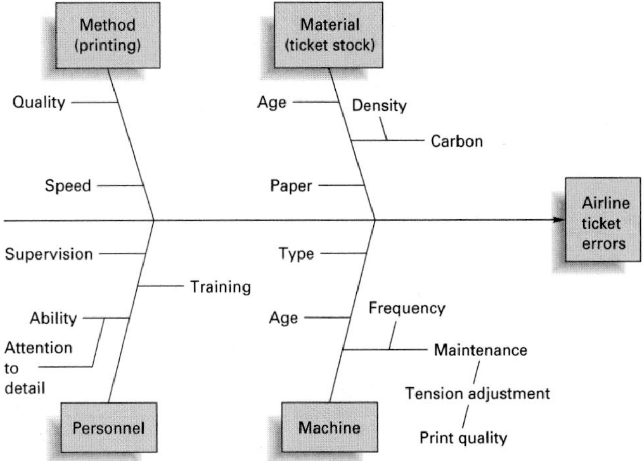

Source: Figure from Gitlow et al., *Quality Management,* p. 313. Copyright © 1995 Richard D. Irwin. Reprinted by permission of McGraw-Hill Companies, Inc.

causes than others, depending on the nature of the errors. If the cause is still not obvious at this point, additional investigation into the *root cause* may be necessary, involving a more in-depth analysis. Often, more detailed information can be obtained by asking *who, what, where, when, why,* and *how* questions about factors that appear to be the most likely sources of problems.

Continuous Improvement on the Free-Throw Line

READING

Timothy Clark and Andrew Clark

In 1924, Walter Shewhart developed a problem-solving method to continually improve quality by reducing variation (the difference between the ideal outcome and the actual situation). To help guide improvement efforts, Shewhart outlined a process referred to as the plan-do-study-act (PDSA) cycle. The PDSA cycle combined with the traditional concepts of decision making and problem solving are what my son and I used to continuously improve his basketball free-throw shooting.

Recognizing the Problem

Identify the Facts I had observed over a three-year period that in basketball games, my son Andrew's free-throw shooting percentage averaged between 45 percent and 50 percent.

Identify and Define the Process Andrew's process for shooting free throws was simple: Go to the free-throw line, bounce the ball four times, aim, and shoot.

The desired outcome was a higher free-throw shooting percentage. An ideal outcome, or perfection, would be one in which 100 percent of the shots fall through the middle of the rim, land at the same spot on the floor every time, and roll straight back in the shooter's direction after landing.

Plot the Points To confirm my observations on the results of the current process, we went to the YMCA and Andrew shot five sets of 10 free throws for a total of 50 shots. His average was 42 percent. Results were recorded on a run chart (see Figure 1). I estimated the process was stable.

FIGURE 1 Free-Throw Shooting Run Chart

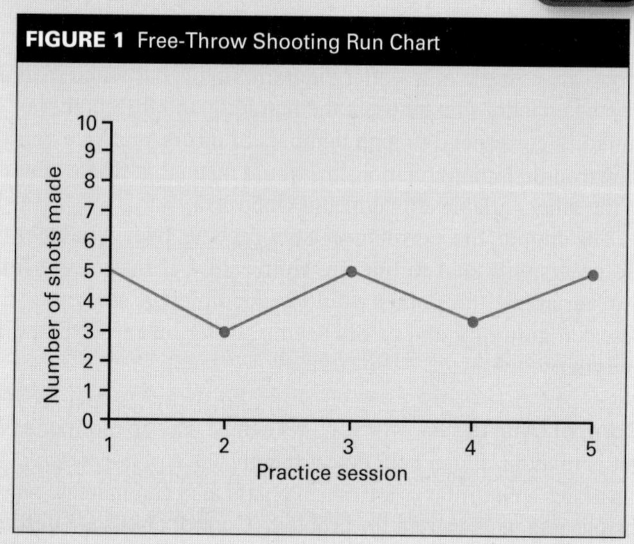

Decision Making

Identify the Causes Causes of variation in any process can be identified through the general categories of people, equipment, materials, methods, environment, and measurement. A cause-and-effect diagram is used to graphically illustrate the relationship between the effect—a low free-throw shooting percentage—and the principal causes (see Figure 2).

In analyzing my son's process, I noticed that he did not stand at the same place on the free-throw line every time. I believed his

FIGURE 2 Free-Throw Shooting Cause-and-Effect Diagram

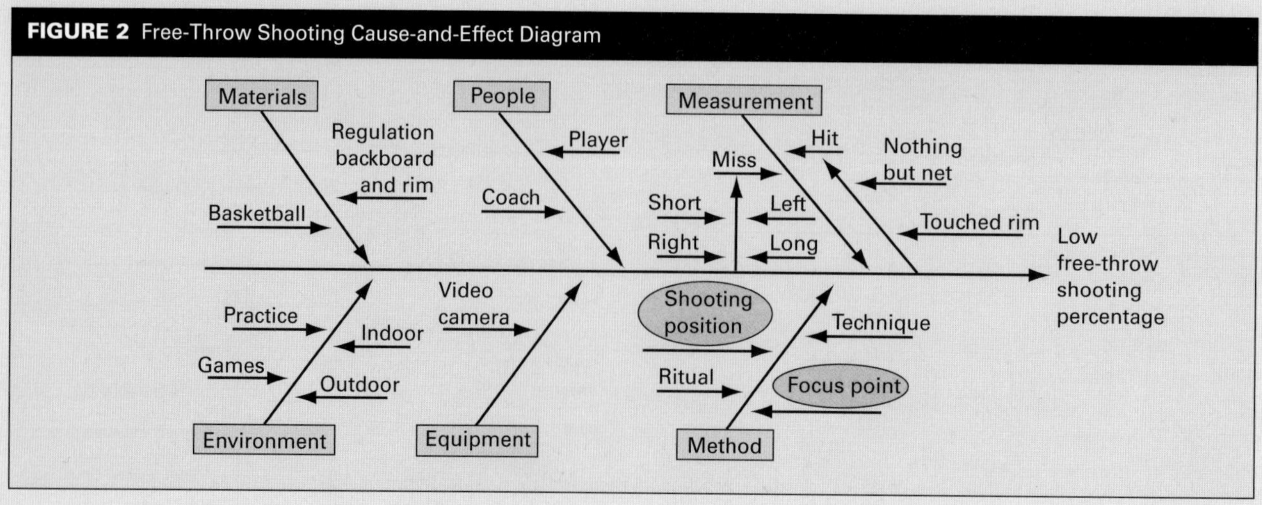

(continued)

inconsistent shooting position affected the direction of the shot. If the shot goes left or right, there is a smaller probability that the ball will have a lucky bounce and go in. I also noticed that he didn't seem to have a consistent focal point.

Develop, Analyze, and Select Alternatives The alternatives selected for Andrew, a right-handed shooter, were for him to line up his right foot on the middle of the free-throw line, focus on the middle of the front part of the rim, and visualize the perfect shot before he released the ball. The modified process is:

1. Stand at the center of the free-throw line.
2. Bounce the ball four times.
3. Focus on the middle of the front part of the rim, and visualize a perfect shot.
4. Shoot.

Develop an Action Plan The course of action at this point was for Andrew to shoot five more sets of 10 free throws to test the effectiveness of the changes.

Problem Solving

Implement the Selected Alternative and Compare Actual with Expected Results The new process resulted in a 36 percent improvement in Andrew's average free-throw percentage at basketball practice, which raised his average to 57 percent (see Figure 3). The new process was first implemented in games toward the end of the 1994 season, and in the last three games, Andrew hit nine of his 13 free throws for a free-throw shooting average of 69 percent.

FIGURE 3 Free-Throw Shots Made Before and After Implementing the PDSA Cycle

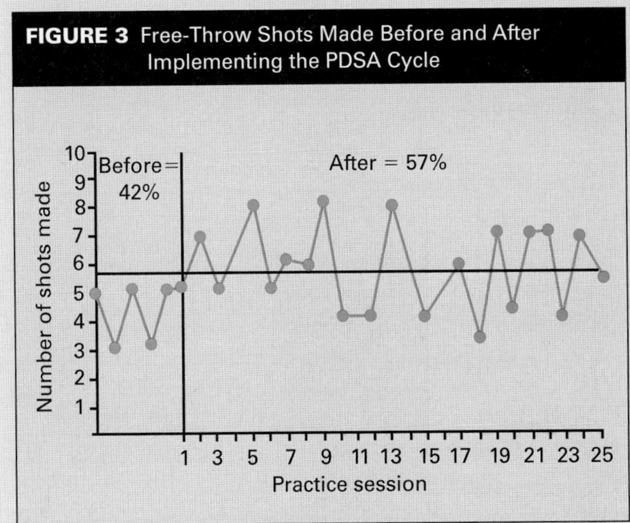

FIGURE 4 Determining Whether the Free-Throw Process Is Stable

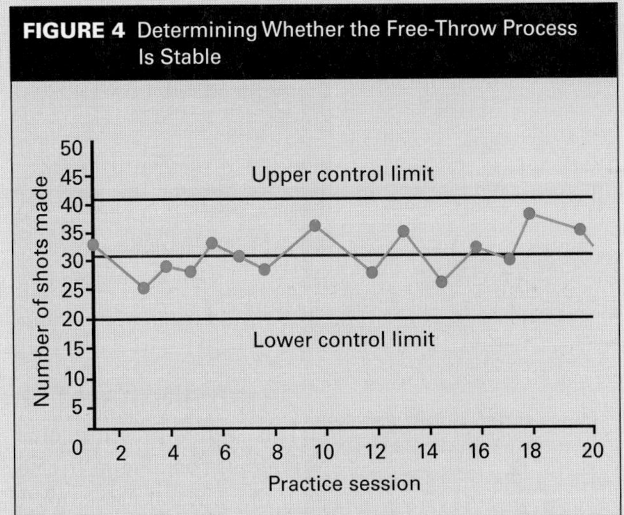

During the 1995 season, Andrew made 37 of 52, or 71 percent. In one extremely close game where the other team was forced to foul, Andrew hit seven of seven, which helped his team win the game. In team practices, the coaches had players shoot two free throws and then rotate. For the entire season, Andrew hit 101 of 169 in team practice for an average of 60 percent.

As we monitored Andrew's process from March to Jan., we plotted the total number of practice shots made out of 50, using Shewhart's number-of-affected-units control chart (see Figure 4).

In the late summer of 1995, Andrew went to a basketball camp where he was advised to change his shooting technique, which reduced his shooting percentage during the 1996 season to 50 percent. We then reinstalled his old process, and his shooting percentage returned to its former level. During the remaining team practices, Andrew hit 14 of 20 for an average of 70 percent.

During the 1996 and 1997 seasons, Andrew was a point guard and had fewer opportunities to shoot free throws, but he made nine of them for an average of 75 percent.

Overall Benefits In addition to the tangible results, Andrew's confidence improved, and he learned how to determine when changes to his shooting technique resulted in improvement. W. Edwards Deming referred to this type of knowledge as profound.

Source: Timothy Clark and Andrew Clark, "Continuous Improvement on the Free-Throw Line," *ASQ Journal,* Copyright © 1997 American Society for Quality. Reprinted with permission from *Quality Progress* magazine.

Run Charts. A **run chart** can be used to track the values of a variable over time. This can aid in identifying trends or other patterns that may be occurring. Figure 9.14 provides an example of a run chart showing a decreasing trend in accident frequency over time. Important advantages of run charts are ease of construction and ease of interpretation.

Run chart Tool for tracking results over a period of time.

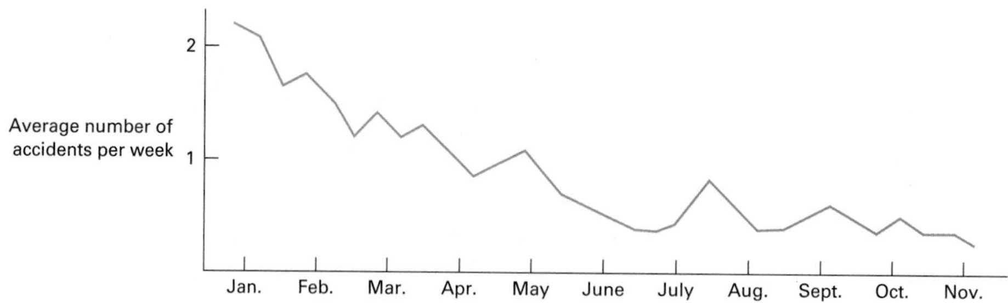

FIGURE 9.14
A run chart shows performance over time

Illustrations of the Use of Graphical Tools

This section presents some illustrations of the use of graphical tools in process or product improvement. Figure 9.15 begins with a check sheet that can be used to develop a Pareto chart of the types of errors found. That leads to a more focused Pareto diagram of the most frequently occurring type of error, followed (moving right) by a cause-and-effect diagram of the second most frequently occurring error. Additional cause-and-effect diagrams, such as errors by location, might also be used.

Figure 9.16 shows how Pareto charts measure the amount of improvement achieved in a before-and-after scenario of errors.

Figure 9.17 illustrates how control charts track two phases of improvement in a process that was initially out of control.

Methods for Generating Ideas

Some additional tools that are useful for problem solving and/or for process improvement are brainstorming, quality circles, and benchmarking.

FIGURE 9.15 Employing graphical tools in problem solving

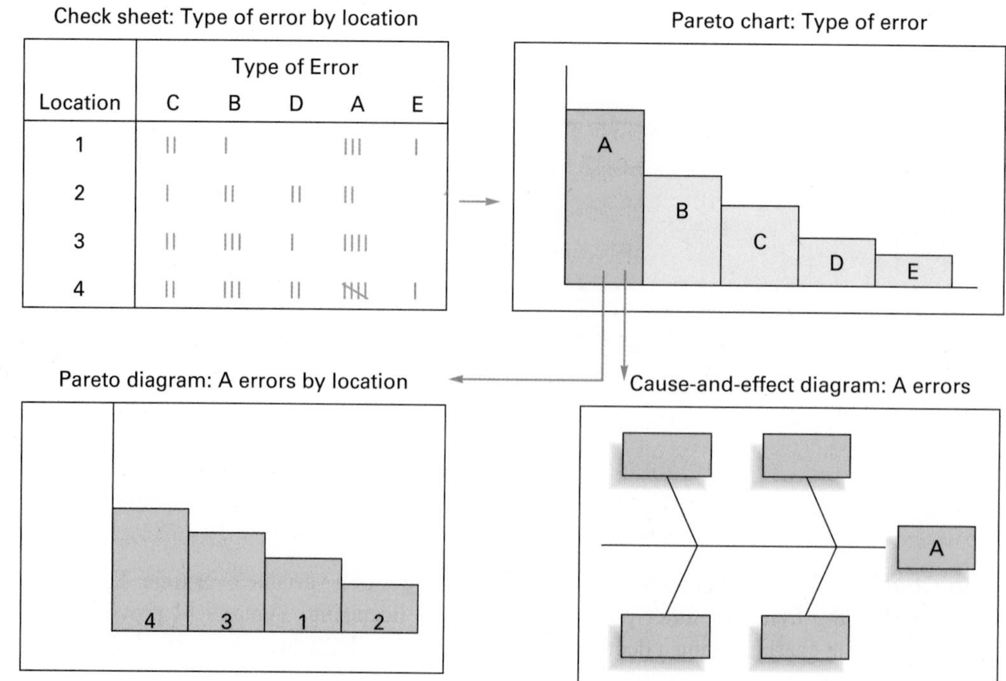

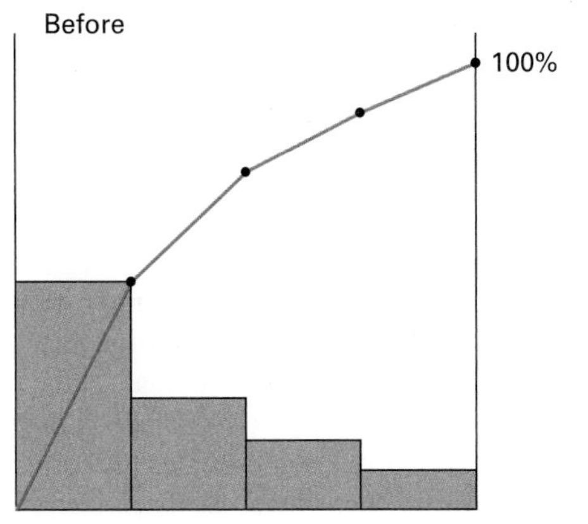

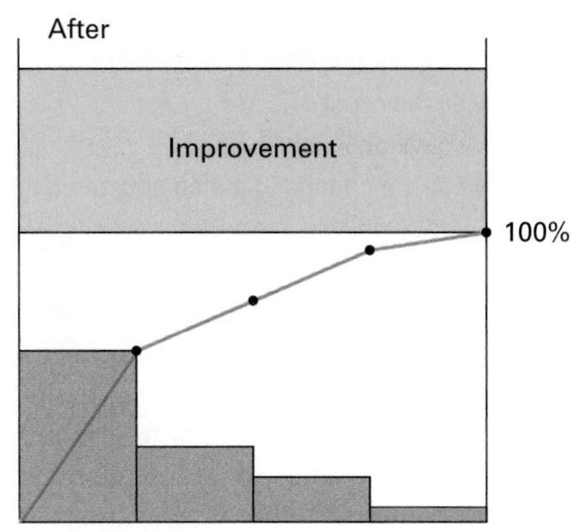

FIGURE 9.16
Comparison of before and after using Pareto charts

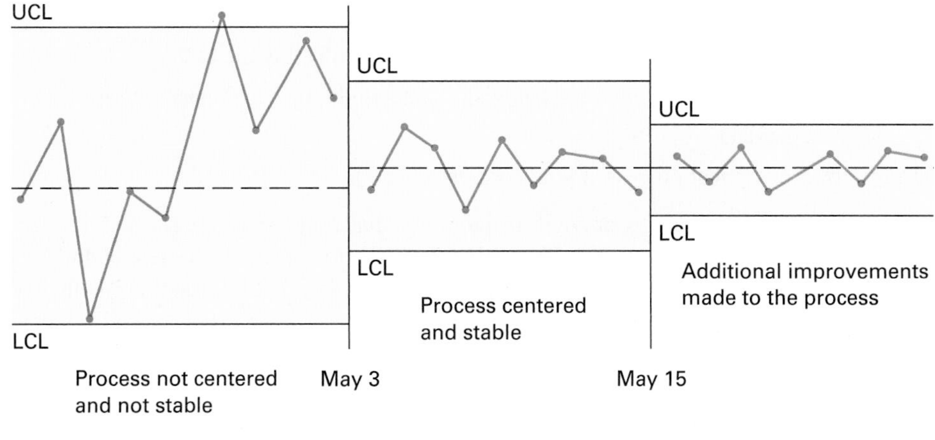

FIGURE 9.17
Using a control chart to track improvements

Brainstorming. **Brainstorming** is a technique in which a group of people share thoughts and ideas on problems in a relaxed atmosphere that encourages unrestrained collective thinking. The goal is to generate a free flow of ideas on identifying problems, and finding causes, solutions, and ways to implement solutions. In successful brainstorming, criticism is absent, no single member is allowed to dominate sessions, and all ideas are welcomed. Structured brainstorming is an approach to assure that everyone participates.

Brainstorming Technique for generating a free flow of ideas in a group of people.

Quality Circles. One way companies have tapped employees for ideas concerning quality improvement is through **quality circles.** The circles comprise a number of workers who get together periodically to discuss ways of improving products and processes. Not only are quality circles a valuable source of worker input, they also can motivate workers, if handled properly, by demonstrating management interest in worker ideas. Quality circles are usually less structured and more informal than teams involved in continuous improvement, but in some organizations quality circles have evolved into continuous improvement teams. Perhaps a major distinction between quality circles and teams is the amount of authority given to the teams. Typically, quality circles have had very little authority to implement any but minor changes; continuous improvement teams are sometimes given a great deal of authority. Consequently, continuous improvement teams have the added motivation generated by *empowerment.*

Quality circles Groups of workers who meet to discuss ways of improving products or processes.

TABLE 9.9
The benchmarking approach

1. What organizations do it the best?
2. How do they do it?
3. How do we do it now?
4. How can we change to match or exceed the best?

Benchmarking Process of measuring performance against the best in the same or another industry.

Benchmarking. **Benchmarking** is an approach that can inject new energy into improvement efforts. Summarized in Table 9.9, benchmarking is the process of measuring an organization's performance on a key customer requirement against the best in the industry, or against the best in any industry. Its purpose is to establish a standard against which performance is judged, and to identify a model for learning how to improve. A benchmark demonstrates the degree to which customers of other organizations are satisfied. Once a benchmark has been identified, the goal is to meet or exceed that standard through improvements in appropriate processes.

The benchmarking process usually involves these steps:

1. Identify a critical process that needs improvement (e.g., order entry, distribution, service after sale).
2. Identify an organization that excels in the process, preferably the best.
3. Contact the benchmark organization, visit it, and study the benchmark activity.
4. Analyze the data.
5. Improve the critical process at your own organization.

Selecting an industry leader provides insight into what competitors are doing; but competitors may be reluctant to share this information. Several organizations are responding to this difficulty by conducting benchmarking studies and providing that information to other organizations without revealing the sources of the data.

Selecting organizations that are world leaders in different industries is another alternative. For example, the Xerox Corporation uses many benchmarks: For employee involvement, Procter & Gamble; for quality process, Florida Power and Light and Toyota; for high-volume production, Kodak and Canon; for billing collection, American Express; for research and development, AT&T and Hewlett-Packard; for distribution, L.L. Bean and Hershey Foods; and for daily sched uling, Cummins Engine.

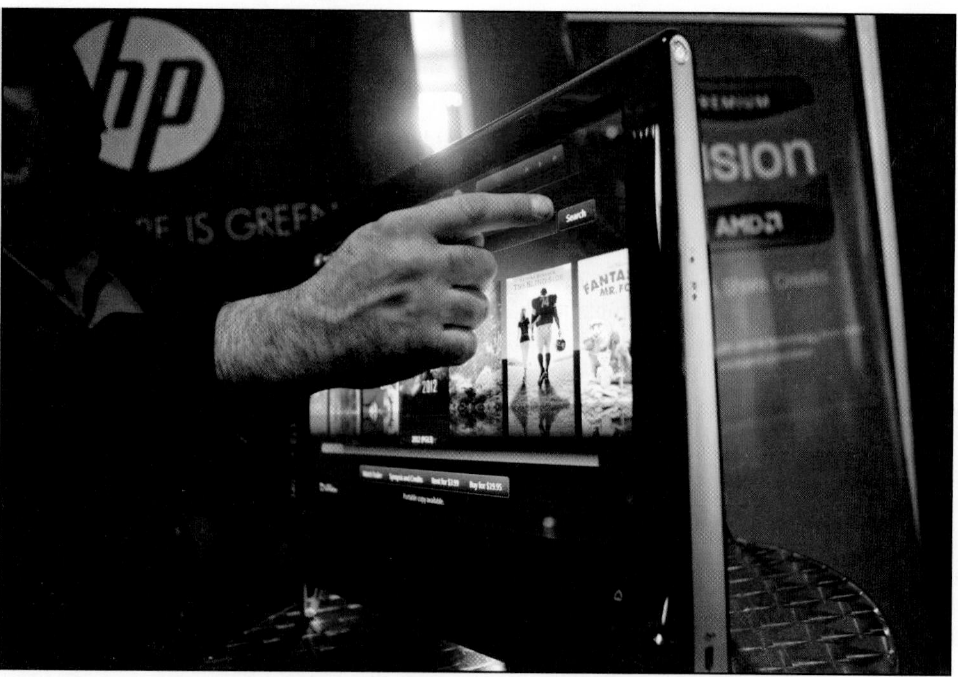

Hewlett-Packard, a world leader in research and development, created the TouchSmart PC. Joint research with universities, customers, and partners meets the scientific and business objectives of HP. This model is a benchmark for other companies.

Benchmarking Corporate Web Sites of Fortune 500 Companies

READING

More and more people are using the Internet. And when these people want information about a company's products or services, they often go to the company's Web site. In a study of the home pages of Fortune 500 companies, 13 factors were deemed critical to quality. Those factors, and the survey results, are shown below:

1. Use of meta tags (e.g., keywords used by search engines) Yes, 70%; no, 30%
2. Meaningful home page title Yes, 97%; no, 3%
3. Unique domain name Yes, 91%; no, 9%
4. Search engine site registration 97% (average)
5. Server reliability 99% (average)
6. Average speed of loading (seconds) 28k, 19.3; 56k, 10.9; T1, 2.6 sec.
7. Average number of bad links .40
8. Average number of spelling errors .16
9. Visibility of contact information Yes, 74%; no, 26%
10. Indication of last update date Yes, 17%; no, 83%
11. A privacy policy Yes, 53%; no, 47%
12. Presence of a search engine Yes, 59%; no, 41%
13. Translation to multiple languages Yes, 11%; no, 89%

The corporations are doing well on most factors, but they need improvement on the last five.

The list is a handy reference other organizations can use to benchmark their existing home pages to see where improvements are needed or to develop effective home pages.

Question Give one reason for the importance of each factor.

Source: Based on Nabil Tamimi, Murli Rajan, and Rose Sebastianelli, "Benchmarking the Home Pages of 'Fortune 500' Companies." Reprinted with permission from *Quality Progress* © 2000 American Society for Quality. No further distribution allowed without permission.

OPERATIONS STRATEGY

All customers are concerned with the quality of goods or services they receive. For this reason alone, business organizations have a vital, strategic interest in achieving and maintaining high quality standards. Moreover, there is a positive link between quality and productivity, giving an additional incentive for achieving high quality and being able to present that image to current and potential customers.

The best business organizations view quality as a never-ending journey. That is, they strive for continual improvement with the attitude that no matter how good quality is, it can always be improved, and there are benefits for doing so.

In order for total quality management to be successful, it is essential that a majority of those in an organization buy in to the idea. Otherwise, there is a risk that a significant portion of the benefits of the approach will not be realized. Therefore, it is important to give this sufficient attention, and to confirm that concordance exists before plunging ahead. A key aspect of this is a top-down approach: Top management needs to be visibly involved and needs to be supportive, both financially and emotionally. Also important is education of managers and workers in the concepts, tools, and procedures of quality. Again, if education is incomplete, there is the risk that TQM will not produce the desired benefits.

And here's a note of caution: Although customer retention rates can have a dramatic impact on profitability, customer satisfaction does not always guarantee customer loyalty. Consequently, organizations may need to develop a retention strategy to deal with this possibility.

It is not enough for an organization to incorporate quality into its operations; the entire supply chain has to be involved. Problems such as defects in purchased parts, long lead times, and late or missed deliveries of goods or services all negatively impact an organization's ability to satisfy its customers. So it is essential to incorporate quality throughout the supply chain.

SUMMARY

This chapter presents philosophies and tools that can be used to achieve high quality and continually improve quality. Quality is the culmination of efforts of the entire organization and its supply chain. It begins with careful assessment of what the customers want, then translating this information into technical specifications to which goods or services must conform. The specifications guide product and service design, process design, production of goods and delivery of services, and service after the sale or delivery.

The consequences of poor quality include loss of market share, liability claims, a decrease in productivity, and an increase in costs. Quality costs include costs related to prevention, appraisal, and failure. Determinants of quality are design, conformance to design, ease of use, and service after delivery.

Modern quality management is directed at preventing mistakes rather than finding them after they occur and reducing process output variation. Currently, the business community shows widespread interest in improving quality and competitiveness.

The chapter includes a description of the key contributors to quality management, and it outlines the ISO 9000, ISO 14000, and ISO 24700 international quality standards.

Three awards of distinction, the Baldrige Award, the European Quality Award, and the Deming Prize, are given annually to organizations that have shown great achievement in quality management.

Total quality management is a never-ending pursuit of quality that involves everyone in an organization. The driving force is customer satisfaction; a key philosophy is continuous improvement. Training of managers and workers in quality concepts, tools, and procedures is an important aspect of the approach. Teams are an integral part of TQM.

Two major aspects of the TQM approach are problem solving and process improvement. Six-sigma programs are a form of TQM. They emphasize the use of statistical and management science tools on selected projects to achieve business results.

KEY POINTS

1. Price and quality are the two primary considerations in every buying transaction, so quality is extremely important.
2. Quality gurus have made important contributions to the way business organizations view quality and achieve quality.
3. Quality certification and quality awards are important because they can provide some degree of assurance to customers about quality.
4. Many tools are available that can be used for problem solving and process improvement.

KEY TERMS

SOLVED PROBLEM

Problem

The county sheriff's department handed out the following tickets on a summer weekend. Make a check sheet and a Pareto diagram for the types of infractions.

Ticket Number	Infraction
1	Excessive speed
2	Expired inspection
3	Improper turn
4	Excessive speed
5	Parking violation
6	Parking violation

Ticket Number	Infraction
7	Excessive speed
8	Parking violation
9	Improper turn
10	Parking violation
11	Expired inspection
12	Parking violation
13	Improper turn
14	Parking violation
15	Excessive speed
16	Parking violation
17	Parking violation
18	Parking violation
19	Excessive speed
20	Parking violation

Solution

Check sheet (list the types of infractions, tally, summarize frequencies):

Infraction	Tally	Frequency
Excessive speed	𝍸	5
Expired inspection	//	2
Improper turn	///	3
Parking violation	𝍸 𝍸	10

Pareto diagram (array infractions from highest frequency to lowest):

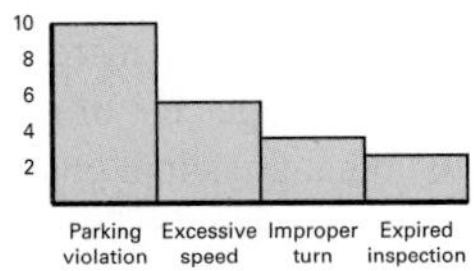

DISCUSSION AND REVIEW QUESTIONS

1. List and briefly explain
   a. The dimensions of service quality.
   b. The determinants of quality.
2. Define the terms *quality of design* and *quality of conformance.*
3. What are some possible consequences of poor quality?
4. Use the dimensions of quality to describe typical characteristics of these products and services:
   a. A television set.
   b. A restaurant meal (product).
   c. A restaurant meal (service).
   d. Painting a house.
   e. Surgery and postsurgery care.
5. Many product reviews are available on the Internet. Two examples are reviews on electronics products such as DVD players and high-definition televisions. There are often both positive and negative reviews.
   a. Do such reviews (positive and negative) influence your purchasing decisions? Why or why not?
   b. Why do you suppose consumers take the time and effort to write such reviews?
   c. There is often a feedback button asking if you found the review helpful. Do you usually respond? Why or why not?
6. Describe the quality–ethics connection.
7. Select one of the quality gurus and briefly describe his major contributions to quality management.

8. a. What is ISO 9000, and why is it important for global businesses to have ISO 9000 certification?
   b. Compare the Baldrige Award and ISO certification. If an organization were going to seek both, which one should it seek first? Why?
9. Briefly explain how a company can achieve lower production costs and increase productivity by improving the quality of its products or services.
10. What are the key elements of the TQM approach? What is the driving force behind TQM?
11. Briefly describe each of the seven quality tools.
12. Briefly define or explain each of these tools:
    a. Brainstorming.
    b. Benchmarking.
    c. Run charts.
13. Explain the plan-do-study-act cycle.
14. List the steps of problem solving.
15. Select four tools and describe how they could be used in problem solving.
16. List the steps of process improvement.
17. Select four tools and describe how they could be used for process improvement.

TAKING STOCK

1. What trade-offs are involved in deciding on whether to offer a product or service guarantee?
2. Who needs to be involved in setting priorities for quality improvement?
3. Name several ways that technology has had an impact on quality.

CRITICAL THINKING EXERCISES

1. A computer repair shop had received a number of complaints on the length of time it took to make repairs. The manager responded by increasing the repair staff by 10 percent. Complaints on repair time quickly decreased, but then complaints on the cost of repairs suddenly increased. Oddly enough, when repair costs were analyzed, the manager found that the average cost of repair had actually decreased relative to what it was before the increase in staff. What are some possible explanations for the complaints, and what actions might the manager contemplate?
2. As a manager, how would you deal with the possibility that customer satisfaction does not always lead to customer retention?
3. What quality-related trade-offs might there be between having a single large, centralized produce-processing facility and having many small, decentralized produce-processing facilities?
4. Give three examples of what would be considered unethical behavior involving management of quality, and state which ethical principle (see Chapter 1) is violated.

PROBLEMS

1. Make a check sheet and then a Pareto diagram for the following car repair shop data:

Ticket No.	Work	Ticket No.	Work	Ticket No.	Work
1	Tires	11	Brakes	21	Lube & oil
2	Lube & oil	12	Lube & oil	22	Brakes
3	Tires	13	Battery	23	Transmission
4	Battery	14	Lube & oil	24	Brakes
5	Lube & oil	15	Lube & oil	25	Lube & oil
6	Lube & oil	16	Tires	26	Battery
7	Lube & oil	17	Lube & oil	27	Lube & oil
8	Brakes	18	Brakes	28	Battery
9	Lube & oil	19	Tires	29	Brakes
10	Tires	20	Brakes	30	Tires

2. An air-conditioning repair department manager has compiled data on the primary reason for 41 service calls for the previous week, as shown in the table. Using the data, make a check sheet for the problem types for each customer type, and then construct a Pareto diagram for each type of customer.

Job Number	Problem/ Customer Type	Job Number	Problem/ Customer Type	Job Number	Problem/ Customer Type
301	F/R	315	F/C	329	O/C
302	O/R	316	O/C	330	N/R
303	N/C	317	W/C	331	N/R
304	N/R	318	N/R	332	W/R
305	W/C	319	O/C	333	O/R
306	N/R	320	F/R	334	O/C
307	F/R	321	F/R	335	N/R
308	N/C	322	O/R	336	W/R
309	W/R	323	F/R	337	O/C
310	N/R	324	N/C	338	O/R
311	N/R	325	F/R	339	F/R
312	F/C	326	O/R	340	N/R
313	N/R	327	W/C	341	O/C
314	W/C	328	O/C		

Key
Problem type:
N = Noisy
F = Equipment failure
W = Runs warm
O = Odor
Customer type:
C = Commercial customer
R = Residential customer

3. Prepare a run chart similar to Figure 9.14 for the occurrences of defective computer monitors based on the following data, which an analyst obtained from the process for making the monitors. Workers are given a 15-minute break at 10:15 a.m. and 3:15 p.m., and a lunch break at noon. What can you conclude?

Interval Start Time	Number of Defects	Interval Start Time	Number of Defects	Interval Start Time	Number of Defects
8:00	1	10:45	0	2:15	0
8:15	0	11:00	0	2:30	2
8:30	0	11:15	0	2:45	2
8:45	1	11:30	1	3:00	3
9:00	0	11:45	3	3:30	0
9:15	1	1:00	1	3:45	1
9:30	1	1:15	0	4:00	0
9:45	2	1:30	0	4:15	0
10:00	3	1:45	1	4:30	1
10:30	1	2:00	1	4:45	3

4. Prepare a run diagram for this emergency call data. Use five-minute intervals (i.e., count the calls received in each five-minute interval. Use intervals of 0–4, 5–9, etc.). *Note:* Two or more calls may occur in the same minute; there were three operators on duty this night. What can you conclude from the run chart?

Call	Time	Call	Time	Call	Time	Call	Time
1	1:03	12	1:36	23	1:56	34	2:08
2	1:06	13	1:39	24	2:00	35	2:11
3	1:09	14	1:42	25	2:00	36	2:12
4	1:11	15	1:43	26	2:01	37	2:12
5	1:12	16	1:44	27	2:02	38	2:13
6	1:17	17	1:47	28	2:03	39	2:14
7	1:21	18	1:48	29	2:03	40	2:14
8	1:27	19	1:50	30	2:04	41	2:16
9	1:28	20	1:52	31	2:06	42	2:19
10	1:29	21	1:53	32	2:07		
11	1:31	22	1:56	33	2:08		

5. Suppose that a table lamp fails to light when turned on. Prepare a simple cause-and-effect diagram to analyze possible causes.

6. Prepare a cause-and-effect diagram to analyze the possible causes of late delivery of parts ordered from a supplier.

7. Prepare a cause-and-effect diagram to analyze why a machine has produced a large run of defective parts.
8. Prepare a scatter diagram for each of these data sets and then express in words the apparent relationship between the two variables. Put the first variable on the horizontal axis and the second variable on the vertical axis.

a.

Age	24	30	22	25	33	27	36	58	37	47	54	28	42	55
Absenteeism rate	6	5	7	6	4	5	4	1	3	2	2	5	3	1

b.

Temperature (°F)	65	63	72	66	82	58	75	86	77	65	79
Error rate	1	2	0	0	3	3	1	5	2	1	3

9. Prepare a flowchart that describes going to the library to study for an exam. Your flowchart should include these items: finding a place at the library to study; checking to see if you have your book, paper, highlighter, and so forth; traveling to the library; and the possibility of moving to another location if the place you chose to study starts to get crowded.
10. College students trying to register for a course sometimes find that the course has been closed, or the section they want has been closed. Prepare a cause-and-effect diagram for this problem.
11. The county sheriff's department responded to an unusually large number of vehicular accidents along a quarter-mile stretch of highway in recent months. Prepare a cause-and-effect diagram for this problem.
12. Suppose you are going to have a prescription filled at a local pharmacy. Referring to the dimensions of service quality for each dimension, give an example of how you would judge the quality of the service.

Chick-n-Gravy Dinner Line

CASE

The operations manager of a firm that produces frozen dinners had received numerous complaints from supermarkets about the firm's Chick-n-Gravy dinners. The manager then asked her assistant, Ann, to investigate the matter and to report her recommendations.

Ann's first task was to determine what problems were generating the complaints. The majority of complaints centered on five defects: underfilled packages, a missing label, spills/mixed items, unacceptable taste, and improperly sealed packages.

Next, she took samples of dinners from the two production lines and examined each sample, making note of any defects that she found. A summary of those results is shown in the table.

The data resulted from inspecting approximately 800 frozen dinners. What should Ann recommend to the manager?

DEFECT OBSERVED

Date	Time	Line	Underfilled	Missing Label	Spill/ Mixed	Unacceptable Taste	Improperly Sealed
5/12	0900	1		✓✓	✓	✓✓✓	
5/12	1330	2			✓✓		✓✓
5/13	1000	2				✓	✓✓✓
5/13	1345	1	✓✓		✓✓		
5/13	1530	2		✓✓	✓✓✓		✓
5/14	0830	1		✓✓✓		✓✓✓	
5/14	1100	2	✓		✓	✓✓	
5/14	1400	1			✓		✓
5/15	1030	1		✓✓✓		✓✓✓✓✓	
5/15	1145	2			✓	✓✓	
5/15	1500	1	✓		✓		
5/16	0845	2				✓✓	✓✓
5/16	1030	1		✓✓✓	✓	✓✓✓	
5/16	1400	1					
5/16	1545	2	✓	✓✓✓✓	✓	✓	✓✓

Tip Top Markets

CASE

Tip Top Markets is a regional chain of supermarkets located in the Southeastern United States. Karen Martin, manager of one of the stores, was disturbed by the large number of complaints from customers at her store, particularly on Tuesdays, so she obtained complaint records from the store's customer service desk for the last nine Tuesdays.

Assume you have been asked to help analyze the data and to make recommendations for improvement. Analyze the data using a check sheet, a Pareto diagram, and run charts. Then construct a cause-and-effect diagram for the leading category on your Pareto diagram.

On July 15, changes were implemented to reduce out-of-stock complaints, improve store maintenance, and reduce checkout lines/pricing problems. Do the results of the last two weeks reflect improvement?

Based on your analysis, prepare a list of recommendations that will address customer complaints.

June 1

out of orange yogurt
bread stale
checkout lines too long
overcharged
double charged
meat smelled strange
charged for item not purchased
couldn't find the sponges
meat tasted strange
store too cold
light out in parking lot
produce not fresh
lemon yogurt past sell date
couldn't find rice
milk past sell date
stock clerk rude
cashier not friendly
out of maple walnut ice cream
something green in meat
didn't like music
checkout lines too slow

June 8

fish smelled funny
out of diet bread
dented can
out of hamburger rolls
fish not fresh
cashier not helpful
meat tasted bad
ATM ate card
slippery floor
music too loud
undercharged
out of roses
meat spoiled
overcharged on two items
store too warm
out of ice
telephone out of order
overcharged
rolls stale
bread past sale date

June 15

wanted smaller size
too cold in store
out of Wheaties
out of Minute Rice
cashier rude
fish tasted fishy
ice cream thawed
double charged on hard rolls
long wait at checkout
wrong price on item
overcharged
fish didn't smell right
overcharged on special
couldn't find aspirin
undercharged
checkout lines too long
out of diet cola
meat smelled bad
overcharged on eggs
bread not fresh
didn't like music
lost wallet
overcharged on bread

June 22

milk past sales date
store too warm
foreign object in meat
store too cold
eggs cracked
couldn't find lard
out of 42 oz. Tide
fish really bad
windows dirty
couldn't find oatmeal
out of Bounty paper towels
overcharged on orange juice
lines too long at checkout
couldn't find shoelaces
out of Smucker's strawberry jam
out of Frosty Flakes cereal
out of Thomas' English Muffins

(continued)

(concluded)

June 29

checkout line too long
out of Dove soap
out of Bisquick
eggs cracked
store not clean
store too cold
cashier too slow
out of skim milk
charged wrong price
restroom not clean
couldn't find sponges
checkout lines slow
out of 18 oz. Tide
out of Campbell's turkey soup
out of pepperoni sticks
checkout lines too long
meat not fresh
overcharged on melon

July 6

out of straws
out of bird food
overcharged on butter
out of masking tape
stockboy was not helpful
lost child
meat looked bad
overcharged on butter
out of Swiss chard
too many people in store
out of bubble bath
out of Dial soap
store too warm
price not as advertised
need to open more checkouts
shopping carts hard to steer
debris in aisles
out of Drano
out of Chinese cabbage
store too warm
floors dirty and sticky
out of Diamond chopped walnuts

July 13

wrong price on spaghetti
water on floor
store looked messy
store too warm
checkout lines too long
cashier not friendly
out of Cheese Doodles
triple charged
out of Saran Wrap
out of Dove Bars
undercharged
out of brown rice
out of mushrooms
overcharged
checkout wait too long
shopping cart broken
couldn't find aspirin
out of Tip Top lunch bags
out of Tip Top straws

July 20

out of cucumbers
checkout lines too slow
found keys in parking lot
lost keys
wrong price on sale item
overcharged on corn
wrong price on baby food
out of 18 oz. Tide
out of Tip Top tissues
checkout lines too long
out of romaine lettuce
out of Tip Top toilet paper
out of red peppers
out of Tip Top napkins
out of apricots
telephone out of order
out of cocktail sauce
water on floor
out of onions
out of squash
out of iceberg lettuce
out of Tip Top paper towels

July 27

out of bananas
reported accident in parking lot
wrong price on cranapple juice
out of carrots
out of fresh figs
out of Tip Top napkins
out of Tip Top straws
windows dirty
out of iceberg lettuce
dislike store decorations
out of Tip Top lunch bags
out of vanilla soy milk
wanted to know who won the lottery
store too warm
oatmeal spilled in bulk section
telephone out of order
out of Tip Top tissues
water on floor
out of Tip Top paper towels
out of Tip Top toilet paper
spaghetti sauce on floor
out of Peter Pan crunchy peanut butter

SELECTED BIBLIOGRAPHY AND FURTHER READINGS

Ahire, S. L. "Linking Operations Management Students Directly to the Real World." *Interfaces* 31, no. 5 (2001), pp. 104–120.

Ansari, Shahid, Janice Bell, Thomas Klammer, and Carol Lawrence. *Measuring and Managing Quality Costs*. New York: McGraw-Hill, 1997.

Besterfield, Dale H., Carol Besterfield-Micha, Glen Besterfield, and Mary Besterfield-Sacre. *Total Quality Management*. 2nd ed. Upper Saddle River, NJ: Prentice Hall, 1999.

Brassard, Michael, and Diane Ritter. *The Memory Jogger II: A Pocket Guide of Tools for Continuous Improvement and Effective Planning*. Methuen, MA: Goal/QPC, 1994.

Butman, John. *Juran: A Lifetime of Influence*. New York: John Wiley & Sons, 1997.

Chakrapani, C. *How to Measure Service Quality and Customer Satisfaction: The Informal Field Guide for Tools and Techniques*. Chicago: American Marketing Association, 1998.

El-Haik, Basem, and David M. Roy. *Service Design for Six Sigma: A Roadmap for Excellence*. Hoboken, NJ: John Wiley and Sons, 2005.

Garvin, David A. *Managing Quality*. New York: Free Press, 1988.

Gitlow, Howard S., Alan J. Oppenheim, Rosa Oppenheim, and David M. Levine. *Quality Management*. 3rd ed. New York: McGraw-Hill, 2005.

Goetsch, David L., and Stanley B. Davis. *Quality Management for Organizational Excellence: Introduction to Total Quality Management*. 6th ed. Upper Saddle River, NJ: Prentice Hall, 2010.

Juran, Joseph M. *Juran's Quality Handbook*. New York: McGraw-Hill, 1999.

Salegna, Gary, and Farzaneh Fazel. "Obstacles to Implementing Quality." *Quality Progress*, July 2000, pp. 53–57.

Scherkenbach, W. W. *The Deming Route to Quality and Productivity: Roadmaps and Roadblocks*. Rockville, MD: Mercury Press/Fairchild Publications, 1990.

Snee, Ronald D., and Roger W. Hoerl. *Six Sigma beyond the Factory Floor: Deployment Strategies for Financial Services, Health Care, and the Rest of the Real Economy*. Upper Saddle River, NJ: Pearson/Prentice Hall, 2005.

Stevenson, William J. "Supercharging Your Pareto Analysis." *Quality Progress*. October 2000, pp. 51–55.

Summers, Donna. *Quality*. 5th ed. Upper Saddle River, NJ: Prentice Hall, 2010.

Trusko, Brett, Carolyn Pexton. Jim Harrington, and Praveen Gupta. *Improving Healthcare Quality and Cost with Six Sigma*. FT Press, 2007.

Yang, Kai, and Basem El-Haik. *Design for Six Sigma*. New York: McGraw-Hill, 2003.

Quality Control

CHAPTER

CHAPTER OUTLINE

LEARNING OBJECTIVES

After completing this chapter, you should be able to:

1 List and briefly explain the elements of the control process.
2 Explain how control charts are used to monitor a process, and the concepts that underlie their use.
3 Use and interpret control charts.
4 Perform run tests to check for nonrandomness in process output.
5 Assess process capability.

This chapter covers quality control. The purpose of quality control is to assure that processes are performing in an acceptable manner. Companies accomplish this by monitoring process output using statistical techniques. **Quality control** is a process that measures output relative to a standard and takes corrective action when output does not meet standards. If the results are acceptable, no further action is required; unacceptable results call for corrective action.

Quality control A process that evaluates output relative to a standard and takes corrective action when output doesn't meet standards.

INTRODUCTION

Quality assurance that relies primarily on inspection of lots (batches) of previously produced items is referred to as *acceptance sampling.* It is described in the chapter supplement. Quality control efforts that occur during production are referred to as *statistical process control,* and these we examine in the following sections.

The best companies emphasize *designing quality into the process,* thereby greatly reducing the need for inspection or control efforts. As you might expect, different business organizations are in different stages of this evolutionary process: The least progressive rely heavily on inspection. Many occupy a middle ground that involves some inspection and a great deal of process control. The most progressive have achieved an inherent level of quality that is sufficiently high that they can avoid wholesale inspection activities and process control activities by mistake prevention. That is the ultimate goal. Figure 10.1 illustrates these phases of quality assurance.

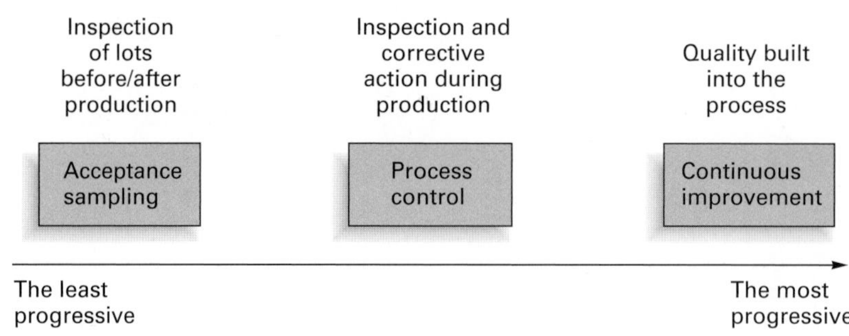

FIGURE 10.1
Approaches to quality assurance

INSPECTION

Inspection Appraisal of goods or services.

Inspection is an appraisal activity that compares goods or services to a standard. Inspection is a vital but often unappreciated aspect of quality control. Although for well-designed processes little inspection is necessary, inspection cannot be completely eliminated. And with increased outsourcing of products and services, inspection has taken on a new level of significance. In lean organizations, inspection is less of an issue than it is for other organizations because lean organizations place extra emphasis on quality in the design of both products and processes. Moreover, in lean operations, workers have responsibility for quality (quality at the source). However, many organizations do not operate in a lean mode, so inspection is important for them. This is particularly true of service operations, where quality continues to be a challenge for management.

Inspection can occur at three points: before production, during production, and after production. The logic of checking conformance before production is to make sure that inputs are acceptable. The logic of checking conformance during production is to make sure that the conversion of inputs into outputs is proceeding in an acceptable manner. The logic of checking conformance of output is to make a final verification of conformance before passing goods on to customers.

Inspection before and after production often involves *acceptance sampling* procedures; monitoring during the production process is referred to as *process control.* Figure 10.2 gives an overview of where these two procedures are applied in the production process.

To determine whether a process is functioning as intended or to verify that a batch or lot of raw materials or final products does not contain more than a specified percentage of defective goods, it is necessary to physically examine at least some of the items in question. The purpose of inspection is to provide information on the degree to which items conform to a standard. The basic issues are

1. How much to inspect and how often.
2. At what points in the process inspection should occur.
3. Whether to inspect in a centralized or on-site location.
4. Whether to inspect attributes (i.e., *count* the number of times something occurs) or variables (i.e., *measure* the value of a characteristic).

Consider, for example, inspection at an intermediate step in the manufacture of personal computers. Because inspection costs are often significant, questions naturally arise on whether one needs to inspect every computer or whether a small sample of computers will suffice. Moreover, although inspections could be made at numerous points in the production process,

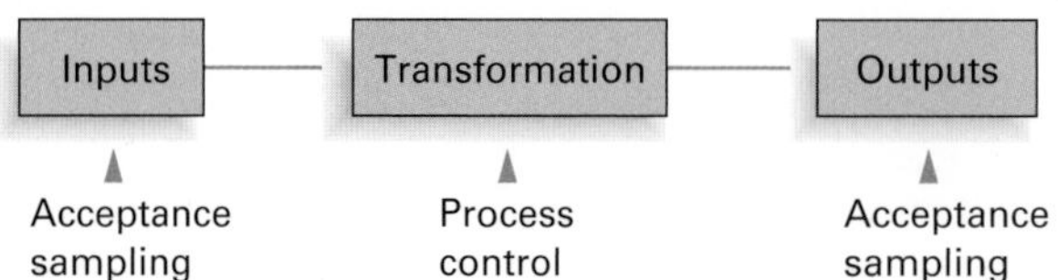

FIGURE 10.2
Acceptance sampling and process control

A Toyota technician prepares to remove the accelerator assembly in a recalled Avalon.

it is not generally cost-effective to make inspections at every point. Hence, the question comes up of which points should be designated for inspections. Once these points have been identified, a manager must decide whether to remove the computers from the line and take them to a lab, where specialized equipment might be available to perform certain tests, or to test them where they are being made. We will examine these points in the following sections.

How Much to Inspect and How Often

The amount of inspection can range from no inspection whatsoever to inspection of each item numerous times. Low-cost, high-volume items such as paper clips, roofing nails, and wooden pencils often require little inspection because (1) the cost associated with passing defective items is quite low and (2) the processes that produce these items are usually highly reliable, so that defects are rare. Conversely, high-cost, low-volume items that have large costs associated with passing defective products often require more intensive inspections. Thus, critical components of a manned-flight space vehicle are closely scrutinized because of the risk to human safety and the high cost of mission failure. In high-volume systems, *automated* inspection is one option that may be employed.

The majority of quality control applications lie somewhere between the two extremes. Most require some inspection, but it is neither possible nor economically feasible to critically examine every part of a product or every aspect of a service for control purposes. The cost of inspection, resulting interruptions of a process or delays caused by inspection, and the manner of testing typically outweigh the benefits of 100 percent inspection. Note that for manual inspection, even 100 percent inspection does not guarantee that all defects will be found and removed. Inspection is a process, and hence, subject to variation. Boredom and fatigue are factors that cause inspection mistakes. Moreover, when destructive testing is involved (items are destroyed by testing), that must be taken into account. However, the cost of letting undetected defects slip through is sufficiently high that inspection cannot be completely ignored. The amount of inspection needed is governed by the costs of inspection and the expected costs of passing defective items. As illustrated in Figure 10.3, if inspection activities increase, inspection costs increase, but the costs of undetected defects decrease. The traditional goal was to minimize the sum of these two costs. In other words, it may not pay to attempt to catch every defect, particularly if the cost of inspection exceeds the penalties associated with letting some defects get through. Current thinking is that every reduction in defective output reduces costs, although not primarily by inspection.

FIGURE 10.3
Traditional view: The amount of inspection is optimal when the sum of the costs of inspection and passing defectives is minimized

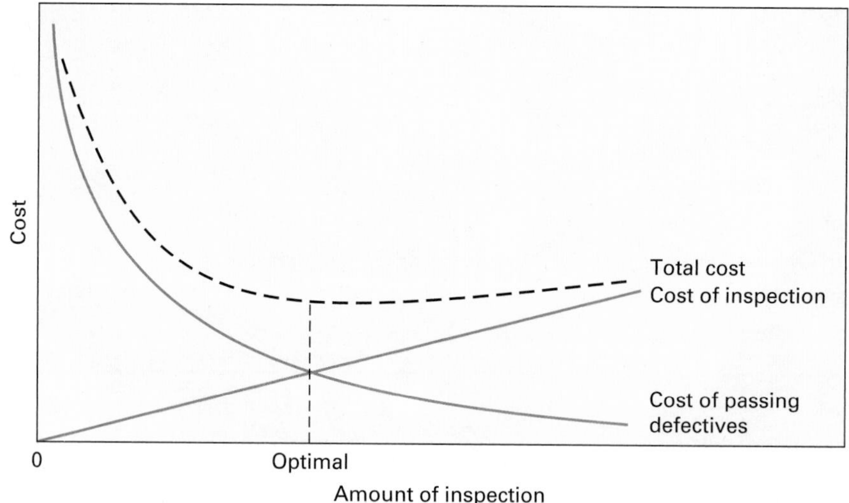

As a rule, operations with a high proportion of human involvement necessitate more inspection effort than mechanical operations, which tend to be more reliable.

The frequency of inspection depends largely on the rate at which a process may go out of control or the number of lots being inspected. A stable process will require only infrequent checks, whereas an unstable one or one that has recently given trouble will require more frequent checks. Likewise, many small lots will require more samples than a few large lots because it is important to obtain sample data from each lot.

Where to Inspect in the Process

Many operations have numerous possible inspection points. Because each inspection adds to the cost of the product or service, it is important to restrict inspection efforts to the points where they can do the most good. In manufacturing, some of the typical inspection points are

1. **Raw materials and purchased parts.** There is little sense in paying for goods that do not meet quality standards and in expending time and effort on material that is bad to begin with. Supplier certification programs can reduce or eliminate the need for inspection.
2. **Finished products.** Customer satisfaction and the firm's image are at stake here, and repairing or replacing products in the field is usually much more costly than doing it at the factory. Likewise, the seller is usually responsible for shipping costs on returns, and payments for goods or service may be held up pending delivery of satisfactory goods or remedial service. Well-designed processes, products and services, quality at the source, and process monitoring can reduce or eliminate the need for inspection.
3. **Before a costly operation.** The point is to not waste costly labor or machine time on items that are already defective.
4. **Before an irreversible process.** In many cases, items can be reworked up to a certain point; beyond that point they cannot. For example, pottery can be reworked prior to firing. After that, defective pottery must be discarded or sold as seconds at a lower price.
5. **Before a covering process.** Painting, plating, and assemblies often mask defects.

Inspection can be used as part of an effort to improve process yield. One measure of process yield is the ratio of output of good product to the total output. Inspection at key points can help guide process improvement efforts to reduce the scrap rate and improve the overall process yield, and reduce or eliminate the need for inspection.

In the service sector, inspection points are incoming purchased materials and supplies, personnel, service interfaces (e.g., service counter), and outgoing completed work (e.g., repaired appliances). Table 10.1 illustrates a number of examples.

TABLE 10.1
Examples of inspection points in service organizations

Type of Business	Inspection Points	Characteristics
Fast food	Cashier	Accuracy
	Counter area	Appearance, productivity
	Eating area	Cleanliness, no loitering
	Building and grounds	Appearance, safety hazards
	Kitchen	Cleanliness, purity of food, food storage, health regulations
	Parking lot	Safety, good lighting
Hotel/motel	Accounting/billing	Accuracy, timeliness
	Building and grounds	Appearance and safety
	Main desk	Appearance, waiting times, accuracy of bills
	Maid service	Completeness, productivity
	Personnel	Appearance, manners, productivity
	Reservations/occupancy	Over/underbooking, percent occupancy
	Restaurants	Kitchen, menus, meals, bills
	Room service	Waiting time, quality of food
	Supplies	Ordering, receiving, inventories
Supermarket	Cashiers	Accuracy, courtesy, productivity
	Deliveries	Quality, quantity
	Produce	Freshness, ample stock
	Aisles and stockrooms	Uncluttered layout
	Inventory control	Stock-outs
	Shelf stock	Ample supply, rotation of perishables
	Shelf displays	Appearance
	Checkouts	Waiting time
	Shopping carts	Good working condition, ample supply, theft/vandalism
	Parking lot	Safety, good lighting
	Personnel	Appearance, productivity
Doctor's office	Waiting room	Appearance, comfortable
	Examination room	Clean, temperature controlled
	Doctor	Neat, friendly, concerned, skillful, knowledgeable
	Doctor's assistant	Neat, friendly, concerned, skillful
	Patient records	Accurate, up-to-date
	Billing	Accurate
	Other	Waiting time minimal, adequate time with doctor

In the Chips at Jays

READING

Neil Steinberg

A potato chip is a delicate thing. Fragile. A pound of pressure will crush it. So when you're moving 250 tons of chips through your plant, as they do every day at Jays Foods, you need to have a system.

"You don't buy potato crumbs, you buy potato chips," said Tom Howe, CEO and co-owner of the Chicago company, at 99th and Cottage Grove. Jays makes 125 different types and brands of chips and several hundred varieties of popcorn, puffs, twists, pretzels and assorted bagged munchies.

Jays combats the tendency of potato chips to crush into flinders with a variety of conveyor belts, radial filling chutes and gently vibrating slides, where masses of chips, a yard deep, are gradually massaged forward, the outer layer of chips shearing away like the face of a glacier.

(continued)

(concluded)

The raw material is far easier to handle. An entire semi-trailer of sturdy North Dakota "chipping" potatoes can be emptied in a matter of minutes, by backing the trailer onto a hydraulic lift, tilting it 45 degrees and letting the potatoes—grown for their thin skins and low moisture—tumble out.

About a dozen semi-trailers' worth of potatoes arrive every day. The potatoes are immediately separated into big and small sizes for a purpose both reasonable and extraordinary: Big potatoes make big chips that go into large bags; small potatoes make small chips for lunch-size bags.

"Nobody wants to open a small bag and find three big potato chips in it," Howe said.

Computers keep track of everything, shunting potatoes to 15,000-pound holding bins. Each bin feeds into a pipe containing a turning screw—a version of the ancient Archimedes screw used to pump water—that moves the potatoes from the bin to conveyor belts, to where they are washed and skinned—the skin scrubbed off by metal bristle brushes.

No machine can detect if a potato is rotten inside. So a pair of human inspectors reach into the passing brown parade and give the potatoes a quick squeeze. Occasionally, they snatch one and slice it open, usually revealing black areas of rot, a skill they attribute to experience.

"I *know,*" said Alicia Jimenez, asked to explain what about a potato tips her off to slice it open and find rot.

The naked potatoes are sent into high-speed chippers—spinning brass rings, each with eight blades inside, straight blades for straight chips, ripple blades for ripple chips.

The blades cut the potatoes, but the potatoes take their revenge. Every three hours the blades are dulled and the line must be stopped so the old rings can be replaced by new rings with sharpened blades.

The sheer quantity of slicing spews big foamy banks of starch from either side of the chipper, which calls to mind a washing machine gone berserk.

Potato chips account for about 55 percent of Jays' business.

The raw chips spend three minutes cooking in hot corn oil, which is constantly circulated and filtered. Then they are salted, and flavorings—barbecue, for instance, or sour cream and onion—are added.

After the chips are fried, there is another quality check, in which workers pluck burned and deformed chips out of the masses passing by. The chips are conveyed on a link grid, wide enough to let broken chips fall through.

The chips also are laser-inspected, rushing, in a single layer, over a complex device called an Opti-Sort Scanner. Chips with dark spots or holes are detected by a laser, which instructs one of 82 small tubes to fire a puff of air that knocks the substandard chip off the line, into a discard bin.

The discards—about 3 percent of production—are gathered up and used: Starch is drawn out and sold to cornstarch makers; the rest goes to hog feed. Just as the stockyards were said to use every part of the pig but the squeal, at Jays every part of the potato is used but the rich, earthy smell.

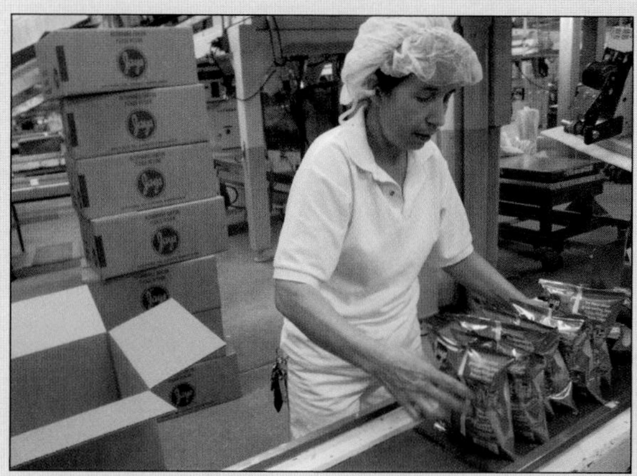

Jays even tried to sell burnt chips to the public once, about 20 years ago. "Consumers kept telling us they liked the brown chips," said Len Japp Jr., recalling the "Brownies" variety. "It went over like a lead balloon." Japp and his father, now 93 and honorary chairman of the board, sold the company to Borden in 1986. "They almost ruined it," Howe said, citing a slump in product quality and neglect of the Jays distribution system. "They lost the connection with the consumer."

By 1994, Jays was on the rocks and the Japps, allied with Howe, bought the company back. "Not too many people have a second chance in life," said Japp, whose children are in the company.

Getting the chips in the bags is another challenge: You can't just fill up bags and seal them; the chips would be smashed. Rather, a conveyor pours chips—gently—onto the central hub of a large, wheel-like device, where the chips scatter into 15 buckets that are, basically, scales. A computer monitors the weight of each bucket and opens up the exact combination that, in this case, will fill a 14-ounce bag. The bags are packed into boxes that read: "HANDLE LIKE EGGS."

While not exactly perishable, potato chips do have a shelf life of about eight weeks, only one day of which is spent at the plant.

"Potatoes that are in this morning will be in our branches tomorrow morning, ready to hit the streets," Howe said. Jays is still a regional brand, sold in Illinois, Indiana, Michigan, Wisconsin and Missouri. But business has grown 50 percent in the past two years.

"We connect to people's lifestyle," Howe said. "People treat themselves with Jays. We're in the fun food business."

Source: Neil Steinberg, "In the Chips," *Chicago Sun-Times,* December 26, 1997.

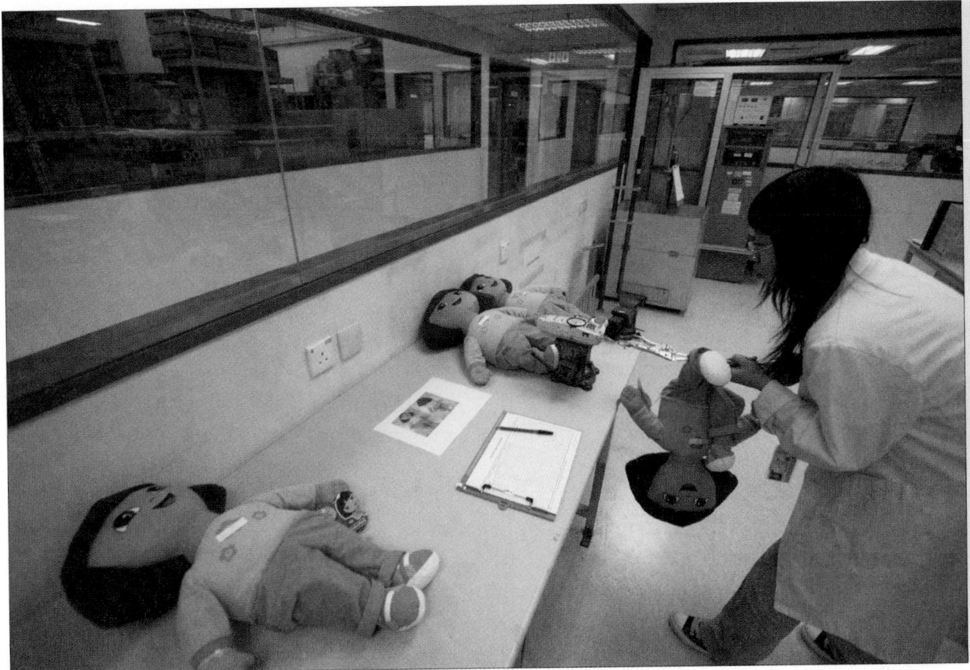

A Mattel technician in China does a pulling test with a Dora the Explorer doll in the name of product safety. Mattel has 10 labs in six countries and has set up strict requirements for vendors because of safety recalls.

Centralized versus On-Site Inspection

Some situations require that inspections be performed *on site.* For example, inspecting the hull of a ship for cracks requires inspectors to visit the ship. At other times, specialized tests can best be performed in a lab (e.g., performing medical tests, analyzing food samples, testing metals for hardness, running viscosity tests on lubricants).

The central issue in the decision concerning on-site or lab inspections is whether the advantages of specialized lab tests are worth the time and interruption needed to obtain the results. Reasons favoring on-site inspection include quicker decisions and avoidance of introduction of extraneous factors (e.g., damage or other alteration of samples during transportation to the lab). On the other hand, specialized equipment and a more favorable test environment (less noise and confusion, lack of vibrations, absence of dust, and no workers "helping" with inspections) offer strong arguments for using a lab.

Some companies rely on self-inspections by operators if errors can be traced back to specific operators. This places responsibility for errors at their source (*quality at the source*).

STATISTICAL PROCESS CONTROL

Quality control is concerned with the **quality of conformance** of a process: Does the output of a process conform to the intent of design? Variations in characteristics of process output provide the rationale for process control. **Statistical process control (SPC)** is used to evaluate process output to decide if a process is "in control" or if corrective action is needed.

Quality of conformance A product or service conforms to specifications.

Statistical process control (SPC) Statistical evaluation of the output of a process.

Process Variability

All processes generate output that exhibits some degree of variability. The issue is whether the output variations are within an acceptable range. This issue is addressed by answering two basic questions about the process variations:

1. Are the variations random? If nonrandom variations are present, the process is considered to be unstable. Corrective action will need to be taken to improve the process by eliminating the causes of nonrandomness and achieve a stable process.
2. Given a stable process, is the inherent variability of process output within a range that conforms to performance criteria? This involves assessment of a process's capability to meet standards. If a process is not capable, this situation will need to be addressed.

Random variation Natural variation in the output of a process, created by countless minor factors.

The natural or inherent process variations in process output are referred to as *chance* or **random variations.** Such variations are due to the combined influences of countless minor factors, each one so unimportant that even if it could be eliminated, the impact on process variations would be negligible. In Deming's terms, this is referred to as *common variability.* The amount of inherent variability differs from process to process. For instance, older machines generally exhibit a higher degree of natural variability than newer machines, partly because of worn parts and partly because new machines may incorporate design improvements that lessen the variability in their output.

Assignable variation In process output, a variation whose cause can be identified. A nonrandom variation.

A second kind of variability in process output is called **assignable variation,** or *nonrandom variation.* In Deming's terms, this is referred to as *special variation.* Unlike natural variation, the main sources of assignable variation can usually be identified (assigned to a specific cause) and eliminated. Tool wear, equipment that needs adjustment, defective materials, human factors (carelessness, fatigue, noise and other distractions, failure to follow correct procedures, and so on) and problems with measuring devices are typical sources of assignable variation.

Sampling and Sampling Distributions

In statistical process control, periodic samples of process output are taken and sample statistics, such as sample means or the number of occurrences of a certain type of outcome, are determined. The sample statistics can be used to judge randomness of process variations. The sample statistics exhibit variation, just as processes do. The variability of sample statistics can be described by its **sampling distribution,** a theoretical distribution that describes the *random* variability of sample statistics. The most frequently used distribution is the normal distribution, for a variety of reasons.

Sampling distribution A theoretical distribution of sample statistics.

Figure 10.4A illustrates a sampling distribution and a process distribution (i.e., the distribution of process variations). Note three important things in Figure 10.4: (1) both distributions have the same mean; (2) the variability of the sampling distribution is less than the variability of the process; and (3) the sampling distribution is normal. This is true even if the process distribution is not normal.

Central limit theorem The distribution of sample averages tends to be normal regardless of the shape of the process distribution.

In the case of sample means, the **central limit theorem** states that as the sample size increases, the distribution of sample averages approaches a normal distribution regardless of the shape of the sampled population. This tends to be the case even for fairly small sample sizes. For other sample statistics, the normal distribution serves as a reasonable approximation to the shape of the actual sampling distribution.

Figure 10.4B illustrates what happens to the shape of the sampling distribution relative to the sample size. The larger the sample size, the narrower the sampling distribution. This means that the likelihood that a sample statistic is close to the true value in the population is higher for large samples than for small samples.

A sampling distribution serves as the theoretical basis for distinguishing between random and nonrandom values of a sampling statistic. Very simply, limits are selected within which

FIGURE 10.4A The sampling distribution of means is normal, and it has less variability than the process distribution, which might not be normal

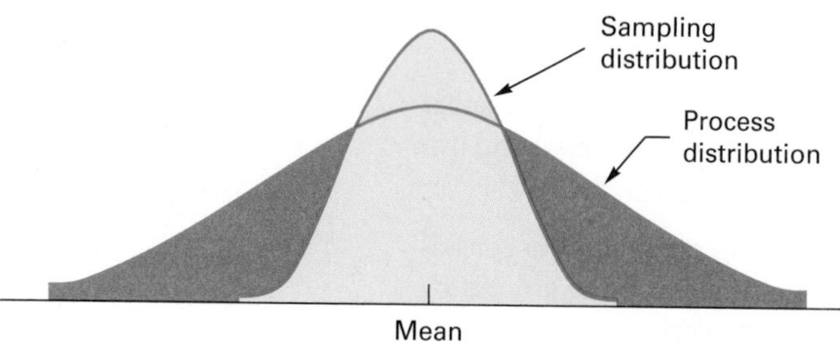

FIGURE 10.4B The larger the sample size, the narrower the sampling distribution

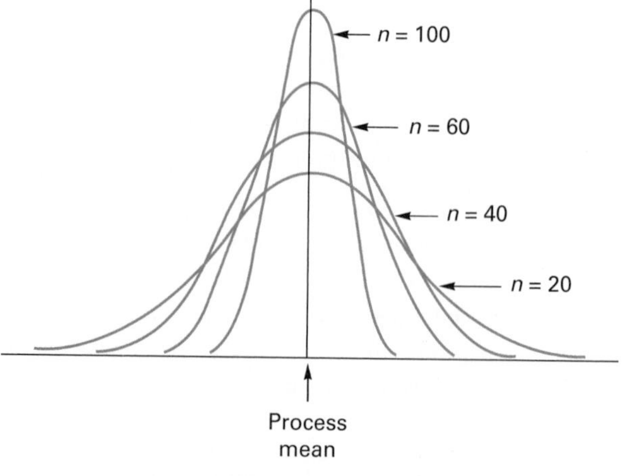

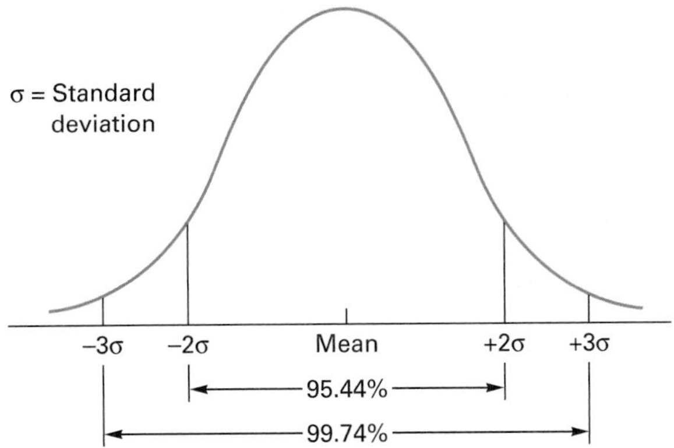

FIGURE 10.5
Percentage of values within given ranges in a normal distribution

most values of a sample statistic should fall if its variations are random. The limits are stated in terms of number of standard deviations from the distribution mean. Typical limits are ±2 standard deviations or ±3 standard deviations. Figure 10.5 illustrates these possible limits and the probability that a sample statistic would fall within those limits if only random variations are present. Conversely, if the value of a sample statistic falls outside those limits, there is only a small probability (1 − 99.74 = .0026 for ±3 limits, and 1 − 95.44 = .0456 for ±2 limits) that the value reflects randomness. Instead, such a value would suggest nonrandomness.

The Control Process

Sampling and corrective action are only a part of the control process. Effective control requires the following steps:

Define. The first step is to define in sufficient detail what is to be controlled. It is not enough, for example, to simply refer to a painted surface. The paint can have a number of important characteristics such as its thickness, hardness, and resistance to fading or chipping. Different characteristics may require different approaches for control purposes.

Measure. Only those characteristics that can be counted or measured are candidates for control. Thus, it is important to consider how measurement will be accomplished.

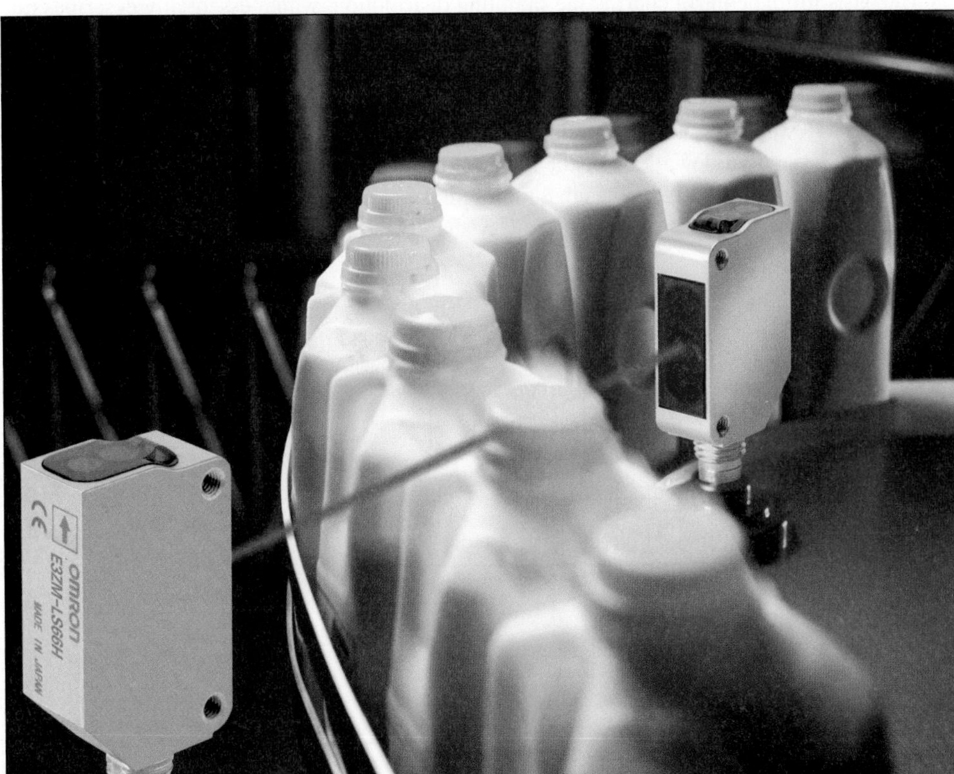

Food and beverage companies use Omron Electronics' fiber optic sensors to monitor processes and to perform quality inspections such as checking beverage content and caps.

Compare. There must be a standard of comparison that can be used to evaluate the measurements. This will relate to the level of quality being sought.

Evaluate. Management must establish a definition of *out of control.* Even a process that is functioning as it should will not yield output that conforms exactly to a standard, simply because of the natural (i.e., random) variations inherent in all processes, manual or mechanical—a certain amount of variation is inevitable. The main task of quality control is to distinguish random from *nonrandom* variability, because nonrandom variability means that a process is out of control.

Correct. When a process is judged out of control, corrective action must be taken. This involves uncovering the cause of nonrandom variability (e.g., worn equipment, incorrect methods, failure to follow specified procedures) and correcting it.

Monitor results. To ensure that corrective action is effective, the output of a process must be monitored for a sufficient period of time to verify that the problem has been eliminated.

In sum, control is achieved by checking a portion of the goods or services, comparing the results to a predetermined standard, evaluating departures from the standard, taking corrective action when necessary, and following up to ensure that problems have been corrected.

Control Charts: The Voice of the Process

Control chart A time-ordered plot of sample statistics, used to distinguish between random and nonrandom variability.

An important tool in statistical process control is the control chart, which was developed by Walter Shewhart. A **control chart** is a *time-ordered* plot of sample statistics. It is used to distinguish between random variability and nonrandom variability. It has upper and lower limits, called *control limits,* that define the range of acceptable (i.e., random) variation for the sample statistic. A control chart is illustrated in Figure 10.6. The purpose of a control chart is to monitor process output to see if it is random. A necessary (but not sufficient) condition for a process to be deemed "in control," or stable, is for all the data points to fall between the upper and lower control limits. Conversely, a data point that falls outside of either limit would be taken as evidence that the process output may be nonrandom and, therefore, not "in control." If that happens, the process would be halted to find and correct the cause of the nonrandom variation. The essence of statistical process control is to assure that the output of a process is random so that *future output* will be random.

The basis for the control chart is the sampling distribution, which essentially describes random variability. There is, however, one minor difficulty relating to the use of a normal sampling distribution. The theoretical distribution extends in either direction to *infinity.* Therefore, *any* value is theoretically possible, even one that is a considerable distance from the mean of the distribution. However, as a practical matter, we know that, say, 99.7 percent of the values will be within ±3 standard deviations of the mean of the distribution. Therefore, we could decide to set the limit, so to speak, at values that represent ±3 standard deviations from the mean, and conclude that any value that was farther away than these limits was a nonrandom variation.

FIGURE 10.6
Example of a control chart

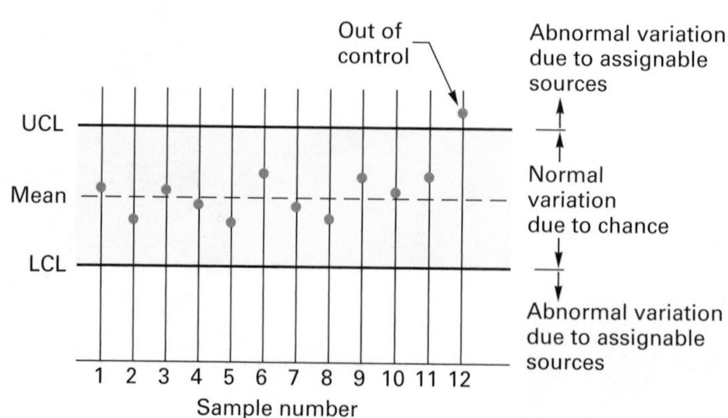

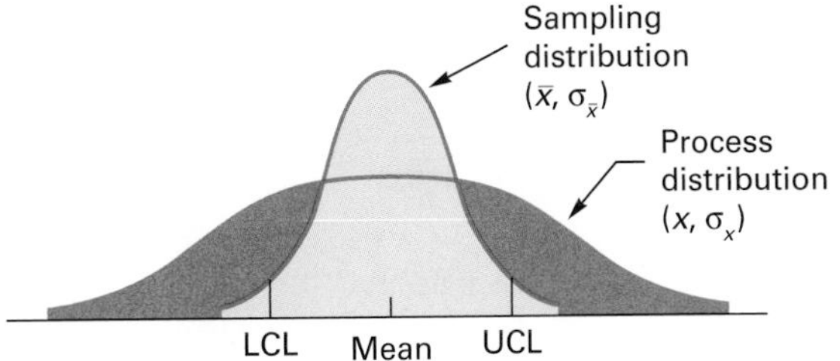

FIGURE 10.7
Control limits are based on the sampling distribution

In effect, these limits are **control limits:** the dividing lines between what will be designated as random deviations from the mean of the distribution and what will be designated as nonrandom deviations from the mean of the distribution. Figure 10.7 illustrates how control limits are based on the sampling distribution.

Control limits The dividing lines between random and nonrandom deviations from the mean of the distribution.

Control charts have two limits that separate random variation and nonrandom variation. The larger value is the *upper control limit* (UCL), and the smaller value is the *lower control limit* (LCL). A sample statistic that falls between these two limits suggests (but does not prove) randomness, while a value outside or on either limit suggests (but does not prove) nonrandomness.

It is important to recognize that because any limits will leave some area in the *tails* of the distribution, there is a small probability that a value will fall outside the limits *even though only random variations are present.* For example, if ±2 sigma (standard deviation) limits are used, they would include 95.5 percent of the values. Consequently, the complement of that number (100 percent − 95.5 percent = 4.5 percent) would not be included. That percentage (or *probability*) is sometimes referred to as the probability of a **Type I error,** where the "error" is concluding that nonrandomness is present when only randomness is present. It is also referred to as an *alpha* risk, where alpha (α) is the sum of the probabilities in the two tails. Figure 10.8 illustrates this concept.

Type I error Concluding a process is not in control when it actually is.

Using wider limits (e.g., ±3 sigma limits) reduces the probability of a Type I error because it decreases the area in the tails. However, wider limits make it more difficult to detect nonrandom variations *if* they are present. For example, the mean of the process might shift (an assignable cause of variation) enough to be detected by two-sigma limits, but not enough to be readily apparent using three-sigma limits. That could lead to a second kind of error, known as a **Type II error,** which is concluding that a process is in control when it is really out of control (i.e., concluding nonrandom variations are not present, when they are). In theory, the costs of making each error should be balanced by their probabilities. However, in practice, two-sigma limits and three-sigma limits are commonly used without specifically referring to the probability of a Type II error.

Type II error Concluding a process is in control when it is not.

Table 10.2 illustrates how Type I and Type II errors occur.

Each sample is represented by a single value (e.g., the sample mean) on a control chart. Moreover, each value is compared to the extremes of the sampling distribution (the control limits) to judge if it is within the acceptable (random) range. Figure 10.9 illustrates this concept.

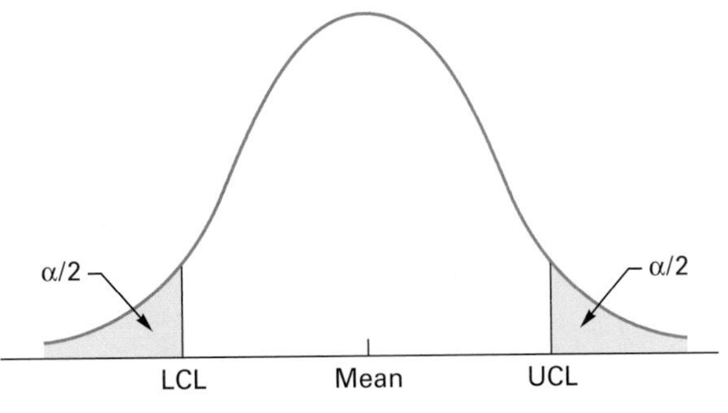

FIGURE 10.8
The probability of a Type I error

TABLE 10.2
Type I and Type II errors

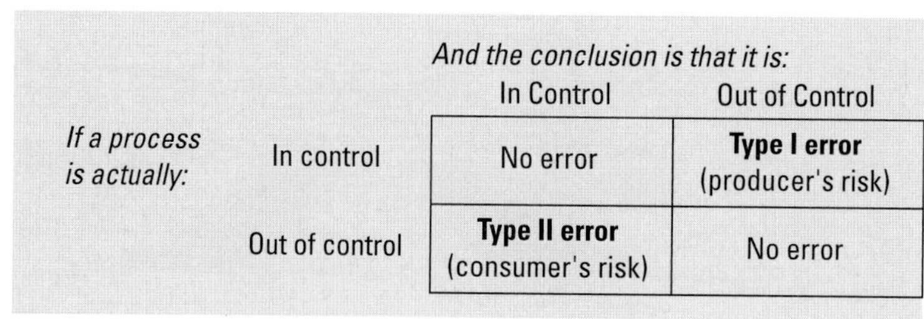

		And the conclusion is that it is: In Control	Out of Control
If a process is actually:	In control	No error	**Type I error** (producer's risk)
	Out of control	**Type II error** (consumer's risk)	No error

FIGURE 10.9
Each observation is compared to the selected limits of the sampling distribution

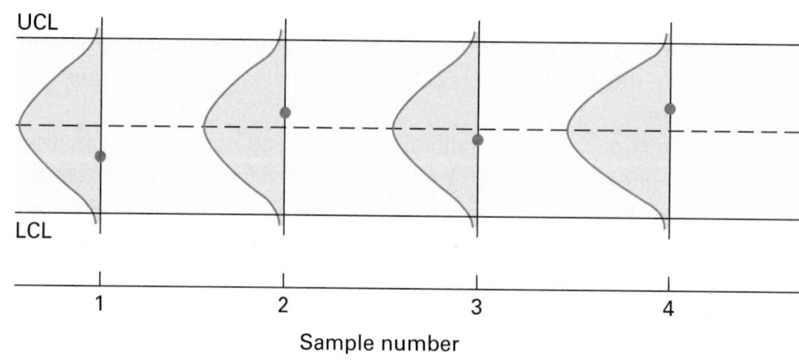

Variables Generate data that are *measured.*

Attributes Generate data that are *counted.*

There are four commonly used control charts. Two are used for **variables,** and two are used for **attributes.** Attribute data are *counted* (e.g., the number of defective parts in a sample, the number of calls per day); variables data are *measured,* usually on a continuous scale (e.g., amount of time needed to complete a task, length or width of a part).

The two control charts for variables data are described in the next section, and the two control charts for attribute data are described in the section following that.

Control Charts for Variables

Mean and range charts are used to monitor variables. Control charts for means monitor the *central tendency* of a process, and range charts monitor the *dispersion* of a process.

Mean control chart Control chart used to monitor the central tendency of a process.

Mean Charts. A **mean control chart,** sometimes referred to as an $\bar{x}$ ("*x*-bar") chart, is based on a normal distribution. It can be constructed in one of two ways. The choice depends on what information is available. Although the value of the standard deviation of a process, σ, is often unknown, if a reasonable estimate is available, one can compute control limits using these formulas:

$$\text{Upper control limit (UCL): } = \bar{\bar{x}} + z\sigma_{\bar{x}} \qquad (10\text{–}1)$$
$$\text{Lower control limit (LCL): } = \bar{\bar{x}} - z\sigma_{\bar{x}}$$

where

$\sigma_{\bar{x}} = \sigma/\sqrt{n}$

$\sigma_{\bar{x}}$ = Standard deviation of distribution of sample means

σ = Estimate of the process standard deviation

n = Sample size

z = Standard normal deviate

$\bar{\bar{x}}$ = Average of sample means

The following example illustrates the use of these formulas.

EXAMPLE 1

www.mhhe.com/stevenson11e

A quality inspector took five samples, each with four observations ($n = 4$), of the length of time for glue to dry. The analyst computed the mean of each sample and then computed the grand mean. All values are in minutes. Use this information to obtain three-sigma (i.e., $z = 3$) control limits for means of future times. It is known from previous experience that the standard deviation of the process is .02 minute.

		SAMPLE				
		1	2	3	4	5
	1	12.11	12.15	12.09	12.12	12.09
Observation	2	12.10	12.12	12.09	12.10	12.14
	3	12.11	12.10	12.11	12.08	12.13
	4	12.08	12.11	12.15	12.10	12.12
	$\bar{X}$	12.10	12.12	12.11	12.10	12.12

SOLUTION

$$\bar{\bar{x}} = \frac{12.10 + 12.12 + 12.11 + 12.10 + 12.12}{5} = 12.11$$

Using Formula 10–1, with $z = 3$, $n = 4$ observations per sample, and $\sigma = .02$, we find

$$\text{UCL:} \quad 12.11 + 3\left(\frac{.02}{\sqrt{4}}\right) = 12.14$$

$$\text{LCL:} \quad 12.11 - 3\left(\frac{.02}{\sqrt{4}}\right) = 12.08$$

Note: If one applied these control limits to the means, one would judge the process to be *in control* because all of the sample means have values that fall within the control limits. The fact that some of the *individual* measurements fall outside of the control limits (e.g., the first observation in Sample 2 and the last observation in Sample 3) is irrelevant. You can see why by referring to Figure 10.7: *Individual* values are represented by the process distribution, a large portion of which lies outside of the control limits for *means.*

If an observation on a control chart is on or outside of either control limit, the process would be stopped to investigate the cause of that value, such as operator error, machine out of adjustment, or similar assignable cause of variation. If no source of error is found, the value could simply be due to chance, and the process would be restarted. However, the output should then be monitored to see if additional values occur that are beyond the control limits, in which case a more thorough investigation would be needed to uncover the source of the problem so that it could be corrected.

If the standard deviation of the process is unknown, another approach is to use the sample *range* as a measure of process variability. The appropriate formulas for control limits are

$$\text{UCL} = \bar{\bar{x}} + A_2\bar{R}$$
$$\text{LCL} = \bar{\bar{x}} - A_2\bar{R} \qquad (10–2)$$

where

A_2 = A factor from Table 10.3
$\bar{R}$ = Average of sample ranges

EXAMPLE 2

www.mhhe.com/stevenson11e

Refer to the data given in Example 1. In order to use Formula 10–2, we need to compute the grand mean for the data and the average sample range. In Example 1, the grand mean is 12.11. The range for each sample is the difference between the largest and smallest sample values. For the first sample, the largest value is 12.11 and the smallest value is 12.08. The range is the difference between these two values, which is $12.11 - 12.08 = .03$. For Sample 2, the range is 12.15 − 12.10 = 0.05. The other ranges can be computed in similar fashion. The average range is:

$$\bar{R} = (.03 + .05 + .06 + .04 + .05)/5 = .046.$$

SOLUTION

$\bar{\bar{x}} = 12.11$, $\bar{R} = .046$, and $A_2 = .73$ for $n = 4$ (from Table 10.3). Using Formula 10–2, we can compute the upper and lower limits for a mean control chart:

$$\text{UCL} = 12.11 + .73(.046) = 12.14 \text{ minutes}$$
$$\text{LCL} = 12.11 + .73(.046) = 12.08 \text{ minutes}$$

Except for rounding, these results are the same as those computed in Example 1.

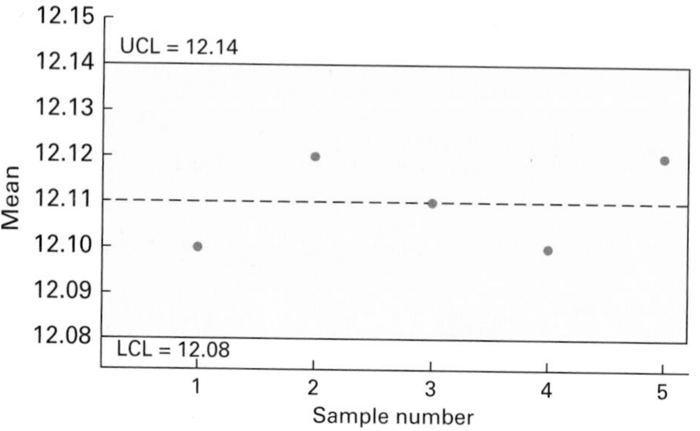

Range control chart Control chart used to monitor process dispersion.

Range Charts. **Range control charts** (R-charts) are used to monitor process dispersion; they are sensitive to changes in process dispersion. Although the underlying sampling distribution is not normal, the concepts for use of range charts are much the same as those for use of mean charts. Control limits for range charts are found using the average sample range in conjunction with these formulas:

$$\text{UCL} = D_4\bar{R}$$
$$\text{LCL} = D_3\bar{R} \qquad (10\text{–}3)$$

where values of D_3 and D_4 are obtained from Table 10.3.[1]

EXAMPLE 3

www.mhhe.com/stevenson11e

Using the average range found in Example 2 and Formula 10–3, we can compute the control limits for a range chart.

SOLUTION

From Table 10.3, for $n = 4$, $D_4 = 2.28$ and $D_3 = 0$. Thus,

$$\text{UCL} = 2.28(.046) = .105 \text{ minutes}$$
$$\text{LCL} = 0(.046) = 0 \text{ minutes}$$

Note that the five sample ranges shown in Example 2 are within these control limits.

Using Mean and Range Charts. Mean control charts and range control charts provide different perspectives on a process. As we have seen, mean charts are sensitive to shifts in the process mean, whereas range charts are sensitive to changes in process dispersion. Because of this difference in perspective, both types of charts might be used to monitor the same process. The logic of using both is readily apparent in Figure 10.10. In Figure 10.10A, the mean

[1]If the process standard deviation is known, control limits for a range chart can be calculated using values from Table 10.3:

$$\text{LCL} = \frac{3D_3\sigma}{A_2\sqrt{n}}, \quad \text{UCL} = \frac{3D_4\sigma}{A_2\sqrt{n}}$$

TABLE 10.3
Factors for three-sigma control limits for $\bar{x}$ and R charts

Number of Observations in Subgroup, n	Factor for $\bar{x}$ Chart, A_2	FACTORS FOR R CHARTS: Lower Control Limit, D_3	Upper Control Limit, D_4
2	1.88	0	3.27
3	1.02	0	2.57
4	0.73	0	2.28
5	0.58	0	2.11
6	0.48	0	2.00
7	0.42	0.08	1.92
8	0.37	0.14	1.86
9	0.34	0.18	1.82
10	0.31	0.22	1.78
11	0.29	0.26	1.74
12	0.27	0.28	1.72
13	0.25	0.31	1.69
14	0.24	0.33	1.67
15	0.22	0.35	1.65
16	0.21	0.36	1.64
17	0.20	0.38	1.62
18	0.19	0.39	1.61
19	0.19	0.40	1.60
20	0.18	0.41	1.59

Source: Adapted from Eugene Grant and Richard Leavenworth, *Statistical Quality Control,* 5th ed. Copyright © 1980 McGraw-Hill Companies, Inc. Used with permission.

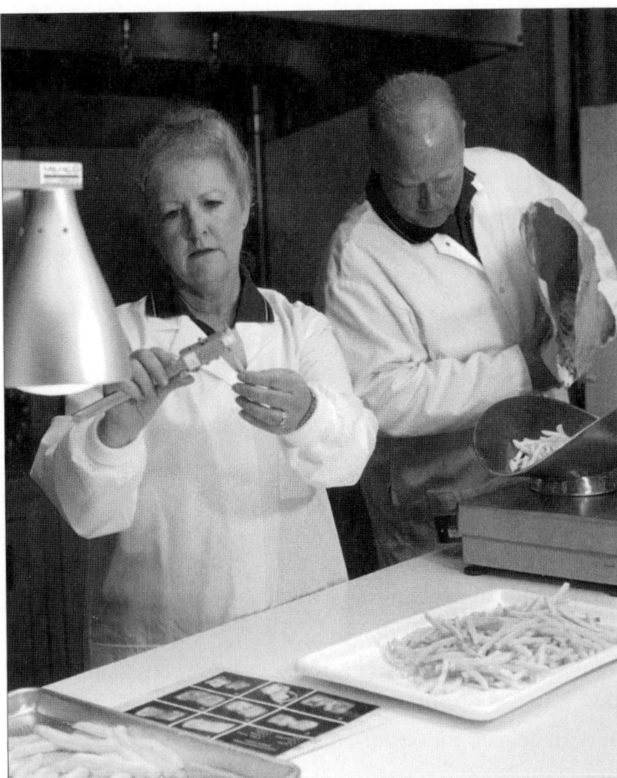

Quality control lab personnel using a caliper to measure french fries and a scale to weigh them. Fast-food restaurants, such as McDonald's, do product testing to ensure uniformity and overall quality of food items to meet customer expectations.

FIGURE 10.10
Mean and range charts used together complement each other

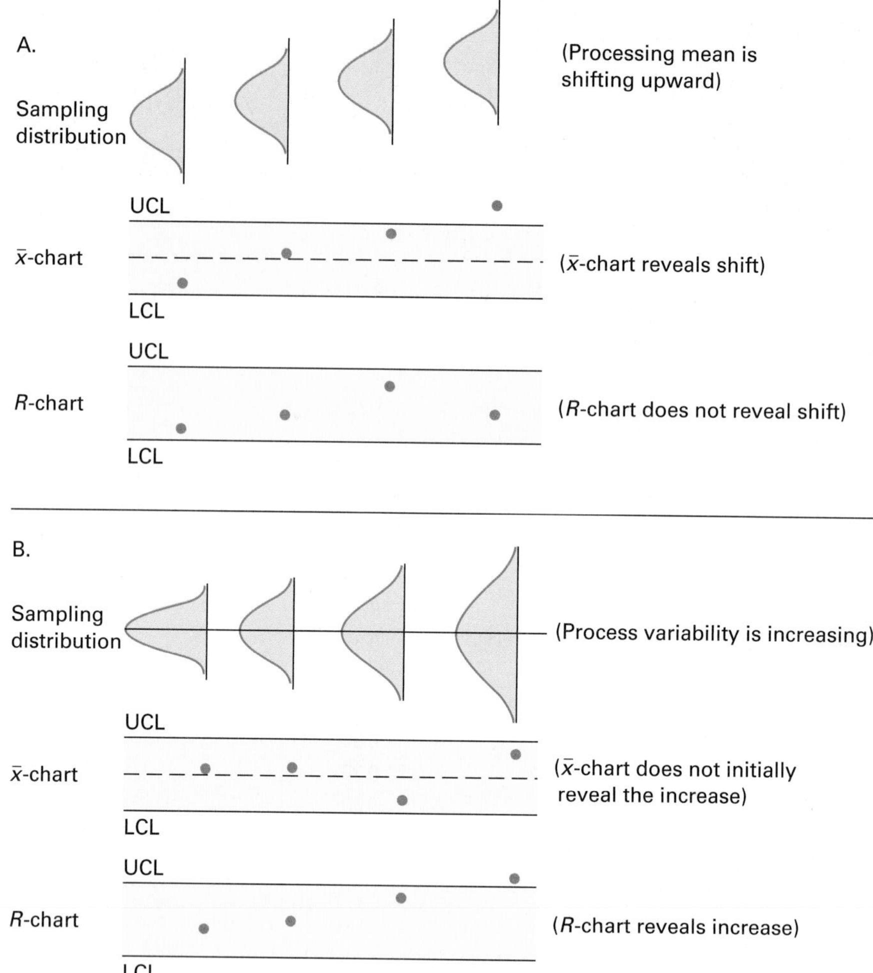

chart picks up the shift in the process mean, but because the dispersion is not changing, the range chart fails to indicate a problem. Conversely, in Figure 10.10B, a change in process dispersion is less apt to be detected by the mean chart than by the range chart. Thus, use of both charts provides more complete information than either chart alone. Even so, a single chart may suffice in some cases. For example, a process may be more susceptible to changes in the process mean than to changes in dispersion, so it might be unnecessary to monitor dispersion. Because of the time and cost of constructing control charts, gathering the necessary data, and evaluating the results, only those aspects of a process that tend to cause problems should be monitored.

Once control charts have been set up, they can serve as a basis for deciding when to interrupt a process and search for assignable causes of variation. To determine initial control limits, one can use the following procedure:

1. Obtain 20 to 25 samples. Compute the appropriate sample statistic(s) for each sample (e.g., mean).
2. Establish preliminary control limits using the formulas.
3. Determine if any points fall outside the control limits.
4. If you find no out-of-control signals, assume that the process is in control. If not, investigate and correct assignable causes of variation. Then resume the process and collect another set of observations upon which control limits can be based.
5. Plot the data on the control chart and check for out-of-control signals.

TABLE 10.4
p-chart or c-chart?

The following tips should help you select the type of control chart, a p-chart or a c-chart, that is appropriate for a particular application:

Use a p-chart:	Use a c-chart:
1. When observations can be placed into one of *two* categories. Examples include items (observations) that can be classified as a. Good or bad. b. Pass or fail. c. Operate or don't operate. 2. When the data consist of multiple samples of n observations each (e.g., 15 samples of $n = 20$ observations each).	When only the number of occurrences per unit of measure can be counted; nonoccurrences cannot be counted. Examples of occurrences and units of measure include a. Scratches, chips, dents, or errors per item. b. Cracks or faults per unit of distance (e.g., meters, miles). c. Breaks or tears, per unit of area (e.g., square yard, square meter). d. Bacteria or pollutants per unit of volume (e.g., gallon, cubic foot, cubic yard). e. Calls, complaints, failures, equipment breakdowns, or crimes per unit of time (e.g., hour, day, month, year).

Control Charts for Attributes

Control charts for attributes are used when the process characteristic is *counted* rather than measured. For example, the number of defective items in a sample is counted, whereas the length of each item is measured. There are two types of attribute control charts, one for the fraction of defective items in a sample (a p-chart) and one for the number of defects per unit (a c-chart). A *p-chart* is appropriate when the data consist of two categories of items. For instance, if glass bottles are inspected for chipping and cracking, both the good bottles and the defective ones can be counted. However, one can count the number of accidents that occur during a given period of time but *not* the number of accidents that did not occur. Similarly, one can count the number of scratches on a polished surface, the number of bacteria present in a water sample, and the number of crimes committed during the month of August, but one cannot count the number of nonoccurrences. In such cases, a *c-chart* is appropriate. See Table 10.4.

p-Chart. A **p-chart** is used to monitor the proportion of defective items generated by a process. The theoretical basis for a p-chart is the binomial distribution, although for large sample sizes, the normal distribution provides a good approximation to it. Conceptually, a p-chart is constructed and used in much the same way as a mean chart.

p-chart Control chart for attributes, used to monitor the proportion of defective items in a process.

The center line on a p-chart is the average fraction defective in the population, p. The standard deviation of the sampling distribution when p is known is

$$\sigma_p = \sqrt{\frac{p(1-p)}{n}}$$

Control limits are computed using the formulas

$$\begin{aligned} UCL_p &= p + z\sigma_p \\ LCL_p &= p - z\sigma_p \end{aligned} \qquad (10\text{–}4)$$

If p is unknown, it can be estimated from samples. That estimate, $\bar{p}$, replaces p in the preceding formulas, and $\hat{\sigma}_p$ replaces σ_p, as illustrated in Example 4.

Note: Because the formula is an approximation, it sometimes happens that the computed LCL is negative. In those instances, zero is used as the lower limit.

EXAMPLE 4

www.mhhe.com/stevenson11e

An inspector counted the number of defective monthly billing statements of a company telephone in each of 20 samples. Using the following information, construct a control chart that will describe 99.74 percent of the chance variation in the process when the process is in control. Each sample contained 100 statements.

Sample	Number of Defectives	Sample	Number of Defectives	Sample	Number of Defectives	Sample	Number of Defectives
1	7	6	11	11	8	16	10
2	10	7	10	12	12	17	8
3	12	8	18	13	9	18	12
4	4	9	13	14	10	19	10
5	9	10	10	15	16	20	21
							220

SOLUTION

To find z, divide .9974 by 2 to obtain .4987, and using that value, refer to Appendix B, Table A to find $z = 3.00$.

$$\bar{p} = \frac{\text{Total number of defectives}}{\text{Total number of observations}} = \frac{220}{20(100)} = .11$$

$$\hat{\sigma}_p = \sqrt{\frac{\bar{p}(1-\bar{p})}{n}} = \sqrt{\frac{.11(1-.11)}{100}} = .0313$$

Control limits are

$$\text{UCL}_p = \bar{p} + z(\hat{\sigma}_p) = .11 + 3.00(.0313) = .2039$$

$$\text{LCL}_p = \bar{p} - z(\hat{\sigma}_p) = .11 - 3.00(.0313) = .0161$$

Plotting the control limits and the sample fraction defective, you can see that the last value is above the upper control limit. The process would be stopped at that point to find and correct the possible cause. Then new data would be collected to establish new control limits. If no cause is found, this could be due to chance. The new limits would remain but future output would be monitored to assure the process remains in control.

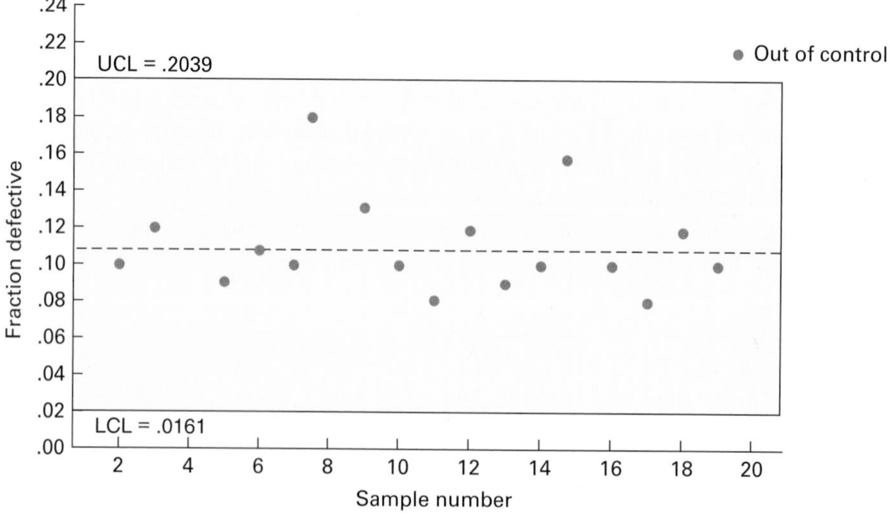

c-Chart. When the goal is to control the number of *occurrences* (e.g., defects) *per unit,* a c-chart is used. Units might be automobiles, hotel rooms, typed pages, or rolls of carpet. The underlying sampling distribution is the Poisson distribution. Use of the Poisson distribution assumes that defects occur over some *continuous* region and that the probability of more than one defect at any particular point is negligible. The mean number of defects per unit is c and

c-chart Control chart for attributes, used to monitor the number of defects per unit.

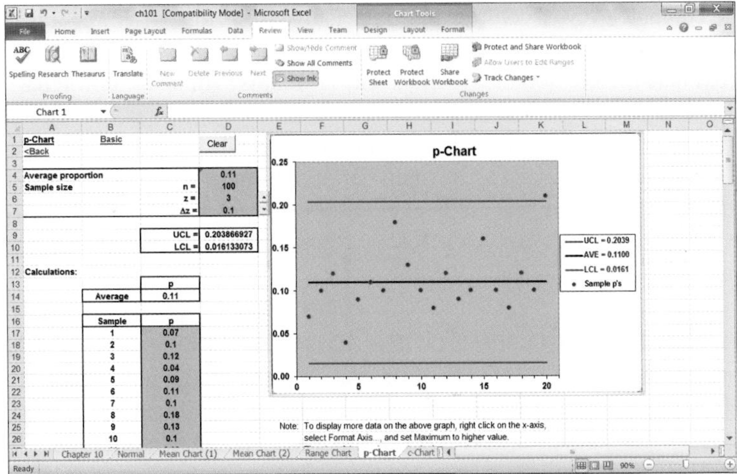

the standard deviation is $\sqrt{c}$. For practical reasons, the normal approximation to the Poisson is used. The control limits are

$$\begin{aligned} \text{UCL}_c &= c + z\sqrt{c} \\ \text{LCL}_c &= c - z\sqrt{c} \end{aligned} \qquad (10–5)$$

If the value of c is unknown, as is generally the case, the sample estimate, $\bar{c}$, is used in place of c, using $\bar{c}$ = Number of defects ÷ Number of samples.

EXAMPLE 5

www.mhhe.com/stevenson11e

Rolls of coiled wire are monitored using a c-chart. Eighteen rolls have been examined, and the number of defects per roll has been recorded in the following table. Is the process in control? Plot the values on a control chart using three standard deviation control limits.

Sample	Number of Defects	Sample	Number of Defects	Sample	Number of Defects
1	3	7	4	13	2
2	2	8	1	14	4
3	4	9	2	15	2
4	5	10	1	16	1
5	1	11	3	17	3
6	2	12	4	18	1
					45

SOLUTION

$\bar{c} = 45/18 = 2.5$ = Average number of defects per coil

$$\begin{aligned} \text{UCL}_c &= \bar{c} + 3\sqrt{\bar{c}} = 2.5 + 3\sqrt{2.5} = 7.24 \\ \text{LCL}_c &= \bar{c} - 3\sqrt{\bar{c}} = 2.5 - 3\sqrt{2.5} = -2.24 \rightarrow 0 \end{aligned}$$

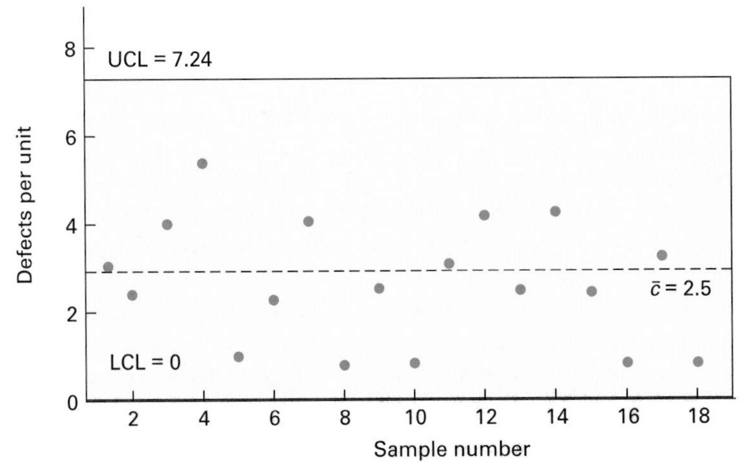

When the computed lower control limit is negative, the effective lower limit is zero. The calculation sometimes produces a negative lower limit due to the use of the normal distribution to approximate the Poisson distribution: The normal is symmetrical, whereas the Poisson is not symmetrical when c is close to zero.

Note that if an observation falls below the lower control limit on a p-chart or a c-chart, the cause should be investigated, just as it would be for a mean or range chart, even though such a point would imply that the process is exhibiting better than expected quality. It may turn out to be the result of an undesirable overuse of resources. On the other hand, it may lead to a discovery that can improve the quality of the process.

Managerial Considerations Concerning Control Charts

Using control charts adds to the cost and time needed to obtain output. Ideally a process is so good that the desired level of quality could be achieved without the use of any control charts. The best organizations strive to reach this level, but many are not yet there, so they employ control charts at various points in their processes. In those organizations, managers must make a number of important decisions about the use of control charts:

1. At what points in the process to use control charts.
2. What size samples to take.
3. What type of control chart to use (i.e., variables or attribute).

The decision about where to use control charts should focus on those aspects of the process that (1) have a tendency to go out of control and (2) are critical to the successful operation of the product or service (i.e., variables that affect product or service characteristics).

Sample size is important for two reasons. One is that cost and time are functions of sample size; the greater the sample size, the greater the cost to inspect those items (and the greater the lost product if destructive testing is involved) and the longer the process must be held up while waiting for the results of sampling. The second reason is that smaller samples are more likely to reveal a change in the process than larger samples because a change is more likely to take place *within* the large sample, but *between* small samples. Consequently, a sample statistic such as the sample mean in the large sample could combine both "before-change" and "after-change" observations, whereas in two smaller samples, the first could contain "before" observations and the second "after" observations, making detection of the change more likely.

In some instances, a manager can choose between using a control chart for variables (a mean chart) and a control chart for attributes (a p-chart). If the manager is monitoring the diameter of a drive shaft, either the diameter could be measured and a mean chart used for control, or the shafts could be inspected using a *go, no-go gauge*—which simply indicates whether a particular shaft is within specification without giving its exact dimensions—and a p-chart could be used. Measuring is more costly and time-consuming per unit than the yes-no inspection using a go, no-go gauge, but because measuring supplies more information than merely counting items as good or bad, one needs a much smaller sample size for a mean chart than a p-chart. Hence, a manager must weigh the time and cost of sampling against the information provided.

Run Tests

Control charts test for points that are too extreme to be considered random (e.g., points that are outside of the control limits). However, even if all points are within the control limits, the data may still not reflect a random process. In fact, any sort of pattern in the data would suggest a nonrandom process. Figure 10.11 illustrates some patterns that might be present.

Run test A test for patterns in a sequence.

Analysts often supplement control charts with a **run test,** which checks for patterns in a sequence of observations. This enables an analyst to do a better job of detecting abnormalities in a process and provides insights into correcting a process that is out of control. A variety of run tests are available; this section describes two that are widely used.

When a process is stable or in statistical control, the output it generates will exhibit random variability over a period of time. The presence of patterns, such as trends, cycles, or bias in

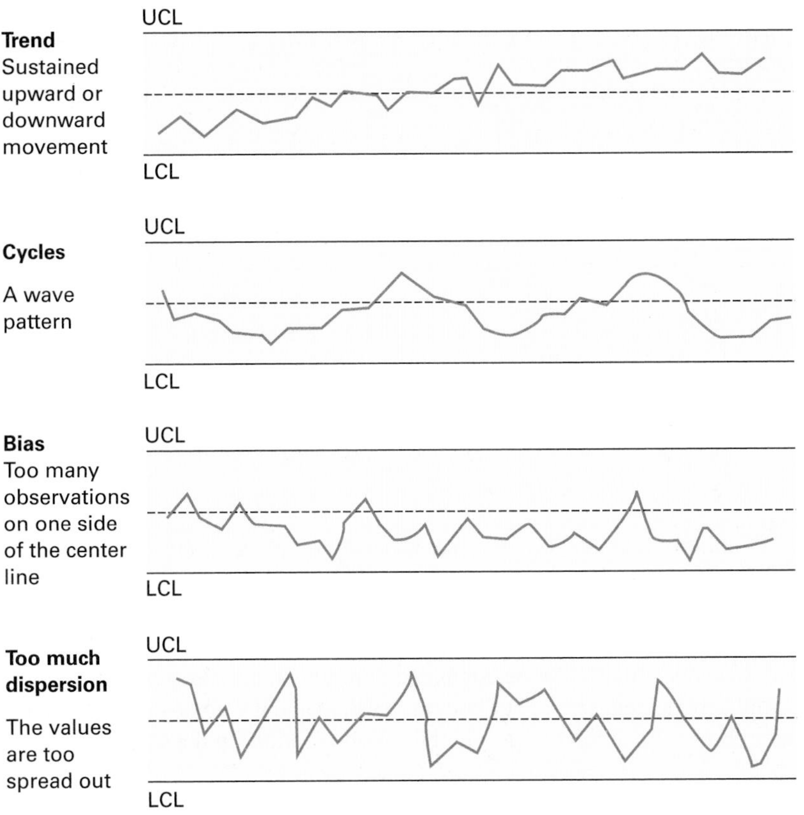

FIGURE 10.11
Some examples of nonrandom patterns in control chart plots

the output indicates that assignable, or nonrandom, causes of variation exist. Hence, a process that produces output with such patterns is not in a state of statistical control. This is true even though all points on a control chart may be within the control limits. For this reason, it is usually prudent to subject control chart data to run tests to determine whether patterns can be detected.

A **run** is defined as a sequence of observations with a certain characteristic, followed by one or more observations with a different characteristic. The characteristic can be anything that is observable. For example, in the series A A A B, there are two runs: a run of three As followed by a run of one B. Underlining each run helps in counting them. In the series A A B B B A, the underlining indicates three runs.

Run Sequence of observations with a certain characteristic.

Two useful run tests involve examination of the number of runs *up and down* and runs above and below the *median.*[2] In order to count these runs, the data are transformed into a series of Us and Ds (for *up* and *down*) and into a series of As and Bs (for *above* and *below* the median). Consider the following sequence, which has a median of 36.5. The first two values are below the median, the next two are above it, the next to last is below, and the last is above. Thus, there are four runs:

25	29	42	40	35	38
B	B	A	A	B	A

In terms of up and down, there are three runs in the same data. The second value is up from the first value, the third is up from the second, the fourth is down from the third, and so on:

25	29	42	40	35	38
—	U	U	D	D	U

(The first value does not receive either a U or a D because nothing precedes it.)

[2]The median and mean are approximately equal for control charts. The use of the median depends on its ease of determination; use the mean instead of the median if it is given.

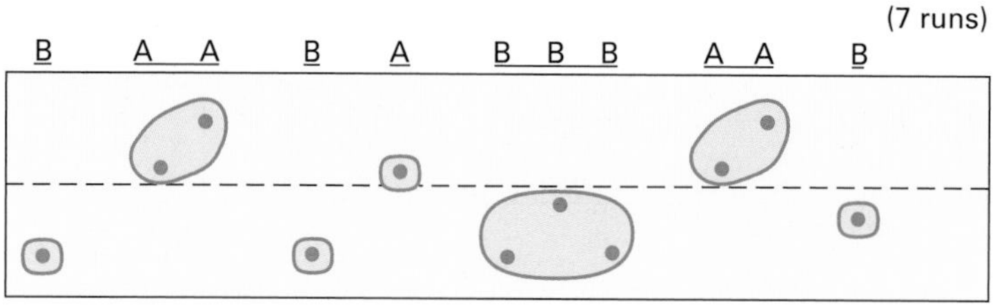

FIGURE 10.12
Counting above/below median runs

(7 runs)
B A A B A B B B A A B

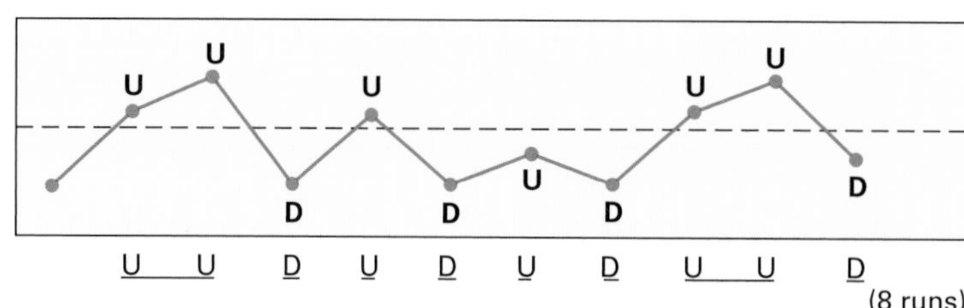

FIGURE 10.13
Counting up/down runs

If a plot is available, the runs can be easily counted directly from the plot, as illustrated in Figures 10.12 and 10.13.

To determine whether any patterns are present in control chart data, one must transform the data into both As and Bs and Us and Ds, and then count the number of runs in each case. These numbers must then be compared with the number of runs that would be expected in a completely random series. For both the median and the up/down run tests, the expected number of runs is a function of the number of observations in the series. The formulas are

$$E(r)_{\text{med}} = \frac{N}{2} + 1 \qquad (10\text{–}6a)$$

$$E(r)_{u/d} = \frac{2N - 1}{3} \qquad (10\text{–}7a)$$

where N is the number of observations or data points, and $E(r)$ is the expected number of runs.

The actual number of runs in any given set of observations will vary from the expected number, due to chance and any patterns that might be present. Chance variability is measured by the standard deviation of runs. The formulas are

$$\sigma_{\text{med}} = \sqrt{\frac{N - 1}{4}} \qquad (10\text{–}6b)$$

$$\sigma_{u/d} = \sqrt{\frac{16N - 29}{90}} \qquad (10\text{–}7b)$$

Distinguishing chance variability from patterns requires use of the sampling distributions for median runs and up/down runs. Both distributions are approximately normal. Thus, for example, 95.5 percent of the time a random process will produce an observed number of runs within two standard deviations of the expected number. If the observed number of runs falls in that range, there are probably no nonrandom patterns; for observed numbers of runs beyond such limits, we begin to suspect that patterns are present. Too few or too many runs can be an indication of nonrandomness.

In practice, it is often easiest to compute the number of standard deviations, z, by which an observed number of runs differs from the expected number. This z value would then be compared to the value ± 2 (z for 95.5 percent) or some other desired value (e.g., ± 1.96 for 95 percent, ± 2.33 for 98 percent). A test z that exceeds the desired limits indicates patterns are present. (See Figure 10.14.) The computation of z takes the form

$$z_{\text{test}} = \frac{\text{Observed number of runs} - \text{Expected number of runs}}{\text{Standard deviation of number of runs}}$$

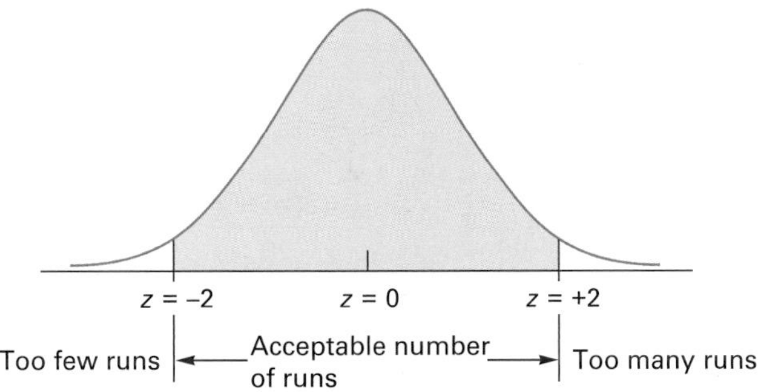

FIGURE 10.14
A sampling distribution for runs is used to distinguish chance variation from patterns

For the median and up/down tests, one can find z using these formulas:

Median: $$z = \frac{r - [(N/2) + 1]}{\sqrt{(N - 1)/4}} \quad (10\text{–}8)$$

Up and down: $$z = \frac{r - [(2N - 1)/3]}{\sqrt{(16N - 29)/90}} \quad (10\text{–}9)$$

where

N = Total number of observations

r = Observed number of runs of either As and Bs or Us and Ds, depending on which test is involved.

It is desirable to apply both run tests to any given set of observations because each test is different in terms of the types of patterns it can detect. Sometimes both tests will pick up a certain pattern, but sometimes only one will detect nonrandomness. If either does, the implication is that some sort of nonrandomness is present in the data.

EXAMPLE 6

Twenty sample means have been taken from a process. The means are shown in the following table. Use median and up/down run tests with $z = 2$ to determine if assignable causes of variation are present. Assume the median is 11.0.

SOLUTION

The means are marked according to above/below the median and up/down. The solid lines represent the runs.

Sample	A/B	Mean	U/D	Sample	A/B	Mean	U/D
1	B	10.0	—	11	B	10.7	D
2	B	10.4	U	12	A	11.3	U
3	B	10.2	D	13	B	10.8	D
4	A	11.5	U	14	A	11.8	U
5	B	10.8	D	15	A	11.2	D
6	A	11.6	U	16	A	11.6	U
7	A	11.1	D	17	A	11.2	D
8	A	11.2	U	18	B	10.6	D
9	B	10.6	D	19	B	10.7	U
10	B	10.9	U	20	A	11.9	U

A/B: 10 runs U/D: 17 runs

The expected number of runs for each test is

$$E(r)_{\text{med}} = \frac{N}{2} + 1 = \frac{20}{2} + 1 = 11$$

$$E(r)_{u/d} = \frac{2N - 1}{3} = \frac{2(20) - 1}{3} = 13$$

The standard deviations are

$$\sigma_{med} = \sqrt{\frac{N-1}{4}} = \sqrt{\frac{20-1}{4}} = 2.18$$

$$\sigma_{u/d} = \sqrt{\frac{16N-29}{90}} = \sqrt{\frac{16(20)-29}{90}} = 1.80$$

The z_{test} values are

$$z_{med} = \frac{10-11}{2.18} = -.46$$

$$z_{u/d} = \frac{17-13}{1.80} = +2.22$$

Although the median test does not reveal any pattern, because its z_{test} value is within the range ± 2, the up/down test does; its value exceeds $+2$. Consequently, nonrandom variations are probably present in the data and, hence, the process is not in control.

If ties occur in either test (e.g., a value equals the median or two values in a row are the same), assign A/B or U/D in such a manner that that z_{test} is as large as possible. If z_{test} still does not exceed ± 2 (± 1.96, etc.), you can be reasonably confident that a conclusion of randomness is justified.

Using Control Charts and Run Tests Together

Although for instructional purposes most of the examples, solved problems, and problems focus on either control charts or run tests, ideally both control charts and run tests should be used to analyze process output, along with a plot of the data. The procedure involves the following three steps:

1. Compute control limits for the process output.
   a. Determine which type of control chart is appropriate (see Table 10.18).
   b. Compute control limits using the appropriate formulas. If no probability is given, use a value of $z = 2.00$ to compute the control limits.
   c. If any sample statistics fall outside of the control limits, the process is not in control. If all values are within the control limits, proceed to Step 2.
2. Conduct median and up/down run tests. Use $z = \pm 2.00$ for comparing the test scores. If either or both test scores are not within $z = \pm 2{,}00$, the output is probably not random. If both test scores are with $z = \pm 2.00$, proceed to Step 3.
3. *Note:* If you are at this point, there is no indication so far that the process output is nonrandom. Plot the sample data and visually check for patterns (e.g., cycling). If you see a pattern, the output is probably not random. Otherwise, conclude the output is random and that the process is in control.

What Happens When a Process Exhibits Possible Nonrandom Variation?

Nonrandom variation is indicated when a point is observed that is outside the control limits, or a run test produces a large z-value (e.g., greater than ± 1.96). Managers should have response plans in place to investigate the cause. It may be a false alarm (i.e., a Type I error), or it may be a real indication of the presence of an assignable cause of variation. If it appears to be a false alarm, resume the process but monitor it for a while to confirm this. If an assignable cause can be found, it needs to be addressed. If it is a good result (e.g., an observation below the lower control limit of a p-chart, a c-chart, or a range chart would indicate unusually good quality), it may be possible to change the process to achieve similar results on an ongoing basis.

The more typical case is that there is a problem that needs to be corrected. Operators can be trained to handle simple problems, while teams may be needed to handle more complex problems. Problem solving often requires the use of various tools, described in Chapter 9, to find the root cause of the problem. Once the cause has been found, changes can be made to reduce the chance of recurrence.

PROCESS CAPABILITY

Once the stability of a process has been established (i.e., no nonrandom variations are present), it is necessary to determine if the process is capable of producing output that is within an acceptable range. The variability of a process becomes the focal point of the analysis.

Three commonly used terms refer to the variability of process output. Each term relates to a slightly different aspect of that variability, so it is important to differentiate these terms.

Specifications or *tolerances* are established by engineering design or customer requirements. They indicate a range of values in which individual units of output must fall in order to be acceptable.

Control limits are statistical limits that reflect the extent to which *sample statistics* such as means and ranges can vary due to randomness alone.

Process variability reflects the natural or inherent (i.e., random) variability in a process. It is measured in terms of the process standard deviation.

Specifications A range of acceptable values established by engineering design or customer requirements.

Process variability Natural or inherent variability in a process.

Control limits and process variability are directly related: Control limits are based on sampling variability, and sampling variability is a function of process variability. On the other hand, there is *no* direct link between specifications and either control limits or process variability. They are specified in terms of the output of a product or service, not in terms of the *process* by which the output is generated. Hence, in a given instance, the output of a process may or may not conform to specifications, even though the process may be statistically in control. That is why it is also necessary to take into account the *capability* of a process. The term **process capability** refers to the inherent variability of process output *relative to* the variation allowed by the design specifications. The following section describes capability analysis.

Process capability The inherent variability of process output relative to the variation allowed by the design specification.

To maximize production of a machine run in a paper mill, it is important that the machine's alignment is correct. If not, performance and quality could be affected, which could result in machine downtime and expensive repairs. The on-board processor calculates the position of the paper in relationship to the machine datum. Two points are then measured on the roller. With the simple press of a button the operator is provided with any deviations on a display panel.

A technician using vernier calipers to measure gears.

Capability Analysis

Capability analysis is the determination of whether the variability inherent in the output of a process that is in control falls within the acceptable range of variability allowed by the design specifications for the process output. If it is within the specifications, the process is said to be "capable." If it is not, the manager must decide how to correct the situation.

Consider the three cases illustrated in Figure 10.15. In the first case, process capability and output specifications are well matched, so that nearly all of the process output can be expected to meet the specifications. In the second case, the process variability is much less than what is called for, so that virtually 100 percent of the output should be well within tolerance. In the third case, however, the specifications are tighter than what the process is capable of, so that even when the process is functioning as it should, a sizable percentage of the output will fail to meet the specifications. In other words, the process could be in control and still generate unacceptable output. Thus, we cannot automatically assume that a process that is in control will provide desired output. Instead, we must specifically check whether a process is *capable* of meeting specifications and not simply set up a control chart to monitor it. A process should be both in control and within specifications *before* production begins—in essence, "Set the toaster correctly at the start. Don't burn the toast and then scrape it!"

In instances such as case C in Figure 10.15, a manager might consider a range of possible solutions: (1) redesign the process so that it can achieve the desired output, (2) use an alternative process that can achieve the desired output, (3) retain the current process but attempt to eliminate unacceptable output using 100 percent inspection, and (4) examine the specifications to see whether they are necessary or could be relaxed without adversely affecting customer satisfaction.

Obviously, process variability is the key factor in process capability. It is measured in terms of the process standard deviation. To determine whether the process is capable, compare ± 3 standard deviations (i.e., 6 standard deviations) of the process to the specifications for the process. For example, suppose the ideal length of time to perform a service is 10 minutes, and an acceptable range of variation around this time is ± 1 minute. If the process has a standard deviation of .5 minute, it would not be capable because ± 3 standard deviations would be ± 1.5 minutes, exceeding the specification of ± 1 minute.

FIGURE 10.15 Process capability and specifications may or may not match

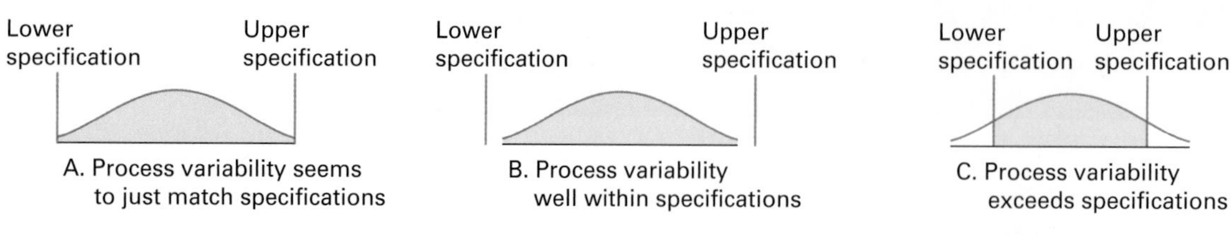

EXAMPLE 7

A manager has the option of using any one of three machines for a job. The processes and their standard deviations are listed below. Determine which machines are capable if the specifications are 10.00 mm and 10.80 mm.

Process	Standard Deviation (mm)
A	.13
B	.08
C	.16

SOLUTION

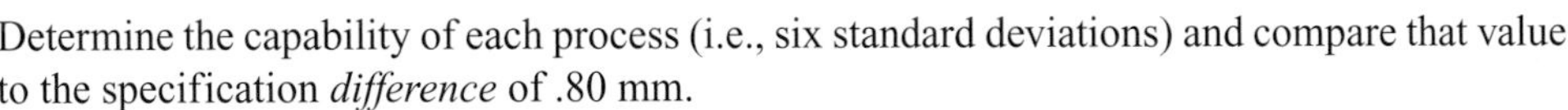

Determine the capability of each process (i.e., six standard deviations) and compare that value to the specification *difference* of .80 mm.

Process	Standard Deviation (mm)	Process Capability
A	.13	.78
B	.08	.48
C	.16	.96

C_p

To assess the capability of a machine or process, a **capability index** can be computed using the following formula:

capability index Used to assess the ability of a process to meet specifications.

$$\text{Process capability index, } C_p = \frac{\text{Specification width}}{\text{Process width}} = \frac{\text{Upper specification} - \text{Lower specification}}{6\sigma} \quad (10\text{–}10)$$

For a process to be deemed to be capable, it must have a capability index of at least 1.00. However, an index of 1.00 would mean that the process is just barely capable. The current trend is to aim for an index of at least 1.33. An index of 1.33 allows some leeway. Consider driving a car into a garage that has a door opening that is 1 inch wider than the car versus driving into a garage where the door opening is 20 inches wider than the car, and you'll understand why this book and many companies use 1.33 as the standard for judging process capability instead of 1.00.

An index of 1.00 implies about 2700 parts per million (ppm) can be expected to not be within the specifications while an index of 1.33 implies only about 30 ppm won't be within specs. Moreover, the greater the capability index, the greater the probability that the output of a process will fall within design specifications.

EXAMPLE 8

Compute the process capability index for each process in Example 7.

SOLUTION

The specification width in Example 7 is .80 mm. Hence, to determine the capability index for each process, divide .80 by the process width (i.e., six standard deviations) of each machine. The results are shown in the following table:

Process	Standard Deviation (mm)	Process Capability	C_p
A	.13	.78	.80/.78 = 1.03
B	.08	.48	.80/.48 = 1.67
C	.16	.96	.80/.96 = 0.83

We can see that only process B is capable because its index is not less than 1.33. (See Figure 10.15 for a visual portrayal of these results.)

For processes that are not capable, several options might be considered, such as performing 100 percent inspection to weed out unacceptable items, improving the process to reduce variability, switching to a capable process, outsourcing, etc.

FIGURE 10.16 Three-sigma versus six-sigma capability

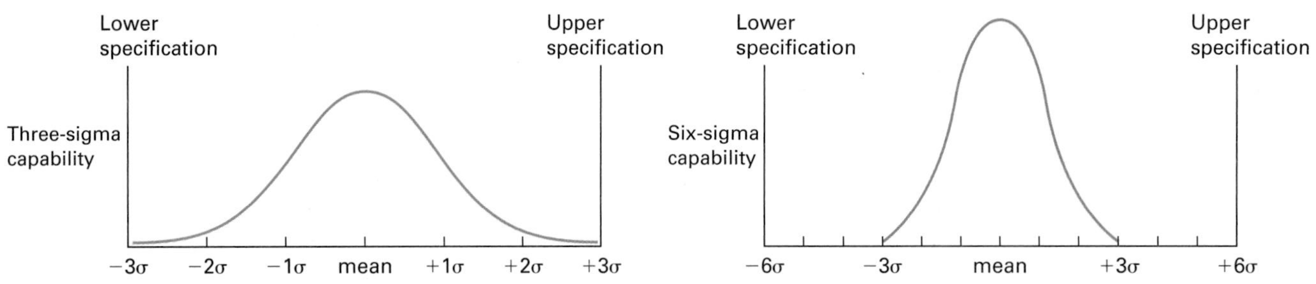

SERVICE

The Motorola Corporation is well known for its use of the term *six sigma,* which refers to its goal of achieving a process variability so small that the design specifications represent six standard deviations above *and* below the process mean. That means a process capability index equal to 2.00, resulting in an extremely small probability of getting any output not within the design specifications. This is illustrated in Figure 10.16.

To get an idea of how a capability index of 2.00 compares to an index of, say, 1.00 in terms of defective items, consider that if the U.S. Postal Service had a capability index of 1.00 for delivery errors of first-class mail, this would translate into about 10,000 misdelivered pieces per day; if the capability index was 2.00, that number would drop to about 1,000 pieces a day.

Care must be taken when interpreting the C_p index, because its computation does not involve the process mean. Unless the target value (i.e., process mean) is *centered* between the upper and lower specifications, the C_p index can be misleading. For example, suppose the specifications are 10 and 11, and the standard deviation of the process is equal to .10. The C_p would seem to be very favorable:

$$\frac{11 - 10}{6(.10)} = 1.67$$

However, suppose that the process mean is 12, with a standard deviation of .10; ± 3 standard deviations would be 11.70 to 12.30, so it is very unlikely that *any* of the output would be within the specifications of 10 to 11!

There are situations in which the target value is not centered between the specifications, either intentionally or unavoidably. In such instances, a more appropriate measure of process capability is the C_{pk} index, because it does take the process mean into account.

C_{pk}

If a process is not centered, a slightly different measure is used to compute its capability. This index is represented by the symbol C_{pk}. It is computed by finding the difference between each of the specification limits and the mean, identifying the smaller difference, and dividing that difference by three standard deviations of the process. Thus, C_{pk} is equal to the *smaller* of

$$\frac{\text{Upper specification} - \text{Process mean}}{3\sigma} \qquad (10\text{–}11)$$

and

$$\frac{\text{Process mean} - \text{Lower specification}}{3\sigma}$$

EXAMPLE 9

A process has a mean of 9.20 grams and a standard deviation of .30 gram. The lower specification limit is 7.50 grams and the upper specification limit is 10.50 grams. Compute C_{pk}.

SOLUTION

1. Compute the index for the lower specification:

$$\frac{\text{Process mean} - \text{Lower specification}}{3\sigma} = \frac{9.20 - 7.50}{3(.30)} = \frac{1.70}{.90} = 1.89$$

2. Compute the index for the upper specification:

$$\frac{\text{Upper specification} - \text{Process mean}}{3\sigma} = \frac{10.50 - 9.20}{3(.30)} = \frac{1.30}{.90} = 1.44$$

The *smaller* of the two indexes is 1.44, so this is the C_{pk}. Because the C_{pk} is more than 1.33, the process is capable.

You might be wondering why a process wouldn't be centered as a matter of course. One reason is that only a range of acceptable values, not a target value, may be specified. A more compelling reason is that the cost of nonconformance is greater for one specification limit than it is for nonconformance for the other specification limit. In that case, it would make sense to have the target value be closer to the spec that has the lower cost of nonconformance. This would result in a noncentered process.

Improving Process Capability

Improving process capability requires changing the process target value and/or reducing the process variability that is inherent in a process. This might involve simplifying, standardizing, making the process mistake-proof, upgrading equipment, or automating. See Table 10.5 for examples.

Improved process capability means less need for inspection, lower warranty costs, fewer complaints about service, and higher productivity. For process control purposes, it means narrower control limits.

Taguchi Cost Function

Gnocchi Taguchi, a Japanese quality expert, holds a nontraditional view of what constitutes poor quality, and hence the cost of poor quality. The traditional view is that as long as output is within specifications, there is no cost. Taguchi believes that any deviation from the target value represents poor quality, and that the farther away from target a deviation is, the greater the cost. Figure 10.17 illustrates the two views. The implication for Taguchi is that reducing the variation inherent in a process (i.e., increasing its capability ratio) will result in lowering the cost of poor quality.

Limitations of Capability Indexes

There are several risks of using a capability index:

1. The process may not be stable, in which case a capability index is meaningless.
2. The process output may not be normally distributed, in which case inferences about the fraction of output that isn't acceptable will be incorrect.
3. The process is not centered but the *Cp* index is used, giving a misleading result.

TABLE 10.5
Process capability improvement

Method	Examples
Simplify	Eliminate steps, reduce the number of parts, use modular design
Standardize	Use standard parts, standard procedures
Make mistake-proof	Design parts that can only be assembled the correct way; have simple checks to verify a procedure has been performed correctly
Upgrade equipment	Replace worn-out equipment; take advantage of technological improvements
Automate	Substitute automated processing for manual processing

FIGURE 10.17
Taguchi and traditional views of the cost of poor quality

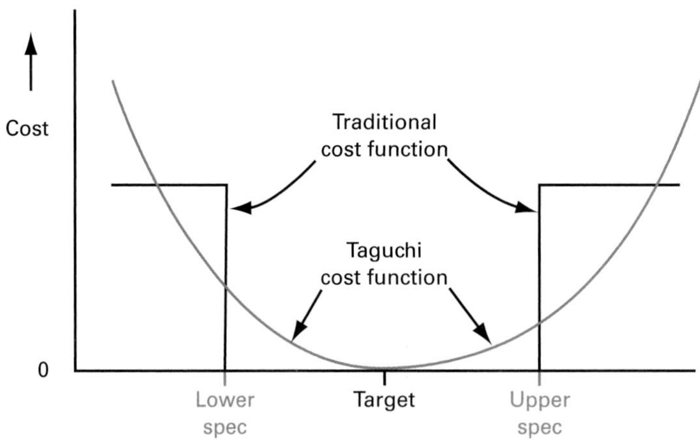

OPERATIONS STRATEGY

Quality is a major consideration for virtually all customers, so achieving and maintaining quality standards is of strategic importance to all business organizations. Quality assurance and product and service design are two vital links in the process. Organizations should continually seek to increase the capability of the processes they use, so that they can move from a position of using inspection or extensive use of control charts to achieve desired levels of quality to one where quality is built into products and processes, so that little or no efforts are needed to assure quality. Processes that exhibit evidence of nonrandomness, or processes that are deemed to not be capable, should be viewed as opportunities for continuous process improvement.

Bar Codes Might Cut Drug Errors in Hospitals

READING

It's estimated that more than 7,000 hospital patients die each year because of drug errors, and many others suffer ill effects from being given the wrong drug or the wrong dosage. Some hospitals are using bar codes attached to patients' wristbands that allow hospital personnel who administer drugs to patients to electronically check to make sure the drug and dosage are appropriate. Before administering a drug, the doctor or nurse scans the bar code attached to the patient to see what drug is needed and when, and then the drug's bar code is scanned to verify that the medication is correct.

But bar codes are not foolproof, as a recent study of hospitals showed. Nurses may develop a workaround that involves using photo copies of a group of patients' bar codes which are then used to obtain drugs for the entire group. The nurse would then have a tray that may contain drugs of different dosages intended for different patients. At that point, the bar code protection has been circumvented.

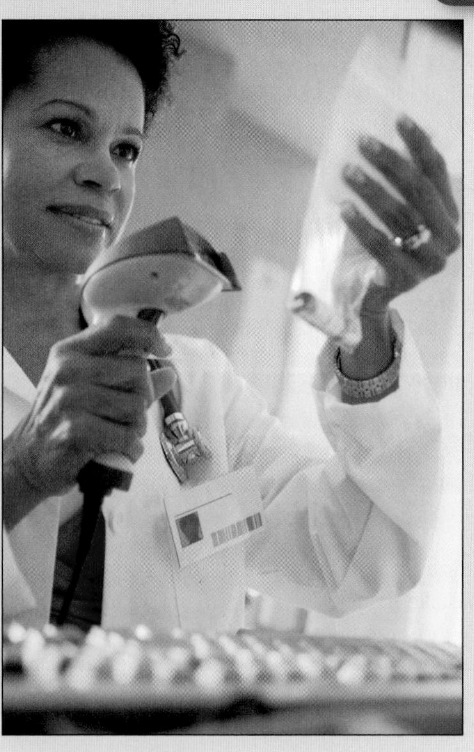

Source: Based on "Bar Codes Might Cut Drug Errors," *Rochester Democrat and Chronicle,* March 14, 2003, p. 9A, and "Bar Codes Are Not Foolproof in Hospitals, says Study," *Rochester Democrat and Chronicle,* July 3, 2008, p. 3A.

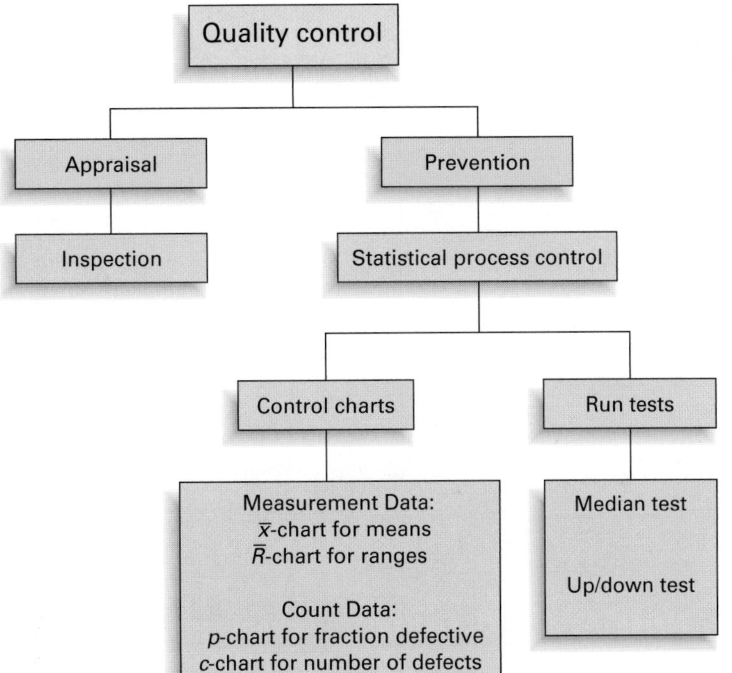

FIGURE 10.18
Overview of quality control

SUMMARY

This chapter describes inspection and statistical process control. Inspection means examining the output of a process to determine whether it is acceptable. Key issues in inspection include where to inspect in the process, how often to inspect, and whether to inspect on-site or in a laboratory.

Statistical process control focuses on detecting departures from randomness in a process. Two basic tools of process control are control charts and run tests. Figure 10.18 gives an overview of quality control. The general theory of control charts is discussed, and four types of control charts—two for variables and two for attributes—and two types of run tests are described in the chapter. The chapter ends with a discussion of process capability. Process capability studies are used to determine if the output of a process will satisfy specifications. They can provide valuable information for managers in terms of reducing costs and avoiding problems created by generating output that is not within specifications. Table 10.6 provides a summary of formulas.

KEY POINTS

1. All processes exhibit random variation. Quality control's purpose is to identify a process that also exhibits nonrandom (correctable) variation on the basis of sample statistics (e.g., sample means) obtained from the process.
2. Control charts and run tests can be used to detect nonrandom variation in sample statistics. It is also advisable to plot the data to visually check for patterns.
3. If a process does not exhibit nonrandom variation, its capability to produce output that meets specifications can be assessed.

KEY TERMS

assignable variation, 426
attributes, 430
capability index, 445
c-chart, 436
central limit theorem, 426
control chart, 428
control limits, 429
inspection, 420
mean control chart, 430
p-chart, 435
process capability, 443
process variability, 443
quality control, 419
quality of conformance, 425
random variation, 426
range control chart, 432
run, 439
run test, 438
sampling distribution, 426
specifications, 443
statistical process control (SPC), 425
Type I error, 429
Type II error, 429
variables, 430

TABLE 10.6
Summary of formulas

CONTROL CHARTS

Name	Symbol	Control Limits
Mean	$\bar{x}$	$\bar{\bar{x}} \pm z\frac{\sigma}{\sqrt{n}}$ or $\bar{\bar{x}} \pm A_2\bar{R}$ n = sample size
Range	R	UCL $= D_4\bar{R}$, LCL $= D_3\bar{R}$
Fraction defective	p	$\bar{p} \pm z\sqrt{\frac{\bar{p}(1-\bar{p})}{n}}$ n = sample size
Number of defects	c	$\bar{c} \pm z\sqrt{\bar{c}}$

RUN TESTS

Name	Number of Runs: Observed	Number of Runs: Expected	Standard Deviation	z
Median	r	$\frac{N}{2}+1$	$\sqrt{\frac{N-1}{4}}$	$\frac{r-[(N/2)+1]}{\sqrt{(N-1)/4}}$
Up/down	r	$\frac{2N-1}{3}$	$\sqrt{\frac{16N-29}{90}}$	$\frac{r-[(2N-1)/3]}{\sqrt{(16N-29)/90}}$

N = number of observations

PROCESS CAPABILITY

Name	Symbol	Formula
Capability index for a centered process	C_p	$\frac{\text{Specification width}}{6\sigma \text{ of process}}$
Capability index for a noncentered process	C_{pk}	Smaller of $\begin{cases} \frac{\text{Mean} - \text{Lower specification}}{3\sigma} \\ \frac{\text{Upper specification} - \text{Mean}}{3\sigma} \end{cases}$

SOLVED PROBLEMS

Problem 1

Process distribution and sampling distribution. An industrial process that makes 3-foot sections of plastic pipe produces pipe with an average inside diameter of 1 inch and a standard deviation of .05 inch.

a. If you randomly select one piece of pipe, what is the probability that its inside diameter will exceed 1.02 inches, assuming the population is normal?

b. If you select a random sample of 25 pieces of pipe, what is the probability that the sample mean will exceed 1.02 inches?

Solution

$\mu = 1.00,\ \sigma = .05$

a. $z = \frac{x-\mu}{\sigma} = \frac{1.02 - 1.00}{.05} = .40$

Using Appendix B, Table A, $P(z > .4) = .5000 - .1554 = .3446$

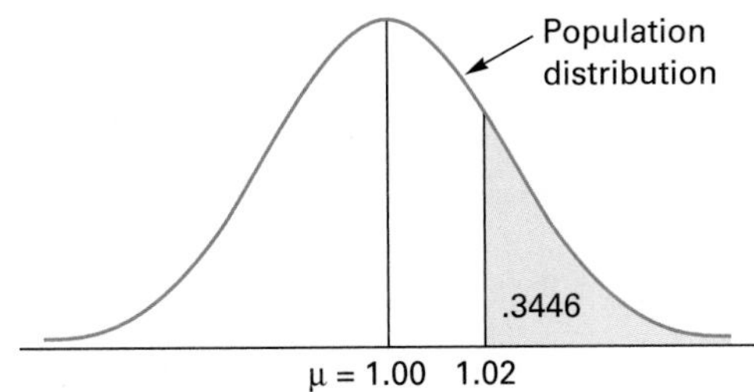

b. $z = \dfrac{\bar{x} - \mu}{\sigma/\sqrt{n}} = \dfrac{1.02 - 1.00}{.05/\sqrt{25}} = 2.00$

Using Appendix B, Table A, $P(z > 2.00) = .5000 - .4772 = .0228$

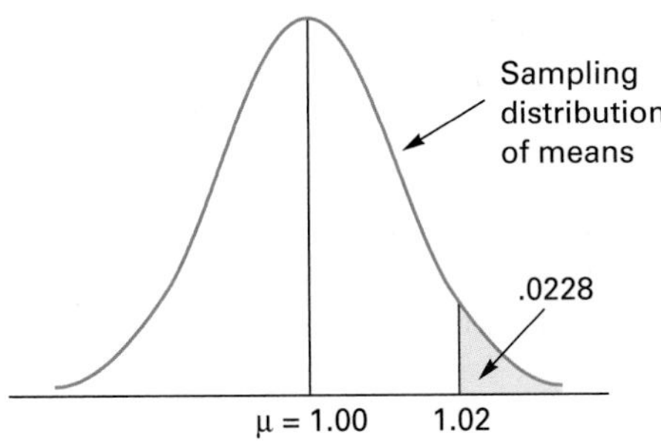

Problem 2

Control charts for means and ranges. Processing new accounts at a bank is intended to average 10 minutes each. Five samples of four observations each have been taken. Use the sample data in conjunction with Table 10.2 to construct upper and lower control limits for both a mean chart and a range chart. Do the results suggest that the process is in control?

	Sample 1	Sample 2	Sample 3	Sample 4	Sample 5
	10.2	10.3	9.7	9.9	9.8
	9.9	9.8	9.9	10.3	10.2
	9.8	9.9	9.9	10.1	10.3
	10.1	10.4	10.1	10.5	9.7
Totals	40.0	40.4	39.6	40.8	40.0

Solution

a. Determine the mean and range of each sample.

$$\bar{x} = \frac{\Sigma x}{n}, \text{ Range} = \text{Largest} - \text{Smallest}$$

Sample	Mean	Range
1	40.0/4 = 10.0	10.2 – 9.8 = .4
2	40.4/4 = 10.1	10.4 – 9.8 = .6
3	39.6/4 = 9.9	10.1 – 9.7 = .4
4	40.8/4 = 10.2	10.5 – 9.9 = .6
5	40.0/4 = 10.0	10.3 – 9.7 = .6

b. Compute the average mean and average range:

$$\bar{\bar{x}} = \frac{10.0 + 10.1 + 9.9 + 10.2 + 10.0}{5} = \frac{50.2}{5} = 10.04$$

$$\bar{R} = \frac{.4 + .6 + .4 + .6 + .6}{5} = \frac{2.6}{5} = .52$$

c. Obtain factors A_2, D_4, and D_3 from Table 10.2 for $n = 4$: $A_2 = .73$, $D_4 = 2.28$, $D_3 = 0$.

d. Compute upper and lower limits:

$$\text{UCL}_{\bar{x}} = \bar{\bar{x}} + A_2\bar{R} = 10.04 + .73(.52) = 10.42$$

$$\text{LCL}_{\bar{x}} = \bar{\bar{x}} - A_2\bar{R} = 10.04 - .73(.52) = 9.66$$

$$\text{UCL}_R = D_4\bar{R} = 2.28(.52) = 1.19$$

$$\text{LCL}_R = D_3\bar{R} = 0(.52) = 0$$

e. Verify that points are within limits. (If they were not, the process would be investigated to correct assignable causes of variation.)

The smallest sample mean is 9.9, and the largest is 10.2. Both are well within the control limits. Similarly, the largest sample range is .6, which is also within the control limits. Hence, the results suggest that the process is in control. Note, however, that for illustrative purposes, the number of samples is deliberately small; 20 or more samples would give a clearer indication of control limits and whether the process is in control.

Problem 3

Type I error (alpha risk). After several investigations of points outside control limits revealed nothing, a manager began to wonder about the probability of a Type I error for the control limits used ($z = 1.90$).

a. Determine the alpha risk (i.e., *P*(Type I error)) for this value of *z*.
b. What *z* would provide an alpha risk of about 2 percent?

Solution

a. Using Appendix B, Table A, find that the area under the curve between $z = 0$ and $z = +1.90$ is .4713. Therefore, the area (probability) of values *within* -1.90 to $+1.90$ is $2(.4713) = .9426$, and the area *beyond* these values is $1 - .9426 = .0574$. Hence, the alpha risk is 5.74 percent.
b. The alpha risk (Type I error probability) is always specified as an *area* in the tail(s) of a distribution. With control charts, you use two-sided control limits. Consequently, half of the risk lies in each tail. Hence, the area in the right tail is 1 percent, or .0100. This means that .4900 should be the area under the curve between $z = 0$ and the value of *z* you are looking for. The closest value is .4901 for $z = 2.33$. Thus, control limits based on $z = \pm 2.33$ provide an alpha risk of about 2 percent.

Problem 4

p-chart and *c-chart.* Using the appropriate control chart, determine two-sigma control limits for each case:

a. An inspector found an average of 3.9 scratches in the exterior paint of each of the automobiles being prepared for shipment to dealers.
b. Before shipping lawn mowers to dealers, an inspector attempts to start each mower and notes any that do not start on the first try. The lot size is 100 mowers, and an average of 4 did not start (4 percent).

Solution

The choice between these two types of control charts relates to whether *two* types of results can be counted (*p*-chart) or whether *only occurrences* can be counted (*c*-chart).

a. The inspector can only count the scratches that occurred, not the ones that did not occur. Consequently, a *c*-chart is appropriate. The sample average is 3.9 scratches per car. Two-sigma control limits are found using the formulas

$$\text{UCL} = \bar{c} + z\sqrt{\bar{c}}$$

$$\text{LCL} = \bar{c} - z\sqrt{\bar{c}}$$

where $\bar{c} = 3.9$ and $z = 2$. Thus,

$$\text{UCL} = 3.9 + 2\sqrt{3.9} = 7.85 \text{ scratches}$$

$$\text{LCL} = 3.9 - 2\sqrt{3.9} = -.05, \text{ so the lower limit is 0 scratches}$$

(*Note:* Round to zero only if the computed lower limit is negative.)

b. The inspector can count both the lawn mowers that started and those that did not start. Consequently, a *p*-chart is appropriate. Two-sigma control limits can be computed using the following:

$$\text{UCL} = \bar{p} + z\sqrt{\frac{\bar{p}(1 - \bar{p})}{n}}$$

$$\text{LCL} = \bar{p} - z\sqrt{\frac{\bar{p}(1 - \bar{p})}{n}}$$

where

$\bar{p} = .04$
$n = 100$
$z = 2$

Thus,

$$\text{UCL} = .04 + 2\sqrt{\frac{.04(96)}{100}} = .079$$

$$\text{LCL} = .04 - 2\sqrt{\frac{.04(.96)}{100}} = .001$$

Problem 5

Run tests. The number of defective items per sample for 11 samples is shown below. Determine if nonrandom patterns are present in the sequence.

	SAMPLE										
	1	2	3	4	5	6	7	8	9	10	11
Number of defectives	22	17	19	25	18	20	21	17	23	23	24

Solution

Since the median isn't given, it must be estimated from the sample data. To do this, array the data from low to high; the median is the middle value. (In this case, there is an odd number of values. For an even number of values, average the middle two to obtain the median.) Thus,

17 17 18 19 20 21 22 23 23 24 25

(5 below) ↑ median (5 above)

The median is 21.

Next, code the observations using A/B and U/D:

Sample	A/B	Number of Defectives	U/D
1	A	22	—
2	B	17	D
3	B	19	U
4	A	25	U
5	B	18	D
6	B	20	U
7	tie	21	U
8	B	17	D
9	A	23	U
10	A	23	tie
11	A	24	U

Note that each test has tied values. How these are resolved can affect the number of observed runs. Suppose that you adhere to this rule: Assign letter (A or B, U or D) so that the resulting difference between the observed and expected number of runs is as large as possible. To accomplish this, it is necessary to initially ignore ties and count the runs to see whether there are too many or too few. Then return to the ties and make the assignments. The rationale for this rule is that it is a conservative method for retaining data; if you conclude that the data are random using this approach, you can be reasonably confident that the method has not "created" randomness. With this in mind, assign a B to sample 7 since the expected number of runs is

$$E(r)_{\text{med}} = N/2 + 1 = 11/2 + 1 = 6.5$$

and the difference between the resulting number of runs, 5, and 6.5 is greater than between 6.5 and 7 (which occurs if A is used instead of B). Similarly, in the up/down test, a U for sample 10 produces six runs, whereas a D produces eight runs. Since the expected number of runs is

$$E(r)_{\text{u/d}} = (2N - 1) \div 3 = (22 - 1) \div 3 = 7$$

it makes no difference which one is used: both yield a difference of 1. For the sake of illustration, a D is assigned.

The computations for the two tests are summarized below. Each test has a z-value that is within the range of ± 2.00. Because neither test reveals nonrandomness, you may conclude that the data are random.

	Runs Observed	*Expected*	σ_r	z	Conclude
Median	5	6.5	1.58	−.95	Random
Up/down	8	7.0	1.28	.78	Random

Problem 6

Process capability. Determine which of these three processes are capable:

Process	Mean	Standard Deviation	Lower Spec	Upper Spec
1	7.5	.10	7.0	8.0
2	4.6	.12	4.3	4.9
3	6.0	.14	5.5	6.7

Solution

Notice that the means of the first two processes are exactly in the center of their upper and lower specs. Hence, the C_p index (Formula 10–10) is appropriate. However, the third process is not centered, so C_{pk} (Formula 10–11) is appropriate.

$$\text{For Processes 1 and 2: } C_p = \frac{\text{Upper spec} - \text{Lower spec}}{6\sigma}$$

In order to be capable, C_p must be at least 1.33.

$$\text{Process 1: } C_p = \frac{8.0 - 7.0}{6(.10)} = 1.67 \text{ (capable)}$$

$$\text{Process 2: } C_p = \frac{4.9 - 4.3}{6(.12)} = .83 \text{ (not capable)}$$

For Process 3, C_{pk} must be at least 1.33. It is the lesser of these two:

$$\frac{\text{Upper spec} - \text{Mean}}{3\sigma} = \frac{6.7 - 6.0}{3(.14)} = 1.67$$

$$\frac{\text{Mean} - \text{Lower spec}}{3\sigma} = \frac{6.0 - 5.5}{3(.14)} = 1.19 \text{ (not capable)}$$

DISCUSSION AND REVIEW QUESTIONS

1. List the steps in the control process.
2. What are the key concepts that underlie the construction and interpretation of control charts?
3. What is the purpose of a control chart?
4. Why is order of observation important in process control?
5. Briefly explain the purpose of each of these control charts:
   a. x-bar
   b. Range
   c. p-chart
   d. c-chart
6. What is a run? How are run charts useful in process control?
7. If all observations are within control limits, does that guarantee that the process is random? Explain.
8. Why is it usually desirable to use both a median run test and an up/down run test on the same data?
9. If both run tests are used, and neither reveals nonrandomness, does that prove that the process is random? Explain.
10. Define and contrast control limits, specifications, and process variability.
11. A customer has recently tightened the specs for a part your company supplies. The specs are now much tighter than the machine being used for the job is capable of. Briefly identify alternatives you might consider to resolve this problem. (See Figure 10.15C.)

12. A new order has come into your department. The capability of the process used for this type of work will enable virtually all of the output to be well within the specs. (See Figure 10.15B.)
    a. What benefits might be derived from this situation?
    b. What alternatives might be considered by the manager?
13. Answer these questions about inspection:
    a. What level of inspection is optimal?
    b. What factors guide the decision of how much to inspect?
    c. What are the main considerations in choosing between centralized inspection and on-site inspection?
    d. What points are potential candidates for inspection?
14. What two basic assumptions must be satisfied in order to use a process capability index?
15. How important is it for managers to maintain and promote ethical behavior in dealing with quality issues? Does your answer depend on the product or service involved?
16. Classify each of the following as either a Type I error or a Type II error:
    a. Putting an innocent person in jail.
    b. Releasing a guilty person from jail.
    c. Eating (or not eating) a cookie that fell on the floor.
    d. Not seeing a doctor as soon as possible after ingesting poison.

TAKING STOCK

1. What trade-offs are involved in each of these decisions?
    a. Deciding whether to use two-sigma or three-sigma control limits.
    b. Choosing between a large sample size and a smaller sample size.
    c. Trying to increase the capability of a process that is barely capable.
2. Who needs to be involved in setting quality standards?
3. Name several ways that technology has had an impact on quality control.

CRITICAL THINKING EXERCISES

1. Analysis of the output of a process has suggested that the variability is nonrandom on several occasions recently. However, each time an investigation has not revealed any assignable causes. What are some of the possible explanations for not finding any causes? What should the manager do?
2. Many organizations use the same process capability standard for all their products or services (e.g., 1.33), but some companies use multiple standards: different standards for different products or services (e.g., 1.00, 1.20, 1.33, and 1.40). What reasons might there be for using a single measure, and what reasons might there be for using multiple standards?
3. Give two examples of unethical behavior for each of these areas: inspection, process control, process capability. For each, name the relevant ethical principle.

PROBLEMS

1. Specifications for a part for a DVD player state that the part should weigh between 24 and 25 ounces. The process that produces the parts has a mean of 24.5 ounces and a standard deviation of .2 ounce. The distribution of output is normal.
    a. What percentage of parts will not meet the weight specs?
    b. Within what values will 95.44 percent of sample means of this process fall, if samples of $n = 16$ are taken and the process is in control (random)?

2. An automatic filling machine is used to fill 1-liter bottles of cola. The machine's output is approximately normal with a mean of 1.0 liter and a standard deviation of .01 liter. Output is monitored using means of samples of 25 observations.
    a. Determine upper and lower control limits that will include roughly 97 percent of the sample means when the process is in control.
    b. Given these sample means: 1.005, 1.001, .998, 1.002, .995, and .999, is the process in control?

3. Checkout time at a supermarket is monitored using a mean and a range chart. Six samples of $n = 20$ observations have been obtained and the sample means and ranges computed:

Sample	Mean	Range	Sample	Mean	Range
1	3.06	.42	4	3.13	.46
2	3.15	.50	5	3.06	.46
3	3.11	.41	6	3.09	.45

a. Using the factors in Table 10.3, determine upper and lower limits for mean and range charts.
b. Is the process in control?

4. Computer upgrades have a nominal time of 80 minutes. Samples of five observations each have been taken, and the results are as listed. Using factors from Table 10.3, determine upper and lower control limits for mean and range charts, and decide if the process is in control.

SAMPLE					
1	2	3	4	5	6
79.2	80.5	79.6	78.9	80.5	79.7
78.8	78.7	79.6	79.4	79.6	80.6
80.0	81.0	80.4	79.7	80.4	80.5
78.4	80.4	80.3	79.4	80.8	80.0
81.0	80.1	80.8	80.6	78.8	81.1

5. Using samples of 200 credit card statements, an auditor found the following:

Sample	1	2	3	4
Number with errors	4	2	5	9

a. Determine the fraction defective in each sample.
b. If the true fraction defective for this process is unknown, what is your estimate of it?
c. What is your estimate of the mean and standard deviation of the sampling distribution of fractions defective for samples of this size?
d. What control limits would give an alpha risk of .03 for this process?
e. What alpha risk would control limits of .047 and .003 provide?
f. Using control limits of .047 and .003, is the process in control?
g. Suppose that the long-term fraction defective of the process is known to be 2 percent. What are the values of the mean and standard deviation of the sampling distribution?
h. Construct a control chart for the process, assuming a fraction defective of 2 percent, using two-sigma control limits. Is the process in control?

6. A medical facility does MRIs for sports injuries. Occasionally a test yields inconclusive results and must be repeated. Using the following sample data and $n = 200$, determine the upper and lower control limits for the fraction of retests using two-sigma limits. Is the process in control?

	SAMPLE												
	1	2	3	4	5	6	7	8	9	10	11	12	13
Number of retests	1	2	2	0	2	1	2	0	2	7	3	2	1

7. The postmaster of a small western town receives a certain number of complaints each day about mail delivery. Determine three-sigma control limits using the following data. Is the process in control?

	DAY													
	1	2	3	4	5	6	7	8	9	10	11	12	13	14
Number of complaints	4	10	14	8	9	6	5	12	13	7	6	4	2	10

8. Given the following data for the number of defects per spool of cable, using three-sigma limits, is the process in control?

	OBSERVATION													
	1	2	3	4	5	6	7	8	9	10	11	12	13	14
Number of defects	2	3	1	0	1	3	2	0	2	1	3	1	2	0

9. After a number of complaints about its directory assistance, a telephone company examined samples of calls to determine the frequency of wrong numbers given to callers. Each sample consisted of 100 calls. Determine 95 percent limits. Is the process stable (i.e., in control)? Explain.

	SAMPLE															
	1	2	3	4	5	6	7	8	9	10	11	12	13	14	15	16
Number of errors	5	3	5	7	4	6	8	4	5	9	3	4	5	6	6	7

10. Specifications for a metal shaft are much wider than the machine used to make the shafts is capable of. Consequently, the decision has been made to allow the cutting tool to wear a certain amount before replacement. The tool wears at the rate of .004 centimeter per piece. The process has a natural variation, σ,

of .02 centimeter and is normally distributed. Specifications are 15.0 to 15.2 centimeters. A three-sigma cushion is set at each end to minimize the risk of output outside of the specifications. How many shafts can the process turn out before tool replacement becomes necessary? (See diagram.)

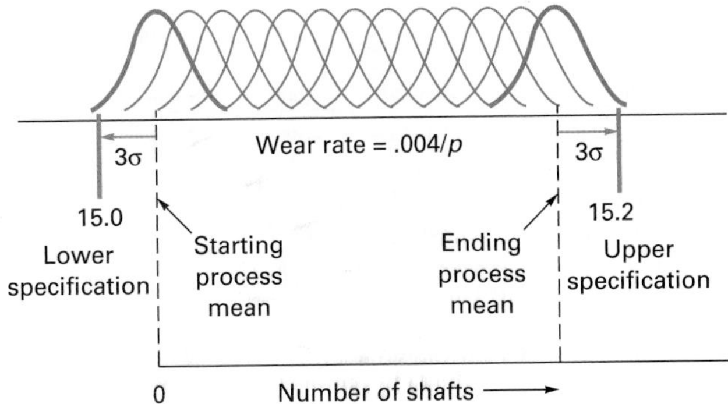

11. Specifications for the computer upgrades in Problem 4 are 78 minutes and 81 minutes. Based on the data given in the problem, are the specifications being met? Estimate the percentage of process output that can be expected to fall within the specifications.

12. The time needed for checking in at a hotel is to be investigated. Historically, the process has had a standard deviation equal to .146. The means of 39 samples of $n = 14$ are

Sample	Mean	Sample	Mean	Sample	Mean	Sample	Mean
1	3.86	11	3.88	21	3.84	31	3.88
2	3.90	12	3.86	22	3.82	32	3.76
3	3.83	13	3.88	23	3.89	33	3.83
4	3.81	14	3.81	24	3.86	34	3.77
5	3.84	15	3.83	25	3.88	35	3.86
6	3.83	16	3.86	26	3.90	36	3.80
7	3.87	17	3.82	27	3.81	37	3.84
8	3.88	18	3.86	28	3.86	38	3.79
9	3.84	19	3.84	29	3.98	39	3.85
10	3.80	20	3.87	30	3.96		

a. Construct an $\bar{x}$-chart for this process with three-sigma limits. Is the process in control?
b. Analyze the data using a median run test and an up/down run test. What can you conclude?

13. For each of the accompanying control charts, analyze the data using both median and up/down run tests with $z = \pm 1.96$ limits. Are nonrandom variations present? Assume the center line is the long-term median.

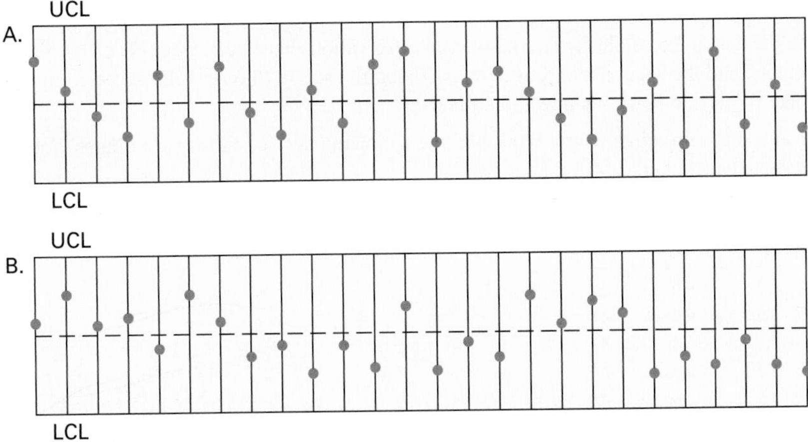

14. Analyze the data in the problems listed below using median and up/down run tests with $z = \pm 2$.

a. Given the following run test results of process output, what do the results of the run tests suggest about the process?

Test	z-score
Median	+1.37
Up/Down	+1.05

b. Twenty means were plotted on a control chart. An analyst counted 14 runs above/below the median, and 8 up/down runs. What do the results suggest about the process?
c. Problem 8.
d. Problem 7.

15. Use both types of run tests to analyze the daily expense voucher listed. Assume a median of $31.

Day	Amount	Day	Amount	Day	Amount	Day	Amount
1	$27.69	16	$29.65	31	$40.54	46	25.16
2	28.13	17	31.08	32	36.31	47	26.11
3	33.02	18	33.03	33	27.14	48	29.84
4	30.31	19	29.10	34	30.38	49	31.75
5	31.59	20	25.19	35	31.96	50	29.14
6	33.64	21	28.60	36	32.03	51	37.78
7	34.73	22	20.02	37	34.40	52	34.16
8	35.09	23	26.67	38	25.67	53	38.28
9	33.39	24	36.40	39	35.80	54	29.49
10	32.51	25	32.07	40	32.23	55	30.81
11	27.98	26	44.10	41	26.76	56	30.60
12	31.25	27	41.44	42	30.51	57	34.46
13	33.98	28	29.62	43	29.35	58	35.10
14	25.56	29	30.12	44	24.09	59	31.76
15	24.46	30	26.39	45	22.45	60	34.90

16. A company has just negotiated a contract to produce a part for another firm. In the process of manufacturing the part, the inside diameter of successive parts becomes smaller and smaller as the cutting tool wears. However, the specs are so wide relative to machine capabilities that it is possible to set the diameter initially at a large value and let the process run for a while before replacing the cutting tool.

The inside diameter decreases at an average rate of .001 cm per part, and the process has a standard deviation of .05 cm. The variability is approximately normal. Assuming a three-sigma buffer at each end, how frequently must the tool be replaced if the process specs are 3 cm and 3.5 cm. (See diagram for Problem 10.)

17. (Refer to Solved Problem 2.) Suppose the process specs are 9.65 and 10.35 minutes. Based on the data given, does it appear that the specs are being met? If not, what should one look for?

18. A production process consists of a three-step operation. The scrap rate is 10 percent for the first step and 6 percent for the other two steps.
a. If the desired daily output is 450 units, how many units must be started to allow for loss due to scrap?
b. If the scrap rate for each step could be cut in half, how many units would this save in terms of the scrap allowance?
c. If the scrap represents a cost of $10 per unit, how much is it costing the company per day for the original scrap rate?

19. (Refer to the data in Example 5.) Two additional observations have been taken. The first resulted in three defects, and the second had four defects. Using the set of 20 observations, perform run tests on the data. What can you conclude about the data?

20. A teller at a drive-up window at a bank had the following service times (in minutes) for 20 randomly selected customers:

SAMPLE			
1	2	3	4
4.5	4.6	4.5	4.7
4.2	4.5	4.6	4.6
4.2	4.4	4.4	4.8
4.3	4.7	4.4	4.5
4.3	4.3	4.6	4.9

a. Determine the mean of each sample.
b. If the process parameters are unknown, estimate its mean and standard deviation.
c. Estimate the mean and standard deviation of the sampling distribution.
d. What would three-sigma control limits for the process be? What alpha risk would they provide?
e. What alpha risk would control limits of 4.14 and 4.86 provide?
f. Using limits of 4.14 and 4.86, are any sample means beyond the control limits? If so, which one(s)?
g. Construct control charts for means and ranges using Table 10.3. Are any samples beyond the control limits? If so, which one(s)?

h. Explain why the control limits are different for means in parts *d* and *g*.
i. If the process has a known mean of 4.4 and a known standard deviation of .18, what would three-sigma control limits be for a mean chart? Are any sample means beyond the control limits? If so, which one(s)?

21. A process that produces computer chips has a mean of .04 defective chip and a standard deviation of .003 chip. The allowable variation is from .03 to .05 defective.
a. Compute the capability index for the process.
b. Is the process capable?

22. Given the following list of processes, the standard deviation for each, and specifications for a job that may be processed on that machine, determine which machines are capable of performing the given jobs.

Process	Standard Deviation (in.)	Job Specification (± in.)
001	.02	.05
002	.04	.07
003	.10	.18
004	.05	.15
005	.01	.04

23. Suppose your manager presents you with the following information about machines that could be used for a job, and wants your recommendation on which one to choose. The specification width is .48 mm. In this instance, you can narrow the set of choices, but you probably wouldn't make a recommendation without an additional piece of information. Explain the logic of the last statement.

Machine	Cost per Unit ($)	Standard Deviation (mm)
A	20	.059
B	12	.060
C	11	.063
D	10	.061

24. Each of the processes listed is noncentered with respect to the specifications for that process. Compute the appropriate capability index for each, and decide if the process is capable.

Process	Mean	Standard Deviation	Lower Spec	Upper Spec
H	15.0	0.32	14.1	16.0
K	33.0	1.00	30.0	36.5
T	18.5	0.40	16.5	20.1

25. An appliance manufacturer wants to contract with a repair shop to handle authorized repairs in Indianapolis. The company has set an acceptable range of repair time of 50 minutes to 90 minutes. Two firms have submitted bids for the work. In test trials, one firm had a mean repair time of 74 minutes with a standard deviation of 4.0 minutes and the other firm had a mean repair time of 72 minutes with a standard deviation of 5.1 minutes. Which firm would you choose? Why?

26. As part of an insurance company's training program, participants learn how to conduct an analysis of clients' insurability. The goal is to have participants achieve a time in the range of 30 to 45 minutes. Test results for three participants were: Armand, a mean of 38 minutes and a standard deviation of 3 minutes; Jerry, a mean of 37 minutes and a standard deviation of 2.5 minutes; and Melissa, a mean of 37.5 minutes and a standard deviation of 1.8 minutes.
a. Which of the participants would you judge to be capable? Explain.
b. Can the value of the C_{pk} exceed the value of C_p for a given participant? Explain.

27. The Good Chocolate Company makes a variety of chocolate candies, including a 12-ounce chocolate bar (340 grams) and a box of six 1-ounce chocolate bars (170 grams).
a. Specifications for the 12-ounce bar are 330 grams to 350 grams. What is the largest standard deviation (in grams) that the machine that fills the bar molds can have and still be considered capable if the average fill is 340 grams?
b. The machine that fills the bar molds for the 6-ounce bars has a standard deviation of .80 gram. The filling machine is set to deliver an average of 1.01 ounces per bar. Specifications for the six-bar box are 160 to 180 grams. Is the process capable? *Hint:* The *variance* for the box is equal to six times the bar *variance.*
c. What is the *lowest* setting in ounces for the filling machine that will provide capability in terms of the six-bar box?

28. The following is a control chart for the average number of minor errors in 22 service reports. What can you conclude from these data? Explain how you reached your conclusion.

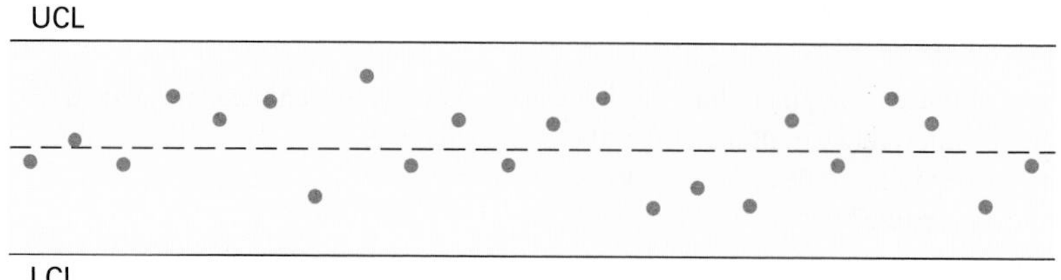

29. Use the three-step process described on p. 442 to decide if the following observations represent a process that is in control.

Observation	1	2	3	4	5	6	7	8	9	10	11	12
No. of errors	1	0	3	2	0	1	3	2	1	0	2	3

Toys, Inc. CASE

Toys, Inc., is a 20-year-old company engaged in the manufacture and sale of toys and board games. The company has built a reputation on quality and innovation. Although the company is one of the leaders in its field, sales have leveled off in recent years. For the most recent six-month period, sales actually declined compared with the same period last year. The production manager, Ed Murphy, attributed the lack of sales growth to "the economy." He was prompted to undertake a number of belt-tightening moves that included cuts in production costs and layoffs in the design and product development departments. Although profits are still flat, he believes that within the next six months, the results of his decisions will be reflected in increased profits.

The vice president of sales, Joe Martin, has been concerned with customer complaints about the company's Realistic line of working-model factories, farms, and service stations. The moving parts on certain models have become disengaged and fail to operate or operate erratically. His assistant, Keith McNally, has proposed a trade-in program by which customers could replace malfunctioning models with new ones. McNally believes that this will demonstrate goodwill and appease dissatisfied customers. He also proposes rebuilding the trade-ins and selling them at discounted prices in the company's retail outlet store. He doesn't think that this will take away from sales of new models. Under McNally's program, no new staff would be needed. Regular workers would perform needed repairs during periods of seasonal slowdowns, thus keeping production level.

When Steve Bukowski, a production assistant, heard Keith's proposal, he said that a better option would be to increase inspection of finished models before they were shipped. "With 100 percent inspection, we can weed out any defective models and avoid the problem entirely."

Take the role of a consultant who has been called in for advice by the company president, Marybeth Corbella. What do you recommend?

Tiger Tools CASE

Tiger Tools, a division of Drillmore Industries, was about to launch a new product. Production Manager Michelle York asked her assistant, Jim Peterson, to check the capability of the oven used in the process. Jim obtained 18 random samples of 20 pieces each. The results of those samples are shown in the following table. After he analyzed the data, he concluded that the process was not capable based on a specification width of 1.44 cm.

Michelle was quite disappointed when she heard this. She had hoped that with the introduction of the new product her operation could run close to full capacity and regain some of its lost luster. The company had a freeze on capital expenditures of more than $10,000, and a replacement oven would cost many times that amount. Jim Peterson worked with the oven crew to see if perhaps different settings could produce the desired results, but they were unable to achieve any meaningful improvements.

Sample	Mean	Range	Sample	Mean	Range
1	45.01	.85	10	44.97	.91
2	44.99	.89	11	45.11	.84
3	45.02	.86	12	44.96	.87
4	45.00	.91	13	45.00	.86
5	45.04	.87	14	44.92	.89
6	44.98	.90	15	45.06	.87
7	44.91	.86	16	44.94	.86
8	45.04	.89	17	45.00	.85
9	45.00	.85	18	45.03	.88

(continued)

(concluded)

Still not ready to concede, Michelle contacted one of her former professors and explained the problem. The professor suggested obtaining another set of samples, this time using a smaller sample size and taking more samples. Michelle then conferred with Jim and they agreed that he would take 27 samples of five observations each. The results are shown in the following table.

Sample	Mean	Range	Sample	Mean	Range
1	44.96	.42	15	45.00	.39
2	44.98	.39	16	44.95	.41
3	44.96	.41	17	44.94	.43
4	44.97	.37	18	44.94	.40
5	45.02	.39	19	44.87	.38
6	45.03	.40	20	44.95	.41
7	45.04	.39	21	44.93	.39
8	45.02	.42	22	44.96	.41
9	45.08	.38	23	44.99	.40
10	45.12	.40	24	45.00	.44
11	45.07	.41	25	45.03	.42
12	45.02	.38	26	45.04	.38
13	45.01	.41	27	45.03	.40
14	44.98	.40			

Questions

Consider the following questions, and then write a brief report to Michelle summarizing your findings.

1. How did Jim conclude that the process was not capable based on his first set of samples? (*Hint:* Estimate the process standard deviation, σ, using $A_2\overline{R} \approx 3\frac{\sigma}{\sqrt{n}}$.)
2. Does the second set of samples show anything that the first set didn't? Explain what and why.
3. Assuming the problem can be found and corrected, what impact do you think this would have on the capability of the process? Compute the potential process capability using the second data set.
4. If small samples can reveal something that large samples might not, why not just take small samples in every situation?

SELECTED BIBLIOGRAPHY AND FURTHER READINGS

Besterfield, Dale H. *Quality Control.* Upper Saddle River, NJ: Prentice Hall, 2009.

Derman, C., and S. M. Ross. *Statistical Aspects of Quality Control.* San Diego: Academic Press, 1997.

Evans, James R., and W. M. Lindsay. *The Management and Control of Quality.* Cincinnati: South-Western College Publications, 1999.

Gitlow, Howard, Alan Oppenheim, and Rosa Oppenheim. *Quality Management: Tools and Methods for Improvement.* 2nd ed. Burr Ridge, IL: Irwin, 1995.

Goetsch, David L., and Stanley B. Davis. *Quality Management: Introduction to Total Quality Management for Production, Processing, and Services.* 3rd ed. Upper Saddle River, NJ: Prentice Hall, 2000.

Grant, Eugene L, and Richard Leavenworth. *Statistical Quality Control.* New York: McGraw-Hill, 1996.

Griffith, Gary K. *The Quality Technician's Handbook.* 4th ed. Upper Saddle River, NJ: Prentice Hall, 2000.

Gyrna, Frank, Jr. *Quality Planning and Analysis.* New York: McGraw-Hill, 2001.

Juran, Joseph M. *Juran's Quality Handbook.* New York: McGraw-Hill, 1999.

Mitra, Amitava. *Fundamentals of Quality Control and Improvement.* 2nd ed. Upper Saddle River, NJ: Prentice Hall, 1998.

Montgomery, Douglas C. *Introduction to Statistical Quality Control.* 5th ed. New York: John Wiley and Sons, 2004.

Ott, Ellis, Edward G. Schilling, and Dean Neubauer. *Process Quality Control.* New York: McGraw-Hill, 2000.

Summers, Donna. *Quality.* 5th ed. Upper Saddle River, NJ: Prentice Hall, 2009.

SUPPLEMENT TO CHAPTER 10

Acceptance Sampling

LEARNING OBJECTIVES

After completing this supplement, you should be able to:

1 Explain the purpose of acceptance sampling.

2 Contrast acceptance sampling and process control.

3 Compare and contrast single- and multiple-sampling plans.

4 Determine the average outgoing quality of inspected lots.

SUPPLEMENT OUTLINE

INTRODUCTION

Acceptance sampling A form of inspection applied to lots or batches of items before or after a process, to judge conformance with predetermined standards.

Acceptance sampling is a form of inspection that is applied to lots or batches of items either before or after a process instead of during the process. In the majority of cases, the lots represent incoming purchased items or final products awaiting shipment to warehouses or customers. The purpose of acceptance sampling is to decide whether a lot satisfies predetermined standards. Lots that satisfy these standards are *passed* or *accepted;* those that do not are *rejected.* Rejected lots may be subjected to 100 percent inspection, or in the case of purchased goods, they may be returned to the supplier for credit or replacement (especially if destructive testing is involved).

Acceptance sampling procedures are most useful when one or more of the following conditions exist:

1. A large number of items must be processed in a short time.
2. The cost consequences of passing defectives are low.
3. Destructive testing is required.
4. Fatigue or boredom caused by inspecting large numbers of items leads to inspection errors.

Acceptance sampling procedures can be applied to both attribute (counts) and variable (measurements) inspection. However, inspection of attributes is perhaps more widely used, so for purposes of illustration, the discussion here focuses exclusively on attribute sampling plans.

SAMPLING PLANS

A key element of acceptance sampling is the sampling plan. **Sampling plans** specify the lot size, *N;* the sample size, *n;* the number of samples to be taken; and the acceptance/rejection criteria. A variety of sampling plans can be used. Some plans call for selection of a single sample, and others call for two or more samples, depending on the nature of the plan. The following paragraphs briefly describe some of the different kinds of plans.

Sampling plans Plans that specify lot size, sample size, number of samples, and acceptance/rejection criteria.

Single-Sampling Plan

In the single plan, one random sample is drawn from each lot, and every item in the sample is examined and classified as either "good" or "defective." If any sample contains more than a specified number of defectives, *c,* that lot is rejected.

Double-Sampling Plan

A double-sampling plan allows for the opportunity to take a second sample if the results of the initial sample are inconclusive. For example, if the quality of the initial sample is high, the lot can be accepted without need for a second sample. If the quality in the initial sample is poor, sampling also can be terminated and the lot rejected. For results between those two cases, a second sample is then taken and the items inspected, after which the lot is either accepted or rejected on the basis of the evidence obtained from both samples. A double-sampling plan specifies the lot size, the size of the initial sample, accept/reject criteria for the initial sample, the size of the second sample, and a single acceptance number for the combined samples.

With a double-sampling plan, two values are specified for the number of defective items, a lower level, c_1, and an upper level, c_2. For instance, the lower level might be two defectives and the upper level might be five defectives. Using those values as decision rules, the first sample is taken. If the number of defective items in the first sample is less than or equal to the lower value (i.e., c_1), the lot is judged to be good and sampling is terminated. Conversely, if the number of defectives exceeds the upper value (i.e., c_2), the lot is rejected. If the number of defectives falls somewhere in between, a second sample is taken and the number of defectives in both samples is compared to a third value, c_3. For example, c_3 might be six. If the combined number of defectives does not exceed that value, the lot is accepted; otherwise, the lot is rejected.

Multiple-Sampling Plan

A multiple-sampling plan is similar to a double-sampling plan except that more than two samples may be required. A sampling plan will specify each sample size and two limits for each sample. The values increase with the number of samples. If, for any sample, the cumulative number of defectives found (i.e., those in the present sample plus those found in all previous samples) exceeds the upper limit specified for that sample, sampling is terminated and the lot is rejected. If the cumulative number of defectives is less than or equal to the lower limit, sampling is terminated and the lot is passed. If the number is between the two limits, another sample is taken. The process continues until the lot is either accepted or rejected.

Choosing a Plan

The cost and time required for inspection often dictate the kind of sampling plan used. The two primary considerations are the number of samples needed and the total number of observations required. Single-sampling plans involve only a single sample, but the sample size is large relative to the total number of observations taken under double- or multiple-sampling plans. Where the cost to obtain a sample is relatively high compared with the cost to analyze the observations, a single-sampling plan is more desirable. For instance, if a sample of moon soil is needed, clearly the cost of returning for a second or third sample far outweighs the cost of analyzing a single large sample. Conversely, where item inspection costs are relatively high, such as destructive testing, it may be better to use double or multiple sampling because the average number of items inspected per lot will be lower. This stems from the fact that a very good or very poor lot quality will often show up initially, and sampling can be terminated.

OPERATING CHARACTERISTIC CURVE

Operating characteristic (OC) curve Probability curve that shows the probabilities of accepting lots with various fractions defective.

An important feature of a sampling plan is how it discriminates between lots of high and low quality. The ability of a sampling plan to discriminate is described by its **operating characteristic (OC) curve.** A typical curve for a single-sampling plan is shown in Figure 10S.1. The curve shows the probability that a given sampling plan will result in lots with various *fractions defective* being accepted. For example, the graph shows that a lot with 3 percent of defectives (a fraction defective of .03) would have a probability of about .90 of being accepted (and a probability of 1.00 − .90 = .10 of being rejected). Note the downward relationship: As lot quality decreases, the probability of acceptance decreases, although the relationship is not linear.

A sampling plan does not provide perfect discrimination between good and bad lots; some low-quality lots will invariably be accepted, and some lots with very good quality will invariably be rejected. Even lots containing more than 20 percent defectives still have some probability of acceptance, whereas lots with as few as 3 percent defectives have some chance of rejection.

The degree to which a sampling plan discriminates between good and bad lots is a function of the steepness of the graph's OC curve: the steeper the curve, the more discriminating the sampling plan. (See Figure 10S.2.) Note the curve for an ideal plan (i.e., one that can discriminate perfectly between good and bad lots). To achieve that, you need to inspect 100 percent of each lot. Obviously, if you are going to do that, theoretically, *all* of the defectives can be eliminated (although errors and boredom might result in a few defectives remaining). However, the point is that 100 percent inspection provides a perspective from which to view the OC curves of other sampling plans.

Be aware that the cost and time needed to conduct 100 percent inspection often rule out 100 percent inspection, as does destructive testing, leaving acceptance sampling as the only viable alternative.

For these reasons, buyers ("consumers") are generally willing to accept lots that contain small percentages of defective items as "good," especially if the cost related to a few defects is low. Often this percentage is in the neighborhood of 1 percent to 2 percent defective. This figure is known as the **acceptable quality level (AQL).**

Acceptable quality level (AQL) The percentage level of defects at which consumers are willing to accept lots as "good."

Because of the inability of random sampling to clearly identify lots that contain more than this specified percentage of defective items, consumers recognize that some lots that actually contain more will be accepted. However, there is usually an upper limit on the percentage of

FIGURE 10S.1 A typical OC curve for proportions

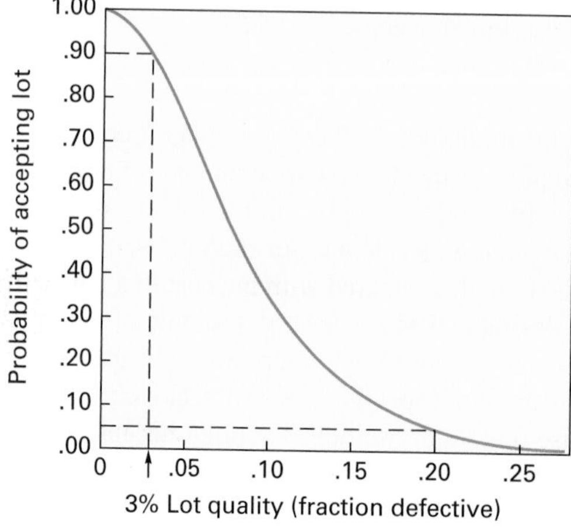

FIGURE 10S.2 The steeper the OC curve, the more discriminating the sampling plan

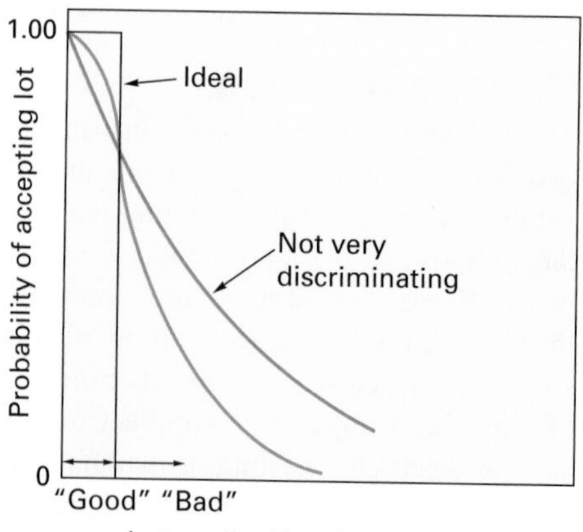

defective items that a consumer is willing to tolerate in accepted lots. This is known as the **lot tolerance percent defective (LTPD).** Thus, consumers want quality equal to or better than the AQL, and are willing to live with some lots with quality as poor as the LTPD, but they prefer not to accept any lots with a defective percentage that exceeds the LTPD. The probability that a lot containing defectives exceeding the LTPD will be accepted is known as the **consumer's risk,** or *beta* (β). The probability that a lot containing the acceptable quality level will be rejected is known as the **producer's risk,** *alpha* (α). Many sampling plans are designed to have a producer's risk of 5 percent and a consumer's risk of 10 percent, although other combinations are also used. It is possible by trial and error to design a plan that will provide selected values for alpha and beta given the AQL and the LTPD. However, standard references such as the government MIL-STD tables are widely used to obtain sample sizes and acceptance criteria for sampling plans. Figure 10S.3 illustrates an OC curve with the AQL, LTPD, producer's risk, and consumer's risk.

Lot tolerance percent defective (LTPD) The upper limit on the percentage of defects that a consumer is willing to accept.

Consumer's risk The probability that a lot containing defects exceeding the LTPD will be accepted.

Producer's risk The probability that a lot containing the acceptable quality level will be rejected.

A certain amount of insight is gained by actually constructing an OC curve. Suppose you want the curve for a situation in which a sample of $n = 10$ items is drawn from lots containing $N = 2{,}000$ items, and a lot is accepted if no more than $c = 1$ defective is found. Because the sample size is small relative to the lot size, it is reasonable to use the binomial distribution to obtain the probabilities that a lot will be accepted for various lot qualities.[1] A portion of the cumulative binomial table found in Appendix B, Table D, is reproduced here to facilitate the discussion.

			FRACTION DEFECTIVE, P											
	n	*x*	.05	.10	.15	.20	.25	.30	.35	.40	.45	.50	.55	.60
	10	0	.5987	.3487	.1969	.1074	.0563	.0282	.0135	.0060	.0025	.0010	.0003	.0001
$c = 1$	→	1	.9139	.7361	.5443	.3758	.2440	.1493	.0860	.0464	.0233	.0107	.0045	.0017
		2	.9885	.9298	.8202	.6778	.5256	.3828	.2616	.1673	.0996	.0547	.0274	.0123
		3	.9990	.9872	.9500	.8791	.7759	.6496	.5138	.3823	.2660	.1719	.1020	.0548

To use the table, select various lot qualities (values of p listed across the top of the table), beginning with .05, and find the probability that a lot with that percentage of defects would be accepted (i.e., the probability of finding zero or one defect in this case). For $p = .05$, the

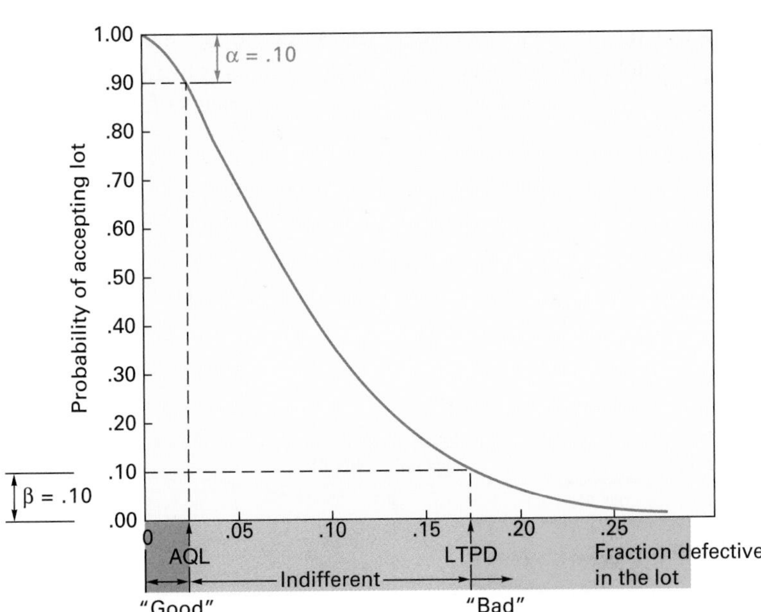

FIGURE 10S.3
The AQL indicates good lots, and the LTPD indicates bad lots

[1]Since sampling is generally performed "without replacement," if the ratio n/N is 5 percent or more, the hypergeometric distribution is more appropriate since the probability of finding a defect would vary from observation to observation. We shall consider only the more general case of the binomial distribution (i.e., $n/N < 5$ percent).

FIGURE 10S.4
OC curve for $n = 10$, $c = 1$

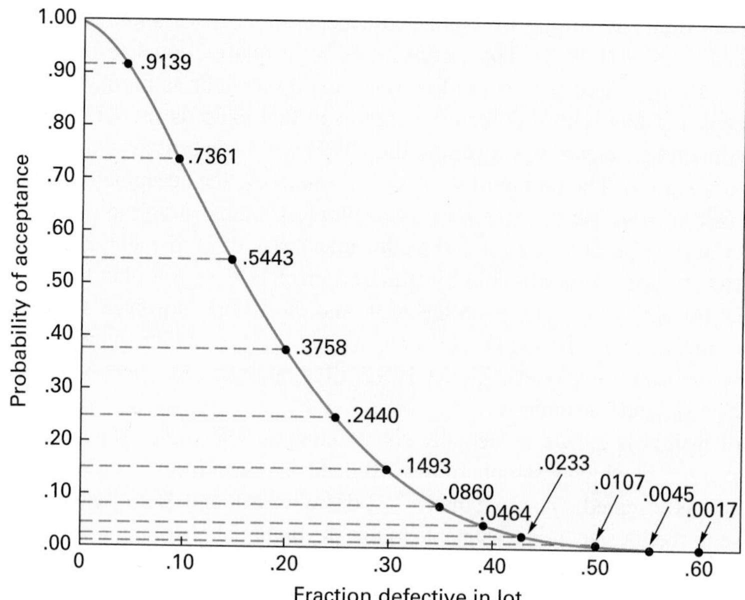

probability of one or no defects is .9139. For a lot with 10 percent defective (i.e., a fraction defective of .10), the probability of one or fewer defects drops to .7361, and for 15 percent defective, the probability of acceptance is .5443. In effect, you simply read the probabilities across the row for $c = 1$. By plotting these points (e.g., .05 and .9139, .10 and .7361) on a graph and connecting them, you obtain the OC curve illustrated in Figure 10S.4.

When $n > 20$ and $p < .05$, the Poisson distribution is useful in constructing operating characteristic curves for proportions. In effect, the Poisson distribution is used to approximate the binomial distribution. The Poisson approximation involves treating the mean of the binomial distribution (i.e., np) as the mean of the Poisson (i.e., μ):

$$\mu = np \qquad (10S\text{–}1)$$

As with the binomial distribution, you select various values of lot quality p, and then determine the probability of accepting a lot (i.e., finding two or fewer defects) by referring to the cumulative Poisson table. Values of p in increments of .01 are often used in this regard. Example 10S–1 illustrates this use of the Poisson table.

EXAMPLE 10S–1

www.mhhe.com/stevenson11e

Use the cumulative Poisson table to construct an OC curve for this sampling plan:

$$N = 5{,}000, \qquad n = 80, \qquad c = 2$$

SOLUTION

Selected Values of p	$\mu = np$	P_{ac} [$P(x \leq 2)$ from Appendix Table C]
.01	80(.01) = 0.8	.953
.02	80(.02) = 1.6	.783
.03	80(.03) = 2.4	.570
.04	80(.04) = 3.2	.380
.05	80(.05) = 4.0	.238
.06	80(.06) = 4.8	.143
.07	80(.07) = 5.6	.082
.08	80(.08) = 6.4	.046

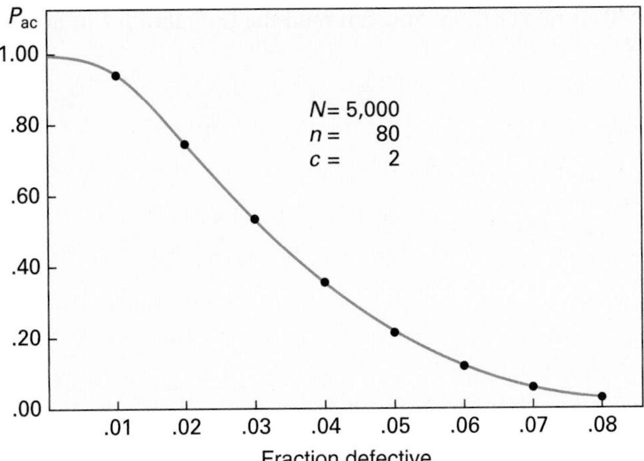

Operating characteristic curves can be constructed for variables sampling plans as well as for attributes sampling plans. To go into detail is beyond the scope of this presentation. The purpose here is merely to illustrate the concept of an OC curve and to show how its construction is based on an underlying *sampling distribution.*

AVERAGE QUALITY OF INSPECTED LOTS

An interesting feature of acceptance sampling is that the level of inspection automatically adjusts to the quality of lots being inspected, assuming rejected lots are subjected to 100 percent inspection. The OC curve reveals that the greater the percentage of defects in a lot, the less likely the lot is to be accepted. Generally speaking, good lots have a high probability and bad lots have a low probability of being accepted. If the lots inspected are mostly good, few will end up going through 100 percent inspection. The poorer the quality of the lots, the greater the number of lots that will come under close scrutiny. This tends to improve overall quality of lots by weeding out defects. In this way, the level of inspection is affected by lot quality.

If all lots have some given fraction defective, p, the **average outgoing quality (AOQ)** of the lots can be computed using the following formula, assuming defective items are replaced with good items:

Average outgoing quality (AOQ) Average of rejected lots (100 percent inspection) and accepted lots (a sample of items inspected).

$$\text{AOQ} = P_{ac} \times p\left(\frac{N - n}{N}\right) \tag{10S–2}$$

where

P_{ac} = Probability of accepting the lot N = Lot size

p = Fraction defective n = Sample size

In practice, the last term is often omitted since it is usually close to 1.0 and therefore has little effect on the resulting values. The formula then becomes

$$\text{AOQ} = P_{ac} \times p \tag{10S–3}$$

Use this formula instead of Formula 10S–2 for computing AOQ values.

Construct the AOQ curve for this situation:

$N = 500, \quad n = 10, \quad c = 1$

SOLUTION

Let values of p vary from .05 to .40 in steps of .05. You can read the probabilities of acceptance, P_{ac} from Appendix B, Table D.

$$AOQ = P_{ac} \times p$$

p	P_{ac}	AOQ
.05	.9139	.046
.10	.7361	.074
.15	.5443	.082
.20	.3758	.075
.25	.2440	.061
.30	.1493	.045
.35	.0860	.030
.40	.0464	.019

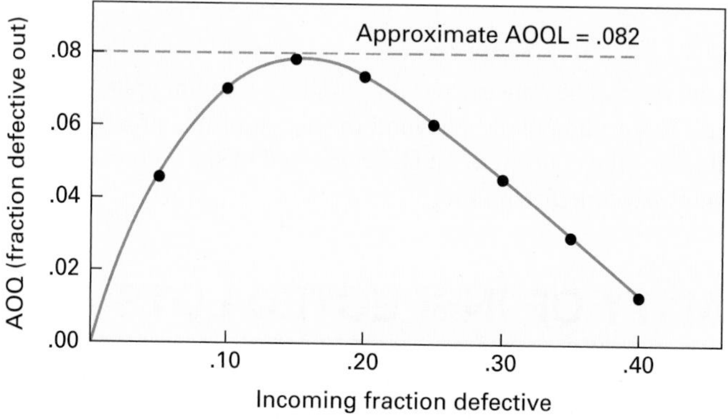

The average outgoing quality limit (AOQL) is just above 8 percent.

By allowing the percentage, p, to vary, a curve such as the one in Example 10S–2 can be constructed in the same way that an OC curve is constructed. The curve illustrates the point that if lots are very good or very bad, the average outgoing quality will be high. The maximum point on the curve becomes apparent in the process of calculating values for the curve.

There are several managerial implications of the graph in Example 10S–2. First, a manager can determine the worst possible outgoing quality. Second, the manager can determine the amount of inspection that will be needed by obtaining an estimate of the incoming quality. Moreover, the manager can use this information to establish the relationship between inspection cost and the incoming fraction defective, thereby underscoring the benefit of implementing process improvements to reduce the incoming fraction defective rather than trying to weed out bad items through inspection.

KEY TERMS

acceptable quality level (AQL), 464
acceptance sampling, 462
average outgoing quality (AOQ), 467
consumer's risk, 465
lot tolerance percent defective (LTPD), 465
operating characteristic (OC) curve, 464
producer's risk, 465
sampling plans, 463

SOLVED PROBLEMS

Problem 1

Inspection. A process for manufacturing shock absorbers for light trucks produces 5 percent defectives. Inspection cost per shock is $0.40, and 100 percent inspection generally catches all defects, due to the nature of the inspection and the small volume produced. Any defects installed on trucks must eventually be replaced at a cost of $12 per shock. Is 100 percent inspection justified?

Solution

Five percent of the output is defective. The expected cost per shock for replacement is thus .05($12) = 60 cents. Since this is greater than the inspection cost per shock of 40 cents, 100 percent inspection is justified.

Problem 2

Acceptance sampling. Shipments of 300 boxes of glassware are received at a warehouse of a large department store. Random samples of five boxes are checked, and the lot is rejected if more than one box reveals breakage. Construct the OC curve for this plan.

Solution

When the sample size is less than 5 percent of the lot size, the binomial distribution can be used to obtain P_{ac} for various lot percentages defective. Here, $n/N = 5/300 = .017$, so the binomial can be used. A portion of the cumulative binomial table is shown below. Note that $c = 1$.

CUMULATIVE BINOMIAL PROBABILITIES

	n	*x*	*p* = FRACTION DEFECTIVE .05	.10	.15	.20	.25	.30
	5	0	.7738	.5905	.4437	.3277	.2373	.1681
$c = 1 \rightarrow$		1	.9774	.9185	.8352	.7373	.6328	.5282
		2	.9988	.9914	.9734	.9421	.8965	.8369
		3	1.0000	.9995	.9978	.9933	.9844	.9692
		4	1.0000	1.0000	.9999	.9997	.9990	.9976
		5	1.0000	1.0000	1.0000	1.0000	1.0000	1.0000

CUMULATIVE BINOMIAL PROBABILITIES

p = FRACTION DEFECTIVE .35	.40	.45	.50	.55	.60	.65	.70	.75	.80
.1160	.0778	.0503	.0313	.0185	.0102	.0053	.0024	.0010	.0003
.4284	.3370	.2562	.1875	.1312	.0870	.0540	.0308	.0156	.0067
.7648	.6826	.5931	.5000	.4069	.3174	.2352	.1631	.1035	.0579
.9460	.9130	.8688	.8125	.7438	.6630	.5716	.4718	.3672	.2627
.9947	.9898	.9815	.9688	.9497	.9222	.8840	.8319	.7627	.6723
1.0000	1.0000	1.0000	1.0000	1.0000	1.0000	1.0000	1.0000	1.0000	1.0000

The table indicates that $P_{ac} = .9774$ when lot quality is 5 percent defective, .9185 for 10 percent defective, .8352 for 15 percent, and so on. The resulting curve is

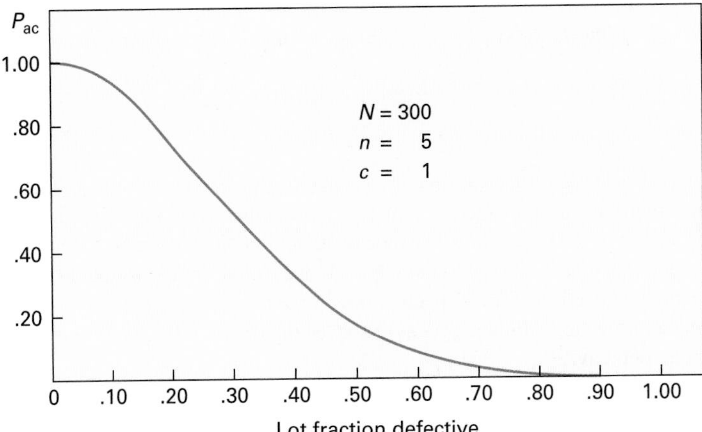

Develop the AOQ curve for the previous problem.

$$\text{AOQ} = P_{ac} \times p$$

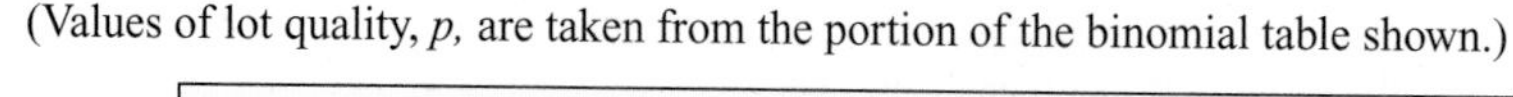

(Values of lot quality, p, are taken from the portion of the binomial table shown.)

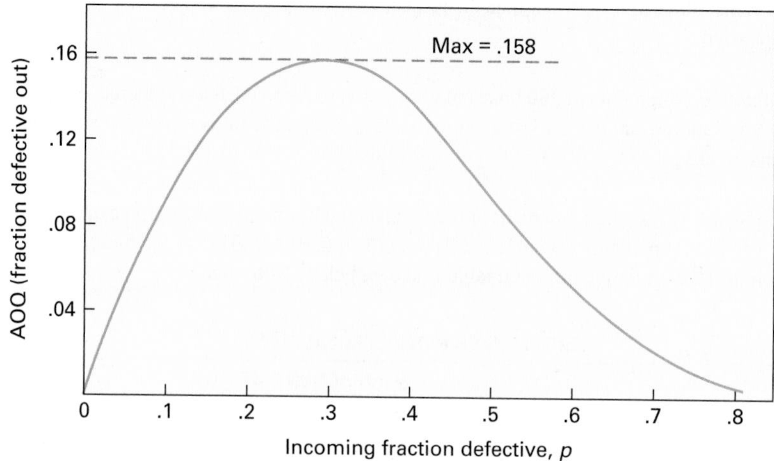

p	P_{ac}	AOQ	p	P_{ac}	AOQ
.05	.9774	.049	.45	.2562	.115
.10	.9185	.092	.50	.1875	.094
.15	.8352	.125	.55	.1312	.072
.20	.7373	.147	.60	.0870	.052
.25	.6328	.158	.65	.0540	.035
.30	.5282	.158	.70	.0308	.022
.35	.4284	.150	.75	.0156	.012
.40	.3370	.135	.80	.0067	.005

DISCUSSION AND REVIEW QUESTIONS

1. What is the purpose of acceptance sampling?
2. How does acceptance sampling differ from process control?
3. What is an operating characteristic curve, and how is it useful in acceptance sampling?
4. What general factors govern the choice between single-sampling plans and multiple-sampling plans?
5. Briefly explain or define each of these terms.
   a. AOQ
   b. AOQL
   c. LTPD
   d. Producer's risk
   e. Consumer's risk

PROBLEMS

1. An assembly operation for trigger mechanisms of a semiautomatic spray gun produces a small percentage of defective mechanisms. Management must decide whether to continue the current practice of 100 percent inspection or to replace defective mechanisms after final assembly when all guns are inspected. Replacement at final assembly costs $30 each; inspection during trigger assembly costs $12 per hour for labor and overhead. The inspection rate is one trigger per minute.
   a. Would 100 percent inspection during trigger assembly be justified if there are (1) 4 percent defective? (2) 1 percent defective?
   b. At what point would management be indifferent between 100 percent inspection of triggers and only final inspection?

2. Random samples of $n = 20$ circuit breakers are tested for damage caused by shipment in each lot of 4,000 received. Lots with more than one defective are pulled and subjected to 100 percent inspection.
   a. Construct the OC curve for this sampling plan.
   b. Construct the AOQ curve for this plan, assuming defectives found during 100 percent inspection are replaced with good parts. What is the approximate AOQL?

3. Auditors use a technique called *discovery sampling* in which a random sample of items is inspected. If any defects are found, the entire lot of items sampled is subjected to 100 percent inspection.

a. Draw an OC curve for the case where a sample of 15 credit accounts will be inspected out of a total of 8,000 accounts.

b. Draw an OC curve for the case where 150 accounts out of 8,000 accounts will be examined. (*Hint:* Use $p = .001, .002, .003, \ldots$)

c. Draw the AOQ curve for the preceding case, and estimate the AOQL.

4. Random samples of lots of textbooks are inspected for defective books just prior to shipment to the warehouse. Each lot contains 3,000 books.

a. On a single graph, construct OC curves for $n = 100$ and (1) $c = 0$, (2) $c = 1$, and (3) $c = 2$. (*Hint:* Use $p = .001, .002, .003, \ldots$)

b. On a single graph, construct OC curves for $c = 2$ and (1) $n = 5$, (2) $n = 20$, and (3) $n = 120$.

5. A manufacturer receives shipments of several thousand parts from a supplier every week. The manufacturer has the option of conducting a 100 percent inspection before accepting the parts. The decision is based on a random sample of 15 parts. If parts are not inspected, defectives become apparent during a later assembly operation, at which time replacement cost is $6.25 per unit. Inspection cost for 100 percent inspection is $1 per unit.

a. At what fraction defective would the manufacturer be indifferent between 100 percent inspection and leaving discovery of defectives until the later assembly operation?

b. For the sample size used, what is the maximum number of sample defectives that would cause the lot to be passed without 100 percent inspection, based on your answer to part *a?*

c. If the shipment actually contains 5 percent defective items:

(1) What is the correct decision?

(2) What is the probability it would be rejected in favor of 100 percent inspection?

(3) What is the probability that it would be accepted without 100 percent inspection?

(4) What is the probability of a Type I error? A Type II error?

d. Answer the questions in part *c* for a shipment that contains 20 percent defective items.

6. (Refer to Problem 5*c*.) Suppose there are two defectives in the sample.

a. If the acceptance number is $c = 1$, what decision should be made? What type of error is possible?

b. If the acceptance number is $c = 3$, what decision should be made? What type of error is possible?

c. Determine the average outgoing quality for each of these percent defective if $c = 1$.

(1) 5 percent.

(2) 10 percent.

(3) 15 percent.

(4) 20 percent.

SELECTED BIBLIOGRAPHY AND FURTHER READINGS

Duncan, A. J. *Quality Control and Industrial Statistics.* 5th ed. Homewood, IL: Richard D. Irwin, 1986.

Enrick, Norbert L. *Quality Reliability and Process Improvement.* 8th ed. New York: Industrial Press, 1985.

Juran, J. M., and F. M.Gryma Jr. *Quality Planning and Analysis.* 2nd ed. New York: McGraw-Hill, 1980.

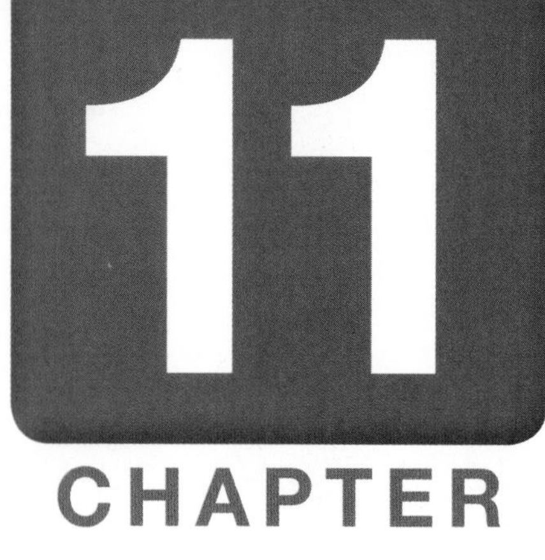

Aggregate Planning and Master Scheduling

CHAPTER OUTLINE

LEARNING OBJECTIVES

After completing this chapter, you should be able to:

1. Explain what aggregate planning is and how it is useful.
2. Identify the variables decision makers have to work with in aggregate planning and some of the possible strategies they can use.
3. Describe some of the graphical and quantitative techniques planners use.
4. Prepare aggregate plans and compute their costs.
5. Describe the master scheduling process and explain its importance.

Seasonal variations in demand are quite common in many industries and public services, such as air-conditioning, fuel, public utilities, police and fire protection, and travel. And these are just a few examples of industries and public services that have to deal with uneven demands. Generally speaking, organizations cannot predict exactly the quantity and timing of demands for specific products or services months in advance under these conditions. Even so, they typically must assess their capacity needs (e.g., labor, inventories) and costs months in advance in order to be able to handle demand. How do they do it? They use a process often referred to as *aggregate planning.* That is the subject of this chapter.

In the spectrum of production planning, **aggregate planning** is intermediate-range capacity planning that typically covers a time horizon of 2 to 12 months, although in some companies it may extend to as much as 18 months. It is particularly useful for organizations that experience seasonal or other fluctuations in demand or capacity. The goal of aggregate planning is to achieve a production plan that will effectively utilize the organization's resources to match expected demand. Planners must make decisions on output rates, employment levels and changes, inventory levels and changes, back orders, and subcontracting in or out.

Aggregate planning Intermediate-range capacity planning, usually covering 2 to 12 months.

Some organizations use the term "sales and operations planning" instead of aggregate planning for intermediate-range planning. Similarly, **sales and operations planning** is defined as making intermediate-range decisions to balance supply and demand, integrating financial and operations planning. Because the plan affects functions throughout the organization, it is typically prepared with inputs from sales (demand forecasts), finance (financial constraints), and operations (capacity constraints). Note that the sales and operations plan is important planning information that will have impacts throughout the supply chain, and it should be shared with supply chain partners, who might also have valuable inputs.

Sales and operations planning Intermediate-range decisions to balance supply and demand, integrating financial and operations planning.

TABLE 11.1
Overview of planning levels (chapter numbers are shown)

Long-Range Plans	Intermediate Plans	Short-Range Plans
Long-term capacity } 5 Location } 8 Layout } 6 Product design } 4 Work system design } 7	(This chapter) General levels of: Employment Output Finished-goods inventories Subcontracting Back orders	Detailed plans: Production lot size, Order quantities } 13 Machine loading, Job assignments, Job sequencing } 16 Work schedules } 16

INTRODUCTION

Intermediate Planning in Perspective

Organizations make capacity decisions on three levels: long term, intermediate term, and short term. Long-term decisions relate to product and service selection (i.e., determining which products or services to offer), facility size and location, equipment decisions, and layout of facilities. These long-term decisions essentially establish the capacity constraints within which intermediate planning must function. Intermediate decisions, as noted above, relate to general levels of employment, output, and inventories, which in turn establish boundaries within which short-range capacity decisions must be made. Thus, short-term decisions essentially consist of deciding the best way to achieve desired results within the constraints resulting from long-term and intermediate-term decisions. Short-term decisions involve scheduling jobs, workers and equipment, and the like. The three levels of capacity decisions are depicted in Table 11.1. Long-term capacity decisions were covered in Chapter 5, and scheduling and related matters are covered in Chapter 16. This chapter covers intermediate capacity decisions.

Many business organizations develop a *business plan* that encompasses both long-term and intermediate-term planning. The business plan establishes guidelines for the organization, taking into account the organization's strategies and policies; forecasts of demand for the organization's products or services; and economic, competitive, and political conditions.

Television manufacturers would not be concerned with various sizes. Instead, planners would treat them all as a single product in aggregate planning.

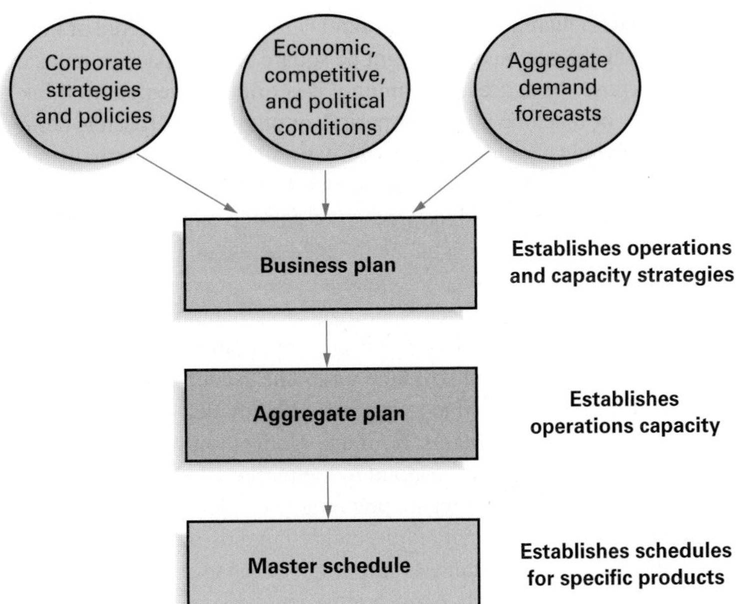

FIGURE 11.1
Planning sequence

A key objective in business planning is to coordinate the intermediate plans of various organization functions, such as marketing, operations, and finance. In manufacturing companies, coordination also includes engineering and materials management. Consequently, all of these functional areas must work together to formulate the aggregate plan. Aggregate planning decisions are strategic decisions that define the framework within which operating decisions will be made. They are the starting point for scheduling and production control systems. They provide input for financial plans; they involve forecasting input and demand management, and they may require changes in employment levels. And if the organization is involved in *time-based competition,* it will be important to incorporate some flexibility in the aggregate plan to be able to handle changing requirements promptly. As noted, the plans must fit into the framework established by the organization's long-term goals and strategies, and the limitations established by long-term facility and capital budget decisions. The aggregate plan will guide the more detailed planning that eventually leads to a *master schedule.* Figure 11.1 illustrates the planning sequence.

Aggregate planning also can serve as an important input to other strategic decisions; for example, management may decide to add capacity when aggregate planning alternatives for temporarily increasing capacity, such as working overtime and subcontracting, are too costly.

The Concept of Aggregation

Aggregate planning is essentially a "big-picture" approach to planning. Planners usually try to avoid focusing on individual products or services—unless the organization has only one major product or service. Instead, they focus on a group of similar products or services, or sometimes an entire product or service line. For example, planners in a company producing television sets would not concern themselves with 40-inch sets versus 46-inch or 55-inch sets. Instead, planners would lump all models together and deal with them as though they were a single product, hence the term *aggregate* planning. Thus, when fast-food companies such as McDonald's, Burger King, or Wendy's plan employment and output levels, they don't try to determine how demand will be broken down into the various menu options they offer; they focus on overall demand and the overall capacity they want to provide.

Now consider how aggregate planning might work in a large department store. Space allocation is often an aggregate decision. That is, a manager might decide to allocate 20 percent of the available space in the clothing department to women's sportswear, 30 percent to juniors, and so on, without regard for what brand names will be offered or how much of juniors will be jeans. The aggregate measure might be square feet of space or racks of clothing.

For purposes of aggregate planning, it is often convenient to think of capacity in terms of labor hours or machine hours per period, or output rates (barrels per period, units per period), without worrying about how much of a particular item will actually be involved. This approach frees planners to make general decisions about the use of resources without having to get into the complexities of individual product or service requirements. Product groupings make the problem of obtaining an acceptable unit of aggregation easier because product groupings may lend themselves to the same aggregate measures.

Why do organizations need to do aggregate planning? The answer is twofold. One part is related to *planning:* It takes time to implement plans. For instance, if plans call for hiring (and training) new workers, that will take time. The second part is strategic: *Aggregation* is important because it is not possible to predict with any degree of accuracy the timing and volume of demand for individual items. So if an organization were to "lock in" on individual items, it would lose the flexibility to respond to the market.

Generally speaking, aggregate planning is connected to the budgeting process. Most organizations plan their financial requirements annually on a department-by-department basis.

Finally, aggregate planning is important because it can help synchronize flow throughout the supply chain; it affects costs, equipment utilization, employment levels, and customer satisfaction.

A key issue in aggregate planning is how to handle variations.

Dealing with Variations

As in other areas of business management, variations in either supply or demand can occur. Minor variations are usually not a problem, but large variations generally have a major impact on the ability to match supply and demand, so they must be dealt with. Most organizations use rolling 3-, 6-, 9-, and 12-month forecasts—forecasts that are updated periodically—rather than relying on a once-a-year forecast. This allows planners to take into account any changes in either expected demand or expected supply and to develop revised plans.

Some businesses tend to exhibit a fair degree of stability, whereas in others, variations are more the norm. In those instances, a number of strategies are used to counter variations. One is to maintain a certain amount of excess capacity to handle increases in demand. This strategy makes sense when the opportunity cost of lost revenue greatly exceeds the cost of maintaining excess capacity. Another strategy is to maintain a degree of flexibility in dealing with changes. That might involve hiring temporary workers and/or working overtime when needed. Organizations that experience seasonal demands typically use this approach. Some of the design strategies mentioned in Chapter 4, such as delayed differentiation and modular design, may also be options. Still another strategy is to wait as long as possible before committing to a certain level of supply capability. This might involve scheduling products or services with known demands first, which allows some time to pass, shortening the time horizon, and perhaps enabling demands for the remaining products or services to become less uncertain.

An Overview of Aggregate Planning

Aggregate planning begins with a forecast of aggregate demand for the intermediate range. This is followed by a general plan to meet demand requirements by setting output, employment, and finished-goods inventory levels or service capacities. Managers might consider a number of plans, each of which must be examined in light of feasibility and cost. If a plan is reasonably good but has minor difficulties, it may be reworked. Conversely, a poor plan should be discarded and alternative plans considered until an acceptable one is uncovered. The production plan is essentially the output of aggregate planning.

Aggregate plans are updated periodically, often monthly, to take into account updated forecasts and other changes. This results in a *rolling planning horizon* (i.e., the aggregate plan always covers the next 12 to 18 months).

TABLE 11.2
Aggregate planning inputs and outputs

Inputs	Outputs
Resources	Total cost of a plan
Workforce/production rates	Projected levels of
Facilities and equipment	Inventory
Demand forecast	Output
Policies on workforce changes	Employment
Subcontracting	Subcontracting
Overtime	Backordering
Inventory levels/changes	
Back orders	
Costs	
Inventory carrying cost	
Back orders	
Hiring/firing	
Overtime	
Inventory changes	
Subcontracting	

Demand and Supply. Aggregate planners are concerned with the *quantity* and the *timing* of expected demand. If total expected demand for the planning period is much different from available capacity over that same period, the major approach of planners will be to try to achieve a balance by altering capacity, demand, or both. On the other hand, even if capacity and demand are approximately equal for the planning horizon as a whole, planners may still be faced with the problem of dealing with uneven demand *within* the planning interval. In some periods, expected demand may exceed projected capacity, in others expected demand may be less than projected capacity, and in some periods the two may be equal. The task of aggregate planners is to achieve rough equality of demand and capacity over the entire planning horizon. Moreover, planners are usually concerned with minimizing the cost of the aggregate plan, although cost is not the only consideration.

Inputs to Aggregate Planning. Effective aggregate planning requires good *information.* First, the available resources over the planning period must be known. Then, a forecast of expected demand must be available. Finally, planners must take into account any policies regarding changes in employment levels (e.g., some organizations view layoffs as extremely undesirable, so they would use that only as a last resort).

Table 11.2 lists the major inputs to aggregate planning.

Companies in the travel industry and some other industries often experience duplicate orders from customers who make multiple reservations but only intend to keep at most one of them. This makes capacity planning all the more difficult.

Aggregate Planning and the Supply Chain

SUPPLY CHAIN

It is essential to take supply chain capabilities into account when doing aggregate planning, to assure that there are no quantity or timing issues that need to be resolved. While this is particularly true if new or changed goods or services are involved, it is also true even when no changes are planned. Supply chain partners should be consulted during the planning stage so that any issues or advice they may have can be taken into account, and they should be informed when plans have been finalized.

Duplicate Orders Can Lead to Excess Capacity

READING

We've all heard about someone who booked seats on two airlines, or reserved two hotel rooms, usually because travel plans weren't firmed up, but the person didn't want to miss out on the trip. Later, the person canceled one set of reservations. This sort of duplicate ordering isn't just limited to the travel industry. The trouble is, companies base their capacity planning on demand estimates, and when there are numerous duplicate orders, it is easy to overestimate demand and end up with excess capacity. In some instances, this has led companies to expand at a time when demand was actually leveling off or even decreasing! The problem is further compounded if companies conclude that canceled orders reflect customers' reluctance to wait, and respond by *adding* capacity when, in fact, order cancellation may actually reflect duplicate ordering.

Some semiconductor companies downplay data on bookings because it is too difficult to distinguish between duplicate orders and actual demand.

Yet it is important to account for double orders. Otherwise, by counting duplicate orders as true demand, you overestimate the demand rate, and by counting the cancellations of duplicate orders as lost sales, you overestimate customers' sensitivity to delay, and then you wind up with excess capacity.

"The optimal level of capacity increases with customers' sensitivity to delay, so estimating customers' sensitivity to delay is a very important part of the puzzle."

Duplicate orders can make capacity planning very difficult. The key is to carefully estimate both the rate of duplicate ordering and the degree of order cancellation that can be attributed to duplicate ordering.

Source: Based on Mor Armony and Erica L. Plambeck, "The Impact of Duplicate Orders on Demand Estimation and Capacity Investment," GSB Research Paper #1740, Graduate School of Business, Stanford University, June 2002.

Demand and Supply Options

Aggregate planning strategies can be described as proactive, reactive, or mixed. *Proactive* strategies involve demand options: They attempt to alter demand so that it matches capacity. *Reactive* strategies involve capacity options: They attempt to alter capacity so that it matches demand. *Mixed* strategies involve an element of each of these approaches.

Demand Options. Demand options include pricing, promotions, using back orders (delaying order filling), and creating new demand.

SERVICE

1. **Pricing.** Pricing differentials are commonly used to shift demand from peak periods to off-peak periods. Some hotels, for example, offer lower rates for weekend stays, and some airlines offer lower fares for night travel. Movie theaters may offer reduced rates for matinees, and some restaurants offer "early bird specials" in an attempt to shift some of the heavier dinner demand to an earlier time that traditionally has less traffic. Some restaurants also offer smaller portions at reduced rates, and most have smaller portions and prices for children. To the extent that pricing is effective, demand will be shifted so that it corresponds more closely to capacity, albeit for an *opportunity cost* that represents the lost profit stemming from capacity insufficient to meet demand during certain periods.

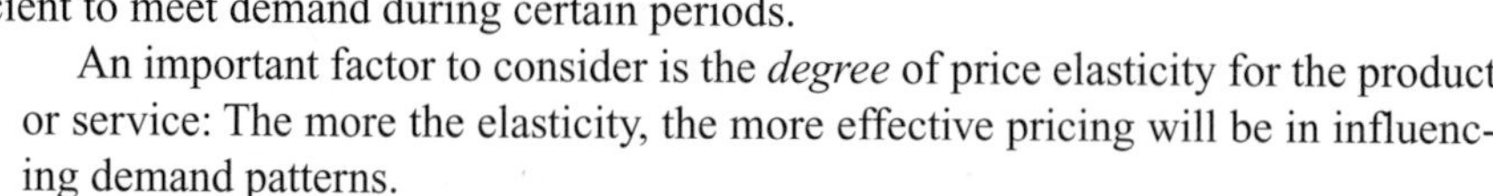

An important factor to consider is the *degree* of price elasticity for the product or service: The more the elasticity, the more effective pricing will be in influencing demand patterns.

2. **Promotion.** Advertising and other forms of promotion, such as displays and direct marketing, can sometimes be very effective in shifting demand so that it conforms more closely to capacity. Obviously, timing of these efforts and knowledge of response rates and response patterns will be needed to achieve the desired results. Unlike pricing policy, there is much less control over the timing of demand, so there is the risk that promotion can worsen the condition it was intended to improve, by bringing in demand at the wrong time, further stressing capacity.

3. **Back orders.** An organization can shift demand fulfillment to other periods by allowing back orders. That is, orders are taken in one period and deliveries promised for a later period. The success of this approach depends on how willing customers are to wait for delivery. Moreover, the costs associated with back

orders can be difficult to pin down since they would include lost sales, annoyed or disappointed customers, and perhaps additional paperwork.

4. **New demand.** Many organizations are faced with the problem of having to provide products or services for peak demand in situations where demand is very uneven. For instance, demand for bus transportation tends to be more intense during the morning and late afternoon rush hours but much lighter at other times. Creating new demand for buses at other times (e.g., trips by schools, clubs, and senior citizen groups) would make use of the excess capacity during those slack times. Similarly, many fast-food restaurants are open for breakfast to use their capacities more fully, and some landscaping firms in northern climates use their equipment during the winter months for snow removal. Manufacturing firms that experience seasonal demands for certain products (e.g., snowblowers) are sometimes able to develop a demand for a complementary product (e.g., lawn mowers, garden equipment) that makes use of the same production processes. They thereby achieve a more consistent use of labor, equipment, and facilities. Another option may be "insourcing" work from another organization.

Supply Options. Supply options include hiring/laying off workers, overtime/slack time, part-time or temporary workers, inventories, and subcontractors.

1. **Hire and lay off workers.** The extent to which operations are labor intensive determines the impact that changes in the workforce level will have on capacity. The resource requirements of each worker also can be a factor. For instance, if a supermarket usually has 10 of 14 checkout lines operating, an additional four checkout workers could be added. Hence, the ability to add workers is constrained at some point by other resources needed to support the workers. Conversely, there may be a lower limit on the number of workers needed to maintain a viable operation (e.g., a skeleton crew).

Union contracts may restrict the amount of hiring and laying off a company can do. Moreover, because laying off can present serious problems for workers, some firms have policies that either prohibit or limit downward adjustments to a workforce. On the other hand, hiring presumes an available supply of workers. This may change from time to time and, at times of low supply, have an impact on the ability of an organization to pursue this approach.

Another consideration is the skill level of workers. Highly skilled workers are generally more difficult to find than lower-skilled workers, and recruiting them involves greater costs. So the usefulness of this option may be limited by the need for highly skilled workers.

Use of hiring and laying off entails certain costs. Hiring costs include recruitment, screening, and training to bring new workers "up to speed." And quality may suffer. Some savings may occur if workers who have recently been laid off are rehired. Layoff costs include severance pay, the cost of realigning the remaining workforce, potential bad feelings toward the firm on the part of workers who have been laid off, and some loss of morale for workers who are retained (i.e., in spite of company assurances, some workers will believe that in time they too will be laid off).

An increasing number of organizations view workers as assets rather than as variable costs, and would not consider this approach. Instead, they might use slack time for other purposes.

2. **Overtime/slack time.** Use of overtime or slack time is a less severe method for changing capacity than hiring and laying off workers, and it can be used across the board or selectively as needed. It also can be implemented more quickly than hiring and laying off and allows the firm to maintain a steady base of employees. The use of overtime can be especially attractive in dealing with seasonal demand peaks by reducing the need to hire and train people who will have to be laid off during the off-season. Overtime also permits the company to maintain a skilled workforce and employees to increase earnings, and companies may save money because fringe and other benefits are generally fixed. Moreover, in situations with crews, it is often necessary to use a full crew rather than to hire one or two additional people. Thus, having the entire crew work overtime would be preferable to hiring extra people.

It should be noted that some union contracts allow workers to refuse overtime. In those cases, it may be difficult to muster a full crew to work overtime or to get an entire production line into operation after regular hours. Although workers often like the additional income overtime can generate, they may not appreciate having to work on short notice or the fluctuations in income that result. Still other considerations relate to the fact that overtime often results in lower productivity, poorer quality, more accidents, and increased payroll costs, whereas idle time results in less efficient use of machines and other fixed assets.

The use of slack when demand is less than capacity can be an important consideration. Some organizations use this time for training. It also can give workers time for problem solving and process improvement, while retraining skilled workers.

3. **Part-time workers.** In certain instances, the use of part-time workers is a viable option—much depends on the nature of the work, training and skills needed, and union agreements. Seasonal work requiring low-to-moderate job skills lends itself to part-time workers, who generally cost less than regular workers in hourly wages and fringe benefits. However, unions may regard such workers unfavorably because they typically do not pay union dues and may lessen the power of unions. Department stores, restaurants, and supermarkets make use of part-time workers. So do parks and recreation departments, resorts, travel agencies, hotels, and other service organizations with seasonal demands. In order to be successful, these organizations must be able to hire part-time employees when they are needed.

Some companies use contract workers, also called *independent contractors,* to fill certain needs. Although they are not regular employees, often they work alongside regular workers. In addition to having different pay scales and no benefits, they can be added or subtracted from the workforce with greater ease than regular workers, giving companies great flexibility in adjusting the size of the workforce.

4. **Inventories.** The use of finished-goods inventories allows firms to produce goods in one period and sell or ship them in another period, although this involves holding or carrying those goods as inventory until they are needed. The cost includes not only storage costs and the cost of money tied up that could be invested elsewhere, but also the cost of insurance, obsolescence, deterioration, spoilage, breakage, and so on. In essence, inventories can be built

Amazon is very aggressive about managing its inventory levels. This may mean that rarely ordered items are not kept in inventory and may require time to source from a supplier. It also means that Amazon tries to move inventory out to customers as quickly as possible.

up during periods when production capacity exceeds demand and drawn down in periods when demand exceeds production capacity.

This method is more amenable to manufacturing than to service industries since manufactured goods can be stored whereas services generally cannot. However, an analogous approach used by services is to make efforts to streamline services (e.g., standard forms) or otherwise do a portion of the service during slack periods (e.g., organize the workplace). In spite of these possibilities, services tend not to make much use of inventories to alter capacity requirements.

5. **Subcontracting.** Subcontracting enables planners to acquire temporary capacity, although it affords less control over the output and may lead to higher costs and quality problems. The question of whether to make or buy (i.e., in manufacturing) or to perform a service or hire someone else to do the work generally depends on factors such as available capacity, relative expertise, quality considerations, cost, and the amount and stability of demand.

Conversely, in periods of excess capacity, an organization may subcontract *in,* that is, conduct work for another organization. As an alternative to subcontracting, an organization might consider *outsourcing:* contracting with another organization to supply some portion of the goods or services on a regular basis.

BASIC STRATEGIES FOR MEETING UNEVEN DEMAND

As you see, managers have a wide range of decision options they can consider for achieving a balance of demand and capacity in aggregate planning. Since the options that are most suited to influencing demand fall more in the realm of marketing than in operations (with the exception of backlogging), we shall concentrate on the capacity options, which are in the realm of operations but include the use of back orders.

SCREENCAM TUTORIAL

Aggregate planners might adopt a number of strategies. Some of the more prominent ones are the following:

1. Maintain a level workforce.
2. Maintain a steady output rate.
3. Match demand period by period.
4. Use a combination of decision variables.

While other strategies might be considered, these will suffice to give you a sense of how aggregate planning operates in a vast number of organizations. The first three strategies are "pure" strategies because each has a single focal point; the last strategy is "mixed" because it lacks the single focus. Under a **level capacity strategy,** variations in demand are met by using some combination of inventories, overtime, part-time workers, subcontracting, and back orders while maintaining a steady rate of output. Matching capacity to demand implies a **chase demand strategy;** the planned output for any period would be equal to expected demand for that period.

Level capacity strategy Maintaining a steady rate of regular-time output while meeting variations in demand by a combination of options.

Chase demand strategy Matching capacity to demand; the planned output for a period is set at the expected demand for that period.

Many organizations regard a level workforce as very appealing. Since workforce changes through hiring and laying off can have a major impact on the lives and morale of employees and can be disruptive for managers, organizations often prefer to handle uneven demand in other ways. Moreover, changes in workforce size can be very costly, and there is always the risk that there will not be a sufficient pool of workers with the appropriate skills when needed. Aside from these considerations, such changes can involve a significant amount of paperwork. Unions tend to favor a level workforce because the freedom to hire and lay off workers diminishes union strengths.

To maintain a constant level of output and still satisfy varying demand, an organization must resort to some combination of subcontracting, backlogging, and use of inventories to absorb fluctuations. Subcontracting requires an investment in evaluating sources of supply as well as possible increased costs, less control over output, and perhaps quality considerations.

SERVICE

Backlogs can lead to lost sales, increased record keeping, and lower levels of customer service. Allowing inventories to absorb fluctuations can entail substantial costs by having money tied up in inventories, having to maintain relatively large storage facilities, and incurring other costs related to inventories. Furthermore, inventories are not usually an alternative for service-oriented organizations. However, there are certain advantages, such as minimum costs of recruitment and training, minimum overtime and idle-time costs, fewer morale problems, and stable use of equipment and facilities.

A chase demand strategy presupposes a great deal of ability and willingness on the part of managers to be flexible in adjusting to demand. A major advantage of this approach is that inventories can be kept relatively low, which can yield substantial savings for an organization. A major disadvantage is the lack of stability in operations—the atmosphere is one of dancing to demand's tune. Also, when forecast and reality differ, morale can suffer, since it quickly becomes obvious to workers and managers that efforts have been wasted. Figure 11.2 provides

FIGURE 11.2 A varying demand pattern and a comparison of a chase demand strategy versus a level strategy

A. A possible uneven demand pattern

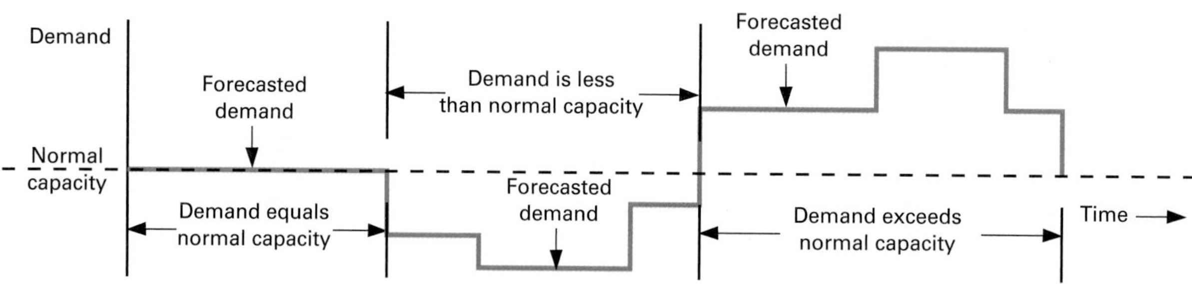

B. Two strategies

Chase demand strategy
(output matches demand)

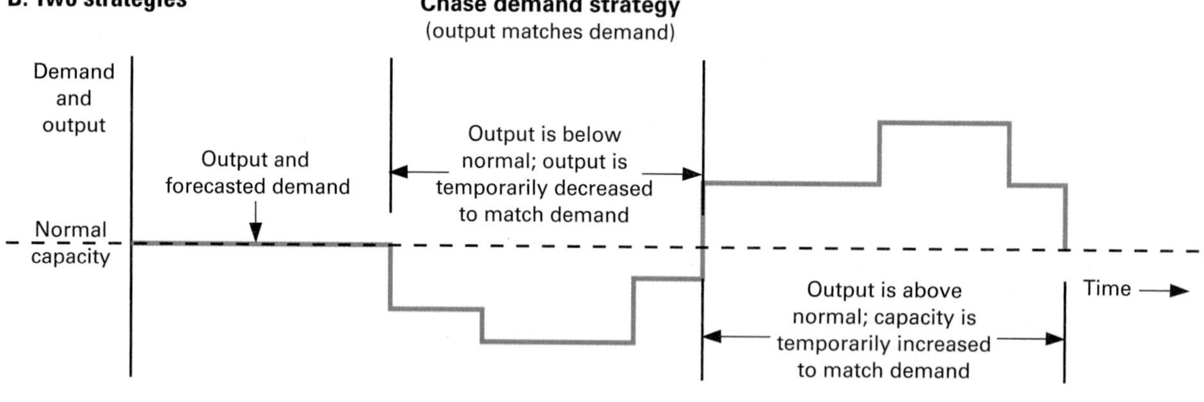

Level output strategy

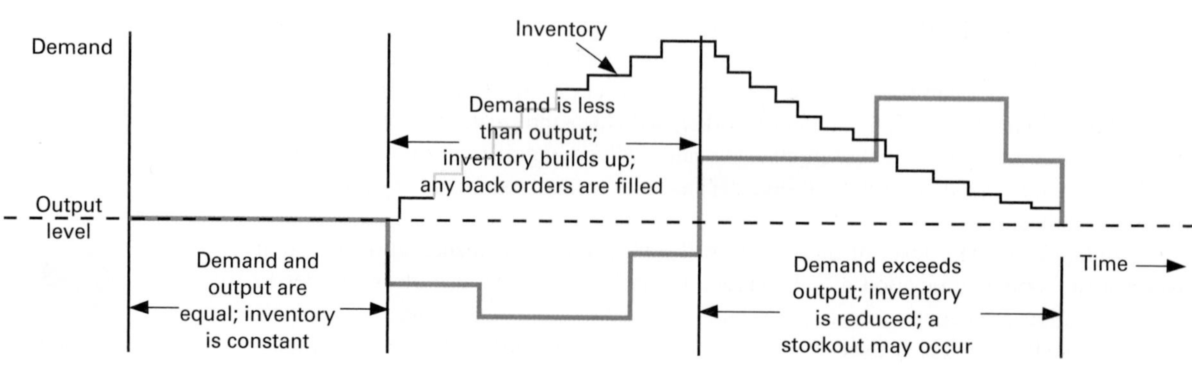

a comparison of the two strategies, using a varying demand pattern to highlight the differences in the two approaches. The same demand pattern is used for each approach. In the upper portion of the figure the pattern is shown. Notice that there are three situations: (1) demand and capacity are equal; (2) demand is less than capacity; and (3) demand exceeds capacity.

The middle portion of the figure illustrates what happens with a chase approach. When normal capacity would exceed demand, capacity is cut back to match demand. Then, when demand exceeds normal capacity, the chase approach is to temporarily increase capacity to match demand.

The bottom portion of the figure illustrates the level-output strategy. When demand is less than capacity, output continues at normal capacity, and the excess output is put into inventory in anticipation of the time when demand exceeds capacity. When demand exceeds capacity, inventory is used to offset the shortfall in output.

Organizations may opt for a strategy that involves some combination of the pure strategies. This allows managers greater flexibility in dealing with uneven demand and perhaps in experimenting with a wide variety of approaches. However, the absence of a clear focus may lead to an erratic approach and confusion on the part of employees.

Choosing a Strategy

Whatever strategy an organization is considering, three important factors are *company policy, flexibility,* and *costs.* Company policy may set constraints on the available options or the extent to which they can be used. For instance, company policy may discourage layoffs except under extreme conditions. Subcontracting may not be a viable alternative due to the desire to maintain secrecy about some aspect of the manufacturing of the product (e.g., a secret formula or blending process). Union agreements often impose restrictions. For example, a union contract may specify both minimum and maximum numbers of hours part-time workers can be used. The degree of flexibility needed to use the chase approach may not be present for companies designed for high, steady output, such as refineries and auto assembly plants.

As a rule, aggregate planners seek to match supply and demand within the constraints imposed on them by policies or agreements and at minimum cost. They usually evaluate alternatives in terms of their overall costs. Table 11.3 compares reactive strategies. In the next section, a number of techniques for aggregate planning are described and presented with some examples of cost evaluation of alternative plans.

TABLE 11.3
Comparison of reactive strategies

Chase approach

Capacities (workforce levels, output rates, etc.) are adjusted to match demand requirements over the planning horizon. A chase strategy works best when inventory carrying costs are high and costs of changing capacity are low.

Advantages:

Investment in inventory is low.

Labor utilization is kept high.

Disadvantage:

The cost of adjusting output rates and/or workforce levels.

Level approach

Capacities (workforce levels, output rates, etc.) are kept constant over the planning horizon. A level strategy works best when inventory carrying costs and backlog costs are relatively low.

Advantage:

Stable output rates and workforce levels.

Disadvantages:

Greater inventory costs.

Increased overtime and idle time.

Resource utilizations that vary over time.

SCREENCAM TUTORIAL

TECHNIQUES FOR AGGREGATE PLANNING

Numerous techniques are available to help with the task of aggregate planning. Generally, they fall into one of two categories: Informal trial-and-error techniques and mathematical techniques. In practice, informal techniques are more frequently used. However, a considerable amount of research has been devoted to mathematical techniques, and even though they are not as widely used, they often serve as a basis for comparing the effectiveness of alternative techniques for aggregate planning. Thus, it will be instructive to briefly examine them as well as the informal techniques.

A general procedure for aggregate planning consists of the following steps:

1. Determine demand for each period.
2. Determine capacities (regular time, overtime, subcontracting) for each period.
3. Identify company or departmental policies that are pertinent (e.g., maintain a safety stock of 5 percent of demand, maintain a reasonably stable workforce).
4. Determine unit costs for regular time, overtime, subcontracting, holding inventories, back orders, layoffs, and other relevant costs.
5. Develop alternative plans and compute the cost for each.
6. If satisfactory plans emerge, select the one that best satisfies objectives. Otherwise, return to step 5.

It can be helpful to use a worksheet or spreadsheet, such as the one illustrated in Table 11.4, to summarize demand, capacity, and cost for each plan. In addition, graphs can be used to guide development of alternatives.

Trial-and-Error Techniques Using Graphs and Spreadsheets

Trial-and-error approaches consist of developing simple tables or graphs that enable planners to visually compare projected demand requirements with existing capacity. Alternatives are usually evaluated in terms of their overall costs. The chief disadvantage of such techniques is that they do not necessarily result in the optimal aggregate plan.

Two examples illustrate the development and comparison of aggregate plans. In the first example, regular output is held steady, with inventory absorbing demand variations. In the second example, a lower rate of regular output is used, supplemented by use of overtime. In both examples, some backlogs are allowed to build up.

These examples and other examples and problems in this chapter are based on the following assumptions:

1. The regular output capacity is the same in all periods. No allowance is made for holidays, different numbers of workdays in different months, and so on. This assumption simplifies computations.
2. Cost (back order, inventory, subcontracting, etc.) is a linear function composed of unit cost and number of units. This often has a reasonable approximation to reality, although there may be only narrow ranges over which this is true. Cost is sometimes more of a step function.
3. Plans are feasible; that is, sufficient inventory capacity exists to accommodate a plan, subcontractors with appropriate quality and capacity are standing by, and changes in output can be made as needed.
4. All costs associated with a decision option can be represented by a lump sum or by unit costs that are independent of the quantity involved. Again, a step function may be more realistic; but for purposes of illustration and simplicity, this assumption is appropriate.
5. Cost figures can be reasonably estimated and are constant for the planning horizon.

TABLE 11.4
Worksheet/spreadsheet

Period	1	2	3	4	5		Total
Forecast							
Output							
Regular time							
Overtime							
Subcontract							
Output – Forecast							
Inventory							
Beginning							
Ending							
Average							
Backlog							
Costs							
Output							
Regular							
Overtime							
Subcontract							
Hire/Lay off							
Inventory							
Back orders							
Total							

6. Inventories are built up and drawn down at a uniform rate and output occurs at a uniform rate throughout each period. However, backlogs are treated as if they exist for an entire period, even though in periods where they initially appear, they would tend to build up toward the end of the period. Hence, this assumption is a bit unrealistic for some periods, but it simplifies computations.

In the examples and problems in this chapter, we use the following relationships to determine the number of workers, the amount of inventory, and the cost of a particular plan.

The number of workers available in any period is calculated as follows:

$$\begin{matrix}\text{Number of} \\ \text{workers in} \\ \text{a period}\end{matrix} = \begin{matrix}\text{Number of} \\ \text{workers at end of} \\ \text{the previous period}\end{matrix} + \begin{matrix}\text{Number of new} \\ \text{workers at start of} \\ \text{the period}\end{matrix} - \begin{matrix}\text{Number of laid-off} \\ \text{workers at start of} \\ \text{the period}\end{matrix}$$

Note: An organization would not hire and lay off simultaneously, so at least one of the last two terms will equal zero.

The amount of inventory at the end of a given period is calculated as follows:

$$\begin{matrix}\text{Inventory} \\ \text{at the end of} \\ \text{a period}\end{matrix} = \begin{matrix}\text{Inventory} \\ \text{at end of the} \\ \text{previous period}\end{matrix} + \begin{matrix}\text{Production} \\ \text{in the} \\ \text{current period}\end{matrix} - \begin{matrix}\text{Amount used to} \\ \text{satisfy demand in the} \\ \text{current period}\end{matrix}$$

The average inventory for a period is equal to

$$\frac{\text{Beginning inventory} + \text{Ending inventory}}{2}$$

The cost of a particular plan for a given period can be determined by summing the appropriate costs:

$$\begin{matrix}\text{Cost for} \\ \text{a period}\end{matrix} = \begin{matrix}\text{Output cost} \\ (\text{Reg} + \text{OT} + \text{Subcontract})\end{matrix} + \begin{matrix}\text{Hire/lay-off} \\ \text{cost}\end{matrix} + \begin{matrix}\text{Inventory} \\ \text{cost}\end{matrix} + \begin{matrix}\text{Back-order} \\ \text{cost}\end{matrix}$$

The appropriate costs are calculated as follows:

Type of Cost	How to Calculate
Output	
Regular	Regular cost per unit × Quantity of regular output
Overtime	Overtime cost per unit × Overtime quantity
Subcontract	Subcontract cost per unit × Subcontract quantity
Hire/lay off	
Hire	Cost per hire × Number hired
Lay off	Cost per layoff × Number laid off
Inventory	Carrying cost per unit × Average inventory
Back order	Back-order cost per unit × Number of back-order units

The following examples are only two of many possible options that could be tried. Perhaps some of the others would result in a lower cost. With trial and error, you can never be completely sure you have identified the lowest-cost alternative unless every possible alternative is evaluated. Of course, the purpose of these examples is to illustrate the process of developing and evaluating an aggregate plan rather than to find the lowest-cost plan. Problems at the end of the chapter cover still other alternatives.

In practice, successful achievement of a good plan depends on the resourcefulness and persistence of the planner. Computer software such as the Excel templates that accompany this book can eliminate the computational burden of trial-and-error techniques.

EXAMPLE 1

www.mhhe.com/stevenson11e

Planners for a company that makes several models of skateboards are about to prepare the aggregate plan that will cover six periods. They have assembled the following information:

Period	1	2	3	4	5	6	Total
Forecast	200	200	300	400	500	200	1,800

Costs
- Output
  - Regular time = \$2 per skateboard
  - Overtime = \$3 per skateboard
  - Subcontract = \$6 per skateboard
- Inventory = \$1 per skateboard per period on average inventory
- Back orders = \$5 per skateboard per period

They now want to evaluate a plan that calls for a steady rate of regular-time output, mainly using inventory to absorb the uneven demand but allowing some backlog. Overtime and subcontracting are not used because they want steady output. They intend to start with zero inventory on hand in the first period. Prepare an aggregate plan and determine its cost using the preceding information. Assume a level output rate of 300 units (skateboards) per period with regular time (i.e., 1,800/6 = 300). Note that the planned ending inventory is zero. There are 15 workers, and each can produce 20 skateboards per period.

SOLUTION

Period	1	2	3	4	5	6	Total
Forecast	200	200	300	400	500	200	1,800
Output							
Regular	300	300	300	300	300	300	1,800
Overtime	—	—	—	—	—	—	
Subcontract	—	—	—	—	—	—	
Output − Forecast	100	100	0	(100)	(200)	100	0
Inventory							
Beginning	0	100	200	200	100	0	
Ending	100	200	200	100	0	0	
Average	50	150	200	150	50	0	600
Backlog	0	0	0	0	100	0	100

Period	1	2	3	4	5	6	Total
Costs							
Output							
Regular	$600	600	600	600	600	600	$3,600
Overtime	—	—	—	—	—	—	
Subcontract	—	—	—	—	—	—	
Hire/Lay off	—	—	—	—	—	—	
Inventory	$ 50	150	200	150	50	0	$ 600
Back orders	$ 0	0	0	0	500	0	$ 500
Total	$650	750	800	750	1,150	600	$4,700

Note that the total regular-time output of 1,800 units equals the total expected demand. Ending inventory equals beginning inventory plus or minus the quantity Output − Forecast. If Output − Forecast is negative, inventory is decreased in that period by that amount. If insufficient inventory exists, a backlog equal to the shortage amount appears, as in period 5. This is taken care of using the excess output in period 6.

The costs were computed as follows. Regular cost in each period equals 300 units × $2 per unit or $600. Inventory cost equals average inventory × $1 per unit. Back-order cost is $5 per unit. The total cost for this plan is $4,700.

Note that the first two quantities in each column are givens. The remaining quantities in the upper portion of the table were determined working down each column, beginning with the first column. The costs were then computed based on the quantities in the upper part of the table.

Very often, graphs can be used to guide the development of alternatives. Some planners prefer cumulative graphs while others prefer to see a period-by-period breakdown of a plan. For instance, Figure 11.3 shows a cumulative graph for a plan with steady output (the slope of the dashed line represents the production rate) and inventory absorption of demand variations. Figure 11.2 is an example of a period-by-period graph. The obvious advantage of a graph is that it provides a visual portrayal of a plan. The preference of the planner determines which of these two types of graphs is chosen.

EXAMPLE 2

After reviewing the plan developed in the preceding example, planners have decided to develop an alternative plan. They have learned that one person is about to retire from the company. Rather than replace that person, they would like to stay with the smaller workforce and use overtime to make up for the lost output. The reduced regular-time output is 280 units per period. The maximum amount of overtime output per period is 40 units. Develop a plan and compare it to the previous one.

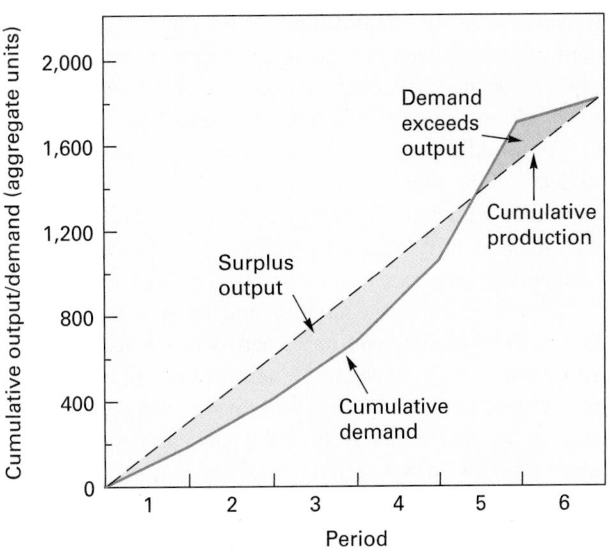

FIGURE 11.3
A cumulative graph

SOLUTION

Period	1	2	3	4	5	6	Total
Forecast	200	200	300	400	500	200	1,800
Output							
Regular	280	280	280	280	280	280	1,680
Overtime	0	0	40	40	40	0	120
Subcontract	—	—	—	—	—	—	
Output – Forecast	80	80	20	(80)	(180)	80	0
Inventory							
Beginning	0	80	160	180	100	0	
Ending	80	160	180	100	0	0	
Average	40	120	170	140	50	0	520
Backlog	0	0	0	0	80	0	80
Costs							
Output							
Regular	$560	560	560	560	560	560	$3,360
Overtime	0	0	120	120	120	0	$ 360
Subcontract	—	—	—	—	—	—	
Hire/Lay off	—	—	—	—	—	—	
Inventory	40	120	170	140	50	0	$ 520
Back orders	$ 0	0	0	0	400	0	$ 400
Total	$600	680	850	820	1,130	560	$4,640

The amount of overtime that must be scheduled has to make up for lost output of 20 units per period for six periods, which is 120. This is scheduled toward the center of the planning horizon since that is where the bulk of demand occurs. Scheduling it earlier would increase inventory carrying costs; scheduling it later would increase the backlog cost.

Overall, the total cost for this plan is $4,640, which is $60 less than the previous plan. Regular-time production cost and inventory cost are down, but there is overtime cost. However, this plan achieves savings in backorder cost, making it somewhat less costly overall than the plan in Example 1.

SCREENCAM TUTORIAL

Mathematical Techniques

A number of mathematical techniques have been developed to handle aggregate planning. They range from mathematical programming models to heuristic and computer search models. This section briefly describes some of the better-known techniques.

Linear Programming. Linear programming (LP) models are methods for obtaining optimal solutions to problems involving the allocation of scarce resources in terms of cost minimization or profit maximization. With aggregate planning, the goal is usually to minimize the sum of costs related to regular labor time, overtime, subcontracting, carrying inventory, and costs associated with changing the size of the workforce. Constraints involve the capacities of the workforce, inventories, and subcontracting.

The problem can be formulated as a transportation-type programming model (described in detail in the supplement to Chapter 8) as a way to obtain aggregate plans that would match capacities with demand requirements and minimize costs. In order to use this approach, planners must identify capacity (supply) of regular time, overtime, subcontracting, and inventory on a period-by-period basis, as well as related costs of each variable.

Table 11.5 shows the notation and setup of a transportation table. Note the systematic way that costs change as you move across a row from left to right. Regular cost, overtime cost, and subcontracting cost are at their lowest when the output is consumed (i.e., delivered, etc.) in the same period it is produced (at the intersection of period 1 row and column for regular cost, at the intersection of period 2 row and column for regular cost, and so on). If goods are made available in one period but carried over to later periods (i.e., moving across a row), holding costs are incurred at the rate of h per period. Thus, holding goods for two periods results in a unit cost of $2h$, whether or not the goods came from regular production, overtime, or subcontracting. Conversely, with back orders, the unit cost increases as you move across a row

TABLE 11.5 Transportation notation for aggregate planning

Period		Period 1	Period 2	Period 3	. . .	Ending inventory period n	Unused capacity	Capacity
	Beginning inventory	0	h	$2h$	. . .	$(n-1)h$	0	I_0
1	Regular time	r	$r+h$	$r+2h$	. . .	$r+(n-1)h$	0	R_1
	Overtime	t	$t+h$	$t+2h$	. . .	$t+(n-1)h$	0	O_1
	Subcontract	s	$s+h$	$s+2h$	. . .	$s+(n-1)h$	0	S_1
2	Regular time	$r+b$	r	$r+h$	. . .	$r+(n-2)h$	0	R_2
	Overtime	$t+b$	t	$t+h$	. . .	$t+(n-2)h$	0	O_2
	Subcontract	$s+b$	s	$s+h$	. . .	$s+(n-2)h$	0	S_2
3	Regular time	$r+2b$	$r+b$	r	. . .	$r+(n-3)h$	0	R_3
	Overtime	$t+2b$	$t+b$	t	. . .	$t+(n-3)h$	0	O_3
	Subcontract	$s+2b$	$s+b$	s	. . .	$s+(n-3)h$	0	S_3
	Demand				. . .			Total

r = Regular production cost per unit
t = Overtime cost per unit
s = Subcontracting cost per unit
h = Holding cost per unit period
b = Back order cost per unit per period
n = Number of periods in planning horizon

from right to left, beginning at the intersection of a row and column for the same period (e.g., period 3). For instance, if some goods are produced in period 3 to satisfy back orders from period 2, a unit back-order cost of b is incurred. And if goods in period 3 are used to satisfy back orders two periods earlier (e.g., from period 1), a unit cost of $2b$ is incurred. Unused capacity is generally given a unit cost of 0, although it is certainly possible to insert an actual cost if that is relevant. Finally, beginning inventory is given a unit cost of 0 if it is used to satisfy demand in period 1. However, if it is held over for use in later periods, a holding cost of h per unit is added for each period. If the inventory is to be held for the entire planning horizon, a total unit cost of h times the number of periods, n, will be incurred.

Example 3 illustrates the setup and final solution of a transportation model of an aggregate planning problem.

EXAMPLE 3

Given the following information set up the problem in a transportation table and solve for the minimum-cost plan:

	PERIOD 1	2	3
Demand	550	700	750
Capacity			
Regular	500	500	500
Overtime	50	50	50
Subcontract	120	120	100
Beginning inventory	100		
Costs			
Regular time	\$60 per unit		
Overtime	\$80 per unit		
Subcontract	\$90 per unit		
Inventory carrying cost	\$1 per unit per month		
Back-order cost	\$3 per unit per month		

SOLUTION

The transportation table and solution are shown in Table 11.6. Some of the entries require additional explanation:

a. In this example, inventory carrying costs are $1 per unit per period (costs are shown in the upper right-hand corner of each cell in the table). Hence, units produced in one period and carried over to a later period will incur a holding cost that is a linear function of the length of time held.

b. Linear programming models of this type require that supply (capacity) and demand be equal. A dummy column has been added (nonexistent capacity) to satisfy that requirement. Since it does not "cost" anything extra to not use capacity in this case, cell costs of $0 have been assigned.

c. No backlogs were needed in this example.

d. The quantities (e.g., 100 and 450 in column 1) are the amounts of output or inventory that will be used to meet demand requirements. Thus, the demand of 550 units in period 1 will be met using 100 units from inventory and 450 obtained from regular-time output.

Where backlogs are not permitted, the cell costs for the backlog positions can be made prohibitively high so that no backlogs will appear in the solution.

The main limitations of LP models are the assumptions of linear relationships among variables, the inability to continuously adjust output rates, and the need to specify a single objective (e.g., minimize costs) instead of using multiple objectives (e.g., minimize cost while stabilizing the workforce).

TABLE 11.6
Transportation solution

Period	Supply from	Demand for: Period 1	Period 2	Period 3	Unused capacity (dummy)	Total capacity available (supply)
	Beginning inventory	[0] 100	[1]	[2]	[0]	100
1	Regular time	[60] 450	[61] 50	[62]	[0]	500
	Overtime	[80]	[81] 50	[82]	[0]	50
	Subcontract	[90]	[91] 30	[92]	[0] 90	120
2	Regular time	[63]	[60] 500	[61]	[0]	500
	Overtime	[83]	[80] 50	[81]	[0]	50
	Subcontract	[93]	[90] 20	[91] 100	[0]	120
3	Regular time	[66]	[63]	[60] 500	[0]	500
	Overtime	[86]	[83]	[80] 50	[0]	50
	Subcontract	[96]	[93]	[90] 100	[0]	100
	Demand	550	700	750	90	2,090

TABLE 11.7
Summary of planning techniques

Technique	Solution Approach	Characteristics
Spreadsheet	Heuristic (trial and error)	Intuitively appealing, easy to understand; solution not necessarily optimal
Linear programming	Optimizing	Computerized; linear assumptions not always valid
Simulation	Heuristic (trial and error)	Computerized models can be examined under a variety of conditions

Simulation Models. A number of **simulation models** have been developed for aggregate planning. (Simulation is described in detail on the textbook Web site.) The essence of simulation is the development of computerized models that can be tested under a variety of conditions in an attempt to identify reasonably acceptable (although not always optimal) solutions to problems.

Simulation models Computerized models that can be tested under different scenarios to identify acceptable solutions to problems.

Table 11.7 summarizes planning techniques.

Aggregate planning techniques other than trial and error do not appear to be widely used. Instead, in the majority of organizations, aggregate planning seems to be accomplished more on the basis of experience along with trial-and-error methods. It is difficult to say exactly why some of the mathematical techniques mentioned are not used to any great extent. Perhaps the level of mathematical sophistication discourages greater use, or the assumptions required in certain models appear unrealistic, or the models may be too narrow in scope. Whatever the reasons, none of the techniques to date have captured the attention of aggregate planners on a broad scale. Simulation is one technique that seems to be gaining favor. Research on improved approaches to aggregate planning is continuing.

SERVICE

AGGREGATE PLANNING IN SERVICES

Aggregate planning for services takes into account projected customer demands, equipment capacities, and labor capabilities. The resulting plan is a time-phased projection of service staff requirements.

Here are examples of service organizations that use aggregate planning:

Hospitals: Hospitals use aggregate planning to allocate funds, staff, and supplies to meet the demands of patients for their medical services. For example, plans for bed capacity, medications, surgical supplies, and personnel needs are based on patient load forecasts.

Airlines: Aggregate planning in the airline industry is fairly complex due to the need to take into account a wide range of factors (planes, flight personnel, ground personnel) and multiple routes and landing/departure sites. Also, capacity decisions must take into account the percentage of seats to be allocated to various fare classes in order to maximize profit or yield.

Restaurants: Aggregate planning in the case of a high-volume product output business such as a restaurant is directed toward smoothing the service rate, determining the size of the workforce, and managing demand to match a fixed capacity. The general approach usually involves building inventory during slack periods and depleting it during peak periods. Because this is very similar to manufacturing, traditional aggregate planning methods

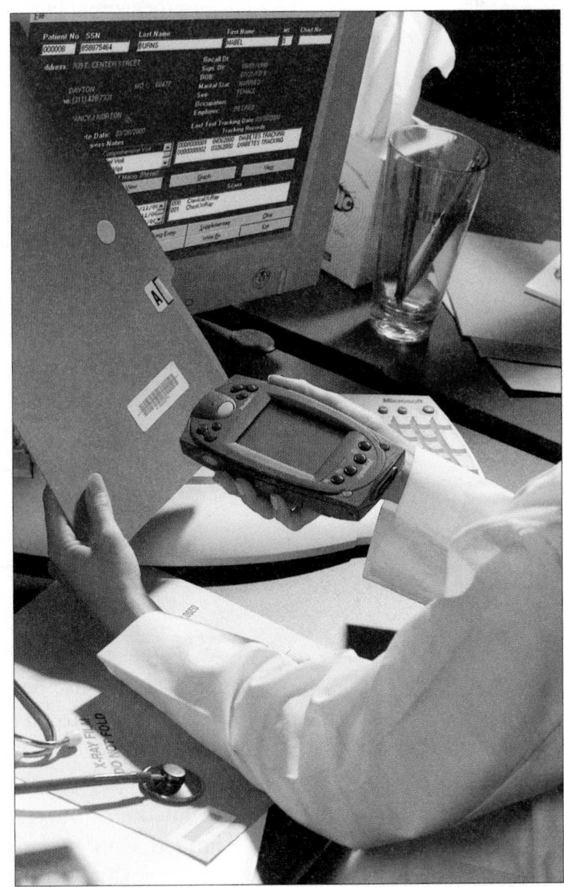

can be applied, although two differences must be taken into account. One difference is that in restaurants, inventory is perishable: Cooked food can be held for only a very short time. Another difference, particularly in fast-food restaurants, is that peak and slack periods occur often and are relatively short-lived.

Other services: Financial, hospitality, transportation, and recreation services provide a high-volume, intangible output. Aggregate planning for these and similar services involves managing demand and planning for human resource requirements. The main goals are to accommodate peak demand and to find ways to effectively use labor resources during periods of low demand.

Aggregate planning for manufacturing and aggregate planning for services share similarities in some respects, but there are some important differences—related in general to the differences between manufacturing and services:

1. **Demand for service can be difficult to predict.** The volume of demand for services is often quite variable. In some situations, customers may *need* prompt service (e.g., police, fire, medical emergency), while in others, they simply *want* prompt service and may be willing to go elsewhere if their wants are not met. These factors place a greater burden on service providers to anticipate demand. Consequently, service providers must pay careful attention to planned capacity levels.
2. **Capacity availability can be difficult to predict.** Processing requirements for services can sometimes be quite variable, similar to the variability of work in a job shop setting. Moreover, the variety of tasks required of servers can be great, again similar to the variety of tasks in a job shop. However, in services, the types of variety are more pervasive than they are in manufacturing. This makes it more difficult to establish simple measures of capacity. For example, what would be the capacity of a person who paints interiors of houses? The number of rooms per day or the number of square feet per hour are possible measures, but rooms come in many different sizes, and because the level of detail (and, thus, the painting implements that can be used) vary tremendously, a suitable measure for planning purposes can be quite difficult to arrive at. Similarly, bank tellers are called upon to handle a wide variety of transactions and requests for information, again making it difficult to establish a suitable measure of their capacity.
3. **Labor flexibility can be an advantage in services.** Labor often comprises a significant portion of service compared to manufacturing. That, coupled with the fact that service providers are often able to handle a fairly wide variety of service requirements, means that to some extent, planning is easier than it is in manufacturing. Of course, manufacturers recognize this advantage, and many are cross-training their employees to achieve the same flexibility. Moreover, in both manufacturing and service systems, the use of part-time workers can be an important option. Note that in self-service systems, the (customer) labor automatically adjusts to changes in demand!
4. **Services occur when they are rendered.** Unlike manufacturing output, most services can't be inventoried. Services such as financial planning, tax counseling, and oil changes can't be stockpiled. This removes the option of building up inventories during a slow period in anticipation of future demand. Moreover, service capacity that goes unused is essentially wasted. Consequently, it becomes even more important to be able to match capacity and demand.

Yield management The application of pricing strategies to allocate capacity among various categories of demand.

Because service capacity is perishable (e.g., an empty seat on an airplane flight can't be saved for use on another flight), aggregate planners need to take that into account when deciding how to match supply and demand. **Yield management** is an approach that seeks to maximize revenue by using a strategy of variable pricing; prices are set relative to capacity availability. Thus, during periods of low demand, price discounts are offered to attract a wider population. Conversely, during peak periods, higher prices are posted to take advantage of limited supply relative to demand. Users of yield management include airlines, restaurants, theaters, hotels, resorts, cruise lines, and parking lots.

DISAGGREGATING THE AGGREGATE PLAN

For the production plan to be translated into meaningful terms for production, it is necessary to *disaggregate* the aggregate plan. This means breaking down the aggregate plan into specific product requirements in order to determine labor requirements (skills, size of workforce), materials, and inventory requirements. This process is described in Chapter 12. At this stage, however, it will be helpful for you to have some understanding of the need for disaggregation and what the term implies.

Working with aggregate units facilitates intermediate planning. However, to put the production plan into operation, one must convert, or decompose, those aggregate units into units of actual products or services that are to be produced or offered. For example, a lawn mower manufacturer may have an aggregate plan that calls for 200 lawn mowers in January, 300 in February, and 400 in March. That company may produce push mowers, self-propelled mowers, and riding mowers. Although all the mowers probably contain some of the same parts and involve some similar or identical operations for fabrication and assembly, there would be some differences in the materials, parts, and operations that each type requires. Hence, the 200, 300, and 400 aggregate lawn mowers that are to be produced during those three months must be translated into specific numbers of mowers of each type prior to actually purchasing the appropriate materials and parts, scheduling operations, and planning inventory requirements.

The result of disaggregating the aggregate plan is a **master production schedule (MPS)**, or simply master schedule, showing the quantity and timing of *specific* end items for a scheduled horizon, which often covers about six to eight weeks ahead. A master schedule shows the planned output for individual products rather than an entire product group, along with the timing of production. The master schedule contains important information for marketing as well as for production. It reveals when orders are scheduled for production and when completed orders are to be shipped.

Figure 11.4 shows an overview of the context of disaggregation.

Figure 11.5 illustrates disaggregating the aggregate plan. The illustration makes a simple assumption in order to clearly show the concept of disaggregation: The totals of the aggregate and the disaggregated units are equal. In reality, that is not always true. As a consequence, disaggregating the aggregate plan may require considerable effort.

Figure 11.5 shows the aggregate plan broken down by units. However, it also can be useful to show the breakdown in *percentages* for different products or product families.

FIGURE 11.4
Moving from the aggregate plan to a master production schedule

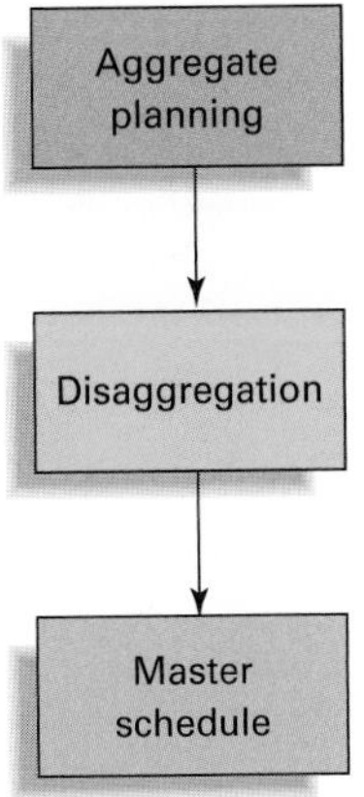

Master production schedule (MPS) This schedule indicates the quantity and timing of planned completed production.

MASTER SCHEDULING

The master schedule is the heart of production planning and control. It determines the quantities needed to meet demand from all sources, and that governs key decisions and activities throughout the organization.

FIGURE 11.5
Disaggregating the aggregate plan

Aggregate plan	***Month***	***Jan.***	***Feb.***	***Mar.***
	Planned output*	200	300	400

**Aggregate units*

Master schedule	***Month***	***Jan.***	***Feb.***	***Mar.***
	Planned output*			
	Push	100	100	100
	Self-propelled	75	150	200
	Riding	25	50	100
	Total	200	300	400

**Actual units*

The master schedule interfaces with marketing, capacity planning, production planning, and distribution planning: It enables marketing to make valid delivery commitments to warehouses and final customers; it enables production to evaluate capacity requirements; it provides the necessary information for production and marketing to negotiate when customer requests cannot be met by normal capacity; and it provides senior management with the opportunity to determine whether the business plan and its strategic objectives will be achieved. The master schedule also drives the material requirements planning (MRP) system that will be discussed in the next chapter.

The capacities used for master scheduling are based on decisions made during aggregate planning. Note that there is a time lapse between the time the aggregate plan is made and the development of a master schedule. Consequently, the outputs shown in a master schedule will not necessarily be identical to those of the aggregate plan for the simple reason that more up-to-date demand information might be available, which the master schedule would take into account.

The central person in the master scheduling process is the master scheduler.

The Master Scheduler

Most manufacturing organizations have (or should have) a master scheduler. The duties of the master scheduler generally include

1. Evaluating the impact of new orders.
2. Providing delivery dates for orders.
3. Dealing with problems:
   a. Evaluating the impact of production delays or late deliveries of purchased goods.
   b. Revising the master schedule when necessary because of insufficient supplies or capacity.
   c. Bringing instances of insufficient capacity to the attention of production and marketing personnel so that they can participate in resolving conflicts.

THE MASTER SCHEDULING PROCESS

A master schedule indicates the quantity and timing (i.e., delivery times) for a product, or a group of products, but it does not show planned *production.* For instance, a master schedule may call for delivery of 50 cases of cranberry-apple juice to be delivered on May 1. But this may not require any production; there may be 200 cases in inventory. Or it may require *some* production: If there were 40 cases in inventory, an additional 10 cases would be needed to achieve the specified delivery amount. Or it may involve production of 50 or more cases: In some instances, it is more economical to produce large amounts rather than small amounts, with the excess temporarily placed in inventory until needed. Thus, the *production lot size* might be 70 cases, so if additional cases were needed (e.g., 50 cases), a run of 70 cases would be made.

The master production schedule is one of the primary outputs of the master scheduling process, as illustrated in Figure 11.6.

Rough-cut capacity planning (RCCP) Approximate balancing of capacity and demand to test the feasibility of a master schedule.

Once a *tentative* master schedule has been developed, it must be validated. This is an extremely important step. Validation is referred to as **rough-cut capacity planning (RCCP).** It involves testing the feasibility of a proposed master schedule relative to available capacities, to assure that no obvious capacity constraints exist. This means checking capacities of production and warehouse facilities, labor, and vendors to ensure that no gross deficiencies

FIGURE 11.6
The master scheduling process

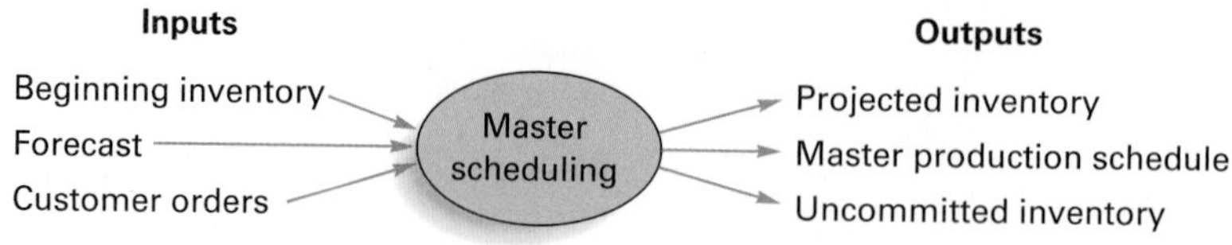

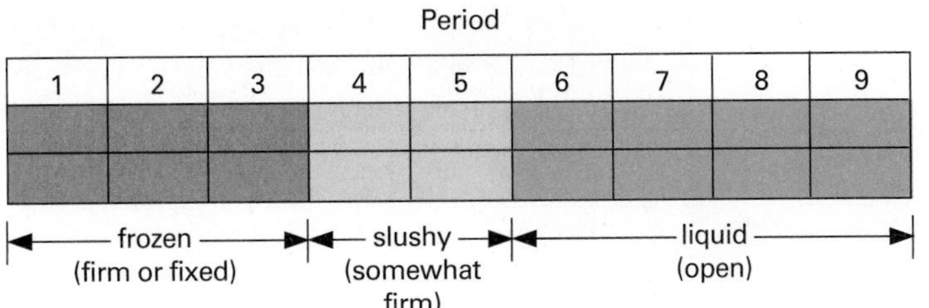

FIGURE 11.7
Time fences in an MPS

exist that will render the master schedule unworkable. The master production schedule then serves as the basis for *short-range* planning. It should be noted that whereas the aggregate plan covers an interval of, say, 12 months, the master schedule covers only a portion of this. In other words, the aggregate plan is disaggregated in stages, or phases, that may cover a few weeks to two or three months. Moreover, the master schedule may be updated monthly, even though it covers two or three months. For instance, the lawn mower master schedule would probably be updated at the end of January to include any revisions in planned output for February and March as well as new information on planned output for April.

Time Fences

Changes to a master schedule can be disruptive, particularly changes to the early, or near, portions of the schedule. Typically, the further out in the future a change is, the less the tendency to cause problems.

High-performance organizations have an effective master scheduling process. A key component of effective scheduling is the use of *time fences* to facilitate order promising and the entry of orders into the system. **Time fences** divide a scheduling time horizon into three sections or phases, sometimes referred to as *frozen, slushy,* and *liquid,* in reference to the firmness of the schedule (see Figure 11.7).

Time fences Points in time that separate phases of a master schedule planning horizon.

Frozen is the near-term phase that is so soon that delivery of a new order would be impossible, or only possible using very costly or extraordinary options such as delaying another order. Authority for new-order entry in this phase usually lies with the VP of manufacturing. The length of the frozen phase is often a function of the total time needed to produce a product, from procuring materials to shipping the order. There is a high degree of confidence in order-promise dates.

Slushy is the next phase, and its time fence is usually a few periods beyond the frozen phase. Order entry in this phase necessitates trade-offs, but is less costly or disruptive than in the frozen phase. Authority for order entry usually lies with the master scheduler. There is relative confidence in order-promise dates, and capacity planning becomes very specific.

Liquid is the farthest out on the time horizon. New orders or cancellations can be entered with ease. Order promise dates are tentative, and will be firmed up with the passage of time when orders are in the firm phase of the schedule horizon.

A key element in the success of the master scheduling process is strict adherence to time fence policies and rules. It is essential that they be adhered to and communicated throughout the organization.

Inputs

The master schedule has three inputs: the beginning inventory, which is the actual quantity on hand from the preceding period; forecasts for each period of the schedule; and customer orders, which are quantities already *committed* to customers. Other factors that might need to be taken into consideration include any hiring or firing restrictions imposed by HR, skill levels, limits on inventory such as available space, whether items are perishable, and whether there are some market lifetime (e.g., seasonal or obsolescence) considerations.

Outputs

The master scheduling process uses this information on a period-by-period basis to determine the projected inventory, production requirements, and the resulting uncommitted inventory,

FIGURE 11.8A
Weekly forecast requirements for industrial pumps

	June				July			
	1	2	3	4	5	6	7	8
Forecast	30	30	30	30	40	40	40	40

FIGURE 11.8B
Eight-week schedule showing forecasts, customer orders, and beginning inventory

Beginning inventory	June				July			
64	1	2	3	4	5	6	7	8
Forecast	30	30	30	30	40	40	40	40
Customer orders (committed)	33	20	10	4	2			

Available-to-promise (ATP) inventory Uncommitted inventory.

which is referred to as **available-to-promise (ATP) inventory.** Knowledge of the uncommitted inventory can enable marketing to make realistic promises to customers about deliveries of new orders.

The master scheduling process begins with a preliminary calculation of projected on-hand inventory. This reveals when additional inventory (i.e., production) will be needed. Consider this example. A company that makes industrial pumps wants to prepare a master production schedule for June and July. Marketing has forecasted demand of 120 pumps for June and 160 pumps for July. These have been evenly distributed over the four weeks in each month: 30 per week in June and 40 per week in July, as illustrated in Figure 11.8A.

Now, suppose that there are currently 64 pumps in inventory (i.e., beginning inventory is 64 pumps), and that there are customer orders that have been committed (booked) and must be filled (see Figure 11.8B).

Figure 11.8B contains the three primary inputs to the master scheduling process: the beginning inventory, the forecast, and the customer orders that have been booked or committed. This information is necessary to determine three quantities: the projected on-hand inventory, the master production schedule, and the uncommitted (ATP) inventory. The first step is to calculate the projected on-hand inventory, one week at a time, until it falls below a specified limit. In this example, the specified limit will be zero. Hence, we will continue until the projected on-hand inventory becomes negative.

The projected on-hand inventory is calculated as follows:

$$\text{Projected on-hand inventory} = \text{Inventory from previous week} - \text{Current week's requirements} \quad (11\text{–}1)$$

where the current week's requirements are the *larger* of forecast and customer orders (committed).

For the first week, projected on-hand inventory equals beginning inventory minus the larger of forecast and customer orders. Because customer orders (33) are larger than the forecast (30), the customer orders amount is used. Thus, for the first week, we obtain

$$\text{Projected on-hand inventory} = 64 - 33 = 31$$

Projected on-hand inventories are shown in Figure 11.9 for the first three weeks (i.e., until the projected on-hand amount becomes negative).

Beginning inventory 64	June				July			
	1	2	3	4	5	6	7	8
Forecast	30	30	30	30	40	40	40	40
Customer orders (committed)	33	20	10	4	2			
Projected on-hand inventory	31	1	−29					

Customer orders are larger than forecast in week 1; projected on-hand inventory is 64 − 33 = 31

Forecast is larger than customer orders in week 2; projected on-hand inventory is 31 − 30 = 1

Forecast is larger than customer orders in week 3; projected on-hand inventory is 1 − 30 = −29

FIGURE 11.9
Projected on-hand inventory is computed week by week until it becomes negative

When the projected on-hand inventory becomes negative, this is a signal that production will be needed to replenish inventory. Hence, a negative projected on-hand inventory will require planned production. Suppose that a production lot size of 70 pumps is used, so that whenever production is called for, 70 pumps will be produced. (The determination of lot size is described in Chapter 13.) Hence, the negative projected on-hand inventory in the third week will require production of 70 pumps, which will meet the projected shortfall of 29 pumps and leave 41 (i.e., 70 − 29 = 41) pumps for future demand.

These calculations continue for the entire schedule. Every time projected inventory becomes negative, another production lot of 70 pumps is added to the schedule. Figure 11.10 illustrates the calculations. The result is the master schedule and projected on-hand inventory for each week of the schedule. These can now be added to the master schedule (see Figure 11.11).

It is now possible to determine the amount of inventory that is uncommitted and, hence, available to promise. Several methods are used in practice. The one we shall employ involves a "look-ahead" procedure: Sum booked customer orders week by week until (but not including) a week in which there is an MPS amount. For example, in the first week, this procedure results in summing customer orders of 33 (week 1) and 20 (week 2) to obtain 53. In the first

Week	Inventory from Previous Week	Requirements*	Net Inventory before MPS		(70) MPS		Projected Inventory
1	64	33	31				31
2	31	30	1				1
3	1	30	−29	+	70	=	41
4	41	30	11				11
5	11	40	−29	+	70	=	41
6	41	40	1				1
7	1	40	−39	+	70	=	31
8	31	40	−9	+	70	=	61

*Requirements equals the larger of forecast and customer orders in each week.

FIGURE 11.10
Determining the MPS and projected on-hand inventory

FIGURE 11.11
Projected on-hand inventory and MPS are added to the master schedule

	June				July			
64	1	2	3	4	5	6	7	8
Forecast	30	30	30	30	40	40	40	40
Customer orders (committed)	33	20	10	4	2			
Projected on-hand inventory	31	1	41	11	41	1	31	61
MPS			70		70		70	70

FIGURE 11.12
The available-to-promise inventory quantities have been added to the master schedule

	June				July			
64	1	2	3	4	5	6	7	8
Forecast	30	30	30	30	40	40	40	40
Customer orders (committed)	33	20	10	4	2			
Projected on-hand inventory	31	1	41	11	41	1	31	61
MPS			70		70		70	70
Available-to-promise inventory (uncommitted)	11		56		68		70	70

week, this amount is subtracted from the beginning inventory of 64 pumps plus the MPS (zero in this example) to obtain the amount that is available to promise. Thus,

$$64 + 0 - (33 + 20) = 11$$

This inventory is uncommitted, and it can be delivered in either week 1 or 2, or part can be delivered in week 1 and part in week 2. (Note that the ATP quantity is only calculated for the first week and for other weeks in which there is an MPS quantity. Hence, it is calculated for weeks 1, 3, 5, 7, 8.) See Figure 11.12.

For weeks other than the first week, the beginning inventory drops out of the computation, and ATP is the look-ahead quantity subtracted from the MPS quantity.

Thus, for week 3, the promised amounts are $10 + 4 = 14$, and the ATP is $70 - 14 = 56$.

For week 5, customer orders are 2 (future orders have not yet been booked). The ATP is $70 - 2 = 68$.

For weeks 7 and 8, there are no customer orders, so for the present, all of the MPS amount is available to promise.

As additional orders are booked, these would be entered in the schedule, and the ATP amounts would be updated to reflect those orders. Marketing can use the ATP amounts to provide realistic delivery dates to customers.

SUMMARY

Aggregate planning establishes general levels of employment, output, and inventories for periods of 2 to 12 months. In the spectrum of planning, it falls between the broad decisions of long-range planning and the very specific and detailed short-range planning decisions. It begins with an overall forecast for the planning horizon and ends with preparations for applying the plans to specific products and services.

The essence of aggregate planning is the aggregation of products or services into one "product" or "service." This permits planners to consider overall levels of employment and inventories without having to become involved with specific details that are better left to short-range planning. Planners often use informal graphic and charting techniques to develop plans, although various mathematical techniques have been suggested. It appears that the complexity and the restrictive assumptions of these techniques limit their widespread use in practice.

After the aggregate plan has been developed, it is disaggregated or broken down into specific product requirements. This leads to a master schedule, which indicates the planned quantities and timing of specific outputs. Inputs to the master schedule are on-hand inventory amounts, forecasts of demand, and customer orders. The outputs are projected production and inventory requirements, and the projected uncommitted inventory, which is referred to as available-to-promise (ATP) inventory.

KEY POINTS

1. An aggregate plan is an intermediate-range plan for a collection of similar products or services that sets the stage for shorter-range plans. See Table 11.8 for a convenient summary of aggregate planning.
2. Master scheduling breaks an aggregate plan into specific shorter-range output quantity and timing requirements.
   a. Rough-cut capacity planning tests the feasibility of a tentative master plan in terms of capacity.
   b. Time fences describe the various time period in terms of the degree to which the master schedule is firm or flexible. Early periods do not generally allow changes, while later periods have more flexibility.
3. It is essential to include the entire supply chain when developing the aggregate plan.

TABLE 11.8
Summary of aggregate planning

Purpose
Decide on the combination of
- Output rates
- Employment levels
- On-hand inventory levels

Objectives
- Minimize cost
- Others, may include
  - Maintain a desirable level of customer service
  - Minimize workforce fluctuations

Possible Strategies
A. Supply Management (reactive)

Level Production
- Allow inventory to absorb variations in demand
- Use back ordering during periods of high demand

Chase Production
- Vary output by varying the number of workers by hiring or layoffs to track demand
- Vary output throughout the use of overtime or idle time
- Vary output using part-time workers
- Use subcontracting to supplement output

Mixed Strategy
- Use a combination of level and chase approaches

B. Demand Management (proactive)
- Influence demand through promotion, pricing, etc.
- Produce goods or services that have complementary demand patterns

Managerial Importance of Aggregate Planning
- Has an effect on
  - Costs
  - Equipment utilization
  - Customer satisfaction
  - Employment levels
  - Synchronization of flow throughout the supply chain

KEY TERMS

aggregate planning, 473
available-to-promise (ATP) inventory, 496
chase demand strategy, 481
level capacity strategy, 481
master production schedule (MPS), 493
rough-cut capacity planning (RCCP), 494
sales and operations planning, 473
simulation models, 491
time fences, 495
yield management, 492

SOLVED PROBLEMS

Problem 1

A manager is attempting to put together an aggregate plan for the coming nine months. She has obtained a forecast of expected demand for the planning horizon. The plan must deal with highly seasonal demand; demand is relatively high in periods 3 and 4 and again in period 8, as can be seen from the following forecasts:

Period	1	2	3	4	5	6	7	8	9	Total
Forecast	190	230	260	280	210	170	160	260	180	1,940

The department now has 20 full-time employees, each of whom can produce 10 units of output per period at a cost of $6 per unit. Inventory carrying cost is $5 per unit per period, and backlog cost is $10 per unit per period. The manager is considering a plan that would involve hiring two people to start working in period 1, one on a temporary basis who would work only through period 5. This would cost $500 in addition to unit production costs.

a. What is the rationale for this plan?

b. Determine the total cost of the plan, including production, inventory, and back-order costs.

Solution

a. With the current workforce of 20 people each producing 10 units per period, regular capacity is 1,800 units. That is 140 units less than expected demand. Adding one worker would increase regular capacity to 1,800 + 90 = 1,890 units. That would still be 50 units short, or just the amount one temporary worker could produce in five periods. Since one of the two seasonal peaks is quite early, it would make sense to start the temporary worker right away to avoid some of the back-order cost.

b. The production plan for this strategy is as follows:

Period	1	2	3	4	5	6	7	8	9	Total
Forecast	190	230	260	280	210	170	160	260	180	1,940
Output										
Regular	220	220	220	220	220	210	210	210	210	1,940
Overtime	—	—	—	—	—	—	—	—	—	—
Subcontract	—	—	—	—	—	—	—	—	—	—
Output − Forecast	30	(10)	(40)	(60)	10	40	50	(50)	30	0
Inventory										
Beginning	0	30	20	0	0	0	0	20	0	
Ending	30	20	0	0	0	0	20	0	0	
Average	15	25	10	0	0	0	10	10	0	70
Backlog	0	0	20	80	70	30	0	30	0	230
Costs										
Output										
Regular @ $6	$1,320	1,320	1,320	1,320	1,320	1,260	1,260	1,260	1,260	$11,640
Overtime										
Subcontract										
Inventory @ $5	$ 75	125	50	0	0	0	50	50	0	$350
Back order @ $10	0	0	200	800	700	300	0	300	0	$ 2,300
Total	$1,395	1,445	1,570	2,120	2,020	1,560	1,310	1,610	1,260	$14,290

The total cost for this plan is $14,290, plus the $500 cost for hiring and for the layoff, giving a total of $14,790. This plan may or may not be good. The manager would need information on other costs and options before settling on one plan.

Although the calculations are relatively straightforward, the backlogs can sometimes seem difficult to obtain. Consider these rules for computing the backlog:

1. Start with the Output − Forecast value. If this is positive and there was a backlog in the preceding period, reduce the backlog by this amount. If the amount exceeds the backlog, the difference becomes the ending inventory for the period. If they are exactly equal, the backlog and the ending inventory will both be equal to zero.
2. If Output − Forecast is negative, subtract it from the beginning inventory. If this produces a negative value, that value becomes the backlog for that period.

You also can use the appropriate Excel template to obtain the solution:

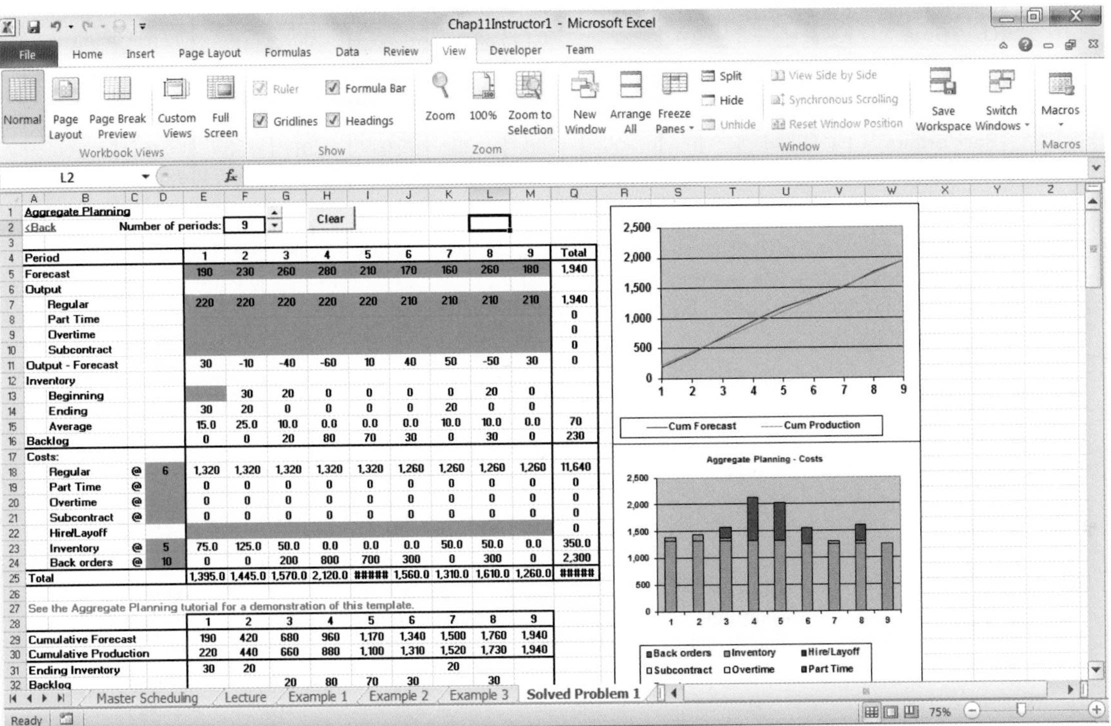

Problem 2

Spring and Summer Fashions, a clothing producer, has generated a forecast for the next eight weeks. Demand is expected to be fairly steady, except for periods 3 and 4, which have higher demands:

Period	1	2	3	4	5	6	7	8	Total
Forecast	1,200	1,200	1,400	3,000	1,200	1,200	1,200	1,200	11,600

The company typically hires seasonal workers to handle the extra workload in periods 3 and 4. The cost for hiring and training a seasonal worker is $50 per worker, and the company plans to hire two additional workers and train them in period 3, for work in period 4, and then lay them off (no cost for layoff). Develop an aggregate plan that uses steady output from regular workers with added output from the two seasonal workers in period 4. The output rate for the seasonal workers is slightly less than that of regular workers, so their cost per unit is higher. The cost per unit for regular workers is $4 per hour, while cost per unit for the seasonal workers is $5 per unit. Backlog cost is $1 per unit per period.

Solution

Period			1	2	3	4	5	6	7	8	Total
Forecast			1,200	1,200	1,400	3,000	1,200	1,200	1,200	1,200	11,600
Output											
Regular			1,200	1,200	1,200	1,200	1,200	1,200	1,200	1,200	9,600
Part Time						2,000					2,000
Overtime											0
Subcontract											0
Output - Forecast			0	0	−200	200	0	0	0	0	0
Inventory											
Beginning			0	0	0	0	0	0	0	0	
Ending			0	0	0	0	0	0	0	0	
Average			0.0	0.0	0.0	0.0	0.0	0.0	0.0	0.0	0
Backlog			0	0	200	0	0	0	0	0	200
Costs :											
Regular	@	4	4,800	4,800	4,800	4,800	4,800	4,800	4,800	4,800	38,400
Part Time	@	5	0	0	0	10,000	0	0	0	0	10,000
OverTime	@		0	0	0	0	0	0	0	0	0
Subcontract	@		0	0	0	0	0	0	0	0	0
Hire/Layoff		50			100						100
Inventory	@		0.0	0.0	0.0	0.0	0.0	0.0	0.0	0.0	0.0
Back orders	@	1	0	0	200	0	0	0	0	0	200
Total			4,800.0	4,800.0	5,100.0	14,800	4,800.0	4,800.0	4,800.0	4,800.0	48,700.0

Problem 3

Prepare a schedule like that shown in Figure 11.11 for the following situation. The forecast for each period is 70 units. The starting inventory is zero. The MPS rule is to schedule production if the projected inventory on hand is negative. The production lot size is 100 units. The following table shows committed orders.

Period	Customer Orders
1	80
2	50
3	30
4	10

Solution

Period	(A) Inventory from Previous Period	(B) Requirements*	(C = A − B) Net Inventory before MPS	MPS	(MPS + C) Projected Inventory
1	0	80	(80)	100	20
2	20	70	(50)	100	50
3	50	70	(20)	100	80
4	80	70	10	0	10

*Requirements equal the larger of forecast and customer orders in each period.

Starting Inv. = 0	1	2	3	4
Forecast	70	70	70	70
Customer orders	80	50	30	10
Projected on-hand inventory	20	50	80	10
MPS	100	100	100	0
ATP	20	50	60	0

DISCUSSION AND REVIEW QUESTIONS

1. What three levels of planning involve operations managers? What kinds of decisions are made at the various levels?
2. What are the three phases of intermediate planning?
3. What is aggregate planning? What is its purpose?

4. Why is there a need for aggregate planning?
5. What are the most common decision variables for aggregate planning in a manufacturing setting? In a service setting?
6. What aggregate planning difficulty that might confront an organization offering a variety of products and/or services would not confront an organization offering one or a few similar products or services?
7. Briefly discuss the advantages and disadvantages of each of these planning strategies:
   a. Maintain a level rate of output and let inventories absorb fluctuations in demand.
   b. Vary the size of the workforce to correspond to predicted changes in demand requirements.
   c. Maintain a constant workforce size, but vary hours worked to correspond to predicted demand requirements.
8. What are the primary advantages and limitations of informal graphic and charting techniques for aggregate planning?
9. Briefly describe the planning techniques listed below, and give an advantage and disadvantage for each:
   a. Spreadsheet
   b. Linear programming
   c. Simulation
10. What are the inputs to master scheduling? What are the outputs?
11. Explain the managerial significance of aggregate planning.

TAKING STOCK

1. What general trade-offs are involved in master scheduling in terms of the frozen portion of the schedule?
2. Who needs to interface with the master schedule and why?
3. How has technology had an impact on master scheduling?

CRITICAL THINKING EXERCISES

1. Service operations often face more difficulty in planning than their manufacturing counterparts. However, service does have certain advantages that manufacturing often does not. Explain service planning difficulty, and the advantages and disadvantages.
2. Name several behaviors related to aggregate planning or master scheduling that you believe would be unethical, and the ethical principle that would be violated for each.

PROBLEMS

1. Refer to Example 1. The president of the firm has decided to shut down the plant for vacation and installation of new equipment in period 4. After installation, the cost per unit will remain the same, but the output rate for regular time will be 450. Regular output is the same as in Example 1 for periods 1, 2, and 3; 0 for period 4; and 450 for each of the remaining periods. Note, though, that the forecast of 400 units in period 4 must be dealt with. Prepare the aggregate plan, and compute its total cost.

2. Refer to Example 1. Suppose that the regular output rate will drop to 290 units per period due to an expected change in production requirements. Costs will not change. Prepare an aggregate plan and compute its total cost for each of these alternatives:
   a. Use overtime at a fixed rate of 20 units per period as needed. Plan for an ending inventory of zero for period 6. Backlogs cannot exceed 90 units per period.
   b. Use subcontracting at a maximum rate of 50 units per period; the usage need not be the same in every period. Have an ending inventory of zero in the last period. Again backlogs cannot exceed 90 units in any period. Compare these two plans.

3. Refer to Example 2. Suppose you can use a combination of overtime and subcontracting, but you cannot use subcontracting in more than two periods. Up to 50 units of subcontracting and either 0 or 40 units of overtime are allowed per period. Subcontracting is $6 per unit, and overtime is $3 per unit. (*Hint:* Use subcontracting only when overtime units are not sufficient to decrease backlogs to 80 units or less.) Plan for an ending inventory balance of 0 for period 6. Prepare a plan that will minimize total cost.

4. Refer to Example 2. Determine whether a plan to use subcontracting at a maximum rate of 50 units per period as needed with no overtime would achieve a lower total cost than the plan shown in Example 2. Again, plan for a zero inventory balance at the end of period 6.

5. Manager T. C. Downs of Plum Engines, a producer of lawn mowers and leaf blowers, must develop an aggregate plan given the forecast for engine demand shown in the table. The department has a normal capacity of 130 engines per month. Normal output has a cost of $60 per engine. The beginning inventory is zero engines. Overtime has a cost of $90 per engine.

a. Develop a chase plan that matches the forecast and compute the total cost of your plan.
b. Compare the costs to a level plan that uses inventory to absorb fluctuations. Inventory carrying cost is $2 per engine per month. Backlog cost is $90 per engine per month.

	Month								
	1	**2**	**3**	**4**	**5**	**6**	**7**	**8**	**Total**
Forecast	120	135	140	120	125	125	140	135	1,040

6. Manager Chris Channing of Fabric Mills, Inc., has developed the forecast shown in the table for bolts of cloth. The figures are in hundreds of bolts. The department has a normal capacity of 275(00) bolts per month, except for the seventh month, when capacity will be 250(00) bolts. Normal output has a cost of $40 per hundred bolts. Workers can be assigned to other jobs if production is less than normal. The beginning inventory is zero bolts.
   a. Develop a chase plan that matches the forecast and compute the total cost of your plan. Overtime is $60 per hundred bolts.
   b. Would the total cost be less with regular production with no overtime, but using a subcontractor to handle the excess above normal capacity at a cost of $50 per hundred bolts? Backlogs are not allowed. The inventory carrying cost is $2 per hundred bolts.

Month	**1**	**2**	**3**	**4**	**5**	**6**	**7**	**Total**
Forecast	250	300	250	300	280	275	270	1,925

7. SummerFun, Inc., produces a variety of recreation and leisure products. The production manager has developed an aggregate forecast:

Month	**Mar**	**Apr**	**May**	**Jun**	**Jul**	**Aug**	**Sep**	**Total**
Forecast	50	44	55	60	50	40	51	350

   Use the following information to develop aggregate plans.

Regular production cost	$80 per unit	Back-order cost	$20 per unit
Overtime production cost	$120 per unit	Beginning inventory	0 units
Regular capacity	40 units per month		
Overtime capacity	8 units per month		
Subcontracting cost	$140 per unit		
Subcontracting capacity	12 units per month		
Holding cost	$10 per unit per month		

   Develop an aggregate plan using each of the following guidelines and compute the total cost for each plan. Which plan has the lowest total cost?
   a. Use regular production. Supplement using inventory, overtime, and subcontracting as needed. No backlogs allowed.
   b. Use a level strategy. Use a combination of backlogs, subcontracting, and inventory to handle variations in demand.

8. Nowjuice, Inc., produces Shakewell® fruit juice. A planner has developed an aggregate forecast for demand (in cases) for the next six months.

Month	**May**	**Jun**	**Jul**	**Aug**	**Sep**	**Oct**
Forecast	4,000	4,800	5,600	7,200	6,400	5,000

   Use the following information to develop aggregate plans.

Regular production cost	$10 per case
Regular production capacity	5,000 cases
Overtime production cost	$16 per case
Subcontracting cost	$20 per case
Holding cost	$1 per case per month
Beginning inventory	0

   Develop an aggregate plan using each of the following guidelines and compute the total cost for each plan. Which plan has the lowest total cost?
   a. Use level production. Supplement using overtime as needed.

b. Use a combination of overtime (500 cases per period maximum), inventory, and subcontracting (500 cases per period maximum) to handle variations in demand.
c. Use overtime up to 750 cases per period and inventory to handle variations in demand.

9. Wormwood, Ltd., produces a variety of furniture products. The planning committee wants to prepare an aggregate plan for the next six months using the following information:

	MONTH					
	1	2	3	4	5	6
Demand	160	150	160	180	170	140
Capacity						
Regular	150	150	150	150	160	160
Overtime	10	10	0	10	10	10

Cost Per Unit	
Regular time	$50
Overtime	75
Subcontract	80
Inventory, per period	4

Subcontracting can handle a maximum of 10 units per month. Beginning inventory is zero. Develop a plan that minimizes total cost. No back orders are allowed.

10. Refer to Solved Problem 1. Prepare two additional aggregate plans. Call the one in the solved problem plan A. For plan B, hire one more worker at a cost of $200. Make up any shortfall using subcontracting at $8 per unit, with a maximum of 20 units per period (i.e., use subcontracting to reduce back orders when the forecast exceeds regular output). Note that the ending inventory in period 9 should be zero. Therefore, Total forecast − Total output = Quantity subcontracted. An additional constraint is that back orders cannot exceed 80 units in any period. For plan C, assume no workers are hired (so regular output is 200 units per period instead of 210 as in plan B). Use subcontracting as needed, but no more than 20 units per period. Compute the total cost of each plan. Which plan has the lowest cost?

11. Refer to Solved Problem 1. Suppose another option is to use part-time workers to assist during seasonal peaks. The cost per unit, including hiring and training, is $11. The output rate is 10 units per worker per period for all workers. A maximum of 10 part-time workers can be used, and the same number of part-time workers must be used in all periods that have part-time workers. The ending inventory in period 9 should be 10 units. The limit on backlogs is 20 units per period. Try to make up backlogs as soon as possible. Compute the total cost for this plan, and compare it to the cost of the plan used in the solved problem. Assume 20 full-time workers.

12. Refer to Solved Problem 1. Prepare an aggregate plan that uses overtime ($9 per unit, maximum output 25 units per period) and inventory variation. Try to minimize backlogs. The ending inventory in period 9 should be zero, and the limit on backlogs is 60 units per period. Note that Total output = Total regular output + Overtime quantity. Compute the total cost of your plan, and compare it to the total cost of the plan used in the solved problem. Assume 20 full-time workers.

13. Refer to Solved Problem 1. Prepare an aggregate plan that uses some combination of laying off ($100 per worker), subcontracting ($8 per unit, maximum of 20 units per period, must use for three consecutive periods), and overtime ($9 per unit, maximum of 25 per period, maximum of 60 for the planning horizon). Compute the total cost, and compare it with any of the other plans you have developed. Which plan has the lowest total cost? Assume you start with 21 workers.

14. Verify the transportation solution shown in Example 3.

15. Refer to Example 3. Suppose that an increase in warehousing costs and other costs brings inventory carrying costs to $2 per unit per month. All other costs and quantities remain the same. Determine a revised solution to this transportation problem.

16. Refer to Example 3. Suppose that regular-time capacity will be reduced to 440 units in period 3 to accommodate a companywide safety inspection of equipment. What will the additional cost of the optimal plan be as compared to the one shown in Example 3? Assume all costs and quantities are the same as given in Example 3 except for the regular-time output in period 3.

17. Solve Problem 16 using an inventory carrying cost of $2 per unit per period.

18. Dundas Bike Components Inc. of Wheelville, Illinois, manufactures bicycle wheels in two different sizes for the Big Bike Co. assembly plant located across town. David Dundas, the firm's owner-manager, has just received Big Bike's order for the next six months.

	Nov.	Dec.	Jan.	Feb.	Mar.	Apr.
20-Inch Wheels	1,000 units	900	600	700	1,100	1,100
24-Inch Wheels	500 units	500	300	500	400	600

a. Under what circumstances will it be possible for David to develop just one aggregate plan rather than two (one for each size wheel)? Explain in two to three sentences without calculations.
b. Currently Dundas employs 28 full-time, highly skilled employees, each of whom can produce 50 wheels per month. Because skilled labor is in short supply in the Wheelville area, David would like to develop a pure level-output plan. There is no inventory of finished wheels on hand at present, but David would like to have 300 on hand at the end of April. Big Bike will tolerate back orders of up to 200 units per month. Show your level plan in tabular form.
c. Calculate the total annual cost of your plan using these costs:

Regular	$5.00	Hiring	$300
Overtime	$7.50	Layoff	$400
Part-time	NA	Inventory	$1.00
Subcontract	NA	Back order	$6.00

19. Prepare a master production schedule for industrial pumps in the manner of Figure 11.11 in the chapter. Use the same inputs as the example, but change the MPS rule from "schedule production when the projected on-hand inventory would be negative without production" to "schedule production when the projected on-hand inventory would be less than 10 without production."

20. Update the master schedule shown in Figure 11.11 given these updated inputs: It is now the end of week 1; customer orders are 25 for week 2, 16 for week 3, 11 for week 4, 8 for week 5, and 3 for week 6. Use the MPS rule of ordering production when projected on-hand inventory would be negative without production.

21. Prepare a master schedule like that shown in Figure 11.11 given this information: The forecast for each week of an eight-week schedule is 50 units. The MPS rule is to schedule production if the projected on-hand inventory would be negative without it. Customer orders (committed) are as follows:

Week	Customer Orders
1	52
2	35
3	20
4	12

Use a production lot size of 75 units and no beginning inventory.

22. Determine the available-to-promise (ATP) quantities for each period for Problem 21.

23. Prepare a schedule like that shown in Figure 11.12 for the following situation: The forecast is 80 units for each of the first two periods and 60 units for each of the next three periods. The starting inventory is 20 units. The company uses a chase strategy for determining the production lot size, except there is an upper limit on the lot size of 70 units. Also, the desired safety stock is 10 units. *Note:* The ATP quantities are based on maximum allowable production and do not include safety stock. Committed orders are as follows:

Period	Customer Orders
1	82
2	80
3	60
4	40
5	20

Eight Glasses a Day (EGAD)

CASE

The EGAD Bottling Company has decided to introduce a new line of premium bottled water that will include several "designer" flavors. Marketing manager Georgianna Mercer is predicting an upturn in demand based on the new offerings and the increased public awareness of the health benefits of drinking more water. She has prepared aggregate forecasts for the next six months, as shown in the following table (quantities are in tankloads):

Month	May	Jun	Jul	Aug	Sept	Oct	Total
Forecast	50	60	70	90	80	70	420

Production manager Mark Mercer (no relation to Georgianna) has developed the following information. (Costs are in thousands of dollars.)

Regular production cost	$1 per tankload
Regular production capacity	60 tankloads
Overtime production cost	$1.6 per tankload
Subcontracting cost	$1.8 per tankload
Holding cost	$2 per tankload per month
Back-ordering cost	$5 per month per tankload
Beginning inventory	0 tankloads

Among the strategies being considered are the following:

1. Level production supplemented by up to 10 tankloads a month from overtime.
2. A combination of overtime, inventory, and subcontracting.
3. Using overtime for up to 15 tankloads a month, along with inventory to handle variations.

Questions

1. The objective is to choose the plan that has the lowest cost. Which plan would you recommend?
2. Presumably, information about the new line has been shared with supply chain partners. Explain what information should be shared with various partners, and why sharing that information is important.

SELECTED BIBLIOGRAPHY AND FURTHER READINGS

Brandimarte, P., and A. Villa (Eds). *Modeling Manufacturing Systems: From Aggregate Planning to Real-Time Control.* New York: Springer, 1999.

Buxey, G. "Production Planning for Seasonal Demand." *International Journal of Operations and Production Management* 13, no. 7 (July 1993), pp. 4–21.

Hopp, Wallace J., and Mark L. Spearman. *Factory Physics.* 3rd ed. New York: Irwin/McGraw-Hill, 2007.

Jacobs, F. Robert, William L. Berry, D. Clay Whybark, and Thomas Vollman. *Manufacturing Planning and Control For Supply Chain Management.* 6th ed. Burr Ridge, IL: McGraw-Hill/Irwin, 2011.

Silver, E. A., D. F. Pyke, and R. Peterson. *Inventory Management and Production Planning and Scheduling.* New York: Wiley, 1998.

Sipper, Daniel, and Robert Bulfin Jr. *Production: Planning, Control, and Integration.* New York: McGraw-Hill, 1997.

Ware, Norman, and Donald Fogarty. "Master Schedule/Master Production Schedule: The Same or Different?" *Production and Inventory Management Journal,* First Quarter 1990, pp. 34–37.

MRP and ERP

CHAPTER OUTLINE

LEARNING OBJECTIVES

After completing this chapter, you should be able to:

1 Describe the conditions under which MRP is most appropriate.
2 Describe the inputs, outputs, and nature of MRP processing.
3 Explain how requirements in a master production schedule are translated into material requirements for lower-level items.
4 Discuss the benefits and requirements of MRP.
5 Explain how an MRP system is useful in capacity requirements planning.
6 Outline the potential benefits and some of the difficulties users have encountered with MRP.
7 Describe MRP II and its benefits.
8 Describe ERP, what it provides, and its hidden costs.

This chapter describes material requirements planning (MRP), manufacturing resource planning (MRP II), and enterprise resource planning (ERP). MRP is a planning and scheduling technique used for batch production of assembled items. The first portion of the chapter is devoted to MRP. The remainder of the chapter is devoted to MRP II and ERP, which involve the use of extensive software to integrate record keeping and information sharing throughout an organization.

INTRODUCTION

A major distinction in the way inventories are managed results from the nature of demand for those items. When demand for items is derived from plans to make certain products, as it is with raw materials, parts, and assemblies used in producing a finished product, those items are said to have **dependent demand.** The parts and materials that go into the production of an automobile are examples of dependent demand because the total quantity of parts and raw materials needed during any time period is a function of the number of cars that will be produced. Conversely, demand for the *finished* cars is independent—a car is not a component of another item.

Dependent demand Demand for items that are subassemblies or component parts to be used in the production of finished goods.

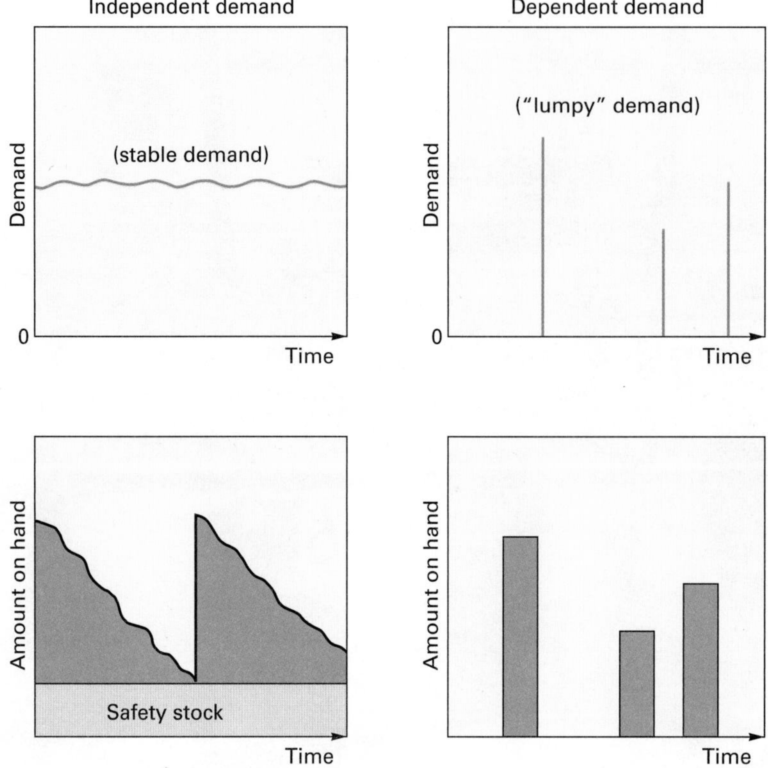

FIGURE 12.1
Comparison of independent and dependent demand

Independent demand is fairly stable once allowances are made for seasonal variations, but dependent demand can be sporadic or "lumpy"; large quantities are used at specific points in time with little or no usage at other times. For example, a firm that produces lawn and garden equipment might make a variety of items, such as trimmers, lawn mowers, and small tractors. Suppose that the various products are produced periodically—in one month, push mowers; in the next month, mulching mowers; and in the third month, tractors. Some components may be used in most of the items (e.g., nuts and bolts, screws). It makes sense to have a continual inventory of these parts because they are always needed. On the other hand, some parts might be used for only one item. Consequently, demand for those parts occurs only when that item is being produced, which might be once every eight or nine weeks; the rest of the time, demand is zero. Thus, demand is "lumpy." Lumpy demand also can be the result of customer ordering rules (e.g., economic order quantity [EOQ] ordering). Because of these tendencies, independent-demand items must be carried on a continual basis, but dependent-demand items need only be stocked just prior to the time they will be needed in the production process. Moreover, the predictability of usage of dependent-demand items means that there is little or no need for safety stock. Figure 12.1 illustrates key differences in independent- and dependent-demand inventories.

AN OVERVIEW OF MRP

Material requirements planning (MRP) A computer-based information system that translates master schedule requirements for end items into time-phased requirements for subassemblies, components, and raw materials.

Material requirements planning (MRP) is a computer-based information system that translates the finished product requirements of the master schedule into time-phased requirements for subassemblies, component parts, and raw materials, working backward from the due date using lead times and other information to determine when and how much to order. Hence, requirements for end items generate requirements for lower-level components, which are broken down by planning periods (e.g., weeks) so that ordering, fabrication, and assembly can be scheduled for timely completion of end items while inventory levels are kept reasonably low.

FIGURE 12.2 Overview of MRP

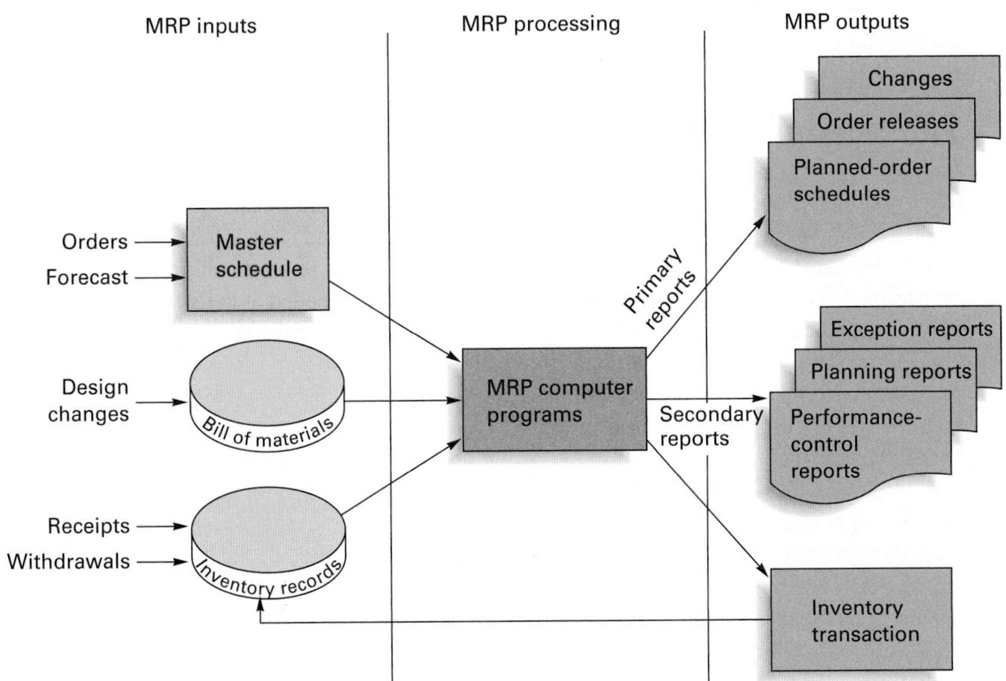

Material requirements planning is as much a philosophy as it is a technique, and as much an approach to scheduling as it is to inventory control.

Historically, ordering and scheduling of assembled products suffered from two difficulties. One was the enormous task of setting up schedules, keeping track of large numbers of parts and components, and coping with schedule and order changes. The other was a lack of differentiation between independent demand and dependent demand. All too often, techniques designed for independent-demand items such as order point systems were used to handle assembled items, which resulted in excessive inventories. Consequently, inventory planning and scheduling presented major problems for manufacturers before the development of MRP.

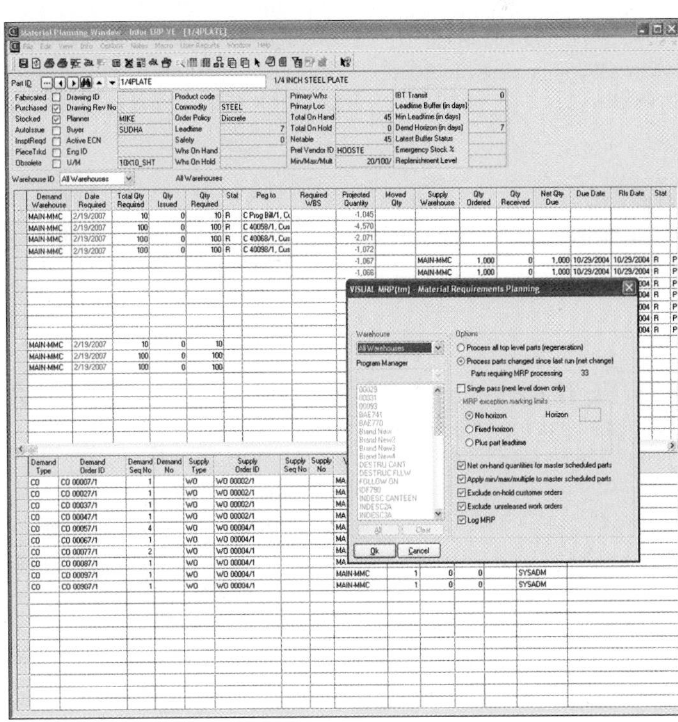

MRP begins with a schedule for finished goods that is converted into a schedule of requirements for the subassemblies, component parts, and raw materials needed to produce the finished items in the specified time frame. Thus, MRP is designed to answer three questions: *What* is needed? *How much* is needed? and *When* is it needed?

The primary inputs of MRP are a bill of materials, which tells the composition of a finished product; a master schedule, which tells how much finished product is desired and when; and an inventory records file, which tells how much inventory is on hand or on order. The planner processes this information to determine the *net* requirements for each period of the planning horizon.

Outputs from the process include planned-order schedules, order releases, changes, performance-control reports, planning reports, and exception reports. These topics are discussed in more detail in subsequent sections. Figure 12.2 provides an overview of an MRP system.

MRP INPUTS

An MRP system has three major sources of information: a master schedule, a bill-of-materials file, and an inventory records file (see Figure 12.2). Let's consider each of these inputs.

The Master Schedule

Master schedule One of three primary inputs in MRP; states which end items are to be produced, when these are needed, and in what quantities.

The **master schedule,** also referred to as the *master production schedule,* states which end items are to be produced, when they are needed, and in what quantities. Figure 12.3 illustrates a portion of a master schedule that shows planned output for end item X for the planning horizon. The schedule indicates that 100 units of X will be needed (e.g., for shipments to customers) at the *start* of week 4 and that another 150 units will be needed at the *start* of week 8.

The quantities in a master schedule come from a number of different sources, including customer orders, forecasts, and orders from warehouses to build up seasonal inventories.

The master schedule separates the planning horizon into a series of time periods or time *buckets,* which are often expressed in weeks. However, the time buckets need not be of equal length. In fact, the near-term portion of a master schedule may be in weeks, but later portions may be in months or quarters. Usually, plans for those more distant time periods are more tentative than near-term requirements.

Cumulative lead time The sum of the lead times that sequential phases of a process require, from ordering of parts or raw materials to completion of final assembly.

Although a master production schedule has no set time period that it must cover, most managers like to plan far enough into the future so they have some general idea of probable upcoming demands for the near term. It is important, though, that the master schedule cover the *stacked* or **cumulative lead time** necessary to produce the end items. This amounts to the sum of the lead times that sequential phases of the production or assembly process require, as illustrated in Figure 12.4, where a total of nine weeks of lead time is needed from ordering parts and raw materials until final assembly is completed. Note that lead times include move and wait times in addition to setup and run times.

The Bill of Materials

Bill of materials (BOM) One of the three primary inputs of MRP; a listing of all of the raw materials, parts, subassemblies, and assemblies needed to produce one unit of a product.

Product structure tree A visual depiction of the requirements in a bill of materials, where all components are listed by levels.

A **bill of materials (BOM)** contains a listing of all of the assemblies, subassemblies, parts, and raw materials that are needed to produce *one* unit of a finished product. Thus, each finished product has its own bill of materials.

The listing in the bill of materials is hierarchical; it shows the quantity of each item needed to complete one unit of its parent item. The nature of this aspect of a bill of materials is clear when you consider a **product structure tree,** which provides a visual depiction of the subassemblies and components needed to assemble a product. Figure 12.5 shows an *assembly diagram* for a chair and a simple product structure tree for the chair. The end item (in this case,

FIGURE 12.3
A master schedule for end item X

	Week number							
Item: X	1	2	3	4	5	6	7	8
Quantity				100				150

FIGURE 12.4
The planning horizon must cover the cumulative lead time

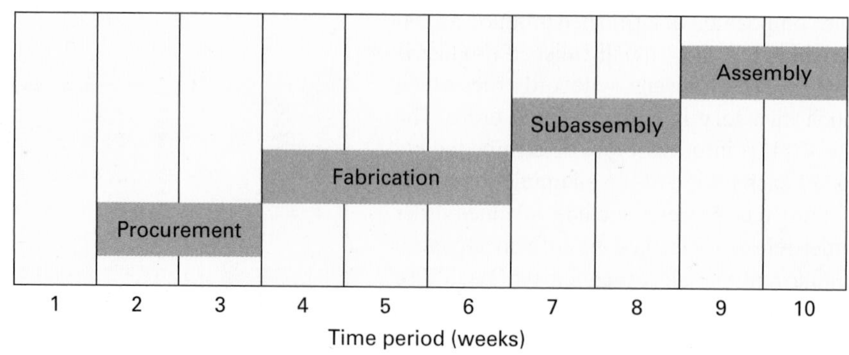

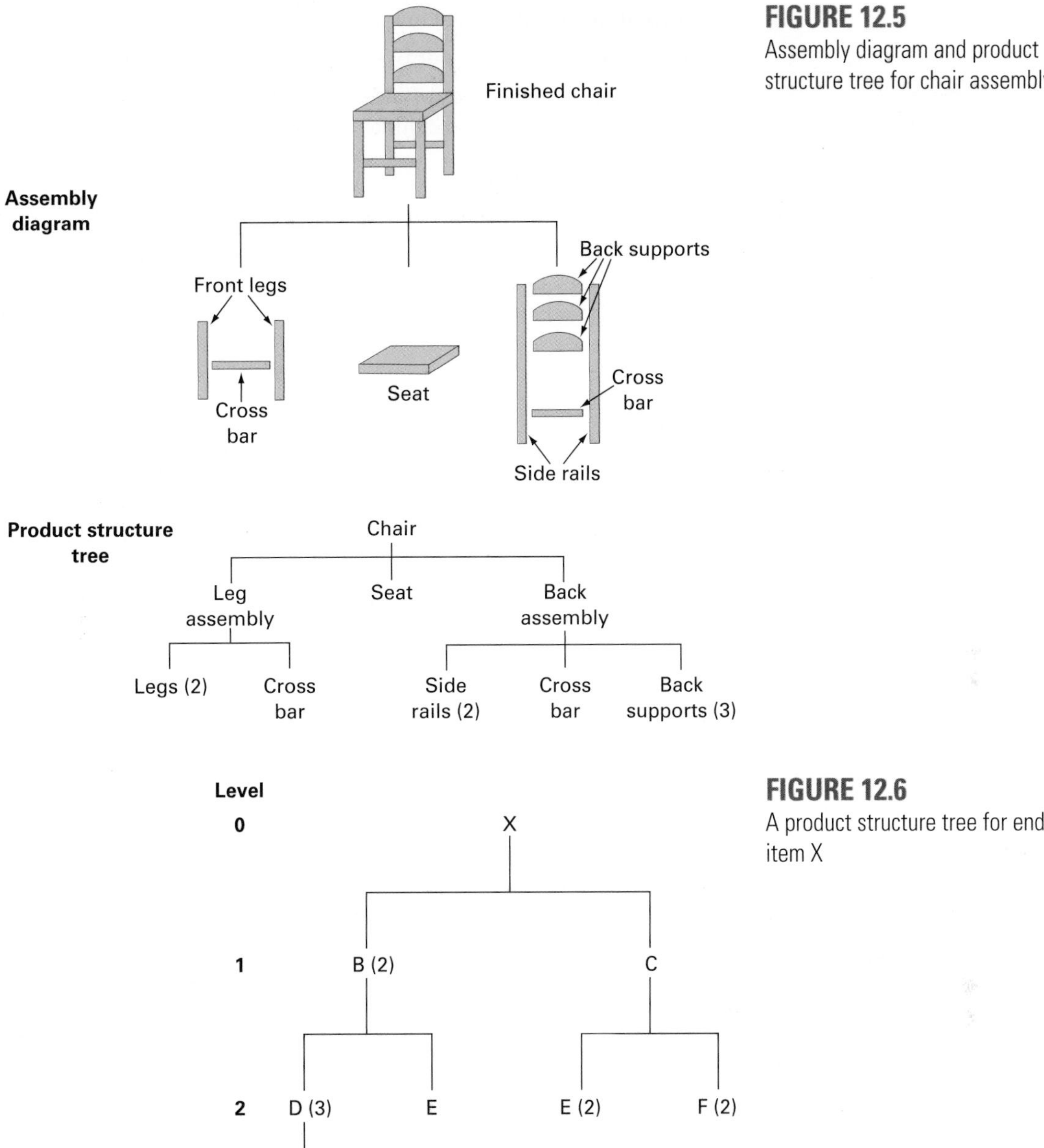

FIGURE 12.5
Assembly diagram and product structure tree for chair assembly

FIGURE 12.6
A product structure tree for end item X

the chair, the finished product) is shown at the top of the tree. Just beneath it are the subassemblies, or major components, that must be put together to make up the end item. Beneath each major component are the necessary lesser components. At each stage moving down the tree are the components (parts, materials) needed to make one unit of the next higher item in the tree.

A product structure tree is useful in illustrating how the bill of materials is used to determine the quantities of each of the ingredients (requirements) needed to obtain a desired number of end items.

Let's consider the product structure tree shown in Figure 12.6. End item X is composed of two Bs and one C. Moreover, each B requires three Ds and one E, and each D requires four Es. Similarly, each C is made up of two Es and two Fs. These *requirements* are listed by *level,* beginning with 0 for the end item, then 1 for the next level, and so on. The items at each level are *components* of the next level up and, as in a family tree, are *parents* of their respective components. Note that the quantities of each item in the product structure tree refer only to the amounts needed to complete the assembly at the next higher level.

EXAMPLE 1

www.mhhe.com/stevenson11e

Use the information presented in Figure 12.6 to do the following:

a. Determine the quantities of B, C, D, E, and F needed to assemble one X.

b. Determine the quantities of these components that will be required to assemble 10 Xs, taking into account the quantities on hand (i.e., in inventory) of various components:

Component	On Hand
B	4
C	10
D	8
E	60

SOLUTION

a.

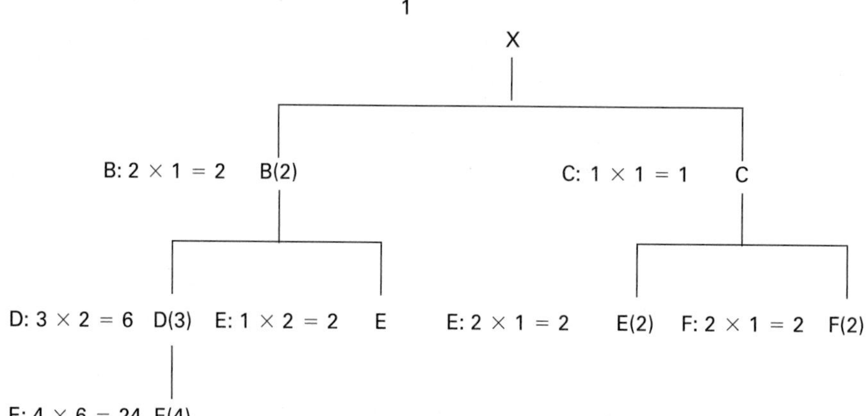

Thus, one X will require

B: 2
C: 1
D: 6
E: 28 (Note that E occurs in three places, with requirements of 24 + 2 + 2 = 28)
F: 2

b.

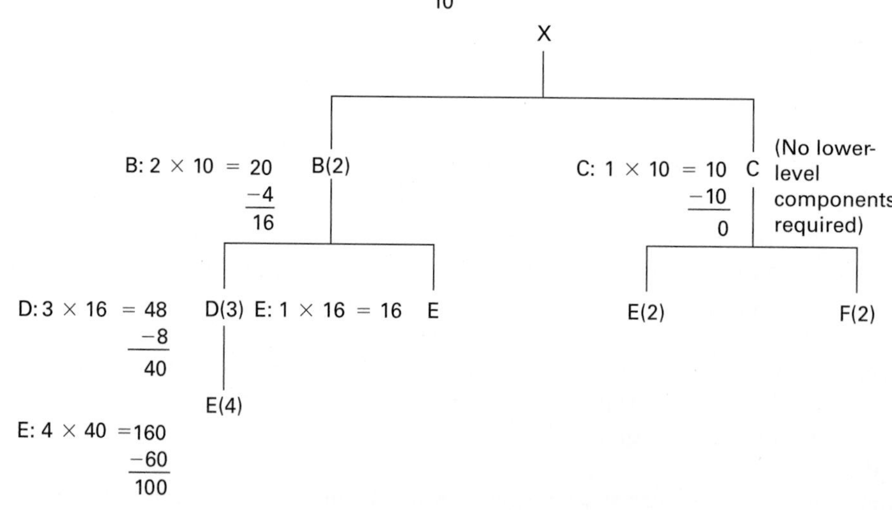

Thus, given the amounts of on-hand inventory, 10 Xs will require

B: 16
C: 0
D: 40
E: 116
F: 0

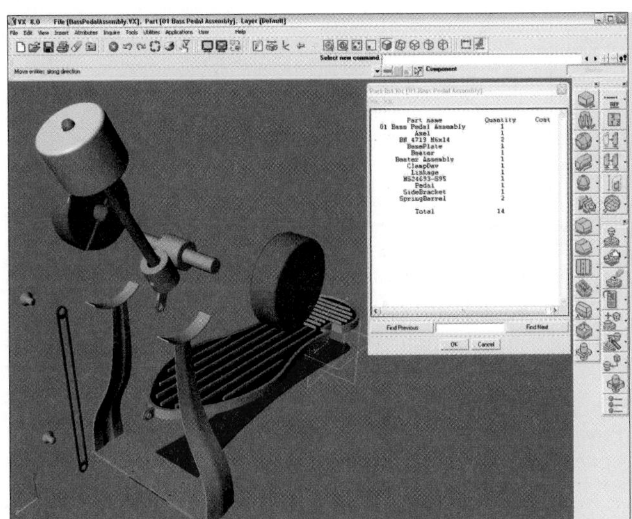

VX Corporation's CAD/CAM software can be used not only for design specification but also to prepare parts lists. This screen shows a parts list for a bass drum pedal along with a three-dimensional view of the product subassemblies.

Determining total requirements is usually more complicated than Example 1 might suggest. For one thing, many products have considerably more components. For another, the issue of *timing* is essential (i.e., when must the components be ordered or made) and must be included in the analysis. Finally, for a variety of reasons, some of the components/subassemblies may be on hand (i.e., currently in inventory). Consequently, in determining total requirements, the amounts on hand must be *netted out* (i.e., subtracted from the apparent requirements) to determine the true requirements as illustrated in Example 1.

When an MRP system calculates requirements, the computer scans a bill of materials by level. When a component such as E in Figure 12.6 appears on more than one level, **low-level coding** is used so that all occurrences of that component appear on the lowest level at which the component appears. In Figure 12.6, conceptually that would be equivalent to lengthening the vertical line for the two appearances of E at level 2 so that all three occurrences line up at level 3 in the tree.

Low-level coding Restructuring the bill of materials so that multiple occurrences of a component all coincide with the lowest level at which the component occurs.

Comment It is extremely important that the bill of materials accurately reflect the composition of a product, particularly since errors at one level become magnified by the multiplication process used to determine quantity requirements. As obvious as this might seem, many companies find themselves with incorrect bill-of-material records. These make it impossible to effectively determine material requirements; moreover, the task of correcting these records can be complex and time-consuming. Accurate records are a prerequisite for effective MRP.

The Inventory Records

Inventory records refer to stored information on the status of each item by time period, called *time buckets.* This includes gross requirements, scheduled receipts, and expected amount on hand. It also includes other details for each item, such as supplier, lead time, and lot size policy. Changes due to stock receipts and withdrawals, canceled orders, and similar events also are recorded in this file.

Inventory records One of the three primary inputs in MRP; includes information on the status of each item by time period.

Like the bill of materials, inventory records must be accurate. Erroneous information on requirements or lead times can have a detrimental impact on MRP and create turmoil when incorrect quantities are on hand or expected delivery times are not met.

MRP PROCESSING

MRP processing takes the end item requirements specified by the master schedule and "explodes" them into *time-phased* requirements for assemblies, parts, and raw materials using the bill of materials offset by lead times. You can see the time-phasing of requirements in the assembly time chart in Figure 12.7. For example, raw materials D, F, and I must be ordered at the start of week 2; part C at the start of week 4; and part H at the start of week 5 in order to be available for delivery as planned.

FIGURE 12.7
Assembly time chart showing material order points needed to meet scheduled availability of the end item

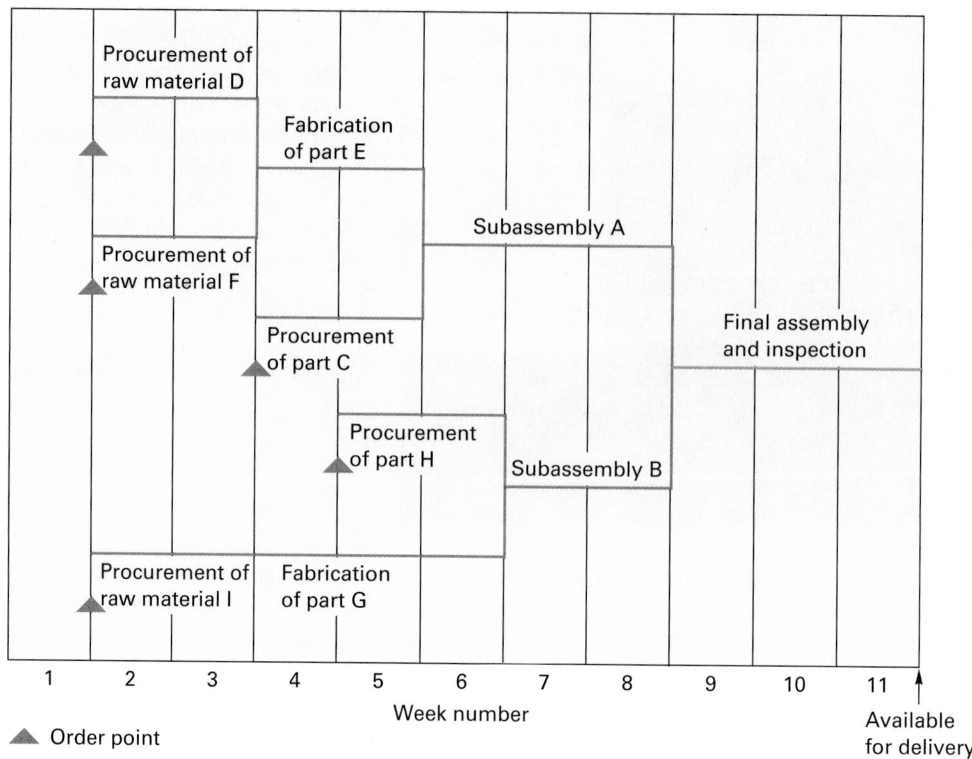

MRP processing combines the time phasing and "explosion" into a sequence of spreadsheet sections, where each section has the following format:

Week Number	Beg. Inv.	1	2	3	4	5	6	7	8
Item:									
Gross requirements									
Scheduled receipts									
Projected on hand									
Net requirements									
Planned-order receipts									
Planned-order releases									

Gross requirements Total expected demand for an item or raw material in a time period.

Scheduled receipts Open orders scheduled to arrive from vendors or elsewhere in the pipeline.

Projected on hand Expected amount of inventory that will be on hand at the beginning of each time period.

Net requirements The actual amount needed in each time period.

Planned-order receipts Quantity expected to be received by the beginning of the period in which it is shown.

The terms in the spreadsheet are defined as follows:

Gross requirements: The total expected demand for an item or raw material *during* each time period without regard to the amount on hand. For end items, these quantities are shown in the master schedule; for components, these quantities are derived from the planned-order releases of their immediate "parents."

Scheduled receipts: Open orders (orders that have been placed and are scheduled to arrive from vendors or elsewhere in the pipeline by the *beginning* of a period).

Projected on hand: The expected amount of inventory that will be on hand at the *beginning* of each time period: scheduled receipts plus available inventory from last period.

Net requirements: The actual amount needed in each time period.

Planned-order receipts: The quantity expected to be received by the *beginning* of the period in which it is shown. Under lot-for-lot ordering, this quantity will equal net requirements. Under lot-size ordering, this quantity may exceed net requirements. Any excess is added to available inventory in the *next* time period for simplicity, although in reality, it would be available in that period.

Planned-order releases: Indicates a *planned* amount to order in each time period; equals planned-order receipts offset by lead time. This amount generates gross requirements at the next level in the assembly or production chain. When an order is executed, it is removed from "planned-order releases" and entered under "scheduled receipts."

Planned-order releases Planned amount to order in each time period; planned-order receipts offset by lead time.

The quantities that are generated by exploding the bill of materials are *gross requirements;* they do not take into account any inventory that is currently on hand or due to be received. The materials that a firm must actually acquire to meet the demand generated by the master schedule are the *net material requirements.*

The determination of the net requirements (*netting*) is the core of MRP processing. One accomplishes it by subtracting from gross requirements the sum of inventory on hand and any scheduled receipts, and then adding in safety stock requirements, if applicable:

$$\text{Net requirements} = \text{Gross requirements} - \text{Available inventory} \quad (12\text{–}1)$$

$$\text{Available inventory} = \text{Projected on hand} - \text{Safety stock} - \text{Inventory allocated to other items} \quad (12\text{–}2)$$

In examples and problems, unless otherwise stated, assume that safety stock and allocated stock are equal to zero. The general computation for net requirements then becomes

$$\text{Net requirements} = \text{Gross requirements} - \text{Projected on-hand inventory} \quad (12\text{–}3)$$

Projected on-hand inventory includes scheduled receipts, which are executed orders for components that are scheduled to be completed in-house or received from suppliers.

The timing and sizes of orders (i.e., materials ordered from suppliers or work started within the firm) are determined by *planned-order releases.* The timing of the receipts of these quantities is indicated by *planned-order receipts.* Depending on ordering policy, the planned-order releases may be multiples of a specified quantity (e.g., 50 units), or they may be equal to the quantity needed at that time. Although there are other possibilities, these two seem to be the most widely used. Example 2 illustrates the difference between these two ordering policies as well as the general concepts of time-phasing material requirements in MRP.

Development of a material requirements plan is based on the product structure tree diagram. Requirements are determined level by level, beginning with the end item (the top of the tree) and working down the tree, because the timing and quantity of each "parent" item become the basis for determining the timing and quantities of the "children" items directly below it. The children items then become the parent items for the next level, and so on.

EXAMPLE 2

www.mhhe.com/stevenson11e

A firm that produces wood shutters and bookcases has received two orders for shutters: one for 100 shutters and one for 150 shutters. The 100-unit order is due for delivery at the start of week 4 of the current schedule, and the 150-unit order is due for delivery at the start of week 8. Each shutter consists of two frames and four slatted wood sections. The wood sections are made by the firm, and fabrication takes one week. The frames are ordered, and lead time is two weeks. Assembly of the shutters requires one week. There is a scheduled receipt of 70 wood sections in (i.e., at the beginning of) week 1. Determine the size and timing of planned-order releases necessary to meet delivery requirements under each of these conditions:

1. Lot-for-lot ordering (i.e., planned-order release equal to net requirements).
2. Lot-size ordering with a lot size of 320 units for frames and 70 units for wood sections.

SOLUTION

a. Develop a master schedule:

Week number	1	2	3	4	5	6	7	8
Quantity				100				150

FIGURE 12.8 MRP schedule with lot-for-lot ordering

Master schedule for shutters:

Week number	Beg. Inv.	1	2	3	4	5	6	7	8
Quantity					100				150

Shutters: LT = 1 week	Beg. Inv.	1	2	3	4	5	6	7	8
Gross requirements					100				150
Scheduled receipts									
Projected on hand									
Net requirements					100				150
Planned-order receipts					100				150
Planned-order releases				100				150	

times 2   times 2

Frames: LT = 2 weeks	Beg. Inv.	1	2	3	4	5	6	7	8
Gross requirements				200				300	
Scheduled receipts									
Projected on hand									
Net requirements				200				300	
Planned-order receipts				200				300	
Planned-order releases		200				300			

times 4   times 4

Wood sections: LT = 1 week	Beg. Inv.	1	2	3	4	5	6	7	8
Gross requirements				400				600	
Scheduled receipts		70							
Projected on hand		70	70	70					
Net requirements				330				600	
Planned-order receipts				330				600	
Planned-order releases			330				600		

b. Develop a product structure tree:

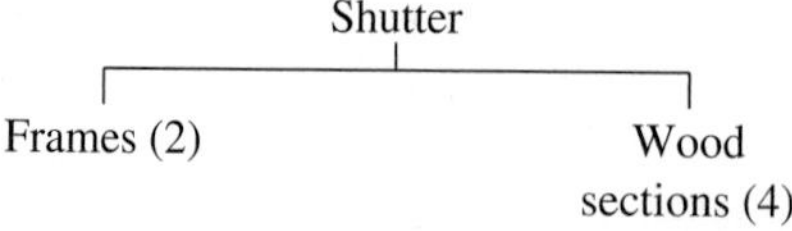

c. Using the master schedule, determine gross requirements for shutters. Next, compute net requirements. Using *lot-for-lot ordering,* determine planned-order receipt quantities and the planned-order release timing to satisfy the master schedule (see Figure 12.8).

The master schedule calls for 100 shutters to be ready for delivery, and no shutters are projected to be on hand at the start of week 4, so the net requirements are also 100 shutters. Therefore, planned receipts for week 4 equal 100 shutters. Because shutter assembly requires one week, this means a planned-order release at the start of week 3. Using the same logic, 150 shutters must be assembled during week 7 in order to be available for delivery at the start of week 8.

FIGURE 12.9 MRP schedule with lot sizes for components

Master schedule for shutters:

Week number	Beg. Inv.	1	2	3	4	5	6	7	8
Quantity					100				150

Shutters: LT = 1 week; Lot size = lot-for-lot	Beg. Inv.	1	2	3	4	5	6	7	8
Gross requirements					100				150
Scheduled receipts									
Projected on hand									
Net requirements					100				150
Planned-order receipts					100				150
Planned-order releases				100				150	

times 2   times 2

Frames: LT = 2 weeks; Lot size = multiples of 320	Beg. Inv.	1	2	3	4	5	6	7	8
Gross requirements				200				300	
Scheduled receipts									
Projected on hand					120	120	120	120	140
Net requirements				200				180	
Planned-order receipts				320				320	
Planned-order releases		320				320			

times 4   times 4

Wood sections: LT = 1 week; Lot size = multiples of 70	Beg. Inv.	1	2	3	4	5	6	7	8
Gross requirements				400				600	
Scheduled receipts		70							
Projected on hand		70	70	70	20	20	20	20	50
Net requirements				330				580	
Planned-order receipts				350				630	
Planned-order releases			350				630		

The planned-order release of 100 shutters at the start of week 3 means that 200 frames (gross requirements) must be available at that time. Because none are expected to be on hand, this generates net requirements of 200 frames and necessitates planned receipts of 200 frames by the start of week 3. With a two-week lead time, this means that the firm must order 200 frames at the start of week 1. Similarly, the planned-order release of 150 shutters at week 7 generates gross and net requirements of 300 frames for week 7 as well as planned receipts for that time. The two-week lead time means the firm must order frames at the start of week 5.

The planned-order release of 100 shutters at the start of week 3 also generates gross requirements of 400 wood sections at that time. However, because 70 wood sections are expected to be on hand, net requirements are $400 - 70 = 330$. This means a planned receipt of 330 by the start of week 3. Since fabrication time is one week, the fabrication must start (planned-order release) at the beginning of week 2.

Similarly, the planned-order release of 150 shutters in week 7 generates gross requirements of 600 wood sections at that point. Because no on-hand inventory of wood sections is projected, net requirements are also 600, and planned-order receipt is 600 units. Again, the one-week lead time means 600 sections are scheduled for fabrication at the start of week 6.

d. Under lot-size ordering, the only difference is the possibility that planned receipts will exceed net requirements. The excess is recorded as projected inventory in the following period. For example, in Figure 12.9, the order size for frames is 320 units. Net requirements for week 3 are 200; thus, there is an excess of 320 − 200 = 120 units, which become projected inventory in the next week. Similarly, net frame requirements of 180 units are 140 less than the 320 order size; again, the excess becomes projected inventory in week 8. The same thing happens with wood sections; an excess of planned receipts in weeks 3 and 7 is added to projected inventory in weeks 4 and 8. Note that the order size must be in *multiples* of the lot size; for week 3 it is 5 times 70, and for week 7 it is 9 times 70.

MRP provides plans for the end item and each of its subassemblies and components. Conceptually, this amounts to what is depicted in Figure 12.10. Practically speaking, however, the number of components in even a relatively simple product would make the width of the resulting spreadsheet far too wide to handle. Consequently, the plans for the individual components are *stacked,* as illustrated in the preceding example. Because of this, it is important to refer to the product tree in order to track relationships between components.

Example 2 is useful for describing some of the main features of MRP processing, but it understates the enormity of the task of keeping track of material requirements, especially in situations where the same subassemblies, parts, or raw materials are used in a number

FIGURE 12.10
Net requirements at each level determine gross requirements at the next

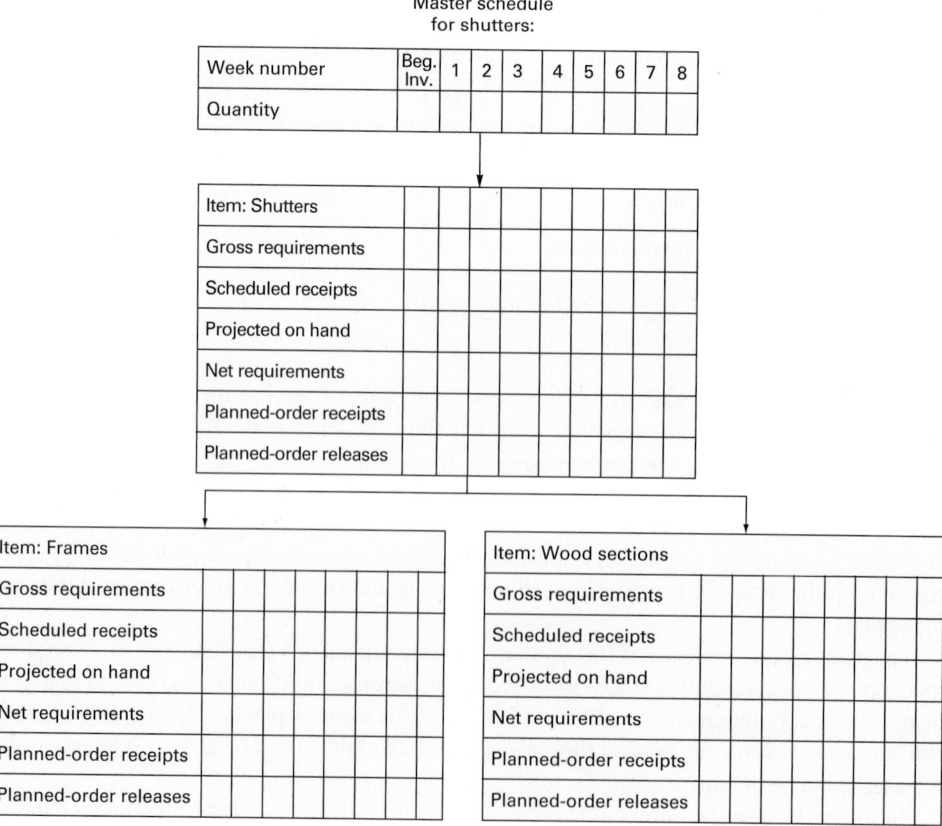

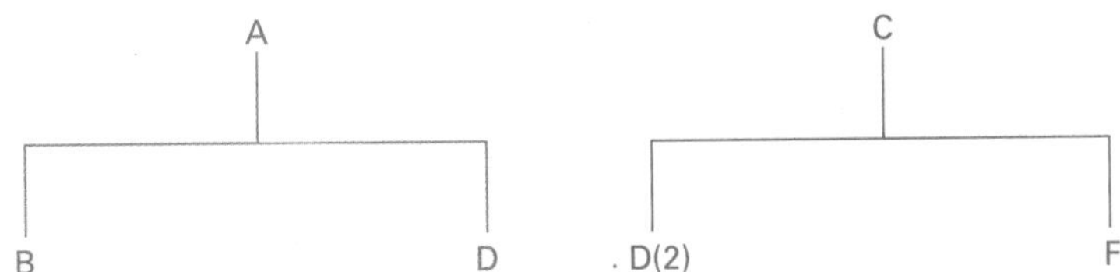

FIGURE 12.11
Two different products have D as a component

of different products. Differences in timing of demands and quantities needed, revisions caused by late deliveries, high scrap rates, and canceled orders all have an impact on processing.

Consider the two product structure trees shown in Figure 12.11. Note that both products have D as a component. Suppose we want to develop a material requirements plan for D given this additional information: There is a beginning inventory of 110 units of D on hand, and all items have lead times of one week. The master schedule calls for 80 units of A in week 4 and 50 units of C in week 5. The plan is shown in Figure 12.12. Note that requirements for B and F are not shown because they are not related to (i.e., neither a "parent" nor a "child" of) D.

The term **pegging** denotes working this process in reverse, that is, identifying the parent items that have generated a given set of material requirements for some item such as D. Although the process may appear simple enough given the product trees and schedules shown in this chapter, when multiple products are involved, the process is more complex. Pegging enables managers to determine which product(s) will be affected if orders are late due to late deliveries, quality problems, or other problems.

Pegging The process of identifying the parent items that have generated a given set of material requirements for an item.

The importance of the computer becomes evident when you consider that a typical firm would have not one but many end items for which it needs to develop material requirements plans, each with its own set of components. Inventories on hand and on order, schedules, order releases, and so on must all be updated as changes and rescheduling occur. Without the aid of a computer, the task would be almost hopeless; with the computer, planners can accomplish all of these things with much less difficulty.

Updating the System

A material requirements plan is not a static document. As time passes, some orders will have been completed, other orders will be nearing completion, and new orders will have been entered. In addition, there may have been changes to orders, such as changes in quantity, delays, missed deliveries of parts or raw materials, and so on. Hence, a material requirements plan is a "living" document, one that changes over time. And what we refer to as "Period 1" (i.e., the current period) is continually moving ahead; so what is now Period 2 will soon be Period 1. In a sense, schedules such as these have a *rolling horizon,* which means that plans are updated and revised so that they reflect the moving horizon over time.

The two basic systems used to update MRP records are *regenerative* and *net change.* A **regenerative system** is updated periodically; a **net-change system** is continuously updated.

Regenerative system Approach that updates MRP records periodically.

Net-change system Approach that updates MRP records continuously.

A regenerative system is essentially a batch-type system, which compiles all changes (e.g., new orders, receipts) that occur within the time interval (e.g., day) and periodically updates the system. Using that information, a revised production plan is developed in the same way that the original plan was developed (e.g., exploding the bill of materials, level by level).

In a net-change system, the production plan is modified to reflect changes as they occur. If some defective purchased parts had to be returned to a vendor, the manager can enter this information into the system as soon as it becomes known. Only the *changes* are exploded through the system, level by level; the entire plan would not be regenerated.

The regenerative system is best suited to fairly stable systems, whereas the net-change system is best suited to systems that have frequent changes. The obvious disadvantage of a

FIGURE 12.12
Material requirements plan for component D

Master schedule

Week number		1	2	3	4	5	6
Quantity of A					80		
Quantity of C						50	

A LT = 1	Beg. Inv.	1	2	3	4	5	6
Gross requirements					80		
Scheduled receipts							
Projected on hand							
Net requirements					80		
Planned-order receipts					80		
Planned-order releases				80			

C LT = 1	Beg. Inv.	1	2	3	4	5	6
Gross requirements						50	
Scheduled receipts							
Projected on hand							
Net requirements						50	
Planned-order receipts						50	
Planned-order releases					50		

times 2

D LT = 1	Beg. Inv.	1	2	3	4	5	6
Gross requirements				80	100		
Scheduled receipts							
Projected on hand	110	110	110	110	30		
Net requirements					70		
Planned-order receipts					70		
Planned-order releases				70			

regenerative system is the potential amount of lag between the time information becomes available and the time it can be incorporated into the material requirements plan. On the other hand, processing costs are typically less using regenerative systems; changes that occur in a given time period could ultimately cancel each other, thereby avoiding the need to modify and then remodify the plan. The disadvantages of the net-change system relate to the costs involved in continuously updating the system and the constant state of flux in a system caused by many small changes. One way around this is to enter minor changes periodically and major changes immediately. The primary advantage of the net-change system is that management can have up-to-date information for planning and control purposes.

MRP OUTPUTS

MRP systems have the ability to provide management with a fairly broad range of outputs. These are often classified as *primary reports,* which are the main reports, and *secondary reports,* which are optional outputs.

Primary Reports. Production and inventory planning and control are part of primary reports. These reports normally include the following:

1. **Planned orders,** a schedule indicating the amount and timing of future orders.
2. **Order releases,** authorizing the execution of planned orders.
3. **Changes** to planned orders, including revisions of due dates or order quantities and cancellations of orders.

Secondary Reports. Performance control, planning, and exceptions belong to secondary reports.

1. **Performance-control reports** evaluate system operation. They aid managers by measuring deviations from plans, including missed deliveries and stockouts, and by providing information that can be used to assess cost performance.
2. **Planning reports** are useful in forecasting future inventory requirements. They include purchase commitments and other data that can be used to assess future material requirements.
3. **Exception reports** call attention to major discrepancies such as late and overdue orders, excessive scrap rates, reporting errors, and requirements for nonexistent parts.

The wide range of outputs generally permits users to tailor MRP to their particular needs.

Planned orders Schedule indicating the amount and timing of future orders.

Order releases Authorization for the execution of planned orders.

Changes Revisions of due dates or order quantities, or cancellations of orders.

Performance-control reports Evaluation of system operation, including deviations from plans and cost information.

Planning reports Data useful for assessing future material requirements.

Exception reports Data on any major discrepancies encountered.

OTHER CONSIDERATIONS

Aside from the main details of inputs, outputs, and processing, managers must be knowledgeable about a number of other aspects of MRP. These include the holding of safety stock, lot-sizing choices, and the possible use of MRP for unfinished products.

Safety Stock

Theoretically, inventory systems with dependent demand should not require safety stock below the end item level. This is one of the main advantages of an MRP approach. Supposedly, safety stock is not needed because the manager can project precise usage quantities once the master schedule has been established because demand is not variable. Practically, however, there may be exceptions. For example, a bottleneck process or one with varying scrap rates can cause shortages in downstream operations. Furthermore, shortages may occur if orders are late or fabrication or assembly times are longer than expected. On the surface, these conditions lend themselves to the use of safety stock to maintain smooth operations; but the problem becomes more complicated when dealing with multiechelon items (i.e., multiple-level arenas such as assembled products) because a shortage of *any* component will prevent manufacture of the final assembly. However, a major advantage of MRP is lost by holding safety stock for all lower-level items.

MRP systems deal with these problems in several ways. The manager's first step is to identify activities or operations that are subject to variability and to determine the extent of that variability. When lead times are variable, the concept of safety *time* instead of safety *stock* is often used. This results in scheduling orders for arrival or completion sufficiently ahead of the time they are needed in order to eliminate or substantially reduce the element of chance in waiting for those items. When quantities tend to vary, some safety stock may be called for, but the manager must carefully weigh the need and cost of carrying extra stock. Frequently, managers elect to carry safety stock for end items, which are subject to random demand, and for selected lower-level operations when safety time is not feasible.

FIGURE 12.13
Demand for part K

	Period				
	1	2	3	4	5
Demand	70	50	1	80	4
Cumulative demand	70	120	121	201	205

It is important in general to make sure that lead times are accurate, particularly when the objective is to have incoming shipments of parts and materials arrive shortly before they are needed. Early arrivals increase on-hand inventory and carrying costs, but late arrivals can raise havoc, possibly delaying all following operations. Knowing this, managers may inflate lead times (i.e., use safety time) and cause early arrivals, defeating the objective of matching the arrival of orders with production schedules.

If safety stock is needed, planned-order release amounts can be increased by the safety stock quantities for the designated components.

Lot Sizing

Lot sizing Choosing a lot size for ordering or production.

Determining a lot size to order or to produce is an important issue in inventory management for both independent- and dependent-demand items. This is called **lot sizing.** For independent-demand items, managers often use economic order sizes and economic production quantities. For dependent-demand systems, however, a much wider variety of plans is used to determine lot sizes, mainly because no single plan has a clear advantage over the others. Some of the most popular plans for lot sizing are described in this section.

A primary goal of inventory management for both independent- and dependent-demand systems is to minimize the sum of ordering cost (or setup cost) and holding cost. With independent demand, that demand is frequently distributed uniformly throughout the planning horizon (e.g., six months, year). Demand tends to be much more lumpy for dependent demand, and the planning horizon shorter (e.g., three months), so that economic lot sizes are usually much more difficult to identify. Consider the situation depicted in Figure 12.13. Period demands vary from 1 to 80 units, and no demand size repeats over the horizon shown.

Managers can realize economies by grouping orders. This would be the case if the additional cost incurred by holding the extra units until they were used led to a savings in setup or ordering cost. This determination can be very complex at times, for several reasons. First, combining period demands into a single order, particularly for middle-level or end items, has a cascading effect down through the product tree: To achieve this grouping, it becomes necessary to also group items at lower levels in the tree and incorporate their setup and holding costs into the decision. Second, the uneven period demand and the relatively short planning horizon require a continual recalculation and updating of lot sizes. Not surprisingly, the methods used to handle lot sizing range from the complex, which attempt to include all relevant costs, to the very simple, which are easy to use and understand. In certain cases, the simple models seem to approach cost minimization although generalizations are difficult. Let's consider some of these models.

Lot-for-Lot Ordering. Perhaps the simplest of all the methods is lot-for-lot ordering. The order or run size for each period is set equal to demand for that period. Example 2 demonstrated this method. Not only is the order size obvious, it also virtually eliminates holding costs for parts carried over to other periods. Hence, lot-for-lot ordering minimizes investment in inventory. Its two chief drawbacks are that it usually involves many different order sizes and thus cannot take advantage of the economies of fixed order size (e.g., standard containers and other standardized procedures), and it requires a new setup for each production run. If setup costs can be significantly reduced, this method may approximate a minimum-cost lot size.

Economic Order Quantity Model. Sometimes economic order quantity (EOQ) models are used. They can lead to minimum costs if usage is fairly uniform. This is sometimes the case for lower-level items that are common to different parents and for raw materials. However, the more lumpy demand is, the less appropriate such an approach is, because the mismatch in supply and demand results in leftover inventories. Since demand tends to be most lumpy at the end item level, EOQ models tend to be less useful for end items than for items and materials at the lowest levels.

Fixed-Period Ordering. This type of ordering provides coverage for some predetermined number of periods (e.g., two or three). In some instances, the span is simply arbitrary; in other cases, a review of historical demand patterns may lead to a more rational designation of a fixed period length. A simple rule is: Order to cover a two-period interval. The rule can be modified when common sense suggests a better way. For example, take a look at the demands shown in Figure 12.13. Using a two-period rule, an order size of 120 units would cover the first two periods. The next two periods would be covered by an order size of 81 units. However, the demands in periods 3 and 5 are so small, it would make sense to combine them both with the 80 units and order 85 units.

MRP IN SERVICES

SERVICE

MRP has applications in services as well as in manufacturing. These applications may involve material goods that form a part of the product–service package, or they may involve mainly service components.

An example of a product–service package is a food catering service, particularly in instances that require preparing and serving meals for large numbers of people. To estimate quantities and costs of an order, the food manager would have to determine the quantities of the ingredients for each recipe on the menu (i.e., a bill of materials), which would then be combined with the number of each meal to be prepared to obtain a material requirements plan for the event.

Similar examples occur for large-scale renovations, such as a sports stadium or a major hotel, where there are multiple repetitions of activities and related materials that must be "exploded" into their components for purposes of cost estimation and scheduling.

BENEFITS AND REQUIREMENTS OF MRP

Benefits

MRP enables managers to easily determine the quantities of every component for a given order size, to know when to release orders for each component, and to be alerted when items need attention. Still other benefits include the following:

1. Low levels of in-process inventories, due to an exact matching of supply to demand.
2. The ability to keep track of material requirements.
3. The ability to evaluate capacity requirements generated by a given master schedule.
4. A means of allocating production time.
5. The ability to easily determine inventory usage by *backflushing.*

Backflushing is a procedure in which an end item's bill of materials (BOM) is periodically exploded to determine the quantities of the various components that were used to make the item, eliminating the need to collect detailed usage information on the production floor.

Backflushing Exploding an end item's BOM to determine the quantities of the components that were used to make the item.

A range of people in a typical manufacturing company are important users of the information provided by an MRP system. Production planners are obvious users of MRP. Production managers, who must balance workloads across departments and make decisions about scheduling work, and plant foremen, who are responsible for issuing work orders and maintaining production schedules, also rely heavily on MRP output. Other users include customer service representatives, who must be able to supply customers with projected delivery dates; purchasing managers; and inventory managers. The benefits of MRP depend in large measure on the use of a computer to maintain up-to-date information on material requirements.

Requirements

In order to implement and operate an effective MRP system, it is necessary to have

1. A computer and the necessary software programs to handle computations and maintain records.
2. Accurate and up-to-date
   a. Master schedules.
   b. Bills of materials.
   c. Inventory records.
3. Integrity of file data.

Accuracy is absolutely essential for a successful MRP system. Inaccuracies in inventory record files or bill-of-material files can lead to unpleasant surprises, ranging from missing parts to ordering too many of some items and too few of others, and failure to stay on schedule, all of which contribute to inefficient use of resources, missed delivery dates, and poor customer service. Companies also need to exert scheduling discipline and have in place standard procedures for maintaining and updating bills of material.

Other common problems associated with using MRP include those due to the assumption of constant lead times, products being produced differently from the bill of materials, and failure to alter a bill of materials when customizing a product.

Similarly, inaccurate forecasts can have serious consequences for producers of assembled items. If forecasts are overly optimistic, companies will experience relatively high holding costs, considering the excess inventory represented by the components and raw materials. Conversely, forecasts that are too low will result in shortages of component parts and require long lead times to acquire the needed components and assemble the products to alleviate the shortages.

MRP II

Manufacturing resources planning (MRP II) Expanded approach to production resource planning, involving other areas of a firm in the planning process and enabling capacity requirements planning.

MRP was developed as a way for manufacturing companies to calculate more precisely what materials were needed to produce a product, and when and how much of those materials were needed. **Manufacturing resources planning (MRP II)** evolved from MRP in the 1980s because manufacturers recognized additional needs. MRP II did not replace or improve MRP. Rather, it expanded the scope of materials planning to include capacity requirements planning, and to involve other functional areas of the organization such as marketing and finance in the planning process.

Material requirements planning is at the heart of the process (see Figure 12.14). The process begins with an aggregation of demand from all sources (e.g., firm orders, forecasts, safety stock requirements). Production, marketing, and finance personnel work toward developing a master production schedule. Although manufacturing people will have a major input in determining that schedule and a major responsibility for making it work, marketing and finance will also have important inputs and responsibilities. The rationale for having these functional areas work together is the increased likelihood of developing a plan that works and with which everyone can live. Moreover, because each of these functional areas has been involved in formulating the plan, they will have reasonably good knowledge of the plan and more reason to work toward achieving it.

In addition to the obvious manufacturing resources needed to support the plan, financing resources will be needed and must be planned for, both in amount and timing. Similarly, marketing resources also will be needed in varying degrees throughout the process. In order for the plan to work, the firm must have all of the necessary resources available as needed. Often, an initial plan must be revised based on an assessment of the availability of various resources. Once these have been decided, the master production schedule can be firmed up.

At this point, material requirements planning comes into play, generating material and schedule requirements. Next, management must make more detailed capacity requirements

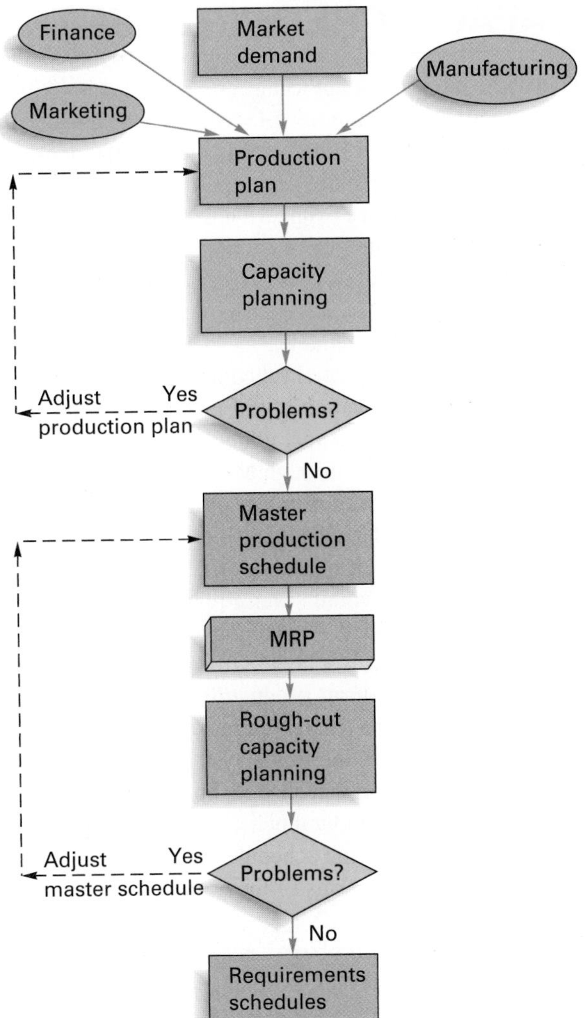

FIGURE 12.14
An overview of MRP II

planning to determine whether these more specific capacity requirements can be met. Again, some adjustments in the master production schedule may be required.

As the schedule unfolds and actual work begins, a variety of reports help managers to monitor the process and to make any necessary adjustments to keep operations on track.

In effect, this is a continuing process, where the master production schedule is updated and revised as necessary to achieve corporate goals. The business plan that governs the entire process usually undergoes changes too, although these tend to be less frequent than the changes made at lower levels (i.e., the master production schedule).

Most MRP II systems have the capability of performing simulation, enabling managers to answer a variety of what-if questions so they can gain a better appreciation of available options and their consequences.

Closed-Loop MRP

When MRP was introduced, it did not have the capability to assess the feasibility of a proposed plan (i.e., if sufficient capacity existed at every level to achieve the plan). Thus, there was no way of knowing before executing a proposed plan if it could be achieved, or after executing the plan if it had been achieved. Consequently, a new plan had to be developed each week. When MRP II systems began to include feedback loops, they were referred to as closed-loop MRP. Closed-loop MRP systems evaluate a proposed material plan relative to available capacity. If a proposed plan is not feasible, it must be revised. The evaluation is referred to as capacity requirements planning.

CAPACITY REQUIREMENTS PLANNING

Capacity requirements planning The process of determining short-range capacity requirements.

One of the most important features of MRP II is its ability to aid managers in capacity planning.

Capacity requirements planning is the process of determining short-range capacity requirements. The necessary inputs include planned-order releases for MRP, the current shop load, routing information, and job times. Key outputs include load reports for each work center. When variances (underloads or overloads) are projected, managers might consider remedies such as alternative routings, changing or eliminating of lot sizing or safety stock requirements, and lot splitting. Moving production forward or backward can be extremely challenging because of precedence requirements and the availability of components.

A firm usually generates a master schedule initially in terms of what is needed but not what is possible. The initial schedule may or may not be feasible given the limits of the production system and availability of materials when end items are translated into requirements for procurement, fabrication, and assembly. Consequently, it is often necessary to run a proposed master schedule through MRP processing in order to obtain a clearer picture of actual requirements, which can then be compared to available capacity and materials. If it turns out that the current master schedule is not feasible, management may make a decision to increase capacity (e.g., through overtime or subcontracting) or to revise the master schedule. In the latter case, this may entail several revisions, each of which is run through the system until a feasible plan is obtained. At that point, the master schedule is *frozen,* at least for the near term, thus establishing a firm schedule from which to plan requirements.

Stability in short-term production plans is very important; without it, changes in order quantity and/or timing can render material requirements plans almost useless. The term *system nervousness* describes the way a system might react to changes. The reaction can sometimes be greater than the original change. For example, a small change near the top of a product tree can reverberate throughout much of the lower parts of the tree, causing major changes to order quantities and production schedules of many components. That, in turn, might cause queues to form at various portions of the system, leading to late orders, increased work in process, and added carrying costs.

Time fences Series of time intervals during which order changes are allowed or restricted; the nearest fence is most restrictive to change, the farthest is least restrictive.

To minimize such problems, many firms establish a series of time intervals, called **time fences,** during which changes can be made to orders. For example, a firm might specify time fences of 4, 8, and 12 weeks, with the nearest fence being the most restrictive and the farthest fence being the least restrictive. Beyond 12 weeks, changes are expected; from 8 to 12 weeks, substitutions of one end item for another may be permitted as long as the components are available and the production plan is not compromised; from 4 to 8 weeks, the plan is fixed, but small changes may be allowed; and the plan is frozen out to the four-week fence.

Some companies use two fences: One is a near-term *demand* fence, and the other is a long-term *planning* fence. For example, the demand fence might be 4 weeks from the present time while the planning fence might be 10 weeks away. In the near term, customer orders receive precedence over the forecast. The time beyond the planning fence is available for inserting new orders into the master schedule. Between the demand fence and the planning fence, management must make trade-offs when changes are introduced unless excess capacity is expected to be available.

In establishing time fences, a manager must weigh the benefits of stability in the production plan against the possible negative impact on the competitive advantage of being able to quickly respond to new orders.

Load reports Department or work center reports that compare known and expected future capacity requirements with projected capacity availability.

Figure 12.15 presents an overview of the capacity planning process. The process begins with a proposed or tentative master production schedule that must be tested for feasibility and possibly adjusted before it becomes permanent. The proposed schedule is processed using MRP to ascertain the material requirements the schedule would generate. These are then translated into resource (i.e., capacity) requirements, often in the form of a series of **load reports** for each department or work center, which compares known and expected future capacity requirements with projected capacity availability. Figure 12.16 illustrates the nature of a load report. It shows expected resource requirements (i.e., usage) for jobs currently being worked on, planned orders, and expected orders for the planning horizon. Given this

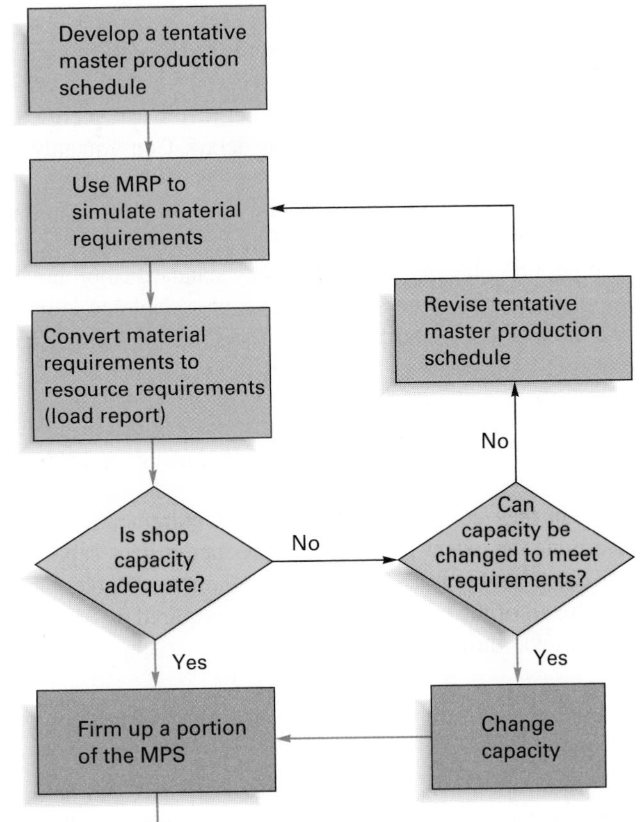

FIGURE 12.15
Using MRP to assist in planning capacity requirements

Source: Stephen Love, *Inventory Control* (New York: McGraw-Hill). Reprinted by permission.

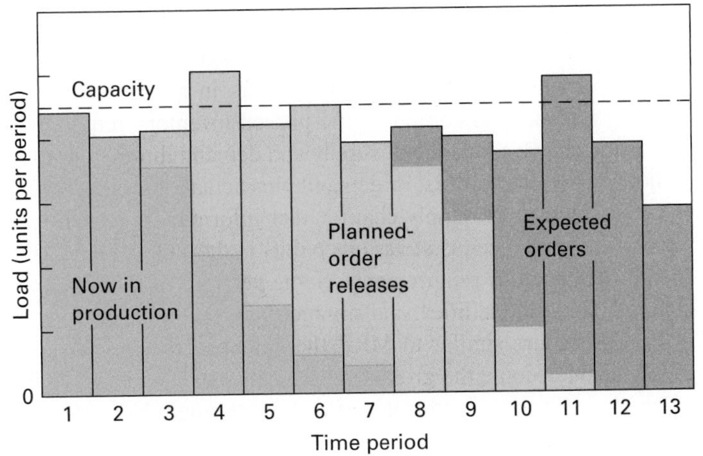

FIGURE 12.16
A hypothetical department load profile

sort of information, the manager can more easily determine whether capacity is sufficient to satisfy these requirements. If there is enough capacity, he or she can freeze the portion of the master production schedule that generates these requirements. In the load profile illustrated in Figure 12.16, planned-order releases in time period 4 will cause an overload. However, it appears possible to accommodate demand by slightly shifting some orders to adjacent periods. Similarly, an overload appears likely in period 11, but that too can be handled by shifting some jobs to adjacent time periods. In cases where capacity is insufficient, a manager may be able to increase capacity (by scheduling overtime, transferring personnel from other areas, or subcontracting some of the work) if this is possible and economical, or else revise the master production schedule and repeat the process until an acceptable production schedule is obtained.

If the master production schedule must be revised, this generally means that the manager must assign priorities to orders, if some orders will be finished later than originally planned.

One note of caution is in order concerning capacity load reports. Often, the load reports are only approximations, and they may not give a true picture because the loading does not take into account scheduling and queuing delays. Consequently, it is possible to experience system backups even though a load report implies sufficient capacity to handle projected loads.

An important aspect of capacity requirements planning is the conversion of quantity requirements into labor and machine requirements. One accomplishes this by multiplying each period's quantity requirements by standard labor and/or machine requirements per unit. For instance, if 100 units of product A are scheduled in the fabrication department, and each unit has a labor standard time of 2 hours and a machine standard time of 1.5 hours, then 100 units of A convert into these capacity requirements:

Labor: $100 \text{ units} \times 2 \text{ hours/unit} = 200 \text{ labor hours}$

Machine: $100 \text{ units} \times 1.5 \text{ hours/unit} = 150 \text{ machine hours}$

One can then compare these capacity requirements with available department capacity to determine the extent to which this product utilizes capacity. For example, if the department has 200 labor hours and 200 machine hours available, labor utilization will be 100 percent because all of the labor capacity will be required by this product. However, machine capacity will be underutilized.

$$\frac{\text{Required}}{\text{Available}} \times 100 = \frac{150 \text{ hours}}{200 \text{ hours}} \times 100 = 75 \text{ percent}$$

Underutilization may mean that unused capacity can be used for other jobs; overutilization indicates that available capacity is insufficient to handle requirements. To compensate, production may have to be rescheduled or overtime may be needed.

Distribution Resource Planning for the Supply Chain

Distribution resource planning (DRP) A method used for planning orders in a supply chain.

Distribution Resource Planning (DRP), also referred to as *distribution requirements planning,* is a method used for planning orders in a supply chain. It extends MRP concepts, enabling a planner to compute time-phased inventory requirements for a supply chain. The goal is to achieve a balance of supply and demand throughout the supply chain.

It begins with a forecast of demand plus actual orders for future periods at the distribution end (e.g., retail) of a supply chain. Other information needed includes the quantity and timing of scheduled receipts at various points in the supply chain as well as on-hand inventories, and any safety stock requirements. Some versions of DRP also include projections for labor, material handling facilities, and storage space that will be needed.

In a procedure similar to MRP, the planned-order release quantities at each level in the supply chain become the gross requirements one level back, as illustrated in Figure 12.17. In effect, the process pulls inventory shipment through the supply chain based on demand.

ERP

Business organizations are complex systems in which various functions such as purchasing, production, distribution, sales, human resources, finance, and accounting must work together to achieve the goals of the organization. However, in the functional structure used by many business organizations, information flows freely within each function, but not so between functions. That makes information sharing among functional areas burdensome.

Enterprise resource planning (ERP) Integration of financial, manufacturing, and human resources on a single computer system.

Enterprise resource planning (ERP) was the next step in an evolution that began with MRP and evolved into MRP II. Like MRP II, it typically has an MRP core. ERP represents an expanded effort to integrate *standardized* record keeping that will permit *information sharing* among different areas of an organization in order to manage the system more effectively.

ERP software provides a system to capture and make data available in real time to decision makers and other users throughout an organization. It also provides a set of tools for planning

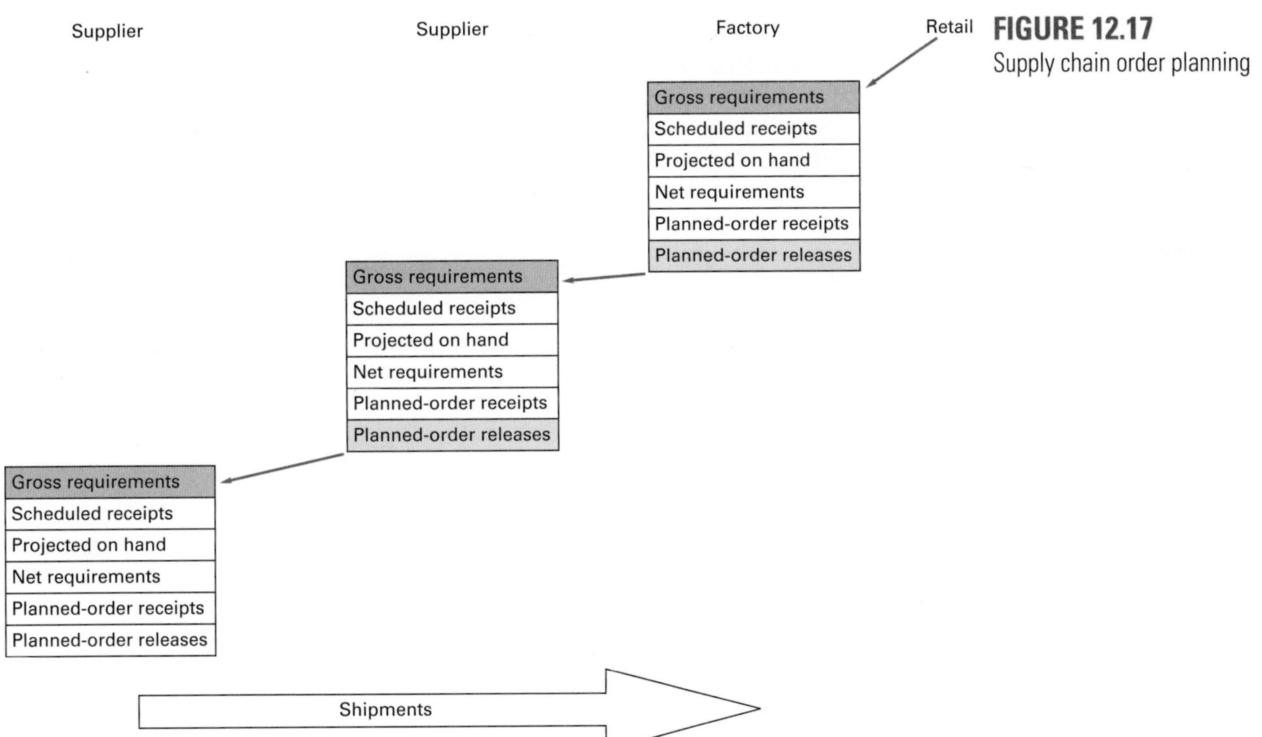

FIGURE 12.17
Supply chain order planning

and monitoring various business processes to achieve the goals of the organization. ERP systems are composed of a collection of integrated modules. There are many modules to choose from, and different software vendors offer different but similar lists of modules. Some are industry specific, and others are general purpose. The modules relate to the functional areas of business organizations. For example, there are modules for accounting and finance, HR, product planning, purchasing, inventory management, distribution, order tracking, finance, accounting, and marketing. Organizations can select the modules that best serve their needs and budgets. Table 12.1 provides an overview of some widely used modules.

TABLE 12.1
An overview of some ERP software modules

Module	Brief Description
Accounting/Finance	A central component of most ERP systems. It provides a range of financial reports, including general ledger, accounts payable, accounts receivable, payroll, income statements, and balance sheets.
Marketing	Supports lead generation, target marketing, direct mail, and sales.
Human Resources	Maintains a complete database of employee information such as date of hire, salary, contact information, performance evaluations, and other pertinent information.
Purchasing	Facilitates vendor selection, price negotiation, making purchasing decisions, and bill payment.
Production Planning	Integrates information on forecasts, orders, production capacity, on-hand inventory quantities, bills of material, work in process, schedules, and production lead times.
Inventory Management	Identifies inventory requirements, inventory availability, replenishment rules, and inventory tracking.
Distribution	Contains information on third-party shippers, shipping and delivery schedules, delivery tracking.
Sales	Information on orders, invoices, order tracking, and shipping.
Supply Chain Management	Facilitates supplier and customer management, supply chain visibility, and event management.

An important feature of the modules is that data entered in one module is automatically routed to other modules, so all data is immediately updated and available to all functional areas.

It should be noted that implementations are costly and time consuming, often lasting many years, and require extensive employee training throughout the organization.

The following reading provides additional insight into ERP.

The ABCs of ERP

READING

Compiled from Reports by Christopher Koch, Derek Slater, and E. Baatz

- What is ERP?
- How can ERP improve a company's business performance?
- How long will an ERP project take?
- What will ERP fix in my business?
- Will ERP fit the way I do business?
- What does ERP really cost?
- When will I get payback from ERP—and how much will it be?
- What are the unforeseen costs of ERP?
- How do you configure ERP software?
- How do companies organize their ERP projects?
- How does ERP fit with electronic commerce?

What Is ERP?

Enterprise resource planning software, or ERP, doesn't live up to its acronym. Forget about planning—it doesn't do that—and forget about resource, a throwaway term. But remember the enterprise part. This is ERP's true ambition. It attempts to integrate all departments and functions across a company onto a single computer system that can serve all those different departments' particular needs.

That is a tall order, building a single software program that serves the needs of people in finance as well as it does the people in human resources and in the warehouse. Each of those departments typically has its own computer system, each optimized for the particular ways that the department does its work. But ERP combines them all together into a single, integrated software program that runs off a single database so that the various departments can more easily share information and communicate with each other.

That integrated approach can have a tremendous payback if companies install the software correctly. Take a customer order, for example. Typically, when a customer places an order, that order begins a mostly paper-based journey from in-basket to in-basket around the company, often being keyed and rekeyed into different departments' computer systems along the way. All that lounging around in in-baskets causes delays and lost orders, and all the keying into different computer systems invites errors. Meanwhile, no one in the company truly knows what the status of the order is at any given point because there is no way for the finance department, for example, to get into the warehouse's computer system to see whether the item has been shipped. "You'll have to call the warehouse," is the familiar refrain heard by frustrated customers.

How Can ERP Improve a Company's Business Performance?

ERP automates the tasks involved in performing a business process—such as order fulfillment, which involves taking an order from a customer, shipping it and billing for it. With ERP, when a customer service representative takes an order from a customer, he or she has all the information necessary to complete the order (the customer's credit rating and order history, the company's inventory levels and the shipping dock's trucking schedule). Everyone else in the company sees the same computer screen and has access to the single database that holds the customer's new order. When one department finishes with the order it is automatically routed via the ERP system to the next department. To find out where the order is at any point, one need only log into the ERP system and track it down. With luck, the order process moves like a bolt of lightning through the organization, and customers get their orders faster and with fewer mistakes than before. ERP can apply that same magic to the other major business processes, such as employee benefits or financial reporting.

That, at least, is the dream of ERP. The reality is much harsher.

Let's go back to those inboxes for a minute. That process may not have been efficient, but it was simple. Finance did its job, the warehouse did its job, and if anything went wrong outside of the department's walls, it was somebody else's problem. Not anymore. With ERP, the customer service representatives are no longer just typists entering someone's name into a computer and hitting the return key. The ERP screen makes them business people. It flickers with the customer's credit rating from the finance department and the product inventory levels from the warehouse. Will the customer pay on time? Will we be able to ship the order on time? These are decisions that customer service representatives have never had to make before and which affect the customer and every other department in the company. But it's not just the customer service representatives who have to wake up. People in the warehouse who used to keep inventory in their heads or on scraps of paper now need to put that information online. If they don't, customer service will see low inventory levels on their screens and tell customers that their requested item is not in stock. Accountability, responsibility and communication have never been tested like this before.

(continued)

How Long Will an ERP Project Take?

Companies that install ERP do not have an easy time of it. Don't be fooled when ERP vendors tell you about a three or six month average implementation time. Those short (that's right, six months is short) implementations all have a catch of one kind or another: the company was small, or the implementation was limited to a small area of the company, or the company only used the financial pieces of the ERP system (in which case the ERP system is nothing more than a very expensive accounting system). To do ERP right, the ways you do business will need to change and the ways people do their jobs will need to change too. And that kind of change doesn't come without pain. Unless, of course, your ways of doing business are working extremely well (orders all shipped on time, productivity higher than all your competitors, customers completely satisfied), in which case there is no reason to even consider ERP.

The important thing is not to focus on how long it will take—real transformational ERP efforts usually run between one to three years, on average—but rather to understand why you need it and how you will use it to improve your business.

What Will ERP Fix in My Business?

There are three major reasons why companies undertake ERP:

To integrate financial data—As the CEO tries to understand the company's overall performance, he or she may find many different versions of the truth. Finance has its own set of revenue numbers, sales has another version, and the different business units may each have their own versions of how much they contributed to revenues. ERP creates a single version of the truth that cannot be questioned because everyone is using the same system.

To standardize manufacturing processes—Manufacturing companies—especially those with an appetite for mergers and acquisitions—often find that multiple business units across the company make the same widget using different methods and computer systems. Standardizing those processes and using a single, integrated computer system can save time, increase productivity and reduce headcount.

To standardize HR information—Especially in companies with multiple business units, HR may not have a unified, simple method for tracking employee time and communicating with them about benefits and services. ERP can fix that.

In the race to fix these problems, companies often lose sight of the fact that ERP packages are nothing more than generic representations of the ways a typical company does business. While most packages are exhaustively comprehensive, each industry has its quirks that make it unique. Most ERP systems were designed to be used by discreet manufacturing companies (who make physical things that can be counted), which immediately left all the process manufacturers (oil, chemical and utility companies that measure their products by flow rather than individual units) out in the cold. Each of these industries has struggled with the different ERP vendors to modify core ERP programs to their needs.

Will ERP Fit the Ways I Do Business?

It's critical for companies to figure out if their ways of doing business will fit within a standard ERP package before the checks are signed and the implementation begins. The most common reason that companies walk away from multimillion-dollar ERP projects is that they discover that the software does not support one of their important business processes. At that point there are two things they can do: They can change the business process to accommodate the software, which will mean deep changes in long-established ways of doing business (that often provide competitive advantage) and shake up important peoples' roles and responsibilities (something that few companies have the stomach for). Or they can modify the software to fit the process, which will slow down the project, introduce dangerous bugs into the system and make upgrading the software to the ERP vendor's next release excruciatingly difficult, because the customizations will need to be torn apart and rewritten to fit with the new version.

Needless to say, the move to ERP is a project of breathtaking scope, and the price tags on the front end are enough to make the most placid CFO a little twitchy. In addition to budgeting for software costs, financial executives should plan to write checks to cover consulting, process rework, integration testing and a long laundry list of other expenses before the benefits of ERP start to manifest themselves. Underestimating the price of teaching users their new job processes can lead to a rude shock down the line. So can failure to consider data warehouse integration requirements and the cost of extra software to duplicate the old report formats. A few oversights in the budgeting and planning stage can send ERP costs spiraling out of control faster than oversights in planning almost any other information system undertaking.

What Does ERP *Really* Cost?

Meta Group recently did a study looking at the Total Cost of Ownership (TCO) of ERP, including hardware, software, professional services, and internal staff costs. The TCO numbers include getting the software installed and the two years afterward, which is when the real costs of maintaining, upgrading and optimizing the system for your business are felt. Among the 63 companies surveyed—including small, medium and large companies in a range of industries—the average TCO was $15 million (the highest was $300 million and lowest was $400,000). While it's hard to draw a solid number from that kind of a range of companies and ERP efforts, Meta came up with one statistic that proves that ERP is expensive no matter what kind of company is using it. The TCO for a "heads-down" user over that period was a staggering $53,320.

When Will I Get Payback from ERP—and How Much Will It Be?

Don't expect to revolutionize your business with ERP. It is a navel gazing exercise that focuses on optimizing the way things are done internally rather than with customers, suppliers or partners. Yet the navel gazing has a pretty good payback if you're willing

(continued)

to wait for it—a Meta Group study of 63 companies found that it took eight months after the new system was in (31 months total) to see any benefits. But the median annual savings from the new ERP system was $1.6 million per year.

The Hidden Costs of ERP

Although different companies will find different land mines in the budgeting process, those who have implemented ERP packages agree that certain costs are more commonly overlooked or underestimated than others. Armed with insights from across the business, ERP pros vote the following areas as most likely to result in budget overrun.

1. **Training.** Training is the near-unanimous choice of experienced ERP implementers as the most elusive budget item. It's not so much that this cost is completely overlooked as it is consistently underestimated. Training expenses are high because workers almost invariably have to learn a new set of processes, not just a new software interface.
2. **Integration and testing.** Testing the links between ERP packages and other corporate software links that have to be built on a case-by-case basis is another often underestimated cost. A typical manufacturing company may have add-on applications for logistics, tax, production planning and bar coding. If this laundry list also includes customization of the core ERP package, expect the cost of integrating, testing and maintaining the system to skyrocket.

   As with training, testing ERP integration has to be done from a process-oriented perspective. Instead of plugging in dummy data and moving it from one application to the next, veterans recommend running a real purchase order through the system, from order entry through shipping and receipt of payment—the whole order-to-cash banana—preferably with the participation of the employees who will eventually do those jobs.
3. **Data conversion.** It costs money to move corporate information, such as customer and supplier records, product design data and the like, from old systems to new ERP homes. Although few CIOs will admit it, most data in most legacy systems is of little use. Companies often deny their data is dirty until they actually have to move it to the new client/server setups that popular ERP packages require. Consequently, those companies are more likely to underestimate the cost of the move. But even clean data may demand some overhaul to match process modifications necessitated—or inspired—by the ERP implementation.
4. **Data analysis.** Often, the data from the ERP system must be combined with data from external systems for analysis purposes. Users with heavy analysis needs should include the cost of a data warehouse in the ERP budget—and they should expect to do quite a bit of work to make it run smoothly. Users are in a pickle here: Refreshing all the ERP data in a big corporate data warehouse daily is difficult, and ERP systems do a poor job of indicating which information has changed from day to day, making selective warehouse updates tough. One expensive solution is custom programming. The upshot is that the wise will check all their data analysis needs before signing off on the budget.
5. **Consultants ad infinitum.** When users fail to plan for disengagement, consulting fees run wild. To avoid this, companies should identify objectives for which [their] consulting partners must aim when training internal staff. Include metrics in the consultants' contract; for example, a specific number of the user company's staff should be able to pass a project-management leadership test—similar to what Big Five consultants have to pass to lead an ERP engagement.
6. **Replacing your best and brightest.** ERP success depends on staffing the project with the best and brightest from the business and IS. The software is too complex and the business changes too dramatic to trust the project to just anyone. The bad news is, a company must be prepared to replace many of those people when the project is over. Though the ERP market is not as hot as it once was, consulting firms and other companies that have lost their best people will be hounding yours with higher salaries and bonus offers than you can afford—or that your HR policies permit. Huddle with HR early on to develop a retention bonus program and to create new salary strata for ERP veterans. If you let them go, you'll wind up hiring them—or someone like them—back as consultants for twice what you paid them in salaries.
7. **Implementation teams can never stop.** Most companies intend to treat their ERP implementations as they would any other software project. Once the software is installed, they figure, the team will be scuttled and everyone will go back to his or her day job. But after ERP, you can't go home again. You're too valuable. Because they have worked intimately with ERP, they know more about the sales process than the salespeople do and more about the manufacturing process than the manufacturing people do. Companies can't afford to send their project people back into the business because there's so much to do after the ERP software is installed. Just writing reports to pull information out of the new ERP system will keep the project team busy for a year at least. And it is in analysis—and, one hopes, insight—that companies make their money back on an ERP implementation. Unfortunately, few IS departments plan for the frenzy of post-ERP installation activity, and fewer still build it into their budgets when they start their ERP projects. Many are forced to beg for more money and staff immediately after the go-live date, long before the ERP project has demonstrated any benefit.
8. **Waiting for ROI.** One of the most misleading legacies of traditional software project management is that the company expects to gain value from the application as soon as it is installed; the project team expects a break, and maybe a pat on the back. Neither expectation applies to ERP. Most don't reveal their value until after companies have had them running for some time and can concentrate on making improvements in the business processes that are affected by the system.

(continued)

And the project team is not going to be rewarded until their efforts pay off.

9. **Post-ERP depression.** ERP systems often wreak havoc in the companies that install them. In a recent Deloitte Consulting survey of 64 Fortune 500 companies, one in four admitted that they suffered a drop in performance when their ERP systems went live. The true percentage is undoubtedly much higher. The most common reason for the performance problems is that everything looks and works differently from the way it did before. When people can't do their jobs in the familiar way and haven't yet mastered the new way, they panic, and the business goes into spasms.

How Do You Configure ERP Software?

Even if a company installs ERP software for the so-called right reasons and everyone can agree on the optimal definition of a customer, the inherent difficulties of implementing something as complex as ERP is like, well, teaching an elephant to do the hootchy-kootchy. The packages are built from database tables, thousands of them, that IS programmers and end users must set to match their business processes; each table has a decision "switch" that leads the software down one decision path or another. By presenting only one way for the company to do each task—say, run the payroll or close the books—a company's individual operating units and far-flung divisions are integrated under one system. But figuring out precisely how to set all the switches in the tables requires a deep understanding of the existing processes being used to operate the business. As the table settings are decided, these business processes are reengineered, ERP's way. Most ERP systems are not shipped as a shell system in which customers must determine at the minutia level how all the functional procedures should be set, making thousands of decisions that affect how their system behaves in line with their own business activities. Most ERP systems are preconfigured, allowing just hundreds— rather than thousands—of procedural settings to be made by the customer.

How Do Companies Organize Their ERP Projects?

Based on our observations, there are three commonly used ways of installing ERP.

The big bang—In this, the most ambitious and difficult of approaches to ERP implementation, companies cast off all their legacy systems at once and implement a single ERP system across the entire company.

Though this method dominated early ERP implementations, few companies dare to attempt it anymore because it calls for the entire company to mobilize and change at once. Most of the ERP implementation horror stories from the late '90s warn us about companies that used this strategy. Getting everyone to cooperate and accept a new software system at the same time is a tremendous effort, largely because the new system will not have any advocates. No one within the company has any experience using it, so no one is sure whether it will work. Also, ERP inevitably involves compromises. Many departments have computer systems that have been honed to match the ways they work. In most cases, ERP offers neither the range of functionality, nor the comfort of familiarity that a custom legacy system can offer. In many cases, the speed of the new system may suffer because it is serving the entire company rather than a single department. ERP implementation requires a direct mandate from the CEO.

Franchising strategy—This approach suits large or diverse companies that do not share many common processes across business units. Independent ERP systems are installed in each unit, while linking common processes, such as financial bookkeeping, across the enterprise.

This has emerged as the most common way of implementing ERP. In most cases, the business units each have their own "instances" of ERP—that is, a separate system and database. The systems link together only to share the information necessary for the corporation to get a performance big picture across all the business units (business unit revenues, for example), or for processes that don't vary much from business unit to business unit (perhaps HR benefits). Usually, these implementations begin with a demonstration or "pilot" installation in a particularly open-minded and patient business unit where the core business of the corporation will not be disrupted if something goes wrong. Once the project team gets the system up and running and works out all the bugs, the team begins selling other units on ERP, using the first implementation as a kind of in-house customer reference. Plan for this strategy to take a long time.

Slam-dunk—ERP dictates the process design in this method, where the focus is on just a few key processes, such as those contained in an ERP system's financials module. The slam-dunk is generally for smaller companies expecting to grow into ERP.

The goal here is to get ERP up and running quickly and to ditch the fancy reengineering in favor of the ERP system's "canned" processes. Few companies that have approached ERP this way can claim much payback from the new system. Most use it as an infrastructure to support more diligent installation efforts down the road. Yet many discover that a slammed-in ERP system is little better than a legacy system, because it doesn't force employees to change any of their old habits. In fact, doing the hard work of process reengineering after the system is in can be more challenging than if there had been no system at all, because at that point few people in the company will have felt much benefit.

How Does ERP Fit with Electronic Commerce?

After all of that work inventing, perfecting and selling ERP to the world, the major ERP vendors are having a hard time shifting gears from making the applications that streamline business practices inside a company to those that face outward to the rest of the world. These days, the hottest areas for outward-looking (that is, Internet) post-ERP work are electronic commerce, planning and

(continued)

(concluded)

managing your supply chain, and tracking and serving customers. Most ERP vendors have been slow to develop offerings for these areas, and they face stiff competition from niche vendors. ERP vendors have the advantage of a huge installed base of customers and a virtual stranglehold on the "back office" functions—such as order fulfillment. Recently ERP vendors have begun to shrink their ambitions and focus on being the back-office engine that powers electronic commerce, rather than trying to own all the software niches that are necessary for a good electronic commerce Web site. Indeed, as the niche vendors make their software easier to hook into electronic commerce Web sites, and as middleware vendors make it easier for IS departments to hook together applications from different vendors, many people wonder how much longer ERP vendors can claim to be the primary platform for the Fortune 500.

Questions

1. What is ERP?
2. What are the three main reasons firms adopt ERP?
3. What are some hidden costs of ERP?
4. How does ERP fit with e-commerce and supply chain management?

Source: Christopher Koch, "ABC: An Introduction to ERP," Cio.com,

SERVICE

ERP in Services

Although ERP was initially developed for manufacturing, it now has a long list of service applications. These include professional services, postal services, retail, banking, health care, higher education, engineering and construction services, logistics services, and real estate management.

In a manufacturing environment, ERP systems generally encompass the major functions such as production planning and scheduling, inventory management, product costing, and distribution. In a service environment, the major functions can differ from one service organization to another. For example, many universities use ERP systems; they typically are used to integrate and access student information, course prerequisites, course schedules, room schedules, human resources, accounting, and financial information. Hospitals' ERP systems include patient records, medication data, treatment plans, and scheduling information (e.g., rooms, equipment, surgery) as well as human resources information.

ERP is now about enterprise applications *integration,* an issue that generally arises with any major technology acquisition. The following reading underscores this point.

The Top 10 ERP Mistakes

READING

Clive Weightman

Although faulty technology often is blamed for problems, it is frequently other shortcomings that create performance-related problems—such as the people employing the ERP application don't fully understand what it is or how it works.

Execution of a successful ERP project provides the backbone for a company's internal and external operations—from integrating back-office financials with business performance data to building a launch platform for an extended enterprise and collaborative commerce. This foundation can serve as the competitive weapon of the future.

Top 10 Mistakes

10. **Believing the journey is complete at "go live."** Treat the day your ERP project goes live as the start of the next phase of your journey, not the finish because an ERP implementation represents much more than simply a project . . . So don't disband the team a month after the project goes live.
9. **Not planning for—and minimizing—the interim performance dip after start up.** Research shows that even the projects that have gone the smoothest in the execution stage suffer a dip in performance after the new system launches. Transactional efficiency, the pace of taking sales orders may slow down, or the speed of pushing products into the warehouse may decline a bit. Recognize that performance is going to suffer some at the outset, but with excellent execution, this effect can be very slim and very short.
8. **Failing to balance the needs and power of integration with seeking quick business hits.** Today, every chief executive officer must deliver results now, not in 15 months from now. Given the challenges of a full ERP implementation, it's difficult for them to promise their board of directors that with the ERP project, they are going to see savings in 24 to 36 months of such-and-such amount. They want to see the return on investment now.
7. **Starting too late to address all things data (architecture, standards, management, cleansing, and so on).** These systems are only as good as the fundamental data that enters them. And that's where a common problem erupts. Far too often, research indicates, companies think about the quality and accuracy of their data too late in the project. The consistency and accuracy of data is [sic] critical.

(continued)

(concluded)

6. **Failing to staff the team with "A" players from business and technical sides of the organization, including program management.** This can be a major challenge. You need top-notch players for these projects—not just technical stars but stellar performers from the business side as well. Indeed, if you have to trade off in terms of quality in one area, never skimp on business talent. You can perhaps trade off on technical expertise because the consultant you retain can bring in skilled technicians.

   And the "A" players should encompass program managers to the most junior members of the team.

5. **Starting without an effective and dedicated senior governance council, including a single executive sponsor.** Any major ERP project overhauls a lot of business processes, roles, responsibilities, standards, and data definitions—and these are changes that cannot be pursued from the bottom up. An effective governing council—a steering group—is essential, as is a single executive sponsor, dedicated and effective, to chair it. The project will trigger difficult, sometimes nasty, issues and a senior executive who is accountable can make those decisions and see that the steering group understands and accepts them.

   The project's executive "angel" must be from the corporate suite and, preferably, not the chief information officer.

4. **Selecting a strong systems integrator and then not heeding its advice.** In selecting an SI, a company should:
   - Consider compatibility. Do you want a firm that wants to come in to do it to you rather than do it with you? Some SI firms favor a "let's solve this together" approach, while others prefer the "here are your marching orders, this is how it's going to be, so let's get down to business." Determine which approach you favor for your firm's culture.
   - Clearly look at the SI's track record. Look beyond its marketing, talk to the software vendors you'll be working with and also talk with industry analysts.
   - Spend considerable time examining the members of the actual team that will be working with you every day. Be sure to put language in the contract that at least binds the team leaders and the firm's partner with you for its duration.

3. **Trying to create a solution incompatible with the company's culture.** In the 1990s, research found that many companies with ERP projects saw them as a silver bullet that would solve all their problems—even if the "style" of solution wasn't compatible with their corporate culture traditions.

   An executive might say he or she wants to operate in a globally centralized fashion—to be more like a Wal-Mart, with the strength and discipline of a global head office. However, this doesn't work if your firm's culture is one of decentralized entrepreneurship. You can't use technology to force change in the culture of your company. So if yours is a very decentralized structure, you'd better opt to install a decentralized ERP application or recognize the enormous change-management mountain you face.

2. **Treating this as a technical project vs. a change that balances people, process, and technology; not using the power of the new, integrated information.** The new technology brings integration and, generally, makes information available instantly. For example, when raw material arrives at a company's receiving dock and is scanned into the system, anyone can access that information and use it.

   Real-time integration and accurate data change people's jobs. A traditional sales order taker can change into a full-service customer agent. For example, with full online access to an integrated ERP backbone, the agent enjoys immediate access to the customer's history and other vital identifiers. The agent can examine real-time open inventory at all warehouses (not just local) and future production schedules. The agent can freeze and commit from this schedule to the customer's immediate needs, among other things.

1. **Embarking on the journey without a solid, approved business case, including mechanisms to update the business case continuously and to ensure the savings are baked into operational budgets.** Since an ERP project is going to take a minimum of 12 months and as much as 36 months to employ, and often costs between $5 million and $50 million out-of-pocket costs, stamina is essential. So you must be absolutely certain why you're embarking on this journey; that is, have a solid business case.

   At the same time, if a solid business case hasn't been made for the project, you won't get the commitment from the entire business team to make the journey successful. Many times when a company pursues an ERP implementation, it isn't simply to cut technology costs, because total technical costs may well increase with the application. Most of the time, the project is undertaken for broader business reasons, so if those reasons aren't clearly expressed, fully understood, and approved in both qualitative and quantitative terms, members of the senior executive team won't give their full support.

   While this is far less of an issue than it was five years ago, a number of major companies still complete the business case for an ERP project, submit a capital appropriation request, eventually get it approved, only to park the business case on the shelf to gather dust while the project proceeds.

   A business case should be a living, breathing document of how to drive out both the original and updated business benefits from the ERP journey for, say, the next 20 years. It must outline how to track the benefits the application will produce, and it must be used for the CEO to bake into the annual operating budgets the cost-reductions and revenue increases that each vice president has committed to. It must make senior and middle executives accountable for the goals so that the anticipated bottom-line benefits are realized. This type of discipline still is relatively rare, in part because many managers think, "Hey, I'm not going to be here to see the end of this."

   But, for an ERP project to succeed, it is critical that this business case is documented and becomes well worn. Just how vital is it? It does head this list of mistakes to avoid!

Source: Condensed from Clive Weightman and Deloitte Consulting, "The Top 10 ERP Mistakes."

Conversion to an ERP system from a traditional operation is a major undertaking that requires a project approach to manage the process. The following reading provides some suggestions for achieving ERP project success.

Tips for Successful ERP Projects

READING

Have a clear, simple corporate vision and objective before you start, and measure and publicize successes as you proceed.

Have a group dedicated to business-process improvements. Also rely on experienced project managers (possibly including internal or external managers who have been certified by the Project Management Institute). Involve key stakeholders as early as possible.

Create a financial analyst position or team to track and analyze project costs and realized benefits.

When choosing a new vendor, put a premium on vertical-industry expertise. Avoid customization, or demand that such requests meet rigorous criteria.

Make sure that data cleansing is addressed as part of the project.

Source: Excerpted from Doug Bartholomew, "The ABC's of ERP," *CFO IT*, September 15, 2004.

OPERATIONS STRATEGY

Acquisition of technology on the order of ERP has strategic implications. Among the considerations are a high initial cost, a high cost to maintain, the need for future upgrades, and the intensive training required. An ERP team is an excellent example of the value of a cross-functional team. Purchasing, which will ultimately place the order, typically does not have the technical expertise to select the best vendor. Information technology can assess various technical requirements, but won't be the user. Various functional users (marketing, operations, and accounting) will be in the best position to evaluate inputs and outputs, and finance must evaluate the effect on the organization's bottom line. Also, it is important to have a member of the purchasing staff involved from the beginning of negotiations on ERP acquisition because this will have major implications for purchasing.

The real-time aspect of ERP makes it valuable as a strategic planning tool. For example, it can improve supply chain management, with stronger links between their customers and their suppliers, and make the organizations more capable of satisfying changing customer requirements.

Because ERP tracks the flow of information and materials through a company, it offers opportunities for collecting information on waste and environmental costs and, hence, opportunities for process improvement.

SUMMARY

MRP is a planning technique that creates a schedule for all the (dependent-demand) items in an end item's bill of materials based on fixed manufacturing lead times. The end item is exploded using the bill of materials, and material requirements plans are developed that show quantity and timing for ordering or producing components.

The main features of MRP are the time-phasing of requirements, calculating component requirements, and planned-order releases. To be successful, MRP requires accurate master production schedules, bills of materials, and inventory data. Firms without reasonably accurate records or schedules have experienced major difficulties in trying to implement MRP-type systems. A potential weakness of MRP is the assumption of constant lead times.

MRP is utilized by most MRP II and ERP systems. MRP II adds software applications designed to better manage the entire manufacturing process involving finance and marketing, and including capacity planning. ERP is the third generation of manufacturing software that encompasses all business functions, including order entry and an option for financial management *integrated* with the manufacturing functions available in MRP II.

KEY POINTS

1. The usage of components in production of assembled items depends on how many of each component are needed per item, and how many items are to be produced. Hence the term *dependent demand.*
2. MRP is a tool used for dependent-demand components, to assist in making the two basic decisions in inventory management: how much of each component to order, and when to order it.
3. MRP II is an enhancement of MRP that gives management the ability to relate financial and other information to an MRP plan.
4. ERP is a software-based enterprise-wide system that allows access to production, sales, accounting, warehouse, and supply chain information.

KEY TERMS

backflushing, 525
bill of materials (BOM), 512
capacity requirements planning, 528
changes, 523
cumulative lead time, 512
dependent demand, 509
distribution resource planning (DRP), 530
enterprise resource planning (ERP), 530
exception reports, 523
gross requirements, 516
inventory records, 515
load reports, 528
lot sizing, 524
low-level coding, 515
manufacturing resources planning (MRP II), 526
master schedule, 512
material requirements planning (MRP), 510
net-change system, 521
net requirements, 516
order releases, 523
pegging, 521
performance-control reports, 523
planned-order receipts, 516
planned-order releases, 517
planned orders, 523
planning reports, 523
product structure tree, 512
projected on hand, 516
regenerative system, 521
scheduled receipts, 516
time fences, 528

SOLVED PROBLEMS

Problem 1

The following product structure tree indicates the components needed to assemble one unit of product W. Determine the quantities of each component needed to assemble 100 units of W.

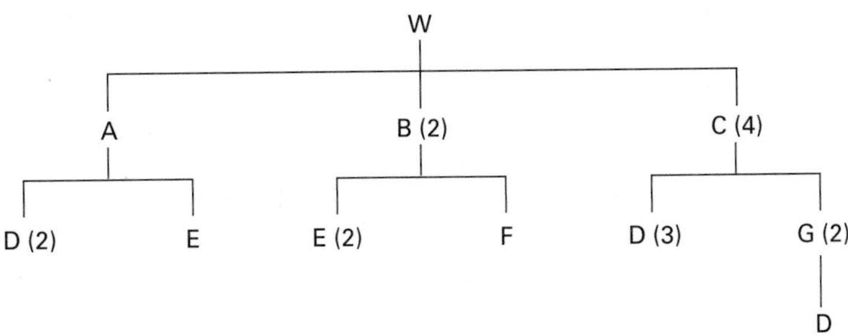

Solution

An easy way to compute and keep track of component requirements is to do it right on the tree, as shown in the following figure. *Note:* For the procedure when there are on-hand inventories, see Example 1, page 514.

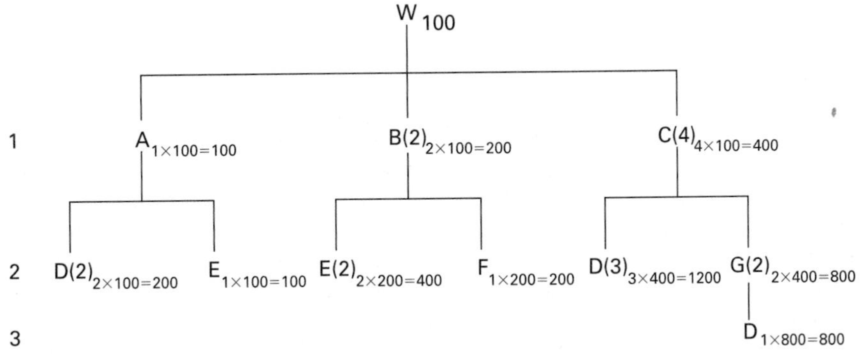

Summary:

Level	Item	Quantity
0	W	100
1	A	100
	B	200
	C	400
2	E	500
	F	200
	G	800
3	D	2,200

Problem 2

The product structure tree for end item E follows. The manager wants to know the material requirements for ordered part R that will be needed to complete 120 units of E by the start of week 5. Lead times for items are one week for level 0 items, one week for level 1 items, and two weeks for level 2 items. There is a scheduled receipt of 60 units of M at the *start* of week 2 and 100 units of R at the *start* of week 1. Lot-for-lot ordering is used.

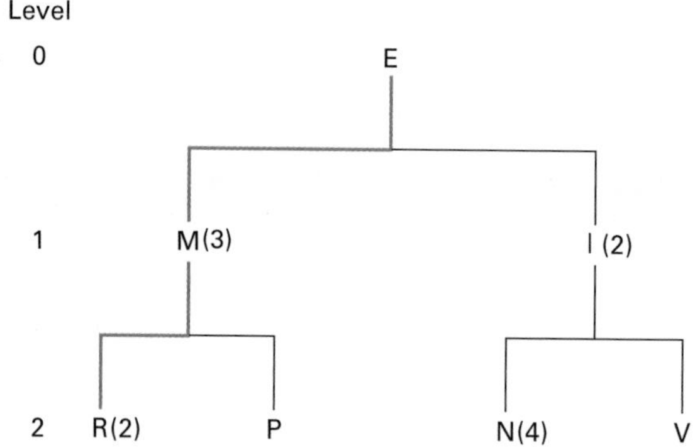

Solution

A partial assembly-time chart that includes R and leads to completion of E by the start of week 5 looks like this:

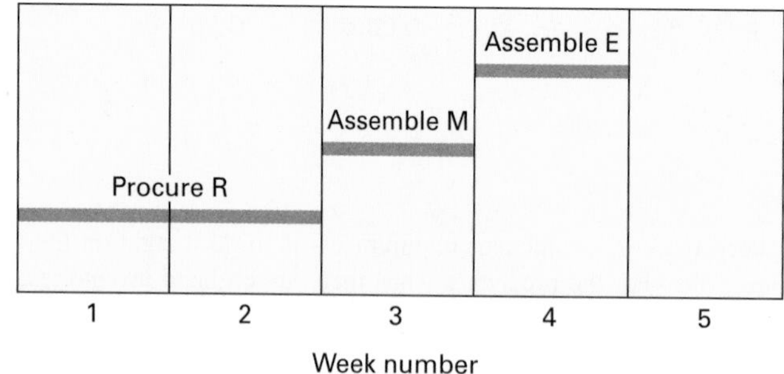

The table entries are arrived at as follows:

Master schedule: 120 units of E to be available at the start of week 5.

Item E: Gross requirements equal the quantity specified in the master production schedule. Since there is no on-hand inventory, net requirements also equal 120 units. Using lot-for-lot ordering, 120 units must be scheduled to be available at the start of week 5. Because there is a one-week lead time for assembly of Es, an order will need to be released (i.e., work started) at the beginning of week 4.

Item M: The *gross* requirements for M are three times the *net* requirements for E, because each E requires three Ms. These must be available at the start of week 4. The net requirements are 60 units fewer due to the 60 units expected to be on hand at that time. Hence, 300 additional units of M must be available at the start of week 4. With the one-week lead time, there must be an order release at the start of week 3.

Item R: Because each M requires two units of R, 600 Rs will be needed to assemble 300 units of M. However, 100 units will be on hand, so only 500 need to be ordered. Because there is a lead time of two weeks, the 500 Rs must be ordered at the start of week 1.

The master schedule for E and requirements plans for E, M, and R follow.

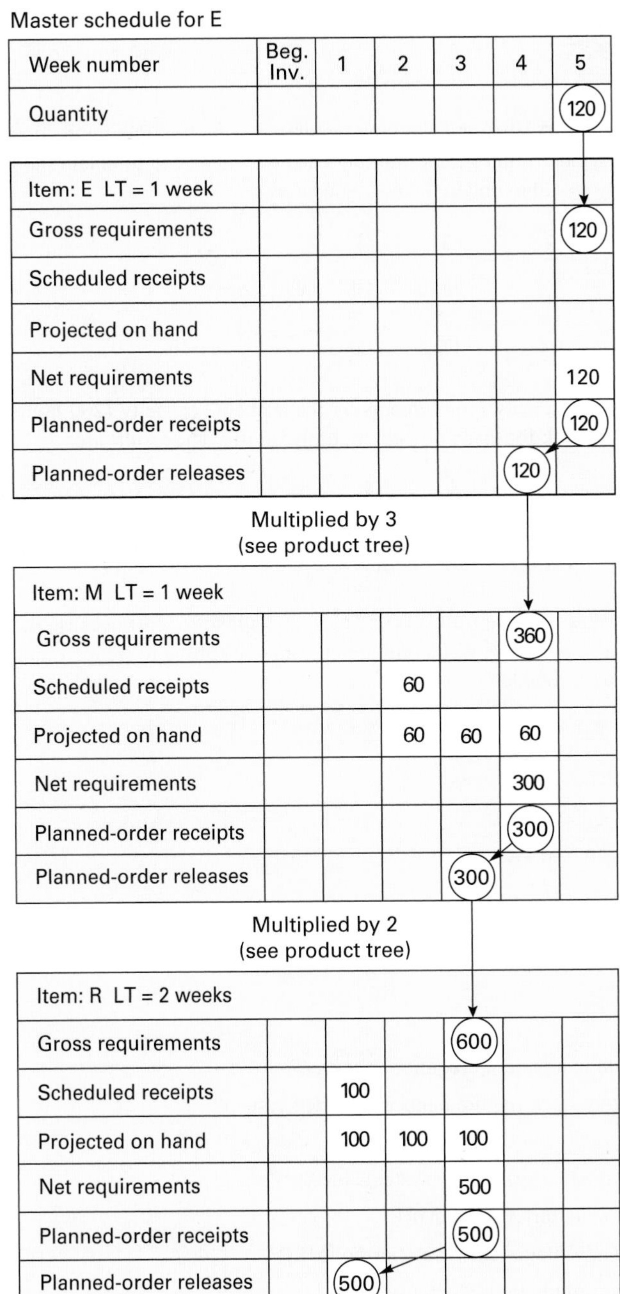

Master schedule for E

Week number	Beg. Inv.	1	2	3	4	5
Quantity						120

Item: E LT = 1 week						
Gross requirements						120
Scheduled receipts						
Projected on hand						
Net requirements						120
Planned-order receipts						120
Planned-order releases					120	

Multiplied by 3 (see product tree)

Item: M LT = 1 week						
Gross requirements					360	
Scheduled receipts			60			
Projected on hand			60	60	60	
Net requirements					300	
Planned-order receipts					300	
Planned-order releases				300		

Multiplied by 2 (see product tree)

Item: R LT = 2 weeks						
Gross requirements				600		
Scheduled receipts		100				
Projected on hand		100	100	100		
Net requirements				500		
Planned-order receipts				500		
Planned-order releases		500				

Problem 3

Capacity requirements planning. Given the following production schedule in units and the production standards for labor and machine time for this product, determine the labor and machine capacity requirements for each week. Then compute the percent utilization of labor and machines in each week if labor capacity is 200 hours per week and machine capacity is 250 hours per week.

Production Schedule:

Week	1	2	3	4
Quantity	200	300	100	150

Standard Times:

Labor	.5 hour/unit
Machine	1.0 hour/unit

Solution

Convert the quantity requirements into labor and machine requirements by multiplying the quantity requirements by the respective standard times (i.e., multiply each quantity by .5 to obtain the labor hours and multiply each quantity by 1.0 to obtain the machine hours):

Week	1	2	3	4
Quantity	200	300	100	150
Labor hours	100	150	50	75
Machine hours	200	300	100	150

To compute utilization, divide the capacity requirements by the available capacity (200 hours per week for labor and 250 hours per week for machine) and multiply by 100. The results are

Week	1	2	3	4
Labor	50%	75%	25%	37.5%
Machine	80%	120%	40%	60%

Note that machine capacity in week 2 is overutilized (i.e., capacity is insufficient) because the utilization exceeds 100 percent. To compensate, some production could be shifted to weeks 1 and/or 3 where labor and machine time are available.

DISCUSSION AND REVIEW QUESTIONS

1. Contrast independent and dependent demand.
2. When is MRP appropriate?
3. Briefly define or explain each of these terms.
   a. Master schedule.
   b. Bill of materials.
   c. Inventory records.
   d. Gross requirements.
   e. Net requirements.
   f. Time-phased plan.
4. How is safety stock included in a material requirements plan?
5. What factors can create safety stock requirements in an MRP system?
6. What is meant by the term *safety time?*
7. Contrast *net-change* systems and *regenerative* systems for MRP.
8. Briefly discuss the requirements for effective MRP.
9. What are some of the main advantages and limitations of MRP?
10. How can the use of MRP contribute to productivity?
11. Briefly describe MRP II and closed-loop MRP.
12. What is lot sizing, what is its goal, and why is it an issue with lumpy demand?
13. Contrast planned-order receipts and scheduled receipts.
14. If seasonal variations are present, is their incorporation into MRP fairly simple or fairly difficult? Explain briefly.
15. How does the purpose of ERP differ from the purpose of MRP II?
16. What are some unforeseen costs of ERP?

TAKING STOCK

1. What trade-offs are involved in the decision to purchase an ERP software package?
2. Who in the organization needs to be involved in designing and implementing MRP II? Who needs to be involved in the decision to purchase an ERP system? Who needs to be trained to use ERP?
3. To what extent has technology such as ERP software improved the ability to manage a business organization? How important are each of the following considerations?
   a. Ease of use.
   b. Complete integration.
   c. Reliability.

CRITICAL THINKING EXERCISES

1. Suppose you work for a furniture manufacturer, one of whose products is the chair depicted in Figure 12.5. Finished goods inventory is held in a central warehouse in anticipation of customer orders. Finished goods are controlled using EOQ/ROP methods. The warehouse manager, Juan Villa, has suggested using the same methods for controlling component inventory. Write him a brief memo outlining your opinion on doing that.
2. Give one example of unethical behavior involving MRP and one involving ERP, and state the ethical principle violated for each example.

PROBLEMS

1. a. Given the following diagram for a product, determine the quantity of each component required to assemble one unit of the finished product.

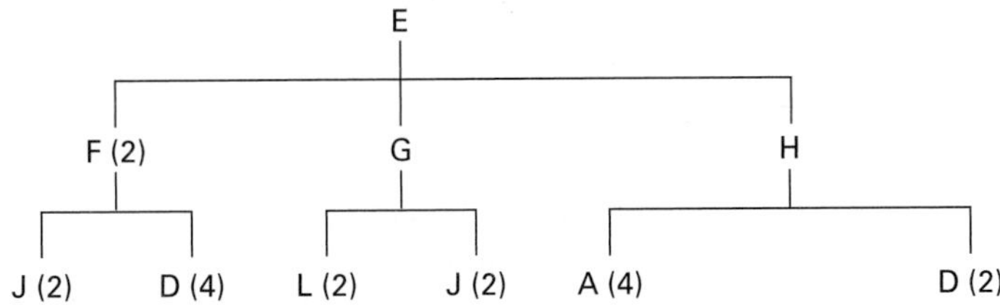

b. Draw a tree diagram for the stapler:

Item	Components
Stapler	Top assembly, base assembly
Top assembly	Cover, spring, slide assembly
Cover	
Spring	
Slide assembly	Slide, spring
Slide	
Spring	
Base assembly	Base, strike plate, rubber pad (2)
Base	
Strike plate	
Rubber pad (2)	

2. The following table lists the components needed to assemble an end item, lead times, and quantities on hand.

Item	End	B	C	D	E	F	G	H
LT (wk)	1	2	3	3	1	2	1	2
Amount on hand	0	10	10	25	12	30	5	0

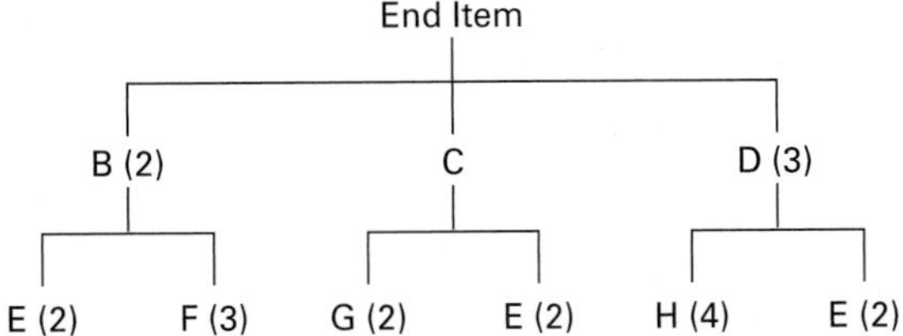

a. If 20 units of the end item are to be assembled, how many additional units of E are needed? (*Hint:* You don't need to develop an MRP plan to determine this.)
b. An order for the end item is scheduled to be shipped at the start of week 11. What is the latest week that the order can be started and still be ready to ship on time? (*Hint:* You don't need to develop an MRP plan for this part either.)

3. The following table lists the components needed to assemble an end item, lead times (in weeks), and quantities on hand.

Item	Lead Time	Amount on Hand	Direct Components
End	1	—	L(2), C(1), K(3)
L	2	10	B(2), J(3)
C	3	15	G(2), B(2)
K	3	20	H(4), B(2)
B	2	30	
J	3	30	
G	3	5	
H	2	—	

a. If 40 units of the end item are to be assembled, how many additional units of B are needed? (*Hint:* You don't need to develop an MRP plan.)
b. An order for the end item is scheduled to be shipped at the start of week 8. What is the latest week that the order can be started and still be ready to ship on time? (*Hint:* You don't need to develop an MRP plan.)

4. Eighty units of end item E are needed at the beginning of week 6. Three cases (30 units per case) of J have been ordered and one case is scheduled to arrive in week 3, one in week 4, and one in week 5. *Note:* J must be ordered by the case, and B must be produced in multiples of 120 units. There are 60 units of B and 20 units of J now on hand. Lead times are two weeks each for E and B, and one week for J.

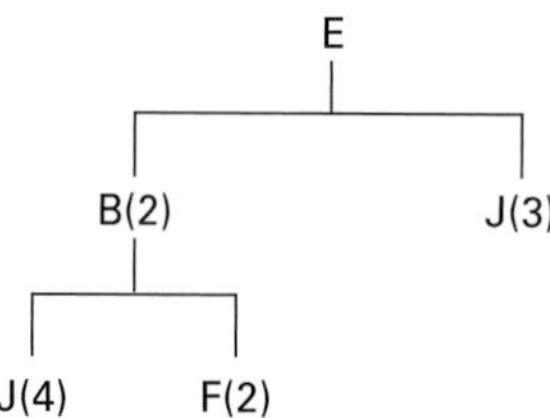

a. Prepare a material requirements plan for component J.
b. Suppose that in week 4 the quantity of E needed is changed from 80 to 70. The planned-order releases through week 3 have all been executed. How many more Bs and Js will be on hand in week 6?

5. End item P is composed of three subassemblies: K, L, and W. K is assembled using 3 Gs and 4 Hs; L is made of 2 Ms and 2 Ns; and W is made of 3 Zs. On-hand inventories are 20 Ls, 40 Gs, and 200 Hs. Scheduled receipts are 10 Ks at the start of week 3, 30 Ks at the start of week 6, and 200 Ws at the start of week 3.

One hundred Ps will be shipped at the start of week 6, and another 100 at the start of week 7. Lead times are two weeks for subassemblies and one week for components G, H, and M. Final assembly of P requires one week. Include an extra 10 percent scrap allowance in each planned order of G. The minimum order size for H is 200 units. Develop each of the following:

a. A product structure tree.
b. An assembly time chart.
c. A master schedule for P.
d. A material requirements plan for K, G, and H using lot-for-lot ordering.

6. A table is assembled using three components, as shown in the accompanying product structure tree. The company that makes the table wants to ship 100 units at the beginning of day 4, 150 units at the beginning of day 5, and 200 units at the beginning of day 7. Receipts of 100 wood sections are scheduled at the beginning of day 2. There are 120 legs on hand. An additional 10 percent of the order size on legs is added for safety stock. There are 60 braces on hand with no safety stock requirement for

braces. Lead times (in days) for all items are shown in the following table. Prepare a material requirements plan using lot-for-lot ordering.

Quantity	Lead Time
1–200	1
201–550	2
551–999	3

Table

Wood sections (2) Braces (3) Legs (4)

7. Eighty units of end item X are needed at the beginning of week 6, and another 30 units are needed at the beginning of week 8. Prepare a material requirements plan for component D. D can only be ordered in whole cases (50 units per case). One case of D is automatically received every other week, beginning in week 1 (i.e., weeks 1, 3, 5, 7). Also, there are 30 units of B and 20 units of D now on hand. Lead times for all items are a function of quantity: one week for up to 100 units, two weeks for 101 to 200 units, three weeks for 201 to 300 units, and four weeks for 301 or more units.

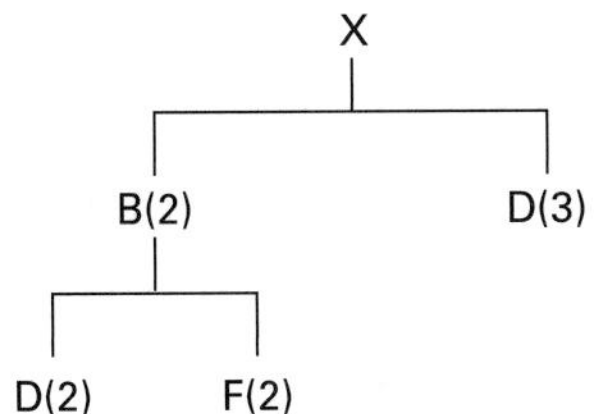

8. Oh No!, Inc., sells three models of radar detector units. It buys the three basic models (E, F, and G) from a Japanese manufacturer and adds one, two, or four lights (component D) to further differentiate the models. D is bought from a domestic producer.

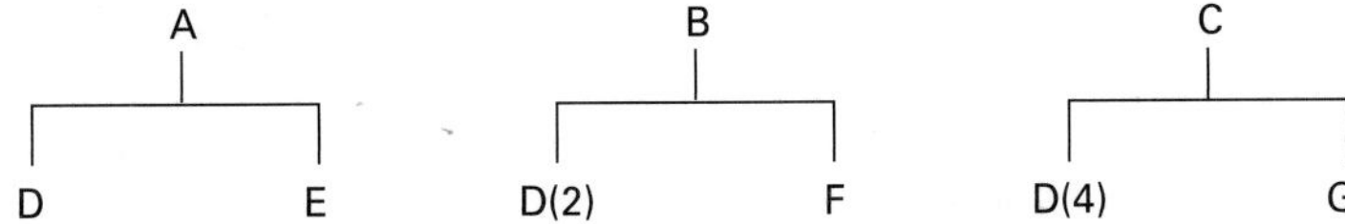

Lead times are one week for all items except C, which is two weeks. There are ample supplies of the basic units (E, F, and G) on hand. There are also 10 units of B, 10 units of C, and 25 units of D on hand. Lot-sizing rules are lot-for-lot ordering for all items except D, which must be ordered in multiples of 100 units. There is a scheduled receipt of 100 units of D in week 1.

The master schedule calls for 40 units of A to be produced in week 4, 60 units of B in week 5, and 30 units of C in week 6. Prepare a material requirements plan for D and its parents.

9. Assume that you are the manager of a shop that assembles power tools. You have just received an order for 50 chain saws, which are to be shipped at the start of week 8. Pertinent information on the saws is

Item	Lead Time (weeks)	On Hand	Components
Saw	2	15	A(2), B(1), C(4)
A	1	10	E(3), D(1)
B	2	5	D(2), F(3)
C	2	65	E(2), D(2)
D	1	20	
E	1	10	
F	2	30	

a. Develop a product structure tree, an assembly time chart, and a master schedule.
b. Develop the material requirements plan for component E using lot-for-lot ordering.
c. Suppose now that capacity to produce part E is limited to a maximum of 100 units per period. Revise the planned-order releases for periods 1 through 4 so that the maximum is not exceeded in any period, keeping in mind an objective of minimizing carrying costs. The quantities need not be equal in every period. Note that the gross requirements for E will remain the same. However, quantities in some of the other rows will change. Determine the new cell values for those rows.

10. Assume that you are the manager of Assembly, Inc. You have just received an order for 40 units of an industrial robot, which is to be delivered at the start of week 7 of your schedule. Using the following information, determine how many units of subassembly G to order and the timing of those orders, given that subassembly G must be ordered in multiples of 80 units and all other components are ordered lot-for-lot. Assume that the components are used only for this particular robot.

Item	Lead Time (weeks)	On Hand	Components
Robot	2	10	B, G, C(3)
B	1	5	E, F
C	1	20	G(2), H
E	2	4	—
F	3	8	—
G	2	15	—
H	1	10	—

11. Determine material requirements plans for parts N and V and subassembly I as described in Solved Problem 2 (see p. 540) for each of the following:

a. Assume that there are currently 100 Ns on hand and scheduled receipts of 40 Is and 10 Vs at the beginning of week 3. No Es are on hand; 120 Es are needed at the start of week 5.

b. Assume on-hand and scheduled receipts as in part *a.* Now suppose that 100 Es are needed at the start of week 5 and 55 at the start of week 7. Also, use multiples of these order sizes: N, 800; V, 200. Use lot-for-lot ordering for I.

c. Using your answer to part *b,* update the MRP for V, using the following additional information for each of these cases: (1) one week has elapsed (making it the start of week 2), and (2) three weeks have elapsed (making it the start of week 4). *Note:* Start your revised plans so that the updated time in each case is designated as week 1.

The updated master schedule now has an order for 100 units of E in week 8 of case 1 (i.e., week 9 under the former master schedule). Assume all orders are released and received as planned.

12. A firm that produces electric golf carts has just received an order for 200 carts, which must be ready for delivery at the start of week 8. Information concerning the product structure, lead times, and quantities on hand is shown in the following table. Use this information to do each of the following:

a. Construct a product tree.

b. Construct an assembly time chart.

c. Develop a material requirements plan that will provide 200 golf carts by week 8 assuming lot-for-lot ordering.

Parts List for Electric Golf Cart	Lead Time	Quantity on Hand
Electric golf cart	1	0
Top	1	40
Base	1	20
Top		
Supports (4)	1	200
Cover	1	0
Base		
Motor	2	300
Body	3	50
Seats (2)	2	120
Body		
Frame	1	35
Controls	1	0
Wheel assemblies (4)	1	240

13. Refer to Problem 12. Assume that unusually mild weather has caused a change in the quantity and timing of orders for golf carts. The revised plan calls for 100 golf carts at the start of week 6, 100 at the start of week 8, and 100 at the start of week 9.

a. Develop a master schedule for this revised plan.
b. Determine the timing and quantities for orders for tops and bases.
c. Assume that equipment problems reduce the firm's capacity for assembling bases to 50 units per week. Revise your material plan for bases to reflect this, but still meet delivery dates.

14. Using the diagram below, do the following:

a. Draw a tree diagram for the scissors.
b. Prepare an MRP for scissors. Lead times are one day for each component and final scissor assembly, but two days for the plastic grips. Six hundred pairs of scissors are needed on Day 6. *Note:* There are 200 straight blades and 350 bent blades on hand, and 40 top blade assemblies on hand.

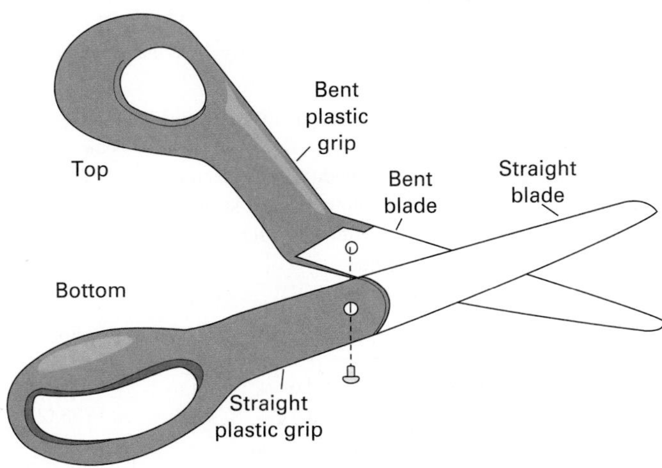

15. A company that manufactures paving material for driveways and parking lots expects the following demand for its product for the next four weeks:

Week number	1	2	3	4
Material (tons)	40	80	60	70

The company's labor and machine standards and available capacities are as follows:

	Labor	**Machine**
Production standard (hours per ton)	4	3
Weekly production capacity (hours)	300	200

a. Determine the capacity utilization for labor and machine for each of the four weeks.
b. In which weeks do you foresee a problem? What options would you suggest to resolve any problems? What costs are relevant in making a decision on choosing an option?

16. A company produces two very similar products that go through a three-step sequence of fabrication, assembly, and packaging. Each step requires one day for a lot to be completely processed and moved to the next department. Processing requirements for the departments (hours per unit) are

	FABRICATION		ASSEMBLY		PACKAGING	
Product	**Labor**	**Machine**	**Labor**	**Machine**	**Labor**	**Machine**
A	2	1	1.5	1	1	.5
B	1	1	1	1	1.5	.5

Department capacities are all 700 hours of labor and 500 hours of machine time, except Friday, when capacities are 200 hours for both labor and machine time. The following production schedule is for next week:

Product	Mon	Tues	Wed	Thurs	Fri
A	200	400	100	300	100
B	300	200	200	200	200

a. Develop a production schedule for each department that shows the capacity requirements for each product and the total load for each day. Ignore changeover time.

b. Evaluate the projected loading for the first three days of the week. Is the schedule feasible? What do you suggest for balancing the load?

17. The MRP Department has a problem. Its computer "died" just as it spit out the following information: Planned order release for item J27 = 640 units in week 2. The firm has been able to reconstruct all the information they lost except the master schedule for end item 565. The firm is fortunate because J27 is used only in 565s. Given the following product structure tree and associated inventory status record information, determine what master schedule entry for 565 was exploded into the material requirements plan that killed the computer.

Part Number	On Hand	Lot Size	Lead Time
565	0	Lot-for-lot	1 week
X43	60	120	1 week
N78	0	Lot-for-lot	2 weeks
Y36	200	Lot-for-lot	1 week
J27	0	Lot-for-lot	2 weeks

565
X43 Y36 (2) N78
J27 (4) X43

18. Develop a material requirements plan for component H. Lead times for the end item and each component except B are one week. The lead time for B is three weeks. Sixty units of A are needed at the start of week 8. There are currently 15 units of B on hand and 130 of E on hand, and 50 units of H are in production and will be completed by the start of week 2.

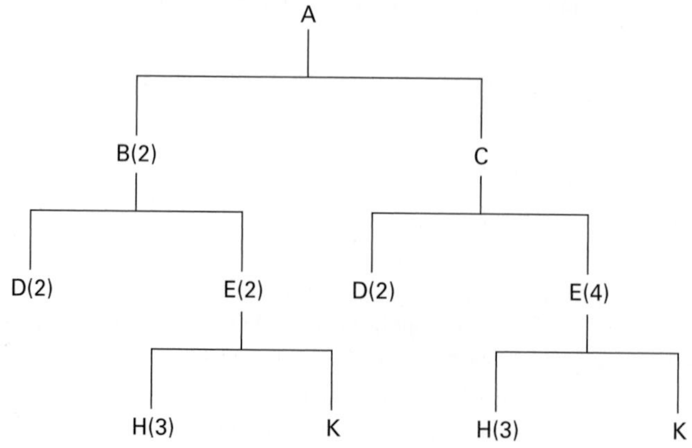

Promotional Novelties

CASE

Promotional Novelties provides a wide range of novelty items for its corporate customers. It has just received an order for 20,000 toy tractor-trailers that will be sold by a regional filling station company as part of a holiday promotion. The order is to be shipped at the beginning of week 8. The tree diagram shows the various components of the trucks.

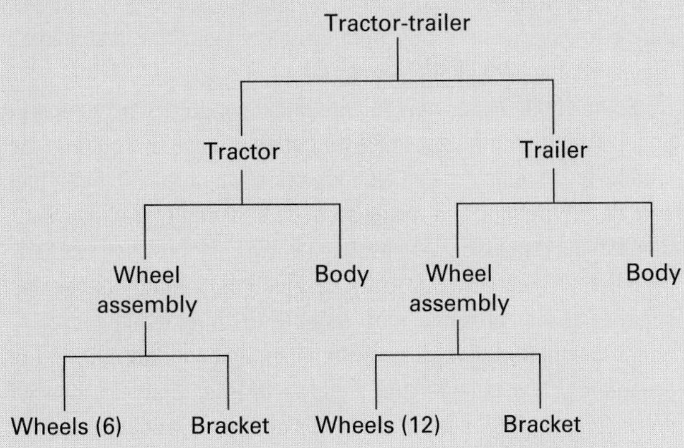

The company can complete final assembly of the tractor-trailers at the rate of 10,000 a week. The tractor and truck bodies are purchased; lead time is three weeks. The wheels are the manager's main concern.

The company has a sufficient supply of brackets on hand. Assembly time is one week each for tractors, trailers, and wheel assembly. However, the wheel department can only produce wheels at the rate of 100,000 a week. The manager plans to use the wheel department to full capacity, starting in week 2 of the schedule, and order additional wheels from a supplier as needed. Ordered wheels come in sets of 6,400. The lead time for delivery from the supplier is expected to be two to three weeks.

Questions

1. How many wheels sets should the manager order?
2. When should the wheels sets be ordered?

DMD Enterprises

CASE

After the dot-com business he tried to start folded, David "Marty" Dawkins decided to pursue his boyhood dream of owning a bike factory. After several false starts, he finally got the small company up and running. The company currently assembles two models Marty designed: the Arrow and the Dart. The company hasn't turned a profit yet, but Marty feels that once he resolves some of the problems he's having with inventory and scheduling, he can increase productivity and reduce costs.

At first, he ordered enough bike parts and subassemblies for four months' worth of production. Parts were stacked all over the place, seriously reducing work space and hampering movement of workers and materials. And no one knew exactly where anything was. In Marty's words, "It was a solid mess!"

He and his two partners eventually managed to work off most of the inventory. They hope to avoid similar problems in the future by using a more orderly approach. Marty's first priority is to develop a materials requirement plan for upcoming periods. He wants to assemble 15 Arrows and 10 Darts each week, for weeks 4 through 8. The product structure trees for the two bikes follow.

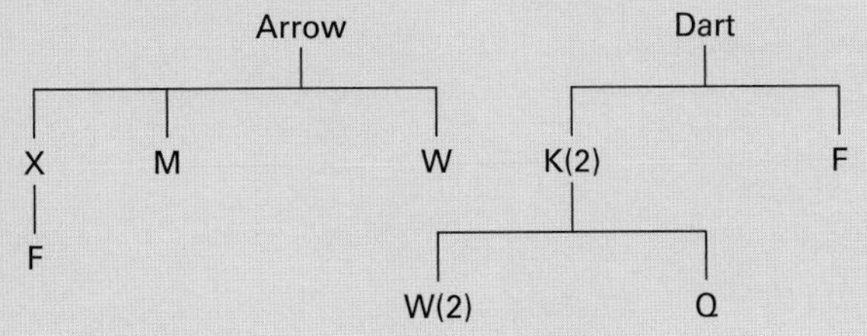

One of Marty's partners, Ann, has organized information on lead times, inventory on hand, and lot-sizing rules (established by suppliers):

Item	Lead Time (weeks)	On Hand	Lot-Sizing Rule
Arrow	2	5	Lot-for-lot
Dart	2	2	Lot-for-lot
X	1	5	Multiples of 25
W	2*	2	Multiples of 12
F	1	10	Multiples of 30
K	1	3	Lot-for-lot
Q	1	15	Multiples of 30
M	1	0	Lot-for-lot

*LT = 3 weeks for orders of 36 or more units on this item.

Scheduled receipts are

Period 1:	20 Arrows and 18 Ws
Period 2:	20 Darts and 15 Fs

As the third partner, it is your job to develop the material requirements plan.

Introduction

www.stickley.com

L.&J.G. Stickley was founded in 1900 by brothers Leopold and George Stickley. Located just outside of Syracuse, New York, the company is a producer of fine cherry, white oak, and mahogany furniture. In the 1980s, the company reintroduced the company's original line of mission oak furniture, which now accounts for nearly 50 percent of the company's sales.

Over the years, the company experienced both good and bad times, and at one point, it employed over 200 people. But by the early 1970s, the business was in disarray; there were only about 20 full-time employees, and the company was on the brink of bankruptcy. The present owners bought the ailing firm in 1974, and under their leadership, the company has prospered and grown, and now has 1,350 employees. Stickley has five retail showrooms in New York State, two in Connecticut, one in North Carolina, and its furniture is sold nationally by some 120 dealers.

Production

The production facility is a large, rectangular building with a 30-foot ceiling. Furniture making is labor intensive, although saws, sanders, and other equipment are very much a part of the process. In fact, electric costs average about $60,000 a month. The company has its own tool room where cutting tools are sharpened, and replacement parts are produced as needed.

Worker skills range from low-skilled material handlers to highly skilled craftsmen. For example, seven master cabinet makers handle customized orders.

The process (see figure on p. 551) begins with various sawing operations where large boards received from the lumber mills are cut into smaller sizes. The company recently purchased a computer-controlled "optimizer" saw that greatly improves sawing productivity, and eliminates some waste. Workers inspect and mark knot locations and other defects they find on each piece of lumber before feeding it into the saw. The computer then determines the optimal set of cuttings, given the location of knots and other defects, and standard lengths needed for subsequent operations. Approximately 20,000 board feet are cut each day. Subsequent sawing operations provide additional cuts for specific jobs.

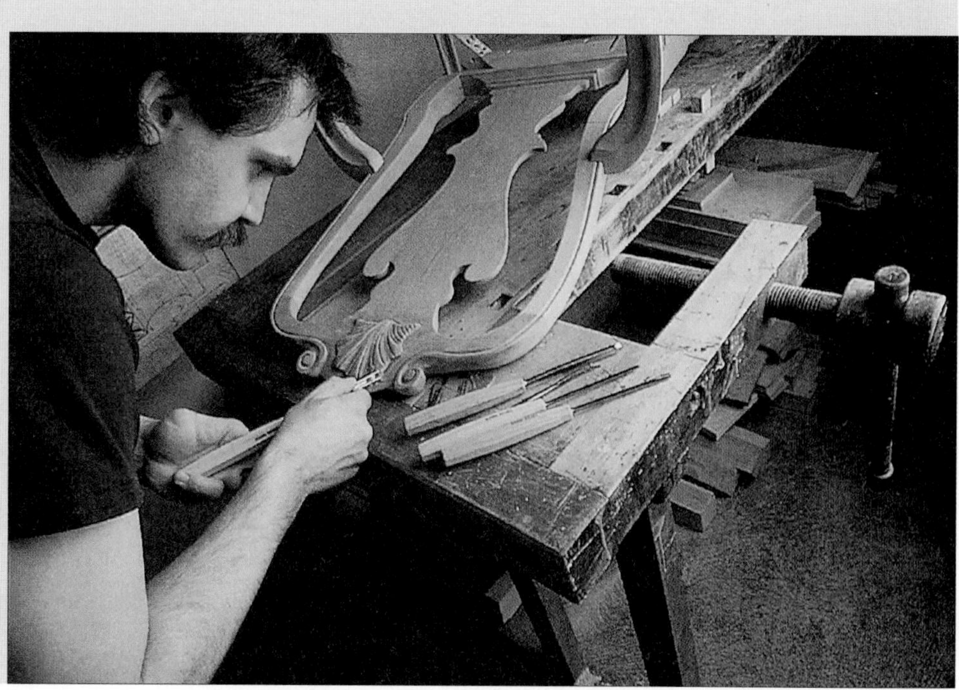

Workers then glue some of the pieces together; they will end up as tops of tables, desks, dressers, or a similar item. Large presses hold 20 to 30 glued sections at a time. Other pieces that will become table or chair legs, chair backs or other items go through various shaping operations. Next comes a series of sanding operations, which remove excess glue from the glued sections, and smooth the surface of both glued pieces and other pieces.

Some of the pieces may require drilling or mortising, an operation in which rectangular holes and other shapes are cut into the wood. The company has a CNC (numerically controlled) router that can be programmed to make grooves and other specialty cuts. Some items require carving, which involves highly skilled workers.

Next, workers assemble the various components, either into subassemblies, or sometimes directly to other components to obtain completed pieces. Each item is stamped with the date of production, and components such as dresser drawers, cabinet doors, and expansion leaves of tables also are stamped to identify their location (e.g., top drawer, left door). Careful records are kept so that if a piece of furniture is ever returned for repairs, complete instructions are available (type of wood, finish, etc.) to enable repair people to closely match the original piece.

The furniture items then usually move to the "white inventory" (unfinished) section, and eventually to the finishing department where workers apply linseed oil or another finish before the items are moved to the finished goods inventory to await shipment to stores or customers.

(continued)

Aggregate Planning

The company uses a level production plan (maintain steady output and steady labor force). Demand is seasonal; it is highest in the first and third quarters. During the second and fourth quarters, excess output goes into inventory; during the first and third quarters, excess demand is met using inventory. The production scheduler uses a schedule that is set for the next 8 to 10 weeks.

(continued)

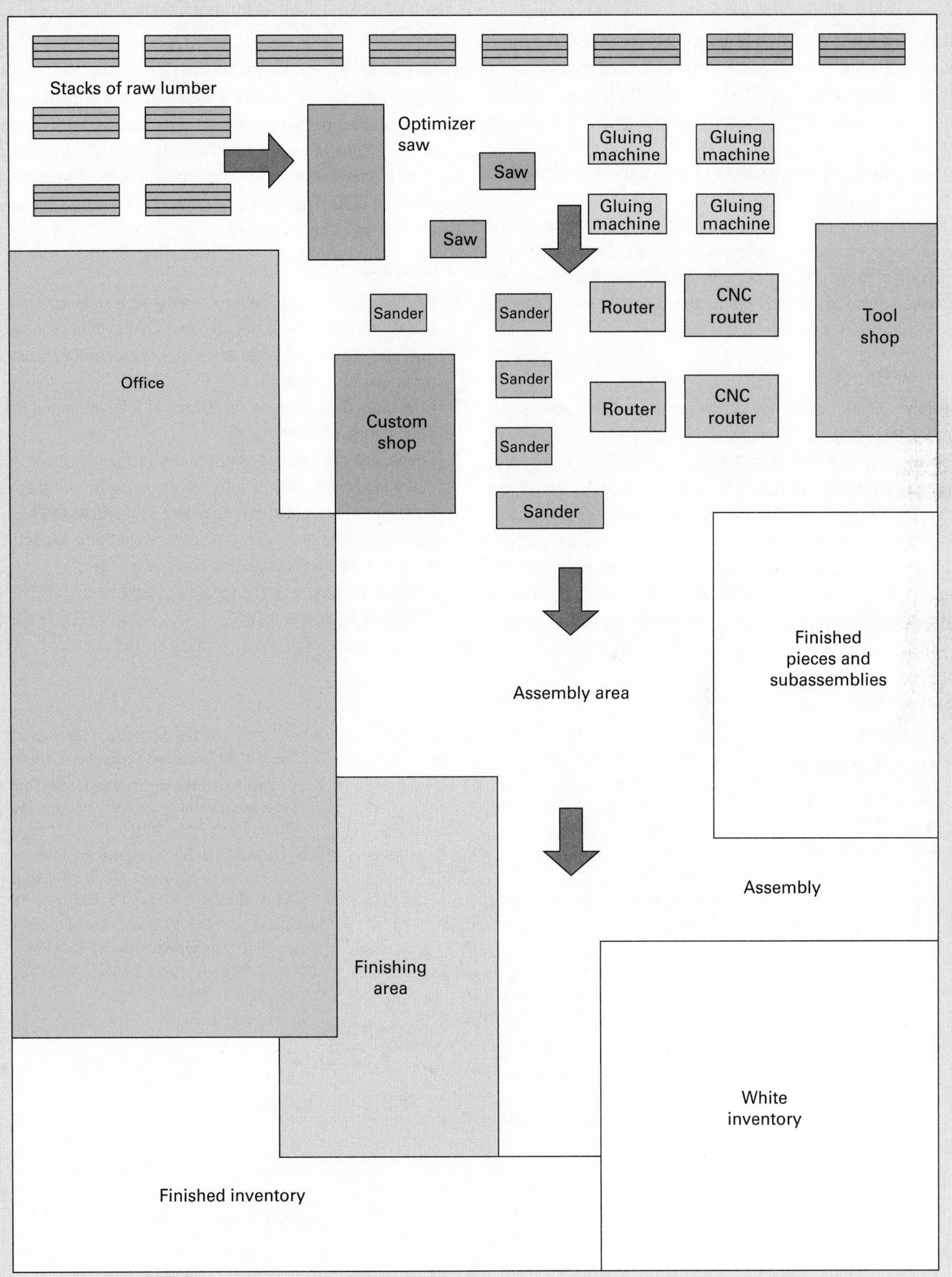

(concluded)

Production Control

Job sequence is determined by the amount of remaining inventory (days' supply on hand), and processing time. Lot sizes are determined by factoring in demand, setup costs, and carrying costs. Typical lot sizes are 25 to 60 pieces. There are many jobs being done concurrently. Each job is accompanied by a set of bar codes that identify the job and the operation. As each operation is completed, the operator removes a bar code sticker and delivers it to the scheduling office where it is scanned into the computer, thereby enabling production control to keep track of progress on a job, and to know its location in the shop.

The company's policy of level output coupled with seasonal demand patterns means that prior to peak demand periods, excess output is used to build up inventories, which is then drawn down when demand exceeds production capacity during periods of peak production.

Inventory

In addition to the "white" inventory and a small finished goods inventory, the company maintains an inventory of furniture pieces (e.g., table and chair legs) and partially assembled items. This inventory serves two important functions. One is to reduce the amount of time needed to respond to customer orders rather than having to go through the entire production process to obtain needed items, and the other is that it helps to smooth production and utilize idle machinery/workers. Because of unequal job times on successive operations, some workstations invariably have slack time while others work at capacity. This is used to build an inventory of commonly used pieces and subassemblies. Moreover, because pieces are being made for inventory, there is flexibility in sequencing. This permits jobs that have similar setups to be produced in sequence, thereby reducing setup time and cost.

Quality

Each worker is responsible for checking his or her quality, as well as the quality of materials received from preceding operations, and to report any deficiencies. In addition, on several difficult operations, quality control people handle inspections and work with operators to correct any deficiencies. The company is considering a TQM approach, but has not yet made a decision on whether to go in that direction.

Questions

1. Which type of production processing—job shop, batch, repetitive, or continuous—is the primary mode of operation at Stickley Furniture? Why? What other type of processing is used to a lesser extent? Explain.
2. How does management keep track of job status and location during production?
3. Suppose the company has just received an order for 40 mission oak dining room sets. Briefly list the kinds of information the company will need to plan, schedule, and process this job.
4. What benefits, and what problems, would you expect, given the company's level production policy?
5. Can you suggest any changes that might be beneficial to the company? What are they?

SELECTED BIBLIOGRAPHY AND FURTHER READINGS

Bennett, Wayne D. "The Big Risk for Small Fry." *CIO Magazine,* May 15, 2000.

Davenport, Tom. "Long Live ERP." *CIO Magazine,* March 1, 2000.

———. *Mission Critical: Realizing the Promise of Enterprise Systems.* Boston: Harvard Business School Press, 2000.

Hopp, Wallace, and Mark L. Spearman. *Factory Physics.* 3rd ed. New York: Irwin/McGraw-Hill, 2007.

Jacobs, F. Robert, William L. Berry, D. Clay Whybark, and Thomas E. Vollman. *Manufacturing Planning and Control for Supply Chain Management.* 6th ed. Burr Ridge, IL: McGraw-Hill/Irwin, 2011.

Jacobs, Robert F., and D. Clay Whybark. *Why ERP? A Primer on SAP Implementation.* New York: Irwin/McGraw-Hill, 2000.

Jeffery, Bill, and Jim Morrison. "ERP, One Step at a Time." *CIO Magazine,* September 1, 2000.

Kapp, Karl M., Bill Latham, and Hester-Ford Latham. *Integrated Learning for ERP Success.* Boca Raton, FL: St. Lucie Press, 2001.

Ptak, Carol A., and Eli Schragenheim. *ERP: Tools, Techniques, and Applications for Integrating the Supply Chain.* Boca Raton, FL: St. Lucie Press, 1999.

Slater, Derek. "The Hidden Costs of Enterprise Software." *CIO Enterprise,* January 15, 1998.

Wheatley, Malcolm. "ERP Training Stinks." *CIO Magazine,* June 1, 2000.

Inventory Management

CHAPTER OUTLINE

LEARNING OBJECTIVES

After completing this chapter, you should be able to:

1 Define the term *inventory,* list the major reasons for holding inventories, and list the main requirements for effective inventory management.
2 Discuss the nature and importance of service inventories.
3 Explain periodic and perpetual review systems.
4 Explain the objectives of inventory management.
5 Describe the A-B-C approach and explain how it is useful.
6 Describe the basic EOQ model and its assumptions and solve typical problems.
7 Describe the economic production quantity model and solve typical problems.
8 Describe the quantity discount model and solve typical problems.
9 Describe reorder point models and solve typical problems.
10 Describe situations in which the single-period model would be appropriate, and solve typical problems.

Inventory management is a core operations management activity. Effective inventory management is important for the successful operation of most businesses and their supply chains. Inventory management impacts operations, marketing, and finance. Poor inventory management hampers operations, diminishes customer satisfaction, and increases operating costs.

SUPPLY CHAIN

Some organizations have excellent inventory management, and many have satisfactory inventory management. Too many, however, have unsatisfactory inventory management, which sometimes is a sign that management does not recognize the importance of inventories. More often than not, though, the recognition is there. What is lacking is an understanding of what needs to be done and how to do it. This chapter presents the concepts and knowledge base for effective inventory management, including

- What types of inventories businesses carry, and why they carry them.
- The costs related to inventory management.
- Why it is essential to be able to keep track of inventory items, both within the organization and throughout the supply chain.
- How the A-B-C approach to inventory increases the effectiveness of inventory management.
- What models are available to answer the question of how much to order, and how to know which model to use.
- The model most retail businesses use to determine how much to order.

- What models are available to answer the question of when to order, and how to know which model to use.
- The two costs that are used to determine how much to order for items that have a limited shelf life.

INTRODUCTION

Inventory A stock or store of goods.

An **inventory** is a stock or store of goods. Firms typically stock hundreds or even thousands of items in inventory, ranging from small things such as pencils, paper clips, screws, nuts, and bolts to large items such as machines, trucks, construction equipment, and airplanes. Naturally, many of the items a firm carries in inventory relate to the kind of business it engages in. Thus, manufacturing firms carry supplies of raw materials, purchased parts, partially finished items, and finished goods, as well as spare parts for machines, tools, and other supplies. Department stores carry clothing, furniture, carpeting, stationery, cosmetics, gifts, cards, and toys. Some also stock sporting goods, paints, and tools. Hospitals stock drugs, surgical supplies, life-monitoring equipment, sheets and pillow cases, and more. Supermarkets stock fresh and canned foods, packaged and frozen foods, household supplies, magazines, baked goods, dairy products, produce, and other items.

The inventory models described in this chapter relate primarily to what are referred to as *independent-demand* items, that is, items that are ready to be sold or used. Chapter 12 described models that are used for *dependent-demand* items, which are components of finished products, rather than the finished products themselves. Thus, a computer would be an independent-demand item, while the components that are used to assemble a computer would be dependent-demand items: The demand for those items would depend on how many of each item is needed for a computer, as well as how many computers are going to be made.

Managing dependent-demand inventory is described in a different chapter because there are basic differences in assumptions and in the character of inventory decisions.

$$$ **READING**

We proceed as follows. First look for a five-by-five-by-three-foot bin of gears or parts that looks like it has been there awhile. Pick up a gear and ask, casually, "How much is this worth?" You then ask, "How many of these are in the bin?" followed by, "How long has this bin been here?" and, "What's your cost of money for this company?" I recall one case in a nameless South American country where the unit cost times the number of parts times the time it had been there times the interest rate resulted in a cost-per-day figure that would insure comfortable retirement for the plant manager on the bank of the Rio de la Plata at one of the better resorts to be found there. The plant manager suddenly realized that what he was holding was not just a chunk of high-test steel, but was *real money*. He then pointed out that *he* now understood the value of the inventory but could I suggest a way to drive the point home to upper management? I suggested that he go to the accounting department and borrow enough money to be equal to the bin's value for as long as it had been sitting there, and pile it on the top of the bin. I further suggested that he do that for every bin on the production line. We rapidly figured out that by the time we had the money piled up on the bin, you would not even be able to *see* the bin. My opinion was that if the upper managers were given a tour of the line with the money piled up, they would *never* forget it.

Source: Gene Woolsey, "On Doing Good Things and Dumb Things in Production and Inventory Control," *Interfaces* 5, no. 3 (May 1975).

THE NATURE AND IMPORTANCE OF INVENTORIES

SUPPLY CHAIN

Inventories are a vital part of business. Not only are they necessary for operations, but they also contribute to customer satisfaction. To get a sense of the significance of inventories, consider the following: Some very large firms have tremendous amounts of inventory. For example, General

Motors was at one point reported to have as much as $40 billion worth of materials, parts, cars, and trucks in its supply chain! Although the amounts and dollar values of inventories carried by different types of firms vary widely, a typical firm probably has about 30 percent of its current assets and perhaps as much as 90 percent of its working capital invested in inventory. One widely used measure of managerial performance relates to *return on investment* (ROI), which is profit after taxes divided by total assets. Because inventories may represent a significant portion of total assets, a reduction of inventories can result in a significant increase in ROI. Furthermore, the ratio of inventories to sales in the manufacturing, wholesale, and retail sectors is one measure that is used to gauge the health of the U.S. economy.

Inventory decisions in service organizations can be especially critical. Hospitals, for example, carry an array of drugs and blood supplies that might be needed on short notice. Being out of stock on some of these could imperil the well-being of a patient. However, many of these items have a limited shelf life, so carrying large quantities would mean having to dispose of unused, costly supplies. On-site repair services for computers, printers, copiers, and fax machines also have to carefully consider which parts to bring to the site to avoid having to make an extra trip to obtain parts. The same goes for home repair services such as electricians, appliance repairers, and plumbers.

The major source of revenues for retail and wholesale businesses is the sale of merchandise (i.e., inventory). In fact, in terms of dollars, the inventory of goods held for sale is one of the largest assets of a merchandising business. Retail stores that sell clothing wrestle with decisions about which styles to carry, and how much of each to stock, knowing full well that fast-selling items will mean greater profits than having to heavily discount goods that didn't sell.

The different kinds of inventories include the following:

Raw materials and purchased parts.

Partially completed goods, called *work-in-process (WIP).*

Finished-goods inventories (manufacturing firms) or merchandise (retail stores).

Tools and supplies.

Maintenance and repairs (MRO) inventory.

Goods-in-transit to warehouses, distributors, or customers (pipeline inventory).

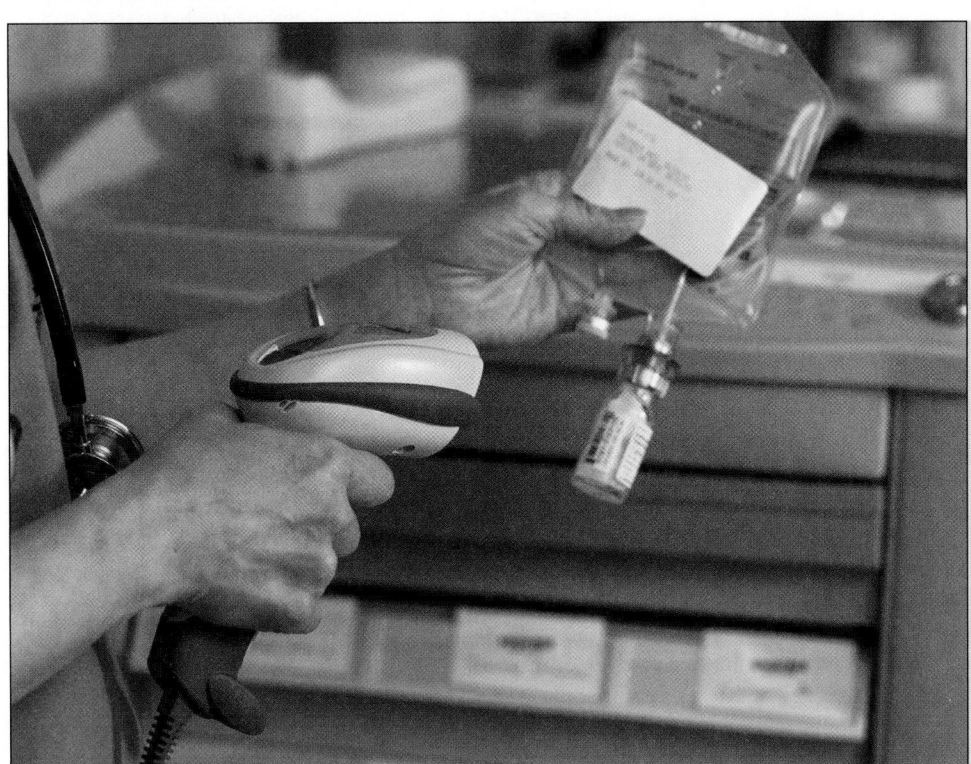

By initiating a program that utilizes barcodes and scanners, such as this one by Motorola, hospitals can control inventory supply areas, as well as keep track of all equipment in use across the enterprise. Stockroom inventory applications track consumable items such as medication and supplies, while check in/out applications track shared or re-usable items such as X-rays, lab results, diagnostic tools, and other medical equipment.

Both manufacturing and service organizations have to take into consideration the space requirements of inventory. In some cases, space limitations may pose restrictions on inventory storage capability, thereby adding another dimension to inventory decisions.

To understand why firms have inventories at all, you need to be aware of the various functions of inventory.

Functions of Inventory

Inventories serve a number of functions. Among the most important are the following:

1. **To meet anticipated customer demand.** A customer can be a person who walks in off the street to buy a new stereo system, a mechanic who requests a tool at a tool crib, or a manufacturing operation. These inventories are referred to as *anticipation stocks* because they are held to satisfy expected (i.e., *average*) demand.

2. **To smooth production requirements.** Firms that experience seasonal patterns in demand often build up inventories during preseason periods to meet overly high requirements during seasonal periods. These inventories are aptly named *seasonal inventories.* Companies that process fresh fruits and vegetables deal with seasonal inventories. So do stores that sell greeting cards, skis, snowmobiles, or Christmas trees.

3. **To decouple operations.** Historically, manufacturing firms have used inventories as buffers between successive operations to maintain continuity of production that would otherwise be disrupted by events such as breakdowns of equipment and accidents that cause a portion of the operation to shut down temporarily. The buffers permit other operations to continue temporarily while the problem is resolved. Similarly, firms have used buffers of raw materials to insulate production from disruptions in deliveries from suppliers, and finished goods inventory to buffer sales operations from manufacturing disruptions. More recently, companies have taken a closer look at buffer inventories, recognizing the cost and space they require, and realizing that finding and eliminating sources of disruptions can greatly decrease the need for decoupling operations.

   Inventory buffers are also important in *supply chains.* Careful analysis can reveal both points where buffers would be most useful and points where they would merely increase costs without adding value.

SUPPLY CHAIN

4. **To protect against stockouts.** Delayed deliveries and unexpected increases in demand increase the risk of shortages. Delays can occur because of weather conditions, supplier stockouts, deliveries of wrong materials, quality problems, and so on. The risk of shortages can be reduced by holding *safety stocks,* which are stocks in excess of expected demand to compensate for *variabilities* in demand and lead time.

5. **To take advantage of order cycles.** To minimize purchasing and inventory costs, a firm often buys in quantities that exceed immediate requirements. This necessitates storing some or all of the purchased amount for later use. Similarly, it is usually economical to produce in large rather than small quantities. Again, the excess output must be stored for later use. Thus, inventory storage enables a firm to buy and produce in *economic lot sizes* without having to try to match purchases or production with demand requirements in the short run. This results in *periodic* orders or order *cycles.*

6. **To hedge against price increases.** Occasionally a firm will suspect that a substantial price increase is about to occur and purchase larger-than-normal amounts to beat the increase. The ability to store extra goods also allows a firm to take advantage of price discounts for larger orders.

7. **To permit operations.** The fact that production operations take a certain amount of time (i.e., they are not instantaneous) means that there will generally be some work-in-process inventory. In addition, intermediate stocking of goods—including raw materials, semifinished items, and finished goods at production sites, as well as goods stored in warehouses—leads to *pipeline* inventories throughout a production-distribution system. Little's Law can be useful in quantifying pipeline inventory. It states that the average amount of inventory in a system is equal to the product of the average rate at which inventory units leave the system (i.e., the average demand rate) and the average time a unit is in the system. Thus, if a unit is in the system for an average of 10 days, and the demand rate is 5 units per day, the average inventory is 50 units: 5 units/day × 10 days = 50 units.

Little's Law The average amount of inventory in a system is equal to the product of the average demand rate and the average time a unit is in the system.

8. **To take advantage of quantity discounts.** Suppliers may give discounts on large orders.

Objectives of Inventory Control

Inadequate control of inventories can result in both under- and overstocking of items. Understocking results in missed deliveries, lost sales, dissatisfied customers, and production bottlenecks; overstocking unnecessarily ties up funds that might be more productive elsewhere. Although overstocking may appear to be the lesser of the two evils, the price tag for excessive overstocking can be staggering when inventory holding costs are high—as illustrated by the reading about the bin of gears at the beginning of the chapter—and matters can easily get out of hand. It is not unheard of for managers to discover that their firm has a 10-year supply of some item. (No doubt the firm got a good buy on it!)

Inventory management has two main concerns. One is the *level of customer service,* that is, to have the right goods, in sufficient quantities, in the right place, at the right time. The other is the *costs of ordering and carrying inventories.*

The overall objective of inventory management is to achieve satisfactory levels of customer service while keeping inventory costs within reasonable bounds. Toward this end, the decision maker tries to achieve a balance in stocking. He or she must make two fundamental decisions: the *timing* and *size* of orders (i.e., when to order and how much to order). The greater part of this chapter is devoted to models that can be applied to assist in making those decisions.

Managers have a number of performance measures they can use to judge the effectiveness of inventory management. The most obvious, of course, is customer satisfaction, which they might measure by the number and quantity of backorders and/or customer complaints. A widely used measure is **inventory turnover,** which is the ratio of annual cost of goods sold to average inventory investment. The turnover ratio indicates how many times a year the inventory is sold. Generally, the higher the ratio, the better, because that implies more efficient use of inventories. However, the desirable number of turns depends on the industry and what the profit margins are. The higher the profit margins, the lower the acceptable number of inventory turns, and vice versa. Also, a product that takes a long time to manufacture, or a long time to sell, will have a low turnover rate. This is often the case with high-end retailers (high profit margins). Conversely, supermarkets (low profit margins) have a fairly high turnover rate. Note, though, that there should be a balance between inventory investment and maintaining good customer service. Managers often use inventory turnover to evaluate inventory management performance; monitoring this metric over time can yield insights into changes in performance.

Inventory turnover Ratio of average cost of goods sold to average inventory investment.

Another useful measure is days of inventory on hand, a number that indicates the expected number of days of sales that can be supplied from existing inventory. Here, a balance is desirable; a high number of days might imply excess inventory, while a low number might imply a risk of running out of stock.

REQUIREMENTS FOR EFFECTIVE INVENTORY MANAGEMENT

Management has two basic functions concerning inventory. One is to establish a system to keep track of items in inventory, and the other is to make decisions about how much and when to order. To be effective, management must have the following:

1. A system to **keep track of the inventory** on hand and on order.
2. A reliable **forecast of demand** that includes an indication of possible *forecast error.*
3. Knowledge of **lead times** and **lead time variability.**
4. Reasonable estimates of inventory **holding costs, ordering costs,** and **shortage costs.**
5. A **classification system** for inventory items.

Let's take a closer look at each of these requirements.

Inventory Counting Systems

Periodic system Physical count of items in inventory made at periodic intervals (weekly, monthly).

Inventory counting systems can be periodic or perpetual. Under a **periodic system,** a physical count of items in inventory is made at periodic intervals (e.g., weekly, monthly) in order to decide how much to order of each item. Many small retailers use this approach: A manager periodically checks the shelves and stockroom to determine the quantity on hand. Then the manager estimates how much will be demanded prior to the next delivery period and bases the order quantity on that information. An advantage of this type of system is that orders for many items occur at the same time, which can result in economies in processing and shipping orders. There are also several disadvantages of periodic reviews. One is a lack of control between reviews. Another is the need to protect against shortages between review periods by carrying extra stock.

Perpetual inventory system System that keeps track of removals from inventory continuously, thus monitoring current levels of each item.

A **perpetual inventory system** (also known as a *continual* system) keeps track of removals from inventory on a continuous basis, so the system can provide information on the current level of inventory for each item. When the amount on hand reaches a predetermined minimum, a fixed quantity, Q, is ordered. An obvious advantage of this system is the control provided by the continuous monitoring of inventory withdrawals. Another advantage is the fixed-order quantity; management can determine an optimal order quantity. One disadvantage of this approach is the added cost of record keeping. Moreover, a physical count of inventories must still be performed periodically to verify records because of possible errors, pilferage, spoilage, and other factors that can reduce the effective amount of inventory. Bank transactions such as customer deposits and withdrawals are examples of continuous recording of inventory changes.

Two-bin system Two containers of inventory; reorder when the first is empty.

Perpetual systems range from very simple to very sophisticated. A **two-bin system,** a very elementary system, uses two containers for inventory. Items are withdrawn from the first bin until its contents are exhausted. It is then time to reorder. Sometimes an order card is placed at the bottom of the first bin. The second bin contains enough stock to satisfy expected demand until the order is filled, plus an extra cushion of stock that will reduce the chance of a stockout if the order is late or if usage is greater than expected. The advantage of this system is that there is no need to record each withdrawal from inventory; the disadvantage is that the reorder card may not be turned in for a variety of reasons (e.g., misplaced, the person responsible forgets to turn it in).

Universal product code (UPC) Bar code printed on a label that has information about the item to which it is attached.

Supermarkets, discount stores, and department stores have always been major users of periodic counting systems. Today, most have switched to computerized checkout systems using a laser scanning device that reads a **universal product code (UPC),** or *bar code,* printed on an item tag or on packaging. A typical grocery product code is illustrated here:

The zero on the left of the bar code identifies this as a grocery item, the first five numbers (14800) indicate the manufacturer (Mott's), and the last five numbers (23208) indicate the specific item (natural-style applesauce). Items in small packages, such as candy and gum, use a six-digit number.

Point-of-sale (POS) systems Record items at time of sale.

Point-of-sale (POS) systems electronically record actual sales. Knowledge of actual sales can greatly enhance forecasting and inventory management: By relaying information about actual demand in real time, these systems enable management to make any necessary changes to restocking decisions. These systems are being increasingly emphasized as an important input to effective supply chain management by making this information available to suppliers.

UPC scanners represent major benefits to supermarkets. In addition to their increase in speed and accuracy, these systems give managers continuous information on inventories, reduce the need for periodic review and order-size determinations, and improve the level of customer service by indicating the price and quantity of each item on the customer's receipt, as in the following illustration:

Poor inventory accuracy leads to too much inventory or shortages. Software systems maintain enormous amounts of data and have a great amount of functionality. Systems can analyze inventory levels, allocate stock plan purchases, and allocate deliveries accordingly. They can identify key suppliers of each stocked item and can give lead times and dock-to-stock times for realistic time-phasing.

```
BRACO CAPELLINI          .79
BUB YUM DBL LIME         .30 T
2/LO FAT MILK H G       1.03
EUROP ROLLS              .91
HUNTS TOMATO             .55
NEWSPAPER                .35
KR CAS BRICK CHEES      1.59
GRAPES-GREEN
  .91 LB @ .89 PER LB    .81
TAX DUE                  .02
TOTAL                   6.35

CASH                   20.00*
CHANGE                 13.65

8/07/10 18:01 21  16  23100  2570
```

Bar coding is important for other sectors of business besides retailing. Manufacturing and service industries benefit from the simplified production and inventory control it provides. In manufacturing, bar codes attached to parts, subassemblies, and finished goods greatly facilitate counting and monitoring activities. Automatic routing, scheduling, sorting, and packaging can also be done using bar codes. In health care, use of bar codes can help to reduce drug dispensing errors.

Radio frequency identification (RFID) tags are also used to keep track of inventory in certain applications.

Radio Frequency Identification (RFID) Tags

READING

Keeping track of inventories in-house and throughout a supply chain is vitally important for manufacturing, service, and retail operations. Bar codes have long been used for that purpose, but they carry only a limited amount of information and require direct line-of-sight to be scanned. Radio frequency identification (RFID) tags are a technological breakthrough in inventory management, providing real-time information that increases the ability to track and process shipping containers, parts in warehouses, items on supermarket shelves, and a whole lot more. They carry much more information than bar codes, and they don't require line-of-sight to be scanned.

(continued)

(concluded)

RFID tags transmit product information or other data to network-connected RFID readers via radio waves. Tags attached to pallets, boxes, or individual items can enable a business to identify, track, monitor, or locate any object that is within range of a reader. For example, the tags are used in "speed passes" for toll roads.

In agriculture, fruit growers might use RFID tags to constantly monitor temperatures around fruit during shipping. This ensures that the fruit is kept at the appropriate temperature. The tags can be used for a wide range of agricultural products, containing information such as cultivation history, as well as whether the fruit is organically grown and what fertilizers or chemicals have been used.

Because major retail chains, such as Walmart and Target, and governmental agencies now require their suppliers to use RFID tags, many companies have already made RFID a priority in their business strategies.

Although RFID technology holds the potential for improved safety, convenience, and inventory management, widespread adoption, particularly in retail operations, could take several years. Until a global standard is established and cheap disposable tags are developed, the main areas of growth continue to be in nonretail operations.

Demand Forecasts and Lead-Time Information

Lead time Time interval between ordering and receiving the order.

Inventories are used to satisfy demand requirements, so it is essential to have reliable estimates of the amount and timing of demand. Similarly, it is essential to know how long it will take for orders to be delivered. In addition, managers need to know the extent to which demand and **lead time** (the time between submitting an order and receiving it) might vary; the greater the potential variability, the greater the need for additional stock to reduce the risk of a shortage between deliveries. Thus, there is a crucial link between forecasting and inventory management.

Inventory Costs

Four basic costs are associated with inventories: purchase, holding, transaction (ordering), and shortage costs.

Purchase cost The amount paid to buy the inventory.

Holding (carrying) cost Cost to carry an item in inventory for a length of time, usually a year.

Purchase cost is the amount paid to a vendor or supplier to buy the inventory. It is typically the largest of all inventory costs.

Holding, or carrying, costs relate to physically having items in storage. Costs include interest, insurance, taxes (in some states), depreciation, obsolescence, deterioration, spoilage, pilferage, breakage, tracking, picking, and warehousing costs (heat, light, rent, security). They also include opportunity costs associated with having funds that could be used elsewhere tied up in inventory. Note that it is the *variable* portion of these costs that is pertinent.

The significance of the various components of holding cost depends on the type of item involved, although taxes, interest, and insurance are generally based on the dollar value of an inventory. Items that are easily concealed (e.g., pocket cameras, transistor radios, calculators) or fairly expensive (cars, TVs) are prone to theft. Fresh seafood, meats and poultry, produce, and baked goods are subject to rapid deterioration and spoilage. Dairy products, salad dressings, medicines, batteries, and film also have limited shelf lives.

Holding costs are stated in either of two ways: as a percentage of unit price or as a dollar amount per unit. Typical annual holding costs range from 20 percent to 40 percent or more of the value of an item. In other words, to hold a $100 item in inventory for one year could cost from $20 to $40.

Ordering costs Costs of ordering and receiving inventory.

Ordering costs are the costs of ordering and receiving inventory. They are the costs that vary with the actual placement of an order. Besides shipping costs, they include determining how much is needed, preparing invoices, inspecting goods upon arrival for quality and quantity, and moving the goods to temporary storage. Ordering costs are generally expressed as a fixed dollar amount per order, regardless of order size.

Setup costs The costs involved in preparing equipment for a job.

Shortage costs Costs resulting when demand exceeds the supply of inventory; often unrealized profit per unit.

When a firm produces its own inventory instead of ordering it from a supplier, machine **setup costs** (e.g., preparing equipment for the job by adjusting the machine, changing cutting tools) are analogous to ordering costs; that is, they are expressed as a fixed charge per production run, regardless of the size of the run.

Shortage costs result when demand exceeds the supply of inventory on hand. These costs can include the opportunity cost of not making a sale, loss of customer goodwill, late charges, backorder costs, and similar costs. Furthermore, if the shortage occurs in an item carried for internal use (e.g., to supply an assembly line), the cost of lost production or downtime is considered a shortage cost. Such costs can easily run into hundreds of dollars a minute or more. Shortage costs are sometimes difficult to measure, and they may be subjectively estimated.

Classification System

An important aspect of inventory management is that items held in inventory are not of equal importance in terms of dollars invested, profit potential, sales or usage volume, or stockout penalties. For instance, a producer of electrical equipment might have electric generators, coils of wire, and miscellaneous nuts and bolts among the items carried in inventory. It would be unrealistic to devote equal attention to each of these items. Instead, a more reasonable approach would be to allocate control efforts according to the *relative importance* of various items in inventory.

The **A-B-C approach** classifies inventory items according to some measure of importance, usually annual dollar value (i.e., dollar value per unit multiplied by annual usage rate), and then allocates control efforts accordingly. Typically, three classes of items are used: A (very important), B (moderately important), and C (least important). However, the actual number of categories may vary from organization to organization, depending on the extent to which a firm wants to differentiate control efforts. With three classes of items, A items generally account for about 10 to 20 percent of the *number* of items in inventory but about 60 to 70 percent of the *annual dollar value.* At the other end of the scale, C items might account for about 50 to 60 percent of the number of items but only about 10 to 15 percent of the dollar value of an inventory. These percentages vary from firm to firm, but in most instances a relatively small number of items will account for a large share of the value

A-B-C approach Classifying inventory according to some measure of importance, and allocating control efforts accordingly.

One way to lower inventory holding costs is to improve space utilization through narrow aisle handling equipment, mezzanines, layout, or other appropriate storage modes. Another is an inventory management system that allows companies to maintain tight control over inventory levels. This allows process planners to optimize material and maintain accurate quantities.

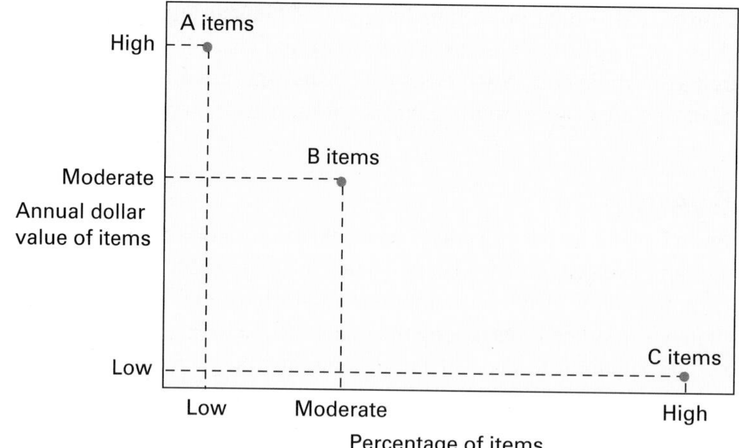

FIGURE 13.1
A typical A-B-C breakdown in relative annual dollar value of items and number of items by category

or cost associated with an inventory, and these items should receive a relatively greater share of control efforts. For instance, A items should receive close attention through frequent reviews of amounts on hand and control over withdrawals, where possible, to make sure that customer service levels are attained. The C items should receive only loose control (two-bin system, bulk orders), and the B items should have controls that lie between the two extremes.

Note that C items are not necessarily *un*important; incurring a stockout of C items such as the nuts and bolts used to assemble manufactured goods can result in a costly shutdown of an assembly line. However, due to the low annual dollar value of C items, there may not be much additional cost incurred by ordering larger quantities of some items, or ordering them a bit earlier.

Figure 13.1 illustrates the A-B-C concept.

To solve an A-B-C problem, follow these steps:

1. For each item, multiply annual volume by unit price to get the annual dollar value.
2. Arrange annual dollar values in descending order.
3. The few (10 to 15 percent) with the highest annual dollar value are A items. The most (about 50 percent) with the lowest annual dollar value are C items. Those in between (about 35 percent) are B items.

EXAMPLE 1

www.mhhe.com/stevenson11e

A manager has obtained a list of unit costs and estimated annual demands for 10 inventory items and now wants to categorize the items on an A-B-C basis. Multiplying each item's annual demand by its unit cost yields its annual dollar value:

Item Number	Annual Demand	×	Unit Cost	=	Annual Dollar Value
1	2,500		$ 360		$ 900,000
2	1,000		70		70,000
3	2,400		500		1,200,000
4	1,500		100		150,000
5	700		70		49,000
6	1,000		1,000		1,000,000
7	200		210		42,000
8	1,000		4,000		4,000,000
9	8,000		10		80,000
10	500		200		100,000
					7,591,000

SOLUTION

Arranging the annual dollars values in descending order can facilitate assigning items to categories:

Item Number	Annual Dollar Value	Classification	Percentage of Items	Percentage of Annual Dollar Value
8	$4,000,000	A	10	52.7
3	1,200,000	B		
6	1,000,000	B	30	40.8
1	900,000	B		
4	150,000	C		
10	100,000	C		
9	80,000	C	60	6.5
2	70,000	C		
5	49,000	C		
7	42,000	C		
			100	100

Note that category A has the fewest number of items but the highest percentage of annual dollar value, while category C has the most items but only a small percentage of the annual dollar value.

Although annual dollar value may be the primary factor in classifying inventory items, a manager may take other factors into account in making exceptions for certain items (e.g., changing the classification of a B item to an A item). Factors may include the risk of obsolescence, the risk of a stockout, the distance of a supplier, and so on.

Managers use the A-B-C concept in many different settings to improve operations. One key use occurs in customer service, where a manager can focus attention on the most important aspects of customer service by categorizing different aspects as very important, important, or of only minor importance. The point is to not overemphasize minor aspects of customer service at the expense of major aspects.

Another application of the A-B-C concept is as a guide to **cycle counting,** which is a physical count of items in inventory. The purpose of cycle counting is to reduce discrepancies between the amounts indicated by inventory records and the actual quantities of inventory on hand. Accuracy is important because inaccurate records can lead to disruptions in operations, poor customer service, and unnecessarily high inventory carrying costs. The counts are conducted more frequently than once a year, which reduces the costs of inaccuracies compared to only doing an annual count, by allowing for investigation and correction of the causes of inaccuracies.

Cycle counting A physical count of items in inventory.

The key questions concerning cycle counting for management are

1. How much accuracy is needed?
2. When should cycle counting be performed?
3. Who should do it?

APICS recommends the following guidelines for inventory record accuracy: ± .2 percent for A items, ± 1 percent for B items, and ± 5 percent for C items. A items are counted frequently, B items are counted less frequently, and C items are counted the least frequently.

Some companies use certain events to trigger cycle counting, whereas others do it on a periodic (scheduled) basis. Events that can trigger a physical count of inventory include an out-of-stock report written on an item indicated by inventory records to be in stock, an inventory report that indicates a low or zero balance of an item, and a specified level of activity (e.g., every 2,000 units sold).

Some companies use regular stockroom personnel to do cycle counting during periods of slow activity while others contract with outside firms to do it on a periodic basis. Use of an outside firm provides an independent check on inventory and may reduce the risk of problems created by dishonest employees. Still other firms maintain full-time personnel to do cycle counting.

INVENTORY ORDERING POLICIES

Inventory ordering policies address the two basic issues of inventory management, which are how much to order and when to order. In the following sections, a number of models are described that are used for these issues.

Cycle stock The amount of inventory needed to meet expected demand.

Safety stock Extra inventory carried to reduce the probability of a stockout due to demand and/or lead time variability.

Inventory that is intended to meet expected demand is known as **cycle stock,** while inventory that is held to reduce the probability of experiencing a stockout (i.e., running out of stock) due to demand and/or lead time variability is known as **safety stock.**

The discussion begins with the issue of how much to order.

HOW MUCH TO ORDER: ECONOMIC ORDER QUANTITY MODELS

Economic order quantity (EOQ) The order size that minimizes total annual cost.

The question of how much to order can be determined by using an **economic order quantity (EOQ)** model. EOQ models identify the optimal order quantity by minimizing the sum of certain annual costs that vary with order size and order frequency. Three order size models are described here:

1. The basic economic order quantity model.
2. The economic production quantity model.
3. The quantity discount model.

SCREENCAM TUTORIAL

Basic Economic Order Quantity (EOQ) Model

The basic EOQ model is the simplest of the three models. It is used to identify a *fixed* order size that will minimize the sum of the annual costs of holding inventory and ordering inventory. The unit purchase price of items in inventory is not generally included in the total cost because the unit cost is unaffected by the order size unless quantity discounts are a factor. If holding costs are specified as a percentage of unit cost, then unit cost is indirectly included in the total cost as a part of holding costs.

The basic model involves a number of assumptions. They are listed in Table 13.1.

Inventory ordering and usage occur in cycles. Figure 13.2 illustrates several inventory cycles. A cycle begins with receipt of an order of Q units, which are withdrawn at a constant rate over time. When the quantity on hand is just sufficient to satisfy demand during lead time, an order for Q units is submitted to the supplier. Because it is assumed that both the usage rate and the lead time do not vary, the order will be received at the precise instant that the inventory on hand falls to zero. Thus, orders are timed to avoid both excess stock and stockouts.

The optimal order quantity reflects a balance between carrying costs and ordering costs: As order size varies, one type of cost will increase while the other decreases. For example, if the order size is relatively small, the average inventory will be low, resulting in low carrying

TABLE 13.1
Assumptions of the basic EOQ model

1. Only one product is involved.
2. Annual demand requirements are known.
3. Demand is spread evenly throughout the year so that the demand rate is reasonably constant.
4. Lead time is known and constant.
5. Each order is received in a single delivery.
6. There are no quantity discounts.

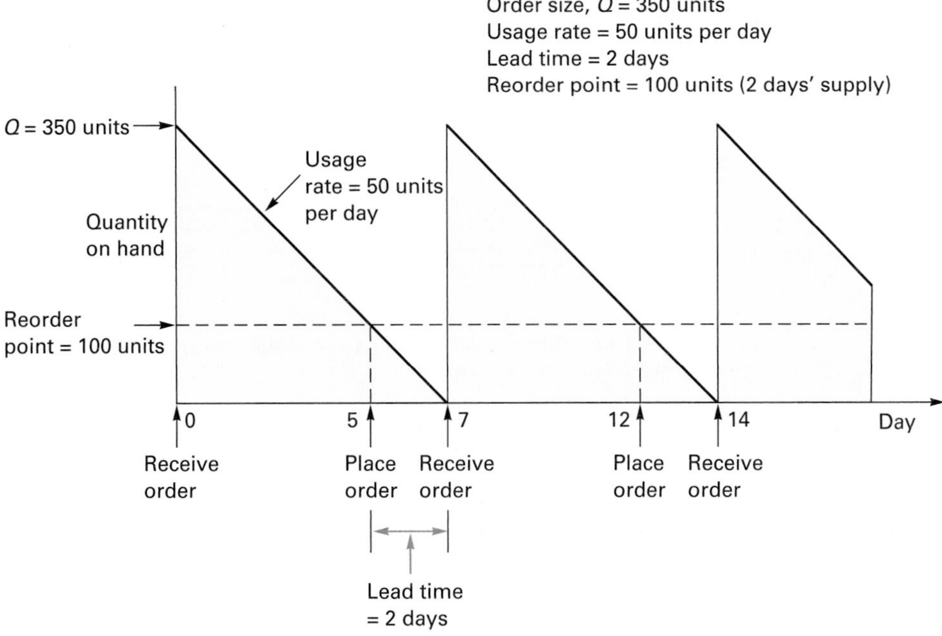

FIGURE 13.2
The inventory cycle: profile of inventory level over time

costs. However, a small order size will necessitate frequent orders, which will drive up annual ordering costs. Conversely, ordering large quantities at infrequent intervals can hold down annual ordering costs, but that would result in higher average inventory levels and therefore increased carrying costs. Figure 13.3 illustrates these two extremes.

Thus, the ideal solution is an order size that causes neither a few very large orders nor many small orders, but one that lies somewhere between. The exact amount to order will depend on the relative magnitudes of carrying and ordering costs.

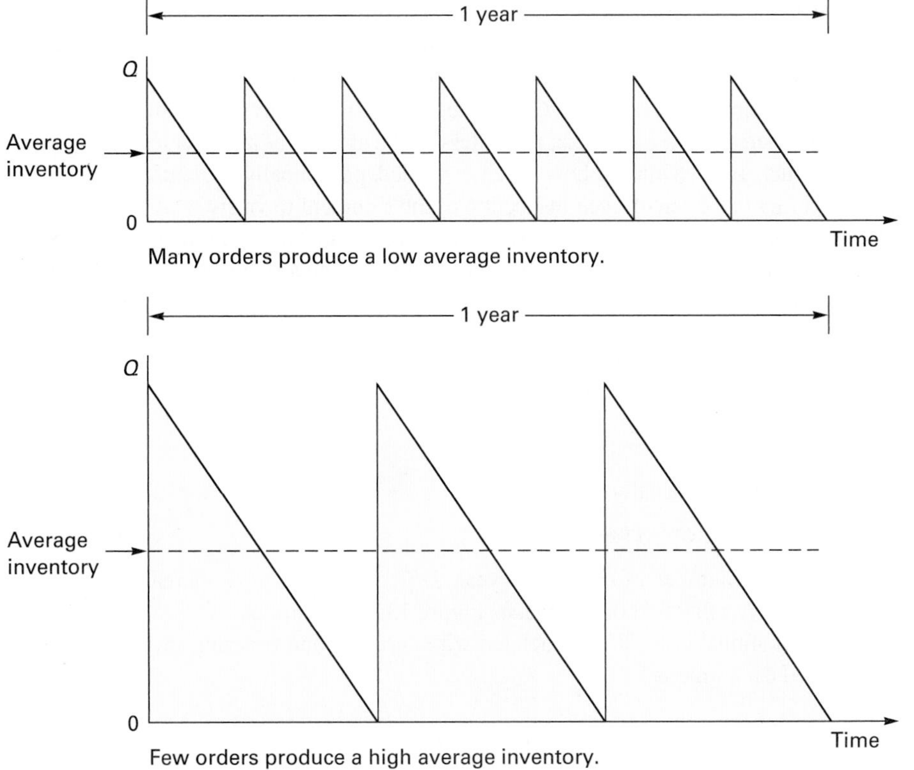

FIGURE 13.3
Average inventory level and number of orders per year are inversely related: As one increases, the other decreases

FIGURE 13.4 Carrying cost, ordering cost, and total cost curve

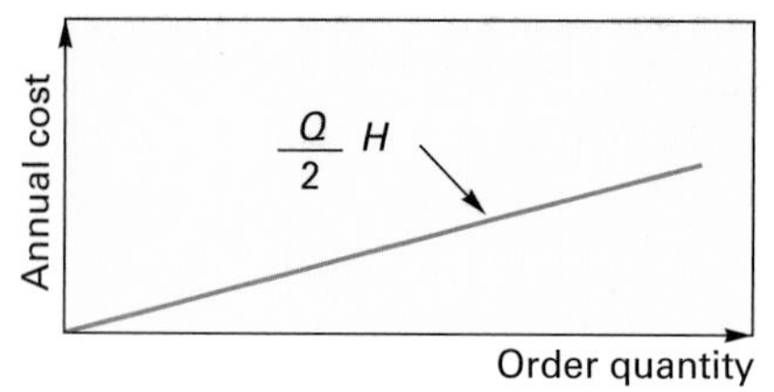

A. Carrying costs are linearly related to order size.

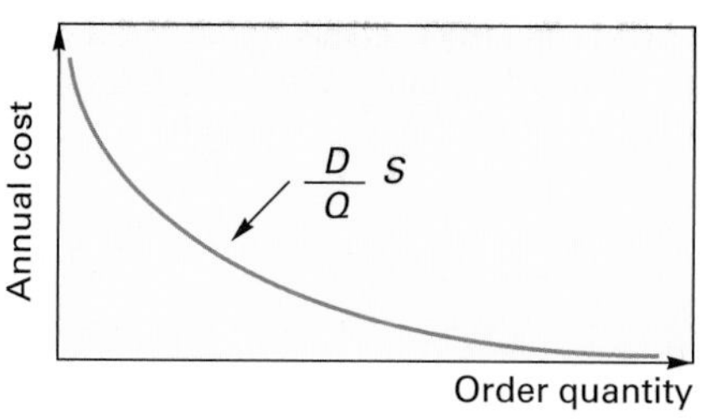

B. Ordering costs are inversely and nonlinearly related to order size.

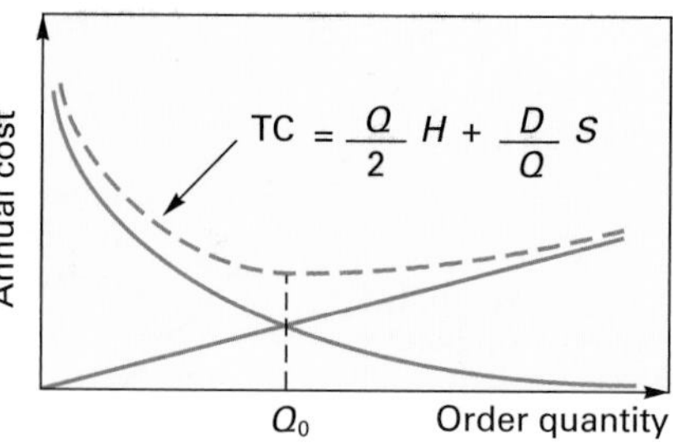

C. The total-cost curve is U-shaped.

Annual carrying cost is computed by multiplying the average amount of inventory on hand by the cost to carry one unit for one year, even though any given unit would not necessarily be held for a year. The average inventory is simply half of the order quantity: The amount on hand decreases steadily from Q units to 0, for an average of $(Q + 0)/2$, or $Q/2$. Using the symbol H to represent the average annual carrying cost per unit, the *total annual carrying cost* is

$$\text{Annual carrying cost} = \frac{Q}{2}H$$

where

Q = Order quantity in units

H = Holding (carrying) cost per unit per year

Carrying cost is thus a linear function of Q: Carrying costs increase or decrease in direct proportion to changes in the order quantity Q, as Figure 13.4A illustrates.

On the other hand, annual ordering cost will decrease as order size increases because, for a given annual demand, the larger the order size, the fewer the number of orders needed. For instance, if annual demand is 12,000 units and the order size is 1,000 units per order, there must be 12 orders over the year. But if $Q = 2{,}000$ units, only six orders will be needed; if $Q = 3{,}000$ units, only four orders will be needed. In general, the number of orders per year will be D/Q, where D = Annual demand and Q = Order size. Unlike carrying costs, ordering costs are relatively insensitive to order size; regardless of the amount of an order, certain activities must be done, such as determining how much is needed, periodically evaluating sources of supply, and preparing the invoice. Even inspection of the shipment to verify quality and quantity characteristics is not strongly influenced by order size since large shipments are sampled rather than completely inspected. Hence, ordering cost is treated as a constant. *Annual ordering cost* is a function of the number of orders per year and the ordering cost per order:

$$\text{Annual ordering cost} = \frac{D}{Q}S$$

where

D = Demand, usually in units per year

S = Ordering cost per order

Because the number of orders per year, D/Q, decreases as Q increases, annual ordering cost is inversely related to order size, as Figure 13.4B illustrates.

The total annual cost (TC) associated with carrying and ordering inventory when Q units are ordered each time is

$$\text{TC} = \underset{\text{cost}}{\overset{\text{Annual}}{\text{carrying}}} + \underset{\text{cost}}{\overset{\text{Annual}}{\text{ordering}}} = \frac{Q}{2}H + \frac{D}{Q}S \qquad (13\text{–}1)$$

(Note that D and H must be in the same units, e.g., months, years.) Figure 13.4C reveals that the total-cost curve is U-shaped (i.e., convex, with one minimum) and that *it reaches its minimum at the quantity where carrying and ordering costs are equal.* An expression for the optimal order quantity, Q_0, can be obtained using calculus.[1] The result is the formula

$$Q_0 = \sqrt{\frac{2DS}{H}} \qquad (13\text{–}2)$$

Thus, given annual demand, the ordering cost per order, and the annual carrying cost per unit, one can compute the optimal (economic) order quantity. The minimum total cost is then found by substituting Q_0 for Q in Formula 13–1.

The length of an order cycle (i.e., the time between orders) is

$$\text{Length of order cycle} = \frac{Q}{D} \qquad (13\text{–}3)$$

EXAMPLE 2

A local distributor for a national tire company expects to sell approximately 9,600 steel-belted radial tires of a certain size and tread design next year. Annual carrying cost is \$16 per tire, and ordering cost is \$75. The distributor operates 288 days a year.

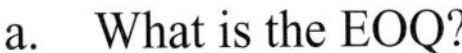

a. What is the EOQ?

b. How many times per year does the store reorder?

c. What is the length of an order cycle?

d. What is the total annual cost if the EOQ quantity is ordered?

SOLUTION

D = 9,600 tires per year

H = \$16 per unit per year

S = \$75

a. $Q_0 = \sqrt{\frac{2DS}{H}} = \sqrt{\frac{2(9{,}600)75}{16}} = 300$ tires.

b. Number of orders per year: $D/Q = \frac{9{,}600 \text{ tires/year}}{300 \text{ tires/order}} = 32$ orders.

c. Length of order cycle: $Q/D = \frac{300 \text{ tires}}{9{,}600 \text{ tires/year}} = 1/32$ of a year, which is $1/32 \times 288$, or nine workdays.

d. $$\begin{aligned} \text{TC} &= \text{Carrying cost} + \text{Ordering cost} \\ &= (Q/2)H + (D/Q)S \\ &= (300/2)16 + (9{,}600/300)75 \\ &= \$2{,}400 + \$2{,}400 \\ &= \$4{,}800 \end{aligned}$$

Note that the ordering and carrying costs are equal at the EOQ, as illustrated in Figure 13.4C.

[1]We can find the minimum point of the total-cost curve by differentiating TC with respect to Q, setting the result equal to zero, and solving for Q. Thus,

1. $\frac{d\text{TC}}{dQ} = H/2 - DS/Q^2$

2. $0 = H/2 - DS/Q^2$, so $Q^2 = \frac{2DS}{H}$ and $Q = \sqrt{\frac{2DS}{H}}$

Note that the second derivative is positive, which indicates a minimum has been obtained.

Carrying cost is sometimes stated as a percentage of the price of an item rather than as a dollar amount per unit. However, as long as the percentage is converted into a dollar amount, the EOQ formula is still appropriate.

EXAMPLE 3

Piddling Manufacturing assembles security monitors. It purchases 3,600 black-and-white cathode ray tubes a year at $65 each. Ordering costs are $31, and annual carrying costs are 20 percent of the purchase price. Compute the optimal quantity and the total annual cost of ordering and carrying the inventory.

SOLUTION

$$D = 3{,}600 \text{ cathode ray tubes per year}$$
$$S = \$31$$
$$H = .20(\$65) = \$13$$
$$Q_0 = \sqrt{\frac{2DS}{H}} = \sqrt{\frac{2(3{,}600)(31)}{13}} \approx 131 \text{ cathode ray tubes}$$
$$\begin{aligned} \text{TC} &= \text{Carrying costs} + \text{Ordering costs} \\ &= (Q_0/2)H + (D/Q_0)S \\ &= (131/2)13 + (3{,}600/131)31 \\ &= \$852 + \$852 = \$1{,}704 \end{aligned}$$

Comment Holding and ordering costs, and annual demand, are typically estimated values rather than values that can be precisely determined, say, from accounting records. Holding costs are sometimes *designated* by management rather than computed. Consequently, the EOQ should be regarded as an *approximate* quantity rather than an exact quantity. Thus, rounding the calculated value is perfectly acceptable; stating a value to several decimal places would tend to give an unrealistic impression of the precision involved. An obvious question is: How good is this "approximate" EOQ in terms of minimizing cost? The answer is that the EOQ is fairly robust; the total cost curve is relatively flat near the EOQ, especially to the right of the EOQ. In other words, even if the order quantity differs from the actual EOQ, total costs will not increase much at all. This is particularly true for quantities larger than the real EOQ, because the total cost curve rises very slowly to the right of the EOQ. (See Figure 13.5.)

Because the total cost curve is relatively flat around the EOQ, there can be some flexibility to modify the order quantity a bit from the EOQ (say, to achieve a round lot or full truckload) without incurring much of an increase in total cost.

Economic Production Quantity (EPQ)

The batch mode is widely used in production. Even in assembly operations, portions of the work are done in batches. The reason for this is that in certain instances, the capacity to produce a part exceeds the part's usage or demand rate. As long as production continues,

FIGURE 13.5
The total cost curve is relatively flat near the EOQ

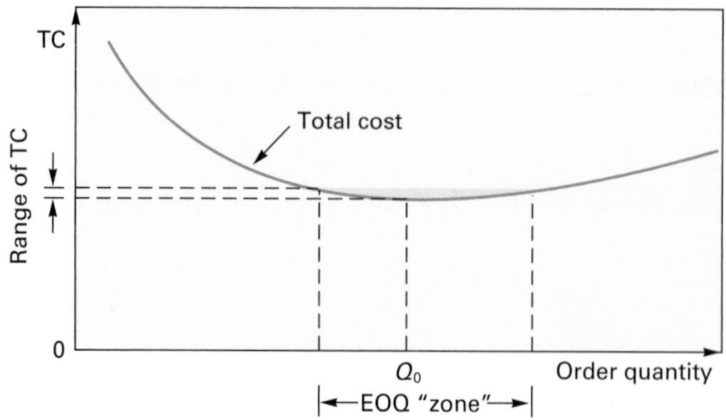

inventory will continue to grow. In such instances, it makes sense to periodically produce such items in batches, or *lots,* instead of producing continually.

The assumptions of the EPQ model are similar to those of the EOQ model, except that instead of orders received in a single delivery, units are received incrementally during production. The assumptions are

1. Only one item is involved.
2. Annual demand is known.
3. The usage rate is constant.
4. Usage occurs continually, but production occurs periodically.
5. The production rate is constant.
6. Lead time does not vary.
7. There are no quantity discounts.

Figure 13.6 illustrates how inventory is affected by periodically producing a batch of a particular item.

During the production phase of the cycle, inventory builds up at a rate equal to the difference between production and usage rates. For example, if the daily production rate is 20 units and the daily usage rate is 5 units, inventory will build up at the rate of $20 - 5 = 15$ units per day. As long as production occurs, the inventory level will continue to build; when production ceases, the inventory level will begin to decrease. Hence, the inventory level will be maximum at the point where production ceases. When the amount of inventory on hand is exhausted, production is resumed, and the cycle repeats itself.

Because the company makes the product itself, there are no ordering costs as such. Nonetheless, with every production run (batch) there are setup costs—the costs required to prepare the equipment for the job, such as cleaning, adjusting, and changing tools and fixtures. Setup costs are analogous to ordering costs because they are independent of the lot (run) size. They are treated in the formula in exactly the same way. The larger the run size, the fewer the number of runs needed and, hence, the lower the annual setup cost. The number of runs or batches per year is D/Q, and the annual setup cost is equal to the number of runs per year times the setup cost, S, per run: $(D/Q)S$.

The total cost is

$$TC_{min} = \text{Carrying cost} + \text{Setup cost} = \left(\frac{I_{max}}{2}\right)H + (D/Q)S \qquad (13\text{–}4)$$

where

I_{max} = Maximum inventory

FIGURE 13.6 EOQ with incremental inventory buildup

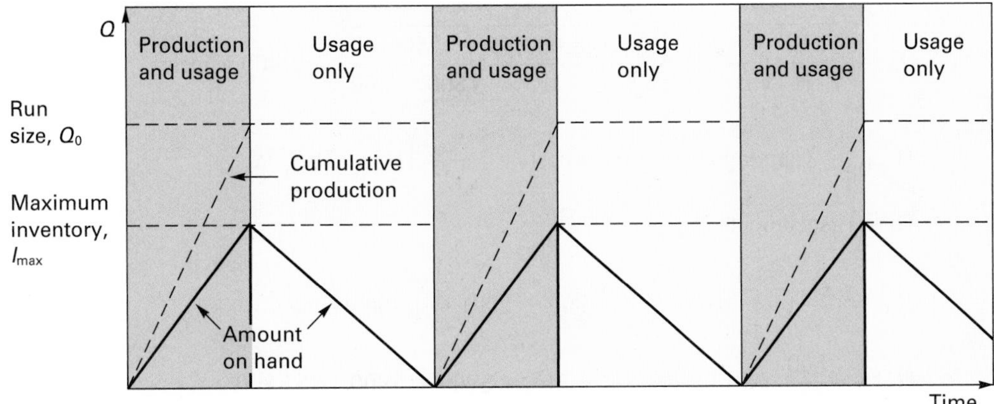

The economic run quantity is

$$Q_p = \sqrt{\frac{2DS}{H}}\sqrt{\frac{p}{p-u}} \qquad (13\text{–}5)$$

where

p = Production or delivery rate
u = Usage rate

The cycle time (the time between orders or between the beginnings of runs) for the economic run size model is a function of the run size and usage (demand) rate:

$$\text{Cycle time} = \frac{Q_p}{u} \qquad (13\text{–}6)$$

Similarly, the run time (the production phase of the cycle) is a function of the run (lot) size and the production rate:

$$\text{Run time} = \frac{Q_p}{p} \qquad (13\text{–}7)$$

The maximum and average inventory levels are

$$I_{max} = \frac{Q_p}{p}(p-u) \quad \text{or} \quad Q_p - \left(\frac{Q_p}{P}\right)u \quad \text{and} \quad I_{average} = \frac{I_{max}}{2} \qquad (13\text{–}8)$$

EXAMPLE 4

www.mhhe.com/stevenson11e

A toy manufacturer uses 48,000 rubber wheels per year for its popular dump truck series. The firm makes its own wheels, which it can produce at a rate of 800 per day. The toy trucks are assembled uniformly over the entire year. Carrying cost is $1 per wheel a year. Setup cost for a production run of wheels is $45. The firm operates 240 days per year. Determine the

a. Optimal run size.
b. Minimum total annual cost for carrying and setup.
c. Cycle time for the optimal run size.
d. Run time.

SOLUTION

D = 48,000 wheels per year
S = \$45
H = \$1 per wheel per year
p = 800 wheels per day
u = 48,000 wheels per 240 days, or 200 wheels per day

a. $$Q_p = \sqrt{\frac{2DS}{H}}\sqrt{\frac{p}{p-u}} = \sqrt{\frac{2(48{,}000)45}{1}}\sqrt{\frac{800}{800-200}} = 2{,}400 \text{ wheels}$$

b. $$TC_{min} = \text{Carrying cost} + \text{Setup cost} = \left(\frac{I_{max}}{2}\right)H + (D/Q_p)S$$

Thus, first compute I_{max}:

$$I_{max} = \frac{Q_p}{p}(p-u) = \frac{2{,}400}{800}(800-200) = 1{,}800 \text{ wheels}$$

$$TC = \frac{1{,}800}{2} \times \$1 + \frac{48{,}000}{2{,}400} \times \$45 = \$900 + \$900 = \$1{,}800$$

Note again the equality of cost (in this example, setup and carrying costs) at the EOQ.

c. $\text{Cycle time} = \dfrac{Q_p}{u} = \dfrac{2{,}400 \text{ wheels}}{200 \text{ wheels per day}} = 12 \text{ days}$

Thus, a run of wheels will be made every 12 days.

d. $\text{Run time} = \dfrac{Q_p}{p} = \dfrac{2{,}400 \text{ wheels}}{800 \text{ wheels per day}} = 3 \text{ days}$

Thus, each run will require three days to complete.

Quantity Discounts

Quantity discounts Price reductions for larger orders.

Quantity discounts are price reductions for larger orders offered to customers to induce them to buy in large quantities. For example, a Chicago surgical supply company publishes the price list shown in Table 13.2 for boxes of gauze strips. Note that the price per box decreases as order quantity increases.

If quantity discounts are offered, the buyer must weigh the potential benefits of reduced purchase price and fewer orders that will result from buying in large quantities against the increase in carrying costs caused by higher average inventories. The buyer's goal with quantity discounts is to select the order quantity that will minimize total cost, where total cost is the sum of carrying cost, ordering cost, *and* purchasing (i.e., product) cost:

$$\begin{aligned} \text{TC} &= \text{Carrying cost} + \text{Ordering cost} + \text{Purchasing cost} \\ &= \left(\frac{Q}{2}\right)H + \left(\frac{D}{Q}\right)S + PD \end{aligned} \tag{13–9}$$

where

P = Unit price

Recall that in the basic EOQ model, determination of order size does not involve the purchasing cost. The rationale for not including unit price is that under the assumption of no quantity discounts, price per unit is the same for all order sizes. Inclusion of unit price in the total-cost computation in that case would merely increase the total cost by the amount P times D. A graph of total annual purchase cost versus quantity would be a horizontal line. Hence, including purchasing costs would merely raise the total-cost curve by the same amount (PD) at every point. That would not change the EOQ. (See Figure 13.7.)

When quantity discounts are offered, there is a separate U-shaped total-cost curve for each unit price. Again, including unit prices merely raises each curve by a constant amount. However, because the unit prices are all different, each curve is raised by a different amount: Smaller unit prices will raise a total-cost curve less than larger unit prices. Note that no one curve applies to the entire range of quantities; each curve applies to only a *portion* of the range. (See Figure 13.8.) Hence, the applicable or *feasible* total cost is initially on the curve with the highest unit price and then drops down, curve by curve, at the *price breaks,* which are the minimum quantities needed to obtain the discounts. Thus, in Table 13.2, the price breaks for gauze strips are at 45 and 70 boxes. The result is a total-cost curve with *steps* at the price breaks.

TABLE 13.2
Price list for extra-wide gauze strips

Order Quantity	Price per Box
1 to 44	$2.00
45 to 69	1.70
70 or more	1.40

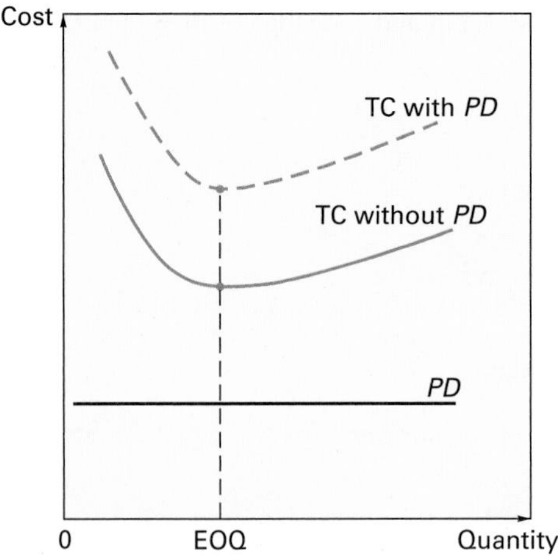

FIGURE 13.7
Adding *PD* doesn't change the EOQ

Even though each curve has a minimum, those points are not necessarily feasible. For example, the minimum point for the \$1.40 curve in Figure 13.8 appears to be about 65 units. However, the price list shown in Table 13.2 indicates that an order size of 65 boxes will involve a unit price of \$1.70. The actual total-cost curve is denoted by the solid lines; only those price–quantity combinations are feasible. The objective of the quantity discount model is to identify the order quantity that will represent the lowest total cost for the entire set of curves.

There are two general cases of the model. In one, carrying costs are constant (e.g., \$2 per unit); in the other, carrying costs are stated as a percentage of purchase price (e.g., 20 percent of unit price). When carrying costs are constant, there will be a single minimum point. All curves will have their minimum point at the same quantity. Consequently, the total-cost curves line up vertically, differing only in that the lower unit prices are reflected by lower total-cost curves as shown in Figure 13.9A. (For purposes of illustration, the horizontal purchasing cost lines have been omitted.)

When carrying costs are specified as a percentage of unit price, each curve will have a different minimum point. Because carrying costs are a percentage of price, lower prices will mean lower carrying costs and larger minimum points. Thus, as price decreases, each curve's minimum point will be to the right of the next higher curve's minimum point. (See Figure 13.9B.)

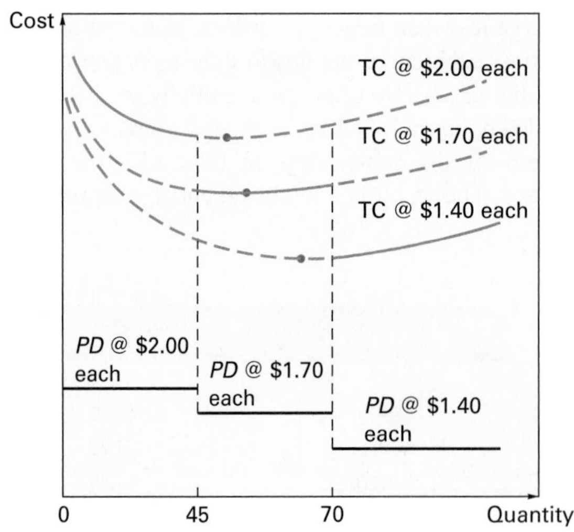

FIGURE 13.8
The total-cost curve with quantity discounts is composed of a portion of the total-cost curve for each price

FIGURE 13.9 Comparison of TC curves for constant carrying costs and carrying costs that are a percentage of unit costs

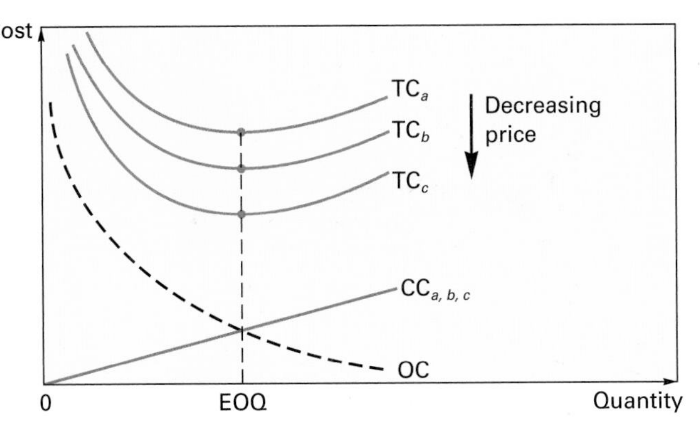

A. When carrying costs are constant, all curves have their minimum points at the same quantity.

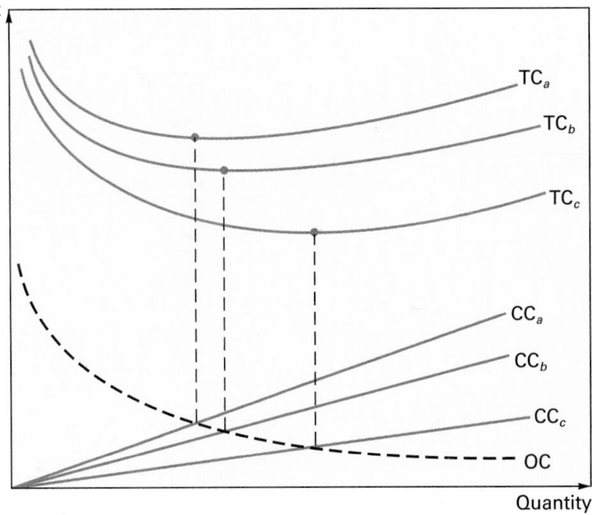

B. When carrying costs are stated as a percentage of unit price, the minimum points do not line up.

The procedure for determining the overall EOQ differs slightly, depending on which of these two cases is relevant. For carrying costs that are constant, the procedure is as follows:

1. Compute the common minimum point.
2. Only one of the unit prices will have the minimum point in its feasible range since the ranges do not overlap. Identify that range.
   a. If the feasible minimum point is on the lowest price range, that is the optimal order quantity.
   b. If the feasible minimum point is in any other range, compute the total cost for the minimum point and for the price breaks of all *lower* unit costs. Compare the total costs; the quantity (minimum point or price break) that yields the lowest total cost is the optimal order quantity.

EXAMPLE 5

The maintenance department of a large hospital uses about 816 cases of liquid cleanser annually. Ordering costs are $12, carrying costs are $4 per case a year, and the new price schedule indicates that orders of less than 50 cases will cost $20 per case, 50 to 79 cases will cost $18 per case, 80 to 99 cases will cost $17 per case, and larger orders will cost $16 per case. Determine the optimal order quantity and the total cost.

SOLUTION

See Figure 13.10:

$D = 816$ cases per year $\quad S = \$12 \quad H = \$4$ per case per year

Range	Price
1 to 49	$20
50 to 79	18
80 to 99	17
100 or more	16

1. Compute the common minimum Q: $= \sqrt{\dfrac{2DS}{H}} = \sqrt{\dfrac{2(816)12}{4}} = 69.97 \approx 70$ cases.

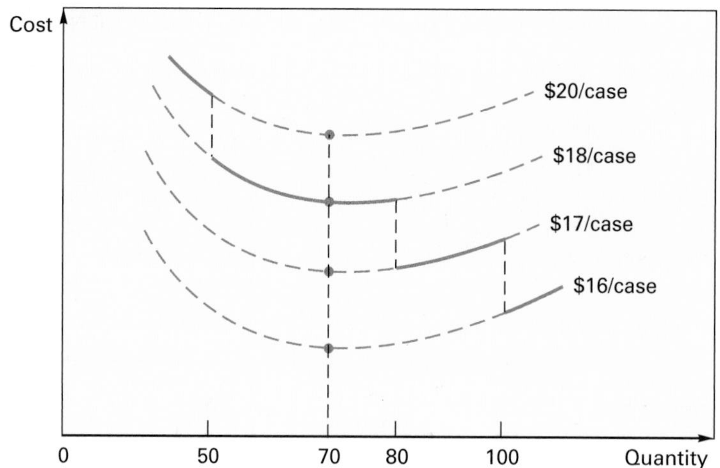

FIGURE 13.10
Total-cost curves for Example 5

2. The 70 cases can be bought at \$18 per case because 70 falls in the range of 50 to 79 cases. The total cost to purchase 816 cases a year, at the rate of 70 cases per order, will be

$$\begin{aligned} TC_{70} &= \text{Carrying cost} + \text{Order cost} + \text{Purchase cost} \\ &= (Q/2)H + (D/Q)S + PD \\ &= (70/2)4 + (816/70)12 + 18(816) = \$14{,}968 \end{aligned}$$

Because lower cost ranges exist, each must be checked against the minimum cost generated by 70 cases at \$18 each. In order to buy at \$17 per case, at least 80 cases must be purchased. (Because the TC curve is rising, 80 cases will have the lowest TC for that curve's feasible region.) The total cost at 80 cases will be

$$TC_{80} = (80/2)4 + (816/80)12 + 17(816) = \$14{,}154$$

To obtain a cost of \$16 per case, at least 100 cases per order are required, and the total cost at that price break will be

$$TC_{100} = (100/2)4 + (816/100)12 + 16(816) = \$13{,}354$$

Therefore, because 100 cases per order yields the lowest total cost, 100 cases is the overall optimal order quantity.

When carrying costs are expressed as a percentage of price, determine the best purchase quantity with the following procedure:

1. Beginning with the lowest unit price, compute the minimum points for each price range until you find a feasible minimum point (i.e., until a minimum point falls in the quantity range for its price).
2. If the minimum point for the lowest unit price is feasible, it is the optimal order quantity. If the minimum point is not feasible in the lowest price range, compare the total cost at the price break for all *lower* prices with the total cost of the feasible minimum point. The quantity that yields the lowest total cost is the optimum.

EXAMPLE 6

excel

www.mhhe.com/stevenson11e

Surge Electric uses 4,000 toggle switches a year. Switches are priced as follows: 1 to 499, 90 cents each; 500 to 999, 85 cents each; and 1,000 or more, 80 cents each. It costs approximately \$30 to prepare an order and receive it, and carrying costs are 40 percent of purchase price per unit on an annual basis. Determine the optimal order quantity and the total annual cost.

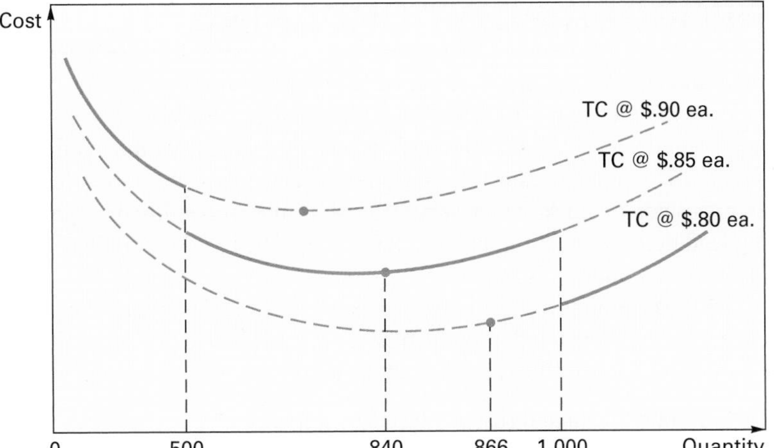

FIGURE 13.11
Total-cost curves for Example 6

SOLUTION

See Figure 13.11:

$D = 4{,}000$ switches per year $\quad S = \$30 \quad H = .40P$

Range	Unit Price	*H*
1 to 499	$.90	.40(.90) = .36
500 to 999	$.85	.40(.85) = .34
1,000 or more	$.80	.40(.80) = .32

Find the minimum point for each price, starting with the lowest price, until you locate a feasible minimum point.

$$\text{Minimum point}_{.80} = \sqrt{\frac{2DS}{H}} = \sqrt{\frac{2(4{,}000)30}{.32}} = 866 \text{ switches}$$

Because an order size of 866 switches will cost $.85 each rather than $.80 each, 866 is not a feasible minimum point for $.80 per switch. Next, try $.85 per unit.

$$\text{Minimum point}_{.85} = \sqrt{\frac{2(4{,}000)30}{.34}} = 840 \text{ switches}$$

This is feasible; it falls in the $.85 per switch range of 500 to 999.

Now compute the total cost for 840, and compare it to the total cost of the minimum quantity necessary to obtain a price of $.80 per switch.

$$\text{TC} = \text{Carrying costs} + \text{Ordering costs} + \text{Purchasing costs}$$

$$= \left(\frac{Q}{2}\right)H + \left(\frac{D}{Q}\right)S + PD$$

$$\text{TC}_{840} = \frac{840}{2}(.34) + \frac{4{,}000}{840}(30) + .85(4{,}000) = \$3{,}686$$

$$\text{TC}_{1{,}000} = \frac{1{,}000}{2}(.32) + \frac{4{,}000}{1{,}000}(30) + .80(4{,}000) = \$3{,}480$$

Thus, the minimum-cost order size is 1,000 switches.

REORDER POINT ORDERING

Reorder point (ROP) When the quantity on hand of an item drops to this amount, the item is reordered.

EOQ models answer the question of how much to order, but not the question of when to order. The latter is the function of models that identify the **reorder point (ROP)** in terms of a *quantity:* The reorder point occurs when the quantity on hand drops to a predetermined amount. That amount generally includes expected demand during lead time and perhaps an extra cushion of stock, which serves to reduce the probability of experiencing a stockout during lead time. Note that in order to know when the reorder point has been reached, *perpetual* inventory monitoring is required.

The goal in ordering is to place an order when the amount of inventory on hand is sufficient to satisfy demand during the time it takes to receive that order (i.e., lead time). There are four determinants of the reorder point quantity:

1. The rate of demand (usually based on a forecast).
2. The lead time.
3. The extent of demand and/or lead time variability.
4. The degree of stockout risk acceptable to management.

SCREENCAM TUTORIAL

If demand and lead time are both constant, the reorder point is simply

$$\text{ROP} = d \times \text{LT} \tag{13–10}$$

where

d = Demand rate (units per day or week)
LT = Lead time in days or weeks

Note: Demand and lead time must be expressed in the same time units.

EXAMPLE 7

www.mhhe.com/stevenson11e

Tingly takes Two-a-Day vitamins, which are delivered to his home by a routeman seven days after an order is called in. At what point should Tingly reorder?

SOLUTION

$$\begin{aligned} \text{Usage} &= 2 \text{ vitamins a day} \\ \text{Lead time} &= 7 \text{ days} \\ \text{ROP} &= \text{Usage} \times \text{Lead time} \\ &= 2 \text{ vitamins per day} \times 7 \text{ days} = 14 \text{ vitamins} \end{aligned}$$

Thus, Tingly should reorder when 14 vitamin tablets are left, which is equal to a seven-day supply of two vitamins a day.

Safety stock Stock that is held in excess of expected demand due to variable demand and/or lead time.

When variability is present in demand or lead time, it creates the possibility that actual demand will exceed expected demand. Consequently, it becomes necessary to carry additional inventory, called **safety stock,** to reduce the risk of running out of inventory (a stockout) during lead time. The reorder point then increases by the amount of the safety stock:

$$\text{ROP} = \begin{matrix}\text{Expected demand} \\ \text{during lead time}\end{matrix} + \text{Safety stock} \tag{13–11}$$

For example, if expected demand during lead time is 100 units, and the desired amount of safety stock is 10 units, the ROP would be 110 units.

Figure 13.12 illustrates how safety stock can reduce the risk of a stockout during lead time (LT). Note that stockout protection is needed only during lead time. If there is a sudden surge at any point during the cycle, that will trigger another order. Once that order is received, the danger of an imminent stockout is negligible.

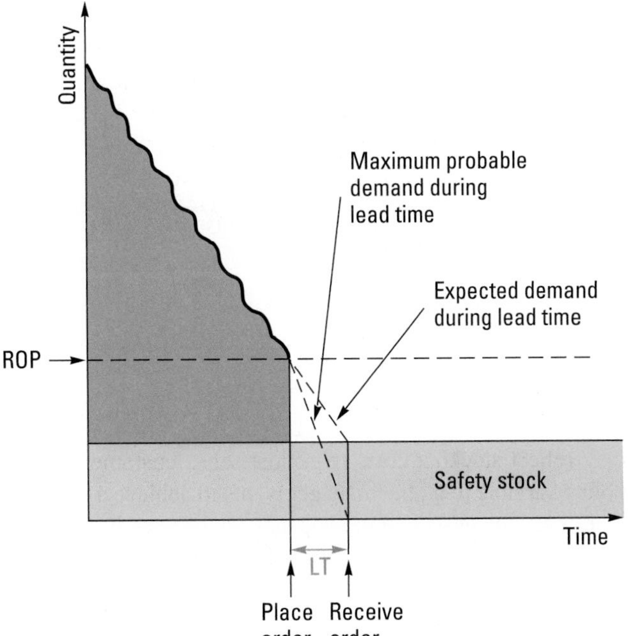

FIGURE 13.12
Safety stock reduces risk of stockout during lead time

Because it costs money to hold safety stock, a manager must carefully weigh the cost of carrying safety stock against the reduction in stockout risk it provides. The customer *service level* increases as the risk of stockout decreases. Order cycle **service level** can be defined as the probability that demand will not exceed supply during lead time (i.e., that the amount of stock on hand will be sufficient to meet demand). Hence, a service level of 95 percent implies a probability of 95 percent that demand will not exceed supply during lead time. An equivalent statement that demand will be satisfied in 95 percent of such instances does *not* mean that 95 percent of demand will be satisfied. The risk of a stockout is the complement of service level; a customer service level of 95 percent implies a stockout risk of 5 percent. That is,

Service level Probability that demand will not exceed supply during lead time.

$$\text{Service level} = 100 \text{ percent} - \text{Stockout risk}$$

Later you will see how the order cycle service level relates to the *annual* service level.

Consider for a moment the importance of stockouts. When a stockout occurs, demand cannot be satisfied at that time. In manufacturing operations, stockouts mean that jobs will be delayed and additional costs will be incurred. If the stockout involves parts for an assembly line, or spare parts for a machine or conveyor belt on the line, the line will have to shut down, typically at a very high cost per hour, until parts can be obtained. For service operations, stockouts mean that services cannot be completed on time. Aside from the added cost that results from the time delay, there is not only the matter of customer dissatisfaction but also the fact that schedules will be disrupted, sometimes creating a "domino effect" on following jobs. In the retail sector, stockouts create a competitive *disadvantage* that can result in customer dissatisfaction and, ultimately, the loss of customers.

The amount of safety stock that is appropriate for a given situation depends on the following factors:

1. The average demand rate and average lead time.
2. Demand and lead time variability.
3. The desired service level.

For a given order cycle service level, the greater the variability in either demand rate or lead time, the greater the amount of safety stock that will be needed to achieve that service level. Similarly, for a given amount of variation in demand rate or lead time, achieving an increase in the service level will require increasing the amount of safety stock. Selection of a service level

FIGURE 13.13
The ROP based on a normal distribution of lead time demand

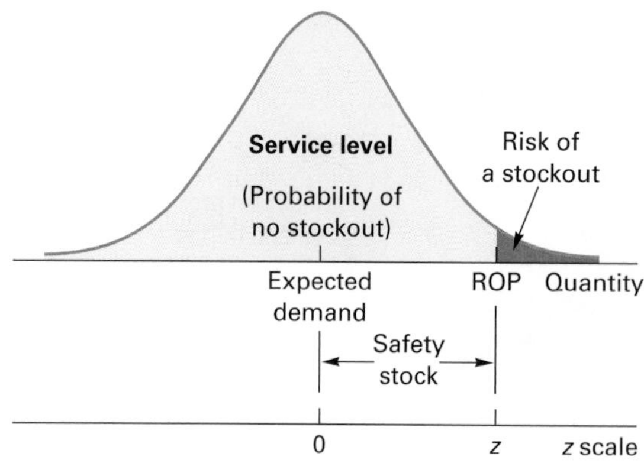

may reflect stockout costs (e.g., lost sales, customer dissatisfaction) or it might simply be a policy variable (e.g., the manager wants to achieve a specified service level for a certain item).

Let us look at several models that can be used in cases when variability is present. The first model can be used if an estimate of expected demand during lead time and its standard deviation are available. The formula is

$$\text{ROP} = \begin{matrix}\text{Expected demand}\\ \text{during lead time}\end{matrix} + z\sigma_{d\text{LT}} \qquad (13\text{–}12)$$

where

z = Number of standard deviations

$\sigma_{d\text{LT}}$ = The standard deviation of lead time demand

The models generally assume that any variability in demand rate or lead time can be adequately described by a normal distribution. However, this is not a strict requirement; the models provide approximate reorder points even where actual distributions depart from normal.

The value of z (see Figure 13.13) used in a particular instance depends on the stockout risk that the manager is willing to accept. Generally, the smaller the risk the manager is willing to accept, the greater the value of z. Use Appendix B, Table B, to obtain the value of z, given a desired service level for lead time.

EXAMPLE 8

www.mhhe.com/stevenson11e

Suppose that the manager of a construction supply house determined from historical records that demand for sand during lead time averages 50 tons. In addition, suppose the manager determined that demand during lead time could be described by a normal distribution that has a mean of 50 tons and a standard deviation of 5 tons. Answer these questions, assuming that the manager is willing to accept a stockout risk of no more than 3 percent:

a. What value of z is appropriate?

b. How much safety stock should be held?

c. What reorder point should be used?

SOLUTION

Expected lead time demand = 50 tons

$\sigma_{d\text{LT}}$ = 5 tons

Risk = 3 percent

a. From Appendix B, Table B, using a service level of $1 - .03 = .9700$, you obtain a value of $z = +1.88$.

b. Safety stock $= z\sigma_{d\text{LT}} = 1.88(5) = 9.40$ tons.

c. ROP = Expected lead time demand + Safety stock $= 50 + 9.40 = 59.40$ tons.

When data on lead time demand are not readily available, Formula 13–12 cannot be used. Nevertheless, data are generally available on daily or weekly demand, and on the length of lead time. Using those data, a manager can determine whether demand and/or lead time is variable, if variability exists in one or both, and the related standard deviation(s). For those situations, one of the following formulas can be used:

If only demand is variable, then $\sigma_{dLT} = \sigma_d\sqrt{LT}$, and the reorder point is

$$\text{ROP} = \bar{d} \times \text{LT} + z\sigma_d\sqrt{\text{LT}} \qquad (13\text{–}13)$$

where

$\bar{d}$ = *Average* daily or weekly demand

σ_d = Standard deviation of demand per day or week

LT = Lead time in days or weeks

If only lead time is variable, then $\sigma_{dLT} = d\sigma_{LT}$, and the reorder point is

$$\text{ROP} = d \times \overline{\text{LT}} + zd\sigma_{\text{LT}} \qquad (13\text{–}14)$$

where

d = Daily or weekly demand

$\overline{\text{LT}}$ = *Average* lead time in days or weeks

σ_{LT} = Standard deviation of lead time in days or weeks

If both demand and lead time are variable, then

$$\sigma_{dLT} = \sqrt{\overline{\text{LT}}\sigma_d^2 + \bar{d}^2\sigma_{\text{LT}}^2}$$

and the reorder point is

$$\text{ROP} = \bar{d} \times \overline{\text{LT}} + z\sqrt{\overline{\text{LT}}\sigma_d^2 + \bar{d}^2\sigma_{\text{LT}}^2} \qquad (13\text{–}15)$$

Note: Each of these models assumes that demand and lead time are *independent.*

EXAMPLE 9

A restaurant uses an average of 50 jars of a special sauce each week. Weekly usage of sauce has a standard deviation of 3 jars. The manager is willing to accept no more than a 10 percent risk of stockout during lead time, which is two weeks. Assume the distribution of usage is normal.

a. Which of the above formulas is appropriate for this situation? Why?

b. Determine the value of z.

c. Determine the ROP.

SOLUTION

$\bar{d}$ = 50 jars per week   LT = 2 weeks

σ_d = 3 jars per week   Acceptable risk = 10 percent, so service level is .90

a. Because only demand is variable (i.e., has a standard deviation), Formula 13–13 is appropriate.

b. From Appendix B, Table B, using a service level of .9000, you obtain $z = +1.28$.

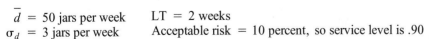

c. $\text{ROP} = \bar{d} \times \text{LT} + z\sigma_d\sqrt{\text{LT}} = 50 \times 2 + 1.28(3)\sqrt{2} = 100 + 5.43 = 105.43$. Because the inventory is discrete units (jars), we round this amount to 106. (Generally, round up.)

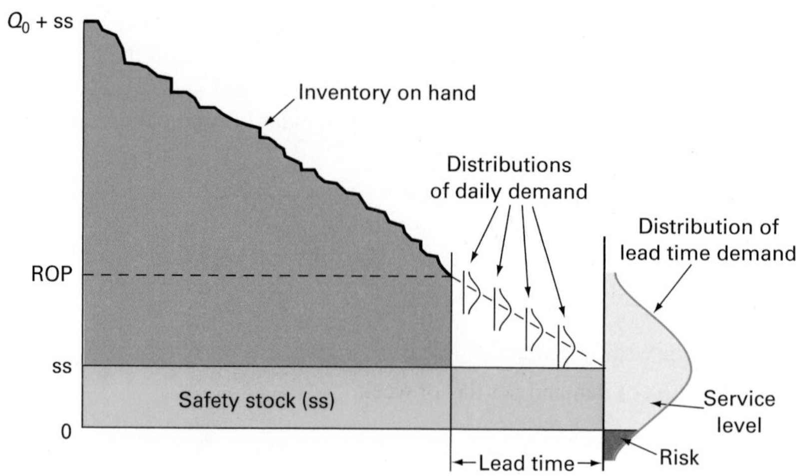

FIGURE 13.14
Lead time demand

Note that a 2-bin ordering system (see p. 560) involves ROP reordering: The quantity in the second bin is equal to the ROP.

The logic of the three formulas for the reorder point may not be immediately obvious. The first part of each formula is the expected demand, which is the product of daily (or weekly) demand and the number of days (or weeks) of lead time. The second part of the formula is z times the standard deviation of lead time demand. For the formula in which only demand is variable, daily (or weekly) demand is assumed to be normally distributed and has the same mean and standard deviation (see Figure 13.14). The standard deviation of demand for the entire lead time is found by summing the *variances* of daily (or weekly) demands, and then finding the square root of that number because, unlike variances, standard deviations are not additive. Hence, if the daily standard deviation is σ_d, the *variance* is σ_d^2, and if lead time is four days, the variance of lead time demand will equal the sum of the four variances, which is $4\sigma_d^2$. The standard deviation of lead time demand will be the square root of this, which is equal to $2\sigma_d$. In general, this becomes $\sqrt{\text{LT}}\sigma_d$ and, hence, the last part of Formula 13–13.

When only lead time is variable, the explanation is much simpler. The standard deviation of lead time demand is equal to the constant daily demand multiplied by the standard deviation of lead time.

When both demand and lead time are variable, the formula appears truly impressive. However, it is merely the result of squaring the standard deviations of the two previous formulas to obtain their variances, summing them, and then taking the square root.

Shortages and Service Levels

The ROP computation does not reveal the expected *amount* of shortage for a given lead time service level. The expected number of units short can, however, be very useful to a manager. This quantity can easily be determined from the same information used to compute the ROP, with one additional piece of information (see Table 13.3). Use of the table assumes that the distribution of lead time demand can be adequately represented by a normal distribution. If it can, the expected number of units short in each order cycle is given by this formula:

$$E(n) = E(z)\sigma_{d\text{LT}} \tag{13–16}$$

where

$E(n)$ = Expected number of units short per order cycle

$E(z)$ = Standardized number of units short obtained from Table 13.3

$\sigma_{d\text{LT}}$ = Standard deviation of lead time demand

TABLE 13.3 Normal distribution service levels and unit normal loss function

Lead Time Service Level	z	$E(z)$	Lead Time Service Level	z	$E(z)$	Lead Time Service Level	z	$E(z)$	Lead Time Service Level	z	$E(z)$
.0082	−2.40	2.403	.2119	−.80	.920	.7881	0.80	.120	.9918	2.40	.0030
.0091	−2.36	2.363	.2236	−.76	.889	.7995	0.84	.112	.9927	2.44	.0020
.0102	−2.32	2.323	.2358	−.72	.858	.8106	0.88	.104	.9934	2.48	.0020
.0113	−2.28	2.284	.2483	−.68	.828	.8212	0.92	.097	.9941	2.52	.0020
.0125	−2.24	2.244	.2611	−.64	.798	.8315	0.96	.089	.9948	2.56	.0020
.0139	−2.20	2.205	.2743	−.60	.769	.8413	1.00	.083	.9953	2.60	.0010
.0154	−2.16	2.165	.2877	−.56	.740	.8508	1.04	.077	.9959	2.64	.0010
.0170	−2.12	2.126	.3015	−.52	.712	.8599	1.08	.071	.9963	2.68	.0010
.0188	−2.08	2.087	.3156	−.48	.684	.8686	1.12	.066	.9967	2.72	.0010
.0207	−2.04	2.048	.3300	−.44	.657	.8770	1.16	.061	.9971	2.76	.0010
.0228	−2.00	2.008	.3446	−.40	.630	.8849	1.20	.056	.9974	2.80	.0008
.0250	−1.96	1.969	.3594	−.36	.597	.8925	1.24	.052	.9977	2.84	.0007
.0274	−1.92	1.930	.3745	−.32	.576	.8997	1.28	.048	.9980	2.88	.0006
.0301	−1.88	1.892	.3897	−.28	.555	.9066	1.32	.044	.9982	2.92	.0005
.0329	−1.84	1.853	.4052	−.24	.530	.9131	1.36	.040	.9985	2.96	.0004
.0359	−1.80	1.814	.4207	−.20	.507	.9192	1.40	.037	.9987	3.00	.0004
.0392	−1.76	1.776	.4364	−.16	.484	.9251	1.44	.034	.9988	3.04	.0003
.0427	−1.72	1.737	.4522	−.12	.462	.9306	1.48	.031	.9990	3.08	.0003
.0465	−1.68	1.699	.4681	−.08	.440	.9357	1.52	.028	.9991	3.12	.0002
.0505	−1.64	1.661	.4840	−.04	.419	.9406	1.56	.026	.9992	3.16	.0002
.0548	−1.60	1.623	.5000	.00	.399	.9452	1.60	.023	.9993	3.20	.0002
.0594	−1.56	1.586	.5160	.04	.379	.9495	1.64	.021	.9994	3.24	.0001
.0643	−1.52	1.548	.5319	.08	.360	.9535	1.68	.019	.9995	3.28	.0001
.0694	−1.48	1.511	.5478	.12	.342	.9573	1.72	.017	.9995	3.32	.0001
.0749	−1.44	1.474	.5636	.16	.324	.9608	1.76	.016	.9996	3.36	.0001
.0808	−1.40	1.437	.5793	.20	.307	.9641	1.80	.014	.9997	3.40	.0001
.0869	−1.36	1.400	.5948	.24	.290	.9671	1.84	.013			
.0934	−1.32	1.364	.6103	.28	.275	.9699	1.88	.012			
.1003	−1.28	1.328	.6255	.32	.256	.9726	1.92	.010			
.1075	−1.24	1.292	.6406	.36	.237	.9750	1.96	.009			
.1151	−1.20	1.256	.6554	.40	.230	.9772	2.00	.008			
.1230	−1.16	1.221	.6700	.44	.217	.9793	2.04	.008			
.1314	−1.12	1.186	.6844	.48	.204	.9812	2.08	.007			
.1401	−1.08	1.151	.6985	.52	.192	.9830	2.12	.006			
.1492	−1.04	1.117	.7123	.56	.180	.9846	2.16	.005			
.1587	−1.00	1.083	.7257	.60	.169	.9861	2.20	.005			
.1685	−.96	1.049	.7389	.64	.158	.9875	2.24	.004			
.1788	−.92	1.017	.7517	.68	.148	.9887	2.28	.004			
.1894	−.88	0.984	.7642	.72	.138	.9898	2.32	.003			
.2005	−.84	0.952	.7764	.76	.129	.9909	2.36	.003			

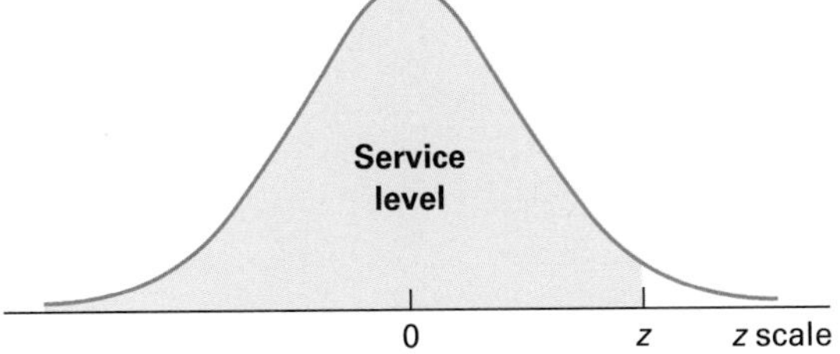

EXAMPLE 10

Suppose the standard deviation of lead time demand is known to be 20 units. Lead time demand is approximately normal.

a. For a lead time service level of 90 percent, determine the expected number of units short for any order cycle.

b. What lead time service level would an expected shortage of two units imply?

SOLUTION

$\sigma_{dLT} = 20$ units

a. Lead time (cycle) service level = .90. From Table 13.3, $E(z) = .048$. Using Formula 13–16, $E(n) = .048(20 \text{ units}) = .96$, or about 1 unit.

b. For the case where $E(n) = 2$, you must solve for $E(z)$ and then use Table 13.3 to determine the lead time service that implies. Thus, $E(n) = E(z)\sigma_{dLT}$, so $E(z) = E(n)/\sigma_{dLT} = 2/20 = .100$. From Table 13.3, this implies a service level of approximately 81.7 percent (interpolating).

The expected number of units short is just that—an expected or *average* amount; the exact number of units short in any given cycle will be an amount close to that. Moreover, if discrete items are involved, the actual number of units short in any cycle will be an integer.

Having determined the expected number of units short for an order cycle, you can determine the expected number of units short per year. It is simply the expected number of units short per cycle multiplied by the number of cycles (orders) per year. Thus,

$$E(N) = E(n)\frac{D}{Q} \qquad (13\text{–}17)$$

where

$E(N)$ = Expected number of units short per year

EXAMPLE 11

Given the following information, determine the expected number of units short per year.

$D = 1{,}000 \quad Q = 250 \quad E(n) = 2.5$

SOLUTION

Using the formula $E(N) = E(n)\frac{D}{Q}$,

$$E(N) = 2.5\left(\frac{1{,}000}{250}\right) = 10.0 \text{ units per year}$$

Fill rate The percentage of demand filled by the stock on hand.

It is sometimes convenient to think of service level in annual terms. One definition of annual service level is the percentage of demand filled directly from inventory. This is also known as the **fill rate.** Thus, if $D = 1{,}000$, and 990 units were filled directly from inventory (shortages totaling 10 units over the year were recorded), the annual service level (fill rate) would be 990/1,000 = 99 percent. The annual service level and the lead time service level can be related using the following formula:

$$SL_{\text{annual}} = 1 - \frac{E(N)}{D} \qquad (13\text{–}18)$$

Using Formulas 13–17 and 13–16,

$$E(N) = E(n)D/Q = E(z)\sigma_{dLT}D/Q$$

Thus,

$$SL_{annual} = 1 - \frac{E(z)\sigma_{dLT}}{Q} \qquad (13\text{–}19)$$

Given a lead time service level of .90, $D = 1{,}000$, $Q = 250$, and $\sigma_{dLT} = 16$, determine (*a*) the annual service level, and (*b*) the amount of cycle safety stock that would provide an annual service level of .98. From Table 13.3, $E(z) = .048$ for a 90 percent lead time service level.

SOLUTION

a. Using Formula 13–19:

$$SL_{annual} = 1 - .048(16)/250 = .997$$

b. Using Formula 13–19 and an annual service level of .98, solve for $E(z)$:

$$.98 = 1 - E(z)(16)/250$$

Solving, $E(z) = .312$. From Table 13.3, with $E(z) = .312$, you can see that this value of $E(z)$ is a little more than the value of .307. So it appears that an acceptable value of z might be .19. The necessary safety stock to achieve the specified annual service level is equal to $z\sigma_{dLT}$. Hence, the safety stock is .19(16) = 3.04, or approximately three units.

Note that in the preceding example, a lead time service level of 90 percent provided an annual service level of 99.7 percent. Naturally, different values of *D, Q,* and σ_{dLT} will tend to produce different results for a cycle service level of 90 percent. Nonetheless, the annual service level will usually be greater than the cycle service level. In addition, since the annual service level as defined relates to the percentage of units short per year, it makes sense to base cycle service levels on a specified annual service level. This means setting the annual level, using Formula 13–19 to solve for $E(z)$, and then using that value to obtain the service level for the order cycles.

HOW MUCH TO ORDER: FIXED-ORDER-INTERVAL MODEL

The **fixed-order-interval (FOI) model** is used when orders must be placed at fixed time intervals (weekly, twice a month, etc.): The timing of orders is set. The question, then, at each order point, is how much to order. Fixed-interval ordering systems are widely used by retail businesses. If demand is variable, the order size will tend to vary from cycle to cycle. This is quite different from an EOQ/ROP approach in which the order size generally remains fixed from cycle to cycle, while the length of the cycle varies (shorter if demand is above average, and longer if demand is below average).

Fixed-order-interval (FOI) model Orders are placed at fixed time intervals.

Reasons for Using the Fixed-Order-Interval Model

In some cases, a supplier's policy might encourage orders at fixed intervals. Even when that is not the case, grouping orders for items from the same supplier can produce savings in shipping costs. Furthermore, some situations do not readily lend themselves to continuous monitoring of inventory levels. Many retail operations (e.g., drugstores, small grocery stores) fall into this category. The alternative for them is to use fixed-interval ordering, which requires only periodic checks of inventory levels.

Determining the Amount to Order

If both the demand rate and lead time are constant, the fixed-interval model and the fixed-quantity model function identically. The differences in the two models become apparent only

FIGURE 13.15
Comparison of fixed-quantity and fixed-interval ordering

A. Fixed quantity

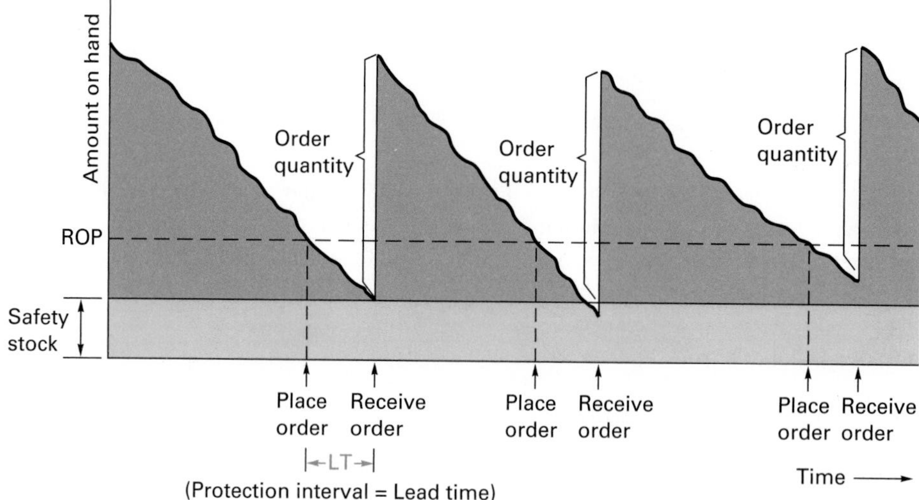

B. Fixed interval

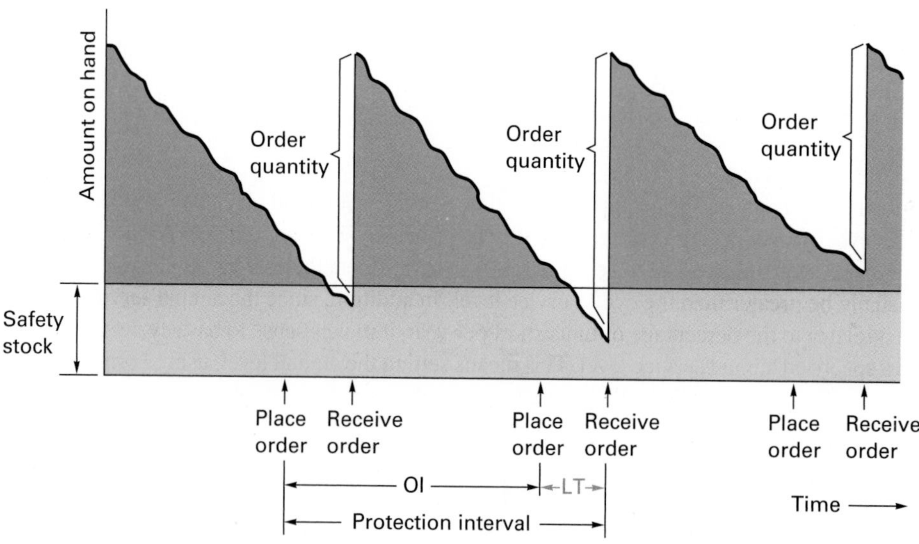

when examined under conditions of variability. Like the ROP model, the fixed-interval model can have variations in demand only, in lead time only, or in both demand and lead time. However, for the sake of simplicity and because it is perhaps the most frequently encountered situation, the discussion here will focus only on *variable demand* and *constant lead time.*

Figure 13.15 provides a comparison of the fixed-quantity and fixed-interval systems. In the fixed-quantity arrangement, orders are triggered by a *quantity* (ROP), while in the fixed-interval arrangement orders are triggered by a *time.* Therefore, the fixed-interval system must have stockout protection for lead time plus the next order cycle, but the fixed-quantity system needs protection only during lead time because additional orders can be placed at any time and will be received shortly (lead time) thereafter. Consequently, there is a greater need for safety stock in the fixed-interval model than in the fixed-quantity model. Note, for example, the large dip into safety stock during the second order cycle with the fixed-interval model.

Both models are sensitive to demand experience just prior to reordering, but in somewhat different ways. In the fixed-quantity model, a higher-than-normal demand causes a *shorter time* between orders, whereas in the fixed-interval model, the result is *a larger order size.* Another difference is that the fixed-quantity model requires close monitoring of inventory levels in order to know *when* the amount on hand has reached the reorder point. The fixed-interval model requires only a periodic review (i.e., physical count) of inventory levels just prior to placing an order to determine how much is needed.

Order size in the fixed-interval model is determined by the following computation:

$$\text{Amount to order} = \text{Expected demand during protection interval} + \text{Safety stock} - \text{Amount on hand at reorder time} \quad (13\text{–}20)$$

$$= \bar{d}(\text{OI} + \text{LT}) + z\sigma_d\sqrt{\text{OI} + \text{LT}} - A$$

where

OI = Order interval (length of time between orders)

A = Amount on hand at reorder time

As in previous models, we assume that demand during the protection interval is normally distributed.

EXAMPLE 13

www.mhhe.com/stevenson11e

Given the following information, determine the amount to order.

$\bar{d}$ = 30 units per day	Desired service level = 99 percent
σ_d = 3 units per day	Amount on hand at reorder time = 71 units
LT = 2 days	OI = 7 days

SOLUTION

z = 2.33 for 99 percent service level

$$\text{Amount to order} = \bar{d}(\text{OI} + \text{LT}) + z\sigma_d\sqrt{\text{OI} + \text{LT}} - A$$

$$= 30(7 + 2) + 2.33(3)\sqrt{7 + 2} - 71 = 220 \text{ units}$$

An issue related to fixed-interval ordering is the risk of a stockout. From the perspective (i.e., the point in time) of placing an order, there are two points in the order cycle at which a stockout could occur. One is shortly after the order is placed, while waiting to receive the current order (refer to Figure 13.15). The second point is near the end of the cycle, while waiting to receive the next order.

To find the initial risk of a stockout, use the ROP formula (13–13), setting ROP equal to the quantity on hand when the order is placed, and solve for z, then obtain the service level for that value of z from Appendix B, Table B, and subtract it from 1.0000 to get the risk of a stockout.

To find the risk of a stockout at the end of the order cycle, use the fixed-interval formula (13–20) and solve for z. Then obtain the service level for that value of z from Appendix B, Table B, and subtract it from 1.0000 to get the risk of a stockout.

Let's look at an example.

EXAMPLE 14

www.mhhe.com/stevenson11e

Given the following information:

LT = 4 days	A = 43 units
OI = 12 days	Q = 171 units
$\bar{d}$ = 10 units/day	
σ_d = 2 units/day	

Determine the risk of a stockout at

a. The end of the initial lead time.

b. The end of the second lead time.

SOLUTION

a. For the risk of stockout for the first lead time, we use Formula 13–13. Substituting the given values, we get $43 = 10 \times 4 + z(2)(2)$. Solving, $z = +.75$. From Appendix B, Table B, the service level is .7734. The risk is $1 - .7734 = .2266$, which is fairly high.

b. For the risk of a stockout at the end of the second lead time, we use Formula 13–20. Substituting the given values we get $171 = 10 \times (4 + 12) + z(2)(4) - 43$. Solving, $z = +6.75$. This value is way out in the right tail of the normal distribution, making the service level virtually 100 percent, and, thus, the risk of a stockout at this point is essentially equal to zero.

Benefits and Disadvantages

The fixed-interval system results in tight control. In addition, when multiple items come from the same supplier, grouping orders can yield savings in ordering, packing, and shipping costs. Moreover, it may be the only practical approach if inventory withdrawals cannot be closely monitored.

On the negative side, the fixed-interval system necessitates a larger amount of safety stock for a given risk of stockout because of the need to protect against shortages during an entire order interval plus lead time (instead of lead time only), and this increases the carrying cost. Also, there are the costs of the periodic reviews.

THE SINGLE-PERIOD MODEL

Single-period model Model for ordering of perishables and other items with limited useful lives.

The **single-period model** (sometimes referred to as the *newsboy problem*) is used to handle ordering of perishables (fresh fruits, vegetables, seafood, cut flowers) and items that have a limited useful life (newspapers, magazines, spare parts for specialized equipment). The *period* for spare parts is the life of the equipment, assuming that the parts cannot be used for other equipment. What sets unsold or unused goods apart is that they are not typically carried over from one period to the next, at least not without penalty. Day-old baked goods, for instance, are often sold at reduced prices; leftover seafood may be discarded; and out-of-date magazines may be offered to used book stores at bargain rates. There may even be some cost associated with disposal of leftover goods.

Analysis of single-period situations generally focuses on two costs: shortage and excess. Shortage cost may include a charge for loss of customer goodwill as well as the opportunity cost of lost sales. Generally, **shortage cost** is simply unrealized profit per unit. That is,

Shortage cost Generally, the unrealized profit per unit.

$$C_{\text{shortage}} = C_s = \text{Revenue per unit} - \text{Cost per unit}$$

If a shortage or stockout relates to an item used in production or to a spare part for a machine, then shortage cost refers to the actual cost of lost production.

Excess cost Difference between purchase cost and salvage value of items left over at the end of a period.

Excess cost pertains to items left over at the end of the period. In effect, excess cost is the difference between purchase cost and salvage value. That is,

$$C_{\text{excess}} = C_e = \text{Original cost per unit} - \text{Salvage value per unit}$$

If there is cost associated with disposing of excess items, the salvage will be negative and will therefore *increase* the excess cost per unit.

The goal of the single-period model is to identify the order quantity, or stocking level, that will minimize the long-run excess and shortage costs.

There are two general categories of problems that we will consider: those for which demand can be approximated using a continuous distribution (perhaps a theoretical one such as a uniform or normal distribution) and those for which demand can be approximated using a discrete distribution (say, historical frequencies or a theoretical distribution such as the Poisson). The kind of inventory can indicate which type of model might be appropriate. For example, demand for petroleum, liquids, and gases tends to vary over some *continuous scale,* thus

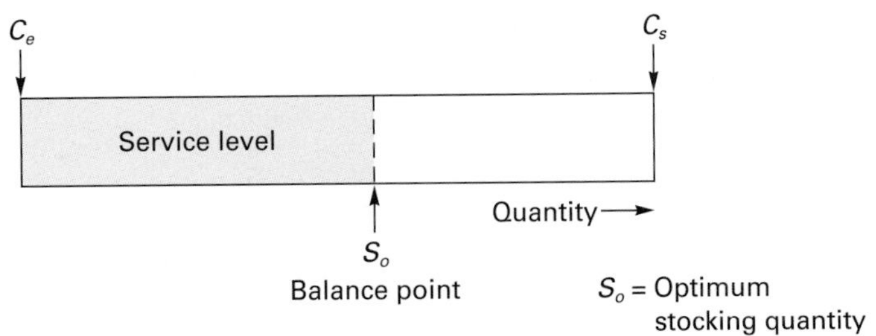

FIGURE 13.16
The optimal stocking level balances unit shortage and excess costs

lending itself to description by a continuous distribution. Demand for tractors, cars, and computers is expressed in terms of the *number of units* demanded and lends itself to description by a discrete distribution.

Continuous Stocking Levels

The concept of identifying an optimal stocking level is perhaps easiest to visualize when demand is *uniform.* Choosing the stocking level is similar to balancing a seesaw, but instead of a person on each end of the seesaw, we have excess cost per unit (C_e) on one end of the distribution and shortage cost per unit (C_s) on the other. The optimal stocking level is analogous to the fulcrum of the seesaw; the stocking level equalizes the cost weights, as illustrated in Figure 13.16.

The *service level* is the *probability* that demand will not exceed the stocking level, and computation of the service level is the key to determining the optimal stocking level, S_o.

$$\text{Service level} = \frac{C_s}{C_s + C_e} \tag{13–21}$$

where

C_s = Shortage cost per unit

C_e = Excess cost per unit

If actual demand exceeds S_o, there is a shortage; hence, C_s is on the right end of the distribution. Similarly, if demand is less than S_o, there is an excess, so C_e is on the left end of the distribution. When $C_e = C_s$, the optimal stocking level is halfway between the endpoints of the distribution. If one cost is greater than the other, S_o will be closer to the larger cost.

EXAMPLE 15

Sweet cider is delivered weekly to Cindy's Cider Bar. Demand varies uniformly between 300 liters and 500 liters per week. Cindy pays 20 cents per liter for the cider and charges 80 cents per liter for it. Unsold cider has no salvage value and cannot be carried over into the next week due to spoilage. Find the optimal stocking level and its stockout risk for that quantity.

SOLUTION

$$\begin{aligned} C_e &= \text{Cost per unit} - \text{Salvage value per unit} \\ &= \$.20 \qquad - \$0 \\ &= \$.20 \text{ per unit} \\ C_s &= \text{Revenue per unit} - \text{Cost per unit} \\ &= \$.80 \qquad - \$.20 \\ &= \$.60 \text{ per unit} \\ \text{SL} &= \frac{C_s}{C_s + C_e} = \frac{\$.60}{\$.60 + \$.20} = .75 \end{aligned}$$

Thus, the optimal stocking level must satisfy demand 75 percent of the time. For the uniform distribution, this will be at a point equal to the minimum demand plus 75 percent of the difference between maximum and minimum demands:

$$S_o = 300 + .75(500 - 300) = 450 \text{ liters}$$

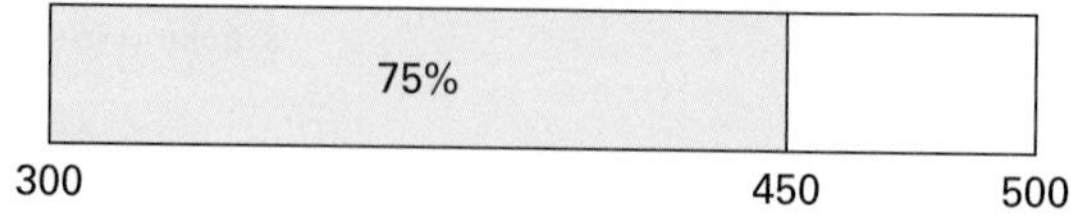

The stockout risk is $1.00 - .75 = .25$.

A similar approach applies when demand is normally distributed.

EXAMPLE 16

Cindy's Cider Bar also sells a blend of cherry juice and apple cider. Demand for the blend is approximately normal, with a mean of 200 liters per week and a standard deviation of 10 liters per week. C_s = 60 cents per liter, and C_e = 20 cents per liter. Find the optimal stocking level for the apple-cherry blend.

SOLUTION

$$SL = \frac{C_s}{C_s + C_e} = \frac{\$.60}{\$.60 + \$.20} = .75$$

This indicates that 75 percent of the area under the normal curve must be to the left of the stocking level. Appendix B, Table B, shows that a value of z between +.67 and +.68, say, +.675, will satisfy this. The optimal stocking level is S_o = mean + $z\sigma$. Thus,

$$S_o = 200 \text{ liters} + .675(10 \text{ liters}) = 206.75 \text{ liters}$$

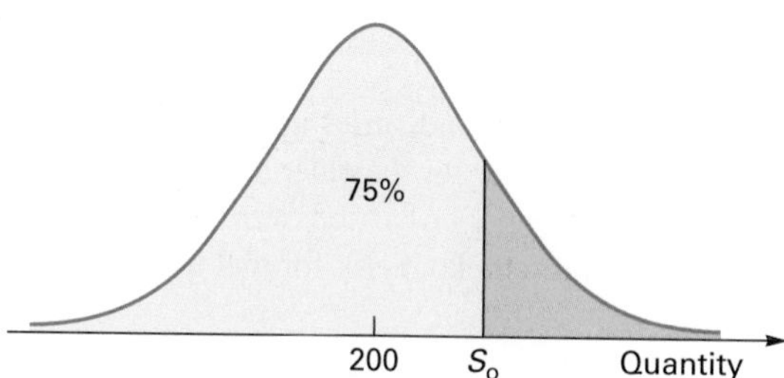

Discrete Stocking Levels

When stocking levels are discrete rather than continuous, the service level computed using the ratio $C_s/(C_s + C_e)$ usually does not coincide with a feasible stocking level (e.g., the optimal amount may be *between* five and six units). The solution is to stock at the *next higher level* (e.g., six units). In other words, choose the stocking level so that the desired service level is equaled or *exceeded.* Figure 13.17 illustrates this concept.

Example 17 illustrates the use of an empirical distribution.

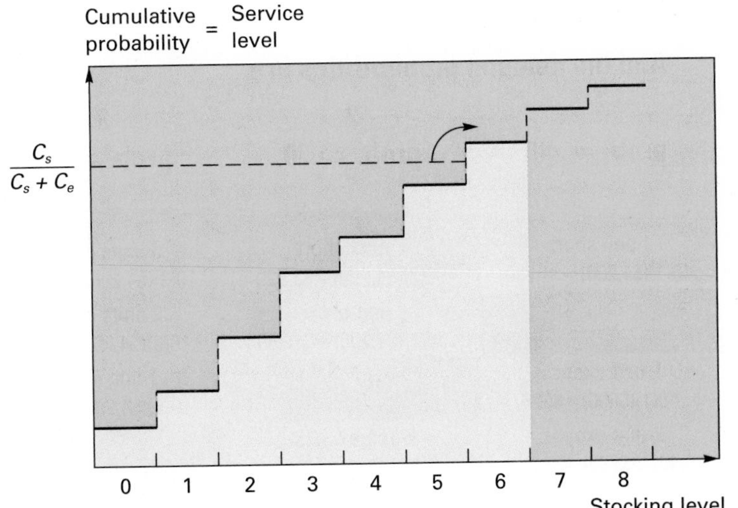

FIGURE 13.17
The service level achievement must equal or exceed the ratio $Cs/(Cs + Ce)$

EXAMPLE 17

www.mhhe.com/stevenson11e

Historical records on the use of spare parts for several large hydraulic presses are to serve as an estimate of usage for spares of a newly installed press. Stockout costs involve downtime expenses and special ordering costs. These average $4,200 per unit short. Spares cost $800 each, and unused parts have zero salvage. Determine the optimal stocking level.

Spares Used	Relative Frequency	Cumulative Frequency
0	.20	.20
1	.40	.60
2	.30	.90
3	.10	1.00
4 or more	.00	
	1.00	

SOLUTION

$$C_s = \$4,200 \qquad C_e = \$800 \qquad \text{SL} = \frac{C_s}{C_s + C_e} = \frac{\$4,200}{\$4,200 + \$800} = .84$$

The cumulative-frequency column indicates the percentage of time that demand did not exceed (was equal to or less than) some amount. For example, demand does not exceed one spare 60 percent of the time, or two spares 90 percent of the time. Thus, in order to achieve a service level of *at least* 84 percent, it will be necessary to stock two spares (i.e., to go to the next higher stocking level).

The logic behind Formula 13–21 can be seen by solving the problem using a *decision table* approach. Table 13.4 illustrates this approach. The table enumerates the expected cost of each combination of stocking level and demand. For instance, if the stocking level is three, and demand turns out to be zero (see the blue-shaded cell), that would result in an excess of three units, at a cost of $800 each. The probability of a demand of zero units is .20, so the expected cost of that cell is .20(3)($800) = $480. Similarly, if no units are stocked and demand is two (see the yellow-shaded cell), the expected cost is the probability of demand being two (i.e., .30) multiplied by two units multiplied by the shortage cost per unit. Thus, the expected cost is .30(2)($4,200) = $2,520. For the cases in which the demand and stocking level are the same (the green-shaded cells), supply = demand, so there is neither a shortage nor an excess, and thus the cost is $0.

TABLE 13.4 Expected cost for each possible outcome

If the stocking level is	And the demand probabilities are: 0 prob. = .20	1 prob. = .40	2 prob. = .30	3 prob. = .10	The expected cost will be
0	*S=D* $0	1 unit short .40(1)($4,200)=$1,680	2 units short .30(2)($4,200)=$2,520	3 units short .10(3)($4,200)=$1,260	$5,460
1	1-unit excess .20(1)($800)=$160	*S=D* $0	1 unit short .30(1)($4,200)=$1,260	2 units short .10(2)($4,200)=$840	$2,260
2	2-unit excess .20(2)($800)=$320	1-unit excess .40(1)($800)=$320	*S=D* $0	1 unit short .10(1)($4,200)=$420	$1,060
3	3-unit excess .20(3)($800)=$480	2-unit excess .40(2)($800)=$640	1-unit excess .30(1)($800)=$240	*S=D* $0	$1,360

The lowest expected cost is $1,060, which occurs for a stocking level of two units, so two is the optimal stocking level, which agrees with the ratio approach.

Example 18 illustrates how to solve a problem when demand is described by a Poisson distribution.

EXAMPLE 18

Demand for long-stemmed red roses at a small flower shop can be approximated using a Poisson distribution that has a mean of four dozen per day. Profit on the roses is $3 per dozen. Leftover flowers are marked down and sold the next day at a loss of $2 per dozen. Assume that all marked-down flowers are sold. What is the optimal stocking level?

SOLUTION

$$C_s = \$3 \qquad C_e = \$2 \qquad \text{SL} = \frac{C_s}{C_s + C_e} = \frac{\$3}{\$3 + \$2} = .60$$

Obtain the cumulative frequencies from the Poisson table (Appendix B, Table C) for a mean of 4.0:

Demand (dozen per day)	Cumulative Frequency
0	.018
1	.092
2	.238
3	.433
4	.629
5	.785
⋮	⋮

Compare the service level to the cumulative frequencies. In order to attain a service level of at least .60, it is necessary to stock four dozen.

One final point about discrete stocking levels: If the computed service level is *exactly* equal to the cumulative probability associated with one of the stocking levels, there are *two* equivalent stocking levels in terms of minimizing long-run cost—the one with equal probability and the next higher one. In the preceding example, if the ratio had been equal to .629, we would be indifferent between stocking four dozen and stocking five dozen roses each day.

OPERATIONS STRATEGY

Inventories often represent a substantial investment. More important, improving inventory processes can offer significant benefits in terms of cost reduction and customer satisfaction. Among the areas that have potential are the following:

Record keeping. It is important to have inventory records that are accurate and up-to-date, so that inventory decisions are based on correct information. Estimates of holding, ordering, and setup costs, as well as demand and lead times, should be reviewed periodically and updated when necessary.

Variation reduction. Lead time variations and forecast errors are two key factors that impact inventory management, and variation reduction in these areas can yield significant improvement in inventory management.

Lean operation. Lean systems are demand driven, which means that goods are pulled through the system to match demand instead of being pushed through without a direct link to demand. Moreover, lean systems feature smaller lot sizes than more traditional systems, based in part on the belief that holding costs are higher than those assigned by traditional systems, and partly as a deliberate effort to reduce ordering and setup costs by simplifying and standardizing necessary activities. An obvious benefit is a decrease in average inventory on hand and, hence, lower carrying costs. Other benefits include fewer disruptions of work flow, reduction in space needs, enhanced ability to spot problems, and increased feasibility to place machines and workers closer together, which allows more opportunities for socialization, communication, and cooperation.

Supply chain management. Working more closely with suppliers to coordinate shipments, reduce lead times, and reduce supply chain inventories can reduce the size and frequency of stockouts while lowering inventory carrying costs. Blanket orders and vendor-managed inventories can reduce transaction costs. Also, consignment agreements, where buyers are not charged for inventory items until the items are sold, may be an option. Storage costs can sometimes be reduced by using cross-docking, whereby inbound trucks with goods arriving at distributor warehouses from suppliers are directly loaded onto outbound trucks for store or dealer delivery, avoiding warehouse handling and storage costs.

SUMMARY

Inventory management is a core operations management activity. Good inventory management is often the mark of a well-run organization. Inventory levels must be planned carefully in order to balance the cost of holding inventory and the cost of providing reasonable levels of customer service. Successful inventory management requires a system to keep track of inventory transactions, accurate information about demand and lead times, realistic estimates of certain inventory-related costs, and a priority system for classifying the items in inventory and allocating control efforts.

Four classes of models are described: EOQ, ROP, fixed-order-interval, and single-period models. The first three are appropriate if unused items can be carried over into subsequent periods. The single-period model is appropriate when items cannot be carried over. EOQ models address the question of how much to order. The ROP models address the question of when to order and are particularly helpful in dealing with situations that include variations in either demand rate or lead time. ROP models involve service level and safety stock considerations. When the time between orders is fixed, the FOI model is useful for determining the order quantity. The single-period model is used for items that have a "shelf life" of one period. The models presented in this chapter are summarized in Table 13.5.

KEY POINTS

1. All businesses carry inventories, which are goods held for future use or potential future use.
2. Inventory represents money that is tied up in goods or materials.
3. Effective inventory decisions depend on having good inventory records, good cost information, and good estimates of demand.

TABLE 13.5 Summary of inventory formulas

Model	Formula	Symbols
1. Basic EOQ	$Q_0 = \sqrt{\frac{2DS}{H}}$ (13–2) $TC = \frac{Q}{2}H + \frac{D}{Q}S$ (13–1) Length of order cycle $= \frac{Q}{D}$ (13–3)	Q_0 = Economic order quantity D = Annual demand S = Order cost per order H = Annual carrying cost per unit Q = Order quantity
2. Economic production quantity	$Q_p = \sqrt{\frac{2DS}{H}}\sqrt{\frac{p}{p-u}}$ (13–5) $TC = \frac{I_{max}}{2}H + \frac{D}{Q}S$ (13–4) Cycle time $= \frac{Q}{u}$ (13–6) Run time $= \frac{Q}{p}$ (13–7) $I_{max} = \frac{Q_0}{p}(p-u)$ (13–8)	Q_p = Optimal run or order size p = Production or delivery rate u = Usage rate I_{max} = Maximum inventory level
3. Quantity discounts	$TC = \frac{Q}{2}H + \frac{D}{Q}S + PD$ (13–9)	P = Unit price
4. Reorder point under: a. Constant demand and lead time b. Variable demand rate c. Variable lead time d. Variable lead time and demand	$ROP = d(LT)$ (13–10) $ROP = \bar{d}LT + z(\sigma_d)\sqrt{LT}$ (13–13) $ROP = d\overline{LT} + z(\sigma_{LT})d$ (13–14) $ROP = \bar{d}\overline{LT} + z\sqrt{\overline{LT}\sigma_d^2 + \bar{d}^2\sigma_{LT}^2}$ (13–15)	ROP = Quantity on hand at reorder point d = Demand rate LT = Lead time $\bar{d}$ = Average demand rate σ_d = Standard deviation of demand rate z = Standard normal deviation $\overline{LT}$ = Average lead time σ_{LT} = Standard deviation of lead time
5. ROP shortages a. Units short per cycle b. Units short per year c. Annual service level	$E(n) = E(z)\sigma_{dLT}$ (13–16) $E(N) = E(n)\frac{D}{Q}$ (13–17) $SL_{annual} = 1 - \frac{E(z)\sigma_{dLT}}{Q}$ (13–19)	$E(n)$ = Expected number short per cycle $E(z)$ = Standardized number short σ_{dLT} = Standard deviation of lead time demand $E(N)$ = Expected number short per year SL_{annual} = Annual service level
6. Fixed interval	$Q = \bar{d}(OI + LT) + z\sigma_d\sqrt{OI + LT} - A$ (13–20)	OI = Time between orders A = Amount on hand at order time
7. Single period	$SL = \frac{C_s}{C_s + C_e}$ (13–21)	SL = Service level C_s = Shortage cost per unit C_e = Excess cost per unit

4. The decision of how much inventory to have on hand reflects a trade-off, for example, how much money to tie up in inventory versus having it available for other uses. Factors related to the decision include purchase costs, holding costs, ordering costs, shortage and backlog costs, available space to store the inventory, and the return that can be had from other uses of the money.
5. As with other areas of operations, variations are present and must be taken into account. Uncertainties can be offset to some degree by holding safety stock, although that adds to the cost of holding inventory.

KEY TERMS

A-B-C approach, 563
cycle counting, 565
cycle stock, 566
economic order quantity (EOQ), 566
excess cost, 588
fill rate, 584
fixed-order-interval (FOI) model, 585
holding (carrying) cost, 562
inventory, 556
inventory turnover, 559
lead time, 562
Little's Law, 558
ordering costs, 562
periodic system, 560
perpetual inventory system, 560
point-of-sale (POS) system, 560
purchase cost, 562
quantity discounts, 573
reorder point (ROP), 578
safety stock, 566, 578
service level, 579
setup costs, 562
shortage costs, 562, 588
single-period model, 588
two-bin system, 560
universal product code (UPC), 560

SOLVED PROBLEMS

Problem 1

Basic EOQ. This type of problem can be recognized when annual demand (D), ordering cost (S), and holding or carrying cost per unit (H) are given. Use Formula 13–2 for order quantity, Formula 13–1 for total cost, and D/Q for number of orders a year.

A toy manufacturer uses approximately 32,000 silicon chips annually. The chips are used at a steady rate during the 240 days a year that the plant operates. Annual holding cost is \$3 per chip, and ordering cost is \$120. Determine

a. The optimal order quantity.

b. The number of workdays in an order cycle.

Solution

$D = 32{,}000$ chips per year $\quad S = \$120$

$H = \$3$ per unit per year

a. $Q_0 = \sqrt{\dfrac{2DS}{H}} = \sqrt{\dfrac{2(32{,}000)120}{3}} = 1{,}600$ chips.

b. $\dfrac{Q}{D} = \dfrac{1{,}600\text{ chips}}{32{,}000\text{ chips/yr.}} = \dfrac{1}{20}$ year (i.e., $\frac{1}{20} \times 240$ days), or 12 days

Problem 2

Economic production quantity. This type of problem can be recognized when a production rate (p) and a usage rate (u) are given in addition to the basic EOQ information. Use Formula 13–5 to compute the optimal run quantity. Production (run) time is Q/p. I_{max} is $(p - u)(Q/p)$. The time between runs is $(I_{max})/u$ – setup time.

The Dine Corporation is both a producer and a user of brass couplings. The firm operates 220 days a year and uses the couplings at a steady rate of 50 per day. Couplings can be produced at a rate of 200 per day. Annual storage cost is \$2 per coupling, and machine setup cost is \$70 per run.

a. Determine the economic run quantity.

b. Approximately how many runs per year will there be?

c. Compute the maximum inventory level.

d. Determine the length of the *pure consumption* portion of the cycle.

Solution

$$D = 50 \text{ units per day} \times 220 \text{ days per year} = 11{,}000 \text{ units per year}$$
$$S = \$70 \text{ per order}$$
$$H = \$2 \text{ per unit per year}$$
$$p = 200 \text{ units per day}$$
$$u = 50 \text{ units per day}$$

a. $$Q_p = \sqrt{\frac{2DS}{H}}\sqrt{\frac{p}{p-u}} = \sqrt{\frac{2(11{,}000)70}{2}}\sqrt{\frac{200}{200-50}} \approx 1{,}013 \text{ units.}$$

b. Number of runs per year: $D/Q_0 = 11{,}000/1{,}013 = 10.86$, or approximately 11.

c. $$I_{max} = \frac{Q_p}{p}(p-u) = \frac{1{,}013}{200}(200-50) = 759.75 \text{ or } 760 \text{ units.}$$

d. $$\text{Length of cycle} = \frac{Q_p}{u} = \frac{1{,}013 \text{ units}}{50 \text{ units per day}} = 20.26 \text{ days}$$

$$\text{Length of run} = \frac{Q_p}{p} = \frac{1{,}013 \text{ units}}{200 \text{ units per day}} = 5.065 \text{ days}$$

$$\text{Length of pure consumption portion} = \text{Length of cycle} - \text{Length of run}$$
$$= 20.26 - 5.065 = 15.20 \text{ days}$$

Problem 3

Quantity discounts. This type of problem can be recognized when a list showing prices for each quantity range is given along with the basic EOQ information.

a. If unit holding cost is constant, use these steps to solve the problem:
   1. Use Formula 13–2 to find Q.
   2. Locate Q in the price schedule.
   3. Compute TC using Formula 13–1 for Q and for all lower-cost price breaks.
b. If unit holding cost is a percentage of unit price, use these steps to solve the problem:
   1. Beginning with the lowest cost, and using the corresponding H for that cost, compute Q using Formula 13–2. Continue moving up in unit cost until a feasible Q is found.
   2. Locate the feasible Q in the price schedule.
   3. Compute TC using Formula 13–9 for Q and for all lower-cost price breaks. Remember to use the corresponding H for each price.

A small manufacturing firm uses roughly 3,400 pounds of chemical dye a year. Currently the firm purchases 300 pounds per order and pays \$3 per pound. The supplier has just announced that orders of 1,000 pounds or more will be filled at a price of \$2 per pound. The manufacturing firm incurs a cost of \$100 each time it submits an order and assigns an annual holding cost of 17 percent of the purchase price per pound.

a. Determine the order size that will minimize the total cost.
b. If the supplier offered the discount at 1,500 pounds instead of 1,000 pounds, what order size would minimize total cost?

$D = 3{,}400$ pounds per year $S = \$100$ per order $H = .17P$

Solution

a. Compute the EOQ for \$2 per pound:

The quantity ranges are

Range	Unit Price
1 to 999	\$3
1,000 +	\$2

$$Q_{\$2/\text{pound}} = \sqrt{\frac{2DS}{H}} = \sqrt{\frac{2(3{,}400)100}{.17(2)}} = 1{,}414 \text{ pounds}$$

Because this quantity is feasible at \$2 per pound, it is the optimum.

b. When the discount is offered at 1,500 pounds, the EOQ for the \$2 per pound range is no longer feasible. Consequently, it becomes necessary to compute the EOQ for \$3 per pound and compare the total cost for that order size with the total cost using the price break quantity (i.e., 1,500).

$$Q_{\$3/\text{pound}} = \sqrt{\frac{2DS}{H}} = \sqrt{\frac{2(3,400)100}{.17(3)}} \approx 1,155 \text{ pounds}$$

$$\text{TC} = \left(\frac{Q}{2}\right)H + \left(\frac{D}{Q}\right)S + PD$$

$$\text{TC}_{1,155} = \left(\frac{1,155}{2}\right).17(3) + \left(\frac{3,400}{1,155}\right)100 + 3(3,400)$$

$$= \$294.53 + \$294.37 + \$10,200 = \$10,789$$

$$\text{TC}_{1,500} = \left(\frac{1,500}{2}\right).17(2) + \left(\frac{3,400}{1,500}\right)100 + 2(3,400)$$

$$= \$255 + \$226.67 + \$6,800 = \$7,282$$

Hence, because it would result in a lower total cost, 1,500 is the optimal order size.

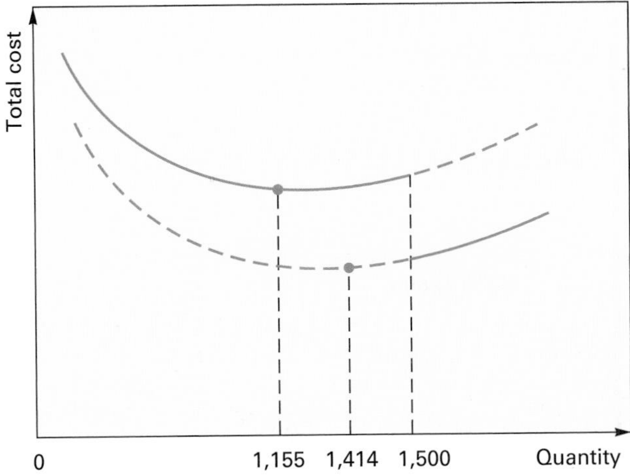

Problem 4

Reorder point. This type of problem can be recognized when the demand rate (d), lead time (LT), and desired service level or stockout risk are given. Use these steps to solve this type of problem:

1. Match the choice of formula to the standard deviation(s) that are given in the problem (e.g., if both demand and lead time standard deviations are given, use Formula 13–15 for the ROP).
2. If the problem asks for the amount of safety stock, use the second part of the appropriate ROP formula.
3. If the "expected demand during lead time" and the "standard deviation of lead time demand" are given, use Formula 13–12.

ROP for variable demand and constant lead time. The housekeeping department of a motel uses approximately 400 washcloths per day. The actual number tends to vary with the number of guests on any given night. Usage can be approximated by a normal distribution that has a mean of 400 and a standard deviation of nine washcloths per day. A linen supply company delivers towels and washcloths with a lead time of three days. If the motel policy is to maintain a stockout risk of 2 percent, what is the minimum number of washcloths that must be on hand at reorder time, and how much of that amount can be considered safety stock?

Solution

$\bar{d}$ = 400 washcloths per day LT = 3 days

σ_d = 9 washcloths per day Risk = 2 percent, so service level = 98 percent

From Appendix B, Table B, the z value that corresponds to an area under the normal curve to the left of z for 98 percent is about +2.055.

$$\text{ROP} = \bar{d}\text{LT} + z\sigma_d\sqrt{\text{LT}} = 400(3) + 2.055(9)\sqrt{3}$$
$$= 1{,}200 + 32.03, \text{ or approximately } 1{,}232 \text{ washcloths}$$

Safety stock is approximately 32 washcloths.

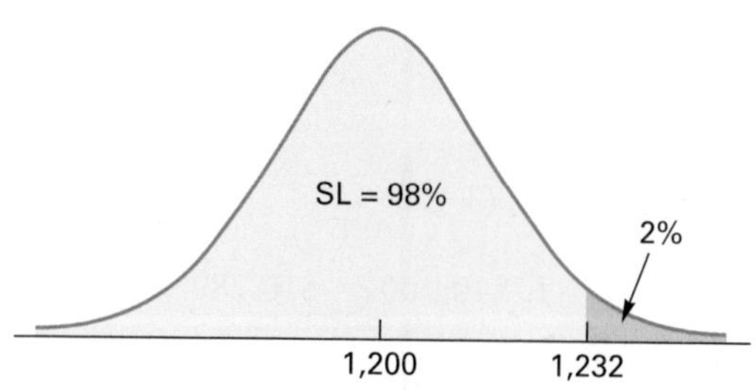

Problem 5

ROP for constant demand and variable lead time. The motel in the preceding example uses approximately 600 bars of soap each day, and this tends to be fairly constant. Lead time for soap delivery is normally distributed with a mean of six days and a standard deviation of two days. A service level of 90 percent is desired.

a. Find the ROP.

b. How many days of supply are on hand at the ROP?

Solution

$$d = 600 \text{ bars per day}$$
$$\text{SL} = 90 \text{ percent, so } z = +1.28 \text{ (from Appendix B, Table B)}$$
$$\overline{\text{LT}} = 6 \text{ days}$$
$$\sigma_{\text{LT}} = 2 \text{ days}$$

a. $\text{ROP} = d\overline{\text{LT}} + z(\sigma_{\text{LT}})d = 600(6) + 1.28(2)(600)$
$= 5{,}136$ bars of soap

b. $\dfrac{\text{ROP}}{d} = \dfrac{5{,}136}{600} = 8.56$ days

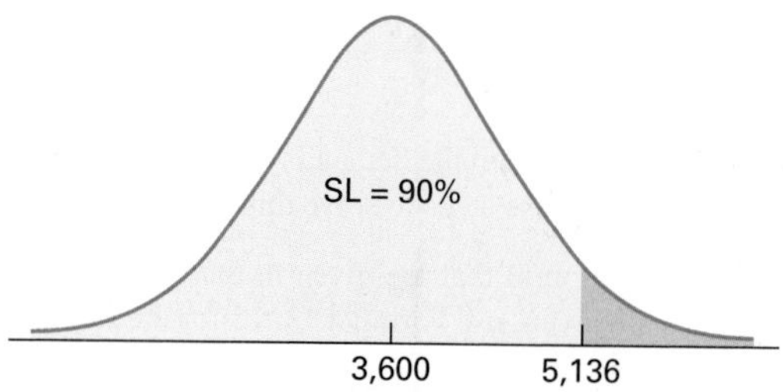

Problem 6

ROP for variable demand rate and variable lead time. The motel replaces broken glasses at a rate of 25 per day. In the past, this quantity has tended to vary normally and have a standard deviation of three glasses per day. Glasses are ordered from a Cleveland supplier. Lead time is normally distributed with an average of 10 days and a standard deviation of 2 days. What ROP should be used to achieve a service level of 95 percent?

Solution

$$\bar{d} = 25 \text{ glasses per day} \qquad \overline{\text{LT}} = 10 \text{ days}$$
$$\sigma_d = 3 \text{ glasses per day} \qquad \sigma_{\text{LT}} = 2 \text{ days}$$
$$\text{SL} = 95 \text{ percent, so } z = +1.65 \text{ (Appendix B, Table B)}$$

$$\text{ROP} = \bar{d}\,\overline{\text{LT}} + z\sqrt{\overline{\text{LT}}\sigma_d^2 + \bar{d}^2\sigma_{\text{LT}}^2}$$
$$= 25(10) + 1.65\sqrt{10(3)^2 + (25)^2(2)^2} = 334 \text{ glasses}$$

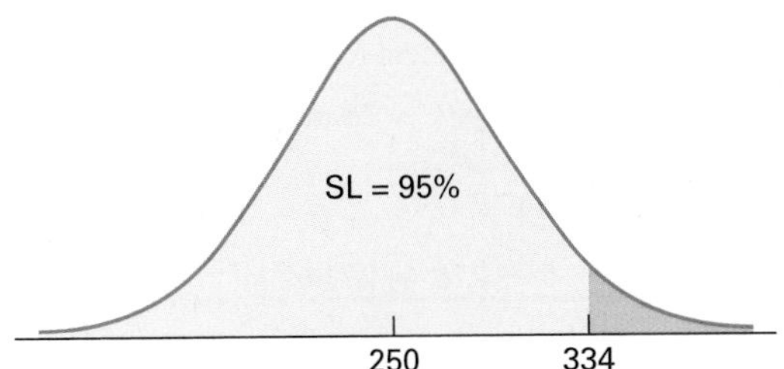

Problem 7

Shortages and service levels. This type of problem can be recognized when the problem asks for the number of units short per order cycle, or per year. Use Formula 13–16 for the expected number of units short per cycle, and formula 13–17 to find the number of units short per year. Use Table 13.3 to obtain the value of $E(z)$.

The manager of a store that sells office supplies has decided to set an annual service level of 96 percent for a certain model of telephone answering equipment. The store sells approximately 300 of this model a year. Holding cost is $5 per unit annually, ordering cost is $25, and $\sigma d_{\text{LT}} = 7$.

a. What average number of units short per year will be consistent with the specified annual service level?

b. What average number of units short per cycle will provide the desired annual service level?

c. What lead time service level is necessary for the 96 percent annual service level?

Solution

$\text{SL}_{\text{annual}} = 96$ percent $\quad D = 300$ units a year $\quad H = \$5 \quad S = \$25 \quad \sigma_{d\text{LT}} = 7$

a. $E(N) = (1 - \text{SL}_{\text{annual}})\, D = (1 - .96)(300) = 12$ units

b. $E(N) = E(n)\dfrac{D}{Q}$. Solving for $E(n)$, you have

$$E(n) = E(N) \div \left(\frac{D}{Q}\right) = 12 \div \left(\frac{300}{Q}\right)$$

$$Q = \sqrt{\frac{2DS}{H}} = \sqrt{\frac{2(300)(25)}{5}} = 54.77 \text{ (round to 55)}$$

Then $E(n) = 12 \div \left(\dfrac{300}{55}\right) = 2.2$.

c. In order to find the lead time service level, you need the value of $E(z)$. Because the value of $E(n)$ is 2.2 and $E(n) = E(z)\sigma_{d\text{LT}}$, you have $2.2 = E(z)(7)$. Solving gives $E(z) = 2.2 \div 7 = .314$. Interpolating in Table 13.3 gives the approximate lead time service level. Thus,

$$\frac{.307 - .314}{.307 - .324} = \frac{.5793 - x}{.5793 - .5636}$$

Solving,

$x = .5728$

[To interpolate, find the two values between which the computed number falls in the $E(z)$ column. Then find the difference between the computed value and one end of the range, and divide by the difference between the two ends of the range. Perform the corresponding calculation on the two service levels using x for the unknown value, and solve for x. Often, simply "eyeballing" the unknown value will suffice.]

Problem 8

Fixed-order-interval. This type of problem can be recognized when an order interval is given (e.g., inventory is ordered every 10 days) along with the demand rate, lead time, and quantity on hand at order time. Use Formula 13–20 to find the optimal order size.

A lab orders a number of chemicals from the same supplier every 30 days. Lead time is five days. The assistant manager of the lab must determine how much of one of these chemicals to order. A check of stock revealed that eleven 25-milliliter (ml) jars are on hand. Daily usage of the chemical is approximately normal with a mean of 15.2 ml per day and a standard deviation of 1.6 ml per day. The desired service level for this chemical is 95 percent.

a. How many jars of the chemical should be ordered?

b. What is the average amount of safety stock of the chemical?

Solution

$\bar{d}$ = 15.2 ml per day	OI = 30 days	SL = 95 percent requires z = 1.65
σ_d = 1.6 ml per day	LT = 5 days	A = 11 jars × 25 ml per jar = 275 ml

a. $\text{Amount to order} = \bar{d}(\text{OI} + \text{LT}) + z\sigma_d\sqrt{\text{OI} + \text{LT}} - A$

$$= 15.2(30 + 5) + 1.65(1.6)\sqrt{30 + 5} - 275 = 272.62 \text{ ml}$$

Convert this to number of jars:

$$\frac{272.62 \text{ ml}}{25 \text{ ml per jar}} = 10.90 \text{ or } 11 \text{ jars}$$

b. $\text{Safety stock} = z\sigma_d\sqrt{\text{OI} + \text{LT}} = 1.65(1.6)\sqrt{30 + 5} = 15.62 \text{ ml.}$

Problem 9

Single-period. This type of problem can be recognized when a probability distribution or empirical distribution for demand for a "perishable" item is given along with unit shortage and excess costs, or information that can be used to calculate them. Use these steps to solve the problem:

1. Compute the optimal service level using Formula 13–21.
2. If the given distribution is uniform or normal, use that to obtain the exact stocking level.
3. If the distribution is Poisson or empirical, SL will fall between two cumulative frequencies. Round up to the higher frequency to find the optimal stocking level. *Note:* If the distribution is empirical, first obtain the cumulative frequencies or probabilities.

A firm that installs cable TV systems uses a certain piece of equipment for which it carries two spare parts. The parts cost $500 each and have no salvage value. Part failures can be modeled by a Poisson distribution with a mean of two failures during the useful life of the equipment. Holding and disposal costs are negligible. Estimate the apparent range of shortage cost.

Solution

C_s is unknown $\quad C_e = \$500$

The Poisson table (Appendix B, Table C) provides these values for a mean of 2.0:

Number of Failures	Cumulative Probability
0	.135
1	.406
2	.677
3	.857
4	.947
5	.983
⋮	⋮

For the optimal stocking level, the service level must usually be rounded up to a feasible stocking level. Hence, you know that the service level must have been between .406 and .677 in order to make two units the optimal level. By setting the service level equal first to .406 and then to .677, you can establish bounds on the possible range of shortage costs.

$$\frac{C_s}{C_s + \$500} = .406, \text{ so } C_s = .406(\$500 + C_s)$$

Solving, you find $C_s = \$341.75$.

Similarly,

$$\frac{C_s}{C_s + \$500} = .677, \text{ so } C_s = .677(\$500 + C_s)$$

Solving, you find $C_s = \$1{,}047.99$. Hence, the apparent range of shortage cost is $341.75 to $1,047.99.

DISCUSSION AND REVIEW QUESTIONS

1. What are the primary reasons for holding inventory?
2. What are the requirements for effective inventory management?
3. Briefly describe each of the costs associated with inventory.
4. What potential benefits and risks do RFID tags have for inventory management?
5. Why might it be inappropriate to use inventory turnover ratios to compare inventory performance of companies that are in different industries?
6. List the major assumptions of the EOQ model.
7. How would you respond to the criticism that EOQ models tend to provide misleading results because values of *D, S,* and *H* are, at best, educated guesses?
8. Explain briefly how a higher carrying cost can result in a decrease in inventory.
9. What is safety stock, and what is its purpose?
10. Under what circumstances would the amount of safety stock held be
    a. Large? b. Small? c. Zero?
11. What is meant by the term *service level?* Generally speaking, how is service level related to the amount of safety stock held?
12. Describe briefly the A-B-C approach to inventory control.
13. The purchasing agent for a company that assembles and sells air-conditioning equipment in a Latin American country noted that the cost of compressors has increased significantly each time they have been reordered. The company uses an EOQ model to determine order size. What are the implications of this price escalation with respect to order size? What factors other than price must be taken into consideration?
14. Explain how a decrease in setup time can lead to a decrease in the average amount of inventory a firm holds, and why that would be beneficial.
15. What is the single-period model, and under what circumstances is it appropriate?
16. Can the optimal stocking level in the single-period model ever be less than expected demand? Explain briefly.
17. What are some ways in which a company can reduce the need for inventories?

TAKING STOCK

1. What trade-offs are involved in each of these aspects of inventory management?
    a. Buying additional amounts to take advantage of quantity discounts.
    b. Treating holding cost as a percentage of unit price instead of as a constant amount.
    c. Conducting cycle counts once a quarter instead of once a year.
2. Who needs to be involved in inventory decisions involving holding costs? Setting inventory levels? Quantity discount purchases?
3. How has technology aided inventory management? How have technological improvements in products such as automobiles and computers impacted inventory decisions?

CRITICAL THINKING EXERCISES

1. To be competitive, many fast-food chains began to expand their menus to include a wider range of foods. Although contributing to competitiveness, this has added to the complexity of operations, including inventory management. Specifically, in what ways does the expansion of menu offerings create problems for inventory management?
2. As a supermarket manager, how would you go about evaluating the criticalness of an inventory shortage?
3. Sam is at the post office to mail a package. After he pays for mailing the package, the clerk asks if he would like to buy some stamps. Sam pauses to think before he answers. He doesn't have a credit card with him. After paying for the package, he has about $30 in his pocket. Analyze this from an inventory standpoint. Identify the relevant considerations.
4. Give two examples of unethical conduct involving inventory management and the ethical principle each one violates.

PROBLEMS

1. The manager of an automobile repair shop hopes to achieve a better allocation of inventory control efforts by adopting an A-B-C approach to inventory control.

a. Given the monthly usages in the following table, classify the items in A, B, and C categories according to dollar usage:

Item	Usage	Unit Cost
4021	90	$1,400
9402	300	12
4066	30	700
6500	150	20
9280	10	1,020
4050	80	140
6850	2,000	10
3010	400	20
4400	5,000	5

b. Determine the percentage of items in each category and the annual dollar value for each category.

2. The following table contains figures on the monthly volume and unit costs for a random sample of 16 items from a list of 2,000 inventory items at a health care facility:

Item	Unit Cost	Usage	Item	Unit Cost	Usage
K34	$10	200	F99	20	60
K35	25	600	D45	10	550
K36	36	150	D48	12	90
M10	16	25	D52	15	110
M20	20	80	D57	40	120
Z45	80	200	N08	30	40
F14	20	300	P05	16	500
F95	30	800	P09	10	30

a. Develop an A-B-C classification for these items.
b. How could the manager use this information?
c. After reviewing your classification scheme, suppose that the manager decides to place item P05 into the A category. What are some possible explanations for this decision?

3. A large bakery buys flour in 25-pound bags. The bakery uses an average of 1,215 bags a year. Preparing an order and receiving a shipment of flour involves a cost of $10 per order. Annual carrying costs are $75 per bag.
a. Determine the economic order quantity.
b. What is the average number of bags on hand?
c. How many orders per year will there be?
d. Compute the total cost of ordering and carrying flour.
e. If holding costs were to increase by $9 per year, how much would that affect the minimum total annual cost?

4. A large law firm uses an average of 40 boxes of copier paper a day. The firm operates 260 days a year. Storage and handling costs for the paper are $30 a year per box, and it costs approximately $60 to order and receive a shipment of paper.
a. What order size would minimize the sum of annual ordering and carrying costs?
b. Compute the total annual cost using your order size from part *a*.
c. Except for rounding, are annual ordering and carrying costs always equal at the EOQ?
d. The office manager is currently using an order size of 200 boxes. The partners of the firm expect the office to be managed "in a cost-efficient manner." Would you recommend that the office manager use the optimal order size instead of 200 boxes? Justify your answer.

5. Garden Variety Flower Shop uses 750 clay pots a month. The pots are purchased at $2 each. Annual carrying costs per pot are estimated to be 30 percent of cost, and ordering costs are $20 per order. The manager has been using an order size of 1,500 flower pots.
a. What additional annual cost is the shop incurring by staying with this order size?
b. Other than cost savings, what benefit would using the optimal order quantity yield?

6. A produce distributor uses 800 packing crates a month, which it purchases at a cost of $10 each. The manager has assigned an annual carrying cost of 35 percent of the purchase price per crate.

Ordering costs are \$28. Currently the manager orders once a month. How much could the firm save annually in ordering and carrying costs by using the EOQ?

7. A manager receives a forecast for next year. Demand is projected to be 600 units for the first half of the year and 900 units for the second half. The monthly holding cost is \$2 per unit, and it costs an estimated \$55 to process an order.
   a. Assuming that monthly demand will be level during each of the six-month periods covered by the forecast (e.g., 100 per month for each of the first six months), determine an order size that will minimize the sum of ordering and carrying costs for each of the six-month periods.
   b. Why is it important to be able to assume that demand will be level during each six-month period?
   c. If the vendor is willing to offer a discount of \$10 *per order* for ordering in multiples of 50 units (e.g., 50, 100, 150), would you advise the manager to take advantage of the offer in either period? If so, what order size would you recommend?

8. A food processor uses approximately 27,000 glass jars a month for its fruit juice product. Because of storage limitations, a lot size of 4,000 jars has been used. Monthly holding cost is 18 cents per jar, and reordering cost is \$60 per order. The company operates an average of 20 days a month.
   a. What penalty is the company incurring by its present order size?
   b. The manager would prefer ordering 10 times each month but would have to justify any change in order size. One possibility is to simplify order processing to reduce the ordering cost. What ordering cost would enable the manager to justify ordering every other day?
   c. Suppose that after investigating ordering cost, the manager is able to reduce it to \$50. How else could the manager justify using an order size that would be consistent with ordering every other day?

9. The Friendly Sausage Factory (FSF) can produce hot dogs at a rate of 5,000 per day. FSF supplies hot dogs to local restaurants at a steady rate of 250 per day. The cost to prepare the equipment for producing hot dogs is \$66. Annual holding costs are 45 cents per hot dog. The factory operates 300 days a year. Find
   a. The optimal run size.
   b. The number of runs per year.
   c. The length (in days) of a run.

10. A chemical firm produces sodium bisulfate in 100-pound bags. Demand for this product is 20 tons per day. The capacity for producing the product is 50 tons per day. Setup costs \$100, and storage and handling costs are \$5 per ton a year. The firm operates 200 days a year. (*Note:* 1 ton = 2,000 pounds.)
   a. How many bags per run are optimal?
   b. What would the average inventory be for this lot size?
   c. Determine the approximate length of a production run, in days.
   d. About how many runs per year would there be?
   e. How much could the company save annually if the setup cost could be reduced to \$25 per run?

11. A company is about to begin production of a new product. The manager of the department that will produce one of the components for the product wants to know how often the machine used to produce the item will be available for other work. The machine will produce the item at a rate of 200 units a day. Eighty units will be used daily in assembling the final product. Assembly will take place five days a week, 50 weeks a year. The manager estimates that it will take almost a full day to get the machine ready for a production run, at a cost of \$300. Inventory holding costs will be \$10 a year.
   a. What run quantity should be used to minimize total annual costs?
   b. What is the length of a production run in days?
   c. During production, at what rate will inventory build up?
   d. If the manager wants to run another job between runs of this item, and needs a minimum of 10 days per cycle for the other work, will there be enough time?
   e. Given your answer to part *d,* the manager wants to explore options that will allow this other job to be performed using this equipment. Name three options the manager can consider.
   f. Suppose the manager decides to increase the run size of the new product. How many additional units would be needed to just accommodate the other job? How much will that increase the total annual cost?

12. A company manufactures hair dryers. It buys some of the components, but it makes the heating element, which it can produce at the rate of 800 per day. Hair dryers are assembled daily, 250 days a year, at a rate of 300 per day. Because of the disparity between the production and usage rates, the heating elements are periodically produced in batches of 2,000 units.

a. Approximately how many *batches* of heating elements are produced annually?
b. If production on a batch begins when there is no inventory of heating elements on hand, how much inventory will be on hand *two days later?*
c. What is the average inventory of elements, assuming each production cycle begins when there are none on hand?
d. The same equipment that is used to make the heating elements could also be used to make a component for another of the firm's products. That job would require four days, including setup. Setup time for making a batch of the heating elements is a half day. Is there enough time to do this job between production of batches of heating elements? Explain.

13. A mail-order house uses 18,000 boxes a year. Carrying costs are 60 cents per box a year, and ordering costs are $96. The following price schedule applies. Determine
    a. The optimal order quantity.
    b. The number of orders per year.

Number of Boxes	Price per Box
1,000 to 1,999	$1.25
2,000 to 4,999	1.20
5,000 to 9,999	1.15
10,000 or more	1.10

14. A jewelry firm buys semiprecious stones to make bracelets and rings. The supplier quotes a price of $8 per stone for quantities of 600 stones or more, $9 per stone for orders of 400 to 599 stones, and $10 per stone for lesser quantities. The jewelry firm operates 200 days per year. Usage rate is 25 stones per day, and ordering costs are $48.
    a. If carrying costs are $2 per year for each stone, find the order quantity that will minimize total annual cost.
    b. If annual carrying costs are 30 percent of unit cost, what is the optimal order size?
    c. If lead time is six working days, at what point should the company reorder?
15. A manufacturer of exercise equipment purchases the pulley section of the equipment from a supplier who lists these prices: less than 1,000, $5 each; 1,000 to 3,999, $4.95 each; 4,000 to 5,999, $4.90 each; and 6,000 or more, $4.85 each. Ordering costs are $50, annual carrying costs per unit are 40 percent of purchase cost, and annual usage is 4,900 pulleys. Determine an order quantity that will minimize total cost.
16. A company will begin stocking remote control devices. Expected monthly demand is 800 units. The controllers can be purchased from either supplier A or supplier B. Their price lists are as follows:

SUPPLIER A		SUPPLIER B	
Quantity	**Unit Price**	**Quantity**	**Unit Price**
1–199	$14.00	1–149	$14.10
200–499	13.80	150–349	13.90
500 +	13.60	350 +	13.70

Ordering cost is $40 and annual holding cost is 25 percent of unit price per unit. Which supplier should be used and what order quantity is optimal if the intent is to minimize total annual costs?

17. A manager just received a new price list from a supplier. It will now cost $1.00 a box for order quantities of 801 or more boxes, $1.10 a box for 200 to 800 boxes, and $1.20 a box for smaller quantities. Ordering cost is $80 per order and carrying costs are $10 per box a year. The firm uses 3,600 boxes a year. The manager has suggested a "round number" order size of 800 boxes. The manager's rationale is that with a U-shaped cost curve that is fairly flat at its minimum, the difference in total annual cost between 800 and 801 units would be small anyway. How would you reply to the manager's suggestion? What order size would you recommend?
18. A newspaper publisher uses roughly 800 feet of baling wire each day to secure bundles of newspapers while they are being distributed to carriers. The paper is published Monday through Saturday. Lead time is six workdays. What is the appropriate reorder point quantity, given that the company desires a service level of 95 percent, if that stockout risk for various levels of safety stock is as follows: 1,500 feet, .10; 1,800 feet, .05; 2,100 feet, .02; and 2,400 feet, .01?

19. Given this information:

Expected demand during lead time = 300 units

Standard deviation of lead time demand = 30 units

Determine each of the following, assuming that lead time demand is distributed normally:

a. The ROP that will provide a risk of stockout of 1 percent during lead time.
b. The safety stock needed to attain a 1 percent risk of stockout during lead time.
c. Would a stockout risk of 2 percent require more or less safety stock than a 1 percent risk? Explain. Would the ROP be larger, smaller, or unaffected if the acceptable risk were 2 percent instead of 1 percent? Explain.

20. Given this information:

Lead-time demand = 600 pounds

Standard deviation of lead time demand = 52 pounds (Assume normality.)

Acceptable stockout risk during lead time = 4 percent

a. What amount of safety stock is appropriate?
b. When should this item be reordered?
c. What risk of stockout would result from a decision not to have any safety stock?

21. Demand for walnut fudge ice cream at the Sweet Cream Dairy can be approximated by a normal distribution with a mean of 21 gallons per week and a standard deviation of 3.5 gallons per week. The new manager desires a service level of 90 percent. Lead time is two days, and the dairy is open seven days a week. (*Hint:* Work in terms of weeks.)

a. If an ROP model is used, what ROP would be consistent with the desired service level? How many days of supply are on hand at the ROP, assuming average demand?
b. If a fixed-interval model is used instead of an ROP model, what order size would be needed for the 90 percent service level with an order interval of 10 days and a supply of 8 gallons on hand at the order time? What is the probability of experiencing a stockout before this order arrives?
c. Suppose the manager is using the ROP model described in part *a*. One day after placing an order with the supplier, the manager receives a call from the supplier that the order will be delayed because of problems at the supplier's plant. The supplier promises to have the order there in two days. After hanging up, the manager checks the supply of walnut fudge ice cream and finds that 2 gallons have been sold since the order was placed. Assuming the supplier's promise is valid, what is the probability that the dairy will run out of this flavor before the shipment arrives?

22. The injection molding department of a company uses an average of 30 gallons of special lubricant a day. The supply of the lubricant is replenished when the amount on hand is 170 gallons. It takes four days for an order to be delivered. Safety stock is 50 gallons, which provides a stockout risk of 9 percent. What amount of safety stock would provide a stockout risk of 3 percent? Assume normality.

23. A company uses 85 circuit boards a day in a manufacturing process. The person who orders the boards follows this rule: Order when the amount on hand drops to 625 boards. Orders are delivered approximately six days after being placed. The delivery time is normal with a mean of six days and a standard deviation of 1.10 days. What is the probability that the supply of circuit boards will be exhausted before the order is received if boards are reordered when the amount on hand drops to 625 boards?

24. One item a computer store sells is supplied by a vendor who handles only that item. Demand for that item recently changed, and the store manager must determine when to replenish it. The manager wants a probability of at least 96 percent of not having a stockout during lead time. The manager expects demand to average a dozen units a day and have a standard deviation of two units a day. Lead time is variable, averaging four days with a standard deviation of one day. Assume normality and that seasonality is not a factor.

a. When should the manager reorder to achieve the desired probability?
b. Why might the model not be appropriate if seasonality were present?

25. The manager of a car wash received a revised price list from the vendor who supplies soap, and a promise of a shorter lead time for deliveries. Formerly the lead time was four days, but now the vendor promises a reduction of 25 percent in that time. Annual usage of soap is 4,500 gallons. The car wash is open 360 days a year. Assume that daily usage is normal, and that it has a standard deviation of 2 gallons per day. The ordering cost is $30 and annual carrying cost is $3 a gallon. The revised price list (cost per gallon) is shown in the following table:

Quantity	Unit Price
1–399	$2.00
400–799	1.70
800 +	1.62

a. What order quantity is optimal?
b. What ROP is appropriate if the acceptable risk of a stockout is 1.5 percent?

26. A small copy center uses five 500-sheet boxes of copy paper a week. Experience suggests that usage can be well approximated by a normal distribution with a mean of five boxes per week and a standard deviation of one-half box per week. Two weeks are required to fill an order for letterhead stationery. Ordering cost is $2, and annual holding cost is 20 cents per box.
a. Determine the economic order quantity, assuming a 52-week year.
b. If the copy center reorders when the supply on hand is 12 boxes, compute the risk of a stockout.
c. If a fixed interval of seven weeks instead of an ROP is used for reordering, what risk does the copy center incur that it will run out of stationery before this order arrives if it orders 36 boxes when the amount on hand is 12 boxes?

27. Ned's Natural Foods sells unshelled peanuts by the pound. Historically, Ned has observed that daily demand is normally distributed with a mean of 80 pounds and a standard deviation of 10 pounds. Lead time also appears normally distributed with a mean of eight days and a standard deviation of one day.
a. What ROP would provide a stockout risk of 10 percent during lead time?
b. What is the expected number of units (pounds) short per cycle?

28. Regional Supermarket is open 360 days per year. Daily use of cash register tape averages 10 rolls. Usage appears normally distributed with a standard deviation of 2 rolls per day. The cost of ordering tape is $1, and carrying costs are 40 cents per roll a year. Lead time is three days.
a. What is the EOQ?
b. What ROP will provide a lead time service level of 96 percent?
c. What is the expected number of units short per cycle with 96 percent? Per year?
d. What is the annual service level?

29. A service station uses 1,200 cases of oil a year. Ordering cost is $40, and annual carrying cost is $3 per case. The station owner has specified an *annual* service level of 99 percent.
a. What level of safety stock is appropriate if lead time demand is normally distributed with a mean of 80 cases and a standard deviation of 5 cases?
b. What is the risk of a stockout during lead time?

30. Weekly demand for diesel fuel at a department of parks depot is 250 gallons. The depot operates 52 weeks a year. Weekly usage is normal and has a standard deviation of 14 gallons. Holding cost for the fuel is $1 a month, and it costs $20 in administrative time to submit an order for more fuel. It takes one-half week to receive a delivery of diesel fuel. Determine the amount of safety stock that would be needed if the manager wants
a. An annual service level of 98 percent. What is the implication of negative safety stock?
b. The expected number of units short per order cycle to be no more than five gallons.

31. A drugstore uses fixed-order cycles for many of the items it stocks. The manager wants a service level of .98. The order interval is 14 days, and lead time is 2 days. Average demand for one item is 40 units per day, and the standard deviation of demand is 3 units per day. Given the on-hand inventory at the reorder time for each order cycle shown in the following table, determine the order quantities for cycles 1, 2, and 3:

Cycle	On Hand
1	42
2	8
3	103

32. A manager must set up inventory ordering systems for two new production items, P34 and P35. P34 can be ordered at any time, but P35 can be ordered only once every four weeks. The company operates 50 weeks a year, and the weekly usage rates for both items are normally distributed. The manager has gathered the following information about the items:

	Item P34	Item P35
Average weekly demand	60 units	70 units
Standard deviation	4 units per week	5 units per week
Unit cost	$15	$20
Annual holding cost	30%	30%
Ordering cost	$70	$30
Lead time	2 weeks	2 weeks
Acceptable stockout risk	2.5%	2.5%

a. When should the manager reorder each item?
b. Compute the order quantity for P34.
c. Compute the order quantity for P35 if 110 units are on hand at the time the order is placed.

33. Given the following list of items,
a. Classify the items as A, B, or C.
b. Determine the economic order quantity for each item (round to the nearest whole unit).

Item	Estimated Annual Demand	Ordering Cost	Holding Cost (%)	Unit Price
H4-010	20,000	50	20	2.50
H5-201	60,200	60	20	4.00
P6-400	9,800	80	30	28.50
P6-401	14,500	50	30	12.00
P7-100	6,250	50	30	9.00
P9-103	7,500	50	40	22.00
TS-300	21,000	40	25	45.00
TS-400	45,000	40	25	40.00
TS-041	800	40	25	20.00
V1-001	33,100	25	35	4.00

34. Demand for jelly doughnuts on Saturdays at Don's Doughnut Shoppe is shown in the following table. Determine the optimal number of doughnuts, in dozens, to stock if labor, materials, and overhead are estimated to be $3.20 per dozen, doughnuts are sold for $4.80 per dozen, and leftover doughnuts at the end of each day are sold the next day at half price. What is the *resulting* service level?

Demand (dozens)	Relative Frequency	Demand (dozens)	Relative Frequency
19	.01	25	.10
20	.05	26	.11
21	.12	27	.10
22	.18	28	.04
23	.13	29	.02
24	.14		

35. A public utility intends to buy a turbine as part of an expansion plan and must now decide on the number of spare parts to order. One part, no. X135, can be purchased for $100 each. Carrying and disposal costs are estimated to be 145 percent of the purchase price over the life of the turbine. A stockout would cost roughly $88,000 due to downtime, ordering, and "special purchase" factors. Historical records based on the performance of similar equipment operating under similar conditions suggest that demand for spare parts will tend to approximate a Poisson distribution with a mean of 3.2 parts for the useful life of the turbine.
a. What is the optimal number of spares to order?
b. Carrying no spare parts would be the best strategy for what range of shortage cost?

36. Skinner's Fish Market buys fresh Boston bluefish daily for $4.20 per pound and sells it for $5.70 per pound. At the end of each business day, any remaining bluefish is sold to a producer of cat food for $2.40 per pound. Daily demand can be approximated by a normal distribution with a mean of 80 pounds and a standard deviation of 10 pounds. What is the optimal stocking level?

37. A small grocery store sells fresh produce, which it obtains from a local farmer. During the strawberry season, demand for fresh strawberries can be reasonably approximated using a normal distribution with a mean of 40 quarts per day and a standard deviation of 6 quarts per day. Excess costs run 35 cents per quart. The grocer orders 49 quarts per day.
   a. What is the implied cost of shortage per quart?
   b. Why might this be a reasonable figure?

38. Demand for devil's food whipped-cream layer cake at a local pastry shop can be approximated using a Poisson distribution with a mean of six per day. The manager estimates it costs $9 to prepare each cake. Fresh cakes sell for $12. Day-old cakes sell for $9 each. What stocking level is appropriate if one-half of the day-old cakes are sold and the rest thrown out?

39. Burger Prince buys top-grade ground beef for $1.00 per pound. A large sign over the entrance guarantees that the meat is fresh daily. Any leftover meat is sold to the local high school cafeteria for 80 cents per pound. Four hamburgers can be prepared from each pound of meat. Burgers sell for 60 cents each. Labor, overhead, meat, buns, and condiments cost 50 cents per burger. Demand is normally distributed with a mean of 400 pounds per day and a standard deviation of 50 pounds per day. What daily order quantity is optimal? (*Hint:* Shortage cost must be in dollars per pound.)

40. Demand for rug-cleaning machines at Clyde's U-Rent-It is shown in the following table. Machines are rented by the day only. Profit on the rug cleaners is $10 per day. Clyde has four rug-cleaning machines.

Demand	Frequency
0	.30
1	.20
2	.20
3	.15
4	.10
5	.05
	1.00

   a. Assuming that Clyde's stocking decision is optimal, what is the implied range of excess cost per machine?
   b. Your answer from part *a* has been presented to Clyde, who protests that the amount is too low. Does this suggest an increase or a decrease in the number of rug machines he stocks? Explain.
   c. Suppose now that the $10 mentioned as profit is instead the excess cost per day for each machine and that the shortage cost is unknown. Assuming that the optimal number of machines is four, what is the implied range of shortage cost per machine?

41. A manager is going to purchase new processing equipment and must decide on the number of spare parts to order with the new equipment. The spares cost $200 each, and any unused spares will have an expected salvage value of $50 each. The probability of usage can be described by this distribution:

Number	0	1	2	3
Probability	.10	.50	.25	.15

If a part fails and a spare is not available, two days will be needed to obtain a replacement and install it. The cost for idle equipment is $500 per day. What quantity of spares should be ordered?
   a. Use the ratio method.
   b. Use the tabular method (see Table 13.4).

42. A Las Vegas supermarket bakery must decide how many wedding cakes to prepare for the upcoming weekend. Cakes cost $33 each to make, and they sell for $60 each. Unsold cakes are reduced to half-price on Monday, and typically one-third of those are sold. Any that remain are donated to a nearby senior center. Analysis of recent demand resulted in the following table:

Demand	0	1	2	3
Probability	.15	.35	.30	.20

How many cakes should be prepared to maximize expected profit?
   a. Use the ratio method.
   b. Use the tabular method (see Table 13.4).

43. Offwego Airlines has a daily flight from Chicago to Las Vegas. On average, 18 ticket holders cancel their reservations, so the company intentionally overbooks the flight. Cancellations can be described by a normal distribution with a mean of 18 passengers and a standard deviation of 4.55 passengers. Profit per passenger is $99. If a passenger arrives but cannot board due to overbooking, the company policy is to provide a cash payment of $200. How many tickets should be overbooked to maximize expected profit?

44. Caring Hospital's dispensary reorders doses of a drug when the supply on hand falls to 18 units. Lead time for resupply is three days. Given the typical usage over the last 10 days, what service level is achieved with the hospital's reorder policy? (*Hint:* Use Formula 13–13.)

Day	1	2	3	4	5	6	7	8	9	10
Units	3	4	7	5	5	6	4	3	4	5

UPD Manufacturing

CASE

UPD Manufacturing produces a range of health care appliances for hospital as well as for home use. The company has experienced a steady demand for its products, which are highly regarded in the health care field. Recently the company has undertaken a review of its inventory ordering procedures as part of a larger effort to reduce costs.

One of the company's products is a blood pressure testing kit. UPD manufactures all of the components for the kit in-house except for the digital display unit. The display units are ordered at six-week intervals from the supplier. This ordering system began about five years ago, because the supplier insisted on it. However, that supplier was bought out by another supplier about a year ago, and the six-week ordering requirement is no longer in place. Nonetheless, UPD has continued to use the six-week ordering policy. According to purchasing manager Tom Chambers, "Unless somebody can give me a reason for changing, I'm going to stick with what we've been doing. I don't have time to reinvent the wheel."

Further discussions with Tom revealed a cost of $32 to order and receive a shipment of display units from the supplier. The company assembles 89 kits a week. Also, information from Sara James, in Accounting, indicated a weekly carrying cost of $.08 for each display unit.

The supplier has been quite reliable with deliveries; orders are received five working days after they are faxed to the supplier. Tom indicated that as far as he was concerned, lead-time variability is virtually nonexistent.

Questions

1. Would using an order interval other than every six weeks reduce costs? If so, what order interval would be best, and what order size would that involve?
2. Would you recommend changing to the optimal order interval? Explain.

Harvey Industries

CASE

Background

Harvey Industries, a Wisconsin company, specializes in the assembly of high-pressure washer systems and in the sale of repair parts for these systems. The products range from small portable high-pressure washers to large industrial installations for snow removal from vehicles stored outdoors during the winter months. Typical uses for high-pressure water cleaning include:

Automobiles	Airplanes
Building maintenance	Barns
Engines	Ice cream plants
Lift trucks	Machinery
Swimming pools	

Industrial customers include General Motors, Ford, Chrysler, Delta Airlines, United Parcel Service, and Shell Oil Company.

Although the industrial applications are a significant part of its sales, Harvey Industries is primarily an assembler of equipment for coin operated self-service car wash systems. The typical car wash is of concrete block construction with an equipment room in the center, flanked on either side by a number of bays. The cars are driven into the bays where the

(continued)

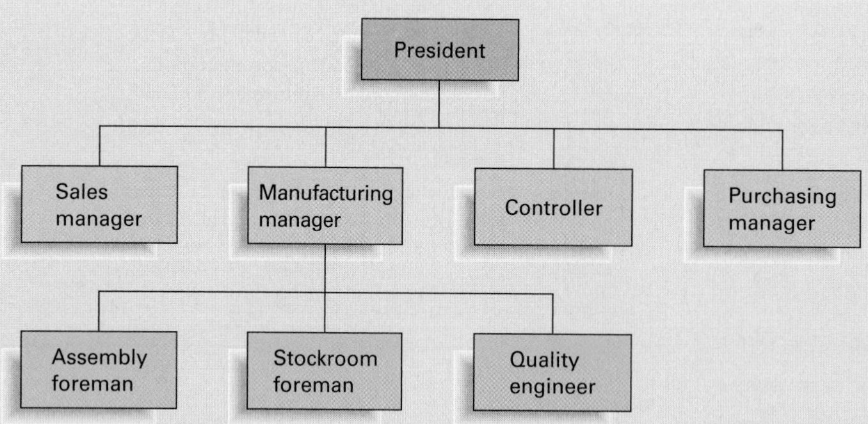

owner can wash and wax the car, utilizing high-pressure hot water and liquid wax. A dollar bill changer is available to provide change for the use of the equipment and the purchase of various products from dispensers. The products include towels, tire cleaner, and upholstery cleaner.

In recent years Harvey Industries has been in financial difficulty. The company has lost money for three of the last four years, with the last year's loss being $17,174 on sales of $1,238,674. Inventory levels have been steadily increasing to their present levels of $124,324.

The company employs 23 people with the management team consisting of the following key employees: president, sales manager, manufacturing manager, controller, and purchasing manager. The abbreviated organization chart reflects the reporting relationship of the key employees and the three individuals who report directly to the manufacturing manager.

Current Inventory Control System

The current inventory control "system" consists of orders for stock replenishment being made by the stockroom foreman, the purchasing manager, or the manufacturing manager whenever one of them notices that the inventory is low. An order for replenishment of inventory is also placed whenever someone (either a customer or an employee in the assembly area) wants an item and it is not in stock.

Some inventory is needed for the assembly of the high-pressure equipment for the car wash and industrial applications. There are current and accurate bills of material for these assemblies. The material needs to support the assembly schedule are generally known well in advance of the build schedule.

The majority of inventory transactions are for repair parts and for supplies used by the car washes, such as paper towels, detergent, and wax concentrate. Because of the constant and rugged use of the car wash equipment, there is a steady demand for the various repair parts.

The stockroom is well organized, with parts stored in locations according to each vendor. The number of vendors is relatively limited, with each vendor generally supplying many different parts. For example, the repair parts from Allen Bradley, a manufacturer of electrical motors, are stocked in the same location. These repair parts will be used to provide service for the many electrical motors that are part of the high-pressure pump and motor assembly used by all of the car washes.

Because of the heavy sales volume of repair parts, there are generally two employees working in the stockroom—a stockroom foreman who reports to the manufacturing manager and an assistant to the foreman. One of these two employees will handle customer orders. Many customers stop by and order the parts and supplies they need. Telephone orders are also received and are shipped by United Parcel Service the same day.

The assembly area has some inventory stored on the shop floor. This inventory consists of low-value items that are used every day, such as nuts, bolts, screws, and washers. These purchased items do not amount to very much dollar volume throughout the year. Unfortunately, oftentimes the assembly area is out of one of these basic items and this causes a significant amount of downtime for the assembly lines.

Paperwork is kept to a minimum. A sales slip listing the part numbers and quantities sold to a customer is generally made out for each sale. If the assembly department needs items that are not stocked on the assembly floor, someone from that department will enter the stockroom and withdraw the necessary material. There is no paperwork made out for the items needed on the assembly floor.

(continued)

(concluded)

There were 973 different part numbers purchased for stock last year and those purchases amounted to $314,673. An analysis of inventory records shows that $220,684 was spent on just 179 of the part numbers.

Fortunately for Harvey Industries, most of the items they purchase are stocked by either the manufacturer or by a wholesaler. When it is discovered that the company is out of stock on an item, it generally takes only two or three days to replenish the stock.

Due to the company's recent losses, its auditing firm became concerned about the company's ability to continue in business. Recently the company sold off excess vacant land adjoining its manufacturing facility to generate cash to meet its financial obligations.

New President

Because of the recent death of the owner, the trust department of a Milwaukee Bank (as trustee for the state) has taken over the company's affairs and has appointed a new company president. The new president has identified many problem areas—one of which is improper inventory control. He has retained you as a consultant to make specific recommendations concerning a revised inventory control system. What are your recommendations and their rationale?

Source: Case "Harvey Industries" by Donald Condit presented at Midwest Case Writer's Association Workshop, 1984.

Grill Rite

CASE

Grill Rite is an old-line company that started out making wooden matches. As that business waned, the company entered the electric barbecue grill market, with five models of grills it sells nationally. For many years the company maintained a single warehouse from which it supplied its distributors.

The plant where the company produces barbecue sets is located in a small town, and many workers have been with the company for many years. During the transition from wooden matches to barbecue grills, many employees gave up their weekends to help with changing over the plant and learning the new skills they would need, without pay. In fact, Mac Wilson, the company president, can reel off a string of such instances of worker loyalty. He has vowed to never lay off any workers, and to maintain a full employment, steady rate of output. "Yes, I know demand for these babies (barbecue grills) is seasonal, but the inventory boys will just have to deal with it. On an annual basis, our output matches sales."

Inventory is handled by a system of four warehouses. There is a central warehouse located near the plant that supplies some customers directly, and the three regional warehouses.

The vice president for sales, Julie Berry, is becoming increasingly frustrated with the inventory system that she says "is antiquated and unresponsive." She points to increasing complaints from regional sales managers about poor customer service, saying customer orders go unfilled or are late, apparently due to shortages at the regional warehouse. Regional warehouse managers, stung by complaints from sales managers, have responded by increasing their order sizes from the main warehouse, and maintaining larger amounts of safety stock. This has resulted in increased inventory holding costs, but it hasn't eliminated the problem. Complaints are still coming in from salespeople about shortages and lost sales. According to managers of the regional warehouses, their orders to the main warehouse aren't being shipped, or when they are, they are smaller quantities than requested. The manager of the main warehouse, Jimmy Joe ("JJ") Sorely, says his policy is to give preference to "filling direct orders from actual customers, rather than warehouse orders that might simply reflect warehouses trying to replenish their safety stock. And besides, I never know when I'll get hit with an order from one of the regional warehouses. I guess they think we've got an unlimited supply." Then he adds, "I thought when we added the warehouses, we could just divide our inventory among the warehouses, and everything would be okay."

When informed of the "actual customers" remark, a regional warehouse manager exclaimed, "We're their biggest customer!"

Julie Berry also mentioned that on more than one occasion she has found that items that were out of stock at one regional warehouse were in ample supply in at least one other regional warehouse.

Take the position of a consultant called in by president Mac Wilson. What recommendations can you make to alleviate the problems the company is encountering?

Farmers Restaurant

CASE

Sarah Lubbers and Chris Rusche

Farmers Restaurant is a full service restaurant offering a variety of breakfast, lunch, and dinner items. Currently, Kristin Davis is the general manager for the Farmers Restaurant located in the Grand Rapids/Wyoming metro area of Michigan. Since becoming manager, Kristin has faced some difficulties with ordering the right amounts of food items for the restaurant. Because of this, there are some weeks the restaurant has a surplus of menu items that are no longer fresh, and must be discarded. At other times, the restaurant has experienced shortages of some items. The fact that inventory accounts for an average cost of 26% of the restaurant's total revenues underscores the importance of managing inventory. Kristin would like to find a way to ensure that she is maintaining the proper amount of inventory. Customer counts at Kristin's restaurant have been declining recently, so one of Kristin's greatest focuses is to keep current customers and attract new customers. She believes that a key aspect of this is having all of the items on the menu in stock.

The restaurant industry is competitive. In the Grand Rapids/Wyoming metro area alone there are over 1,600 restaurants. Some of Farmers Restaurant's most serious competitors are IHOP, Applebee's, and Big Boy, all of which are located within 20 miles of the Farmers Restaurant, so customers have many alternatives from which to choose.

Online inventory systems are used to assist restaurant managers in determining on-hand inventory and gauging how well the restaurant is controlling food costs. The fiscal week for Farmers Restaurant starts on Thursday and ends on Wednesday of the following week. Each Wednesday, the manager physically counts the inventory on hand and enters the data into the online inventory system. The computer software system then compares the on-hand inventory for that week, the amount of food ordered, and the inventory on hand for the end of the previous week with the sales for the current week. By doing so, it is able to determine a total food cost. The manager compares this cost with the benchmark cost to see how well the restaurant has been managing its inventory. This is one of the most important numbers to managers at the Farmers Restaurant because it accounts for approximately 30% of total costs in terms of a store's cost structure.

The computer software system also compares the total cost of food on hand with the total amount of sales for that week and computes a percentage of on-hand inventories. As a guideline, the company has set a standard of having between 29% and 36% for its on-hand inventory level. The company feels that this level of inventory is an appropriate average to ensure quality food that is fresh and within expiration. Lastly, it is better to keep the inventory at a minimum level to ensure the accuracy and ease of inventory counts.

The Farmers Restaurant Kristin manages has been running above average in terms of food costs. For this reason, her boss has become concerned with the performance of the ordering system she is using at her restaurant. Kristin has been using her intuition to decide how much product to order despite the fact that the product order sheets provide a moving average usage of each product. Kristin bases her inventory management on her intuition because she does not understand how to utilize the moving average forecasting technique when placing orders. An additional complication with ordering inventory is that each item is packed in multiple quantities, so she cannot order the exact amount that she needs. Her boss requested that she create a more accurate way of ordering food and to report back to him in one month. Kristin is worried that if she cuts inventory levels too low she will run out of products which may result in a decrease in customer counts.

After Kristin met with her boss, she began to think about what changes she could make. She knows that inventory has been a weak point for her, but she remembers one of her employees talking about inventory management from one of his college courses. Kristin decides to ask the employee if he would be willing to help her try and come up with a better way for her to order products. Kristin tells him how the ordering system works, shows him the ordering form, and relates the above information.

Suppose you have been asked to work with Kristin to improve inventory ordering.

Questions

1. Describe the importance of inventory management as it relates to the Farmers Restaurant.
2. What ordering system would be best for this situation?
3. Given the following information, provide an example of how much of Farmers Sausage Gravy Mix should be ordered. You are doing the order for Thursday. Also, Kristin would like a service level of 95%, and you have found that there is a standard deviation of 3.5 units per week, and a moving average weekly demand of 35 servings. The gravy mix comes in packs of two servings. There are currently three packs in inventory.
4. Given the above information and an on-hand inventory of 12, determine the risk of stock out at the end of initial lead time and at the end of the second lead time. The lead time is 2 days and orders are placed once a week.
5. The supplier Kristin uses is located in Ohio. Why might Kristin consider dealing with a nearby supplier instead of the one in Ohio? What reasons might there be for not switching suppliers?

Bruegger's Bagel Bakery

OPERATIONS TOUR

Bruegger's Bagel Bakery makes and sells a variety of bagels, including plain, onion, poppyseed, and cinnamon raisin, as well as assorted flavors of cream cheese. Bagels are the major source of revenue for the company.

The bagel business is a $3 billion industry. Bagels are very popular with consumers. Not only are they relatively low in fat, they are filling, and they taste good! Investors like the bagel industry because it can be highly profitable: it only costs about $.10 to make a bagel, and they can be sold for $.50 each or more. Although some bagel companies have done poorly in recent years, due mainly to poor management, Bruegger's business is booming; it is number one nationally, with over 450 shops that sell bagels, coffee, and bagel sandwiches for takeout or on-premise consumption. Many stores in the Bruegger's chain generate an average of $800,000 in sales annually.

Production of bagels is done in batches, according to flavor, with each flavor being produced on a daily basis. Production of bagels at Bruegger's begins at a processing plant, where the basic ingredients of flour, water, yeast, and flavorings are combined in a special mixing machine. After the dough has been thoroughly mixed, it is transferred to another machine that shapes the dough into individual bagels. Once the bagels have been formed, they are loaded onto refrigerated trucks for shipping to individual stores. When the bagels reach a store, they are unloaded from the trucks and temporarily stored while they rise. The final two steps of processing involve boiling the bagels in a kettle of water and malt for one minute, and then baking the bagels in an oven for approximately 15 minutes.

The process is depicted in the figure.

Quality is an important feature of a successful business. Customers judge the quality of bagels by their appearance (size, shape, and shine), taste, and consistency. Customers are also sensitive to the service they receive when they make their purchases. Bruegger's devotes careful attention to quality at every stage of operation, from choosing suppliers of ingredients, careful monitoring of ingredients, and keeping equipment in good operating condition to monitoring output at each step in the process. At the stores, employees are instructed to watch for deformed bagels and to remove them when they find them. (Deformed bagels are returned to a processing plant where they are sliced into bagel chips, packaged, and then taken back to the stores for sale, thereby reducing the scrap rate.) Employees who work in the stores are carefully chosen and then trained so that they are competent to operate the necessary equipment in the stores and to provide the desired level of service to customers.

The company operates with minimal inventories of raw materials and inventories of partially completed bagels at the plant and very little inventory of bagels at the stores. One reason for this is to maintain a high degree of freshness in the final product by continually supplying fresh product to the stores. A second reason is to keep costs down; minimal inventories mean less space is needed for storage.

Questions

1. Bruegger's maintains relatively little inventory at either its plants or its retail stores. List the benefits and risks of this policy.
2. Quality is very important to Bruegger's.
   a. What features of bagels do customers look at to judge their quality?
   b. At what points in the production process do workers check bagel quality?
   c. List the steps in the production process, beginning with purchasing ingredients, and ending with the sale, and state how quality can be positively affected at each step.
3. Which inventory models could be used for ordering the ingredients for bagels? Which model do you think would be most appropriate for deciding how many bagels to make in a given batch?
4. Bruegger's has bagel-making machines at its plants. Another possibility would be to have a bagel-making machine at each store. What advantages does each alternative have?

PSC, Inc.

OPERATIONS TOUR

PSC designs and produces a variety of laser bar code scanning devices. The products include handheld bar code readers, high-speed fixed-position industrial scanners, and retail checkout scanners as well as a full line of accessories, software, and supplies to support its products. Headquartered in Eugene, Oregon, the company has manufacturing facilities in Eugene and Paris, France, with roughly 1,200 employees worldwide.

Products

Bar code scanners are designed for a variety of situations that can involve long-range scanning, reading small bar codes, and performing high-speed scans. They are used extensively in industry, business, and government to manage and control the entire supply chain, which includes suppliers, production, warehousing, distribution, retail sales, and service. Examples of bar code readers include the familiar point-of-sale scanners encountered at supermarkets and other retail stores. They come in a variety of forms, ranging from handheld to built-in models. High-speed, unattended scanners are used for automated material handling and sorting. Typical installations include high-volume distribution centers such as JC Penney's catalog operation and airport baggage handling systems. The company also produces "reader engines" that it supplies to other companies for use in their products. These may be as small as 1.2 cubic inches. One application for an "engine product" is found in lottery ticket validation machines. Use of bar code readers has greatly increased the speed and accuracy of data collection, resulting in increased productivity, improved production and inventory tracking and control, and improved market information.

Operations

Forecasting Forecasting is not a significant activity at PSC due to several factors. There is high standardization of scanner components, which creates stability in usage requirements. Supplier lead times are relatively short, often only a few days. Orders are typically small; 70 percent of all orders are for 10 units or less. There is a fair degree of production flexibility, particularly in terms of product customization. As a result of these factors, the company relies mainly on short-term, moving average forecasts.

Product Design PSC has developed a robust design in many of its products, enabling them to perform effectively under a broad range of operating conditions. For example, many of its handheld scanners can operate at temperatures ranging from −22° F to 120° F, and can withstand drops onto concrete surfaces from heights up to six feet and still function. This has enabled the company to offer warranties ranging from 24 to 36 months, far exceeding the industry standard of 3 to 12 months.

Layout PSC has developed an efficient production layout that consists of assembly lines and work centers. The assembly lines handle standardized production and subassemblies and the work centers handle final assembly and customization of products. Assembly lines are U-shaped to facilitate communication among workers. The work centers are designed for production flexibility; they can be reconfigured in about four hours. Work centers are staffed by teams of three to six cross-trained workers who are responsible for an order from start to finish.

The Production Process Production involves a combination of assembly line and batch processing that provides high volume and flexibility to customized individual orders. Because of the high standardization among the internal components of different scanners, many of the subassemblies can be produced on assembly lines. Customization is done primarily on the external portion of various products according to customer specification.

The production process for scanner engines is depicted in the process flowchart shown in the figure. The process begins when an order is received from a customer. The order is then configured according to customer specifications. Next it is entered into the computer to obtain a bill of materials (BOM), and the order is transmitted to production control so that it can be scheduled for production. A "traveler" packet containing product specifications and the BOM is created. It will accompany the order throughout the process.

The traveler is sent to the "kitting" area where standard parts and any customized parts are obtained and placed into a bin ("kit") and then placed in a flow rack until the assigned work center is ready for the job (i.e., a pull system).

The next phase of the process transforms unprogrammed, panelized circuit boards into programmed boards. The boards first pass through a screen printer which uses a stencil to coat the boards with a solder paste. Next the boards pass through a chip mounter which enters values for the smaller, passive components of the circuit board at a rate of 25,000 parts per hour. A second mounter enters values for the larger, programmable components at a rate of 7,000 parts per hour. The slower rate for the larger components is offset by the fact that there are fewer of those components. The process ends up being balanced, and no bottlenecks occur.

The programmed boards move by conveyor to a station for visual inspection. Rejects are returned to the chip mounter area, and boards that pass are sent through an oven to solidify the solder, making the programming permanent. The circuit boards are then removed from the panels and placed into the kit. The kits

(continued)

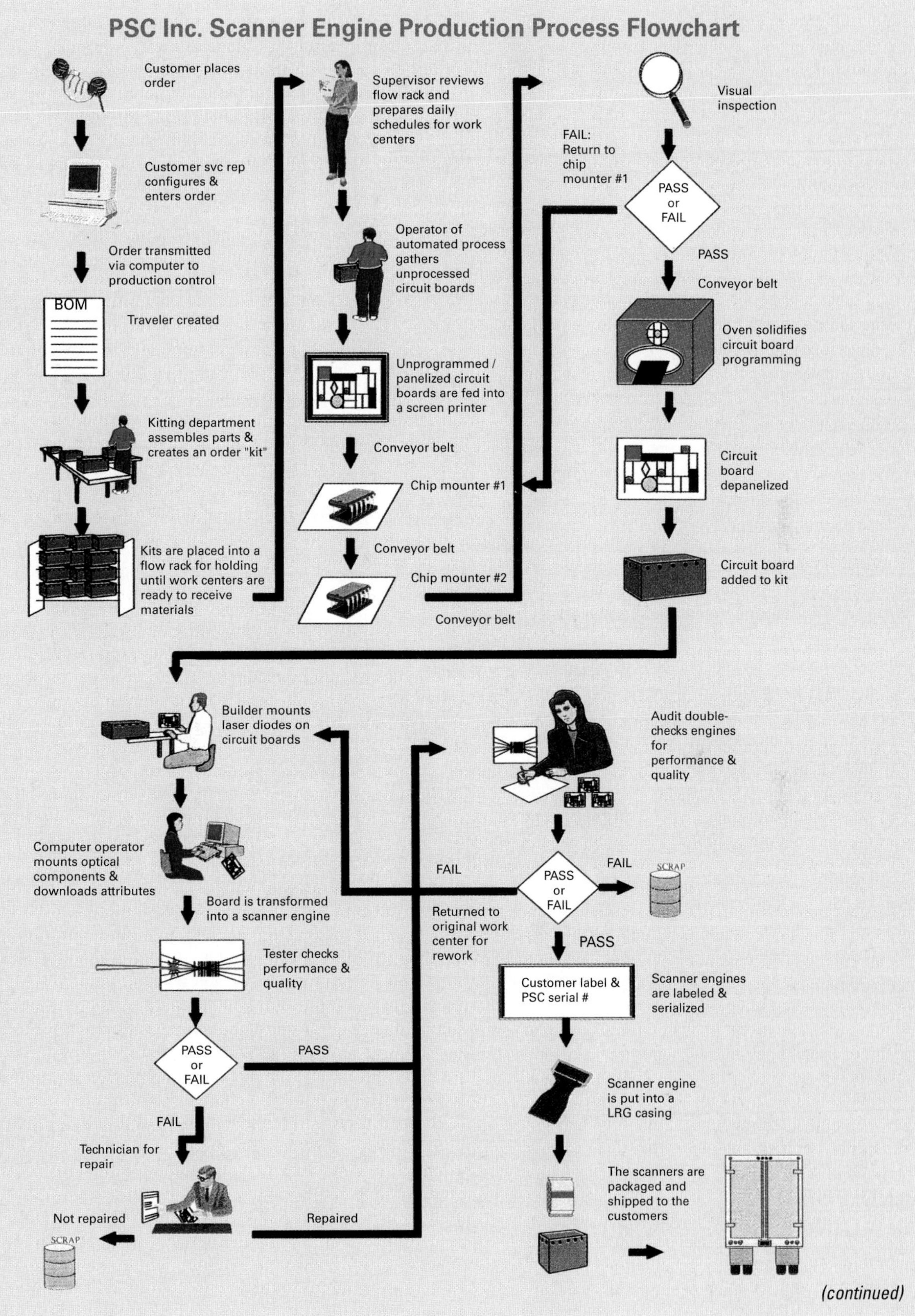
PSC Inc. Scanner Engine Production Process Flowchart
Customer places order
Customer svc rep configures & enters order
Order transmitted via computer to production control
BOM
Traveler created
Kitting department assembles parts & creates an order "kit"
Kits are placed into a flow rack for holding until work centers are ready to receive materials
Supervisor reviews flow rack and prepares daily schedules for work centers
Operator of automated process gathers unprocessed circuit boards
Unprogrammed / panelized circuit boards are fed into a screen printer
Conveyor belt
Chip mounter #1
Conveyor belt
Chip mounter #2
Conveyor belt
Visual inspection
FAIL: Return to chip mounter #1
PASS or FAIL
PASS
Conveyor belt
Oven solidifies circuit board programming
Circuit board depanelized
Circuit board added to kit
Builder mounts laser diodes on circuit boards
Computer operator mounts optical components & downloads attributes
Board is transformed into a scanner engine
Tester checks performance & quality
PASS or FAIL
PASS
FAIL
Technician for repair
Not repaired
SCRAP
Repaired
Audit double-checks engines for performance & quality
FAIL
PASS or FAIL
FAIL
SCRAP
Returned to original work center for rework
PASS
Customer label & PSC serial #
Scanner engines are labeled & serialized
Scanner engine is put into a LRG casing
The scanners are packaged and shipped to the customers

(continued)

(concluded)

are then taken to designated work centers for customization and placement in scanner engines.

Work centers typically have builders, computer operators, and a tester. A builder mounts the laser diodes on the circuit board and passes it to a computer operator who downloads the customer specifications into the microprocessor of the scan engine. The operator also mounts the optical components and adjusts them for the design of the scanner (e.g., long-range scanning). Next, the engine goes to the tester, who checks to make sure that the scanner is capable of reading bar codes and laser characteristics. Engines that fail are sent for repair and later retested. If the engine fails a second time, it is either returned for further repair or scrapped. Engines which pass are placed in an electrostatic bag which protects them from static electricity that could damage the programming.

Engines are then sent to Audit for another check for performance quality.

Engines that pass are incorporated into the final product, a serial number is added, along with a label, and the product is sent to the packing area and then shipped to the customer.

Inventory The company uses a variety of methods for inventory management, and it attempts to minimize the amount of inventory. A computer determines component requirements and generates purchase orders for the components for each order, and then appropriate orders for various components from vendors are prepared. However, the company maintains a stock of standard components that are replenished using a reorderpoint system. The company has adopted point-of-use replenishment for some areas of operations, having deliveries come directly to the production floor. Finished products are immediately shipped to the customer, which enhances the company's delivery performance and avoids finished goods inventory.

Suppliers Approximately 40 vendors supply parts and materials to PSC, each of which has been subjected to a multiple-step supplier certification program that includes the supplier's completing a self-evaluation questionnaire; an on-site visit of supplier facilities by a team from PSC made up of people from engineering, purchasing, and operations; a probation period; and rating of products using government MIL-STD 105 specifications. Vendor performance is tracked on product quality, delivery, and service.

When an item is removed from inventory, it is scanned into the computer, and this information is transmitted directly to suppliers, along with purchase orders to restock components.

Quality Quality is strongly emphasized at PSC. Employees are trained in quality concepts and the use of quality tools. Training is incorporated on-the-job so that employees can see the practical applications of what they are learning. Employees are responsible for performing in-process quality checks (quality at the source), and to report any defects they discover to their supervisor. Defects are assigned to one of three categories for problem solving:

- Operator/training error. The supervisor notifies a trainer who then provides appropriate retraining.
- Process/equipment problem. The supervisor notifies the manufacturing engineer who is then responsible for diagnosing the cause and correcting the problem.
- Parts/material problem. The supervisor notifies quality assurance, who then notifies the vendor to correct the problem. Defective parts are either scrapped or returned to the vendor.

Lean Production

PSC strives to operate on lean production principles. In addition to emphasizing high levels of quality, production flexibility, low levels of inventories, and having some deliveries come right to the production floor, its organization structure is fairly flat, and it uses a team approach. Still another feature of lean production is that many of PSC's workers are multiskilled. The company encourages employees to master new skills through a pay-for-skill program, and bases hourly pay rates on the number of skills a worker can perform.

Business Strategy

The company has developed what it believes is a strong strategy for success. Strategic initiatives include anticipating customer demand for miniaturization and the ability to customize products; expanding its proprietary technology; and expanding internationally into Western Europe (now accounts for about 35 percent of sales) and the Pacific rim (now accounts for about 10 percent of sales). Several plants or groups are ISO certified, which has been important for European sales. The company intends to continue to expand its product lines through acquisition of other companies.

SELECTED BIBLIOGRAPHY AND FURTHER READINGS

Hopp, Wallace J., and Mark L. Spearman. *Factory Physics.* 3rd ed. New York: Irwin/McGraw-Hill, 2007.

Peterson, R., and E. A. Silver. *Decision Systems for Inventory Management and Production Planning.* 2nd ed. New York: John Wiley & Sons, 1998.

Zipkin, Paul. *Foundations of Inventory Management.* New York: Irwin/McGraw-Hill, 2000.

JIT and Lean Operations

CHAPTER OUTLINE

LEARNING OBJECTIVES

After completing this chapter, you should be able to:

1. Explain what is meant by the term *lean operations system.*
2. List each of the goals of a lean system and explain its importance.
3. List and briefly describe the building blocks of lean.
4. Identify the benefits of a lean system.
5. Outline the considerations important in converting a traditional mode of operations to a lean system.
6. Point out some of the obstacles that might be encountered when converting to a lean system.
7. Describe value stream mapping.

As business organizations strive to maintain competitiveness in an ever-changing global economy, they are increasingly seeking new and better ways of operating. For some, this means changing from the traditional ways of operating to what is now referred to as lean operation. A **lean operation** is a flexible system of operation that uses considerably fewer resources (i.e., activities, people, inventory, and floor space) than a traditional system. Moreover, lean systems tend to achieve greater productivity, lower costs, shorter cycle times, and higher quality than nonlean systems.

Lean operation A flexible system that uses minimal resources and produces high-quality goods or services.

Lean systems are sometimes referred to as **just-in-time (JIT)** systems owing to their highly coordinated activities and delivery of goods that occur just as they are needed. The lean approach was pioneered by Toyota's founder, Taiichi Ohno, and Shigeo Shingo as a much faster and less costly way of producing automobiles. Following its success, today the lean approach is being applied in a wide range of manufacturing and service operations.

Just-in-time (JIT) A highly coordinated processing system in which goods move through the system, and services are performed, just as they are needed.

Lean is both a philosophy and a methodology that focuses on eliminating waste (non-value-added activities) and streamlining operations by closely coordinating all activities. Lean systems have three basic elements: They are demand driven, are focused on waste reduction, and have a culture that is dedicated to excellence and continuous improvement.

This chapter describes the lean production approach, including the basic elements of these systems and what it takes to make them work effectively. It also points out the benefits of these systems and the potential obstacles that companies may encounter when they attempt to convert from a traditional system to a lean production system.

INTRODUCTION

Lean operations began as lean manufacturing in the mid-1900s. It was developed by the Japanese automobile manufacturer Toyota. The development in Japan was influenced by the limited resources available at the time. Not surprisingly, the Japanese were very sensitive to waste and inefficiency. Widespread interest in lean manufacturing occurred after a book about automobile production, *The Machine That Changed the World,* by James Womack, Daniel Jones, and Daniel Roos, was published in 1990. As described in the book, Toyota's focus was on the elimination of all waste from every aspect of the process. Waste was defined as anything that interfered with, or did not add value to, the process of producing automobiles.

A stunning example of the potential of lean manufacturing was illustrated by the successful adoption of lean methods in the mid-1980s in a Fremont, California, auto plant. The plant was originally operated by General Motors (GM). However, GM closed the plant in 1982 because of its low productivity and high absenteeism. A few years later the plant was reopened as a joint venture of Toyota and GM, called NUMMI (New United Motor Manufacturing, Inc.). About 80 percent of the former plant workers were rehired, but the white-collar jobs were shifted from directing to supporting workers, and small teams were formed and trained to design, measure, and improve their performance. The result? By 1985 productivity and quality improved dramatically, exceeding all other GM plants, and absenteeism was negligible.

As other North American companies attempted to adopt the lean approach, they began to realize that in order to be successful, they needed to make major organizational and cultural changes. They also recognized that mass production, which emphasizes the efficiency of individual operations and leads to unbalanced systems and large inventories, was outmoded. Instead, they discovered that lean methods involve demand-based operations, flexible operations with rapid changeover capability, effective worker behaviors, and continuous improvement efforts.

Some of the philosophies used by NUMMI and other lean manufacturers are described in the next section.

The Toyota Approach

Many of the methods that are common to lean operations were developed as part of Japanese car maker Toyota's approach to manufacturing. You can get a sense of that approach from some of the terms commonly associated with lean operations:

Muda Waste and inefficiency.

Pull system Replacing material or parts based on demand.

Kanban A manual system that signals the need for parts or materials.

- **Muda:** Waste and inefficiency. Perhaps the driving philosophy. Waste and inefficiency can be minimized by using the following tactics.
- **Pull system:** Replacing material or parts based on demand; produce only what is needed.
- **Kanban:** A manual system used for controlling the movement of parts and materials that responds to *signals* of the need (i.e., demand) for delivery of parts or materials. This applies both to delivery to the factory and delivery to each workstation. The result is the delivery of a steady stream of containers of parts throughout the workday. Each container holds a small supply of parts or materials. New containers are delivered to replace empty containers.

Heijunka Workload leveling.

Kaizen Continuous improvement of the system.

Jidoka Quality at the source (autonomation).

- **Heijunka:** Variations in production volume lead to waste. The workload must be leveled; volume and variety must be averaged to achieve a steady flow of work.
- **Kaizen:** Continuous improvement of the system. There is always room for improvement, so this effort must be ongoing.
- **Jidoka:** Quality at the source. A machine automatically stops when it detects a bad part. A worker then stops the line. Also known as *autonomation.*
- **Team concept:** Use small teams of workers for process improvement.

In the mid-1920s, the Ford assembly plant in River Rouge, Michigan, was a state-of-the-art industrial complex employing over 75,000 workers. In 1982, Eiji Toyoda, head of the Toyota Company, toasted Ford's then-president Philip Caldwell, saying, "There is no secret to how we learned to do what we do—we learned it at the Rouge."

Toyota Recalls

READING

In recent years Toyota has been plagued by more than a few recalls of its popular vehicles. This was somewhat surprising, given Toyota's reputation as a world leader in quality and lean production. Various news reports pointed to the following as possible causes: overdoing its quest for cost reduction; failure to heed early reports of problems and address them, possibly due to a refusal to admit there were problems; and increased difficulty in overseeing the entire system from Japan as overseas sales expanded.

In some respects, the just-in-time concept was operational over 60 years ago at Henry Ford's great industrial complex in River Rouge, Michigan.

Toyota learned a great deal from studying Ford's operations and based its lean approach on what it saw. However, Toyota was able to accomplish something that Ford couldn't: a system that could handle some variety.

A widely held view of JIT/lean production is that it is simply a system for scheduling production that results in low levels of work-in-process and inventory. But in its truest sense, JIT/lean production represents a *philosophy* that encompasses every aspect of the process, from design to after the sale of a product. The philosophy is to pursue a system that functions well with minimal levels of inventories, minimal waste, minimal space, and minimal transactions. Truly, a *lean* system. As such, it must be a system that is not prone to disruptions and is flexible in terms of the product variety and range of volume that it can handle.

In lean systems, quality is ingrained in both the product and the process. Companies that use lean operations have achieved a level of quality that enables them to function with small batch sizes and tight schedules. Lean systems have high reliability; major sources of inefficiency and disruption have been eliminated, and workers have been trained not only to function in the system but also to continuously improve it.

The ultimate goal of a lean operation is to achieve a system that matches supply to customer demand; supply is synchronized to meet customer demand in a smooth, uninterrupted flow. Figure 14.1 provides an overview of the goals and building blocks of a lean system. The following pages provide more details about the supporting goals and building blocks.

FIGURE 14.1
An overview of the goals and building blocks of lean systems

Source: Adapted from Thomas E. Vollmann, William L. Berry, and D. Clay Whybark, *Manufacturing Planning and Control Systems,* 5th ed. Copyright 2005 Irwin/McGraw-Hill Companies, Inc. Used with permission.

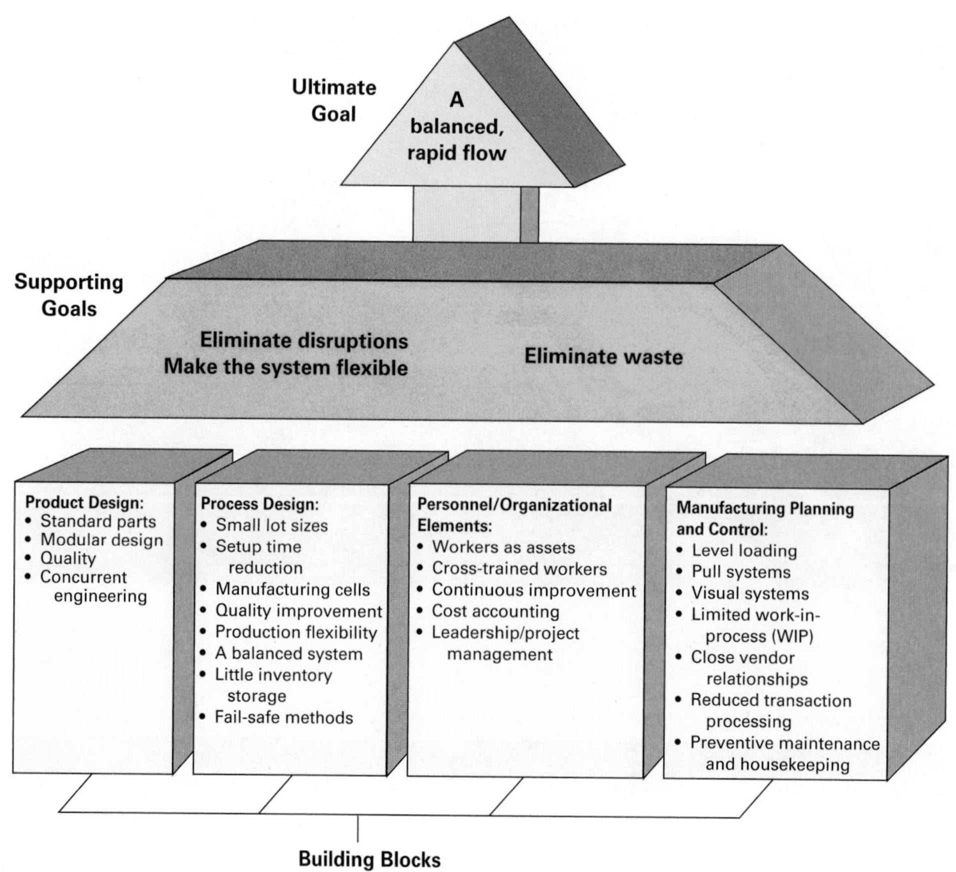

SUPPORTING GOALS

The ultimate goal of lean is a *balanced* system, that is, one that achieves a smooth, rapid flow of materials and/or work through the system. The idea is to make the process time as short as possible by using resources in the best possible way. The degree to which the overall goal is achieved depends on how well certain supporting goals are achieved. Those goals are to

1. Eliminate disruptions.
2. Make the system flexible.
3. Eliminate waste, especially excess inventory.

Disruptions have a negative influence on the system by upsetting the smooth flow of products through the system, and they should be eliminated. Disruptions are caused by a variety of factors, such as poor quality, equipment breakdowns, changes to the schedule, and late deliveries. Quality problems are particularly disruptive because in lean systems there is no extra inventory that can be used to replace defective items. All disruptions should be eliminated where possible. This will reduce the uncertainty that the system must deal with.

A *flexible system* is one that is robust enough to handle a mix of products, often on a daily basis, and to handle changes in the level of output while still maintaining balance and throughput speed. This enables the system to deal with some uncertainty. Long setup times and long lead times negatively impact the flexibility of the system. Hence, reduction of setup and lead times is very important in a lean system.

Waste represents unproductive resources; eliminating waste can free up resources and enhance production. *Inventory* is an idle resource, taking up space and adding cost to the system. It should be minimized as much as possible. In the lean philosophy, there are seven wastes:

1. **Inventory**—beyond minimal quantities, an idle resource, takes up floor space, and adds to cost.
2. **Overproduction**—involves excessive use of manufacturing resources.
3. **Waiting time**—requires space, adds no value.
4. **Unnecessary transporting**—increases handling, increases work-in-process inventory.
5. **Processing waste**—makes unnecessary production steps, scrap.
6. **Inefficient work methods**—reduce productivity, increase scrap, increase work-in-process inventory.
7. **Product defects**—require rework costs and possible lost sales due to customer dissatisfaction.

The existence of these wastes is an indication that improvement is possible. The list of wastes also can identify potential targets for continuous improvement efforts.

The *kaizen* philosophy for eliminating waste is based on the following tenets:[1]

1. Waste is the enemy, and to eliminate waste it is necessary to get the hands dirty.
2. Improvement should be done gradually and continuously; the goal is not big improvements done intermittently.
3. Everyone should be involved: top managers, middle managers, and workers.
4. *Kaizen* is built on a cheap strategy, and it does not require spending great sums on technology or consultants.
5. It can be applied anywhere.
6. It is supported by a visual system: a total transparency of procedures, processes, and values, making problems and wastes visible to all.
7. It focuses attention where value is created.
8. It is process oriented.
9. It stresses that the main effort of improvement should come from new thinking and a new work style.
10. The essence of organizational learning is to learn while doing.

BUILDING BLOCKS

The design and operation of a lean system provide the foundation for accomplishing the aforementioned goals. As shown in Figure 14.1, the building blocks are:

1. Product design.
2. Process design.
3. Personnel/organizational elements.
4. Manufacturing planning and control.

Speed and simplicity are two common threads that run through these building blocks.

Product Design

Four elements of product design are important for a lean production system:

1. Standard parts.
2. Modular design.

[1]Adapted from Jorge Nascimento Rodrigues with Masaaki Imai, "Masaaki Imai: The Father of Kaizen," www.gurusonline.tv/uk/conteudos/imai.asp.

3. Highly capable production systems with quality built in.
4. Concurrent engineering.

The first two elements relate to speed and simplicity.

The use of *standard parts* means that workers have fewer parts to deal with, and training times and costs are reduced. Purchasing, handling, and checking quality are more routine and lend themselves to continual improvement. Another important benefit is the ability to use standard processing.

Modular design is an extension of standard parts. Modules are clusters of parts treated as a single unit. This greatly reduces the number of parts to deal with, simplifying assembly, purchasing, handling, training, and so on. Standardization has the added benefit of reducing the number of different parts contained in the bill of materials for various products, thereby simplifying the bill of materials.

Lean requires highly capable production systems. Quality is the sine qua non ("without which not") of lean. It is crucial to lean systems because poor quality can create major disruptions. Quality must be embedded in goods and processes. The systems are geared to a smooth flow of work; the occurrence of problems due to poor quality creates disruption in this flow. Because of small lot sizes and the absence of buffer stock, production must cease when problems occur, and it cannot resume until the problems have been resolved. Obviously, shutting down an entire process is costly and cuts into planned output levels, so it becomes imperative to try to avoid shutdowns and to quickly resolve problems when they do appear.

Lean systems use a comprehensive approach to quality. Quality is designed into the product and the production process. High quality levels can occur because lean systems produce standardized products that lead to standardized job methods, employ workers who are very familiar with their jobs, and use standardized equipment. Moreover, the cost of product design quality (i.e., building quality in at the *design* stage) can be spread over many units, yielding a low cost per unit. It is also important to choose appropriate quality levels in terms of the final customer and of manufacturing capability. Thus, product design and process design must go hand in hand.

Engineering changes can be very disruptive to smooth operations. Concurrent engineering practices (described in Chapter 4) can substantially reduce these disruptions.

Process Design

Eight aspects of process design are particularly important for lean production systems:

1. Small lot sizes.
2. Setup time reduction.
3. Manufacturing cells.
4. Quality improvement.
5. Production flexibility.
6. A balanced system.
7. Little inventory storage.
8. Fail-safe methods.

Small Lot Sizes. In the lean philosophy, the ideal lot size is one unit, a quantity that may not always be realistic owing to practical considerations requiring minimum lot sizes (e.g., machines that process multiple items simultaneously, heat-treating equipment that processes multiple items simultaneously, and machines with very long setup times). Nevertheless, the goal is still to reduce the lot size as much as possible. Small lot sizes in both the production process and deliveries from suppliers yield a number of benefits that enable lean systems to operate effectively. First, with small lots moving through the system, in-process inventory is considerably less than it is with large lots. This reduces carrying costs, space requirements, and clutter in the workplace. Second, inspection and

A = units of product A
B = units of product B
C = units of product C

Small-lot approach

AAA BBBBBBB CC AAA BBBBBBB CC AAA BBBBBBB CC AAA BBBBBBB CC

Time →

Large-lot approach

AAAAAAAAAAAA BBBBBBBBBBBBBBBBBBBBBBBBB CCCCCCCCC AAAAAAAAAAA

Time →

FIGURE 14.2
Small-versus large-lot run sizes

rework costs are less when problems with quality occur, because there are fewer items in a lot to inspect and rework.

Small lots also permit greater flexibility in scheduling. Repetitive systems typically produce a small variety of products. In traditional systems, this usually means long production runs of each product, one after the other. Although this spreads the setup cost for a run over many items, it also results in long cycles over the entire range of products. For instance, suppose a firm has three product versions, A, B, and C. In a traditional system, there would be a long-run of version A (e.g., covering two or three days or more), then a long-run of version B, followed by a long-run of version C before the sequence would repeat. In contrast, a lean system, using small lots, would frequently shift from producing A to producing B and C. This flexibility enables lean systems to respond more quickly to changing customer demands for output: lean systems can produce just what is needed, when it is needed. The contrast between small and large lot sizes is illustrated in Figure 14.2. A summary of the benefits of small lot sizes is presented in Table 14.1.

It is important to note that the use of small lot sizes is not in conflict with the economic order quantity (EOQ) approach. The fact is that two aspects of the lean philosophy support small EOQ lot sizes. One is that inventory holding cost is deemed to be high, but because this cost is based on the average inventory, inventory costs can be lowered by reducing the lot size, which reduces average inventory. Second, reducing the setup cost is emphasized. Thus, both higher holding costs and lower setup costs act to reduce the optimal lot size.

Setup Time Reduction. Small lots and changing product mixes require frequent setups. Unless these are quick and relatively inexpensive, the time and cost to accomplish them can be prohibitive. Moreover, long setup times require holding more inventory than with short setup times. Hence, there is strong emphasis on reducing setup times. In JIT, workers are often trained to do their own setups. Moreover, programs to reduce setup time and cost are used to achieve the desired results; a deliberate effort is required, and workers are usually a valuable part of the process.

TABLE 14.1
Benefits of small lot sizes

Benefits of small lot sizes
Reduced inventory, lower carrying costs
Less space required to store inventory
Less rework if defects occur
Less inventory to "work off" before implementing product improvements
Increased visibility of problems
Increased production flexibility
Increased ease of balancing operations

General Mills Turns to NASCAR to Reduce Changeover Time

READING

Karen Mills

MINNEAPOLIS—When General Mills wanted to cut the time it takes to make a product changeover at a Betty Crocker plant, it turned to NASCAR for help. The food company sent a team to work with a pit crew "because nobody can change over a car faster than these guys can," said Randy Darcy, senior vice president of General Mills' supply chain operations.

After studying the NASCAR crew, General Mills cut to 12 minutes—from as long as 412 hours—the time it takes to switch production lines from one Betty Crocker meal to another. One thing the mechanics learned from working with the NASCAR pit crew was to videotape each of the changeovers, then critique everything that happened.

Source: Excerpted from Karen Mills, "General Mills Looks Outside the Box for Innovation." Copyright © The Associated Press. Used with permission.

Single-minute exchange of die (SMED) A system for reducing changeover time.

Shigeo Shingo made a very significant contribution to lean operation with the development of what is called the **single-minute exchange of die (SMED)** system for reducing changeover time. It involves first categorizing changeover activities as either "internal" or "external" activities. Internal activities are those that can only be done while a machine is stopped (i.e., not running). Hence, they contribute to long changeover times. External activities are those that do not involve stopping the machine; they can be done before or after the changeover. Hence, they do not affect changeover time. After activities have been categorized, a simple approach to achieving quick changeovers is to convert as many internal activities as possible to external activities and then streamline the remaining internal activities.

The potential benefits that can be achieved using the SMED system were impressively illustrated in 1982 at Toyota, when the changeover time for a machine was reduced from 100 minutes to 3 minutes! The principles of the SMED system can be applied to any changeover operation.

Setup tools and equipment and setup procedures must be simple and standardized. Multipurpose equipment or attachments can help to reduce setup time. For instance, a machine with multiple spindles that can easily be rotated into place for different job requirements can drastically reduce job changeover time. Moreover, *group technology* (described in Chapter 6) may be used to reduce setup cost and time by capitalizing on similarities in recurring operations. For instance, parts that are similar in shape, materials, and so on, may require very similar setups. Processing them in sequence on the same equipment can reduce the need to completely change a setup; only minor adjustment may be necessary.

Manufacturing Cells. One characteristic of lean production systems is multiple *manufacturing cells.* The cells contain the machines and tools needed to process families of parts having similar processing requirements. In essence, the cells are highly specialized and efficient production centers. Among the important benefits of manufacturing cells are reduced changeover times, high utilization of equipment, and ease of cross-training operators.

Quality Improvement. The occurrence of quality defects during the process can disrupt the orderly flow of work. Consequently, problem solving is important when defects occur. Moreover, there is a never-ending quest for *quality improvement,* which often focuses on finding and eliminating the causes of problems so they do not continually crop up.

Autonomation Automatic detection of defects during production.

Lean production systems sometimes minimize defects through the use of **autonomation** (note the extra syllable *on* in the middle of the word). Also referred to as *jidoka,* it involves the automatic detection of defects during production. It can be used with machines or manual operations. It consists of two mechanisms: one for detecting defects when they occur and another for a human stopping production to correct the cause of the defects. Thus, the halting of production forces immediate attention to the problem, after which an investigation of the problem is conducted, and corrective action is taken to resolve the problem.

TABLE 14.2
Guidelines for increasing production flexibility

1. Reduce downtime due to changeovers by reducing changeover time.
2. Use preventive maintenance on key equipment to reduce breakdowns and downtime.
3. Cross-train workers so they can help when bottlenecks occur or other workers are absent. Train workers to handle equipment adjustments and minor repairs.
4. Use many small units of capacity; many small cells make it easier to shift capacity temporarily and to add or subtract capacity than a few units of large capacity.
5. Use offline buffers. Store infrequently used safety stock away from the production area to decrease congestion and to avoid continually turning it over.
6. Reserve capacity for important customers.

Source: Adapted from Edward M. Knod Jr. and Richard J. Schonberger, *Operations Management: Meeting Customers' Demands,* 7th ed. (New York: McGraw-Hill, 2001)

Work Flexibility. The overall goal of a lean system is to achieve the ability to process a mix of products or services in a smooth flow. One potential obstacle to this goal is bottlenecks that occur when portions of the system become overloaded. The existence of bottlenecks reflects inflexibilities in a system. Process design can increase *production flexibility* and reduce bottlenecks in a variety of ways. Table 14.2 lists some of the techniques used for this purpose.

A Balanced System. Line balancing of production lines (i.e., distributing the workload evenly among workstations) helps to achieve a rapid flow of work through the system. Time needed for work assigned to each workstation must be less than or equal to the cycle time. The cycle time is set equal to what is referred to as the *takt time.* (*Takt* is the German word for musical meter.) ***Takt* time** is the cycle time needed in a production system to match the pace of production to the demand rate. It is sometimes said to be the heartbeat of a lean production system.

***Takt* time** The cycle time needed to match customer demand for final product.

Takt time is often set for a work shift. The procedure for obtaining the *takt* time is:

1. Determine the net time available per shift by subtracting any nonproductive time from total shift time.
2. If there is more than one shift per day, multiply the net time per shift by the number of shifts to obtain the net available time per day.
3. Compute *takt* time by dividing the net available time by demand.

EXAMPLE 1

Given the following information, compute the *takt* time: Total time per shift is 480 minutes per day, and there are two shifts per day. There are two 20-minute rest breaks and a 30-minute lunch break per shift. Daily demand is 80 units.

SOLUTION

1. Compute net time available per shift:

Total time	480 minutes
Rest breaks	−40 minutes
Lunch	−30 minutes
	410 minutes per shift

2. Compute the net time available per day:

   410 minutes per shift
   × 2 shifts/day
   820 minutes per day

3. Compute the *takt* time:

$$\textit{Takt}\text{ time} = \frac{\text{Net time available per day}}{\text{Daily demand}} = \frac{820 \text{ minutes per day}}{80 \text{ units per day}} \quad (14\text{–}1)$$

$$= 10.25 \text{ minutes per cycle}$$

FIGURE 14.3 Large rocks (problems) are hidden by a high water level (inventory) in A. Lower water level (B) reveals rocks (problems such as bottlenecks, waste, poor timing). Once the large rocks are removed, the water level (inventory) can be lowered (C).

A

B

C

Once the *takt* time for the system has been determined, it can be used to determine the time that should be allotted to each workstation in the production process. Using the *takt* time results in minimizing work-in-process (WIP) inventory in instances where demand is stable and the system capacity matches demand. For unstable demand, additional inventory is needed to offset demand variability.

Inventory Storage. Lean systems are designed to *minimize* inventory storage. Recall that in the lean philosophy, inventory storage is a waste. Inventories are buffers that tend to cover up recurring problems that are never resolved, partly because they aren't obvious and partly because the presence of inventory makes them seem less serious. When a machine breaks down, it won't disrupt the system if there is a sufficient inventory of the machine's output to feed into the next workstation. The use of inventory as the "solution" can lead to increasing amounts of inventory if breakdowns increase. A better solution is to investigate the *causes* of machine breakdowns and focus on eliminating them. Similar problems with quality, unreliable vendors, and scheduling also can be solved by having ample inventories to fall back on. However, carrying all that extra inventory creates a tremendous burden in cost and space and allows problems to go unresolved.

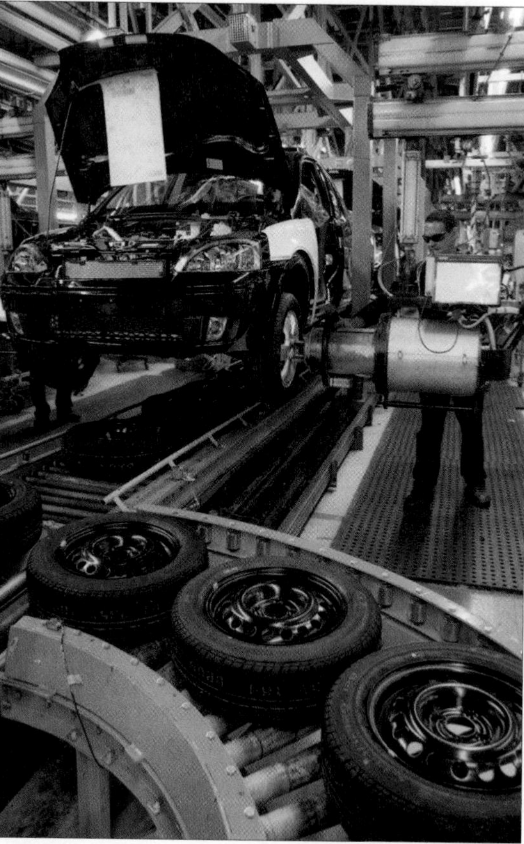
A worker attaches wheels and hubcaps to a GM Montana Sport pick-up truck on an assembly line in Brazil.

The lean approach is to pare down inventories gradually in order to uncover the problems. Once they are uncovered and solved, the system removes more inventory, finds and solves additional problems, and so on. A useful analogy is a boat on a pond that has large, hidden rocks. (See Figure 14.3.) The rocks represent problems that can hinder production (the boat). The water in the pond that covers the rocks is the inventory in the system. As the water level is slowly lowered, the largest rocks are the first to appear (those problems are the first to be identified). At that point, efforts are undertaken to remove these rocks from the water (resolve these problems). Once that has been accomplished, additional water is removed from the pond, revealing the next layer of rocks, which are then worked on. As more rocks are removed, the need for water to cover them diminishes. Likewise, as more of the major production problems are solved, there is less need to rely on inventory or other buffers.

Low inventories are the result of a *process* of successful problem solving, one that has occurred over time. Furthermore, because it is unlikely that all problems will be found and resolved, it is necessary to be able to deal quickly with problems when they do occur. Hence, there is a continuing need to identify and solve problems within a short time span to prevent new problems from disrupting the smooth flow of work through the system.

One way to minimize inventory storage in a lean system is to have deliveries from suppliers go directly to the production floor, which completely eliminates the need to store incoming parts and materials. At the other end of the process, completed units are shipped out as soon as they are ready, which minimizes storage of finished goods. Coupled with low work-in-process inventory, these features result in systems that operate with very little inventory.

Among the advantages of lower inventory are less carrying cost, less space needed, less tendency to rely on buffers, less rework if defects occur, and less need to "work off" current inventory before implementing design improvements. But carrying less inventory also has some risks: The primary one is that if problems arise, there is no safety net. Another is missed opportunities if the system is unable to respond quickly to them.

Pedal Pushers

READING

Tim Stevens

Across the street from the Fred Meyer store, behind a NAPA Auto Parts outlet in Eugene, Oregon, lies one of those gems you'd surely miss if you weren't looking for it. It's Green Gear Cycling Inc., manufacturer of Bike Friday, the largest-selling custom-made folding bike in the world. The bike fits into a car trunk, a tight storage space, or an optional suitcase to travel on a plane like regular baggage. (The suitcase even can be converted into a trailer to haul gear.) "Like Robinson Crusoe's man Friday, the Bike Friday is always there when you need it," says Alan Scholz, CEO.

Green Gear's operations are as distinctive as its product. A relatively small company ($3 million in sales, 30 employees, 17,000 sq. ft. of production space), Green Gear uses advanced manufacturing principles—adopted from Toyota Motor Corp. and others normally associated with considerably larger facilities. Management is split between Alan Scholz, who handles the business side, and his younger brother Hanz, product design and development manager.

Because of the uniqueness of its products, the company is able to command a premium price for them, and customers pay in advance. "It's not unusual for someone to call us with plane ticket in hand and say they are going on a trip, [and] can we have a bike ready for them in so many days," says Alan Scholz. "We can accommodate those kinds of requests, from decision-to-buy to riding in three days. Most bike manufacturers have terrible margins and huge lead times. They have no levers. We give people what they want, when they want it. If you do that, people are willing to pay you for it."

This year the company will build about 2,000 bikes to customer weight, measurements, and equipment specifications, at an average selling price of $1,700 including the optional case. Twenty-five percent of sales are to overseas customers, primarily in Japan, the UK, Australia, and Europe. On the list of Bike Friday riders are a nuclear weapons inspector who ordered a cycle specifically for his assignment in Iraq; David Robinson, former center for the NBA's San Antonio Spurs; comedian Dick Smothers; Tour de France winner Greg LeMond; and a woman who is only 52 in. tall, demonstrating the range of vehicles produced. Bike Friday can be offered about 2.5 million different ways depending on size, components, and color. Folding, custom-made recumbent and tandem bikes also are available.

Build-to-Order Basics

Built individually, each Green Gear cycle begins its life as a bundle of tubes, components, and other structures. These are processed through a build-to-order, flow-manufacturing configuration that is organized in a series of cells, a production system the company deployed from the very start. "If you are a batch manufacturer, it's like pulling teeth to get lean and build in production cells," says Scholz. "If you start off that way, the people you hire just think that's the way it's done."

In the first cell, a U-shaped configuration, an operator works multiple pieces of dedicated equipment, all set to run automatically so that he can multitask. Here tubing is cut and shaped into frame

(continued)

(concluded)

members before moving to a welding cell. The cells are designed so that any one cell can do some of the work of the previous or next cell if production runs behind or ahead.

"It works like a track relay with a transition area," says Hanz Scholz. "We've set up everything with single-process–specific tools so there is no process changeover time, which is part of the Toyota Production System (TPS)." The flow motto is "touch it once, do it now." Once work on a bike has begun, it flows through the process without hesitation at any point.

Takt time, the time between completion of bikes at the end of the process, is adjusted based on how sales are going—another TPS concept based on producing to demand, not projection. "We look at sales velocity and set the takt time to deliver units at that rate," says Hanz Scholz. In May of this year the rate averaged one bike every 1.5 hours across the mix of different models (it takes about nine hours to build one bike). When a 50-bike order came in from a Japanese distributor, however, takt time was slashed to 27 minutes. Takt-time reductions typically are accomplished with personnel from sales, service, and management departments supplemented with temps brought in to assist production.

Operating in a one-at-a-time flow system rather than in batches maximizes the chances for continuous improvement, according to Alan Scholz, who applies kaizen principles of continuous improvement to each bike. "For us, every bike is a batch, so we have 150 to 200 chances per month to make process improvements. A small manufacturer operating in a large-batch mode can be put out of business if he ruins just one. If you can make improvements as you find them, you can survive as a small manufacturer." When a quality problem is discovered, the operator switches on a red light and all procedures stop until the production cell is adjusted to eliminate the problem.

Stocking parts to cover the many variations of the bicycle would be far too costly for the company so, in lean-manufacturing style, inventory is handled kanban fashion, with parts reordered as they are used and minimum buffer stocks maintained based on vendor response time. Parts are pulled one bike at a time, three days before the ship date established by the customer, "just like Dell," says Scholz. "In fact the only difference between us and Dell is that you can't design a Bike Friday on the Internet . . . yet." (Michael Dell's wife Susan is a Bike Friday owner.)

"What's unique is that a company our size is handling inventory this way," says Scholz. "Many small companies feel it is too risky to operate like this, but we are proof that it can be successful." The kanban system replenishes inventory a little more often, "but it's a system that doesn't just order parts, it orders the right parts." Replenishing often so the company can operate at low inventory levels is an integral part of the cash-flow management expertise that helps make the company a success.

The company is in the process of moving to a "perpetual inventory" system that is expected to save thousands of dollars more in inventory. Parts will be reordered based on bikes sold, much as Kmart reorders based on sales rung at the cash register. "It's based on an MRP-type system, but without a lot of the things MRP requires," says Scholz. "Again, small companies tend not to have MRP because it costs too much." Green Gear's IS person is creating a system, based on a Microsoft Access database, to allow sales to "talk" to production. "The way it talks to production is through inventory. We'll be replacing inventory with information," Scholz notes.

Customers for Life

Lessons from Green Gear's success with lean manufacturing are applied to customer service and sales as well. Each sales consultant sits at a highly customized computer workstation, but with no desk. "That way it can't get cluttered up," says Hanz Scholz, "and for whatever they are doing, it encourages the 'touch it once, do it now' philosophy." Formerly housed in walled offices, the sales force now works in an open-office area. "If you have walls, you have barriers to the learning process," he adds. "Since we made the move, a lot of the fluctuations disappeared. Now all are selling in a similar way." And, since the change in September, sales are up 50%.

Green Gear practices a "Customers for Life" strategy it adopted from a luxury car dealer in Dallas. The dealer figured a customer that bought exclusively from him would spend in the neighborhood of $300,000 over his or her lifetime. "So," says Alan Scholz, "why nit-pick a $10 part?" A study of Bike Friday customers who have owned their bikes for more than three years shows there were repeat buys for other family members, adding a mountain bike or recumbent to the original "road" purchase, or upgrading to new technology. The company predicts a value of $10,000 to $25,000 for a lifetime customer. Therefore, it provides extra service at no cost when a bike comes in for repairs, or replaces a tire for free.

Source: Excerpted from Tim Stevens, "Pedal Pushers," *Industry Week*, July 17, 2000. Copyright © 2000 Penton Media, Inc. Used with permission.

Poka-yoke Safeguards built into a process to reduce the possibility of errors.

Fail-Safe Methods. Failsafing refers to building safeguards into a process to reduce or eliminate the potential for errors during a process. The term that was used initially was *baka-yoke,* which meant "foolproofing." However, due to its offensive connotation, the term was changed to **poka-yoke,** which means "mistake proofing." Some examples of failsafing include an alarm that sounds if the weight of a packaged item is too low, indicating missing components; putting assembly components in "egg cartons" to ensure that no parts are left out; and designing parts that can only be attached in the correct position. There are several everyday examples in vehicles, including signals that warn that the key is still in the ignition if the car door is opened, warn if a door is ajar, warn if seatbelts are not fastened, or warn if the fuel level is low. Other examples include an ATM signal if a card is left in a machine, detectors at department stores that signal if a monitoring tag hasn't been removed from an item, electrical fuses and circuit breakers that interrupt electrical supply if a circuit is overloaded, computers and other devices that won't operate if an incorrect password is used, and so on. Much of the credit for poka-yoke thinking is attributed to the work of Shigeo Shingo, who extensively promoted the use of failsafing in operations.

Personnel/Organizational Elements

There are five elements of personnel and organization that are particularly important for lean systems:

1. Workers as assets.
2. Cross-trained workers.
3. Continuous improvement.
4. Cost accounting.
5. Leadership/project management.

Workers as Assets. A fundamental tenet of the lean philosophy is that *workers are assets.* Well-trained and motivated workers are the heart of a lean system. They are given more authority to make decisions than their counterparts in more traditional systems, but they are also expected to do more.

"People" Firms Boost Profits, Study Shows

READING

Companies that treat employees as valuable assets, invest in training programs and use innovative workplace practices are more profitable than those that don't, a study found.

The two-year look at the workplace strategies of American companies was conducted by the management consulting firm Ernst & Young LLP for the Labor Department.

"This is a path-breaking study that shows the surest way to profits and productivity is to treat employees as assets to be developed rather than costs to be cut," Labor Secretary Robert Reich said at a press conference.

For the study, researchers at Harvard and Wharton business schools in partnership with the Ernst & Young Center for Business Innovation, reviewed over 100 papers examining business practices of thousands of U.S. companies.

The report focused on the economic benefits to companies of such Japanese-inspired concepts of labor-management cooperation as Just-In-Time inventory, which moves components to factories only as they are needed.

Among the findings:

- Economic benefits to companies were greatest when they successfully integrated innovations in management and technology with the appropriate employee training and "empowerment" programs.
- Companies investing in employee development enjoy significantly higher market values on average than their industry peers.
- Companies that were first among their competitors in implementing new management practices reaped the largest rewards.

According to the study, Motorola, Inc. estimates it earns $30 for every $1 invested in employee training, while Xerox Corp. found that in cooperation with its employee union it has reduced manufacturing costs by 30 percent and halved the time needed to develop new products.

Source: "People Firms Boost Profits, Study Shows."

Cross-Trained Workers. Workers are *cross-trained* to perform several parts of a process and operate a variety of machines. This adds to system flexibility because workers are able to help one another when bottlenecks occur or when a coworker is absent. It also helps line balancing.

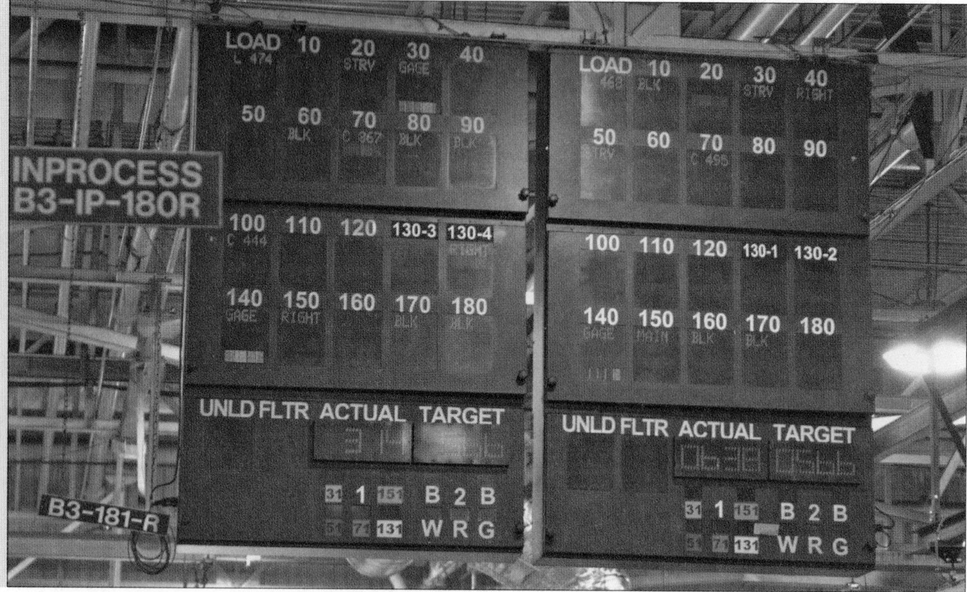

The Andon board in the GM Powertrain Engine facility is a visual communication tool. It advises employees of the real-time status of each machine within the manufacturing lines, enabling the production system to be run more effectively.

Continuous Improvement. Workers in a lean system have greater responsibility for quality than workers in traditional systems, and they are expected to be involved in problem solving and *continuous improvement.* Lean system workers receive extensive training in statistical process control, quality improvement, and problem solving.

Problem solving is a cornerstone of any lean system. Of interest are problems that interrupt, or have the potential to interrupt, the smooth flow of work through the system. When such problems surface, it becomes important to resolve them quickly. This may entail increasing inventory levels *temporarily* while the problem is investigated, but the intent of problem solving is to eliminate the problem, or at least greatly reduce the chances of it recurring.

Andon System of lights used at each workstation to signal problems or slowdowns.

Problems that occur during production must be dealt with quickly. Some companies use a light system to signal problems; in Japan, such a system is called *andon.* Each workstation is equipped with a set of three lights. A green light means no problems, an amber light means a worker is falling a little bit behind, and a red light indicates a serious problem. The purpose of the light system is to keep others in the system informed and to enable workers and supervisors to immediately see when and where problems are occurring.

Japanese companies have been very successful in forming teams composed of workers and managers who routinely work on problems. Moreover, workers are encouraged to report problems and potential problems to the teams.

It is important that all levels of management actively support and become involved in problem solving. This includes a willingness to provide financial support and to recognize achievements. It is desirable to formulate goals with the help of workers, publicize the goals, and carefully document accomplishments. Goals give workers something tangible to strive for; recognition can help maintain worker interest and morale.

A central theme of a true lean approach is to work toward continual improvement of the system—reducing inventories, reducing setup cost and time, improving quality, increasing the output rate, and generally cutting waste and inefficiency. Toward that end, problem solving becomes a way of life—a "culture" that must be assimilated into the thinking of management and workers alike. It becomes a never-ending quest for improving operations as all members of the organization strive to improve the system.

One challenge to continuous improvement is that once the "easy" improvements have been made, it becomes more difficult to keep workers motivated to continue to look for further improvements.

Workers in lean systems have more stress than their counterparts in more traditional systems. Stress comes not only from their added authority and responsibility but also from the high-paced system they work in, where there is little slack and a continual push to improve.

Cost Accounting. Another feature of some lean systems is the method of allocating overhead. Traditional accounting methods sometimes distort overhead allocation because they allocate it on the basis of direct labor hours. However, that approach does not always accurately reflect the consumption of overhead by different jobs. In addition, the number of direct labor hours in some industries has declined significantly over the years and now frequently accounts for a relatively small portion of the total cost. Conversely, other costs now represent a major portion of the total cost. Therefore, labor-intensive jobs (i.e., those that use relatively large proportions of direct labor) may be assigned a disproportionate share of overhead, one that does not truly reflect actual costs. That in turn can cause managers to make poor decisions. Furthermore, the need to track direct labor hours can itself involve considerable effort.

One alternative method of allocating overhead is **activity-based costing.** This method is designed to more closely reflect the actual amount of overhead consumed by a particular job or activity. Activity-based costing first identifies traceable costs and then assigns those costs to various types of activities such as machine setups, inspection, machine hours, direct labor hours, and movement of materials. Specific jobs are then assigned overhead based on the percentage of activities they consume.

Activity-based costing Allocation of overhead to specific jobs based on their percentage of activities.

Leadership/Project Management. Another feature of lean systems relates to *leadership.* Managers are expected to be leaders and facilitators, not order givers. Lean encourages two-way communication between workers and managers.

Manufacturing Planning and Control

Seven elements of manufacturing planning and control are particularly important for lean systems:

1. Level loading.
2. Pull systems.
3. Visual systems.
4. Limited work-in-process (WIP).
5. Close vendor relationships.
6. Reduced transaction processing.
7. Preventive maintenance and housekeeping.

Level Loading. Lean systems place a strong emphasis on achieving stable, level daily mix schedules. Toward that end, the master production schedule is developed to provide *level capacity loading.* That may entail a rate-based production schedule instead of the more familiar quantity-based schedule. Moreover, once established, production schedules are relatively fixed over a short time horizon, and this provides certainty to the system. Even so, some adjustments may be needed in day-to-day schedules to achieve level capacity requirements. Suppliers like level loading because it means smooth demand for them.

A level production schedule requires smooth production. When a company produces different products or product models, it is desirable to produce in small lots (to minimize work-in-process inventory and to maintain flexibility) and to spread the production of the different products throughout the day to achieve smooth production. The extreme case would be to produce one unit of one product, then one of another, then one of another, and so on. While this approach would allow for maximum smoothness, it would generally not be practical because it would generate excessive setup costs.

Mixed-model sequencing begins with daily production requirements of each product or model. For instance, suppose a department produces three models, A, B, and C, with these daily requirements:

Model	Daily Quantity
A	10
B	15
C	5

Three issues then need to be resolved. One is which sequence to use (C-B-A, A-C-B, etc.), another is how many times (i.e., cycles) the sequence should be repeated daily, and the third is how many units of each model to produce in each cycle.

The choice of sequence can depend on several factors, but the key one is usually the setup time or cost, which may vary depending on the sequence used. For instance, if two of the models, say A and C, are quite similar, the sequences A-C and C-A may involve only minimal setup changes, whereas the setup for model B may be more extensive. Choosing a sequence that has A-C or C-A will result in about 20 percent fewer setups over time than having B produced between A and C on every cycle.

The number of cycles per day depends on the daily production quantities. If every model is to be produced in every cycle, which is often the goal, determining the smallest integer that can be evenly divided into each model's daily quantity will indicate the number of cycles. This will be the fewest number of cycles that will contain one unit of the model with the lowest quantity requirements. For models A, B, and C shown in the preceding table, there should be five cycles (5 can be evenly divided into each quantity). High setup costs may cause a manager to use fewer cycles, trading off savings in setup costs and level production. If dividing by the smallest daily quantity does not yield an integer value for each model, a manager may opt for using the smallest production quantity to select a number of cycles, but then produce more of some items in some cycles to make up the difference.

Sometimes a manager determines the number of units of each model in each cycle by dividing each model's daily production quantity by the number of cycles. Using five cycles per day would yield the following:

Model	Daily Quantity	Units per Cycle
A	10	10/5 = 2
B	15	15/5 = 3
C	5	5/5 = 1

These quantities may be unworkable due to restrictions on lot sizes. For example, Model B may be packed four to a carton, so producing three units per cycle would mean that at times finished units (inventory) would have to wait until sufficient quantities were available to fill a crate. Similarly, there may be standard production lot sizes for some operations. A heat-treating process might involve a furnace that can handle six units at a time. If the different models require different furnace temperatures, they could not be grouped. What would be necessary here is an analysis of the trade-off between furnace lot size and the advantages of level production.

EXAMPLE 2

Determine a production plan for these three models using the sequence A-B-C:

Model	Daily Quantity
A	7
B	16
C	5

SOLUTION

The smallest daily quantity is 5, but dividing the other two quantities by 5 does not yield integers. The manager might still decide to use five cycles. Producing one unit of Models A and C and three units of Model B in each of the five cycles would leave the manager short two units of Model A and one unit of Model B. The manager might decide to intersperse those units like this to achieve nearly level production:

Cycle	1	2	3	4	5
Pattern	A B(3) C	A(2) B(3) C	A B(4) C	A(2) B(3) C	A B(3) C
Extra unit(s)		A	B	A	

If the requirement for Model A had been 8 units a day instead of 7, the manager might decide to use the following pattern:

Cycle	1	2	3	4	5
Pattern	A(2) B(3) C	A B(3) C	A(2) B(4) C	A B(3) C	A(2) B(3) C
Extra unit(s)	A		A B		A

Pull Systems. The terms *push* and *pull* are used to describe two different systems for moving work through a production process. In traditional production environments, a **push system** is used: When work is finished at a workstation, the output is *pushed* to the next station; or, in the case of the final operation, it is pushed on to final inventory. Conversely, in a **pull system,** control of moving the work rests with the following operation; each workstation *pulls* the output from the preceding station as it is needed; output of the final operation is pulled by customer demand or the master schedule. Thus, in a pull system, work moves on in response to demand from the next stage in the process, whereas in a push system, work moves on as it is completed, without regard to the next station's readiness for the work. Consequently, work may pile up at workstations that fall behind schedule because of equipment failure or the detection of a problem with quality.

Push system Work is pushed to the next station as it is completed.

Pull system A workstation pulls output from the preceding station as it is needed.

Communication moves backward through the system from station to station. Each workstation (i.e., customer) communicates its need for more work to the preceding workstation (i.e., supplier), thereby assuring that supply equals demand. Work moves "just in time" for the next operation; the flow of work is thereby coordinated, and the accumulation of excessive inventories between operations is avoided. Of course, some inventory is usually present because operations are not instantaneous. If a workstation waited until it received a request from the next workstation before starting its work, the next station would have to wait for the preceding station to perform its work. Therefore, by design, each workstation produces just enough output to meet the (anticipated) demand of the next station. This can be accomplished by having the succeeding workstation communicate its need for input sufficiently ahead of time to allow the preceding station to do the work. Or there can be a small buffer of

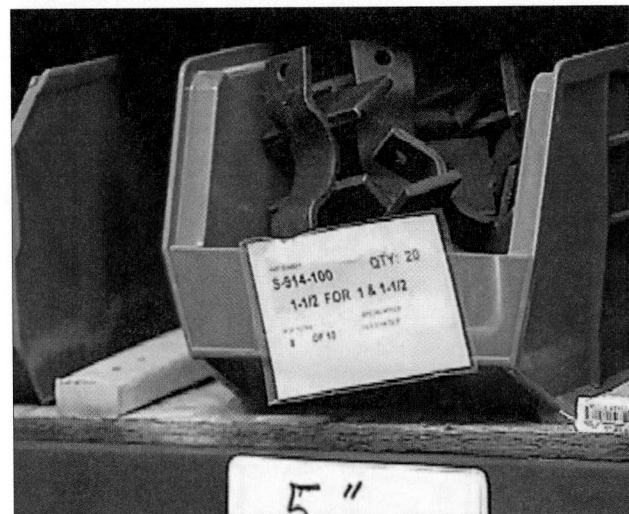

At TriState Industries, a kanban system is in effect to move work through the production system. Shown here, a kanban card provides the authorization to move or work on parts.

Special carts were designed that, when filled, act as a visual signal that they are ready to be moved to the next work cell. An empty cart indicates that it is time to produce, in order to refill the cart.

stock between stations; when the buffer decreases to a certain level, this signals the preceding station to produce enough output to replenish the buffer supply. The size of the buffer supply depends on the cycle time at the preceding workstation. If the cycle time is short, the station will need little or no buffer; if the cycle time is long, it will need a considerable amount of buffer. However, production occurs only in response to *usage* of the succeeding station; work is still pulled by the demand generated by the next operation.

Pull systems aren't necessarily appropriate for all manufacturing operations because they require a fairly steady flow of repetitive work. Large variations in volume, product mix, or product design will undermine the system.

Kanban Card or other device that communicates demand for work or materials from the preceding station.

Visual Systems. In a pull system work flow is dictated by "next-step demand." A system can communicate such demand in a variety of ways, including a shout or a wave, but by far the most commonly used device is the **kanban** card. *Kanban* is a Japanese word meaning "signal" or "visible record." When a worker needs materials or work from the preceding station, he or she uses a kanban card. In effect, the kanban card is the *authorization* to move or work on parts. In kanban systems, no part or lot can be moved or worked on without one of these cards.

There are two main types of kanbans:

1. **Production kanban (p-kanban):** signals the need to produce parts.
2. **Conveyance kanban (c-kanban):** signals the need to deliver parts to the next work center.

The system works this way: A kanban card is affixed to each container. When a workstation needs to replenish its supply of parts, a worker goes to the area where these parts are stored and withdraws one container of parts. Each container holds a predetermined quantity. The worker removes the kanban card from the container and posts it in a designated spot where it will be clearly visible, and the worker moves the container to the workstation. The posted kanban is then picked up by a stock person who replenishes the stock with another container, and so on down the line. Demand for parts triggers a replenishment, and parts are supplied as usage dictates. Similar withdrawals and replenishments—all controlled by kanbans—occur all the way up and down the line from vendors to finished-goods inventories. If supervisors decide the system is too loose because inventories are building up, they may decide to tighten the system and withdraw some kanbans. Conversely, if the system seems too tight, they may introduce additional kanbans to bring the system into balance. Vendors also can influence the number of containers. Moreover, trip times can affect the number: Longer trip times may lead to fewer but larger containers, while shorter trip times may involve a greater number of small containers.

It is apparent that the number of kanban cards in use is an important variable. One can compute the ideal number of kanban cards using this formula:

$$N = \frac{DT(1 + X)}{C} \quad (14\text{–}2)$$

where

N = Total number of containers (1 card per container)

D = Planned usage rate of using work center

T = Average waiting time for replenishment of parts plus average production time for a container of parts

X = Policy variable set by management that reflects possible inefficiency in the system (the closer to 0, the more efficient the system)

C = Capacity of a standard container (should be no more than 10 percent of daily usage of the part)

Note that D and T must use the same units (e.g., minutes, days).

EXAMPLE 3

Usage at a work center is 300 parts per day, and a standard container holds 25 parts. It takes an average of .12 day for a container to complete a circuit from the time a kanban card is received until the container is returned empty. Compute the number of kanban cards (containers) needed if $X = .20$.

SOLUTION

$N = ?$

$D = 300$ parts per day

$T = .12$ day

$C = 25$ parts per container

$X = .20$

$$N = \frac{300(.12)(1 + .20)}{25} = 1.728;\ \text{round to 2 containers}$$

Note: Rounding up will cause the system to be looser, and rounding down will cause it to be tighter. Usually, rounding up is used.

Although the goals of MRP and kanban are essentially the same (i.e., to improve customer service, reduce inventories, and increase productivity), their approaches are different. Neither MRP nor kanban is a stand-alone system—each exists within a larger framework. MRP is a computerized system; kanban is a manual system that may be part of a lean system, although lean can exist without kanban.

Kanban is essentially a two-bin type of inventory: Supplies are replenished semiautomatically when they reach a predetermined level. MRP is more concerned with projecting requirements and with planning and scheduling operations.

A major benefit of the kanban system is its simplicity; a major benefit of MRP is its ability to handle complex planning and scheduling. In addition, MRP II enables management to answer what-if questions for capacity planning.

The philosophies that underlie kanban systems are quite different from those traditionally held by manufacturers. Nonetheless, both approaches have their merits, so it probably would not make sense in most instances to switch from one method of operation to the other. Moreover, to do so would require a tremendous effort. It is noteworthy that at the same time that Western manufacturers are studying kanban systems, some Japanese manufacturers are studying MRP systems. This suggests the possibility that either system could be improved by incorporating selected elements of the other. That would take careful analysis to determine which elements to incorporate as well as careful implementation of selected elements, and close monitoring to assure that intended results were achieved.

Whether manufacturers should adopt the kanban method is debatable. Some form of it may be useful, but kanban is merely an information system; by itself it offers little in terms of helping manufacturers become more competitive or productive. By the same token, MRP alone will not achieve those results either. Instead, it is the overall approach to manufacturing that is crucial; it is the commitment and support of top management and the continuing efforts of all levels of management to find new ways to improve their manufacturing planning and control techniques, and to adapt those techniques to fit their particular circumstances, that will determine the degree of success.

Comment The use of either kanban or MRP does not preclude the use of the other. In fact, it is not unusual to find the two systems used in the same production facility. Some Japanese manufacturers, for example, are turning to MRP systems to help them plan production. Both approaches have their advantages and limitations. MRP systems provide the capability to explode the bill of materials to project timing and material requirements that can then be used to plan production. But the MRP assumption of fixed lead times and infinite capacity can often result in significant problems. At the shop floor level, the discipline of a kanban system, with materials pull, can be very effective. But kanban works best when there is a uniform flow through the shop; a variable flow requires buffers and this reduces the advantage of a pull system.

In effect, some situations are more conducive to a visual approach, others to an MRP approach. Still others can benefit from a hybrid of the two. Hybrid systems like kanban/ MRP can be successful if MRP is used for planning and kanban is used as the execution system.

Limited Work-in-Process (WIP). Movement of materials and work-in-process (WIP) in a lean system is carefully coordinated, so that they arrive at each step in a process just as they are needed. Controlling the amount of WIP in a production system can yield substantial benefits. One is lower carrying costs due to lower WIP inventory. Another is the increased flexibility that would be lost if there were large amounts of WIP in the system. In addition, low WIP aids scheduling and saves costs of rework and scrapping if there are design changes.

Controlling WIP also results in low cycle-time variability. WIP is determined by cycle time and the arrival rate of jobs. According to Little's law, WIP = Cycle time × Arrival rate. If both WIP and the arrival rate of jobs are held constant, the cycle time will also be constant. In a push system, the arrival rate of jobs is not held constant, so there is the possibility of large WIP buildups, which results in high variability in cycle times. This forces companies to quote longer lead times to customers to allow for variable cycle times.

There are two general approaches to controlling WIP; one is kanban and the other is constant work-in-process (CONWIP). Kanban's control of WIP focuses on individual workstations, while CONWIP'S focus is on the system as a whole. With CONWIP, when a job exits the system, a new job is allowed to enter. This results in a constant level of work-in-process.

Kanban works best in an environment that is stable and predictable. CONWIP offers an advantage if there is variability in a line, perhaps due to a breakdown in an operation or a quality problem. With kanban, upstream work is blocked and processing will stop fairly quickly, while with CONWIP upstream stations can continue to operate for a somewhat longer time. Then, after the reason for stoppage has been corrected, there will be less need to make up lost production than if the entire line had been shut down, as it would be under kanban. Also, in a mixed product environment, CONWIP can be easier than kanban because kanban focuses on specific part numbers whereas CONWIP does not.

Close Vendor Relationships. Lean systems typically have *close relationships with vendors,* who are expected to provide frequent small deliveries of high-quality goods. Traditionally, buyers have assumed the role of monitoring the quality of purchased goods, inspecting shipments for quality and quantity, and returning poor-quality goods to the vendor for rework. JIT systems have little slack, so poor-quality goods cause a disruption in the smooth flow of work. Moreover, the inspection of incoming goods is viewed as inefficient because it does not add value to the product. For these reasons, the burden of ensuring quality shifts to the vendor. Buyers work with vendors to help them achieve the desired quality levels and to impress upon them the importance of consistent, high-quality goods. The ultimate goal of the buyer is to be able to *certify* a vendor as a producer of high-quality goods. The implication of certification is that a vendor can be relied on to deliver high-quality goods without the need for buyer inspection.

Suppliers also must be willing and able to ship in small lots on a regular basis. Ideally, suppliers themselves will be operating under JIT systems. Buyers can often help suppliers convert to JIT production based on their own experiences. In effect, the supplier becomes part of an extended JIT system that integrates the facilities of buyer and supplier. Integration is easier when a supplier is dedicated to only one or a few buyers. In practice, a supplier is likely to have many different buyers, some using traditional systems and others using JIT. Consequently, compromises may have to be made by both buyers and suppliers.

Traditionally, a spirit of cooperation between buyer and seller has not been present; buyers and vendors have had a somewhat adversarial relationship. Buyers have generally regarded price as a major determinant in sourcing, and they have typically used *multiple-source* purchasing, which means having a list of potential vendors and buying from several to avoid getting locked into a sole source. In this way, buyers play vendors off against each other to get better pricing arrangements or other concessions. The downside is that vendors cannot rely on a long-term relationship with a buyer, and they feel no loyalty to a particular buyer. Furthermore, vendors have often sought to protect themselves from losing a buyer by increasing the number of buyers they supply.

Under JIT purchasing, good vendor relationships are very important. Buyers take measures to reduce their lists of suppliers, concentrating on maintaining close working relationships with a few good ones. Because of the need for frequent, small deliveries, many buyers attempt to find local vendors to shorten the lead time for deliveries and to reduce lead time variability. An added advantage of having vendors nearby is quick response when problems arise.

JIT purchasing is enhanced by long-term relationships between buyers and vendors. Vendors are more willing to commit resources to the job of shipping according to a buyer's JIT system given a long-term relationship. Moreover, price often becomes secondary to other aspects of the relationship (e.g., consistent high quality, flexibility, frequent small deliveries, and quick response to problems).

SUPPLY CHAIN

Supplier Tiers A key feature of many lean production systems is the relatively small number of suppliers used. In traditional production, companies often deal with hundreds or even thousands of suppliers in a highly centralized arrangement not unlike a giant wheel with many spokes. The company is at the hub of the wheel, and the spokes radiate out to suppliers, each of whom must deal directly with the company. In traditional systems, a supplier does not know the other suppliers or what they are doing. Each supplier works to specifications provided by the buyer. Suppliers have very little basis (or motivation) for suggesting improvements. Moreover, as companies play one supplier off against others, the sharing of information is more risky than rewarding. In contrast, lean production companies may employ a tiered approach for suppliers: They use relatively few first-tier suppliers who work directly with the company or who supply major subassemblies. The first-tier suppliers are responsible for dealing with second-tier suppliers who provide components for the subassemblies, thereby relieving the final buyer from dealing with large numbers of suppliers.

The automotive industry provides a good example of this situation. Suppose a certain car model has an electric seat. The seat and motor together might entail 250 separate parts. A traditional producer might use more than 30 suppliers for the electric seat, but a lean producer might use a single (first-tier) supplier who has the responsibility for the entire seat unit. The company would provide specifications for the overall unit, but leave to the supplier the details of the motor, springs, and so on. The first-tier supplier, in turn, might subcontract the motor to a second-tier supplier, the track to another second-tier supplier, and the cushions and fabric to still another. The second-tier suppliers might subcontract some of their work to third-tier suppliers, and so on. Each tier has only to deal with those just above it or just below it. Suppliers on each level are encouraged to work with each other, and they are motivated to do so because that increases the probability that the resulting item (the seat) will meet or exceed the final buyer's expectations. In this "team of suppliers" approach, all suppliers benefit from a successful product, and each supplier bears full responsibility for the quality of its portion of the product. Figure 14.4 illustrates the difference between the traditional approach and the tiered approach.

Reduced Transaction Processing. Traditional manufacturing systems often have many built-in transactions that do not add value. In their classic article, "The Hidden Factory,"[2] Jeffrey G. Miller and Thomas Vollmann identify a laundry list of transaction processing that comprises a "hidden factory" in traditional manufacturing planning and control systems, and point out the tremendous cost burden that results. The transactions can be classified as logistical, balancing, quality, or change transactions.

[2]Excerpted from Jeffrey Miller and Thomas Vollmann, "The Hidden Factory," *Harvard Business Review*, September/October 1985, pp. 141–50.

FIGURE 14.4 Traditional supplier network compared to supplier tiers

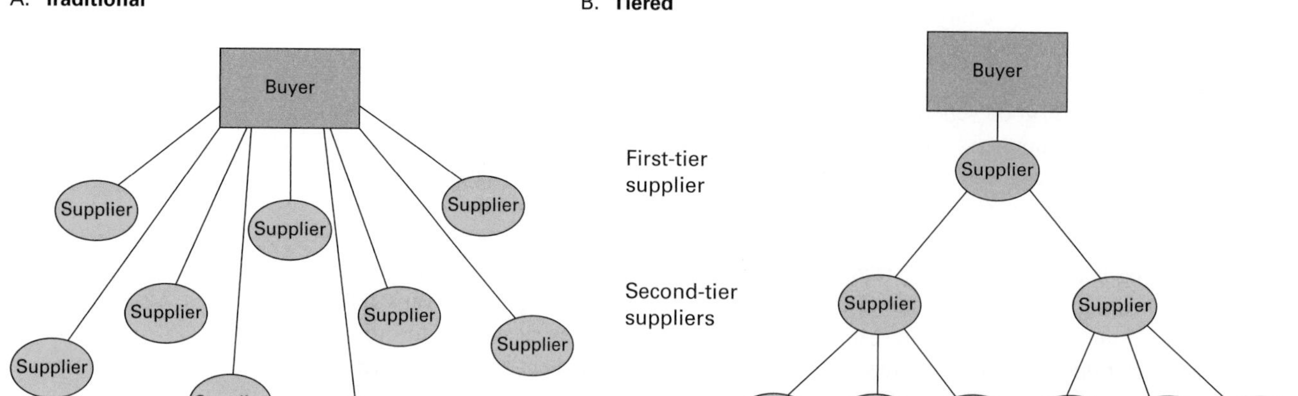

Logistical transactions include ordering, execution, and confirmation of materials transported from one location to another. Related costs cover shipping and receiving personnel, expediting orders, data entry, and data processing.

Balancing transactions include forecasting, production planning, production control, procurement, scheduling, and order processing. Associated costs relate to the personnel involved in these and supporting activities.

Quality transactions include determining and communicating specifications, monitoring, recording, and followup activities. Costs relate to appraisal, prevention, internal failures (e.g., scrap, rework, retesting, delays, administration activities) and external failures (e.g., warranty costs, product liability, returns, potential loss of future business).

Change transactions primarily involve engineering changes and the ensuing changes generated in specifications, bills of material, scheduling, processing instructions, and so on. Engineering changes are among the most costly of all transactions.

Lean systems cut transaction costs by reducing the number and frequency of transactions. For example, suppliers deliver goods directly to the production floor, bypassing the storeroom entirely, thereby avoiding the transactions related to receiving the shipment into inventory storage and later moving the materials to the production floor. In addition, vendors are certified for quality, eliminating the need to inspect incoming shipments for quality. The unending quest for quality improvement that pervades lean systems eliminates many of the above-mentioned quality transactions and their related costs. The use of bar coding (not exclusive to lean systems) can reduce data entry transactions and increase data accuracy.

Preventive Maintenance and Housekeeping. Because lean systems have very little in-process inventory, equipment breakdowns can be extremely disruptive. To minimize breakdowns, companies use **preventive maintenance** programs, which emphasize maintaining equipment in good operating condition and replacing parts that have a tendency to fail before they fail. Workers are often responsible for maintaining their own equipment.

Preventive maintenance Maintaining equipment in good operating condition and replacing parts that have a tendency to fail before they actually do fail.

Even with preventive maintenance, occasional equipment failures will occur. Companies must be prepared for this, so they can quickly return equipment to working order. This may mean maintaining supplies of critical spare parts and making other provisions for emergency situations, perhaps maintaining a small force of repair people or training workers to do certain repairs themselves. Note that when breakdowns do occur, they indicate potential opportunities to be exploited in a lean environment.

Housekeeping involves keeping the workplace clean as well as keeping it free of any materials that are not needed for production, because those materials take up space and may cause disruptions to the work flow.

Housekeeping Maintaining a workplace that is clean and free of unnecessary materials.

TABLE 14.3
Comparison of lean and traditional production philosophies

Factor	Traditional	Lean
Inventory	Much, to offset forecast errors, late deliveries	Minimal necessary to operate
Deliveries	Few, large	Many, small
Lot sizes	Large	Small
Setups, runs	Few, long runs	Many, short runs
Vendors	Long-term relationships are unusual	Partners
Workers	Necessary to do the work	Assets

Housekeeping is part of what is often referred to as the five S's, which are five behaviors intended to make the workplace effective:

1. **Sort.** Decide which items are needed to accomplish the work, and keep only those items.
2. **Straighten.** Organize the workplace so that the needed items can be accessed quickly and easily.
3. **Sweep.** Keep the workplace clean and ready for work. Perform equipment maintenance regularly.
4. **Standardize.** Use standard instructions and procedures for all work.
5. **Self-discipline.** Make sure that employees understand the need for an uncluttered workplace.

Among the benefits of the five S's are increased productivity, improved employee morale, decreased risk of accidents, and improved appearance for visitors. Employees and managers must appreciate the rationale for the five S's. Otherwise, they may view them as unnecessary and a waste of effort.

Lean systems have been described and compared with traditional manufacturing systems in the preceding pages. Table 14.3 provides a brief overview of those comparisons.

VALUE STREAM MAPPING

Business processes often become bloated with inefficiencies and waste, and over time, these inefficiencies become ingrained in the processes. Rooting out the inefficiencies and wastes using techniques such as value stream mapping offers tremendous opportunities to greatly improve these processes.

Value stream mapping is a visual tool to systematically examine the flow of materials and information involved in bringing a product or service to a consumer. The technique originated at Toyota, where it is referred to as "Material and Information Flow Mapping." The systematic attack on waste can lead to uncovering factors related to poor quality and management problems.

Value stream mapping A visual tool to systematically examine the flow of materials and information.

A value stream map provides an overview of the activities that comprise a process. Its purpose is to help identify waste and opportunities for improvement. Data collected during the mapping process might include times (e.g., cycle time, setup time, changeover time, touch time, lead time), distances traveled (e.g., by parts, workers, paperwork), mistakes (e.g., product defects, data entry errors), inefficient work methods (e.g., extra motions, excessive lifting or moving, repositioning), and waiting lines (e.g., workers waiting for parts or equipment repairs, orders waiting to be processed). Information flows are also included in the mapping process.

Once a value stream map is completed, data analysis can uncover improvement opportunities by asking key questions, such as:

Where are the process bottlenecks?

Where do errors occur?

Which processes have to deal with the most variation?

Where does waste occur?

All business organizations, whether they are primarily engaged in service or manufacturing, can benefit by applying lean principles to their office operations. This includes purchasing, accounting, order entry, and other office functions. Office wastes might include:

1. **Inventory**—excess suppliers and equipment.
2. **Overprocessing**—excess paperwork and redundant approvals.
3. **Waiting times**—orders waiting to be processed, requests for information awaiting answers.
4. **Unnecessary transportation**—inefficient routing.
5. **Processing waste**—using more resources than necessary to accomplish a task.
6. **Inefficient work methods**—poor layout design, unnecessary steps, inadequate training.
7. **Mistakes**—order entry errors, lost files, miscommunications.

Process Improvement Using the 5W2H Approach

5W2H approach A method of asking questions about a process that includes what, why, where, when, who, how, and how much.

Asking certain questions about a process can lead to cost and waste reduction. The **5W2H approach** (five questions that begin with *w,* and two questions that begin with *h*) is outlined in Table 14.4.

Lean and Six Sigma

Some believe that lean and six sigma are two alternate approaches for process improvement. However, another view is that the two approaches are complementary and, when used together, can lead to superior results.

TABLE 14.4
The 5W2H approach

Category	5W2H	Typical Questions	Goal
Subject	What?	What is being done?	Identify the focus of analysis.
Purpose	Why?	Why is this necessary?	Eliminate unnecessary tasks.
Location	Where?	Where is it being done? Why is it done there? Would it be better to do it someplace else?	Improve the location.
Sequence	When?	When is it done? Would it be better to do it at another time?	Improve the sequence.
People	Who?	Who is doing it? Could someone else do it better?	Improve the sequence or output.
Method	How?	How is it being done? Is there a better way?	Simplify tasks, improve output.
Cost	How much?	How much does it cost now? What would the new cost be?	Select an improved method.

Source: Adapted from Alan Robinson, ed., *Continuous Improvement in Operations: A Systematic Approach to Waste Reduction,* p. 246. Copyright © 1991 Productivity Press. www.productivitypress.com.

Lean strives to eliminate non-value-added activities, using simple tools to find and eliminate them. It focuses on maximizing process velocity, and it employs tools to analyze and improve process flow. However, variation exists in all processes. Understanding and reducing variation are important for quality improvement. Lean principles alone cannot achieve statistical process control, and six sigma alone cannot achieve improved process speed and flow. Using the two approaches in combination integrates lean principles and six sigma statistical tools for variation reduction to achieve a system that has both a balanced flow and quality.

JIT Deliveries and the Supply Chain

SUPPLY CHAIN

Direct suppliers must be able to support frequent just-in-time deliveries of small batches of parts. That may lead to an increase in transportation costs if trucks carry partial loads, and perhaps to congestion at loading docks. Moreover, the JIT delivery requirement may extend to other portions of the supply chain, in which case close coordination among supply chain partners is critical. Also, JIT delivery results in pressure for on-time deliveries to avoid production interruptions due to stockouts.

Nearby Suppliers Match Ford's Mix

READING

Ford Motor Company took a page out of Toyota's just-in-time book at its Chicago plant by having some of its suppliers locate very close to its assembly plant. It leased production facilities on its 155 acres to about 10 key suppliers. Suppliers' parts and components feed directly into Ford's assembly operation, carefully coordinated to match the sequence of vehicles Ford is producing, which can range from small cars to SUVs. Not only are suppliers nearby in case problems arise, the shortened travel distance and lead times yield tremendous savings in the pipeline inventories of parts and materials.

Lean and ERP

Lean systems focus on pacing production and synchronizing delivery of incoming supply. SAP's Lean Planning and Operations module extends ERP to lean operation by providing lean planning and scheduling capability linked to customer demand. It enables leveling of schedules and synchronization of supply chain activities with paced company operations.

TRANSITIONING TO A LEAN SYSTEM

The success of lean systems in Japan and the United States has attracted keen interest among other traditional manufacturers.

Planning a Successful Conversion

To increase the probability of successful transition, companies should adopt a carefully planned approach that includes the following elements:

1. Make sure top management is committed to the conversion and that they know what will be required. Make sure that management is involved in the process and knows what it will cost, how long it will take to complete the conversion, and what results can be expected.
2. Study the operations carefully; decide which parts will need the most effort to convert.
3. Obtain the support and cooperation of workers. Prepare training programs that include sessions in setups, maintenance of equipment, cross-training for multiple tasks, cooperation, and problem solving. Make sure workers are fully informed about what lean is and why it is desirable. Reassure workers that their jobs are secure.
4. Begin by trying to reduce setup times while maintaining the current system. Enlist the aid of workers in identifying and eliminating existing problems (e.g., bottlenecks, poor quality).

5. Gradually convert operations, beginning at the *end* of the process and working *backward.* At each stage, make sure the conversion has been relatively successful before moving on. Do not begin to reduce inventories until major problems have been resolved.
6. As one of the last steps, convert suppliers to JIT and be prepared to work closely with them. Start by narrowing the list of vendors, identifying those who are willing to embrace the lean philosophy. Give preference to vendors who have long-term track records of reliability. Use vendors located nearby if quick response time is important. Establish long-term commitments with vendors. Insist on high standards of quality and adherence to strict delivery schedules.
7. Be prepared to encounter obstacles to conversion.

Obstacles to Conversion

Converting from a traditional system to a lean system may not be smooth. For example, *cultures* vary from organization to organization. Some cultures relate better to the lean philosophy than others. If a culture doesn't relate, it can be difficult for an organization to change its culture within a short time. Also, manufacturers that operate with large amounts of inventory to handle varying customer demand may have difficulty acclimating themselves to less inventory.

Some other obstacles include the following:

1. Management may not be totally committed or may be unwilling to devote the necessary resources to conversion. This is perhaps the most serious impediment because the conversion is probably doomed without serious commitment.
2. Workers and/or management may not display a cooperative spirit. The system is predicated on cooperation. Managers may resist because lean shifts some of the responsibility from management to workers and gives workers more control over the work. Workers may resist because of the increased responsibility and stress.
3. It can be very difficult to change the culture of the organization to one consistent with the lean philosophy.
4. Suppliers may resist for several reasons:
   a. Buyers may not be willing to commit the resources necessary to help them adapt to the lean systems.
   b. They may be uneasy about long-term commitments to a buyer.
   c. Frequent, small deliveries may be difficult, especially if the supplier has other buyers who use traditional systems.
   d. The burden of quality control will shift to the supplier.
   e. Frequent engineering changes may result from continuing lean improvements by the buyer.

SUPPLY CHAIN

A Cooperative Spirit

Lean systems require a cooperative spirit among workers, management, and vendors. Unless that is present, it is doubtful that a truly effective lean system can be achieved. The Japanese have been very successful in this regard, partly because respect and cooperation are ingrained in the Japanese culture. In Western cultures, workers, managers, and vendors have historically been strongly at odds with each other. Consequently, a major consideration in converting to a lean system is whether a spirit of mutual respect and cooperation can be achieved. This requires an appreciation of the importance of cooperation and a tenacious effort by management to instill and maintain that spirit.

Finally, it should be noted that not all organizations lend themselves to a lean approach. Lean is best used for repetitive operations under fairly stable demand.

The Downside of a Lean System

Despite the many advantages of lean production systems, an organization must take into account a number of other considerations when planning a conversion.

The key considerations are the time and cost requirements for successful conversion, which can be substantial. But it is absolutely essential to eliminate the major sources of disruption in the system. Management must be prepared to commit the resources necessary to achieve a high level of quality and to function on a tight schedule. That means attention to even the smallest of details during the design phase and substantial efforts to debug the system to the point where it runs smoothly. Beyond that, management must be capable of responding quickly when problems arise, and both management and workers must be committed to the continuous improvement of the system. Although each case is different, a general estimate of the time required for conversion is one to three years.

John Deere, the well-known tractor supply company, bolstered profits during the recession by using a JIT approach to reduce inventory levels. However, when demand picked up as the economy strengthened, a shortage of parts led to stretched out delivery dates. Long lead times to replenish parts meant that in some cases harvesting equipment farmers wanted wouldn't be available until *after* harvest time! As a result, some farmers turned to Deere competitors to purchase needed equipment.

LEAN SERVICES

SERVICE

The discussion of lean systems has focused on manufacturing simply because that is where it was developed, and where it has been used most often. Nonetheless, services can and do benefit from many lean concepts. When just-in-time is used in the context of services, the focus is often on the time needed to perform a service—because speed is often an important order winner for services. Some services do have inventories of some sort, so inventory reduction is another aspect of lean that can apply to services. Examples of speedy delivery ("available when requested") are Domino's Pizza, FedEx and Express Mail, fast-food restaurants, and emergency services. Other examples include just-in-time publishing and work cells at fast-food restaurants.

In addition to speed, lean services emphasize consistent, high-quality, standard work methods; flexible workers; and close supplier relationships.

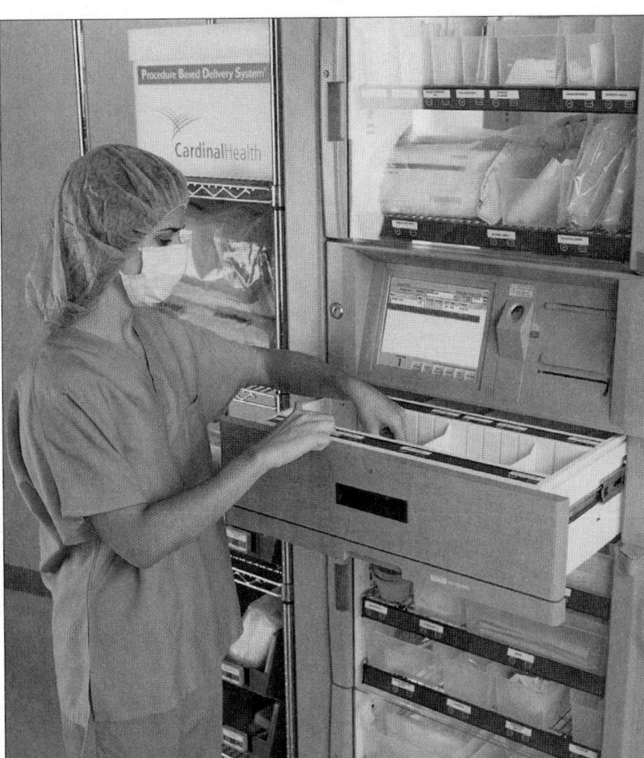

The Pyxis® ProcedureStation™ system provides rapid access to inventory in the operating room, cath and cardiac labs, and other specialty departments. Usage, inventory, and replenishment information are transmitted electronically, creating an efficient supply management and workflow process.

Process improvement and problem solving can contribute to streamlining a system, resulting in increased customer satisfaction and higher productivity. The following are the ways lean benefits can be achieved in services:

- **Eliminate disruptions.** For example, try to avoid having workers who are servicing customers also answer telephones.
- **Make the system flexible.** This can cause problems unless approached carefully. Often, it is desirable to standardize work because that can yield high productivity. On the other hand, being able to deal with variety in task requirements can be a competitive advantage. One approach might be to train workers so that they can handle more variety. Another might be to assign work according to specialties, with certain workers handling different types of work according to their specialty.

To Build a Better Hospital, Virginia Mason Takes Lessons from Toyota Plants READING

When you think of a hospital, what comes to mind? Patients, emergency rooms, technology and medical advancements. Making the sick and injured well again.

When officials at Virginia Mason think of hospitals, they think of cars. A car manufacturing plant, to be exact.

Beginning in 2000 the hospital's leaders looked at their infrastructure and saw it was designed around them, not the patient, said Dr. Gary Kaplan, Virginia Mason's chairman and chief executive officer.

For example, you hurry up and be on time, only to wait for the physician to see you.

They began looking for a better way to improve quality, safety and patient satisfaction. After two years of searching, they discovered the Toyota Production System, also known as lean manufacturing. Developed in part by Japanese businessman Taiichi Ohno, the idea is to eliminate waste and defects in production. Virginia Mason has tailored the Japanese model to fit health care.

Kaplan and other Virginia Mason managers took their first trip to Japan in 2002 where they visited manufacturing plants such as Toyota and Yamaha. Nearly 200 employees have toured plants in Japan and a ninth trip is planned for this summer. While Virginia Mason couldn't say exactly how much they paid over the years to send the staff overseas, officials liken it to leadership training other companies pay for their employees. They say the benefits offset the costs.

" 'People are not cars' is very common for me to hear," Kaplan said. "We get so wrapped up in the seriousness and specialness of health care, but we also have to open our eyes to other industries—we're way behind in information specialists and taking waste out of our process. Toyota is obsessed with the customer and customer satisfaction . . . all those things Toyota was about was what we wanted."

So what does that mean?

There are seven wastes, according to the production system. One is wasting time, such as patients waiting for a doctor or for test results to come back. Others are inventory waste—having more materials and information than is necessary—and overproduction waste, producing more than is necessary.

Take, for example, stockpiling brochures and pamphlets in storage closets. They take up space. There is wasted cost to make so many pamphlets that aren't needed.

The hospital and all of its campuses in the Seattle area implemented a Kanban system, which signals the need to restock. Kanban, which means "visual card" in Japanese, uses exactly that—a card put near the bottom of a pile of tongue dispensers, gauze strips or brochures, for example. When a nurse or physician sees the card, he or she knows it's time to refill. Supplies don't run out, but they also aren't over-ordered.

The hospital created standardized instrument trays for surgeries and procedures, which saved several hundred dollars by no longer setting out extra instruments no one used. Unused but opened instruments have to be thrown away.

It takes a series of simple steps to make improvements, said Janine Wentworth, an administrative director who returned from a two-week trip to Japan last month. One example is the development of a flip chart showing the level of mobility in physical therapy patients. The chart shows the appropriate picture of what the patient can do, and each nurse or physician who comes in the room doesn't have to waste time searching charts or asking questions.

Wentworth also wants to implement a production plan to hire more staff before a shortage exists based on turnover rates on any given hospital floor.

Another adaptation from the Toyota model is a patient safety alert system. At the manufacturing plant, if there's a problem, the whole line is stopped and the problem is fixed immediately. Virginia Mason's practice had been to identify and fix problems after the fact, perhaps leading to mistakes recurring many times before a solution was found. The alert system allows nurses and physicians to signal a problem when it happens and fix it immediately. Virginia Mason's Kirkland site has about 10 alerts each day.

(continued)

(concluded)

The Kirkland campus implemented the Toyota model in 2003. They've reduced appointment and telephone delays by having medical assistants handle incoming calls, instead of medically untrained operators.

Also, instead of doctors waiting until the end of the day to go through a stack of patient records, they now write comments and recommendations immediately after seeing the patient before going to see the next one. The time saved increases the time a physician can spend with a patient. Dr. Kim Pittenger, medical director at Virginia Mason Kirkland, said most of the cost of medical care involves clogs in the flow of information—paper forms, lab results, phone messages, often leading to irritated patients. Working the backlog down costs more than if you never let things pile up in the first place, he said.

He said not everyone has agreed with the new system and a few physicians have left Virginia Mason because of it.

"To some it seems like obsessive-compulsive disorder run amok, but it's part of a solution that eliminates mistakes," Pittenger said.

Other hospitals, including Swedish Medical Center, have incorporated the lean system into parts of their operation.

Virginia Mason said overall benefits include an 85 percent reduction in how long patients wait to get lab results back, and lowering inventory costs by $1 million. They've redesigned facilities to make patient and staff work flow more productive. The hospital reduced overtime and temporary labor expenses by $500,000 in one year and increased productivity by 93 percent. While direct cost savings aren't passed on to patients with the new system, less waiting, increased safety and more efficient care are.

Kaplan's vision is to have patients start their appointment in the parking garage with a smart card that triggers their entire appointment process. No more waiting rooms, just move directly from the garage to an examination room.

Total flow—no waiting, no waste and it's all about the patient.

"We have more than enough resources in health care," Kaplan said. "We just need to stop wasting it and only do what's appropriate and value-added and we'd save billions."

Source: Cherie Black, "To Build a Better Hospital, Virginia Mason Takes Lessons from Toyota Plant," *Seattle Post-Intelligencer,* March 15, 2008.

- **Reduce setup times and processing times.** Have frequently used tools and spare parts readily available. Additionally, for service calls, try to estimate what parts and supplies might be needed so they will be on hand, and avoid carrying huge inventories.
- **Eliminate waste.** This includes errors and duplicate work. Keep the emphasis on quality and uniform service.
- **Minimize work-in-process.** Examples include orders waiting to be processed, calls waiting to be answered, packages waiting to be delivered, trucks waiting to be unloaded or loaded, applications waiting to be processed.
- **Simplify the process.** This works especially when customers are part of the system (self-service systems including retail operations, ATMs and vending machines, service stations, etc.).

JIT service can be a major competitive advantage for companies that can achieve it. An important key to JIT service is the ability to provide service when it is needed. That requires flexibility on the part of the provider, which generally means short setup times, and it requires clear communication on the part of the requester. If a requester can determine when it will need a particular service, a JIT server can schedule deliveries to correspond to those needs, eliminating the need for continual requests, and reducing the need for provider flexibility—and therefore probably reducing the cost of the JIT service.

Although lean concepts are applicable to service organizations, the challenge of implementing lean in service is that there are still relatively few lean service applications that service companies can reference to see how to apply the underlying lean principles. Consequently, it can be difficult to build a strong commitment among workers to achieve a lean service system.

JIT II

SUPPLY CHAIN

In some instances, companies allow *suppliers* to manage restocking of inventory obtained from the suppliers. A supplier representative works right in the company's plant, making sure there is an appropriate supply on hand. The term *JIT II* is used to refer to this practice. JIT II was popularized by the Bose Corporation. It is often referred to as *vendor-managed inventory (VMI)*. You can also read more about vendor-managed inventories in the supply chain management chapter (Chapter 15).

OPERATIONS STRATEGY

The lean operation offers new perspectives on operations that must be given serious consideration by managers in repetitive systems who wish to be competitive.

Potential adopters should carefully study the requirements and benefits of lean production systems, as well as the difficulties and strengths of their current systems, before making a decision on whether to convert. Careful estimates of time and cost to convert, and an assessment of how likely workers, managers, and suppliers are to cooperate in such an approach, are essential.

The decision to convert can be sequential, giving management an opportunity to gain firsthand experience with portions of lean operations without wholly committing themselves. For instance, improving vendor relations, reducing setup times, improving quality, and reducing waste and inefficiency are desirable goals in themselves. Moreover, a level production schedule is a necessary element of a lean system, and achieving that will also be useful under a traditional system of operation.

It is prudent to carefully weigh the risks and benefits of a just-in-time approach to inventories. A just-in-time approach can make companies and even countries vulnerable to disruptions in their supply chains. For example, low stockpiles of flu vaccine at hospitals lower their costs but leave the health system at risk if there is a flu outbreak. Also, severe weather such as hurricanes, floods, and tornadoes, and other natural disasters caused by earthquakes can cut off supply routes, leaving community services as well as companies desperately in need of supplies.

Supplier management is critical to a JIT operation. Generally, suppliers are located nearby to facilitate delivery on a daily or even hourly basis. Moreover, suppliers at every stage must gauge the ability of their production facilities to meet demand requirements that are subject to change.

SUMMARY

Lean operation is an alternative to traditional operation that an increasing number of organizations are adopting. The ultimate goal of a lean system is to achieve a balanced, smooth flow of operations. Supporting goals include eliminating disruptions to the system, making the system flexible, and eliminating waste. The building blocks of a lean production system are product design, process design, personnel and organization, and manufacturing planning and control.

Lean systems require the elimination of sources of potential disruption to the even flow of work. High quality is essential because problems with quality can disrupt the process. Quick, low-cost setups, special layouts, allowing work to be pulled through the system rather than pushed through, and a spirit of cooperation are important features of lean systems. So, too, are problem solving aimed at reducing disruptions and making the system more efficient, and an attitude of working toward continual improvement.

Key benefits of lean systems are reduced inventory levels, high quality, flexibility, reduced lead times, increased productivity and equipment utilization, reduced amounts of scrap and rework, and reduced space requirements. The risks stem from the absence of buffers, such as extra personnel and inventory stockpiles to fall back on if something goes wrong. The possible results of risks include lost sales and lost customers.

Just-in-time (JIT) is a system of lean production used mainly in repetitive operations, in which goods move through the system and tasks are completed just in time to maintain the schedule. JIT systems require very little inventory because successive operations are closely coordinated. Careful planning and much effort are needed to achieve a smoothly functioning system in which all resources needed for production come together at precisely the right time throughout the process. Raw materials and purchased parts must arrive when needed, fabricated parts and subassemblies must be ready when needed for final assembly, and finished goods must be delivered to customers

TABLE 14.5
Overview of lean

Lean systems are designed to operate with fewer resources than traditional systems.
Elements of lean operation include:
- Smooth flow of work (the ultimate goal).
- Elimination of waste.
- Continuous improvement.
- Elimination of anything that does not add value.
- Simple systems that are easy to manage.
- Use of product layouts that minimize time spent moving materials and parts.
- Quality at the source: Each worker is responsible for the quality of his or her output.
- *Poka-yoke:* fail-safe tools and methods to prevent mistakes.
- Preventive maintenance to reduce the risk of equipment breakdown.
- Good housekeeping: an orderly and clean workplace.
- Setup time reduction.
- Cross-trained workers.
- A pull system.

There are seven types of waste:
- Inventory.
- Overproduction.
- Waiting time.
- Excess transportation.
- Processing waste.
- Inefficient work methods.
- Product or service defects.

when needed. Special attention must be given to reducing the risk of disruptions to the system as well as rapid response to resolving any disruptions that do occur. Usually, a firm must redesign its facilities and rework labor contracts to implement lean operation. Teamwork and cooperation are important at all levels, as are problem-solving abilities of workers and an attitude of continuous improvement.

Table 14.5 provides an overview of lean.

KEY POINTS

1. Lean systems produce high-quality goods or services using fewer resources than traditional operations systems.
2. Lean thinking helps business organizations to become more productive, reduce costs, and be more market-responsive.
3. Lean operations are designed to eliminate waste (value stream mapping), minimize inventory (JIT deliveries), maximize work flow (small batches with quick changeovers), make only what is needed (demand pull), empower work teams, do it right the first time (quality at the source), and continually improve.

KEY TERMS

activity-based costing, 633
andon, 632
autonomation, 626
5W2H approach, 642
heijunka, 620
housekeeping, 640
jidoka, 620
just-in-time (JIT), 619
kaizen, 620
kanban, 620, 636
lean operation, 619
muda, 620
poka-yoke, 630
preventive maintenance, 640
pull system, 620, 635
push system, 635
single-minute exchange of die (SMED), 626
takt time, 627
value stream mapping, 641

SOLVED PROBLEMS

Problem 1

Determine the number of containers needed for a workstation that uses 100 parts per hour if the time for a container to complete a cycle (move, wait, empty, return, fill) is 90 minutes and a standard container holds 84 parts. An inefficiency factor of .10 is currently being used.

Solution

$N = ?$

$D = 100$ parts per hour

$T = 90$ minutes (1.5 hours)

$C = 84$ parts

$X = .10$

$$N = \frac{D(T)(1 + X)}{C} = \frac{100(1.5)(1 + .10)}{84} = 1.96; \text{ round to 2 containers}$$

Problem 2

Determine the number of cycles per day and the production quantity per cycle for this set of products. The department operates five days a week. Assume the sequence A-B-C-D will be used.

Product	Weekly Quantity
A	20
B	40
C	30
D	15

Solution

Convert weekly quantities to daily quantities. The smallest *daily* quantity is 3 units. Producing in multiples of 3 units leaves A and B a few units short:

Product	Daily Quantity = Weekly Quantity ÷ 5	Units Short Using 3 Cycles
A	20 ÷ 5 = 4	1
B	40 ÷ 5 = 8	2
C	30 ÷ 5 = 6	—
D	15 ÷ 5 = 3	—

Use three cycles, producing all four products in every cycle. Produce units that are short by adding units to some cycles. Disperse the additional units as evenly as possible. There are several possibilities. One is

Cycle	1	2	3
Pattern	A B(3) C(2) D	A B(3) C(2) D	A(2) B(2) C(2) D
Extra unit(s)	B	B	A

DISCUSSION AND REVIEW QUESTIONS

1. Some key elements of production systems are listed in Table 14.3. Explain briefly how lean systems differ from traditional production systems for each of those elements.
2. What is the ultimate goal of a lean system? What are the supporting goals? What are the building blocks?
3. Describe the philosophy that underlies JIT (i.e., what is JIT intended to accomplish?).
4. What are some of the main obstacles that must be overcome in converting from a traditional system to lean?
5. Briefly discuss vendor relations in lean systems in terms of the following issues:
   a. Why are they important?
   b. How do they tend to differ from the more adversarial relations of the past?
   c. Why might suppliers be hesitant about JIT purchasing?

6. Certain Japanese have claimed that Henry Ford's assembly line provided some of the rationale for lean. What features of assembly lines are common to lean systems?
7. What is the kanban aspect of JIT?
8. Contrast push and pull methods of moving goods and materials through production systems.
9. What are the main benefits of a lean system?
10. What are the benefits and risks of small lot sizes?

TAKING STOCK

1. What trade-offs are involved in shifting from a traditional operations system to a lean system for:
   a. A manufacturing firm?
   b. A service firm?
2. Who in the organization is affected by a decision to shift from a traditional operations system to a lean system?
3. To what extent has technology had an impact on lean systems?

CRITICAL THINKING EXERCISES

1. In operations management, as in life, a balanced approach is often the best policy. One of the best examples of the benefits of this in operations management is the lean approach. Explain the basic factors that must be in place in order to achieve a balanced lean system.
2. Give three examples of unethical behavior involving lean operations and state the relevant ethical principle that would be violated.

PROBLEMS

1. A manager wants to determine the number of containers to use for incoming parts for a kanban system to be installed next month. The process will have a usage rate of 80 pieces per hour. Because the process is new, the manager has assigned an inefficiency factor of .35. Each container holds 45 pieces and it takes an average of 75 minutes to complete a cycle. How many containers should be used? As the system improves, will more or fewer containers be required? Why?

2. A JIT system uses kanban cards to authorize movement of incoming parts. In one portion of the system, a work center uses an average of 100 parts per hour while running. The manager has assigned an inefficiency factor of .20 to the center. Standard containers are designed to hold six dozen parts each. The cycle time for parts containers is about 105 minutes. How many containers are needed?

3. A machine cell uses 200 pounds of a certain material each day. Material is transported in vats that hold 20 pounds each. Cycle time for the vats is about two hours. The manager has assigned an inefficiency factor of .08 to the cell. The plant operates on an eight-hour day. How many vats will be used?

4. Determine the number of cycles per day and the production quantity per cycle for this set of vehicles:

Product	Daily Quantity
A	21
B	12
C	3
D	15

Use the sequence A-B-C-D.

5. Given this set of daily service operations, and assuming a processing order of A-B-C-D-E:
   a. Give one reason that each arrangement might be preferred over the other.
   b. Determine the number of repetitions for each service if four cycles are used.
   c. Determine the number of repetitions for each service if two cycles are used.

Service Operation	Number of Daily Reps
A	22
B	12
C	4
D	18
E	8

6. Determine the number of cycles per day and a production quantity per cycle for this set of products that achieves fairly level production:

Product	Daily Quantity
F	9
G	8
H	5
K	6

Assume the production sequence will be F-G-H-K.

7. Compute the *takt* time for a system where the total time per shift is 480 minutes, there is one shift, and workers are given two 15-minute breaks and 45 minutes for lunch. Daily demand is 300 units.

8. What cycle time would match capacity and demand if demand is 120 units a day, there are two shifts of 480 minutes each, and workers are given three half-hour breaks during each shift, one of which is for lunch or dinner?

9. Compute the *takt* time for a service system that intended to perform a standardized service. The system will have a total work time of 440 minutes per day, two 10-minute breaks, and an hour for lunch. The service system must process 90 jobs a day.

Level Operations

CASE

Level Operations is a small company located in eastern Pennsylvania. It produces a variety of security devices and safes. The safes come in several different designs. Recently, a number of new customers have placed orders, and the production facility has been enlarged to accommodate increased demand for safes. Production manager Stephanie Coles is currently working on a production plan for the safes. She needs a plan for each day of the week. She has obtained the following information from the marketing department on projected demand for the next five weeks:

Model	S1	S2	S7	S8	S9
Weekly Quantity	120	102	48	90	25

The department operates five days a week. One complexity is that partially completed safes are not permitted; each cycle must turn out finished units.

After discussions with engineering, Stephanie determined that the best production sequence for each cycle is S7-S8-S9-S1-S2.

Question

What might Stephanie determine as the best production quantity per cycle for each day of the week?

Boeing

OPERATIONS TOUR

The Boeing Company, headquartered in Chicago, Illinois, is one of the two major producers of aircraft in the global market. The other major producer is European Airbus.

Boeing produces three models in Everett, Washington: 747s, 767s, and 777s. The planes are all produced in the same building. At any one time, there may be as many as six planes in various stages of production. Obviously the building has to be fairly large to accommodate such a huge undertaking. In fact, the building is so large that it covers over 98 acres and it is four stories high, making it the largest building by volume in the world. It is so large that all of Disneyland would fit inside, and still leave about 15 acres for indoor parking! The windowless building has six huge doors along one side, each about 100 yards wide and 40 yards high (the size of a football field)—large enough to allow a completed airplane to pass through.

Boeing sells airplanes to airlines and countries around the globe. There isn't a set price for the planes; the actual price depends on what features the customer wants. Once the details have been settled and an order submitted, the customer requirements are sent to the design department.

Design

Designers formerly had to construct a mock-up to determine the exact dimensions of the plane and to identify any assembly problems that might occur. That required time, materials, labor, and space. Now they use computers (CAD) to design airplanes, avoiding the cost of the mock-ups and shortening the development time.

The Production Process

Once designs have been completed and approved by the customer, production of the plane is scheduled, and parts and materials are ordered. Parts come to the plant by rail, airplane, and

(continued)

(concluded)

truck, and are delivered to the major assembly area of the plane they will be used for. The parts are scheduled so they arrive at the plant just prior to when they will be used in assembly, and immediately moved to storage areas close to where they will be used. Time-phasing shipments to arrive as parts are needed helps to keep inventory investment low and avoids having to devote space to store parts that won't be used immediately. There is a trade-off, though, because if any parts are missing or damaged and have to be reordered, that could cause production delays. When missing or defective parts are discovered, they are assigned priorities according to how critical the part is in terms of disruption of the flow of work. The parts with the highest priorities are assigned to expediters who determine the best way to replace the part. The expediters keep track of the progress of the parts and deliver them to the appropriate location as soon as they arrive. In the meantime, a portion of the work remains unfinished, awaiting the replacement parts, and workers complete other portions of the assembly. If the supplier is unable to replace the part in a time frame that will not seriously delay assembly, as a last resort, Boeing has a machine shop that can make the necessary part.

The partially assembled portions of the plane, and in later stages, the plane itself, move from station to station as the work progresses, staying about five days at each station. Giant overhead cranes are used to move large sections from one station to the next, although once the wheel assemblies have been installed, the plane is towed to the remaining stations.

Finished planes are painted in one of two separate buildings. Painting usually adds 400 to 600 pounds to the weight of a plane. The painting process involves giving the airplane a negative charge and the paint a positive charge so that the paint will be attracted to the airplane.

Testing and Quality Control

Boeing has extensive quality control measures in place throughout the entire design and production process. Not only are there quality inspectors, individual employees inspect their own work and the work previously done by others on the plane. Buyers' inspectors also check on the quality of the work.

There are 60 test pilots who fly the planes. Formerly planes were tested to evaluate their flight worthiness in a wind tunnel, which required expensive testing and added considerably to product development time. Now new designs are tested using a computerized wind tunnel before production even begins, greatly reducing both time and cost. And in case you're wondering, the wings are fairly flexible; a typical wing can flap by as much as 22 feet before it will fracture.

Re-engineering

Boeing is re-engineering its business systems. A top priority is to upgrade its computer systems. This will provide better links to suppliers, provide more up-to-date information for materials management, and enable company representatives who are at customer sites to create a customized aircraft design on their laptop computer.

Another aspect of the re-engineering involves a shift to lean production. Key goals are to reduce production time and reduce inventory.

Boeing wants to reduce the time that a plane spends at each work station from 5 days to 3 days, a reduction of 40 percent. Not only will that mean that customers can get their planes much sooner, it will also reduce labor costs and inventory costs, and improve cash flow. One part of this will be accomplished by moving toward late-stage customization, or delayed differentiation. That would mean standardizing the assembly of planes as long as possible before adding custom features. This, and other time-saving steps, will speed up production considerably, giving it a major competitive advantage. It also wants to reduce the tremendous amount of inventory it carries (a 747 jumbo jet has about 6 million parts, including 3 million rivets). One part of the plan is to have suppliers do more predelivery work by assembling the parts into kits that are delivered directly to the staging area where they will be installed on the aircraft instead of delivering separate parts to inventory. That would cut down on inventory carrying costs and save time.

Boeing is also hoping to reduce the number of suppliers it has, and to establish better links and cooperation from suppliers. Currently Boeing has about 3,500 suppliers. Compare that with GM's roughly 2,500 suppliers, and you get an idea of how large this number is.

SELECTED BIBLIOGRAPHY AND FURTHER READINGS

Chalice, Robert. *Improving Healthcare Using Toyota Lean Production Methods: 46 Steps for Improvement.* 2nd ed. Milwaukee: ASQ Quality Press, 2007.

El-Haik, Basem, and David M. Roy. *Service Design for Six Sigma: A Roadmap for Excellence.* New York: Wiley-Interscience, 2005.

Hariharan, Arun. "CEO's Guide to Six Sigma Success." *ASQ Six Sigma Forum Magazine,* May 2006, pp. 16–25.

Hopp, Wallace J., and Mark Spearman. *Factory Physics: Foundations of Manufacturing Management.* 3rd ed. New York: Irwin/McGraw-Hill, 2007.

Jacobs, F. Robert, William L. Berry, D. Clay Whybark, and Thomas E. Vollmann. *Manufacturing Planning and Control Systems for Supply Chain Management.* 6th ed. New York: Irwin/McGraw-Hill, 2011.

Liker, Jeffrey. *The Toyota Way: 14 Management Principles from the World's Greatest Manufacturer.* New York: McGraw-Hill, 2004.

Mann, David. *Creating a Lean Culture: Tools to Sustain Lean Conversions.* New York: Productivity Press, 2005.

Monden, Yasuhiro. "What Makes the Toyota Production System Really Tick?" *Industrial Engineering* 13, no. 1 (January 1981), pp. 38–46.

Rich, Nick, Nicola Bateman, Ann Esain, Lynn Massey, and Donna Samuel. *Lean Evolution: Lessons from the Workplace.* New York: Cambridge University Press, 2006.

Shingo, Shigeo. *Non-Stock Production: The Shingo System for Continuous Improvement.* New York: Productivity Press, 2006.

Swank, Cynthia Karen. "The Lean Service Machine." *Harvard Business Review,* October 2003, pp. 123–129.

Taghizadegan, Salman. *Essentials of Lean Six Sigma.* Burlington, MA: Butterworth-Heinemann, 2006.

Womack, James P., and Daniel T. Jones. "Lean Consumption." *Harvard Business Review,* March 2005, pp. 58–68.

Womack, James P., and Daniel T. Jones. *Lean Thinking: Banish Waste and Create Wealth in Your Corporation.* New York: Free Press, 2003.

Womack, James P., Daniel T. Jones, and Daniel Roos. *The Machine that Changed the World.* New York: Simon & Schuster, 1991, 2007.

Zipkin, Paul H. *Foundations of Inventory Management.* New York: Irwin/McGraw-Hill, 2000.

SUPPLEMENT TO CHAPTER 14

Maintenance

LEARNING OBJECTIVES

After completing this supplement, you should be able to:

1. Explain the importance of maintenance in production systems.
2. Describe the range of maintenance activities.
3. Discuss preventive maintenance and the key issues associated with it.
4. Explain breakdown maintenance and name the key issues associated with it.
5. State how the Pareto phenomenon pertains to maintenance decisions.

SUPPLEMENT OUTLINE

Maintaining the production capability of an organization is an important function in any production system. **Maintenance** encompasses all those activities that relate to keeping facilities and equipment in good working order and making necessary repairs when breakdowns occur, so that the system can perform as intended.

Maintenance All activities that maintain facilities and equipment in good working order so that a system can perform as intended.

Maintenance activities are often organized into two categories: (1) buildings and grounds and (2) equipment maintenance. Buildings and grounds is responsible for the appearance and functioning of buildings, parking lots, lawns, fences, and the like. Equipment maintenance is responsible for maintaining machinery and equipment in good working condition and making all necessary repairs.

INTRODUCTION

The goal of maintenance is to keep the production system in good working order at minimal cost. There are several reasons for wanting to keep equipment and machines in good operating condition, such as to

1. Avoid production or service disruptions.
2. Not add to production or service costs.

3. Maintain high quality.
4. Avoid missed delivery dates.

When breakdowns occur, there are a number of adverse consequences:

1. Operations capacity is reduced, and orders are delayed.
2. There is no output, but overhead continues, increasing the cost per unit.
3. There are quality issues; output may be damaged.
4. There are safety issues; employees or customers may be injured.

Breakdown maintenance Reactive approach; dealing with breakdowns or problems when they occur.

Preventive maintenance Proactive approach; reducing breakdowns through a program of lubrication, adjustment, cleaning, inspection, and replacement of worn parts.

Decision makers have two basic options with respect to maintenance. One option is *reactive:* It is to deal with breakdowns or other problems when they occur. This is referred to as **breakdown maintenance.** The other option is *proactive:* It is to reduce breakdowns through a program of lubrication, adjustment, cleaning, inspection, and replacement of worn parts. This is referred to as **preventive maintenance.**

Decision makers try to make a trade-off between these two basic options that will minimize their combined cost. With no preventive maintenance, breakdown and repair costs would be tremendous. Furthermore, hidden costs, such as lost output and the cost of wages while equipment is not in service, must be factored in. So must the cost of injuries or damage to other equipment and facilities or to other units in production. However, beyond a certain point, the cost of preventive maintenance activities exceeds the benefit.

As an example, if a person never had the oil changed in his or her car, never had it lubricated, and never had the brakes or tires inspected, but simply had repairs done when absolutely necessary, preventive costs would be negligible but repair costs would be quite high, considering the wide range of parts (engine, steering, transmission, tires, brakes, etc.) that could fail. In addition, property damage and injury costs might be incurred, plus there would be the uncertainty of when failure might occur (e.g., on the expressway during rush hour, or late at night). On the other hand, having the oil changed and the car lubricated every morning would obviously be excessive because automobiles are designed to perform for much longer periods without oil changes and lubrications. The best approach is to seek a balance between preventive maintenance and breakdown maintenance. The same concept applies to maintaining production systems: Strike a balance between prevention costs and breakdown costs. This concept is illustrated in Figure 14S.1.

The age and condition of facilities and equipment, the degree of technology involved, the type of production process, and similar factors enter into the decision of how much preventive maintenance is desirable. Thus, in the example of a new automobile, little preventive maintenance may be needed since there is slight risk of breakdowns. As the car ages and becomes

FIGURE 14S.1
Total maintenance cost as a function of preventive maintenance effort

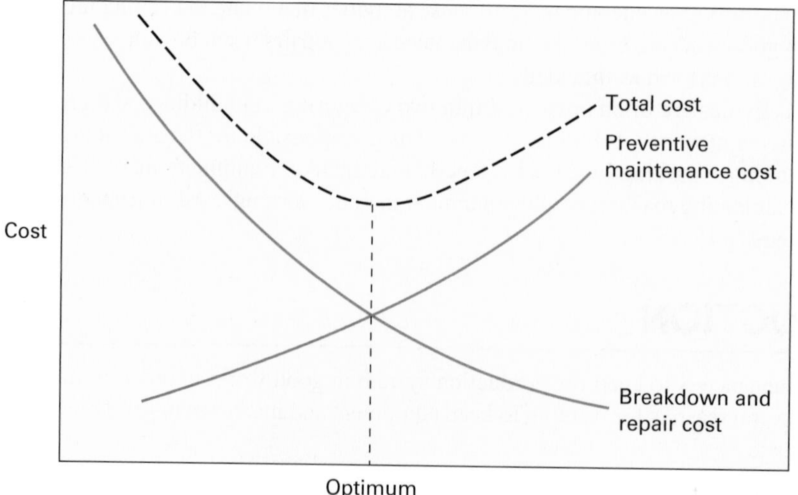

worn through use, the desirability of preventive maintenance increases because the risk of breakdown increases. Thus, when tires and brakes begin to show signs of wear, they should be replaced before they fail; dents and scratches should be periodically taken care of before they begin to rust; and the car should be lubricated and have its oil changed after exposure to high levels of dust and dirt. Also, inspection and replacement of critical parts that tend to fail suddenly should be performed before a road trip to avoid disruption of the trip and costly emergency repair bills.

PREVENTIVE MAINTENANCE

The goal of preventive maintenance is to reduce the incidence of breakdowns or failures in the plant or equipment to avoid the associated costs. Those costs can include loss of output; idle workers; schedule disruptions; injuries; damage to other equipment, products, or facilities; and repairs, which may involve maintaining inventories of spare parts, repair tools and equipment, and repair specialists.

Preventive maintenance is *periodic*. It can be scheduled according to the availability of maintenance personnel and to avoid interference with operating schedules. Managers usually schedule preventive maintenance using some combination of the following:

1. The result of planned inspections that reveal a need for maintenance.
2. According to the calendar (passage of time).
3. After a predetermined number of operating hours.

An important issue in preventive maintenance is the frequency of preventive maintenance. As the time between periodic maintenance increases, the cost of preventive maintenance decreases while the risk (and cost) of breakdowns increases. As noted, the goal is to strike a balance between the two costs (i.e., to minimize total cost).

Determining the amount of preventive maintenance to use is a function of the expected frequency of breakdown, the cost of a breakdown (including actual repair costs as well as potential damage or injury, lost production, and so on). The following two examples illustrate this.

EXAMPLE 14S–1

eXcel

www.mhhe.com/stevenson11e

The frequency of breakdown of a machine per month is shown in the table. The cost of a breakdown is $1,000 and the cost of preventive maintenance is $1,250 per month. If preventive maintenance is performed, the probability of a machine breakdown is negligible. Should the manager use preventive maintenance, or would it be cheaper to repair the machine when it breaks down?

Number of breakdowns	0	1	2	3
Frequency of occurrence	.20	.30	.40	.10

SOLUTION

The expected number of breakdowns without preventive maintenance is 1.40:

Number of Breakdowns	×	Frequency of Occurrence	=	Expected Number of Breakdowns
0		.20		0
1		.30		.30
2		.40		.80
3		.10		.30
		1.00		1.40

Expected cost using repair policy is 1.40 breakdowns/month × $1,000/breakdown = $1,400. Preventive maintenance would cost $1,250.

Therefore, preventive maintenance would yield a savings of $150/month.

EXAMPLE 14S–2

Another approach that might be used relates to the time before a breakdown occurs. Suppose that the average time before breakdown is normally distributed and has a mean of 3 weeks and a standard deviation of .60 week. If breakdown cost averages $1,000 and preventive maintenance costs $250, what is the optimal maintenance interval?

SOLUTION

Begin by computing the ratio of preventive cost to the breakdown cost:

$$\frac{\text{Preventive cost}}{\text{Breakdown cost}} = \frac{\$250}{\$1{,}000} = .25$$

Find the number of standard deviations from the mean represented by an area under the normal curve equal to .25 using Appendix B, Table B. It is $-.67$. Use this value of z to compute the maintenance interval:

$$\text{Mean} + z \text{ standard deviations} = 3 - .67(.60) = 2.598 \text{ (round to 2.6 weeks)}$$

Predictive maintenance An attempt to determine when best to perform preventive maintenance activities.

Total productive maintenance JIT approach where workers perform preventive maintenance on the machines they operate.

Ideally, preventive maintenance will be performed just prior to a breakdown or failure because this will result in the longest possible use of facilities or equipment without a breakdown. **Predictive maintenance** is an attempt to determine when to perform preventive maintenance activities. It is based on historical records and analysis of technical data to predict when a piece of equipment or part is about to fail. The better the predictions of failures are, the more effective preventive maintenance will be. A good preventive maintenance effort relies on complete records for each piece of equipment. Records must include information such as date of installation, operating hours, dates and types of insurance, and dates and types of repairs.

Some companies have workers perform preventive maintenance on the machines they operate, rather than use separate maintenance personnel for that task. Called **total productive maintenance,** this approach is consistent with JIT systems and lean operations, where employees are given greater responsibility for quality, productivity, and the general functioning of the system.

In the broadest sense, preventive maintenance extends back to the design and selection stage of equipment and facilities. Maintenance problems are sometimes *designed into* a system. For example, equipment may be designed in such a way that it needs frequent maintenance, or maintenance may be difficult to perform (e.g., the equipment has to be partially dismantled in order to perform routine maintenance). An extreme example of this was a certain car model that required the engine block to be lifted slightly in order to change the spark plugs! In such cases, maintenance is very likely to be performed less often than if its performance were less demanding. In other instances, poor design can cause equipment to wear out at an early age or experience a much higher than expected breakdown rate. *Consumer Reports,* for example, publishes annual breakdown data on automobiles. The data indicate that some models tend to break down with a much higher frequency than other models.

One possible reason for maintenance problems being designed into a product is that designers have accorded other aspects of design greater importance. Cost is one such aspect. Another is appearance; an attractive design may be chosen over a less attractive one even though it will be more demanding to maintain. Customers may contribute to this situation; the buying public probably has a greater tendency to select an attractive design over one that offers ease of maintenance.

Obviously, durability and ease of maintenance can have long-term implications for preventive maintenance programs. Training of employees in proper operating procedures and in how to keep equipment in good operating order—and providing the incentive to do so—are also important. More and more, U.S. organizations are taking a cue from the Japanese and transferring routine maintenance (e.g., cleaning, adjusting, inspecting) to the users of equipment, in an effort to give them a sense of responsibility and awareness of the equipment they use and to cut down on abuse and misuse of the equipment.

BREAKDOWN PROGRAMS

The risk of a breakdown can be greatly reduced by an effective preventive maintenance program. Nonetheless, occasional breakdowns still occur. Even firms with good preventive practices have some need for breakdown programs. Of course, organizations that rely less on preventive maintenance have an even greater need for effective ways of dealing with breakdowns.

Unlike preventive maintenance, management cannot schedule breakdowns but must deal with them on an irregular basis (i.e., as they occur). Among the major approaches used to deal with breakdowns are the following:

1. **Standby or backup equipment** that can be quickly pressed into service.
2. **Inventories of spare parts** that can be installed as needed, thereby avoiding lead times involved in ordering parts, and *buffer inventories,* so that other equipment will be less likely to be affected by short-term downtime of a particular piece of equipment.
3. **Operators** who are able to perform at least minor repairs on their equipment.
4. **Repair people** who are well trained and readily available to diagnose and correct problems with equipment.

The degree to which an organization pursues any or all of these approaches depends on how important a particular piece of equipment is to the overall operations system. At one extreme is equipment that is the focal point of a system (e.g., printing presses for a newspaper, or vital operating parts of a car, such as brakes, steering, transmission, ignition, and engine). At the other extreme is equipment that is seldom used because it does not perform an important function in the system, and equipment for which substitutes are readily available.

The implication is clear: Breakdown programs are most effective when they take into account the degree of importance a piece of equipment has in the operations system, and the ability of the system to do without it for a period of time. The Pareto phenomenon exists in such situations: A relatively few pieces of equipment will be extremely important to the functioning of the system, thereby justifying considerable effort and/or expense; some will require moderate effort or expense; and many will justify little effort or expense.

REPLACEMENT

When breakdowns become frequent and/or costly, the manager is faced with a trade-off decision in which costs are an important consideration: What is the cost of replacement compared with the cost of continued maintenance? This question is sometimes difficult to resolve, especially if future breakdowns cannot be readily predicted. Historical records may help to project future experience. Another factor is technological change; newer equipment may have features that favor replacement over either preventive or breakdown maintenance. On the other hand, the removal of old equipment and the installation of new equipment may cause disruptions to the system, perhaps greater than the disruptions caused by breakdowns. Also, employees may have to be trained to operate the new equipment. Finally, forecasts of future demand for the use of the present or new equipment must be taken into account. The demand for the replacement equipment might differ because of the different features it has. For instance, demand for output of the current equipment might be two years, while demand for output of the replacement equipment might be much longer.

These decisions can be fairly complex, involving a number of different factors. Nevertheless, most of us are faced with a similar decision with our personal automobiles: When is it time for a replacement?

SUMMARY

Maintaining the productive capability of an organization is an important function. Maintenance includes all of the activities related to keeping facilities and equipment in good operating order and maintaining the appearance of buildings and grounds.

The goal of maintenance is to minimize the total cost of keeping the facilities and equipment in good working order. Maintenance decisions typically reflect a trade-off between preventive maintenance, which seeks to reduce the incidence of breakdowns and failures, and breakdown maintenance, which seeks to reduce the impact of breakdowns when they do occur.

KEY TERMS

DISCUSSION AND REVIEW QUESTIONS

1. What is the goal of a maintenance program?
2. List the costs associated with equipment breakdown.
3. What are three different ways preventive maintenance is scheduled?
4. Explain the term *predictive maintenance* and the importance of good records.
5. List the major approaches organizations use to deal with breakdowns.
6. Explain how the Pareto phenomenon applies to
   a. Preventive maintenance.
   b. Breakdown maintenance.
7. Discuss the key points of this supplement as they relate to maintenance of an automobile.
8. What advantages does preventive maintenance have over breakdown maintenance?
9. Explain why having a good preventive maintenance program in place is necessary prior to implementing a lean system.
10. Discuss the relationship between preventive maintenance and quality.

PROBLEMS

1. The probability that equipment used in a hospital lab will need recalibration is given in the following table. A service firm is willing to provide maintenance and provide any necessary calibrations for a fee of $650 per month. Recalibration costs $500 per time. Which approach would be most cost-effective, recalibration as needed or the service contract?

Number of Recalibrations	0	1	2	3	4
Probability of Occurrence	.15	.25	.30	.20	.10

2. The frequency of breakdown of a machine that issues lottery tickets is given in the following table. Repairs cost an average of $240. A service firm is willing to provide preventive maintenance under either of two options: #1 is $500 and covers all necessary repairs, and #2 is $350 and covers any repairs after the first one. Which option would have the lowest expected cost: pay for all repairs, service option #1, or service option #2?

Number of Breakdowns/Month	0	1	2	3	4
Frequency of Occurrence	.10	.30	.30	.20	.10

3. Determine the optimum preventive maintenance frequency for each of the pieces of equipment if breakdown time is normally distributed:

Equipment	Average Time (days) between Breakdowns	Standard Deviation
A201	20	2
B400	30	3
C850	40	4

Equipment	Preventive Maintenance Cost	Breakdown Cost
A201	$300	$2,300
B400	$200	$3,500
C850	$530	$4,800

SELECTED BIBLIOGRAPHY AND FURTHER READINGS

Hall, Robert W. "Total Productive Maintenance—Essential to Maintain Progress." *Target* 3, no. 3 (Fall 1987), pp. 4–11.

Hora, Michael E. "The Unglamorous Game of Managing Maintenance." *Business Horizons* 30, no. 3 (May–June 1987), pp. 67–75.

Mann, Lawrence, Jr. *Maintenance Management.* Rev. ed. Lexington, MA: Lexington Books, 1983.

Nolden, Carol. "Predictive Maintenance: Route to Zero Unplanned Downtime." *Plant Engineering* 41, no. 4 (February 1987), pp. 38–43.

Supply Chain Management

CHAPTER OUTLINE

LEARNING OBJECTIVES

After completing this chapter, you should be able to:

1 Discuss the key issues of supply chain management.
2 Name the recent trends in supply chain management.
3 Summarize the motivations and risks of outsourcing as a strategy.
4 State some of the complexities that are involved with global supply chains.
5 List some of the strategic, tactical, and operational responsibilities of supply chain management.
6 Give examples of some advantages of e-business.
7 Explain the importance of supplier partnerships.
8 Discuss the issues involved in managing returns.
9 List the requirements of an effective supply chain.
10 Name some of the challenges in creating an effective supply chain.

The Wegmans supermarket chain (see the Wegmans Operations Tour in Chapter 1) is often mentioned as being the best-run supermarket chain in the United States. It's now being mentioned for its leadership in supply chain management in the grocery industry. Wegmans employs about 37,000 people. When a Wegmans spokesperson was asked how many of its people work in its supply chain, the spokesperson replied "37,000."

The fact of the matter is that most if not all of the people who work in any business organization are somehow involved with the supply chain. And no matter where your career takes you, in every job you do, you'll be involved in one (or more) supply chain(s).

In this chapter you will learn about recent trends in supply chain management, key supply chain processes and management responsibilities, procurement, logistics, managing returns, managing risks, and creating an effective supply chain. You can get an indication of the importance of supply chains from this statistic: According to one estimate, the value of inventories in supply chains of U.S. companies is over a trillion dollars.[1]

SUPPLY CHAIN

INTRODUCTION

A **supply chain** is the sequence of organizations—their facilities, functions, and activities—that are involved in producing and delivering a product or service. The sequence begins with basic suppliers of raw materials and extends all the way to the final customer. Facilities include warehouses, factories, processing centers, distribution centers, retail outlets, and offices. Functions

Supply chain A sequence of organizations—their facilities, functions, and activities—that are involved in producing and delivering a product or service.

[1] "What in the World is the Global Supply Chain?" Video, Council of Supply Chain Management Professionals, 2005.

Supply chain management The strategic coordination of the supply chain for the purpose of *integrating* supply and demand management.

Logistics The part of a supply chain involved with the forward and reverse flow of goods, services, cash, and information.

and activities include forecasting, purchasing, inventory management, information management, quality assurance, scheduling, production, distribution, delivery, and customer service.

Supply chain management is the strategic coordination of business functions within a business organization and throughout its supply chain for the purpose of *integrating* supply and demand management. Supply chain managers are people at various levels of the organization who are responsible for managing supply and demand both within and across business organizations. They are involved with planning and coordinating activities that include sourcing and procurement of materials and services, transformation activities, and logistics. **Logistics** is the part of a supply chain involved with the forward and reverse flow of goods, services, cash, and information. Logistics management includes management of inbound and outbound transportation, material handling, warehousing, inventory, order fulfillment and distribution, third-party logistics, and reverse logistics (the return of goods from customers).

Every business organization is part of at least one supply chain, and many are part of multiple supply chains. Often the number and type of organizations in a supply chain are determined by whether the supply chain is manufacturing or service oriented. Figure 15.1 illustrates several

FIGURE 15.1 Typical supply chains

a. A typical manufacturing supply chain.

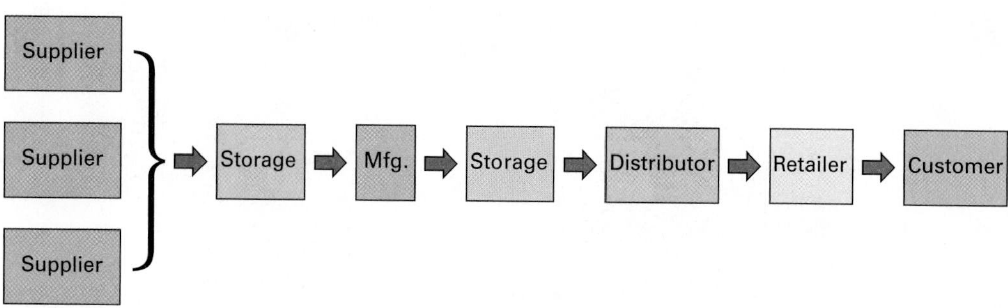

b. A typical service supply chain.

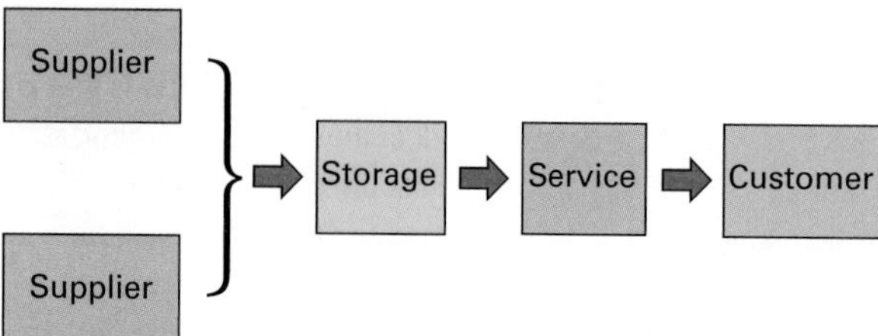

c. Goods and services flow clockwise in this diagram, and cash flows counter-clockwise.

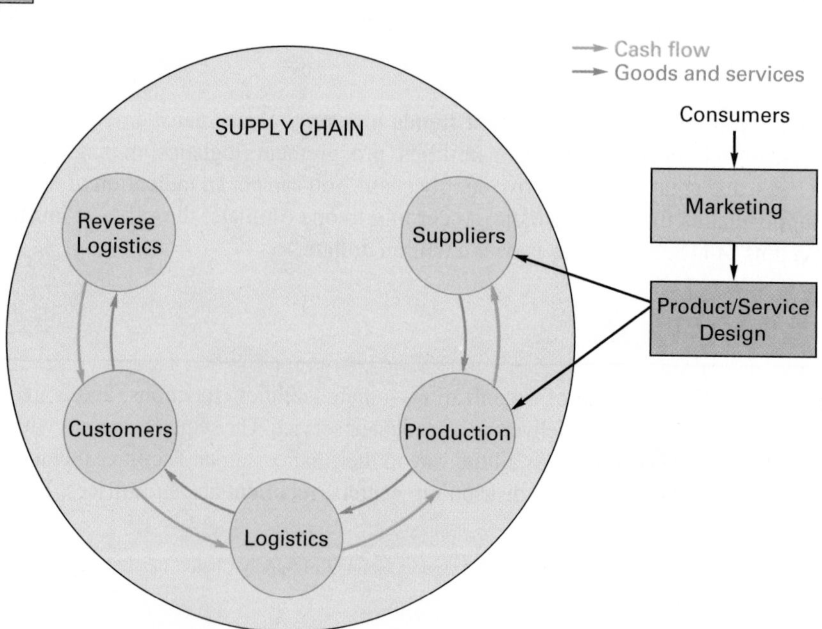

FIGURE 15.2 A farm-to-market supply chain

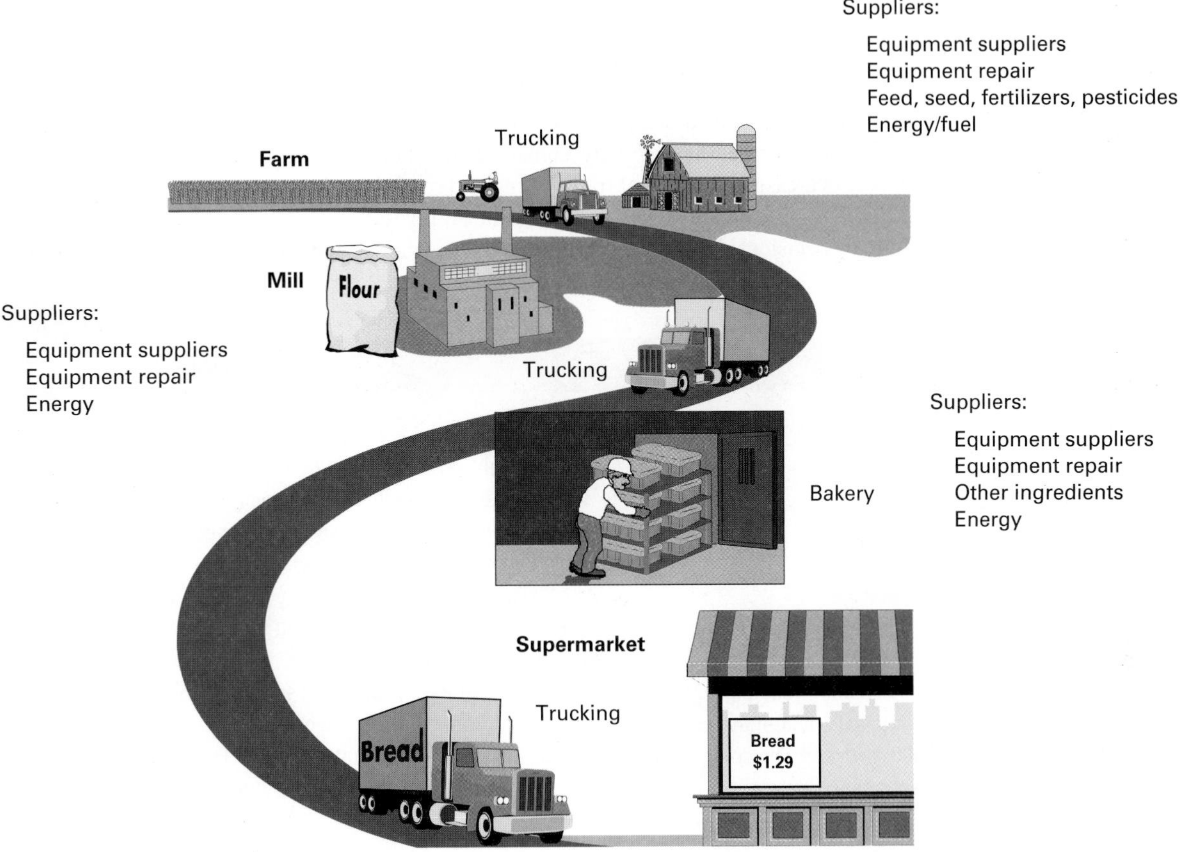

perspectives of supply chains. Figure 15.2 shows a more detailed version of the farm-to-market supply chain that was shown in Chapter 1, with key suppliers at each stage included.

Supply chains are sometimes referred to as *value chains,* a term that reflects the concept that value is added as goods and services progress through the chain. Supply or value chains typically comprise separate business organizations, rather than just a single organization. Moreover, the supply or value chain has two components for each organization: a supply component and a demand component. The supply component starts at the beginning of the chain and ends with the internal operations of the organization. The demand component of the chain starts at the point where the organization's output is delivered to its immediate customer and ends with the final customer in the chain. The *demand chain* is the sales and distribution portion of the value chain. The length of each component depends on where a particular organization is in the chain; the closer the organization is to the final customer, the shorter its demand component and the longer its supply component.

Supply chains are the lifeblood of any business organization. They connect suppliers, producers, and final customers in a network that is essential to the creation and delivery of goods and services. Managing the supply chain is the process of planning, implementing, and controlling supply chain operations. The basic components are strategy, procurement, supply management, demand management, and logistics. The goal of supply chain management is to match supply to demand as effectively and efficiently as possible. Key issues relate to:

1. Determining the appropriate level of outsourcing.
2. Managing procurement.
3. Managing suppliers.
4. Managing customer relationships.
5. Being able to quickly identify problems and respond to them.

An important aspect of supply chain management is *flow management.* The three types of flow that need to be managed are product and service flow, information flow, and financial flow. Product and service flow involves the movement of goods or services from suppliers to customers as well as handling customer service needs and product returns. Information flow involves sharing forecast and sales data, transmitting orders, tracking shipments, and updating order status. Financial flow involves credit terms, payments, and consignment and title ownership arrangements. Technological advances have greatly enhanced the ability to effectively manage these flows. A dramatic decrease in the cost of transmitting and receiving information and the increased ease and speed of communication have facilitated the ability to coordinate supply chain activities and make timely decisions. In effect, a supply chain is a complex supply network.

Veggie Tales

READING

Think food distribution is a low-tech enterprise? Just try getting a box of lettuce and other perishables across the country without sophisticated software and systems.

When people hear the name "Sysco," they probably think of Cisco, the San Jose–based maker of routers and other high-tech gear. But Houston-based food distributor Sysco, which each year ships 21.5 million tons of produce, meats, prepared meals, and other food-related products, is pretty technologically savvy too. The company supplies goods to one in three U.S. restaurants, cafeterias, and sports stadiums—anyplace that serves food. To get all that food safely to the right venue at the right time, Sysco maintains a complex web of software, databases, scanning systems, and robotics that surely would impress Silicon Valley types (including executives from that homonymic company).

Sysco's supply-chain logistics are especially complex because a single jar of caviar can't be handled the same way as a box of frozen onion rings or an 80-pound tub of flour. That rules out most off-the-shelf inventory-management software. So Sysco uses customized tech tools to crank out a logistical plan every day and then execute it. That way a restaurant that wants Fuji apples doesn't get Macintoshes instead, or an elementary school cafeteria doesn't

From Farm to Fork

Sysco tracks its produce and records precise information about the product's condition from the moment it leaves the farm to the instant a customer takes delivery. Here's a look at the life of a head of lettuce once it is farmed.

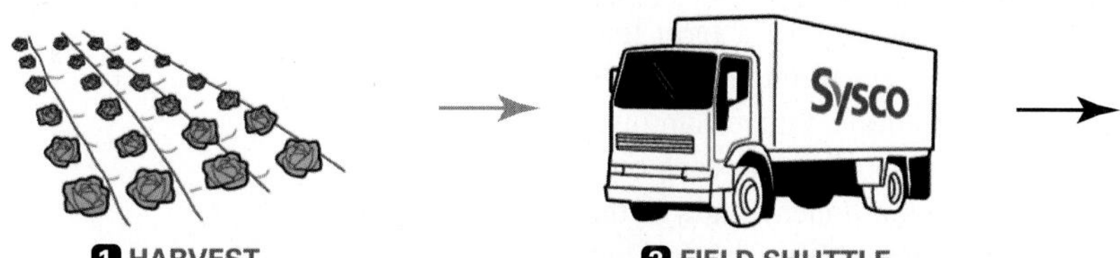

1 HARVEST
Lettuce from a Sysco-approved field near Salinas, Calif., is harvested. The temperature of the vegetable pulp ranges from 46° to 60°F.

2 FIELD SHUTTLE
Lettuce is loaded onto field shuttle trucks, which are kept at a chilly 38° to 42°F. It travels to a cooling location in Salinas, less than an hour's drive from the field.

3 PRECOOLING
A Sysco supplier in Salinas uses vacuum technology to rapidly precool the lettuce; this ensures maximum shelf life. The temperature of the lettuce pulp plunges to 34° to 36°F.

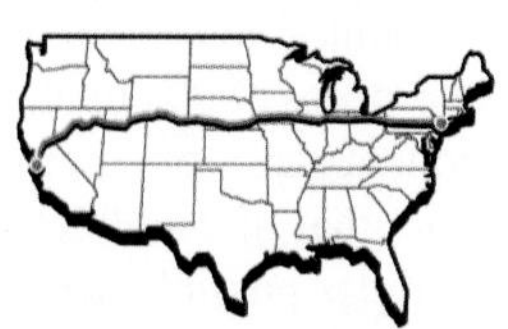

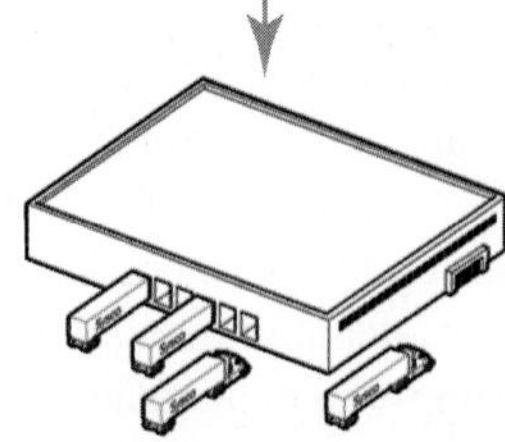

4 STORAGE
The produce then is stored at a separate cooling facility (at Salinas) with an ambient temperature of 34° to 38° F, where it awaits shipment, usually later that day.

5 TRANSPORT
Boxes of lettuce are loaded onto a refrigerated truck (usually run by an independent carrier). The trip from Salinas to Sysco's sorting center in Jersey City takes two to four days.

6 FINAL DELIVERY
Lettuce is selected by Sysco workers in Jersey City and loaded into the cooler section of a three-temperature-zone truck for delivery to the customer's door.

(continued)

end up with meals meant for the assisted-living facility down the street. In the process, the company has found ways to cut costs and speed delivery times, which is helping Sysco weather a downturn that is forcing many of its restaurant customers to cut back or close altogether.

Food Sorting the Sysco Way

On a recent afternoon around 5:40, a whirring noise picks up, punctuated by honks as men drive forklifts across the floor of Sysco's 450,000-square-foot facility in Jersey City, N.J. This is where restaurant supplies and food are sorted and loaded before reaching their final destination. (Sysco refers to each of its sorting centers as an "operating company.") Every driver is wearing a wireless scanner made by Symbol, a unit of Motorola, plus a printer on his hip with exact instructions on what to load on his forklift. Sysco has software that calculates exactly how each pallet—a forklift can accommodate three of the large portable platforms—should be arranged, based on the weight of its items, its location, and its destination.

"It's like the game of Tetris," says the facility's vice president of operations, Robert Heim, who says hello to everyone who drives by.

The "selectors," as the men are called, point their scanners at a bar code above an item, grab it, and put it on a pallet. The facility is arranged so that people work methodically in one direction, never doubling back, which could create chaos. The aisles are organized according to weight and temperature; heavier cans that weigh 40 to 50 pounds are put on one side of the warehouse, while lighter items, like boxes of potato chips, go on the other. It's all about maximum efficiency.

At this location 11,000 items turn over every 17 days. To achieve that, each product—even the napkins and silverware—has a kind of expiration date on it, because Sysco wants everything to move out in a particular order. If an item passes its "expiration," the inventory-management software alerts workers to pull it. Or if supplies of it are running low, they are replenished.

Fuller Trucks Hit the Roads

Thanks to the geographic spread and diversity of its customers, Sysco's trucks are seemingly everywhere. To make sure the trucks are as full as can be, Sysco in 2000 began revamping its supply-chain operations. In the past Sysco had its food suppliers—such as Kraft and Kellogg—ship directly to operating centers like the one in Jersey City. The problem was that suppliers were sending a separate truck to each operating company. Not only did each truck take 2½ hours to unload, but they often arrived only half full. The upshot: Sysco, which covers these suppliers' delivery costs, was wasting time and money. Today a centralized supply-chain group in Houston, with the help of software from Manhattan Associates, directs shipments from suppliers to one of two new redistribution centers, where Sysco workers consolidate and pack into trucks large quantities of supplies before sending them on to the appropriate operating companies. In some cases the redistribution centers can get pallets for customers packed and ready, so the operating companies need to assemble only a few more pallets before sending the truck out for delivery. The result: Fewer trucks on the road—each one fuller—and Sysco spends less time turning products around. Sysco says that in the first three quarters of last year it increased shipped cases per employee (a key metric of efficiency) 5%.

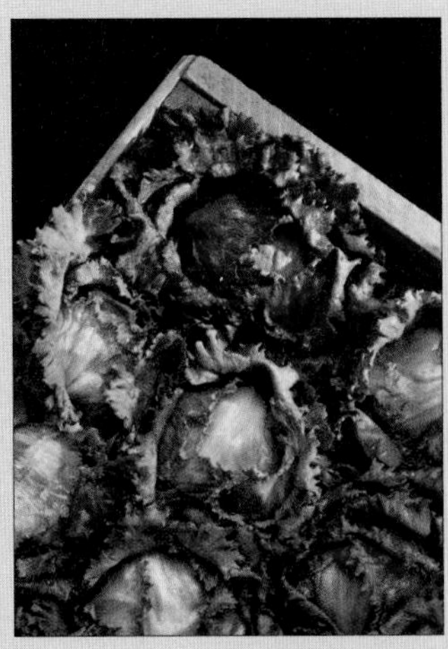

Sysco has also saved money by revamping its truck routes. That became imperative last year when fuel prices skyrocketed. It uses Roadnet, a software program developed by UPS, to determine the most efficient routes for its trucks. In the past nine months, the company says, diesel usage is down almost 8% from a year earlier. It also is trying to get all its units to coordinate by moving to an SAP software platform, which should take a few more years to complete.

Total Recall

Sysco's technology not only helps the company run more efficiently, it can aid government agencies after outbreaks related to tainted food. When the Food and Drug Administration ordered the recall of salmonella-contaminated peanut products supplied by Peanut Corp. of America last year, Sysco quickly identified six operating companies that potentially carried tainted goods. The company says it also used its tracking software to help the FDA investigate the sources of contamination by triangulating information about its shipments, eateries that had reported outbreaks, and the suspected ingredients. Using that kind of information, Sysco also helped health officials identify sources of contamination during the 2006 spinach E. coli outbreak.

TRENDS IN SUPPLY CHAIN MANAGEMENT

Although different industries and different businesses vary widely in terms of where they are in the evolution of their supply chain management, many businesses emphasize the following:

- Measuring supply chain ROI.
- "Greening" the supply chain.
- Reevaluating outsourcing.

Supply chain disruptions can reduce revenue and threaten production and distribution. A risk from accidents is shown here with containers falling from the deck of a damaged cargo ship off the Mumbai coast after a collision between two cargo ships

- Integrating IT.
- Managing risks.
- Adopting lean principles.

Measuring supply chain ROI enables managers to incorporate economics into outsourcing and other decisions, giving them a rational basis for managing their supply chains.

Greening the supply chain is generating interest for a variety of reasons, including corporate responsibility, regulations, and public pressure. This may involve redesigning products and services; reducing packaging; near-sourcing to reduce pollution from transportation (one estimate is that marine shipping alone causes about 60,000 premature deaths annually worldwide due to lung cancer and cardiopulmonary disease)[2]; choosing "green" suppliers; managing returns; and implementing end-of-life programs, particularly for appliances and electronic equipment.

Reevaluating outsourcing. Companies are taking a second look at outsourcing, especially global suppliers. Business organizations outsource for a variety of reasons. Often decisions to outsource have been based on lower prices resulting from lower labor costs. Other potential benefits include: the ability to focus on core strengths, converting fixed costs to variable costs, freeing up capital to devote to other needs, shifting some risks to suppliers, taking advantage of supplier expertise, and ease of expansion outside the home country. Some potential difficulties, depending on the nature of what is outsourced and the length of the supply chain, include inflexibility due to longer lead times for delivery of goods with distant suppliers, increased transportation costs, language and cultural differences, loss of jobs, loss of control, lower productivity, loss of ability to do the work internally and loss of business knowledge, knowledge transfer, concerns about intellectual property security, and increased effort needed to manage the supply chain.

Integrating IT produces real-time data that can enhance strategic planning and help businesses to control costs, measure quality and productivity, respond quickly to problems, and improve supply chain operations.

Managing risks is getting increasing attention from many companies in light of recent events. Risk management involves identifying risks, assessing their likelihood of occurring and their potential impacts, prioritizing the risks, and then developing strategies to manage those risks. Strategies can involve risk avoidance, risk reduction, risk transference to another

[2]James J. Corbett, James J. Winebrake, Erin H. Green, Prasad Kasibhatla, Veronika Eyring, and Axel Lauer, "Mortality from Ship Emissions: A Global Assessment," *Environmental Science & Technology* 41, no. 24 (December 15, 2007), pp. 8512–8518.

supply chain party, or some combination of these strategies. For example, risk avoidance may mean not operating in a certain country, or not dealing with a certain supplier or transporter. Risk reduction may involve increasing inventory levels at various points in the supply chain. Risk transference may mean having contractual agreements that make suppliers responsible for compliance with quality standards.

Many businesses are turning to **lean principles** to improve the performance of their supply chains. In too many instances, traditional supply chains are a collection of loosely connected steps, and business processes are not linked to suppliers' or customers' needs. Applying lean principles to supply chains can overcome this weakness by eliminating non-value-added processes; improving product flow by using pull systems rather than push systems; using fewer suppliers and supplier certification programs, which can nearly eliminate the need for inspection of incoming goods; and adopting the lean attitude of never ceasing to improve the system.

As a result of these current and possible future trends, organizations are likely to give serious thought to reconfiguring their supply chains to reduce risks, improve flow, increase profits, and generally increase customer satisfaction.

GLOBAL SUPPLY CHAINS

As businesses increasingly make use of outsourcing and pursue opportunities beyond their domestic markets, their supply chains are becoming increasingly global. For example, product design often uses inputs from around the world, and products are sold globally. Some manufacturing operations may be outsourced to countries that have low labor or material costs, and some services may be outsourced to countries such as China and India, where young, well-educated people are willing to work for wages much lower than those domestic employees earn.

As businesses recognize the strategic importance of effective supply chain management, they are also discovering that global supply chains have additional complexities that were either negligible or nonexistent in domestic operations. These complexities include language and cultural differences, currency fluctuations, armed conflicts, increased transportation costs and lead times, and the increased need for trust and cooperation among supply chain partners. Furthermore, managers must be able to identify and analyze factors that differ from country to country which can impact the success of the supply chain, including local capabilities; financial, transportation, and communication infrastructures; governmental, environmental, and regulatory issues; and political issues.

These and other factors have made risk management an important aspect of global supply chain management. To compensate for this, some firms have increased the amount of inventory at various points in their supply chains, thereby losing some of the benefits of global sourcing.

Risks can relate to supply (e.g., supplier failure, quality issues, sustainability issues, transportation issues, pirates, terrorism), costs (e.g., increasing commodity costs), and demand (e.g., decreasing demand, demand volatility, and transportation issues). Still other risks can involve intellectual rights issues, contract compliance issues, competitive pressure, forecasting errors, and inventory management.

A positive factor of globalization has been the set of technological advances in communications: the ability to link operations around the world with real-time information exchange. Consequently, information technology has a key role in integrating operations across global supply chains.

ERP and Supply Chain Management

Supply chain management that integrates ERP is a formal approach to effectively plan and manage all the resources of a business enterprise. Implementation of ERP involves establishing operating systems and operating performance measurements to enable them to manage business operations and meet business and financial objectives. ERP encompasses supply chain management activities such as planning for demand and managing supply, inventory replenishment, production, warehousing, and transportation. ERP software also plays a key role in centralizing transaction data.

Ethics and the Supply Chain

There are many examples of unethical behavior involving supply chains. They include bribing government or company officials to secure permits or favorable status; "exporting smokestacks" to developing countries; claiming a "green" supply chain when in reality the level of "green" is only minimal; ignoring health, safety, and environmental standards; violating basic rights of workers (e.g., paying substandard wages; using sweatshops, forced labor, or child labor); mislabeling country of origin; and selling goods abroad that are banned at home.

Every company should develop an ethical supply chain code to guide behavior. A code should cover behaviors that involve customers, suppliers, suppliers' behaviors, contract negotiation, recruiting, and the environmental issues.

A major risk of unethical behavior is that when such behavior is exposed in the media, consumers tend to blame the major company or brand in the supply chain associated with the ethical infractions that were actually committed by legally independent companies in the supply chain. The problem is particularly difficult to manage when supply chains are global, as they often are in manufacturing operations. Unfortunately, many companies lack the ability to quickly contact most or all of the companies in their supply chain, and communicate with suppliers on critical issues of ethics and compliance. Although monitoring of supply chain activities is essential, it is only one aspect of maintaining an ethical supply chain. With global manufacturing and distribution, supply chain scrutiny should include all supply chain activities from purchasing, manufacturing, assembly, and transportation, to service and repair operations, and eventually to proper disposal of products at the end of their useful life.

Key steps companies can take to reduce the risk of damages due to unethical supplier behavior are to choose those that have a reputation for good ethical behavior; incorporate compliance with labor standards in supplier contracts; develop direct, long-term relationships with ethical suppliers; and address quickly any problems that occur.

MANAGEMENT RESPONSIBILITIES

Generally speaking, corporate management responsibilities have legal, economic, and ethical aspects. Legal responsibilities include being knowledgeable about laws and regulations of the countries where supply chains exist, obeying the laws, and operating to conform to regulations. Economic responsibilities include supplying products and services to meet demand as efficiently as possible. Ethical responsibilities include conducting business in ways that are consistent with the moral standards of society.

More specific areas of responsibility relate to organizational strategy, tactics, and operations.

SOME SUPPLY CHAIN STRATEGIES

There are many different strategies a business organization can choose from. Here is a sample of some of those strategies:

Responsive/agile. A flexible supply chain that has the ability to quickly respond to changes in product requirements or volume of demand as well as adapt to supply chain disruptions.

Lean supply chain. Focused on eliminating non-value-added activities to create an efficient, low-cost supply chain.

Near-sourcing. Using nearby suppliers shortens the supply chain, reducing transportation time and cost, reducing supply chain inventory, reducing the risk of disruptions, and increasing responsiveness.

Strategic Responsibilities

Top management has certain strategic responsibilities that have a major impact on the success not only of supply chain management but also of the business itself. These strategies include:

Supply chain strategy alignment: Aligning supply and distribution strategies with organizational strategy and deciding on the degree to which outsourcing will be employed.

Network configuration: Determining the number and location of suppliers, warehouses, production/operations facilities, and distribution centers.

Information technology: Integrating systems and processes throughout the supply chain to share information, including forecasts, inventory status, tracking of shipments, and events.

Products and services: Making decisions on new product and services selection and design.

TABLE 15.1
Key tactical and operational responsibilities

Tactical Responsibilities

Forecasting: Prepare and evaluate forecasts.

Sourcing: Choose suppliers and some make-or-buy decisions.

Operations planning: Coordinate the external supply chain and internal operations.

Managing inventory: Decide where in the supply chain to store the various types of inventory (raw materials, semifinished goods, finished goods).

Transportation planning: Match capacity with demand.

Collaborating: Work with supply chain partners to coordinate plans.

Operational Responsibilities

Scheduling: Short-term scheduling of operations and distribution.

Receiving: Management of inbound deliveries from suppliers.

Transforming: Conversion of inputs into outputs.

Order fulfilling: Linking production resources and/or inventory to specific customer orders.

Managing inventory: Maintenance and replenishment activities.

Shipping: Management of outbound deliveries to distribution centers and/or customers.

Information sharing: Exchange of information with supply chain partners.

Controlling: Control of quality, inventory, and other key variables and implementing corrective action, including variation reduction, when necessary.

Capacity planning: Assessing long-term capacity needs, including when and how much will be needed and the degree of flexibility to incorporate.

Strategic partnerships: Partnership choices, level of partnering, and degree of formality.

Distribution strategy: Deciding whether to use centralized or decentralized distribution, and deciding whether to use the organization's own facilities and equipment for distribution or to use third-party logistics providers.

Uncertainty and risk reduction: Identifying potential sources of risk and deciding the amount of risk that is acceptable.

Key Tactical and Operational Responsibilities

The key tactical and operational responsibilities are outlined in Table 15.1.

Purchasing is "critical to supply chain efficiency because it is the job of purchasing to select suppliers and then establish mutually beneficial relationships with them. Without good suppliers and without superior purchasing, supply chains cannot compete in today's marketplace." Purchasing is also very involved in product design and development work. Many "manufacturers have found out that manufacturing costs can be reduced, product quality maximized, and new products brought to market at a much faster rate if purchasing brings key suppliers into the product design and development at the earliest stage of the process." And purchasing is directly involved in the implementation of e-commerce systems.

Source: Based on Kevin R. Fitzgerald, "Purchasing Occupies Key Position in Supply Chains," *Supply Chain Yearbook 2000* (New York: Cahners Business Information, 2000), p. 21.

PROCUREMENT

The purchasing department of an organization is responsible for obtaining the materials, parts, supplies, and services needed to produce a product or provide a service. You can get some idea of the importance of purchasing when you consider that, in manufacturing, upwards of 60 percent of the cost of finished goods comes from purchased parts and materials. Furthermore, the percentages for purchased inventories are even higher for retail and wholesale companies, sometimes exceeding 90 percent. Nonetheless, the importance of purchasing is more than just the cost of goods purchased; other important factors include the *quality* of goods and services and the *timing* of deliveries of goods or services, both of which can have a significant impact on operations.

Among the duties of purchasing are identifying sources of supply, negotiating contracts, maintaining a database of suppliers, obtaining goods and services that meet or exceed operations requirements in a timely and cost-efficient manner, and managing suppliers.

Purchasing Interfaces

Purchasing has interfaces with a number of other functional areas, as well as with outside suppliers. It is the connecting link between the organization and its suppliers. In this capacity, it exchanges information with suppliers and functional areas. The interactions between purchasing and these other areas are briefly summarized in the following paragraphs.

Operations constitute the main source of requests for purchased materials, and close cooperation between these units and the purchasing department is vital if quality, quantity, and delivery goals are to be met. Cancellations, changes in specifications, or changes in quantity or delivery times must be communicated immediately for purchasing to be effective.

The purchasing department may require the assistance of the *legal* department in contract negotiations, in drawing up bid specifications for nonroutine purchases, and in helping interpret legislation on pricing, product liability, and contracts with suppliers.

Accounting is responsible for handling payments to suppliers and must be notified promptly when goods are received in order to take advantage of possible discounts. In many firms, *data processing* is handled by the accounting department, which keeps inventory records, checks invoices, and monitors vendor performance.

Design and engineering usually prepare material specifications, which must be communicated to purchasing. Because of its contacts with suppliers, purchasing is often in a position to pass information about new products and materials improvements on to design personnel. Also, design and purchasing people may work closely to determine whether changes in specifications, design, or materials can reduce the cost of purchased items (see the following section on value analysis).

Receiving checks incoming shipments of purchased items to determine whether quality, quantity, and timing objectives have been met, and it moves the goods to temporary storage. Purchasing must be notified when shipments are late; accounting must be notified when shipments are received so that payments can be made; and both purchasing and accounting must be apprised of current information on continuing vendor evaluation.

Suppliers or vendors work closely with purchasing to learn what materials will be purchased and what kinds of specifications will be required in terms of quality, quantity, and deliveries. Purchasing must rate vendors on cost, reliability, and so on (see the later section on vendor analysis). Good supplier relations can be important on rush orders and changes, and vendors provide a good source of information on product and material improvements.

Figure 15.3 depicts the purchasing interfaces.

The Purchasing Cycle

Purchasing cycle Series of steps that begin with a request for purchase and end with notification of shipment received in satisfactory condition.

The **purchasing cycle** begins with a request from within the organization to purchase material, equipment, supplies, or other items from outside the organization, and the cycle ends when the purchasing department is notified that a shipment has been received in satisfactory condition. The main steps in the cycle are these:

1. **Purchasing receives the requisition.** The requisition includes (*a*) a description of the item or material desired, (*b*) the quantity and quality necessary, (*c*) desired delivery dates, and (*d*) who is requesting the purchase.
2. **Purchasing selects a supplier.** The purchasing department must identify suppliers who have the capability of supplying the desired goods. If no suppliers are currently listed in the files, new ones must be sought. Vendor ratings may be referred to in choosing among vendors, or perhaps rating information can be relayed to the vendor with the thought of upgrading future performance.
3. **Purchasing places the order with a vendor.** If the order involves a large expenditure, particularly for a one-time purchase of equipment, for example, vendors will usually be asked to bid on the job, and operating and design personnel may be asked to assist in negotiations with a vendor. Large-volume, continuous-usage items may be covered by blanket

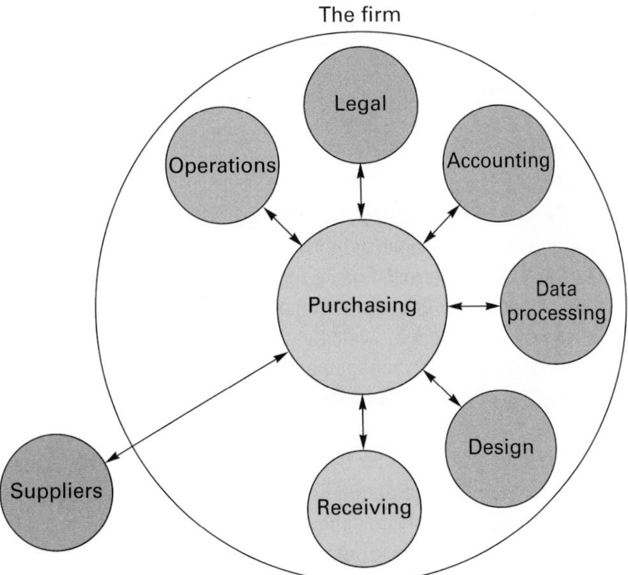

FIGURE 15.3
Purchasing interfaces

purchase orders, which often involve annual negotiation of prices with deliveries subject to request throughout the year. Moderate-volume items may also have blanket purchase orders, or they may be handled on an individual basis. Small purchases may be handled directly between the operating unit requesting a purchased item and the supplier, although some control should be exercised over those purchases so they don't get out of hand.

4. **Monitoring orders.** Routine follow-up on orders, especially large orders or those with lengthy lead times, allows the purchasing department to project potential delays and relay that information to the operating units. Conversely, the purchasing department must communicate changes in quantities and delivery needs of the operating units to suppliers to allow them time to change their plans.
5. **Receiving orders.** Receiving must check incoming shipments for quality and quantity. It must notify purchasing, accounting, and the operating unit that requested the goods. If the goods are not satisfactory, they may have to be returned to the supplier or subjected to further inspection.

Centralized versus Decentralized Purchasing

Purchasing can be centralized or decentralized. Centralized purchasing means that purchasing is handled by one special department. Decentralized purchasing means that individual departments or separate locations handle their own purchasing requirements.

Centralized purchasing may be able to obtain lower prices than decentralized units if the higher volume created by combining orders enables it to take advantage of quantity discounts offered on large orders. Centralized purchasing may also be able to obtain better service and closer attention from suppliers. In addition, centralized purchasing often enables companies to assign certain categories of items to specialists, who tend to be more efficient because they are able to concentrate their efforts on relatively few items instead of spreading themselves across many items.

Centralized purchasing Purchasing is handled by one special department.

Decentralized purchasing has the advantage of awareness of differing "local" needs and being better able to respond to those needs. Decentralized purchasing usually can offer quicker response than centralized purchasing. Where locations are widely scattered, decentralized purchasing may be able to save on transportation costs by buying locally, which has the added attraction of creating goodwill in the community.

Decentralized purchasing Individual departments or separate locations handle their own purchasing requirements.

Some organizations manage to take advantage of both centralization and decentralization by permitting individual units to handle certain items while centralizing purchases of other items. For example, small orders and rush orders may be handled locally or by departments, while centralized purchases would be used for high-volume, high-value items for which discounts are applicable or specialists can provide better service than local buyers or departments.

TABLE 15.2
Guidelines for ethical behavior in purchasing

PRINCIPLES
Integrity in Your Decisions and Actions
Value for Your Employer
Loyalty to Your Profession

STANDARDS

1. **Perceived Impropriety.** Prevent the intent and appearance of unethical or compromising conduct in relationships, actions, and communications.
2. **Conflicts of Interest.** Ensure that any personal, business, or other activity does not conflict with the lawful interests of your employer.
3. **Issues of Influence.** Avoid behaviors or actions that may negatively influence, or appear to influence, supply management decisions.
4. **Responsibilities to Your Employer.** Uphold fiduciary and other responsibilities using reasonable care and granted authority to deliver value to your employer.
5. **Supplier and Customer Relationships.** Promote positive supplier and customer relationships.
6. **Sustainability and Social Responsibility.** Champion social responsibility and sustainability practices in supply management.
7. **Confidential and Proprietary Information.** Protect confidential and proprietary information.
8. **Reciprocity.** Avoid improper reciprocal agreements.
9. **Applicable Laws, Regulations, and Trade Agreements.** Know and obey the letter and spirit of laws, regulations, and trade agreements applicable to supply management.
10. **Professional Competence.** Develop skills, expand knowledge, and conduct business that demonstrates competence and promotes the supply management profession.

Ethics in Purchasing

Ethical behavior is important in all aspects of business. This is certainly true in purchasing, where the temptations for unethical behavior can be enormous. Buyers often hold great power, and salespeople are often eager to make a sale. Unless both parties act in an ethical manner, the potential for abuse is very real. Furthermore, with increased globalization, the challenges are particularly great because a behavior regarded as customary in one country might be regarded as unethical in another country.

The National Association of Purchasing Management has established a set of guidelines for ethical behavior. (See Table 15.2.) As you read through the list, you get insight into the scope of ethics issues in purchasing.

IBM's Supply Chain Social Responsibility

READING

From its inception almost a century ago, IBM has been based on a set of fundamental values. IBM's values shape and define our company and permeate all of our relationships—between our company's people and our shareholders, our clients, the communities where our people live and work, and among our network of suppliers.

Within our supply chain relationships, we know that our company's sizable purchasing power is a unique resource that we must manage responsibly, and we do. IBM spends nearly $2 billion a year with diverse suppliers, for example, greater than any other technology company. Yet more than managing our spending, we have a responsibility to hold ourselves—and our suppliers—to high standards of behavior. This means complying with all applicable laws and regulations. But it goes beyond that. It entails a strong commitment to work with suppliers to encourage sound practices and develop sound global markets.

We have always maintained an open channel of communications with suppliers to set expectations. Today, in an increasingly interconnected world market, the expectations for all players across the entire supply chain go up. Therefore, we are both reaffirming our existing policies and instituting some new practices, which are spelled out in the following Supplier Conduct Principles. These principles establish for our suppliers the minimum standards we expect from them as a condition of doing business with IBM. IBM will have the right to take action with suppliers that fail to comply with these principles, including terminating our relationship with them.

Source: Reprinted courtesy of International Business Machines Corporation.

E-BUSINESS

The commercial blossoming of the Internet has led to an explosion of Internet-related activities, many of which have a direct impact on organizations' supply chains, even if those organizations aren't themselves users of the Internet. **E-business** refers to the use of electronic technology to facilitate business transactions. E-business, or e-commerce, involves the interaction of different business organizations as well as the interaction of individuals with business organizations. Applications include Internet buying and selling, e-mail, order and shipment tracking, and electronic data interchange. In addition, companies use e-business to promote their products or services, and to provide information about them. Delivery firms have seen the demand for their services increase dramatically due to e-business. Among them are giants UPS and FedEx.

E-business The use of electronic technology to facilitate business transactions.

SERVICE

Table 15.3 lists some of the numerous advantages of e-business.

There are two essential features of e-business: the Web site and order fulfillment. Companies may invest considerable time and effort in front-end design (the Web site), but the back end (order fulfillment) is at least as important. It involves order processing, billing, inventory management, warehousing, packing, shipping, and delivery.

Many of the problems that occur with Internet selling are supply related. The ability to order quickly creates an expectation in customers that the remainder of the process will proceed smoothly and quickly. But the same capability that enables quick ordering also enables demand fluctuations that can inject a certain amount of chaos to the system, almost guaranteeing that there won't be a smooth or quick delivery. Oftentimes the rate at which orders come in via the Internet greatly exceeds an organization's ability to fulfill them. Not too long ago, Toys "R" Us had that experience during the busy Christmas season; it ended up offering thousands of disappointed customers a $100 coupon to make up for it.

In the early days of Internet selling, many organizations thought they could avoid bearing the costs of holding inventories by acting solely as intermediaries, having their suppliers ship directly to their customers. Although this approach worked for some companies, it failed for others, usually because suppliers ran out of certain items. This led some companies to rethink the strategy.

TABLE 15.3
Advantages of e-business

Companies and publishers have a global presence and the customer has global choices and easy access to information.

Companies can improve competitiveness and quality of service by allowing access to their services any place, any time. Companies also have the ability to monitor customers' choices and requests electronically.

Companies can analyze the interest in various products based on the number of hits and requests for information.

Companies can collect detailed information about clients' preferences, which enables mass customization and personalized products. An example is the purchase of PCs over the Web, where the buyer specifies the final configuration.

Supply chain response times are shortened. The biggest impact is on products that can be delivered directly on the Web, such as forms of publishing and software distribution.

The roles of the intermediary and sometimes the traditional retailer or service provider are reduced or eliminated entirely in a process called *disintermediation.* This process reduces costs and adds alternative purchasing options.

Substantial cost savings and substantial price reductions related to the reduction of transaction costs can be realized. Companies that provide purchasing and support through the Web can save significant personnel costs.

E-commerce allows the creation of virtual companies that distribute only through the Web, thus reducing costs. Amazon.com and other net vendors can afford to sell for a lower price because they do not need to maintain retail stores and, in many cases, warehouse space.

The playing field is leveled for small companies that lack significant resources to invest in infrastructure and marketing.

Source: Reprinted by permission from David Simchi-Levi, Philip Kaminsky, and Edith Simchi-Levi, *Designing and Managing the Supply Chain: Concepts, Strategies, and Case Studies* (New York: Irwin/McGraw-Hill, 2000), p. 235.

Industry giants such as Amazon.com and Barnesandnoble.com built huge warehouses around the country so they could maintain greater control over their inventories. Still others are outsourcing fulfillment, turning over that portion of their business to third-party fulfillment operators such as former catalog fulfillment company Fingerhut, now a unit of Federated Department Stores.

Using third-party fulfillment means losing control over fulfillment. It might also result in fulfillers substituting their standards for the company they are serving, and using the fulfiller's shipping price structure. On the other hand, an e-commerce company may not have the resources or infrastructure to do the job itself. Another alternative might be to form a strategic partnership with a bricks-and-mortar company. This can be a quick way to jump-start an e-commerce business. In any case, somewhere in the supply chain there has to be a bricks-and-mortar facility.

A growing portion of e-business involves business-to-business (B2B) commerce rather than business-to-consumer commerce. To facilitate business-to-business commerce, B2B marketplaces are created. Table 15.4 describes B2B marketplace enablers.

B2B exchanges can improve supply chain visibility to trading partners from a single point of access, facilitating the development of common standards and data formats for schedules, product codes, location codes, and performance criteria. And e-businesses focusing on transportation services can benefit from having an efficient hub for collaboration between shippers and transportation providers, helping to translate customer shipment forecasts into more predictable demand for equipment, and enabling carriers to deploy their equipment more effectively.

Desperately Seeking E-Fulfillment

READING

Fingerhut is now a major e-commerce fulfillment player, thanks as much to its massive data warehouse of customer information as to its four million square feet of high-tech warehouse space.

In addition to handling its own business, Fingerhut handles the back end of other high-volume retailers, such as Walmart and eToys. Their massive warehouse in St. Cloud, MN, can process as many as 30,000 items per hour.

Big shippers like UPS and FedEx have also successfully branched into e-commerce fulfillment. In addition to their traditional shipping niche, they'll warehouse your inventory for you, handle all back-end tasks, and offer complete solutions including Web site design, development, and hosting. Their e-commerce edge came not only from their overnight, single-order delivery infrastructure, but also from having already developed package-tracking software.

Hiring a fulfillment giant is de rigueur these days for huge "click and bricks" retailers like Walmart and Pier One, who have to switch in a hurry from their old operating model of moving big pallets of goods to stores to moving single items to individuals.

Third-party fulfillers are treasured for their efficiencies and advanced technology. But some can be unresponsive and not always capable of supporting [clients'] software. There has also been some grumbling in *Barron's* that the big third-party fulfillers are doomed middlemen, a mere transitory phase for e-commerce.

Source: Excerpted from Judith Silverstein, "Desperately Seeking E-Fulfillment," *Digital Chicago*, November/December 1999, pp. 29 and 30.

Behind the scenes of e-commerce: Order processing and fulfillment at Fingerhut.

Type	Description
Financial	Provide financial and other resources for Web-enhanced commerce.
Technology	Provide software, applications, and expertise necessary to create B2B marketplace.

TABLE 15.4
B2B marketplace enablers

Source: Adapted from *Forbes,* July 2000.

E-Procurement at IBM

READING

"In 1999, IBM did what would seem to be a near impossible task. It began doing business with 12,000 suppliers over the Internet—sending purchase orders, receiving invoices and paying suppliers, all using the World Wide Web as its transaction-processing network."

Setting up 12,000 suppliers to do business on the Internet was relatively easy compared to the resistance of suppliers to link to IBM via EDI (electronic data interchange). Suppliers who didn't have large contracts with IBM balked at EDI because of the expense of special software and a VAN (value-added network) that were needed to do EDI. No such problem with using the Internet: Suppliers don't need special software or a costly VAN to do business with IBM.

The Internet's simplicity reduces costs for IBM and its suppliers. IBM estimated that it saved $500 million in 1999 by moving procurement to the Web, and believes that is only the tip of the iceberg. Much of the savings came from eliminating intermediaries. IBM uses the Web to manage multiple tiers of suppliers and as a tool to work with suppliers to improve quality and reduce costs.

But cost reduction was not the only reason IBM switched to Internet procurement. Web-based procurement is a key part of its supplier management strategy: IBM sees great value in using the Internet to collaborate with suppliers and tap into their expertise much more rapidly than previously. "The Internet will also allow IBM to collaborate with suppliers over scheduling issues. If the company wants to increase production of a certain product it will be able to check with component suppliers and determine if suppliers can support the increase. If there are schedule cutbacks, [it] will be able to notify suppliers almost instantaneously and excess inventory can be avoided."

And although supply chains are viewed as sequential, IBM doesn't necessarily want to manage them that way. Rather, it wants to use the Internet to manage multiple tiers of suppliers simultaneously. An example of this is how it deals with CMs (contract manufacturers). The company sends forecasts and purchase orders to the CMs for the printed circuit boards they supply. It also gives all the component manufacturers the requirements and they ship parts directly to the CM. The company estimates it saved in excess of $150 million in 1999. "The savings were the difference between contract manufacturers' price for components used on the boards and IBM's price that it had negotiated with component suppliers."

Because the Internet is becoming crucial to IBM's supplier-management strategies, IBM is trying to make it easier for suppliers to do business over the Web. The company has developed a Web-based portal to provide a single entry point to IBM. As is the case with most large companies, IBM has multiple interfaces with its suppliers, including engineering, quality, as well as purchasing, and typically suppliers have to connect to separate URLs (universal resource locators) in a company. IBM's portal provides a single point of entry for suppliers, making it easier for suppliers to do business with IBM and increasing the speed of the supply chain. Speed is vitally important in the electronics industry due to very short product life cycles. If products don't get to the market quickly, most of the profit opportunity is lost.

Still another benefit envisioned by IBM will be the ability to form strategic alliances with some of its suppliers. In the past, the fact that many suppliers used by IBM for its production processes were as far as 12,000 miles away made it difficult to build strategic alliances with them. IBM believes that using the Internet will strengthen relations and enable it to develop alliances.

"The Internet also will play an important role in IBM's general procurement . . . IBM was doing EDI with core production suppliers, but not with . . . other forms of general procurement. Purchasers were still faxing and phoning orders, which is timely and costly."

Additional cost savings come from small volume, one-of-a-kind special purchases, because of the speed and ease of using the Internet.

Web-based procurement will eliminate mistakes that occur during the procurement process due to having to type or enter prices and other figures on paper documents.

Questions

1. How did IBM achieve cost reductions by using the Internet for procurement?
2. What advantage did IBM's use of the Internet have for small suppliers?
3. Aside from cost reduction, what major value does IBM envision for its interaction with suppliers?
4. How does use of the Internet for procurement reduce mistakes? Indicate how using the Internet made that benefit possible.
5. How does having a Web-based portal help IBM's suppliers?

Source: Based on James Carbone, "E-Procurement at IBM: POs Are Just the Beginning," *Purchasing* 128, no. 4 (March 23, 2000), p. S50.

SUPPLIER MANAGEMENT

Reliable and trustworthy suppliers are a vital link in an effective supply chain. Timely deliveries of goods or services and high quality are just two of the ways that suppliers can contribute to effective operations. A purchasing manager may function as an "external operations manager," working with suppliers to coordinate supplier operations and buyer needs.

In this section, various aspects of supplier management are described, including supplier audits, supplier certification, and supplier partnering. The section starts with an aspect that can have important ramifications for the entire organization: choosing suppliers.

Choosing Suppliers

In many respects, choosing a vendor involves taking into account many of the same factors associated with making a major purchase (e.g., a car or stereo system). A company considers price, quality, the supplier's reputation, past experience with the supplier, and service after the sale. The main difference is that a company, because of the quantities it orders and operations requirements, often provides suppliers with detailed specifications of the materials or parts it wants instead of buying items off the shelf, although most organizations buy standard items that way. The main factors a company takes into account when it selects a vendor are outlined in Table 15.5.

Because different factors are important for different situations, purchasing must decide, with the help of operations, the importance of each factor (i.e., how much weight to give to each factor), and then rate potential vendors according to how well they can be expected to perform against this list. This process is called **vendor analysis**, and it is conducted periodically, or whenever there is a significant change in the weighting assigned to the various factors.

Vendor analysis Evaluating the sources of supply in terms of price, quality, reputation, and service.

Supplier Audits

Periodic audits of suppliers are a means of keeping current on suppliers' production (or service) capabilities, quality and delivery problems and resolutions, and suppliers' performance

TABLE 15.5
Choosing a supplier

Factor	Typical Questions
Quality and quality assurance	What procedures does the supplier have for quality control and quality assurance? Are quality problems and corrective actions documented?
Flexibility	How flexible is the supplier in handling changes in delivery schedules, quantity, and product or service changes?
Location	Is the supplier nearby?
Price	Are prices reasonable given the entire package the supplier will provide? Is the supplier willing to negotiate prices? Is the supplier willing to cooperate to reduce costs?
Product or service changes	How much advance notification does the supplier require for product or service changes?
Reputation and financial stability	What is the reputation of the supplier? How financially stable is the supplier?
Lead times and on-time delivery	What lead times can the supplier provide? What procedures does the supplier have for assuring on-time deliveries? What procedures does the supplier have for documenting and correcting problems?
Other accounts	Is the supplier heavily dependent on other customers, causing a risk of giving priority to those needs over ours?

on other criteria. If an audit reveals problem areas, a buyer can attempt to find a solution before more serious problems develop. Among the factors typically covered by a supplier audit are management style, quality assurance, materials management, the design process used, process improvement policies, and procedures for corrective action and follow-up.

Supplier audits are also an important first step in supplier certification programs.

Supplier Certification

Supplier certification is a detailed examination of the policies and capabilities of a supplier. The certification process verifies that a supplier meets or exceeds the requirements of a buyer. This is generally important in supplier relationships, but it is particularly important when buyers are seeking to establish a long-term relationship with suppliers. Certified suppliers are sometimes referred to as *world class* suppliers. One advantage of using certified suppliers is that the buyer can eliminate much or all of the inspection and testing of delivered goods. And although problems with supplier goods or services might not be totally eliminated, there is much less risk than with noncertified suppliers.

Rather than develop their own certification program, some companies rely on standard industry certifications such as ISO 9000, perhaps the most widely used international certification.

Supplier Relationship Management

Purchasing has the ultimate responsibility for establishing and maintaining good supplier relationships. The type of relationship is often related to the length of a contract between buyers and sellers. Short-term contracts involve competitive bidding. Companies post specifications and potential suppliers bid on the contracts. Suppliers are kept at arm's length, and the relationship is minimal. Business may be conducted through computerized interaction. Medium-term contracts often involve ongoing relationships. Long-term contracts often evolve into partnerships, with buyers and sellers cooperating on various issues that tend to benefit both parties. Increasingly, business organizations are establishing long-term relationships with suppliers in certain situations that are based on *strategic* considerations.

Some business organizations use *supplier forums* to educate potential suppliers about the organization's policies and requirements and to enhance opportunities for receiving contracts. Others use supplier forums to share information, strengthen cooperation, and encourage joint thinking. And some organizations use a *supplier code of conduct* that requires suppliers to maintain safe working conditions, treat workers with respect and dignity, and have production processes that do not harm workers, customers, or the environment.

Business organizations are becoming increasingly aware of the importance of building good relationships with their suppliers. In the past, too many firms regarded their suppliers as adversaries and dealt with them on that basis. One lesson learned from the Japanese is that numerous benefits derive from good supplier relations, including supplier flexibility in terms of accepting changes in delivery schedules, quality, and quantities. Moreover, suppliers can often help identify problems and offer suggestions for solving them. Thus, simply choosing and switching suppliers on the basis of price is a very shortsighted approach to handling an ongoing need.

Keeping good relations with suppliers is increasingly recognized as an important factor in maintaining a competitive edge. Many companies are adopting a view of suppliers as partners. This viewpoint stresses a stable relationship with relatively few reliable suppliers who can provide high-quality supplies, maintain precise delivery schedules, and remain flexible relative to changes in productive specifications and delivery schedules. A comparison of the contrasting views of suppliers is provided in Table 15.6.

Supplier Partnerships

More and more business organizations are seeking to establish partnerships with other organizations in their supply chains. This implies fewer suppliers, longer-term relationships, sharing of information (forecasts, sales data, problem alerts), and cooperation in planning. Among the possible benefits are higher quality, increased delivery speed and reliability, lower inventories, lower costs, higher profits, and, in general, improved operations.

TABLE 15.6
Supplier as adversary versus supplier as partner

Aspect	Adversary	Partner
Number of suppliers	Many; play one off against the others	One or a few
Length of relationship	May be brief	Long-term
Low price	Major consideration	Moderately important
Reliability	May not be high	High
Openness	Low	High
Quality	May be unreliable; buyer inspects	At the source; vendor certified
Volume of business	May be low due to many suppliers	High
Flexibility	Relatively low	Relatively high
Location	Widely dispersed	Nearness is important for short lead times and quick service

There are a number of obstacles to supplier partnerships, not the least of which is that because many of the benefits go to the buyer, suppliers may be hesitant to enter into such relationships. Suppliers may have to increase their investment in equipment, which might put a strain on cash flow. Another possibility is that the cultures of the buyer and supplier might be quite different and not lend themselves to such an arrangement.

Strategic Partnering

Strategic partnering Two or more business organizations that have complementary products or services join so that each may realize a strategic benefit.

Strategic partnering occurs when two or more business organizations that have complementary products or services that would *strategically* benefit the others agree to join so that each may realize a strategic benefit. One way this occurs is when a supplier agrees to hold inventory for a customer, thereby reducing the customer's cost of holding the inventory, in exchange for the customer's agreeing to a long-term commitment, thereby relieving the supplier of the costs that would be needed to continually find new customers, negotiate prices and services, and so on.

NestléUSA and Ocean Spray Form Strategic Operations Alliance

READING

Glendale, CA—01/25/02—The NestléUSA—Beverage Division and Ocean Spray Cranberries, Inc., announced today that they have formed a long-term strategic operations alliance that will enable both companies to significantly increase manufacturing and supply chain efficiency, while maintaining high quality products for their respective juice businesses.

"Ocean Spray shares many of our same business values, in particular their commitment to high quality manufacturing standards," said Mike Mitchell, President and General Manager of NestléUSA—Beverage Division. "By capitalizing upon each other's best practices, we feel both Nestlé and Ocean Spray will be better equipped to grow in this highly aggressive juice category in which we compete."

Within the strategic operations alliance, Nestlé will transition over time its manufacturing of Libby's Juicy Juice and Libby's Kerns Nectars to Ocean Spray facilities. The companies will also pursue collaborative procurement of common raw and packaging materials, and common operating supplies, as well as shared logistics to increase process efficiency across the supply chain.

"This alliance between two great companies creates a powerful synergy," said Ocean Spray President and Chief Operating Officer Randy Papadellis. "By bringing Nestlé juice production into our plants and joining forces with them on purchasing and distribution, we will establish an economy of scale that will boost the profitability of both companies."

With Ocean Spray leading the category of shelf stable juices and Libby's Juicy Juice being the leader in 100% juice for kids, the operations alliance is expected to create added value of mutual benefit. The strategic operations alliance will be governed by a leadership team and an executive operating committee, both comprised of members from each company.

Source: www.Nestleusa.com, www.NestleNewsroom.com.

INVENTORY MANAGEMENT

Inventories are a key component of supply chains. Although inventory management is discussed in more detail in several other chapters, certain aspects of inventory management are particularly important for supply chain management. They relate to the location of inventories in the supply chain, the speed at which inventory moves through the supply chain, and dealing with the effect of demand variability on inventories.

The location of inventories is an important factor for effective material flow through the chain and for order fulfillment. Often trade-offs must be made. One approach is to use centralized inventories, which generally results in lower overall inventory than there would be if decentralized inventories were used, because with decentralized inventories, one location may be understocked while another location is overstocked. Conversely, decentralized locations can provide faster delivery and generally lower shipping costs.

The rate at which material moves through a supply chain is referred to as **inventory velocity**. The greater the velocity, the lower the inventory holding costs and the faster orders are filled and goods are turned into cash.

Inventory velocity The speed at which goods move through a supply chain.

Without careful management, demand variations can easily cause inventory fluctuations to get out of control. Variations in demand at the consumer end of a supply chain tend to ripple backwards through the chain. Moreover, periodic ordering and reaction to shortages can magnify variations, causing inventories to oscillate in increasingly larger swings. This is known as the **bullwhip effect**, because the pattern of demand variation is analogous to the motion of a bullwhip response to slight jerking of the handle. Consequently, shortages and surpluses occur throughout the chain, resulting in higher costs and lower customer satisfaction, unless preventive action is taken. The bullwhip effect is illustrated in Figure 15.4.

Bullwhip effect Inventory oscillations become progressively larger looking backward through the supply chain.

The causes of inventory variability can be not only demand variability but also factors such as quality problems, labor problems, unusual weather conditions, and delays in shipments of goods. Adding to this can be communication delays, incomplete communications, and lack of coordination of activities among organizations in the supply chain.

Still other factors can contribute to the bullwhip effect. They include forecast inaccuracies, overreaction to stockouts (customers often order more than they need after experiencing a shortage), order batching to save on ordering and transportation costs (e.g., full truckloads, economic lot sizes), sales incentives and promotions, and service and product mix changes, which can create uneven demand patterns, and liberal return policies.

Good supply chain management can overcome the bullwhip effect by *strategic buffering* and inventory replenishment based on needs. An example of strategic buffering would be holding the bulk of retail inventory at a distribution center rather than at retail outlets. That way, inventories of specific retail outlets can be replenished as needed based on point-of-sale information from retail outlets as well as information on retail outlet inventories.

This is sometimes accomplished using **vendor-managed inventory (VMI)**. Vendors track goods shipped to distributors and retail outlets, and monitor retail supplies, enabling the vendors to replenish inventories when supplies are low. The practice is common in the retail sector, and is also used in other phases of supply chains. VMI lets companies reduce overhead by shifting responsibility for owning, managing, and replenishing inventory to vendors. Not only do assets decrease, the amount of working capital needed to operate a business also decreases.

Vendor-managed inventory (VMI) Vendors monitor goods and replenish retail inventories when supplies are low.

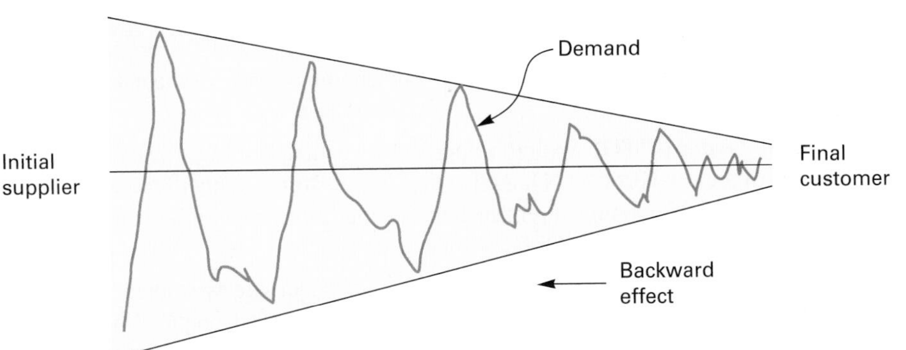

FIGURE 15.4
The bullwhip effect: demand variations begin at the customer end of the chain and become increasingly large as they radiate backward through the chain

Passengers line up for Eurostar tickets at Gare du Nord train station in Paris. Eurostar reported that its entire service between London, Paris, and Brussels was fully booked as stranded airline passengers searched for alternative methods of travel after volcanic ash from Iceland grounded more than half of Europe's airspace in 2010.

SERVICE

ORDER FULFILLMENT

Order fulfillment The processes involved in responding to customer orders.

Order fulfillment refers to the processes involved in responding to customer orders. Fulfillment time can be an important criterion for customers. It is often a function of the degree of customization required. Here are some common approaches:

- **Engineer-to-Order (ETO).** With this approach, products are designed and built according to customer specifications. This approach is frequently used for large-scale construction projects, custom homebuilding, home remodeling, and for products made in job shops. The fulfillment time can be relatively lengthy because of the nature of the project, as well as the presence of other jobs ahead of the new one.
- **Make-to-Order (MTO).** With this approach, a standard product design is used, but production of the final product is linked to the final customer's specifications. This approach is used by aircraft manufacturers such as Boeing. Fulfillment time is generally less than with ETO fulfillment, but still fairly long.
- **Assemble-to-Order (ATO).** With this approach, products are assembled to customer specifications from a stock of standard and modular components. Computer manufacturers such as Dell operate using this approach. Fulfillment times are fairly short, often a week or less.

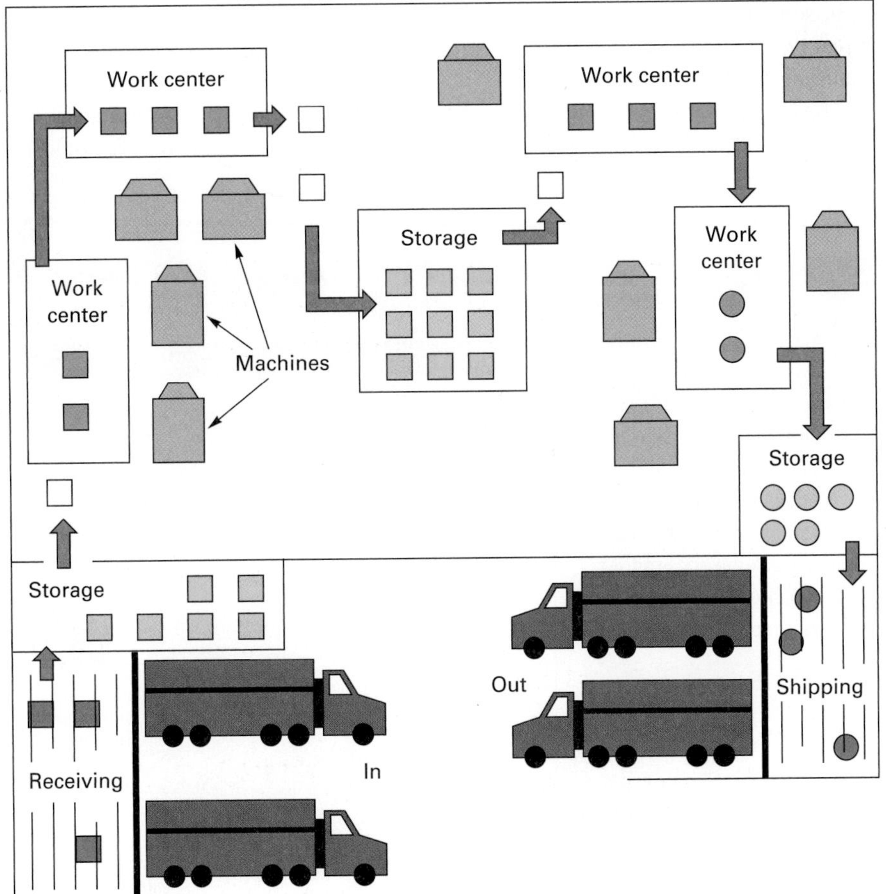

FIGURE 15.5
Movement within a facility

- **Make-to-Stock (MTS).** With this approach, production is based on a forecast, and products are sold to the customer from finished goods stock. This approach is used in department stores and supermarkets. The order fulfillment time is immediate. A variation of this is e-commerce; although goods have already been produced, there is a lag in fulfillment to allow for shipping.

LOGISTICS

Logistics refers to the movement of materials, services, cash, and information in a supply chain. Materials include all of the physical items used in a production process. In addition to raw materials and work in process, there are support items such as fuels, equipment, parts, tools, lubricants, office supplies, and more. Logistics includes movement within a facility, overseeing incoming and outgoing shipments of goods and materials, and information flow throughout the supply chain.

Logistics The movement of materials, services, cash, and information in a supply chain.

Movement within a Facility

Movement of goods within a manufacturing facility is part of production control. Figure 15.5 shows the many steps where materials move within a manufacturing facility:

1. From incoming vehicles to receiving.
2. From receiving to storage.
3. From storage to the point of use (e.g., a work center).
4. From one work center to the next or to temporary storage.
5. From the last operation to final storage.
6. From storage to packaging/shipping.
7. From shipping to outgoing vehicles.

In some instances, the goods being moved are supplies; in other instances, the goods are actual products or partially completed products; and in still other instances, the goods are raw materials or purchased parts.

Movement of materials must be coordinated to arrive at the appropriate destinations at appropriate times. Workers and supervisors must take care so that items are not lost, stolen, or damaged during movement.

Wegmans' Shipping System

OPERATIONS TOUR

The Wegmans supermarket chain (see the Wegmans Operations Tour at the end of Chapter 1) has been cited as a leader in supply chain management in the grocery industry. Its distribution system provides a number of examples of strategies and tactics that contribute to its success in managing its supply chain.

Wegmans operates a number of warehouses that are used to supply its stores. Some warehouses stock grocery items, while others stock frozen foods, and still others stock bakery products, seasonal items, and/or produce. Even though all stores and warehouses are owned by Wegmans, the warehouses service the stores on a B2B basis.

Distribution

Individual stores' orders are generated automatically on a daily basis. These are directed to the appropriate warehouses. Order fulfillment begins when a warehouse downloads a store's order to its information system. There are a variety of methods used to replenish stores' inventories. Several of these avoid the need for warehouse storage, saving the company storage and handling costs. Those methods are

1. **Cross dock:** A full inbound pallet is redirected to an outbound shipment.
2. **Cross distribution:** An inbound pallet is broken down into cases right on the dock, and then the cases are immediately distributed to outbound pallets.
3. **Vendor-managed inventory:** Vendors of some non–store brand items such as bread and soft drinks handle replenishment, and those items come directly from the vendor's warehouse to the stores.

Warehoused replenishment items are handled as full pallets, or broken down into cases, depending on quantities ordered:

1. **Block pick:** An entire pallet of goods in the warehouse is placed on an outbound truck.
2. **Case pick:** Individual cases or packages are pulled from inventory, placed on pallets and shrink wrapped, and then placed on outbound trucks.

Computerized information on incoming orders is checked against incoming shipments of stocks to determine which items can be filled using cross docking or cross distribution right in the loading area. These items are then subtracted from a store's order. The remaining items are filled from warehouse supplies.

FIGURE 1 Distribution Diagram

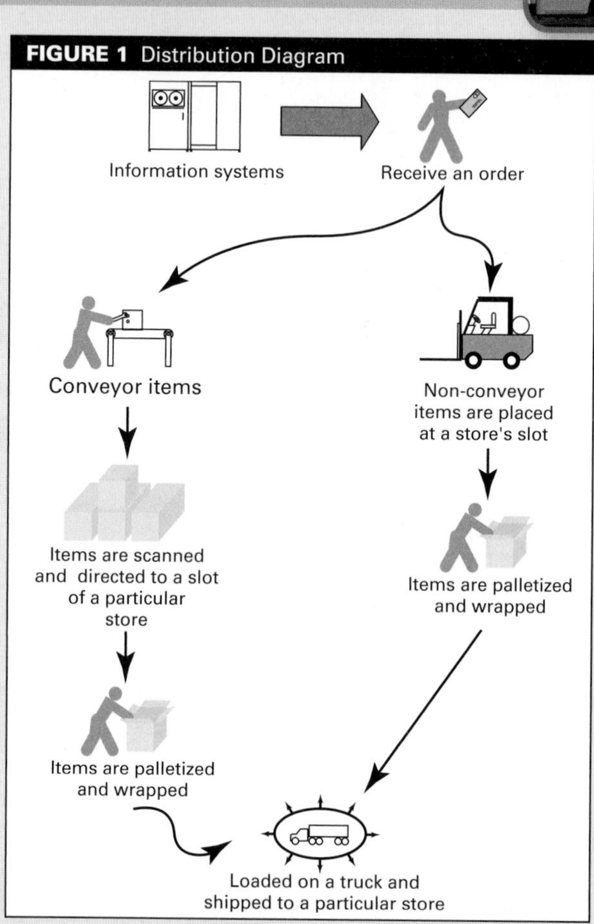
Information systems
Receive an order
Conveyor items
Non-conveyor items are placed at a store's slot
Items are scanned and directed to a slot of a particular store
Items are palletized and wrapped
Items are palletized and wrapped
Loaded on a truck and shipped to a particular store

Warehoused Items

Here is a brief description of retrieval of warehoused items in a dry goods (canned, boxed, etc.) warehouse: The system is semiautomated, and only a few workers are needed to process orders and monitor the system.

Warehoused items are classified for either conveyor belt or non–conveyor belt handling. Items are designated for conveyor belt handling based on their packaging and volume. If volume is low and packaging can withstand the conveyor belt, it will be assigned to the conveyor belt. If the packaging cannot withstand the conveyor belt, the items will be individually case-picked. Non–conveyor belt items that are high volume are automatically moved in bulk from their warehouse locations to a staging area to await loading onto an outbound truck.

(continued)

(concluded)

When orders for conveyor belt items are received, a worker is given bar code labels that contain the number of the ordering store. The worker then goes to the section where an item is stored, affixes the appropriate store bar code, and places the item on the conveyor belt. As items move along the conveyer, their bar codes are scanned and they are sorted according to store number. After scanning and sorting, items move to staging areas where they are placed on pallets and shrink wrapped, and then placed in a slot designated for the appropriate store. The figure illustrates the handling of low-volume items.

Collaboration with Vendors

A desire to improve conveyer belt transporting has led Wegmans to collaborate with vendors in an effort to improve packaging design. Occasionally goods will fall off the belt, and those items have to be inspected to see if they have been damaged. Damaged goods not only are costly, but they are also lost from inventory and must be replaced. Improved packaging also increases the number of goods that can be handled with the conveyer system.

Forecasting

In 2002 Wegmans implemented its program of consistent, low pricing. This program reduced the number of promotional and sale items, reduced much of the volatility in demand, and made forecasting and inventory planning easier.

New Approaches

In 2003 Wegmans began exploring the use of auto-ID tags. The tags are very small micro chips, no bigger than a grain of salt. The tags are somewhat similar to bar codes, but offer greater potential for supply chain management because they can be more quickly read (e.g., multiple items can be scanned at once and, unlike bar codes, no line-of-sight is required for a reading), and scanning devices can be placed in warehouses and even on supermarket shelves that would warn when stocks of individual items are running low. The tags initially cost about $1 each, and currently cost about five cents each, making them cost effective for tracking shipments and bulk quantities of items, but still too costly to use on individual store items. However, they hold great promise for increasing supply chain visibility and event management capabilities.

Incoming and Outgoing Shipments

Overseeing the shipment of incoming and outgoing goods comes under the heading of **traffic management.** This function handles schedules and decisions on shipping method and times, taking into account costs of various alternatives, government regulations, the needs of the organization relative to quantities and timing, and external factors such as potential shipping delays or disruptions (e.g., highway construction, truckers' strikes).

Traffic management Overseeing the shipment of incoming and outgoing goods.

Computer tracking of shipments often helps to maintain knowledge of the current status of shipments as well as to provide other up-to-date information on costs and schedules.

Tracking Goods: RFID

Advances in technology are revolutionizing the way businesses track goods in their supply chains. **Radio frequency identification (RFID)** is a technology that uses radio waves to identify objects, such as goods in supply chains. This is done through the use of an RFID tag that is attached to an object. The tag has an integrated circuit and an antenna that project information or other data to network-connected RFID readers using radio waves. RFID tags can be attached to pallets, cases, or individual items. They provide unique identification, enabling businesses to identify, track, monitor, or locate practically any object in the supply chain that is within range of a tag reader. These tags are similar to bar codes, but they have the advantage of conveying much more information, and they do not require a line-of-sight for reading that bar codes require. And unlike

Radio frequency identification (RFID) A technology that uses radio waves to identify objects, such as goods in supply chains.

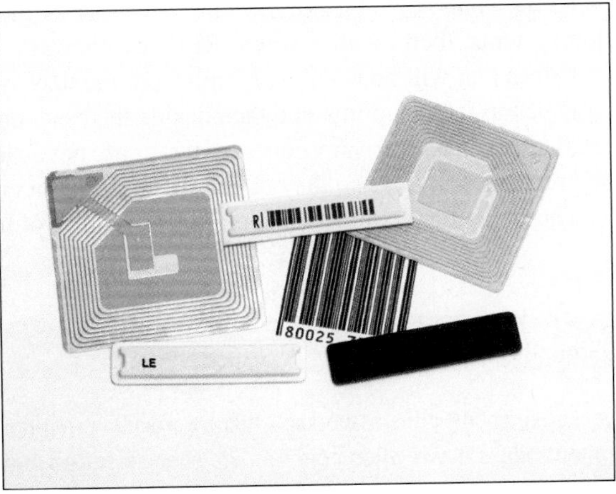

bar codes, which must be scanned individually and usually manually, multiple RFID tags can be read simultaneously and automatically. Furthermore, an RFID tag provides more precise information than a bar code: Tags contain detailed information on each object, whereas bar codes convey only an object's classification, such as its stockkeeping unit (SKU). This enables management to know where every object is in the supply chain. RFID has the potential to fundamentally change the way companies track inventory and share information, and dramatically improve the management of supply chains. This technology increases supply chain visibility, improves inventory management, improves quality control, and enhances relationships with suppliers and customers.

Springdale Farm

READING

The Springdale Farm is a demonstration farm located near Rochester, New York. One area of the farm is dedicated to advances in dairy cow management that involves a unique application of RFID technology. The farm has a milking parlor that features a robotic milking system that has been "trained" on a cow-by-cow basis so that it automatically adapts to the physical aspects of each particular cow. When a cow enters the milking parlor, it is immediately identified by its RFID tag, and the milking machine adjusts itself and then attaches itself to the cow for milking. The system includes a self-cleaning, laser-guided robot plus an automatic feeder, all managed by a software program tied into RFID tags worn by the cows. The accompanying software keeps track of data regarding the cow's health, history, milk production, and milk quality. It also allows the cows to be milked whenever they want, without human intervention, freeing workers to focus on other aspects of the operation of the farm. When a cow enters the milking parlor, it is bathed, and then the milking equipment automatically attaches itself to the cow and begins milking. Meanwhile, the cow is given a snack especially formulated for that cow. When the milking is complete, the machine detaches from the cow, the snack is withdrawn, the front door swings open, and the cow exits.

RFID eliminates the need for manual counting and bar-code scanning of goods at receiving docks, in warehouses, and on retail shelves. This eliminates errors and greatly speeds up the process. Tags could reduce employee and customer theft by placing readers at building exits and in parking lots. Still other advantages include increased accuracy in warehouse "picking" of items for shipping or for use in assembly operations, increased accuracy in dispensing drugs to patients in hospitals, and reduced surgical errors.

RFID may enable small, agile businesses to compete with larger, more bureaucratic businesses that may be slow to adopt this new technology. Conversely, large businesses may be better able to afford the costs involved. These include the costs of the tags themselves as well as the cost of affixing individual tags, the cost of readers, and the cost of computer hardware and software to transmit and analyze the data generated.

The potential benefits for supply chain management are huge, and widespread adoption of RFID technology by retailers and manufacturers is predicted. In order to take advantage of RFID technology, businesses must first assess the capabilities of their existing information systems, then identify where RFID can have the greatest impact, estimate the time and resources that will be needed to implement the new system, estimate the risks and rewards of early versus late adoption, and then decide the best course of action. Important concerns at the retail level relate to privacy concerns if tags are not deactivated after items have been purchased and placement of tags so they do not hide important customer information on products.

The following reading provides an explanation of how an RFID system would work.

RFID Tags: Keeping the Shelves Stocked

READING

The supply chain of the consumer packaged goods industry works well when sales are steady, but it often breaks down when confronted by a sudden surge in demand. RFID tags could change that by providing real-time information about what's happening on store shelves. Here's how the system would work:

(continued)

(concluded)

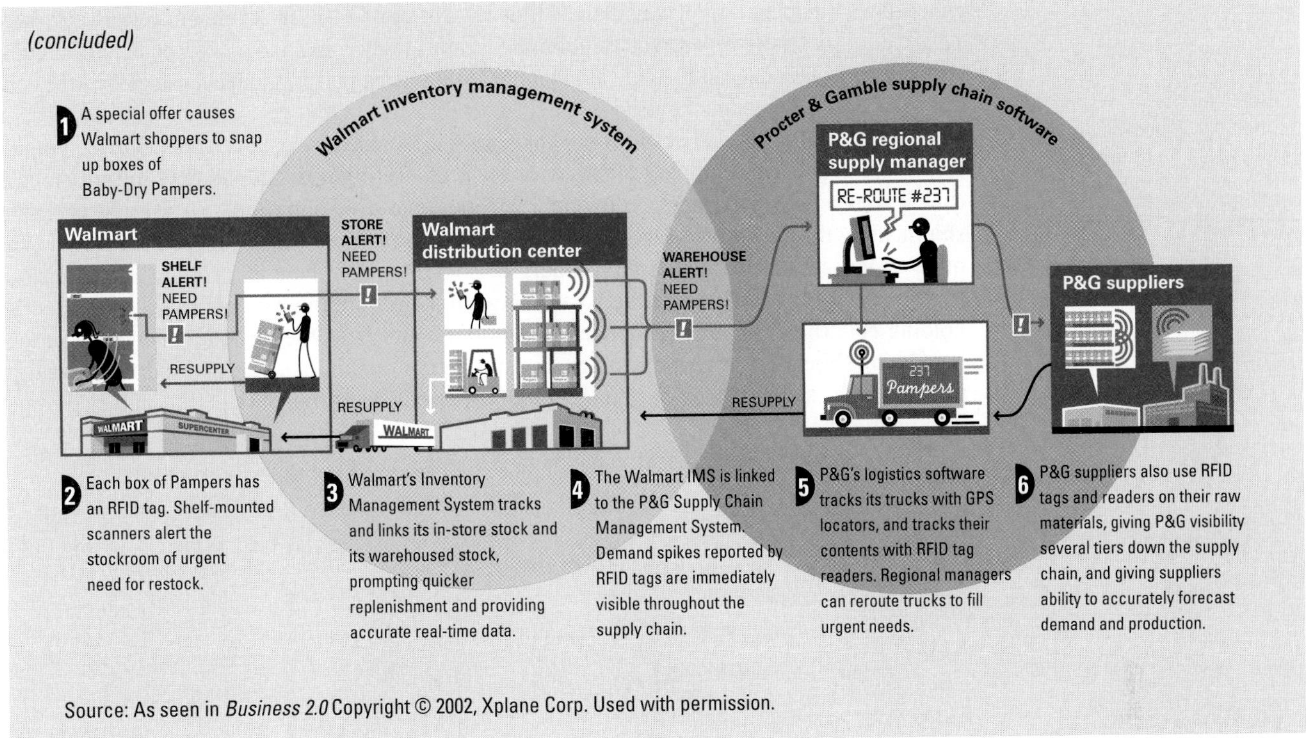
Walmart inventory management system
Procter & Gamble supply chain software
1 A special offer causes Walmart shoppers to snap up boxes of Baby-Dry Pampers.
Walmart
SHELF ALERT! NEED PAMPERS!
RESUPPLY
STORE ALERT! NEED PAMPERS!
Walmart distribution center
RESUPPLY
WAREHOUSE ALERT! NEED PAMPERS!
P&G regional supply manager
RE-ROUTE #237
237 Pampers
RESUPPLY
P&G suppliers
2 Each box of Pampers has an RFID tag. Shelf-mounted scanners alert the stockroom of urgent need for restock.
3 Walmart's Inventory Management System tracks and links its in-store stock and its warehoused stock, prompting quicker replenishment and providing accurate real-time data.
4 The Walmart IMS is linked to the P&G Supply Chain Management System. Demand spikes reported by RFID tags are immediately visible throughout the supply chain.
5 P&G's logistics software tracks its trucks with GPS locators, and tracks their contents with RFID tag readers. Regional managers can reroute trucks to fill urgent needs.
6 P&G suppliers also use RFID tags and readers on their raw materials, giving P&G visibility several tiers down the supply chain, and giving suppliers ability to accurately forecast demand and production.

Source: As seen in *Business 2.0* Copyright © 2002, Xplane Corp. Used with permission.

Active RFID vs. Passive RFID

READING

Allan Griebenow

RFID tag technology falls into two broad categories—passive or active. Active RFID has an on-board power supply (e.g., a battery) while passive relies on capturing and "re-using" a small portion of the wake-up signal's energy to transmit its RFID tag I.D. back to the receiver. This is a "good news, bad news" situation. The "good news" is that passive tags can be manufactured and sold at a much lower price point today than active tags. This is a critical element in many RFID supply chain applications requiring the tagging of millions of units. The "bad news" is that passive tags often struggle to provide reliable reads given the performance limitations of a technology using only a small amount of power to push its signal off metal surfaces, through layers of palletized products, etc. Also, passive tags sometimes struggle to provide a highly reliable signal when supply chain goods are in motion. Active tags therefore have an innate performance advantage over passive tags when it comes to providing a consistently robust, penetrating signal. So higher value "things" at the pallet level and above often require active tags. Considering the total cost of ownership, an active tag's higher cost is offset by a lower cost reader and processor infrastructure making the cost justification easier. Containers, trucks, and trailers are the best examples of high value items that require active tags.

In summary, passive and active RFID capabilities are related, but they are distinctly different technologies which should be matched to the application's technical and economic requirements. Automatically identifying personnel, assets, and vehicles are "active" applications and the cornerstones of automated visibility, security, and quality improvements in the enterprise. In the supply chain, for example, total visibility, security and quality can only be attained by utilizing both.

Source: Excerpted from: www.rfidsb.com/index.php?page=rfidsb&c_ID=156. Copyright © 2008 Axcess International, Inc. Used with permission.

Evaluating Shipping Alternatives

Evaluation of shipping alternatives is an important component of supply chain management. Considerations include not only shipping costs, but also coordination of shipments with other supply chain activities, flexibility, speed, and environmental issues. Shipping options can involve trains, trucks, planes, and boats. Relevant factors include cost, time, availability, materials being shipped, and sometimes environmental considerations. At times options may be limited due to one or more of these factors. For example, heavy materials such as coal and iron ore would not be shipped by plane. High costs in some cases may rule out certain options. Also, time–cost trade-offs can be important. Organizations using a low-cost strategy often opt for slower, lower cost options, whereas organizations using a responsive strategy more often opt for quicker, higher cost options.

A situation that often arises in some businesses is the need to make a choice between rapid (but more expensive) shipping alternatives such as overnight or second-day air and slower (but less expensive) alternatives. In some instances, an overriding factor justifies sending a shipment by the quickest means possible, so there is little or no choice involved. However, in other instances, urgency is not the primary consideration, so there is a choice. The decision in such cases often focuses on the cost savings of slower alternatives versus the incremental holding cost (here, the annual dollar amount that could be earned by the revenue from the item being shipped) that would result from using the slower alternative. An important assumption is that the seller gets paid upon receipt of the goods by the buyer (e.g., through electronic data interchange).

The incremental holding cost incurred by using the slower alternative is computed as

$$\text{Incremental holding cost} = \frac{H(d)}{365} \tag{15–1}$$

where

H = Annual earning potential of shipped item

d = Difference (in days) between shipping alternatives

EXAMPLE 1

Determine which shipping alternative, one day or three days, is best when the holding cost of an item is $1,000 per year, the one-day shipping cost is $40, and the three-day shipping cost is

a. $35

b. $30

SOLUTION

H = $1,000 per year
Time savings = 2 days using 1-day shipping
Holding cost for additional 2 days = $1,000 × (2/365) = $5.48

a. Cost savings = $5. Because the actual savings of $5 is less than the holding cost ($5.48), use the one-day alternative.

b. Cost savings = $10. Because the actual savings of $10 exceeds the savings in holding cost of $5.48, use the three-day alternative.

3-PL

Third-party logistics (3-PL) The outsourcing of logistics management.

Third-party logistics (3-PL) is the term used to describe the outsourcing of logistics management. Companies are turning over warehousing and distribution to companies that specialize in these areas. Among the potential benefits of this are taking advantage of specialists' knowledge, their well-developed information system, and their ability to obtain more favorable shipping rates, and enabling the company to focus more on its core business.

Rise of the 3PL

READING

Over 40 percent of companies plan to outsource more software from third-party logistics providers (3PLs) over the next five years, according to "Beyond Software: Maximizing Value Via Outsourcing," a new strategic report developed by ARC Advisory Group and *SUPPLY CHAIN TECHNOLOGY NEWS*. Outsourcing is becoming the preferred choice for many companies, as evidenced by the strong growth of 3PLs and the increasing number of solution vendors that are offering hosted solutions.

(continued)

(concluded)

Major companies such as Ford Motor, Procter & Gamble, General Mills, DuPont and CVS are all outsourcing various logistics-related tasks from transportation management to global trade management to fleet management. In the case of Ford, for instance, the automaker uses a 3PL to manage its import and export trade processes throughout North America.

ARC and *SCTN* conducted a survey of manufacturers and retailers to better understand their perspective of this emerging trend.

"Since software is generally coupled with specific business processes, it's not surprising that companies are . . . expecting 3PLs to provide a certain level of IT sophistication," explains ARC analyst Adrian Gonzalez, author of the report. "Hence, technology is becoming a competitive differentiator for 3PLs, especially for small and midsize players that want to level the playing field with 'the big boys.' Technology also enables 3PLs to scale their operations without incurring additional overhead, assets and other costs. Simply stated, it allows them to do more with less."

Key findings of the report indicate that:

- Large companies are more inclined to outsource than smaller ones, but both want to maintain some level of control, particularly for solutions/business process that directly impact customer and supplier relationships.
- When companies decide to outsource, they generally prefer to bundle the technology with managed services, primarily from a 3PL (as opposed to a software vendor).
- If a company decides to outsource just the technology, a software vendor is preferred over a 3PL.

Questions

1. Why do you think that large companies are more inclined to outsource than smaller ones?
2. How important is technology in the 3PL decision? Why do you think this is?

Source: Excerpted from "The Rise of the 3PL," www.totalmedia.com.

CREATING AN EFFECTIVE SUPPLY CHAIN

Creating an effective supply chain requires a thorough analysis of all aspects of the supply chain. Strategic sourcing is a term that is sometimes used to describe the process. **Strategic sourcing** is a systematic process for analyzing the purchase of products and services to reduce costs by reducing waste and non-value-added activities, increase profits, reduce risks, and improve supplier performance. Strategic sourcing differs from more traditional sourcing in that it emphasizes total cost rather than purchase price. Total cost includes storage costs, repair costs, disposal costs, and sustainability costs in addition to purchase price. It also seeks to consolidate purchasing power to achieve lower prices, relies on fewer suppliers and collaborative relationships, works to eliminate redundancies, and employs cross-functional teams to help overcome traditional organizational barriers.

Strategic sourcing Analyzing the procurement process to lower costs by reducing waste and non-value-added activities, increase profits, reduce risks, and improve supplier performance.

Strategic sourcing looks at current procurement in terms of what is bought, where and from what suppliers it is bought, and what other sources of supply are available; a sourcing strategy then is designed to minimize a combination of costs and risks. The process is repeated periodically. A system for tracking results and making changes when needed is also established.

Creating a supply chain typically involves the following steps:

1. **Plan.** Develop a strategy for managing all the resources that go into meeting expected customer demand for a product or service, including a set of metrics to monitor the supply chain.
2. **Source.** Select suppliers that will provide the goods and services needed to create products or support services. Also, develop a system for delivery, receiving, and verifying shipments or services. Structure payment along with metrics for monitoring and, if necessary, improving relationships.
3. **Make.** Design the processes necessary for providing services or producing, testing, and packaging goods. Monitor quality, service levels or production output, and worker productivity.
4. **Deliver.** Establish systems for coordinating receipt of shipments from vendors; develop a network of warehouses; select carriers to transport goods to customers; set up an invoicing system to receive payments; and devise a communication system for two-way flow of information among supply chain partners.
5. **Manage returns.** Create a responsive and flexible network for receiving defective and excess products from customers.

Achieving an effective supply chain requires integration of all aspects of the supply chain. The goal is to have a cooperative relationship among supply chain partners that will facilitate planning and coordination of activities. To accomplish this, there must be:

Trust. It is essential for major trading partners to trust each other, and feel confident that partners share similar goals and that they will take actions that are mutually beneficial.

Effective communication. Effective supply chain communication requires integrated technology and standardized ways and means of communicating among partners.

Information velocity The speed at which information is communicated in a supply chain.

Supply chain visibility A major trading partner can connect to its supply chain to access data in real time.

Event management The ability to detect and respond to unplanned events.

Information velocity. **Information velocity** is important; the faster information flows (two-way), the better.

Supply chain visibility. **Supply chain visibility** means that a major trading partner can connect to any part of its supply chain to access data in real time on inventory levels, shipment status, and similar key information. This requires data sharing.

Event management capability. **Event management** is the ability to detect and respond to unplanned events such as delayed shipment or a warehouse running low on a certain item. An event management system should have four capabilities: *monitoring* the system; *notifying* when certain planned or unplanned events occur; *simulating* potential solutions when an unplanned event occurs; and *measuring* the long-term performance of suppliers, transporters, and other supply chain partners in the supply chain.

Fill rate The percentage of demand filled from stock on hand.

Performance metrics. Performance metrics are necessary to confirm that the supply chain is functioning as expected, or that there are problems that must be addressed. There are a variety of measures that can be used, which relate to such things as late deliveries, inventory turnover, response time, quality issues, and so on. In the retail sector, the **fill rate** (the percentage of demand filled from stock on hand) is often very important.

Table 15.7 lists some other key performance measures.

Managing Returns

Products are returned to companies or third-party handlers for a variety of reasons, and in a variety of conditions. Among them are the following:

- Defective products.
- Recalled products.
- Obsolete products.
- Unsold products returned from retailers.
- Parts replaced in the field.
- Items for recycling.
- Waste.

TABLE 15.7
Supply chain performance measures

Financial	Operations	Order fulfillment
Return on assets	Productivity	Order accuracy
Cost	Quality	Time to fill orders
Cash flow		Percentage of incomplete orders shipped
Profits		Percentage of orders delivered on time
Suppliers	**Inventory**	**Customers**
Quality	Average value	Customer satisfaction
On-time delivery	Turnover	Percentage of customer complaints
Cooperation	Weeks of supply	
Flexibility		

An Amazon.com employee inspects returned products at a distribution warehouse in Nevada. The returned goods are inspected for restocking if in pristine condition, forwarded to a repair center if necessary, inventoried, and disposed if defective.

The importance of returns is underscored by the fact that in the United States, the annual value of returns is estimated to be in the neighborhood of $100 billion. In the past, most items—except unsold products—were typically discarded. More recently, companies are recognizing that substantial value can be reclaimed from returned items. For example, defective parts can be repaired or replaced, and products can be resold as reconditioned. Obsolete products may have usable parts or subassemblies, or they may have value in other markets. Parts replaced in the field may in fact not be defective at all; it is estimated that about a third of such parts are not defective and may be reusable as "reconditioned" replacement parts. Recyclable items can be sold to recyclers and might be usable for energy production; other waste and unusable products and parts might require disposal according to sometimes stringent guidelines. For example, governments, particularly in Europe, are increasingly enacting legislation making original manufacturers responsible for acquiring and disposing of their products at the end of their products' useful lives.

To make a determination as to the appropriate disposition of returned items, the items must be sorted, inspected, or tested and directed to the appropriate destination for repair and reuse, recycling, or disposal. Often, transportation is required. **Reverse logistics** is the process of physically transporting returned items. This involves either retrieving items from the field or moving items from the point of return to a facility where they will be inspected and sorted and then transporting to their final destination.

Reverse logistics The process of transporting returned items.

Two key elements of managing returns are *gatekeeping* and *avoidance.* **Gatekeeping** oversees the acceptance of returned goods with the intent of reducing the cost of returns by screening returns at the point of entry into the system and refusing to accept goods that should not be returned or goods that are returned to the wrong destination. Effective gatekeeping enables organizations to control the rate of returns without negatively impacting customer service. **Avoidance** refers to finding ways to minimize the number of items that are returned. It can involve product design and quality assurance. It may also involve monitoring forecasts during promotional programs to avoid overestimating demand to minimize returns of unsold product.

Gatekeeping Screening returned goods to prevent incorrect acceptance of goods.

Avoidance Finding ways to minimize the number of items that are returned.

The condition of returned products as well as the timing of returns may vary, making it difficult to plan for the reverse flow. On the other hand, returns can provide valuable information, such as how and why failures occurred, which can improve product quality and/or product design and minimize future returns for that reason. They can also help identify some sources of customer dissatisfaction, which can have design benefits.

It is likely that the importance of this aspect of supply chain management will grow due to shortened product life cycles, increasing returns from increasing Internet commerce sales from dissatisfied customers, replacement of consumer electronics that are in working order as newer models become available, pressures on manufacturers to reduce costs, and increasing consumer and government environmental concerns. The term **closed-loop supply chain** is used to describe a situation where a manufacturer controls both the forward and reverse logistics.

Closed-loop supply chain A manufacturer controls both the forward and reverse shipment of product.

Challenges

Barriers to Integration of Separate Organizations. Organizations, and their functional areas, have traditionally had an inward focus. They set up buffers between themselves and their suppliers. Changing that attitude can be difficult. The objective of supply chain management is to be efficient across the entire supply chain.

One difficulty in achieving this objective is that different components of the supply chain often have conflicting objectives. For example, to reduce their inventory holding costs, some companies opt for frequent small deliveries of supplies. This can result in increased holding costs for suppliers, so the cost is merely transferred to suppliers. Similarly, within an organization, functional areas often make decisions with a narrow focus, doing things that "optimize" results under their control; in so doing, however, they may suboptimize results for the overall organization. To be effective, organizations must adopt a *systems approach* to both the internal and external portions of their supply chains, being careful to make decisions that are consistent with optimizing the supply chain.

Another difficulty is that for supply chain management to be successful, organizations in the chain must allow other organizations access to their data. There is a natural reluctance to do this in many cases. One reason can be lack of trust; another can be unwillingness to share proprietary information in general; and another can be that an organization, as a member of multiple chains, fears exposure of proprietary information to competitors.

Getting CEOs, Boards of Directors, Managers, and Employees "Onboard." CEOs and boards of directors need to be convinced of the potential payoffs from supply chain management. And because much of supply chain management involves a change in the way business has been practiced for an extended period of time, getting managers and workers to adopt new attitudes and practices that are consistent with effective supply chain operations poses a real challenge.

Dealing with Trade-offs. Authors Hau Lee and C. Billington list a number of trade-offs that must be taken into account in structuring a supply chain:[3]

1. **Lot size–inventory trade-off.** Producing or ordering large lot sizes yields benefits in terms of quantity discounts and lower annual setup costs, but it increases the amount of safety stock carried by suppliers and, hence, the carrying cost. It also can create the bullwhip effect.

It is caused by the way inventories are replenished at various points along a supply chain. For a variety of reasons, organizations tend to periodically order batches of an item from their suppliers. This creates "lumpy" demand for suppliers and, hence, high-variability demand, which causes suppliers to carry relatively large amounts of safety stock. Starting with the final customer and moving backward through the supply chain, batch sizes tend to increase, thereby increasing the level of safety stock carried. What is so striking about this phenomenon is that any demand variations that exist at the customer end of the supply chain get magnified as orders are generated back through the supply chain.

[3]Excerpted from Hau Lee and C. Billington, "Managing Supply Chain Inventory," *Sloan Management Review*, Spring 1992, pp. 65–68, by permission of publisher. Copyright © 1992 by *Sloan Management Review*. All rights reserved.

2. **Inventory–transportation cost trade-off.** Suppliers prefer to ship full truckloads instead of partial loads in order to spread shipping costs over as many units as possible. This leads to higher holding costs for customers. Solutions include combining orders to realize full truckloads, downsizing truck capacity, and shipping late in the process along with *cross-docking*. **Cross-docking** is a technique whereby goods arriving at a warehouse from a supplier are unloaded from the supplier's truck and immediately loaded on one or more outbound trucks, thereby avoiding storage at the warehouse completely. Walmart is among the companies that have used this technique successfully to reduce inventory holding costs and lead times.

Cross-docking A technique whereby goods arriving at a warehouse from a supplier are unloaded from the supplier's truck and loaded onto outbound trucks, thereby avoiding warehouse storage.

3. **Lead time–transportation cost trade-off.** Suppliers usually prefer to ship in full loads, as mentioned previously. But waiting for sufficient orders and/or production to achieve a full load increases lead time. In addition to the preceding suggestions, improved forecasting information to suppliers might improve the timing of their production and orders to their suppliers.

4. **Product variety–inventory trade-off.** Higher product variety generally means smaller lot sizes, which results in higher setup costs, as well as higher transportation and inventory management costs. One possible means of reducing some costs is **delayed differentiation,** which means producing standard components and subassemblies, then waiting until late in the process to add differentiating features. For example, an automobile producer may produce and ship cars without radios, allowing customers to select from a range of radios that can be installed by the dealer, thereby eliminating that variety from much of the supply chain.

Delayed differentiation Production of standard components and subassemblies, which are held until late in the process to add differentiating features.

5. **Cost–customer service trade-off.** Producing and shipping in large lots reduces costs, but it increases lead times, as previously noted. One approach to reducing lead time is to ship directly from a warehouse to the customer, bypassing a retail outlet. Reducing one or more steps in a supply chain by cutting out one or more intermediaries is referred to as **disintermediation.** Although transportation costs are higher, storage costs are lower.

Disintermediation Reducing one or more steps in a supply chain by cutting out one or more intermediaries.

Small Businesses. Small businesses may be reluctant to embrace supply chain management because it can involve specialized, complicated software as well as sharing sensitive information with outside companies. Nonetheless, in order for them to survive, they may have to do so.

Variability and Uncertainty. Variations create uncertainty, thereby causing inefficiencies in a supply chain. Variations occur in incoming shipments from suppliers, internal operations, deliveries of products or services to customers, and customer demands. Increases in product and service *variety* add to uncertainty, because organizations have to deal with a broader range and frequent changes in operations. Hence, when deciding to increase variety, organizations should consider this trade-off.

Although variations exist throughout most supply chains, decision makers often treat the uncertainties as if they were certainties and make decisions on that basis. In fact, systems are often designed on the basis of certainty, so they may not be able to cope with uncertainty. Unfortunately, uncertainties are detrimental to effective management of supply chains because they result is various undesirable occurrences, such as inventory buildups, bottleneck delays, missed delivery dates, and frustration for employees and customers at all stages of a supply chain.

Response Time. Response time is an important issue in supply chain management. Long lead times impair the ability of a supply chain to quickly respond to changing conditions, such as changes in the quantity or timing of demand, changes in product or service design, and quality or logistics problems. Therefore, it is important to work to reduce long product lead times and long collaborative lead times, and a plan should be in place to deal with problems when they arise.

Table 15.8 lists some potential solutions to supply chain problems and possible drawbacks.

TABLE 15.8
Benefits and possible drawbacks of potential improvements to a supply chain

Problem	Potential Improvement	Benefits	Possible Drawbacks
Large inventories	Smaller, more frequent deliveries, cross-docking	Reduced holdings costs	Traffic congestion, increased ordering costs, increased supplier costs
Long lead times	Delayed differentiation	Quick response	May not be feasible
	Disintermediation	Quick response	May need to absorb functions
Large number of parts	Modular construction	Fewer parts to keep track of, simpler ordering	Less variety
Cost, quality	Outsourcing	Reduced cost, higher quality, fewer internal problems, remaining operations more focused	Loss of control
Variability	Shorter lead times, better forecasts, reduction in product/service variety	Better able to match supply and demand	Less variety

STRATEGY

Effective supply chains are critical to the success of business organizations. Development of supply chains should be accorded strategic importance. Achieving an effective supply chain requires integration of all aspects of the chain. Supplier relationships are a critical component of supply chain management. Collaboration and joint planning and coordination are keys to supply chain success. In that regard, a systems view of the supply chain is essential.

Many businesses are employing principles of lean operations and six sigma methodology to improve supply chain performance. However, lean supply chains can increase supply chain risk and may necessitate increased inventories to offset those risks.

SUMMARY

A supply chain consists of all of the organizations, facilities, functions, and activities involved in producing a product or providing a service. The chapter provides a list of strategic, tactical, and operational responsibilities related to supply chain management. The chapter covers key issues, recent trends, procurement, ethical behavior, e-business, supplier management, inventory management, returns management, and risk management.

The basic components of supply chain management are strategy formulation, procurement, supply management, demand management, and logistics management. The key issues in supply chain management relate to determining the appropriate level of outsourcing, managing procurement, managing suppliers, managing customer relationships, being able to quickly identify problems and respond to them, and managing risk.

The goal of supply chain management is to match supply and demand as effectively and efficiently as possible. Because supply chains are made up of multiple organizations, cooperation and collaboration among supply chain partners is very important. Supply chain functioning benefits from mutual trust, information sharing, and collaborative forecasting and planning.

Recent trends in supply chain management relate to managing risk, reevaluating outsourcing, managing inventories, and applying lean principles to improve supply chain performance.

KEY POINTS

1. Supply chains are a vital part of every business organization and need to be managed effectively to achieve a balance of supply and demand.
2. Among important trends in supply chain management are measuring ROI, "greening" the supply chain, reevaluating outsourcing, integrating IT, managing risks, and adopting lean principles.
3. It is important for businesses to encourage their supply chain partners to act ethically.
4. Effective supply chains involve trust, communication, a rapid, two-way flow of information, visibility, and event management capability.

KEY TERMS

avoidance, 691
bullwhip effect, 681
centralized purchasing, 673
closed-loop supply chain, 692
cross-docking, 693
decentralized purchasing, 673
delayed differentiation, 693
disintermediation, 693
e-business, 675
event management, 690
fill rate, 690
gatekeeping, 691
information velocity, 690
inventory velocity, 681
logistics, 664, 683
order fulfillment, 682
purchasing cycle, 672
reverse logistics, 691
radio frequency identification (RFID), 685
strategic partnering, 680
strategic sourcing, 689
supply chain, 663
supply chain management, 664
supply chain visibility, 690
third-party logistics (3-PL), 688
traffic management, 685
vendor analysis, 678
vendor-managed inventory (VMI), 681

DISCUSSION AND REVIEW QUESTIONS

1. What is a supply chain?
2. What are some recent trends in supply chain management?
3. What are the elements of supply chain management?
4. What are the strategic, tactical, and operations responsibilities in supply chain management?
5. What is the bullwhip effect, and why does it occur? How can it be overcome?
6. Explain the increasing importance of the procurement function.
7. What is meant by the term *inventory velocity* and why is this important? What is *information velocity,* and why is it important?
8. Explain strategic partnering.
9. What impact has e-business had on supply chain management?
10. What are some of the advantages of e-business?
11. What are some of the trade-offs that might be factors in designing a supply chain?
12. Why is managing returns important?
13. Explain the importance of supply chain visibility.
14. Describe what purchasing managers do.
15. Describe how purchasing interacts with two other functional areas of an organization.
16. Discuss the importance of RFID for supply chain management.
17. Discuss centralization versus decentralization in purchasing. What are the advantages of each?
18. Describe vendor analysis.
19. Describe supplier certification and explain why it can be important.
20. Compare viewing suppliers as adversaries with viewing them as partners.
21. Explain the benefit of cross-docking.

TAKING STOCK

1. What trade-offs are involved in (*a*) sharing information with other organizations in a supply chain and (*b*) the acquisition of information-processing technology?
2. Who needs to be involved in (*a*) decisions on technology acquisition for supply chain management and (*b*) supply chain management?
3. Name three different ways that technology has improved the ability to manage supply chains.

CRITICAL THINKING EXERCISES

1. Explain why each of these is critical for a successful supply chain operation:
   a. Integrated technology
   b. Information sharing
   c. Trust among trading partners
   d. Real-time information availability
   e. Event management capability
   f. Procurement
2. Given the complexities and risks involved with supply chains, might it make sense for a business organization to vertically integrate and be its own supply chain?
3. From a systems viewpoint, what are some of the environmental issues involved in a decision by a company to outsource manufacturing operations to a foreign country?
4. Select three of the examples of unethical behavior on p.670, other than those that violate basic human rights, and indicate which principle in Table 15.2 would be violated.

PROBLEMS

1. A manager at Strateline Manufacturing must choose between two shipping alternatives: two-day freight and five-day freight. Using five-day freight would cost $135 less than using two-day freight. The primary consideration is holding cost, which is $10 per unit a year. Two thousand items are to be shipped. Which alternative would you recommend? Explain.
2. Determine which shipping alternative would be most economical to ship 80 boxes of parts when each box has a price of $200 and holding costs are 30 percent of price, given this shipping information: overnight, $300, two-day, $260, six-day, $180.
3. A manager must make a decision on shipping. There are two shippers, A and B. Both offer a two-day rate: A for $500 and B for $525. In addition, A offers a three-day rate of $460 and a nine-day rate of $400, and B offers a four-day rate of $450 and a seven-day rate of $410. Annual holding costs are 35 percent of unit price. Three hundred boxes are to be shipped, and each box has a price of $140. Which shipping alternative would you recommend? Explain.

MasterTag

CASE

Nicole Foster

When MasterTag was founded in 1949, its founder, Ludwig Schmidt, set out to be a manufacturer of plastic fishing bobbers. Then, in 1950, Mr. Schmidt was approached by a local greenhouse owner and was asked if he could produce a line of horticultural labels for plants. At the time, these labels were made of wood. Mr. Schmidt adapted his machines to produce these labels and has been manufacturing the plastic "tags" for plants ever since. Over the years, the labels have increased in quality and now feature full-color pictures of the plants along with the name and planting and care instructions.

Many of MasterTag's largest customers are seed companies that sell the seeds to commercial growers. The large seed companies typically place one or two large orders with MasterTag at the beginning of the growing season. The seed companies then sell their seeds and the labels to their customers who grow

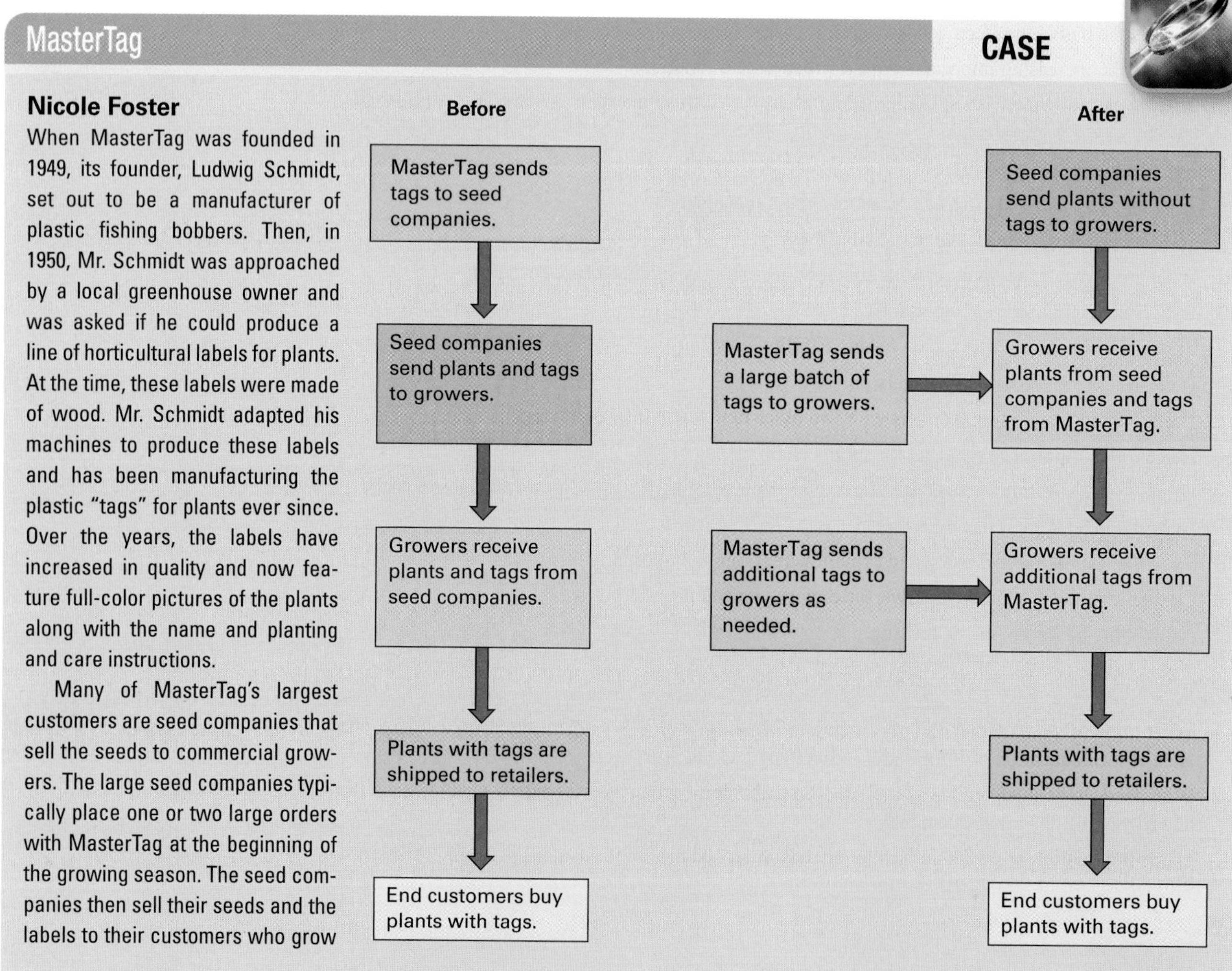

(continued)

(concluded)

the plants and sell them to the end consumer. For various reasons, the seed companies do not like ordering tags, but do so because their customers demand labels with their seeds.

However, there are several problems with this ordering process. The main issue stems from the fact that the exact quantities of tags that will be needed is difficult to predict due to possible crop failures and the introduction of new items. To avoid a shortage of tags, seed companies order and ship a large quantity of tags to their customers. Tags are ordered early to allow for the time needed to incorporate the tags with the seeds. Seed companies usually end up each year with huge numbers of leftover tags. In fact, MasterTag's largest customers often end up with millions of leftover tags.

When MasterTag's management became aware of all the unused labels and unhappy customers, they decided they must come up with a better solution for achieving a match between supply and demand of the tags. One possible solution would be to make an initial, fairly large batch, which would be produced and shipped directly to the growers instead of the seed companies, as is now being done. Later, when the grower results became available, a second batch would be produced using information from growers on how many additional tags are needed. The second batch would then be made and shipped to the growers. (See figure for Before and After.)

Questions

1. Explain the key benefit of the revised approach, and the reason for the benefit.
2. MasterTag has not yet decided to implement this plan. List the pros and cons you think should be considered.

B&L Inc.

CASE

Brian Wilson, materials manager at B&L Inc. in Lancaster, Pennsylvania, was considering a proposal from his purchasing agent to outsource manufacturing for an outrigger bracket. It was the end of April and Mr. Wilson had to evaluate the proposal and make a decision regarding whether to proceed.

B&L Inc. Background

B&L Inc. manufactured trailers for highway transport trucks. The company comprised three divisions: the Trailer, Sandblast & Paint, and Metal Fabricating Divisions. Each division operated as a separate profit center, but manufacturing operations between each were highly integrated. The Metal Fabricating Division produced most of the component parts of the trailers, the Trailer Division performed the assembly operations, and the Sandblast & Paint Division was responsible for completing the sandblasting and final painting operation. B&L manufactured approximately 40 trailers per year, with about two-thirds produced during the period from November to April.

The Outrigger Bracket

The outrigger bracket, part number T-178, was an accessory that could be used to secure oversized containers. The bracket consisted of four component parts welded together, and each trailer sold by B&L had 20 brackets—10 per side.

The Metal Fabricating Division was presently manufacturing the outrigger bracket. The subassembly parts—T-67, T-75, T-69, and T-77—were processed on a burn table, which cut the raw material to size. Although the burn table could work with eight stations, this machine had only been operating with one station. The final assembly operation, T-70, was performed at a manual welding station.

Manufacturing lead time for the outrigger bracket was two weeks. However, the Metal Fabricating Division had been able to coordinate supply and production with assembly operations. Consequently, finished inventory levels of the outrigger bracket were kept to a minimum. B&L's inventory holding costs were 20 percent per annum.

The Outsourcing Decision

In an effort to reduce costs, the purchasing agent, Alison Beals, who reported to Brian Wilson, solicited quotes from three local companies to supply the outrigger bracket. Mayes Steel Fabricators (Mayes), a current supplier to B&L for other components, offered the lowest bid, with a cost of $108.20, FOB B&L.

Brian met with the controller, Mike Carr, who provided a breakdown of the manufacturing costs for the outrigger bracket. Looking at the spreadsheet, Mike commented: "These are based on estimates of our costs from this year's budget. Looking at the material, labor, and overhead costs, I would estimate that the fixed costs for this part are in the area of about 20 percent. Keep in mind that it costs us about $75 to place an order with our vendors." Exhibit 1 provides B&L's internal cost breakdown and details from the quote from Mayes.

EXHIBIT 1 Manufacturing Costs and Mayes Quote: Outrigger Bracket T-178

Parts	Mayes Steel Fabricators	B&L Manufacturing Costs
T-67	$14.60	$17.92
T-75	21.10	17.92
T-69	18.50	45.20
T-77	13.00	10.37
T-70	41.00	58.69
Total	$108.20	$150.10

(continued)

(concluded)

Brian expected that B&L would have to arrange for extra storage space if he decided to outsource the outrigger bracket to Mayes, who had quoted delivery lead time of four weeks. Because Mayes was local and had a good track record, Brian didn't expect the need to carry much safety stock, but the order quantity issue still needed to be resolved.

B&L was operating in a competitive environment and Brian had been asked by the division general manager to look for opportunities to reduce costs. As he sat down to review the information, Brian knew that he should make a decision quickly if it was possible to cut costs by outsourcing the outrigger bracket.

Analyze the information and make a recommendation.

Source: Johnson, P. Fraser, Michiel R. Leenders, and Anna E. Flynn. *Purchasing and Supply Management,* 14th ed. New York: McGrawHill/Irwin, 2011, pp. 131–7.

SELECTED BIBLIOGRAPHY AND FURTHER READINGS

Benton, W. C. *Purchasing and Supply Chain Management.* New York: McGraw-Hill, 2007.

Blumberg, Donald F. *Introduction to Management of Reverse Logistics and Closed Loop Supply Chain Processes,* Boca Raton, FL: CRC Press, 2005.

Bowersox, Donald J., David J. Closs, and M. Bixby Cooper. *Supply Chain Logistics Management.* 3rd ed. New York: Irwin/McGraw-Hill, 2010.

Burt, David N., Donald W. Dobler, and Stephen Starling. *World Class Supply Management: The Key to Supply Chain Management.* 7th ed. New York: McGraw-Hill, 2002.

Chen, Injazz, and Antony Paulraj. "Towards a Theory of Supply Chain Management: The Constructs and Measurement." *Journal of Operations Management* 22, no. 2 (2004).

Corbett, James J., James J. Winebrake, Erin H. Green, Prasad Kasibhatia, Veronika Eyring, and Axel Lauer. "Mortality from Ship Emissions: A Global Assessment." *Environmental Science & Technology* 41, no. 24(December 15, 2007), pp. 8512–8518.

Corbett, James J., and James J. Winebrake. "Sustainable Movement of Goods: Energy and Environmental Implications of Trucks, Trains, Ships, and Planes." *Environmental Management,* November 2007, pp. 8–12.

Fitzgerald, Kevin R. "Purchasing Occupies Key Position in Supply Chains." *Supply Chain Yearbook 2000.* New York: Cahners Business Information, 2000, p. 21.

Flapper, Simme Douwe P., Jo A.E.E. van Nunen, and Luk N. Van Wassenhove (Eds.). *Managing Closed-Loop Supply Chains.* New York: Springer, 2005.

Guide, V. Daniel R., Jr., and Luk N. Van Wassenhove. "The Reverse Supply Chain." *Harvard Business Review* 80, (2), pp. 25–26, 2002.

Handfield, Robert B., and Ernest L. Nichols Jr. *Introduction to Supply Chain Management.* Upper Saddle River, NJ: Prentice Hall, 1999.

Hickey, Kathleen. "MacDonald's Tall Order." *Traffic World,* January 2004, p. 1.

Hira, Ronald. *Outsourcing America.* New York: American Management Association, 2006.

Hoppe, Wallace. *Supply Chain Science.* New York: McGraw-Hill, 2008.

Lee, Hau L. "The Triple-A Supply Chain." *Harvard Business Review,* October 2004.

RFID Journal.com

Simchi-Levi, David, Philip Kaminsky, and Edith Simchi-Levi. *Designing and Managing the Supply Chain: Concepts, Strategies, and Case Studies.* New York: Irwin/McGraw-Hill, 2000.

Webster, Scott. *Principles and Tools for Supply Chain Management.* New York: McGraw-Hill, 2008.

Scheduling

CHAPTER OUTLINE

LEARNING OBJECTIVES

After completing this chapter, you should be able to:

1. Explain what scheduling involves and the importance of good scheduling.
2. Describe scheduling needs in high-volume and intermediate-volume systems.
3. Describe scheduling needs in job shops.
4. Use and interpret Gantt charts, and use the assignment method for loading.
5. Give examples of commonly used priority rules.
6. Summarize some of the unique problems encountered in service systems, and describe some of the approaches used for scheduling service systems.

Airline travel can be difficult when flights are delayed or canceled due to weather problems. And even though it may be clear and dry in some areas, flights in those places can still be affected by weather in other areas. Because of all the interdependencies, a problem in one area, especially around major hub airports like Chicago, Atlanta, and New York, has a cascading effect with impacts throughout the nation. This results in massive scheduling problems. Flight arrivals and departures have to be rescheduled which then means flight crews, terminal gates, connections, and baggage and freight also must be rescheduled. Airline and air traffic control software scheduling systems include and optimize thousands of variables.

Within an organization, **scheduling** pertains to establishing the timing of the use of specific resources of that organization. It relates to the use of equipment, facilities, and human activities. Scheduling occurs in every organization, regardless of the nature of its activities. For example, manufacturers must schedule production, which means developing schedules for workers, equipment, purchases, maintenance, and so on. Hospitals must schedule admissions, surgery, nursing assignments, and support services such as meal preparation, security, maintenance, and cleaning. Educational institutions must schedule classrooms, instruction, and students. And lawyers, doctors, dentists, hairdressers, and auto repair shops must schedule appointments.

In the decision-making hierarchy, scheduling decisions are the final step in the transformation process before actual output occurs. Many decisions about system design and operation have been made long before scheduling decisions. They include the capacity of the system, product or service design, equipment selection, selection and training of workers, and aggregate planning and master scheduling. Consequently, scheduling decisions must be made within the constraints established by many other decisions, making them fairly narrow in scope and latitude. Figure 16.1 depicts scheduling hierarchies for manufacturing and service scheduling.

Scheduling Establishing the timing of the use of equipment, facilities, and human activities in an organization.

FIGURE 16.1
Scheduling hierarchies

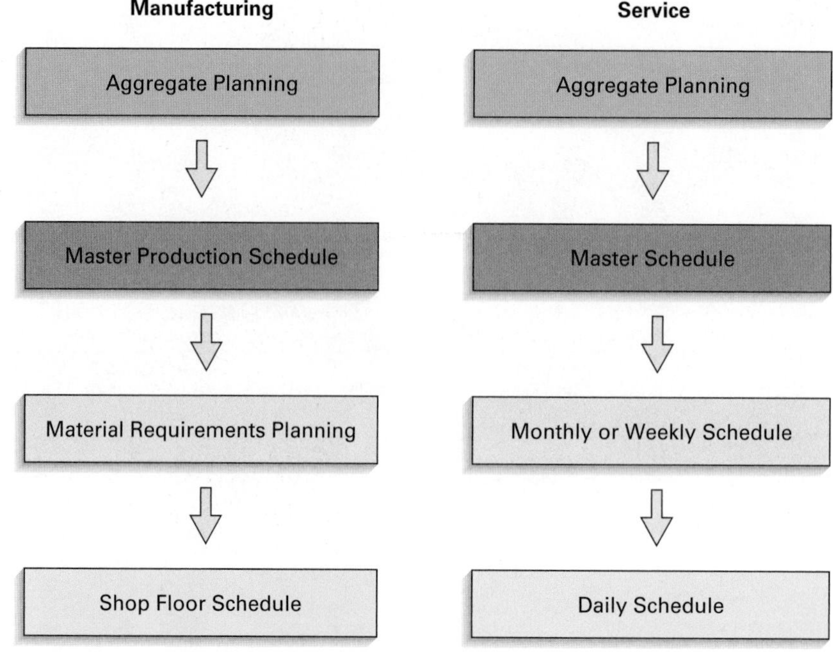

Effective scheduling can yield cost savings, increases in productivity, and other benefits. For example, in hospitals, effective scheduling can save lives and improve patient care. In educational institutions, it can reduce the need for expansion of facilities. In competitive environments, effective scheduling can give a company a competitive advantage in terms of customer service (shorter wait time for their orders) if its competitors are less effective with their scheduling.

Generally, the objectives of scheduling are to achieve trade-offs among conflicting goals, which include efficient utilization of staff, equipment, and facilities, and minimization of customer waiting time, inventories, and process times.

This chapter covers scheduling in both manufacturing and service environments. Although the two environments have many similarities, some basic differences are important.

SCHEDULING OPERATIONS

Scheduling tasks are largely a function of the volume of system output. High-volume systems require approaches substantially different from those required by job shops, and project scheduling requires still different approaches. In this chapter, we will consider scheduling for high-volume systems, intermediate-volume systems, and low-volume (job shop) scheduling. Project scheduling is discussed in Chapter 17.

Scheduling in High-Volume Systems

Scheduling encompasses allocating workloads to specific work centers and determining the sequence in which operations are to be performed. High-volume systems are characterized by standardized equipment and activities that provide identical or highly similar operations on customers or products as they pass through the system. The goal is to obtain a smooth rate of flow of goods or customers through the system in order to get a high utilization of labor and equipment. High-volume systems, where jobs follow the same sequence, are often referred to as **flow systems**; scheduling in these systems is referred to as **flow-shop**

Flow system High-volume system in which jobs all follow the same sequence.

Flow-shop scheduling Scheduling for flow systems.

scheduling, although flow-shop scheduling also can be used in medium-volume systems. Examples of high-volume products include autos, personal computers, radios and televisions, stereo equipment, toys, and appliances. In process industries, examples include petroleum refining, sugar refining, mining, waste treatment, and the manufacturing of fertilizers. Examples of services include cafeteria lines, news broadcasts, and mass inoculations. Because of the highly repetitive nature of these systems, many of the loading and sequence decisions are determined during the design of the system. The use of highly specialized tools and equipment, the arrangement of equipment, the use of specialized material-handling equipment, and the division of labor are all designed to enhance the flow of work through the system, since all items follow virtually the same sequence of operations.

At the Wakefield, U.K. factory, Rexam produces 5,000 cans per minute and delivers them to its main customer, Coca-Cola Bottling. To meet Coke's lean manufacturing requirements, Rexam needed to spray cans the same every single time. They added a spray monitor system to immediately identify spray malfunctions. The early diagnostics of the spray monitor system can save Rexam from coating hundreds of cans improperly. The objectives in upgrading were to improve quality, reduce variation, and reduce costs.

A major aspect in the design of flow systems is *line balancing,* which concerns allocating the required tasks to workstations so that they satisfy technical (sequencing) constraints and are balanced with respect to equal work times among stations. Highly balanced systems result in the maximum utilization of equipment and personnel as well as the highest possible rate of output. Line balancing is discussed in Chapter 6.

In setting up flow systems, designers must consider the potential discontent of workers in connection with the specialization of job tasks in these systems; high work rates are often achieved by dividing the work into a series of relatively simple tasks assigned to different workers. The resulting jobs tend to be boring and monotonous and may give rise to fatigue, absenteeism, turnover, and other problems, all of which tend to reduce productivity and disrupt the smooth flow of work. These problems and potential solutions are elaborated on in Chapter 7, which deals with the design of work systems.

In spite of the built-in attributes of flow systems related to scheduling, a number of scheduling problems remain. One stems from the fact that few flow systems are *completely* devoted to a single product or service; most must handle a variety of sizes and models. Thus, an automobile manufacturer will assemble many different combinations of cars—two-door and four-door models, some with air-conditioning and some not, some with deluxe trim and others with standard trim, some with CD players, some with tinted glass, and so on. The same can be said for producers of appliances, electronic equipment, and toys. Each change involves slightly different inputs of parts, materials, and processing requirements that must be scheduled into the line. If the line is to operate smoothly, a supervisor must coordinate the flow of materials and the work, which includes the inputs, the processing, and the outputs, as well as purchases. In addition to achieving a smooth flow, it is important to avoid excessive buildup of inventories. Again, each variation in size or model will tend to have somewhat different inventory requirements, so that additional scheduling efforts will be needed.

One source of scheduling concern is possible disruptions in the system that result in less than the desired output. These can be caused by equipment failures, material shortages, accidents, and absences. In practice, it is usually impossible to increase the rate of output to compensate for these factors, mainly because flow systems are designed to operate at a given rate. Instead, strategies involving subcontracting or overtime are often required, although subcontracting on short notice is not always feasible. Sometimes work that is partly completed can be made up off the line.

The reverse situation can also impose scheduling problems although these are less severe. This happens when the desired output is less than the usual rate. However, instead of slowing the ensuing rate of output, it is usually necessary to operate the system at the usual rate, but for fewer hours. For instance, a production line might operate temporarily for seven hours a day instead of eight.

High-volume systems usually require automated or specialized equipment for processing and handling. Moreover, they perform best with a high, uniform output. Shutdowns and startups are generally costly, and especially costly in process industries. Consequently, the following factors often determine the success of such a system:

- **Process and product design.** Here, cost and manufacturability are important, as is achieving a smooth flow through the system.
- **Preventive maintenance.** Keeping equipment in good operating order can minimize breakdowns that would disrupt the flow of work.
- **Rapid repair when breakdowns occur.** This can require specialists as well as stocks of critical spare parts.
- **Optimal product mixes.** Techniques such as linear programming can be used to determine optimal blends of inputs to achieve desired outputs at minimal costs. This is particularly true in the manufacture of fertilizers, animal feeds, and diet foods.
- **Minimization of quality problems.** Quality problems can be extremely disruptive, requiring shutdowns while problems are resolved. Moreover, when output fails to meet quality standards, not only is there the loss of output but also a waste of the labor, material, time, and other resources that went into it.
- **Reliability and timing of supplies.** Shortages of supplies are an obvious source of disruption and must be avoided. On the other hand, if the solution is to stockpile supplies, that can lead to high carrying costs. Shortening supply lead times, developing reliable supply schedules, and carefully projecting needs are all useful.

Scheduling in Intermediate-Volume Systems

Intermediate-volume system outputs fall between the standardized type of output of the high-volume systems and made-to-order output of job shops. Like the high-volume systems, intermediate-volume systems typically produce standard outputs. If manufacturing is involved, the products may be for stock rather than for special order. However, the volume of output in such cases is not large enough to justify continuous production. Instead, it is more economical to process these items *intermittently*. Thus, intermediate-volume work centers periodically shift from one job to another. In contrast to a job shop, the run (batch) sizes are relatively large. Examples of products made in these systems include canned foods, baked goods, paint, and cosmetics.

The three basic issues in these systems are the *run size* of jobs, the *timing* of jobs, and the *sequence* in which jobs should be processed.

Sometimes, the issue of run size can be determined by using a model such as the economic run size model discussed in Chapter 13 on inventory management. The run size that would minimize setup and inventory costs is

$$Q_0 = \sqrt{\frac{2DS}{H}}\sqrt{\frac{p}{p-u}}, \qquad \text{where } S = \text{Setup cost} \tag{16–1}$$

Setup cost may be an important consideration. Setup costs may depend on the order in which jobs are processed; similar jobs may require less setup change between them. For example, jobs in a print shop may be sequenced by ink color to reduce the number of setups needed. This opens up the possibility of reducing setup cost and time by taking processing sequence into account. It also makes sequencing more complex, and it requires estimating job setup costs for every sequence combination.

In another vein, companies are working to reduce setup times and, hence, experience less downtime for equipment changeover. Tactics include offline setups, snap-on parts, modular setups, and flexible equipment designed to handle a variety of processing requirements.

Another difficulty arises because usage is not always as smooth as assumed in the model. Some products will tend to be used up faster than expected and have to be replenished sooner. Also, because multiple products are to be processed, it is not always possible to schedule production to correspond with optimum run times.

Another approach frequently used is to base production on a master schedule developed from customer orders and forecasts of demand. Companies engaged in assembly operations would then use an MRP approach (described in Chapter 12) to determine the quantity and projected timing of jobs for components. The manager would then compare projected requirements with projected capacity and develop a feasible schedule from that information. Companies engaged in producing processed rather than assembled goods (e.g., food products, such as canned goods and beverages; publishing, such as magazines; paints and cleaning supplies) would use a somewhat different approach; the *time-phasing* information provided by MRP would not be an important factor.

SCHEDULING IN LOW-VOLUME SYSTEMS

The characteristics of low-volume systems (job shops) are considerably different from those of high- and intermediate-volume systems. Products are made to order, and orders usually differ considerably in terms of processing requirements, materials needed, processing time, and processing sequence and setups. Because of these circumstances, **job-shop scheduling** is usually fairly complex. This is compounded by the impossibility of establishing firm schedules prior to receiving the actual job orders.

Job-shop scheduling Scheduling for low-volume systems with many variations in requirements.

Job-shop processing gives rise to two basic issues for schedulers: how to distribute the workload among work centers and what job processing sequence to use.

Loading

Loading refers to the assignment of jobs to processing (work) centers. Loading decisions involve assigning specific jobs to work centers and to various machines in the work centers. In cases where a job can be processed only by a specific center, loading presents little difficulty. However, problems arise when two or more jobs are to be processed and there are a number of work centers capable of performing the required work. In such cases, the operations manager needs some way of assigning jobs to the centers.

Loading The assignment of jobs to processing centers.

When making assignments, managers often seek an arrangement that will minimize processing and setup costs, minimize idle time among work centers, or minimize job completion time, depending on the situation.

Gantt Charts. Visual aids called **Gantt charts** are used for a variety of purposes related to loading and scheduling. They derive their name from Henry Gantt, who pioneered the use of charts for industrial scheduling in the early 1900s. Gantt charts can be used in a number of different ways, two of which are illustrated in Figure 16.2, which shows scheduling classrooms for a university and scheduling hospital operating rooms for a day.

Gantt chart Chart used as visual aid for loading and scheduling purposes.

The purpose of Gantt charts is to organize and visually display the actual or intended use of resources in a *time framework.* In most cases, a time scale is represented horizontally,

FIGURE 16.2
Examples of charts used for scheduling

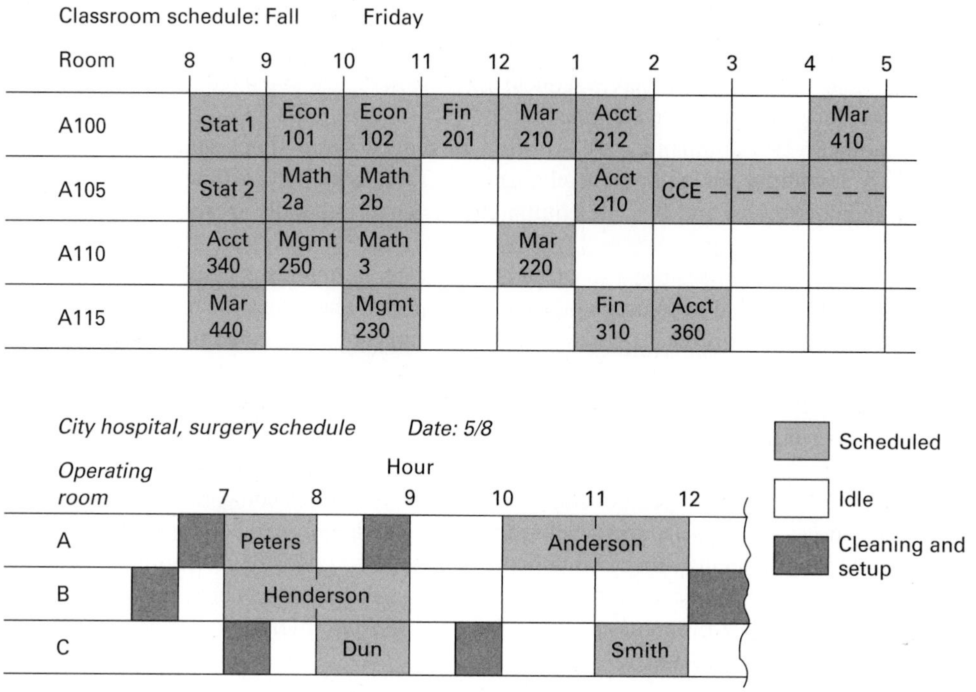

Classroom schedule: Fall Friday

Room	8	9	10	11	12	1	2	3	4
A100	Stat 1	Econ 101	Econ 102	Fin 201	Mar 210	Acct 212			Mar 410
A105	Stat 2	Math 2a	Math 2b			Acct 210	CCE —	— — —	— — —
A110	Acct 340	Mgmt 250	Math 3		Mar 220				
A115	Mar 440		Mgmt 230			Fin 310	Acct 360		

City hospital, surgery schedule *Date: 5/8*

Operating room	Hour: 7 – 12
A	Peters, Anderson
B	Henderson
C	Dun, Smith

Scheduled
Idle
Cleaning and setup

and resources to be scheduled are listed vertically. The use and idle times of resources are reflected in the chart.

Managers may use the charts for trial-and-error schedule development to get an idea of what different arrangements would involve. Thus, a tentative surgery schedule might reveal insufficient allowance for surgery that takes longer than expected and can be revised accordingly. Use of the chart for classroom scheduling would help avoid assigning two different classes to the same room at the same time.

There are a number of different types of Gantt charts. Two of the most commonly used are the *load chart* and the *schedule chart.*

Load chart A Gantt chart that shows the loading and idle times for a group of machines or list of departments.

A **load chart** depicts the loading and idle times for a group of machines or a list of departments. Figure 16.3 illustrates a typical load chart. This chart indicates that work center 3 is completely loaded for the entire week, center 4 will be available after noon on Tuesday, and the other two centers have idle time scattered throughout the week. This information can help a manager rework loading assignments to better utilize the centers. For instance, if all centers perform the same kind of work, the manager might want to free one center for a long job or a rush order. The chart also shows when certain jobs are scheduled to start and finish, and where to expect idle time.

Infinite loading Jobs are assigned to work centers without regard to the capacity of the work center.

Finite loading Jobs are assigned to work centers taking into account the work center capacity and job processing times.

Two different approaches are used to load work centers: *infinite* loading and *finite* loading. **Infinite loading** assigns jobs to work centers without regard to the capacity of the work center. As you can see in the diagram below, this can lead to overloads in some time periods and underloads in others. The priority sequencing rules described in this chapter use infinite loading. One possible result of infinite loading is the formation of queues in some (or all) work centers. That requires a second step to correct the imbalance. **Finite loading** projects actual job starting and stopping times at each work center, taking into account the capacities of each work center and the processing times of jobs, so that capacity is not exceeded. One output of finite loading is a detailed projection of hours each work center will operate. Schedules based on finite loading may have to be updated often, perhaps daily, due to processing delays at work centers and the addition of new jobs or cancellation of current jobs. The following diagram illustrates these two approaches:

A.

Work center	Mon.	Tues.	Wed.	Thurs.	Fri.
1	Job 3			Job 4	
2		Job 3	Job 7		(not available)
3	Job 1	(not available)	(not available)	Job 6	Job 7
4	Job 10				

Processing

Center not available (e.g., maintenance)

B.

FIGURE 16.3

A. Sample Gantt load chart.
B. The same Gantt chart using the Lekin software, developed at New York University, includes multiple scheduling routines along with graphics.

Source: © Pinedo and Feldman. Used with permission.

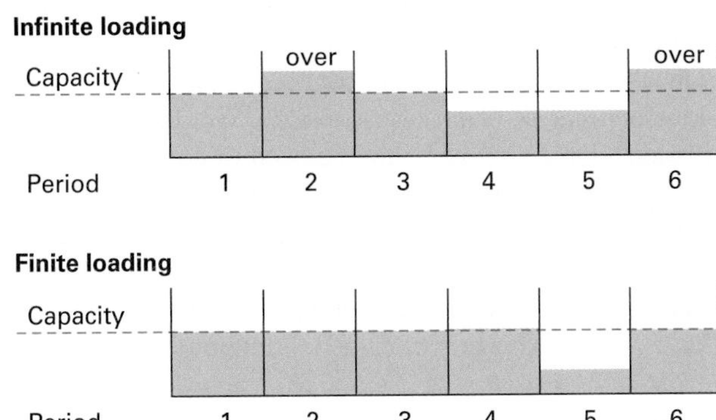

With infinite loading, a manager may need to make some response to overloaded work centers. Among the possible responses are shifting work to other periods or other centers, working overtime, or contracting out a portion of the work. Note that the last two options in effect increase capacity to meet the work load.

Finite loading may reflect a fixed upper limit on capacity. For example, a bus line will have only so many buses. Hence, the decision to place into service a particular number of buses fixes capacity. Similarly, a manufacturer might have one specialized machine that it operates

FIGURE 16.4
Progress chart for landscaping job

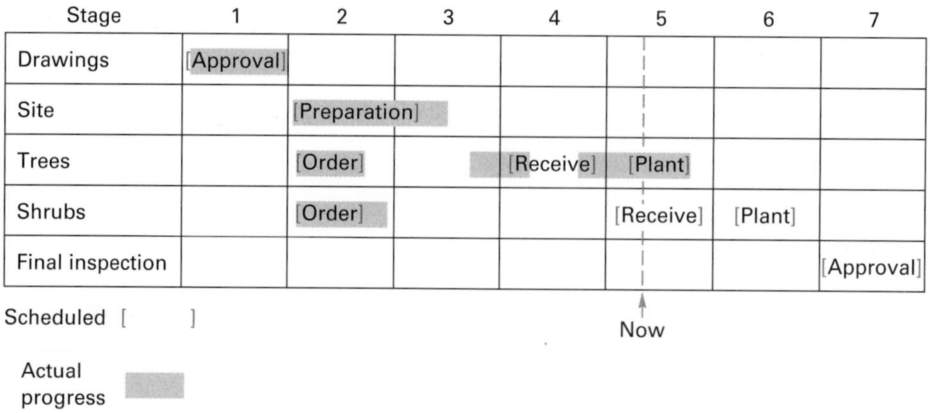

Stage	1	2	3	4	5	6	7
Drawings	[Approval]						
Site		[Preparation]					
Trees		[Order]		[Receive]	[Plant]		
Shrubs		[Order]			[Receive]	[Plant]	
Final inspection							[Approval]

Scheduled [ ]

Now

Actual progress

around the clock. Thus, it is operated at the upper limit of its capacity, so finite loading would be called for.

Forward scheduling Scheduling ahead from a point in time.

Backward scheduling Scheduling backward from a due date.

There are two general approaches to scheduling: forward scheduling and backward scheduling. **Forward scheduling** means scheduling ahead from a point in time; **backward scheduling** means scheduling backward from a due date. Forward scheduling is used if the issue is "How long will it take to complete this job?" Backward scheduling would be used if the issue is "When is the latest the job can be started and still be completed by the due date?" Forward scheduling enables the scheduler to determine the earliest possible completion time for each job and, thus, the amount of lateness or the amount of slack can be determined. That information can be combined with information from other jobs in setting up a schedule for all current jobs.

Schedule chart A Gantt chart that shows the orders or jobs in progress and whether they are on schedule.

A manager often uses a **schedule chart** to monitor the progress of jobs. The vertical axis on this type of Gantt chart shows the orders or jobs in progress, and the horizontal axis shows time. The chart indicates which jobs are on schedule and which are behind or ahead.

A typical schedule chart is illustrated in Figure 16.4. It shows the current status of a landscaping job with planned and actual starting and finishing times for the five stages of the job. The chart indicates that approval and the ordering of trees and shrubs was on schedule. The site preparation was a bit behind schedule. The trees were received earlier than expected, and planting is ahead of schedule. However, the shrubs have not yet been received. The chart indicates some slack between scheduled receipt of shrubs and shrub planting, so if the shrubs arrive by the end of the week, it appears the schedule can still be met.

Despite the obvious benefits of Gantt charts and the fact that they are widely used, they possess certain limitations, the chief one being the need to repeatedly update a chart to keep it current. In addition, a chart does not directly reveal costs associated with alternative loadings. Finally, a job's processing time may vary depending on the work center; certain stations or work centers may be capable of processing some jobs faster than other stations. Again, that situation would increase the complexity of evaluating alternative schedules.

In addition to Gantt charts, managers often rely on input/output reports to manage work flow.

Input/output (I/O) control Managing work flow and queues at work centers.

Input/Output Control. **Input/output (I/O) control** refers to monitoring the work flow and queue lengths at work centers. The purpose of I/O control is to manage work flow so that queues and waiting times are kept under control. Without I/O control, demand may exceed processing capacity, causing an overload at a center. Conversely, work may arrive slower than the rate a work center can handle, leaving the work center underutilized. Ideally, a balance can be struck between the input and output rates, thereby achieving effective use of work center capacities without experiencing excessive queues at the work centers. A simple example of I/O control is the use of stoplights on some expressway on-ramps. These regulate the flow of entering traffic according to the current volume of expressway traffic.

		Period					
		1	2	3	4	5	6
Input	Planned	100	100	90	90	90	90
	Actual	120	95	80	88	93	94
	Deviation	+20	−5	−10	−2	+3	+4
	Cum. dev.	+20	+15	+5	+3	+6	+10
Output	Planned	110	110	100	100	100	95
	Actual	110	105	95	101	103	96
	Deviation	0	−5	−5	+1	+3	+1
	Cum. dev.	0	−5	−10	−9	−6	−5

Backlog	40*	50	40	25	12	2	0

FIGURE 16.5
A sample input/output report for a work center showing input and output in hours of processing time

Note: Figures represent standard hours of processing time.

*Given, not derived from the data.

Figure 16.5 illustrates an input/output report for a work center. A key portion of the report is the backlog of work waiting to be processed. The report also reveals deviations-from-planned for both inputs and outputs, thereby enabling a manager to determine possible sources of problems.

The deviations in each period are determined by subtracting "planned" from "actual." For example, in the first period, subtracting the planned input of 100 hours from the actual input of 120 hours produces a deviation of +20 hours. Similarly, in the first period, the planned and actual outputs are equal, producing a deviation of 0 hours.

The backlog for each period is determined by subtracting the "actual output" from the "actual input" and adjusting the backlog from the previous period by that amount. For example, in the second period actual output exceeds actual input by 10 hours. Hence, the previous backlog of 50 hours is reduced by 10 hours to 40 hours.

Another approach that can be used to assign jobs to resources is the *assignment method.*

Assignment Method of Linear Programming. The **assignment model** is a special-purpose linear programming model that is useful in situations that call for assigning tasks or other work requirements to resources. Typical examples include assigning jobs to machines or workers, territories to salespeople, and repair jobs to repair crews. The idea is to obtain an optimum *matching* of tasks and resources. Commonly used criteria include costs, profits, efficiency, and performance.

Assignment model A linear programming model for optimal assignment of tasks and resources.

Table 16.1 illustrates a typical problem, where four jobs are to be assigned to four workers. The problem is arranged in a format that facilitates evaluation of assignments. The numbers in the body of the table represent the value or cost associated with each job–worker combination. In this case, the numbers represent costs. Thus, it would cost $8 for worker A to do job 1, $6 for worker B to do job 1, and so on. If the problem involved minimizing the cost for job 1 alone, it would clearly be assigned to worker C, since that combination has the lowest cost. However, that assignment does not take into account the other jobs and their costs, which is important since the lowest-cost assignment for any one job may not be consistent with a minimum-cost assignment when all jobs are considered.

SCREENCAM TUTORIAL

If there are to be n matches, there are $n!$ different possibilities. In this case, there are $4! = 24$ different matches. One approach is to investigate each match and select the one with the lowest cost. However, if there are 12 jobs, there would be 479 million different matches! A much simpler approach is to use a procedure called the **Hungarian method** to identify the lowest-cost solution.

Hungarian method Method of assigning jobs by a one-for-one matching to identify the lowest-cost solution.

To be able to use the Hungarian method, a one-for-one matching is required. Each job, for example, must be assigned to only one worker. It is also assumed that every worker is capable of handling every job, and that the costs or values associated with each assignment

TABLE 16.1
A typical assignment problem showing job times for each job/worker combination

		WORKER			
		A	B	C	D
Job	1	8	6	2	4
	2	6	7	11	10
	3	3	5	7	6
	4	5	10	12	9

combination are known and fixed (i.e., not subject to variation). The number of rows and columns must be the same. Solved Problem 1 at the end of the chapter shows what to do if they aren't the same.

Once the relevant cost information has been acquired and arranged in tabular form, the basic procedure of the Hungarian method is as follows:

1. Subtract the smallest number in each row from every number in the row. This is called a *row reduction.* Enter the results in a new table.
2. Subtract the smallest number in each column of the new table from every number in the column. This is called a *column reduction.* Enter the results in another table.
3. Test whether an optimum assignment can be made. You do this by determining the *minimum* number of lines (horizontal or vertical) needed to cross out (cover) all zeros. If the number of lines equals the number of rows, an optimum assignment is possible. In that case, go to step 6. Otherwise go on to step 4.
4. If the number of lines is less than the number of rows, modify the table in this way:
   a. Subtract the smallest uncovered number from every uncovered number in the table.
   b. Add the smallest uncovered number to the numbers at *intersections* of cross-out lines.
   c. Carry over numbers crossed out but not at intersections of cross-out lines carry over to the next table.
5. Repeat steps 3 and 4 until an optimal table is obtained.
6. Make the assignments. Begin with rows or columns with only one zero. Match items that have zeros, using only one match for each row and each column. Eliminate both the row and the column after the match.

EXAMPLE 1

www.mhhe.com/stevenson11e

Determine the optimum assignment of jobs to workers for the following data (from Table 16.1):

		WORKER				
		A	B	C	D	Row Minimum
Job	1	8	6	2	4	2
	2	6	7	11	10	6
	3	3	5	7	6	3
	4	5	10	12	9	5

SOLUTION

a. Subtract the smallest number in each row from every number in the row, and enter the results in a new table. The result of this row reduction is

		WORKER			
		A	B	C	D
Job	1	6	4	0	2
	2	0	1	5	4
	3	0	2	4	3
	4	0	5	7	4
Column Minimum		0	1	0	2

b. Subtract the smallest number in each column from every number in the column, and enter the results in a new table. The result of this column reduction is

		WORKER			
		A	B	C	D
Job	1	6	3	0	0
	2	0	0	5	2
	3	0	1	4	1
	4	0	4	7	2

c. Determine the *minimum* number of lines needed to cross out all zeros. (Try to cross out as many zeros as possible when drawing lines.)

		WORKER			
		A	B	C	D
Job	1	6	3	0	0
	2	0	0	5	2
	3	0	1	4	1
	4	0	4	7	2

d. Since only three lines are needed to cross out all zeros and the table has four rows, this is not the optimum. Note that the smallest uncovered value is 1.

e. Subtract the smallest uncovered value from every uncovered number that hasn't been crossed out, and add it to numbers that are at the intersections of covering lines. The results are as follows:

		WORKER			
		A	B	C	D
Job	1	7	3	0	0
	2	1	0	5	2
	3	0	0	3	0
	4	0	3	6	1

f. Determine the minimum number of lines needed to cross out all zeros (four). Since this equals the number of rows, you can make the optimum assignment.

		WORKER			
		A	B	C	D
Job	1	7	3	0	0
	2	1	0	5	2
	3	0	0	3	0
	4	0	3	6	1

g. Make assignments: Start with rows and columns with only one zero. Match jobs with machines that have a zero cost.

		WORKER			
		A	B	C	D
Job	1	7	3	0	0
	2	1	0	5	2
	3	0	0	3	0
	4	0	3	6	1

Assignment	Cost
1-C	$ 2
2-B	7
3-D	6
4-A	5
	$20

As you can see, the process is relatively simple. The simplicity of the Hungarian method belies its usefulness when the assumptions are met. Not only does it provide a rational method for making assignments, it guarantees an optimal solution, often without the use of a computer, which is necessary only for fairly large problems. When profits instead of costs are involved, the profits can be converted to *relative costs* by subtracting every number in the table from the largest number and then proceeding as in a minimization problem.

It is worth knowing that one extension of this technique can be used to prevent undesirable assignments. For example, union rules may prohibit one person's assignment to a particular job, or a manager might wish to avoid assigning an unqualified person to a job. Whatever the reason, specific combinations can be avoided by assigning a relatively high cost to that combination. In the previous example, if we wish to avoid combination 1-A, assigning a cost of $50 to that combination will achieve the desired effect, because $50 is much greater than the other costs.

Sequencing

Sequencing Determining the order in which jobs at a work center will be processed.

Workstation An area where one or a few workers and/or machines perform similar work.

Although loading decisions determine the machines or work centers that will be used to process specific jobs, they do not indicate the *order* in which the jobs waiting at a given work center are to be processed. **Sequencing** is concerned with determining job processing order. Sequencing decisions determine both the order in which jobs are processed at various work centers and the order in which jobs are processed at individual **workstations** *within* the work centers.

If work centers are lightly loaded and if jobs all require the same amount of processing time, sequencing presents no particular difficulties. However, for heavily loaded work centers, especially in situations where relatively lengthy jobs are involved, the order of processing can be very important in terms of costs associated with jobs waiting for processing and in terms of idle time at the work centers. In this section, we will examine some of the ways in which jobs are sequenced.

Priority rules Simple heuristics used to select the order in which jobs will be processed.

Job time Time needed for setup and processing of a job.

Typically, a number of jobs will be waiting for processing. **Priority rules** are simple heuristics used to select the order in which the jobs will be processed. Some of the most common are listed in Table 16.2. The rules generally rest on the assumption that job setup cost and time are *independent* of processing sequence. In using these rules, job processing times and due dates are important pieces of information. **Job time** usually includes setup and processing times. Jobs that require similar setups can lead to reduced setup times if the sequencing rule takes this into account (the rules described here do not). Due dates may be the result of delivery times promised to customers, material requirements planning (MRP) processing, or managerial decisions. They are subject to revision and must be kept current to give meaning to sequencing choices. Also, it should be noted that due dates associated with all rules except slack per operation (S/O) and critical ratio (CR) are for the operation about to be performed; due dates for S/O and CR are typically final due dates for orders rather than intermediate, departmental deadlines.

Local priority rules Focus on information pertaining to a single workstation when establishing a job sequence.

Global priority rules Incorporate information from multiple workstations when establishing a job sequence.

The priority rules can be classified as either *local* or *global*. **Local priority rules** take into account information pertaining only to a single workstation; **global priority rules** take into account information pertaining to multiple workstations. First come, first served (FCFS), shortest processing time (SPT), and earliest due date (EDD) are local rules; CR and S/O are global rules. Rush can be either local or global. As you might imagine, global rules require more effort than local rules. A major complication in global sequencing is that not all jobs require the same processing or even the same order of processing. As a result, the set of jobs is different for different workstations. Local rules are particularly useful for bottleneck operations, but they are not limited to those situations.

TABLE 16.2
Possible priority rules

First come, first served (FCFS): Jobs are processed in the order in which they arrive at a machine or work center.
Shortest processing time (SPT): Jobs are processed according to processing time at a machine or work center, shortest job first.
Earliest due date (EDD): Jobs are processed according to due date, earliest due date first.
Critical ratio (CR): Jobs are processed according to smallest ratio of time remaining until due date to processing time remaining.
Slack per operation (S/O): Jobs are processed according to average slack time (time until due date minus remaining time to process). Compute by dividing slack time by number of remaining operations, including the current one.
Rush: Emergency or preferred customers first.

TABLE 16.3
Assumptions of priority rules

The set of jobs is known; no new jobs arrive after processing begins; and no jobs are canceled.
Setup time is independent of processing sequence.
Setup time is deterministic.
Processing times are deterministic rather than variable.
There will be no interruptions in processing such as machine breakdowns, accidents, or worker illness.

A number of assumptions apply when using the priority rules; Table 16.3 lists them. In effect, the priority rules pertain to *static* sequencing: For simplicity, it is assumed that there is no variability in either setup or processing times, or in the set of jobs. The assumptions make the scheduling problem manageable. In practice, jobs may be delayed or canceled, and new jobs may arrive, requiring schedule revisions.

The effectiveness of any given sequence is frequently judged in terms of one or more *performance measures.* The most frequently used performance measures follow:

- **Job flow time** is the amount of time it takes from when a job arrives until it is complete. It includes not only actual processing time but also any time waiting to be processed, transportation time between operations, and any waiting time related to equipment breakdowns, unavailable parts, quality problems, and so on. The average flow time for a group of jobs is equal to the total flow time for the jobs divided by the number of jobs.

Job flow time The amount of time from when a job arrives until it is finished.

- **Job lateness** is the amount of time the job completion date is expected to exceed the date the job was due or promised to a customer. It is the difference between the actual completion time and the due date. If only differences for jobs with completion times that exceed due dates are recorded, and zeros are assigned to jobs that are early, the term used is job *tardiness.*

Job lateness The difference between the actual completion date and the due date.

- **Makespan** is the total time needed to complete a *group* of jobs. It is the length of time between the start of the first job in the group and the completion of the last job in the group. If processing involves only one work center, makespan will be the same regardless of the priority rule being used.

Makespan Total time needed to complete a group of jobs from the beginning of the first job to the completion of the last job.

- **Average number of jobs.** Jobs that are in a shop are considered to be work-in-process inventory. The average work-in-process for a group of jobs can be computed using the following formula:

  $$\text{Average number of jobs} = \text{Total flow time} \div \text{Makespan}$$

  If the jobs represent equal amounts of inventory, the average number of jobs will also reflect the average work-in-process inventory.

Of the priority rules, rush scheduling is quite simple and needs no explanation. The other rules and performance measures are illustrated in the following two examples.

EXAMPLE 2

Processing times (including setup times) and due dates for six jobs waiting to be processed at a work center are given in the following table. Determine the sequence of jobs, the average flow time, average tardiness, and average number of jobs at the work center, for each of these rules:

a. FCFS
b. SPT
c. EDD
d. CR

Job	Processing Time (days)	Due Date (days from present time)
A	2	7
B	8	16
C	4	4
D	10	17
E	5	15
F	12	18

Assume jobs arrived in the order shown.

SOLUTION

a. The FCFS sequence is simply A-B-C-D-E-F. The measures of effectiveness are as follows (see table):

(1) *Average flow time:* 120/6 = 20 days.

(2) *Average tardiness:* 54/6 = 9 days.

(3) The *makespan* is 41 days. *Average number of jobs at the work center:* 120/41 = 2.93.

Job Sequence	(1) Processing Time	(2) Flow Time	(3) Due Date	(2) − (3) Days Tardy [0 if negative]
A	2	2	7	0
B	8	10	16	0
C	4	14	4	10
D	10	24	17	7
E	5	29	15	14
F	12	41	18	23
	41	120		54

The flow time column indicates *cumulative* processing time, so summing these times and dividing by the total number of jobs processed indicates the average time each job spends at the work center. Similarly, find the average number of jobs at the center by summing the flow times and dividing by the total processing time.

b. Using the SPT rule, the job sequence is A-C-E-B-D-F (see the following table). The resulting values for the three measures of effectiveness are

(1) *Average flow time:* 108/6 = 18 days.

(2) *Average tardiness:* 40/6 = 6.67 days.

(3) *Average number of jobs at the work center:* 108/41 = 2.63.

Job Sequence	(1) Processing Time	(2) Flow Time	(3) Due Date	(2) − (3) Days Tardy [0 if negative]
A	2	2	7	0
C	4	6	4	2
E	5	11	15	0
B	8	19	16	3
D	10	29	17	2
F	12	41	18	23
	41	108		40

c. Using earliest due date as the selection criterion, the job sequence is C-A-E-B-D-F. The measures of effectiveness are as follows (see table):

(1) *Average flow time:* 110/6 = 18.33 days.

(2) *Average tardiness:* 38/6 = 6.33 days.

(3) *Average number of jobs at the work center:* 110/41 = 2.68.

Job Sequence	(1) Processing Time	(2) Flow Time	(3) Due Date	(2) − (3) Days Tardy [0 if negative]
C	4	4	7	0
A	2	6	4	0
E	5	11	15	0
B	8	19	16	3
D	10	29	17	12
F	12	41	18	23
	41	110		38

d. Using the critical ratio we find

Job Sequence	Processing Time	Due Date	Critical Ratio Calculation
A	2	7	(7 − 0)/ 2 = 3.5
B	8	16	(16 − 0)/ 8 = 2.0
C	4	4	(4 − 0)/ 4 = 1.0 (lowest)
D	10	17	(17 − 0)/10 = 1.7
E	5	15	(15 − 0)/ 5 = 3.0
F	12	18	(18 − 0)/12 = 1.5

At day 4 [C completed], the critical ratios are

Job Sequence	Processing Time	Due Date	Critical Ratio Calculation
A	2	7	(7 − 4)/ 2 = 1.5
B	8	16	(16 − 4)/ 8 = 1.5
C	—	—	—
D	10	17	(17 − 4)/10 = 1.3
E	5	15	(15 − 4)/ 5 = 2.2
F	12	18	(18 − 4)/12 = 1.17 (lowest)

At day 16 [C and F completed], the critical ratios are

Job Sequence	Processing Time	Due Date	Critical Ratio Calculation
A	2	7	(7 − 16)/ 2 = −4.5 (lowest)
B	8	16	(16 − 16)/ 8 = 0.0
C	—	—	—
D	10	17	(17 − 16)/10 = 0.1
E	5	15	(15 − 16)/ 5 = −0.2
F	—	—	—

At day 18 [C, F, and A completed], the critical ratios are

Job Sequence	Processing Time	Due Date	Critical Ratio Calculation
A	—	—	—
B	8	16	(16 − 18)/ 8 = −0.25
C	—	—	—
D	10	17	(17 − 18)/10 = −0.10
E	5	15	(15 − 18)/ 5 = −0.60 (lowest)
F	—	—	—

At day 23 [C, F, A, and E completed], the critical ratios are

Job Sequence	Processing Time	Due Date	Critical Ratio Calculation
A	—	—	—
B	8	16	(16 − 23)/ 8 = −0.875 (lowest)
C	—	—	—
D	10	17	(17 − 23)/10 = −0.60
E	—	—	—
F	—	—	—

The job sequence is C-F-A-E-B-D, and the resulting values for the measures of effectiveness are as follows:

(1) *Average flow time:* 133/6 = 22.17 days.

(2) *Average tardiness:* 58/6 = 9.67 days.

(3) *Average number of jobs at the work center:* 133/41 = 3.24.

Sequence	(1) Processing Time	(2) Flow Time	(3) Due Date	(2) − (3) Days Tardy
C	4	4	4	0
F	12	16	18	0
A	2	18	7	11
E	5	23	15	8
B	8	31	16	15
D	10	41	17	24
	41	133		58

The results of these four rules are summarized in Table 16.4.

In Example 2, the SPT rule was the best according to two of the measures of effectiveness and a little worse than the EDD rule on average tardiness. The CR rule was the worst in every case. For a different set of numbers, the EDD rule (or perhaps another rule not mentioned here) might prove superior to SPT in terms of average job tardiness or some other measure of effectiveness. However, SPT is always superior in terms of minimizing flow time and, hence, in terms of minimizing the average number of jobs at the work center and completion time. This results in faster job completion, which has the potential to generate more revenue.

Generally speaking, the FCFS rule and the CR rule turn out to be the least effective of the rules.

SERVICE

The primary limitation of the FCFS rule is that long jobs will tend to delay other jobs. If a process consists of work on a number of machines, machine idle time for downstream workstations will increase. However, for service systems in which customers are directly involved,

TABLE 16.4
Comparison of the four rules for Example 2

Rule	Average Flow Time (days)	Average Tardiness (days)	Average Number of Jobs at the Work Center
FCFS	20.00	9.00	2.93
SPT	18.00	6.67	2.63
EDD	18.33	6.33	2.68
CR	22.17	9.67	3.24

the FCFS rule is by far the dominant priority rule, mainly because of the inherent fairness but also because of the inability to obtain realistic estimates of processing time for individual jobs. The FCFS rule also has the advantage of simplicity. If other measures are important when there is high customer contact, companies may adopt the strategy of moving processing to the "backroom" so they don't necessarily have to follow FCFS.

Because the SPT rule always results in the lowest (i.e., optimal) average completion (flow) time, it can result in lower in-process inventories. And because it often provides the lowest (optimal) average tardiness, it can result in better customer service levels. Finally, since it always involves a lower average number of jobs at the work center, there tends to be less congestion in the work area. SPT also minimizes downstream idle time. However, due dates are often uppermost in managers' minds, so they may not use SPT because it doesn't incorporate due dates.

The major disadvantage of the SPT rule is that it tends to make long jobs wait, perhaps for rather long times (especially if new, shorter jobs are continually added to the system). That can be troubling if long jobs are from the company's best customers. Various modifications may be used in an effort to avoid this. For example, after waiting for a given time period, any remaining jobs are automatically moved to the head of the line. This is known as the *truncated* SPT rule.

The EDD rule directly addresses due dates and minimizes lateness. Although it has intuitive appeal, its main limitation is that it does not take processing time into account. One possible consequence is that it can result in some jobs waiting a long time, which adds to both in-process inventories and shop congestion.

The CR rule is easy to use and has intuitive appeal. Although it had the poorest showing in Example 2 for all three measures, it usually does quite well in terms of minimizing job tardiness. Therefore, if job tardiness is important, the CR rule might be the best choice among the rules.

Let's take a look now at the S/O (slack per operation) rule.

EXAMPLE 3

excel

www.mhhe.com/stevenson11e

Use the S/O rule to schedule the following jobs. Note that processing time includes the time remaining for the current and subsequent operations. In addition, you will need to know the number of operations remaining, including the current one.

Job	Remaining Processing Time	Due Date	Remaining Number of Operations
A	4	14	3
B	16	32	6
C	8	8	5
D	20	34	2
E	10	30	4
F	18	30	2

SOLUTION

Determine the difference between the due date and the processing time for each operation. Divide the difference by the number of remaining operations, and rank them from low to high. This yields the sequence of jobs:

Job	(1) Remaining Processing Time	(2) Due Date	(3) (2) − (1) Slack	(4) Remaining Number of Operations	(5) (3) ÷ (4) Ratio	(6) Rank
A	4	14	10	3	3.33	3
B	16	32	16	6	2.67	2
C	8	8	0	5	0	1
D	20	34	14	2	7.00	6
E	10	30	20	4	5.00	4
F	18	30	12	2	6.00	5

The indicated sequence (see column 6) is C-B-A-E-F-D.

Using the S/O rule, the designated job sequence may change after any given operation, so it is important to reevaluate the sequence after each operation. Note that any of the previously mentioned priority rules could be used on a station-by-station basis for this situation; the only difference is that the S/O approach incorporates downstream information in arriving at a job sequence.

In reality, many priority rules are available to sequence jobs, and some other rule might provide superior results for a given set of circumstances. The purpose in examining these few rules is to provide insight into the nature of sequencing rules. Each shop or organization should consider carefully its own circumstances and the measures of effectiveness it feels are important, when selecting a rule to use.

The following section describes a special-purpose algorithm that can be used to sequence a set of jobs that must all be processed at the same two machines or work centers.

Sequencing Jobs through Two Work Centers[1]

Johnson's rule Technique for minimizing makespan for a group of jobs to be processed on two machines or at two work centers.

Johnson's rule is a technique that managers can use to minimize the makespan for a group of jobs to be processed on two machines or at two successive work centers (sometimes referred to as a two-machine flow shop).[2] It also minimizes the total idle time at the work centers. For the technique to work, several conditions must be satisfied:

- Job time (including setup and processing) must be known and constant for each job at each work center.
- Job times must be independent of the job sequence.
- All jobs must follow the same two-step work sequence.
- A job must be completed at the first work center before the job moves on to the second work center.

Application of Johnson's rule begins with a listing of all jobs to be scheduled, and how much time will be required by each job at each workstation. The sequence is determined by following these steps:

1. Select the job with the shortest time. If the shortest time is at the first work center, schedule that job first; if the time is at the second work center, schedule the job last. Break ties arbitrarily.
2. Eliminate the job and its time from further consideration.
3. Repeat steps 1 and 2, working toward the center of the sequence, until all jobs have been scheduled.

Successful application of these steps identifies the sequence with the minimum makespan, or all work is completed as soon as possible. However, precisely *when* a certain job will be completed (its flow time) or when idle time will occur is not apparent by inspecting the sequence. To determine such detailed performance information, it is generally easiest to create a Gantt chart illustrating the finished sequence, as demonstrated in Example 4.

When significant idle time at the second work center occurs, job splitting at the first center just prior to the occurrence of idle time may alleviate some of it and also shorten throughput time. In Example 4, this is not a concern. The last solved problem at the end of this chapter illustrates the use of job splitting.

[1]For a description of a heuristic that can be used for the case where a set of jobs is to be processed through more than two work centers, see Thomas Vollmann et al., *Manufacturing Planning and Control Systems,* 5th ed. (New York: Irwin/McGraw-Hill, 2004).

[2]S. M. Johnson, "Optimal Two- and Three-Stage Production with Setup Times Included," *Naval Research Quarterly* 1 (March 1954), pp. 61–68.

EXAMPLE 4

eXcel

www.mhhe.com/stevenson11e

A group of six jobs is to be processed through a two-machine flow shop. The first operation involves cleaning and the second involves painting. Determine a sequence that will minimize the total completion time for this group of jobs. Processing times are as follows:

	PROCESSING TIME (hours)	
Job	**Work Center 1**	**Work Center 2**
A	5	5
B	4	3
C	8	9
D	2	7
E	6	8
F	12	15

To employ Johnson's rule, create a "blank" sequence first, such as:

1st	2nd	3rd	4th	5th	6th

SOLUTION

a. Select the job with the shortest processing time. It is job D, with a time of two hours.

b. Since the time is at the first center, schedule job D first. Eliminate job D from further consideration.

1st	2nd	3rd	4th	5th	6th
D					

c. Job B has the next shortest time. Since it is at the second work center, schedule it last and eliminate job B from further consideration. We now have

1st	2nd	3rd	4th	5th	6th
D					B

d. The remaining jobs and their times are

Job	1	2
A	5	5
C	8	9
E	6	8
F	12	15

Note that there is a tie for the shortest remaining time; job A has the same time at each work center. It makes no difference, then, whether we place it toward the beginning or the end of the sequence. Suppose it is placed arbitrarily toward the end. We now have

1st	2nd	3rd	4th	5th	6th
D				A	B

e. The shortest remaining time is six hours for job E at work center 1. Thus, schedule that job toward the beginning of the sequence (after job D):

1st	2nd	3rd	4th	5th	6th
D	E			A	B

f. Job C has the shortest time of the remaining two jobs. Since it is for the first work center, place it third in the sequence. Finally, assign the remaining job (F) to the fourth position and the result is

1st	2nd	3rd	4th	5th	6th
D	E	C	F	A	B

g. Construct a Gantt chart to reveal flow time and idle time information. Be very careful not to schedule the beginning of work at center 2 *before* work at center 1 has been completed for any given job. Traditionally, it is assumed that center 1 must finish and pass the job to center 2, which can cause idle time in center 2's schedule, such as in the case of job F below:

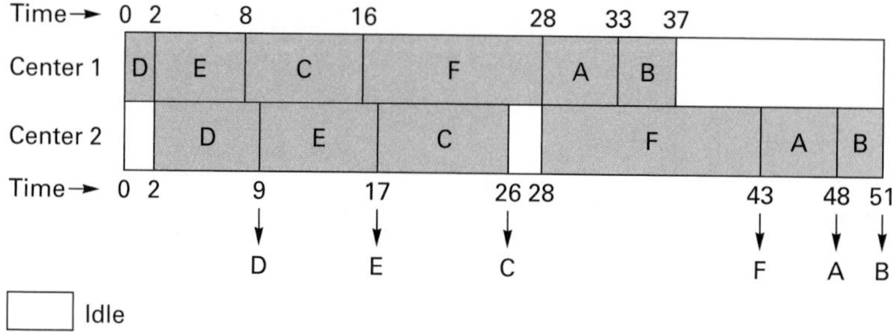

Thus, the group of jobs will take 51 hours to complete. The second work center will wait two hours for its first job and also wait two hours after finishing job C. Center 1 will be finished in 37 hours. Of course, idle periods at the beginning or end of the sequence could be used to do other jobs or for maintenance or setup/teardown activities.

Sequencing Jobs When Setup Times Are Sequence-Dependent

The preceding discussion and examples assumed that machine setup times are independent of processing order, but in many instances that assumption is not true. Consequently, a manager may want to schedule jobs at a workstation taking those dependencies into account. The goal is to minimize total setup time.

Consider the following table, which shows workstation machine setup times based on job processing order. For example, if job A is followed by job B, the setup time for B will be six hours. Furthermore, if job A is completed first, followed by job B, job C will then follow job B and have a setup time of four hours. If a job is done first, its setup time will be the amount shown in the setup time column to the right of the job. Thus, if job A is done first, its setup time will be three hours.

			Resulting following job setup time (hrs.) is		
		Setup time (hrs.)	**A**	**B**	**C**
If the preceding job is	**A**	3	—	6	2
	B	2	1	—	4
	C	2	5	3	—

The simplest way to determine which sequence will result in the lowest total setup time is to list each possible sequence and determine its total setup time. In general, the number of different alternatives is equal to $n!$, where n is the number of jobs. Here, n is 3, so $n! = 3 \times 2 \times 1 = 6$. The six alternatives and their total setup times are as follows:

Sequence	Setup Times	Total
A-B-C	3 + 6 + 4 = 13	
A-C-B	3 + 2 + 3 = 8	
B-A-C	2 + 1 + 2 = 5 (best)	
B-C-A	2 + 4 + 5 = 11	
C-A-B	2 + 5 + 6 = 13	
C-B-A	2 + 3 + 1 = 6	

Hence, to minimize total setup time, the manager would select sequence B-A-C.

This procedure is relatively simple to do manually when the number of jobs is two or three. However, as the number of jobs increases, the list of alternatives quickly becomes larger. For example, six jobs would have 720 alternatives. In such instances, a manager would employ a computer to generate the list and identify the best alternative(s). (Note that more than one alternative may be tied for the lowest setup time.)

Why Scheduling Can Be Difficult

Scheduling can be difficult for a number of reasons. One is that, in reality, an operation must deal with variability in setup times, processing times, interruptions, and changes in the set of jobs. Another major reason is that, except for small job sets, there is no method for identifying the optimal schedule, and it would be virtually impossible to sort through the vast number of possible alternatives to obtain the best schedule. As a result, scheduling is far from an exact science and, in many instances, is an ongoing task for a manager.

Computer technology reduces the burden of scheduling and makes real-time scheduling possible.

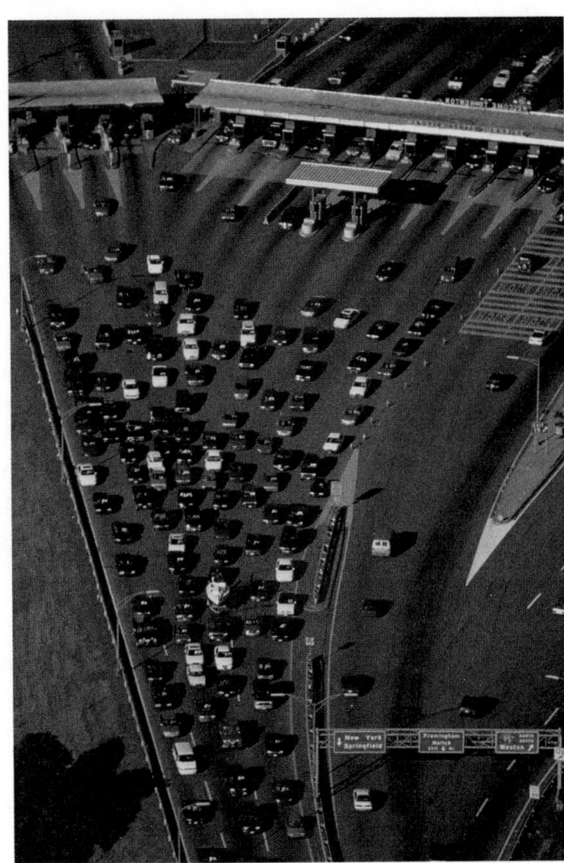

Minimizing Scheduling Difficulties

There are a number of actions that managers can consider to minimize scheduling problems:

- Setting realistic due dates.
- Focusing on bottleneck operations: First, try to increase the capacity of the operations. If that is not possible or feasible, schedule the bottleneck operations first, and then schedule the nonbottleneck operations around the bottleneck operations.
- Considering lot splitting for large jobs. This usually works best when there are relatively large differences in job times. Note that this doesn't apply to single-unit jobs.

The Theory of Constraints

Another approach to scheduling was developed and promoted by Eli Goldratt.[3] He first described it in his book *The Goal.* Goldratt avoided much of the complexity often associated with scheduling problems by simply focusing on *bottleneck* operations (i.e., those for which there was insufficient capacity—in effect, a work center with zero idle time). He reasoned the output of the system was limited by the output of the bottleneck operation(s); therefore, it was essential to schedule the nonbottleneck operations in a way that minimized the idle time of the bottleneck operation(s). Thus, idle time of nonbottleneck operations was not a factor in overall productivity of the system, as long as the bottleneck operations were used effectively. These observations have been refined into a series of scheduling principles which include:

- An hour lost at a bottleneck operation is an hour lost by the system. The bottleneck operation determines the overall capacity of the system.
- Saving time through improvements of a nonbottleneck will not increase the ultimate output of the system.
- Activation of a resource is not the same as utilization of a resource. Because a nonbottleneck operation is active does not necessarily mean it is being useful.

These principles are also the foundation of a specific scheduling technique for intermittent production systems, one that many firms have found simpler and less time-consuming to use than traditional analytical techniques. This technique uses a *drum-buffer-rope* conceptualization to manage the system. The "drum" is the schedule; it sets the pace of production. The goal is to schedule to make maximum use of bottleneck resources. The "buffer" refers to potentially constraining resources outside of the bottleneck. The role of the buffer is to keep a small amount of inventory ahead of the bottleneck operation to minimize the risk of having it be idle. The "rope" represents the synchronizing of the sequence of operations to ensure effective use of the bottleneck operations. The goal is to avoid costly and time-consuming multiple setups, particularly of capacity-constrained resources, so they do not become bottlenecks too.

The drum-buffer-rope approach provides a basis for developing a schedule that achieves maximum output and shorter lead times while avoiding carrying excess inventory. Use of the drum-buffer-rope approach generally results in operations capable of consistent on-time delivery, reduced inventory, and shorter lead times, as well as a reduction in disruptions that require expediting.

Process batch The economical quantity to produce upon the activation of a given operation.

Transfer batch The quantity to be transported from one operation to another, assumed to be smaller than the first operation's process batch.

Theory of constraints Production planning approach that emphasizes balancing flow throughout a system, and pursues a perpetual five-step improvement process centered around the system's currently most restrictive constraint.

Goldratt also developed a system of varying batch sizes to achieve the greatest output of bottleneck operations. He used the term **process batch** to denote the basic lot size for a job and the term **transfer batch** to denote a portion of the basic lot that could be used during production to facilitate utilization of bottleneck operations. In effect, a lot could be split into two or more parts. Splitting a large lot at one or more operations preceding a bottleneck operation would reduce the waiting time of the bottleneck operation.

Traditional management has emphasized maximizing output of every operation. In contrast to that approach, the **theory of constraints** has as its goal maximizing flow through the entire system, which it does by emphasizing balancing the flow through the various operations. It begins with identifying the bottleneck operation. Next, there is a five-step procedure to improve the performance of the bottleneck operation:

1. Determine what is constraining the operation.
2. Exploit the constraint (i.e., make sure the constraining resource is used to its maximum).
3. Subordinate everything to the constraint (i.e., focus on the constraint).

[3]Eli Goldratt, *The General Theory of Constraints* (New Haven, CT: Avraham Y. Institute, 1989).

4. Determine how to overcome (eliminate) the constraint.
5. Repeat the process for the next highest constraint.

(Note the similarity to the plan-do-study-act (PDSA) approach discussed in Chapter 9.)

The goal, of course, is to make *money.* The theory of constraints uses three metrics to assess the effectiveness of improvements:

- **Throughput:** the rate at which the system generates *money* through sales (i.e., the contribution margin, or sales revenue less variable costs; labor costs are considered to be part of operating expense).
- **Inventory:** Inventory represents *money* tied up in goods and materials used in a process.
- **Operating expense:** all the *money* the system spends to convert inventory into throughput; this includes utilities, scrap, depreciation, and so on.

Goldratt's ideas are applicable to both manufacturing and service environments.

SCHEDULING SERVICES

SERVICE

Scheduling service systems presents certain problems not generally encountered in manufacturing systems. This is due primarily to (1) the inability to store or inventory services and (2) the random nature of customer requests for service. In some situations, the second difficulty can be moderated by using appointment or reservation systems, but the inability to store services in most cases is a fact of life that managers must contend with.

The approach used to schedule services generally depends on whether customer contact is involved. In back-office operations, where there is little or no customer contact—such as processing mail-order requests, loan approvals, and tax preparation—the same priority rules described in the preceding pages are used. The goal is to maximize worker efficiency, and work is often processed in batches. A key factor can be the due date, say for rush orders, orders where the customer has paid a premium for faster than normal delivery. That is similar to the situation that occurs in front-office operations, where there is a high degree of customer contact, and efficiency may become secondary to keeping customer waiting times to reasonable levels, so scheduling the workforce to meet demand becomes a priority. Having too few workers causes waiting lines to form, but having more workers than needed increases labor costs, which can have a substantial impact on profits, particularly in service systems where labor is the major cost involved.

An ideal situation is one that has a smooth flow of customers through the system. This would occur if each new customer arrives at the precise instant that the preceding customer's service is completed, as in a physician's office, or in air travel if the demand just equals the number of available seats. In each of these situations customer waiting time would be minimized, and the service system staff and equipment would be fully utilized. Unfortunately, the random nature of customer requests for service that generally prevails in service systems makes it nearly impossible to provide service capability that matches demand. Moreover, if service times are subject to variability—say, because of differing processing requirements—the inefficiency of the system is compounded. The inefficiencies can be reduced if arrivals can be scheduled (e.g., appointments), as in the case of doctors and dentists. However, in many situations appointments are not possible (supermarkets, gas stations, theaters, hospital emergency rooms, repair of equipment breakdowns). Chapter 18, on waiting lines, focuses on those kinds of situations. There, the emphasis is on intermediate-term decisions related to service capacity. In this section, we will concern ourselves with short-term *scheduling,* in which much of the capacity of a system is essentially fixed, and the goal is to achieve a certain degree of customer service by efficient utilization of that capacity.

Scheduling in service systems may involve scheduling (1) customers, (2) the workforce, and (3) equipment. Scheduling customers often takes the form of appointment systems or reservation systems.

Appointment Systems

Appointment systems are intended to control the timing of customer arrivals in order to minimize customer waiting while achieving a high degree of capacity utilization. A doctor can use an appointment system to schedule patients' office visits during the afternoon, leaving the mornings free for hospital duties. Similarly, an attorney can schedule client meetings around court appearances. Even with appointments, however, problems can still arise due to lack of punctuality on the part of patients or clients, no-shows, and the inability to completely control the length of contact time (e.g., a dentist might run into complications in filling a tooth and have to spend additional time with a patient, thus backing up later appointments). Some of this can be avoided by trying to match the time reserved for a patient or client with the specific needs of that case rather than setting appointments at regular intervals. Even with the problems of late arrivals and no-shows, the appointment system is a tremendous improvement over random arrivals.

Reservation Systems

Reservation systems are designed to enable service systems to formulate a fairly accurate estimate of the demand on the system for a given time period and to minimize customer disappointment generated by excessive waiting or inability to obtain service. Reservation systems are widely used by resorts, hotels and motels, restaurants, and some modes of transportation (e.g., airlines, car rentals). In the case of restaurants, reservations enable management to spread out or group customers so that demand matches service capabilities. Late arrivals and no-shows can disrupt the system. One approach to the no-show problem is to use decision theory (described in the supplement to Chapter 5). The problem also can be viewed as a single-period inventory problem, as described in Chapter 11.

Yield Management

Many companies, especially in the travel and tourist industries, operate with fixed capacities. Examples include hotels and motels, which operate with a fixed number of rooms to rent each night; airlines, which operate with a fixed number of seats to sell on any given flight; and cruise lines, which operate with a fixed number of berths to sell for any given cruise. The number of rooms, seats, or berths can be thought of as perishable inventory. For example, unsold seats on a flight cannot be carried over to the next flight; they are lost. The same is true for hotel rooms and cruise berths. Of course that unsold inventory does not generate income, so companies with fixed capacities must develop strategies to deal with sales.

Yield management The application of pricing strategies to allocate capacity among various categories of demand.

Yield management is the application of pricing strategies to allocate capacity among various categories of demand with the goal of maximizing the revenue generated by the fixed capacity. Demand for fixed capacity usually consists of customers who make advance reservations and walk-ins. Customers who make advance reservations are typically price-sensitive, while walk-ins are often price-insensitive. Companies must decide on the percentage of their limited inventory to allocate to reservations, trading off lower revenue per unit for increased certainty of sales, and how much to allocate to walk-ins, where demand is less certain but revenue per unit is higher.

The basic yield management concept is applicable to railroads as well as airlines. Yield management is multidisciplinary because it blends elements of marketing, operations, and financial management.

The ability to predict demand is critical to the success of yield management, so forecasting plays a key role in the process. Seasonal variations are generally important, so forecasts must incorporate seasonality and plans must also be somewhat flexible to allow for ever-present random variations.

Servicing Passenger Planes

READING

Robert L. Crandall
Former CEO—American Airlines

Before takeoff and after landing, you've probably noticed lots of people and various types of vehicles and equipment busily moving around on the ground outside with no apparent game plan, particularly at larger airports. Actually, all that activity is carefully orchestrated, and because the people involved are an important part of our team, I'd like to tell you what the hustle and bustle is all about.

When a flight lands and approaches the terminal, ramp personnel guide the aircraft to its parking position and after it comes to a stop, put chocks under its wheels. As soon as that's been done, other workers hook up ground-based power and air conditioning. Electric power comes from what looks like a large, industrial-strength extension cord plugged into the lower portion of the nose section. Heated or cooled air goes into the cabin via the big yellow hoses that run from the airplane either to the terminal, in cities where we have central air-handling facilities or, in others, to mobile air-handling units.

On the airplane, meanwhile, flight attendants open the door and as passengers begin deplaning, a mechanic squeezes past them to get a debriefing from the cockpit and check to see if any maintenance work must be done.

Once all deplaning passengers are off, the cabin cleaners go into high gear on most flights, cleaning our seatback pockets, tidying up the cabin, cleaning the lavatories, doing a light vacuuming, repositioning safety belts for each seat's next occupant, and so forth. (A more thorough cleaning is done each night.)

Simultaneously, out on the ramp, our people are unloading baggage, freight, and mail from the airplane's belly compartments and beginning the process of sorting by various categories and destinations. In addition to the bags and cargo that have reached their destination, which must be delivered promptly to passengers and shippers, some must be transferred to other American or American Eagle flights, and still others must be transferred to other carriers. Complicating matters further, baggage, freight, and mail are often handled in different facilities on the airport property.

If a meal has been served or is planned for the outbound flight, catering trucks pull up to service the First Class and main cabin galleys. Another special truck services the lavatory holding tanks, and in the midst of all this, mechanics are dealing with any problems reported by the crew and doing their own walk-around inspections.

Once all that is complete, customers start to board the aircraft for its next flight and everything happens in reverse. Ground workers start loading baggage in the forward belly and freight and mail in the rear. Fuel trucks pull up to refuel most flights. The airplanes must be "watered" as well; fresh water is pumped aboard from either a water truck or servicing equipment built into the gate itself. During cold-weather months, deicing trucks add another element of ramp activity as they spray fluid on the airplane's wings and fuselage.

Most of the work on the ramp is done by our own people, principally fleet-service personnel, but there are also various services, like catering, which are performed by contractors.

All this simultaneous activity can create conflicts. Baggage carts unloading the forward hold can encroach on the ground space needed by the trucks catering the First Class cabin, for example, and fuelers perform their function in the space needed by those unloading freight and mail. The ramp crew chiefs are the conductors, orchestrating the entire production, overseeing the detail, and seeing to it that all gets done without mishap—and on time.

It's a delicate balancing act, and although our customers rarely come in contact with the folks working on the ramp, they are an important part of a team that aims to serve every customer well and keep our operation running safely and on time.

Source: Robert L. Crandall, "Servicing Passenger Planes," *American Way*, March 15, 1995.

Scheduling the Workforce

Scheduling customers is demand management. Scheduling the workforce is capacity management. This approach works best when demand can be predicted with reasonable accuracy. This is often true for restaurants, theaters, rush-hour traffic, and similar instances that have repeating patterns of intensity of customer arrivals. Scheduling hospital personnel, police, and telephone operators for catalog sales, credit card companies, and mutual fund companies also comes under this heading. An additional consideration is the extent to which variations in customer demands can be met with workforce flexibility. Thus, capacity can be adjusted by having cross-trained workers who can be temporarily assigned to help out on bottleneck operations during periods of peak demand.

Various constraints can affect workforce scheduling flexibility, including legal, behavioral, technical—such as workers' qualifications to perform certain operations—and budget constraints. Union or federal work rules and vacations can make scheduling more complicated.

Cyclical Scheduling

In many services (e.g., hospitals, police departments, fire departments, restaurants, and supermarkets) the scheduling requirements are fairly similar: Employees must be assigned to work shifts or time slots, and have days off, on a repeating or cyclical basis. Here is a method for determining both a schedule and the minimum number of workers needed.

Generally a basic work pattern is set (e.g., work five consecutive days, have two consecutive days off), and a list of staffing needs for the schedule cycle (usually one week) is given. For example:

Day	Mon	Tue	Wed	Thu	Fri	Sat	Sun
Staff needed	**2**	**4**	**3**	**4**	**6**	**5**	**5**

A fairly simple but effective approach for determining the minimum number of workers needed is the following: Begin by repeating the staff needs for worker 1. Then,

1. Make the first worker's assignment such that the two days with the lowest need (i.e., lowest sum) are designated as days off. Here Monday–Tuesday has the two lowest consecutive requirements. Circle those days. (Note, in some instances, Sun–Mon might yield the two lowest days.) In case of a tie, pick the pair with the lowest adjacent requirement. If there is still a tie, pick arbitrarily.

Day	Mon	Tue	Wed	Thu	Fri	Sat	Sun
Staff needed	**2**	**4**	**3**	**4**	**6**	**5**	**5**
Worker 1	2	4	3	4	6	5	5

2. Subtract one from each day's requirement, except for the circled days. Assign the next employee, again using the two lowest consecutive days as days off. Circle those days.

Day	Mon	Tue	Wed	Thu	Fri	Sat	Sun
Staff needed	**2**	**4**	**3**	**4**	**6**	**5**	**5**
Worker 1	2	4	3	4	6	5	5
Worker 2	2	4	2	3	5	4	4

3. Repeat the preceding step for each additional worker until all staffing requirements have been met. However, don't subtract from a value of zero.

Day	Mon	Tue	Wed	Thu	Fri	Sat	Sun
Staff needed	**2**	**4**	**3**	**4**	**6**	**5**	**5**
Worker 1	2	4	3	4	6	5	5
Worker 2	2	4	2	3	5	4	4
Worker 3	1	3	2	3	4	3	3
Worker 4	1	3	1	2	3	2	2 (tie)
Worker 5	1	2	0	1	2	1	2
Worker 6	0	1	0	1	1	0	1 (multiple ties)
Worker 7	0	1	0	0	0	0	0 (tie)
No. working:	**2**	**4**	**3**	**4**	**6**	**5**	**5**

To identify the days each worker is working, go across each worker's row to find the nonzero values that are not circled, signifying that the worker is assigned for those days. Similarly, to find the workers who are assigned to work for any particular day, go down that day's column to find the nonzero values that are not circled. *Note:* Worker 6 will only work four days, and worker 7 will only work *one* day.

Scheduling Multiple Resources

In some situations, it is necessary to coordinate the use of more than one resource. For example, hospitals must schedule surgeons, operating room staffs, recovery room staffs, admissions, special equipment, nursing staffs, and so on. Educational institutions must schedule faculty, classrooms, audiovisual equipment, and students. As you might guess, the greater the number of resources to be scheduled simultaneously, the greater the complexity and the less likely that an optimum schedule can be achieved. The problem is further complicated by the variable nature of such systems. For example, educational institutions frequently change their course offerings, student enrollments change, and students exhibit different course-selection patterns.

Some schools and hospitals are using computer software to assist them in devising acceptable schedules, although many appear to be using intuitive approaches with varying degrees of success.

Airlines are another example of service systems that require the scheduling of multiple resources. Flight crews, aircraft, baggage handling equipment, ticket counters, gate personnel, boarding ramps, and maintenance personnel all have to be coordinated. Furthermore, government regulations on the number of hours a pilot can spend flying place an additional restriction on the system. Another interesting variable is that, unlike most systems, the flight crews and the equipment do not remain in one location. Moreover, the crew and the equipment are not usually scheduled as a single unit. Flight crews are often scheduled so that they return to their base city every two days or more, and rest breaks must be considered. On the other hand, the aircraft may be in almost continuous use except for periodic maintenance and repairs. Consequently, flight crews commonly follow different trip patterns than that of the aircraft.

There are also other activities that must be scheduled, some of which are described by American Airlines Chairman Robert L. Crandall in the reading on servicing passenger planes.

Service systems are prone to slowdowns when variability in demand for services causes bottlenecks. Part of the difficulty lies in predicting which operations will become bottlenecks. Moreover, bottlenecks may shift with the passage of time, so that different operations become bottleneck operations—further complicating the problem.

OPERATIONS STRATEGY

Scheduling can either help or hinder operations strategy. If scheduling is done well, goods or services can be made or delivered in a timely manner. Resources can be used to best advantage and customers will be satisfied. Scheduling not performed well will result in inefficient use of resources and possibly dissatisfied customers.

The implication is clear: Management should not overlook the important role that scheduling plays in the success of an organization and the supply chain, giving a competitive advantage if done well or disadvantage if done poorly. Time-based competition depends on good scheduling. Coordination of materials, equipment use, and employee time is an important function of operations management. It is not enough to have good design, superior quality, and the other elements of a well-run organization if scheduling is done poorly—just as it is not enough to own a well-designed and well-made car, with all the latest features for comfort and safety, if the owner doesn't know how to drive it!

SUMMARY

Scheduling involves the timing and coordination of operations. Such activities are fundamental to virtually every organization. Scheduling problems differ according to whether a system is designed for high volume, intermediate volume, or low volume. Scheduling problems are particularly complex for job shops (low volume) because of the variety of jobs these systems are required to process.

The two major problems in job-shop scheduling are assigning jobs to machines or work centers, and designating the sequence of job processing at a given machine or work center. Gantt load charts are frequently employed to help managers visualize workloads, and they are useful for describing and analyzing sequencing alternatives. In addition, both heuristic and optimizing methods are used to develop loading and sequencing plans. For the most part, the optimization techniques can be used only if certain assumptions can be made.

Customer requirements in service systems generally present very different circumstances than those encountered in manufacturing systems. Some services can use appointments and reservations for scheduling purposes, although not all systems are amenable to this. When multiple resources are involved, the task of balancing the system can be fairly complex.

KEY POINTS

1. Scheduling occurs in every business organization.
2. Scheduling decisions are made within constraints established by decisions on capacity, product or service design, process selection and layout, aggregate planning, and master scheduling.
3. Scheduling decisions occur just prior to the conversion of inputs into outputs.
4. Effective scheduling can reduce costs and increase productivity.

KEY TERMS

assignment model, 709
backward scheduling, 708
finite loading, 706
flow-shop scheduling, 702
flow system, 702
forward scheduling, 708
Gantt chart, 705
global priority rules, 712
Hungarian method, 709
infinite loading, 706
input/output (I/O) control, 708
job flow time, 713
job lateness, 713
job-shop scheduling, 705
job time, 712
Johnson's rule, 718
load chart, 706
loading, 705
local priority rules, 712
makespan, 713
priority rules, 712
process batch, 722
schedule chart, 708
scheduling, 701
sequencing, 712
theory of constraints, 722
transfer batch, 722
workstation, 712
yield management, 724

SOLVED PROBLEMS

Problem 1

The assignment method. The following table contains information on the cost to run three jobs on four available machines. Determine an assignment plan that will minimize costs.

		MACHINE			
		A	B	C	D
	1	12	16	14	10
Job	2	9	8	13	7
	3	15	12	9	11

Solution

In order for us to be able to use the assignment method, the numbers of jobs and machines must be equal. To remedy this situation, add a *dummy* job with costs of 0, and then solve as usual.

		MACHINE			
		A	B	C	D
	1	12	16	14	10
Job	2	9	8	13	7
	3	15	12	9	11
(dummy)	4	0	0	0	0

a. Subtract the smallest number from each row. The results are

		MACHINE			
		A	B	C	D
	1	2	6	4	0
Job	2	2	1	6	0
	3	6	3	0	2
	4	0	0	0	0

b. Subtract the smallest number in each column. (Because of the dummy zeros in each column, the resulting table will be unchanged.)

c. Determine the minimum number of lines needed to cross out the zeros. One possible way is

		MACHINE			
		A	B	C	D
Job	1	2	6	4	0
	2	2	1	6	0
	3	6	3	0	2
	4	0	0	0	0

d. Because the number of lines is less than the number of rows, modify the numbers.

(1) Subtract the smallest uncovered number (1) from each uncovered number.
(2) Add the smallest uncovered number to numbers at line intersections.
The result is

		MACHINE			
		A	B	C	D
Job	1	1	5	4	0
	2	1	0	6	0
	3	5	2	0	2
	4	0	0	1	1

e. Test for optimality:

		MACHINE			
		A	B	C	D
Job	1	1	5	4	0
	2	1	0	6	0
	3	5	2	0	2
	4	0	0	1	1

Because the minimum number of lines equals the number of rows, an optimum assignment can be made.

f. Assign jobs to machines. Start with rows 1 and 3, since they each have one zero, and columns A and C, also with one zero each. After each assignment, cross out all the numbers in that row *and* column. The result is

		MACHINE			
		A	B	C	D
Job	1	1	5	4	**0**
	2	1	**0**	6	0
	3	5	2	**0**	2
	4	**0**	0	1	1

Notice that there is only one assignment in each row, and only one assignment in each column.

g. Compute total costs, referring to the original table

1-D	$10
2-B	8
3-C	9
4-A	0
	$27

h. The implication of assignment 4-A is that machine A will not be assigned a job. It may remain idle or be used for another job.

Problem 2

Priority rules. Job times (including processing and setup) are shown in the following table for five jobs waiting to be processed at a work center:

Job	Job Time (hours)	Due Date (hours)
a	12	15
b	6	24
c	14	20
d	3	8
e	7	6

Determine the processing sequence that would result from each of these priority rules:

a. SPT b. EDD

Solution

Assume job times are independent of processing sequence.

	a. SPT		b. EDD	
Job	**Job Time**	**Processing Order**	**Hour Due**	**Processing Order**
a	12	4	15	3
b	6	2	24	5
c	14	5	20	4
d	3	1	8	2
e	7	3	6	1

Problem 3

Priority rules. Using the job times and due dates from Solved Problem 2, determine each of the following performance measures for first-come, first-served processing order:

a. Makespan.

b. Average flow time.

c. Average tardiness.

d. Average number of jobs at the workstation.

Solution

Job	Job Time	Flow Time	Hour Due	Hours Tardy
a	12	12	15	0
b	6	18	24	0
c	14	32	20	12
d	3	35	8	27
e	7	42	6	36
Total		139		75

a. Makespan $= 42$ hours

b. Average flow time $= \dfrac{\text{Total flow time}}{\text{Number of jobs}} = \dfrac{139}{5} = 27.80$ hours

c. Average tardiness $= \dfrac{\text{Total hours tardy}}{\text{Number of jobs}} = \dfrac{75}{5} = 15$ hours

d. Average number of jobs at workstation $= \dfrac{\text{Total flow time}}{\text{Makespan}} = \dfrac{139}{42} = 3.31$

Problem 4

S/O rule. Using the following information, determine an order processing sequence using the S/O priority rule.

Order	Processing Time Remaining (days)	Due Date (days)	Number of Operations Remaining
A	20	30	2
B	11	18	5
C	10	6	2
D	16	23	4

Assume times are independent of processing sequence.

Solution

Order	(1) Remaining Processing Time	(2) Due Date	(3) (2) − (1) Slack	(4) Number of Operations	(5) Ratio	(6) Rank (sequence)
A	20	30	10	2	5.00	4
B	11	18	7	5	1.40	2
C	10	6	−4	2	−2.00	1
D	16	23	7	4	1.75	3

(Note that one ratio is negative. When negatives occur, assign the *lowest* rank to the *most negative* number.)

Problem 5

Sequencing jobs through two work centers. Use Johnson's rule to obtain the optimum sequence for processing the jobs shown through work centers A and B.

Job	JOB TIMES (hours) Work Center A	Work Center B
a	2.50	4.20
b	3.80	1.50
c	2.20	3.00
d	5.80	4.00
e	4.50	2.00

Solution

a. Identify the smallest time: job b (1.50 hours at work center B). Because the time is for B, schedule this job last.

b. The next smallest time is job e (2.00 hours at B). Schedule job e next to last.

c. Identify the smallest remaining job time: job c (2.20 hours at center A). Since the time is in the A column, schedule job c first. At this point, we have:
c, ______, ______, e, b

d. The smallest time for the remaining jobs is 2.50 hours for job a at center A. Schedule this job after job c. The one remaining job (job d) fills the remaining slot. Thus, we have
c-a-d-e-b

Problem 6

For Solved Problem 5, determine what effect splitting jobs c, d, e, and b in work center A would have on the idle time of work center B and on the throughput time. Assume that each job can be split into two equal parts.

Solution

We assume that the processing sequence remains unchanged and proceed on that basis. The solution from the previous problem is shown in the following chart. The next chart shows reduced idle time at center B when splitting is used.

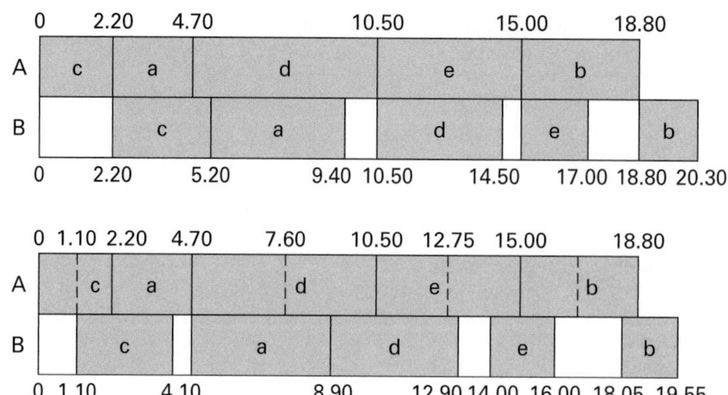

An inspection of these two figures reveals that throughput time has decreased from 20.30 hours to 19.55 hours. In addition, the original idle time was 5.6 hours. After splitting certain jobs, it was reduced to 4.85 hours, so some improvement was achieved. Note that processing times at B are generally less than at A for jobs toward the end of the sequence. As a result, jobs such as e and b at B were scheduled so that they were *centered* around the finishing times of e and b, respectively, at A, to avoid having to break the jobs due to waiting for the remainder of the split job from A. Thus, the greatest advantage from job splitting generally comes from splitting earlier jobs when Johnson's rule is used for sequencing.

DISCUSSION AND REVIEW QUESTIONS

1. Why is scheduling fairly simple for repetitive systems but fairly complex for job shops?
2. What are the main decision areas of job-shop scheduling?
3. What are Gantt charts? How are they used in scheduling? What are the advantages of using Gantt charts?
4. What are the basic assumptions of the assignment method of linear programming?
5. Briefly describe each of these priority rules:
   a. FCFS b. SPT c. EDD d. S/O e. Rush
6. Why are priority rules needed?
7. What problems not generally found in manufacturing systems do service systems present in terms of scheduling the use of resources?
8. Explain forward and backward schedulings and each one's advantage.
9. How are scheduling and productivity related?
10. What factors would you take into account in deciding whether to split a job?
11. Explain the term *makespan.*

TAKING STOCK

1. What general trade-offs are involved in sequencing decisions? In scheduling decisions?
2. Who needs to be involved in setting schedules?
3. How has technology had an impact on scheduling?

CRITICAL THINKING EXERCISES

1. One approach that can be effective in reducing the impact of production bottlenecks in a job shop or batch operations setting is to use smaller lot sizes.
   a. What is the impact of a production bottleneck?
   b. Explain how small lot sizes can reduce the impact of bottleneck operations.

c. What are the key trade-offs in using small lot sizes for the purpose of reducing the bottleneck effect?
d. In some cases, the location of a bottleneck will shift (i.e., sometimes it is at workstation 3, another time it is at workstation 12). Furthermore, there can be more than one bottleneck operation at the same time. How would these situations impact scheduling using small lot sizes?

2. Doctors' and dentists' offices frequently schedule patient visits at regularly spaced intervals. What problems can this create? Can you suggest an alternative approach to reduce these problems? Under what circumstances would regularly spaced appointments constitute a reasonable approach to patient scheduling?
3. Name 3 examples of unethical behavior involving scheduling and state the ethical principle each violates.

PROBLEMS

1. Use the assignment method to determine the best way to assign workers to jobs, given the following cost information. Compute the total cost for your assignment plan.

		JOB		
		A	B	C
Worker	1	5	8	6
	2	6	7	9
	3	4	5	3

2. Rework problem 1, treating the numbers in the table as profits instead of costs. Compute the total profit.
3. Assign trucks to delivery routes so that total costs are minimized, given the cost data shown. What is the total cost?

		ROUTE				
		A	B	C	D	E
Truck	1	4	5	9	8	7
	2	6	4	8	3	5
	3	7	3	10	4	6
	4	5	2	5	5	8
	5	6	5	3	4	9

4. Develop an assignment plan that will minimize processing costs, given the information shown, and interpret your answer.

		WORKER		
		A	B	C
Job	1	12	8	11
	2	13	10	8
	3	14	9	14
	4	10	7	12

5. Use the assignment method to obtain a plan that will minimize the processing costs in the following table under these conditions:
   a. The combination 2-D is undesirable.
   b. The combinations 1-A and 2-D are undesirable.

		WORKER				
		A	B	C	D	E
Job	1	14	18	20	17	18
	2	14	15	19	16	17
	3	12	16	15	14	17
	4	11	13	14	12	14
	5	10	16	15	14	13

6. The following table contains information concerning four jobs that are awaiting processing at a work center.

Job	Job Time (days)	Due Date (days)
A	14	20
B	10	16
C	7	15
D	6	17

a. Sequence the jobs using (1) FCFS, (2) SPT, (3) EDD, and (4) CR. Assume the list is by order of arrival.
b. For each of the methods in part *a,* determine (1) the average job flow time, (2) the average tardiness, and (3) the average number of jobs at the work center.
c. Is one method superior to the others? Explain.

7. Using the information presented in the following table, identify the processing sequence that would result using (1) FCFS, (2) SPT, (3) EDD, and (4) CR. For each method, determine (1) average job flow time, (2) average job tardiness, and (3) average number of jobs in the system. Jobs are listed in order of arrival. (*Hint:* First determine the total job time for each job by computing the total processing time for the job and then adding in the setup time. All times and due dates are in hours.)

Job	Processing Time per Unit	Units per Job	Setup Time	Due Date
a	.14	45	0.7	4
b	.25	14	0.5	10
c	.10	18	0.2	12
d	.25	40	1.0	20
e	.10	75	0.5	15

8. The following table shows orders to be processed at a machine shop as of 8:00 a.m. Monday. The jobs have different operations they must go through. Processing times are in days. Jobs are listed in order of arrival.
a. Determine the processing sequence at the first work center using each of these rules: (1) FCFS, (2) S/O.
b. Compute the effectiveness of each rule using each of these measures: (1) average completion time, (2) average number of jobs at the work center.

Job	Processing Time (days)	Due Date (days)	Remaining Number of Operations
A	8	20	2
B	10	18	4
C	5	25	5
D	11	17	3
E	9	35	4

9. A wholesale grocery distribution center uses a two-step process to fill orders. Tomorrow's work will consist of filling the seven orders shown. Determine a job sequence that will minimize the time required to fill the orders.

	TIME (hours)	
Order	Step 1	Step 2
A	1.20	1.40
B	0.90	1.30
C	2.00	0.80
D	1.70	1.50
E	1.60	1.80
F	2.20	1.75
G	1.30	1.40

10. The times required to complete each of eight jobs in a two-machine flow shop are shown in the table that follows. Each job must follow the same sequence, beginning with machine A and moving to machine B.

a. Determine a sequence that will minimize makespan time.
b. Construct a chart of the resulting sequence, and find machine B's idle time.
c. For the sequence determined in part *a,* how much would machine B's idle time be reduced by splitting the last two jobs in half?

	TIME (hours)	
Job	**Machine A**	**Machine B**
a	16	5
b	3	13
c	9	6
d	8	7
e	2	14
f	12	4
g	18	14
h	20	11

11. Given the operation times provided:

a. Develop a job sequence that minimizes idle time at the two work centers.
b. Construct a chart of the activities at the two centers, and determine each one's idle time, assuming no other activities are involved.

	JOB TIMES (minutes)					
	A	**B**	**C**	**D**	**E**	**F**
Center 1	20	16	43	60	35	42
Center 2	27	30	51	12	28	24

12. A shoe repair operation uses a two-step sequence that all jobs in a certain category follow. For the group of jobs listed,

a. Find the sequence that will minimize total completion time.
b. Determine the amount of idle time for workstation B.
c. What jobs are candidates for splitting? Why? If they were split, how much would idle time and makespan time be reduced?

	JOB TIMES (minutes)				
	A	**B**	**C**	**D**	**E**
Workstation A	27	18	70	26	15
Workstation B	45	33	30	24	10

13. The following schedule was prepared by the production manager of Marymount Metal Shop:

	CUTTING		POLISHING	
Job	**Start**	**Finish**	**Start**	**Finish**
A	0	2	2	5
B	2	6	6	9
C	6	11	11	13
D	11	15	15	20
E	15	17	20	23
F	17	20	23	24
G	20	21	24	28

Determine a schedule that will result in earlier completion of all jobs on this list.

14. The production manager must determine the processing sequence for seven jobs through the grinding and deburring departments. The same sequence will be followed in both departments. The manager's goal is to move the jobs through the two departments as quickly as possible. The foreman of the deburring department wants the SPT rule to be used to minimize the work-in-process inventory in his department.

Job	PROCESSING TIME (hours) Grinding	Deburring
A	3	6
B	2	4
C	1	5
D	4	3
E	9	4
F	8	7
G	6	2

a. Prepare a schedule using SPT for the grinding department.
b. What is the flow time in the grinding department for the SPT sequence? What is the total time needed to process the seven jobs in both the grinding and deburring departments?
c. Determine a sequence that will minimize the total time needed to process the jobs in both departments. What flow time will result for the grinding department?
d. Discuss the trade-offs between the two alternative sequencing arrangements. At what point would the production manager be indifferent concerning the choice of sequences?

15. A foreman has determined processing times at a work center for a set of jobs and now wants to sequence them. Given the information shown, do the following:
   a. Determine the processing sequence using (1) FCFS, (2) SPT, (3) EDD, and (4) CR. For each sequence, compute the average job tardiness, the average flow time, and the average number of jobs at the work center. The list is in FCFS order.
   b. Using the results of your calculations in part *a,* show that the average flow time and the average number of jobs measures are equivalent for all four sequencing rules.
   c. Determine the processing sequence that would result using the S/O rule.

Job	Job Time (days)	Due Date	Operations Remaining
a	4.5	10	3
b	6.0	17	4
c	5.2	12	3
d	1.6	27	5
e	2.8	18	3
f	3.3	19	1

16. Given the information in the following table, determine the processing sequence that would result using the S/O rule.

Job	Remaining Processing Time (days)	Due Date	Remaining Number of Operations
a	5	8	2
b	6	5	4
c	9	10	4
d	7	12	3
e	8	10	2

17. Given the following information on job times and due dates, determine the optimal processing sequence using (1) FCFS, (2) SPT, (3) EDD, and (4) CR. For each method, find the average job flow time and the average job tardiness.

Job	Job Time (hours)	Due Date (hours)
a	3.5	7
b	2.0	6
c	4.5	18
d	5.0	22
e	2.5	4
f	6.0	20

18. The Budd Gear Co. specializes in heat-treating gears for automobile companies. At 8:00 a.m., when Budd's shop opened today, five orders (listed in order of arrival) were waiting to be processed.

Order	Order Size (units)	Per Unit Time in Heat Treatment (minutes/unit)	Due Date (min. from now)
A	16	4	160
B	6	12	200
C	10	3	180
D	8	10	190
E	4	1	220

a. If the due date rule is used, what sequence should be used?
b. What will be the average job tardiness?
c. What will be the average number of jobs in the system?
d. Would the SPT rule produce better results in terms of lateness?

19. The following table contains order-dependent setup times for three jobs. Which processing sequence will minimize the total setup time?

			Following Job's Setup Time (hrs.)		
		Setup Time (hrs.)	A	B	C
Preceding Job	A	2	—	3	5
	B	3	8	—	2
	C	2	4	3	—

20. The following table contains order-dependent setup times for three jobs. Which processing sequence will minimize the total setup time?

			Following Job's Setup Time (hrs.)		
		Setup Time (hrs.)	A	B	C
Preceding Job	A	2.4	—	1.8	2.2
	B	3.2	0.8	—	1.4
	C	2.0	2.6	1.3	—

21. The following table contains order-dependent setup times for four jobs. For safety reasons, job C cannot follow job A, nor can job A follow job C. Determine the processing sequence that will minimize the total setup time. (*Hint:* There are 12 alternatives.)

			Following Job's Setup Time (hrs.)			
		Setup Time (hrs.)	A	B	C	D
Preceding Job	A	2	—	5	x	4
	B	1	7	—	3	2
	C	3	x	2	—	2
	D	2	4	3	6	—

22. Given this information on planned and actual inputs and outputs for a service center, determine the work backlog for each period. The beginning backlog is 12 hours of work. The figures shown are standard hours of work.

		PERIOD				
		1	2	3	4	5
Input	Planned	24	24	24	24	20
	Actual	25	27	20	22	24
Output	Planned	24	24	24	24	23
	Actual	24	22	23	24	24

23. Given the following data on inputs and outputs at a work center, determine the cumulative deviation and the backlog for each time period. The beginning backlog is 7.

Input

	PERIOD 1	2	3	4	5	6
Planned	200	200	180	190	190	200
Actual	210	200	179	195	193	194

Output

	PERIOD 1	2	3	4	5	6
Planned	200	200	180	190	190	200
Actual	205	194	177	195	193	200

24. Determine the minimum number of workers needed, and a schedule for the following staffing requirements, giving workers two consecutive days off per cycle (not including Sunday).

Day	Mon	Tue	Wed	Thu	Fri	Sat
Staff needed	2	3	1	2	4	3

25. Determine the minimum number of workers needed, and a schedule for the following staffing requirements, giving workers two consecutive days off per cycle (not including Sunday).

Day	Mon	Tue	Wed	Thu	Fri	Sat
Staff needed	3	4	2	3	4	5

26. Determine the minimum number of workers needed, and a schedule for the following staffing requirements, giving workers two consecutive days off per cycle (not including Sunday).

Day	Mon	Tue	Wed	Thu	Fri	Sat
Staff needed	4	4	5	6	7	8

Hi-Ho, Yo-Yo, Inc.

CASE

It was a little past 9:00 on a Monday morning when Jeff Baker walked into your office with a box of donuts.

"I've been talking with Anne about a problem we have with short-term capacity in our pad printing operation. You know, that's where we print the logo on the Custom lines of yo-yos. We have received more orders than usual for July, and I want to release the orders to pad printing in a way that will enable us to meet our due date commitments in the best way possible. Would you have time to look at the order list (attached) and see what kind of schedule we should follow to do that? By the way, you have established quite a reputation in your short stay here. You have a talent for really explaining why your recommendations are the best approach in a way that all of us 'over-the-hill' managers can understand. Please be sure to do that for me too. I want to understand why your recommendation is the best schedule and what the tradeoffs are for other possible schedules—and none of that philosophical college mumbo-jumbo. Remember, I came up through the ranks. I don't have one of those sheepskins on my wall," he says with a laugh.

Since your schedule was back to normal after that MRP report you did for Anne, you agreed to look at the information. After that compliment, how could you say no? "Try to get back to me within a couple of days," Jeff said as he left your office.

After a few minutes with your old operations management text, you call the production control office to confirm the pad printing schedule. They confirm that pad printing runs one eight-hour shift per day. They tell you that due to a make-up day for flooding in June, pad printing will be running 23 days in July, beginning Friday, July 1 (they will work three Saturdays on July 9, 16, and 23, and take a one-day holiday for July 4). You thank them for the information and then you begin to develop your plan.

Even though Jeff lacks a college degree, from what you have seen, he is very sharp. And obviously he knows good work when he sees it since he liked, and apparently understood, your past work. You resolve to cover all the bases but in a way that is as clear as possible.

(continued)

(concluded)

PAD PRINTING ORDER LIST

Job	Date Order Received	Set-up Time	Production Time	Due Date
A	6/4	2 hrs.	6 days	11 July
B	6/7	4 hrs.	2 days	8 July
C	6/12	2 hrs.	8 days	25 July
D	6/14	4 hrs.	3 days	19 July
E	6/15	4 hrs.	9 days	29 July

Note: Setup time is to set up the pad printer at the start of the job. Setup includes thoroughly cleaning the printing heads and ink reservoirs, installing the new pad(s) and ink supply, and carefully aligning the machine. Setup at the beginning of a new day with the same job is insignificant.

Examine the following rules and write a report to Jeff Baker summarizing your findings and advise him on which rule to use. Rules: FCFS, SPT, DD, and CR.

Source: Victor E. Sower, "Hi-Ho, Yo-Yo, Inc." Copyright © 2006 Victor E. Sower, Ph.D, C.D.E.

SELECTED BIBLIOGRAPHY AND FURTHER READINGS

Bushong, J. Gregory, and John C. Talbott. "An Application of the Theory of Constraints." *The CPA in Industry,* April 1999.

Goldratt, Eli, and Jeff Cox. *The Goal: A Process of Ongoing Improvement.* Great Barrington, MA: North River Press, 1992.

Hopp, Wallace J., and Mark L. Spearman. *Factory Physics.* 2nd ed. New York: Irwin/McGraw-Hill, 2001.

Jacobs, F. Robert, William L. Berry, D. Clay Whybark, and Thomas E.Vollmann. *Manufacturing Planning and Control Systems.* 6th ed. New York: Irwin/McGraw-Hill, 2011.

Metters, Richard, and Vicente Vargus. "A Comparison of Production Scheduling Policies on Costs, Service Levels, and Scheduling Changes." *Production and Operations Management* 17, no. 8 (1999), pp. 76–91.

Pinedo, Michael. *Planning and Scheduling in Manufacturing and Services.* New York: Springer, 2005.

17 CHAPTER

Project Management

CHAPTER OUTLINE

LEARNING OBJECTIVES

After completing this chapter, you should be able to:

1. Discuss the behavioral aspects of projects in terms of project personnel and the project manager.
2. Explain the nature and importance of a work breakdown structure in project management.
3. Give a general description of PERT/CPM techniques.
4. Construct simple network diagrams.
5. List the kinds of information that a PERT or CPM analysis can provide.
6. Analyze networks with deterministic times.
7. Analyze networks with probabilistic times.
8. Describe activity "crashing" and solve typical problems.

Projects are a unique aspect of business operations that require a special management approach. Unlike many other aspects of business, which tend to operate more routinely, projects often have uncertainties and risks that tend to make managing them more challenging, such as the Hoover Dam bridge.

Examples of projects are many. Some are huge, such as building the space station, rescue and cleanup operations after major natural disasters, and hosting the Olympic games. Others are smaller in scope, but still quite involved, such as producing a major motion picture, putting on a Broadway play, or producing a music video. They involve a tremendous amount of planning and coordinating set design, set building, script writing, camera crews, directors, actors or hosts, costumes, advertising, and more to accomplish project objectives while meeting budget and time constraints.

Consider the Olympic Games. They involve much more than the festivities, the excitement, national pride, and competition among athletes. They all involve a tremendous amount of planning, preparation, and coordinating work that needs to get done before and during the games. Athletes' living quarters and training facilities must be provided, competition schedules must be developed, arrangements for televising events must be made, equipment and crews must be coordinated, transportation and hotel accommodations must be made, and many other activities that go on behind the scenes must be planned and managed so that everything goes off smoothly.

The Microsoft Corporation periodically releases new or updated software. Each release is the result of many people working countless hours writing code, testing programs, and revising code. Design, production, and marketing efforts also have to be coordinated. The reputation and profits of the company are closely related to successful software development.

Not all projects are successful, and the consequences of project failure can be costly, and even catastrophic. ERP installation projects (see Chapter 12) are expensive and time-consuming, and more than a few companies have terminated their projects after spending large sums of money. Hurricane Katrina, which devastated the U.S. gulf coast in 2005, provides many examples of project failure: the rescue, relief, and cleanup operations all left much to be desired.

This chapter introduces the basic concepts of project management. It includes a discussion of some behavioral aspects of project management, along with some of the difficulties project managers are apt to encounter. The main portion of the chapter is devoted to a description of graphical and computational methods that are used for planning and scheduling projects.

INTRODUCTION

Projects Unique, one-time operations designed to accomplish a specific set of objectives in a limited time frame.

Managers typically oversee a variety of operations. Some of these involve routine, repetitive activities, but others involve *nonroutine* activities. Under the latter heading are **projects:** unique, one-time operations designed to accomplish a set of objectives in a limited time frame. Other examples of projects include constructing a shopping complex, merging two companies, putting on a play, and designing and running a political campaign. Examples of projects within business organizations include designing new products or services, designing advertising campaigns, designing information systems, reengineering a process, designing databases, software development, and designing Web pages.

Projects may involve considerable cost. Some have a long time horizon, and some involve a large number of activities that must be carefully planned and coordinated. Most are expected to be completed based on time, cost, and performance targets. To accomplish this, goals must be established and priorities set. Tasks must be identified and time estimates made. Resource requirements also must be projected and budgets prepared. Once under way, progress must be monitored to assure that project goals and objectives will be achieved.

The project approach enables an organization to focus attention and concentrate efforts on accomplishing a narrow set of performance objectives within a limited time and budget framework. This can produce significant benefits compared with other approaches that might be considered. Even so, projects present managers with a host of problems that differ in many respects from those encountered with more routine activities. The problems of planning and coordinating project activities can be formidable for large projects, which typically have thousands of activities that must be carefully planned and monitored if the project is to proceed according to schedule and at a reasonable cost.

Projects can have strategic importance for organizations. For example, good project management can be instrumental in successfully implementing an enterprise resource planning (ERP) system or converting a traditional operation to a lean operation. And good project management is very important when virtual teams are used.

Table 17.1 provides an overview of project management.

PROJECT LIFE CYCLE

The size, length, and scope of projects vary widely according to the nature and purpose of the project. Nevertheless, all projects have something in common: They go through a life cycle, which typically consists of four phases.

1. **Definition.** This has two parts: (*a*) *concept,* at which point the organization recognizes the need for a project or responds to a request for a proposal from a potential customer or client, and (*b*) *feasibility analysis,* which examines the expected costs, benefits, and risks of undertaking the project.
2. **Planning,** which spells out the details of the work and provides estimates of the necessary human resources, time, and cost.
3. **Execution,** during which the project itself is done. This phase often accounts for the majority of time and resources consumed by a project.
4. **Termination,** during which closure is achieved. Termination can involve reassigning personnel and dealing with any leftover materials, equipment (e.g., selling or transferring equipment), and any other resources associated with the project.

It should be noted that the phases can overlap, so that one phase may not be fully complete before the next phase begins. This can reduce the time necessary to move through the life cycle, perhaps generating some competitive advantage and cost saving. Although subsequent decisions in an earlier phase may result in waste for some portion of the activity in a following phase, careful coordination of activities can minimize that risk.

Figure 17.1 illustrates the phases in a project life cycle.

TABLE 17.1
Overview of project management

What is project management? A team-based approach for managing projects.

How is it different from general operations management?

1. Limited time frame.
2. Narrow focus, specific objectives.
3. Less bureaucratic.

Why is it used?

1. Special needs that don't lend themselves to functional management.
2. Pressures for new or improved products or services, cost reduction.

What are the key metrics?

1. Time.
2. Cost.
3. Performance objectives.

What are the key success factors?

1. Top-down commitment.
2. A respected and capable project manager.
3. Enough time to plan.
4. Careful tracking and control.
5. Good communications.

What are the major administrative issues?

1. Executive responsibilities:
   a. Project selection.
   b. Selection of a project manager.
   c. Organizational structure. (To whom will the project manager report?)
2. Organizational alternatives:
   a. Manage within functional unit.
   b. Assign a coordinator.
   c. Use a matrix organization with a project leader.

What are the main tools?

1. *Work breakdown structure.* An initial planning tool that is needed to develop a list of activities, activity sequences, and a realistic budget.
2. *Network diagram.* A "big picture" visual aid that is used to estimate project duration, identify activities that are critical for timely project completion, identify areas where slack time exists, and develop activity schedules.
3. *Gantt charts.* A visual aid used to plan and monitor individual activities.
4. *Risk management.* Analyses of potential failures or problems, assessment of their likelihood and consequences, and contingency plans.

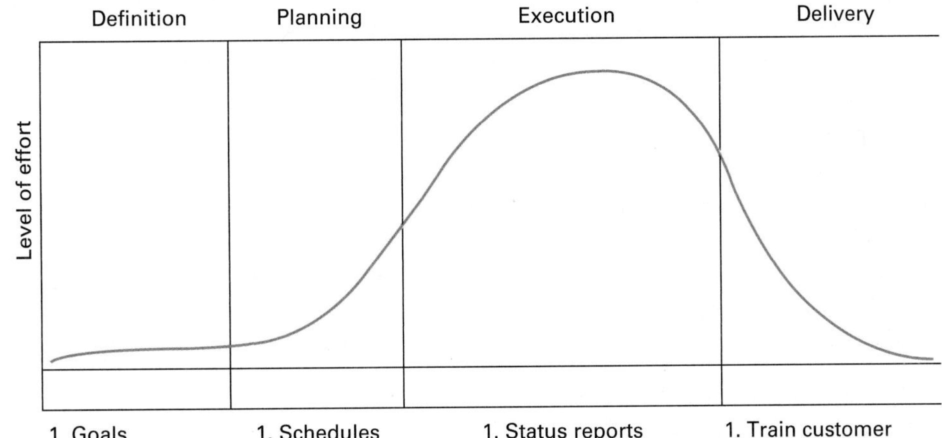

FIGURE 17.1
Project life cycle

Source: Adapted from Clifford F. Gray and Erik W. Larson, *Project Management: The Managerial Process*, 2nd ed., p. 6. Copyright © 2003 McGraw-Hill Companies, Inc. Used with permission.

BEHAVIORAL ASPECTS OF PROJECT MANAGEMENT

Project management differs from management of more traditional activities mainly because of its limited time framework and the unique set of activities involved, which gives rise to a host of unique problems. This section describes more fully the nature of projects and their behavioral implications. Special attention is given to the role of the project manager.

The Nature of Projects

As projects go through their life cycle, a variety of skill requirements are involved. The circumstances are analogous to constructing a house. Initially an idea is presented and its feasibility is assessed, then plans must be drawn up and approved by the owner and possibly a town building commission or other regulatory agency. Then a succession of activities occurs, each with its own skill requirements, starting with the site preparation, then laying the foundation, erecting the frame, roofing, constructing exterior walls, wiring and plumbing, installing kitchen and bathroom fixtures and appliances, interior finishing work, and painting and carpeting work. Similar sequences occur on large construction projects, in R&D work, in the aerospace industry, and in virtually every other instance where projects are being carried out.

Projects typically bring together people with diverse knowledge and skills, most of whom remain associated with the project for less than its full life. Some people go from project to project as their contributions become needed, and others are "on loan," either on a full-time or part-time basis, from their regular jobs. The latter is usually the case when a special project exists within the framework of a more traditional organization. However, some organizations are involved with projects on a regular basis; examples include consulting firms, architects, writers and publishers, and construction firms. In those organizations, it is not uncommon for some individuals to spend virtually all of their time on projects.

Some organizations use a *matrix organization* that allows them to integrate the activities of a variety of specialists within a functional framework. For instance, they have certain people who prepare proposals, others who concentrate exclusively on engineering, others who devote their efforts to marketing, and so on.

In a matrix organization, functional and project managers share workers and facilities. Project managers negotiate with functional managers for people to work on a project. Those selected will be temporarily assigned to the project manager. However, they are still responsible to their functional manager. They may work part-time or full-time on the project. When their work is done, they return to their functional department.

A matrix organization works quite well with people who can function with two managers. It can create synergy when people from various functional areas are brought together to work on a project. However, some people do not function well under such a structure, and may be stressed working in that environment. Matrix organizations typically do not allow long-term working relationships to develop. Furthermore, using multiple managers for one employee may result in uncertainty regarding employee evaluation and accountability.

Key Decisions in Project Management

Much of the success of projects depends on key managerial decisions over a sequence of steps:

- Deciding which projects to implement.
- Selecting the project manager.
- Selecting the project team.
- Planning and designing the project.
- Managing and controlling project resources.
- Deciding if and when a project should be terminated.

The U2 360 Tour is named after the 360-degree staging and audience configuration it uses for shows. To accommodate this, the stage set makes use of a massive four-legged supporting rig that has been nicknamed "The Claw." The tour crew consists of 137 touring crews supplemented by over 120 hired locally. Moving the massive set from venues takes as long as 3½ days. First, sound and light equipment is packed into the fleet of trucks during the four hours following the concert; the remainder of the time is spent deconstructing the steel structures.

Deciding Which Projects to Implement. This involves determining the criteria that will be used to decide which projects to pursue. Typical factors include budget, availability of appropriate knowledge and skill personnel, and cost–benefit considerations. Of course, other factors may override these criteria, factors such as availability of funds, safety issues, government-mandated actions, and so on.

Selecting the Project Manager. The project manager is the central person in the project. The following section on project managers discusses this topic.

Selecting the Project Team. The team can greatly influence the ultimate success or failure of a project. Important considerations include not only a person's knowledge and skill base, but also how well the person works with others (particularly those who have already been chosen for the project), enthusiasm for the project, other projects the person is involved in, and how likely those other projects might be to interfere with work on this project.

Planning and Designing the Project. Project planning and design require decisions on project performance goals, a timetable for project completion, the scope of the project, what work needs to be done, how it will be done, if some portions will be outsourced, what resources will be needed, a budget, and when and how long resources will be needed.

Managing and Controlling Project Resources. This involves managing personnel, equipment, and the budget; establishing appropriate metrics for evaluating the project; monitoring progress; and taking corrective action when needed. Also necessary are designing an information system and deciding what project documents should be generated, their contents and format, when and by whom they will be needed, and how often they should be updated.

Deciding If and When a Project Should Be Terminated. Sometimes it is better to terminate a project than to invest any more resources. Important considerations here are the likelihood of success, termination costs, and whether resources could be better used elsewhere.

The Project Manager

The project manager bears the ultimate responsibility for the success or failure of the project. He or she must be capable of working through others to accomplish the objectives of the project. The project manager is responsible for effectively managing each of the following:

1. The **work,** so that all of the necessary activities are accomplished in the desired sequence, and performance goals are met.
2. The **human resources,** so that those working on the project have direction and motivation.

3. **Communications,** so that everybody has the information needed to do the work.
4. **Quality,** so that performance objectives are realized.
5. **Time,** so that the project is completed on schedule.
6. **Costs,** so that the project is completed within budget.

Several of these responsibilities are often portrayed in what is known as a "project management triangle":

The Project Management Triangle

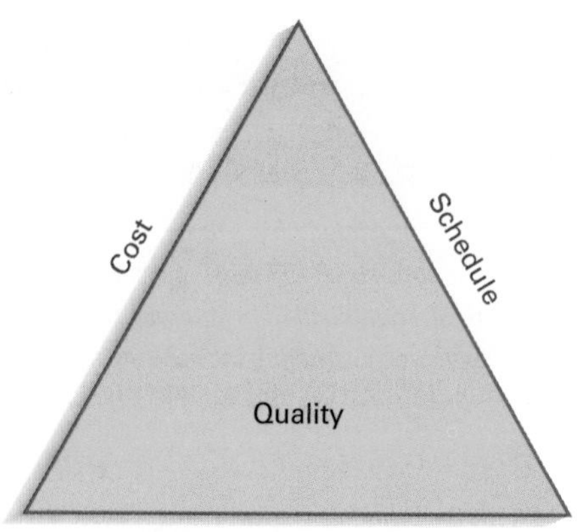

To effectively manage a project, a project manager must employ a certain set of skills. The skills include the ability to motivate and direct team members; make trade-off decisions; expedite the work when necessary; put out fires; and monitor time, budget, and technical details. For projects that involve fairly well-defined work, those skills will often suffice. However, for projects that are less well defined, and thus have a higher degree of uncertainty, the project manager also must employ strong leadership skills. These include the ability to adapt to changing circumstances that may involve changes to project goals, technical requirements, and project team composition. As a leader, the project manager not only must be able to deal with these issues; he or she also must recognize the need for change, decide what changes are necessary, and work to accomplish them.

The job of project manager can be both difficult and rewarding. The manager must coordinate and motivate people who sometimes owe their allegiance to other managers in their functional areas. In addition, the people who work on a project frequently possess specialized knowledge and skills that the project manager lacks. Nevertheless, the manager is expected to guide and evaluate their efforts. Project managers often must function in an environment that is beset with uncertainties. Even so, budgets and time constraints are usually imposed, which can create additional pressures on project personnel. Finally, the project manager may not have the authority needed to accomplish all the objectives of the project. Instead, the manager sometimes must rely on persuasion and the cooperation of others to realize project goals.

Ethical issues often arise in connection with projects. Examples include the temptation to understate costs or to withhold information in order to get a project approved, pressure to alter or make misleading statements on status reports, falsifying records, compromising workers' safety, and approving substandard work. It is the responsibility of managers at all levels to maintain and enforce ethical standards. Moreover, employees often take their cue from managers' behavior, so it is doubly important for managers to model ethical behavior. The Project Management Institute (PMI) has a Web site (www.pmi.org) that includes a code of ethics for project managers, in addition to other useful information about project management.

The position of project manager has high visibility. The rewards of the job of project manager come from the creative challenges of the job, the benefits of being associated with a successful project (including promotion and monetary compensation), and the personal satisfaction of seeing it through to its conclusion.

Behavioral Issues

Project metrics related to cost, schedule, and quality are important indicators of how well a project is doing. Behavioral metrics are also important, and should not be overlooked. People make the project happen. However, behavioral issues can interfere with the success of a project if they are not carefully managed. Decentralized decision making, the stress of achieving project milestones on time and within budget, and surprises can contribute to behavioral problems.

Because project work is often based on team efforts, workers are usually evaluated on the basis of the team's overall contribution relative to project metrics, and not on an individual basis. The team must be able to function as a unit, so interpersonal skills are very important, as are coping skills. And conflict resolution can be an important part of a project manager's job. Some problems can be avoided by the project manager by carefully selecting team members when possible; leadership; motivation; maintaining an environment of integrity, trust, and professionalism; and being supportive of team efforts.

Project Champions

Some companies make use of **project champions.** These are people, usually within the company, who promote and support the project. They can be instrumental in facilitating the work of the project manager by "talking up" the project to other managers who might be asked to share resources with the project team as well as employees who might be asked to work on parts of the project. The work that a project champion does can be critical to the success of a project, so it is important for team members to encourage and communicate with the project champion.

Project champion A person who promotes and supports a project.

Project Managers Have Never Been More Critical

READING

Bob Weinstein

Not many people can eloquently describe the changing role of project managers as well as Jonathan Gispan, who teaches the skill to managers at the Lockheed Martin Corporation division in King of Prussia, PA. Gispan spent 38 years of his career working at GE Aerospace as a project manager.

Project managers have never been more critical, according to this veteran techie. The function's core responsibilities haven't changed, but the players and playing field are very different than they were five years ago.

Gispan views the project manager as the focal point of a complex relationship matrix that includes customers, workers, vendors and bosses. "Project managers make things happen," he says. "Not only do they manage a project from start to finish, they also manage the people who make it happen."

The job requires a jack-of-all-trades who can both understand a problem and solve it. "Project managers must successfully manage the total lifecycle of a project," says Gispan. "The job requires a super-organized person who knows how to get a project completed quickly and inexpensively and boasts the advanced communication skills necessary to work closely with vendors, project teams and senior management."

Project managers have always had to deal with changing relationships. The big change, according to Gispan, is the speed of change, which has made the project manager's job more difficult. "The changes taking place now are faster and more dramatic than in the past," he says. "Customers are less inclined to give you money for development work, for example. They'd rather save money by using off-the-shelf capabilities. Budgets that used to be reasonably substantial and healthy are now tight."

Gispan adds that corporate mergers and consolidations have complicated the picture. Project managers must deal with complex, often labyrinthine decision-making structures. Getting quick decisions requires work and persistence.

Further complicating the situation is a high worker attrition rate. "A decade ago, the attrition rate was about 3 percent; today it has jumped to almost 10 percent," Gispan explains. "It means project managers have to constantly put together new teams."

Through it all, the project manager must be clear-headed and keep tight rein on projects. It sounds intimidating, yet Gispan sees it as a positive. "The current marketplace keeps you on your toes," he says. "Even though everything is changing at what seems like an overwhelming pace, it is best to view change as a motivator that allows you to keep pace with technology and get better at your job. The idea is not merely to cope with change but to thrive in it. It is more of an attitude than anything else."

What does it take to be a project manager? "You need a good technical base," says Karen Nichols, project manager at EWP Engineering, Inc., a consulting engineering company in Salt Lake City, UT. "That translates to at least five to seven years in the trenches."

That's for starters. "But you also need to know how the business side of the equation works," says Nichols. "This is tough for some technical people because it requires the ability to understand how the two different sides of the business mesh. Project managers must also be familiar with accounting methods as well as sales and marketing strategies. In short, they must know how to manage a project so it makes a profit."

If you think you have what it takes, ask to work with a project manager. "It won't take you long to find out whether you have an aptitude and natural feel for the work," says Nichols. "Not everyone is happy—or capable of—juggling many balls in the air at once."

Once you get your feet wet, you can move up quickly, adds Gispan. "After you've proven to management that you're organized and can manage several tasks, it won't be long before you are managing everything associated with a program. Get good at it and you'll move up the ranks from project manager to general manager where you are running several company businesses."

And, don't be confused by job titles. Each company has its own unique title for the project manager role. Whatever the title, a project manager is easy to spot. "It's the person who negotiates with all the key players and makes things happen," says Gispan. "Technology companies would perish without them."

Source: Bob Weinstein, "Project Managers Have Never Been More Critical," *Rochester Democrat and Chronicle,* February 18, 1999.

Certification

The Project Management Institute (PMI) administers a globally recognized, examination-based professional certification program. The certification program maintains ISO 9001 certification in Quality Management Systems. There are two levels of certification: Associate and Project Management Professional. Candidates for the Associate and Professional levels must meet specific education and experience requirements and agree to adhere to a code of professional conduct. The Project Management Professional must demonstrate an ongoing professional commitment to the field of project management by satisfying PMI's Continuing Certification Requirements Program.[1]

The Pros and Cons of Working on Projects

People are selected to work on special projects because the knowledge or abilities they possess are needed. In some instances, however, their supervisors may be reluctant to allow them to interrupt their regular jobs, even on a part-time basis, because it may require training a new person to do a job that will be temporary. Moreover, managers don't want to lose the output of good workers. The workers themselves are not always eager to participate in projects because it may mean working for two bosses who impose differing demands, it may disrupt friendships and daily routines, and it presents the risk of being replaced on the current job. Furthermore, there may be fear of being associated with an unsuccessful project because of the adverse effect it might have on career advancement. In too many instances, when a major project is phased out and the project team disbanded, team members tend to drift away from the organization for lack of a new project and the difficulty of returning to former jobs. This tendency is more pronounced after lengthy projects and is less likely to occur when a team member works on a part-time basis.

In spite of the potential risks, people are attracted by the potential rewards of being involved in a project. One is the dynamic environment that surrounds a project, often a marked contrast to the staid environment of a routine in which some may feel trapped. Some individuals seem to thrive in more dynamic environments; they welcome the challenge of working under pressure and solving new problems. Then, too, projects may present opportunities to meet new people and to increase future job opportunities, especially if the project is successful. In addition, association with a project can be a source of status among fellow workers. Finally, working on projects frequently inspires a team spirit, increasing morale and motivation to achieve successful completion of project goals.

WORK BREAKDOWN STRUCTURE

Work breakdown structure (WBS) A hierarchical listing of what must be done during a project.

Because large projects usually involve a very large number of activities, planners need some way to determine exactly what will need to be done so that they can realistically estimate how long it will take to complete the various elements of the project and how much it will cost. They often accomplish this by developing a **work breakdown structure (WBS)**, which is a hierarchical listing of what must be done during the project. This methodology establishes a logical framework for identifying the required activities for the project (see Figure 17.2). The first step in developing the work breakdown structure is to identify the major elements of the project. These are the Level 2 boxes in Figure 17.2. The next step is to identify the major supporting activities for each of the major elements—the Level 3 boxes. Then, each major supporting activity is broken down into a list of the activities that will be needed to accomplish it—the Level 4 boxes. (For purposes of illustration, only a portion of the Level 4 boxes are shown.) Usually there are many activities in the Level 4 lists. Large projects involve additional levels, but Figure 17.2 gives you some idea of the concept of the work breakdown structure.

Developing a good work breakdown structure can require substantial time and effort due to the uncertainties associated with a project and/or the size of the project. Typically the portion

[1]www.pmi.org.

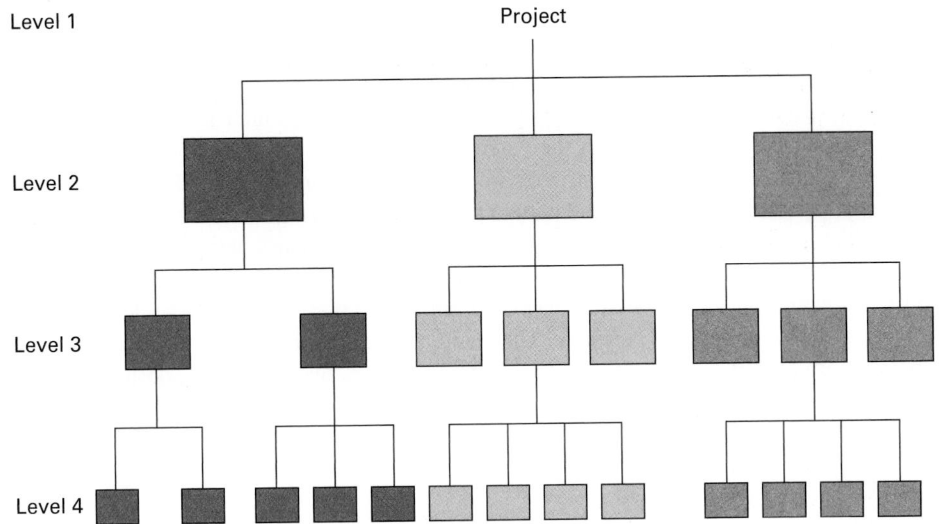

FIGURE 17.2
Schematic of a work breakdown structure

of time spent on developing the work breakdown structure greatly exceeds the time spent on actually developing a project schedule. The importance of a work breakdown structure is underscored by the fact that the activity list that results serves as the focal point for planning and doing the project. Moreover, the work breakdown structure is the basis for developing time and cost estimates.

PLANNING AND SCHEDULING WITH GANTT CHARTS

The Gantt chart (see Chapter 16) is a popular visual tool for planning and scheduling *simple* projects. It enables a manager to initially schedule project activities and then to monitor progress over time by comparing planned progress to actual progress. Figure 17.3 illustrates a

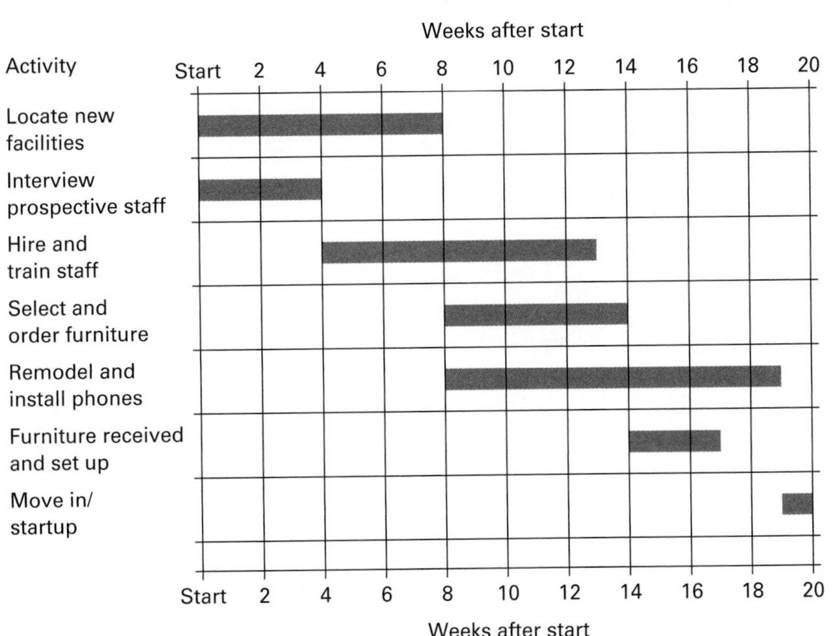

FIGURE 17.3
Gantt chart for bank example

Gantt chart for a bank's plan to establish a new direct marketing department. To prepare the chart, the vice president in charge of the project had to first identify the major activities that would be required. Next, time estimates for each activity were made, and the sequence of activities was determined. Once completed, the chart indicated which activities were to occur, their planned duration, and when they were to occur. Then, as the project progressed, the manager was able to see which activities were on schedule and which were behind schedule. However, Gantt charts fail to reveal certain relationships among activities that can be crucial to effective project management. For instance, if one of the early activities in a project suffers a delay, it would be important for the manager to be able to easily determine which later activities would result in a delay. Conversely, some activities may safely be delayed without affecting the overall project schedule. The Gantt chart does not directly reveal this. On more complex projects, it is often used in conjunction with a *network diagram,* defined in the following section, for scheduling purposes.

PERT AND CPM

PERT Program evaluation and review technique, for planning and coordinating large projects.

CPM Critical path method, for planning and coordinating large projects.

PERT (program evaluation and review technique) and **CPM** (critical path method) are two of the most widely used techniques for planning and coordinating large-scale projects. By using PERT or CPM, managers are able to obtain

1. A graphical display of project activities.
2. An estimate of how long the project will take.
3. An indication of which activities are the most critical to timely project completion.
4. An indication of how long any activity can be delayed without delaying the project.

Although PERT and CPM were developed independently, they have a great deal in common. Moreover, many of the initial differences between them have disappeared as users borrowed certain features from one technique for use with the other. For practical purposes, the two techniques now are the same; the comments and procedures described will apply to CPM analysis as well as to PERT analysis of projects.

The Network Diagram

Network (precedence) diagram Diagram of project activities that shows sequential relationships by use of arrows and nodes.

Activity-on-arrow (AOA) Network diagram convention in which arrows designate activities.

Activity-on-node (AON) Network diagram convention in which nodes designate activities.

Activities Project steps that consume resources and/or time.

Events The starting and finishing of activities, designated by nodes in the AOA convention.

One of the main features of PERT and related techniques is their use of a **network** or **precedence diagram** to depict major project activities and their sequential relationships. There are two slightly different conventions for constructing these network diagrams. Under one convention, the *arrows* designate activities; under the other convention, the *nodes* designate activities. These conventions are referred to as **activity-on-arrow (AOA)** and **activity-on-node (AON)**. **Activities** consume resources and/or *time.* The nodes in the AOA approach represent the activities' starting and finishing points, which are called **events.** Events are points in time. Unlike activities, they consume neither resources nor time. The nodes in an AON diagram represent activities.

Both conventions are illustrated in Figure 17.4, using the bank example that was depicted in the Gantt chart in Figure 17.3. Compare the two. In the AOA diagram, the arrows represent activities and they show the sequence in which certain activities must be performed (e.g., Interview precedes Hire and train); in the AON diagram, the arrows show only the sequence in which certain activities must be performed while the nodes represent the activities. Activities in AOA networks can be referred to in either of two ways. One is by their endpoints (e.g., activity 2-4) and the other is by a letter assigned to an arrow (e.g., activity *c*). Both methods are illustrated in this chapter. Activities in AON networks are referred to by a letter (or number) assigned to a node. Although these two approaches are slightly different, they both show sequential relationships—something Gantt charts don't. Note that the AON diagram has a starting node, S, which is actually not an activity but is added in order to have a single starting node.

Despite these differences, the two conventions are remarkably similar, so you should not encounter much difficulty in understanding either one. In fact, there are convincing arguments

FIGURE 17.4 A simple project network diagram

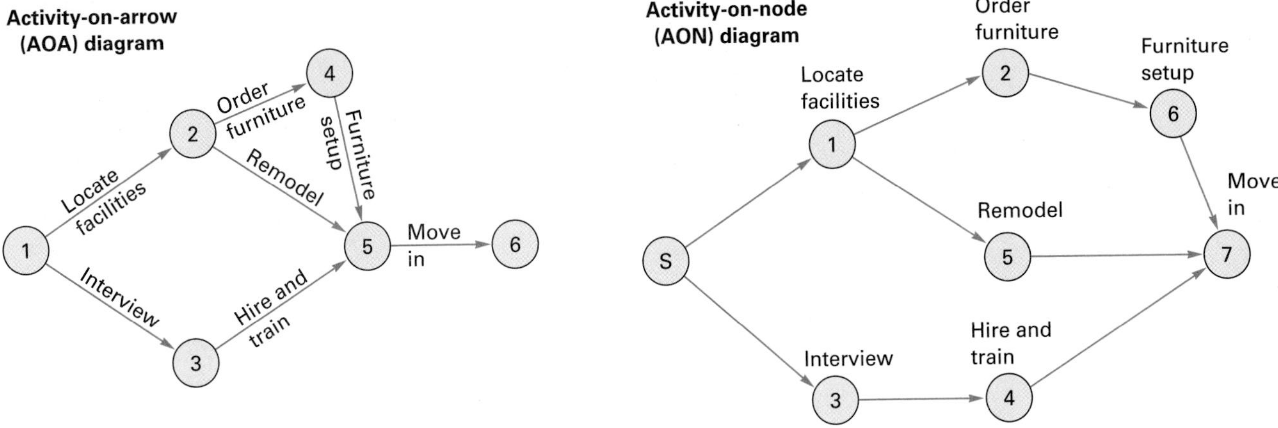

for having some familiarity with *both* approaches. Perhaps the most compelling is that both approaches are widely used. Moreover, a contractor doing work for the organization may be using the other approach, so employees of the organization who deal with the contractor on project matters would benefit from knowledge of the other approach. However, any particular organization would typically use only one approach, and employees would have to work with that approach.

Of particular interest to managers are the *paths* in a network diagram. A **path** is a sequence of activities that leads from the starting node to the ending node. For example, in the AOA diagram, the sequence 1-2-4-5-6 is a path. In the AON diagram, S-1-2-6-7 is a path. Note that in both diagrams there are three paths. One reason for the importance of paths is that they reveal *sequential relationships.* The importance of sequential relationships cannot be overstated: If one activity in a sequence is delayed (i.e., late) or done incorrectly, the start of all following activities on that path will be delayed.

Path A sequence of activities that leads from the starting node to the finishing node.

Another important aspect of paths is the length of a path: How long will a particular sequence of activities take to complete? The length (of time) of any path can be determined by summing the expected times of the activities on that path. The path with the longest time is of particular interest because it governs project completion time. In other words, expected project duration equals the expected time of the longest path. Moreover, if there are any delays along the longest path, there will be corresponding delays in project completion time. Attempts to shorten project completion must focus on the longest sequence of activities. Because of its influence on project completion time, the longest path is referred to as the **critical path,** and its activities are referred to as **critical activities.**

Critical path The longest path; determines expected project duration.

Critical activities Activities on the critical path.

Paths that are shorter than the critical path can experience some delays and still not affect the overall project completion time as long as the ultimate path time does not exceed the length of the critical path. The allowable slippage for any path is called **slack,** and it reflects the difference between the length of a given path and the length of the critical path. The critical path, then, has zero slack time.

Slack Allowable slippage for a path; the difference between the length of a path and the length of the critical path.

Network Conventions

Developing and interpreting network diagrams requires some familiarity with networking conventions. Table 17.2 illustrates some of the most basic and most common features of network diagrams. This will provide sufficient background for understanding the basic concepts associated with precedence diagrams and allow you to solve typical problems.

A special feature that is sometimes used in AOA networks to clarify relationships is a *dummy activity.* In order to recognize the need to use a dummy activity using the AOA approach when presented with a list of activities and the activities each precedes, examine the "Immediate Predecessor" list. Look for instances where multiple activities are listed, such as *a, b* in the following list. If *a* or *b* appears separately in the list (as *a* does here), a dummy will be needed to clarify the relationship (see the last diagram in Table 17.2).

Activity	Immediate Predecessor
a	—
b	—
c	a, b
d	a,

Here are two more AOA conventions:

For reference purposes, nodes are numbered typically from left to right, with lower numbers assigned to preceding nodes and higher numbers to following nodes:

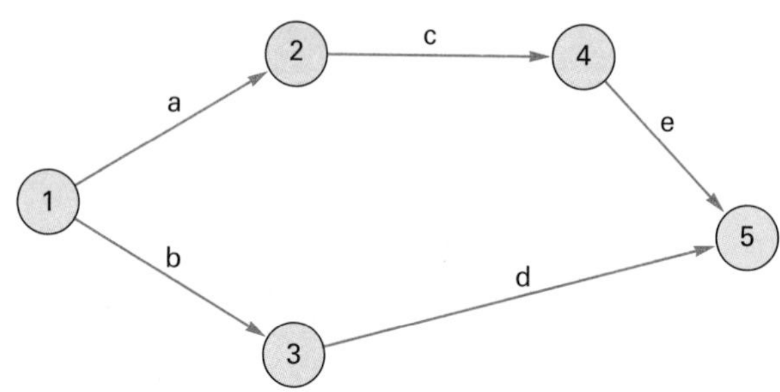

TABLE 17.2 Network conventions

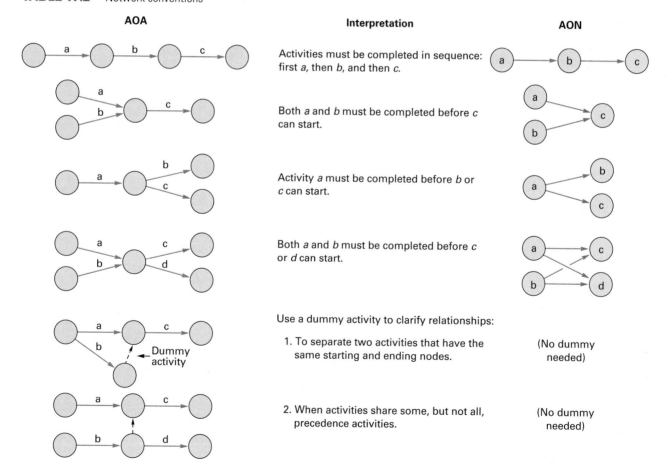

AOA	Interpretation	AON
a, b, c	Activities must be completed in sequence: first *a*, then *b*, and then *c*.	a, b, c
a, b, c	Both *a* and *b* must be completed before *c* can start.	a, b, c
a, b, c	Activity *a* must be completed before *b* or *c* can start.	a, b, c
a, b, c, d	Both *a* and *b* must be completed before *c* or *d* can start.	a, b, c, d
	Use a dummy activity to clarify relationships:	
a, b, c, Dummy activity	1. To separate two activities that have the same starting and ending nodes.	(No dummy needed)
a, b, c, d	2. When activities share some, but not all, precedence activities.	(No dummy needed)

Starting and ending arrows are sometimes used during development of a network for increased clarity:

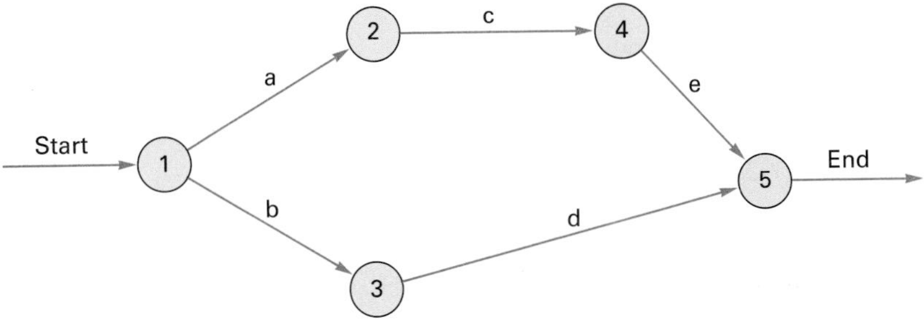

DETERMINISTIC TIME ESTIMATES

The main determinant of the way PERT and CPM networks are analyzed and interpreted is whether activity time estimates are *probabilistic* or *deterministic.* If time estimates can be made with a high degree of confidence that actual times are fairly certain, we say the estimates are **deterministic.** If actual times are subject to variation, we say the estimates are **probabilistic.** Probabilistic time estimates must include an indication of the extent of probable variation.

Deterministic Time estimates that are fairly certain.

Probabilistic Estimates of times that allow for variation.

This section describes analysis of networks with deterministic time estimates. A later section deals with probabilistic times.

One of the best ways to gain an understanding of the nature of network analysis is to consider a simple example.

EXAMPLE 1

Given the additional information on the bank network of Figure 17.4 shown in Figure 17.5, determine

a. The length of each path.
b. The critical path.
c. The expected length of the project.
d. The amount of slack time for each path.

SOLUTION

a. As shown in the following table, the path lengths are 18 weeks, 20 weeks, and 14 weeks.
b. Path 1-2-5-6 is the longest path (20 weeks), so it is the critical path.
c. The expected length of the project is equal to the length of the critical path (i.e., 20 weeks).

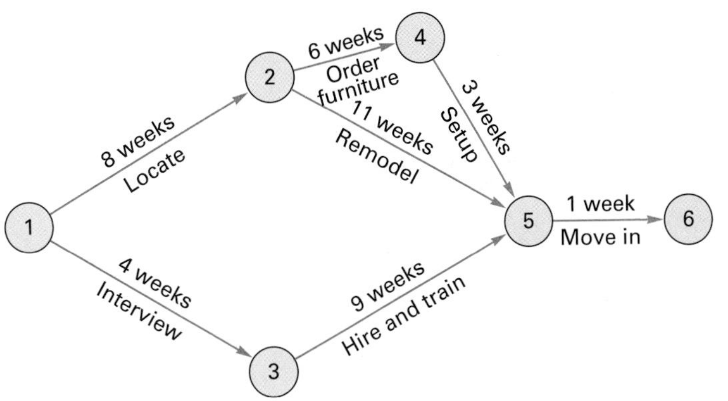

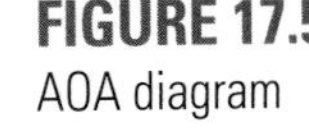

FIGURE 17.5
AOA diagram

SCREENCAM TUTORIAL

d. We find the slack for each path by subtracting its length from the length of the critical path, as shown in the last column of the table. (*Note:* It is sometimes desirable to know the slack time associated with activities. The next section describes a method for obtaining those slack times.)

Path	Length (weeks)	Slack
1-2-4-5-6	8 + 6 + 3 + 1 = 18	20 − 18 = 2
1-2-5-6	8 + 11 + 1 = 20*	20 − 20 = 0
1-3-5-6	4 + 9 + 1 = 14	20 − 14 = 6

*Critical path length.

A COMPUTING ALGORITHM

SCREENCAM TUTORIAL

Many real-life project networks are much larger than the simple network illustrated in the preceding example; they often contain hundreds or even thousands of activities. Because the necessary computations can become exceedingly complex and time-consuming, large networks are generally analyzed by computer programs instead of manually. Planners use an algorithm to develop four pieces of information about the network activities:

ES, the earliest time activity can start, assuming all preceding activities start as early as possible.

EF, the earliest time the activity can finish.

LS, the latest time the activity can start and not delay the project.

LF, the latest time the activity can finish and not delay the project.

Once these values have been determined, they can be used to find

1. Expected project duration.
2. Slack time.
3. The critical path.

Activity-on-Arrow

The three examples that follow illustrate how to compute those values using the precedence diagram of Example 1.

EXAMPLE 2

www.mhhe.com/stevenson11e

Compute the earliest starting time and earliest finishing time for each activity in the diagram shown in Figure 17.5.

SOLUTION

Begin by placing brackets at the two ends of each starting activity:

We want to determine and place in the brackets for each activity the earliest starting time, ES, and the earliest finishing time, EF, for every activity, and put them in brackets, as follows:

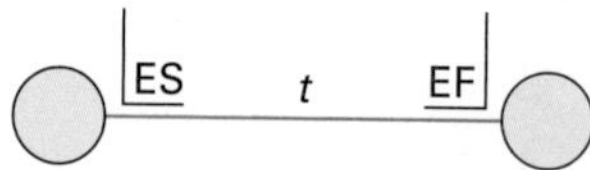

Do this for all activities, beginning at the left side of the precedence diagram and moving to the right side.

Once ES has been determined for each activity, EF can be found by adding the activity time, t, to ES: ES + t = EF.

Use an ES of 0 for all starting activities. Thus, activities 1-2 and 1-3 are assigned ES values of 0. This permits computation of the EF for each of these activities:

$$EF_{1\text{-}2} = 0 + 8 = 8 \quad \text{and} \quad EF_{1\text{-}3} = 0 + 4 = 4$$

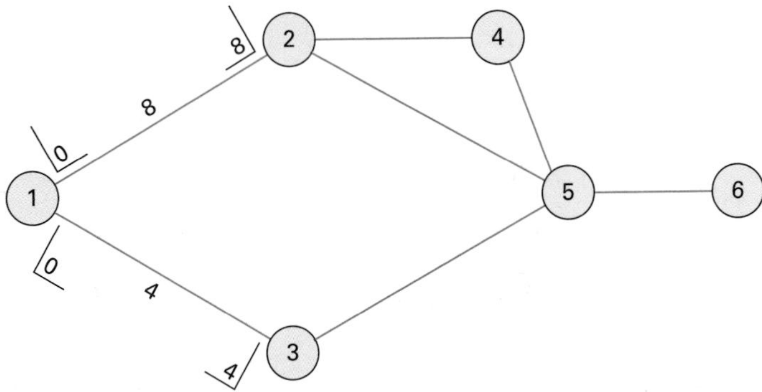

The EF time for an activity becomes the ES time for the next activity to follow it in the diagram. Hence, because activity 1-2 has an EF time of 8, both activities 2-4 and 2-5 have ES times of 8. Similarly, activity 3-5 has an ES time of 4.

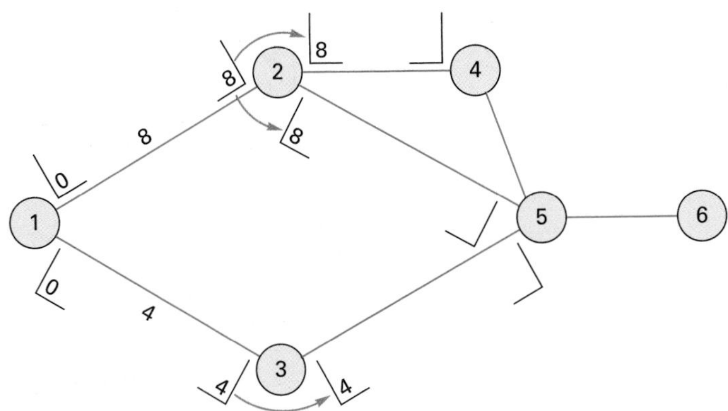

This permits calculation of the EF times for these activities: $EF_{2\text{-}4} = 8 + 6 = 14$; $EF_{2\text{-}5} = 8 + 11 = 19$; and $EF_{3\text{-}5} = 4 + 9 = 13$.

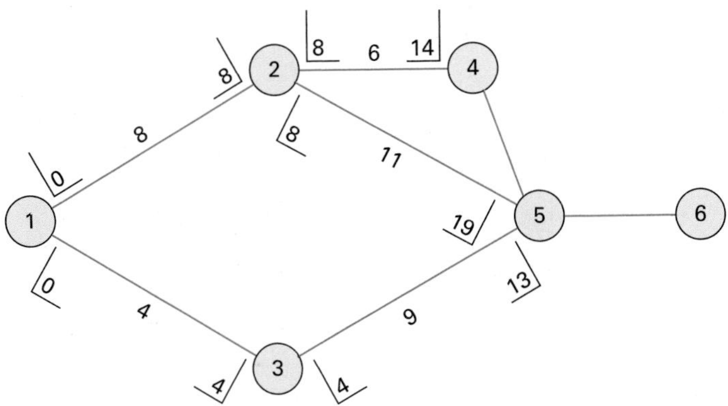

The ES for activity 4-5 is the EF time of activity 2-4, which is 14. Using this value, we find the EF for activity 4-5 is 17; $EF_{4\text{-}5} = 14 + 3 = 17$.

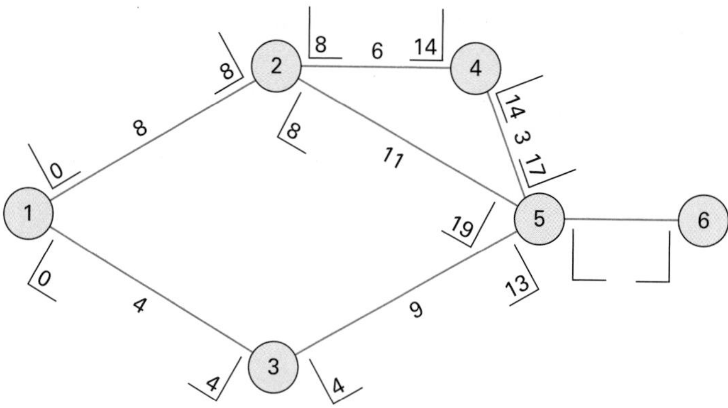

In order to determine the ES for activity 5-6, we must realize that activity 5-6 cannot start until *every* activity that precedes it is finished. Therefore, the *largest* of the EF times for the three activities that precede activity 5-6 determines $ES_{5\text{-}6}$. Hence, the ES for activity 5-6 is 19.

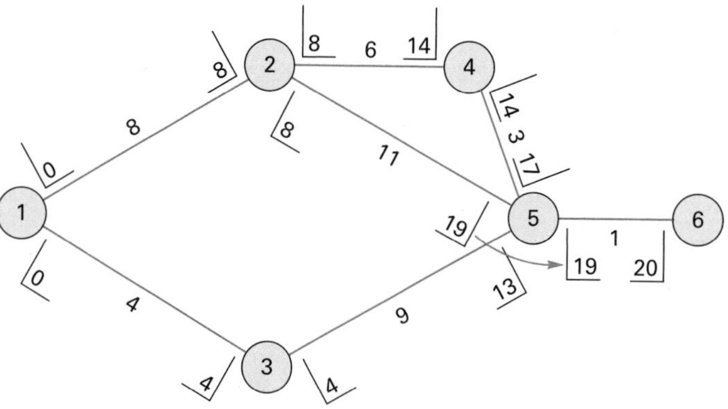

Then the EF for the last activity, 5-6, is 20; $EF_{5\text{-}6} = 19 + 1 = 20$. Note that the latest EF is the project duration. Thus, the expected length of the project is 20 weeks.

Computation of earliest starting and finishing times is aided by two simple rules:

1. The earliest finish time for any activity is equal to its earliest start time plus its expected duration, *t*:

   $$EF = ES + t \tag{17–1}$$

2. ES for activities at nodes with one entering arrow is equal to EF of the entering arrow. ES for activities leaving nodes with multiple entering arrows is equal to the largest EF of the entering arrow.

Computation of the latest starting and finishing times is aided by the use of two rules:

1. The latest starting time for each activity is equal to its latest finishing time minus its expected duration:

   $$LS = LF - t \tag{17–2}$$

2. For nodes with one leaving arrow, LF for arrows entering that node equals the LS of the leaving arrow. For nodes with multiple leaving arrows, LF for arrows entering that node equals the smallest LS of leaving arrows.

Finding ES and EF times involves a *forward pass* through the network; finding LS and LF times involves a *backward pass* through the network. Hence, we must begin with the EF of the last activity and use that time as the LF for the last activity. Then we obtain the LS for the last activity by subtracting its expected duration from its LF.

RULES FOR THE COMPUTING ALGORITHM

(*Note:* For an AON diagram, if a starting node or ending node does not have a time associated with it, ignore that node.)

Forward Pass

For each path, start at the left side of the diagram and work toward the right side.

For each beginning activity: ES = 0.

For each activity: ES + Activity time = EF.

For the following activity: ES = EF of preceding activity.

Note: If an activity has multiple immediate preceding activities, set its ES equal to the largest EF of its immediate predecessors.

Backward Pass

For each path, start at the right side of the diagram and work toward the left side.

Use the largest EF as the LF for all ending activities.

For each activity: LS = LF − Activity time.

For the preceding activity: LF = LS of following activity.

Note: If an activity has multiple immediately following activities, set the activity's LF equal to the smallest LS of the following activities.

EXAMPLE 3

Compute the latest finishing and starting times for the precedence diagram developed in Example 2.

SOLUTION

We must add the LS and LF times to the brackets on the diagram.

Begin by setting the LF time of the last activity equal to the EF of that activity. Thus,

$$LF_{5\text{-}6} = EF_{5\text{-}6} = 20 \text{ weeks}$$

Obtain the LS time for activity 5-6 by subtracting the activity time, t, from the LF time:

$$LS_{5\text{-}6} = LF_{5\text{-}6} - t = 20 - 1 = 19$$

Mark these values on the diagram:

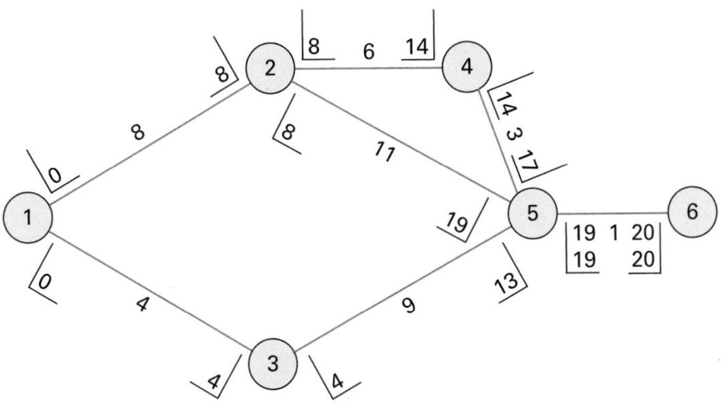

The LS time of 19 for activity 5-6 now becomes the LF time for each of the activities that precedes activity 5-6. This permits determination of the LS times for each of those activities: Subtract the activity time from the LF to obtain the LS time for the activity. The LS time for activity 3-5 is 19 − 9 = 10.

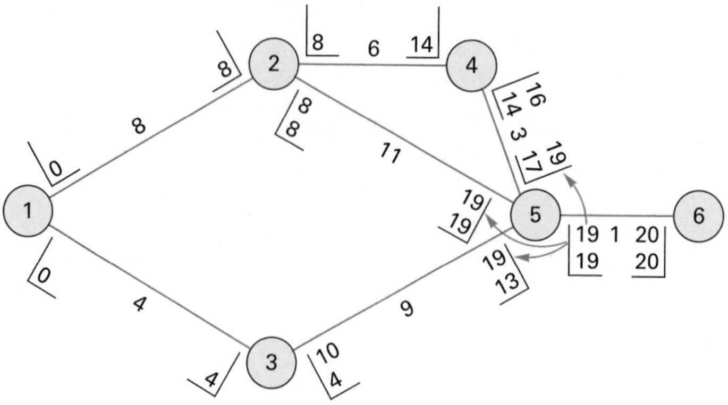

Next, the LS for activity 4-5, which is 16, becomes the LF for activity 2-4, and the LS for activity 3-5, which is 10, becomes the LF for activity 1-3. Using these values, you find the LS for each of these activities by subtracting the activity time from the LF time.

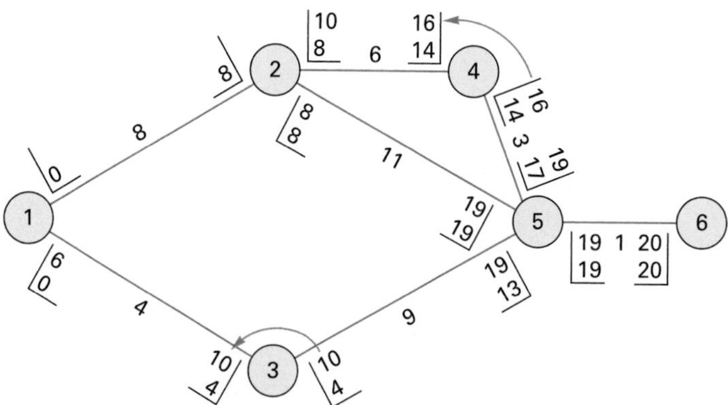

The LF for activity 1-2 is the *smaller* of the two LS times of the activities that 1-2 precedes. Hence, the LF time for activity 1-2 is 8. The reason you use the smaller time is that activity 1-2 must finish at a time that permits all following activities to start no later than their LS times.

Once you have determined the LF time of activity 1-2, find its LS time by subtracting the activity time of 8 from the LF time of 8. Hence, the LS time is 0.

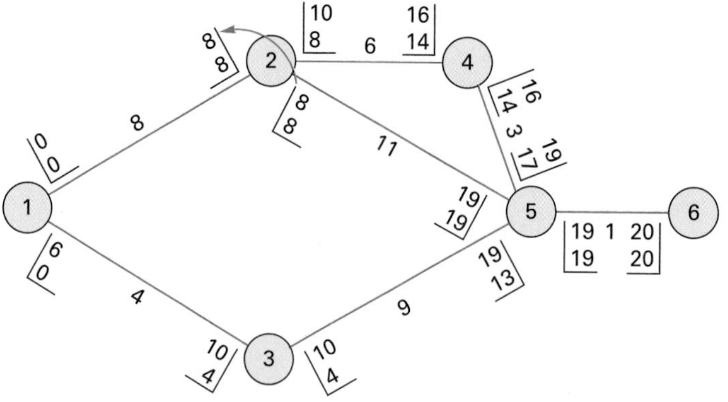

Activity-on-Node

The computing algorithm is performed in essentially the same manner in the AON approach. Figure 17.6 shows the node diagram, and Figures 17.7A, B, and C illustrate the computing algorithm.

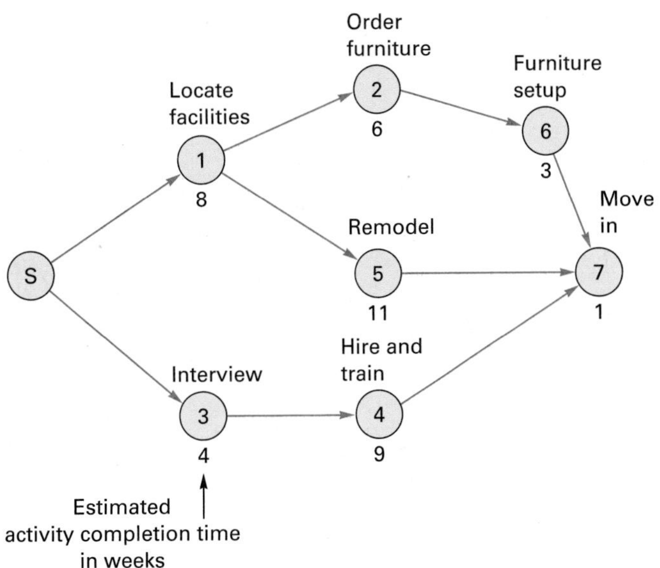

FIGURE 17.6
AON diagram

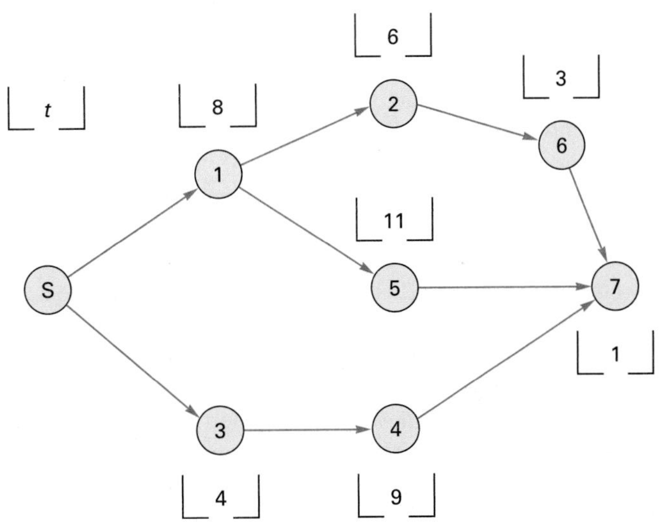

FIGURE 17.7A
AON diagram with brackets added

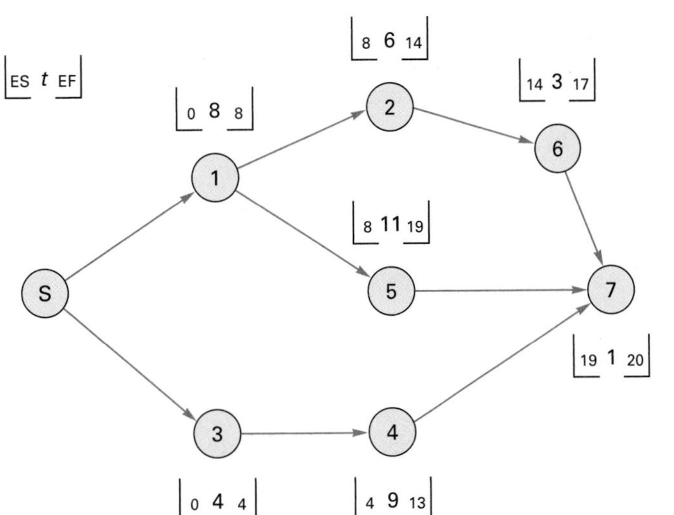

FIGURE 17.7B
Forward pass

FIGURE 17.7C
Backward pass

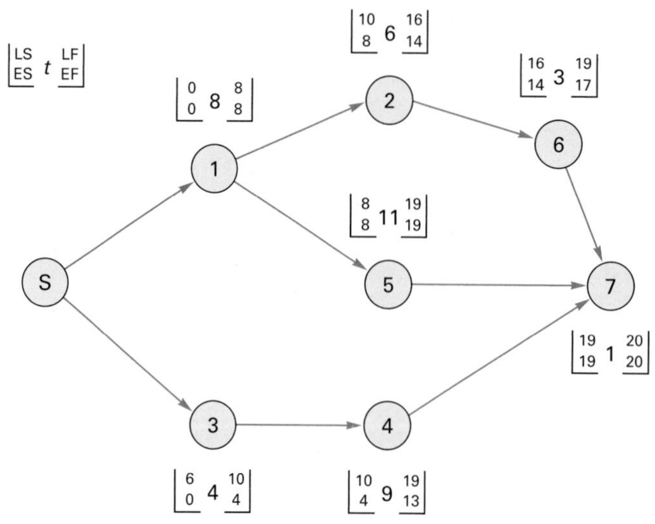

Computing Slack Times

The slack time can be computed in either of two ways:

$$\text{Slack} = \text{LS} - \text{ES} \qquad \text{or} \qquad \text{LF} - \text{EF} \tag{17–3}$$

The critical path using this computing algorithm is denoted by activities with zero slack time. Thus, the table in Example 4 indicates that activities 1-2, 2-5, and 5-6 are all critical activities, which agrees with the results of the intuitive approach demonstrated in Example 1.

Knowledge of slack times provides managers with information for planning allocation of scarce resources and for directing control efforts toward those activities that might be most susceptible to delaying the project. In this regard, it is important to recognize that the activity slack times are based on the assumption that all of the activities on the same path will be started as early as possible and not exceed their expected times. Furthermore, if two activities are both on the same path (e.g., activities 2-4 and 4-5 in the preceding example) and have the same slack (e.g., two weeks), this will be the *total* slack available to both. In essence, the activities have *shared slack.* Hence, if the first activity uses all the slack, there will be zero slack for all following activities on that same path.

EXAMPLE 4

www.mhhe.com/stevenson11e

Compute slack times for the preceding example.

SOLUTION

Either the starting times or the finishing times can be used. Suppose we choose the starting times. Using ES times computed in Example 2 and LS times computed in Example 3, slack times are

Activity	LS	ES	(LS − ES) Slack
1-2	0	0	0
1-3	6	0	6
2-4	10	8	2
2-5	8	8	0
3-5	10	4	6
4-5	16	14	2
5-6	19	19	0

Activities that have a slack of zero are on the critical path. Hence, the critical path is 1-2-5-6.

As noted earlier, this algorithm lends itself to computerization. A computer printout for this problem would appear something like the one shown in Table 17.3.

TABLE 17.3
Computer printout

		SCHEDULE				
		EARLY		LATE		
Activity	Time	ES	EF	LS	LF	Slack
1-2	8.00	0.00	8.00	0.00	8.00	0.00
1-3	4.00	0.00	4.00	6.00	10.00	6.00
2-4	6.00	8.00	14.00	10.00	16.00	2.00
2-5	11.00	8.00	19.00	8.00	19.00	0.00
3-5	9.00	4.00	13.00	10.00	19.00	6.00
4-5	3.00	14.00	17.00	16.00	19.00	2.00
5-6	1.00	19.00	20.00	19.00	20.00	0.00

THE CRITICAL PATH SEQUENCE IS:

SNODE	FNODE	TIME
1	2	8.00
2	5	11.00
5	6	1.00
		20.00

PROBABILISTIC TIME ESTIMATES

The preceding discussion assumed that activity times were known and not subject to variation. While that condition exists in some situations, there are many others where it does not. Consequently, those situations require a probabilistic approach.

The probabilistic approach involves *three* time estimates for each activity instead of one:

1. **Optimistic time:** The length of time required under optimum conditions; represented by t_o.
2. **Pessimistic time:** The length of time required under the worst conditions; represented by t_p.
3. **Most likely time:** The most probable amount of time required; represented by t_m.

Optimistic time The length of time required under optimal conditions.

Pessimistic time The length of time required under the worst conditions.

Most likely time The most probable length of time that will be required.

Beta distribution Used to describe the inherent variability in activity time estimates.

Managers or others with knowledge about the project can make these time estimates.

The **beta distribution** is generally used to describe the inherent variability in time estimates (see Figure 17.8). Although there is no real theoretical justification for using the beta distribution, it has certain features that make it attractive in practice: The distribution can be symmetrical or skewed to either the right or the left according to the nature of a particular activity; the mean and variance of the distribution can be readily obtained from the three time estimates listed above; and the distribution is unimodal with a high concentration of probability surrounding the most likely time estimate.

Of special interest in network analysis are the average or expected time for each activity, t_e, and the variance of each activity time, σ_i^2. The expected time of an activity, t_e, is a weighted average of the three time estimates:

$$t_e = \frac{t_o + 4t_m + t_p}{6} \tag{17–4}$$

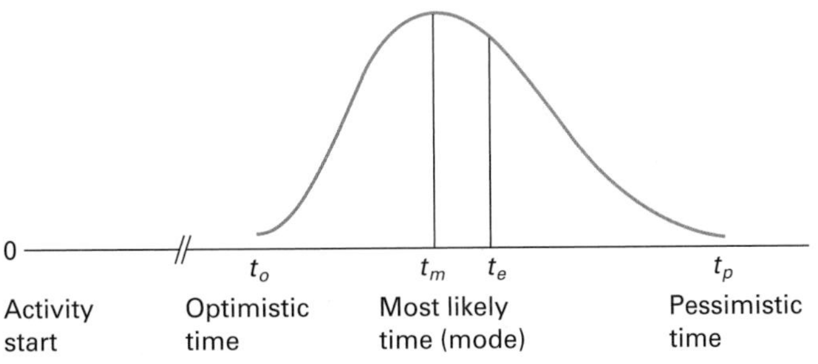

FIGURE 17.8
A beta distribution is used to describe probabilistic time estimates

The expected duration of a path (i.e., the path mean) is equal to the sum of the expected times of the activities on that path:

$$\text{Path mean} = \Sigma \text{ of expected times of activities on the path} \tag{17–5}$$

The standard deviation of each activity's time is estimated as one-sixth of the difference between the pessimistic and optimistic time estimates. (Analogously, nearly all of the area under a normal distribution lies within three standard deviations of the mean, which is a range of six standard deviations.) We find the variance by squaring the standard deviation. Thus,

$$\sigma^2 = \left[\frac{(t_p - t_o)}{6}\right]^2 \quad \text{or} \quad \frac{(t_p - t_o)^2}{36} \tag{17–6}$$

The size of the variance reflects the degree of uncertainty associated with an activity's time: The larger the variance, the greater the uncertainty.

It is also desirable to compute the standard deviation of the expected time for *each path.* We can do this by summing the variances of the activities on a path and then taking the square root of that number; that is,

$$\sigma_{\text{path}} = \sqrt{\Sigma(\text{Variances of activities on path})} \tag{17–7}$$

Example 5 illustrates these computations.

EXAMPLE 5

www.mhhe.com/stevenson11e

The network diagram for a project is shown in the accompanying figure, with three time estimates for each activity. Activity times are in weeks. Do the following:

a. Compute the expected time for each activity and the expected duration for each path.
b. Identify the critical path.
c. Compute the variance of each activity and the variance and standard deviation of each path.

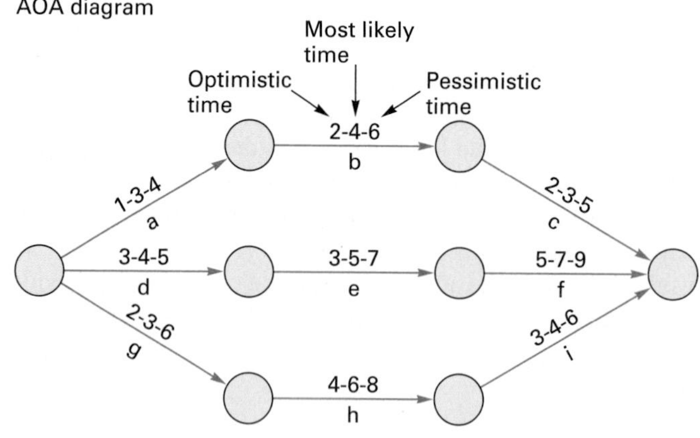

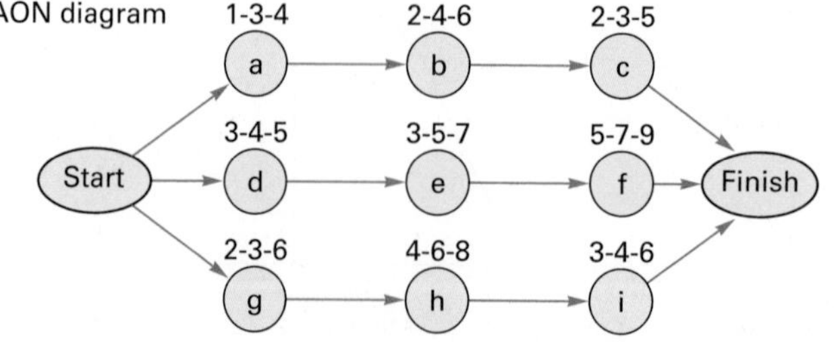

SOLUTION

a.

Path	Activity	TIMES t_o	t_m	t_p	$t_e = \frac{t_o + 4t_m + t_p}{6}$	Path Total
a-b-c	a	1	3	4	2.83	
	b	2	4	6	4.00	10.00
	c	2	3	5	3.17	
d-e-f	d	3	4	5	4.00	
	e	3	5	7	5.00	16.00
	f	5	7	9	7.00	
g-h-i	g	2	3	6	3.33	
	h	4	6	8	6.00	13.50
	i	3	4	6	4.17	

b. The path that has the longest expected duration is the critical path. Because path d-e-f has the largest path total, it is the critical path.

c.

Path	Activity	TIMES t_o	t_m	t_p	$s^2_{act} = \frac{(t_p - t_o)^2}{36}$	σ^2_{path}	σ_{path}
a-b-c	a	1	3	4	$(4 - 1)^2/36 = 9/36$		
	b	2	4	6	$(6 - 2)^2/36 = 16/36$	34/36 = 0.944	0.97
	c	2	3	5	$(5 - 2)^2/36 = 9/36$		
d-e-f	d	3	4	5	$(5 - 3)^2/36 = 4/36$		
	e	3	5	7	$(7 - 3)^2/36 = 16/36$	36/36 = 1.00	1.00
	f	5	7	9	$(9 - 5)^2/36 = 16/36$		
g-h-i	g	2	3	6	$(6 - 2)^2/36 = 16/36$		
	h	4	6	8	$(8 - 4)^2/36 = 16/36$	41/36 = 1.139	1.07
	i	3	4	6	$(6 - 3)^2/36 = 9/36$		

Knowledge of the expected path times and their standard deviations enables a manager to compute probabilistic estimates of the project completion time, such as these:

The probability that the project will be completed by a specified time.

The probability that the project will take longer than its scheduled completion time.

These estimates can be derived from the probability that various paths will be completed by the specified time. This involves the use of the normal distribution. Although activity times are represented by a beta distribution, the path distribution is represented by a normal distribution. The central limit theorem tells us that the summing of activity times (random variables) results in a normal distribution. This is illustrated in Figure 17.9. The rationale for using a normal distribution is that sums of random variables (activity times) will tend to be normally distributed, regardless of the distributions of the variables. The normal tendency improves as the number of random variables increases. However, even when the number of items being summed is fairly small, the normal approximation provides a reasonable approximation to the actual distribution.

FIGURE 17.9 Activity distributions and the path distribution

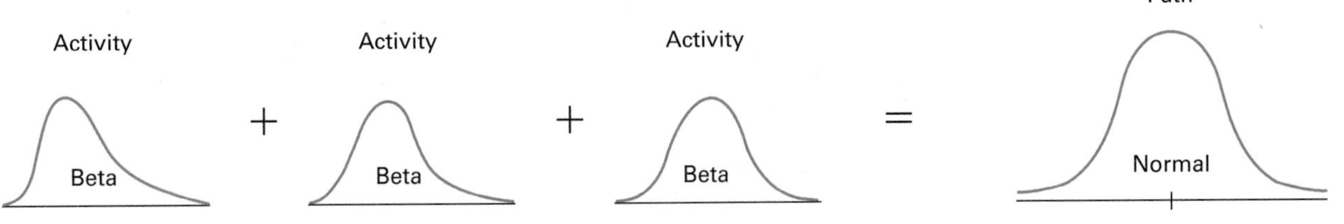

DETERMINING PATH PROBABILITIES

The probability that a given path will be completed in a specified length of time can be determined using the following formula:

$$z = \frac{\text{Specified time} - \text{Path mean}}{\text{Path standard deviation}} \tag{17–8}$$

The resulting value of z indicates how many standard deviations of the path distribution the specified time is beyond the expected path duration. The more positive the value, the better. (A negative value of z indicates that the specified time is *earlier* than the expected path duration.) Once the value of z has been determined, it can be used to obtain the probability that the path will be completed by the specified time from Appendix B, Table B. Note that the probability is equal to the area under the normal curve to the left of z, as illustrated in Figure 17.10.

If the value of z is $+3.00$ or more, the path probability is close to 100 percent (for $z = +3.00$, it is .9987). Hence, it is very likely the activities that make up the path will be completed by the specified time. For that reason, a useful rule of thumb is to treat the path probability as being equal to 100 percent if the value of z is $+3.00$ or more.

> Rule of thumb: If the value of z is $+3.00$ or more, treat the probability of path completion by the specified time as 100 percent.

A project is not completed until *all* of its activities have been completed, not only those on the critical path. It sometimes happens that another path ends up taking more time to complete than the critical path, in which case the project runs longer than expected. Hence, it can be risky to focus exclusively on the critical path. Instead, one must consider the possibility that at least one other path will delay timely project completion. This requires determining the probability that *all* paths will finish by a specified time. To do that, find the probability that each path will finish by the specified time, and then multiply those probabilities. The result is the probability that the *project* will be completed by the specified time.

Independence Assumption that path duration times are independent of each other; requiring that activity times be independent, and that each activity is on only one path.

It is important to note the assumption of **independence.** It is assumed that path duration times are independent of each other. In essence, this requires two things: Activity times are independent of each other, and each activity is only on one path. For activity times to be independent, the time for one must not be a function of the time of another; if two activities were always early or late together, they would not be considered independent. The assumption of independent *paths* is usually considered to be met if only a *few* activities in a large project are on multiple paths. Even then, common sense should govern the decision of whether the independence assumption is justified.

EXAMPLE 6

www.mhhe.com/stevenson11e

Using the information from Example 5, answer the following questions:

a. Can the paths be considered independent? Why?

b. What is the probability that the project can be completed within 17 weeks of its start?

c. What is the probability that the project will be completed within 15 weeks of its start?

d. What is the probability that the project will *not* be completed within 15 weeks of its start?

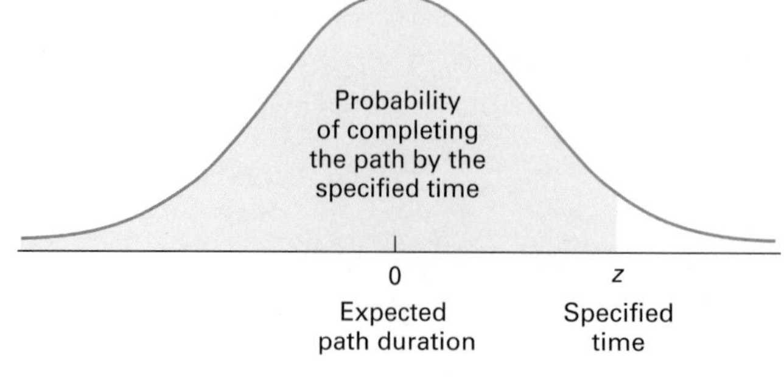

FIGURE 17.10
The path probability is the area under a normal curve to the left of z

SOLUTION

a. Yes, the paths can be considered independent, since no activity is on more than one path and you have no information suggesting that any activity times are interrelated.

b. To answer questions of this nature, you must take into account the degree to which the path distributions "overlap" the specified completion time. This overlap concept is illustrated in the accompanying figure, which shows the three path distributions, each centered on that path's expected duration, and the specified completion time of 17 weeks. The shaded portion of each distribution corresponds to the probability that the part will be completed within the specified time. Observe that paths a-b-c and g-h-i are well enough to the left of the specified time, so that it is highly likely that both will be finished by week 17, but the critical path overlaps the specified completion time. In such cases, you need consider only the distribution of path d-e-f in assessing the probability of completion by week 17.

To find the probability for a path you must first compute the value of z using Formula 17–8 for the path. For example, for path d-e-f, we have

$$z = \frac{17 - 16}{1.00} = +1.00$$

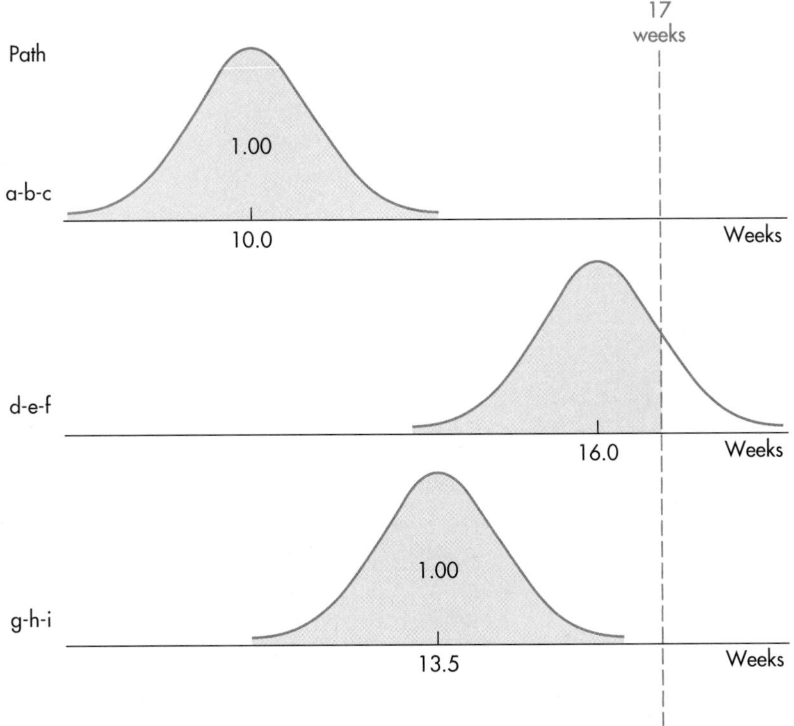

Turning to Appendix B, Table B, with $z = +1.00$, you will find that the area under the curve to the left of z is .8413. The computations are summarized in the following table. *Note:* If the value of z exceeds +3.00, treat the probability of completion as being equal to 1.000.

Path	$z = \frac{17 - \text{Expected path duration}}{\text{Path standard deviation}}$	Probability of Completion in 17 Weeks
a-b-c	$\frac{17 - 10}{0.97} = +7.22$	1.00
d-e-f	$\frac{17 - 16}{1.00} = +1.00$	.8413
g-h-i	$\frac{17 - 13.5}{1.07} = +3.27$	1.00

$$P(\text{Finish by week 17}) = P(\text{Path a-b-c finish}) \times P(\text{Path d-e-f finish}) \times P(\text{Path g-h-i finish})$$
$$= 1.00 \times .8413 \times 1.00 = .8413$$

c. For a specified time of 15 weeks, the z values are

Path	$z = \dfrac{15 - \text{Expected path duration}}{\text{Path standard deviation}}$	Probability of Completion in 15 Weeks
a-b-c	$\dfrac{15 - 10.00}{.97} = +5.15$	1.00
d-e-f	$\dfrac{15 - 16.00}{1.00} = -1.00$	.1587
g-h-i	$\dfrac{15 - 13.50}{1.07} = +1.40$	.9192

Paths d-e-f and g-h-i have z values that are less than +3.00.

From Appendix B, Table B, the area to the *left* of $z = -1.00$ is .1587, and the area to the *left* of $z = +1.40$ is .9192. The path distributions are illustrated in the figure. The joint probability of all finishing before week 15 is the product of their probabilities: 1.00(.1587)(.9192) = .1459.

d. The probability of not finishing before week 15 is the complement of the probability obtained in part *c:* 1 − .1459 = .8541.

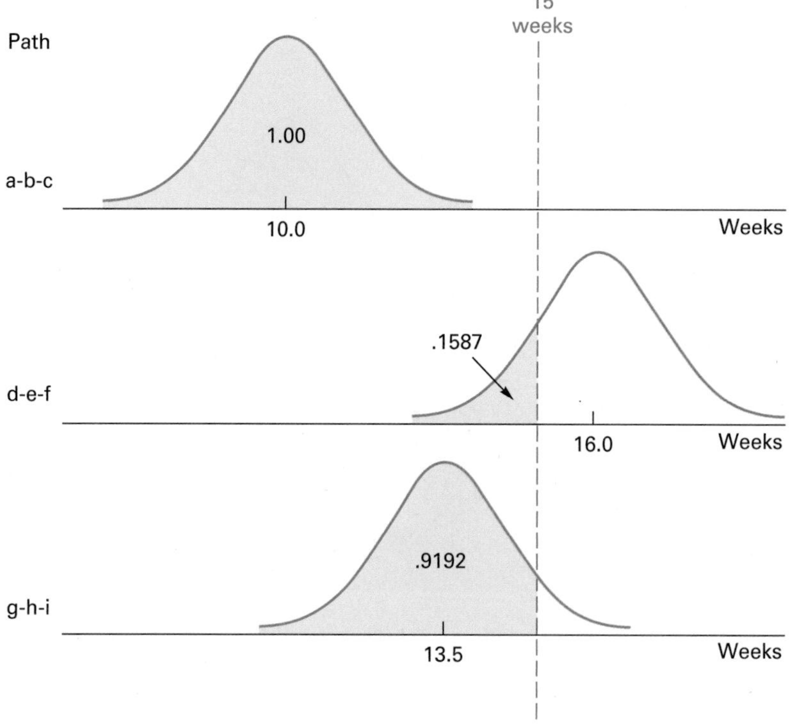

SIMULATION

We have examined a method for computing the probability that a project would be completed in a specified length of time. That discussion assumed that the paths of the project were *independent;* that is, the same activities are not on more than one path. If an activity were on more than one path and it happened that the completion time for that activity far exceeded its expected time, all paths that included that activity would be affected and, hence, their times would not be independent. Where activities are on multiple paths, one must consider if the preceding approach can be used. For instance, if only a few activities are on multiple paths, particularly if the paths are *much* shorter than the critical path, that approach may still be reasonable. Moreover, for purposes of illustration, as in the text problems and examples, the paths are treated as being independent when, in fact, they may not be.

In practice, when *dependent* cases occur, project planners often use *simulation.* It amounts to a form of repeated sampling wherein many passes are made through the project network. In each pass, a randomly selected value for each activity time is made based on the characteristics of the activity's probability distribution (e.g., its mean, standard deviation, and distribution type). After each pass, the expected project duration is determined by adding the times along each path and designating the time of the longest path as the project duration. After a large number of such passes (e.g., several hundred), there is enough information to prepare a frequency distribution of the project duration times. Planners can use this distribution to make a probabilistic assessment of the actual project duration, allowing for some activities that are on more than one path. Problem 19 in the simulation supplement to Chapter 18 located on the text Web site illustrates this.

BUDGET CONTROL

Budget control is a critical aspect of a project. Costs can exceed budget for a number of reasons, and unless corrective action is taken, serious cost overruns can occur, possibly putting the project in jeopardy. Cost overruns can occur for various reasons. One possibility is that initial estimates might have been overly optimistic. Another is that unforeseen events such as weather or supplier issues, work or parts that were substandard and had to be remedied, or some other event added costs.

Table 17.4 illustrates the project cost status for a hypothetical project that is in progress. For this project, the first three activities have been completed. Activity A was $1,000 under budget, Activity B was right at its budgeted amount, and Activity C was over budget by $3,500. The remaining activities are incomplete, but each has a projected cost and a projected difference. Unless there is a change during the remaining life of the project, the cost overrun is projected to be $4,000. The project manager will have to decide if that amount is acceptable, or whether corrective action should be initiated. Although managers' intuitive feeling may be to focus on the activities that are over budget, they would likely review all activities to see where potential savings are possible. Of course, the project cost status would be updated, usually on a daily or weekly basis, to keep the project manager informed.

TIME–COST TRADE-OFFS: CRASHING

Estimates of activity times for projects usually are made for some given level of resources. In many situations, it is possible to reduce the length of a project by injecting additional resources. The impetus to shorten projects may reflect efforts to avoid late penalties, to take advantage

TABLE 17.4
Project cost status for a hypothetical project

Activity	Budgeted Cost	Percent Complete	Actual or Projected Cost	(Over/Under) Actual–Budget
A	$25,000	100%	$24,000	$1,000
B	15,000	100	15,000	0
C	22,000	100	25,500	−3,500
D	10,000	75	10,500	−500
E	30,000	50	29,000	1,000
F	20,000	40	22,000	−2,000
G	8,000	25	8,000	0
				−$4,000

The 2012 Olympic Stadium construction site in London, England. When completed it will have a capacity of 80,000 during the Games: 25,000 permanent seats in its permanent lower tier, and a lightweight steel and concrete upper tier holding a further 55,000 spectators. The upper tier can be dismantled after the Games.

of monetary incentives for timely or early completion of a project, or to free resources for use on other projects. In new product development, shortening may lead to a strategic benefit: beating the competition to the market. In some cases, however, the desire to shorten the length of a project merely reflects an attempt to reduce the costs associated with running the project, such as facilities and equipment costs, supervision, and labor and personnel costs. Managers often have various options at their disposal that will allow them to shorten, or **crash**, certain activities. Among the most obvious options are the use of additional funds to support additional personnel or more efficient equipment, and the relaxing of some work specifications. Hence, a project manager may be able to shorten a project by increasing *direct* expenses to speed up the project, thereby realizing savings on indirect project costs. The goal in evaluating time–cost trade-offs is to identify activities that will reduce the sum of the project costs.

Crash Shortening activity durations.

In order to make a rational decision on which activities, if any, to crash and on the extent of crashing desirable, a manager needs certain information:

1. Regular time and crash time estimates for each activity.
2. Regular cost and crash cost estimates for each activity.
3. A list of activities that are on the critical path.

Activities on the critical path are potential candidates for crashing, because shortening noncritical activities would not have an impact on total project duration. From an economic standpoint, activities should be crashed according to crashing costs: Crash those with the lowest crash costs first. Moreover, crashing should continue as long as the cost to crash is less than the benefits derived from crashing. Figure 17.11 illustrates the basic cost relationships.

Crashing analysis requires estimates of regular and crash times and costs for each activity, path lengths, and identification of critical activities. The general procedure for crashing is

1. Crash the project one period at a time.
2. Crash the least expensive activity that is on the critical path.
3. When there are multiple critical paths, find the sum of crashing the least expensive activity on each critical path. If two or more critical paths share common activities, compare the least expensive cost of crashing a common activity shared by critical paths with the sum for the separate critical paths.

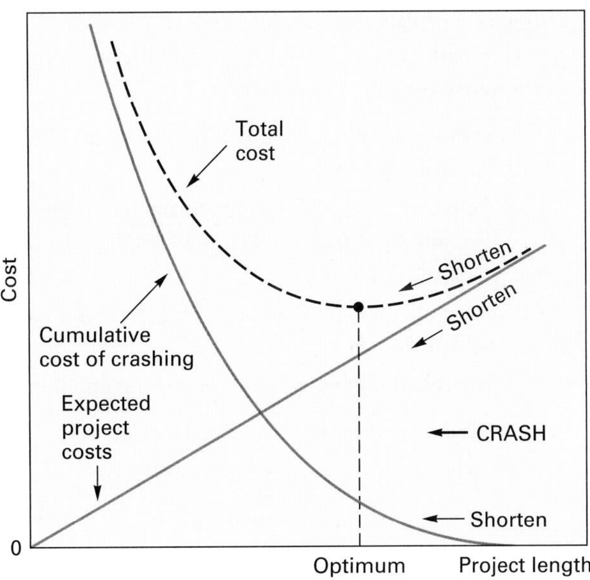

FIGURE 17.11
Crashing activities*

*Crashing activities reduce indirect project costs and increase direct costs; the optimum amount of crashing results in minimizing the sum of these two types of costs.

SCREENCAM TUTORIAL

www.mhhe.com/stevenson11e

Using the following information, develop the optimal time–cost solution. Project costs are $1,000 per day.

Activity	Normal Time	Crash Time	Cost per Day to Crash
a	6	6	—
b	10	8	$500
c	5	4	300
d	4	1	700
e	9	7	600
f	2	1	800

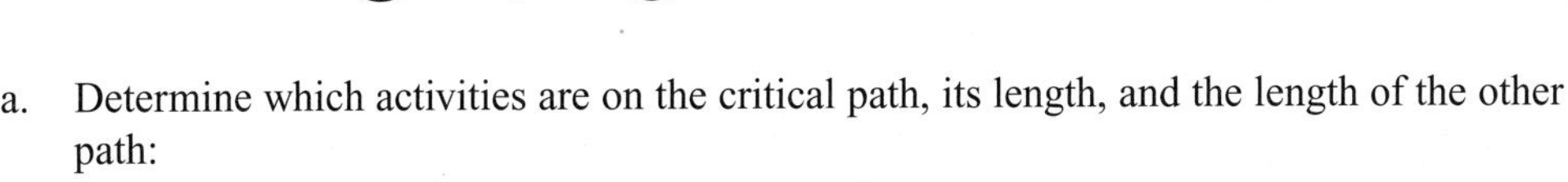

a. Determine which activities are on the critical path, its length, and the length of the other path:

Path	Length
a-b-f	18
c-d-e-f	20 (critical path)

b. Rank the critical path activities in order of lowest crashing cost, and determine the number of days each can be crashed.

Activity	Cost per Day to Crash	Available Days
c	$300	1
e	600	2
d	700	3
f	800	1

c. Begin shortening the project, one day at a time, and check after each reduction to see which path is critical. (After a certain point, another path may equal the length of the shortened critical path.) Thus:

(1) Shorten activity *c* one day at a cost of $300. The length of the critical path now becomes 19 days.

(2) Activity *c* cannot be shortened any more. Shorten activity *e* one day at a cost of $600. The length of path c-d-e-f now becomes 18 days, which is the same as the length of path a-b-f.

(3) The paths are now both critical; further improvements will necessitate shortening both paths.

The remaining activities for crashing and their costs are:

Path	Activity	Crash Cost (per day)
a-b-f	a	No reduction possible
	b	$500
	f	800
c-d-e-f	c	No further reduction possible
	d	$700
	e	600
	f	800

At first glance, it would seem that crashing *f* would not be advantageous, because it has the highest crashing cost. However, *f* is on *both* paths, so shortening *f* by one day would shorten *both* paths (and hence, the project) by one day for a cost of $800. The option of shortening the least expensive activity on each path would cost $500 for *b* and $600 for *e,* or $1,100. Thus shorten *f* by one day. The project duration is now 17 days.

(4) At this point, no additional improvement is feasible. The cost to crash *b* is $500 and the cost to crash *e* is $600, for a total of $1,100, and that would exceed the indirect project costs of $1,000 per day.

(5) The crashing sequence is summarized below:

	LENGTH AFTER CRASHING *n* DAYS:			
Path	$n = 0$	1	2	3
a-b-f	18	18	18	17
c-d-e-f	20	19	18	17
Activity crashed		c	e	f
Cost		$300	$600	$800

An important benefit of the sequential crashing procedure just described is that it provides the ability to quote different budget costs for different project times.

ADVANTAGES OF USING PERT AND POTENTIAL SOURCES OF ERROR

PERT and similar project scheduling techniques can provide important services for the project manager. Among the most useful features are these:

1. Use of these techniques forces the manager to organize and quantify available information and to recognize where additional information is needed.
2. The techniques provide a graphic display of the project and its major activities.
3. They identify (*a*) activities that should be closely watched because of the potential for delaying the project and (*b*) other activities that have slack time and so can be delayed without affecting project completion time. This raises the possibility of reallocating resources to shorten the project.

No analytical technique is without potential errors. Among the more important sources of errors are the following:

1. When developing the project network, managers may unwittingly omit one or more important activities.
2. Precedence relationships may not all be correct as shown.
3. Time estimates may include a fudge factor; managers may feel uncomfortable about making time estimates because they appear to commit themselves to completion within a certain time period.
4. There may be a tendency to focus solely on activities that are on the critical path. As the project progresses, other paths may become critical. Furthermore, major risk events may not be on the critical path.

CRITICAL CHAIN PROJECT MANAGEMENT

Critical chain project management (CCPM) is an approach to project management that includes an emphasis on the resources required to execute project tasks. It was developed by Eli Goldratt, who also developed the theory of constraints (see Chapter 16). Goldratt identifies certain aspects of projects that he believes managers need to be aware of to better manage projects:

1. Time estimates are often pessimistic and with attention can be made more realistic (i.e., shortened).
2. When activities are finished ahead of schedule, that fact may go unreported, so managers may be unaware of resources that could potentially be used to shorten the critical path.

The critical chain of a project is analogous to the critical path of a network. However, the critical chain approach takes into account not only sequential task relationships, but also resource constraints that can result in tasks being delayed when they must wait for a resource that is being used on another task.

A key feature of the critical chain approach is the use of various buffers. *Feeding (time)* buffers are positioned at points in the network where noncritical sections of the network feed into the critical chain path to reduce the risk of delaying critical chain activities. Their purpose is to insulate the critical chain from variation in noncritical chains' activities. Not every intersection will require a time buffer; only those sections that have a relatively small degree of slack time will provide benefit from a time buffer. *A project (time) buffer* at the end of the project is used to reduce the risk that time variations on the critical chain will interfere with timely project completion. *Capacity (resource) buffers* are used when multiple projects are ongoing to help manage the impact of variation of resource requirements among projects.

Regular updates of activity status relative to planned completion times can enable the project manager to see where actual or potential problems can arise, as well as where buffers can be reduced or eliminated, to reconfigure buffers.

OTHER TOPICS IN PROJECT MANAGEMENT

This section touches briefly on several other project management topics, including six-sigma projects, virtual project teams, and managing multiple projects.

One increasingly popular use of project management is for *six-sigma projects.* Although six-sigma projects tend to have a narrow focus, they still involve all of the typical elements and requirements of general project management. Six-sigma projects are discussed in more detail in Chapter 9.

As companies globalize operations, they are increasingly using **virtual project teams.** All the basic elements of a project are present, but some or all of the team members are geographically separated. Recent advances in communication technology have made this feasible. A key benefit is the ability to tap into human talents and perspectives that would

Virtual project teams Some or all of the team members are geographically separated.

otherwise be difficult or impossible to use. A key disadvantage can be the inability to realize synergies that can arise from closer contact among team members. Also, there are risks if there are language or cultural differences among team members, so communications have to be managed more carefully.

The existence of *multiple projects* can create added layers of pressure and complexity to project management. Resources often need to be shared across projects, and problems on one project may create issues for other projects, and can require reassessing priorities. When multiple projects are ongoing within an organization, resources needed for one project may be in use on another project, which could delay the project waiting for the resources to become available. Hence, it is important for managers to cross-check project schedules to avoid such conflicts. Project management software can help avoid conflicts when there are shared resources. In a related issue, *project slippage* can occur as a project nears completion if resources are transferred to new projects too quickly.

PROJECT MANAGEMENT SOFTWARE

Technology has had a number of benefits for project management. Among those benefits are the use of computer-aided design (CAD) to produce updated prototypes on construction and product-development projects; software such as Lotus Notes to keep team members who are in separate locations in close contact; and the ability for remote viewing of projects, allowing those in different locations a firsthand view of progress and problems.

There are a variety of specialized software programs available to help manage projects. As an example, let's consider Microsoft Project.[2] It can be used to effectively create schedules, estimate costs, and track progress. Users can

- **Assign resources.** Assign resources to tasks and adjust them as necessary.
- **Compare project plan versions.** Track version changes in project plans.
- **Evaluate changes.** Evaluate the impact of schedule and resources changes.
- **Track performance.** Track progress and monitor variances between target and actual project goals such as cost, start date, and finish date, and maintain historical records.

Microsoft Project facilitates communication by enabling users to share a project plan with others in the organization, generate predefined reports, format and print custom reports, and easily present project status.

Microsoft Project can be customized to accommodate specific needs by allowing choice of data to display in a project schedule, the custom fields, and modification of formulas, toolbars, and reports. Microsoft Project is an integral part of the Microsoft Office System, making it easy to use products like Microsoft Office PowerPoint and Microsoft Office Visio to present project status.

There are many advantages to using a project management software package. Among them are the following:

- It imposes a methodology and a common project management terminology.
- It provides a logical planning structure.
- It can enhance communication among team members.
- It can flag the occurrence of constraint violations.
- It automatically formats reports.
- It can generate multiple levels of summary reports and detailed reports.
- It enables what-if scenarios.
- It can generate various chart types, including basic Gantt charts.

[2]www.microsoft.com/office/project/prodinfo/standard/overview.mspx.

One thing to keep in mind is that project management is more than choosing the right software. There is much that a project manager must do. Recall the key decisions that were discussed early in the chapter.

OPERATIONS STRATEGY

Projects can present both strategic opportunities and strategic risks, so it is critical for management to devote adequate attention and resources to projects.

Projects are often used in situations that have some degree of uncertainty, which can result in delays, budget overruns, and failure to meet technical requirements. To minimize the impact of these possibilities, management must ensure that careful planning, wise selection of project managers and team members, and monitoring of the project occur.

Computer software and tools such as PERT can greatly assist project management. However, care must be taken to avoid focusing exclusively on the critical path. The obvious reason is that as the project progresses, other paths may become critical. But another, less obvious, reason is that key risk events may not be on the critical path. Even so, if they occur, they can have a major impact on the project.

It is not uncommon for projects to fail, either completely or partially. When that happens, it can be beneficial to examine the probable reasons for the failure, and decide what possible decisions or actions, if any, might have contributed to the failure. These become "lessons learned" that may be applicable to future projects to decrease the likelihood of failure.

RISK MANAGEMENT

Risks are inherent in projects. They relate to the occurrence of events that can have undesirable consequences, such as delays, increased costs, and an inability to meet technical specifications. In some instances, there is the risk that events will occur that will cause a project to be terminated. Although careful planning can reduce risks, no amount of planning can eliminate chance events due to unforeseen, or uncontrollable, circumstances.

The probability of occurrence of risk events is highest near the beginning of a project and lowest near the end. However, the cost associated with risk events tends to be lowest near the beginning of a project and highest near the end. (See Figure 17.12.)

Good risk management entails identifying as many potential risks as possible, analyzing and assessing those risks, working to minimize the probability of their occurrence, and establishing contingency plans (and funds) for dealing with any that do occur. Much of this takes place before the start of a project, although it is not unusual for this process to be repeated during the project as experience grows and new information becomes available.

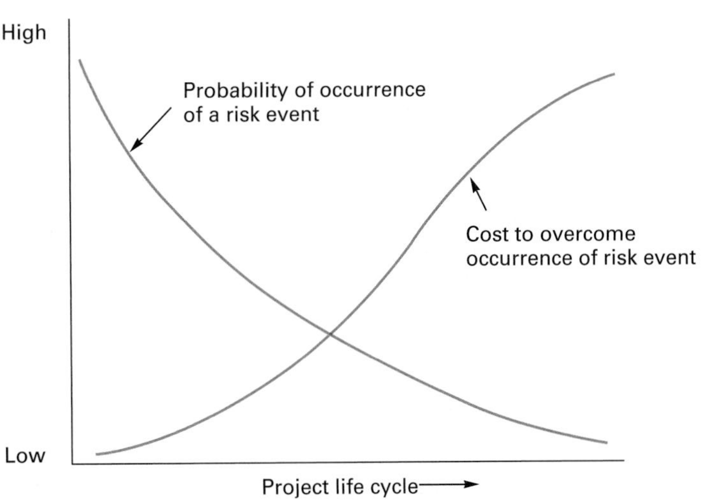

FIGURE 17.12
Risk event probability and cost

Source: Adapted from Clifford Gray and Erik W. Larson, *Project Management: The Managerial Process,* 4th ed., p. 198. Copyright © 2008 McGraw-Hill Companies, Inc. Used with permission.

FIGURE 17.13
A risk matrix

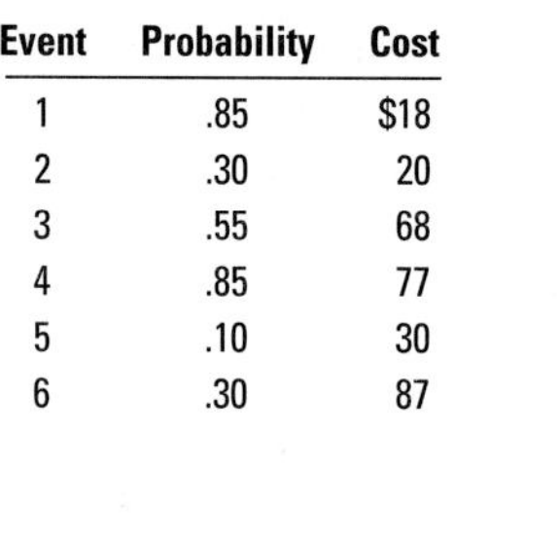

Event	Probability	Cost
1	.85	$18
2	.30	20
3	.55	68
4	.85	77
5	.10	30
6	.30	87

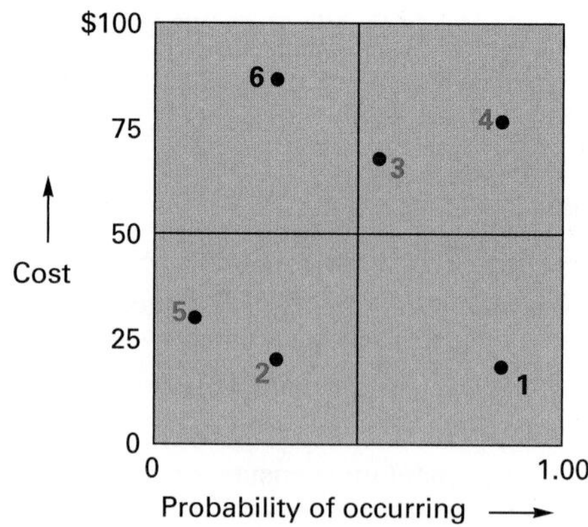

The first step is to identify the risks. Typically, there are numerous sources of risks, although the more experience an organization has with a particular type of work, the fewer and more identifiable the risks. Everyone associated with the project should have responsibility for the task of identifying risks. Brainstorming sessions and questionnaires can be useful in this regard.

Once risks have been identified, each risk must be evaluated to determine its probability of occurrence and the potential consequences if it does occur. Both quantitative and qualitative approaches have merit. Managers and workers can contribute to this effort, and experts might be called on. Experience with previous projects can be useful. Many tools might be applied, including scenario analysis, simulation, and PERT (described earlier in the chapter).

Risk reduction can take a number of forms. Much depends on the nature and scope of a project. "Redundant" (backup) systems can sometimes be used to reduce the risk of failure. For example, an emergency generator could supply power in the event of an electrical failure. Another approach is frequent monitoring of critical project dimensions with the goal of catching and eliminating problems in their early stages, before they cause extensive damage. Risks can sometimes be transferred, say by outsourcing a particular component of a project. Risk-sharing is another possibility. This might involve partnering, which can spread risks among partners; this approach may also reduce risk by enlarging the sphere of sources of ideas for reducing the risk.

A project leader may have to contend with multiple risks that have different costs and different probabilities of occurring. A simple matrix such as the one illustrated in Figure 17.13 can be used to put the risks into perspective.

Events in the upper right-hand quadrant (events 3 and 4) have the highest probability of occurring, and also high costs. They should be given the greatest attention. Conversely, events in the lower left-hand quadrant (events 2 and 5) have relatively low probabilities and low costs, so they should be given the least attention. Events in the other two quadrants (events 6 and 1) should get moderate attention due either to high cost (event 6) or high probability of occurrence (event 1).

SUMMARY

Projects are composed of a unique set of activities established to realize a given set of objectives in a limited time span. Projects go through a life cycle that involves definition, planning, execution, and delivery/termination. The nonroutine nature of project activities places a set of demands on the project manager that are different in many respects from those the manager of more routine operations activities experiences, both in planning and coordinating the work and in the human problems encountered. Ethical conduct and risk management are among the key issues project managers must deal with.

PERT and CPM are two commonly used techniques for developing and monitoring projects. Although each technique was developed independently and for expressly different purposes, time and practice have erased most of the original differences, so that now there is little distinction between the two. Either provides the manager with a rational approach to project planning and a graphical display of project activities. Both depict the sequential relationships that exist among activities and reveal to managers which activities must be completed on time to achieve timely project completion. Managers can use that information to direct their attention toward the most critical activities.

Two slightly different conventions can be used for constructing a network diagram. One designates the arrows as activities; the other designates the nodes as activities.

The task of developing and updating project networks quickly becomes complex for projects of even moderate size, so computer software is important. Among the advantages of using project management software are the provision for a logical planning structure, enhanced communication, and automatically formatted charts and reports.

In some instances, it may be possible to shorten, or crash, the length of a project by shortening one or more of the project activities. Typically, such gains are achieved by the use of additional resources, although in some cases, it may be possible to transfer resources among project activities. Generally, projects are shortened to the point where the cost of additional reduction would exceed the benefit of additional reduction, or to a specified time.

KEY POINTS

1. Projects are unique, limited duration sets of tasks designed to accomplish a set of objectives.
2. The key project metrics are cost, time, and performance.
3. Table 17.1 and Figure 17.1 provide valuable insights into the nature of projects and project management.
4. The project manager and the project team can be major factors in achieving project goals.
5. Work breakdown structures, Gantt charts, and precedence diagrams are useful tools for managing projects.

KEY TERMS

activities, 750
activity-on-arrow (AOA), 750
activity-on-node (AON), 750
beta distribution, 761
CPM, 750
crash, 768
critical activities, 751
critical path, 751
deterministic, 753
events, 750
independence, 764
most likely time, 761
network (precedence) diagram, 750
optimistic time, 761
path, 751
PERT, 750
pessimistic time, 761
precedence diagram, 750
probabilistic, 753
project champion, 747
projects, 742
slack, 751
virtual project teams, 771
work breakdown structure (WBS), 748

SOLVED PROBLEMS

Problem 1

The following table contains information related to the major activities of a research project. Use the information to do the following:

a. Draw a precedence diagram using AOA.
b. Find the critical path.
c. Determine the expected length of the project.

Activity	Immediate Predecessor	Expected Time (days)
a	—	5
c	a	8
d	c	2
b	a	7
e	—	3
f	e	6
i	b, d	10
m	f, i	8
g	—	1
h	g	2
k	h	17
end	k, m	

Solution

a. In constructing networks, these observations can be useful.

(1) Activities with no predecessors are at the beginning (left side) of the network.

(2) Activities with multiple predecessors are located at path intersections.

Complete the diagram in sections. Go down the activity list in order to avoid overlooking any activities.

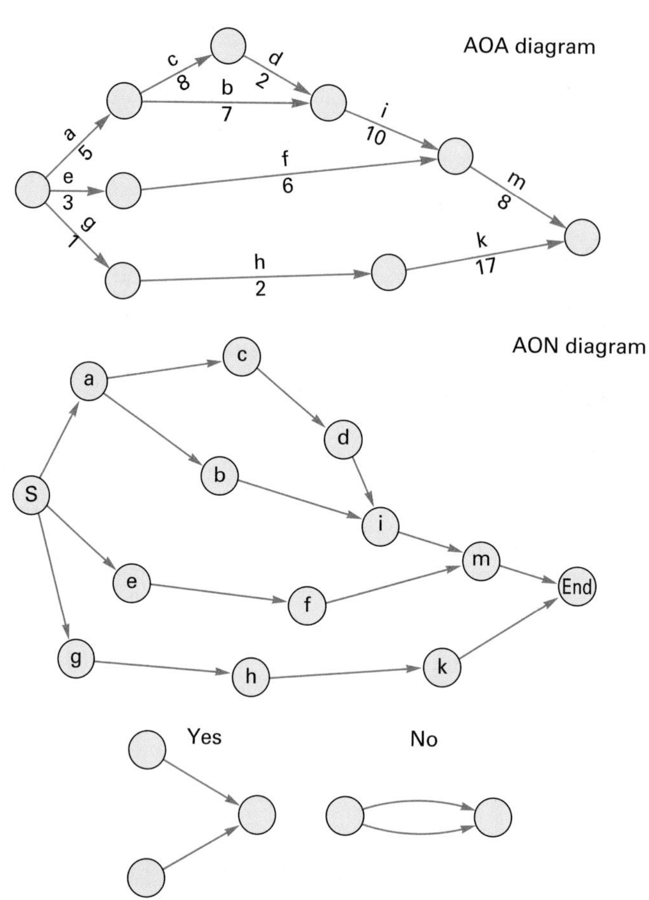

Here are some additional hints for constructing a precedence diagram.

(1) Use pencil.

(2) Start and end with a single node.

(3) Avoid having paths cross each other.

(4) Have activities go from left to right.

(5) Use only one arrow between any pair of nodes.

b. and c.

Path	Length (days)
a-c-d-i-m*	5 + 8 + 2 + 10 + 8 = 33†
a-b-i-m	5 + 7 + 10 + 8 = 30
e-f-m	3 + 6 + 8 = 17
g-h-k	1 + 2 + 17 = 20

*Critical path.

†Expected project duration.

Problem 2

Using the computing algorithm, determine the slack times for the following AOA diagram. Identify the activities that are on the critical path.

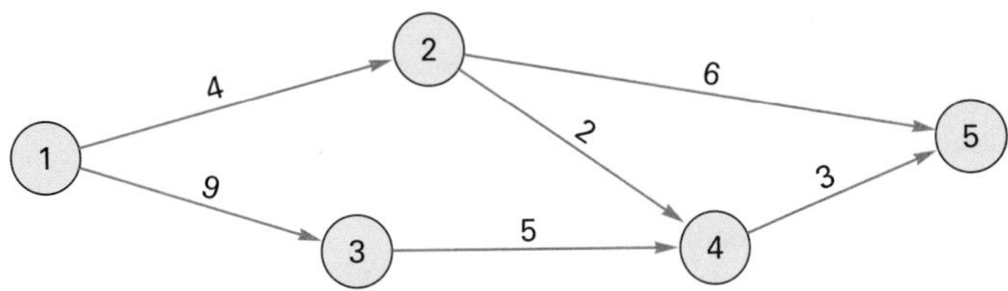

Solution

The task of determining ES, EF, LS, and LF times can be greatly simplified by setting up two brackets for each activity, as illustrated:

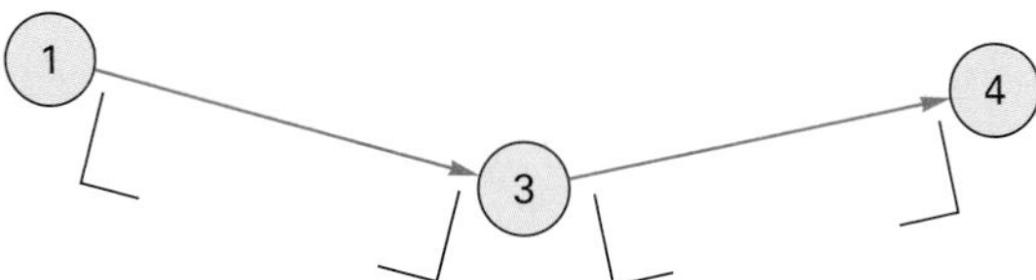

The bracket at the left of each activity will eventually be filled in with the earliest and latest *starting* times, and the bracket at the right end of each activity will be filled in with the earliest and latest *finishing* times:

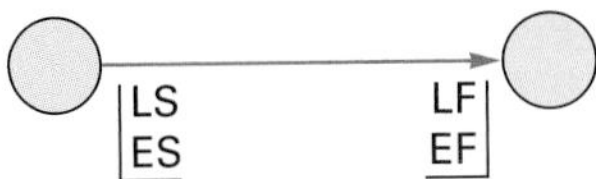

This is accomplished in a two-step process. First, determine the earliest starting times and earliest finishing times, working from left to right, as shown in the following diagram.

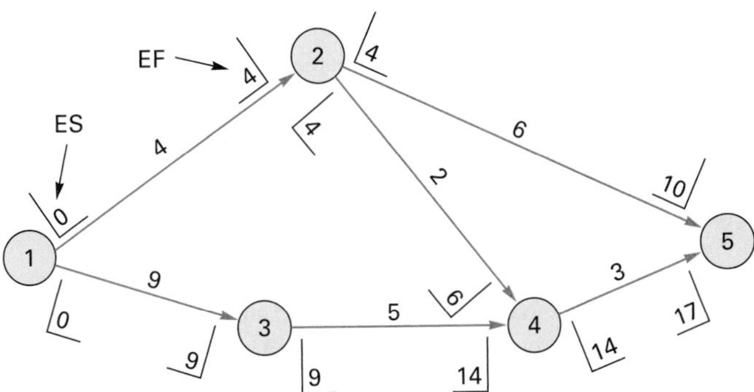

Thus, activity 1-2 can start at 0. With a time of 4, it can finish at 0 + 4 = 4. This establishes the earliest start for all activities that begin at node 2. Hence, 2-5 and 2-4 can start no earlier than time 4. Activity 2-5 has an early finish of 4 + 6 = 10, and activity 2-4 has an early finish of 4 + 2 = 6. At this point, it is impossible to say what the earliest start is for 4-5; that will depend on which activity, 3-4 or 2-4, has the latest EF. Consequently, it is necessary to compute ES and EF along the lower path. Assuming an ES of 0 for activity 1-3, its EF will be 9, so activity 3-4 will have an ES of 9 and an EF of 9 + 5 = 14.

Considering that the two activities entering node 4 have EF times of 6 and 14, the earliest that activity 4-5 can start is the *larger* of these, which is 14. Hence, activity 4-5 has an ES of 14 and an EF of 14 + 3 = 17.

Now compare the EFs of the activities entering the final node. The larger of these, 17, is the expected project duration.

The LF and LS times for each activity can now be determined by working backward through the network (from right to left). The LF for the two activities entering node 5 is 17—the project duration. In other words, to finish the project in 17 weeks, these last two activities must both finish by that time.

In the case of activity 4-5, the LS necessary for an LF of 17 is 17 − 3 = 14. This means that both activities 2-4 and 3-4 must finish no later than 14. Hence, their LF times are 14. Activity 3-4 has an LS time of 14 − 5 = 9, making the LF of activity 1-3 equal to 9, and its LS equal to 9 − 9 = 0.

Activity 2-4, with an LF time of 14, has an LS time of 14 − 2 = 12. Activity 2-5 has an LF of 17 and therefore an LS of 17 − 6 = 11. Thus, the latest activity 2-5 can start is 11, and the latest 2-4 can start is 12 in order to finish by week 17. Since activity 1-2 precedes *both* of these activities, it can finish no later than the *smaller* of these, which is 11. Hence, activity 1-2 has an LF of 11 and an LS of 11 − 4 = 7.

The ES, EF, LF, and LS times are shown on the following network.

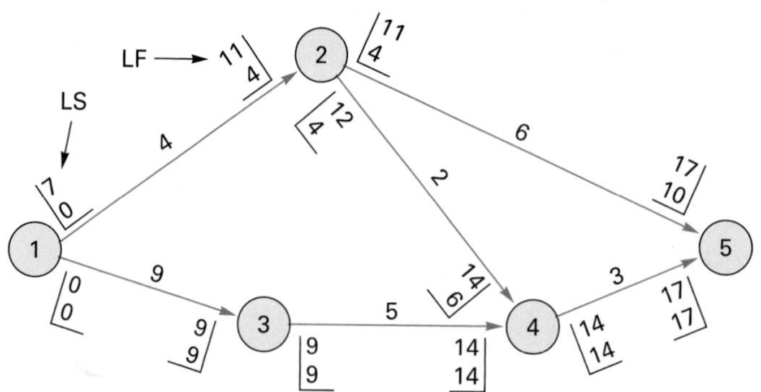

The slack time for any activity is the difference between *either* LF and EF *or* LS and ES. Thus,

Activity	LS	ES	Slack	or	LF	EF	Slack
1-2	7	0	7		11	4	7
2-5	11	4	7		17	10	7
2-4	12	4	8		14	6	8
1-3	0	0	0		9	9	0
3-4	9	9	0		14	14	0
4-5	14	14	0		17	17	0

The activities with zero slack times indicate the critical path. In this case the critical path is 1-3-4-5. When working problems of this nature, keep in mind the following:

- The ES time for leaving activities of nodes with multiple entering activities is the largest EF of the entering activities.
- The LF for an entering activity for nodes with multiple leaving activities is the smallest LS of the leaving activities.

Problem 3

Expected times and variances for the major activities of an R&D project are depicted in the following PERT chart. Determine the probability that project completion time will be

a. 50 weeks or less.

b. More than 50 weeks.

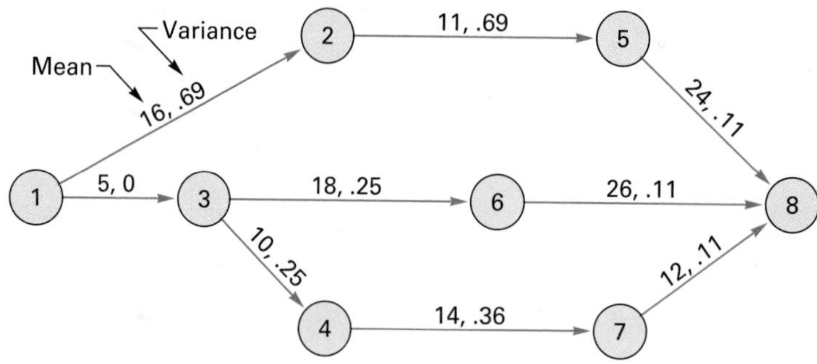

Solution

Compute the mean and standard deviation for each path:

Path	Expected Time (weeks)	Standard Deviation (weeks)
1-2-5-8	16 + 11 + 24 = 51	$\sqrt{.69 + .69 + .11} = 1.22$
1-3-6-8	5 + 18 + 26 = 49	$\sqrt{.00 + .25 + .11} = .60$
1-3-4-7-8	5 + 10 + 14 + 12 = 41	$\sqrt{.00 + .25 + .36 + .11} = .85$

a. Compute the z for each path for the length specified. For any path that has a z of $+3.00$ or more, treat its probability of completion before the specified time as 1.00. Use

$$z = \frac{50 - t_{\text{path}}}{\sigma_{\text{path}}}$$

The probability that each path will be completed in 50 weeks or less is shown in the corresponding diagram. (Probabilities are from Appendix B, Table B.) The probability that the project will be completed in 50 weeks or less depends on all three paths being completed in that time. Because z for path 1-3-4-7-8 is greater than $+3.00$, it is treated as having a probability of completion in 50 weeks of 100 percent. It is less certain that the other two paths will be completed in that time. The probability that *both* will not exceed 50 is the *product* of their individual probabilities of completion. Thus, .2061(.9525)(1.00) = .1963.

b. The probability that the project *will* exceed 50 weeks is the complement of this number, which is 1.000 − .1963 = .8037. (Note that it is *not* the product of the path probabilities.)

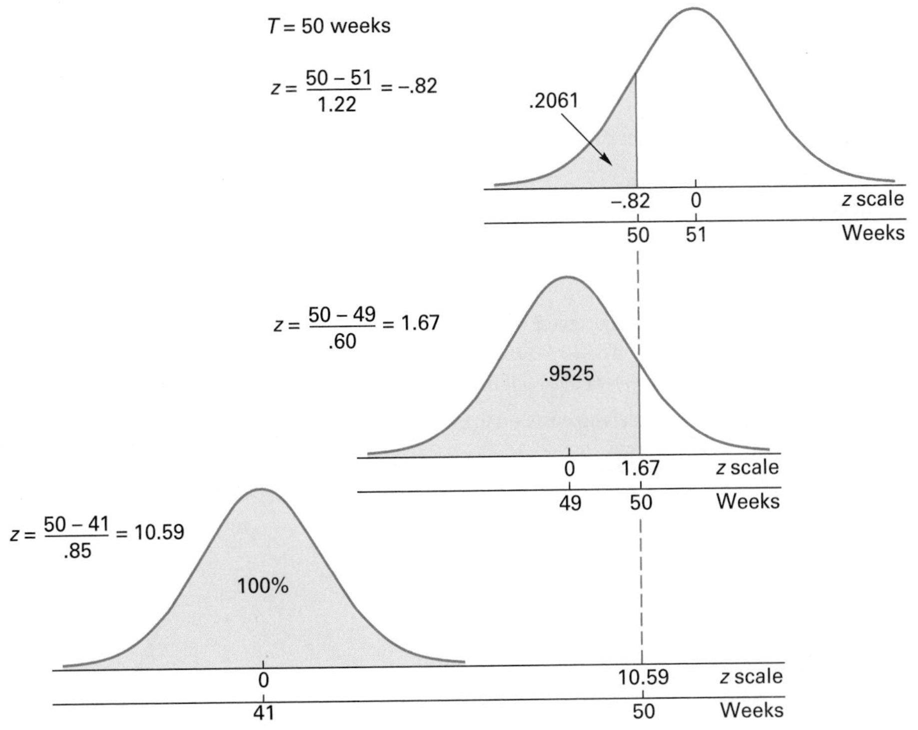

Problem 4

Costs for a project are $12,000 per week for as long as the project lasts. The project manager has supplied the cost and time information shown. Use the information to

a. Determine an optimum crashing plan.
b. Graph the total costs for the plan.

Activity	Crashing Potential (weeks)	Cost per Week to Crash
a	3	$11,000
b	3	3,000 first week, $4,000 others
c	2	6,000
d	1	1,000
e	3	6,000
f	1	2,000

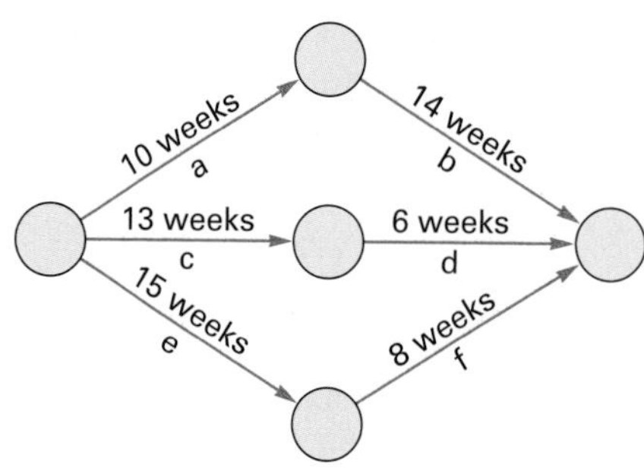

Solution

a. (1) Compute path lengths and identify the critical path:

Path	Duration (weeks)
a-b	24 (critical path)
c-d	19
e-f	23

(2) Rank critical activities according to crash costs:

Activity	Cost per Week to Crash
b	$ 3,000
a	11,000

Activity b should be shortened one week since it has the lower crashing cost. This would reduce indirect costs by $12,000 at a cost of $3,000, for a net savings of $9,000. At this point, paths a-b and e-f would both have a length of 23 weeks, so both would be critical.

(3) Rank activities by crashing costs on the two critical paths:

Path	Activity	Cost per Week to Crash
a-b	b	$ 4,000
	a	11,000
e-f	e	6,000
	f	2,000

Choose one activity (the least costly) on each path to crash: b on a-b and f on e-f, for a total cost of $4,000 + $2,000 = $6,000 and a net savings of $12,000 − $6,000 = $6,000.

(4) Check to see which path(s) might be critical: a-b and e-f would be 22 weeks in length, and c-d would still be 19 weeks.

(5) Rank activities on the critical paths:

Path	Activity	Cost per Week to Crash
a-b	b	$ 4,000
	a	11,000
e-f	e	6,000
	f	(no further crashing possible)

Crash b on path a-b and e on e-f for a cost of $4,000 + $6,000 = $10,000, for a net savings of $12,000 − $10,000 = $2,000.

(6) At this point, no further improvement is possible: paths a-b and e-f would be 21 weeks in length, and one activity from each path would have to be shortened. This would mean activity a at $11,000 and e at $6,000 for a total of $17,000, which exceeds the $12,000 potential savings in costs.

b. The following table summarizes the results, showing the length of the project after crashing n weeks:

Path	$n = 0$	1	2	3
a-b	24	23	22	21
c-d	19	19	19	19
e-f	23	23	22	21
Activity crashed		b	b,f	b,e
Crashing costs ($000)		3	6	10

A summary of costs for the preceding schedule would look like this:

Project Length	Cumulative Weeks Shortened	Cumulative Crashing Costs ($000)	Indirect Costs ($000)	Total Costs ($000)
24	0	0	24(12) = 288	288
23	1	3	23(12) = 276	279
22	2	3 + 6 = 9	22(12) = 264	273
21	3	9 + 10 = 19	21(12) = 252	271
20	4	19 + 17 = 36	20(12) = 240	276

The graph of total costs is as follows:

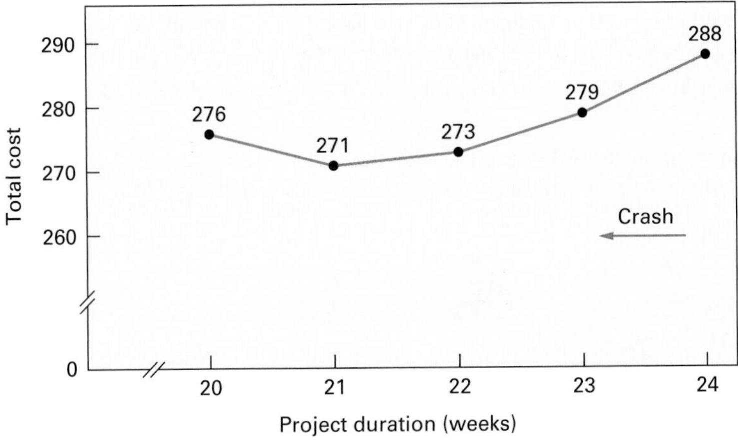

DISCUSSION AND REVIEW QUESTIONS

1. A project manager may need two skill sets—those of a manager and those of a leader. Explain.
2. Explain the term *project champion* and list some ways to keep a champion involved with the project.
3. List the steps in risk management.
4. Give some examples of ethical issues that may arise on projects. What can a project manager do to minimize such issues?
5. What are the key advantages of using project management software?
6. What is a work breakdown structure, and how is it useful for project planning?
7. Identify the term being described for each of the following:
   a. A sequence of activities in a project.
   b. The longest time sequence of activities in a project.
   c. Used when two activities have the same starting and finishing points.
   d. The difference in time length of any path and the critical path.
   e. The statistical distribution used to describe variability of an activity time.
   f. The statistical distribution used to describe path variability.
   g. Shortening an activity by allocating additional resources.
8. List the main advantages of PERT. List the main limitations.
9. Why might a probabilistic estimate of a project's completion time based solely on the variance of the *critical path* be misleading? Under what circumstances would it be acceptable?

10. Define each of these terms, and indicate how each is determined.
    a. Expected activity time.
    b. Variance of an activity time.
    c. Standard deviation of a path's time.
11. Why might a person wish to be involved with a critical path activity? What are some of the reasons one might have for not wanting this association?
12. What are some of the potential benefits of working on a special project in one's firm? What are some of the risks?
13. What are some aspects of the project manager's job that make it more demanding than the job of a manager working in a more routine organizational framework?
14. What is the main benefit of a project organization over more traditional forms of operations management for project work?

TAKING STOCK

1. What trade-offs are associated with time and cost estimates for a proposed project?
2. Who needs to be involved in assessing the cost of a project?
3. Name and explain briefly two ways that technology has had an impact on project management.

CRITICAL THINKING EXERCISES

1. Project management techniques have been used successfully for a wide variety of efforts, including the many NASA space missions, huge construction projects, implementation of major systems such as ERP, production of movies, development of new products and services, theatrical productions, and much more. Why not use them for managing the operations function of any business?
2. Give three examples of unethical conduct involving projects and the ethical principle each one violates.

PROBLEMS

1. For each of the following network diagrams, determine both the critical path and the expected project duration. The numbers on the arrows represent expected activity times.

a. AOA diagram

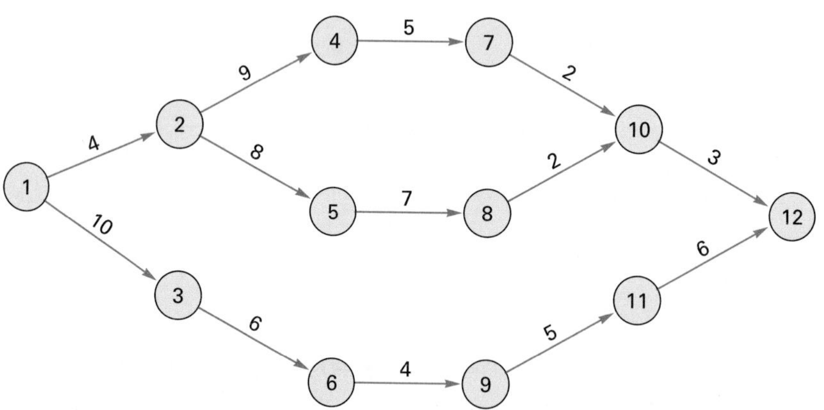

b. AON diagram

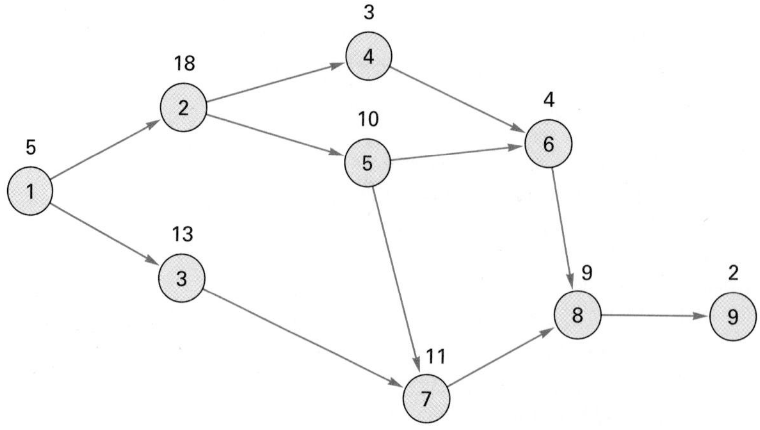

c. AOA diagram

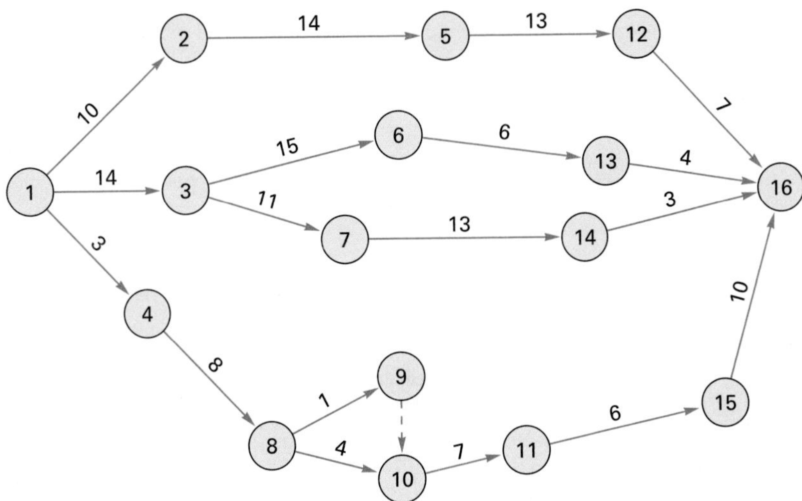

d. AON diagram

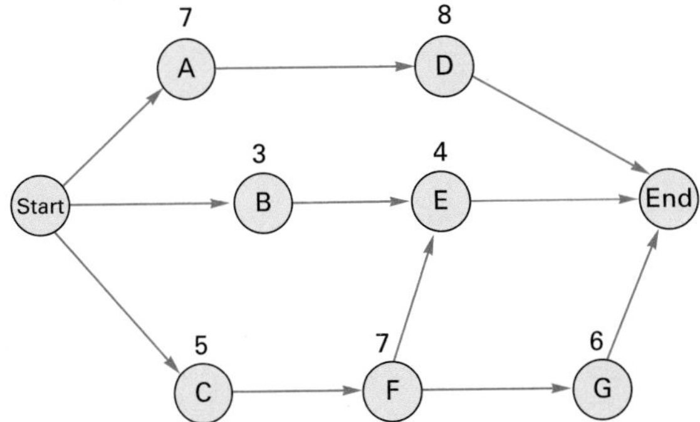

2. Chris received new word processing software for her birthday. She also received a check, with which she intends to purchase a new computer. Chris's college instructor assigned a paper due next week. Chris decided that she will prepare the paper on the new computer. She made a list of the activities she will need to do and their estimated times.

a. Arrange the activities into two logical sequences.

b. (1) Construct an AOA network diagram.
   (2) Construct an AON diagram.

c. Determine the critical path and the expected duration time.

d. What are some possible reasons for the project to take longer than the expected duration?

Estimated Time (hrs.)	Activity (abbreviation)
0.8	Install software (Inst)
0.4	Outline the paper (Out)
0.2	Submit paper to instructor (Sub)
0.6	Choose a topic (Ch)
0.5	Use grammar-checking routine and make corrections (Ck)
3.0	Write the paper using the word-processing software (Write)
2.0	Shop for a new computer (Sh)
1.0	Select and purchase computer (Sel)
2.0	Do library research on chosen topic (Lib)

3. Prepare a Gantt chart for each of the following in the style of the chart shown on p. 749.

a. The bank location problem (see Figure 17.4, p. 751). *Hint:* Use the early start (ES) times given in Table 17.3 on p. 761.

b. Solved Problem number 2 on p. 776.

4. a. Develop a list of activities and their immediate predecessors similar to the lists in this problem for this diagram:

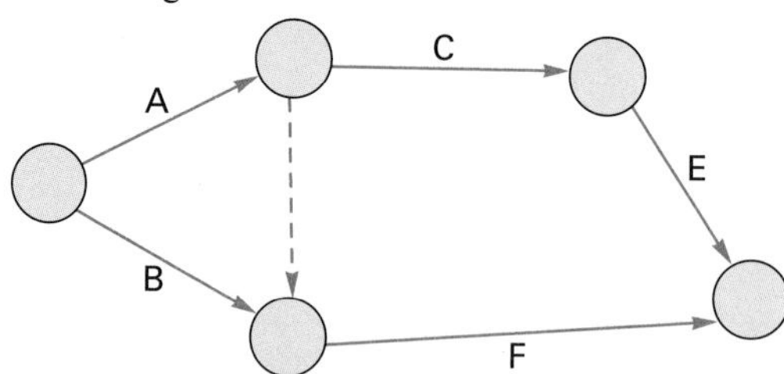

b. Construct an activity-on-arrow precedence diagram for each of the following cases. Note that each case requires the use of a dummy activity.

c. Construct an AON diagram for each case.

(1) Activity	Immediate Predecessor	(2) Activity	Immediate Predecessor
A	—	J	—
B	—	K	—
C	—	L	J
D	A	M	L
E	B	N	J
F	B	P	N
G	C	Q	—
H	F	R	K
I	F, G	S	Q
K	D, E	V	R, S, T
End	H, I, K	T	Q
		W	T
		End	M, P, V, W

5. For each of the problems listed, determine the following quantities for each activity: the earliest start time, latest start time, earliest finish time, latest finish time, and slack time. List the critical activities, and determine the expected duration of the project.
   a. Problem 1*a*.
   b. Problem 1*b*.
   c. Problem 3.

6. Reconsider the network diagram of Problem 1*a*. Suppose that after 12 weeks, activities 1-2, 1-3, and 2-4 have been finished; activity 2-5 is 75 percent finished; and activity 3-6 is half finished. How many weeks after the original start time should the project be finished?

7. Three recent college graduates have formed a partnership and have opened an advertising firm. Their first project consists of activities listed in the following table.
   a. Draw the precedence diagram.
   b. What is the probability that the project can be completed in 24 days or less? In 21 days or less?
   c. Suppose it is now the end of the seventh day and that activities A and B have been completed while activity D is 50 percent completed. Time estimates for the completion of activity D are 5, 6, and 7. Activities C and H are ready to begin. Determine the probability of finishing the project by day 24 and the probability of finishing by day 21.

		TIME IN DAYS		
Activity	Immediate Predecessor	Optimistic	Most Likely	Pessimistic
A	—	5	6	7
B	—	8	8	11
C	A	6	8	11
D	—	9	12	15
E	C	5	6	9
F	D	5	6	7
G	F	2	3	7
H	B	4	4	5
I	H	5	7	8
End	E, G, I			

d. The partners have decided that shortening the project by two days would be beneficial, as long as it doesn't cost more than about $20,000. They have estimated the daily crashing costs for each activity in thousands, as shown in the following table. Which activities should be crashed, and what further analysis would they probably want to do?

Activity	First Crash	Second Crash
C	$8	$10
D	10	11
E	9	10
F	7	9
G	8	9
H	7	8
I	6	8

8. The new director of special events at a large university has decided to completely revamp graduation ceremonies. Toward that end, a PERT chart of the major activities has been developed. The chart has five paths with expected completion times and variances as shown in the table. Graduation day is 16 weeks from now. Assuming the project begins now, what is the probability that the project will be completed before
   a. Graduation time?
   b. The end of week 15?
   c. The end of week 13?

Path	Expected Duration (weeks)	Variance
A	10	1.21
B	8	2.00
C	12	1.00
D	15	2.89
E	14	1.44

9. What is the probability that the following project will take more than 10 weeks to complete if the activity means and standard deviations are as shown below?

Activity	Mean	Standard Deviation
1-2	5	1.3
2-3	4	1.0
1-3	8	1.6

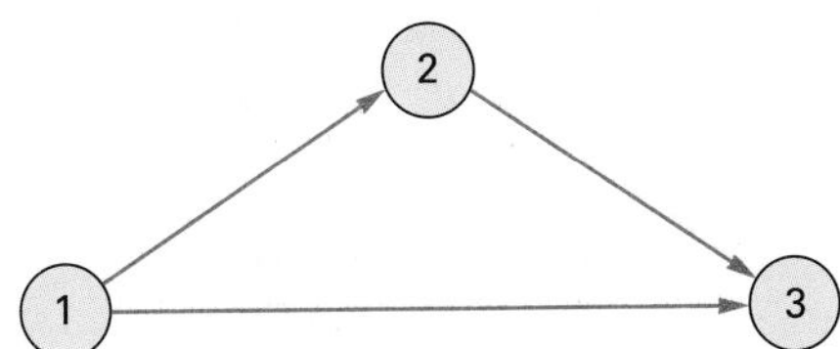

10. The project described in the following table has just begun. It is scheduled to be completed in 11 weeks.
    a. If you were the manager of this project, would you be concerned? Explain.
    b. If there is a penalty of $5,000 a week for each week the project is late, what is the probability of incurring a penalty of at least $5,000?

Activity	Estimated Time (weeks)	Standard Deviation (wks.)
1-2	4	0.70
2-4	6	0.90
1-3	3	0.62
3-4	9	1.90

11. The following precedence diagram reflects three time estimates for each activity. Determine:
    a. The expected completion time for each path and its variance.
    b. The probability that the project will require more than 49 weeks.
    c. The probability that the project can be completed in 46 weeks or less.

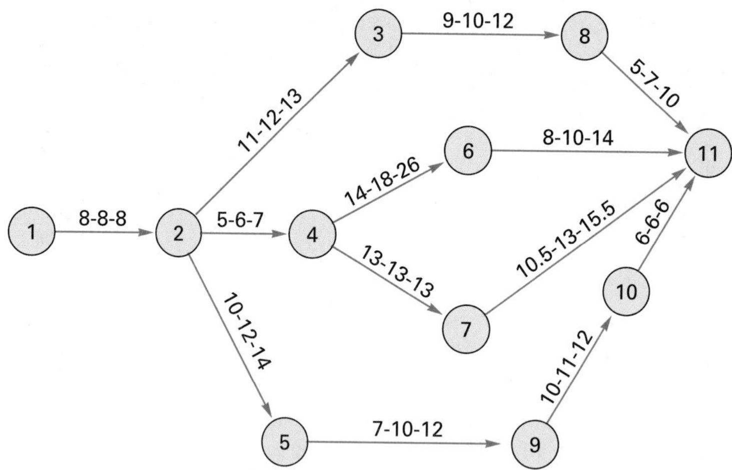

12. A project manager has compiled a list of major activities that will be required to install a computer information system in her firm. The list includes estimated completion times for activities and precedence relationships.

Activity	Immediate Predecessor	Estimated Times (weeks)
A	—	2-4-6
D	A	6-8-10
E	D	7-9-12
H	E	2-3-5
F	A	3-4-8
G	F	5-7-9
B	—	2-2-3
I	B	2-3-6
J	I	3-4-5
K	J	4-5-8
C	—	5-8-12
M	C	1-1-1
N	M	6-7-11
O	N	8-9-13
End	H, G, K, O	

a. Construct an activity-on-node diagram for this project.

b. If the project is finished within 26 weeks of its start, the project manager will receive a bonus of $1,000; and if the project is finished within 27 weeks of its start, the bonus will be $500. Find the probability of each bonus.

13. Here is a list of activity times for a project as well as crashing costs for its activities. Determine which activities should be crashed and the total cost of crashing if the goal is to shorten the project by three weeks as cheaply as possible.

Activity	Duration (weeks)	First Crash	Second Crash
1-2	5	$ 8	$10
2-4	6	7	9
4-7	3	14	15
1-3	3	9	11
3-4	7	8	9
1-5	5	10	15
5-6	5	11	13
6-7	5	12	14

14. The project manager of a task force planning the construction of a domed stadium had hoped to be able to complete construction prior to the start of the next college football season. After reviewing construction time estimates, it now appears that a certain amount of crashing will be needed to ensure project completion before the season opener. Given the following time and cost estimates, determine a minimum-cost crashing schedule that will shave five weeks off the project length. *Note:* No activity can be crashed more than two weeks.

Activity	Immediate Predecessor	Normal Time (weeks)	CRASHING COSTS First Week	Second Week
A	—	12	$15,000	$20,000
B	A	14	10,000	10,000
C	—	10	5,000	5,000
D	C	17	20,000	21,000
E	C	18	16,000	18,000
F	C	12	12,000	15,000
G	D	15	24,000	24,000
H	E	8	—	—
I	F	7	30,000	—
J	I	12	25,000	25,000
K	B	9	10,000	10,000
M	G	3	—	—
N	H	11	40,000	—
P	H, J	8	20,000	20,000
End	K, M, N, P			

15. A construction project has indirect costs totaling $40,000 per week. Major activities in the project and their expected times are shown in this precedence diagram:

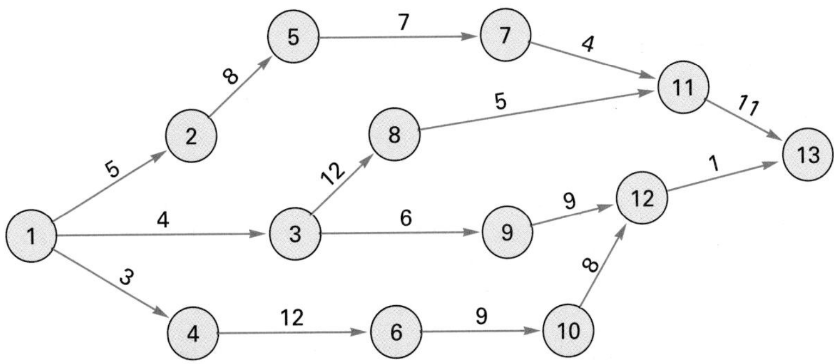

Crashing costs for each activity are

Activity	CRASHING COSTS ($000) First Week	Second Week	Third Week
1-2	$18	$22	$—
2-5	24	25	25
5-7	30	30	35
7-11	15	20	—
11-13	30	33	36
1-3	12	24	26
3-8	—	—	—
8-11	40	40	40
3-9	3	10	12
9-12	2	7	10
12-13	26	—	—
1-4	10	15	25
4-6	8	13	—
6-10	5	12	—
10-12	14	15	—

a. Determine the optimum time–cost crashing plan.

b. Plot the total-cost curve that describes the least expensive crashing schedule that will reduce the project length by six weeks.

16. Chuck's Custom Boats (CCB) builds luxury yachts to customer order. CCB has landed a contract with a mysterious New York lawyer (Mr. T). Relevant data are shown on the next page. The complication is that Mr. T wants delivery in 32 weeks or he will impose a penalty of $375 for each week his yacht is late. *Note:* No activity can be crashed more than two weeks.

Activity	Immediate Predecessor	Normal Time (weeks)	CRASHING COSTS 1st Week	2nd Week
K	—	9	$410	$415
L	K	7	125	—
N	K	5	45	45
M	L	4	300	350
J	N	6	50	—
Q	J, M	5	200	225
P	Q	8	—	—
Y	Q	7	85	90
Z	P	6	90	—
End	Y, Z			

Develop a crashing schedule.

17. Given the accompanying network diagram, with times shown in days,
   a. Determine the expected duration of the project.
   b. Compute the probability that the project will take at least 18 days.

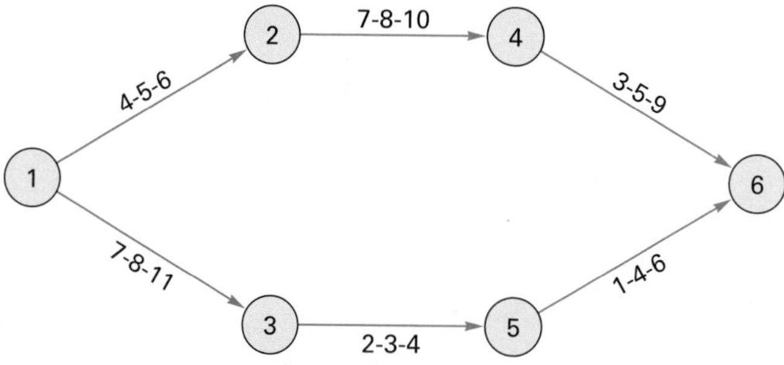

18. Create a risk matrix in the style of Figure 17.13 for this project. Use a vertical scale of $0 to $80. Which event should the project manager be most concerned about?

Event	Probability	Cost ($000)
1	.25	15
2	.35	25
3	.20	55
4	.80	10
5	.10	77
6	.40	55
7	.60	50

19. Create a risk matrix for this project:

Event	Cost ($000)	Probability
Equipment breakdown	40	.20
Vendor is late with key segment	200	.60
Subcontractor has labor issues	140	.30
Weather problems	15	Unknown
Funding delays	50	.40 to .60
Testing delays	20	.40

Explain your reasoning for your placement of the events weather problems and funding delays.

"The mission of the project which you will head is to get our new Mexican subsidiary ready for take-over by Mexican managers. My hope is that you will be able to do this in about two years," explained Robert Linderman, president of Linderman Industries, Inc., to Carl Conway, newly appointed manager for "Operation Mexicano." Conway had been hired specifically for this assignment because of his experience in managing large defense projects in the aerospace industry.

"The first thing that I will have to do is put a project team together," said Conway. "I imagine that you have in mind my drawing people from the functional divisions."

"Yes, I have already sent memoranda to the division managers informing them that you will be asking for some of their key people to work under you for about two years," said Linderman. "In addition, I have advised them to be prepared to process work orders from Operation Mexicano with the personnel and equipment of their organizations. Later on in the project's life, you will begin to get Mexican personnel, both managers and technicians, in to your organization. These people will have Mexican supervisors, but until the mission is accomplished, they also will report to you. I will have to admit that you are going to have some complex authority relationships, especially as you personally will be responsible to the president of the subsidiary, Felix Delgado, as well as to me."

Conway began to make his plans for the project team. The plant building was available and empty in Mexico City, and it was important to get equipment purchased and installed as soon as possible. A plant layout would have to be prepared, but before that could be done there would have to be a manufacturing plan. Therefore, he needed to recruit an industrial engineer, a production planner, and an equipment buyer. They, in turn, would have to build their own staffs.

He made an appointment with Sam Sargis, corporate manager of industrial engineering. "I have had a preliminary talk with Bob Cates about his joining Operation Mexicano, and he is quite interested," Carl said. "Will you release him to me?"

"Why, I'm grooming Cates to take over my job when I retire," replied Sargis. "He is my best man. Let me pick someone else for you, or better still, you just tell me what industrial engineering work you want done, and I will have it done for you."

"Sorry, I want Cates," said Carl firmly. "And besides, you are not due to retire for five years. This will be good experience for him."

For production planning, Carl had in mind Bert Mill, an older man with extensive experience in managing production operations, but Mill rejected his offer. "I talked it over with my wife," he said, "and we feel that at my age I shouldn't take a chance on not having a job to come back to when Operation Mexicano is finished."

Carl next talked to Emil Banowetz, who was assistant to Jim Burke, the vice president for manufacturing, and Banowetz decided that he would like to join the project team. However, Burke told Conway that if Banowetz were forcibly taken away from him, he would give Mr. Linderman his resignation, so Carl decided to back down. He finally accepted a man that Burke recommended.

Filling the equipment buyer's slot was easy. The director of procurement phoned Carl and said that a senior buyer, Humberto Guzman, had requested permission to ask for the assignment, and that he strongly recommended him. Guzman has been purchasing agent for a large mining company in Mexico for about 10 years.

Carl had about the same experiences in getting the people he wanted for the functions of engineering, quality control, cost, marketing, and advertising as he did for the first three positions; in other words, he won some confrontations with the division managers and lost some. For personnel, he got Dr. Juan Perez, who was slated to be personnel director of the subsidiary company, to affiliate temporarily with the project team.

The first brush that Project Mexicano had in getting a functional division to do work for it came when Carl's engineering man, Frank Fong, reported to him that the engineering vice president, who was formerly Fong's boss, refused to authorize top priority to the changing of dimensions in the production drawings to the metric system. Carl had to take this issue to Linderman, who ruled in his favor. The defeated vice president, of course, did not take kindly to the decision.

The next incident revolved around Carl's desire to have a pilot run of products made with metric measurements for shipment to Mexico. The purpose was to test the market acceptance of the Linderman articles. Jim Burke stated flatly that there was no way that his production workers could be trained to work with metric drawings. Carl quickly saw that this was an issue that he was not going to win, so he had his buyer, Guzman, work with the newly appointed manufacturing manager for the subsidiary in getting a run of the products subcontracted in Mexico City.

Bob Cates made a special trip from Mexico City to present Carl with an interesting problem. The Mexican industrial engineer, whom Bob was supposed to be training, had his own ideas about plant layout. When they differed from Bob's as they usually did, he would take his complaint directly to Felix Delgado, the president of the Mexican subsidiary. Because Delgado's competence was primarily in finance, he would not know how to decide the argument and would simply table it. Carl took examples of some of the disagreements to Bob's former boss, Sam Sargis, who quite unexpectedly ruled against Bob's proposed methods. Carl saw that there was bad feeling by Sargis against Bob for leaving his department, which boded ill for Bob's return. To solve the immediate problem, however, Carl asked Dr. Perez to try to reconcile the situation in Mexico City.

Despite these problems, and many more of a similar nature, Project Mexicano was successful, and the transition to Mexican management was made in just a little over two years. By a curious twist, through Dr. Perez's intercession Felix Delgado became very impressed by Bob Cates and convinced him to accept the job of

(continued)

(concluded)

director of industrial engineering for the Mexican company. Humberto Guzman also stayed on to head the procurement operation.

Other members of the project team were not so fortunate. Linderman Industries was laying off personnel when the project ended, and only the project production man was able to get a job in the company at as high a level as the one he had when he joined the team. The cost expert elected to leave Linderman because he said the glamour of Project Mexicano had spoiled him for any routine job.

Carl Conway had a difficult decision of his own to make. Robert Linderman said that he was extremely pleased with his performance and that something good would open up in the company for him soon. In the meantime, there was a staff assignment available for him. Carl had seen enough project managers in the aerospace industry who had figuratively rotted on staff assignments when their projects were completed to be somewhat wary.

Questions

1. Was Linderman Industries' adoption of project organization an appropriate one for getting the Mexican subsidiary started?
2. In consideration of Robert Linderman's letting the division managers know that the project manager would be asking for some of their key people, why would Conway have any difficulty in getting the ones he wanted?
3. Would you expect that many people would turn down a chance to join a project organization, as Bert Mill did?
4. Why would Conway take his problem with the engineering vice president to Linderman and have it resolved in his favor, yet back down in two disputes with the manufacturing vice president?
5. What could Linderman Industries have done to assure good jobs for the people coming off Project Mexicano, including Carl Conway, the project manager?

Source: Clayton Reeser and Marvin Loper, *Management: The Key to Organizational Effectiveness,* rev. ed. Copyright © 1978.

Time, Please

CASE

B. "Smitty" Smith is a project manager for a large consumer electronics corporation. Although she has been with the company only four years, she has demonstrated an uncanny ability to bring projects in on time, meet technical specifications, and be close to budget. Her latest assignment is a project that will involve merging two existing technologies. She and her team have almost finished developing the proposal that will be presented to a management committee for approval. All that remains to be done is to develop a time estimate for the project. The team has to construct a network diagram for the project. It has three paths. The expected durations and standard deviations for the paths are listed in the following table.

Path	Expected Duration (weeks)	Standard Deviation
A	10	4
B	14	2
C	13	2

What project durations (in weeks) should Smitty include in the proposal for these risks of not delivering the project on time: 5 percent, 10 percent, 15 percent? What are the pros and cons of quoting project times aggressively? Conservatively?

SELECTED BIBLIOGRAPHY AND FURTHER READINGS

Angus, Robert B., Norman A. Gundersen, and Thomas P. Cullinane. *Planning, Performing, and Controlling Projects: Principles and Applications.* 2nd ed. Upper Saddle River, NJ: Prentice Hall, 2000.

Chapman, Chris, and Stephen Ward. *Project Risk Management.* New York: John Wiley & Sons, 1997.

Cleland, David I. *Project Managers' Portable Handbook.* New York: McGraw-Hill, 2000.

DeWeaver, Mary Feeherry, and Lori Ciprian Gillespie. *Real World Project Management.* New York: Quality Resources, 1997.

Ghattas, R. G., and Sandra L. McKee. *Practical Project Management.* Upper Saddle River, NJ: Prentice Hall, 2001.

Gido, Jack, and James P. Clements. *Successful Project Management.* Cincinnati: South-Western, 1999.

Goldratt, Eliyahu M. *Critical Chain.* Great Barrington, MA: North River Press, 1997.

Goncalves, Marcus. *Managing Virtual Projects.* New York: McGraw-Hill, 2005.

Graham, Robert J., and Randall L. Englund. *Creating an Environment for Successful Projects: The Quest to Manage Project Management.* San Francisco: Jossey-Bass, 1997.

Gray, Clifford F., and Erik W. Larson. *Project Management: The Managerial Process.* 3rd ed. New York: McGraw-Hill/Irwin, 2005.

Kanabar, Vijay. *Project Risk Management: A Step-by-Step Guide to Reducing Project Risk.* Boston: Copley Publishing Group, 1997.

Kerzner, Harold. *Project Management: A Systems Approach for Planning, Scheduling, and Controlling.* 7th ed. New York: Wiley, 2001.

Larson, Melissa. "Manage Your Projects before They Manage You." *Quality,* September 1997, pp. 64–67.

Lientz, Bennet P., and Kathryn P. Rea. *Breakthrough Project Management.* New York: Academic Press, 1999.

Mantel, Samuel, Jack R. Meredith, Scott M. Shafer, and Margaret Sutton. *Project Management in Practice.* New York: Wiley, 2001.

Matta, Nadim F., and Ronald N. Ashkenas. "Why Good Projects Fail Anyway." *Harvard Business Review,* September 2003, pp. 109–14.

Newbold, R. C. *Project Management in the Fast Lane: Applying the Theory of Constraints.* Boca Raton, FL: St. Lucie Press, 1998.

Project Management Institute Standards Committee. *A Guide to the Project Management Body of Knowledge.* 4th ed. Upper Darby, PA: Project Management Institute Communications, 2008.

Smith-Daniels, Dwight. "Teaching Project Management to MBAs: The Means to How Many Ends?" *Decision Line,* May 1997, pp. 11–13.

Stevenson, William J., and Ceyhun Ozgur. *Introduction to Management Science with Spreadsheets.* 3rd ed. New York: McGraw-Hill/Irwin, 2007.

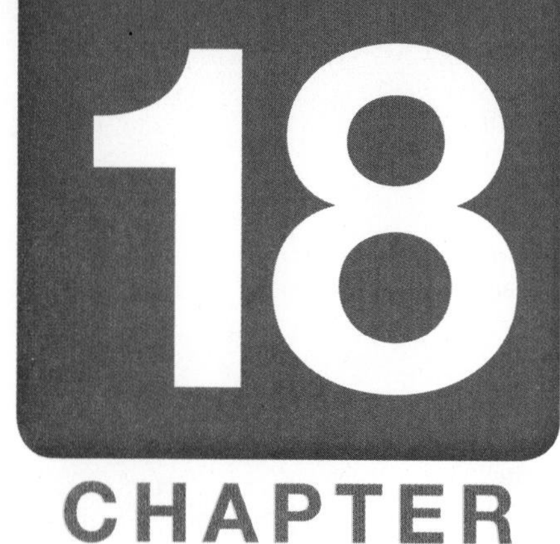

CHAPTER 18 Management of Waiting Lines

CHAPTER OUTLINE

LEARNING OBJECTIVES

After completing this chapter, you should be familiar with waiting line terminology, be able to solve typical problems using the models presented in this chapter, and answer these questions:

1. What imbalance does the existence of a waiting line reveal?
2. What causes waiting lines to form, and why is it impossible to eliminate them completely?
3. What metrics are used to help managers analyze waiting lines?
4. What are some psychological approaches to managing waiting lines, and why might a manager want to use them?
5. What very important lesson does the constant service time model provide for managers?

The mission of Walt Disney theme parks is to "make people happy," and the folks at Disney World in Orlando are masters at doing that. They realize that waiting in lines at attractions does not add to the enjoyment of their customers. They also realize that customers waiting in lines are not generating the revenue that they would if they visited restaurants and souvenir shops. Hence, they have several reasons for wanting to reduce waiting times. Lately they have been using a reservation system called FastPass at some attractions that allow customers to reserve visit times instead of having to wait in line. This is a win-win solution: Customers are happier because they don't have to wait in line, and the park's potential for additional revenue is increased. You will learn more about Disney's approaches to waiting lines later in the chapter.

Waiting lines occur when there is a temporary imbalance between supply (capacity) and demand. Waiting lines add to the cost of operation and they reflect negatively on customer service, so it is important to balance the cost of having customers wait with the cost of providing service capacity. Customer waiting lines occur when there is too little capacity to handle demand, but having more capacity than what is needed to handle demand means that there is idle (unproductive) capacity. From a managerial perspective, the key is to determine the balance that will provide an adequate level of service at a reasonable cost.

SERVICE

Waiting lines abound in all sorts of service systems. They are *non-valued-added* occurrences. In lean systems, waiting is one of the seven wastes. For customers, having to wait for service can range from being acceptable (usually short waits), to being annoying (longer waits), to being a matter of life and death (e.g., in emergencies). For businesses, the costs of waiting come from lower productivity and competitive disadvantage. For society, the costs are wasted resources (e.g., fuel consumption of cars stuck in traffic) and reduced quality of life. Hence, it is important for system designers and managers of existing service systems to fully appreciate the impact of waiting lines.

Passengers wait to buy tickets at Termini train station in Rome.

Designers must weigh the cost of providing a given level of service capacity against the potential (implicit) cost of having customers wait for service. This planning and analysis of service capacity frequently lends itself to **queuing theory**, which is a mathematical approach to the analysis of waiting lines. Queuing theory is directly applicable to a wide range of service operations, including call centers, banks, post offices, restaurants, theme parks, telecommunications systems, and traffic management.

Queuing theory Mathematical approach to the analysis of waiting lines.

The foundation of modern queuing theory is based on studies about automatic dialing equipment made in the early part of the 20th century by Danish telephone engineer A. K. Erlang. Prior to World War II, very few attempts were made to apply queuing theory to business problems. Since that time, queuing theory has been applied to a wide range of problems.

The mathematics of queuing can be complex; for that reason, the emphasis here will not be on the mathematics but the concepts that underlie the use of queuing in analyzing waiting-line problems. We shall rely on the use of formulas and tables for analysis.

Waiting lines are commonly found wherever customers arrive *randomly* for services. Some examples of waiting lines we encounter in our daily lives include the lines at supermarket checkouts, fast-food restaurants, airport ticket counters, theaters, post offices, and toll booths. In many situations, the "customers" are not people but orders waiting to be filled, trucks waiting to be unloaded, jobs waiting to be processed, or equipment awaiting repairs. Still other examples include ships waiting to dock, planes waiting to land, and cars waiting at a stop sign.

One reason that queuing analysis is important is that customers regard waiting negatively. Customers may tend to associate this with poor service quality, especially if the wait is long. Similarly, in an organizational setting, having work or employees wait is the sort of waste that workers in lean systems strive to reduce.

The discussion of queuing begins with an examination of what is perhaps the most fundamental issue in waiting-line theory: Why is there waiting?

WHY IS THERE WAITING?

Many people are surprised to learn that waiting lines tend to form even though a system is basically underloaded. For example, a fast-food restaurant may have the capacity to handle an average of 200 orders per hour and yet experience waiting lines even though the average number of orders is only 150 per hour. The key word is *average*. In reality, customers arrive at random intervals rather than at evenly spaced intervals, and some orders take longer to fill than others. In other words, both arrivals and service times exhibit a high degree of variability. And because services cannot be performed ahead of time and stored until needed, the system at times becomes temporarily overloaded, giving rise to waiting lines. However, at other times, the system is idle because there are no customers. It follows that in systems where variability is minimal or nonexistent (e.g., because arrivals can be scheduled and service time is constant), waiting lines do not ordinarily form. JIT/lean systems strive to achieve this.

MANAGERIAL IMPLICATIONS OF WAITING LINES

Managers have a number of very good reasons to be concerned with waiting lines. Chief among those reasons are the following:

1. The cost to provide waiting space.
2. A possible loss of business should customers leave the line before being served or refuse to wait at all.
3. A possible loss of goodwill.
4. A possible reduction in customer satisfaction.
5. The resulting congestion that may disrupt other business operations and/or customers.

New Yorkers Do Not Like Waiting in Line

READING

According to a new Visa survey conducted with 1,000 adults standing in lines throughout New York City, most consumers would actually prefer to clean their bathroom (42 percent), sit in traffic (20 percent) or go to the dentist (18 percent) than stand in line.

Source: ItsaSurvey.com (www.itsasurvey.com/artman2/publish/consumers/Americans_Do_Not_Like_Waiting_in_Line_They_Like_Credit_Cards_for_Faster_Purchases.shtml).

GOAL OF WAITING-LINE MANAGEMENT

In a queuing system customers enter a waiting line of a service facility, receive service when their turn comes, and then leave the system. The number of customers in the system (awaiting service or being served) will vary randomly over time. The goal of waiting-line management is essentially to minimize total costs. There are two basic categories of cost in a queuing situation: those associated with customers waiting for service and those associated with capacity. Thus,

$$\text{TC} = \text{Customer waiting cost} + \text{Capacity cost}$$

Capacity costs are the costs of maintaining the ability to provide service. Examples include the number of bays at a car wash, the number of checkouts at a supermarket, the number of repair people to handle equipment breakdowns, and the number of lanes on a highway. When a service facility is idle, capacity is lost since it cannot be stored. The costs of customer waiting include the salaries paid to employees while they wait for service (mechanics waiting for tools, the drivers of trucks waiting to unload), the cost of the space for waiting (size of doctor's waiting room, length of driveway at a car wash, fuel consumed by planes waiting to land), and any loss of business due to customers refusing to wait and possibly going elsewhere in the future.

A practical difficulty frequently encountered is pinning down the cost of customer waiting time, especially since major portions of that cost are not a part of accounting data. One

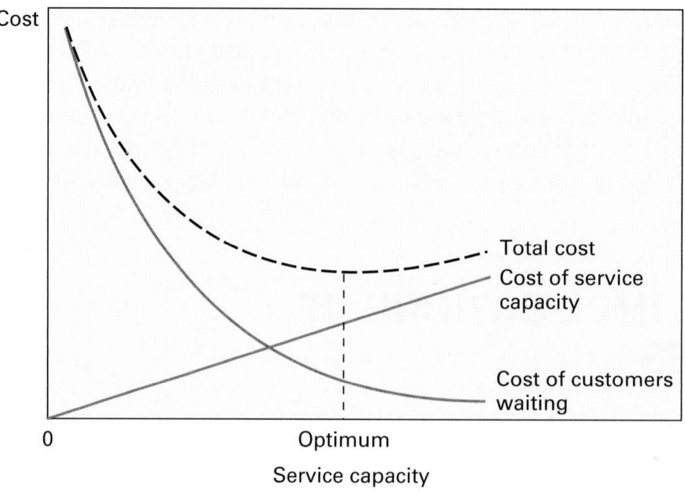

FIGURE 18.1
The goal of waiting-line management is to minimize the sum of two costs: customer waiting costs and service capacity costs

approach often used is to treat waiting times or line lengths as a policy variable: A manager simply specifies an acceptable level of waiting and directs that capacity be established to achieve that level.

The goal of waiting-line management is to balance the cost of providing a level of service capacity with the cost of customers waiting for service. Figure 18.1 illustrates this concept. Note that as capacity increases, its cost increases. For simplicity, the increase is shown as a linear relationship. Although a step function is often more appropriate, use of a straight line does not significantly distort the picture. As capacity increases, the number of customers waiting and the time they wait tend to decrease, thereby decreasing waiting costs. As is typical in trade-off relationships, total costs can be represented as a U-shaped curve. The goal of analysis is to identify a level of service capacity that will minimize total cost. (Unlike the situation in the inventory EOQ model, the minimum point on the total cost curve is *not* usually where the two cost lines intersect.)

In situations where those waiting in line are *external* customers (as opposed to employees), the existence of waiting lines can reflect negatively on an organization's *quality* image. Consequently, some organizations are focusing their attention on providing faster service—speeding up the rate at which service is delivered rather than merely increasing the number of servers. The effect of this is to shift the total cost curve downward if the cost of customer waiting decreases by more than the cost of the faster service.

CHARACTERISTICS OF WAITING LINES

There are numerous queuing models from which an analyst can choose. Naturally, much of the success of the analysis will depend on choosing an appropriate model. Model choice is affected by the characteristics of the system under investigation. The main characteristics are

1. Population source.
2. Number of servers (channels).
3. Arrival and service patterns.
4. Queue discipline (order of service).

Figure 18.2 depicts a simple queuing system.

Population Source

Infinite-source situation Customer arrivals are unrestricted.

The approach to use in analyzing a queuing problem depends on whether the potential number of customers is limited. There are two possibilities: *infinite-source* and *finite-source* populations. In an **infinite-source situation,** the *potential* number of customers greatly exceeds

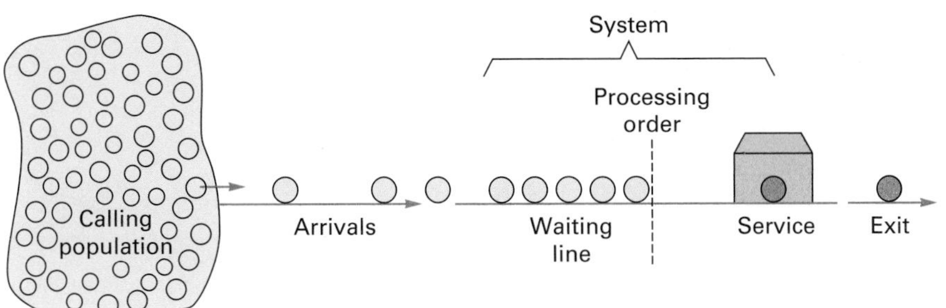

FIGURE 18.2
A simple queuing system

system capacity. Infinite-source situations exist whenever service is *unrestricted.* Examples are supermarkets, drugstores, banks, restaurants, theaters, amusement centers, and toll bridges. Theoretically, large numbers of customers from the "calling population" can request service at any time. When the potential number of customers is limited, a **finite-source situation** exists. An example is the repairman responsible for a certain number of machines in a company. The potential number of machines that might need repairs at any one time cannot exceed the number of machines assigned to the repairer. Similarly, an operator may be responsible for loading and unloading a bank of four machines, a nurse may be responsible for answering patient calls for a 10-bed ward, a secretary may be responsible for taking dictation from three executives, and a company shop may perform repairs as needed on the firm's 20 trucks.

Finite-source situation The number of potential customers is limited.

Number of Servers (Channels)

The capacity of queuing systems is a function of the capacity of each server and the number of servers being used. The terms *server* and **channel** are synonymous, and it is generally assumed that each channel can handle one customer at a time. Systems can be either *single-* or *multiple-channel.* (A group of servers working together as a team, such as a surgical team, is treated as a single-channel system.) Examples of single-channel systems are small grocery stores with one checkout counter, some theaters, single-bay car washes, and drive-in banks with one teller. Multiple-channel systems (those with more than one server) are commonly found in banks, at airline ticket counters, at auto service centers, and at gas stations.

Channel A server in a service system.

A related distinction is the number of steps or *phases* in a queuing system. For example, at theme parks, people go from one attraction to another. Each attraction constitutes a separate phase where queues can (and usually do) form.

Figure 18.3 illustrates some of the most common queuing systems. Because it would not be possible to cover all of these cases in sufficient detail in the limited amount of space available here, our discussion will focus on *single-phase* systems.

Arrival and Service Patterns

Waiting lines are a direct result of arrival and service variability. They occur because random, highly variable arrival and service patterns cause systems to be temporarily overloaded. In many instances, the variabilities can be described by theoretical distributions. In fact, the most commonly used models assume that arrival and service *rates* can be described by a Poisson distribution or, equivalently, that the interarrival *time* and service *time* can be described by a negative exponential distribution. Figure 18.4 illustrates these distributions.

The Poisson distribution often provides a reasonably good description of customer arrivals per unit of time (e.g., per hour). Figure 18.5A illustrates how Poisson-distributed arrivals (e.g., accidents) might occur during a three-day period. In some hours, there are three or four arrivals; in other hours one or two arrivals; and in some hours no arrivals.

The negative exponential distribution often provides a reasonably good description of customer service times (e.g., first aid care for accident victims). Figure 18.5B illustrates how exponential service times might appear for the customers whose arrivals are illustrated in Figure 18.5A. Note that most service times are very short—some are close to zero—but a few require a relatively long service time. That is typical of a negative exponential distribution.

FIGURE 18.3
Four common variations of queuing systems

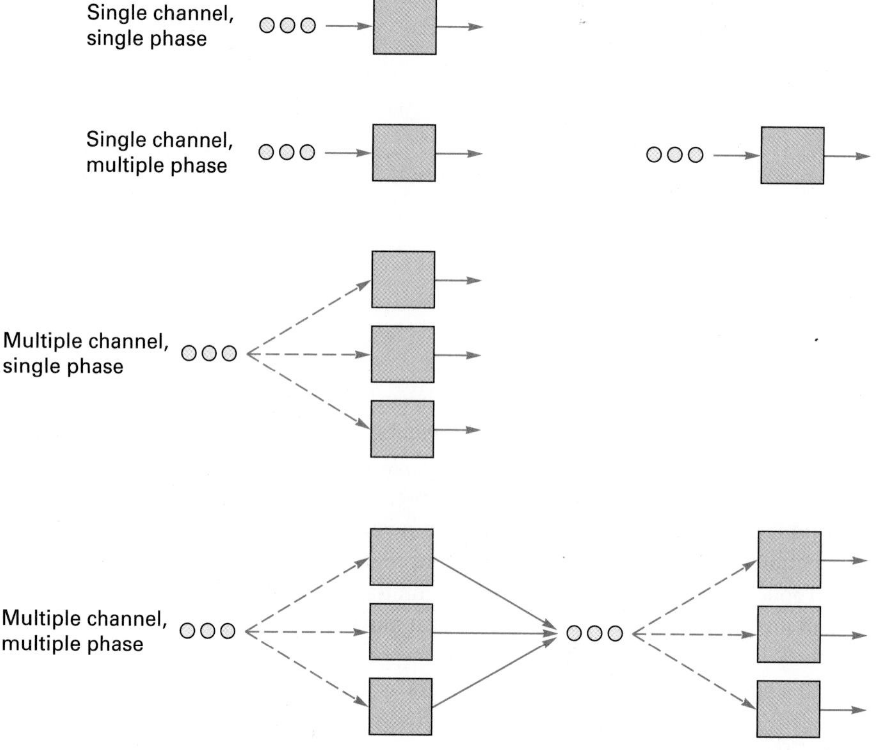

FIGURE 18.4 Poisson and negative exponential distributions

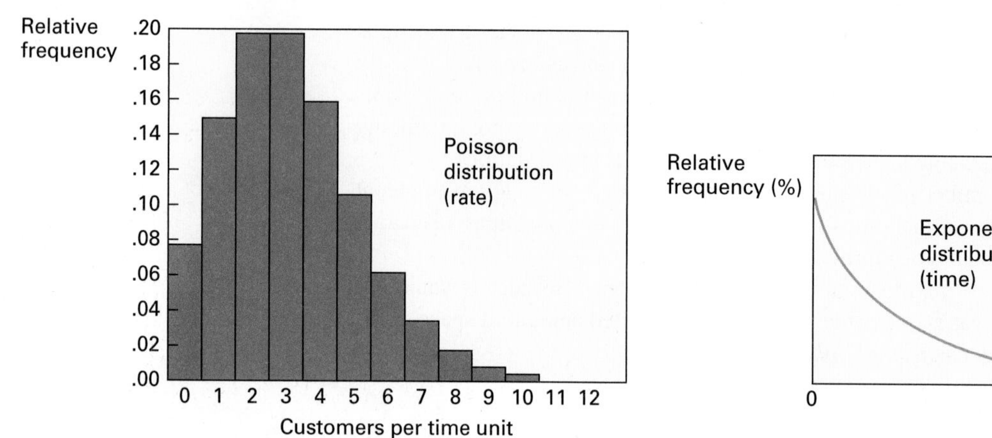

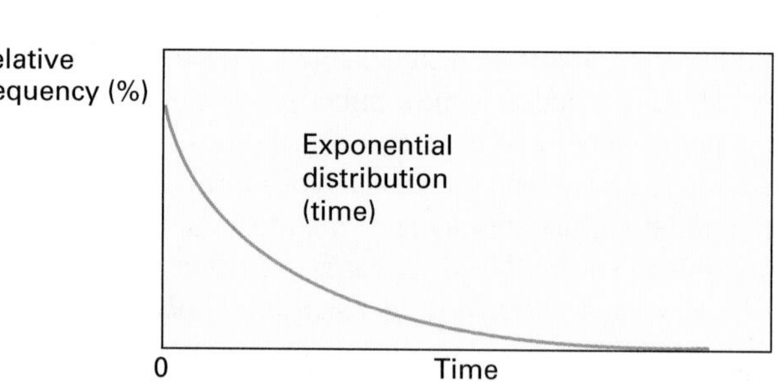

Waiting lines are most likely to occur when arrivals are bunched or when service times are particularly lengthy, and they are very likely to occur when both factors are present. For instance, note the long service time of customer 7 on day 1, in Figure 18.5B. In Figure 18.5A, the seventh customer arrived just after 10 o'clock and the next two customers arrived shortly after that, making it very likely that a waiting line formed. A similar situation occurred on day 3 with the last three customers: The relatively long service time for customer 13 (Figure 18.5B) and the short time before the next two arrivals (Figure 18.5A, day 3) would create (or increase the length of) a waiting line.

It is interesting to note that the Poisson and negative exponential distributions are alternate ways of presenting the same basic information. That is, if service time is exponential, then the service rate is Poisson. Similarly, if the customer arrival rate is Poisson, then the interarrival time (i.e., the time between arrivals) is exponential. For example, if a service facility can

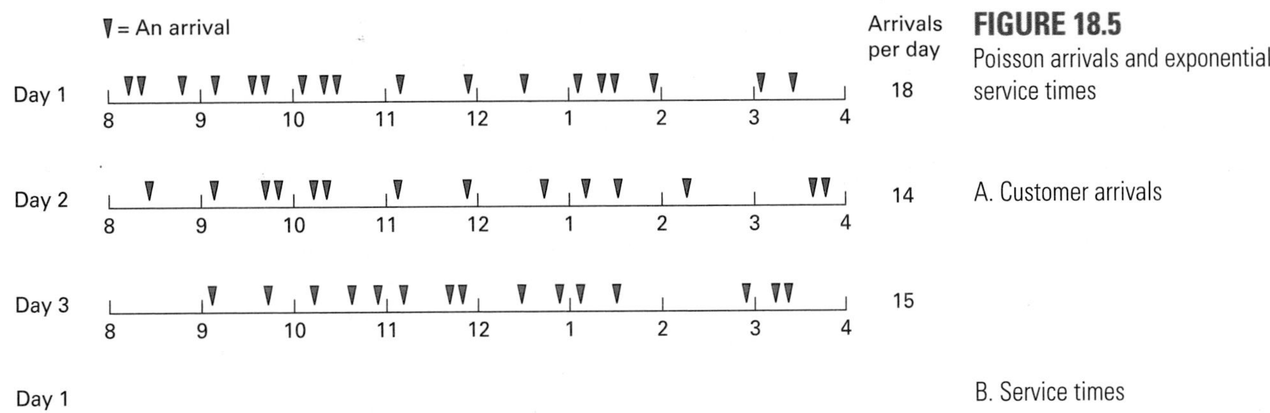

FIGURE 18.5
Poisson arrivals and exponential service times

A. Customer arrivals

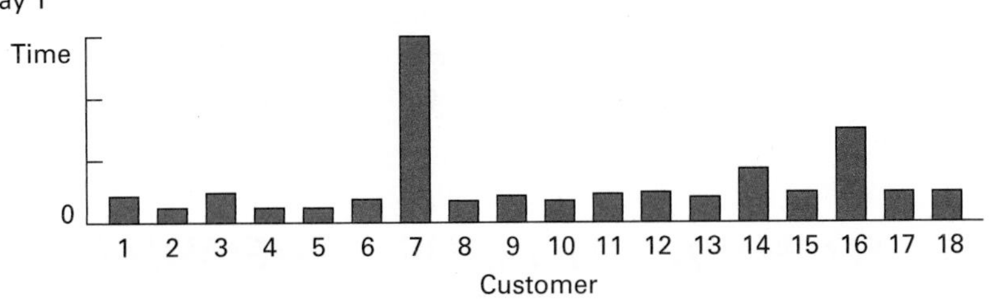

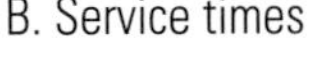

B. Service times

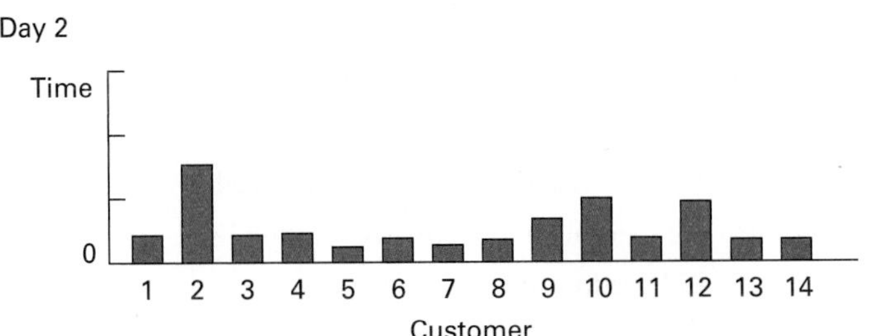

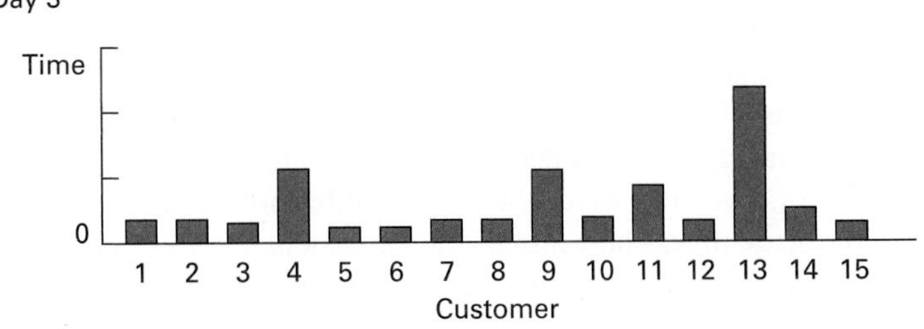

process 12 customers per hour (rate), average service time is five minutes. And if the arrival rate is 10 per hour, then the average time between arrivals is six minutes.

The models described here generally require that arrival and service rates lend themselves to description using a Poisson distribution or, equivalently, that interarrival and service times lend themselves to description using a negative exponential distribution. In practice, it is necessary to verify that these assumptions are met. Sometimes this is done by collecting data and plotting them, although the preferred approach is to use a chi-square goodness-of-fit test for that purpose. A discussion of the chi-square test is beyond the scope of this text, but most basic statistics textbooks cover the topic.

Research has shown that these assumptions are often appropriate for customer arrivals but less likely to be appropriate for service. In situations where the assumptions are not reasonably satisfied, the alternatives would be to (1) develop a more suitable model, (2) search for a better (and usually more complex) existing model, or (3) resort to computer simulation. Each of these alternatives requires more effort or cost than the ones presented here.

The models in this chapter assume customers are patient, that is, that customers enter the waiting line and remain until they are served. Other possibilities are that (1) waiting customers grow impatient and leave the line (*reneging*); (2) customers switch to another line (*jockeying*); or (3) upon arriving, customers decide the line is too long and, therefore, do not enter the line (*balking*).

Queue Discipline

Queue discipline The order in which customers are processed.

Queue discipline refers to the order in which customers are processed. All but one of the models to be described shortly assume that service is provided on a *first-come, first-served* basis. This is perhaps the most commonly encountered rule. There is first-come service at banks, stores, theaters, restaurants, four-way stop signs, registration lines, and so on. Examples of systems that do not serve on a first-come basis include hospital emergency rooms, rush orders in a factory, and mainframe computer processing of jobs. In these and similar situations, customers do not all represent the same waiting costs; those with the highest costs (e.g., the most seriously ill) are processed first, even though other customers may have arrived earlier.

MEASURES OF WAITING-LINE PERFORMANCE

The operations manager typically looks at five measures when evaluating existing or proposed service systems. They relate to potential customer dissatisfaction and costs:

1. The average number of customers waiting, either in line or in the system.
2. The average time customers wait, either in line or in the system.
3. System utilization, which refers to the percentage of capacity utilized.
4. The implied cost of a given level of capacity and its related waiting line.
5. The probability that an arrival will have to wait for service.

Of these measures, system utilization bears some elaboration. It reflects the extent to which the servers are busy rather than idle. On the surface, it might seem that the operations manager would want to seek 100 percent utilization. However, as Figure 18.6 illustrates, increases in system utilization are achieved at the expense of increases in both the length of the waiting line and the average waiting time. In fact, these values become exceedingly large as utilization approaches 100 percent. The implication is that under normal circumstances, 100 percent utilization is not a realistic goal. Even if it were, 100 percent utilization of service personnel is not good; they need some slack time. Thus, instead, the operations manager should try to achieve a system that minimizes the sum of waiting costs and capacity costs.

FIGURE 18.6
The average number waiting in line and the average time customers wait in line increase exponentially as the system utilization increases

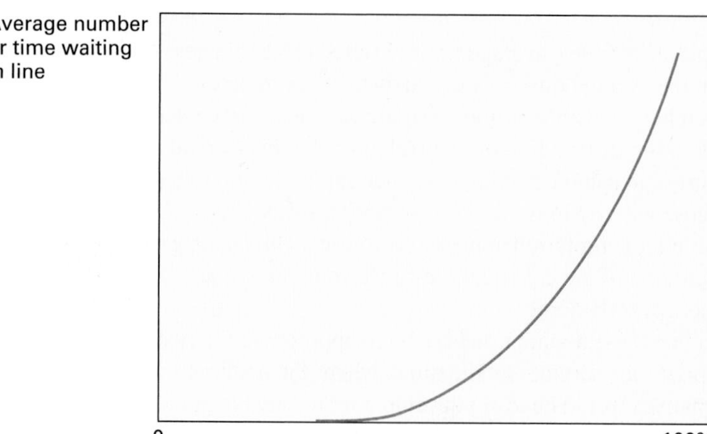

QUEUING MODELS: INFINITE-SOURCE

Many queuing models are available for a manager or analyst to choose from. The discussion here includes four of the most basic and most widely used models. The purpose is to provide an exposure to a range of models rather than an extensive coverage of the field. All assume a Poisson arrival rate. Moreover, the models pertain to a system operating under *steady-state* conditions; that is, they assume the average arrival and service rates are stable. The four models described are

1. Single server, exponential service time.
2. Single server, constant service time.
3. Multiple servers, exponential service time.
4. Multiple priority service, exponential service time.

Note that the terms "server" and "channel" mean the same thing. To facilitate your use of waiting-line models, Table 18.1 provides a list of the symbols used for the infinite-source models.

Basic Relationships

Certain basic relationships hold for all infinite-source models. Knowledge of these can be very helpful in deriving desired performance measures, given a few key values. Here are the basic relationships:

Note: The arrival and service rates, represented by λ and μ, must be in the same units (e.g., customers per hour, customers per minute).

System utilization: This reflects the ratio of demand (as measured by the arrival rate) to supply or capacity (as measured by the product of the number of servers, M, and the service rate, μ).

$$\rho = \frac{\lambda}{M\mu} \tag{18–1}$$

The average number of customers being served:

$$r = \frac{\lambda}{\mu} \tag{18–2}$$

TABLE 18.1
Infinite-source symbols

Symbol	Represents
λ	Customer arrival rate
μ	Service rate per server
L_q	The average number of customers waiting for service
L_s	The average number of customers in the system (waiting and/or being served)
r	The average number of customers being served
ρ	The system utilization
W_q	The average time customers wait in line
W_s	The average time customers spend in the system (waiting in line and service time)
$1/\mu$	Service time
P_0	The probability of zero units in the system
P_n	The probability of n units in the system
M	The number of servers
L_{max}	The maximum expected number waiting in line

For nearly all queuing systems, there is a relationship between the average time a unit spends in the system or queue and the average number of units in the system or queue. According to Little's law, for a stable system, the average number of customers in line or in the system is equal to the average customer arrival rate multiplied by the average time in line or in the system. That is,

$$L_s = \lambda W_s \quad \text{and} \quad L_q = \lambda W_q$$

The implications of this are important to analysis of waiting lines. The relationships are independent of any probability distribution and require no assumptions about which customers arrive or are serviced, or the order in which they are served. It also means that knowledge of any two of the three variables can be used to obtain the third variable. For example, knowing the arrival rate and the average number in line, one can solve for the average waiting time.

The average *number* of customers

Waiting in line for service: L_q [Model dependent. Obtain using a table or formula.]

In the system (line plus being served): $L_s = L_q + r$ (18–3)

The average *time* customers are

Waiting in line: $W_q = \frac{L_q}{\lambda}$ (18–4)

In the system: $W_s = W_q + \frac{1}{\mu} = \frac{L_s}{\lambda}$ (18–5)

All infinite-source models require that system utilization be less than 1.0; the models apply only to underloaded systems.

The average number waiting in line, L_q, is a key value because it is a determinant of some of the other measures of system performance, such as the average number in the system, the average time in line, and the average time in the system. Hence, L_q will usually be one of the first values you will want to determine in problem solving.

Figure 18.7 can help you relate the symbols to the basic relationships in a queuing system.

EXAMPLE 1

www.mhhe.com/stevenson11e

Customers arrive at a bakery at an average rate of 18 per hour on weekday mornings. The arrival distribution can be described by a Poisson distribution with a mean of 18. Each clerk can serve a customer in an average of three minutes; this time can be described by an exponential distribution with a mean of 3.0 minutes.

a. What are the arrival and service *rates?*

b. Compute the average number of customers being served at any time.

c. Suppose it has been determined that the average number of customers waiting in line is 8.1. Compute the average number of customers in the system (i.e., waiting in line or being served), the average time customers wait in line, and the average time in the system.

d. Determine the system utilization for $M = 1$, 2, and 3 servers.

FIGURE 18.7
Basic relationships

	Line	+	Service	=	System
Customers ⟶	000	→	[0]	→	0000
Average number waiting:	L_q	+	$\frac{\lambda}{\mu}$	=	L_s
Average time waiting:	$W_q = \frac{L_q}{\lambda}$	+	$\frac{1}{\mu}$	=	W_s

SOLUTION

a. The arrival rate is given in the problem: $\lambda = 18$ customers per hour. Change the service *time* to a comparable hourly rate. Thus,

60 minutes per hour/3minutes per customer $= \mu = 20$ customers per hour

b. $r = \dfrac{\lambda}{\mu} = \dfrac{18}{20} = .90$ customer.

c. Given: $L_q = 8.1$ customers.

$L_s = L_q + r = 8.1 + .90 = 9.0$ customers

$$W_q = \frac{L_q}{\lambda} = \frac{8.1}{18} = .45 \text{ hour}$$

W_s = Waiting in line plus service

$$= W_q + \frac{1}{\mu} = .45 + \frac{1}{20} = .50 \text{ hour}$$

d. System utilization is $\rho = \dfrac{\lambda}{M\mu}$.

$$\text{For } M = 1,\ \rho = \frac{18}{1(20)} = .90$$

$$\text{For } M = 2,\ \rho = \frac{18}{2(20)} = .45$$

$$\text{For } M = 3,\ \rho = \frac{18}{3(20)} = .30$$

Note that as the system capacity as measured by $M\mu$ increases, the system utilization for a given arrival rate decreases.

Single Server, Exponential Service Time, M/M/1[1]

The simplest model involves a system that has one server (or a single crew). The queue discipline is first-come, first-served, and it is assumed that the customer arrival rate can be approximated by a Poisson distribution and service time by a negative exponential distribution. There is no limit on length of queue.

Table 18.2 lists the formulas for the single-server model, which should be used in conjunction with Formulas 18–1 through 18–5.

TABLE 18.2
Formulas for basic single-server model

Performance Measure	Equation	
Average number in line	$L_q = \dfrac{\lambda^2}{\mu(\mu - \lambda)}$	(18–6)
Probability of zero units in the system	$P_0 = 1 - \left(\dfrac{\lambda}{\mu}\right)$	(18–7)
Probability of *n* units in the system	$P_n = P_0\left(\dfrac{\lambda}{\mu}\right)^n$	(18–8a)
Probability of less than *n* units in the system	$P_{<n} = 1 - \left(\dfrac{\lambda}{\mu}\right)^n$	(18–8b)

[1]This notation is commonly used to specify waiting-line models. The first symbol refers to arrivals, the second to service, and the third to the number of servers. M stands for a rate that can be described by a Poisson distribution or, equivalently, a time that can be described by an exponential distribution. Hence, M/M/1 indicates a Poisson arrival rate, a Poisson service rate, and one server. The symbol D is used to denote a deterministic (i.e., constant) service rate. Thus the notation M/D/I would indicate the arrival rate is Poisson and the service rate is constant. Finally, the notation M/M/S would indicate multiple servers.

EXAMPLE 2

www.mhhe.com/stevenson11e

An airline is planning to open a satellite ticket desk in a new shopping plaza, staffed by one ticket agent. It is estimated that requests for tickets and information will average 15 per hour, and requests will have a Poisson distribution. Service time is assumed to be exponentially distributed. Previous experience with similar satellite operations suggests that mean service time should average about three minutes per request. Determine each of the following:

a. System utilization.
b. Percentage of time the server (agent) will be idle.
c. The expected number of customers waiting to be served.
d. The average time customers will spend in the system.
e. The probability of zero customers in the system and the probability of four customers in the system.

SOLUTION

$\lambda = 15$ customers per hour

$$\mu = \frac{1}{\text{Service time}} = \frac{1 \text{ customer}}{3 \text{ minutes}} \times 60 \text{ minutes per hour}$$
$$= 20 \text{ customers per hour}$$

a. $\rho = \dfrac{\lambda}{M\mu} = \dfrac{15}{1(20)} = .75$

b. Percentage idle time $= 1 - \rho = 1 - .75 = .25$, or 25 percent

c. $L_q = \dfrac{\lambda^2}{\mu(\mu - \lambda)} = \dfrac{15^2}{20(20 - 15)} = 2.25$ customers

d. $W_s = \dfrac{L_q}{\lambda} + \dfrac{1}{\mu} = \dfrac{2.25}{15} + \dfrac{1}{20} = .20$ hour, or 12 minutes

e. $P_0 = 1 - \dfrac{\lambda}{\mu} = 1 - \dfrac{15}{20} = .25$ and $P_4 = P_0\left(\dfrac{\lambda}{\mu}\right)^4 = .25\left(\dfrac{15}{20}\right)^4 = .079$

Single Server, Constant Service Time, M/D/1

As noted previously, waiting lines are a consequence of random, highly variable arrival and service rates. If a system can reduce or eliminate the variability of either or both, it can shorten waiting lines noticeably. A case in point is a system with constant service time. The effect of a constant service time is to cut in half the average number of customers waiting in line:

$$L_q = \frac{\lambda^2}{2\mu(\mu - \lambda)} \qquad (18\text{–}9)$$

The average time customers spend waiting in line is also cut in half. Similar improvements can be realized by smoothing arrival times (e.g., by use of appointments).

EXAMPLE 3

www.mhhe.com/stevenson11e

Wanda's Car Wash & Dry is an automatic, five-minute operation with a single bay. On a typical Saturday morning, cars arrive at a mean rate of eight per hour, with arrivals tending to follow a Poisson distribution. Find

a. The average number of cars in line.
b. The average time cars spend in line and service.

SOLUTION

$\lambda = 8$ cars per hour
$\mu = 1$ per 5 minutes, or 12 per hour

a. $L_q = \dfrac{\lambda^2}{2\mu(\mu - \lambda)} = \dfrac{8^2}{2(12)(12 - 8)} = .667$ car

b. $W_s = \dfrac{L_q}{\lambda} + \dfrac{1}{\mu} = \dfrac{.667}{8} + \dfrac{1}{12} = .167$ hour, or 10 minutes

Multiple Servers, M/M/S

A multiple-server system exists whenever two or more servers are working *independently* to provide service to customer arrivals. Use of the model involves the following assumptions:

1. A Poisson arrival rate and exponential service time.
2. Servers all work at the same average rate.
3. Customers form a single waiting line (in order to maintain first-come, first-served processing).

Formulas for the multiple-server model are listed in Table 18.3. Obviously, the multiple-server formulas are more complex than the single-server formulas, especially the formulas for L_q and P_0. These formulas are shown primarily for completeness; you can actually determine their values using Table 18.4, which gives values of L_q and P_0 for selected values of λ/μ and M.

To use Table 18.4, compute the value of λ/μ and round according to the number of decimal places given for that ratio in the table. Then simply read the values of L_q and P_0 for the appropriate number of channels, M. For instance, if $\lambda/\mu = 0.50$ and $M = 2$, the table provides a value of 0.033 for L_q and a value of .600 for P_0. These values can then be used to compute other measures of system performance. Note that the formulas in Table 18.3 and the values in Table 18.4 yield *average* amounts (i.e., expected values). Note also that Table 18.4 can be used for some single-channel problems (i.e., $M = 1$) as well.

TABLE 18.3
Multiple-server queuing formulas

Performance Measure	Equation	
Average number in line	$L_q = \dfrac{\lambda\mu\left(\dfrac{\lambda}{\mu}\right)^M}{(M-1)!(M\mu - \lambda)^2} P_0$	(18–10)
Probability of zero units in the system	$P_0 = \left[\displaystyle\sum_{n=0}^{M-1} \dfrac{\left(\dfrac{\lambda}{\mu}\right)^n}{n!} + \dfrac{\left(\dfrac{\lambda}{\mu}\right)^M}{M!\left(1 - \dfrac{\lambda}{M\mu}\right)}\right]^{-1}$	(18–11)
Average waiting time for an arrival not immediately served	$W_a = \dfrac{1}{M\mu - \lambda}$	(18–12)
Probability that an arrival will have to wait for service	$P_w = \dfrac{W_q}{W_a}$	(18–13)

TABLE 18.4
Infinite-source values for L_q and P_0 given λ/μ and M

λ/μ	M	L_q	P_0
0.15	1	0.026	.850
	2	0.001	.860
0.20	1	0.050	.800
	2	0.002	.818
0.25	1	0.083	.750
	2	0.004	.778
0.30	1	0.129	.700
	2	0.007	.739
0.35	1	0.188	.650
	2	0.011	.702
0.40	1	0.267	.600
	2	0.017	.667
0.45	1	0.368	.550
	2	0.024	.633
	3	0.002	.637
0.50	1	0.500	.500
	2	0.033	.600
	3	0.003	.606
0.55	1	0.672	.450
	2	0.045	.569
	3	0.004	.576
0.60	1	0.900	.400
	2	0.059	.538
	3	0.006	.548
0.65	1	1.207	.350
	2	0.077	.509
	3	0.008	.521
0.70	1	1.633	.300
	2	0.098	.481
	3	0.011	.495
0.75	1	2.250	.250
	2	0.123	.455
	3	0.015	.471
0.80	1	3.200	.200
	2	0.152	.429
	3	0.019	.447
0.85	1	4.817	.150
	2	0.187	.404
	3	0.024	.425
	4	0.003	.427
0.90	1	8.100	.100
	2	0.229	.379
	3	0.030	.403
	4	0.004	.406
0.95	1	18.050	.050
	2	0.277	.356
	3	0.037	.383
	4	0.005	.386
1.0	2	0.333	.333
	3	0.045	.364
	4	0.007	.367
1.1	2	0.477	.290
	3	0.066	.327
	4	0.011	.332
1.2	2	0.675	.250
	3	0.094	.294
	4	0.016	.300
	5	0.003	.301
1.3	2	0.951	.212
	3	0.130	.264
	4	0.023	.271
	5	0.004	.272
1.4	2	1.345	.176
	3	0.177	.236
	4	0.032	.245
	5	0.006	.246
1.5	2	1.929	.143
	3	0.237	.211
	4	0.045	.221
	5	0.009	.223
1.6	2	2.844	.111
	3	0.313	.187
	4	0.060	.199
	5	0.012	.201
1.7	2	4.426	.081
	3	0.409	.166
	4	0.080	.180
	5	0.017	.182
1.8	2	7.674	.053
	3	0.532	.146
	4	0.105	.162
	5	0.023	.165
1.9	2	17.587	.026
	3	0.688	.128
	4	0.136	.145
	5	0.030	.149
	6	0.007	.149
2.0	3	0.889	.111
	4	0.174	.130
	5	0.040	.134
	6	0.009	.135
2.1	3	1.149	.096
	4	0.220	.117
	5	0.052	.121
	6	0.012	.122
2.2	3	1.491	.081
	4	0.277	.105
	5	0.066	.109
	6	0.016	.111
2.3	3	1.951	.068
	4	0.346	.093
	5	0.084	.099
	6	0.021	.100
2.4	3	2.589	.056
	4	0.431	.083
	5	0.105	.089
	6	0.027	.090
	7	0.007	.091
2.5	3	3.511	.045
	4	0.533	.074
	5	0.130	.080
	6	0.034	.082
	7	0.009	.082
2.6	3	4.933	.035
	4	0.658	.065
	5	0.161	.072
	6	0.043	.074
	7	0.011	.074
2.7	3	7.354	.025
	4	0.811	.057
	5	0.198	.065
	6	0.053	.067
	7	0.014	.067
2.8	3	12.273	.016
	4	1.000	.050
	5	0.241	.058
	6	0.066	.060
	7	0.018	.061
2.9	3	27.193	.008
	4	1.234	.044
	5	0.293	.052
	6	0.081	.054
	7	0.023	.055
3.0	4	1.528	.038
	5	0.354	.047
	6	0.099	.049
	7	0.028	.050
	8	0.008	.050
3.1	4	1.902	.032
	5	0.427	.042
	6	0.120	.044
	7	0.035	.045
	8	0.010	.045
3.2	4	2.386	.027
	5	0.513	.037
	6	0.145	.040
	7	0.043	.040
	8	0.012	.041
3.3	4	3.027	.023
	5	0.615	.033
	6	0.174	.036
	7	0.052	.037
	8	0.015	.037

(continued)

TABLE 18.4
(Concluded)

λ/μ	M	L_q	P_0	λ/μ	M	L_q	P_0	λ/μ	M	L_q	P_0
3.4	4	3.906	.019	4.3	7	0.289	.130	5.2	6	4.301	.003
	5	0.737	.029		8	0.097	.013		7	1.081	.005
	6	0.209	.032		9	0.033	.014		8	0.368	.005
	7	0.063	.033		10	0.011	.014		9	0.135	.005
	8	0.019	.033	4.4	5	5.268	.006		10	0.049	.005
3.5	4	5.165	.015		6	1.078	.010		11	0.018	.006
	5	0.882	.026		7	0.337	.012	5.3	6	5.303	.003
	6	0.248	.029		8	0.114	.012		7	1.249	.004
	7	0.076	.030		9	0.039	.012		8	0.422	.005
	8	0.023	.030		10	0.013	.012		9	0.155	.005
	9	0.007	.030	4.5	5	6.862	.005		10	0.057	.005
3.6	4	7.090	.011		6	1.265	.009		11	0.021	.005
	5	1.055	.023		7	0.391	.010		12	0.007	.005
	6	0.295	.026		8	0.134	.011	5.4	6	6.661	.002
	7	0.019	.027		9	0.046	.011		7	1.444	.004
	8	0.028	.027		10	0.015	.011		8	0.483	.004
	9	0.008	.027	4.6	5	9.289	.004		9	0.178	.004
3.7	4	10.347	.008		6	1.487	.008		10	0.066	.004
	5	1.265	.020		7	0.453	.009		11	0.024	.005
	6	0.349	.023		8	0.156	.010		12	0.009	.005
	7	0.109	.024		9	0.054	.010	5.5	6	8.590	.002
	8	0.034	.025		10	0.018	.010		7	1.674	.003
	9	0.010	.025	4.7	5	13.382	.003		8	0.553	.004
3.8	4	16.937	.005		6	1.752	.007		9	0.204	.004
	5	1.519	.017		7	0.525	.008		10	0.077	.004
	6	0.412	.021		8	0.181	.009		11	0.028	.004
	7	0.129	.022		9	0.064	.009		12	0.010	.004
	8	0.041	.022		10	0.022	.009	5.6	6	11.519	.001
	9	0.013	.022	4.8	5	21.641	.002		7	1.944	.003
3.9	4	36.859	.002		6	2.071	.006		8	0.631	.003
	5	1.830	.015		7	0.607	.008		9	0.233	.004
	6	0.485	.019		8	0.209	.008		10	0.088	.004
	7	0.153	.020		9	0.074	.008		11	0.033	.004
	8	0.050	.020		10	0.026	.008		12	0.012	.004
	9	0.016	.020	4.9	5	46.566	.001	5.7	6	16.446	.001
4.0	5	2.216	.013		6	2.459	.005		7	2.264	.002
	6	0.570	.017		7	0.702	.007		8	0.721	.003
	7	0.180	.018		8	0.242	.007		9	0.266	.003
	8	0.059	.018		9	0.087	.007		10	0.102	.003
	9	0.019	.018		10	0.031	.007		11	0.038	.003
4.1	5	2.703	.011		11	0.011	.007		12	0.014	.003
	6	0.668	.015	5.0	6	2.938	.005	5.8	6	26.373	.001
	7	0.212	.016		7	0.810	.006		7	2.648	.002
	8	0.070	.016		8	0.279	.006		8	0.823	.003
	9	0.023	.017		9	0.101	.007		9	0.303	.003
4.2	5	3.327	.009		10	0.036	.007		10	0.116	.003
	6	0.784	.013		11	0.013	.007		11	0.044	.003
	7	0.248	.014	5.1	6	3.536	.004		12	0.017	.003
	8	0.083	.015		7	0.936	.005	5.9	6	56.300	.000
	9	0.027	.015		8	0.321	.006		7	3.113	.002
	10	0.009	.015		9	0.117	.006		8	0.939	.002
4.3	5	4.149	.008		10	0.042	.006		9	0.345	.003
	6	0.919	.012		11	0.015	.006		10	0.133	.003

EXAMPLE 4

www.mhhe.com/stevenson11e

Alpha Taxi and Hauling Company has seven cabs stationed at the airport. The company has determined that during the late-evening hours on weeknights, customers request cabs at a rate that follows the Poisson distribution with a mean of 6.6 per hour. Service time is exponential with a mean of 50 minutes per customer. Assume that there is one customer per cab. Find each of the performance measures listed in Table 18.3 and the system utilization.

SOLUTION

$\lambda = 6.6$ per hour $\quad M = 7$ cabs (servers)

$$\mu = \frac{1 \text{ customer per trip}}{50 \text{ minutes per trip} \div 60 \text{ minutes per hour}}$$

$$= 1.2 \text{ customers per hour per cab}$$

$\lambda/\mu = 5.5$

From Table 18.4 with $M = 7$,

$$L_q = 1.674 \text{ customers} \quad \text{and} \quad P_0 = .003$$

$$W_a = \frac{1}{M\mu - \lambda} = \frac{1}{7(1.2) - 6.6} = .556 \text{ hour, or } 33.36 \text{ minutes}$$

$$W_q = \frac{L_q}{\lambda} = \frac{1.674}{6.6} = .2536 \text{ hour, or } 15.22 \text{ minutes}$$

$$P_W = \frac{W_q}{W_a} = \frac{.2536}{.556} = .456$$

$$\rho = \frac{\lambda}{M\mu} = \frac{6.6}{7(1.2)} = .786$$

www.mhhe.com/stevenson11e

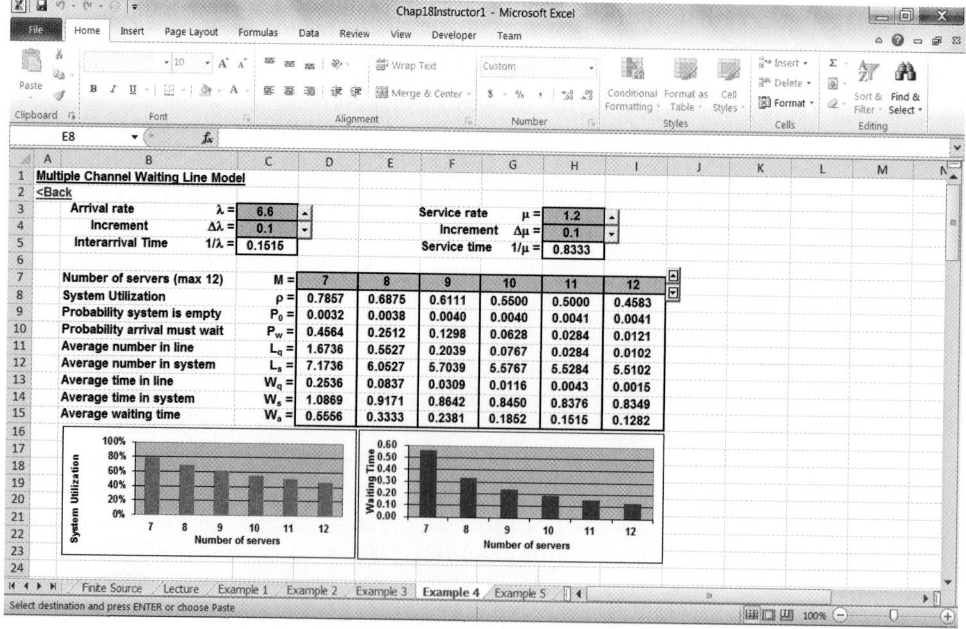
Multiple Channel Waiting Line Model

<Back

Arrival rate	$\lambda =$ 6.6		Service rate	$\mu =$ 1.2	
Increment	$\Delta\lambda =$ 0.1		Increment	$\Delta\mu =$ 0.1	
Interarrival Time	$1/\lambda =$ 0.1515		Service time	$1/\mu =$ 0.8333	

Number of servers (max 12)	M =	7	8	9	10	11	12
System Utilization	$\rho =$	0.7857	0.6875	0.6111	0.5500	0.5000	0.4583
Probability system is empty	$P_0 =$	0.0032	0.0038	0.0040	0.0040	0.0041	0.0041
Probability arrival must wait	$P_w =$	0.4564	0.2512	0.1298	0.0628	0.0284	0.0121
Average number in line	$L_q =$	1.6736	0.5527	0.2039	0.0767	0.0284	0.0102
Average number in system	$L_s =$	7.1736	6.0527	5.7039	5.5767	5.5284	5.5102
Average time in line	$W_q =$	0.2536	0.0837	0.0309	0.0116	0.0043	0.0015
Average time in system	$W_s =$	1.0869	0.9171	0.8642	0.8450	0.8376	0.8349
Average waiting time	$W_a =$	0.5556	0.3333	0.2381	0.1852	0.1515	0.1282

The Excel template also can be used to solve Example 4. After entering $\lambda = 6.6$ and $\mu = 1.2$ at the top of the template, the queuing statistics for 7 servers are shown in the first column of the table in the template. The template also provides queuing statistics for 8 through 12 servers for comparison, although these are not required for this example. In addition, the template can be used to increment λ, μ, or the number of servers to further investigate the queuing system.

The process also can be worked in reverse; that is, an analyst can determine the capacity needed to achieve specified levels of various performance measures. This approach is illustrated in the following example.

EXAMPLE 5

Alpha Taxi and Hauling also plans to have cabs at a new rail station. The expected arrival rate is 4.8 customers per hour, and the service rate (including return time to the rail station) is expected to be 1.5 per hour. How many cabs will be needed to achieve an average time in line of 20 minutes or less?

SOLUTION

$\lambda = 4.8$ customers per hour

$\mu = 1.5$ customers per hour

$M = ?$

$$r = \frac{\lambda}{\mu} = \frac{4.8}{1.5} = 3.2 \text{ customers}$$

W_q (desired) $= 20$ minutes, or .333 hour

Using $L_q = \lambda \times W_q$, you can solve for L_q: 4.8/hour (.333 hour) = 1.6 units. Thus, the average number waiting should not exceed 1.6 customers. Referring to Table 18.4, with $r = 3.2$, $L_q = 2.386$ for $M = 4$ and 0.513 for $M = 5$. Hence, five cabs will be needed.

Finally, note that in a situation where there are multiple servers, each with a separate line (e.g., a supermarket), each line would be treated as a single-server system.

Cost Analysis

The design of a service system often reflects the desire of management to balance the cost of capacity with the expected cost of customers waiting in the system. (Note that customer waiting cost refers to the costs incurred by the organization due to customer waiting.) For example, in designing loading docks for a warehouse, the cost of docks plus loading crews must be balanced against the cost of trucks and drivers that will be in the system, both while waiting to be unloaded and while actually being unloaded. Similarly, the cost of having a mechanic wait for tools at a tool crib must be balanced against the cost of servers at the crib. In cases where the customers are not employees (e.g., retail sales), the costs can include lost sales when customers refuse to wait, the cost of providing waiting space, and the cost of added congestion (lost business, shoplifting).

The optimal capacity (usually in terms of number of channels) is one that minimizes the sum of customer waiting costs and capacity or server costs. Thus, the goal is

$$\text{Minimize} \quad \begin{matrix}\text{Total}\\ \text{cost}\end{matrix} = \begin{matrix}\text{Customer}\\ \text{waiting cost}\end{matrix} + \begin{matrix}\text{Capacity}\\ \text{cost}\end{matrix}$$

The simplest approach to a cost analysis involves computing *system* costs, that is, computing the costs for customers in the system and total capacity cost. Capacity cost typically is a function of the number of servers.

An iterative process is used to identify the capacity size that will minimize total costs. Capacity is incremented one unit at a time (e.g., increase the number of channels by one) and the total cost is computed at each increment. Because the total cost curve is U-shaped, usually the total cost will initially decrease as capacity is increased and then it will eventually begin to increase. Once it begins to increase, additional increases in capacity will cause it to continue to increase. Hence, once that occurs, the optimal capacity size can be readily identified. Figure 18.8 illustrates this

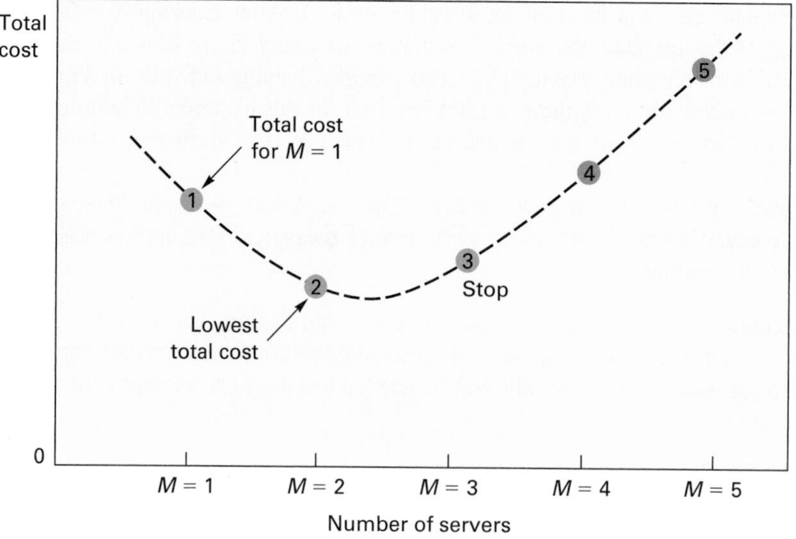

FIGURE 18.8
As the number of servers is increased, the optimal number of servers becomes apparent when the total cost begins to increase

approach. Find the total cost for $M = 1$, then $M = 2$, $M = 3$, and continue as long as the total costs continue to decline. However, as soon as the total cost begins to rise, as it does at $M = 3$ in Figure 18.8, the search can be stopped. The optimal solution is apparent; it is $M = 2$. There would be no need to continue computing total costs for additional servers because, as you can see, the total costs will continue to increase as more servers are added. *Note:* Although in many instances the starting point is $M = 1$, the general rule is to begin at the smallest number of servers for which the system is underloaded (i.e., the system utilization is < 1.00).

The computation of customer waiting costs is based on the average *number* of customers in the *system.* This is perhaps not intuitively obvious; instead, it might seem that customer waiting *time* in the system would be more appropriate. However, that approach would pertain to only *one* customer—it would not convey information concerning *how many* customers would wait that long. Obviously, an average of five customers waiting would involve a lower waiting cost than an average of nine. Therefore, it is necessary to focus on the *number* waiting. Moreover, if on average two customers are in the system, this is equivalent to having *exactly* two customers in the system at all times, even though in reality there will be times when zero, one, two, three, or more customers are in the system.

EXAMPLE 6

www.mhhe.com/stevenson11e

Trucks arrive at a warehouse at a rate of 15 per hour during business hours. Crews can unload the trucks at a rate of five per hour. The high unloading rate is due to cargo being containerized. Recent changes in wage rates have caused the warehouse manager to reexamine the question of how many crews to use. The new rates are: Crew and dock cost is \$100 per hour; truck and driver cost is \$120 per hour.

SOLUTION

(L_q values are from Table 18.4, using $\frac{\lambda}{\mu} = \frac{15}{5} = 3.0$.)

Number of Crews	Crew and Dock Cost	$\left[L_s = L_q + \frac{\lambda}{\mu}\right]$ Average Number in System	$[L_s \times \$120]$ Driver/Truck Cost	Total Cost
4	\$400	1.528 + 3.0 = 4.528	\$543.36	\$943.36
5	500	.354 + 3.0 = 3.354	402.48	902.48 (minimum)
6	600	.099 + 3.0 = 3.099	371.88	971.88
7	700	.028 + 3.0 = 3.028	363.36	1,063.36

Five crews will minimize the total cost. Because the total cost will continue to increase once the minimum is reached, it is not really necessary to compute total costs for crew sizes larger than six, because total cost increased as the crew size was increased from five to six, indicating that a crew of five is optimal.

One additional point should be made concerning cost analysis. Because both customer waiting costs and capacity costs often reflect estimated amounts, the apparent optimal solution may not represent the true optimum. One ramification of this is that when computations are shown to the nearest penny, or even the nearest dollar, the total cost figures may seem to imply a higher degree of precision than is really justified by the cost estimates. This is compounded by the fact that arrival and service rates may either be approximations or not be exactly represented by the Poisson/exponential distribution. Another ramification is that if cost estimates can be obtained as *ranges* (e.g., customer waiting cost is estimated to range between $40 and $50 per hour), total costs should be computed using both ends of the range to see whether the optimal solution is affected. If it is, management must decide whether to expend additional effort to obtain more precise cost estimates or choose one of the two indicated optimal solutions. Management would most likely choose to employ the latter strategy if there were little disparity between total costs of various capacity levels close to the indicated optimal solutions.

Maximum Line Length

Another question that often comes up in capacity planning is the amount of space to allocate for waiting lines. Theoretically, with an infinite population source, the waiting line can become infinitely long. This implies that no matter how much space is allocated for a waiting line, one can never be completely sure that the space requirements won't exceed that amount. Nonetheless, as a practical matter, one can determine a line length that will not be exceeded a specified proportion of the time. For instance, an analyst may wish to know the length of line that will probably not be exceeded 98 percent of the time, or perhaps 99 percent of the time, and use that number as a planning value.

The approximate line length that will satisfy a specified percentage can be determined by solving the following equation for L_{max}:

$$L_{max} = \frac{\log K}{\log \rho} \text{ or } \frac{\ln K}{\ln \rho} \quad (18\text{–}14)$$

where

$$K = \frac{1 - \frac{\text{Specified}}{\text{percentage}}}{L_q(1 - \rho)}$$

The resulting value of L_{max} will not usually be an integer. Generally, round *up* to the next integer and treat the value as L_{max}. However, as a practical matter, if the computed value of L_{max} is less than .10 above the next lower integer, round down. Thus, 15.2 would be rounded to 16, but 15.06 would be rounded to 15.

EXAMPLE 7

Determine the maximum length of a waiting line for specified probabilities of 95 percent and 98 percent, for a system in which $M = 2$, $\lambda = 8$ per hour, and $\mu = 5$ per hour.

SOLUTION

$$r = \frac{8}{5} = 1.6 \quad \text{and} \quad \rho = \frac{8}{2(5)} = .80$$

From Table 18.4, $L_q = 2.844$ customers. For 95 percent, using Formula 18–14:

$$K = \frac{1 - .95}{2.844(1 - .80)} = .088$$

$$L_{max} = \frac{\ln .088}{\ln .80} = \frac{-2.4304}{-.2231} = 10.89, \text{ which rounds to } 11$$

For 98 percent:

$$K = \frac{1 - .98}{2.844(1 - .80)} = .35$$

$$L_{max} = \frac{\ln .035}{\ln .80} = \frac{-3.352}{-.2231} = 15.02, \text{ which rounds to } 15$$

Multiple Priorities

In many queuing systems, processing occurs on a first-come, first-served basis. However, there are situations in which that rule is inappropriate. The reason is that the waiting cost or penalty incurred is not the same for all customers. In a hospital emergency waiting room, a wide variety of injuries and illnesses needs treatment. Some may be minor (e.g., sliver in finger) and others may be much more serious, even life-threatening. It is more reasonable to treat the most serious cases first, letting the nonserious cases wait until all serious cases have been treated. Similarly, computer processing of jobs often follows rules other than first-come, first-served (e.g., shortest job first). In such cases, a **multiple-priority model** is useful for describing customer waiting times.

Multiple-priority model Customers are processed according to some measure of importance.

In these systems, arriving customers are assigned to one of several *priority classes,* or categories, according to a predetermined assignment method (e.g., in a hospital emergency room, heart attacks, serious injuries, and unconscious persons are assigned to the highest priority class; sprains, minor cuts, bruises, and rashes are assigned to the lowest class; and other problems are assigned to one or more intermediate classes). Customers are then processed by class, highest class first. Within each class, processing is first-come, first-served. Thus, all customers in the highest class would be processed before those in the next lower class, then processing would move to that class, and then to the next lower class. Exceptions would occur only if a higher-priority customer arrived; that customer would be processed *after* the customer currently being processed (i.e., service would not be *preemptive*).

This model incorporates all of the assumptions of the basic multiple-server model except that it uses priority serving instead of first-come, first-served. Arrivals to the system are assigned a priority as they arrive (e.g., highest priority = 1, next priority class = 2, next priority class = 3, and so on). An existing queue might look something like this:

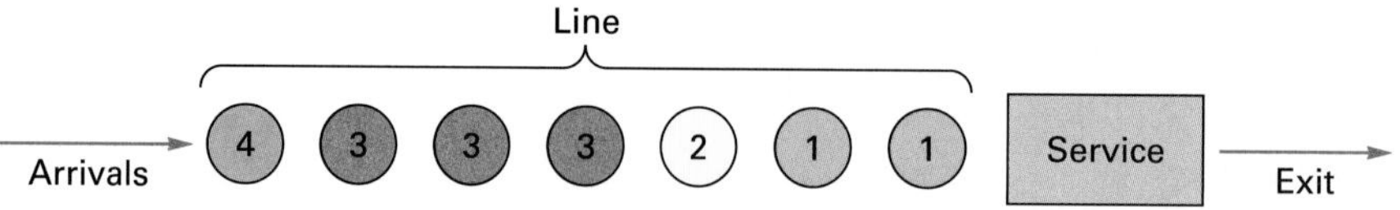

Within each class, waiting units are processed in the order they arrived (i.e., first-come, first-served). Thus, in this sequence, the first 1 would be processed as soon as a server was available. The second 1 would be processed when that server or another one became available. If, in the interim, another 1 arrived, it would be next in line *ahead of the first 2.* If there were no new arrivals, the only 2 would be processed by the next available server. At that point, if a new 1 or 2 arrived, it would be processed ahead of the 3s and the 4. Conversely, if a new 4 arrived, it would take its place at the end of the line.

Obviously, a unit with a low priority could conceivably wait a rather long time for processing. In some cases, units that have waited more than some specified time are reassigned to a higher priority.

Table 18.5 gives the appropriate formulas for this multiple-channel priority service model. However, due to the extent of computations involved, it is best to use the appropriate Excel template on the Web site for computations.

EXAMPLE 8

A machine shop handles tool repairs in a large company. As each job arrives in the shop, it is assigned a priority based on urgency of the need for that tool. Requests for repair can be described by a Poisson distribution. Arrival rates are: $\lambda_1 = 2$ per hour, $\lambda_2 = 2$ per hour, and $\lambda_3 = 1$ per hour. The service rate is one tool per hour for each server, and there are six servers in the shop. Determine the following information.

a. The system utilization.

b. The average time a tool in each of the priority classes will wait for service.

c. The average time a tool spends in the system for each priority class.

d. The average number of tools waiting for repair in each class.

TABLE 18.5
Multiple-server priority service model

Performance Measure	Formula	Formula Number
System utilization	$\rho = \frac{\lambda}{M\mu}$	(18–15)
Intermediate values (L_q from Table 18.4)	$A = \frac{\lambda}{(1-\rho)L_q}$	(18–16)
	$B_k = 1 - \sum_{c=1}^{k} \frac{\lambda_c}{M\mu}$	(18–17)
	$(B_0 = 1)$	
Average waiting time in line for units in *k*th priority class	$W_k = \frac{1}{A \cdot B_{k-1} \cdot B_k}$	(18–18)
Average time in the system for units in the *k*th priority class	$W = W_k + \frac{1}{\mu}$	(18–19)
Average number waiting in line for units in the *k*th priority class	$L_k = \lambda_k \times W_k$	(18–20)

SOLUTION

$$\lambda = \Sigma\lambda_k = 2 + 2 + 1 = 5 \text{ customers per hour}$$

$$M = 6 \text{ servers}$$

$$\mu = 1 \text{ customer per hour}$$

Using the Excel template, the solution would appear as follows.

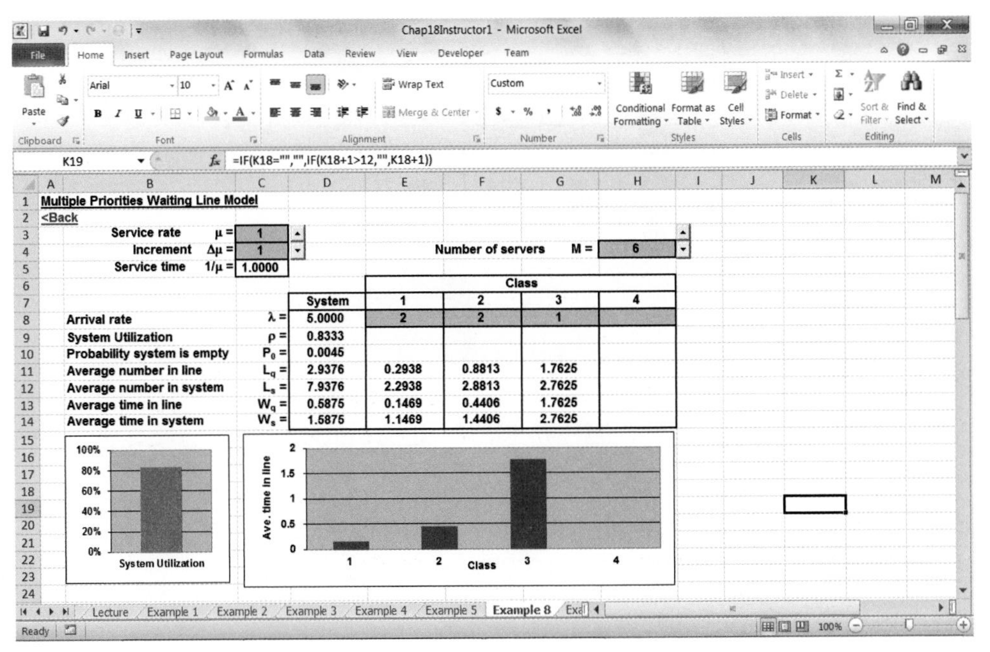

www.mhhe.com/stevenson11e

Revising Priorities. If any of the waiting times computed in Example 8 is deemed too long by management (e.g., a waiting time of .147 hour for tools in the first class might be too long), there are several options. One is to increase the number of servers. Another is to attempt to increase the service rate, say, by introducing new methods. If such options are not feasible, another approach is to reexamine the membership of each of the priority classifications because if some repair requests in the first priority class, for example, can be reassigned to the second priority class, this will tend to decrease the average waiting times for repair jobs in the highest priority classification, simply because the arrival rate of those items will be lower.

EXAMPLE 9

www.mhhe.com/stevenson11e

The manager of the repair shop, after consulting with the managers of the departments that use the shop's services, has revised the list of tools that are given the highest priorities. This is reflected by revised arrival rates. Suppose that the revised rates are: $\lambda_1 = 1.5$, $\lambda_2 = 2.5$, and λ_3 remains unchanged at 1.0. Determine the following information:

a. The system utilization.

b. The average waiting time for units in each priority class.

SOLUTION

$\lambda = \Sigma\lambda_k = 1.5 + 2.5 + 1.0 = 5.0$ customers per hour

$M = 6$ servers

$\mu = 1$ customer per hour

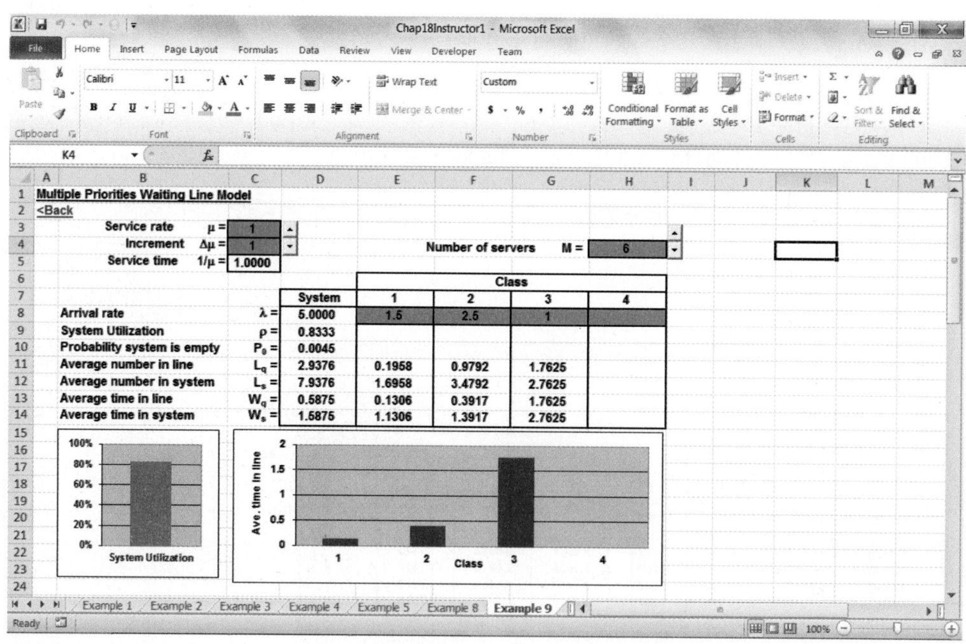

Multiple Priorities Waiting Line Model

<Back

Service rate μ = 1; Increment $\Delta\mu$ = 1; Service time $1/\mu$ = 1.0000; Number of servers M = 6

		System	Class 1	Class 2	Class 3	Class 4
Arrival rate	λ =	5.0000	1.5	2.5	1	
System Utilization	ρ =	0.8333				
Probability system is empty	P_0 =	0.0045				
Average number in line	L_q =	2.9376	0.1958	0.9792	1.7625	
Average number in system	L_s =	7.9376	1.6958	3.4792	2.7625	
Average time in line	W_q =	0.5875	0.1306	0.3917	1.7625	
Average time in system	W_s =	1.5875	1.1306	1.3917	2.7625	

a. As shown in the template, the system utilization is still 0.8333.

b. $W_1 = 0.1306$, $W_2 = 0.3917$, $W_3 = 1.7625$.

Example 9 offers several interesting results. One is that through reduction of the arrival rate of the highest priority class, the average waiting time for units in that class has decreased. In other words, removing some members of the highest class and placing them into the next lower class reduced the average waiting time for units that remained in the highest class. Note that the average waiting time for the second priority class also was reduced, even though units were added to that class. Although this may appear counterintuitive, it is necessary to recognize that the *total* waiting time (when all arrivals are taken into account) will remain unchanged. We can see this by noticing that the average *number* waiting (see Example 8, part *d*) is .294 + .884 + 1.765 = 2.943. In Example 9, using the average waiting times just computed, the average number waiting in all three classes is

$$\sum_{k=1}^{3} \lambda_k W_k = 1.5(.131) + 2.5(.393) + 1.0(1.765) = 2.944$$

Aside from a slight difference due to rounding, the totals are the same.

Another interesting observation is that the average waiting time for customers in the third priority class did not change from the preceding example. The reason for this is that the *total* arrival rate for the two higher-priority classes did not change, and the average arrival rate for this class did not change. Hence, units assigned to the lowest class must still contend with a combined arrival rate of 4 for the two higher-priority classes.

QUEUING MODEL: FINITE-SOURCE

The finite-source model is appropriate for cases in which the calling population is limited to a relatively small number of potential calls. For instance, one person may be responsible for handling breakdowns on 15 machines; thus, the size of the calling population is 15. However, there may be more than one server or channel; for example, due to a backlog of machines awaiting repairs, the manager might authorize an additional person to work on repairs.

As in the infinite-source models, arrival rates are required to be Poisson and service times exponential. A major difference between the finite- and infinite-source models is that the arrival rate of customers in a finite situation is *affected by* the length of the waiting line; the arrival rate decreases as the length of the line increases simply because there is a decreasing proportion of the population left to generate calls for service. The limit occurs when *all* of the population is waiting in line; at that point the arrival rate is zero since no additional units can arrive.

Because the mathematics of the finite-source model can be complex, analysts often use finite-queuing tables in conjunction with simple formulas to analyze these systems. Table 18.6 contains a list of the key formulas and definitions. You will find it helpful to study the diagram of a cycle that is presented in the table.

Table 18.7 is an abbreviated finite-queuing table used to obtain values of D and F. (Most of the formulas require a value for F.) In order to use the finite-queuing table, follow this procedure:

1. Identify the values for
   a. N, population size.
   b. M, number of servers/channels.
   c. T, average service time.
   d. U, average time between calls for service per customer.
2. Compute the service factor, $X = T/(T + U)$.
3. Locate the section of the finite-queuing tables for N.
4. Using the value of X as the point of entry, find the values of D and F that correspond to M.
5. Use the values of N, M, X, D, and F as needed to determine the values of the desired measures of system performance.

TABLE 18.6 Finite-source queuing formulas and notation

Performance Measure	Formulas		Notation[†]
Service factor	$X = \frac{T}{T+U}$	(18–21)	D = Probability that a customer will have to wait in line
Average number waiting	$L = N(1 - F)$	(18–22)	F = Efficiency factor: 1 − Percentage waiting in line
Average waiting time	$W = \frac{L(T+U)}{N-L} = \frac{T(1-F)}{XF}$	(18–23)	H = Average number of customers being served
Average number running	$J = NF(1 - X)$	(18–24)	J = Average number of customers not in line or in service
Average number being served	$H = FNX$	(18–25)	L = Average number of customers waiting for service
Number in population	$N = J + L + H$	(18–26)	M = Number of service channels
			N = Number of potential customers
			T = Average service time
			U = Average time between customer service requirements per customer
			W = Average time customers wait in line
			X = Service factor

Cycle

	Not waiting or being served	Waiting	Being served
Average number:	J	L	H
Average time:	U	W	T

$$F = \frac{J+H}{J+L+H}\ ^*$$

*The purpose of this formula is to provide an understanding of F. Because the value of F is needed to compute J, L, and H, the formulas cannot be used to actually compute F. The finite queuing tables must be used for that purpose.

†Adapted from L. G. Peck and R. N. Hazelwood, *Finite Queuing Tables* (New York: John Wiley & Sons, 1958). Reprinted by permission.

EXAMPLE 10

www.mhhe.com/stevenson11e

One operator loads and unloads a group of five machines. Service time is exponentially distributed with a mean of 10 minutes per cycle. Machines run for an average of 70 minutes between loading and unloading, and this time is also exponential. Find:

a. The average number of machines waiting for the operator.
b. The expected number of machines running.
c. Average downtime.
d. The probability that a machine will not have to wait for service.

SOLUTION

$N = 5$

$T = 10$ minutes

$M = 1$

$U = 70$ minutes

$$X = \frac{T}{T+U} = \frac{10}{10+70} = .125$$

TABLE 18.7
Finite-queuing tables

X	M	D	F
Population 5			
.012	1	.060	.999
.019	1	.095	.998
.025	1	.125	.997
.030	1	.149	.996
.034	1	.169	.995
.036	1	.179	.994
.040	1	.199	.993
.042	1	.208	.992
.044	1	.218	.991
.046	1	.228	.990
.050	1	.247	.989
.052	1	.257	.988
.054	1	.266	.987
.056	2	.018	.999
	1	.276	.985
.058	2	.019	.999
	1	.285	.984
.060	2	.020	.999
	1	.295	.983
.062	2	.022	.999
	1	.304	.982
.064	2	.023	.999
	1	.314	.981
.066	2	.024	.999
	1	.323	.979
.068	2	.026	.999
	1	.333	.978
.070	2	.027	.999
	1	.342	.977
.075	2	.031	.999
	1	.365	.973
.080	2	.035	.998
	1	.388	.969
.085	2	.040	.998
	1	.410	.965
.090	2	.044	.998
	1	.432	.960
.095	2	.049	.997
	1	.454	.955
.100	2	.054	.997
	1	.475	.950
.105	2	.059	.997
	1	.496	.945
.110	2	.065	.996
	1	.516	.939
.115	2	.017	.995
	1	.537	.933
.120	2	.076	.995
	1	.556	.927
.125	2	.082	.994
	1	.575	.920
.130	2	.089	.933
	1	.594	.914
.135	2	.095	.933
	1	.612	.907
.140	2	.102	.992
	1	.630	.900
.145	3	.011	.999
	2	.109	.991
	1	.647	.892
.150	3	.012	.999
	2	.115	.990
	1	.664	.885
.155	3	.013	.999
	2	.123	.989
	1	.680	.877
.160	3	.015	.999
	2	.130	.988
	1	.695	.869
.165	3	.016	.999
	2	.137	.987
	1	.710	.861
.170	3	.017	.999
	2	.145	.985
	1	.725	.853
.180	3	.021	.999
	2	.161	.983
	1	.752	.836
.190	3	.024	.998
	2	.117	.980
	1	.778	.819
.200	3	.028	.998
	2	.194	.976
	1	.801	.801
.210	3	.032	.998
	2	.211	.973
	1	.822	.783
.220	3	.036	.997
	2	.229	.969
	1	.842	.765
.230	3	.041	.997
	2	.247	.965
	1	.860	.747
.240	3	.046	.996
	2	.265	.960
	1	.876	.730
.250	3	.052	.995
	2	.284	.955
	1	.890	.712
.260	3	.058	.994
	2	.303	.950
	1	.903	.695
.270	3	.064	.994
	2	.323	.944
	1	.915	.677
.280	3	.071	.993
	2	.342	.938
	1	.925	.661
.290	4	.007	.999
	3	.079	.992
	2	.362	.932
	1	.934	.644
.300	4	.008	.999
	3	.086	.990
	2	.382	.926
	1	.942	.628
.310	4	.009	.999
	3	.094	.989
	2	.402	.919
	1	.950	.613
.320	4	.010	.999
	3	.103	.988
	2	.422	.912
	1	.956	.597
.330	4	.012	.999
	3	.112	.986
	2	.442	.904
	1	.962	.583
.340	4	.013	.999
	3	.121	.985
	2	.462	.896
	1	.967	.569
.360	4	.017	.998
	3	.141	.981
	2	.501	.880
	1	.975	.542
.380	4	.021	.998
	3	.163	.976
	2	.540	.863
	1	.981	.516
.400	4	.026	.997
	3	.186	.972
	2	.579	.845
	1	.986	.493
.420	4	.031	.997
	3	.211	.966
	2	.616	.826
	1	.989	.471
.440	4	.037	.996
.440	3	.238	.960
	2	.652	.807
	1	.992	.451
.460	4	.045	.995
	3	.266	.953
	2	.686	.787
	1	.994	.432
.480	4	.053	.994
	3	.296	.945
	2	.719	.767
	1	.996	.415
.500	4	.063	.992
	3	.327	.936
	2	.750	.748
	1	.997	.399
.520	4	.073	.991
	3	.359	.927
	2	.779	.728
	1	.998	.384
.540	4	.085	.989
	3	.392	.917
	2	.806	.708
	1	.998	.370
.560	4	.098	.986
	3	.426	.906
	2	.831	.689
	1	.999	.357
.580	4	.113	.984
	3	.461	.895
	2	.854	.670
	1	.999	.345
.600	4	.130	.981
	3	.497	.883
	2	.875	.652
	1	.999	.333
.650	4	.179	.972
	3	.588	.850
	2	.918	.608
	1	.999	.308
.700	4	.240	.960
	3	.678	.815
	2	.950	.568
	1	.999	.286
.750	4	.316	.944
	3	.763	.777
	2	.972	.532
.800	4	.410	.924
	3	.841	.739
	2	.987	.500

(continued)

TABLE 18.7
(Continued)

X	M	D	F	X	M	D	F	X	M	D	F	X	M	D	F
.850	4	.522	.900	.064	1	.547	.940	.135	2	.415	.952	.220	5	.030	.998
	3	.907	.702	.066	2	.126	.995		1	.907	.699		4	.124	.990
	2	.995	.470		1	.562	.936	.140	4	.028	.999		3	.366	.954
.900	4	.656	.871	.068	3	.020	.999		3	.132	.991		2	.761	.815
	3	.957	.666		2	.133	.994		2	.437	.947		1	.993	.453
	2	.998	.444		1	.577	.931		1	.919	.680	.230	5	.037	.998
.950	4	.815	.838	.070	3	.022	.999	.145	4	.032	.999		4	.142	.988
	3	.989	.631		2	.140	.994		3	.144	.990		3	.400	.947
Population 10					1	.591	.926		2	.460	.941		2	.791	.794
.016	1	.144	.997	.075	3	.026	.999		1	.929	.662		1	.995	.434
.019	1	.170	.996		2	.158	.992	.150	4	.036	.998	.240	5	.044	.997
.021	1	.188	.995		1	.627	.913		3	.156	.989		4	.162	.986
.023	1	.206	.994	.080	3	.031	.999		2	.483	.935		3	.434	.938
.025	1	.224	.993		2	.177	.990		1	.939	.644		2	.819	.774
.026	1	.232	.992		1	.660	.899	.155	4	.040	.998		1	.996	.416
.028	1	.250	.991	.085	3	.037	.999		3	.169	.987	.250	6	.010	.999
.030	1	.268	.990		2	.196	.988		2	.505	.928		5	.052	.997
.032	2	.033	.999		1	.692	.883		1	.947	.627		4	.183	.983
	1	.285	.988	.090	3	.043	.998	.160	4	.044	.998		3	.469	.929
.034	2	.037	.999		2	.216	.986		3	.182	.986		2	.844	.753
	1	.301	.986		1	.722	.867		2	.528	.921		1	.997	.400
.036	2	.041	.999	.095	3	.049	.998		1	.954	.610	.260	6	.013	.999
	1	.320	.984		2	.237	.984	.165	4	.049	.997		5	.060	.996
.038	2	.046	.999		1	.750	.850		3	.195	.984		4	.205	.980
	1	.337	.982	.100	3	.056	.998		2	.550	.914		3	.503	.919
.040	2	.050	.999		2	.258	.981		1	.961	.594		2	.866	.732
	1	.354	.980		1	.776	.832	.170	4	.054	.997		1	.998	.384
.042	2	.055	.999	.105	3	.064	.997		3	.209	.982	.270	6	.015	.999
	1	.371	.978		2	.279	.978		2	.571	.906		5	.070	.995
.044	2	.060	.998		1	.800	.814		1	.966	.579		4	.228	.976
	1	.388	.975	.110	3	.072	.997	.180	5	.013	.999		3	.537	.908
.046	2	.065	.998		2	.301	.974		4	.066	.996		2	.886	.712
	1	.404	.973		1	.822	.795		3	.238	.978		1	.999	.370
.048	2	.071	.998	.115	3	.081	.996		2	.614	.890	.280	6	.018	.999
	1	.421	.970		2	.324	.971		1	.975	.890		5	.081	.994
.050	2	.076	.998		1	.843	.776	.190	5	.016	.999		4	.252	.972
	1	.437	.967	.120	4	.016	.999		4	.078	.995		3	.571	.896
.052	2	.082	.997		3	.090	.995		3	.269	.973		2	.903	.692
	1	.454	.963		2	.346	.967		2	.654	.873		1	.999	.357
.054	2	.088	.997		1	.861	.756		1	.982	.522	.290	6	.022	.999
	1	.470	.960	.125	4	.019	.999	.200	5	.020	.999		5	.093	.993
.056	2	.094	.997		3	.100	.994		4	.092	.994		4	.278	.968
	1	.486	.956		2	.369	.962		3	.300	.968		3	.603	.884
.058	2	.100	.996		1	.878	.737		2	.692	.854		2	.918	.672
	1	.501	.953	.130	4	.022	.999		1	.987	.497		1	.999	.345
.060	2	.106	.996		3	.110	.994	.210	5	.025	.999	.300	6	.026	.998
	1	.517	.949		2	.392	.958		4	.108	.992		5	.106	.991
.062	2	.113	.996		1	.893	.718		3	.333	.961		4	.304	.963
	1	.532	.945	.135	4	.025	.999		2	.728	.835		3	.635	.872
.064	2	.119	.995		3	.121	.993		1	.990	.474				

(continued)

TABLE 18.7
(Concluded)

X	M	D	F	X	M	D	F	X	M	D	F	X	M	D	F
.300	2	.932	.653	.400	6	.105	.991	.500	3	.972	.598	.650	7	.353	.954
	1	.999	.333		5	.292	.963		2	.999	.400		6	.651	.878
.310	6	.031	.998		4	.591	.887	.520	8	.026	.998		5	.882	.759
	5	.120	.990		3	.875	.728		7	.115	.989		4	.980	.614
	4	.331	.957		2	.991	.499		6	.316	.958		3	.999	.461
	3	.666	.858	.420	7	.034	.993		5	.606	.884	.700	9	.040	.997
	2	.943	.635		6	.130	.987		4	.864	.752		8	.200	.979
.320	6	.036	.998		5	.341	.954		3	.980	.575		7	.484	.929
	5	.135	.988		4	.646	.866		2	.999	.385		6	.772	.836
	4	.359	.952		3	.905	.700	.540	8	.034	.997		5	.940	.711
	3	.695	.845		2	.994	.476		7	.141	.986		4	.992	.571
	2	.952	.617	.440	7	.045	.997		6	.363	.949	.750	9	.075	.994
.330	6	.042	.997		6	.160	.984		5	.658	.867		8	.307	.965
	5	.151	.986		5	.392	.943		4	.893	.729		7	.626	.897
	4	.387	.945		4	.698	.845		3	.986	.555		6	.870	.792
	3	.723	.831		3	.928	.672	.560	8	.044	.996		5	.975	.666
	2	.961	.600		2	.996	.454		7	.171	.982		4	.998	.533
.340	7	.010	.999	.460	8	.011	.999		6	.413	.939	.800	9	.134	.988
	6	.049	.997		7	.058	.995		5	.707	.848		8	.446	.944
	5	.168	.983		6	.193	.979		4	.917	.706		7	.763	.859
	4	.416	.938		5	.445	.930		3	.991	.535		6	.939	.747
	3	.750	.816		4	.747	.822	.580	8	.057	.995		5	.991	.625
	2	.968	.584		3	.947	.646		7	.204	.977		4	.999	.500
.360	7	.014	.999		2	.998	.435		6	.465	.927	.850	9	.232	.979
	6	.064	.995	.480	8	.015	.999		5	.753	.829		8	.611	.916
	5	.205	.978		7	.074	.994		4	.937	.684		7	.879	.818
	4	.474	.923		6	.230	.973		3	.994	.517		6	.978	.705
	3	.798	.787		5	.499	.916	.600	9	.010	.999		5	.998	.588
	2	.978	.553		4	.791	.799		8	.072	.994	.900	9	.387	.963
.380	7	.019	.999		3	.961	.621		7	.242	.972		8	.785	.881
	6	.083	.993		2	.998	.417		6	.518	.915		7	.957	.777
	5	.247	.971	.500	8	.020	.999		5	.795	.809		6	.995	.667
	4	.533	.906		7	.093	.992		4	.953	.663	.950	9	.630	.938
	3	.840	.758		6	.271	.966		3	.996	.500		8	.934	.841
	2	.986	.525		5	.553	.901	.650	9	.021	.999		7	.994	.737
.400	7	.026	.998		4	.830	.775		8	.123	.988				

Source: L. G. Peck and R. N. Hazelwood, *Finite Queuing Tables* (New York: John Wiley & Sons, 1958). Reprinted by permission.

From Table 18.7, with $N = 5$, $M = 1$, and $X = .125$, $D = .575$ and $F = .920$.

a. Average number waiting, $L = N(1 - F) = 5(1 - .920) = .40$ machine.

b. Expected number running, $J = NF(1 - X) = 5(.920)(1 - .125) = 4.025$ machines.

c. Downtime = Waiting time + Service time:

$$\text{Waiting time, } W = \frac{L(T + U)}{N - L} = \frac{.40(10 + 70)}{5 - .40} = 6.957 \text{ minutes}$$

Downtime = 6.957 minutes + 10 minutes = 16.957 minutes

d. Probability of not waiting = 1 − Probability of waiting

$= 1 - D$

$= 1 - .575 = .425$

Using the Excel template, the solution to Example 10 would appear as follows:

www.mhhe.com/stevenson11e

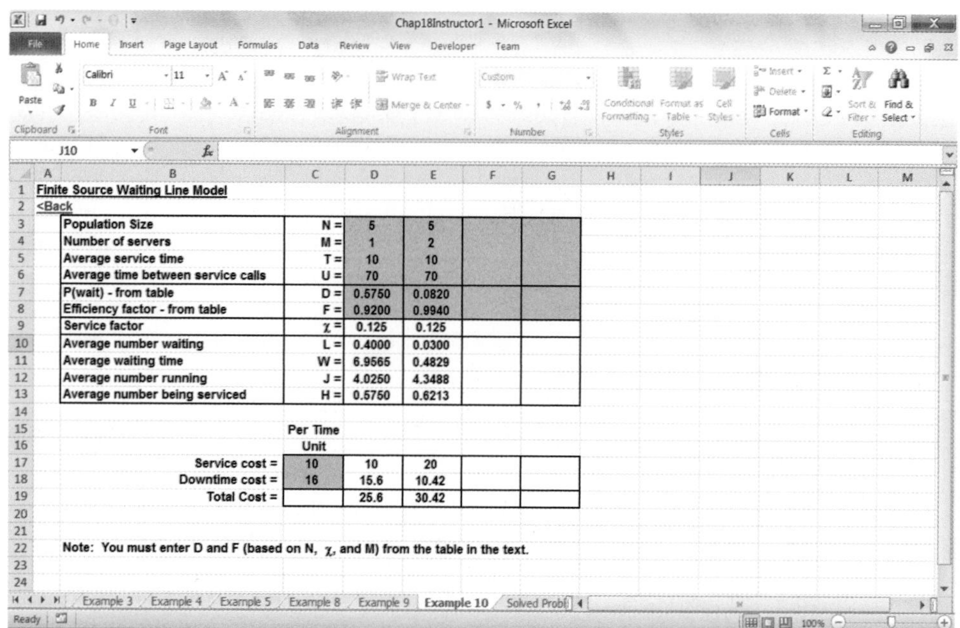

	A	B	C	D	E
1	Finite Source Waiting Line Model				
2	<Back				
3		Population Size	N =	5	5
4		Number of servers	M =	1	2
5		Average service time	T =	10	10
6		Average time between service calls	U =	70	70
7		P(wait) - from table	D =	0.5750	0.0820
8		Efficiency factor - from table	F =	0.9200	0.9940
9		Service factor	χ =	0.125	0.125
10		Average number waiting	L =	0.4000	0.0300
11		Average waiting time	W =	6.9565	0.4829
12		Average number running	J =	4.0250	4.3488
13		Average number being serviced	H =	0.5750	0.6213
15–16			Per Time Unit		
17		Service cost =	10	10	20
18		Downtime cost =	16	15.6	10.42
19		Total Cost =		25.6	30.42

Note: You must enter D and F (based on N, χ, and M) from the table in the text.

EXAMPLE 11

Suppose that in Example 10 operators are paid $10 per hour, and machine downtime costs $16 per hour. Should the department add another operator if the goal is cost optimization?

SOLUTION

Compare the total cost of the present system with the expected total cost of the proposed system:

M	Average Number Down, $N - J$	Average Down Cost (per hour), $(N - J)$ \$16	Operator Cost (per hour)	Total Cost (per hour)
1	.975	$15.60	$10	$25.60
2	.651	10.42	20	30.42

Hence, the present system is superior because its total cost is less than the expected total cost using two operators.

Hotels Exploring Easier Customer Check-ins

READING

Salina Kahn

The hotel front desk is no longer the only place where travelers check in and get their room keys.

More hotels are shortening front desk lines by doing that outside their front door—on airport shuttle buses and even at airports.

Hotels have long allowed guests to register via the phone or the Internet and then pick up a key at a special counter or kiosk in the lobby. Now hotels are accelerating express check-in by using wireless technology to program electronic card keys outside the hotel.

The improvements should be popular: 81 percent of business travelers say express check-in and checkout services are very desirable, according to the 1999 Business Travel Monitor by Yesawich, Pepperdine & Brown and Yankelovich Partners.

Hilton plans to use the technology to provide curbside check-in at hotels in Honolulu, New York and Anaheim, Calif., early next year, says John Luke, Hilton vice president.

Starwood Hotels and Resorts will test curbside check-in at the Boston Park Plaza within 60 days.

(continued)

(concluded)

Other hotels where guests check in before they reach the lobby:

- The Fairmont Vancouver Airport Hotel accepts reservations, checks bags and hands out keys from two "satellite lobbies" in the airport.
- Park Place Entertainment plans to open a check-in counter at McCarran International Airport in Las Vegas early next year.
- Hilton Boston Logan Airport began in September to allow guests to register on the shuttle bus ride from the airport to the hotel.
- The Loews Portofino Bay Hotel in Orlando, Fla., provides curb-side check-in.

Source: Salina Kahn, "Hotels Exploring Easier Customer Check-ins," *Rochester Democrat and Chronicle,* Nov. 7, 1999, p. 1E.

CONSTRAINT MANAGEMENT

Managers may be able to reduce waiting times by actively managing one or more system constraints. Typically, in the short term, the facility size and the number of servers are fixed resources. However, some other options might be considered:

Use temporary workers. Using temporary or part-time workers during busy periods may be possible. Trade-offs might involve training costs, quality issues, and perhaps slower service than would be provided by regular workers.

Shift demand. In situations where demand varies by time of day, or time of week, variable pricing strategies can be effective in smoothing demand more evenly on the system. Theaters use this option with lower prices to shift demand from busy times to slower times. Restaurants offer "early-bird specials" to accomplish this. Some retail businesses offer coupons that are valid only for certain (slow) days or times.

Standardize the service. We saw the effect of constant service on waiting lines compared to nonconstant service (the number and time in line were cut in half). The more service can be standardized, the greater the impact on waiting lines.

Look for a bottleneck. One aspect of a process may be largely responsible for a slow service rate; improving that aspect of the process might yield a disproportionate increase in the service rate. Employees often have insights that can be exploited.

THE PSYCHOLOGY OF WAITING

Despite management's best efforts, in some instances it is not feasible to shorten waiting times. Nevertheless, steps can be taken in certain situations that make the situation more acceptable to those waiting in line, particularly when the waiting line consists of people. The importance of doing so should not be underestimated.

Studies have shown a difference—sometimes a remarkable difference—between the *actual time* customers spend waiting and their *perceived time.* Several factors can influence the differences. One is the reason for being in line (e.g., waiting for police or fire personnel, waiting at the emergency room, having other appointments or a plane or train to catch). Aside from those situations, where the level of anxiety can make even short waits seem long, in many instances management can reduce their customers' perception of the waiting time.

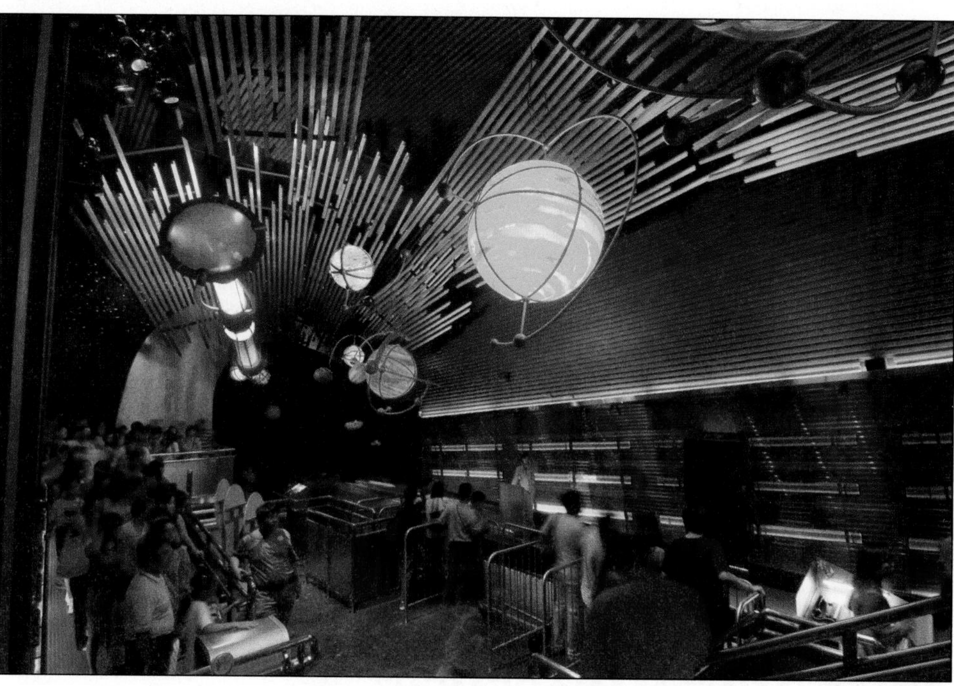

Customers are entertained while waiting in line for a space ride at an amusement park.

David H. Maister on the Psychology of Waiting

READING

David H. Maister's classic article on the psychology of waiting included these pearls of wisdom about waiting that can serve as a guide to system designers and to those operating a system in which waiting lines of people occur

- Occupied time feels shorter than unoccupied time
- People want to get started
- Anxiety makes waits seem longer
- Uncertain waits are longer than known, finite waits
- Unexplained waits are longer than explained waits
- Unfair waits are longer than equitable waits
- The more valuable the service, the longer the customer will wait
- Solo waits feel longer than group waits

Source: David H. Maister, "The Psychology of Waiting Lines," davidmaister.com, blog, September 8, 2008. Retrieved October 24, 2010.

If those waiting in line have nothing else to occupy their thoughts, they often tend to focus on the fact that they are waiting in line and usually perceive the waiting time to be longer than the actual waiting time. Conversely, if something else occupies them while they wait, their perception of the waiting time is often less than their actual waiting time. Examples of distractions include in-flight snacks, meals or videos, and magazines and televisions in waiting rooms. Giving customers something to do while waiting, such as filling out forms, can make their wait seem productive. Of course, some customers provide their own distractions (e.g., they talk on their cell phones, text message, or play games on hand-held electronic devices). Another factor can be the level of comfort available (e.g., standing versus sitting, waiting outside in the weather versus inside or under cover). Also, informing customers how long the wait will be can reduce anxiety. For example, call centers sometimes announce the expected waiting time before a service representative will be available, and restaurants usually are able to tell patrons how long they will wait to be seated.

Several of these approaches are employed at Disney theme parks, as illustrated in the following reading.

Managing Waiting Lines at Disney World

READING

Walt Disney theme parks are leaders in effectively managing waiting lines. Disney people present seminars on managing waiting lines. Their success can serve as a benchmark and provide valuable insights for a wide range of services.

Disney's methods are particularly relevant when circumstances make it impossible to quickly add capacity to alleviate waiting times. Here are some of the tactics Disney employs to achieve customer satisfaction:

1. **Provide distractions.** Disney characters may entertain customers, videos provide safety information and build anticipation for the event, vendors move along some lines selling food and drinks, and other vendors sell souvenirs.
2. **Provide alternatives for those willing to pay a premium.** Disney offers its FastPass system, which allows customers to pay to reserve a time when they will be allowed to bypass the regular waiting line, sometimes using a separate entrance. This has the potential for increasing customer satisfaction by enabling customers to enjoy more events, as well as the potential to generate additional revenue as customers visit food concessions and souvenir shops. Another tactic is to sell passes that allow customers to enter the park earlier.
3. **Keep customers informed.** Signs are clearly posted that give approximate waiting times from that point, allowing the customers to make a decision of whether to join the line and setting expectations.
4. **Exceed expectations.** Waiting times are kept to less than estimated times, thereby exceeding customers' expectations. Also, the event is to be worth the wait.
5. **Other tactics.** Disney maintains a comfortable waiting environment: Waiting lines are often inside, protected from weather conditions. Lines are kept moving, giving the impression of making progress. Attendants and signs direct customers to sections of the park that are less busy.

Source: Based in part on "Queuing Featuring Disney World," McGraw-Hill Video Series.

The implication in these ideas is that imagination and creativity can often play an important role in system design and that mathematical approaches are not the only ones worth considering.

OPERATIONS STRATEGY

Managers must carefully assess the costs and benefits of various alternatives for capacity of service systems. Working to increase the processing rate may be a worthwhile option instead of increasing the number of servers. New processing equipment and/or processing methods may contribute to this goal. One important factor to consider is the possibility of reducing variability in processing times by increasing the degree of standardization of the service being provided. In fact, managers of all services would be wise to pursue this goal, not only for the benefits of reduced waiting times but also for benefits of standardizing server training and hence reducing those costs and times, and the potential for increased quality due to the decreased variety in service requirements.

Other approaches might involve efforts to shift some arrivals to "off-times" by using reservations systems, "early-bird" specials, senior discounts, or some of the approaches used by Disney to manage customer waiting.

SUMMARY

Analysis of waiting lines can be an important aspect of the design of service systems. Waiting lines have a tendency to form in such systems even though, in a macro sense, the system is underloaded. The arrival of customers at random times and variability of service times combine to create temporary overloads. When this happens, waiting lines appear. By the same token, at other times the servers are idle.

A major consideration in the analysis of queuing systems is whether the number of potential customers is limited (finite source) or whether entry to the system is unrestricted (infinite source). Five basic queuing models are described, four dealing with infinite-source populations and one dealing with finite-source populations. In general, the models assume that customer arrival rates can be described by a Poisson distribution and that service time can be described by a negative exponential distribution.

Choosing the Appropriate Model

Infinite-Source Model. Use when entry to the system is unrestricted (open to the public).

The *basic relationship formulas* can be used with an infinite source model. There are formulas for system utilization, the average number or average time waiting for service, the average number being served, and the average number or time in the system. Refer to Figure 18.7 on p. 802 to help you connect with the appropriate formula. The formulas are on p. 802.

Single-channel model: Use when there is *one* server, team, or crew. See p. 803.
Single-channel, constant service time. See p. 804.
Multiple-channel model. Use when there are *two or more* independent servers, teams, or crews. See p. 805
Multiple-priority model. Use when service order is based on priority class. See p. 813.

Finite-Source Model. Use when entry to the system is restricted to system members. See p. 816.

KEY POINTS

1. Waiting line occur because there is an imbalance between supply and demand in service systems.
2. One cause of imbalances is variability in service times and/or customer arrival times.
3. Two important approaches to managing waiting lines are reducing variability where possible by standardizing a process and/or altering the perceived waiting time.

KEY TERMS

channel, 797
finite-source situation, 797
infinite-source situation, 796
multiple-priority model, 812
queue discipline, 800
queuing theory, 794

SOLVED PROBLEMS

Use this approach for infinite-source problems:

1. Note the number of servers. If there is only one server, $M = 1$. Use the basic relationship formulas in Figure 18.7 and the single-server formulas in Table 18.1. If service is constant, use Formula 18–9 for L_q. For $M > 1$, use the basic relationship formulas in Figure 18.7, the multiple-server values in Table 18.4 for L_q and P_0, and Formulas 18–12 and 18–13.
2. Determine the customer arrival rate and the service rate. If the arrival or service *time* is given instead of a rate, convert the time to a rate. For example, a service time of 10 minutes would convert to a service rate, μ, of

   $\mu = [1/(10 \text{ minutes/customer})]\ (60 \text{ minutes/hour}) = 6 \text{ customers/hour}$
3. If multiple priorities are involved, use the Excel template on the Web site (preferred approach) or the formulas in Table 18.5.

Problem 1

Infinite source. One of the features of a new machine shop will be a well-stocked tool crib. The manager of the shop must decide on the number of attendants needed to staff the crib. Attendants will receive $9 per hour in salary and fringe benefits. Mechanics' time will be worth $30 per hour, which includes salary and fringe benefits plus lost work time caused by waiting for parts. Based on previous experience, the manager estimates requests for parts will average 18 per hour with a service capacity of 20 requests per hour per attendant. How many attendants should be on duty if the manager is willing to assume that arrival and service rates will be Poisson-distributed? (Assume the number of mechanics is very large, so an infinite-source model is appropriate.)

Solution

$\lambda = 18$ per hour
$\mu = 20$ per hour

The solution requires a trial-and-error approach that reveals the total cost of feasible alternatives (i.e., a utilization less than 100 percent) and selection of the lowest-cost alternative. Note that the total-cost curve will always be U-shaped; increase the number of servers until the total cost shows an increase over the previous value. The optimum will be the number of servers that produced the previous total cost value. Thus,

Number of Servers, *M*	L_q*	$L_q + \frac{\lambda}{\mu} = L_s$	\$9*M*: Server Cost (per hour)	\$30 L_s: Mechanic Cost (per hour)	Total Cost (per hour)
1	8.1	8.1 + 0.9 = 9.0	\$ 9	\$270	\$279
2	0.229	0.229 + 0.9 = 1.129	\$18	\$ 33.87	\$ 52†
3	0.03	0.03 + 0.9 = 0.93	\$27	\$ 27.9	\$ 55†

*L_q from Table 18.4, with $r = \lambda/\mu = 18/20 = .9$.

†Rounded.

Hence, two servers will produce the lowest total cost.

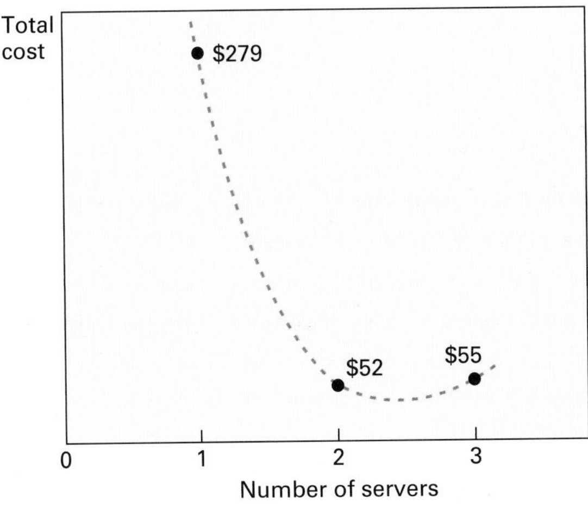

Problem 2

Infinite source. The following is a list of service times for three different operations:

Operation	Service Time
A	8 minutes
B	1.2 hours
C	2 days

a. Determine the service rate for each operation.

b. Would the calculated rates be different if these were interarrival times rather than service times?

Solution

a. The service rate is the reciprocal of service time. Thus, the rates are

A: 1/8 customer per minute = .125 customer per minute, or .125/min × 60 min/hr = 7.5 customers per hour

B: 1/1.2 customer per hour = .833 customer per hour

C: 1/2 customer per day = .50 customer per day

b. No. In either case, the rate is simply the reciprocal of the time.

Problem 3

Finite source. A group of 10 machines is loaded and unloaded by one of three servers. The machines run for an average of six minutes per cycle, and average time to unload and reload is nine minutes. Each time can be described by an exponential distribution. While running, the machines produce at a rate that would yield 16 units per hour if they did not have to pause to wait for a server and be loaded and unloaded. What is the average hourly output of each machine when waiting and serving are taken into account?

Solution

$T = 9$ minutes

$U = 6$ minutes; $x = \dfrac{T}{T+U} = \dfrac{9}{9+6} = .60$

$M = 3$ servers; from Table 18.7, $F = .500$

$N = 10$ machines

a. Compute the average number of machines running:

$$J = NF(1 - X) = 10(.500)(.40) = 2$$

b. Determine the percentage of machines running, and multiply by output while running:

$$\frac{J}{N} \times (16 \text{ per hour}) = \frac{2}{10} \times (16 \text{ per hour}) = 3.2 \text{ per hour}$$

DISCUSSION AND REVIEW QUESTIONS

1. In what kinds of situations is queuing analysis most appropriate?
2. Why do waiting lines form even though a service system is underloaded?
3. What are the most common measures of system performance in a queuing analysis?
4. What effect would decreasing arrival and service variability have on the effective capacity of a system?
5. What approaches do supermarkets use to offset variations in customer traffic intensity?
6. Contrast *finite* and *infinite* population sources.
7. Under what circumstances would a multiple-priority waiting system be appropriate?
8. In a multiple-channel system, what is the rationale for having customers wait in a single line, as is now being done in many banks and post offices, rather than multiple lines? (*Hint:* The average waiting time is unaffected.)
9. What happens to the length of a waiting line in a highly variable (queuing) setting if a manager attempts to achieve a high percentage of capacity utilization?

TAKING STOCK

1. What general trade-offs are involved in waiting line decisions?
2. Who needs to be involved in assessing the cost of customers waiting for service if the customers are (a) the general public and (b) employees of the organization?
3. How has technology had an impact on analyzing waiting line systems? How has technology improved waiting line performance?

CRITICAL THINKING EXERCISES

1. What benefits do psychological approaches to waiting lines have over other approaches?
2. Consider this situation: A manager is contemplating making changes to a single-server system that is expected to double the service rate, and still have just one server.
   a. Would you (intuitively) think that doubling the service rate of a single-server system would cut the average waiting time in line in half?
   b. For the sake of analysis, suppose the current system has an arrival rate of 8 customers per hour and a service rate of 10 customers per hour. If the service rate is doubled, what impact will that have on the average number waiting in line?
   c. What are some managerial implications of your analysis?
3. There are certain instances where pooling of operations can be desirable. For example, a large factory may have two or more locations where mechanics can obtain special tools or equipment they occasionally need. The separate locations mean less travel time for workers, but sometimes there will be a waiting line at one location while servers are idle at another location. What factors should an analysis of this sort of situation take into account in deciding on whether to keep separate locations or pool servers and equipment at one central location?

4. The owner of Eat Now Restaurant implemented an expanded menu early last year. The menu was a success, drawing many more customers, who seemed to like the increased variety of menu choices over that of the previous menu. But good news soon became bad news as long waiting lines began to deter customers, and business dropped off. Because of space and other limitations, there didn't seem to be any viable options to consider. Then a customer mentioned a technique called mass customization that was being used in the company he worked for. He said it really streamlined processing, and maybe it could work for the restaurant.

   Describe how that approach might work at the restaurant and why that could be expected to reduce waiting times. What costs would be involved in transitioning to such a system? What other approaches could be used to reduce waiting times?
5. Describe two examples of unethical behavior related to waiting line management and state which ethical principles they violate.

PROBLEMS

1. Repair calls are handled by one repairman at a photocopy shop. Repair time, including travel time, is exponentially distributed, with a mean of two hours per call. Requests for copier repairs come in at a mean rate of three per eight-hour day (assume Poisson). Determine:
   a. The average number of customers awaiting repairs.
   b. System utilization.
   c. The amount of time during an eight-hour day that the repairman is not out on a call.
   d. The probability of two or more customers in the system.

2. A vending machine dispenses hot chocolate or coffee. Service time is 30 seconds per cup and is constant. Customers arrive at a mean rate of 80 per hour, and this rate is Poisson-distributed. Determine:
   a. The average number of customers waiting in line.
   b. The average time customers spend in the system.
   c. The average number in the system.

3. Many of a bank's customers use its automatic teller machine to transact business after normal banking hours. During the early evening hours in the summer months, customers arrive at a certain location at the rate of one every other minute. This can be modeled using a Poisson distribution. Each customer spends an average of 90 seconds completing his or her transactions. Transaction time is exponentially distributed. Determine:
   a. The average time customers spend at the machine, including waiting in line and completing transactions.
   b. The probability that a customer will not have to wait upon arriving at the automatic teller machine.
   c. The average number waiting to use the machine.

4. A small town with one hospital has two ambulances to supply ambulance service. Requests for ambulances during nonholiday weekends average .45 per hour and tend to be Poisson-distributed. Travel and assistance time averages two hours per call and follows an exponential distribution. Find:
   a. System utilization.
   b. The average number of customers waiting.
   c. The average time customers wait for an ambulance.
   d. The probability that *both* ambulances will be busy when a call comes in.

5. The following information pertains to telephone calls to a motel switchboard on a typical Tuesday.

Period	Incoming Rate (calls per minute)	Service Rate (calls per minute per operator)	Number of Operators
Morning	1.8	1.5	2
Afternoon	2.2	1.0	3
Evening	1.4	0.7	3

   a. Determine the average time callers wait to have their calls answered for each period and the probability that a caller will have to wait for each period.
   b. For each case in the previous problem, determine the maximum line length for a probability of 96 percent.

6. Trucks are required to pass through a weighing station so that they can be checked for weight violations. Trucks arrive at the station at the rate of 40 an hour between 7:00 p.m. and 9:00 p.m. Currently two inspectors are on duty during those hours, each of whom can inspect 25 trucks an hour.
   a. How many trucks would you expect to see at the weighing station, including those being inspected?
   b. If a truck was just arriving at the station, about how many minutes could the driver expect to be at the station?
   c. What is the probability that both inspectors would be busy at the same time?
   d. How many minutes, on average, would a truck that is not immediately inspected have to wait?
   e. What condition would exist if there was only one inspector?
   f. What is the maximum line length for a probability of .97?
7. The manager of a regional warehouse must decide on the number of loading docks to request for a new facility in order to minimize the sum of dock costs and driver-truck costs. The manager has learned that each driver-truck combination represents a cost of $300 per day and that each dock plus loading crew represents a cost of $1,100 per day.
   a. How many docks should be requested if trucks arrive at the rate of three per day, each dock can handle five trucks per day, and both rates are Poisson?
   b. An employee has proposed adding new equipment that would speed up the loading rate to 4.2856 trucks per day. The equipment would cost $100 per day for each dock. Should the manager invest in the new equipment?
8. The parts department of a large automobile dealership has a counter used exclusively for mechanics' requests for parts. The time between requests can be modeled by a negative exponential distribution that has a mean of five minutes. A clerk can handle requests at a rate of 15 per hour, and this can be modeled by a Poisson distribution that has a mean of 15. Suppose there are two clerks at the counter.
   a. On average, how many mechanics would be at the counter, including those being served?
   b. What is the probability that a mechanic would have to wait for service?
   c. If a mechanic has to wait, how long would the average wait be?
   d. What percentage of time are the clerks idle?
   e. If clerks represent a cost of $20 per hour and mechanics a cost of $30 per hour, what number of clerks would be optimal in terms of minimizing total cost?
9. One field representative services five customers for a computer manufacturer. Customers request assistance at an average (Poisson-distributed) rate of once every four working days. The field representative can handle an average (Poisson-distributed) of one call per day. Determine:
   a. The expected number of customers waiting.
   b. The average length of time customers must wait from the initial request for service until the service has been completed.
   c. The percentage of time the service rep will be idle.
   d. By how much would your answer to part *a* be reduced if a second field rep were added?
10. Two operators handle adjustments for a group of 10 machines. Adjustment time is exponentially distributed and has a mean of 14 minutes per machine. The machines operate for an average of 86 minutes between adjustments. While running, each machine can turn out 50 pieces per hour. Find:
    a. The probability that a machine will have to wait for an adjustment.
    b. The average number of machines waiting for adjustment.
    c. The average number of machines being serviced.
    d. The expected hourly output of each machine, taking adjustments into account.
    e. Machine downtime represents a cost of $70 per hour; operator cost (including salary and fringe benefits) is $15 per hour. What is the optimum number of operators?
11. One operator services a bank of five machines. Machine running time and service time are both exponential. Machines run for an average of 90 minutes between service requirements, and service time averages 35 minutes. The operator receives $20 per hour in salary and fringe benefits, and machine downtime costs $70 per hour per machine.
    a. If each machine produces 60 pieces per hour while running, find the average hourly output of each machine, when waiting and service times are taken into account.
    b. Determine the optimum number of operators.

12. A milling department has 10 machines. Each operates an average of eight hours before requiring adjustment, which takes an average of two hours. While running, each machine can produce 40 pieces an hour.
    a. With one adjuster, what is the net average hourly output per machine?
    b. If machine downtime cost is \$80 per hour and adjuster cost is \$30 per hour, how many adjusters would be optimal?
13. Trucks arrive at the loading dock of a wholesale grocer at the rate of 1.2 per hour. A single crew consisting of two workers can load a truck in about 30 minutes. Crew members receive \$10 per hour in wages and fringe benefits, and trucks and drivers reflect an hourly cost of \$60. The manager is thinking of adding another member to the crew. The service rate would then be 2.4 trucks per hour. Assume rates are Poisson.
    a. Would the third crew member be economical?
    b. Would a fourth member be justifiable if the resulting service capacity were 2.6 trucks per hour?
14. Customers arriving at a service center are assigned to one of three categories, with category 1 given the highest priority. Records indicate that an average of nine customers arrive per hour and that one-third are assigned to each category. There are two servers, and each can process customers at the rate of five per hour. Arrival and service rates can be described by Poisson distributions.
    a. What is the utilization rate for this system?
    b. Determine the average waiting time for units in each class.
    c. Find the average number of customers in each class that are waiting for service.
15. A manager must determine requirements for waiting space for customers. A priority system is used to process customers, who are assigned to one of two classes when they enter the processing center. The highest-priority class has an arrival rate of four per hour; the other class has an arrival rate of two per hour. Both can be described as Poisson-distributed. There are two servers, and each can process customers in an average of 15 minutes.
    a. What is the system utilization?
    b. Determine the number of customers of each class that are waiting for service.
    c. Determine the average waiting time for each class.
    d. If the manager could alter the assignment rules so that arrival rates of the two classes were equal, what would be the revised average waiting time for each priority class?
16. A priority waiting system assigns arriving customers to one of four classes. Arrival rates (Poisson) of the classes are shown in the following table:

Class	Arrivals per Hour
1	2
2	4
3	3
4	2

    Five servers process the customers, and each can handle three customers per hour.
    a. What is the system utilization?
    b. What is the average wait for service by customers in the various classes? How many are waiting in each class, on average?
    c. If the arrival rate of the second priority class could be reduced to three units per hour by shifting some arrivals into the third priority class, how would your answers to part *b* change?
    d. What observations can you make based on your answers to part *c?*
17. Referring to Problem 16, suppose that each server could handle four customers per hour. Answer the questions posed in the problem. Explain why the impact of reassigning customers is much less than in Problem 16.
18. During the morning hours at a catalog sales department, telephone calls come in at the rate (Poisson) of 40 per hour. Calls that cannot be answered immediately are put on hold. The system can handle eight callers on hold. If additional calls come in, they receive a busy signal. The three customer service representatives who answer the calls spend an average of three minutes with a customer.
    a. What is the probability that a caller will get a busy signal? (*Hint:* Solve for log K or ln K using trial and error.)
    b. What is the probability that a customer will be put on hold?

Big Bank

CASE

The operations manager of a soon-to-open branch of a large bank is in the process of configuring teller operations. Currently some branches have a separate teller line for customers who have a single transaction, while other branches don't have separate lines. The manager wants to avoid complaints about long waits that have been received at some branches. Because the demographics differ from location to location, a system that works at one branch won't necessarily work at another.

The manager has obtained data on processing times from the bank's home office and is ready to explore different options for configuring operations. (Fortunately she has her textbook and CD from when she took an operations management course at a nearby university.)

An average of 80 customers are processed during the noon hour. The average processing time for customers with a single transaction is 90 seconds, while the processing time for customers with multiple transactions is 4 minutes. Sixty percent of the customers are expected to have multiple transactions.

One time that will get special attention is the noon hour on Friday. The plan is to have five tellers available. Under consideration are the following options:

a. Have one waiting line and have the first person in line go to the next available teller.
b. Have two waiting lines: one teller for customers who have a single transaction and four tellers who would handle customers who have multiple transactions.

Questions

If you were the manager, which option would you select? Why? Explain the disparity between the results for the two options. What assumptions did you make in your analysis?

Stopped at a Light? Why Not Read This, You May Have Time

READING

Anna Wilde Mathews

At the corner of Fairfax County Parkway and Fair Lakes Parkway, drivers see red.

More than four minutes of it.

Hanging over this crowded intersection in northern Virginia's booming suburbs is one of the longest stoplights in the country. Washington-bound commuters curse it. Highflying tech executives making their way to appointments feel grounded. Prepared motorists bring breakfast to nibble while they wait. Occasionally, a gaggle of geese waddles across the road to a nearby pond, slowing things even more.

"You come out here sometimes, and it brings tears to your eyes, it's so bad," says Jeris J. White, the state transportation manager and former professional-football player who tackles traffic delays here.

Spread of Red It's happening everywhere—red lights are getting longer. And longer. Cities and towns are quietly, albeit reluctantly, giving the green light to longer traffic signals. Through the 1970s, the typical wait at a red light was 45 seconds or so. The wait started growing in the 1980s and 1990s. Today, 90-second spans aren't uncommon, and some are inching near the three-minute mark. Many of these long lights are their longest only at rush hour, but that's little solace to impatient travelers.

Law-abiding drivers stuck at the two-minute-36-second red light at the corner of DuPont Parkway and Frenchtown Road south of Wilmington, Del., take coffee breaks, work on crossword puzzles and, now and then, do some automotive hugging.

"You see couples getting a little more amorous than you'd expect at a traffic light," says Paul Rada, manager of the nearby Quality Inn. "You've got to do something." Mr. Rada himself has read the comics and eaten his lunch sitting at the light, he says. The truly desperate will "jump out of cars and hit the pedestrian button," hoping it will trigger a light change, adds Larry Koczak, a local mail carrier.

Reasons for the lengthening lights vary: More traffic. Wider streets. More lanes dedicated to left turns. And disagreement among traffic engineers who feel just as stuck as the drivers who endure these lights. "It's crept up gradually," says Scott Wainwright, a Montgomery County, Md., official who chairs a national engineering committee on traffic signals.

Longer red lights are intended to help keep busy intersections clear of anything approaching gridlock. In part, that's because several seconds go to waste every time traffic has to start again when red turns to green.

Yielding to Temptation

But longer lights can encourage antsy drivers to race through yellow lights and run reds, causing accidents and pileups that, in addition to risking injury and death, clog traffic even more. Each year, more than 1.8 million crashes occur at intersections, killing more than 7,800 people, the Federal Highway Administration says.

The federal government has launched a special "Stop Red Light Running" initiative, and localities are cracking down with hidden

(continued)

(concluded)

cameras that snap automatic pictures of scofflaws. For safety's sake, many cities have built more time into stoplight cycles so, for a few seconds, lights at all sides of a given intersection are red—an "all-red" delay designed to clear stragglers and minimize collisions.

All-reds are a source of controversy among traffic engineers. Peter Parsonson, professor of civil engineering at Georgia Tech in Atlanta, says they add an extra margin of safety. But at Marquette University in Milwaukee, David Kuemmel, who is in the department of civil and environmental engineering, argues that the all-red sequence is being used "indiscriminately."

The way to stop frustrated drivers from going through lights is not to make them wait longer, Mr. Kuemmel says. "That's a pet peeve of mine. It's an incentive for motorists to run the red light." The disagreements are further complicated by the lack of conclusive research on the link between light length and crashes.

Many roads are sprouting more left-turn-only lanes, with their own green-arrow turn indicators to keep vehicles that want to turn from backing up forever. But that stretches the light-cycle length. And with extra lanes making streets wider, pedestrians need more time to cross, requiring longer greens to accommodate them.

Even in Las Vegas

"In the old days, when you had two-lane roads, things were different," says Gerry de Camp, a transportation consultant and former manager of the Las Vegas area computer traffic system. Now, he says, "you can have a three-lane left turn, plus a bus lane, and a 12-foot shoulder, yadda, yadda, yadda." Las Vegas has a red light that stretches to two minutes and 45 seconds, although Mr. DeCamp says he tried to keep it from getting any longer. "I wasn't proud of it," he says. "I preferred not to advertise it."

In Northern Virginia, Mr. White, who played cornerback for nine years for the Washington Redskins and other teams, has gone from stopping opposing teams to trying to get vehicles moving. He looks more like a referee on a recent weekday evening as he stands at the Fairfax County intersection, stopwatch in hand, timing a seemingly endless procession of glowing headlights and taillights.

"This is brutal," he says, peering down a line of vehicles that stretches down Fair Lakes Parkway to the horizon, waiting for the light to change. One white sedan waits four minutes and 41 seconds to make a left turn; Mr. White explains why: Southbound traffic on the seven-lane Fairfax County Parkway hasn't eased enough to trigger a change in the computer-controlled light. The light is set to switch automatically only when traffic thins on that road, which typically carries a heavier load than the intersecting one.

"You see any end in sight?" he asks. There is none, for now.

The crossroads appears deceptively rural, with trees and grass at each corner and the nearby pond. But it rests amid gleaming new condominiums, a shopping mall and an office park, and the roads are lined with signs urging drivers to stop and see the latest housing developments under construction.

Standing on one corner, Mr. White offers running sports-style commentary on the traffic flow, groaning occasionally at a bad move. "The truck is going to run the red!" he shouts. "The truck ran the red!"

A Long Red

He varies the light cycles at different times of the day, and uses the longest cycles only during peak rush-hour traffic. But at those times, he says, he has little choice but to keep the Fair Lakes Parkway red light so as to prevent miles-long backups on the Fairfax County Parkway.

Suddenly, Fair Lakes seems to be clearing up. Cars flow smoothly through the intersection and, by the time the light changes to red, none are left waiting. "This is beautiful!" Mr. White cheers. "We cleared the whole side street out. If it's still that way at 6:30 or so, we can open the champagne."

But Mr. White thinks the light still is too long, and he hopes to do something about it. As part of a computer-plotted plan to smooth traffic flows through 76 local intersections, the longest possible red light here will drop from four minutes and 47 seconds to three minutes and 15 seconds.

It'll still be one of the longest reds anywhere, and Mr. White can't be sure the change will stick. "The goal is to move the traffic," he says. "If it doesn't hold up, we'll change it" back.

Source: Anna Wilde Mathews, "Stopped at a Light?" *The Wall Street Journal,* June 13, 2000, pp. A1 & A12.

SELECTED BIBLIOGRAPHY AND FURTHER READINGS

Buffa, Elwood. *Operations Management.* 3rd ed. New York: John Wiley & Sons, 1972.

Griffin, W. *Queuing: Basic Theory and Applications.* Columbus, OH: Grid Publishing, 1978.

Hillier, Frederick S., and Gerald J. Lieberman. *Introduction to Operations Research.* 3rd ed. San Francisco: Holden-Day, 1980.

Katz, K. L., B. M. Larson, and R. C. Larson. "Prescriptions for the Waiting-in-Line Blues: Entertain, Enlighten, and Engage." *Sloan Management Review* 32, no. 2 (Winter 1991), pp. 44–53.

Stevenson, William J., and Ceyhun Ozgur. *Introduction to Management Science with Spreadsheets.* New York: McGraw-Hill/Irwin, 2006.

Linear Programming

CHAPTER OUTLINE

LEARNING OBJECTIVES

After completing this chapter, you should be able to:

1. Describe the type of problem that would lend itself to solution using linear programming.
2. Formulate a linear programming model from a description of a problem.
3. Solve simple linear programming problems using the graphical method.
4. Interpret computer solutions of linear programming problems.
5. Do sensitivity analysis on the solution of a linear programming problem.

Linear programming is a powerful quantitative tool used by operations managers and other managers to obtain optimal solutions to problems that involve restrictions or limitations, such as budgets and available materials, labor, and machine time. These problems are referred to as *constrained optimization* problems. There are numerous examples of linear programming applications to such problems, including

- Establishing locations for emergency equipment and personnel that will minimize response time.
- Determining optimal schedules for airlines for planes, pilots, and ground personnel.
- Developing financial plans.
- Determining optimal blends of animal feed mixes.
- Determining optimal diet plans.
- Identifying the best set of worker–job assignments.
- Developing optimal production schedules.
- Developing shipping plans that will minimize shipping costs.
- Identifying the optimal mix of products in a factory.
- Performing production and service planning.

INTRODUCTION

Linear programming (LP) techniques consist of a sequence of steps that will lead to an optimal solution to linear-constrained problems, if an optimum exists. There are a number of different linear programming techniques; some are special-purpose (i.e., used to find solutions for specific types of problems) and others are more general in scope. This chapter covers the two general-purpose solution techniques: graphical linear programming and computer solutions. Graphical linear programming provides a visual portrayal of many of the important concepts of linear programming. However, it is limited to problems with only two variables. In practice, computers are used to obtain solutions for problems, some of which involve a large number of variables.

LINEAR PROGRAMMING MODELS

eXcel
www.mhhe.com/stevenson11e

SCREENCAM TUTORIAL

Linear programming models are mathematical representations of constrained optimization problems. These models have certain characteristics in common. Knowledge of these characteristics enables us to recognize problems that can be solved using linear programming. In addition, it also can help us formulate LP models. The characteristics can be grouped into two categories: components and assumptions. First, let's consider the components.

Four components provide the structure of a linear programming model:

1. Objective function.
2. Decision variables.
3. Constraints.
4. Parameters.

Objective function Mathematical statement of profit (or cost, etc.) for a given solution.

Decision variables Amounts of either inputs or outputs.

Constraints Limitations that restrict the available alternatives.

Linear programming algorithms require that a single goal or *objective,* such as the maximization of profits, be specified. The two general types of objectives are maximization and minimization. A maximization objective might involve profits, revenues, efficiency, or rate of return. Conversely, a minimization objective might involve cost, time, distance traveled, or scrap. The **objective function** is a mathematical expression that can be used to determine the total profit (or cost, etc., depending on the objective) for a given solution.

Decision variables represent choices available to the decision maker in terms of amounts of either inputs or outputs. For example, some problems require choosing a combination of inputs to minimize total costs, while others require selecting a combination of outputs to maximize profits or revenues.

Constraints are limitations that restrict the alternatives available to decision makers. The three types of constraints are less than or equal to ($\leq$), greater than or equal to ($\geq$), and simply equal to ($=$). A $\leq$ constraint implies an upper limit on the amount of some scarce resource (e.g., machine hours, labor hours, materials) available for use. A $\geq$ constraint specifies a minimum that must be achieved in the final solution (e.g., must contain at least 10 percent real fruit juice, must get at least 30 MPG on the highway). The $=$ constraint is more restrictive in the sense that it specifies *exactly* what a decision variable should equal (e.g., make 200 units of product A). A linear programming model can consist of one or more constraints. The constraints of a given problem define the set of all feasible combinations of decision variables; this set is referred to as the **feasible solution space.** Linear programming algorithms are designed to search the feasible solution space for the combination of decision variables that will yield an optimum in terms of the objective function.

Feasible solution space The set of all feasible combinations of decision variables as defined by the constraints.

Parameters Numerical constants.

An LP model consists of a mathematical statement of the objective and a mathematical statement of each constraint. These statements consist of symbols (e.g., x_1, x_2) that represent the decision variables and numerical values, called **parameters.** The parameters are fixed values; the model is solved *given* those values.

Example 1 illustrates an LP model.

EXAMPLE 1

Here is an LP model of a situation that involves the production of three possible products, each of which will yield a certain profit per unit, and each requires a certain use of two resources that are in limited supply: labor and materials. The objective is to determine how much of each product to make to achieve the greatest possible profit while satisfying all constraints.

Decision variables
$$\begin{cases} x_1 = \text{Quantity of product 1 to produce} \\ x_2 = \text{Quantity of product 2 to produce} \\ x_3 = \text{Quantity of product 3 to produce} \end{cases}$$

Maximize $5x_1 + 8x_2 + 4x_3$ (profit) (Objective function)

Subject to

Labor	$2x_1 + 4x_2 + 8x_3 \leq 250$ hours	
Material	$7x_1 + 6x_2 + 5x_3 \leq 100$ pounds	(Constraints)
Product 1	$x_1 \geq 10$ units	

$$x_1, x_2, x_3 \geq 0 \quad \text{(Nonnegativity constraints)}$$

First, the model lists and defines the decision variables. These typically represent *quantities*. In this case, they are quantities of three different products that might be produced.

Next, the model states the objective function. It includes every decision variable in the model and the contribution (profit per unit) of each decision variable. Thus, product x_1 has a profit of $5 per unit. The profit from product x_1 for a given solution will be 5 times the value of x_1 specified by the solution; the total profit from all products will be the sum of the individual product profits. Thus, if $x_1 = 10$, $x_2 = 0$, and $x_3 = 6$, the value of the objective function would be

$$5(10) + 8(0) + 4(6) = 74$$

The objective function is followed by a list (in no particular order) of three constraints. Each constraint has a right-hand-side numerical value (e.g., the labor constraint has a right-hand-side value of 250) that indicates the amount of the constraint and a relation sign that indicates whether that amount is a maximum ($\leq$), a minimum ($\geq$), or an equality ($=$). The left-hand side of each constraint consists of the variables subject to that particular constraint and a coefficient for each variable that indicates how much of the right-hand-side quantity *one unit* of the decision variable represents. For instance, for the labor constraint, one unit of x_1 will require two hours of labor. The sum of the values on the left-hand side of each constraint represents the amount of that constraint used by a solution. Thus, if $x_1 = 10$, $x_2 = 0$, and $x_3 = 6$, the amount of labor used would be

$$2(10) + 4(0) + 8(6) = 68 \text{ hours}$$

Because this amount does not exceed the quantity on the right-hand side of the constraint, it is said to be *feasible.*

Note that the third constraint refers to only a single variable; x_1 must be at least 10 units. Its implied coefficient is 1, although that is not shown.

Finally, there are the nonnegativity constraints. These are listed on a single line; they reflect the condition that no decision variable is allowed to have a negative value.

In order for LP models to be used effectively, certain *assumptions* must be satisfied:

1. **Linearity:** The impact of decision variables is linear in constraints and the objective function.
2. **Divisibility:** Noninteger values of decision variables are acceptable.
3. **Certainty:** Values of parameters are known and constant.
4. **Nonnegativity:** Negative values of decision variables are unacceptable.

Model Formulation

An understanding of the components of linear programming models is necessary for model formulation. This helps provide organization to the process of assembling information about a problem into a model.

Naturally, it is important to obtain valid information on what constraints are appropriate, as well as on what values of the parameters are appropriate. If this is not done, the usefulness of the model will be questionable. Consequently, in some instances, considerable effort must be expended to obtain that information.

In formulating a model, use the format illustrated in Example 1. Begin by identifying the decision variables. Very often, decision variables are "the quantity of" something, such as

x_1 = the quantity of product 1. Generally, decision variables have profits, costs, times, or a similar measure of value associated with them. Knowing this can help you identify the decision variables in a problem.

Constraints are restrictions or requirements on one or more decision variables, and they refer to available amounts of resources such as labor, material, or machine time, or to minimal requirements, such as "Make at least 10 units of product 1." It can be helpful to give a name to each constraint, such as "labor" or "material 1." Let's consider some of the different kinds of constraints you will encounter.

1. A constraint that refers to one or more decision variables. This is the most common kind of constraint. The constraints in Example 1 are of this type.

2. A constraint that specifies a ratio. For example, "The ratio of x_1 to x_2 must be at least 3 to 2." To formulate this, begin by setting up the following ratio:

$$\frac{x_1}{x_2} \geq \frac{3}{2}$$

Then, cross multiply, obtaining

$$2x_1 \geq 3x_2$$

This is not yet in a suitable form because all variables in a constraint must be on the left-hand side of the inequality (or equality) sign, leaving only a constant on the right-hand side. To achieve this, we must subtract the variable amount that is on the right side from both sides. That yields

$$2x_1 - 3x_2 \geq 0$$

(Note that the direction of the inequality remains the same.)

3. A constraint that specifies a percentage for one or more variables relative to one or more other variables. For example, "x_1 cannot be more than 20 percent of the mix." Suppose that the mix consists of variables x_1, x_2, and x_3. In mathematical terms, this would be

$$x_1 \leq .20(x_1 + x_2 + x_3)$$

As always, all variables must appear on the left-hand side of the relationship. To accomplish that, we can expand the right-hand side, and then subtract the result from both sides. Expanding yields

$$x_1 \leq .20x_1 + .20x_2 + .20x_3$$

Subtracting yields

$$.80x_1 - .20x_2 - .20x_3 \leq 0$$

Once you have formulated a model, the next task is to solve it. The following sections describe two approaches to problem solution: graphical solutions and computer solutions.

GRAPHICAL LINEAR PROGRAMMING

Graphical linear programming Graphical method for finding optimal solutions to two-variable problems.

Graphical linear programming is a method for finding optimal solutions to two-variable problems. This section describes that approach.

Outline of Graphical Procedure

The graphical method of linear programming plots the constraints on a graph and identifies an area that satisfies all of the constraints. The area is referred to as the *feasible solution space.* Next, the objective function is plotted and used to identify the optimal point in the feasible solution space. The coordinates of the point can sometimes be read directly from the graph, although generally an algebraic determination of the coordinates of the point is necessary.

The general procedure followed in the graphical approach is as follows:

1. Set up the objective function and the constraints in mathematical format.
2. Plot the constraints.
3. Identify the feasible solution space.
4. Plot the objective function.
5. Determine the optimum solution.

The technique can best be illustrated through solution of a typical problem. Consider the problem described in Example 2.

EXAMPLE 2

General description: A firm that assembles computers and computer equipment is about to start production of two new types of microcomputers. Each type will require assembly time, inspection time, and storage space. The amounts of each of these resources that can be devoted to the production of the microcomputers is limited. The manager of the firm would like to determine the quantity of each microcomputer to produce in order to maximize the profit generated by sales of these microcomputers.

Additional information: In order to develop a suitable model of the problem, the manager has met with design and production personnel. As a result of those meetings, the manager has obtained the following information:

	Type 1	Type 2
Profit per unit	$60	$50
Assembly time per unit	4 hours	10 hours
Inspection time per unit	2 hours	1 hour
Storage space per unit	3 cubic feet	3 cubic feet

The manager also has acquired information on the availability of company resources. These (daily) amounts are as follows:

Resource	Amount Available
Assembly time	100 hours
Inspection time	22 hours
Storage space	39 cubic feet

The manager met with the firm's marketing manager and learned that demand for the microcomputers was such that whatever combination of these two types of microcomputers is produced, all of the output can be sold.

In terms of meeting the assumptions, it would appear that the relationships are *linear:* The contribution to profit per unit of each type of computer and the time and storage space per unit of each type of computer are the same regardless of the quantity produced. Therefore, the total impact of each type of computer on the profit and each constraint is a linear function of the quantity of that variable. There may be a question of *divisibility* because, presumably, only whole units of computers will be sold. However, because this is a recurring process (i.e., the computers will be produced daily; a noninteger solution such as 3.5 computers per day will result in 7 computers every other day), this does not seem to pose a problem. The question of *certainty* cannot be explored here; in practice, the manager could be questioned to determine if there are any other possible constraints and whether the values shown for assembly times, and so forth, are known with certainty. For the purposes of discussion, we will assume certainty. Last, the assumption of *nonnegativity* seems justified; negative values for production quantities would not make sense.

Because we have concluded that linear programming is appropriate, let us now turn our attention to constructing a model of the microcomputer problem. First, we must define the decision variables. Based on the statement "The manager . . . would like to determine the quantity of each microcomputer to produce," the decision variables are the quantities of each type of computer. Thus,

$$x_1 = \text{quantity of type 1 to produce}$$
$$x_2 = \text{quantity of type 2 to produce}$$

Next, we can formulate the objective function. The profit per unit of type 1 is listed as \$60, and the profit per unit of type 2 is listed as \$50, so the appropriate objective function is

$$\text{Maximize} \quad Z = 60x_1 + 50x_2$$

where Z is the value of the objective function, given values of x_1 and x_2. Theoretically, a mathematical function requires such a variable for completeness. However, in practice, the objective function often is written without the *Z,* as sort of a shorthand version. (That approach is underscored by the fact that computer input does not call for *Z:* It is understood. The output of a computerized model does include a *Z,* though.)

Now for the constraints. There are three resources with limited availability: assembly time, inspection time, and storage space. The fact that availability is limited means that these constraints will all be ≤ constraints. Suppose we begin with the assembly constraint. The type 1 microcomputer requires 4 hours of assembly time per unit, whereas the type 2 microcomputer requires 10 hours of assembly time per unit. Therefore, with a limit of 100 hours available, the assembly constraint is

$$4x_1 + 10x_2 \leq 100 \text{ hours}$$

Similarly, each unit of type 1 requires 2 hours of inspection time, and each unit of type 2 requires 1 hour of inspection time. With 22 hours available, the inspection constraint is

$$2x_1 + 1x_2 \leq 22$$

(Note: The coefficient of 1 for x_2 need not be shown. Thus, an alternative form for this constraint is $2x_1 + x_2 \leq 22$.) The storage constraint is determined in a similar manner:

$$3x_1 + 3x_2 \leq 39$$

There are no other system or individual constraints. The nonnegativity constraints are

$$x_1, x_2 \geq 0$$

In summary, the mathematical model of the microcomputer problem is

$$x_1 = \text{quantity of type 1 to produce}$$
$$x_2 = \text{quantity of type 2 to produce}$$
$$\text{Maximize} \quad 60x_1 + 50x_2$$

Subject to

Assembly	$4x_1 + 10x_2 \leq 100$ hours
Inspection	$2x_1 + 1x_2 \leq 22$ hours
Storage	$3x_1 + 3x_2 \leq 39$ cubic feet
	$x_1, x_2 \geq 0$

The next step is to plot the constraints.

Plotting Constraints

Begin by placing the nonnegativity constraints on a graph, as in Figure 19.1. The procedure for plotting the other constraints is simple:

1. Replace the inequality sign with an equal sign. This transforms the constraint into an *equation of a straight line.*
2. Determine where the line intersects each axis.

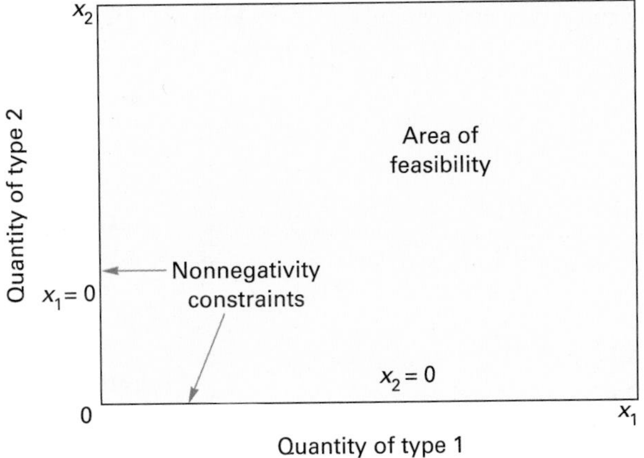

FIGURE 19.1
Graph showing the nonnegativity constraints

a. To find where it crosses the x_2 axis, set x_1 equal to zero and solve the equation for the value of x_2.
b. To find where it crosses the x_1 axis, set x_2 equal to zero and solve the equation for the value of x_1.

3. Mark these intersections on the axes, and connect them with a straight line. (*Note:* If a constraint has only one variable, it will be a vertical line on a graph if the variable is x_1, or a horizontal line if the variable is x_2.)
4. Indicate by shading (or by arrows at the ends of the constraint line) whether the inequality is greater than or less than. (A general rule to determine which side of the line satisfies the inequality is to pick a point that is not on the line, such as 0,0, solve the equation using these values, and see whether it is greater than or less than the constraint amount.)
5. Repeat steps 1–4 for each constraint.

Consider the assembly time constraint:

$$4x_1 + 10x_2 \leq 100$$

Removing the inequality portion of the constraint produces this straight line:

$$4x_1 + 10x_2 = 100$$

Next, identify the points where the line intersects each axis, as step 2 describes. Thus with $x_2 = 0$, we find

$$4x_1 + 10(0) = 100$$

Solving, we find that $4x_1 = 100$, so $x_1 = 25$ when $x_2 = 0$. Similarly, we can solve the equation for x_2 when $x_1 = 0$:

$$4(0) + 10x_2 = 100$$

Solving for x_2, we find $x_2 = 10$ when $x_1 = 0$.

Thus, we have two points: $x_1 = 0, x_2 = 10$, and $x_1 = 25, x_2 = 0$. We can now add this line to our graph of the nonnegativity constraints by connecting these two points (see Figure 19.2).

Next we must determine which side of the line represents points that are less than 100. To do this, we can select a test point that is not on the line, and we can substitute the x_1 and x_2 values of that point into the left-hand side of the equation of the line. If the result is less than 100, this tells us that all points on that side of the line are less than the value of the line (e.g., 100). Conversely, if the result is greater than 100, this indicates that the other side of the line represents the set of points that will yield values that are less than 100. A relatively simple test point to use is the origin (i.e., $x_1 = 0, x_2 = 0$). Substituting these values into the equation yields

$$4(0) + 10(0) = 0$$

FIGURE 19.2 Plot of the first constraint (assembly time)

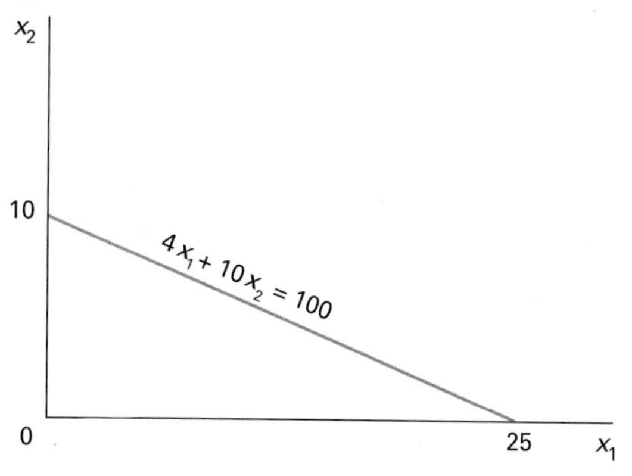

FIGURE 19.3 The feasible region, given the first constraint and the nonnegativity constraints

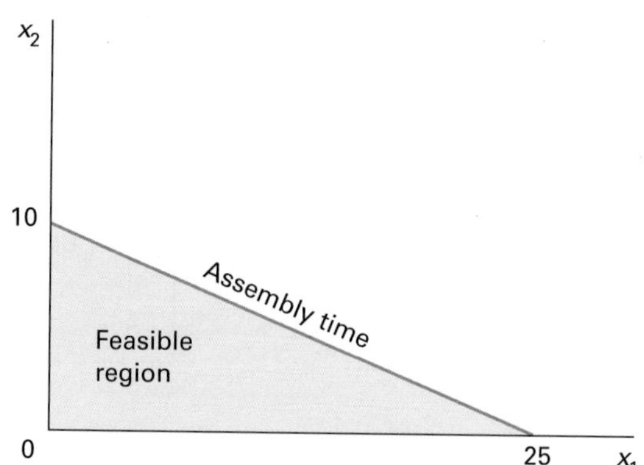

Obviously this is less than 100. Hence, the side of the line closest to the origin represents the "less than" area (i.e., the feasible region).

The feasible region for this constraint and the nonnegativity constraints then becomes the shaded portion shown in Figure 19.3.

For the sake of illustration, suppose we try one other point, say $x_1 = 10, x_2 = 10$. Substituting these values into the assembly constraint yields

$$4(10) + 10(10) = 140$$

Clearly this is greater than 100. Therefore, all points on this side of the line are greater than 100 (see Figure 19.4).

Continuing with the problem, we can add the two remaining constraints to the graph. For the inspection constraint:

1. Convert the constraint into the equation of a straight line by replacing the inequality sign with an equality sign:

   $$2x_1 + 1x_2 \leq 22 \quad \text{becomes} \quad 2x_1 + 1x_2 = 22$$

2. Set x_1 equal to zero and solve for x_2:

   $$2(0) + 1x_2 = 22$$

   Solving, we find $x_2 = 22$. Thus, the line will intersect the x_2 axis at 22.
3. Next, set x_2 equal to zero and solve for x_1:

   $$2x_1 + 1(0) = 22$$

   Solving, we find $x_1 = 11$. Thus, the other end of the line will intersect the x_1 axis at 11.
4. Add the line to the graph (see Figure 19.5).

Note that the area of feasibility for this constraint is below the line (Figure 19.5). Again the area of feasibility at this point is shaded in for illustration, although when graphing problems, it is more practical to refrain from shading in the feasible region until all constraint lines have been drawn. However, because constraints are plotted one at a time, using a small arrow at the end of each constraint to indicate the direction of feasibility can be helpful.

The storage constraint is handled in the same manner:

1. Convert it into an equality:

   $$3x_1 + 3x_2 = 39$$

2. Set x_1 equal to zero and solve for x_2:

   $$3(0) + 3x_2 = 39$$

FIGURE 19.4 The point (10, 10) is above the constraint line

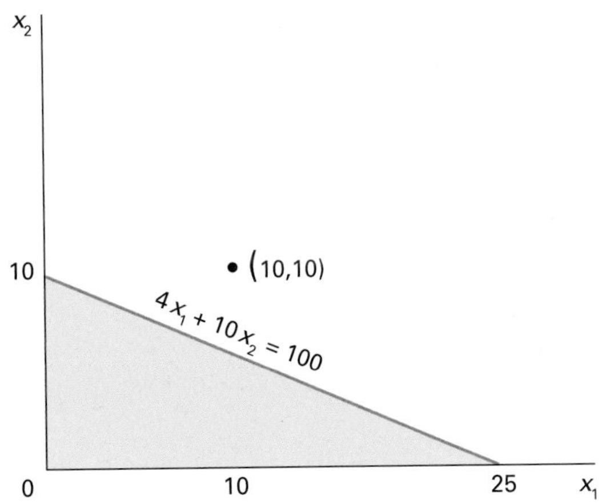

FIGURE 19.5 Partially completed graph, showing the assembly, inspection, and nonnegativity constraints

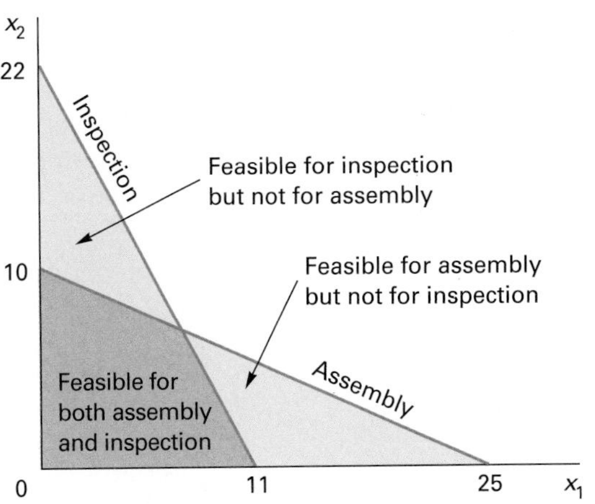

Solving, $x_2 = 13$. Thus, $x_2 = 13$ when $x_1 = 0$.

3. Set x_2 equal to zero and solve for x_1:

$$3x_1 + 3(0) = 39$$

Solving, $x_1 = 13$. Thus, $x_1 = 13$ when $x_2 = 0$.

4. Add the line to the graph (see Figure 19.6).

Identifying the Feasible Solution Space

The feasible solution space is the set of all points that satisfies *all* constraints. (Recall that the x_1 and x_2 axes form nonnegativity constraints.) The heavily shaded area shown in Figure 19.6 is the feasible solution space for our problem.

The next step is to determine which point in the feasible solution space will produce the optimal value of the objective function. This determination is made using the objective function.

Plotting the Objective Function Line

Plotting an objective function line involves the same logic as plotting a constraint line: Determine where the line intersects each axis. Recall that the objective function for the microcomputer problem is

$$60x_1 + 50x_2$$

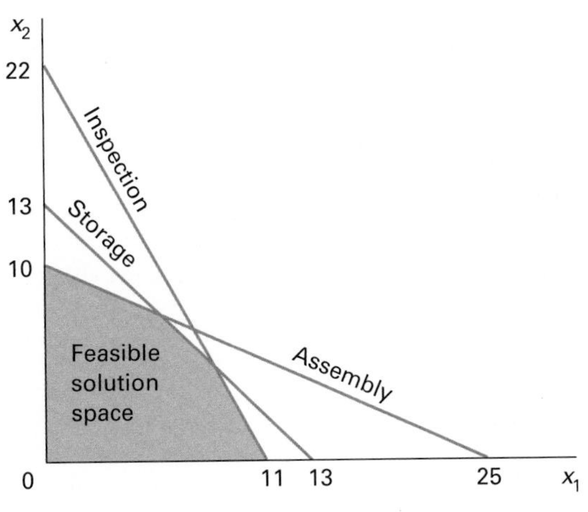

FIGURE 19.6 Completed graph of the microcomputer problem showing all constraints and the feasible solution space

This is not an equation because it does not include an equal sign. We can get around this by simply setting it equal to some quantity. Any quantity will do, although one that is evenly divisible by both coefficients is desirable.

Suppose we decide to set the objective function equal to 300. That is,

$$60x_1 + 50x_2 = 300$$

We can now plot the line on our graph. As before, we can determine the x_1 and x_2 intercepts of the line by setting one of the two variables equal to zero, solving for the other, and then reversing the process. Thus, with $x_1 = 0$, we have

$$60(0) + 50x_2 = 300$$

Solving, we find $x_2 = 6$. Similarly, with $x_2 = 0$, we have

$$60x_1 + 50(0) = 300$$

Solving, we find $x_1 = 5$. This line is plotted in Figure 19.7.

The profit line can be interpreted in the following way. It is an *isoprofit* line; every point on the line (i.e., every combination of x_1 and x_2 that lies on the line) will provide a profit of \$300. We can see from the graph many combinations that are both on the \$300 profit line and within the feasible solution space. In fact, considering noninteger as well as integer solutions, the possibilities are infinite.

Suppose we now consider another line, say the \$600 line. To do this, we set the objective function equal to this amount. Thus,

$$60x_1 + 50x_2 = 600$$

Solving for the x_1 and x_2 intercepts yields these two points:

x_1 intercept	x_2 intercept
$x_1 = 10$	$x_1 = 0$
$x_2 = 0$	$x_2 = 12$

This line is plotted in Figure 19.8, along with the previous \$300 line for purposes of comparison.

Two things are evident in Figure 19.8 regarding the profit lines. One is that the \$600 line is *farther* from the origin than the \$300 line; the other is that the two lines are *parallel.* The lines are parallel because they both have the same slope. The slope is not affected by the right side of the equation. Rather, it is determined solely by the coefficients 60 and 50. It would be

FIGURE 19.7 Microcomputer problem with \$300 profit line added

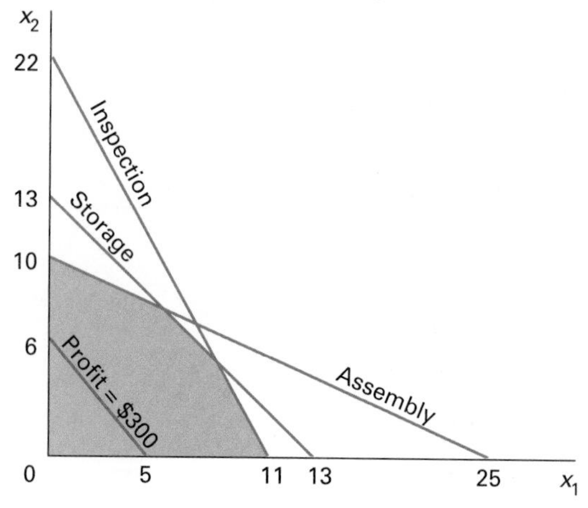

FIGURE 19.8 Microcomputer problem with profit lines of \$300 and \$600

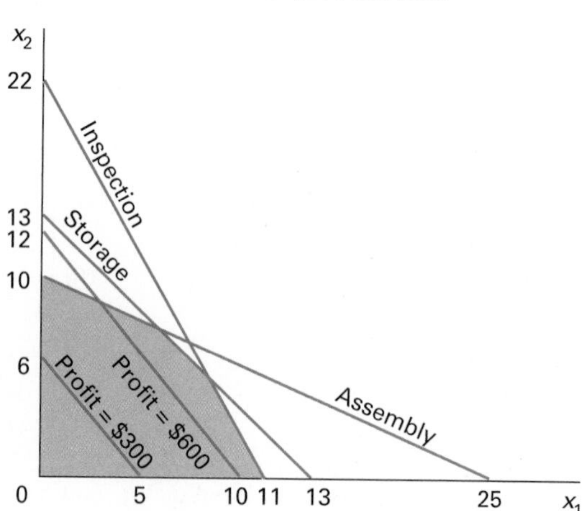

FIGURE 19.9 Microcomputer problem with profit lines of \$300, \$600, and \$900

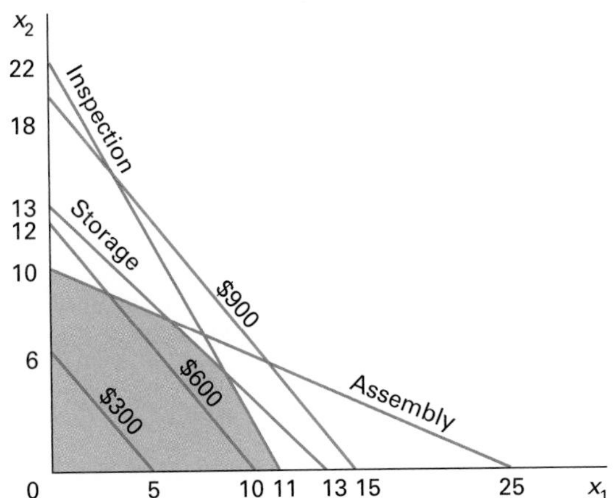

FIGURE 19.10 Finding the optimal solution to the microcomputer problem

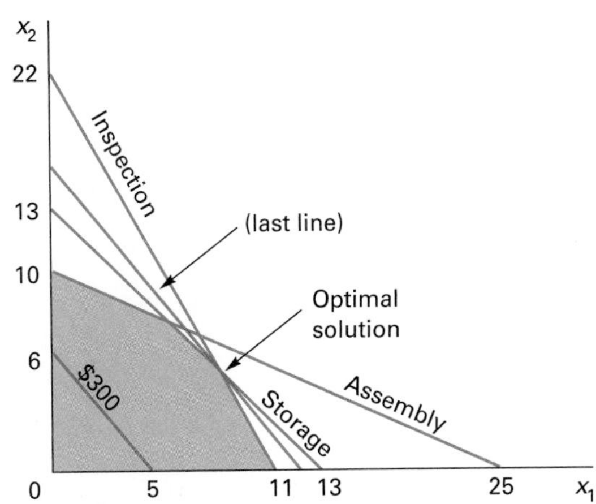

correct to conclude that regardless of the quantity we select for the value of the objective function, the resulting line will be parallel to these two lines. Moreover, if the amount is greater than 600, the line will be even farther away from the origin than the \$600 line. If the value is less than 300, the line will be closer to the origin than the \$300 line. And if the value is between 300 and 600, the line will fall between the \$300 and \$600 lines. This knowledge will help in determining the optimal solution.

Consider a third line, one with the profit equal to \$900. Figure 19.9 shows that line along with the previous two profit lines. As expected, it is parallel to the other two, and even farther away from the origin. However, the line does not touch the feasible solution space at all. Consequently, there is no feasible combination of x_1 and x_2 that will yield that amount of profit. Evidently, the maximum possible profit is an amount between \$600 and \$900, which we can see by referring to Figure 19.9. We could continue to select profit lines in this manner, and eventually, we could determine an amount that would yield the greatest profit. However, there is a much simpler alternative. We can plot just one line, say the \$300 line. We know that all other lines will be parallel to it. Consequently, by moving this one line parallel to itself we can "test" other profit lines. We also know that as we move away from the origin, the profits get larger. What we want to know is how far the line can be moved out from the origin and still be touching the feasible solution space, and the values of the decision variables at that point of greatest profit (i.e., the optimal solution). Locate this point on the graph by placing a straight edge along the \$300 line (or any other convenient line) and sliding it away from the origin, being careful to keep it parallel to the line. This approach is illustrated in Figure 19.10.

Once we have determined where the optimal solution is in the feasible solution space, we must determine the values of the decision variables at that point. Then, we can use that information to compute the profit for that combination.

Note that the optimal solution is at the intersection of the inspection boundary and the storage boundary (see Figure 19.10). In other words, the optimal combination of x_1 and x_2 must satisfy both boundary (equality) conditions. We can determine those values by solving the two equations *simultaneously.* The equations are

Inspection	$2x_1 + 1x_2 = 22$
Storage	$3x_1 + 3x_2 = 39$

The idea behind solving two *simultaneous equations* is to algebraically eliminate one of the unknown variables (i.e., to obtain an equation with a single unknown). This can be accomplished by multiplying the constants of one of the equations by a fixed amount and then adding (or subtracting) the modified equation from the other. (Occasionally, it is easier to multiply each equation by a fixed quantity.) For example, we can eliminate x_2 by multiplying the inspection equation by 3 and then subtracting the storage equation from the modified inspection equation. Thus,

$$3(2x_1 + 1x_2 = 22) \quad \text{becomes} \quad 6x_1 + 3x_2 = 66$$

Subtracting the storage equation from this produces

$$\begin{array}{r} 6x_1 + 3x_2 = 66 \\ -(3x_1 + 3x_2 = 39) \\ \hline 3x_1 + 0x_2 = 27 \end{array}$$

Solving the resulting equation yields $x_1 = 9$. The value of x_2 can be found by substituting $x_1 = 9$ into either of the original equations or the modified inspection equation. Suppose we use the original inspection equation. We have

$$2(9) + 1x_2 = 22$$

Solving, we find $x_2 = 4$.

Hence, the optimal solution to the microcomputer problem is to produce nine type 1 computers and four type 2 computers per day. We can substitute these values into the objective function to find the optimal profit:

$$\$60(9) + \$50(4) = \$740$$

Hence, the last line—the one that would last touch the feasible solution space as we moved away from the origin parallel to the $300 profit line—would be the line where profit equaled $740.

In this problem, the optimal values for both decision variables are integers. This will not always be the case; one or both of the decision variables may turn out to be noninteger. In some situations noninteger values would be of little consequence. This would be true if the decision variables were measured on a continuous scale, such as the amount of water, sand, sugar, fuel oil, time, or distance needed for optimality, or if the contribution per unit (profit, cost, etc.) were small, as with the number of nails or ball bearings to make. In some cases, the answer would simply be rounded down (maximization problems) or up (minimization problems) with very little impact on the objective function. Here, we assume that noninteger answers are acceptable as such.

Let's review the procedure for finding the optimal solution using the objective function approach:

1. Graph the constraints.
2. Identify the feasible solution space.
3. Set the objective function equal to some amount that is divisible by each of the objective function coefficients. This will yield integer values for the x_1 and x_2 intercepts and simplify plotting the line. Often, the product of the two objective function coefficients provides a satisfactory line. Ideally, the line will cross the feasible solution space close to the optimal point, and it will not be necessary to slide a straight edge because the optimal solution can be readily identified visually.
4. After identifying the optimal point, determine which two constraints intersect there. Solve their equations simultaneously to obtain the values of the decision variables at the optimum.
5. Substitute the values obtained in the previous step into the objective function to determine the value of the objective function at the optimum.

Redundant Constraints

Redundant constraint A constraint that does not form a unique boundary of the feasible solution space.

In some cases, a constraint does not form a unique boundary of the feasible solution space. Such a constraint is called a **redundant constraint.** Two such constraints are illustrated in Figure 19.11. Note that a constraint is redundant if it meets the following test: Its removal would not alter the feasible solution space.

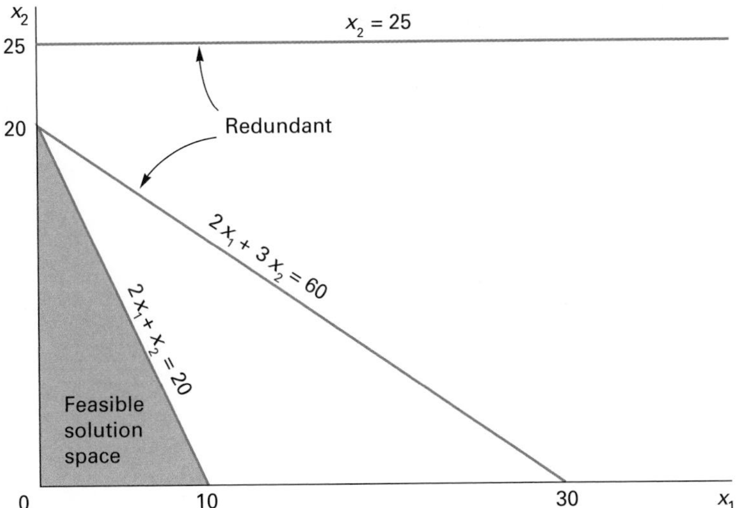

FIGURE 19.11
Examples of redundant constraints

When a problem has a redundant constraint, at least one of the other constraints in the problem is more restrictive than the redundant constraint.

Solutions and Corner Points

The feasible solution space in graphical linear programming is typically a polygon. Moreover, the solution to any problem will be at one of the corner points (intersections of constraints) of the polygon. It is possible to determine the coordinates of each corner point of the feasible solution space, and use those values to compute the value of the objective function at those points. Because the solution is always at a corner point, comparing the values of the objective function at the corner points and identifying the best one (e.g., the maximum value) is another way to identify the optimal corner point. Using the graphical approach, it is much easier to plot the objective function and use that to identify the optimal corner point. However, for problems that have more than two decision variables, and the graphical method isn't appropriate, the "enumeration" approach is used to find the optimal solution.

With the **enumeration approach,** the coordinates of each corner point are determined, and then each set of coordinates is substituted into the objective function to determine its value at that corner point. After all corner points have been evaluated, the one with the maximum or minimum value (depending on whether the objective is to maximize or minimize) is identified as the optimal solution.

Enumeration approach
Substituting the coordinates of each corner point into the objective function to determine which corner point is optimal.

Thus, in the microcomputer problem, the corner points are $x_1 = 0, x_2 = 10, x_1 = 11, x_2 = 0$ (by inspection; see Figure 19.10), and $x_1 = 9, x_2 = 4$ and $x_1 = 5, x_2 = 8$ (using simultaneous equations, as illustrated on pages 843–844). Substituting into the objective function, the values are \$500 for (0,10); \$740 for (9,4); \$660 for (11,0), and \$700 for (5,8). Because (9,4) yields the highest value, that corner point is the optimal solution.

In some instances, the objective function will be *parallel* to one of the constraint lines that forms a *boundary of the feasible solution space.* When this happens, *every* combination of x_1 and x_2 on the segment of the constraint that touches the feasible solution space represents an optimal solution. Hence, there are multiple optimal solutions to the problem. Even in such a case, the solution will also be a corner point—in fact, the solution will be at *two* corner points: those at the ends of the segment that touches the feasible solution space. Figure 19.12 illustrates an objective function line that is parallel to a constraint line.

Minimization

Graphical minimization problems are quite similar to maximization problems. There are, however, two important differences. One is that at least one of the constraints must be of the = or ≥ variety. This causes the feasible solution space to be away from the origin. The other difference is that the optimal point is the one closest to the origin. We find the optimal corner point by sliding the objective function (which is an *isocost* line) *toward* the origin instead of away from it.

FIGURE 19.12
Some LP problems have multiple optimal solutions

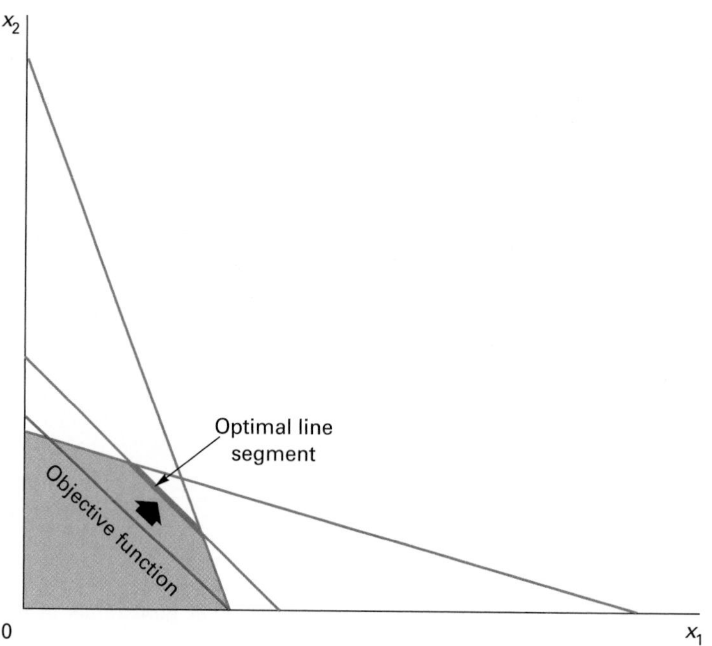

EXAMPLE 3

Solve the following problem using graphical linear programming.

$$\begin{aligned} \text{Minimize} \quad & Z = 8x_1 + 12x_2 \\ \text{Subject to} \quad & 5x_1 + 2x_2 \geq 20 \\ & 4x_1 + 3x_2 \geq 24 \\ & x_2 \geq 2 \\ & x_1, x_2 \geq 0 \end{aligned}$$

SOLUTION

1. Plot the constraints (shown in Figure 19.13).
   a. Change constraints to equalities.
   b. For each constraint, set $x_1 = 0$ and solve for x_2, then set $x_2 = 0$ and solve for x_1.
   c. Graph each constraint. Note that $x_2 = 2$ is a horizontal line parallel to the x_1 axis and 2 units above it.
2. Shade the feasible solution space (see Figure 19.13).
3. Plot the objective function.
   a. Select a value for the objective function that causes it to cross the feasible solution space. Try $8 \times 12 = 96$; $8x_1 + 12x_2 = 96$ (acceptable).
   b. Graph the line (see Figure 19.14).
4. Slide the objective function toward the origin, being careful to keep it parallel to the original line.
5. The optimum (last feasible point) is shown in Figure 19.14. The x_2 coordinate ($x_2 = 2$) can be determined by inspection of the graph. Note that the optimum point is at the intersection of the line $x_2 = 2$ and the line $4x_1 + 3x_2 = 24$. Substituting the value of $x_2 = 2$ into the latter equation will yield the value of x_1 at the intersection:

   $$4x_1 + 3(2) = 24 \qquad x_1 = 4.5$$

   Thus, the optimum is $x_1 = 4.5$ units and $x_2 = 2$.
6. Compute the minimum cost:
   $$8x_1 + 12x_2 = 8(4.5) + 12(2) = 60$$

FIGURE 19.13 The constraints define the feasible solution space

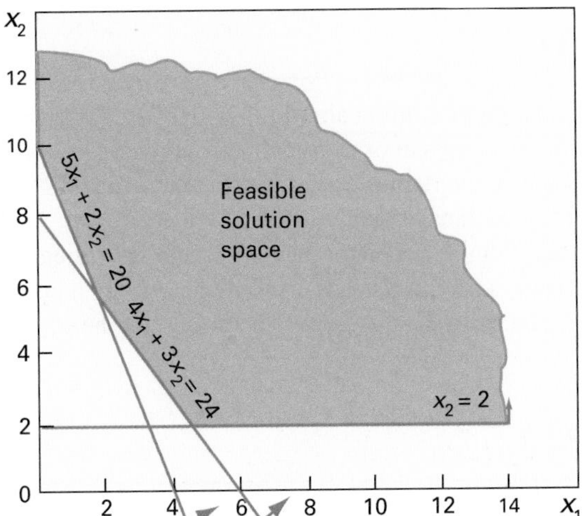

FIGURE 19.14 The optimum is the last point the objective function touches as it is moved toward the origin

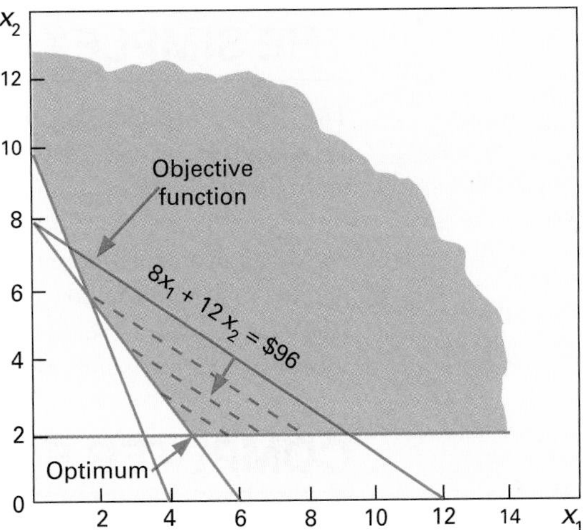

Slack and Surplus

If a constraint forms the optimal corner point of the feasible solution space, it is called a **binding constraint.** In effect, it limits the value of the objective function; if the constraint could be relaxed (less restrictive), an improved solution would be possible. For constraints that are not binding, making them less restrictive will have no impact on the solution.

Binding constraint A constraint that forms the optimal corner point of the feasible solution space.

If the optimal values of the decision variables are substituted into the left-hand side of a binding constraint, the resulting value will exactly equal the right-hand value of the constraint. However, there will be a difference with a nonbinding constraint. If the left-hand side is greater than the right-hand side, we say that there is **surplus;** if the left-hand side is less than the right-hand side, we say that there is **slack.** Slack can only occur in a $\leq$ constraint; it is the amount by which the left-hand side is less than the right-hand side when the optimal values of the decision variables are substituted into the left-hand side. And surplus can only occur in a $\geq$ constraint; it is the amount by which the left-hand side exceeds the right-hand side of the constraint when the optimal values of the decision variables are substituted into the left-hand side.

Surplus When the values of decision variables are substituted into a $\geq$ constraint the amount by which the resulting value exceeds the right-hand-side value.

Slack When the values of decision variables are substituted into a $\leq$ constraint the amount by which the resulting value is less than the right-hand-side value.

For example, suppose the optimal values for a problem are $x_1 = 10$ and $x_2 = 20$. If one of the constraints is

$$3x_1 + 2x_2 \leq 100$$

substituting the optimal values into the left-hand side yields

$$3(10) + 2(20) = 70$$

Because the constraint is $\leq$, the difference between the values of 100 and 70 (i.e., 30) is *slack.* Suppose the optimal values had been $x_1 = 20$ and $x_2 = 20$. Substituting these values into the left-hand side of the constraint would yield $3(20) + 2(20) = 100$. Because the left-hand side equals the right-hand side, this is a binding constraint; slack is equal to zero.

Now consider this constraint:

$$4x_1 + x_2 \geq 50$$

Suppose the optimal values are $x_1 = 10$ and $x_2 = 15$; substituting into the left-hand side yields

$$4(10) + 15 = 55$$

Because this is a $\geq$ constraint, the difference between the left- and right-hand-side values is *surplus.* If the optimal values had been $x_1 = 12$ and $x_2 = 2$, substitution would result in the left-hand side being equal to 50. Hence, the constraint would be a binding constraint, and there would be no surplus (i.e., surplus would be zero).

THE SIMPLEX METHOD

Simplex A linear programming algorithm that can solve problems having more than two decision variables.

The **simplex** method is a general-purpose linear programming algorithm widely used to solve large-scale problems. Although it lacks the intuitive appeal of the graphical approach, its ability to handle problems with more than two decision variables makes it extremely valuable for solving problems often encountered in operations management.

Although manual solution of linear programming problems using simplex can yield a number of insights on how solutions are derived, space limitations preclude describing it here. However, it is available on the Web site that accompanies this book. The discussion here will focus on computer solutions.

COMPUTER SOLUTIONS

The microcomputer problem will be used to illustrate computer solutions. We repeat it here for ease of reference.

Maximize $60x_1 + 50x_2$ where x_1 = the number of type 1 computers

x_2 = the number of type 2 computers

Subject to

Assembly	$4x_1 + 10x_2 \leq$	100 hours
Inspection	$2x_1 + 1x_2 \leq$	22 hours
Storage	$3x_1 + 3x_2 \leq$	39 cubic feet
	$x_1, x_2 \geq$	0

Solving LP Models Using MS Excel

SCREENCAM TUTORIAL

Solutions to linear programming models can be obtained from spreadsheet software such as Microsoft's Excel. Excel has a routine called Solver that performs the necessary calculations.

To use Solver:

1. First, enter the problem in a worksheet, as shown in Figure 19.15. What is not obvious from the figure is the need to enter a formula for each cell where there is a zero (Solver automatically inserts the zero after you input the formula). The formulas are for the value of the objective function and the constraints, in the appropriate cells. Before you enter the formulas, designate the cells where you want the optimal values of x_1 and x_2. Here, cells D4 and E4 are used. To enter a formula, click on the cell that the formula will pertain to, and then enter the formula, starting with an equal sign. We want the optimal value of the objective function to appear in cell G4. For G4, enter the formula

```
=60*D4+50*E4
```

The constraint formulas, using cells C7, C8, and C9, are

for C7: `=4*D4+10*E4`

for C8: `=2*D4+1*E4`

for C9: `=3*D4+3*E4`

2. Now, to access Solver in Excel 2010 or 2007, click Data at the top of the worksheet, and in that ribbon, click on Solver in the Analysis group. In Excel 2010 the Solver menu will appear as illustrated in Figure 19.16. Begin by setting the Objective (i.e., indicating the cell where you want the optimal value if the objective function to appear). Note, if the activated cell is the cell designated for the value of Z when you click on Solver, Solver will automatically set that cell as the Objective.

	A	B	C	D	E	F	G
1	Microcomputer Problem						
2							
3		**Variables**		Type 1	Type 2		**Total Profit**
4							0
5							
6		**Constraints**		**RHS**			
7		Assembly	0	100			
8		Inspection	0	22			
9		Storage	0	39			

G4 f_x =60*D4+50*E4

FIGURE 19.15
MS Excel worksheet for microcomputer problem

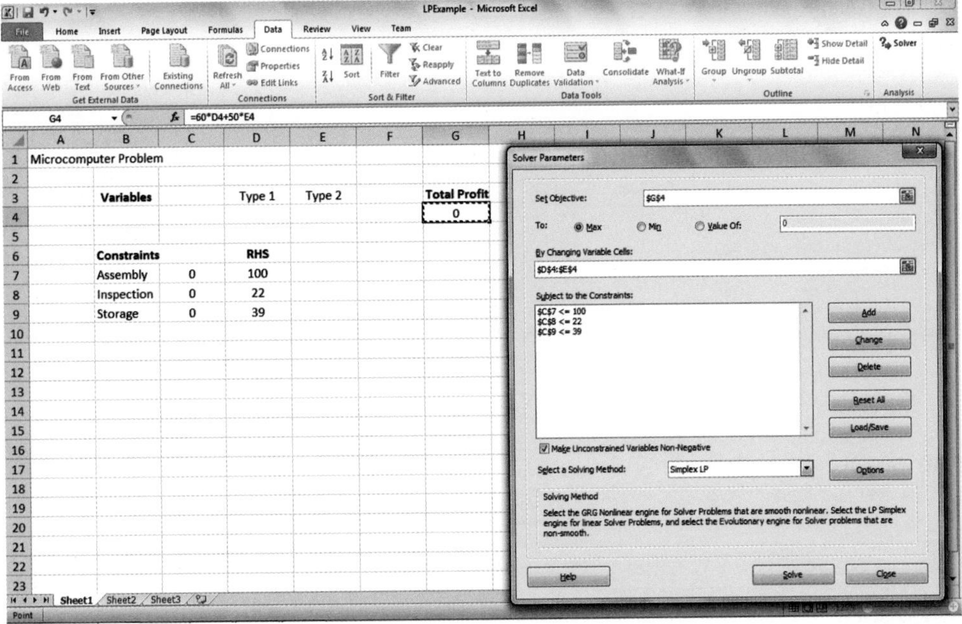

FIGURE 19.16
MS Excel Solver parameters for microcomputer problem

Select the Max radio button if it isn't already selected. The Changing Variable Cells are the cells where you want the optimal values of the decision variables to appear. Here, they are cells D4 and E4. We indicate this by the range D4:E4 (Solver will add the $signs).

Finally, add the constraints by clicking on Add . . . When that menu appears, for each constraint, enter the cell that contains the formula for the left-hand-side of the constraint, then select the appropriate inequality sign, and then enter the right-hand-side amount of the cell that has the right-hand-side amount. Here the right-hand-side amounts are used. After you have entered each constraint, either click on Add to add another constraint or click on OK to return to the Solver menu. (Notes: Constraints can be entered in any order, and if cells are used for the right-hand-side, then constraints with the same inequality could be combined). For the nonnegativity constraints simply check the checkbox to

Make Unconstrained Variables Non-Negative. Also select Simplex LP as the Solving Method. Click on Solve.

3. The Solver Results menu will then appear, indicating that a solution has been found, or that an error has occurred. If there has been an error, go back to the Solver Parameters menu and check to see that your constraints refer to the correct changing cells, and that the inequality directions are correct. Make the corrections and click on Solve.

Assuming everything is correct, in the Solver Results menu, in the Reports box, highlight both Answer and Sensitivity, and then click OK.

4. Solver will incorporate the optimal values of the decision variables and the objective function in your original layout on your worksheet (see Figure 19.17). We can see that the optimal values are type 1 = 9 units and type 2 = 4 units, and the total profit is 740. The answer report will also show the optimal values of the decision variables (upper part of Figure 19.18),

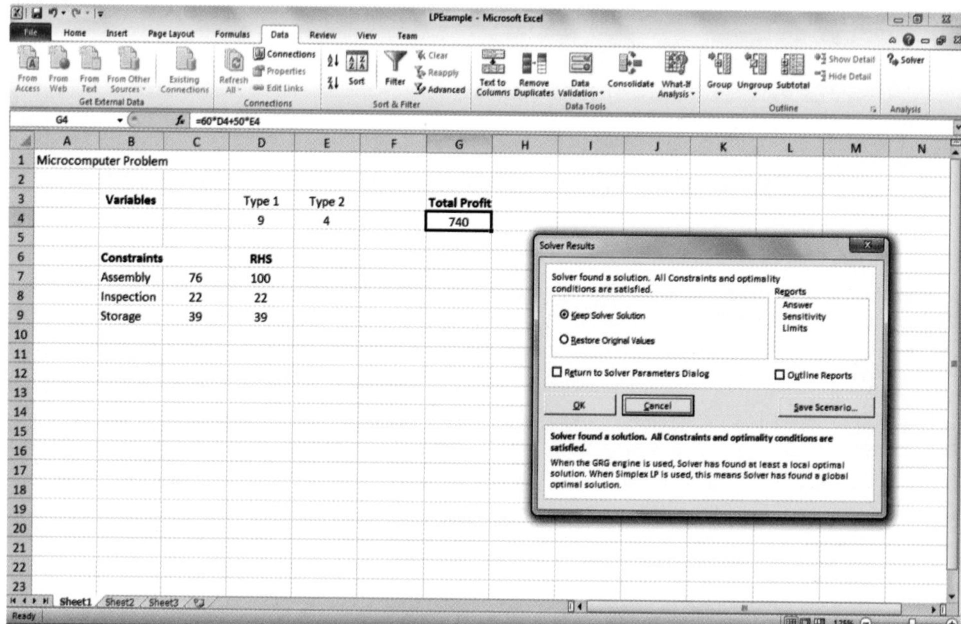

FIGURE 19.17
MS Excel worksheet solution for microcomputer problem

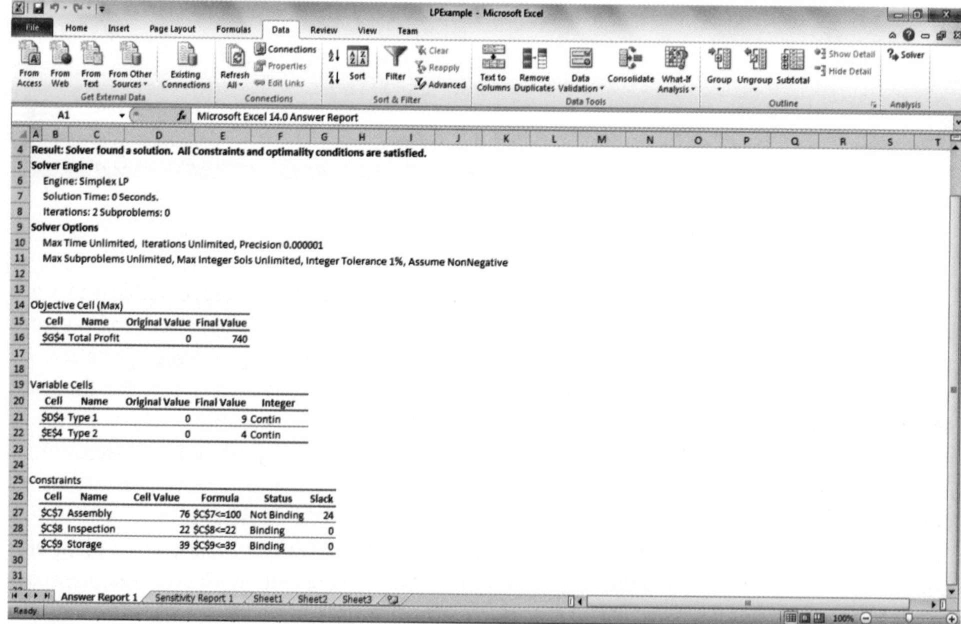

FIGURE 19.18
MS Excel Answer Report for microcomputer problem

and some information on the constraints (lower part of Figure 19.18). Of particular interest here is the indication of which constraints have slack and how much slack. We can see that the constraint entered in cell C7 (assembly) has a slack of 24, and that the constraints entered in cells C8 (inspection) and C9 (storage) have slack equal to zero, indicating that they are binding constraints.

SENSITIVITY ANALYSIS

Sensitivity analysis is a means of assessing the impact of potential changes to the parameters (the numerical values) of an LP model. Such changes may occur due to forces beyond a manager's control; or a manager may be contemplating making the changes, say, to increase profits or reduce costs.

Sensitivity analysis Assessing the impact of potential changes to the numerical values of an LP model.

There are three types of potential changes:

1. Objective function coefficients.
2. Right-hand values of constraints.
3. Constraint coefficients.

SCREENCAM TUTORIAL

We will consider the first two of these here. We begin with changes to objective function coefficients.

Objective Function Coefficient Changes

A change in the value of an objective function coefficient can cause a change in the optimal solution of a problem. In a graphical solution, this would mean a change to another corner point of the feasible solution space. However, not every change in the value of an objective function coefficient will lead to a changed solution; generally there is a *range of values for which the optimal values of the decision variables will not change.* For example, in the microcomputer problem, if the profit on type 1 computers increased from $60 per unit to, say, $65 per unit, the optimal solution would still be to produce nine units of type 1 and four units of type 2 computers. Similarly, if the profit per unit on type 1 computers decreased from $60 to, say, $58, producing nine of type 1 and four of type 2 would still be optimal. These sorts of changes are not uncommon; they may be the result of such things as price changes in raw materials, price discounts, cost reductions in production, and so on. Obviously, when a change does occur in the value of an objective function coefficient, it can be helpful for a manager to know if that change will affect the optimal values of the decision variables. The manager can quickly determine this by referring to that coefficient's **range of optimality**, which is the range in possible values of that objective function coefficient over which the optimal values of the decision variables will not change. Before we see how to determine the range, consider the implication of the range. The range of optimality for the type 1 coefficient in the microcomputer problem is 50 to 100. That means that as long as the coefficient's value is in that range, the optimal values will be 9 units of type 1 and 4 units of type 2. Conversely, *if a change extends beyond the range of optimality, the solution will change.*

Range of optimality Range of values over which the solution quantities of all the decision variables remain the same.

Similarly, suppose, instead, the coefficient (unit profit) of type 2 computers was to change. Its range of optimality is 30 to 60. As long as the change doesn't take it outside of this range, nine and four will still be the optimal values. Note, however, even for changes that are *within* the range of optimality, the optimal value of the objective function *will* change. If the type 1 coefficient increased from $60 to $61, and nine units of type 1 is still optimum, profit would increase by $9: nine units times $1 per unit. Thus, for a change that is within the range of optimality, a revised value of the objective function must be determined.

Now let's see how we can determine the range of optimality using computer output.

Using MS Excel. There is a table for the Changing Cells (see Figure 19.19). It shows the value of the objective function that was used in the problem for each type of computer (i.e., 60 and 50), and the allowable increase and allowable decrease for each coefficient. By subtracting the allowable decrease from the original value of the coefficient, and adding the

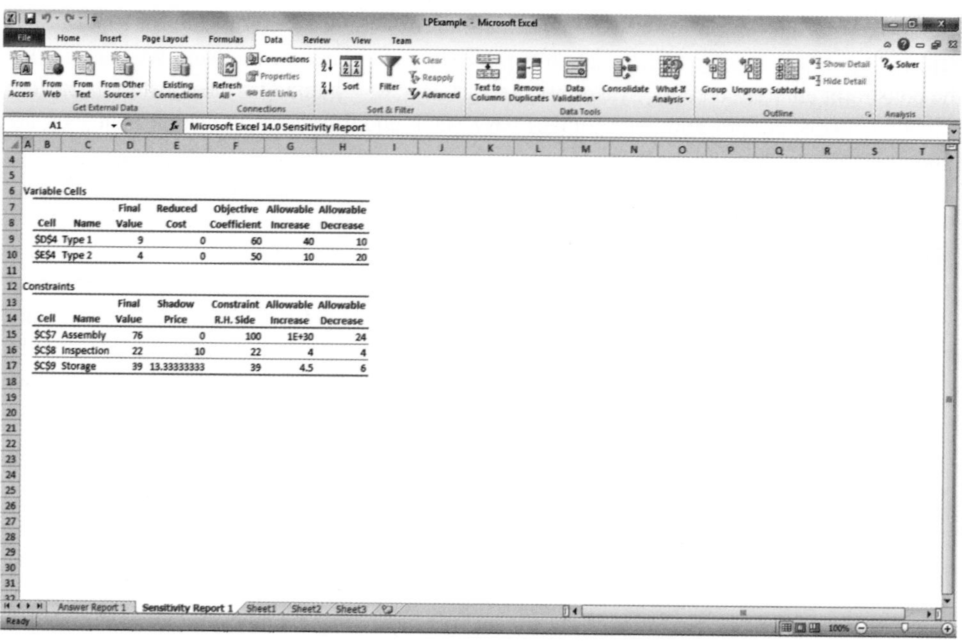

Microsoft Excel 14.0 Sensitivity Report

Variable Cells

Cell	Name	Final Value	Reduced Cost	Objective Coefficient	Allowable Increase	Allowable Decrease
D4	Type 1	9	0	60	40	10
E4	Type 2	4	0	50	10	20

Constraints

Cell	Name	Final Value	Shadow Price	Constraint R.H. Side	Allowable Increase	Allowable Decrease
C7	Assembly	76	0	100	1E+30	24
C8	Inspection	22	10	22	4	4
C9	Storage	39	13.33333333	39	4.5	6

FIGURE 19.19
MS Excel sensitivity report for microcomputer problem

allowable increase to the original value of the coefficient, we obtain the range of optimality for each coefficient. Thus, we find for type 1:

$$60 - 10 = 50 \quad \text{and} \quad 60 + 40 = 100$$

Hence, the range for the type 1 coefficient is 50 to 100. For type 2:

$$50 - 20 = 30 \quad \text{and} \quad 50 + 10 = 60$$

Hence the range for the type 2 coefficient is 30 to 60.

In this example, both of the decision variables are *basic* (i.e., nonzero). However, in other problems, one or more decision variables may be *nonbasic* (i.e., have an optimal value of zero). In such instances, unless the value of that variable's objective function coefficient increases by more than its *reduced cost,* it won't come into solution (i.e., become a basic variable). Hence, the range of optimality (sometimes referred to as the *range of insignificance*) for a nonbasic variable is from negative infinity to the sum of its current value and its reduced cost.

Now let's see how we can handle multiple changes to objective function coefficients, that is, a change in more than one coefficient. To do this, divide each coefficient's change by the allowable change in the same direction. Thus, if the change is a decrease, divide that amount by the allowable decrease. Treat all resulting fractions as positive. Sum the fractions. If the sum does not exceed 1.00, then multiple changes are within the range of optimality and will not result in any change to the optimal values of the decision variables.

Changes in the Right-Hand-Side (RHS) Value of a Constraint

In considering right-hand-side (RHS) changes, it is important to know if a particular constraint is binding on a solution. A constraint is binding if substituting the values of the decision variables of that solution into the left-hand side of the constraint results in a value that is equal to the RHS value. In other words, that constraint stops the objective function from achieving a better value (e.g., a greater profit or a lower cost). Each constraint has a corresponding **shadow price,** which is a marginal value that indicates the amount by which the value of the objective function would change if there were a one-unit change in the RHS value of that constraint. If a constraint is nonbinding, its shadow price is zero, meaning that

Shadow price Amount by which the value of the objective function would change with a one-unit change in the RHS value of a constraint.

increasing or decreasing its RHS value by one unit will have no impact on the value of the objective function. Nonbinding constraints have either slack (if the constraint is ≤) or surplus (if the constraint is ≥). Suppose a constraint has 10 units of slack in the optimal solution, which means 10 units that are unused. If we were to increase or decrease the constraint's RHS value by one unit, the only effect would be to increase or decrease its slack by one unit. But there is no profit associated with slack, so the value of the objective function wouldn't change. On the other hand, if the change is to the RHS value of a binding constraint, then the optimal value of the objective function would change. Any change in a binding constraint will cause the optimal values of the decision variables to change, and hence, cause the value of the objective function to change. For example, in the microcomputer problem, the inspection constraint is a binding constraint; it has a shadow price of 10. That means if there was one hour less of inspection time, total profit would decrease by \$10, or if there was one more hour of inspection time available, total profit would increase by \$10. In general, multiplying the amount of change in the RHS value of a constraint by the constraint's shadow price will indicate the change's impact on the optimal value of the objective function. However, this is only true over a limited range called the **range of feasibility**. In this range, the value of the shadow price remains constant. Hence, as long as a change in the RHS value of a constraint is within its range of feasibility, the shadow price will remain the same, and one can readily determine the impact on the objective function.

Range of feasibility Range of values for the RHS of a constraint over which the shadow price remains the same.

Let's see how to determine the range of feasibility from computer output.

Using MS Excel. In the sensitivity report there is a table labeled "Constraints" (see Figure 19.19). The table shows the shadow price for each constraint, its RHS value, and the allowable increase and allowable decrease. Adding the allowable increase to the RHS value and subtracting the allowable decrease will produce the range of feasibility for that constraint. For example, for the inspection constraint, the range would be

$$22 + 4 = 26; \quad 22 - 4 = 18$$

Hence, the range of feasibility for inspection is 18 to 26 hours. Similarly, for the storage constraint, the range is

$$39 - 6 = 33 \quad \text{to} \quad 39 + 4.5 = 43.5$$

The range for the assembly constraint is a little different; the assembly constraint is nonbinding (note the shadow price of 0) while the other two are binding (note their nonzero shadow prices). The assembly constraint has a slack of 24 (the difference between its RHS value of 100 and its final value of 76). With its slack of 24, its RHS value could be decreased by as much as 24 (to 76) before it would become binding. Conversely, increasing its right-hand side will only produce more slack. Thus, no amount of increase in the RHS value will make it binding, so there is no upper limit on the allowable increase. Excel indicates this by the large value (1E + 30) shown for the allowable increase. So its range of feasibility has a lower limit of 76 and no upper limit.

If there are changes to more than one constraint's RHS value, analyze these in the same way as multiple changes to objective function coefficients. That is, if the change is an increase, divide that amount by that constraint's allowable increase; if the change is a decrease, divide the decrease by the allowable decrease. Treat all resulting fractions as positives. Sum the fractions. As long as the sum does not exceed 1.00, the changes are within the range of feasibility for multiple changes, and the shadow prices won't change.

Table 19.1 summarizes the impacts of changes that fall within either the range of optimality or the range of feasibility.

Now let's consider what happens if a change goes beyond a particular range. In a situation involving the range of optimality, a change in an objective function that is beyond the range of optimality will result in a new solution. Hence, it will be necessary to recompute the solution. For a situation involving the range of feasibility, there are two cases to consider. The first case would be increasing the RHS value of a ≤ constraint to beyond the upper limit of its

TABLE 19.1
Summary of the impact of changes within their respective ranges

Changes to objective function coefficients that are within the range of optimality	
Component	**Result**
Values of decision variables	No change
Value of objective function	Will change

Changes to RHS values of constraints that are within the range of feasibility	
Component	**Result**
Value of shadow price	No change
List of basic variables	No change
Values of basic variables	Will change
Value of objective function	Will change

range of feasibility. This would produce slack equal to the amount by which the upper limit is exceeded. Hence, if the upper limit is 200, and the increase is 220, the result is that the constraint has a slack of 20. Similarly, for a ≥ constraint, going below its lower bound creates a surplus for that constraint. The second case for each of these would be exceeding the opposite limit (the lower bound for a ≤ constraint, or the upper bound for a ≥ constraint). In either instance, a new solution would have to be generated.

SUMMARY

Linear programming is a powerful tool used for constrained optimization situations. Components of LP problems include an objective function, decision variables, constraints, and numerical values (parameters) of the objective function and constraints.

The size of real-life problems and the burden of manual solution make computer solutions the practical way to solve real-life problems. Even so, much insight can be gained through the study of simple, two-variable problems and graphical solutions.

KEY POINTS

1. Optimizing techniques such as linear programming help business organizations make the best use of limited resources such as materials, time, and energy, to maximize profits or to minimize costs.
2. As with all techniques, it is important to confirm that the underlying assumptions on which the technique is based are reasonably satisfied by the model in order to achieve valid results.
3. Although the graphical technique has limited use due to the fact that it can only handle two-variable problems, it is very useful in conveying many of the important concepts associated with linear programming techniques.

KEY TERMS

binding constraint, 847
constraints, 834
decision variables, 834
enumeration approach, 845
feasible solution space, 834
graphical linear programming, 836
objective function, 834
parameters, 834
range of feasibility, 853
range of optimality, 851
redundant constraint, 844
sensitivity analysis, 851
shadow price, 852
simplex, 848
slack, 847
surplus, 847

SOLVED PROBLEMS

Problem 1

A small construction firm specializes in building and selling single-family homes. The firm offers two basic types of houses, model A and model B. Model A houses require 4,000 labor hours, 2 tons of stone, and 2,000 board feet of lumber. Model B houses require 10,000 labor hours, 3 tons of stone, and 2,000 board feet of lumber. Due to long lead times for ordering supplies and the scarcity of skilled and semiskilled workers in the area, the firm will be forced to rely on its present resources for the upcoming building season. It has 400,000 hours of labor, 150 tons of stone, and 200,000 board feet of lumber. What mix of model A and B houses should the firm construct if model A yields a profit of $3,000 per unit and model B yields $6,000 per unit? Assume that the firm will be able to sell all the units it builds.

Solution

1. Formulate the objective function and constraints:[1]

   Maximize $Z = 3{,}000A + 6{,}000B$

   Subject to

$$\begin{array}{lrl} \text{Labor} & 4{,}000A + 10{,}000B & \leq 400{,}000 \text{ labor hours} \\ \text{Stone} & 2A + 3B & \leq 150 \text{ tons} \\ \text{Lumber} & 2{,}000A + 2{,}000B & \leq 200{,}000 \text{ board feet} \\ & A, B & \geq 0 \end{array}$$

2. Graph the constraints and objective function, and identify the optimum corner point (see graph). Note that the lumber constraint is *redundant:* It does not form a boundary of the feasible solution space.

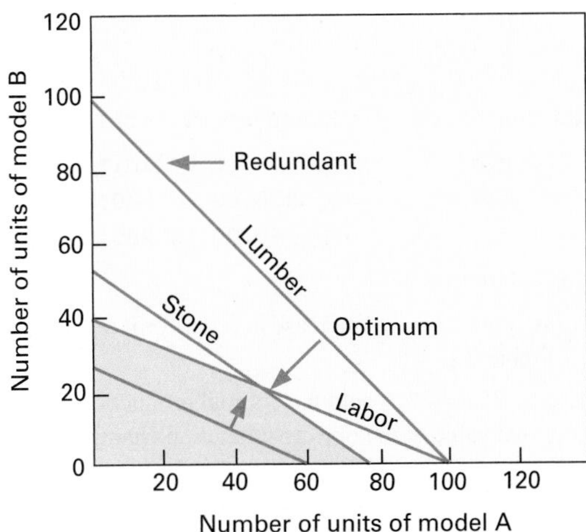

3. Determine the optimal quantities of models A and B, and compute the resulting profit. Because the optimum point is at the intersection of the stone and labor constraints, solve those two equations for their common point:

$$\begin{array}{rl} \text{Labor } 4{,}000A + 10{,}000B = & 400{,}000 \\ -2{,}000 \times (\text{Stone } 2A + 3B = & 150) \\ \hline 4{,}000B = & 100{,}000 \\ B = & 25 \end{array}$$

   Substitute $B = 25$ in one of the equations, and solve for A:

   $2A + 3(25) = 150 \qquad A = 37.5$

   $Z = 3{,}000(37.5) + 6{,}000(25) = 262{,}500$

4. We could have used the enumeration approach to find the optimal corner point. The corner points and the value of the objective function at each corner point are:

   $A = 0, B = 40$ (found by inspection); $Z = 3{,}000(0) + 6{,}000(40) = 240{,}000$

   $A = 37.5, B = 25$ (found using simultaneous equations); $Z = 262{,}500$ (see step 3)

   $A = 80, B = 0$ (found by inspection); $Z = 3{,}000(80) + 6{,}000(0) = 240{,}000$

   The best value of Z is 262,500 (because this is a maximization problem), so that indicates that the optimal corner point is $A = 37.5$, $B = 25$.

[1]For the sake of consistency, we will assign to the horizontal axis the first decision variable mentioned in the problem. In this case, variable A will be represented on the horizontal axis and variable B on the vertical axis.

Problem 2

This LP model was solved by computer:

Maximize $15x_1 + 20x_2 + 14x_3$ where x_1 = quantity of product 1
x_2 = quantity of product 2
x_3 = quantity of product 3

Subject to

Labor	$5x_1 + 6x_2 + 4x_3 \leq 210$ hours
Material	$10x_1 + 8x_2 + 5x_3 \leq 200$ pounds
Machine	$4x_1 + 2x_2 + 5x_3 \leq 170$ minutes
	$x_1, x_2, x_3 \geq 0$

The following information was obtained from the output. The ranges were also computed based on the output, and they are shown as well.

Total profit = 548.00

Variable	Value	Reduced Cost	Range of Optimality
Product 1	0	10.6	unlimited to 25.60
Product 2	5	0	9.40 to 22.40
Product 3	32	0	12.50 to 50.00

Constraint	Slack	Shadow Price	Range of Feasibility
Labor	52	0.0	158.00 to unlimited
Material	0	2.4	170.00 to 270.91
Machine	0	0.4	50.00 to 200.00

a. Which decision variables are basic (i.e., in solution)?

b. By how much would the profit per unit of product 1 have to increase in order for it to have a nonzero value (i.e., for it to become a basic variable)?

c. If the profit per unit of product 2 increased by \$2 to \$22, would the optimal production quantities of products 2 and 3 change? Would the optimal value of the objective function change?

d. If the available amount of labor decreased by 12 hours, would that cause a change in the optimal values of the decision variables or the optimal value of the objective function? Would anything change?

e. If the available amount of material increased by 10 pounds to 210 pounds, how would that affect the optimal value of the objective function?

f. If profit per unit on product 2 increased by \$1 and profit per unit on product 3 decreased by \$.50, would that fall within the range of multiple changes? Would the values of the decision variables change? What would be the revised value of the objective function?

Solution

a. Products 2 and 3 are in solution (i.e., have nonzero values); the optimal value of product 2 is 5 units, and the optimal value of product 3 is 32 units.

b. The amount of increase would have to equal its *reduced cost* of \$10.60.

c. No, because the change would be within its range of optimality, which has an upper limit of \$22.40. The objective function value would increase by an amount equal to the quantity of product 2 and its increased unit profit. Hence, it would increase by 5(\$2) = \$10 to \$558.

d. Labor has a slack of 52 hours. Consequently, the only effect would be to decrease the slack to 40 hours.

e. The change is within the range of feasibility. The objective function value will increase by the amount of change multiplied by material's shadow price of \$2.40. Hence, the objective function value would increase by 10(\$2.40) = \$24.00. (*Note:* If the change had been a *decrease* of 10 pounds, which is also within the range of feasibility, the value of the objective function would have *decreased* by this amount.)

f. To determine if the changes are within the range for multiple changes, we first compute the ratio of the amount of each change to the end of the range *in the same direction.* For product 2, it is \$1/\$2.40 = .417; for product 3, it is −\$.50/ − \$1.50 = .333. Next, we compute the sum of these ratios: .417 + .333 = .750. Because this does not exceed 1.00, we conclude that these changes are within the range. This means that the optimal values of the decision variables will not change. We can compute the change to the value of the objective function by multiplying each product's optimal quantity by its changed profit per unit: 5(\$1) + 32(−\$.50) = −\$11. Hence, with these changes, the value of the objective function would decrease by \$11; its new value would be \$548 − \$11 = \$537.

DISCUSSION AND REVIEW QUESTIONS

1. For which decision environment is linear programming most suited?
2. What is meant by the term *feasible solution space?* What determines this region?
3. Explain the term *redundant constraint.*
4. What is an isocost line? An isoprofit line?
5. What does sliding an objective function line toward the origin represent? Away from the origin?
6. Briefly explain these terms:
   a. Basic variable.
   b. Shadow price.
   c. Range of feasibility.
   d. Range of optimality.

PROBLEMS

1. Solve these problems using graphical linear programming and answer the questions that follow. Use simultaneous equations to determine the optimal values of the decision variables.

a. Maximize $Z = 4x_1 + 3x_2$
Subject to

Material	$6x_1 + 4x_2 \le 48$ lb
Labor	$4x_1 + 8x_2 \le 80$ hr
	$x_1, x_2 \ge 0$

b. Maximize $Z = 2x_1 + 10x_2$
Subject to

Durability	$10x_1 + 4x_2 \ge 40$ wk
Strength	$1x_1 + 6x_2 \ge 24$ psi
Time	$1x_1 + 2x_2 \le 14$ hr
	$x_1, x_2 \ge 0$

c. Maximize $Z = 6A + 3B$ (revenue)
Subject to

Material	$20A + 6B \le 600$ lb
Machinery	$25A + 20B \le 1{,}000$ hr
Labor	$20A + 30B \le 1{,}200$ hr
	$A, B \ge 0$

(1) What are the optimal values of the decision variables and *Z?*
(2) Do any constraints have (nonzero) slack? If yes, which one(s) and how much slack does each have?
(3) Do any constraints have (nonzero) surplus? If yes, which one(s) and how much surplus does each have?
(4) Are any constraints redundant? If yes, which one(s)? Explain briefly.

2. Solve these problems using graphical linear programming and then answer the questions that follow. Use simultaneous equations to determine the optimal values of the decision variables.

a. Minimize $Z = 1.80S + 2.20T$
Subject to

Potassium	$5S + 8T \ge 200$ gr
Carbohydrate	$15S + 6T \ge 240$ gr
Protein	$4S + 12T \ge 180$ gr
T	$T \ge 10$gr
	$S, T \ge 0$

b. Minimize $Z = 2x_1 + 3x_2$
Subject to

D	$4x_1 + 2x_2 \ge 20$
E	$2x_1 + 6x_2 \ge 18$
F	$1x_1 + 2x_2 \le 12$
	$x_1, x_2 \ge 0$

(1) What are the optimal values of the decision variables and *Z?*
(2) Do any constraints have (nonzero) slack? If yes, which one(s) and how much slack does each have?
(3) Do any constraints have (nonzero) surplus? If yes, which one(s) and how much surplus does each have?
(4) Are any constraints redundant? If yes, which one(s)? Explain briefly.

3. An appliance manufacturer produces two models of microwave ovens: H and W. Both models require fabrication and assembly work; each H uses four hours of fabrication and two hours of assembly, and each W uses two hours of fabrication and six hours of assembly. There are 600 fabrication hours available this week and 480 hours of assembly. Each H contributes $40 to profits, and each W contributes $30 to profits. What quantities of H and W will maximize profits?
   a. Use the objective function approach.
   b. Use the enumeration approach.
4. A small candy shop is preparing for the holiday season. The owner must decide how many bags of deluxe mix and how many bags of standard mix of Peanut/Raisin Delite to put up. The deluxe mix has ⅔ pound raisins and ⅓ pound peanuts, and the standard mix has ½ pound raisins and ½ pound peanuts per bag. The shop has 90 pounds of raisins and 60 pounds of peanuts to work with.
   Peanuts cost $.60 per pound and raisins cost $1.50 per pound. The deluxe mix will sell for $2.90 per pound, and the standard mix will sell for $2.55 per pound. The owner estimates that no more than 110 bags of one type can be sold.
   a. If the goal is to maximize profits, how many bags of each type should be prepared?
   b. What is the expected profit?
5. A retired couple supplement their income by making fruit pies, which they sell to a local grocery store. During the month of September, they produce apple and grape pies. The apple pies are sold for $1.50 to the grocer, and the grape pies are sold for $1.20. The couple is able to sell all of the pies they produce owing to their high quality. They use fresh ingredients. Flour and sugar are purchased once each month. For the month of September, they have 1,200 cups of sugar and 2,100 cups of flour. Each apple pie requires 1½ cups of sugar and 3 cups of flour, and each grape pie requires 2 cups of sugar and 3 cups of flour.
   a. Determine the number of grape and the number of apple pies that will maximize revenues if the couple working together can make an apple pie in six minutes and a grape pie in three minutes. They plan to work no more than 60 hours.
   b. Determine the amounts of sugar, flour, and time that will be unused.
6. Solve each of these problems by computer and obtain the optimal values of the decision variables and the objective function.
   a. Maximize $4x_1 + 2x_2 + 5x_3$
      Subject to

$$\begin{aligned} 1x_1 + 2x_2 + 1x_3 &\le 25 \\ 1x_1 + 4x_2 + 2x_3 &\le 40 \\ 3x_1 + 3x_2 + 1x_3 &\le 30 \\ x_1, x_2, x_3 &\ge 0 \end{aligned}$$

   b. Maximize $10x_1 + 6x_2 + 3x_3$
      Subject to

$$\begin{aligned} 1x_1 + 1x_2 + 2x_3 &\le 25 \\ 2x_1 + 1x_2 + 4x_3 &\le 40 \\ 1x_1 + 2x_2 + 3x_3 &\le 40 \\ x_1, x_2, x_3 &\ge 0 \end{aligned}$$

7. For Problem 6*a*, determine the following:
   a. The range of feasibility for each constraint.
   b. The range of optimality for the coefficients of the objective function.
8. For Problem 6*b*:
   a. Find the range of feasibility for each constraint, and interpret your answers.
   b. Determine the range of optimality for each coefficient of the objective function. Interpret your results.
9. A small firm makes three similar products, which all follow the same three-step process, consisting of milling, inspection, and drilling. Product A requires 12 minutes of milling, 5 minutes for inspection, and 10 minutes of drilling per unit; product B requires 10 minutes of milling, 4 minutes for inspection, and 8 minutes of drilling per unit; and product C requires 8 minutes of milling, 4 minutes for inspection, and 16 minutes of drilling. The department has 20 hours available during the next period for milling, 15 hours for inspection, and 24 hours for drilling. Product A contributes $2.40 per unit to profit, product B contributes $2.50 per unit, and product C contributes $3.00

per unit. Determine the optimal mix of products in terms of maximizing contribution to profits for the period. Then, find the range of optimality for the profit coefficient of each variable.

10. Formulate and then solve a linear programming model of this problem, to determine how many containers of each product to produce tomorrow to maximize profits. The company makes four juice products using orange, grapefruit, and pineapple juice.

Product	Retail Price per Quart
Orange juice	$1.00
Grapefruit juice	.90
Pineapple juice	.80
All-in-One	1.10

The All-in-One juice has equal parts of orange, grapefruit, and pineapple juice. Each product is produced in a one-quart size (there are four quarts in a gallon). On hand are 400 gallons of orange juice, 300 gallons of grapefruit juice, and 200 gallons of pineapple juice. The cost per gallon is $2.00 for orange juice, $1.60 for grapefruit juice, and $1.40 for pineapple juice.

In addition, the manager wants grapefruit juice to be used for no more than 30 percent of the number of containers produced. She wants the ratio of the number of containers of orange juice to the number of containers of pineapple juice to be at least 7 to 5.

11. A wood products firm uses available time at the end of each week to make goods for stock. Currently, two products on the list of items are produced for stock: a chopping board and a knife holder. Both items require three operations: cutting, gluing, and finishing. The manager of the firm has collected the following data on these products:

		TIME PER UNIT (minutes)		
Item	Profit/Unit	Cutting	Gluing	Finishing
Chopping board	$2	1.4	5	12
Knife holder	$6	0.8	13	3

The manager has also determined that, during each week, 56 minutes are available for cutting, 650 minutes are available for gluing, and 360 minutes are available for finishing.

a. Determine the optimal quantities of the decision variables.
b. Which resources are not completely used by your solution? How much of each resource is unused?

12. The manager of the deli section of a grocery superstore has just learned that the department has 112 pounds of mayonnaise, of which 70 pounds is approaching its expiration date and must be used. To use up the mayonnaise, the manager has decided to prepare two items: a ham spread and a deli spread. Each pan of the ham spread will require 1.4 pounds of mayonnaise, and each pan of the deli spread will require 1.0 pound. The manager has received an order for 10 pans of ham spread and 8 pans of the deli spread. In addition, the manager has decided to have at least 10 pans of each spread available for sale. Both spreads will cost $3 per pan to make, but ham spread sells for $5 per pan and deli spread sells for $7 per pan.

a. Determine the solution that will minimize cost.
b. Determine the solution that will maximize profit.

13. A manager wants to know how many units of each product to produce on a daily basis in order to achieve the highest contribution to profit. Production requirements for the products are shown in the following table.

Product	Material 1 (pounds)	Material 2 (pounds)	Labor (hours)
A	2	3	3.2
B	1	5	1.5
C	6	—	2.0

Material 1 costs $5 a pound, material 2 costs $4 a pound, and labor costs $10 an hour. Product A sells for $80 a unit, product B sells for $90 a unit, and product C sells for $70 a unit. Available resources each day are 200 pounds of material 1; 300 pounds of material 2; and 150 hours of labor.

The manager must satisfy certain output requirements: The output of product A should not be more than one-third of the total number of units produced; the ratio of units of product A to units of product B should be 3 to 2; and there is a standing order for 5 units of product A each day. Formulate a linear programming model for this problem, and then solve.

14. A chocolate maker has contracted to operate a small candy counter in a fashionable store. To start with, the selection of offerings will be intentionally limited. The counter will offer a regular mix of candy made up of equal parts of cashews, raisins, caramels, and chocolates, and a deluxe mix that is one-half cashews and one-half chocolates, which will be sold in one-pound boxes. In addition, the candy counter will offer individual one-pound boxes of cashews, raisins, caramels, and chocolates.

A major attraction of the candy counter is that all candies are made fresh at the counter. However, storage space for supplies and ingredients is limited. Bins are available that can hold the amounts shown in the table:

Ingredient	Capacity (pounds per day)
Cashews	120
Raisins	200
Caramels	100
Chocolates	160

In order to present a good image and to encourage purchases, the counter will make at least 20 boxes of each type of product each day. Any leftover boxes at the end of the day will be removed and given to a nearby nursing home for goodwill.

The profit per box for the various items has been determined as follows:

Item	Profit per Box
Regular	$.80
Deluxe	.90
Cashews	.70
Raisins	.60
Caramels	.50
Chocolates	.75

a. Formulate the LP model.
b. Solve for the optimal values of the decision variables and the maximum profit.

15. Given this linear programming model, solve the model and then answer the questions that follow.

Maximize $12x_1 + 18x_2 + 15x_3$ where x_1 = the quantity of product 1 to make etc.
Subject to

Machine	$5x_1 + 4x_2 + 3x_3 \leq 160$ minutes
Labor	$4x_1 + 10x_2 + 4x_3 \leq 288$ hours
Materials	$2x_1 + 2x_2 + 4x_3 \leq 200$ pounds
Product 2	$x_2 \leq 16$ units
	$x_1, x_2, x_3 \geq 0$

a. Are any constraints binding? If so, which one(s)?
b. If the profit on product 3 were changed to $22 a unit, what would the values of the decision variables be? The objective function? Explain.
c. If the profit on product 1 were changed to $22 a unit, what would the values of the decision variables be? The objective function? Explain.
d. If 10 hours less of labor time were available, what would the values of the decision variables be? The objective function? Explain.
e. If the manager decided that as many as 20 units of product 2 could be produced (instead of 16), how much additional profit would be generated?
f. If profit per unit on each product increased by $1, would the optimal values of the decision variables change? Explain. What would the optimal value of the objective function be?

16. A garden store prepares various grades of pine bark for mulch: nuggets (x_1), mini-nuggets (x_2), and chips (x_3). The process requires pine bark, machine time, labor time, and storage space. The following model has been developed.

Maximize $9x_1 + 9x_2 + 6x_3$ (profit)

Subject to

Bark	$5x_1 + 6x_2 + 3x_3 \leq 600$ pounds
Machine	$2x_1 + 4x_2 + 5x_3 \leq 600$ minutes
Labor	$2x_1 + 4x_2 + 3x_3 \leq 480$ hours
Storage	$1x_1 + 1x_2 + 1x_3 \leq 150$ bags
	$x_1, x_2, x_3 \geq 0$

a. What is the marginal value of a pound of pine bark? Over what range is this price value appropriate?
b. What is the maximum price the store would be justified in paying for additional pine bark?
c. What is the marginal value of labor? Over what range is this value in effect?
d. The manager obtained additional machine time through better scheduling. How much additional machine time can be effectively used for this operation? Why?
e. If the manager can obtain *either* additional pine bark or additional storage space, which one should she choose and how much (assuming additional quantities cost the same as usual)?
f. If a change in the chip operation increased the profit on chips from \$6 per bag to \$7 per bag, would the optimal quantities change? Would the value of the objective function change? If so, what would the new value(s) be?
g. If profits on chips increased to \$7 per bag and profits on nuggets decreased by \$.60, would the optimal quantities change? Would the value of the objective function change? If so, what would the new value(s) be?
h. If the amount of pine bark available decreased by 15 pounds, machine time decreased by 27 minutes, and storage capacity increased by five bags, would this fall in the range of feasibility for multiple changes? If so, what would the value of the objective function be?

Son, Ltd

CASE

Son, Ltd., manufactures a variety of chemical products used by photoprocessors. Son was recently bought out by a conglomerate, and managers of the two organizations have been working together to improve the efficiency of Son's operations.

Managers have been asked to adhere to weekly operating budgets and to develop operating plans using quantitative methods whenever possible. The manager of one department has been given a weekly operating budget of \$11,980 for production of three chemical products, which for convenience shall be referred to as Q, R, and W. The budget is intended to pay for direct labor and materials. Processing requirements for the three products, on a per unit basis, are shown in the table.

The company has a contractual obligation for 85 units of product R per week.

Material A costs \$4 per pound, as does material B. Labor costs \$8 an hour.

Product Q sells for \$122 a unit, product R sells for \$115 a unit, and product W sells for \$76 a unit.

The manager is considering a number of different proposals regarding the quantity of each product to produce. The manager is primarily interested in maximizing contribution. Moreover, the manager wants to know how much labor will be needed, as well as the amount of each material to purchase.

Questions Prepare a report that addresses the following issues:

1. The optimal quantities of products and the necessary quantities of labor and materials.
2. One proposal is to make equal amounts of the products. What amount of each will maximize contribution, and what quantities of labor and materials will be needed? How much less will total contribution be if this proposal is adopted?
3. How would you formulate the constraint for material A if it was determined that there is a 5 percent waste factor for material A and equal quantities of each product are required?

Product	Labor (hours)	Material A (pounds)	Material B (pounds)
Q	5	2	1
R	4	2	—
W	2	½	2

Custom Cabinets, Inc.©

CASE

Custom Cabinets, Inc. (CCI), manufactures two major lines of kitchen and bathroom cabinets. The SemiCustom Line consists of cabinets that are variations on a standard design. These cabinets are made to order. The StandardLine is a lower priced line of cabinets that use standardized designs and materials. StandardLine cabinets are made to stock. The company has been in business for many years and has consistently performed well financially.

It was obvious that something big was up as the management staff began to gather for a meeting called by CCI General Manager John Fleming. There was little of the usual light banter, and more significantly, there were no coffee and donuts. The CCI culture celebrates even small achievements with coffee and donuts. Their absence was not a good omen.

John began rather somberly. "As you know we are almost 2 months into our second fiscal quarter. Frankly, the financial results don't look very good. You are aware, I'm sure, of how the stock market has been punishing companies that fail to at least meet their sales and profit targets. We are in danger of having to announce that we met our sales goals but fell short of our profit goals. This will be a real jolt to our shareholders, and since, except for the interns, we are all in the company's stock purchase plan, that means it will hurt us too. We only have one month to turn this around. We don't want to take any shortcut approaches to meeting our goals—we want the results to reflect the real results of our operation.

The headquarters brass talked with a consultant who analyzed our records. Her opinion is that we need to address operations efficiency. In her words, we have to learn to get more out of our existing resources. She leaves the details to us to figure out. Our biggest personnel resource to assign to this problem is our group of management interns from Nearby University. I've talked to the interns and alerted them that for the next month or so they are to work directly with Bill Chavez, our Operations Manager, on this project. The goal is to be sure that we get the maximum bang for our resource buck during the next month's operations. We have to get the most profit possible to make the quarter's results look at least respectable. Needless to say, I want each of you to give the intern group your fullest cooperation."

Now you understand why the interns were invited to the staff meeting. You've just been on board for a few weeks and have just begun to understand the company's operations. That means the boss can't be looking to you for engineering solutions. Your expertise is operations management, not engineering.

As the meeting broke up, Bill Chavez asked you (the interns) to stay for a follow-up meeting with him. "I've been very impressed with the work that you have done in your short time with CCI. You obviously get an excellent education at Nearby U. I asked Tom to assign you to me because I think you are our best hope of pulling out some really good profit numbers. You don't have any preconceived ideas about what will and will not work, so I expect you to come up with ideas that are more innovative than the old hands.

"I spent most of the morning with the other department heads gathering information that I think you might need (that information is enclosed with this case). If you need additional information send me an e-mail or stop in my office. If I can get the information you need, I will do so. We're counting on you. Don't let us down. I'll let you guys figure out when and where to meet. Needless to say you have full access to all our computer resources should you need them.

"There are a few things you need to keep in mind. Our SemiCustom Line is hot because of our excellent customer service. We never fail to deliver a SemiCustom unit on time. We also need to meet our customer orders on the StandardLine units, but we can cut the stockage levels if necessary. We can't, however, exceed the stockage levels. Making excess inventory is no way to be more efficient. If necessary, we could work 10 percent overtime in assembly and 5 percent overtime in finishing. Each overtime hour will add $5.00 per hour to our labor cost. I've checked with all our suppliers. We can get up to 50,000 additional board-feet of wood by paying a $0.50 per board-foot upcharge and 10,000 additional square feet of laminate for an upcharge of $0.15 per square foot. There is no reasonable prospect of obtaining more of the other materials at any price. Because of the way our profit center is set up, we get credit for building to the authorized stockage level as if it were a final sale."

As you were leaving the meeting, Barbara Wilson invited you to the break room for a cup of coffee. Barbara is the Lead Production Scheduler and has worked for Custom Cabinets for a long time. You have been told that she knows everything about how things work here and is a good person to know. "I heard about your assignment," she began. "Let me tell you some things about your boss, Bill Chavez. He is a great guy to work for and he really knows his stuff. He is not one of the college guys who act as if they know everything—no offense. He worked his way up. He is very intelligent, but doesn't have the educational background that you do. In the past, new college graduates have made some mistakes in writing reports for Bill. He likes for everything in the report to be written in words he can understand. He likes you to include computer printouts in an appendix to the report (he likes to see all the backup detail), but wants you to explain in the body of the report why they are necessary and what they mean. If he doesn't understand what you are recommending and why, he won't ask questions. He will just discard the report, and that will be the last assignment you will ever do for him. I figured that the least I could do would be to buy you a cup of coffee and try to help you get off to a good start on this project."

(continued)

ENCLOSURE A
BILLS OF MATERIALS AND LABOR

	Wood bd.-ft.	Trim lin. ft.	Granite sq. ft.	Solid Surface sq. ft.	Laminate sq. ft.	Assbly. Labor hrs.	Finish Labor hrs.
SemiCustom Line							
SC-A	125	27	175	0	0	37	7
SC-B	160	42	243	0	0	57	12
SC-C	140	35	0	160	0	30	5
SC-D	200	52	0	140	0	35	7
StandardLine							
S-10	60	21	0	112	0	21	3
S-20	110	28	0	0	135	25	5
S-30	200	50	0	0	254	30	7
S-40	180	43	0	0	176	27	5
Available	400,000	140,000	45,000	150,000	400,000	100,000	25,000

ENCLOSURE B
ORDERS AND PROFITS

	Profit/Unit @ Standard	Customer Orders Next Month	Build-to-Stock Authorization Next Month
SemiCustom Line			
SC-A	$325	117	0
SC-B	$575	92	0
SC-C	$257	130	0
SC-D	$275	150	0
StandardLine			
S-10	$175	475	400
S-20	$210	363	350
S-30	$260	510	450
S-40	$230	412	475

Source: © Victor E. Sower, 2006.

Questions

1. Should there be additional overtime, and if so, how much?
2. Should additional laminate be purchased. and if so, how much?
3. Should additional wood be purchased, and if so, how much?
4. What is the maximum profit that can be achieved?

SELECTED BIBLIOGRAPHY AND FURTHER READINGS

Hillier, Frederick S., Mark S. Hillier, and Gerald Lieberman. *Introduction to Management Science.* Burr Ridge, IL: Irwin/McGraw-Hill, 2000.

Ragsdale, Cliff T. *Spreadsheet Modeling and Decision Analysis.* 5th ed. Thompson-Southwestern Publishing, 2007.

Stevenson, W. J., and Ceyhun Ozgur. *Introduction to Management Science with Spreadsheets.* New York: McGraw-Hill, 2006.

Taylor, Bernard. *Introduction to Management Science.* 10th ed. Upper Saddle River, NJ: Pearson Prentice Hall, 2009.

APPENDIX A Answers to Selected Problems

Chapter 2: Competitiveness, Strategy, and Productivity

1. Anniversary = 37.5 meals per worker.
   Wedding = 40 meals per worker.
2. Smaller crew sizes had the higher productivity.
3. Week 1: 3.03.
   Week 2: 2.99.
   Week 3: 2.89.
   Week 4: 2.84.
4. a. Before: Labor productivity = 16 carts per worker per hour.
   After: Labor productivity = 21 carts per worker per hour.
   b. Before: Multifactor productivity = .89 cart per dollar.
   After: Multifactor productivity = .93 cart per dollar.
5. 11.1%.
6. 4.3%.
8. Current: $5; A = $6.30; B = $6.71

Chapter 3: Forecasting

1. a. blueberry = 33, cinnamon = 35, cupcakes = 47.
   b. Demand did not exceed supply.
2. b. (1) 20.86, (2) 19, (3) 19.26, (4) 20, (5) 20.4.
3. a. 88.16 percent.
   b. 88.54 percent.
4. a. 22. b. 20.75. c. 20.72.
5. a. Increasing by 15,000 bottles per year.
   b. 320 (i.e., 320,000 bottles).
6. $500 - 20t$.
7. a. $Ft = 208.48 + 19.06t$. b. 588.40, 607.40. c. Week 32.
8. a. $Ft = 195.47 + 7.00t$. b. 307.22.
   $F_{16} = 307.47$ $F_{18} = 321.47$
   $F_{17} = 314.17$ $F_{19} = 328.47$
11. Q_1: 127.6; Q_2: 143.5; Q_3: 105; Q_4: 273.65; Q_1 = 275.
12. a. Fri. = 0.79, Sat. = 1.34, Sun. = 0.87.
    b. Fri. = 0.756, Sat. = 1.341, Sun. = 0.874.

15.

Day	a. Relative	b. Relative
1	0.901	0.887
2	0.838	0.831
3	0.884	0.876
4	1.020	1.022
5	1.430	1.438
6	1.480	1.483
7	0.450	0.464

17. b.

Jan.	800
Feb.	810
Mar.	900
Apr.	810

19.

	SR1	SR2	SR3	SR4
a.	0.509	0.836	1.164	1.491
b.	1.0	1.0	1.0	1.0

22. a.

	MSE	MAD
Forecast 1	10.44	2.8
Forecast 2	42.44	3.6
Naive	156	10.7

b. $MAPE_1$ = .36%.
$MAPE_2$ = .46%.

23. b. $147,000.
24. b. $17.90.
25. b. −0.985.
26. b. $Y = 66.33 + .584x$.
    d. 90.27.
27. a. $r = +.96$.
    b. $Y = -0.672 + 6.158x$.
    c. About 12 mowers.
28. a. $MAD_5 = 5$.
    $MAD_6 = 5.9$.
    $MAD_7 = 4.73$.
    $MAD_8 = 3.911$.
    $MAD_9 = 4.238$.
    etc.
    b. $TS_5 = 1.40$.
    $TS_6 = -0.17$.
    $TS_7 = -0.63$.
    $TS_8 = -0.26$.
    $TS_9 = -1.42$.
    etc.
30. a. Initial MAD = 4.727. The tracking signal for month 15 is 4.088, so at that point, the forecast would be suspect.
    b. Σ errors = −1, Σ errors^2 = 345. Control limits: 0 ± 12.38 (in limits). Plot reveals cycles in errors.

Chapter 4 Supplement: Reliability

1. a. .81. b. .9801. c. .9783.
2. .9033.
3. .9726.
4. .93.
5. a. .9315. b. .9953. c. .994.
6. a. .7876. b. .90 component.
7. a. Plan 2 (.9934).
8. a. .0021. b. .0023.
9. a. .996.
10. .995.
11. .006.
12. a. (1) .2725.
    (2) .2019.
    (3) .1353.
    b. (1) .6671.
    (2) .3935.
    (3) .1813.
    c. (1) 21 months.
    (2) 57 months.
    (3) 90 months.
    (4) 138 months.
13. a. .6321. b. Three months or 90 days.
14. a. .3012. b. .1813. c. .5175.
15. a. .2231. b. .8647.
    c. .0878. d. .0302.
16. a. .2266. b. .4400. c. .3830.
17. a. (1) .9772.
    (2) .5000.
    (3) .0013.
    b. Approximately zero.

18. a. 4.97 years. b. 5.18 years.
19. a. .93. b. .98.

Chapter 5: Strategic Capacity Planning for Products and Services

1. a. Utilization = 70%.
   Efficiency = 87.5%.
   b. Utilization = 67%.
   Efficiency = 80%.
2. 20 jobs per week.
3. a. 46,000 units.
   b. (1) $3,000. (2) $8,200.
   c. 126,000 units. d. 25,556 units.
4. a. A: 8,000 units. b. 10,000 units.
   B: 7,500 units.
   c. A: $20,000.
   B: $18,000.
5. a. 39,683 units.
   b. $1.71 (rounded up).
6. a. A: $82.
   B: $92.
   C: $100.
   c. A: 0 to less than 178.
   B: Never.
   C: 178+ .
   d. 1/3 day, 2/3 evening.
7. Vendor best for $Q < 63{,}333$. For larger quantities, produce in-house at $4 per unit.
8. a. Vendor B best for 10,000 and 20,000.
9. 3 cells.
10. a. Buy 2 Bs. b. Buy 2 Bs.
11. a. one: $Q = 80$. two: $Q = 152$.
13. a. 11 units/hr.
14. a. 5 units/hr. b. 10 units/hr.

Chapter 5 Supplement: Decision Theory

1. a. Expand (80).
   b. Do nothing (50).
   c. Indifferent between do nothing and subcontract (55).
   d. Subcontract (10).
2. a. Expand (62). c. $9 (000).
3. Do nothing: $P(\text{high}) < .50$.
   Subcontract: $.50 < P(\text{high}) < .67$.
   Expand: $P(\text{high}) > .67$.
4. a.

Build small
Demand low (.4) — $400,000 (1)
Demand high (.6)
Maintain — $ 50,000 (2)
Expand — $450,000 (3)
Build large
Demand low (.4) — $–10,000 (4)
Demand high (.6) — $800,000 (5)

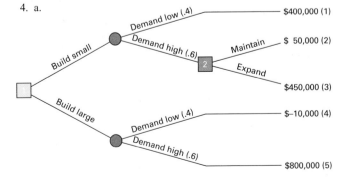

   b. $164,000.
   c. Large 0 to .46.
   Small .46 to 1.00.

5. Subcontract: $1.23.
   Expand: $1.57.
   Build: $1.35.
6. a. Relocate.
   b. Renew.
   c. Relocate.
   d. Relocate.
7. a. Renew.
   b. EVPI = $1,575,000.
   c. Yes.
9. a. Build large: $53.6 million.
   b. Build small: $42 million.
   c. $12.4.
   d. Build small for $P(\text{high}) < .721$.
   Build large for $P(\text{high}) > .721$.
10. Buy two ($113.5).
11. A: 49.
12. b. maximin: small.
    maximax: large.
    Laplace: large.
    minimax regret: large.
13. a. New staff.
    b. Redesign.
    c. New staff.
    d. New staff or redesign.
16. b. Alternative C.
    c. $P(2) > .625$.
    d. $P(1) < .375$.
17. b. Alternative B.
    c. $P(2) < .444$.
    d. $P(1) > .556$.

Chapter 6: Process Selection and Facility Layout

1. a. Minimum is 2.4 minutes, maximum is 18 minutes.
   b. 25 units to 187.5 units. c. Eight.
   d. 3.6 minutes. e. (1) 50 units.
   (2) 30 units.
2. a.

Station	Tasks	Time
1	a	1.4
2	b, e	1.3
3	d, c, f	1.8
4	g, h	1.5

3. a.

Station	Tasks	Time
1	f, a, g	14
2	d, b, c	13
3	e, h	13
4	i	5

4. a. (3) 11.54%. (4) 323 c opiers per day.
   b. (1) 2.3 minutes. (3) 182.6 copiers per day.
   (4) 91.3 copiers units per day.
5. b. 2 minutes. c. Three stations.
6. c. (1) 11.1%. (2) 11.1%. (3) 11.1%.
7. b. CT = .84 min. or 50.4 sec.
   c. $n = 3.83$ (round to 4) stations.

10. 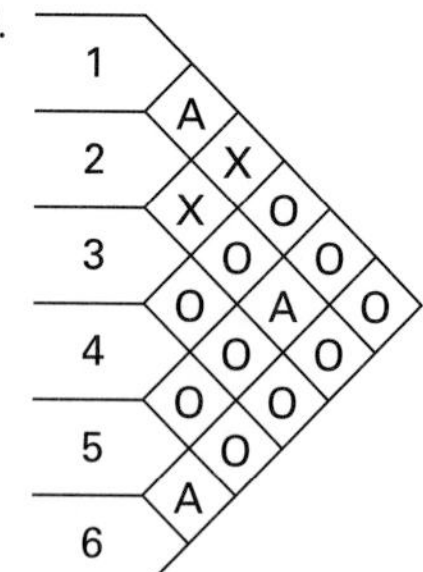

11.

1	5	4
3	8	7
6	2	

13.

3	1	8
9	7	4
5	2	6

14. a.

A #1	B #4	C #2
	D #3	

TC = $14,150.

16. A: 3; B: 5; C: 1; D: 4; E: 6; F: 2.
17. A: 1; B: 2; C: 5; D: 4; E: 9; F: 8; G: 6; H: 10; I: 7; J: 3.

Chapter 7: Work Design and Measurement

1. 15.08 minutes.
2. a. 1.2 minutes.
   b. 1.14 minutes.
   c. 1.27 minutes.
3.

Element	OT	NT	ST
1.......	0.46	0.414	0.476
2.......	1.505	1.280	1.472
3.......	0.83	0.913	1.050
4.......	1.16	1.160	1.334

4.

Element	Average
1.........	4.1
2.........	1.5
3.........	3.3
4.........	2.8

7. 5.85 minutes.
8. 7.125 minutes.
10. 57 observations.
11. 37 cycles.
12. a. 12%.
    b. 163 observations.
13. 377 observations.

Chapter 7 Supplement: Learning Curves

1. a. 178.8 hours.
   b. 1,121.4 hours.
   c. 2,914.8 hours.
2. a. 41.47 hours.
   b. 60.55 hours.
   c. 72.20 hours.
3. a. 56.928 days.
   b. 42.288 days.
   c. 37.512 days.
5. a. P = 85 percent.
   b. 26.21 minutes.
6. 87.9 minutes.
7. 201.26 hours.
8. a. 11.35 hours.
   b. 13.05 hours.
   c. 13.12 hours.
9. a. $80.31.
   b. 10 units.
10. B and C.
12. 30.82 hours.
13. No.
14. 18.76 hours.
15. Art: 20; Sherry: 4; Dave: 10.
16. 7 repetitions.
17. Beverly: 6; Max: 22; Antonio: 4.
19. 8.232 hours.

Chapter 8: Location Planning and Analysis

1. Kansas City: $256,000.
2. a. A: 16,854; B: 17,416; C: 17,753.
   b. C: $14,670.
3. a. 120 units.
   b. A: 0 to 119; B: 121+.
4. a. B: 0 to 33; C: 34 to 400; A: 400+.
5. C ($270,000).
6. Biloxi ($160,000).
7. a. (1) outside; (2) city. b. 230 cars.
9. A.
11. a. B = C > A.
    b. B > C > A.
12. (5,4) is optimal.
13. (6,7).
14. (5.97, 5.95).
15. (3.24, 2.30).

Chapter 8 Supplement: The Transportation Model

1. $X_{12} = 15.$ $X_{13} = 75$
   $X_{21} = 105.$
   $X_{31} = 45.$ $X_{32} = 60.$
   TC = $1,050.

2.

	A	B	C	Dummy
1		500		
2	400			
N1		100	350	50

	A	B	C	Dummy
1		500		
2	400			
N2		100	350	50

3.

	A	B	C
1			210
2	140		
3	80	60	10
Tol.		160	

	A	B	C
1			210
2	60	80	
3		140	10
Cin.	160		

Chapter 9: Management of Quality

2.

	Res.	Com.
Noisy	10	3
Failed	7	2
Odor	5	7
Warm	3	4

Chapter 10: Quality Control

1. a. .0124.
   b. 24.40 ounces and 24.60 ounces.
2. a. LCL: 0.996 liter.
   UCL: 1.004 liters.
   b. Not in control.
3. a. Mean: LCL is 3.019, UCL is 3.181.
   Range: LCL is 0.1845, UCL is 0.7155.
   b. Yes.
4. Mean: LCL is 78.88 cm.
   UCL is 81.04 cm.
   Range: LCL is 0 cm.
   UCL is 3.95 cm.
   Process in control.
5. a.

1	2	3	4
.020	.010	.025	.045

   b. 2.5 percent.
   c. Mean = .025, standard deviation = .011.
   d. LCL = .0011, UCL = .0489.
   e. .0456.
   f. Yes.
   g. Mean = .02, standard deviation = .01.
   h. LCL = 0, UCL = .04.
6. LCL: 0.
   UCL: .0234.
   Sample #10 is outside of the UCL.
7. Yes, UCL = 16.266, LCL = 0.
8. Yes, UCL = 5.17, LCL = 0.
9. No, UCL = .10, LCL = .01. Yes.
10. 20 pieces.
11. One in 30 is "out." Tolerances seem to be met. Approximately 97% will be acceptable.
12. a. LCL: 3.73.
    UCL: 3.97.
    Out of control.
    b. Random variations.
13.

	Test	NUMBER OF RUNS Observed	Expected	Standard Deviation	z	Conclude
a.	Med . . .	18	14	2.50	1.6	Okay
	U/D	17	17	2.07	0	Okay
b.	Med. . . .	8	14	2.50	−2.40	Nonrandom
	U/D	22	17	2.07	2.41	Nonrandom

14. a. Random because both scores are less than ±2
    b. Random because both scores are less than ±2
    c. Med: z = 1.11.
    U/D: z = 0.68.
    d. Med: z = −1.11.
    U/D: z = −1.36.
15. Med: z = −2.34.
    U/D: z = −1.45.
16. 200 pieces.
18. a. 566 units.
    b. 62 units.
    c. $1,160.
19. Med: z = +0.9177.
    U/D: z = +0.5561.
20. b. 4.5, .192.
    c. 4.5, .086.
    d. 4.242 to 4.758.
    f. None.
21. a. 1.11. b. No.
22. Process 005 is capable.

24. C_{pk}: $H = .94$, $k = 1.00$, $T = 1.33$.
26. Melissa.
27. a. 2.506.
    b. $C_{pk} = 1.41$.
    c. .987 ounces.

Chapter 10 Supplement: Acceptance Sampling

1. a. (1) Yes. (2) Yes. b. .0067.
2. b. .0390.
3. c. .0024.
5. a. 0.16.
    b. 2.
    c. (1) Accept.
       (2) .0362.
       (3) .9638.
       (4) p(Type I) = .0362.
       p(Type II) = 0.

Chapter 11: Aggregate Planning and Master Scheduling

1. b. $6,350.
2. a. $4,670.
    b. $4,800.
3. b. $4,640.
4. $4,970.
7. a. $31,250.
    b. $31,520.
8. a. $350,800.
    b. $356,200.
    c. $353,700.
10. B: $14,340.
    C: $14,370.
11. $13,475.
12. $13,885.
13. $12,930.
15. $124,960.
16. $126,650; additional cost: $1,920.

Chapter 12: MRP and ERP

1. F = 2, G = 1, H = 1, J = 6, D = 10, L = 2, A = 4.
2. a. E = 138.
    b. Week 5.
3. a. 360.
    b. Day 1 (now).

4. a.

Master Schedule	Beg. Inv.	1	2	3	4	5	6
Week							
Quantity							80

E LT = 2	Beg. Inv.	1	2	3	4	5	6
Gross requirements							80
Scheduled receipts							
Projected on hand							
Net requirements							80
Planned-order receipts							80
Planned-order releases					80		

B (2) LT = 2	Beg. Inv.	1	2	3	4	5	6
Gross requirements					160		
Scheduled receipts							
Projected on hand	60	60	60	60	60	20	20
Net requirements					100		
Planned-order receipts					120		
Planned-order releases			120				

J (4) and J (3) LT = 1	Beg. Inv.	1	2	3	4	5	6
Gross requirements			480		240		
Scheduled receipts				30	30	30	
Projected on hand	20	20	20	50	80	50	50
Net requirements			460		160		
Planned-order receipts			480		180		
Planned-order releases		480		180			

b.

Master Schedule	Week	Beg. Inv.	1	2	3	4	5	6
	Quantity							70

E LT = 2	Beg. Inv.	1	2	3	4	5	6
Gross requirements							70
Scheduled receipts							
Projected on hand							
Net requirements							70
Planned-order receipts							70
Planned-order releases					70		

B(2) LT = 1	Beg. Inv.	1	2	3	4	5	6
Gross requirements					140		
Scheduled receipts							
Projected on hand	60	60	60	60	60	40	40
Net requirements					80		
Planned-order receipts					120		
Planned-order releases			120				

J(4) and J(3) LT = 1	Beg. Inv.	1	2	3	4	5	6
Gross requirements			480		210		
Scheduled receipts				30	30	30	
Projected on hand	20	20	20	50	80	80	80
Net requirements			460		130		
Planned-order receipts			480		180		
Planned-order releases		480		180			

There will be an additional 20 units of B and 30 units of J.

5. c.

Master Schedule	Weeks	Beg. Inv.	1	2	3	4	5	6	7
	Quantity							100	100

P LT = 1 wk.	Beg. Inv.	1	2	3	4	5	6	7
Gross requirements							100	100
Scheduled receipts								
Projected on hand								
Net requirements							100	100
Planned-order receipts							100	100
Planned-order releases						100	100	

K LT = 2 wk.	Beg. Inv.	1	2	3	4	5	6	7
Gross requirements						100	100	
Scheduled receipts				10			30	
Projected on hand				10	10	10		
Net requirements						90	70	
Planned-order receipts						90	70	
Planned-order releases				90	70			

G (3) LT = 1 wk.	Beg. Inv.	1	2	3	4	5	6	7
Gross requirements				270	210			
Scheduled receipts								
Projected on hand	40	40	40	40				
Net requirements				230	210			
Planned-order receipts				253	231			
Planned-order releases			253	231				

H (4) LT = 1 wk.	Beg. Inv.	1	2	3	4	5	6	7
Gross requirements				360	280			
Scheduled receipts								
Projected on hand	200	200	200	200	40			
Net requirements				160	240			
Planned-order receipts				200	240			
Planned-order releases			200	240				

6.

Master Schedule	Beg. Inv.	1	2	3	4	5	6	7
Day	Beg. Inv.	1	2	3	4	5	6	7
Quantity					100	150		200

Table	Beg. Inv.	1	2	3	4	5	6	7
Gross requirements					100	150		200
Scheduled receipts								
Projected on hand								
Net requirements					100	150		200
Planned-order receipts					100	150		200
Planned-order releases				100	150		200	

Wood Sections (2)	Beg. Inv.	1	2	3	4	5	6	7
Gross requirements				200	300		400	
Scheduled receipts			100					
Projected on hand			100	100				
Net requirements				100	300		400	
Planned-order receipts				100	300		400	
Planned-order releases			400		400			

Braces (3)	Beg. Inv.	1	2	3	4	5	6	7
Gross requirements				300	450		600	
Scheduled receipts								
Projected on hand	60	60	60	60				
Net requirements				240	450		600	
Planned-order receipts				240	450		600	
Planned-order releases		240	450	600				

Legs (4)	Beg. Inv.	1	2	3	4	5	6	7
Gross requirements				400	600		800	
Scheduled receipts								
Projected on hand	120	120	120	120				
Net requirements				280	600		800	
Planned-order receipts				308	660		880	
Planned-order releases		968		880				

10. Order 160 units in week 2.
11. a. Master Schedule for E.

Week number	1	2	3	4	5	6	7	8
Quantity					120			

Item: E LT = 1 week								
Gross requirements					120			
Scheduled receipts								
Projected on hand								
Net requirements					120			
Planned-order receipts					120			
Planned-order releases				120				

Item: I (2) LT = 1 week	1	2	3	4	5	6	7	8
Gross requirements				240				
Scheduled receipts			40					
Projected on hand			40	40				
Net requirements				200				
Planned-order receipts				200				
Planned-order releases			200					

Item: N (4) LT = 2 weeks	1	2	3	4	5	6	7	8
Gross requirements			800					
Scheduled receipts								
Projected on hand	100	100	100					
Net requirements			700					
Planned-order receipts			700					
Planned-order releases	700							

Item: V LT = 2 weeks	1	2	3	4	5	6	7	8
Gross requirements			200					
Scheduled receipts			10					
Projected on hand								
Net requirements			190					
Planned-order receipts			190					
Planned-order releases	190							

13. c. Master Schedule for golf carts.

Week number	1	2	3	4	5	6	7	8	9
Quantity						100		100	100

Item: Golf cart LT = 1 week									
Gross requirements						100		100	100
Scheduled receipts									
Projected on hand									
Net requirements						100		100	100
Planned-order receipts						100		100	100
Planned-order releases					100		100	100	

Item: Bases LT = 1 week									
Gross requirements					100		100	100	
Scheduled receipts									
Projected on hand 20	20	20	20	50	100	50	100	50	
Net requirements					0		0	50	
Planned-order receipts			30	50	50	50	50	50	
Planned-order releases		30	50	50	50	50	50		

15. Labor: 53.3% 106.7% 80% 93.3%
    Machine: 60% 120% 90% 105%

Chapter 13: Inventory Management

1. a.

Item	Category
4021	A
9402	C
4066	B
6500	C
9280	C
4050	C
6850	B
3010	C
4400	B

   b. A: 11%, 55.26%.
   B: 33%, 28.95%.
   C: 56%, 15.79%.

2. a.

Item	Category
K34	C
K35	A
K36	B
M10	C
M20	C
Z45	A
F14	B
F95	A
F99	C
D45	B
D48	C
D52	C
D57	B
N08	C
P05	B
P09	C

3. a. 18 bags.
   b. 9 bags.
   c. 67.5.
   d. $1,350
   e. Increase by $78.71
4. a. 204 packages.
   b. $6,118.82.
   c. Yes.
   d. No; TC = $6,120; only save $1.18.
5. a. $105.29.
6. $364.
7. a. 1–6: 75 units; 7–12: 91 units.
   b. EOQ requirement.
   c. 1–6: 50 units; 7–12: 100 units.
8. a. $1.32.
   b. $24.30.
9. a. 4,812.
   b. 15.59 (approx. 16).
   c. .96.
10. a. 10,328 bags.
   b. 3,098 bags.
   c. 10.33 days.
   d. 7.75 (approx. 8).
   e. $774.50.
11. a. 1,414 units.
   b. 7.07 days.
   c. 120 units.
   d. No.
   f. Approximately 54 units, $168.
12. a. 37.5 batches.
   b. 1,000 units.
   c. 625 units.
   d. No.
13. a. 5,000 boxes.
   b. 3.6 orders.
14. a. 600 stones.
   b. 600 stones.
   c. 150 stones on hand.
15. Indifferent between 495 and 1,000 pulleys.
16. A, 500 units.
18. 6,600 feet.
19. a. 370 units.
   b. 70 units.
   c. Both smaller.
20. a. 91 pounds.
   b. ROP = 691 pounds.
   c. 50%.
21. a. 8.39 gallons.
   b. 34 gallons, .1423.
   c. risk = .4168.
22. 70.14 gallons.
23. .1093.
24. ROP = 70.14.
25. a. 400 gallons.
   b. 45.02 gallons.
26. a. 72 boxes.
   b. .0023.
   c. .0228.
27. a. 749 pounds.
   b. 4.073 pounds.
28. a. 134 rolls.
   b. 36 rolls.
   c. .055 per cycle $\sigma_{d\text{LT}} = \sqrt{\text{LT}}\sigma_d$].
   d. .9996.
29. 0.40 cases.
30. a. −0.40 gal.
   b. −1.98 gal.
31.

Cycle	Order Quantity
1	623
2	657
3	562

32. a. P34: Every 5.1 weeks.
   P35: Every 4 weeks.
   b. 306 units.
   c. 334 units.
34. 25 dozen.
35. a. Nine spares. b. $C_s \le \$10.47$.
36. 78.9 pounds.
37. $4.89 per quart.
38. Five cakes.
39. 421.5 pounds.
40. a. $0.53 to $1.76.
   c. $56.67 to $190.00.
41. 3 spares.
42. 2 cakes.
43. 16 tickets.
44. 97.26%.

Chapter 14: JIT and Lean Operations

1. 3.
2. 3.
3. 3.
4. 3 cycles.
5. 2 cycles:

	Cycle 1	Cycle 2
A	11	11
B	6	6
C	2	2
D	8	8
E	4	4

7. 1.35 minutes.
8. 6.50 minutes.
9. 4 minutes.

Chapter 14 Supplement: Maintenance

1. Expected recalibration cost = $925 a month.
   Use the service contract.
2. Expected repair cost = $456 a month.
   Option #1: $500.
   Option #2: $566.

3.

Equipment	Ratio	Interval (days)
A201	.1304	17.76
B400	.0571	25.26
C850	.1104	35.12

Chapter 15: Supply Chain Management

1. Use 2-day freight.
2. Use 6-day.
3. Ship 2-day using A.

Chapter 16: Scheduling

1. 1-A, 2-B, 3-C, TC = 15.
2. 1-B, 2-C, 3-A, TC = 21.
3. 1-A, 2-E, 3-D, 4-B, 5-C; or 1-A, 2-D, 3-E, 4-B, 5-C.
4. 1-B, 2-C, 4-A, TC = 26.
5. a. 1-A, 2-B, 3-C, 4-D, 5-E.
   b. 1-E, 2-B, 3-C, 4-D, 5-A.
6. b.

	FCFS	SPT	EDD	CR
Av. flow time........	26.5	19.75	21	24.75
Av. job tardiness	11	6	6	9.25
Av. no. of jobs.......	2.86	2.14	2.27	2.68

7. FCFS: a-b-c-d-e.
   SPT: c-b-a-e-d.
   EDD: a-b-c-e-d.
   CR: a-b-c-e-d.

	FCFS	SPT	EDD	CR
Av. flow time	17.40	14.80	16.80	20.60
Av. job tardiness........	5.20	5.40	4.60	8.80
Av. no. of jobs	2.72	2.31	2.63	3.23

9. B-A-G-E-F-D-C.
10. a. e-b-g-h-d-c-a-f.
    c. 2 hours.
11. a. B-A-C-E-F-D.
12. a. b-a-c-d-e.
    b. 37 minutes.
    c. both reduced by 17 minutes.
13. G-A-E-D-B-C-F.
14. a., b. Grinding flow time is 93 hours. Total time is 37 hours.
    c. Grinding flow time is 107 hours. Total time is 35 hours.
15. a.

	FCFS	SPT	EDD	CR
Av. flow time	15.25	11.12	15.60	15.60
Av. job tardiness.....	1.7	2.33	0.55	0.55
Av. no. of jobs	3.91	2.85	4.00	4.00

    c. a-c-b-e-d-f.
16. b-c-e-a-d.
19. A-B-C.
20. C-B-A.
21. B-C-D-A.

Chapter 17: Project Management

1. a. 1-3-6-9-11-12: 31.
   b. 1-2-5-7-8-9: 55.
   c. 1-2-5-12-16: 44.
4. a.

Activity	Immed. Pred.
A	–
B	–
C	A
D	A,B
E	C

5. a. Summary:

Activity	ES	EF	LF	LS	Slack
1-2.......	0	4	11	7	7
2-4.......	4	13	21	12	8
4-7.......	13	18	26	21	8
7-10......	18	20	28	26	8
10-12......	21	24	31	28	7
2-5.......	4	12	19	11	7
5-8.......	12	19	26	19	7
8-10......	19	21	28	26	7
1-3.......	0	10	10	0	0
3-6.......	10	16	16	10	0
6-9.......	16	20	20	16	0
9-11......	20	25	25	20	0
11-12......	25	31	31	25	0

   b. Summary:

Activity	ES	EF	LF	LS	Slack
1	0	5	5	0	0
2	5	23	23	5	0
3	5	18	33	20	15
4	23	26	40	37	14
5	23	33	33	23	0
6	33	37	44	40	7
7	33	44	44	33	0
8	44	53	53	44	0
9	53	55	55	53	0

6. 30 weeks.
7. b. 24 days: .9686; 21 days: .2350.
   c. 24 days: .9328; 21 days: .0186.
   d. Crash activities F, C, and G one day each.
8. a. .6881.
   b. .3984.
   c. .0203.
9. .3479.
10. b. .52.
11. b. .030.
    c. .2085.

12.

Path	Mean	Standard Deviation
a-d-e-h	24.34	1.354
a-f-g	15.50	1.258
b-i-j-k	14.83	1.014
c-m-n-o	26.17	1.658

27 weeks: .6742; 26 weeks: .4099.

14. Crash schedule (1 week each): C, C, F, F, E, P.
15. a. Crash four weeks:
    (1) 7-11, (2) 1-2, (3) 7-11 and 6-10, (4) 11-13 and 4-6.
17. a. 18.5 days.
    b. .67.

Chapter 18: Management of Waiting Lines

1. a. 2.25 customers.
   b. 75 percent.
   c. Two hours.
   d. .5625.
2. a. 0.67 customer.
   b. One minute.
   c. 1.33 customers.
3. a. 6 minutes.
   b. 0.25.
   c. 2.25 customers.
4. a. 45 percent.
   b. .229.
   c. .509 hour.
   d. .28.
5. a. Morning: 0.375 minute; .45.
   Afternoon: 0.678 minute; .54.
   Evening: 0.635 minute; .44.
   b. M: 4; A: 8; E: 5.
6. a. 4.444 trucks.
   b. 6.67 minutes.
   c. .711.
   d. 6 minutes.
   e. The system would be overloaded.
   f. 13.186.
7. a. One dock.
   b. No.
8. a. 0.952 mechanic.
   b. 0.228.
   c. 0.056 hr.
   d. 0.60.
   e. Two.
9. a. 0.995 customer.
   b. 2.24 days.
   c. 19.9 percent.
   d. 0.875 customer.
10. a. .437.
    b. 0.53 machine.
    c. 1.33 machines.
    d. 40.72 pieces.
    e. Three.
11. a. 28.56 pieces.
    b. Two.
12. a. 15.9 pieces.
    b. Three.
13. Three.
14. a. .90.
    b. W_1 = .12 hour.
    W_2 = .3045 hour.
    W_3 = 2.13 hours.
    c. L_1 = .365.
    L_2 = .914.
    L_3 = 6.395.
15. a. .75.
    b. L_1 = .643.
    L_2 = 1.286.
18. a. approx. 0.0116.
    b. approx. 0.433.

Chapter 19: Linear Programming

1. a. (1) $x_1 = 2, x_2 = 9, Z = 35$.
   (2) No.
   (3) No.
   (4) No.
   b. (1) $x_1 = 1.5, x_2 = 6.25, Z = 65.5$.
   (2) No.
   (3) Yes, S has surplus of 15.
   (4) No.
   c. (1) $A = 24, B = 20, Z =$ \$204.
   (2) Yes. Labor, 120 hr.
   (3) No.
   (4) No.
2. a. $S = 8, T = 20, Z =$ \$58.40.
   b. (1) $x_1 = 4.2, x_2 = 1.6, Z = 13.2$.
   (2) Yes. $F = 4.6$.
   (3) No.
   (4) No.
3. $H = 132$ units, $W = 36$ units, Profit = \$6,360.
4. Deluxe = 90 bags, Standard = 60 bags, Profit = \$243.
5. 500 apple, 200 grape, Revenue = \$990. Fifty cups of sugar will be unused.
6. a. $x_1 = 4, x_2 = 0, x_3 = 18$.
   $s_1 = 3, s_2 = 0, s_3 = 0$.
   $Z = 106$.
   b. $x_1 = 15, x_2 = 10, x_3 = 0$.
   $s_1 = 0, s_2 = 0, s_3 = 5$.
   $Z = 210$.
9. $A = 0, B = 80, C = 50$.
   $Z = 350$.
   C_A (insignificance): \$$-\infty$ to \$3.04.
   C_B (optimality): \$1.95 to \$3.75.
   C_C (optimality): \$2.00 to \$5.00.
11. a. board = 0, holder = 50.
    b. Cutting = 16 minutes, gluing = 0 minutes, finishing = 210 minutes.

12. a. Ham = 37.14, deli = 18, cost = $165.42.
    b. Ham = 20, deli = 84, profit = $376.
14. Z = $433.
15. a. Machine and materials are binding.
    b. No change.
    c. No change.
    d. Only s_2 would change. It would be 46.
    e. None.
    f. Yes; $844.
16. a. $1.50; range is 510 to 750.
    b. $1.50/pound.
    c. $0; range 375 to infinity.
    d. None.
    e. 150 pounds of pine bark.
    f. Optimal quantities would not change; Z would increase by $75.
    g. Yes, $1,155.
    h. Yes, $1,125.

APPENDIX B Tables

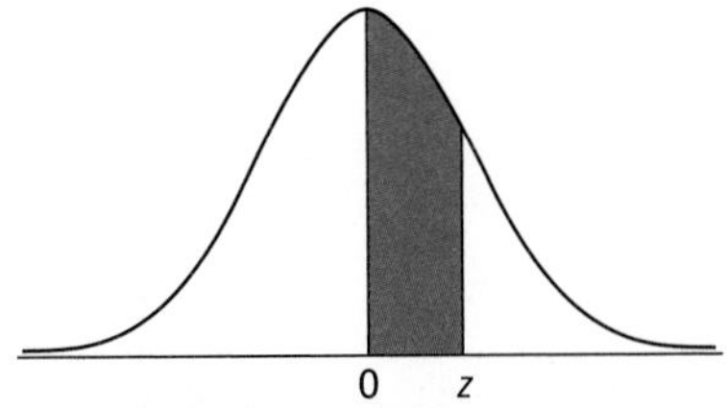

Table A Areas under the normal curve, 0 to z

z	.00	.01	.02	.03	.04	.05	.06	.07	.08	.09
0.0	.0000	.0040	.0080	.0120	.0160	.0199	.0239	.0279	.0319	.0359
0.1	.0398	.0438	.0478	.0517	.0557	.0596	.0636	.0675	.0714	.0753
0.2	.0793	.0832	.0871	.0910	.0948	.0987	.1026	.1064	.1103	.1141
0.3	.1179	.1217	.1255	.1293	.1331	.1368	.1406	.1443	.1480	.1517
0.4	.1554	.1591	.1628	.1664	.1700	.1736	.1772	.1808	.1844	.1879
0.5	.1915	.1950	.1985	.2019	.2054	.2088	.2123	.2157	.2190	.2224
0.6	.2257	.2291	.2324	.2357	.2389	.2422	.2454	.2486	.2517	.2549
0.7	.2580	.2611	.2642	.2673	.2703	.2734	.2764	.2794	.2823	.2852
0.8	.2881	.2910	.2939	.2967	.2995	.3023	.3051	.3078	.3106	.3133
0.9	.3159	.3186	.3212	.3238	.3264	.3289	.3315	.3340	.3365	.3389
1.0	.3413	.3438	.3461	.3485	.3508	.3531	.3554	.3577	.3599	.3621
1.1	.3643	.3665	.3686	.3708	.3729	.3749	.3770	.3790	.3810	.3830
1.2	.3849	.3869	.3888	.3907	.3925	.3944	.3962	.3980	.3997	.4015
1.3	.4032	.4049	.4066	.4082	.4099	.4115	.4131	.4147	.4162	.4177
1.4	.4192	.4207	.4222	.4236	.4251	.4265	.4279	.4292	.4306	.4319
1.5	.4332	.4345	.4357	.4370	.4382	.4394	.4406	.4418	.4429	.4441
1.6	.4452	.4463	.4474	.4484	.4495	.4505	.4515	.4525	.4535	.4545
1.7	.4554	.4564	.4573	.4582	.4591	.4599	.4608	.4616	.4625	.4633
1.8	.4641	.4649	.4656	.4664	.4671	.4678	.4686	.4693	.4699	.4706
1.9	.4713	.4719	.4726	.4732	.4738	.4744	.4750	.4756	.4761	.4767
2.0	.4772	.4778	.4783	.4788	.4793	.4798	.4803	.4808	.4812	.4817
2.1	.4821	.4826	.4830	.4834	.4838	.4842	.4846	.4850	.4854	.4857
2.2	.4861	.4864	.4868	.4871	.4875	.4878	.4881	.4884	.4887	.4890
2.3	.4893	.4896	.4898	.4901	.4904	.4906	.4909	.4911	.4913	.4916
2.4	.4918	.4920	.4922	.4925	.4927	.4929	.4931	.4932	.4934	.4936
2.5	.4938	.4940	.4941	.4943	.4945	.4946	.4948	.4949	.4951	.4952
2.6	.4953	.4955	.4956	.4957	.4959	.4960	.4961	.4962	.4963	.4964
2.7	.4965	.4966	.4967	.4968	.4969	.4970	.4971	.4972	.4973	.4974
2.8	.4974	.4975	.4976	.4977	.4977	.4978	.4979	.4979	.4980	.4981
2.9	.4981	.4982	.4982	.4983	.4984	.4984	.4985	.4985	.4986	.4986
3.0	.4987	.4987	.4987	.4988	.4988	.4989	.4989	.4989	.4990	.4990

Table B

1. Areas under the standardized normal curve, from $-\infty$ to $-z$

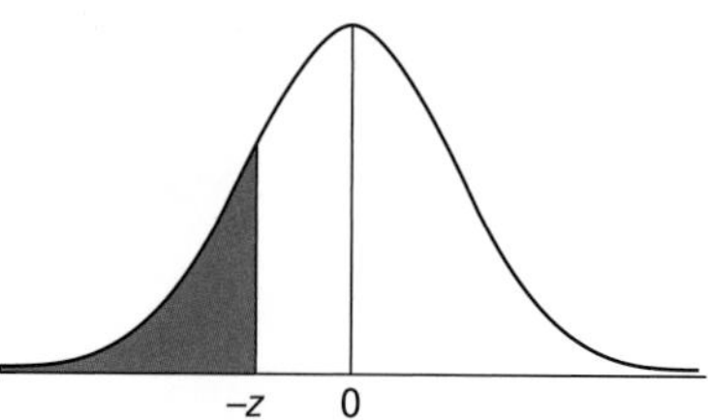

.09	.08	.07	.06	.05	.04	.03	.02	.01	.00	z
.0002	.0003	.0003	.0003	.0003	.0003	.0003	.0003	.0003	.0003	−3.4
.0003	.0004	.0004	.0004	.0004	.0004	.0004	.0005	.0005	.0005	−3.3
.0005	.0005	.0005	.0006	.0006	.0006	.0006	.0006	.0007	.0007	−3.2
.0007	.0007	.0008	.0008	.0008	.0008	.0009	.0009	.0009	.0010	−3.1
.0010	.0010	.0011	.0011	.0011	.0012	.0012	.0013	.0013	.0013	−3.0
.0014	.0014	.0015	.0015	.0016	.0016	.0017	.0018	.0018	.0019	−2.9
.0019	.0020	.0021	.0021	.0022	.0023	.0023	.0024	.0025	.0026	−2.8
.0026	.0027	.0028	.0029	.0030	.0031	.0032	.0033	.0034	.0035	−2.7
.0036	.0037	.0038	.0039	.0040	.0041	.0043	.0044	.0045	.0047	−2.6
.0048	.0049	.0051	.0052	.0054	.0055	.0057	.0059	.0060	.0062	−2.5
.0064	.0066	.0068	.0069	.0071	.0073	.0075	.0078	.0080	.0082	−2.4
.0084	.0087	.0089	.0091	.0094	.0096	.0099	.0102	.0104	.0107	−2.3
.0110	.0113	.0116	.0119	.0122	.0125	.0129	.0132	.0136	.0139	−2.2
.0143	.0146	.0150	.0154	.0158	.0162	.0166	.0170	.0174	.0179	−2.1
.0183	.0188	.0192	.0197	.0202	.0207	.0212	.0217	.0222	.0228	−2.0
.0233	.0239	.0244	.0250	.0256	.0262	.0268	.0274	.0281	.0287	−1.9
.0294	.0301	.0307	.0314	.0322	.0329	.0336	.0344	.0351	.0359	−1.8
.0367	.0375	.0384	.0392	.0401	.0409	.0418	.0427	.0436	.0446	−1.7
.0455	.0465	.0475	.0485	.0495	.0505	.0516	.0526	.0537	.0548	−1.6
.0559	.0571	.0582	.0594	.0606	.0618	.0630	.0643	.0655	.0668	−1.5
.0681	.0694	.0708	.0721	.0735	.0749	.0764	.0778	.0793	.0808	−1.4
.0823	.0838	.0853	.0869	.0885	.0901	.0918	.0934	.0951	.0968	−1.3
.0985	.1003	.1020	.1038	.1056	.1075	.1093	.1112	.1131	.1151	−1.2
.1170	.1190	.1210	.1230	.1251	.1271	.1292	.1314	.1335	.1357	−1.1
.1379	.1401	.1423	.1446	.1469	.1492	.1515	.1539	.1562	.1587	−1.0
.1611	.1635	.1660	.1685	.1711	.1736	.1762	.1788	.1814	.1841	−0.9
.1867	.1894	.1922	.1949	.1977	.2005	.2033	.2061	.2090	.2119	−0.8
.2148	.2177	.2206	.2236	.2266	.2296	.2327	.2358	.2389	.2420	−0.7
.2451	.2483	.2514	.2546	.2578	.2611	.2643	.2676	.2709	.2743	−0.6
.2776	.2810	.2843	.2877	.2912	.2946	.2981	.3015	.3050	.3085	−0.5
.3121	.3156	.3192	.3228	.3264	.3300	.3336	.3372	.3409	.3446	−0.4
.3483	.3520	.3557	.3594	.3632	.3669	.3707	.3745	.3783	.3821	−0.3
.3859	.3897	.3936	.3974	.4013	.4052	.4090	.4129	.4168	.4207	−0.2
.4247	.4286	.4325	.4364	.4404	.4443	.4483	.4522	.4562	.4602	−0.1
.4641	.4681	.4721	.4761	.4801	.4840	.4880	.4920	.4960	.5000	−0.0

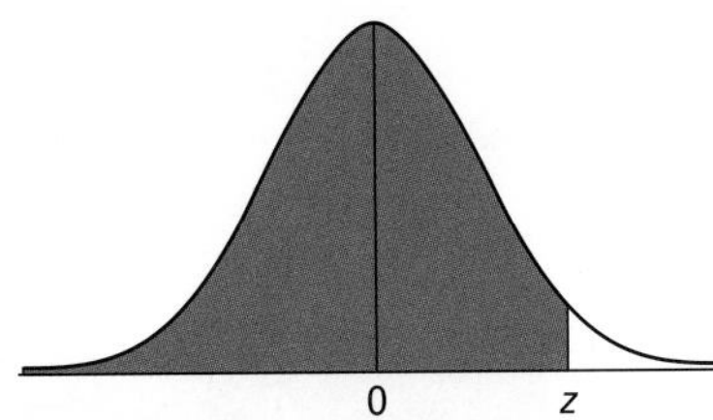

Table B
(concluded)
2. Areas under the standardized normal curve, from $-\infty$ to $+z$

z	.00	.01	.02	.03	.04	.05	.06	.07	.08	.09
.0	.5000	.5040	.5080	.5120	.5160	.5199	.5239	.5279	.5319	.5359
.1	.5398	.5438	.5478	.5517	.5557	.5596	.5636	.5675	.5714	.5753
.2	.5793	.5832	.5871	.5910	.5948	.5987	.6026	.6064	.6103	.6141
.3	.6179	.6217	.6255	.6293	.6331	.6368	.6406	.6443	.6480	.6517
.4	.6554	.6591	.6628	.6664	.6700	.6736	.6772	.6808	.6844	.6879
.5	.6915	.6950	.6985	.7019	.7054	.7088	.7123	.7157	.7190	.7224
.6	.7257	.7291	.7324	.7357	.7389	.7422	.7454	.7486	.7517	.7549
.7	.7580	.7611	.7642	.7673	.7703	.7734	.7764	.7794	.7823	.7852
.8	.7881	.7910	.7939	.7967	.7995	.8023	.8051	.8078	.8106	.8133
.9	.8159	.8186	.8212	.8238	.8264	.8289	.8315	.8340	.8365	.8389
1.0	.8413	.8438	.8461	.8485	.8508	.8531	.8554	.8577	.8599	.8621
1.1	.8643	.8665	.8686	.8708	.8729	.8749	.8770	.8790	.8810	.8830
1.2	.8849	.8869	.8888	.8907	.8925	.8944	.8962	.8980	.8997	.9015
1.3	.9032	.9049	.9066	.9082	.9099	.9115	.9131	.9147	.9162	.9177
1.4	.9192	.9207	.9222	.9236	.9251	.9265	.9279	.9292	.9306	.9319
1.5	.9332	.9345	.9357	.9370	.9382	.9394	.9406	.9418	.9429	.9441
1.6	.9452	.9463	.9474	.9484	.9495	.9505	.9515	.9525	.9535	.9545
1.7	.9554	.9564	.9573	.9582	.9591	.9599	.9608	.9616	.9625	.9633
1.8	.9641	.9649	.9656	.9664	.9671	.9678	.9686	.9693	.9699	.9706
1.9	.9713	.9719	.9726	.9732	.9738	.9744	.9750	.9756	.9761	.9767
2.0	.9772	.9778	.9783	.9788	.9793	.9798	.9803	.9808	.9812	.9817
2.1	.9821	.9826	.9830	.9834	.9838	.9842	.9846	.9850	.9854	.9857
2.2	.9861	.9864	.9868	.9871	.9875	.9878	.9881	.9884	.9887	.9890
2.3	.9893	.9896	.9898	.9901	.9904	.9906	.9909	.9911	.9913	.9916
2.4	.9918	.9920	.9922	.9925	.9927	.9929	.9931	.9932	.9934	.9936
2.5	.9938	.9940	.9941	.9943	.9945	.9946	.9948	.9949	.9951	.9952
2.6	.9953	.9955	.9956	.9957	.9959	.9960	.9961	.9962	.9963	.9964
2.7	.9965	.9966	.9967	.9968	.9969	.9970	.9971	.9972	.9973	.9974
2.8	.9974	.9975	.9976	.9977	.9977	.9978	.9979	.9979	.9980	.9981
2.9	.9981	.9982	.9982	.9983	.9984	.9984	.9985	.9985	.9986	.9986
3.0	.9987	.9987	.9987	.9988	.9988	.9989	.9989	.9989	.9990	.9990
3.1	.9990	.9991	.9991	.9991	.9992	.9992	.9992	.9992	.9993	.9993
3.2	.9993	.9993	.9994	.9994	.9994	.9994	.9994	.9995	.9995	.9995
3.3	.9995	.9995	.9995	.9996	.9996	.9996	.9996	.9996	.9996	.9997
3.4	.9997	.9997	.9997	.9997	.9997	.9997	.9997	.9997	.9997	.9998

Table C
Cumulative Poisson probabilities

$$P(x \le c) = \sum_{x=0}^{x=c} \frac{\mu^{x} \cdot e^{-\mu}}{x!}$$

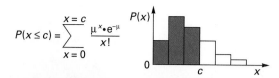

$\mu \backslash x$	0	1	2	3	4	5	6	7	8	9
0.05	.951	.999	1.000							
0.10	.905	.995	1.000							
0.15	.861	.990	.999	1.000						
0.20	.819	.982	.999	1.000						
0.25	.779	.974	.998	1.000						
0.30	.741	.963	.996	1.000						
0.35	.705	.951	.994	1.000						
0.40	.670	.938	.992	.999	1.000					
0.45	.638	.925	.989	.999	1.000					
0.50	.607	.910	.986	.998	1.000					
0.55	.577	.894	.982	.998	1.000					
0.60	.549	.878	.977	.997	1.000					
0.65	.522	.861	.972	.996	.999	1.000				
0.70	.497	.844	.966	.994	.999	1.000				
0.75	.472	.827	.960	.993	.999	1.000				
0.80	.449	.809	.953	.991	.999	1.000				
0.85	.427	.791	.945	.989	.998	1.000				
0.90	.407	.772	.937	.987	.998	1.000				
0.95	.387	.754	.929	.984	.997	1.000				
1.0	.368	.736	.920	.981	.996	.999	1.000			
1.1	.333	.699	.900	.974	.995	.999	1.000			
1.2	.301	.663	.880	.966	.992	.998	1.000			
1.3	.273	.627	.857	.957	.989	.998	1.000			
1.4	.247	.592	.833	.946	.986	.997	.999	1.000		
1.5	.223	.558	.809	.934	.981	.996	.999	1.000		
1.6	.202	.525	.783	.921	.976	.994	.999	1.000		
1.7	.183	.493	.757	.907	.970	.992	.998	1.000		
1.8	.165	.463	.731	.891	.964	.990	.997	.999	1.000	
1.9	.150	.434	.704	.875	.956	.987	.997	.999	1.000	
2.0	.135	.406	.677	.857	.947	.983	.995	.999	1.000	
2.2	.111	.355	.623	.819	.928	.975	.993	.998	1.000	
2.4	.091	.308	.570	.779	.904	.964	.988	.997	.999	1.000
2.6	.074	.267	.518	.736	.877	.951	.983	.995	.999	1.000
2.8	.061	.231	.470	.692	.848	.935	.976	.992	.998	.999

Table C (concluded)

$\mu\backslash x$	0	1	2	3	4	5	6	7	8	9	10	11	12	13	14	15	16	17	18	19	20
3.0	.050	.199	.423	.647	.815	.916	.966	.988	.996	.999	1.000										
3.2	.041	.171	.380	.603	.781	.895	.955	.983	.994	.998	1.000										
3.4	.033	.147	.340	.558	.744	.871	.942	.977	.992	.997	.999	1.000									
3.6	.027	.126	.303	.515	.706	.844	.927	.969	.988	.996	.999	1.000									
3.8	.022	.107	.269	.474	.668	.816	.909	.960	.984	.994	.998	.999	1.000								
4.0	.018	.092	.238	.433	.629	.785	.889	.949	.979	.992	.997	.999	1.000								
4.2	.015	.078	.210	.395	.590	.753	.868	.936	.972	.989	.996	.999	1.000								
4.4	.012	.066	.185	.359	.551	.720	.844	.921	.964	.985	.994	.998	.999	1.000							
4.6	.010	.056	.163	.326	.513	.686	.818	.905	.955	.980	.992	.997	.999	1.000							
4.8	.008	.048	.143	.294	.476	.651	.791	.887	.944	.975	.990	.996	.999	1.000							
5.0	.007	.040	.125	.265	.441	.616	.762	.867	.932	.968	.986	.995	.998	.999	1.000						
5.2	.006	.034	.109	.238	.406	.581	.732	.845	.918	.960	.982	.993	.997	.999	1.000						
5.4	.005	.029	.095	.213	.373	.546	.702	.822	.903	.951	.978	.990	.996	.999	1.000						
5.6	.004	.024	.082	.191	.342	.512	.670	.797	.886	.941	.972	.988	.995	.998	.999	1.000					
5.8	.003	.021	.072	.170	.313	.478	.638	.771	.867	.929	.965	.984	.993	.997	.999	1.000					
6.0	.003	.017	.062	.151	.285	.446	.606	.744	.847	.916	.957	.980	.991	.996	.999	.999	1.000				
6.2	.002	.015	.054	.134	.259	.414	.574	.716	.826	.902	.949	.975	.989	.995	.998	.999	1.000				
6.4	.002	.012	.046	.119	.235	.384	.542	.687	.803	.886	.939	.969	.986	.994	.997	.999	1.000				
6.6	.001	.010	.040	.105	.213	.355	.511	.658	.780	.869	.927	.963	.982	.992	.997	.999	.999	1.000			
6.8	.001	.009	.034	.093	.192	.327	.480	.628	.755	.850	.915	.955	.978	.990	.996	.998	.999	1.000			
7.0	.001	.007	.030	.082	.173	.301	.450	.599	.729	.830	.901	.947	.973	.987	.994	.998	.999	1.000			
7.2	.001	.006	.025	.072	.156	.276	.420	.569	.703	.810	.887	.937	.967	.984	.993	.997	.999	.999	1.000		
7.4	.001	.005	.022	.063	.140	.253	.392	.539	.676	.788	.871	.926	.961	.980	.991	.996	.998	.999	1.000		
7.6	.001	.004	.019	.055	.125	.231	.365	.510	.648	.765	.854	.915	.954	.976	.989	.995	.998	.999	1.000		
7.8	.000	.004	.016	.048	.112	.210	.338	.481	.620	.741	.835	.902	.945	.971	.986	.993	.997	.999	1.000		
8.0	.000	.003	.014	.042	.100	.191	.313	.453	.593	.717	.816	.888	.936	.966	.983	.992	.996	.998	.999	1.000	
8.2	.000	.003	.012	.037	.089	.174	.290	.425	.566	.692	.796	.873	.926	.960	.979	.990	.995	.998	.999	1.000	
8.4	.000	.002	.010	.032	.079	.157	.267	.400	.537	.666	.774	.857	.915	.952	.975	.987	.994	.997	.999	1.000	
8.6	.000	.002	.009	.030	.070	.142	.246	.373	.509	.640	.752	.849	.909	.949	.973	.986	.993	.997	.999	1.000	
8.8	.000	.002	.007	.024	.062	.128	.226	.348	.482	.614	.729	.822	.889	.935	.964	.981	.990	.995	.998	.999	1.000
9.0	.000	.001	.006	.021	.055	.116	.207	.324	.456	.587	.706	.803	.876	.926	.959	.978	.989	.995	.998	.999	1.000
9.5	.000	.001	.004	.015	.040	.089	.165	.269	.392	.522	.645	.752	.836	.898	.940	.967	.982	.991	.996	.998	.999

$$P(x \le c) = \sum_{x=0}^{c} \binom{n}{x} p^x (1-p)^{n-x}$$

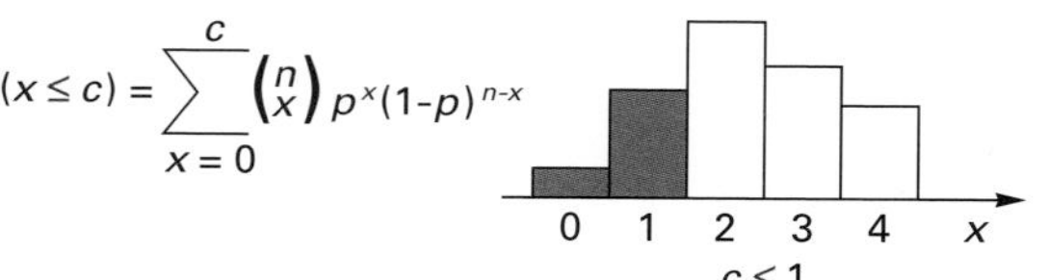

Table D Cumulative binomial probabilities

n	x	.05	.10	.15	.20	.25	.30	.35	.40	.45	.50	.55	.60	.65	.70	.75	.80	.85	.90
1	0	.9500	.9000	.8500	.8000	.7500	.7000	.6500	.6000	.5500	.5000	.4500	.4000	.3500	.3000	.2500	.2000	.1500	.1000
	1	1.0000	1.0000	1.0000	1.0000	1.0000	1.0000	1.0000	1.0000	1.0000	1.0000	1.0000	1.0000	1.0000	1.0000	1.0000	1.0000	1.0000	1.0000
2	0	.9025	.8100	.7225	.6400	.5625	.4900	.4225	.3600	.3025	.2500	.2025	.1600	.1225	.0900	.0625	.0400	.0225	.0100
	1	.9975	.9900	.9775	.9600	.9375	.9100	.8775	.8400	.7975	.7500	.6975	.6400	.5775	.5100	.4375	.3600	.2775	.1900
	2	1.0000	1.0000	1.0000	1.0000	1.0000	1.0000	1.0000	1.0000	1.0000	1.0000	1.0000	1.0000	1.0000	1.0000	1.0000	1.0000	1.0000	1.0000
3	0	.8574	.7290	.6141	.5120	.4219	.3430	.2746	.2160	.1664	.1250	.0911	.0640	.0429	.0270	.0156	.0080	.0034	.0010
	1	.9928	.9720	.9393	.8960	.8438	.7840	.7183	.6480	.5748	.5000	.4253	.3520	.2818	.2160	.1563	.1040	.0608	.0280
	2	.9999	.9990	.9966	.9920	.9844	.9730	.9571	.9360	.9089	.8750	.8336	.7840	.7254	.6570	.5781	.4880	.3859	.2710
	3	1.0000	1.0000	1.0000	1.0000	1.0000	1.0000	1.0000	1.0000	1.0000	1.0000	1.0000	1.0000	1.0000	1.0000	1.0000	1.0000	1.0000	1.0000
4	0	.8145	.6561	.5220	.4096	.3164	.2401	.1785	.1296	.0915	.0625	.0410	.0256	.0150	.0081	.0039	.0016	.0005	.0001
	1	.9860	.9477	.8905	.8192	.7383	.6517	.5630	.4752	.3910	.3125	.2415	.1792	.1265	.0837	.0508	.0272	.0120	.0037
	2	.9995	.9963	.9880	.9728	.9492	.9163	.8735	.8208	.7585	.6875	.6090	.5248	.4370	.3483	.2617	.1808	.1095	.0523
	3	1.0000	.9999	.9995	.9984	.9961	.9919	.9850	.9744	.9590	.9375	.9085	.8704	.8215	.7599	.6836	.5904	.4780	.3439
	4	1.0000	1.0000	1.0000	1.0000	1.0000	1.0000	1.0000	1.0000	1.0000	1.0000	1.0000	1.0000	1.0000	1.0000	1.0000	1.0000	1.0000	1.0000
5	0	.7738	.5905	.4437	.3277	.2373	.1681	.1160	.0778	.0503	.0313	.0185	.0102	.0053	.0024	.0010	.0003	.0001	.0000
	1	.9774	.9185	.8352	.7373	.6328	.5282	.4284	.3370	.2562	.1875	.1312	.0870	.0540	.0308	.0156	.0067	.0022	.0005
	2	.9988	.9914	.9734	.9421	.8965	.8369	.7648	.6826	.5931	.5000	.4069	.3174	.2352	.1631	.1035	.0579	.0266	.0086
	3	1.0000	.9995	.9978	.9933	.9844	.9692	.9460	.9130	.8688	.8125	.7438	.6630	.5716	.4718	.3672	.2627	.1648	.0815
	4	1.0000	1.0000	.9999	.9997	.9990	.9976	.9947	.9898	.9815	.9688	.9497	.9222	.8840	.8319	.7627	.6723	.5563	.4095
	5	1.0000	1.0000	1.0000	1.0000	1.0000	1.0000	1.0000	1.0000	1.0000	1.0000	1.0000	1.0000	1.0000	1.0000	1.0000	1.0000	1.0000	1.0000
6	0	.7351	.5314	.3771	.2621	.1780	.1176	.0754	.0467	.0277	.0156	.0083	.0041	.0018	.0007	.0002	.0001	.0000	.0000
	1	.9672	.8857	.7765	.6554	.5339	.4202	.3191	.2333	.1636	.1094	.0692	.0410	.0223	.0109	.0046	.0016	.0004	.0001
	2	.9978	.9842	.9527	.9011	.8306	.7443	.6471	.5443	.4415	.3438	.2553	.1792	.1174	.0705	.0376	.0170	.0059	.0013
	3	.9999	.9987	.9941	.9830	.9624	.9295	.8826	.8208	.7447	.6563	.5585	.4557	.3529	.2557	.1694	.0989	.0473	.0159
	4	1.0000	.9999	.9996	.9984	.9954	.9891	.9777	.9590	.9308	.8906	.8364	.7667	.6809	.5798	.4661	.3446	.2235	.1143
	5	1.0000	1.0000	1.0000	.9999	.9998	.9993	.9982	.9959	.9917	.9844	.9723	.9533	.9246	.8824	.8220	.7379	.6229	.4686
	6	1.0000	1.0000	1.0000	1.0000	1.0000	1.0000	1.0000	1.0000	1.0000	1.0000	1.0000	1.0000	1.0000	1.0000	1.0000	1.0000	1.0000	1.0000

Table D (continued)

n	x	.05	.10	.15	.20	.25	.30	.35	.40	.45	.50	.55	.60	.65	.70	.75	.80	.85	.90
7	0	.6983	.4783	.3206	.2097	.1335	.0824	.0490	.0280	.0152	.0078	.0037	.0016	.0006	.0002	.0001	.0000	.0000	.0000
	1	.9556	.8503	.7166	.5767	.4449	.3294	.2338	.1586	.1024	.0625	.0357	.0188	.0090	.0038	.0013	.0004	.0001	.0000
	2	.9962	.9743	.9262	.8520	.7564	.6471	.5323	.4199	.3164	.2266	.1529	.0963	.0556	.0288	.0129	.0047	.0012	.0002
	3	.9998	.9973	.9879	.9667	.9294	.8740	.8002	.7102	.6083	.5000	.3917	.2898	.1998	.1260	.0706	.0333	.0121	.0027
	4	1.0000	.9998	.9988	.9953	.9871	.9712	.9444	.9037	.8471	.7734	.6836	.5801	.4677	.3529	.2436	.1480	.0738	.0257
	5	1.0000	1.0000	.9999	.9996	.9987	.9962	.9910	.9812	.9643	.9375	.8976	.8414	.7662	.6706	.5551	.4233	.2834	.1497
	6	1.0000	1.0000	1.0000	1.0000	.9999	.9998	.9994	.9984	.9963	.9922	.9848	.9720	.9510	.9176	.8665	.7903	.6794	.5217
	7	1.0000	1.0000	1.0000	1.0000	1.0000	1.0000	1.0000	1.0000	1.0000	1.0000	1.0000	1.0000	1.0000	1.0000	1.0000	1.0000	1.0000	1.0000
8	0	.6634	.4305	.2725	.1678	.1001	.0576	.0319	.0168	.0084	.0039	.0017	.0007	.0002	.0001	.0000	.0000	.0000	.0000
	1	.9428	.8131	.6572	.5033	.3671	.2553	.1691	.1064	.0632	.0352	.0181	.0085	.0036	.0013	.0004	.0001	.0000	.0000
	2	.9942	.9619	.8948	.7969	.6785	.5518	.4278	.3154	.2201	.1445	.0885	.0498	.0253	.0113	.0042	.0012	.0002	.0000
	3	.9996	.9950	.9786	.9437	.8862	.8059	.7064	.5941	.4770	.3633	.2604	.1737	.1061	.0580	.0273	.0104	.0029	.0004
	4	1.0000	.9996	.9971	.9896	.9727	.9420	.8939	.8263	.7396	.6367	.5230	.4059	.2936	.1941	.1138	.0563	.0214	.0050
	5	1.0000	1.0000	.9998	.9988	.9958	.9887	.9747	.9502	.9115	.8555	.7799	.6848	.5722	.4482	.3215	.2031	.1052	.0381
	6	1.0000	1.0000	1.0000	.9999	.9996	.9987	.9964	.9915	.9819	.9648	.9368	.8936	.8309	.7447	.6329	.4967	.3428	.1869
	7	1.0000	1.0000	1.0000	1.0000	1.0000	.9999	.9998	.9993	.9983	.9961	.9916	.9832	.9681	.9424	.8999	.8322	.7275	.5695
	8	1.0000	1.0000	1.0000	1.0000	1.0000	1.0000	1.0000	1.0000	1.0000	1.0000	1.0000	1.0000	1.0000	1.0000	1.0000	1.0000	1.0000	1.0000
9	0	.6302	.3874	.2316	.1342	.0751	.0404	.0207	.0101	.0046	.0020	.0008	.0003	.0001	.0000	.0000	.0000	.0000	.0000
	1	.9288	.7748	.5995	.4362	.3003	.1960	.1211	.0705	.0385	.0195	.0091	.0038	.0014	.0004	.0001	.0000	.0000	.0000
	2	.9916	.9470	.8591	.7382	.6007	.4628	.3373	.2318	.1495	.0898	.0498	.0250	.0112	.0043	.0013	.0003	.0000	.0000
	3	.9994	.9917	.9661	.9144	.8343	.7297	.6089	.4826	.3614	.2539	.1658	.0994	.0536	.0253	.0100	.0031	.0006	.0001
	4	1.0000	.9991	.9944	.9804	.9511	.9012	.8283	.7334	.6214	.5000	.3786	.2666	.1717	.0988	.0489	.0196	.0056	.0009
	5	1.0000	.9999	.9994	.9969	.9900	.9747	.9464	.9006	.8342	.7461	.6386	.5174	.3911	.2703	.1657	.0856	.0339	.0083
	6	1.0000	1.0000	1.0000	.9997	.9987	.9957	.9888	.9750	.9502	.9102	.8505	.7682	.6627	.5372	.3993	.2618	.1409	.0530
	7	1.0000	1.0000	1.0000	1.0000	.9999	.9996	.9986	.9962	.9909	.9805	.9615	.9295	.8789	.8040	.6997	.5638	.4005	.2252
	8	1.0000	1.0000	1.0000	1.0000	1.0000	1.0000	.9999	.9997	.9992	.9980	.9954	.9899	.9793	.9596	.9249	.8658	.7684	.6126
	9	1.0000	1.0000	1.0000	1.0000	1.0000	1.0000	1.0000	1.0000	1.0000	1.0000	1.0000	1.0000	1.0000	1.0000	1.0000	1.0000	1.0000	1.0000
10	0	.5987	.3487	.1969	.1074	.0563	.0282	.0135	.0060	.0025	.0010	.0003	.0001	.0000	.0000	.0000	.0000	.0000	.0000
	1	.9139	.7361	.5443	.3758	.2440	.1493	.0860	.0464	.0233	.0107	.0045	.0017	.0005	.0001	.0000	.0000	.0000	.0000
	2	.9885	.9298	.8202	.6778	.5256	.3828	.2616	.1673	.0996	.0547	.0274	.0123	.0048	.0016	.0004	.0001	.0000	.0000
	3	.9990	.9872	.9500	.8791	.7759	.6496	.5138	.3823	.2660	.1719	.1020	.0548	.0260	.0106	.0035	.0009	.0001	.0000
	4	.9999	.9984	.9901	.9672	.9219	.8497	.7515	.6331	.5044	.3770	.2616	.1662	.0949	.0473	.0197	.0064	.0014	.0001
	5	1.0000	.9999	.9986	.9936	.9803	.9527	.9051	.8338	.7384	.6230	.4956	.3669	.2485	.1503	.0781	.0328	.0099	.0016
	6	1.0000	1.0000	.9999	.9991	.9965	.9894	.9740	.9452	.8980	.8281	.7340	.6177	.4862	.3504	.2241	.1209	.0500	.0128
	7	1.0000	1.0000	1.0000	.9999	.9996	.9984	.9952	.9877	.9726	.9453	.9004	.8327	.7384	.6172	.4744	.3222	.1798	.0702
	8	1.0000	1.0000	1.0000	1.0000	1.0000	.9999	.9995	.9983	.9955	.9893	.9767	.9536	.9140	.8507	.7560	.6242	.4557	.2639
	9	1,0000	1.0000	1.0000	1.0000	1.0000	1.0000	1.0000	.9999	.9997	.9990	.9975	.9940	.9865	.9718	.9437	.8926	.8031	.6513
	10	1.0000	1.0000	1.0000	1.0000	1.0000	1.0000	1.0000	1.0000	1.0000	1.0000	1.0000	1.0000	1.0000	1.0000	1.0000	1.0000	1.0000	1.0000

Table D (concluded)

n	x	p .05	.10	.15	.20	.25	.30	.35	.40	.45	.50	.55	.60	.65	.70	.75	.80	.85	.90
15	0	.4633	.2059	.0874	.0352	.0134	.0047	.0016	.0005	.0001	.0000	.0000	.0000	.0000	.0000	.0000	.0000	.0000	.0000
	1	.8290	.5490	.3186	.1671	.0802	.0353	.0142	.0052	.0017	.0005	.0001	.0000	.0000	.0000	.0000	.0000	.0000	.0000
	2	.9638	.8159	.6042	.3980	.2361	.1268	.0617	.0271	.0107	.0037	.0011	.0003	.0001	.0000	.0000	.0000	.0000	.0000
	3	.9945	.9444	.8227	.6482	.4613	.2969	.1727	.0905	.0424	.0176	.0063	.0019	.0005	.0001	.0000	.0000	.0000	.0000
	4	.9994	.9873	.9383	.8358	.6865	.5155	.3519	.2173	.1204	.0592	.0255	.0093	.0028	.0007	.0001	.0000	.0000	.0000
	5	.9999	.9978	.9832	.9389	.8516	.7216	.5643	.4032	.2608	.1509	.0769	.0338	.0124	.0037	.0008	.0001	.0000	.0000
	6	1.0000	.9997	.9964	.9819	.9434	.8689	.7548	.6098	.4522	.3036	.1818	.0950	.0422	.0152	.0042	.0008	.0001	.0000
	7	1.0000	1.0000	.9994	.9958	.9827	.9500	.8868	.7869	.6535	.5000	.3465	.2131	.1132	.0500	.0173	.0042	.0006	.0000
	8	1.0000	1.0000	.9999	.9992	.9958	.9848	.9578	.9050	.8182	.6964	.5478	.3902	.2452	.1311	.0566	.0181	.0036	.0003
	9	1.0000	1.0000	1.0000	.9999	.9992	.9963	.9876	.9662	.9231	.8491	.7392	.5968	.4357	.2784	.1484	.0611	.0168	.0022
	10	1.0000	1.0000	1.0000	1.0000	.9999	.9993	.9972	.9907	.9745	.9408	.8796	.7827	.6481	.4845	.3135	.1642	.0617	.0127
	11	1.0000	1.0000	1.0000	1.0000	1.0000	.9999	.9995	.9981	.9937	.9824	.9576	.9095	.8273	.7031	.5387	.3518	.1773	.0556
	12	1.0000	1.0000	1.0000	1.0000	1.0000	1.0000	.9999	.9997	.9989	.9963	.9893	.9729	.9383	.8732	.7639	.6020	.3958	.1841
	13	1.0000	1.0000	1.0000	1.0000	1.0000	1.0000	1.0000	1.0000	.9999	.9995	.9983	.9948	.9858	.9647	.9198	.8329	.6814	.4510
	14	1.0000	1.0000	1.0000	1.0000	1.0000	1.0000	1.0000	1.0000	1.0000	1.0000	.9999	.9995	.9984	.9953	.9866	.9648	.9126	.7941
	15	1.0000	1.0000	1.0000	1.0000	1.0000	1.0000	1.0000	1.0000	1.0000	1.0000	1.0000	1.0000	1.0000	1.0000	1.0000	1.0000	1.0000	1.0000
20	0	.3585	.1216	.0388	.0115	.0032	.0008	.0002	.0000	.0000	.0000	.0000	.0000	.0000	.0000	.0000	.0000	.0000	.0000
	1	.7358	.3917	.1756	.0692	.0243	.0076	.0021	.0005	.0001	.0000	.0000	.0000	.0000	.0000	.0000	.0000	.0000	.0000
	2	.9245	.6769	.4049	.2061	.0913	.0355	.0121	.0036	.0009	.0002	.0000	.0000	.0000	.0000	.0000	.0000	.0000	.0000
	3	.9841	.8670	.6477	.4114	.2252	.1071	.0444	.0160	.0049	.0013	.0003	.0000	.0000	.0000	.0000	.0000	.0000	.0000
	4	.9974	.9568	.8298	.6296	.4148	.2375	.1182	.0510	.0189	.0059	.0015	.0003	.0000	.0000	.0000	.0000	.0000	.0000
	5	.9997	.9887	.9327	.8042	.6172	.4164	.2454	.1256	.0553	.0207	.0064	.0016	.0003	.0000	.0000	.0000	.0000	.0000
	6	1.0000	.9976	.9781	.9133	.7858	.6080	.4166	.2500	.1299	.0577	.0214	.0065	.0015	.0003	.0000	.0000	.0000	.0000
	7	1.0000	.9996	.9941	.9679	.8982	.7723	.6010	.4159	.2520	.1316	.0580	.0210	.0060	.0013	.0002	.0000	.0000	.0000
	8	1.0000	.9999	.9987	.9900	.9591	.8867	.7624	.5956	.4143	.2517	.1308	.0565	.0196	.0051	.0009	.0001	.0000	.0000
	9	1.0000	1.0000	.9998	.9974	.9861	.9520	.8782	.7553	.5914	.4119	.2493	.1275	.0532	.0171	.0039	.0006	.0000	.0000
	10	1.0000	1.0000	1.0000	.9994	.9961	.9829	.9468	.8725	.7507	.5881	.4086	.2447	.1218	.0480	.0139	.0026	.0002	.0000
	11	1.0000	1.0000	1.0000	.9999	.9991	.9949	.9804	.9435	.8692	.7483	.5857	.4044	.2376	.1133	.0409	.0100	.0013	.0001
	12	1.0000	1.0000	1.0000	1.0000	.9998	.9987	.9940	.9790	.9420	.8684	.7480	.5841	.3990	.2277	.1018	.0321	.0059	.0004
	13	1.0000	1.0000	1.0000	1.0000	1.0000	.9997	.9985	.9935	.9786	.9423	.8701	.7500	.5834	.3920	.2142	.0867	.0219	.0024
	14	1.0000	1.0000	1.0000	1.0000	1.0000	1.0000	.9997	.9984	.9936	.9793	.9447	.8744	.7546	.5836	.3828	.1958	.0673	.0113
	15	1.0000	1.0000	1.0000	1.0000	1.0000	1.0000	1.0000	.9997	.9985	.9941	.9811	.9490	.8818	.7625	.5852	.3704	.1702	.0432
	16	1.0000	1.0000	1.0000	1.0000	1.0000	1.0000	1.0000	1.0000	.9997	.9987	.9951	.9840	.9556	.8929	.7748	.5886	.3523	.1330
	17	1.0000	1.0000	1.0000	1.0000	1.0000	1.0000	1.0000	1.0000	1.0000	.9998	.9991	.9964	.9879	.9645	.9087	.7939	.5951	.3231
	18	1.0000	1.0000	1.0000	1.0000	1.0000	1.0000	1.0000	1.0000	1.0000	1.0000	.9999	.9995	.9979	.9924	.9757	.9308	.8244	.6083
	19	1.0000	1.0000	1.0000	1.0000	1.0000	1.0000	1.0000	1.0000	1.0000	1.0000	1.0000	1.0000	.9998	.9992	.9968	.9885	.9612	.8784
	20	1.0000	1.0000	1.0000	1.0000	1.0000	1.0000	1.0000	1.0000	1.0000	1.0000	1.0000	1.0000	1.0000	1.0000	1.0000	1.0000	1.0000	1.0000

APPENDIX C Working with the Normal Distribution

The normal distribution is a theoretical distribution that approximates many real-life phenomena. It is widely used in many disciplines, including operations management. Consequently, having the ability to work with normal distributions is a skill that will serve you well.

The normal curve is symmetrical and bell-shaped, as illustrated in Figure C.1. Although the theoretical distribution extends in both directions, to plus or minus infinity, most of the distribution lies close to its mean, so values of a variable that is normally distributed will occur relatively close to the distribution mean.

FIGURE C.1 The normal distribution

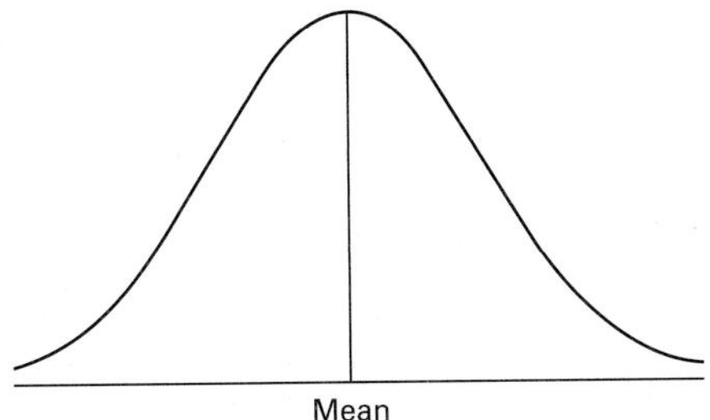

z Values

It is customary to refer to a value of a normally distributed random variable in terms of the number of standard deviations the value is from the mean of the distribution. This is known as its *z* value, or *z* score. In Figure C.2 you can see the normal distribution in terms of some selected *z* values. This particular distribution is referred to as the standard normal distribution. Notice that the *z* values to the left of (i.e., below) the mean are negative. Thus, a *z* value of -1.25 refers to a value that is 1.25 standard deviations below the distribution mean.

FIGURE C.2 The standard normal distribution with selected values of *z*

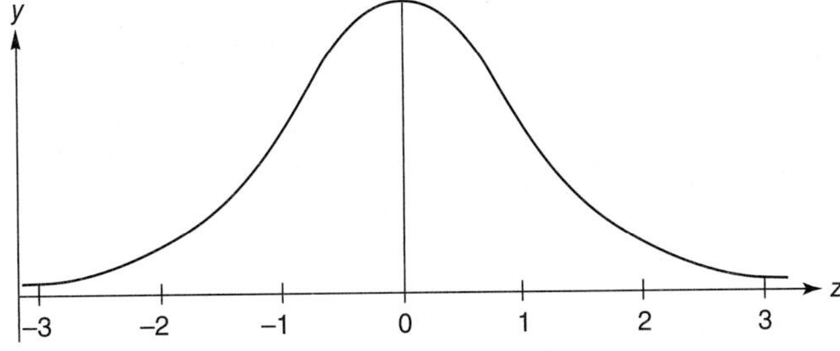

When working with a variable that is normally distributed, it is often necessary to convert an actual value of the variable to a *z* value. The *z* value can be computed using the following formula:

$$z = \frac{x - \mu}{\sigma}$$

where x = A specified value of a variable
μ = The distribution mean
σ = The distribution standard deviation

EXAMPLE 1

A normal distribution has a mean of 20 and a standard deviation of 2. What is the z value of 17.5?

SOLUTION

$x = 17.5$
$\mu = 20$
$\sigma = 2$

Using the formula for z, we find:

$$z = \frac{x - \mu}{\sigma}$$

$$z = \frac{17.5 - 20}{2} = -1.25$$

z Values and Probabilities

Once the z value is known, it can be used to obtain various probabilities by referring to a table of the normal distribution, such as the probability that a value will occur by chance that is greater than, or less than, that value. Note that the probability of *exactly* that value is zero, because there are an infinite number of values that could occur, so the probability of specifying in advance that any one particular value will occur is essentially equal to zero. z values can also be used to find the probability that a value will occur that is between $\pm z$. Two such cases are shown in Figure C.3. Note that the total area underneath the curve represents 100 percent of the probability, so knowing that the probability that a value will occur that is within the range, say, of $z = \pm 2$ is .9544, we can say that the probability that a value will occur that is outside of the range (e.g., either less than $z = -2$ or greater than $z = +2$) is equal to $1.0000 - .9544 = .0456$.

FIGURE C.3 Areas under the normal curve between $z = \pm 2\sigma$ and $z = \pm 3\sigma$

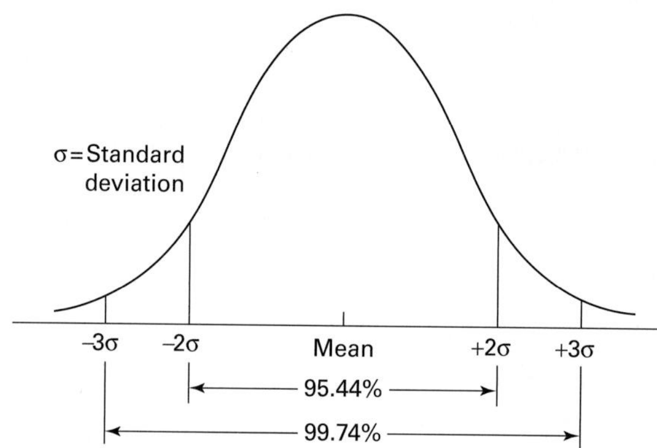

Tables of the Normal Distribution

Virtually all applications of the normal distribution involve working with a table of normal distribution probabilities. Tables make the process of obtaining probabilities and z values quite simple. This book has two slightly different normal distribution tables. Appendix B Table A has values for the right half of the distribution for the area under the curve (note the figure at the top of the table), which is the probability from the mean of the distribution ($z = 0$) to any other value of z, up to $z = +3.09$. Statistics books always have this version of the table, so you may already be familiar with it. A second table of normal probabilities is presented in Appendix B Tables B1 and B2. They show the area under the curve from negative infinity to any point z (see the figure at the top of the table), up to $z = +3.49$. In both tables, the values of z are shown in two parts. The integer and first decimal are shown along the side of the table, while the second decimal is shown across the top.

EXAMPLE 2

Using Appendix B Table B.2, find the area under the curve to the left of $z = 1.12$.

SOLUTION

$z = 1.12$ becomes 1.1
.02
———
1.12

Find the row where $z = 1.1$ down the left-hand side of the table. Find the .02 column across the top of the table. The probability is at the intersection of the 1.1 row and the .02 column.

z	.00	.01	.02	.03	.04	.05	.06	.07	.08	.09
.0	.5000	.5040	.5080	.5120	.5160	.5199	.5239	.5279	.5319	.5359
.1	.5398	.5438	.5478	.5517	.5557	.5596	.5636	.5675	.5714	.5753
.2	.5793	.5832	.5871	.5910	.5948	.5987	.6026	.6064	.6103	.6141
.3	.6179	.6217	.6255	.6293	.6331	.6368	.6406	.6443	.6480	.6517
.4	.6554	.6591	.6628	.6664	.6700	.6736	.6772	.6808	.6844	.6879
.5	.6915	.6950	.6985	.7019	.7054	.7088	.7123	.7157	.7190	.7224
.6	.7257	.7291	.7324	.7357	.7389	.7422	.7454	.7486	.7517	.7549
.7	.7580	.7611	.7642	.7673	.7703	.7734	.7764	.7794	.7823	.7852
.8	.7881	.7910	.7939	.7967	.7995	.8023	.8051	.8078	.8106	.8133
.9	.8159	.8186	.8212	.8238	.8264	.8289	.8315	.8340	.8365	.8389
1.0	.8413	.8438	.8461	.8485	.8508	.8531	.8554	.8577	.8599	.8621
1.1	.8643	.8665	.8686	.8708	.8729	.8749	.8770	.8790	.8810	.8830
1.2	.8849	.8869	.8888	.8907	.8925	.8944	.8962	.8980	.8997	.9015
1.3	.9032	.9049	.9066	.9082	.9099	.9115	.9131	.9147	.9162	.9177
1.4	.9192	.9207	.9222	.9236	.9251	.9265	.9279	.9292	.9306	.9319

Note: You will find versions of both tables at the very end of the book for easy reference. The last table repeats Appendix B Table A. The other table repeats Appendix B Table B.2., the positive values of z. For problems that involve negative values of z, refer to the portion of Appendix B Table B.1. on p. 880.

Finding a Probability of Observing a Value That Is Within $\pm z$ of the Mean or Outside of $\pm z$

Use Appendix B Table A for this type of problem:

EXAMPLE 3

Find the area under the curve that is *within* two standard deviations of the mean.

SOLUTION

What the problems is asking for:

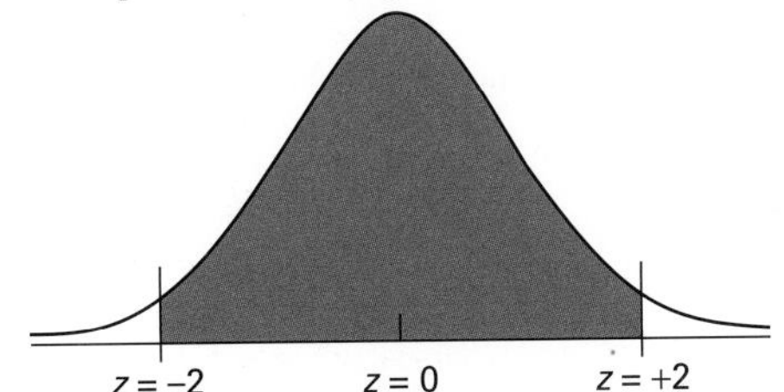

Appendix B Table A provides the right half of the area:

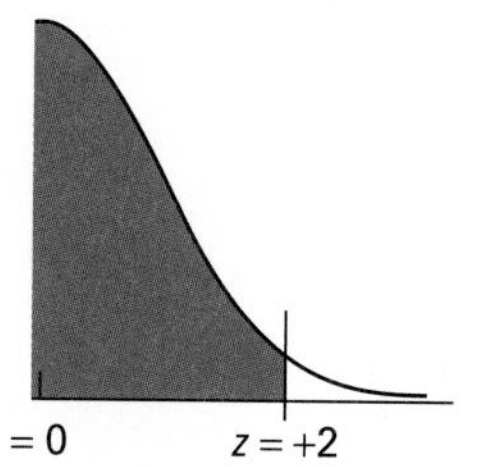

The shaded area is .4772

To find the total area between $\pm z = 2$, double the amount in the right half: 2(.4772) = .9544.

EXAMPLE 4

Find the area under the curve that is *outside* of two standard deviations from the mean.

SOLUTION

What the problem is asking for:

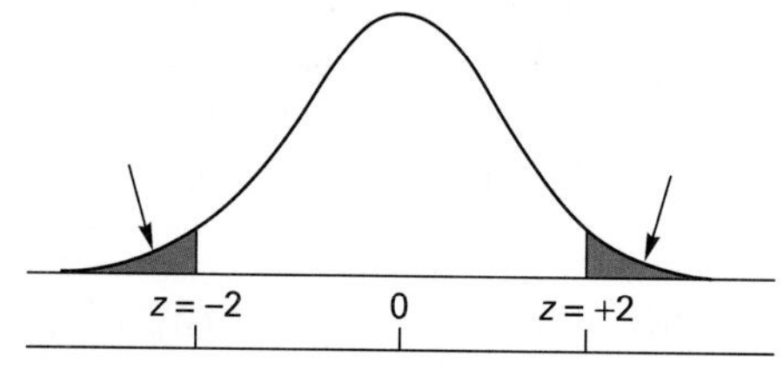

Appendix B Table A provides the right half of the area between the mean and $z = +2$. To find the area in the right tail, subtract the amount between the mean and $z = +2$ from .5000:

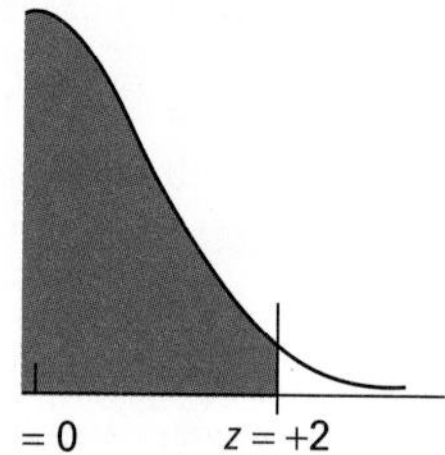

Area under the right side of the curve:	.5000
Subtract the area from $z = 0$ to $z = +2.00$:	−.4772
The area to the right of $z = +2.00$ is:	.0228

The same amount will be in each tail, so the total area in both tails is 2(.0228) = .0456.

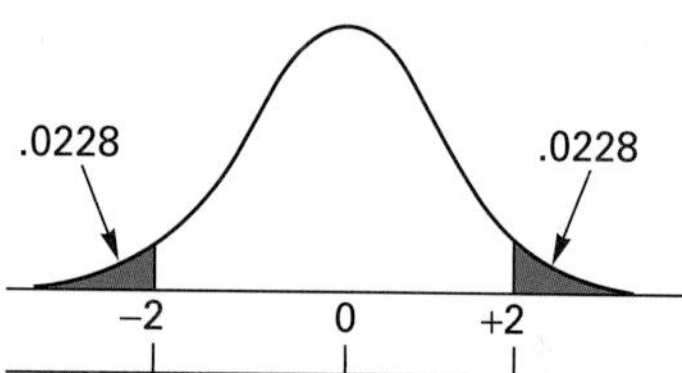

Another way to arrive at the same answer is to note that the area *within* two standard deviations of the mean is .9544, as shown previously, so the area outside of that is 1.0000 − .9544 = .0456.

Finding an Area (Probability) That Is to the Left or to the Right of *z*

Use Appendix B Table B.2 for this type of problem (e.g., "What is the probability that the time will not exceed 22 weeks?").

EXAMPLE 5

A normal distribution has a mean of 20 and a standard deviation of 1.0. Find the probabilities:

a. A value that is 22 or less.

b. A value that is 22 or more.

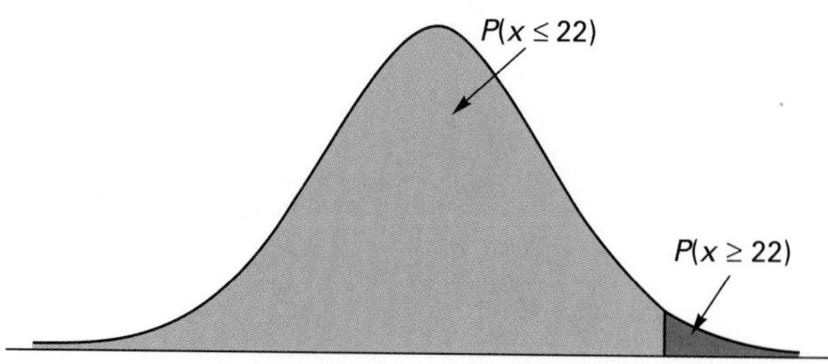

SOLUTION

First, determine the value of z for 22:

$$z = \frac{x - \mu}{\sigma} = \frac{22 - 20}{1} = +2.00$$

a. From Appendix B Table B, the area (probability) to the left of $z = +2.00$ is .9772.

b. Because the total area under the curve is 100 percent, or 1.0000, the area to the right of $z = +2.00$ is simply $1.0000 - .9772 = .0228$.

Points to Remember

1. The area under a normal curve represents probability.
2. The area under the curve is 100 percent, or 1.0000.
3. The area on either side of the mean is equal to half of the total, which is 50 percent, or .5000.
4. The curve extends to ± infinity, but 99.74 percent of the values will occur within ±3 standard deviations of the mean.
5. It is best to use Appendix B Table A for problems involving $\pm z$ (i.e., Chapters 7 and 10), and to use Appendix B Table B for problems involving one-sided probabilities such as the probability that x will be no more than a given (i.e., Chapters 4S, 13, and 17).
6. The probability of an exact value (e.g., 22 in Example 5) is zero. Therefore, $P(x \leq 22) = P(x < 22)$.

Test Yourself

1. Suppose a normal distribution has a mean of 40 and a standard deviation of 5. Find the value of z for each of these values:
   a. 48 b. 30
   c. 34 d. 52.5
2. Using Appendix B Table A, find the area between $\pm z$ when z is:
   a. 1.00 b. 1.96
   c. 2.10 d. 2.50
3. Find the probability of observing a value that is beyond $\pm z$ when z is:
   a. 1.00 b. 1.80
   c. 1.88 d. 2.54
4. Use the appropriate Appendix B Table to find the probability of a value that does not exceed a z value of:
   a. .40 b. 1.27
   c. −1.32 d. 2.75
5. Find the probability of observing a value that is more than a z value of:
   a. .77 b. 1.65
   c. −1.32 d. 2.75

Answers

1. a. +1.60 b. −2.00
   c. −1.20 d. +2.50
2. a. .6826 b. .9500
   c. .9642 d. .9876
3. a. .3174 b. .0718
   c. .0602 d. .0110
4. a. .6554 b. .8980
   c. .0934 d. .9970
5. a. .2206 b. .0495
   c. .9066 d. .0030

Photo Credits

Chapter 1

page 3, US Coast Guard/Handout/Corbis
page 8, Rick Wilking/Reuters/Corbis
page 11, Comstock Images/Alamy
page 12, Courtesy of Trek Bicycle Corporation
page 22, Rykoff Collection/Corbis
page 28, Photo by Getty Images for Puma
page 29, Photo by Mario Tama/Getty Images
page 31, © AP Photo/Kent Gilbert
page 34, Courtesy of Wegmans Food Markets, Inc.
page 34, Courtesy of Wegmans Food Markets, Inc.
page 35, Courtesy of Wegmans Food Markets, Inc.
page 35, Courtesy of Wegmans Food Markets, Inc.

Chapter 2

page 41, Corbis
page 43, © Sherwin Crasto/Reuters/Corbis
page 45, Ken James/Bloomberg via Getty images
page 51, The McGraw-Hill Companies, Inc./Christopher Kerrigan, photographer
page 55, Courtesy of Apple Inc.
page 57, Louie Psihoyos/Getty Images

Chapter 3

page 73, © Getty Images
page 74, AP Photo/Peter Cosgrove
page 78, www.CartoonStock.com
page 94, Jack Hollingsworth/Corbis
page 103, Chris Ratcliffe/Bloomberg via Getty Images

Chapter 4

page 133, Jeff Corwin/Getty Images
page 136, Courtesy of Dutch Boy
page 138, Courtesy of Pinnacle Foods Corporation.
page 140, © AP Photo/David Adame
page 144, Courtesy of Kraft Foods Inc.
page 146, © Jack Star/Photolink/Getty Images
page 148, Courtesy of Nike
page 148, Design: Peter Stathis
page 150, © 2008 Dell Inc. All Rights Reserved
page 159, © Kevin Horan/Getty Images

Chapter 5

page 183, Mark Peterson/Redux
page 183, Grant Faint/Getty Images
page 185, Thomas Coex/APF/Getty Images
page 188, © Mark Richards/PhotoEdit
page 188, © Brand X Pictures/PunchStock
page 196, © Royalty-Free/Corbis
page 196, © Royalty-Free/Corbis

Chapter 6

page 235, AP Photo/Eckenhard Schulz
page 237, © Royalty-Free/Corbis
page 237, © Don Tremain/Getty Images
page 237, © Keith Dannemiller/Corbis
page 237, © Royalty-Free/CORBIS
page 244, © Brand X Pictures/PunchStock
page 245, © FRANCK ROBICHON/epa/Corbis
page 246, Department of Energy Digital Archive
page 253, Courtesy of Cunard Line
page 257, © Reuters/Corbis

Chapter 7

page 285, Corbis
page 288, © Jared McMillen/Aurora Photos/Corbis
page 291, Courtesy of Humantech Inc.
page 296, Courtesy of Peak Ergonomics www.HealthyWorkSolutions.com
page 296, Courtesy of Peak Ergonomics www.HealthyWorkSolutions.com
page 300, none

Chapter 8

page 333, Yu Chu Di/Redlink/Corbis
page 334, Comstock Images/Alamy
page 337, Erica Simona Leeds 2007
page 340, Eightfish/Getty
page 345, Tom Dixon Studios

Chapter 9

page 371, Monty Rakusen/Getty
page 377, © Alex Segre/Alamy
page 383, Reprinted with permission of Alcatel-Lucent USA Inc.
page 384, AP Photo/Richard Drew
page 386, NIST public domain
page 389, Jay Mallin/Bloomberg via Getty Images
page 392, AP Photo/Paul Sakuma
page 408, Ryan Anson/ Bloomberg via Getty Images

Chapter 10

page 419, © Peter Ginter/Getty Image
page 421, Tim Boyle/Bloomberg via Getty Images
page 424, Chicago Sun-Times
page 425, © Chang W. Lee/The New York Times/Redux
page 427, Courtesy of Omron Industrial Automation
page 433, © David R. Frazier/PhotoEdit
page 443, © Royalty-Free/Corbis
page 444, Lester Lefkowitz/Getty Images
page 448, Corbis Super RF/Alamy

Chapter 11

page 473, Courtesy of Canon USA
page 474, Adam Berry/Bloomberg via Getty Images
page 480, AP Photo/Scott Sady
page 491, Courtesy of Motorola

Chapter 12

page 509, Michael Rosenfeld/Getty Images
page 515, Courtesy of VX Corporation
page 550, Courtesy of L. & J.G. Stickley

Chapter 13

page 555, © Monty Rakusen/Getty Images
page 557, Courtesy of Motorola
page 561, Ryan McVay/Getty Images
page 563, 2007 Getty Images Inc.

Chapter 14

page 619, LENNOX MCLENDON/ASSOCIATED PRESS
page 621, Courtesy of Ford Motor Company
page 628, Marcos Issa/Bloomberg via Getty Images
page 632, General Motors LLC, used with permission GM Media Archive
page 635, Tri State Industries, footage courtesy of Mac Lean Media, Inc.
page 635, Tri State Industries, footage courtesy of Mac Lean Media, Inc.
page 645, Courtesy of Cardinal Health

Chapter 15

page 663, Eightfish/Getty Images
page 667, Scott Bauer/USDA
page 668, DANISH SIDDIQUI/Reuters/Landov
page 676, © Jim Hansen Photography
page 682, © IAN LANGSDON/epa/Corbis
page 685, Steven Puetzer/Getty Images
page 691, Mark Richards/PhotoEdit

Chapter 16

page 701, Altrendo Travel/Getty Images
page 703, Courtesy Rexam PLC.
page 721, Alex MacLean/Getty Images
page 724, Mark Wilson/Getty Images

Chapter 17

page 741, Jamey Stillings
page 745, Matt Kent/Getty Images
page 745, Kevin Mazur/Getty Images
page 768, Justin Kase zfivez/Alamy

Chapter 18

page 793, Jeff Greenberg/Photoedit
page 794, Andreas Solaro/Getty Images
page 805, Stephen Chernin/Getty Images
page 821, Yotel
page 822, Atlantide Phototravel/Corbis

Chapter 19

page 833, Jon Feingersh/Getty Images

Company Index

Subject Index

Note: Boldface entries indicate key terms and the page numbers where they are defined; page numbers followed by n refer to notes.

OPERATIONS

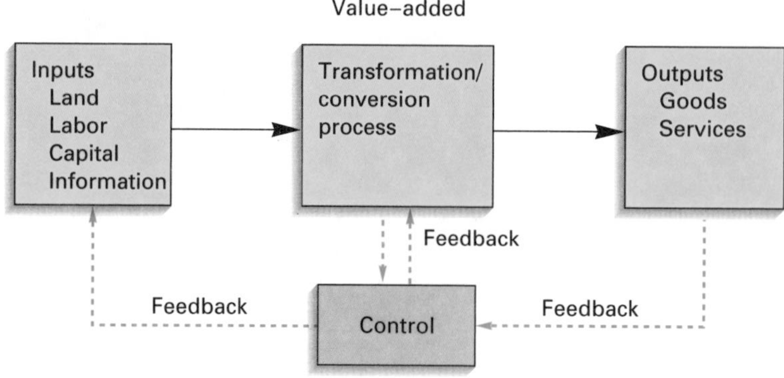

TYPICAL SUPPLY CHAINS

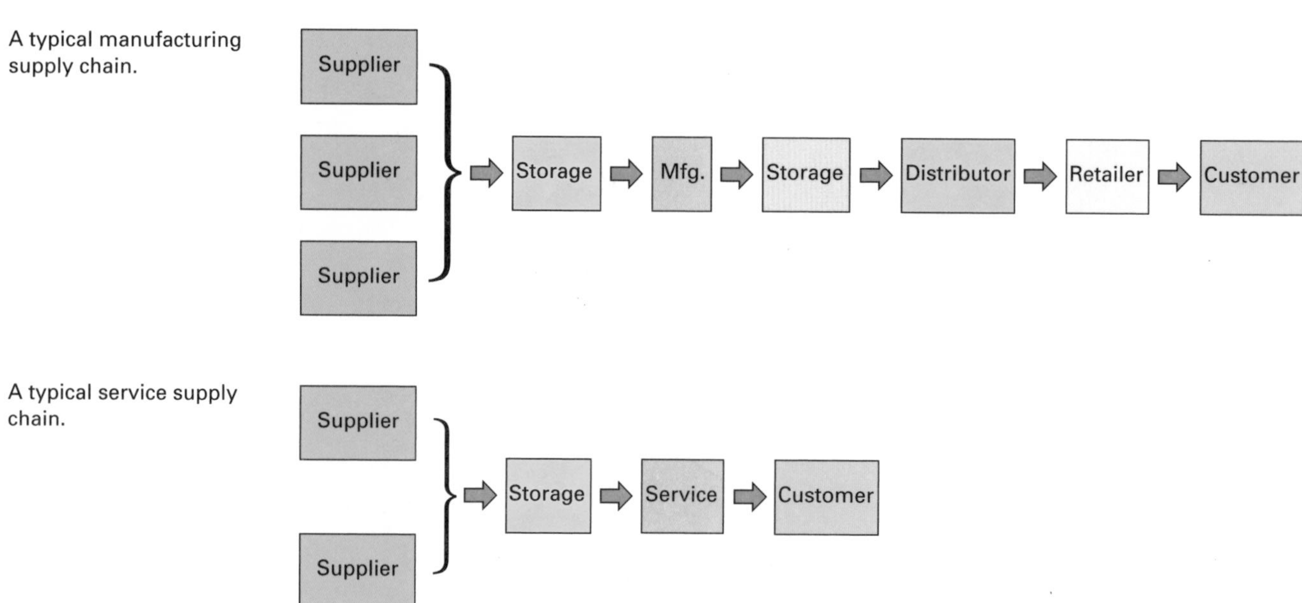